RON SHANDLER's

Baseball Forecaster

2003

Seventeenth Edition

Shandler Enterprises, LLC
Roanoke, VA

Shandler Enterprises LLC
P.O. Box 20303
Roanoke, VA 24018

Offices 540-772-6315
Fax 540-772-1969
Customer service 800-422-7820

E-mail shandler@baseballhq.com
Internet http://www.baseballhq.com
http://www.baseballforecaster.com
http://www.rotohq.com

Cover design by JonResh@ViperPress.com
Cover photography by Ron Shandler

ISBN 1-891566-03-2
Printed in the United States of America

Acknowledgments

Lately it seems that people keep coming up to me to say how lucky I am to write about baseball for a living. I suppose I do live a charmed life, of sorts. I have a wonderful family, a nice house in the country and I even bought a new car this year. However, while my name may grace the cover of this book (and thousands of you will finally get to see what this stat geek looks like), there are many others whose influence impacts the product you hold in your hands, either directly or indirectly.

My sincerest gratitude to:

Paul Petera, for his expert and expedient data compilation and stat-crunching. The minor league data, PQS logs and tons more are all a product of his tireless efforts.

Matt Dodge, for his terrific work on Baseball HQ's bullpen indicator charts, which debut here this year.

Deric McKamey, who contributes a level of minor league analysis not found *anywhere else*. There are several fine writers of this genre out there, but nobody integrates pure scouting and statistical analysis like Deric does.

Rick Wilton, whose injury reports are just a small part of this book, but whose support and friendship are immeasurable.

The *information sources that I relied on* to help fill in missing data, to jog my memory when I drew a mental blank about a player and to add color to the commentaries... Rotowire.com, ESPN.com, BaseballAmerica.com, the *Baseball America Almanac*, and *The Sporting News Baseball Register*. Thanks also to *Kevin Goldstein*, who contributed one small data file that made a big difference in this year's MLE charts.

The *forefathers of both the baseball analysis and fantasy baseball industries* – Bill James, Pete Palmer, Steve Mann, Glen Waggoner and Alex Patton – who've given us a reason to follow this sport despite the inability of its caretakers to see beyond the tips of their billfolds.

The participants in the LABR and Tout Wars experts leagues, the speakers at our conferences, and the principals of the Fantasy Sports Trade Association, who have become *valued colleagues*, sounding boards and friends... Greg Ambrosius, Jeff Barton, Jim Callis, Jim Dressel, Jeff Erickson, John Hunt, Peter Kreutzer, Gene McCaffrey, Lenny Melnick, Bill Meyer, Steve Moyer, Rob Neyer, Mat Olkin, Rich Pike, David Rawnsley, Peter Schoenke, John Sickels, Scott Wilderman, Rick Wolf, John Zaleski and Irwin Zwilling. If you ever wanted a Who's Who List of the best writers, analysts and vendors in this industry – this is it.

The *incredible group of writers and analysts for the BaseballHQ.com web site*, who've taken the building blocks from this book and have helped create a metropolis... Matt Bruce, John Burnson, Matt Carter, Patrick Davitt, Doug Dennis, Michael Duncan, Jon Enriquez, Brent Hershey, Allen Hirsch, Jeff Howard, Terry Linhart, Al Melchior, Scott Monroe, Rich Murawski, Ray Murphy, Harold Nichols, Stephen Nickrand, Frank Noto, Doug Ohlandt, Josh Paley, Michael Sanderson, Mike Shears and Rod Truesdell.

Finally...

Thank *you*. You've spent your hard-earned money for this book of numbers and I sincerely appreciate your continued confidence in me for yet another year.

And... the *ladies of my life*, Sue, Darielle and Justina for their unending support during the seven weeks that I go MIA each fall. My girls (now 11 and 10) recently came to the conclusion that their Dad must be famous, so they have started giving out my books to their friends at school, who are now also under this same misconception. These friends come home with the girls and are then led into my office where they stand about 10 feet from my desk, and just stare. You will never fully appreciate the dark underbelly of fame until you have a bunch of 10 and 11-year-olds staring you down in complete silence. I keep asking Sue why she doesn't set the record straight for these kids, but she's always too busy rolling on the floor laughing.

Life's good.

Acknowledgments

CONTENTS

I. PILGRIMAGE

We are all on a journey to a destination that does not exist.

Since the beginnings of fantasy baseball, and before, we've all wanted to find the Holy Grail of Information – the perfect projections model. If we could unlock the secrets of player performance, and project the future with absolute accuracy, we would finally have the ultimate competitive edge in our leagues.

So, everyone with a calculator has been waging an annual assault on quantitative theory. Each year, more and more University of Baseball graduates are finding new ways to slice, dice and reassemble every line drive into right field and flare over shortstop. We've taken performance down to its lowest common denominator and then reconstructed arcane and convoluted formulas that allege this week's new revelation.

And wouldn't you know it, it seems like we *do* get closer to the Grail each year.

I've been flexing my Excel muscle on the prognosticating bandwagon as well. I'm the guy who added the concept of "component skills analysis" to the fantasy baseball landscape. This is the process of analyzing the individual elements of a player's skill set and then using the findings to project more familiar measures, like ERA and batting average. It is a process that is fundamental to the analytical arsenal we've developed here, but more than that, it gives us fantasy geeks something to play with.

It sounds simple and straightforward, but arriving at this particular destination has not been a straight journey. We've not gone from Point A to Point B and recorded the miles traveled. Everything you read here has been a step along a winding, evolutionary path that has been ongoing for about 17 years.

The *Baseball Forecaster* started out as a purely sabermetric tome; it didn't even contain player projections until its 5th edition. BPV was once PVal, an early 1990's version of the formula. In 1993 came the first mention of raw skills and something called "creative discrepancy analysis." And in the 1994 edition of the book, I boldly announced that "numbers are everything."

Over the past few years or so, I've come to realize that, not only are numbers not everything, most of them hardly even matter at all, especially the numbers that we play our fantasy games with. Precision and accuracy in baseball prognosticating is a fool's quest. There are far too many unexpected variables and noise, things that occur daily that render our expectations null and void. Still, each year, we see more and more web sites coming out with projections, and self-proclaimed accuracy levels that would drive bookmakers out of business...

...if we could believe any of their claims. Which we can't. You see, as long as human beings play this game, both on and off the field, the Grail will forever be beyond our grasp. And the harsh reality of all this is – *there really is no Grail.*

There will never be a perfect projections model. We will never achieve 100% accuracy. But that's okay. It's the journey that's important, not the destination. And we can potentially do better if we focus on making Point A to Point B a more meaningful trip. Let everyone else swim the oceans in search of some nonexistent Grail.

I've come to realize that the best we can ever hope for is to accurately forecast general tendencies. Using the library of research results built by myself and others, we've created a series of rules and have developed percentage plays for performance. I could not tell you that Edgar Renteria would hit exactly .305 last year, but I could tell you that, based on his outstanding contact rate and batting eye, players with similar characteristics were almost always .300 hitters. If that probability was 80%, then that's what you hang your hat on, even though Renteria hadn't hit .300 since 1996.

And that should be enough. Actually, it *has* to be enough. Any tout who exactly projected a .305 batting average was just lucky with his dart throws that day.

Of course, you also must remember the flipside: When you follow an 80% percentage play, you will still lose 20% of the time. Those 20% worth of outlying players are what skeptics like to use as proof that all prognosticators are frauds. HQ writer John Burnson once wrote: "The issue is not the success rate for one player, but the success rate for all players. No system is 100% reliable, and in trying to capture the outliers, you weaken the middle and thereby lose more predictive pull than you gain. At some level, everyone is an exception!"

So, long-term success dictates that you always chase the 80% and accept the fact that you will be wrong 20% of the time. Or, whatever that percentage play happens to be.

For our own fantasy league purposes, playing the percentages can take on an even less precise spin. The alternate reality of our game model suggests that the best projections are just the ones that are far enough away from the field of expectation to alter decision-making. In other words, it doesn't matter if I project Player X to hit 20 HRs and he only hits 10. It matters that I projected 20 HRs, and everyone else projected 30.

Understand, though, that we do still need some numbers. It's just not the numbers you think we need, and they are not used in the way that you'd expect them to be used. That's what the *Baseball Forecaster* is all about.

This evolutionary process we've been on has often taken us far from the path to the Grail. We've found formulas and correlations that work in one year and not another. Sometimes, we misread the results. Other times, the rules simply change. The Grail is a moving target.

For many years, I've hung my hat on batting eye ratio (BB/K) as a predictor of future batting average. The truth is that batting eye is a marvelous descriptor of current performance, but the correlations are weaker when attempting to use it as a leading indicator. Several writers have looked at this recently. Peter Kreutzer (MLB.com and AskRotoman.com) wrote:

"Ron Shandler has been writing about the skills of players for years, and I dare say that they have had a profound effect on the way fantasy baseball is played. His LIMA Plan, which applies the same principles to pitchers, is the single most important roto strategy since the Sweeney Plan. It is also the most pertinent to real baseball, which is kind of cool. What it isn't is predictive of a player's developing skills.

"As valuable as Eye Ratio may be for evaluating a player's talents (and shortcomings), an improvement from one year to the next is absolutely not indicative that a player is going to improve the next year.

"I ran a survey of the years 1997-2001, finding three consecutive years where hitters had 200 or more at bats. I then compared Eye Ratio change in the first two years to the change between Years 2 and 3.

"The outcome: Totally random. Absolutely no correlation."

When I first looked at this correlation in the early 1990's, there was more reason to be optimistic, but Peter's findings now become incredibly important. They help us take that next step in our journey. Late last season, I wrote a column on Baseball HQ that tried to explain the nightmare that Alfonso Soriano was to sabermetric prognosticators. My conclusion: "We need the Sorianos." The Yankee second-baseman, who put up MVP-caliber numbers with the most impossibly horrible batting eye ratio, served an important role in perpetuating the educational process.

We can't be afraid to face these demons. John Burnson wasn't, and as you'll soon see, has come up with what could arguably be considered the most important new indicator in many years.

In 2001, *Baseball Weekly* writer Mat Olkin made a presentation at our Arizona Fall League Symposium that looked at batters' fly ball tendencies and their relevance in projecting swings in home run output. Intuitively, this seemed like a no-brainer – hit more fly balls means the potential to hit more home runs – but Mat's early work was inconclusive. When I asked him to contribute his findings to this book, he was hesitant. He wrote me:

"I'd be glad to, but I would want to be very explicit that the connection between G:F and power growth is still very much in the hypothesis stage… More rigorous research may well show that there's nothing to it… I know you usually hold your methods to a higher standard than that. If you're thinking of presenting this as an indicator with predictive value, I'm not sure the evidence is there yet. But if you're thinking of presenting this as an avenue that might merit further exploration, I'll sign on to that."

His note made me realize how important it is to keep ourselves open to all possibilities, even if they are not yet proven. I responded: "Everything we do here is a work in progress. We've yet to find the Holy Grail, so anything we get our hands on that might move us one step closer is worth exploring. Often, these speculations provide a springboard for someone else to find the next missing link."

And that is how we take another step forward in the pilgrimage to reach our non-existent destination.

The quest continues now. 2002 was a great year for component skills analysis. In this book are several essays with some new perspectives on the topic. First is a piece I wrote for Baseball HQ that provides a different angle in looking at batting eye ratios. Mat Olkin's work has opened up the door for us to start looking at ground ball and fly ball tendencies, and their predictability for both batters and pitchers. Later in the book, I'll introduce you to qERA, which first made its appearance this past summer at Baseball HQ. This fascinating new tool approaches starting pitching from a new angle, and gives the word "component" a new meaning.

And then there's Alfonso Soriano. Batting eye might call him a fluke, but John Burnson's new Expected Batting Average asserts that we've been looking at the wrong component skills. xBA says that Soriano might well be for real, despite his apparent inability to tell the difference between a ball and a strike.

There will be more. Much more.

* * *

Welcome to the 17th Edition of the *Baseball Forecaster*. If you missed the news, there will be labor peace in the sport for at least another four or five years. That means we'll be able to watch Barry Bonds make his assault on the career home run record without interruption. It means that we will eventually have an answer to the question, "Will I be able to call the Expos my home team soon?" And it means that I'll be around long enough to write about Jesse Orosco's retirement. I think.

Despite my becoming disenchanted with the numbers as of late, the Forecaster is, in fact, a book of numbers. Its purpose is to instill a bit of order into apparently random data. It is an analytical tool, nothing more. It charts trends, reveals patterns and points to possible directions. It makes no absolute statements, but it does often reveal strong tendencies. There are some words, but they are just one man's analysis. The power of this book is in the numbers and what you see when *you* read them.

How to Use This Book

My philosophy regarding fantasy baseball analysis was once unique, but not so much anymore since I started winning these experts leagues. Now, everybody is embracing component skills analysis, and in some cases proclaiming it as their own. That's fun. Still, there are ideas here that will likely challenge your own beliefs. Keep an open mind. These tools do work, but you may have to throw away some preconceptions in order to embrace the possibilities. In the end, concepts like strand rates, and base performance values, and the LIMA Plan have helped fantasy leaguers win their leagues. That's the bottom line. What you choose to do is your own decision.

The place to start your journey is in the next section, *The Tools of Victory*. It is here that you will read about some of the foundation principles of my approach. Probably the most valuable reference section of the book is the **Forecaster's Toolbox**. This provides all of the rules and research results I use to draw conclusions about player performance. It contains the concepts for this book that have been developed over the past 17 years.

A quick scan through the **Sabermetric Glossary**, which is in the back of the book, is also a good thing to do. You don't need to memorize the formulas, but a cursory knowledge can't hurt. At minimum, you should know where to go in case you run across an unfamiliar gauge. There are lots of them. Be prepared, but don't be intimidated. Not all of these formulas will have relevance for the particular game you play. As you read through the player commentaries, you'll get a sense of the ones that are best to have a working knowledge of.

It's good to have this foundation, because it will provide you with a far greater analytical arsenal when you jump into the meat of the book. That meat — the **Batter** and **Pitcher** sections — contains an incredible wealth of data.

I include a brief commentary for each player, but these just touch the surface. To be honest, in cranking out this book in seven weeks, sometimes I just miss stuff. For instance, our PQS logs include valuable perspectives on starting pitching; it would have been great to include info from these logs for every pitcher, especially the pitch counts, but there was neither space nor time. I've included ground ball to fly ball ratios for everyone as well, but since this tool is so new, I was often hesitant to draw definitive conclusions from the data. By the time you read this, however, perhaps your comfort level will have risen.

And finally, the 2003 baseball landscape is already changing. The potential impact a new manager like Lou Piniella might have on Tampa, for instance, is also fodder for analysis that was not weighed. But you can, and should.

So consider the data as your own personal resource and use my notes just to provide some small direction. Then it will be up to you to do the rest of the legwork, and undoubtedly, you will uncover many more insights. *Forecaster* veterans would likely say that this self-guided excursion is the best part of owning the book.

The Minor League section will help you more properly evaluate those players with little or no major league experience. Deric McKamey's **Top Prospects** charts the trends for 54 minor leaguers most likely to have an impact in 2003. There will likely be dozens more that will make an appearance in the majors, and for those we provide complete **Major League Equivalencies**. One of the great in-season advantages of the *Forecaster* is that, when an unknown name gets a call-up, you can check back on his past equivalent performances and see if it is someone worth pursuing. Of course, BaseballHQ.com subscribers get Deric's analyses on these guys all season long.

The *Draft Guide History* section has been in this book since 1988, and finds great value in providing player rankings and trends in a variety of categories. For those who play in simulation games, we have batters and pitchers ranked together in the **Runs Above Replacement** section.

Finally, there's the *2002 Greatest Hits*, which are some of the top columns I wrote for Baseball HQ in 2002. There are some important essays in this year's collection, especially for those people who have been wondering what the fuss is about this LIMA Plan thing.

What's New

For the Forecaster's old friends, welcome back. Once again, we've got a bunch of new stuff this year...

1. In our never-ending quest to avoid drafting the Matt Andersons and unearth the Eric Gagnes, we take a deeper look into the indicators that might foretell future save opportunities. The **Bullpen Indicator Charts** debuted on Baseball HQ in 2001 to much fanfare, and have helped us understand save opportunity decisions just a little bit better. The charts in this book take a three-year scan of all relief pitchers who compiled at least one save or three holds in 2002.

2. Mat Olkin's early research on **ground ball to fly ball ratios** made me realize that this is an area that might hold much analytical insight, for batters *and* pitchers. We've included five years worth of this data – at the major league level only – and have begun to see some consistencies and inconsistencies that merit further research. It starts here, but there is certainly more work to do.

3. During the course of 2002, in the Baseball HQ Think Tank forum, John Burnson began his own personal journey of discovery. Taking the elements of batting average apart, he created a new formula — **Expected Batting Average** — which opens up new opportunities for prognosticators. Its accuracy is pretty amazing, but it is the outliers that are particularly insightful. xBA appears in the player boxes.

4. In the May 19, 1995 issue of the *Baseball Forecaster* newsletter, I introduced the concept of Pure Quality Starts (PQS). We've found many applications for PQS over the years, and it has provided great insight into the trends of starting pitchers. Last summer, I discovered a new perspective, and came up with a gauge that attempts to get a better handle on ERA. This PQS ERA, or **qERA** for short, is included in the pitching logs.

5. Over the past few years, we've been slowly integrating **platoon data** – specifically, batting averages versus left-handed and right-handed batters and pitchers – into each player box. For several years we presented only the previous season's splits. Last year, we squeezed in three years of data. This year we go the full five years.

6. Projecting pitching wins is darned near impossible. We long ago ran a study that showed which variables had the most relevance when projecting wins, and determined that team offense held the greatest impact. To provide a bit of insight, this year's pitcher boxes include **average run support per game data** from 2002.

7. In last year's book, we began reprinting the **pitching logs** that appear on Baseball HQ. That section spanned nearly 20 pages, with minutia that took micro-analysis to its limits. Since we try hard to look at the bigger picture here, I've condensed the format for these charts so that they will:

a) provide you with *three* years worth of trend data
b) provide you with more analytical information about each pitcher's season
c) take up less space in the book so we could more easily accommodate future expansion.

For those of you who need the minutia, that will always remain accessible in the Baseball HQ archives.

Other Stuff

The voluminous amount of information in each year's *Forecaster* is compiled and written over the course of seven weeks. In a project as large as this, there inevitably will be a few little things that slip through the cracks. Errors. Omissions. Unintentional oversights. We have set up a **Content Update page,** which is available online at http://www.baseballforecaster.com/bfupdates.shtml. This page will contain information to help you get the most out of your reading experience. If nobody finds anything wrong, the page will remain blank.

The content in this book also changes over time, through no fault of its own. More specifically, as we get closer to Opening Day, we'll have a better handle on how playing time is going to be allocated, so our projections can become more and more accurate. As a buyer of this book, you are privy to a **Free 2003 Projections Update**, which will be available online only, at the BaseballForecaster.com web site. This update, in the form of text and spreadsheet data files, will be posted on February 28, 2003.

This free update is *only available online* and only for those who own this Book. When you access the web site, have the book in front of you as it will ask for a password that appears somewhere in these pages. We'll be changing those codes pretty regularly too because there are still a few people who like to get something for nothing, and I still do need to pay my mortgage.

Beyond the Forecaster

Imagine being able to take the concepts and information in this book, and update them constantly during the year. Imagine having daily player analyses, with write-ups eight times as comprehensive as the snippets in these pages. Imagine the projections being updated weekly, as well as the pitching logs and bullpen charts. Imagine being able to search for a player at any time during the season, and have his complete statistical record – including current season stats and balance of year projections – available at the click of your mouse. Imagine being able to profile your own fantasy team and see at a glance whether its current or projected BPI's are up to snuff, or evaluate a trade proposal in the same way. Imagine getting complete scouting reports for *hundreds* of top prospects as well as daily analyses of every major league call-up. Imagine having access to a complete staff of fantasy baseball experts who you can ask about your own team issues.

That's the tip of the iceberg at **BaseballHQ.com**.

Just the tip.

Subscription information appears at the back of this book, but we have something special for *Forecaster* book buyers this year as well.

Last year, we offered a premium subscription to the BaseballForecaster.com web site. That contained electronic versions of some of the charts in the book, weekly fantasy draft guides and my weekly column from Baseball HQ (that included my sleepers and gambles lists, among other things). We're not going to do that this year. However, we will be offering *complete access to Baseball HQ* from March 1 through April 15 – at a discount to book buyers — which will provide you with a ton more information for almost the same price. This special rate will be available beginning in mid-February. Details will be posted at BaseballForecaster.com, or you can write us at support@baseballhq.com in the spring for more details.

We also have a sister site, called **RotoHQ.com**, which is the largest library of fantasy strategy essays and tools known to man. We'll be adding a bunch of new content in January, including a series I ran last summer on game theory, which was very popular. More details about RotoHQ, including ordering information, can also be found in the back of the book.

Finally, our conferences. Our big annual event is the **Fantasy Baseball Symposium at the Arizona Fall League**. In early November each year, we assemble some of the top writers in the industry, and along with many of you, meet down in Phoenix for three days of seminars, scouting and socializing. It's always my favorite weekend of the year. Information about next year's event, scheduled for November 7-9, 2003, will be posted at BaseballHQ.com around the All Star Break.

Last year we began taking the Phoenix show on the road. Our new **First Pitch Forums** made stops in Chicago and New York for open forum Q&A sessions with some of the industry's top analysts. We're planning to expand our sites in 2003. Once again, Baseball HQ is the place to find out the FPF schedule, which will be posted just after the first of the year.

All of that keeps my plate pretty full.

If you have questions or comments, feel free to drop me a personal e-mail at ron@baseballhq.com. As my long-time readers can attest, I do read every e-mail and respond to as many as I can, as quickly as I can. However, with this full plate, I don't have time to do things like analyze your roster or rank your keeper list (though we do have writers at Baseball HQ who can handle that), and sometimes e-mails do end up growing cobwebs in the deep recesses of my In Box. This morning, for instance, I opened my personal e-mail to find 126 messages, of which 78 were immediately deleted by my spam filter, 12 were e-zines I subscribe to, 32 were business issues I needed to address, and four were questions about whether I would have accepted the Red Sox consultancy position if Bill James hadn't. (I wouldn't.)

And today was a slow day.

Enough of this drivel; let's get started.

— Ron Shandler

Batting Eye: Playing the Percentages

by Ron Shandler

For years I have been talking about the correlation between batting eye and batting average. But the recent challenges to that assertion, which cite a high variability in results, force us to question just how strong the correlation really is.

Given two sets of numbers, our BPI analyses have become almost no-brainers...

PLAYER	bb%	ct%	Eye
Player A	15%	88%	1.48
Player B	8%	65%	0.27

Based on these numbers alone, which player would you rather have on your team? The obvious answer would be Player A. Those BPI's belong to John Olerud, who batted .300 last year. Player B? Chad Hermansen, who batted .207. But the numbers don't always tell you what you think they should...

PLAYER	bb%	ct%	Eye
Player C	5%	92%	0.63
Player D	5%	92%	0.63

You would think that these two players would have put up fairly comparable batting averages. These BPIs certainly do not indicate anything like a 52 point difference in BA, yet Toby Hall (C) batted .258 and Einar Diaz (D) just .206.

The correlation between batting eye and batting average is usually clear, but the percentage play in using this information is not as clear.

Batting Eye	BA	bb%	ct%
1.51 +	.314	15%	90%
1.01 - 1.50	.300	13	87
0.76 - 1.00	.288	11	85
0.51 - 0.75	.278	10	82
0.26 - 0.50	.269	7	81
0.00 - 0.25	.259	4	79

This chart has been a valued part of our analytical arsenal. The data represents the last five years and includes all players who posted at least 300 AB in any year. And the numbers make us feel good — the better the batting eye, the better the batting average. Even the walk and contact rates fall right in line.

But all is not what it seems. The mean values correlate up and down the scale, but the range of values within each group is wider than you could imagine...

Batting Eye	BA	Range
1.51 +	.314	.250-.379
1.01 - 1.50	.300	.215-.372
0.76 - 1.00	.288	.202-.366
0.51 - 0.75	.278	.199-.351
0.26 - 0.50	.269	.192-.347
0.00 - 0.25	.259	.184-.306

Yes, we'd expect there to be outliers, but the fact that there is such a wide range forces us to qualify our expectations. Perhaps we might say, "The higher the batting eye, the greater we can maximize our BA upside and minimize our BA downside." That's what this chart shows.

If I take a hitter with a batting eye of over 1.50, there is virtually no chance that he will bat under .250. If I take a hitter with an eye ratio under 0.25, there is little chance of him hitting over .300. But is that good enough?

This is where we can start trying to use percentage plays. First we need to determine the percentage at which you feel comfortable following the play? Certainly not at 50%. I've bandied the 80% figure around from time to time in other analyses, but most of us would probably venture a percentage play for a bit less. For me, the minimum level that would constitute an acceptable percentage play would be about 66%. If something has at least a two-thirds chance of occurring, I'll take that.

If we apply that 66% percentage play to the above chart, we get smaller ranges. We can now say, there is at least a 66% probability that a player with a certain batting eye will have a batting average within the stated range.

Batting Eye	BA	Range
1.51 +	.314	.297-.372
1.01 - 1.50	.300	.267-.327
0.76 - 1.00	.288	.257-.321
0.51 - 0.75	.278	.253-.304
0.26 - 0.50	.269	.244-.300
0.00 - 0.25	.259	.228-.290

The ranges, however, are still very wide. If I draft a player with a 1.05 eye ratio, there is still a 66% chance that he'll bat under .270. If I draft a player with a 0.45 eye ratio, it is still within the 66% percentage play that he'll put up a .300 season.

And this may be the best that we can expect. For those who took *Intro to Statistics 101* in college, you might recall the use of standard deviations, which measure how confident we are that a data point is within a reasonable range of reality. When it comes to batting average in general, standard deviations state (within a 95% confidence interval) that a true .290 hitter, for instance, could bat anywhere between .254 and .326 in a given year and still be considered a true .290 hitter.

So we may not be able to get away from these wide ranges.

But there is another part of playing percentages. It's called maximizing gains and minimizing risk. We may have to come to terms with the reality that there is a high variability in the BA to Eye relationship, however, we can look to the far ends of the performance spectrum to get a better handle on upside and downside potential.

What are the odds that a player drafted with a 1.25 eye ratio will bat .300? What are the odds that he might bat under .250? Here is where we can gain some more insight...

		Pct who bat	
Batting Eye	BA	.300+	.250-
1.51 +	.314	59%	4%
1.01 - 1.50	.300	51%	9%
0.76 - 1.00	.288	32%	14%
0.51 - 0.75	.278	18%	17%
0.26 - 0.50	.269	14%	26%
0.00 - 0.25	.259	7%	39%

There are no clear 66% winners here, but the spread is worth noting. At the high end — batting eye ratios over 1.5 — you have nearly a 6 in 10 chance at drafting a .300 hitter... *and at the same time,* less than a 1 in 20 chance of having that draft pick post a sub-.250 BA.

Same numbers, different spin... With an eye ratio over 1.5, you are nearly 15 times more likely to end up with a .300 hitter than a .250 hitter. On the low end, with an eye ratio under 0.26, you are over five times more likely to draft a poor hitter than a .300 hitter, and less than a 10% chance overall of drafting the latter.

Of course, in the middle is a vast wasteland of batting averages. Draft someone with an eye ratio between 0.51 and 0.75 and you could get just about anything, and equal chances at a .300 gem or .250 bum. It still makes sense to target higher eye ratios overall because the correlation exists, but the results of our picks will fall in line less often than we had previously expected.

Or, we can just go back to our original conclusion... "The higher the batting eye, the greater we can maximize our BA upside and minimize our BA downside."

At minimum, this set of numbers allows us to get a slightly better handle on a relationship that, up until now, we've almost taken for granted. The percentage play is stronger at the far ends of the batting eye spectrum, but the overall play is still to go after the guys with the better ratio of walks to strikeouts.

Expected Batting Average

by John Burnson

Why does Alfonso Soriano's bat sing? In 2002, Soriano hit .300, yet he walked rarely (23 BB in 719 PA) and struck out repeatedly (157 K). The resulting Batting Eye of 0.15 is usually associated with a batting average that is 50 points below Soriano's. Are we missing something?

In this writer's opinion, yes – or, rather, we are missing a few things, and paying too much mind to another.

To find the truth, we need a model for expected batting average (xBA). At present, our best rule of thumb is to use prior year's BA, but we seek a more instructive guide.

To start with, batting average is a ratio of two variables:

$$\text{BA} = \frac{\text{Hits}}{\text{At-bats}}$$

We can rewrite BA as the product of two other ratios:

$$\text{BA} = \frac{\text{Balls in play}}{\text{At-bats}} \times \frac{\text{Hits}}{\text{Balls in play}}$$

In other words, batting average is the percentage of balls put in play multiplied by the chance that a ball in play falls for a hit. Our motive for breaking up BA in this way is that the first piece is known to us – it's simply contact rate (CT%). A scan of batter's logs indicates that CT% is a steady indicator over a batter's recent past, so it catches our eye as a component of a formula for xBA.

Unlike the first ratio, the second ratio – hits per balls in play – is new. Let's call it hitter's hit rate (H%). Our equation for xBA now looks like this:

$$\text{xBA} = \text{CT\%} * \text{H\%}$$

The next task is to project H%. Roughly speaking, the likelihood of a hit depends on (1) the speed of the ball (so that it can elude the fielders), (2) the distance of the ball (so that it is a long way from first base), and (3) the speed of the batter (so that he can outrun the throw). The first two factors are captured in PX – this is a weighted ratio of doubles, triples, and homers per at-bat. The third factor, the batter's speed, is measured by SX (Speed Score Index), which is an average of four speed-related terms.

With this logic, we arrive at an equation of this form:

$$\text{H\%} = f(\text{PX}, \text{SX})$$

...where f(PX, SX) is a function of PX and SX. Our next step is to define this function. Plots of H% vs. PX and SX indicate that linear models (i.e., equations of the form H% = a * PX + b) can fit both relationships. The relationship is weaker for SX but it is still positive – that is, power matters a lot for BA, speed matters less but it still matters.

Using a linear model for both variables yields this:

$$\text{H\%} = (A * \text{PX}) + (B * \text{SX}) + C$$

...where A, B, and C are all constants. We can use regression analysis to find the values for these constants that best fit the observed hit rates.

Our results for 2002 were consistent with those of years past. Plugging our regression results for H% into our equation, here is the best-fit formula for xBA for 2002:

$$\text{AL: xBA} = \text{CT\%} * [(.00077 * \text{PX}) + (.00005 * \text{SX}) + .245]$$

$$\text{NL: xBA} = \text{CT\%} * [(.00065 * \text{PX}) + (.00012 * \text{SX}) + .252]$$

How does xBA fare? We offer two pieces of evidence. First, in our articles about xBA at Baseball HQ this season, we posted the Top 5 under- and overachievers in BA in each league as of the three-quarters mark of the season. We can now assess these selections:

	AL [--- Through Aug 14 ---]				[-- Rest of year --]		
Player	AB	BA	xBA	Diff	AB	BA	Chng
Lawton	363	.240	.305	+65	53	.208	-32
Fullmer	317	.271	.336	+65	112	.339	+68
Diaz, E	309	.210	.273	+63	[Injured]		
Easley	210	.210	.269	+59	94	.255	+45
Mondesi	428	.231	.290	+59	141	.234	+3
TOTAL		.234				.260	+26
Williams,B	461	.325	.279	-46	151	.358	+33
Martinez,E	191	.309	.261	-48	137	.234	-75
Phelps,J	126	.270	.220	-50	139	.345	+75
Suzuki,I	480	.346	.293	-53	167	.251	-95
Wilson,D	267	.296	.241	-55	92	.293	-3
TOTAL		.320				.296	-24

	NL [--- Through Aug 14 ---]				[-- Rest of year --]		
Player	AB	BA	xBA	Diff	AB	BA	Chng
Perez, E	114	.211	.291	+80	40	.175	-36
Stairs, M	168	.238	.309	+71	102	.255	+17
Brown, A	172	.192	.262	+70	36	.333	+141
Stynes, C	140	.229	.286	+57	55	.273	+44
Grace, M	250	.248	.301	+53	48	.271	+23
TOTAL		.226				.260	+34
Wilson,C	263	.278	.230	-48	105	.229	-49
Castillo,L	466	.311	.261	-50	140	.286	-25
Redmond	192	.328	.275	-53	64	.234	-94
Hernandz,J	398	.274	.217	-57	127	.331	+57
Franco,M	124	.355	.295	-60	81	.259	-96
TOTAL		.301				.275	-26

Our equation correctly predicted the direction of change in BA for 79% of the players. Moreover, the aggregate change for each group was 25 points. The magnitude and consistency of these moves is impressive, especially in light of the small samples and short time frames.

These results show that xBA has utility *within* seasons. What about *across* seasons? Certainly, we expect xBA to be more reliable within a season, because the underlying indicators (CT%, PX, SX) are themselves more stable. Still, the main insight – that BA is a function of those indicators – should aid us in longer-term forecasts as well.

We investigated two pairs of seasons, 2000-2001 and 2001-2002. The findings were nearly identical: Our equation had an overall edge of 55:45 vs. prior year's BA at predicting the following year's BA, and xBA correctly predicted the direction of change in 65% of these cases. When the discrepancy between xBA and prior year's BA was large (at least 30 points), our equation's predictive edge grew to almost 2:1 vs. prior year's BA, and xBA predicted the direction of change in 80% of these cases.

Here are the results for this latter group for 2001-2002 (the better prediction for each player is in bold):

AL	[---- 2001	-----]	2002
	BA	xBA	BA
Batista, T	**.238**	.274	.244
Boone, B	.331	**.294**	.278
Catalanotto, F	.330	**.296**	.269
Clark, T	.287	**.253**	.207
Conine, J	.311	**.267**	.273
Cordova, M	.301	**.269**	.253
Flaherty, J	.238	**.272**	.260
Fryman, T	.263	**.232**	.217
Gibbons, J	**.236**	.283	.247
Grieve, B	**.264**	.222	.251
Hairston Jr., J	.233	**.270**	.268
Hatteberg, S	.245	**.275**	.280
Jimenez, D	.276	**.238**	.252
Magee, W	.213	**.267**	.271
Mayne, B	.285	**.244**	.236
Mientkiewicz, D	.306	**.267**	.261
O'Leary, T	.240	**.270**	.286
Ortiz, D	.234	**.272**	.272
Palmiero, R	**.273**	.308	.273
Posada, J	**.277**	.241	.268
Ramirez, M	**.306**	.268	.349
Thome, J	**.291**	.244	.304

NL	[---- 2001	-----]	2002
	BA	xBA	BA
Alfonzo, E	.243	**.282**	.308
Ausmus, B	.232	**.265**	.257
Barrett, M	**.250**	.280	.263
Berkman, L	.331	**.301**	.292
Blanco, H	**.210**	.248	.204
Bonds, B	.328	**.368**	.370
Cora, A	.217	**.258**	.291
Edmonds, J	**.304**	.266	.311
Giambi, Je	.283	**.252**	.259
Grissom, M	.221	**.253**	.277
Helms, W	.222	**.256**	.243
Houston, T	**.289**	.241	.281
Loretta, M	**.289**	.255	.304
Nevin, P	.306	**.268**	.285
Pierre, J	.327	**.292**	.287
Reese, P	.224	**.255**	.264
Relaford, D	.302	**.266**	.267
Walker, L	**.350**	.305	.338

Both before and during the 2002 season, we would have been better served with xBA than prior year's BA. In the quest for BA, power, speed, and contact rate prevail.

And *now* we can say why Soriano hits better than .250:

(1) He's dang strong.

(2) He's dang fast.

Alfonso Soriano, 2002

BA	PX	SX	CT%	xBA
.300	153	141	77%	.285

Our equation indicates that Soriano *was* batting over his head in 2002, but by only 15 points instead of the 35 points suggested by his Eye ratio. In fact, if Soriano can continue to display these PX and SX numbers, he should keep hitting for a good average.

Eagle-eyed readers might notice something odd about this model: *There is no mention of Batting Eye. This absence is intentional.* Part of the reason was logistical – Batting Eye did not fit neatly into our equation. The larger reason, though, was that we don't know what it means.

It is true that Batting Eye correlates well with batting average. There are two problems with drawing conclusions from this finding. First, *correlation does not mean causation.* Second, even if there is causation, *it could flow either way* – in other words, it could be that a higher BA leads to a higher Batting Eye.

How could this be? The case of Samuel J. Sosa:

Sammy Sosa

	Eye	CT%	PX
1997	0.26	73	144
1998	0.43	73	197
1999	0.46	73	190
2000	0.54	72	178
2001	0.76	73	225

That's a nice progression of Batting Eye, isn't it? Given this improving "Eye," one might think that Sosa would make contact more often at the plate. And yet, Sosa's contact rate hasn't budged. The conclusion is that Sosa is *not* getting more selective. Why, then, is his Eye improving? Could it be simply that a greater proportion of pitches to Sosa are balls? And why would that be?

For one possible answer, note the jumps in Eye from 1997 to 1998, when Sosa's PX shot up 53 points, and again from 2000 to 2001, when his PX shot up 47 points. It's reasonable to surmise that a pitcher will deal more cautiously with a guy with a 225 PX than a guy with a 144 PX. We can't *prove* that Eye rises with PX (rather than the converse), but the steadiness of contact rate in the face of improving "Eye" gives that explanation credence.

Let's look at a hitter who points up a different puzzle:

Brady Anderson

	BB/K	BB%	BA	PX
1997	0.80	12	.288	116
1998	0.96	14	.236	113
1999	0.91	15	.282	114
2000	0.89	15	.257	98
2001	0.78	12	.202	58

In 2001, Brady Anderson had a BA of .202. Given his PX of 58, that result is understandable in light of our model. And yet, he had a walk rate of 12%! Why are pitchers walking a guy who is hitting .202? Could it be that, with the exception of powerhouses like Sosa, pitchers don't tailor their approach to batters? If so, to whose credit (if anyone's) is Anderson's high Eye?

As we say, we are more confused than anything. We believe that we can make a case that a high Batting Eye is a *consequence* of a strong batting average rather than a *cause,* because power drives BA and pitchers respect power. However, there are cases like Brady Anderson's where Batting Eye seems wholly irrespective of power (or anything else). In any event, we do not believe that a low Batting Eye necessarily caps the batting average of Alfonso Soriano or anyone else. You can have the guy who takes a walk; give us the guy who hits with authority.

Fly Ball Tendency and Power

by Mat Olkin

It's damned difficult to hit a ground ball over a fence.

Safe to say *that one won't provoke heated* debate, eh? If you take it one small step further, though, it raises a worthwhile question: Is there a connection between a hitter's ground ball-fly ball tendencies and his power production? More specifically, is there a link between ground-ball/fly-ball ratio and home runs?

Sorry, but I don't have the answer – no definitive answer, anyway. I haven't researched the issue in a way that anyone would call "rigorous" or "scientific." All I'm saying is this: I've looked at the numbers, a lot – enough to think I may have spotted something others have overlooked – and *it seems to me there's something there.*

But I'm not saying there necessarily *is anything there. More exhaustive research may well prove that* there's nothing to it, like the supposed canals on Mars. All I'm saying is it's worth taking a closer look. Otherwise, you run the risk of remaining in the dark. Then you may wake up one day to discover that your planet's network of man-made waterways has been put to shame by your little green neighbors.

Before we get into the nuts and bolts, though, a word on terms. A hit is a hit no matter whose data you use, but ground balls and fly balls are somewhat murkier. First, not all balls in play are scored as either a ground ball or a fly ball, at least under STATS Inc.'s system. Some balls in play fall under neither category (including line drives, bunts and perhaps some others). Plus, there's obviously a certain degree of subjectivity involved in deciding whether to score a medium-arc fly as a line drive or a fly ball.

There also are differences between the ground/fly ratios compiled by different statistical services. The ratios presented by STATS (which appear on *ESPN.com* and in the soon-to-be-defunct *STATS Player Profiles) almost never* agree completely with those put out by the Elias Sports Bureau (which appear in *USA Today Sports Weekly*, formerly *Baseball Weekly*). This may be due to differences in their respective scorers' subjective judgments, and/or the two companies may use different scoring criteria. I don't know, and I don't really care, either. I mention it only to prevent confusion. Either company's numbers are sufficient. The data presented here is STATS' data, just so you know.

Anyway, in looking at the connection between ground/fly ratio and home run power, I've become pretty well convinced of several things:

1. Extreme ground-ball hitters generally do not hit for much power. It is very rare for a hitter with a ground/fly ratio over 1.80 to hit as many as 25 homers in a season. If you take the group of players who *do have good* home run power, you'll find it consists of extreme fly-ball hitters (like Barry Bonds), players whose ground-fly ratio is roughly average (Magglio Ordonez), and some who hit more ground balls than average (Shawn Green). That's as far as it goes, though. It's almost impossible for a hitter with a ground/fly ratio over 1.80 to hit enough fly balls to hit a decent number of homers.

Last year Jacque Jones was something of an exception to that rule. He hit 27 homers, and his ground/fly ratio was 1.86. Consider this, though: He hit only 131 balls that STATS scored as "fly balls." In other words, 21% of his fly balls left the park. The major league home run leader, Alex Rodriguez, hit nearly twice as many fly balls as Jones, but the percentage of his fly balls that left the park was *not dramatically higher (26%).* Conclusion: Jones will have a hard time maintaining his home run output unless he starts hitting more fly balls. And as we said, he's been one of the few exceptions.

Don't take this to mean that a low G/F ratio necessarily guarantees power production, though. Some players, like Jerry Hairston Jr., have no problem getting the ball into the air, but simply lack the strength to reach the fences consistently.

These are the batting-title qualifiers with the most extreme ground/fly ratios last year, along with their home run totals. The highest G/F:

Player	G/F	HR
Luis Castillo	3.39	2
Juan Pierre	3.20	1
Ichiro Suzuki	2.48	8
Rey Ordonez	2.23	1
Derek Jeter	2.23	18

As you can see, the guys who take a slap-and-scoot approach show up at this end of the spectrum.

But wait – didn't Jeter almost reach 25 homers once? Yes, he did, when he hit a career-high 24 in 1999. His G/F that year was 1.63, the lowest of his career. It's been 1.96 or higher every season since, and his home run totals during that time have been 15, 21 and 18.

The lowest G/F ratios last year:

Player	G/F	HR
Frank Thomas	.40	28
Rafael Palmeiro	.48	43
Tony Batista	.54	31
Brian Giles	.58	38
Kevin Young	.60	16

Young had an uninspiring rookie season in 1993, batting .236 with six homers, and didn't reestablish himself until 1997, when he hit 18 homers in 97 games. In hindsight, the only real positive he displayed as a rookie was a low G/F ratio (.82).

2. Most batters' ground/fly ratios stay pretty steady over time. If a guy comes up as a fly-ball hitter, the chances are pretty good that he always will be one, more or less. Most year-to-year changes are small and random, as they are in any other statistical category. A large, sudden change in G/F, on the other hand, can signal a conscious change in plate approach.

Taking #1 and #2 together, what logically follows is:

3. If a guy comes up and has high ground/fly ratios in his first few years, he probably isn't ever going to hit for all that much power.

Based on this, we shouldn't expect too much power growth from guys like Aaron Rowand, Michael Barrett and Milton Bradley, and we've got a reason to think guys like David Ortiz, Junior Spivey and Chris Woodward might show better development than you'd otherwise expect.

4. When a batter's power suddenly jumps, his ground/fly ratio often drops at the same time.

Illustrations:

Aubrey Huff

Yr	G/F	HR
01	2.04	8
02	1.31	23

Aramis Ramirez

Yr	G/F	HR
98	1.17	6
00	1.16	6
01	0.88	34

Randy Winn

Yr	G/F	HR
98	2.89	1
99	2.65	2
00	1.73	1
01	1.91	6
02	1.46	14

Alfonso Soriano

Yr	G/F	HR
01	0.97	18
02	0.78	39

Jeff Kent

Yr	G/F	HR
95	1.05	20
96	1.27	12
97	0.73	29
98	0.70	31

More often, the ratio will stay the same. It almost *never* will go up as power output rises, though — it will either drop or stay the same.

5. Every once in a while, a hitter's ratio will drop significantly even as his power production remains level. In these rare cases, impending power development is likely, since the two factors almost always follow each other closely.

Illustrations:

Carl Everett

Yr	G/F	HR
95	1.65	12
96	2.34	1
97	*1.22*	14
98	1.10	15
99	1.00	*25*
00	0.88	34

Mike Bordick

Yr	G/F	HR
97	1.42	7
98	*1.12*	18
99	1.05	10
00	1.06	*20*

Edgardo Alfonzo

Yr	G/F	HR
95	1.45	4
96	1.23	4
97	1.23	10
98	*0.76*	17
99	0.72	27
00	0.70	25

Richard Hidalgo

Yr	G/F	HR
98	1.15	7
99	0.79	15
00	0.58	44

Luis Gonzalez

Yr	G/F	HR
98	1.02	23
99	1.11	26
00	*0.86*	31
01	0.78	*57*

This one is especially intriguing, for obvious reasons.

A word of warning: The world is always more complex that we'd like it to be. Don't reduce the issue to low-good/high-bad. Certain hitters seem to be more effective when their ratio stays within a certain range; Frank Thomas became a more extreme fly-ball hitter last year, but it certainly didn't seem to help. Gene McCaffrey and John Menna of *Wise Guy Baseball* have even suggested that when a hitter like Luis Castillo or Juan Pierre raises his G/F ratio, that may be a *positive* sign, since players of that type must try to hit the ball on the ground in order to succeed.

One final thought: G/F ratio might even help explain Ben Grieve. When he first came up, he had it all, both from a traditional viewpoint (bloodlines, high draft position, nice left-handed swing) and from a sabermetric angle (youth, power and walks, good performance in the minors).

His first two full big league seasons were very promising, but he stagnated a bit in 2000. At that point, the A's soured on him – which was especially surprising for an organization that rarely fails to appreciate power and walks – and dealt him away. Since then, he's regressed, at the point in his career when he ought to be reaching his peak.

Take a look at his G/F ratios, though. As a rookie, he hit 18 homers, but his ratio was 2.08, disturbingly high for a budding power hitter. The next year, he made good progress in both areas, upping his home run total to 28 while cutting his G/F ratio to 1.42. That marked a huge improvement in his ratio, one of a magnitude rarely seen. That didn't necessarily mean he'd improved it enough, though -- it was still too high for comfort. His future as a power hitter depended on his ability to cut it further, or at the very least prevent it from creeping back up.

It didn't happen. The next year it went back up to 1.51, and he hit one fewer homer. At that point, the A's very well might have decided that Grieve had gone as far as he was going to go, power-wise. I'm not saying they necessarily were watching his G/F ratio *per se,* or that they already had postulated a connection between G/F and power growth. But they probably were well aware that he was hitting far too many ground balls for a hitter of his type. It was kind of hard to miss, especially when he was hitting into a major league-leading 32 ground-ball double plays.

If they thought his power wouldn't develop, the results certainly have vindicated that belief. He hasn't topped 20 homers in either of the two years since he was dealt, and his G/F ratio has ballooned back up above 2.00. So while Grieve seemed to have it all when he first came up, it's fair to say that if we'd looked closer, we might have discovered that he was missing one critical ingredient: an uppercut.

II.
The TOOLS of VICTORY

>At 07:05 AM 10/4/2002 -0400, you wrote:
>Ron, I have been left with a sour taste in my mouth.
>These players even threatening to strike has left me
>questioning whether or not I want to return to
>baseball. Since they set the strike date, I have found
>I just do not give a damn about them anymore. I'm
>seriously questioning whether I want to continue
>playing fantasy baseball.
>
>I have always enjoyed your insight and feel you guys
>have been instrumental in my winning several
>championships. But I'm disillusioned!
>
>Good luck in the future,
>Brian M.
>
>

Brian... I've heard this lament more times than I care to think about, and feel a lot of these same things myself. The one thing that keeps me going is knowing that our fantasy baseball hobby does little to add to MLB's already burgeoning coffers. We can enjoy using their news and numbers, providing ourselves with needed diversion during these troubling times, with little direct benefit to them.

For me, it's like being able to go out and enjoy a Woody Allen movie without having to like him as a person.

Hope you find the spirit again,
Ron

Foundation Philosophies

This is where it all begins.

Forecasting baseball performance is far from an exact science, but it's neither an exercise in crystal ball logic that some people would lead you to believe.

The process might be considered equal parts science, art and perspective. That last element could well be the most important one. As each year passes, it is becoming apparent that the actual numbers don't have much to do with winning at fantasy baseball. The perspective of what the numbers mean and how to use them is what provides the greatest advantage.

That's what this book is all about.

These foundation philosophies are the building blocks to your next championship, whether you play Rotisserie, Scoresheet, Challenge games, or just about any other fantasy format...

Global Forecasting Tenets

There are many misconceptions about the field of forecasting, be it financial forecasting, sales forecasting, baseball forecasting, or even weather forecasting. We need to review some foundation concepts so that we're all starting on a level playing field.

Law of Reality: Forecasting is not an exact science. It is the process of determining likely end results. Nobody can make absolute statements about the future. But, by using forecasting tools, we can draw scientific conclusions as to the most likely outcome of a series of events.

Corollary to the Law of Reality: In any given set of circumstances, the proper course of action is determined by subsequent events.

Law of Baseball Reality: Baseball performance forecasting is inherently a high-risk exercise with a very modest accuracy rate. Any hype of high accuracy rates on traditional statistical measures (HRs, AVG, ERA, etc.) is pure promotional puffery (read: lies). Accuracy rates for raw skill evaluators are higher.

Law of Forecasting Noise: Bad stats mean bad projections. If a gauge like pitching wins is loaded with noise, then the only way to accurately project it is to be able to accurately project every element of that noise. You'd have to project the pitcher's skill, the skills of his supporting offense, defense and bullpen, and the tendencies of his manager. A single win requires the input of *all* those elements, most of which have absolutely nothing to do with pitching skill. So, it's better to focus on statistical categories that measure something more isolated, and thus can be projected with a higher level of accuracy.

Law of Playing Time Forecasting: Playing time projections are an exercise in futility. Beyond the small group of players who have guaranteed jobs each year, that leaves hundreds of others whose roles may or may not be nailed down at any subsequent time. Playing time is the most volatile element of the entire baseball forecasting process, and routinely invalidates hundreds of projections annually.

EDITOR NOTE: Rather than making arbitrary decisions about who will play and who won't, this book focuses on performance. The playing time projections presented here are merely to help you better evaluate each player's talent. To what extent they will be able to use that talent won't be determined until much later.

Law of Perpetuity: Forecasting is a dynamic, cyclical, ongoing process. Conditions are constantly changing and we must react to those changes by adjusting our expectations. A pre-season baseball projection is just an isolated snapshot in time. Once the first batter steps to the plate on Opening Day, that projection has become obsolete. Its value to fantasy leaguers is merely to provide a starting point, a baseline for what is about to occur.

During the season, if a projection appears to have been invalidated by current performance, the process continues. It is then that we need to ask... What went wrong? What conditions have changed? In fact, has *anything* changed? We need to analyze the situation and revise our expectation, if necessary. This process must be ongoing, all year long.

Law of the Process: The outcomes of forecasted events should not be confused with the process itself. Outcomes may be the components that are the most closely scrutinized, but as long as the process is sound, the forecast has done its job.

Corollary to the Law of the Process (The Forecaster's Universal Cop-out): There are no bad forecasts, only bad outcomes.

Component Skills Analysis (CSA)

CSA is one of the foundation concepts of the *Baseball Forecaster*. First introduced in the 1993 edition, it has evolved over time and now has become an accepted — and often imitated — method of evaluating performance.

What is skill? Familiar gauges like home runs and ERA have long been used to measure raw skill. In fact, these gauges only measure the outcome of an individual event, or series of events. They represent statistical output.

Raw skill is the talent beneath the stats, the individual elements of a player's makeup. For batters, skill is the ability to see and follow pitches, the ability to make contact with the ball and the ability to hit with authority. For pitchers, skill is the ability to get the ball over the plate, the ability to fool or dominate hitters and the ability to prevent batted balls from being hit with authority.

Players use these skills to create the individual events that we record using measures like HR and ERA. Why are these events not skills unto themselves? In tracking a batter's home run trend, for instance, what we are really trying to track is his power skills. And power skills are comprised of not only home runs, but *every* event that displays a batter's power — doubles, triples, fly outs, and even long foul balls.

From the perspective of a round bat meeting a round ball, it may be only a fraction of an inch at the point of contact that makes the difference between a homerun or a long foul ball. When a ball is hit safely, often it is only a few inches that separate a HR from a double. Yet we tend to neglect these facts in our analyses, although the outcomes — the doubles, the triples, the long fly balls — may be no less a measure of that batter's raw power skill. Similarly, we must look at the component events that contribute to other raw skills, such as speed and pitching effectiveness.

In order for us to get a better read on raw skill, we use formulas that contain relevant raw statistical categories. Among these are linear weighted power (which includes weighted levels of HRs, doubles, and triples), batting eye, pitching command, and many others.

Why is all this important? Analysts complain about the lack of predictability of many traditional statistical gauges. The reason they find it difficult is that they are trying to project performance using gauges that are loaded with external noise. Raw skills gauges are more pure and follow better defined trends over the course of a player's career.

The next step in CSA is to assemble these peripheral evaluators in such a way that they can provide a more accurate view of performance. By creating a structure, sequence and organization to these gauges, we can paint a picture that can be used to validate our observations, analyze their relevance and project a likely future direction.

As a fantasy leaguer, accurate projections are our ultimate goal. The beauty of CSA is it allows us to identify variances between statistical output and raw skill gauges, and from that, project changes in performance within a season or from one season to another. How it works...

In a perfect world, if a player's raw skills improve, then so should his statistical output. If his skills decline, then his stats should follow suit as well. Well, sometimes a player's skill may increase while the traditional stat category we use to measure that skill may decline. These variances may be due to a variety of factors, from the performances of other players on his team to the random impact of luck.

CSA is based on the philosophy that events tend to move towards universal order. This has been proven in other areas of baseball analysis... Players' performance tends to move towards their career averages, team Won/Loss records tend to move towards their statistical levels. CSA states that these variances will correct themselves over time. Statistical levels will eventually approach their associated raw skill levels. And from this, we can identify players whose performance may change.

A batter whose HR output drops while his batting eye ratio and linear weighted power level increases has a high probability of improving his future HR output. A pitcher whose ERA improves while his command ratio and strikeout rate fall off is a good bet to see a spike in his ERA.

Skills Ownership

Once a player displays a skill, he owns it. That display could occur at any time... earlier in his career, back in the minors, or even in winter ball play. And while that skill may lie dormant after its initial display, the potential is always there for him to tap back into that skill at some point, barring injury or age. That dormant skill can reappear at any time given the right set of circumstances.

Caveats...

1. The initial display of skill must have occurred over an extended period of time. An isolated 1-hit shut-out in Single-A ball amidst a 5.00 ERA season is not enough. The shorter the display of skill in the past, the more likely it can be attributed to random chance. The longer the display, the more likely that any re-emergence of that skill is for real. Typically, you'd want to see a consistent level of performance over at least a several month period.
2. Once a player displays a vulnerability or skills deficiency, he owns that as well. That vulnerability could be an old injury problem, an inability to hit breaking pitches, or just a tendency to go into prolonged slumps.
3. The probability of a player addressing and correcting a skills deficiency declines with each year that deficiency continues to exist.

Completeness of Information

Nearly all baseball publications separate a player's statistical experiences in the major leagues from the minor leagues. While this may be an appropriate approach for the sake of official record-keeping, it is not an accurate measure of a player's complete performance for the year.

Bill James has proven that minor league statistics, at Double-A level or above, are accurate indicators of future potential. If we can agree that this is true, then we should be including them in the pool of historical data.

By limiting an analysis of a player's performance trends to major league numbers only, we ignore a wealth of valuable data. This data adds more depth to a player's historical trends, especially those with limited major league experience. So we include major league equivalencies as a part of each batter's and pitcher's yearly stats in this book..

The Forecaster's Scientific Method

This is a process for accumulating and using information. It requires us to be able to distinguish between important data and noise, and to integrate everything we read, see and hear into a cohesive plan of attack. Stray at any of the following steps, and you put your efforts — and fantasy team — in danger.

1. Employ the correct quantitative perspective. The language of fantasy baseball is numbers, however the particular numbers used by most games are faulty. They are neither accurate measures of skill nor can be projected for the future. So we are forced to find a balance between the numbers we play with and the numbers that have relevance.

We do this by using the traditional gauges as a benchmark but to be aware of the underlying raw skills indicators. And never get married to any fixed set of numbers.

2. Create preliminary projections that are based on general tendencies, not hard numbers. It is a waste of time to create a projections model that states how many HRs each player will hit and every pitcher's ERA. The reason is that there are so many variables impacting a single projection as to render its accuracy moot.

In this book, we do provide hard numbers, but these are merely to provide a performance baseline. From here, what we need to do is create a general expectation about future performance. The questions we need to ask, in order, are:

- Do the BPI's support the player's current level of production?
- Does a trend in the BPI's point to an increase or decrease in his levels?
- Are several BPI's in agreement about the direction, or is there conflict?
- Are there other variables that may influence a player's future statistical output?

3. Get a handle on the world in which these numbers live. News is the lifeblood in which we assemble and run our teams, but most everything we read in the media is faulty. News information is comprised of other people's opinions... a manager who believes that a certain player has what it takes to be a regular, a scout whose observation is that a player has potential, a team physician whose diagnosis is that a player is healthy enough to play. These words from experts have some element of truth, especially in reference to current events, but cannot be wholly relied upon to provide an accurate expectation of future events.

The truth is that the news we rely on is really only part news and the rest noise. Our biggest challenge is to be able to distinguish between the two, so you need to develop an appropriate cynicism for what you read.

Four areas to be keenly aware of:

a. Full, prompt disclosure is something that is essentially non-existent. We will never know the entire truth. Players, management and the media have absolute control over what we are allowed to know. And so, as long as we do not know all the variables, we cannot dismiss the possibility that any one variable does exist... no matter how outrageous it seems, no matter how often the media assures it, deplores it, or ignores it. So, if a player is struggling for no apparent reason, and there are complete denials about health issues, don't dismiss the possibility that an injury does, in fact, exist. Hear that, Jason Kendall??

b. Fluidity of decision-making: Nothing lasts forever in major league baseball. In fact, everything lasts for a shorter time than you can possibly imagine.

The term, "firm decision," is an oxymoron. One decision begets a series of events that leads to another decision. And then another. Any reported action that could easily be reversed based on subsequent events is mostly noise (e.g. a rookie being handed a starting role prior to spring training, etc.). Decisions made in spring training are more benched in reality, but still faulty. If a player looks good in 75 ABs or 15 IP against a mixture of major and minor league competition, is that really an accurate barometer of future major league success? For some managers, that's more than enough. Until, of course, the first 0 for 14 slump.

c. Medical reporting: Much of the prognosis reporting that goes on is pure speculation. Every player's ability to rehab from an injury is different. 15-day disabled list stays last 15 days only about half the time. Plus, ballclubs routinely refrain from reporting all information for fear that any perception of serious injury will significantly reduce a player's marketplace value. Player agents also have a say in what information gets leaked out about their players.

d. Direct quotes: Statements from players, scouts, coaches, managers and national columnists provide little more than isolated opinion and virtually no meaningful information. Always question whether there could be a hidden motive for someone making a particular statement. You'll be amazed at how noisy things can get.

We need the media to provide us with context for our statistical analyses, and the *real* news they provide is valuable intelligence. But separating the news from the noise is difficult. In most cases, the only thing you can trust is how that player actually performs.

4. Integrate your information. Start with each player's general performance tendencies. Look at leading indicators and trends, and form a preliminary conclusion about the likely direction a player's performance may take. Then appropriately evaluate the news information. Use the validated news information in concert with your preliminary performance expectations to determine which expectations are real, could be prone to change, or invalid.

5. Develop a set of performance expectations. Real performance forecasting is a process of looking at a set of leading indicator statistics, integrating them with validated news information, and drawing educated conclusions. It is a living, breathing process that generates a set of general expectations. Statistical projections, by themselves, are canned, inert numbers with little value. You need to look beyond these raw numbers. That includes the projections provided in this book.

The power of the process is to be able to work within ranges of expectation. A fixed performance forecast might say a player will hit 25 HRs, but more valuable information would be a projection that says a player has "developing power skills and could hit 15-25% more home runs than in the previous year." This approach provides far more flexibility in drafting and managing your fantasy teams.

Forecaster's Toolbox

Over time, baseball analysts have amassed a large pool of research to help us understand how and why a player's performance changes from one year to another. The baseball prognosticating process, which relies on this research, has evolved into one where the best success can often be found by learning to play the percentages. This critical intelligence does not provide absolutes, but strong tendencies that we can use in evaluating talent.

The following tools, rules and findings represent the work of many authors. Much of our own research is here. There are findings of other baseball analysts. Bill James was the founding father of the seeds of this research, and many of his findings appear as well.

There are two types of information here. There are analytical tools, which are methods to put events and performances into some type of context. And there are actual research results. Generally, we only include the results of each particular piece of research, rather than take up space with all the methodologies and minutia. The back-up data has appeared in our other publications and on BaseballHQ.com in the past. Our purpose here is to give you the tools you need to make evaluations, and quickly. So pardon the lack of support data. Rest assured we're not making this stuff up.

Also remember that, since these research findings represent tendencies, not absolutes, they will occasionally be wrong. If we tell you that 96% of batters with eye ratios under 0.50 will not hit .300, don't send us hate mail if the spray hitter you passed on in the draft falls into the other 4%. It happens. It's not our fault. Consider this a universal disclaimer.

But beyond that, there is great value here. Consider this your own personal analytical arsenal. Use it to figure out why players perform how they do. Use it to help project what players might do in the future. Use it to help explain deviations from those expectations.

And use it to gain some perspective.

The Baker's Dozen

This is a list of criteria that helps us analyze changes in a player's performance. Often, when a player puts up numbers that vary from expectation, it is this Baker's Dozen that can help us determine whether the surprise is for real or a fluke.

1. The player's age... Is he at the stage of development when we might expect a change in performance?

2. Health status... Is he coming off an injury, reconditioned and healthy for the first time in years, or a habitual resident of the disabled list?

3. Minor league performance... Has he ever shown the potential for greater things at some level of the minors? Or does his minor league history show a poor skill set that might indicate a potential relapse?

4. Historical trends... Have his raw skill levels been on an upswing or downswing?

5. Hidden indicators within traditional stats... Looking beyond batting averages and ERAs, what do his support ratios look like?

6. Change in ballpark, team, league... Pitchers going to Colorado will see their ERA spike. Pitchers going to Shea Stadium will see their ERA improve. Stuff like that.

7. Change in team performance... Has a player's performance been affected by overall team chemistry or the environment fostered by a winning or losing club?

8. Change in batting stance, pitching style... Has a change in performance been due to an adjustment made during the off-season?

9. Change in usage, lineup position, etc.... Has a change in RBI opportunities been a result of moving further up or down in the batting order? Has pitching effectiveness been impacted by moving from the bullpen to the rotation?

10. Change in managerial strategy (opportunity)... Does his sudden change in performance have less to do with ability than with playing time, or perhaps not having a well-defined role?

11. Coaching effects... Has the coaching staff changed the way a player approaches his conditioning, or how he approaches the game itself?

12. Off-season activity... Has a player spent the winter frequenting workout rooms or banquet tables?

13. Personal factors... Has the player undergone a family crisis? Experienced spiritual rebirth? Given up red meat?

Using the Baker's Dozen to Analyze Surprises

By looking at each of the criteria in the Baker's Dozen, we can categorize unexpected performances. There are seven categories:

1. Career year: These are players who have established a certain level of performance over several years, then suddenly put up exceptional numbers. Career years may be explained from the list of criteria, but are usually one-shot deals.

2. Maturation: These players have also established a certain level of performance over time, but the performance spike is truly indicative of their potential and will likely be maintained.

3. Off year: These are players who have established a certain level of performance over several years, then suddenly drop off. This could be a performance blip, an adjustment period or an injury-induced decline. These players have the potential to bounce back.

4. Comedown: These players have also established a certain level of performance over time, but their performance drop is indicative of a new level at which they will likely plateau. The typical thirtysomething syndrome.

5. Opportunity: Sometimes a surprise isn't a change in performance at all but the effect a change in playing time has on performance. Often, a solid role player gets thrust into a full-time job and suddenly puts up extraordinary numbers. This can work both ways — a player may rise to the occasion, or find that the regular day-to-day grind has an adverse effect on his numbers. Opportunity surprises are created by events like injuries or changes in managerial strategy and can last as long as the opportunity lasts.

6. No surprise: We sometimes form unrealistic expectations about certain players due to media hype or short-term performance levels. Rookies fall into this category, for instance, but the failure of unproven commodities should not be unexpected. In addition, frequently injured players who've lowered our expectations, then bounce back to previous productivity levels when healthy, should not be surprises either (except, perhaps, that they managed to stay healthy).

7. Aberration: These are the performances that simply cannot be adequately explained by the Baker's Dozen. Chance occurrences do happen, and sometimes in bunches. There are stretches in a player's career when a spray hitter might see a few week's worth of fat, juicy homer balls, or a pitcher might face a string of wiffle bats. It just happens, then it stops. Most times, it will never happen again.

Using the Baker's Dozen to Assess Forecast Risk

While forecasts are constructed with the best possible data available, there are many factors that can impact a player exceeding or falling short of expectation. One of the ways we deal with this is to assign each of our projections a risk level. The less certainty we can see in a data set, the higher the forecast risk.

The Baker's Dozen impacts how confident we are about any set of numbers. Using this list as a starting point, we can identify several variables that must be considered in evaluating the riskiness of any player's forecast.

1. Is he a batter or a pitcher? As pitchers' traditional stats tend toward marked fluctuations, projections of those stats would have to be considered higher risk.

2. Is he a rookie or veteran? The greater the pool of major league history to draw from, the greater our ability to construct a viable forecast. Length of service is important, as is length of consistent service. So players who bounce up and down from the majors to the minors are higher risk players. And rookies are all high risk.

3. Is his performance history consistent or erratic? Naturally, consistent performers are easier to project and garner lower risk levels. Players that mix mediocrity, or worse, with occasional flashes of brilliance generate higher risk projections.

4. Is he injury prone or generally healthy? Players with a history of health problems — whether or not they are healthy right now — will generate higher risk projections.

5. Is his role or usage stable or unstable? Any change in a player's role or usage will increase the risk of his projection being off. These changes could include a move from the bullpen into the rotation, a move to another position in the batting order, or the move from full-timer to a platoon role.

6. Is the manager's strategies and tendencies consistent or inconsistent? Tougher to nail down, but important in considering risk. There are many unstable bullpen situations each year which make projecting saves a difficult task. Similarly, a speedster not knowing whether he will be at the top or middle of a lineup will impact his projected stolen base opportunities.

7. Is the player's environment stable or changing? Any player who has recently switched uniforms or has a history of frequent moves to different teams, or leagues, drops a notch in forecast confidence level.

The player forecast boxes evaluate these criteria for each player and assign them a risk rating. The scale we use is Very Low, Low, Moderate, High, Very High and X HIGH (Extremely High). You may be surprised at the paucity of lower risk players, but that is the reality of forecasting performance. It is inherently a high-risk game.

As a fantasy leaguer, you have to determine just how much risk you are willing to take on draft day and during the season. Do you go high risk/high payoff or do you play it conservative with all low risk picks? It really has to be a mix, but how much of a mix is up to you.

It often depends on the type of league you're in. Leagues that allow limited player movement require a more conservative approach. Unfortunately, it is a double-edged sword because fantasy league titles are often won with sleepers — those high risk picks. So, you have to carefully minimize your risk, perhaps by taking chances with some higher risk batters and sticking to low risk pitchers.

Batting Toolbox

Batting Eye as a Leading Indicator

The raw ability to distinguish between balls and strikes — strike zone judgment — is a good descriptor of a batter's potential batting average, and in some cases, can be used as a predictor of future performance. Research findings:

1. There is a high correlation between a batter's eye ratio and his batting average.

	Batting Average				
Batting Eye	**1998**	**1999**	**2000**	**2001**	**2002**
0.00 - 0.25	.251	.257	.253	.240	.251
0.26 - 0.50	.261	.269	.268	.257	.254
0.51 - 0.75	.271	.277	.273	.264	.266
0.76 - 1.00	.283	.283	.289	.277	.282
1.01 and over	.292	.299	.306	.304	.293

2. Any batter with an eye ratio over 1.50 has about a 4% chance of hitting under .250 over 500 at bats.

3. Of all .300 hitters, those with ratios of at least 1.00 have a 65% chance of repeating as .300 hitters. Those with ratios under 1.00 have less than a 50% chance of repeating.

4. Sub-.250 batters with eye ratios under 1.00 are not likely to mature into .300 hitters the following year. Only 12% of those with ratios between 0.50 and 0.99, and only 4% of those with ratios under 0.50 will hit .300 in year #2.

5. Batters with eye ratios under 0.50 are a high risk group. They may hit over .300 at some point in their careers (some batters can hack their way to anything), but pitchers eventually figure out that they do not have to give these free-swingers anything good to hit. At that point, it takes a large scale adjustment on the part of the batter to return to the .300 plateau.

In a study covering 1995-2000, there were only 37 batters that had hit .300 or better with an eye ratio of 0.50 or less over at least 300 AB in a single season. Of this group, 30% exhibited the unique ability to accomplish this feat on a consistent basis. For the other 70%, a .300-plus BA and sub-0.50 eye ratio was a short-term aberration.

Contact Rate as a Leading Indicator

It follows intuitively that the more often a batter makes contact with the ball, the higher the likelihood that he will hit safely. Not rocket science here, but good to see that the numbers do typically bear this out. This past year was a bit of an anomaly at the high end, however.

	Batting Average		
Contact Rate	2000	2001	2002
0% - 60%	.143	.170	.185
61% - 65%	.212	.228	.233
66% - 70%	.250	.233	.242
71% - 75%	.262	.255	.247
76% - 80%	.263	.259	.261
81% - 85%	.275	.277	.268
86% - 90%	.293	.278	.279
Over 90%	.294	.291	.272

Batting Eye and Power

We often ignore the batting eye ratio when evaluating power because so many batters achieve their lofty HR numbers by opening up their swing, thereby increasing their strikeout totals and depressing their eye ratio. However, this path to power success is a riskier one.

During the four-year study period, any batter who slammed 30 HRs in a season had less than a 3 in 10 chance of improving his power skills in the following year. But by adding in the eye ratios of each batter, the power decline can be better defined...

	YEAR 2	
Batting eye	PX increased	PX declined
Less than 0.50	13%	87%
0.50 - 0.99	24%	76%
1.00 and over	31%	69%

Batters with lower eye ratios were more likely to experience a power drop-off in the year following a 30-HR campaign. We can use this information to our advantage when tracking a batter's power trends from year to year. Here are the various scenarios and explanations:

Power increases and batting eye increases: This is the most favorable scenario. The batter is seeing the ball better, exhibiting improved plate discipline, and the end result is an improvement in his power skills. These power surges are often long-term.

Power increases and batting eye decreases: The most likely scenario when a batter displays a spike in power. He opens up his swing and begins to drive the ball, the fallout often being an increase in strikeouts and a drop in batting average. The danger is that opposing pitchers often figure out that they do not have to give him anything good to hit. These batters are prone to prolonged streaks and slumps.

Power decreases and batting eye increases: This scenario occurs when a batter is trying to become more selective at the plate, often in response to a slump. In most cases, the power outage is short-term and the skills eventually return.

Power decreases and batting eye decreases: The least favorable scenario. The batter is slumping, but rather than working on being more selective at the plate, he begins to press, chase bad pitches, and the slump deepens. Large chunks of seasons can be lost when this scenario occurs.

Power Breakouts

It is not an easy task to predict which batters are going to put up an extraordinary power season. What we can do is categorize these power breakouts:

1. Increase in playing time. An unexpected increase in HR output might not be a product of any change in skills but the direct result of an increase in playing time, which may be expected or unexpected.

2. History of power skills. A player may have displayed power skills sometime in the past, be it in his early major league career or prior. (Once a player displays a skill, he owns it.)

3. Distribution of extra base hits. There is not much difference in skill between a double and a HR. A HR breakout may merely be a random redistribution of already demonstrated extra base hit power.

4. Normal skills growth. The power spike may be a normal occurrence along a batter's growth curve. A batter's breakout year may have been easily predicted from a review of his power index (PX) trend.

5. Situational breakouts. No matter how impressive the homer-hitting feats of a player like Vinny Castilla have been in the past, the fact that he played half his games in Coors Field discounted any true spike in power skills (even more noted since his departure from thin air). Similar for any player moving into a more power-conducive venue, or moving *out* of a pitcher-friendly venue.

6. Fly ball tendency. Early research shows that a batter who increases his fly ball tendency may be trackable as a potential surger in power output.

7. The unexplained. Sometimes, a power spike makes no logical sense — Brady Anderson hitting 50 HRs, for instance. These power surges hold the lowest probability for a comparable follow-up performance.

Handedness Notes

1. While pure southpaws account for about 27% of total ABs (RHers about 55% and switch-hitters about 18%), they hit 31% of the triples and take 30% of the walks.

2. The average lefty posts a batting average about 10 points higher than the average RHer. The on base averages of pure LHers are nearly 20 points higher than RHers, but only 10 points higher than switch-hitters.

3. LHers tend to have a better batting eye ratio than RHers, but about the same as switch-hitters.

4. Pure righties and lefties have virtually identical power skills. Switch-hitters, however, tend to have less power, on average.

5. Switch-hitters tend to have the best speed, followed by LHers, and then RHers.

6. On an overall production basis, LHers have about an 8% advantage over RHers and about a 14% edge over switch-hitters.

Batting Average Perception

Early season batting average strugglers who surge later in the year get no respect because they have to live with the weight of their early numbers all season long. Conversely, quick starters who fade late get far more accolades than they deserve.

For instance, take Moises Alou's 2002 month by month batting averages. Perception, which is typically based purely on a player's cumulative season level, was that he had a terrible year. Reality is different. How many people knew he batted over .300 in three of the six months, and .304 from June 1 on?

Month	BA	Cum BA
April	.133	.133
May	.211	.192
June	.316	.247
July	.259	.250
August	.318	.268
September	.314	.275

League Switching

Since the AL is a breaking ball league, right-handed NL hitters coming over to the AL tend to struggle at first until they adjust. Some never do.

AL free-swingers often have a difficult time when coming over to the NL and being fed a steady diet of fastballs.

Optimal Ages

Players develop at different paces, but in general terms, age can be helpful to determine where they should be along the developmental curve. From Bill James' research it has been accepted that batters tend to peak at about age 27. But further research has helped to refine these tendencies.

"26 With Experience" *(John Benson):* While batters may peak at about age 27, the players most likely to exhibit the most dramatic spike in performance are those aged 26 who have several years of major league experience.

Power: Batting power skills tend to grow consistently between ages 24 and 29. Many batters experience a power peak at about age 30-31. Catchers often experience a power spike in the mid-30's.

Speed: Baserunning and speed are skills of the young. When given the choice of two speedsters of fairly equivalent abilities and opportunity, always go after the younger one. A sharp drop-off in speed skills typically occurs at age 34.

Batting eye: For batters who continue to play into their 30's, this is a skill that can develop and grow throughout their career. A decline in this level, which can occur at any age, often indicates a decline in overall skills.

Point of No Return: Unproven batters will not likely experience a performance spike after age 28. Much of this has to do with opportunity.

Thirtysomethings *(Ed Spaulding)*: Batters tend to lose points on their batting average, steal fewer bases (and with a lower success rate) and draw more walks. While players on the outside of the defensive spectrum (1B, 3B, LF, RF, DH) often have their best seasons in their 30's, players in the middle (2B, SS, CF) tend to fade. Many former stars move to new positions (Ripken, Molitor, Banks, etc.).

Catchers *(Ed Spaulding)*: Many catchers — particularly second line catchers — have their best seasons late in their careers. Some possible reasons why:

1. Catchers, like shortstops, often get to the big leagues for defensive reasons and not their offensive skills. These skills take longer to develop.

2. The heavy emphasis on learning the catching/defense/pitching side of the game detracts from their time to learn about, and practice, hitting.

3. Injuries often curtail their ability to show offensive skills, though these injuries (typically jammed fingers, bruises on the arms, rib injuries from collisions) often don't lead to time on the disabled list.

4. The time spent behind the plate has to impact the ability to recognize, and eventually hit, all kinds of pitches.

September Performance Declines *(Harold Brooks)*

Overall, batting average (-.002), on base average (-.002) and slugging average (-.006) decline after the end of August. Those who play every day of the season are more prone to decline. Throwing infielders (2B, 3B, SS) appear to suffer more than outfielders. As little as five days off during the season alleviates any of the problems in September, and with 10 days off, the chances of a September fade are very small.

Park elevations

On average, the higher the elevation of the ballpark, the higher the run and HR production — regardless of any other park dimension or characteristic. The following chart includes all major and minor league ballparks (1995):

		FACTOR	
Elevation	**Mean**	**Run**	**HR**
Over 2000 ft.	3418	120	125
750-1999 ft.	951	102	107
100-750 ft.	463	99	97
Under 100 ft.	42	93	94

Pitching Toolbox

The Global Fallacy

"There's no way to project pitchers accurately from year to year." — Bill James.

"Your most valuable commodity is a starting pitcher you can count on. The only problem is, you can't count on any of them." — Peter Golenbock

"Where else in the realm of fantasy sports can you have worse odds on success than from the wonderful world of the pitcher?" — Rod Beaton

"Starting pitchers are the most unreliable, unpredictable, unpleasant group of people in the world, statistically speaking that is." — John Benson

"No one, not the most astute major league scout nor the world's top number cruncher, can correctly project the statistical output of more than a couple of dozen of the game's 400 hurlers." — Steve Mann

While it's difficult to argue with the collective wisdom of these top baseball writers, their perception is tainted. Unreliable pitching performance is a fallacy driven by the practice of attempting to project performance using pitching gauges that are poor evaluators of talent.

In the *1991 Baseball Sabermetric*, Phil Birnbaum wrote an essay on the perception of pitching inconsistency from year to year. He showed how small changes in batting statistics were equivalent to large changes in pitching stats, and how pitching numbers are heavily influenced by the supporting offense, defense, bullpen and random chance.

Birnbaum showed a player's batting line for two different years. In the first, this player hit .237 with 11 HRs and 52 RBIs. The second year he hit .264 with 15 HRs and 65 RBIs. Birnbaum notes, "you notice the improvement but you recognize that this is the same player; in fact, you might think these are pretty similar seasons." Yet, if these two lines represented the stats allowed by a pitcher, the first would have equated to an ERA of 3.29, the second, 4.55.

Birnbaum concludes that, although a pitcher's statistics tend to show great inconsistencies from year to year, his talent does not fluctuate any more than a batter's does.

Fundamental Skills and Base Performance Indicators

How can we better evaluate pitching talent? There are three statistical categories generally unaffected by external factors. These three categories capture the outcome of an individual at bat that is solely the result of a pitcher versus batter match-up. A good or bad offense, defense or bullpen have no effect on these three stats.

Walks Allowed
Strikeouts
Homeruns Allowed

Even with only three stats to look at, there is a wealth of insight that these measures can provide. In fact, these three stats alone can measure several fundamental pitching skills.

The first skill is a pitcher's ability to get the ball over the plate. By looking at his ratio of strikeouts to walks (K/BB), his Command Ratio, we can get a fairly accurate picture of whether he has good command or is wild and hittable.

Another fundamental skill is a pitcher's ability to dominate hitters. Keeping batters off-stride and getting them to swing through pitches is another quality that breeds success. We look at a pitcher's Dominance Rate (K/9 IP).

The third fundamental skill is a pitcher's ability to keep the ball in the park. In today's game of rising power, this fundamental skill is becoming more and more important. We look at a pitcher's Homerun Rate (HR/9 IP).

These three fundamental skills are the core components of the Base Performance Value (BPV) gauge (see the Glossary for a complete description). BPV also includes one more skill — the pitcher's ability to prevent hits. However, since this skill is impacted by the defense's ability to reach and successfully field the balls hit to them, and not entirely a measure of pure pitching skill, its role in the BPV formula is only as an adjustment measure.

Using BPV is a much better way to track skills trends over time. BPV values do not fluctuate as wildly from year to year, and provide an excellent leading indicator to changes in a pitcher's traditional stat categories, like ERA.

Command Ratio as a Leading Indicator

The raw ability to get the ball over the plate — command of the strike zone — is one of the best leading indicators for future pitching performance. The command ratio (K/BB) can be used to project future potential in earned run average and other skills gauges as well.

In general, pitchers who maintain a command ratio of 2.5 have a high probability of long-term success. For fantasy drafting purposes, it is best to avoid pitchers with ratios of less than 2.0. Bullpen closers should be avoided if they have a command ratio under 2.5.

Research indicates that there is a high correlation between a pitcher's command ratio and his ERA (minimum 30 IP).

	Earned Run Average				
Command	**1998**	**1999**	**2000**	**2001**	**2002**
0.0 - 1.0	5.80	5.99	6.11	6.84	6.05
1.1 - 1.5	5.17	4.97	5.04	5.02	4.79
1.6 - 2.0	4.58	4.56	4.59	4.63	4.59
2.1 - 2.5	4.13	3.95	4.23	4.22	3.98
2.6 - 3.0	4.09	4.08	4.19	4.07	3.60
3.1 and over	3.41	3.46	3.54	3.45	3.15

Research also suggests that there is a strong correlation between a pitcher's command ratio and his propensity to win ballgames. Some results from a recent study:

Overall, pitchers with better command do tend to win more games. Over three quarters of those with ratios over 3.0 posted winning records and the collective W/L record of those command artists was nearly .600.

The command/winning correlation held up in both leagues, although the effect was much more pronounced in the NL. Over four times more NL hurlers than AL hurlers had command ratios over 3.0, and it appears that higher command ratios are required in the NL to maintain good winning percentages. While a ratio between 2.0 and 2.9 might be good enough for a winning record for over 70% of AL pitchers, that level of command in the NL will generate an above-.500 mark only slightly more than half the time.

In short, in order to have at least a 70% chance of drafting a pitcher with a winning record, you must target NL pitchers with at least a 3.0 command ratio. To achieve the same odds in the AL, a 2.0 command ratio will suffice.

Good Command versus Bad Command

While we can maximize our chances for assembling a good pitching staff by targeting pitchers with good command, we still have to be a little bit careful.

There are some pitchers that have excellent command, but still fare poorly. These pitchers are typically hard-throwers, but who have little movement on their pitches. Batters find that they don't need to wait on pitches and can usually make contact a high percentage of the time. The end result is a depressed control ratio (fewer walks allowed as batters make more contact) which, in turn, artificially pumps up a pitcher's command ratio. Poor opposition batting averages, and often poor strand rates also result.

These pitchers may still have good upside potential, especially those whose strikeout rates remain high. However, their development may be slower than other comparable pitchers, and their year-to-year consistency may be low. As such, their risk to you will be somewhat greater.

Strand Rates as a Leading Indicator

Strand Rate finds great utility in explaining variances between a pitcher's ERA and his performance indicators.

Pitchers with strand rates over 80% almost always have exemplary ERAs. Starters and middle relievers who post this level in a given season have an 80% likelihood of watching their ERA rise in the following year. Bullpen short relievers who post an 80% strand rate have a 50% chance of repeating at that level in the following season.

Pitchers with strand rates under 65% almost always have inflated ERAs, but have an 89% likelihood of watching their ERA improve in the following year. In addition, 83% will improve their ERA by more than one run.

Pitching and Defense *(Voros McCracken)*

In 2000, Voros McCracken published a study that concluded that "there is little if any difference among major league pitchers in their ability to prevent hits on balls hit in the field of play."

His assertion was that, while a Randy Johnson would have a better ability to prevent a batter from getting wood on a ball, or perhaps keeping the ball in the park, once that ball was hit in the field of play, the probability of it falling for a hit was virtually no different than for any other pitcher.

Among the findings in his study were:

1. There is little correlation between what a pitcher does one year in the stat and what he will do the next. This is not true with other significant stats (BB, K, HR).
2. You can better predict a pitcher's hits per balls in play from the rate of the rest of the pitcher's team than from the pitcher's own rate.

This last point brings a team's defense into the picture. It begs the question, when a batter gets a hit, is it because the pitcher made a bad pitch, the batter took a good swing, or the defense was not positioned correctly to field it? McCracken's findings take the onus away from the pitcher and put it on the shoulders of the batter and defense. The pitcher's role in the entire event is insignificant.

Pitchers will often post hit rates per balls in play (H%) that are far off from the league average, but then revert to the mean the following year. As such, we can use it in much the same way we use strand rate to project the direction of a pitcher's ERA. For instance, if a pitcher with an elevated H% (indicating that more hits are falling than normal) and a depressed strand rate (indicating that baserunners were scoring more often than normal), random chance could reverse both of these occurrences. One could then conclude that this pitcher's ERA would likely improve.

This is not the final say on the matter. McCracken's research is controversial and has raised some flags in the sabermetric community. However, it is intriguing, and a scan through the player boxes does reveal many cases that support his conclusions.

Projecting Wins

Using regression analyses, we can rank the importance of the variables that impact pitching win totals. In order:

1. Team offense (run support)
2. Pitching Effectiveness (base performance value)
3. Run Prevention (strand rate)
4. Bullpen support (inherited runners stranded %)
5. Managerial Tendencies (quick hooks/slow hooks)
6. Team Defense (fielding percentage)

As such, when a fantasy player needs to draft or beef up in the win category, the most prudent approach is always to target teams with good offensive support before looking at pitching performance data.

Optimal Ages

As with batters, pitchers develop at different rates, but in general terms, a look at their age can be helpful to determine where they should be along the developmental curve. From Bill James' research it has been accepted that pitchers tend to peak at about age 30. But further research has helped to refine these tendencies.

While peaks vary, most all pitchers (who are still around) tend to experience a sharp drop-off in their skills at age 38.

Starting pitchers *(Rick Wilton)*: Their first productive season in the majors (10 wins, 150 IP, sub-4.00 ERA) is at age 25 or 26. Starters who experience a career year after age 31 are far less likely to repeat that performance than those who achieve their career year at a younger age.

Relief aces *(Rick Wilton)*: Their first 20-save season arrives at about age 26. About three of every four relievers who begin a run of 20-save seasons in their 20's will likely sustain that level for about four years, with their value beginning to decline at the beginning of the third year.

Many aces achieve a certain level of maturity in their 30's and can experience a run of 20-save seasons between ages 33 and 36. For some, this may be their first time in the role of bullpen closer. However, those who achieve their first 20-save season after age 34 are unlikely to repeat.

Thirtysomethings *(Ed Spaulding)*: Older pitchers, as they lose velocity and movement on the ball, must rely on more variety and better location. Thus, if strikeouts are a priority, you don't want many pitchers over 30. The over-30 set that tends to be surprising includes finesse types (Morgan, Moyer), career minor leaguers who break through for 2-3 seasons, often in relief (Telford, Vosberg, Shaw), and knuckleballers (a young knuckleballer is 31).

Career Year Drop-off *(Rick Wilton)*

Research shows that a pitcher's post-career year drop-off, on average, looks like this...

- ERA increases by 1.00
- WHIP increases by 0.14.
- Nearly 6 fewer wins

Usage Warning Flags

Research evidence suggests that there is a finite number of innings in a pitcher's arm. This number varies by pitcher, by development cycle, and by pitching style and repertoire. There are several gauges we can use to measure a pitcher's potential for future arm problems and/or reduced effectiveness. When this occurs in pitchers under the age of 28, we call it "early burnout."

One gauge we can use is simply a year-to-year tracking of innings pitched levels. Sharp increases in usage from one year to the next, such as when a pitcher moves from the bullpen to the rotation, can cause burnout symptoms. Rule of thumb... any pitcher who increases his workload by 50 IP or more from year #1 to year #2 is a candidate to experience symptoms of burnout in year #3.

Another gauge we can use is Batters Faced per Game. Consistent BF/Gs of 28.0 or higher, combined with consistent seasonal IP totals of 200 or more may indicate high burnout potential. A BF/G level of over 30.0 combined with a projected IP total of 200 during any given season indicates a high likelihood of a late season fade.

Short relievers who post in excess of 100 IP in a season, while averaging fewer than 2 IP per outing, have a high likelihood of experiencing a performance letdown and/or health problems in the following year.

Particularly vulnerable are pitchers under the age of 25.

When focusing solely on minor league pitchers, research results are striking:

Stamina: Virtually every minor league pitcher who has had a BF/G of 28.5 or more in one season will experience a drop-off in BF/G the following year. Many will be unable to ever duplicate that previous level of durability.

Performance: Most pitchers experience an associated drop-off in their BPVs in the years following the 28.5 BF/G season. Some are able to salvage their effectiveness later on by moving to the bullpen.

In the player charts, we measure these warning flags under "BURN," or Burnout Potential. This level is indicated as None, Low, Moderate, High or Very High, and is determined by counting how many high risk seasons that pitcher has experienced within the past five years.

Catchers' Effect on Pitching *(Thomas Hanrahan)*

A typical catcher handles a pitching staff better after having been with a club for a few years. Research has shown that there is an improvement in team ERA of approximately 0.33 runs per game from a catcher's rookie season to his prime years with a club. Therefore, if a team has a veteran who has been catching for several seasons and are thinking of calling up a backstop from the minors, they can expect their short-term pitching results to drop off.

The Knuckleballers Rule

Knuckleballers don't follow any of the rules.

League Switching

American League left-handers often experience some early dominance upon coming over to the NL. This advantage over hitters normally lasts about one season. Pitchers then return to their previous performance levels.

Projecting Breakout Performances

Research has provided us with a set of criteria that can be used to identify candidates that have the potential to experience large-scale ERA improvement. For pitchers that have consistently posted ERAs at or above the league average, target those that...

- will be between 24 and 28 years of age (and eliminate anyone over 29)
- have a minimum of two full years of major league experience
- have a history of command ratios over 2.0 (although the most previous year may be below 2.0)
- have had consistent strikeout rates of 6.0 or above
- have had consistent opposition on base averages under .350
- have had strand rates of 70% or less and the promise of improved bullpen support in the next season.
- have had BPVs that showed potential for 50-plus levels, either via rising trends or minor league success.

Very few pitchers will meet all eight criteria; target those who meet the most criteria, with a minimum of five.

Origin of Closers

History has long maintained that ace closers are not easily recognizable early on in their careers, so that every season does see its share of the unexpected. Jorge Julio, Damaso Marte, Juan Acevedo, Danys Baez, Francisco Cordero, Scott Williamson, Braden Looper, Eric Gagne... who would have thought it a year ago at this time?

Some accepted facts...

- You cannot find major league closers from pitchers who were closers in the minors.
- Closers begin their careers as starters.
- Closers are converted set-up men.
- Closers are pitchers who were unable to develop a third effective pitch.

All four statements are true. But the reality is a lot more simple... closers are a product of circumstance.

Are the minor leagues a place to look at all?

From a 1996 study... From 1990-1995, there were 104 incidences of 20-save performances in Double-A and Triple-A, which were accomplished by 89 different pitchers.

Of those 89, only 23 ever made it to the majors.

Of those 23, only 7 ever closed any game.

Of those 7, only 3 ever became full-time closers: John Wetteland, Mark Wohlers and Ricky Bottalico.

Three pitchers out of 89, a successful conversion rate of 3%. Not exactly a fertile ground.

The Rule of TOG

The task of finding future closing potential comes down to looking at three things, which we call the Rule of TOG:

Talent: The raw skills to mow down hitters for short periods of time. Pinpoint control, dominance and command are paramount. Optimal BPVs over 100, but not under 75.

Opportunity: The single most important element, and the one the pitcher has the least control over.

Guile: Gamesmanship, the innate mental makeup that allows a pitcher to make the most use of his talent in high-pressure situations. Guile is tough to project; we often can only assess it after the fact, when a pitcher is given an opportunity and either succeeds or fails. A good rule of thumb is to use a pitcher's saves success rate, or the percent of opportunities successfully converted. Proof of guile can be considered for those that convert at least 80% of their save opportunities.

The league's top closers possess all three qualities. The absence of any of the three significantly raises the risk of not accumulating saves.

There are pitchers that have *Talent and Guile, but not the Opportunity*. Often, these pitchers have proven that they can successfully close out games but are not given the full-time chance to do so, for a variety of reasons (e.g. being blocked by a solid frontliner in the pen, being lefthanded, etc.) They are good to own because they will not likely hurt your pitching staff, but you cannot count on them for saves. In 2002, these were pitchers like Buddy Groom, Alan Embree, Cliff Politte and Octavio Dotel.

There are pitchers that have *Talent and Opportunity, but not the Guile*. Any pitcher with talent is good to own, and these pitchers have saves upside if they manage to overcome the obstacles to success. Failure, however, might incur some short-term impact to ERA and WHIP. In 2002, pitchers that were given some closing opportunities, had the skill, but fell short on Guile included Hideki Irabu and Vladimir Nunez.

Finally, there are pitchers that have *Opportunity and Guile, but not the Talent*. MLB managers decide on who to give the ball to in the 9th inning based on their own perceptions about what skills are required to succeed. Sometimes the only criteria is "he has to be a hard-thrower who keeps the ball on the ground," even if those tendencies demonstrate little pure command or produce elevated opposition on base averages.

Those without any real command or dominance may have some initial short-term success, but their long-term prognosis is poor and they are high risks to your roster. In 2002, pitchers that amassed 10 or more saves without closer-worthy BPIs included Kelvim Escobar, Juan Acevedo, Mike DeJean and Esteban Yan. Classic examples of the short life span of these types of pitchers include Matt Karchner and Heath Slocumb.

Handedness Notes

1. Left-handed pitchers tend to peak about a year after right-handed pitchers.

2. While southpaws account for about 26% of total IPs, they post only 15% of the total saves. Typically, the few left-handers on a staff are reserved for specialized roles so few are given the job of frontline closer.

3. RHers have slightly better command and a slightly better HR rate.

4. But there is no statistically significant variance in LHer versus RHer ERAs.

5. On an overall productivity basis, RHers only have about a 6% advantage over LHers.

Minor League Toolbox

Minor League Information Management

(Terry Linhart)

The increased attention that the minor leagues are getting has created some dangerous analytical by-products.

Hype. With the minor leagues still largely uncovered by the media, one reporter's short-term observations can make their way into the mainstream as fact. This growing subjective information base is often not rooted in fact at all, yet drives perception about prospects.

There is a **rush** to scour the lower minors statistically for the next great phenom before anyone else does. But statistics alone do not tell the whole story. Often, there is an exaggerated emphasis on short-term performance in an environment (major league player development) that is supposed to focus on the long-term. Two poor outings don't mean a 21-year-old pitcher is washed up.

Other common factors that affect statistics:

League variances: Some leagues historically favor hitters or pitchers.

Ballpark variances: Dimensions and altitude create hitters parks and pitchers parks, but a factor rarely mentioned is that many ballparks in the lower minors are inconsistent in their field quality. Minor league clubs have limited resources to maintain their field conditions, and this can artificially depress defensive statistics while inflating gauges like batting average.

Widely variant skills: Some players' skills are so superior to the caliber of competition at their level that you can't truly get a picture of what they're going to do from their statistics alone.

Player development assignments: Many pitchers are told to work on secondary pitches while moving through the minors, throwing curveballs and change-ups on 3-2 or 2-2 counts to gain confidence in the pitch. The result is an increased number of walks affecting their command ratio. Again, the bigger picture is the long-term development for a major league club. They may be able to get hitters out with a sharp, moving fastball, but are trying to work on keeping hitters off-stride.

Pitching rotations: The #3, #4, and #5 pitchers in the lower minors are truly longshots to make the majors. They often possess only two pitches and can barely go five innings. The most obvious weakness is the inability to disguise the off-speed pitches with their delivery and arm speed. Hitters can see inflated statistics in these leagues.

Recommendations:

Look past the headline notes to uncover those players with major league skills.

Pick your sources carefully, focusing on those writers who avoid the pitfalls and either see minor leaguers play or talk to people in baseball who do.

Use statistics appropriately, looking for major league skills (batting eye, pitching command, etc.), but not as the sole basis for decision-making.

Minor League Level versus Age

When evaluating minor league talent, you must look at the age of the prospect in relation to the median age of the league he is in:

Low level A	Between 19-20
Upper level A	Around 20
Double-A	21
Triple-A	22

These are the ideal ages for prospects at the particular level. If a prospect is younger than most and he holds his own against older and more experienced players, elevate his status. If a prospect is older than the median, reduce his status. These adjustments are taken into account in the Major League Equivalents section.

Law of Promotion *(Deric McKamey)*

Defense is what gets a minor league prospect to the majors; offense is what keeps him there.

Call-up Success Rates I

The overall probability that a promoted minor leaguer will immediately succeed at the major league level can vary depending upon the level of Triple-A experience that player has amassed at the time of call-up. Research conclusions:

The odds of a batter achieving immediate major league success, no matter what his minor league experience, remains slightly more than 50-50.

However, over 80% of all minor league pitchers promoted with less than a full year at Triple-A will struggle in their first year in the majors. Those pitchers who do have a full year of Triple-A experience increase their probability of success to a level equal to that of batters (about 50-50).

Another way to look at it... Pitchers with a full year at Triple-A are 3.5 times more likely to perform well in the majors in year #1 than those without a full year at Triple-A.

Call-up Success Rates II

Historical BPIs have some value in determining which minor league pitching call-ups fare well.

Based on a recent study, the percentage of hurlers that were good investments in the year that they were called up varied by the level of their historical BPIs *prior* to that year.

Pitchers who had:	Fared well	Fared poorly
Good indicators	79%	21%
Marginal or poor indicators	18%	82%

The minor league data used to classify these pitchers were MLE levels from the previous two years, not the season in which they were called up. What is the significance of this? Typically, it is solid current year performance in the minors that merits the call-up in the first place, but those minor league numbers had little bearing on who fared well. Early season performance in the minors is not a good indicator of short-term major league success, for two reasons:

1. The performance data set is too small, typically just a few month's worth of statistics. For pitchers, this is not nearly enough data to draw any reasonable conclusions.

2. For those pitchers putting up those stats at a new minor league level, there has not been enough time for the scouting reports to make their rounds, so we do not know if they have truly mastered that level yet.

Projecting Second Year Success

One of the most accurate indicators of a rookie's future potential is his performance during the second half of his debut season in the majors.

First year players often get off to particularly fast or slow starts. During their second tour of the league is when we get to see what they're truly made of. Have the slow starters adjusted to the level of play and brought their game up a notch? Has the rest of the league figured out the fast starters and taken them down a peg? That 2nd half "adjustment" performance level is the one you want to look at when projecting the sophomore campaign and beyond.

It also stands to reason that this phenomenon should occur at every level of professional baseball play.

When a player gets promoted to, say Triple-A, he is, in fact, a "rookie" during his first year at that level. An analysis of his second half Triple-A performance gives us a better indication of his true ability there.

And... premature major league call-ups often negate that ability to evaluate a player's true potential.

It happens all the time. A hotshot Double-A player opens the new season in Triple-A. After putting up solid numbers for a month or two, he gets a call to the big club... and then struggles. We wonder why. The fact is, at the point of call-up, we do not have enough evidence that the player has mastered the Triple-A level. We don't know whether the rest of the league would have caught up to him during his second tour of the league. But now he's an underperformer in the bigs. When someone says that a player needs a full season in Triple-A, there's a valid reason for it.

Older Prospects

There is a hidden wealth of potential talent in older prospects — age 26, 27 or higher — who, for whatever reason (untimely injury, circumstance, bad luck, etc.), don't reach the majors until they've lost their Official Prospect Status. Downgrading potential with age is an old-school approach to prospecting, but you do not have to buy into it.

Skills growth and decline is universal, whether it occurs at the major league level or in the minors. So a high skills journeyman in Triple-A is just as likely to peak at age 27, or thereabouts, as a major leaguer of the same age. The question becomes one of opportunity — will the parent club see fit to reap the benefits of that peak performance?

Most clubs approach the calling up of a minor leaguer in the same way as they approach all their future investments. They are often more likely to take a chance on a 23-year-old who might return long-term dividends than a 29-year-old whose return is likely far lower... even if it is to fill a short-term roster opening. However, for those short-term openings — *especially* for those short-term openings — it is often a lower risk move to go with an older player at peak than a younger player still learning the craft.

Since many organizations do continue to ignore potential sources of talent from within their systems, prospecting these players for your fantasy team is, admittedly, a high risk endeavor. For every Dave Roberts and Jason Simontacchi who makes an impact, there are many more Roberto Petagines who might have made an impact but are never given a full opportunity.

In order to uncover next season's "Bull Durham" prospects, look for a player who is/has:

- Optimally, age 27-28 for overall peak skills, age 30-31 for power skills, or age 28-31 for pitchers.
- At least two seasons of experience at Triple-A. Career Double-A players are generally not good picks.
- Solid base skills levels.
- Shallow organizational depth at their position.
- Notable winter league or spring training performance.

Players who meet these conditions can often slip onto a 25-man roster by Opening Day, or become an early call-up.

What should you do with these players? In general, these are typically not draftable players, but worthwhile reserve or Rotisserie-Ultra picks.

Team Toolbox

Not surprisingly, the following principles all come from the annals of Bill James and his *Baseball Abstracts* from the 1980's.

Johnson Effect *(Bryan Johnson)*: Teams whose actual won/loss record exceeds or falls short of their statistically projected record in one season will tend to revert to the level of their projection in the following season.

Law of Competitive Balance: The level at which a team (or player) will address its problems is inversely related to its current level of success. Losing teams/low performing players will tend to make changes to improve; winning teams/high performing players will not. This law is the explanation for the existence of the Plexiglass Principle and the Whirlpool Principle.

Plexiglass Principle: If a player or team improves markedly in one season, it will likely decline in the next. The opposite is also true but with a slightly lower frequency (because a poorer performing player will get fewer opportunities to rebound).

Whirlpool Principle: All team and player performances are forcefully drawn to the center. For teams, that center is a .500 record. For players, it represents their career average level of performance.

Japanese Baseball Toolbox

Japan's Pacific and Central Leagues are generally considered to be equivalent to very good Triple-A level ball, and the pitching may be even better.

As good as this league is, Japanese statistics are difficult to convert to a major league equivalent due to a variety of differences in the way the game is played there:

1. Japanese baseball's guiding philosophy centers on risk avoidance. Mistakes are not tolerated. Since fewer risks are taken, runners rarely take extra bases, batters focus on making contact rather than driving the ball, and managers play for one run at a time, rather than going for a big inning. As a result, offenses score fewer runs than they should given the number of hits produced. And pitching stats tend to look better than the talent behind them.

2. Stadiums in Japan have much shorter fences. Normally this would mean more HRs, but given #1 above, it is the American players who make up the majority of Japan's power elite. This skews offensive statistics.

3. There are more artificial turf fields, which increases the number of groundball singles.

4. The quality of umpiring is questionable. Far fewer errors are called (again, the cultural philosophy of low tolerance for mistakes).

5. Teams have smaller pitching staffs, often no more than about seven deep. Three-man pitching rotations are common, there is no relief specialization, and the best starters often work out of the pen between starts. Despite superior conditioning, Japanese pitchers tend to burn out early, often before age 30.

Still, despite all this, it is difficult to see how this player would be anything but an instant success in the Majors...

Matsui,Hideki	
Pos	CF
Age	28 Peak
Bats	L
Pwr	-
Spd	No change
BAvg	- -
Risk	Very Low

	Tm	AB	R	H	HR	RBI	SB	Avg	R$	OB	Slg	OPS	bb%	ct%	Eye	xBA	PX	SX	RC/G	RAR
93	JPN	184	27	41	11	27	1	223	$4	289	451	740	8	73	0.34	259	139	51	4.53	-0.6
94	JPN	503	70	148	20	66	6	294	$17	366	475	841	10	80	0.56	270	106	84	6.60	32.0
95	JPN	501	76	142	22	80	9	283	$18	362	481	843	11	81	0.67	285	119	67	6.38	29.0
96	JPN	487	97	153	38	99	7	314	$31	401	622	1024	13	80	0.72	307	180	74	9.82	85.7
97	JPN	484	93	144	37	103	9	298	$30	418	564	982	17	83	1.19	300	153	63	9.32	73.3
98	JPN	487	103	142	34	100	3	292	$25	416	563	979	18	79	1.03	295	160	69	8.99	73.7
99	JPN	471	100	143	42	95	0	304	$26	418	631	1049	16	79	0.94	303	183	41	10.15	89.4
00	JPN	474	116	150	42	108	5	316	$31	441	654	1095	18	77	0.98	311	190	70	11.65	117.2
01	JPN	481	107	160	36	104	3	333	$32	466	617	1083	20	80	1.25	296	159	67	11.96	129.2
02	JPN	500	112	167	50	107	3	334	$38	458	692	1150	19	79	1.10	317	207	52	13.05	142.5

Other Diamonds

A-Rod 10-Step Path to Stardom *(The "Little Ballplayer Who Cried Wolf" Syndrome)***:** Not all well-hyped prospects hit the ground running like Vladimir Guerrero. More often they follow an alternative path...

1. Prospect puts up phenomenal minor league numbers.
2. The media machine gets oiled up.
3. Prospect gets called up, but struggles, Year 1.
4. Prospect gets demoted.
5. Prospect tears it up in Triple-A, Year 2.
6. Prospect gets called up, but struggles, Year 2.
7. Prospect gets demoted.
8. The media turns their backs and fantasy leaguers reduce their expectations.
9. Prospect tears it up in Triple-A, Year 3. The public shrugs its collective shoulders.
10. Prospect is promoted in Year 3 and explodes. Some lucky fantasy leaguer lands a franchise player for under $5.

Some players that are currently stuck at one of the interim steps, and may or may not ever reach Step 10, include Hank Blalock, Peter Bergeron and Dee Brown. Did Karim Garcia reach Step 10 in 2002? We'll see in 2003.

A-Rod's Rangers Rationalization: Money can't buy happiness, but it sure can make misery easier to live with.

The Bones-Olivares List: Pitcher with BPIs so incredibly poor that you have to wonder how they can possibly draw a major league paycheck year after year.

Denver Doctrine: Coors does not turn bad hitters into good hitters; it only turns good hitters into better hitters.

The Dave Eiland Catch-22 *(John Sickels)*: There are minor league pitchers who would hold their own for a strong winning team because they are good enough to keep a game close, however, strong teams rarely promote this type of pitcher, so they end up losing for bad teams that can't provide the necessary offensive support.

Expos Law of Destiny: Glory may be fleeting, but obscurity lasts forever.

Foreign Player 10-Step Research Process: A series of questions that fantasy leaguers use to evaluate foreign born players. This year's subject is Kazuhisa Ishii. Past years' subjects have included Ariel Prieto, Osvaldo Fernandez, Hideki Irabu, Roberto Ramirez, Rolando Arrojo, Geraldo Guzman and Tsuyoshi Shinjo.

1. Who is Kazuhisa Ishii?
2. Are there any numbers available for Ishii?
3. Does any scouting information for Ishii appear in any of the pre-season guides?
4. Is Ishii's potential really better than Hideo Nomo?
5. How long has Ishii been dormant during contract negotiations?
6. What role will Ishii have on his team?
7. Who will Ishii take playing time away from?
8. Should I pick up Ishii?
9. Will Ishii get any better?
10. How can I get rid of Ishii?

George Brett Path to Retirement: Get out while you're still putting up good numbers and the public perception of you is favorable. *(See Steve Carlton Path to Retirement.)*

Japan/Korea/Mexico Law of Perception: Foreign talent always seems better than home-grown talent.

Lance Painter Lesson: Six months of solid performance can be screwed up by one bad outing. (In 2000, Painter finished with an ERA of 4.76. However, prior to his final appearance of the year — in which he pitched 1 inning and gave up 8 earned runs — his ERA was 3.70.)

Law of Micro-management: The length of a team's transaction list is inversely proportional to its success.

Laws of Team Co-Dependency:

1. The one player that fails causes other players to fail.
2. No matter how many pieces have been assembled correctly, one mistake will cause the entire team to malfunction.
3. A $60 million team will be rendered useless by a $200,000 relief pitcher.

Official Colorado Procedures Manual for Recently Acquired Batters:

1. Arrive at Coors. Unpack.
2. Abandon plate patience. Swing at everything.
3. Post career best numbers.
4. Sign lucrative free agent contract somewhere else.
5. Ride out career.
6. Retire wealthy.

Steve Carlton Path to Retirement: Hang around the major leagues long enough for your numbers to become so wretched that people begin to forget your past successes.

Among the many players who have taken this path include Ken Caminiti, David Cone, Bobby Bonilla, Eric Davis, Doc Gooden, Orel Hershiser, Howard Johnson, Mark Langston, Don Mattingly, Hal Morris, Jack Morris, Dale Murphy, Tim Raines, Dave Stewart and of course, Steve Carlton. Current players who look to be on the same course include Brady Anderson, Jeff Fassero, Mark Grace, Barry Larkin, Denny Neagle, Shane Reynolds and Greg Vaughn. *(See George Brett Path to Retirement.)*

Steve Moyer's Rationale for Not Trading Me Chan Ho Park in Mid-1999: If you hold on and he sucks, you've got an excuse. If you dump him and he comes around, you've got a nightmare.

Strawberry Postulate: It may be that your sole purpose in life is simply to serve as a warning to others.

Timlin Syndrome: A dreaded draft day malady in which you are unable to resist acquiring a player that has burned you multiple times in the past.

The Final Pitch

"Forecasting is a business art, a marriage of quantitative technique and creative process, seeking not just truth but also beauty and elegance." — Unknown

"The best forecast combines sophisticated information management with good common sense." — Unknown

"Baseball is like this. Have one good year and you can fool them for five more, because for five more years they expect you to have another good one." — Frankie Frisch

III.
MAJOR LEAGUES

The Batters

QUALIFICATION: All batters who accumulated at least 100 at bats in the majors in 2002 have been included. Nearly all who accumulated between 50 and 100 AB in 2002 are also included. A handful of players with fewer than 50 AB in 2002 are included if we believe that they will have an impact in 2003. Remember that low AB totals raise the risk of any analysis or projection, so be cautious when reviewing any player who had fewer than 100 ABs in 2002.

This book is designed to be an historical analysis, so players who will likely have a vital role in 2003, but spent the better part of 2002 on the sidelines or in the minors, are not included. We cover some of them briefly on page 146 and others in the Top Prospects section. All of these players will appear on BaseballHQ.com over the winter as their 2003 roles and projected impacts become clearer.

POSITIONS: Up to three positions are listed for each batter and represent those for which he appeared a minimum of 20 games in 2002.

AGE: Each batter's current age is shown, along with a description of the associated stage in his career.

BATS: Shows which side of the plate he bats from — right (R), left (L) or switch-hitter (S).

SNAPSHOT ANALYSES: This section takes a look at a batter's potential change in performance from 2002 on a graphical +/- scale. The scale runs from "- - - - -" representing high potential for decline to "+ + + + +" representing high potential for improvement. Note that this is *not* the *amount* of performance change; it represents the *probability* of change.

Power skills (PWR): Looks at a batter's age versus power output, growth/decline in power skills versus growth/decline in batting eye, and his year-to-year consistency in determining his potential for change from 2002.

Speed skills (SPD): Looks at a runner's age versus SB output, growth/decline in batting eye (you can't use speed skills unless you get on base), and year-to-year consistency.

Batting average (BAVG): Looks at a hitter's batting eye versus batting average, and LH/RH platoon variance.

Note that each player's 2003 projection may or may not reflect these indicators. We evaluate every projection and often overrule the BPIs if we feel the situation warrants it.

LIMA Grade: Rating that evaluates how well a batter would fit into a team using the LIMA Plan. Best grades go to batters who have excellent base skills (BPV), are expected to see a good amount of playing time, and are in the $10-$30 Rotisserie value range. Lowest grades will go to poor skills, few at bats and values under $5 or over $30.

FORECAST RISK: Refer to the description in the Forecaster's Toolbox.

PLAYER STAT LINES: The past five year's statistics represent the total accumulated in the majors as well as in Triple-A and Double-A ball during each year. All minor league stats used have been converted to their equivalent major league performance level. Levels below AA are not included. See the note in the Foundation Philosophies section for the rationale behind using minor league statistics in this manner.

TEAM DESIGNATIONS: An asterisk (*) appearing with a team name means that major league equivalent Triple-A and/or Double-A numbers are included in that year's stat line. A designation of "a/a" means the stats were accumulated at both Triple-A and Double-A levels that year. "JPN" means Japan, "MEX" means Mexico, "KOR" means Korea, "TWN" means Taiwan and "ind" means independent league.

The designation "2TM" appears whenever a player was on more than one major league team, crossing leagues, in a season. "2AL" and "2NL" represent more than one team in the same league. Complete season stats are presented for players who crossed leagues during the season.

SABERMETRIC CATEGORIES: Descriptions of all the sabermetric categories appear in the glossary. The decimal point has been suppressed on several categories to conserve space.

New categories for 2003...

vLH / vRH: Complete 5-year scan (where available) of each player's batting average versus left-handed and right-handed pitchers. Data shown is at the major league level only.

xBA: Expected batting average

G/F: Ground ball to fly ball ratio. Data shown is at the major league level only.

2003 FORECASTS: It is far too early to be making definitive projections for 2003, especially on playing time. Focus on the skill levels and trends, then consult Baseball HQ for playing time revisions as players change teams and roles become finalized. A free projections update will also be available online at BaseballForecaster.com in March.

Forecasts are computed from a player's trends over the past five years. Adjustments were made for leading indicators and variances between skill and output. After reviewing the leading indicators, you might opt to make further adjustments.

Although each year's numbers include all playing time at the Double-A level or above, the 2003 forecast only represents potential playing time at the major league level, and again is highly preliminary.

CAPSULE COMMENTARIES: For each player, a brief analysis of their BPIs and the potential impact on performance in 2003 is provided. For those who played only a portion of 2002 at the major league level, and whose isolated MLB stats are significantly different from their full-season total, their MLB stats are listed here. Note that these commentaries generally look at performance related issues only. Playing time expectations may impact these analyses, so you will have to adjust accordingly, especially as we get closer to Opening Day. Upside (UP) and downside (DN) statistical potential appears for some players. These are less grounded in hard data and more speculative of longer-term potential.

Abernathy,Brent		Tm	AB	R	H	HR	RBI	SB	Avg	vLH	vRH	R$	OB	Slg	OPS	bb%	ct%	Eye	xBA	PX	SX	G/F	RC/G	RAR
Pos 2B	98		0	0	0	0	0	0	0								0							
Age 25 Pre-Peak	99	aa	577	83	148	9	48	26	256			$12	308	376	684	7	94	1.19	305	85	98		3.85	-5.8
Bats R	00	aaa	449	51	120	4	41	19	267			$10	313	363	676	6	92	0.86	289	68	92		3.70	-6.9
Pwr No change	01	TAM	* 556	83	154	9	54	18	277	320	253	$15	327	396	722	7	90	0.75	286	84	93	1.04	4.71	7.2
Spd +++++	02	TAM	463	46	112	2	40	10	242	203	250	$5	281	311	592	5	90	0.54	261	51	107	1.47	3.05	-14.9
BAvg +++	1st Half		291	30	75	2	22	6	258			$4	296	333	630	5	90	0.55	263	56	92		3.43	-6.1
LIMA B	2nd Half		172	16	37	0	18	4	215			$1	254	273	527	5	90	0.53	256	43	120		2.47	-8.5
Risk Moderate	03	Proj	450	53	113	4	42	14	251			$7	295	341	636	6	91	0.68	276	64	106		3.50	-9.6

Big time sophomore slump. Lost over 100 points in BA vs LHers and completely tanked in the 2nd half. Most likely projection is somewhere between '01 and '02.The seeds are there for a rebound.

Abreu,Bobby		Tm	AB	R	H	HR	RBI	SB	Avg	vLH	vRH	R$	OB	Slg	OPS	bb%	ct%	Eye	xBA	PX	SX	G/F	RC/G	RAR
Pos RF	98	PHI	497	68	155	17	74	19	312	320	310	$26	411	497	908	14	73	0.63	256	122	119	1.33	7.96	49.1
Age 29 Past Peak	99	PHI	546	118	183	20	93	27	335	298	348	$34	446	549	995	17	79	0.96	283	130	165	1.53	10.14	94.3
Bats L	00	PHI	576	103	182	25	79	28	316	243	339	$32	417	554	971	15	80	0.86	294	142	154	1.20	9.24	77.2
Pwr ++	01	PHI	588	118	170	31	110	36	289	258	301	$37	398	543	940	15	77	0.77	288	155	128	1.14	8.14	49.0
Spd --	02	PHI	572	102	176	20	85	31	308	302	310	$33	414	521	935	15	80	0.89	284	138	130	1.26	8.45	58.8
BAvg --	1st Half		264	52	83	6	41	14	314			$15	433	504	936	17	82	1.15	288	130	133		8.95	32.3
LIMA C+	2nd Half		308	50	93	14	44	17	302			$19	398	536	933	14	78	0.71	280	145	122		8.01	26.5
Risk Very Low	03	Proj	575	105	176	26	95	31	306			$35	411	542	953	15	78	0.83	287	146	131		8.66	72.9

Started slow at the plate and everyone was labeling this an off-year. Reality is that, despite the drop in HR/RBI, '02 was a better skills year than '01. G/F ratio says no, but another 30-100-35 season is a decent pct play.

Agbayani,Benny		Tm	AB	R	H	HR	RBI	SB	Avg	vLH	vRH	R$	OB	Slg	OPS	bb%	ct%	Eye	xBA	PX	SX	G/F	RC/G	RAR
Pos CF	98	aaa	337	35	79	9	42	12	234			$7	316	383	698	11	83	0.70	277	96	104		4.27	-3.8
Age 31 Past Peak	99	NYM	* 377	60	111	20	69	10	294	398	279	$18	370	541	911	11	80	0.59	291	148	105	1.25	7.29	34.8
Bats R	00	NYM	350	59	101	15	60	5	289	275	293	$14	384	480	864	13	81	0.79	280	115	64	1.10	6.88	28.5
Pwr +	01	NYM	296	28	82	6	27	4	277	333	259	$7	355	399	754	11	75	0.49	238	77	67	1.23	5.13	11.4
Spd No change	02	2TM	* 318	38	71	12	53	2	223	209	241	$5	308	387	695	11	76	0.51	247	101	61	1.46	4.27	-6.7
BAvg +++++	1st Half		144	11	31	4	23	0	215			$0	280	347	627	8	74	0.34	229	87	12		3.38	-6.9
LIMA C	2nd Half		174	27	40	8	30	2	230			$3	330	420	750	13	78	0.67	261	113	84		5.07	0.9
Risk Moderate	03	Proj	250	31	63	9	37	3	252			$6	337	412	750	11	77	0.56	257	99	65		5.03	2.5

4-27-.227 in 154 AB at COL and BOS. Was batting .300 on April 20, then began to plummet, culminating in a hamstring DL stint. Odds are it nagged him all year. There's still talent here and could be a serviceable 4th OFer.

Alfonzo,Edgardo		Tm	AB	R	H	HR	RBI	SB	Avg	vLH	vRH	R$	OB	Slg	OPS	bb%	ct%	Eye	xBA	PX	SX	G/F	RC/G	RAR
Pos 3B	98	NYM	557	94	155	17	78	8	278	234	293	$18	354	427	781	10	86	0.84	288	100	87	0.76	5.69	21.2
Age 29 Past Peak	99	NYM	628	123	191	27	108	9	304	268	314	$27	387	502	889	12	86	1.00	301	124	80	0.72	7.63	64.8
Bats R	00	NYM	544	109	176	25	94	3	324	298	330	$26	424	542	966	15	87	1.36	314	134	63	0.70	9.32	89.7
Pwr No change	01	NYM	457	64	111	17	49	5	243	211	251	$8	319	403	722	10	86	0.82	286	97	70	0.58	4.70	0.2
Spd -	02	NYM	490	78	151	16	56	6	308	364	290	$19	386	459	845	11	89	1.13	286	96	69	0.71	7.09	37.9
BAvg -	1st Half		273	35	82	4	24	3	300			$8	392	396	787	13	90	1.46	271	67	52		6.29	14.4
LIMA A	2nd Half		217	43	69	12	32	3	318			$12	378	539	917	9	88	0.78	303	132	72		8.08	23.1
Risk Low	03	Proj	500	84	157	20	75	6	314			$23	391	488	879	11	88	1.01	293	108	67		7.62	49.4

His MIA power started to come around in the 2nd half, and as he enters his peak power years, he could bounce back to pre-'01 levels. Will likely go for under $20 but could earn $25, or more.

Alicea,Luis		Tm	AB	R	H	HR	RBI	SB	Avg	vLH	vRH	R$	OB	Slg	OPS	bb%	ct%	Eye	xBA	PX	SX	G/F	RC/G	RAR
Pos 2B 3B	98	TEX	259	51	71	6	33	4	274	302	269	$6	365	425	790	13	85	0.93	283	96	114	1.05	5.76	14.1
Age 37 Decline	99	TEX	164	33	33	3	17	2	201	290	147	($1)	318	317	635	15	80	0.88	256	79	79	1.18	3.64	-2.2
Bats S	00	TEX	540	85	159	6	63	1	294	316	289	$10	364	404	768	10	86	0.79	267	67	95	0.97	5.57	27.9
Pwr No change	01	KC	387	44	106	4	32	8	274	253	280	$7	315	367	682	6	86	0.41	259	60	98	1.23	4.06	-2.7
Spd ----	02	KC	237	28	54	1	23	2	228	205	233	$1	320	291	611	12	86	0.94	243	46	80	1.61	3.31	-6.2
BAvg +++++	1st Half		115	12	24	0	11	1	209			($0)	316	287	603	14	91	1.80	268	56	106		3.26	-3.3
LIMA C	2nd Half		122	16	30	1	12	1	246			$1	324	295	619	10	80	0.58	221	36	52		3.36	-2.9
Risk Very High	03	Proj	250	33	63	2	25	3	252			$3	328	334	662	10	85	0.75	251	56	84		3.92	-2.2

While he's maintained his plate patience, his skills are in clear decline. His BA may rebound a bit, but he'll still be pretty much undraftable.

Alomar Jr.,Sandy		Tm	AB	R	H	HR	RBI	SB	Avg	vLH	vRH	R$	OB	Slg	OPS	bb%	ct%	Eye	xBA	PX	SX	G/F	RC/G	RAR
Pos CA	98	CLE	409	45	96	6	44	0	235	250	230	$1	267	352	619	4	89	0.40	281	82	52	1.29	3.12	-11.8
Age 36 Decline	99	CLE	* 199	34	59	8	39	1	296	353	291	$8	336	503	839	6	86	0.44	306	129	77	1.22	6.22	12.5
Bats R	00	CLE	356	44	103	7	42	2	289	351	273	$7	320	404	724	4	88	0.39	275	71	69	1.57	4.69	4.9
Pwr --	01	CHW	220	17	54	4	21	1	245	273	239	$2	284	345	630	5	92	0.71	273	63	44	1.62	3.33	-4.0
Spd No change	02	2TM	283	29	79	7	37	0	279	247	292	$6	301	410	711	3	88	0.27	276	86	37	1.46	4.46	4.3
BAvg --	1st Half		116	13	33	4	18	0	284			$3	297	448	745	2	93	0.25	302	100	57		4.79	2.8
LIMA D	2nd Half		167	16	46	3	19	0	275			$2	305	383	688	4	85	0.28	259	76	23		4.23	1.4
Risk X HIGH	03	Proj	250	26	68	6	30	1	272			$5	301	396	697	4	89	0.39	284	80	49		4.23	2.1

Always on the lookout for those late career HR spikes and a player with previous pop now in COL would be a good candidate. But G/F ratio and middling PX levels say to bet against.

Alomar,Roberto		Tm	AB	R	H	HR	RBI	SB	Avg	vLH	vRH	R$	OB	Slg	OPS	bb%	ct%	Eye	xBA	PX	SX	G/F	RC/G	RAR
Pos 2B	98	BAL	588	86	166	14	56	18	282	311	271	$17	348	418	766	9	88	0.84	289	91	90	1.54	5.50	25.8
Age 35 Decline	99	CLE	563	138	182	24	120	37	323	338	318	$39	424	533	957	15	83	1.03	301	129	135	1.18	9.44	102.0
Bats S	00	CLE	610	111	189	19	89	39	310	318	307	$33	375	475	851	9	87	0.78	296	103	126	1.54	7.25	63.6
Pwr No change	01	CLE	575	113	193	20	100	30	336	279	356	$37	417	541	958	12	88	1.13	312	122	167	1.27	9.31	93.9
Spd -----	02	NYM	590	73	157	11	53	16	266	205	290	$14	331	376	707	9	86	0.69	266	70	105	1.51	4.64	2.6
BAvg No change	1st Half		312	41	81	6	25	8	260			$6	319	359	678	8	83	0.52	253	63	89		4.16	-3.3
LIMA A+	2nd Half		278	32	76	5	28	8	273			$7	344	396	740	10	89	0.97	280	77	111		5.22	6.3
Risk Low	03	Proj	575	90	164	15	73	14	285			$19	358	436	794	10	87	0.86	286	94	119		5.93	33.6

Shea is not kind to hitters, for sure, but a look at his BA vsLH trend and you'll know to raise the red flag. MInor 2nd half rebound means '03 won't be quite as bad, but odds are against a return to '01 levels.

Alou,Moises		Tm	AB	R	H	HR	RBI	SB	Avg	vLH	vRH	R$	OB	Slg	OPS	bb%	ct%	Eye	xBA	PX	SX	G/F	RC/G	RAR
Pos LF	98	HOU	584	104	182	38	124	11	312	288	318	$37	398	582	980	13	85	0.97	321	169	104	0.79	9.11	80.4
Age 36 Decline	99	HOU	0	0	0	0	0	0	0								0							
Bats R	00	HOU	454	82	161	30	114	3	355	370	350	$33	421	623	1044	10	90	1.16	337	155	58	0.78	10.66	77.1
Pwr No change	01	HOU	513	79	170	27	108	5	331	424	309	$31	398	554	952	10	89	1.00	315	133	63	1.00	8.86	49.7
Spd ---	02	CHC	484	50	133	15	61	8	275	322	260	$15	339	419	758	9	87	0.77	279	90	72	1.08	5.40	-16.9
BAvg No change	1st Half		223	24	55	6	23	4	247			$4	311	368	679	9	86	0.68	265	72	78		4.23	-15.9
LIMA A	2nd Half		261	26	78	9	38	4	299			$11	362	464	826	9	89	0.87	289	106	49		6.56	0.3
Risk Moderate	03	Proj	450	61	128	20	79	6	284			$19	354	480	835	10	88	0.90	301	119	69		6.46	24.3

2nd half surge salvaged some small shred of dignity, but it was not nearly enough. At 36, with his injury history and declining trends, the percentage play is to consider this a new level at which he will plateau.

Anderson,Brady		Tm	AB	R	H	HR	RBI	SB	Avg	vLH	vRH	R$	OB	Slg	OPS	bb%	ct%	Eye	xBA	PX	SX	G/F	RC/G	RAR
Pos CF	98	BAL	479	84	113	18	51	21	236	179	258	$12	339	420	759	14	84	0.96	292	113	118	0.89	5.17	5.0
Age 39 Decline	99	BAL	564	109	159	24	81	36	282	237	291	$28	386	477	863	15	81	0.91	286	114	140	0.84	7.27	46.6
Bats L	00	BAL	506	89	130	19	50	16	257	260	256	$13	371	421	792	15	80	0.89	266	98	77	0.85	5.79	17.7
Pwr +	01	BAL	430	50	87	8	45	12	202	185	206	$2	300	300	600	12	82	0.78	247	58	97	0.98	3.23	-24.0
Spd ----	02	CLE	80	4	13	1	5	4	163	111	169	($0)	316	250	566	18	71	0.78	213	66	53	0.81	3.22	-4.6
BAvg +++++	1st Half		80	4	13	1	5	4	163			($0)	316	250	566	18	71	0.78	213	66	53		3.22	-4.6
LIMA C	2nd Half		0	0	0	0	0	0	0			($0)					0							-0.0
Risk Moderate	03	Proj	100	13	22	3	10	4	220			$2	340	351	691	15	78	0.84	248	87	69		4.51	-1.3

There is an outside chance he could still resurface, but not worth pursuing in any case.

Anderson,Garret

	Tm	AB	R	H	HR	RBI	SB	Avg	vLH	vRH	R$	OB	Slg	OPS	bb%	ct%	Eye	xBA	PX	SX	G/F	RC/G	RAR
Pos LF	98 ANA	622	62	183	15	79	8	294	292	295	$18	326	455	781	4	87	0.36	295	104	97	1.64	5.46	5.7
Age 30 Past Peak	99 ANA	620	88	188	21	80	3	303	280	312	$19	339	469	809	5	87	0.42	289	103	59	1.53	5.88	13.2
Bats L	00 ANA	647	92	185	35	117	7	286	333	266	$25	311	519	831	4	87	0.28	315	135	79	1.11	5.70	9.7
Pwr +	01 ANA	672	83	194	28	123	13	289	288	289	$29	316	478	794	4	85	0.27	287	116	77	1.09	5.43	14.1
Spd ---	02 ANA	638	93	195	29	123	6	306	284	316	$31	337	539	876	4	87	0.38	325	159	80	0.95	6.70	33.7
BAvg ---	1st Half	326	54	97	15	60	6	298			$16	326	534	860	4	86	0.30	319	159	109		6.40	14.2
LIMA C+	2nd Half	312	39	98	14	63	0	314			$15	348	545	892	5	89	0.48	330	158	37		7.02	19.6
Risk Moderate	03 Proj	650	88	204	34	129	7	314			$34	343	552	895	4	87	0.34	318	150	72		7.04	37.1

Signs that he may be on the verge of a career year include the up-trending BPIs, the drop in G/F ratio and his age. I was never a big fan here, but I would not be surprised to see him post a 40-HR season.

Anderson,Marlon

	Tm	AB	R	H	HR	RBI	SB	Avg	vLH	vRH	R$	OB	Slg	OPS	bb%	ct%	Eye	xBA	PX	SX	G/F	RC/G	RAR
Pos 2B	98 PHI	* 618	85	173	14	71	21	280		350	$21	306	434	739	4	89	0.34	303	104	151	2.50	4.77	10.5
Age 29 Past Peak	99 PHI	452	48	114	5	54	13	252	297	245	$7	290	361	651	5	87	0.39	277	75	114	1.53	3.77	-7.2
Bats L	00 PHI	* 559	57	149	7	58	22	267	190	234	$14	322	383	705	8	89	0.77	287	73	120	2.20	4.27	-3.1
Pwr No change	01 PHI	522	69	153	11	61	8	293	327	285	$16	338	421	759	6	86	0.47	277	84	80	1.89	5.23	20.5
Spd +++++	02 PHI	539	64	139	8	48	5	258	220	269	$7	312	380	692	7	87	0.59	275	81	105	1.64	4.31	-3.3
BAvg No change	1st Half	284	37	77	5	23	1	271			$4	312	408	721	6	87	0.46	279	88	100		4.58	0.7
LIMA A+	2nd Half	255	27	62	3	25	4	243			$2	311	349	660	9	87	0.74	269	72	93		4.01	-4.0
Risk High	03 Proj	500	59	134	8	51	9	268			$10	319	392	711	7	87	0.58	279	81	106		4.53	6.5

This is a weak skills set, and past the point when we could expect much growth. A BA rebound is likely, but not much else.

Aurilia,Rich

	Tm	AB	R	H	HR	RBI	SB	Avg	vLH	vRH	R$	OB	Slg	OPS	bb%	ct%	Eye	xBA	PX	SX	G/F	RC/G	RAR
Pos SS	98 SF	413	54	110	9	49	3	266	275	263	$9	318	407	724	7	85	0.50	284	101	72	0.80	4.60	11.7
Age 31 Past Peak	99 SF	558	68	157	22	80	2	281	296	276	$16	333	444	777	7	87	0.61	288	98	39	0.89	5.38	30.6
Bats R	00 SF	509	67	138	20	79	1	271	286	267	$14	341	444	785	10	82	0.60	279	102	46	0.89	5.55	32.5
Pwr ++	01 SF	636	114	206	37	97	1	324	322	325	$32	370	572	943	7	82	0.57	316	144	70	0.87	8.12	87.6
Spd No change	02 SF	538	76	138	15	61	1	257	241	261	$9	304	413	717	6	83	0.41	271	102	61	0.68	4.43	7.4
BAvg -	1st Half	230	33	59	6	25	0	257			$3	293	426	719	5	85	0.35	284	115	59		4.42	3.1
LIMA A+	2nd Half	308	43	79	9	36	1	256			$5	312	403	715	8	82	0.45	261	92	59		4.43	4.3
Risk Low	03 Proj	550	81	153	24	92	1	278			$19	330	476	806	7	84	0.49	289	120	62		5.68	32.7

The remnant effects of spring elbow surgery. Expect a rebound.

Ausmus,Brad

	Tm	AB	R	H	HR	RBI	SB	Avg	vLH	vRH	R$	OB	Slg	OPS	bb%	ct%	Eye	xBA	PX	SX	G/F	RC/G	RAR
Pos CA	98 HOU	412	62	111	6	45	10	269	267	270	$10	353	357	709	11	85	0.88	264	56	114	1.42	4.82	10.9
Age 34 Decline	99 DET	458	62	126	9	54	12	275	264	277	$11	348	415	763	10	84	0.72	278	87	117	1.52	5.17	14.8
Bats R	00 DET	523	75	139	7	51	11	266	321	246	$8	351	365	717	12	85	0.87	261	64	93	1.45	4.83	10.0
Pwr No change	01 HOU	422	45	98	5	34	4	232	186	241	$1	283	341	624	7	85	0.47	268	73	100	1.01	3.39	-2.6
Spd No change	02 HOU	447	57	115	6	50	2	257	307	245	$6	315	353	669	8	84	0.54	254	63	72	1.66	3.98	-3.0
BAvg No change	1st Half	199	33	54	3	19	1	271			$3	332	377	709	8	82	0.51	252	62	116		4.49	1.8
LIMA B	2nd Half	248	24	61	3	31	1	246			$2	302	335	637	7	85	0.56	255	64	38		3.59	-4.6
Risk Low	03 Proj	400	50	101	5	41	4	253			$5	315	355	670	8	85	0.60	262	68	86		4.02	0.5

His speed game is gone, and with it, the bonus value he used to provide at catcher. His declining walk rate likely signals that a .250 BA is going to be home territory from now on.

Baerga,Carlos

	Tm	AB	R	H	HR	RBI	SB	Avg	vLH	vRH	R$	OB	Slg	OPS	bb%	ct%	Eye	xBA	PX	SX	G/F	RC/G	RAR
Pos DH	98 NYM	511	46	136	7	53	0	266			$7	299	364	663	4	89	0.44	281	74	30		3.87	-23.3
Age 34 Decline	99 2TM	* 449	39	96	6	32	4	214			($2)	252	286	539	5	90	0.49	265	47	52		2.44	-38.6
Bats S	00	0	0	0	0	0	0	0								0							
Pwr +	01 ind	203	38	64	9	44	3	315			$11	362	522	885	7	83	0.43	288	118	128		7.26	12.0
Spd No change	02 BOS	182	17	52	2	19	6	286	224	308	$6	312	379	691	4	89	0.35	272	74	77	2.74	4.53	-6.0
BAvg --	1st Half	130	16	40	2	16	6	308			$6	343	431	774	5	89	0.50	288	96	87		5.92	1.1
LIMA F	2nd Half	52	1	12	0	3	0	231			($0)	231	250	481	0	88	0.00	229	18	1		1.91	-5.5
Risk High	03 Proj	100	10	25	1	12	1	250			$1	280	313	593	4	87	0.33	251	47	57		3.12	-7.1

Had some value in the 1st half, but that went away after he came back from his hamstring injury and lost any semblance of semi-regular playing time. G/F ratio likely means a surprise HR spike is not in the cards.

Bagwell,Jeff

	Tm	AB	R	H	HR	RBI	SB	Avg	vLH	vRH	R$	OB	Slg	OPS	bb%	ct%	Eye	xBA	PX	SX	G/F	RC/G	RAR
Pos 1B	98 HOU	540	124	164	34	111	19	304	402	279	$36	421	557	978	17	83	1.21	310	162	94	0.90	9.26	71.7
Age 34 Decline	99 HOU	562	143	171	42	126	30	304	354	289	$40	450	591	1041	21	77	1.17	291	169	86	0.78	10.65	106.5
Bats R	00 HOU	590	152	183	47	132	9	310	366	297	$37	416	615	1031	15	80	0.92	311	174	80	0.79	9.95	89.5
Pwr +	01 HOU	600	126	173	39	130	11	288	296	287	$33	395	568	964	15	78	0.79	295	165	110	1.05	8.68	46.3
Spd -----	02 HOU	571	94	166	31	98	7	291	333	281	$27	397	518	916	15	77	0.78	269	136	71	0.89	8.00	43.9
BAvg --	1st Half	281	43	72	12	40	3	256			$8	363	459	822	14	75	0.67	257	127	66		6.16	4.1
LIMA A	2nd Half	290	51	94	19	58	4	324			$19	430	576	1006	16	79	0.90	281	144	66		10.13	43.4
Risk Very Low	03 Proj	575	114	161	33	114	5	280			$26	392	522	914	16	78	0.85	281	144	71		7.78	46.9

We'd expect there to be some deterioration of skills at this age. Outward stats don't show it, but declining eye ratio and '02's xBA show that there is more downside on the horizon. Don't overvalue.

Bako,Paul

	Tm	AB	R	H	HR	RBI	SB	Avg	vLH	vRH	R$	OB	Slg	OPS	bb%	ct%	Eye	xBA	PX	SX	G/F	RC/G	RAR
Pos CA	98 DET	* 353	28	95	4	36	1	269	174	290	$4	316	357	673	6	73	0.25	218	59	52	1.86	4.09	0.0
Age 30 Past Peak	99 HOU	* 262	17	62	3	20	1	237	167	264	($0)	308	351	659	9	75	0.41	240	81	54	1.60	3.85	-1.6
Bats R	00 2NL	221	18	50	2	20	0	226	148	237	($1)	310	308	618	11	71	0.42	218	56	36	1.98	3.47	-4.3
Pwr No change	01 ATL	137	19	29	2	15	1	212	208	212	($0)	312	343	655	13	75	0.59	246	91	87	1.66	3.88	1.3
Spd No change	02 MIL	234	24	55	4	20	0	235	167	245	$0	295	329	624	8	80	0.43	238	59	46	1.74	3.33	-6.3
BAvg No change	1st Half	113	12	31	3	12	0	274			$2	344	389	733	10	79	0.50	237	63	61		4.86	2.4
LIMA F	2nd Half	121	12	24	1	8	0	198			($2)	248	273	521	6	82	0.36	240	56	44		2.19	-7.4
Risk Very High	03 Proj	200	21	45	3	18	0	225			($0)	298	327	625	9	77	0.46	238	69	56		3.42	-3.6

Stable skills set, but not one worth owning.

Barajas,Rod

	Tm	AB	R	H	HR	RBI	SB	Avg	vLH	vRH	R$	OB	Slg	OPS	bb%	ct%	Eye	xBA	PX	SX	G/F	RC/G	RAR
Pos CA	98	0	0	0	0	0	0	0								0							
Age 27 Peak	99 aa	510	58	139	10	71	2	273			$10	296	408	704	3	89	0.30	290	92	66	0.33	4.34	3.7
Bats R	00 aaa	416	33	82	9	56	3	197			($1)	218	317	535	3	88	0.23	283	79	49	1.00	2.15	-24.5
Pwr +	01 ARI	* 268	26	63	10	33	2	235	214	141	$4	265	403	668	4	83	0.24	278	104	47	0.48	3.62	0.3
Spd No change	02 ARI	* 170	14	42	4	24	1	247	196	252	$3	293	382	675	6	85	0.42	268	92	34	0.56	3.99	-1.1
BAvg -	1st Half	76	6	13	1	7	0	171			($2)	241	250	491	8	82	0.50	237	54	23		2.03	-5.1
LIMA D	2nd Half	94	8	29	3	17	1	309			$4	337	489	826	4	87	0.33	293	122	33		6.28	5.8
Risk Very High	03 Proj	150	13	36	4	21	1	240			$2	275	380	656	5	85	0.33	275	93	40		3.62	-1.6

Wanna take a flyer? I would not normally recommend this skills set, but our two new tools, xBA and G/F ratio paint an intriguing upside. A .275 BA and a bit of pop potential might be worth a buck, no?

Barrett,Michael

	Tm	AB	R	H	HR	RBI	SB	Avg	vLH	vRH	R$	OB	Slg	OPS	bb%	ct%	Eye	xBA	PX	SX	G/F	RC/G	RAR
Pos CA	98 aa	476	70	143	16	77	6	300			$19	338	481	819	5	91	0.63	316	121	77	1.75	5.92	26.9
Age 26 Pre-Peak	99 MON	433	53	127	8	52	0	293	267	303	$9	342	436	778	7	91	0.82	301	99	49	1.32	5.52	19.6
Bats R	00 MON	* 391	47	98	3	39	1	251	160	237	$2	311	335	646	8	89	0.77	277	62	52	1.48	3.75	-3.9
Pwr ++	01 MON	472	42	118	6	38	2	250	254	249	$3	288	367	654	5	89	0.46	283	83	59	2.04	3.71	1.6
Spd No change	02 MON	376	41	99	12	49	6	263	261	264	$10	334	418	752	10	83	0.62	267	97	63	1.71	5.08	10.5
BAvg No change	1st Half	198	23	56	7	25	1	283			$6	360	449	810	11	86	0.86	278	102	50		5.96	11.2
LIMA B+	2nd Half	178	18	43	5	24	5	242			$4	304	382	686	8	79	0.43	253	91	65		4.19	-0.0
Risk Low	03 Proj	400	43	109	14	56	5	273			$12	329	442	771	8	85	0.58	285	107	58		5.30	16.3

Was 6-23-.322 on May 1, but it went all downhill from there. Still, there are signs of growth here, and at age 26, he could take the next step up.

Batista,Tony		Yr	Tm	AB	R	H	HR	RBI	SB	Avg	vLH	vRH	R$	OB	Slg	OPS	bb%	ct%	Eye	xBA	PX	SX	G/F	RC/G	RAR
Pos	3B	98	ARI	293	46	80	18	41	1	273	320	247	$11	315	519	834	6	82	0.35	301	155	62	0.84	5.84	11.9
Age	29 Past Peak	99	2TM	519	77	144	31	100	4	277	230	296	$21	327	518	845	7	82	0.40	293	142	68	0.64	6.24	28.1
Bats	R	00	TOR	620	96	163	41	114	5	263	235	273	$22	302	519	822	5	80	0.29	297	143	74	0.79	5.47	18.3
Pwr	+	01	2AL	579	70	138	25	87	5	238	203	248	$13	278	435	713	5	80	0.28	273	115	98	0.76	4.16	-5.0
Spd	-----	02	BAL	615	90	150	31	87	5	244	234	247	$18	301	457	758	8	83	0.47	292	137	68	0.54	4.75	3.7
BAvg	No change	1st Half		293	48	81	18	50	4	276			$13	333	536	869	8	84	0.54	317	165	78		6.36	16.4
LIMA	A+	2nd Half		322	42	69	13	37	1	214			$4	271	385	656	7	81	0.41	270	111	50		3.53	-10.2
Risk	Moderate	03	Proj	600	84	158	31	90	5	263			$20	311	477	788	6	82	0.38	285	130	69		5.26	12.0

Interesting test case for xBAs... Low BAs, consistently higher xBAs. Perhaps his 1st half performance was a sign of a return to pre-'01 levels, but other BPIs are soft. Let's take a shot at a slight BA rebound.

Bautista,Danny		Yr	Tm	AB	R	H	HR	RBI	SB	Avg	vLH	vRH	R$	OB	Slg	OPS	bb%	ct%	Eye	xBA	PX	SX	G/F	RC/G	RAR
Pos	RF	98	ATL	144	17	36	3	17	1	250	259	237	$2	285	389	674	5	85	0.33	287	106	54	1.71	3.92	-4.6
Age	30 Past Peak	99	FLA	* 340	51	95	11	45	5	279	277	293	$10	304	438	742	3	87	0.27	290	98	93	1.59	4.70	-4.0
Bats	R	00	2NL	351	54	100	11	59	6	285	267	295	$12	332	476	808	7	86	0.50	299	112	147	1.50	5.82	6.2
Pwr	+++	01	ARI	222	26	67	5	26	3	302	239	343	$7	343	437	780	6	86	0.45	278	84	87	1.52	5.56	-0.8
Spd	No change	02	ARI	154	22	50	6	23	4	325	362	308	$9	370	500	870	7	86	0.52	285	99	112	2.11	7.05	7.7
BAvg	--	1st Half		154	22	50	6	23	4	325			$9	370	500	870	7	86	0.52	285	99	112		7.05	7.7
LIMA	C+	2nd Half		0	0	0	0	0	0	0			($0)					0							-0.0
Risk	X HIGH	03	Proj	250	35	71	5	35	4	284			$8	326	413	739	6	86	0.45	277	81	114		4.90	0.0

Shoulder surgery prematurely ended a potential career year. Always be cautious with injury rehabs.

Bellhorn,Mark		Yr	Tm	AB	R	H	HR	RBI	SB	Avg	vLH	vRH	R$	OB	Slg	OPS	bb%	ct%	Eye	xBA	PX	SX	G/F	RC/G	RAR
Pos	2B 3B 1B	98	aaa	309	49	72	8	38	5	233			$4	342	392	733	14	76	0.69	258	105	109	1.00	4.91	7.8
Age	28 Peak	99	aa	57	10	14	1	7	0	246			$0	348	333	682	14	74	0.60	221	57	40		4.41	0.4
Bats	S	00	aaa	436	99	104	21	65	17	239			$14	360	454	814	16	74	0.72	261	116	183	1.33	6.06	27.6
Pwr	No change	01	OAK	* 230	34	44	10	31	2	191	118	140	$1	265	365	630	9	62	0.26	203	96	111	0.63	3.30	-7.1
Spd	No change	02	CHC	445	86	115	27	56	7	258	303	241	$15	367	512	879	15	68	0.53	244	147	112	0.79	6.83	34.7
BAvg	No change	1st Half		142	25	34	10	26	5	239			$6	361	521	882	16	58	0.46	216	168	73		6.95	11.8
LIMA	A+	2nd Half		303	61	81	17	30	2	267			$9	369	508	878	14	72	0.58	255	137	114		6.78	22.9
Risk	X HIGH	03	Proj	500	91	117	22	67	9	234			$11	338	431	769	14	67	0.48	232	115	129		5.25	19.0

Doing all he can to lock up a full-time gig, but his BPIs paint a scary picture. Platoon splits, poor contact rate, xBA all describe a skills set with downside. He might hit 30 HRs but battle the Mendoza Line.

Belliard,Ron		Yr	Tm	AB	R	H	HR	RBI	SB	Avg	vLH	vRH	R$	OB	Slg	OPS	bb%	ct%	Eye	xBA	PX	SX	G/F	RC/G	RAR
Pos	2B 3B	98	aaa	512	87	147	10	55	25	287			$19	355	430	785	10	89	0.95	300	98	133	3.00	5.71	25.3
Age	28 Peak	99	MIL	* 565	70	158	9	64	13	280	273	304	$13	356	400	764	12	88	1.10	284	82	83	1.41	5.45	21.0
Bats	R	00	MIL	571	83	150	8	54	7	263	282	257	$8	355	389	744	13	85	0.98	278	79	115	1.61	5.14	12.8
Pwr	+	01	MIL	364	69	96	11	36	5	264	284	259	$8	328	453	782	9	82	0.54	290	123	119	1.29	5.40	16.6
Spd	No change	02	MIL	289	30	61	3	26	2	211	200	217	($2)	257	287	545	6	84	0.39	247	55	54	1.69	2.42	-18.2
BAvg	+++	1st Half		151	18	36	0	11	2	238			($0)	290	298	588	7	87	0.58	257	52	65		3.05	-6.7
LIMA	C	2nd Half		138	12	25	3	15	0	181			($2)	221	275	496	5	80	0.26	237	58	40		1.83	-11.1
Risk	Moderate	03	Proj	250	33	62	4	24	3	248			$3	308	366	674	8	84	0.54	265	79	76		3.95	-1.2

2nd half culminated his descent into oblivion. Nearly every key indicator is on a 4-year freefall. The good news is there's only one way to go from here. The bad news is the risk is too great to even take a flyer at this point.

Bell,David		Yr	Tm	AB	R	H	HR	RBI	SB	Avg	vLH	vRH	R$	OB	Slg	OPS	bb%	ct%	Eye	xBA	PX	SX	G/F	RC/G	RAR
Pos	3B	98	2AL	429	48	117	10	49	0	273	261	278	$7	316	422	738	6	85	0.42	278	100	41	0.85	4.66	1.4
Age	30 Past Peak	99	SEA	597	92	160	21	78	7	268	220	280	$14	333	432	765	9	85	0.64	283	100	79	1.00	5.23	13.4
Bats	R	00	SEA	454	57	112	11	47	2	247	287	234	$4	310	381	692	8	85	0.64	274	83	60	0.86	4.16	-4.6
Pwr	+++	01	SEA	470	62	122	15	64	2	260	256	261	$10	301	415	716	6	87	0.47	282	100	50	0.65	4.44	-0.1
Spd	No change	02	SF	552	82	144	20	73	1	261	263	260	$13	327	429	756	9	86	0.68	279	104	55	0.83	5.06	6.5
BAvg	No change	1st Half		280	48	70	11	39	0	250			$6	314	421	735	8	86	0.68	282	103	61		4.68	-0.0
LIMA	A	2nd Half		272	34	74	9	34	1	272			$7	340	437	777	9	85	0.67	276	104	51		5.47	6.7
Risk	Low	03	Proj	500	68	130	16	64	2	260			$10	319	417	736	8	86	0.61	281	99	52		4.76	3.3

Consistent skills set, his last two seasons are virtually indistinguishable, despite the apparent power growth. Quite likely won't hit 20 HRs again.

Bell,Jay		Yr	Tm	AB	R	H	HR	RBI	SB	Avg	vLH	vRH	R$	OB	Slg	OPS	bb%	ct%	Eye	xBA	PX	SX	G/F	RC/G	RAR
Pos	3B	98	ARI	549	79	138	20	67	3	251	255	250	$12	348	432	779	13	77	0.63	263	118	79	0.90	5.41	16.3
Age	37 Decline	99	ARI	589	132	170	38	112	7	289	339	268	$28	376	557	932	12	78	0.62	286	155	114	0.84	7.86	65.5
Bats	R	00	ARI	565	87	151	18	68	7	267	347	239	$13	348	437	785	11	84	0.80	287	102	103	0.83	5.64	22.5
Pwr	---	01	ARI	428	59	106	13	46	0	248	224	256	$6	347	400	746	13	82	0.82	267	96	37	0.98	5.12	6.1
Spd	No change	02	ARI	* 71	6	12	2	13	0	169	130	192	($1)	253	310	563	10	86	0.80	270	92	18	1.06	2.63	-4.6
BAvg	+++++	1st Half		22	3	4	0	2	0	182			($1)	280	318	598	12	95	3.00	319	118	44		3.09	-1.1
LIMA	C+	2nd Half		49	3	8	2	11	0	163			($0)	241	306	547	9	82	0.56	248	80	2		2.44	-3.5
Risk	Very High	03	Proj	250	43	67	6	35	2	268			$6	359	411	769	12	80	0.71	261	91	89		5.52	7.9

PX and G/F trends say the power days are gone. So even if he is perfectly healthy and lands another full-time job, 15 HRs could be a stretch.

Beltran,Carlos		Yr	Tm	AB	R	H	HR	RBI	SB	Avg	vLH	vRH	R$	OB	Slg	OPS	bb%	ct%	Eye	xBA	PX	SX	G/F	RC/G	RAR
Pos	CF	98	aa	240	49	72	10	40	8	300			$12	354	533	887	8	86	0.61	322	145	180	0.94	7.25	19.5
Age	25 Pre-Peak	99	KC	663	112	194	22	108	27	293	273	298	$29	339	454	793	6	81	0.37	275	93	143	1.46	5.72	18.6
Bats	S	00	KC	372	49	92	7	44	13	247	310	233	$7	312	366	678	9	81	0.51	257	70	139	1.43	4.32	-5.1
Pwr	No change	01	KC	617	106	189	24	101	31	306	315	303	$34	360	514	874	8	81	0.43	288	121	181	1.36	7.39	46.7
Spd	----	02	KC	637	114	174	29	105	35	273	244	283	$34	346	501	847	10	79	0.53	289	147	160	1.39	6.49	32.6
BAvg	-	1st Half		302	53	80	12	46	18	265			$15	337	480	817	10	78	0.49	282	141	170		6.06	11.4
LIMA	A	2nd Half		335	61	94	17	59	17	281			$19	354	519	873	10	80	0.56	295	154	142		6.88	21.4
Risk	High	03	Proj	625	107	170	20	89	35	272			$28	337	451	789	9	80	0.50	278	113	167		5.82	18.0

Four reasons to be cautious:
- At a more normal 550 AB, his stats aren't nearly as impressive.
- Platoon splits show vulnerability.
- G/F ratios indicate possible power downside.
- Other BPIs just average.

Beltre,Adrian		Yr	Tm	AB	R	H	HR	RBI	SB	Avg	vLH	vRH	R$	OB	Slg	OPS	bb%	ct%	Eye	xBA	PX	SX	G/F	RC/G	RAR
Pos	3B	98	LA	* 441	61	112	18	71	21	254	175	226	$19	327	444	772	10	85	0.72	299	128	100	1.05	5.26	10.6
Age	25 Pre-Peak	99	LA	538	84	148	15	67	18	275	230	290	$17	349	428	776	10	80	0.58	268	95	116	1.16	5.53	18.5
Bats	R	00	LA	510	71	148	20	85	12	290	277	294	$21	360	475	835	10	84	0.70	292	112	81	1.07	6.42	32.6
Pwr	+	01	LA	475	59	126	13	60	13	265	265	265	$14	306	411	717	6	83	0.34	271	88	117	1.09	4.50	-2.5
Spd	-----	02	LA	587	70	151	21	75	7	257	302	245	$15	301	426	727	6	84	0.39	274	100	91	0.99	4.46	-3.9
BAvg	--	1st Half		296	31	70	7	29	2	236			$2	289	365	654	7	85	0.50	266	80	67		3.52	-10.6
LIMA	A	2nd Half		291	39	81	14	46	5	278			$12	314	488	802	5	82	0.29	282	121	110		5.57	7.8
Risk	Low	03	Proj	550	70	157	26	91	10	285			$24	334	493	827	7	83	0.43	288	122	90		5.99	24.2

Reasons why we might want to put him back on our radar:
- Terrific 2nd half
- xBAs better and more stable than BAs
- Declining G/F ratios might indicate power growth.

Benard,Marvin		Yr	Tm	AB	R	H	HR	RBI	SB	Avg	vLH	vRH	R$	OB	Slg	OPS	bb%	ct%	Eye	xBA	PX	SX	G/F	RC/G	RAR
Pos	RF	98	SF	286	41	92	3	36	11	322	237	335	$13	394	434	827	11	86	0.87	283	89	90	1.61	6.80	16.5
Age	32 Past Peak	99	SF	562	100	163	16	64	27	290	263	297	$22	353	457	811	9	83	0.57	282	107	126	1.29	5.83	12.8
Bats	L	00	SF	560	102	147	12	55	22	263	216	273	$14	337	396	734	10	83	0.65	271	82	140	1.62	4.94	-5.4
Pwr	No change	01	SF	392	70	104	15	44	10	265	390	251	$12	316	439	755	7	83	0.44	282	103	115	1.16	4.89	-9.4
Spd	++	02	SF	123	16	34	1	13	5	276	389	257	$4	315	407	722	5	79	0.27	259	90	153	1.06	4.74	-2.5
BAvg	--	1st Half		115	16	34	1	13	5	296			$4	336	435	771	6	81	0.32	269	96	156		5.55	0.5
LIMA	B+	2nd Half		8	0	0	0	0	0	0			($1)	0	0	0	0	50	0.00		0			0.00	-1.2
Risk	Low	03	Proj	350	57	99	10	39	9	283			$12	341	457	798	8	83	0.50	282	109	125		5.65	8.1

Knee surgery ended his season early, but it was starting out to be pretty similar to 2001. If healthy, should post comparable numbers, except perhaps for his speed.

Benjamin,Mike

		Tm	AB	R	H	HR	RBI	SB	Avg	vLH	vRH	R$	OB	Slg	OPS	bb%	ct%	Eye	xBA	PX	SX	G/F	RC/G	RAR
Pos 3B	98	BOS	349	46	95	4	39	3	272	333	338	$5	302	372	675	4	79	0.21	247	75	69	1.47	4.11	-4.6
Age 37 Decline	99	PIT	368	42	91	1	37	10	247	261	239	$4	286	364	650	5	76	0.22	248	82	163	1.09	3.76	-7.7
Bats R	00	PIT	233	28	63	2	19	5	270	325	242	$4	306	391	697	5	81	0.27	266	86	101	1.24	4.11	-2.1
Pwr No change	01	PIT	0	0	0	0	0	0	0								0							
Spd No change	02	PIT	120	7	18	0	3	0	150	128	160	($5)	197	183	380	6	74	0.23	204	22	75	1.26	0.95	-13.6
BAvg +++++	1st Half		70	3	10	0	1	0	143			($3)	178	157	335	4	74	0.17	197	12	42		0.65	-8.4
LIMA F	2nd Half		50	4	8	0	2	0	160			($2)	222	220	442	7	74	0.31	215	35	133		1.45	-5.0
Risk Moderate	03	Proj	100	9	21	0	6	1	210			($1)	253	291	544	5	76	0.25	233	58	98		2.31	-6.8

The issue is not so much how bad this season was but how any team would see fit to endure 120 AB of it.

Bennett,Gary

		Tm	AB	R	H	HR	RBI	SB	Avg	vLH	vRH	R$	OB	Slg	OPS	bb%	ct%	Eye	xBA	PX	SX	G/F	RC/G	RAR
Pos CA	98	aaa	313	27	70	7	32	0	224			$1	275	342	616	7	88	0.58	275	82		1.86	3.25	-7.6
Age 31 Past Peak	99	PHI	88	7	24	1	21	0	273	273	273	$2	304	352	657	4	88	0.36	265	57		2.11	3.89	-0.4
Bats R	00	PHI	* 391	46	108	11	48	1	276	364	192	$8	354	440	794	11	86	0.87	296	109	33	1.10	5.89	22.7
Pwr No change	01	2NL	* 198	21	49	4	22	0	247	185	260	$2	304	374	677	7	81	0.43	259	82	46	1.50	4.06	2.9
Spd No change	02	COL	291	26	77	4	26	1	265	365	237	$4	301	354	655	5	85	0.33	250	57	57	2.06	3.67	-4.6
BAvg --	1st Half		139	11	36	3	12	1	259			$2	304	345	649	6	80	0.32	231	52	31		3.59	-2.6
LIMA D	2nd Half		152	15	41	1	14	0	270			$2	297	362	659	4	89	0.35	268	61	81		3.75	-2.0
Risk X HIGH	03	Proj	250	25	65	4	25	0	260			$3	308	369	678	7	85	0.46	262	72	46		4.04	0.5

This is not the type of player who would ever likely surprise you offensively, except... When you're down to your last spot and have $1 to spend, any COL player is a better pct play than the alternative.

Bergeron,Peter

		Tm	AB	R	H	HR	RBI	SB	Avg	vLH	vRH	R$	OB	Slg	OPS	bb%	ct%	Eye	xBA	PX	SX	G/F	RC/G	RAR
Pos CF	98	aa	550	83	138	6	51	33	251			$15	326	344	669	10	86	0.80	271	62	144		4.15	-8.3
Age 25 Pre-Peak	99	a/a	356	56	106	6	33	20	298			$14	369	441	810	10	83	0.68	280	96	124	1.67	5.53	10.5
Bats L	00	MON	518	80	127	5	31	11	245	218	251	$3	321	349	671	10	81	0.58	256	67	122	2.23	3.80	-10.0
Pwr --	01	MON	* 581	79	125	3	23	24	215	250	200	$2	273	279	552	7	78	0.37	232	40	143	1.98	2.51	-25.4
Spd --	02	MON	* 463	69	116	1	32	16	251	200	184	$6	330	305	635	11	78	0.55	227	35	126	2.39	3.60	-20.3
BAvg No change	1st Half		285	51	71	1	21	13	249			$5	335	316	651	11	73	0.48	218	42	161		3.96	-9.3
LIMA C	2nd Half		178	18	45	0	11	3	253			$1	321	287	608	9	87	0.78	240	24	69		3.05	-10.7
Risk Very High	03	Proj	250	35	61	1	15	8	244			$2	315	314	630	9	81	0.54	242	45	125		3.40	-7.8

0-7-10-.187 in 123 AB at MON. Slightly better in AAA, but not enough to warrant a F/T MLB job. BPIs and trends don't offer much hope, but he's young and has shown promise before. You can't ever write these guys off.

Berger,Brandon

		Tm	AB	R	H	HR	RBI	SB	Avg	vLH	vRH	R$	OB	Slg	OPS	bb%	ct%	Eye	xBA	PX	SX	G/F	RC/G	RAR
Pos CF	98		0	0	0	0	0	0	0								0							
Age 28 Peak	99		0	0	0	0	0	0	0								0							
Bats R	00	aa	86	8	13	2	7	5	151			($0)	207	244	451	7	66	0.21	201	54	96		1.58	-7.9
Pwr ++	01	aa	486	75	122	32	84	10	251			$19	297	516	814	6	83	0.40	307	151	109	0.20	5.21	11.4
Spd --	02	KC	* 395	43	94	16	53	10	238	214	192	$11	287	418	704	6	83	0.40	280	115	97	0.83	4.21	-8.1
BAvg -	1st Half		182	17	38	8	21	3	209			$3	262	396	657	7	81	0.37	276	122	56		3.56	-7.3
LIMA C+	2nd Half		213	26	56	8	32	7	263			$8	308	437	745	6	85	0.42	282	108	115		4.82	-0.4
Risk Very High	03	Proj	200	26	49	10	30	5	245			$7	293	456	749	6	83	0.40	291	128	90		4.63	-1.7

6-17-.201 in 134 AB at KC. At 28, he's experiencing his peak AND trying to make the jump to the majors at the same time. So far, not so good. OB says he's not worth watching. xBA says otherwise. End-game flyer.

Berg,Dave

		Tm	AB	R	H	HR	RBI	SB	Avg	vLH	vRH	R$	OB	Slg	OPS	bb%	ct%	Eye	xBA	PX	SX	G/F	RC/G	RAR
Pos 2B 3B	98	FLA	182	18	57	2	21	3	313	290	327	$6	399	407	806	13	75	0.57	237	75	47	1.06	6.70	14.9
Age 32 Past Peak	99	FLA	304	42	87	3	25	2	286	241	303	$5	344	382	726	8	81	0.46	253	70	61	1.14	4.89	5.6
Bats R	00	FLA	210	23	53	1	21	3	252	270	245	$2	332	343	675	11	78	0.54	247	68	75	0.98	4.32	-0.9
Pwr +	01	FLA	215	26	52	4	16	0	242	211	253	$1	288	363	651	6	82	0.36	260	80	59	0.67	3.60	-2.2
Spd No change	02	TOR	374	42	101	4	39	0	270	264	272	$6	318	382	700	7	85	0.46	266	86	51	0.97	4.34	2.5
BAvg --	1st Half		173	16	41	4	15	0	237			$2	279	364	643	5	83	0.33	259	85	46		3.53	-3.1
LIMA D+	2nd Half		201	26	60	0	24	0	299			$4	350	398	748	7	87	0.59	273	87	56		5.12	6.2
Risk Moderate	03	Proj	250	29	66	3	24	1	264			$3	319	373	692	8	82	0.46	257	81	57		4.30	0.7

374 AB won't likely happen again, which means in 2003 he returns to undraftable status.

Berkman,Lance

		Tm	AB	R	H	HR	RBI	SB	Avg	vLH	vRH	R$	OB	Slg	OPS	bb%	ct%	Eye	xBA	PX	SX	G/F	RC/G	RAR
Pos CF LF	98	a/a	484	78	130	21	83	5	269			$17	367	473	840	13	84	0.97	298	136	55		6.48	29.6
Age 27 Peak	99	HOU	* 319	42	84	9	52	10	263	154	250	$10	345	411	756	11	82	0.68	271	98	73	1.16	5.36	9.9
Bats S	00	HOU	353	76	105	21	67	6	297	218	320	$18	394	561	955	14	79	0.77	300	159	85	1.14	8.55	48.4
Pwr +	01	HOU	577	110	191	34	126	7	331	308	337	$37	423	620	1043	14	79	0.76	307	178	88	1.02	10.19	119.7
Spd ---	02	HOU	578	106	169	42	128	8	292	240	307	$35	403	578	981	16	80	0.91	293	166	72	0.95	8.97	78.4
BAvg -	1st Half		286	48	81	25	68	4	283			$18	399	601	1000	16	83	1.10	310	181	45		9.12	40.4
LIMA C+	2nd Half		292	58	88	17	60	4	301			$17	407	555	962	15	77	0.76	277	151	90		8.82	37.8
Risk Moderate	03	Proj	575	108	173	46	120	8	301			$36	402	623	1025	14	79	0.83	309	188	80		9.59	100.0

Does he keep rising, or level out? Eye and G/F trends point skyward, but BA vsLH and 2nd half fade suggest we may need to temper our expectations a bit. Still... UP: 50 HRs

Biggio,Craig

		Tm	AB	R	H	HR	RBI	SB	Avg	vLH	vRH	R$	OB	Slg	OPS	bb%	ct%	Eye	xBA	PX	SX	G/F	RC/G	RAR
Pos 2B	98	HOU	646	123	210	20	88	50	325	343	320	$44	386	503	889	9	83	0.57	292	128	130	1.38	7.91	75.3
Age 37 Decline	99	HOU	639	123	188	16	73	28	294	307	290	$24	380	457	837	12	83	0.82	286	115	90	1.40	6.51	45.9
Bats R	00	HOU	377	67	101	8	35	12	268	235	275	$9	370	393	762	14	81	0.84	259	72	138	1.59	5.70	15.6
Pwr ---	01	HOU	617	118	180	20	70	7	292	222	306	$20	360	455	816	10	84	0.66	281	102	95	1.25	6.18	43.8
Spd -	02	HOU	577	96	146	15	58	16	253	183	271	$13	313	404	716	8	81	0.45	267	98	125	1.31	4.63	2.4
BAvg -	1st Half		282	42	69	6	30	9	245			$6	311	379	690	9	80	0.48	260	91	109		4.35	-1.4
LIMA A	2nd Half		295	54	77	9	28	7	261			$7	314	427	742	7	81	0.42	273	105	127		4.92	3.8
Risk Moderate	03	Proj	450	80	117	12	47	10	260			$11	331	414	744	10	82	0.58	272	98	119		5.04	13.3

5-year decline in BA vsLH may mean it's time to consider more of a platoon role here. At 37, it's not likely going to get any better than this.

Blalock,Hank

		Tm	AB	R	H	HR	RBI	SB	Avg	vLH	vRH	R$	OB	Slg	OPS	bb%	ct%	Eye	xBA	PX	SX	G/F	RC/G	RAR
Pos 3B	98		0	0	0	0	0	0	0								0							
Age 22 Growth	99		0	0	0	0	0	0	0								0							
Bats L	00		0	0	0	0	0	0	0								0							
Pwr No change	01	aa	272	44	87	11	54	3	320			$14	399	529	929	12	89	1.24	313	128	87		8.19	31.9
Spd No change	02	TEX	* 534	69	148	10	69	2	277	67	248	$12	338	412	750	8	84	0.58	274	101	55	0.95	5.18	10.3
BAvg -	1st Half		247	30	74	3	29	2	300			$7	352	437	789	7	83	0.47	275	109	69		5.93	10.4
LIMA A	2nd Half		287	39	74	7	40	0	258			$6	326	390	716	9	86	0.71	274	94	35		4.60	0.4
Risk High	03	Proj	400	57	112	11	63	3	280			$12	351	443	794	10	86	0.80	289	110	67		5.76	14.7

3-17-.211 in 147 AB at TEX. Flopped in his 1st exposure to the bigs, but it's tough for a 21-year-old to please all the flag wavers. BPIs took a step back in '02, but '01 shows the potential. Give him time.

Blanco,Henry

		Tm	AB	R	H	HR	RBI	SB	Avg	vLH	vRH	R$	OB	Slg	OPS	bb%	ct%	Eye	xBA	PX	SX	G/F	RC/G	RAR
Pos CA	98	aaa	134	14	26	3	16	2	194			$0	270	321	591	9	83	0.61	268	89	58		3.04	-4.2
Age 31 Past Peak	99	COL	* 320	35	79	8	36	1	247	222	238	$3	321	391	712	10	86	0.78	281	90	64	0.64	4.46	4.2
Bats R	00	MIL	284	29	67	7	31	0	236	306	216	$2	322	394	716	11	79	0.60	270	109	20	0.71	4.40	2.9
Pwr -	01	MIL	314	33	66	6	31	3	210	164	224	$0	287	344	631	10	77	0.47	250	86	96	0.57	3.45	-1.4
Spd No change	02	ATL	221	17	45	6	22	0	204	211	202	($1)	270	335	605	8	77	0.39	238	81	38	0.79	2.97	-8.5
BAvg +++	1st Half		90	6	17	2	7	0	189			($1)	247	300	547	7	78	0.35	234	72	13		2.49	-4.7
LIMA F	2nd Half		131	11	28	4	15	0	214			$0	285	359	643	9	76	0.42	240	86	55		3.31	-3.6
Risk Very High	03	Proj	200	18	42	5	21	1	210			($0)	283	348	632	9	78	0.46	250	89	52		3.33	-4.1

Yuck. I thought it was tough to keep falling once you're already on the floor, but he keeps proving me wrong.

Blum,Geoff

Pos	3B
Age	29 Past Peak
Bats	S
Pwr	+
Spd	+
BAvg	-
LIMA	C+
Risk	High

Yr	Tm	AB	R	H	HR	RBI	SB	Avg	vLH	vRH	R$	OB	Slg	OPS	bb%	ct%	Eye	xBA	PX	SX	G/F	RC/G	RAR
98	aa	162	20	40	5	17	2	247			$3	315	444	759	9	83	0.57	294	127	126		4.95	2.1
99	MON	* 401	58	98	16	50	6	244	190	250	$8	328	431	760	11	86	0.86	293	113	93	0.82	5.17	9.3
00	MON	343	40	97	11	45	1	283	292	280	$9	333	449	782	7	83	0.43	280	102	51	0.93	5.31	9.5
01	MON	453	57	107	9	50	9	236	263	229	$6	302	351	653	9	79	0.46	251	77	73	1.01	3.71	-13.7
02	HOU	368	45	104	10	52	2	283	185	304	$11	367	440	807	12	81	0.70	264	98	86	1.03	6.23	18.4
1st Half		158	19	43	3	21	1	272			$4	343	424	767	10	80	0.55	264	106	68		5.47	3.9
2nd Half		210	26	61	7	31	1	290			$7	384	452	837	13	81	0.82	263	92	90		6.83	14.8
03	Proj	250	31	69	6	32	2	276			$6	350	417	767	10	81	0.60	263	90	79		5.46	7.2

I'mproving plate patience might help him maintain his BA near this level, but platoon split will most surely cost him playing time. 821 AB in 2 years has been a gift, thanks to injuries and prospect failures.

Bocachica,Hiram

Pos	LF
Age	27 Peak
Bats	R
Pwr	+
Spd	No change
BAvg	No change
LIMA	C
Risk	Very High

Yr	Tm	AB	R	H	HR	RBI	SB	Avg	vLH	vRH	R$	OB	Slg	OPS	bb%	ct%	Eye	xBA	PX	SX	G/F	RC/G	RAR
98	a/a	438	54	108	6	43	24	247			$11	307	377	683	8	82	0.48	273	92	140		4.06	-13.2
99	aa	477	66	116	9	48	23	243			$10	310	358	668	9	88	0.79	279	70	123		3.65	-22.6
00	aaa	482	77	131	18	66	8	272			$14	316	456	772	6	83	0.38	288	113	81	1.00	4.50	-11.0
01	LA	133	15	31	2	9	4	233	260	217	$1	282	376	658	6	75	0.27	253	100	113	0.88	3.70	-8.6
02	2TM	168	26	37	8	17	3	220	275	182	$2	264	405	669	6	76	0.24	253	112	83	0.85	3.39	-11.8
1st Half		56	10	13	3	7	1	232			$0	295	446	742	8	68	0.28	237	132	77		4.69	-1.8
2nd Half		112	16	24	5	10	2	214			$0	248	384	632	4	79	0.22	261	102	83		2.82	-9.7
03	Proj	150	22	35	5	15	4	233			$2	281	412	693	6	77	0.29	268	112	109		3.79	-7.7

In leagues where every HR counts, he can be a useful end-gamer, just so long as you're stocked well with .300 hitters.

Bonds,Barry

Pos	LF
Age	38 Decline
Bats	L
Pwr	No change
Spd	- - - - -
BAvg	-
LIMA	C
Risk	Moderate

Yr	Tm	AB	R	H	HR	RBI	SB	Avg	vLH	vRH	R$	OB	Slg	OPS	bb%	ct%	Eye	xBA	PX	SX	G/F	RC/G	RAR
98	SF	552	120	167	37	122	28	303	280	313	$41	435	609	1044	19	83	1.41	329	196	136	0.63	10.32	105.6
99	SF	355	91	93	34	83	15	262	266	260	$23	388	617	1005	17	83	1.18	327	200	122	0.62	9.10	48.3
00	SF	480	129	147	49	106	11	306	230	340	$34	442	688	1130	20	84	1.52	346	209	112	0.57	12.15	116.4
01	SF	476	129	156	73	137	13	328	312	334	$51	510	863	1373	27	80	1.90	376	292	84	0.56	18.50	236.8
02	SF	403	117	149	46	110	9	370	384	363	$44	577	799	1376	33	88	4.21	371	244	78	0.65	21.62	259.4
1st Half		206	62	71	25	50	3	345			$20	563	791	1354	33	88	4.29	374	248	85		20.09	119.8
2nd Half		197	55	78	21	60	6	396			$25	592	807	1400	33	88	4.13	367	241	56		23.38	140.7
03	Proj	450	124	145	43	110	7	322			$36	515	692	1206	28	85	2.67	345	213	75		15.27	188.8

Another season for the ages, but where does he go from here? With a 38-year-old, you HAVE to start tempering expectations.

Boone,Aaron

Pos	3B
Age	30 Past Peak
Bats	R
Pwr	+ + +
Spd	+ + + + +
BAvg	+ + +
LIMA	A
Risk	High

Yr	Tm	AB	R	H	HR	RBI	SB	Avg	vLH	vRH	R$	OB	Slg	OPS	bb%	ct%	Eye	xBA	PX	SX	G/F	RC/G	RAR
98	CIN	* 513	73	124	8	61	21	242	208	313	$12	300	359	659	8	81	0.43	264	86	127	0.90	3.89	-9.7
99	CIN	* 513	61	144	14	77	19	281	219	297	$19	323	441	763	6	84	0.39	282	100	119	1.03	5.09	10.0
00	CIN	291	44	83	12	43	6	285	302	382	$11	340	471	810	8	82	0.46	286	114	73	0.79	6.01	14.4
01	CIN	381	54	112	14	62	6	294	306	290	$16	344	483	827	7	81	0.41	282	118	87	1.00	6.14	17.1
02	CIN	606	83	146	26	87	32	241	233	243	$23	305	439	744	8	82	0.50	282	122	114	1.01	4.75	1.2
1st Half		291	31	65	11	39	11	223			$7	283	375	657	8	82	0.45	261	87	89		3.56	-10.1
2nd Half		315	52	81	15	48	21	257			$16	326	498	824	9	82	0.55	300	155	127		6.01	13.2
03	Proj	600	85	164	29	99	23	273			$28	331	488	819	8	82	0.47	289	131	102		5.90	25.1

xBA says his low batting avg was a fluke. We should see some rebound there. His PX trend is exciting, and at 30, his power skills may not have peaked yet.

Boone,Bret

Pos	2B
Age	34 Decline
Bats	R
Pwr	+ +
Spd	No change
BAvg	-
LIMA	A
Risk	Moderate

Yr	Tm	AB	R	H	HR	RBI	SB	Avg	vLH	vRH	R$	OB	Slg	OPS	bb%	ct%	Eye	xBA	PX	SX	G/F	RC/G	RAR
98	CIN	583	76	155	24	95	6	266	230	277	$20	322	458	780	8	82	0.46	288	130	63	1.31	5.26	19.1
99	ATL	608	102	153	20	63	14	252	280	241	$12	305	416	721	7	82	0.42	276	106	91	1.11	4.37	1.3
00	SD	463	61	116	19	74	8	251	235	257	$12	324	421	745	10	79	0.52	266	98	78	0.98	4.87	6.1
01	SEA	623	118	206	37	141	5	331	444	296	$38	371	578	949	6	82	0.36	294	146	75	1.13	8.19	73.9
02	SEA	608	88	169	24	107	12	278	295	272	$25	336	462	798	8	83	0.52	285	120	95	1.68	5.68	29.4
1st Half		301	45	70	11	50	6	233			$8	300	395	695	9	84	0.60	276	102	103		4.05	-0.7
2nd Half		307	43	99	13	57	6	322			$17	372	528	899	7	82	0.44	293	138	81		7.71	33.9
03	Proj	600	92	164	22	100	10	273			$21	329	449	778	8	82	0.47	278	112	93		5.35	21.3

Excellent 2nd half salvaged a poor start, but at 34, these periodic lapses will become tougher to climb over.

Bordick,Mike

Pos	SS
Age	37 Decline
Bats	R
Pwr	- -
Spd	- -
BAvg	+ + +
LIMA	B
Risk	High

Yr	Tm	AB	R	H	HR	RBI	SB	Avg	vLH	vRH	R$	OB	Slg	OPS	bb%	ct%	Eye	xBA	PX	SX	G/F	RC/G	RAR
98	BAL	465	59	121	13	51	6	260	184	285	$9	317	411	728	8	86	0.60	283	99	62	1.12	4.50	7.3
99	BAL	631	93	175	10	77	14	277	402	252	$15	334	403	737	8	84	0.53	273	81	127	1.05	5.01	14.9
00	2TM	583	88	166	20	80	9	285	307	277	$18	340	443	783	8	83	0.49	277	96	72	1.06	5.49	26.6
01	BAL	229	32	57	7	30	9	249	333	217	$7	301	397	698	7	84	0.47	274	95	86	0.98	4.21	-1.8
02	BAL	367	37	85	8	36	7	232	236	230	$5	299	365	664	9	83	0.56	265	91	94	0.88	3.78	-10.3
1st Half		223	22	52	3	18	5	233			$3	305	359	664	9	83	0.62	266	88	119		3.95	-5.1
2nd Half		144	15	33	5	18	2	229			$3	288	375	663	8	82	0.46	262	95	49		3.50	-5.2
03	Proj	400	49	96	8	47	5	240			$6	300	359	659	8	83	0.51	261	81	68		3.68	-1.5

His offensive value has waned to the point that he's no more than an end-game pick right now.

Bradley,Milton

Pos	CF
Age	25 Pre-Peak
Bats	S
Pwr	No change
Spd	- - -
BAvg	No change
LIMA	A+
Risk	X HIGH

Yr	Tm	AB	R	H	HR	RBI	SB	Avg	vLH	vRH	R$	OB	Slg	OPS	bb%	ct%	Eye	xBA	PX	SX	G/F	RC/G	RAR
98		0	0	0	0	0	0	0								0							
99	aa	346	53	105	9	43	12	303			$14	356	465	821	7	85	0.54	287	102	115		5.62	10.9
00	MON	* 496	71	131	8	40	11	264	261	204	$8	334	375	709	9	83	0.63	268	74	76	1.57	4.11	-4.7
01	2TM	* 488	57	115	8	44	29	236	156	247	$12	317	361	678	11	75	0.48	243	81	135	1.90	4.17	-4.2
02	CLE	* 359	52	90	9	42	8	251	293	230	$9	319	396	715	9	82	0.57	268	97	110	1.70	4.43	-5.0
1st Half		168	19	40	3	14	4	238			$3	312	345	657	10	79	0.50	238	67	112		3.73	-6.1
2nd Half		191	33	50	6	28	4	262			$6	325	440	765	9	86	0.67	296	123	103		5.11	1.4
03	Proj	550	77	140	12	59	15	255			$13	324	395	720	9	81	0.55	265	93	111		4.45	-7.8

Signs of life in the second half presage him taking his game to the next level. Still some concerns, however, about his BA vsRH and low OB, which will limit his upside in the short-term.

Bragg,Darren

Pos	RF
Age	33 Decline
Bats	L
Pwr	No change
Spd	+ + + +
BAvg	No change
LIMA	C
Risk	Very High

Yr	Tm	AB	R	H	HR	RBI	SB	Avg	vLH	vRH	R$	OB	Slg	OPS	bb%	ct%	Eye	xBA	PX	SX	G/F	RC/G	RAR
98	BOS	409	51	114	8	57	5	279	246	248	$10	346	423	769	9	76	0.42	252	98	85	1.78	5.41	3.4
99	STL	273	38	71	6	26	3	260	230	269	$4	363	377	740	14	75	0.66	240	75	69	1.51	5.31	1.9
00	COL	149	16	33	3	21	4	221	63	241	$2	301	342	643	10	72	0.41	234	76	92	1.82	3.70	-7.3
01	2TM	* 359	48	93	9	28	9	259	333	259	$7	342	401	743	11	71	0.44	232	91	90	2.13	4.91	-5.3
02	ATL	* 287	46	75	4	21	9	261	308	263	$5	350	387	736	12	77	0.59	248	88	111	1.20	5.01	-3.7
1st Half		158	29	43	2	13	5	272			$4	375	405	780	14	81	0.87	264	91	126		5.55	0.8
2nd Half		129	17	32	2	8	4	248			$2	317	364	681	9	72	0.36	228	84	79		4.37	-4.2
03	Proj	200	28	51	4	17	5	255			$4	338	381	718	11	74	0.48	238	84	94		4.73	-1.1

Lefties off the bench always have some value, but his is marginal. xBAs are soft and G/F ratios might limit his power upside. 2nd half fade is not so good either.

Branyan,Russ

Pos	LF 3B
Age	27 Peak
Bats	L
Pwr	+
Spd	No change
BAvg	No change
LIMA	B+
Risk	High

Yr	Tm	AB	R	H	HR	RBI	SB	Avg	vLH	vRH	R$	OB	Slg	OPS	bb%	ct%	Eye	xBA	PX	SX	G/F	RC/G	RAR
98	aa	163	32	46	14	42	1	282			$10	400	638	1038	16	67	0.59	275	213	106		9.63	25.7
99	aaa	395	43	76	25	57	7	192			$6	275	413	688	10	60	0.28	206	120	67	0.50	3.79	-17.3
00	CLE	* 422	72	99	35	90	1	235	200	242	$14	310	533	843	10	64	0.30	243	157	84	0.59	5.75	7.5
01	CLE	315	48	73	20	54	1	232	325	218	$8	314	486	800	11	58	0.29	208	146	76	0.56	5.34	6.3
02	2TM	378	50	86	24	56	4	228	233	226	$4	319	458	777	12	60	0.34	209	133	61	0.88	5.09	-7.8
1st Half		208	23	45	11	26	2	216			$3	297	404	701	10	64	0.32	210	109	39		4.07	-10.9
2nd Half		170	27	41	13	30	2	241			$6	345	524	869	14	55	0.36	205	162	87		6.48	4.2
03	Proj	350	52	86	24	61	3	246			$12	334	505	839	12	60	0.33	220	147	78		6.01	6.0

There has been virtually no skills growth, not a good sign for someone entering his peak. Had a promising, albeit short streak when he came to CIN, which might indicate some upside if he got more consistent PT.

Brown,Adrian	Yr	Tm	AB	R	H	HR	RBI	SB	Avg	vLH	vRH	R$	OB	Slg	OPS	bb%	ct%	Eye	xBA	PX	SX	G/F	RC/G	RAR
Pos CF	98	PIT	•463	65	124	2	26	24	268	395	239	$11	315	337	652	6	89	0.65	275	50	143	3.04	3.96	-6.2
Age 29 Past Peak	99	PIT	•282	42	77	4	20	10	273	250	289	$6	367	365	733	13	84	0.93	260	56	111	3.11	5.16	7.0
Bats R	00	PIT	308	64	97	4	28	13	315	365	305	$12	374	432	806	9	89	0.85	289	77	141	2.46	6.57	20.8
Pwr No change	01	PIT	31	3	6	1	2	2	194			$0	265	290	555	9	90	1.00	268	48	73	2.00	2.50	-1.4
Spd +++++	02	PIT	•392	48	98	3	33	27	250	154	237	$11	315	332	646	9	88	0.76	265	56	124	1.86	3.63	-16.4
BAvg +++	1st Half		171	16	32	1	15	7	187			($1)	265	263	528	10	86	0.75	257	49	118		2.18	-15.0
LIMA C+	2nd Half		221	32	66	2	18	20	299			$12	354	385	739	8	89	0.76	271	61	120		5.13	1.1
Risk Very High	03	Proj	250	38	68	2	20	14	272			$8	338	361	699	9	88	0.80	270	60	125		4.52	1.1

1-21-10-.216 in 208 AB at PIT. Injuries have derailed his career, but at 29, there is still talent here. 2nd half shows upside, and with expectations low right now, a late-round bid could net you a bunch of SBs.

Brown,Dee	Yr	Tm	AB	R	H	HR	RBI	SB	Avg	vLH	vRH	R$	OB	Slg	OPS	bb%	ct%	Eye	xBA	PX	SX	G/F	RC/G	RAR
Pos CF	98		0	0	0	0	0	0	0								0							
Age 25 Pre-Peak	99	aa	235	48	77	10	46	8	328			$14	399	532	931	11	86	0.88	303	119	121		7.60	22.6
Bats L	00	aaa	479	63	126	20	59	17	263			$16	305	455	760	6	83	0.36	289	111	121	2.00	4.98	5.7
Pwr No change	01	KC	•417	43	103	9	45	5	247	258	241	$6	288	357	645	5	80	0.28	242	72	54	1.81	3.57	-17.4
Spd +++++	02	KC	•509	59	128	15	68	8	251	91	275	$13	303	395	698	7	79	0.36	254	95	80	0.47	4.18	-10.8
BAvg --	1st Half		271	24	62	4	29	3	229			$3	277	317	594	6	83	0.39	247	65	49		2.96	-15.8
LIMA C	2nd Half		238	35	66	11	39	5	277			$10	333	483	817	8	74	0.33	260	129	109		5.86	7.3
Risk Very High	03	Proj	200	26	51	7	27	4	255			$5	306	413	719	7	80	0.37	263	100	86		4.41	-3.0

1-7-.235 in 51 AB at KC. In reality, his skills set was soft even in those years that generated all the hot prospect buzz. With neither plate patience nor on base ability, there is a low ceiling here.

Brown,Roosevelt	Yr	Tm	AB	R	H	HR	RBI	SB	Avg	vLH	vRH	R$	OB	Slg	OPS	bb%	ct%	Eye	xBA	PX	SX	G/F	RC/G	RAR
Pos CF LF	98	aa	163	16	38	5	20	2	233			$2	282	387	668	6	84	0.42	280	104	49		3.73	-4.4
Age 27 Peak	99	CHC	•457	53	132	22	79	8	289		226	$19	330	525	855	6	83	0.36	301	150	72	0.86	6.27	25.9
Bats L	00	CHC	•363	57	98	9	47	9	270	250	356	$10	327	419	746	8	86	0.60	290	100	81	0.64	4.95	6.1
Pwr ++	01	CHC	•447	70	130	21	87	3	291	353	242	$19	320	517	837	4	83	0.26	301	140	74	1.35	5.75	24.3
Spd No change	02	CHC	204	14	43	3	23	2	211	200	212	($0)	291	314	604	10	75	0.46	229	73	35	1.65	3.13	-11.9
BAvg +++	1st Half		97	8	17	2	10	1	175			($1)	238	299	537	8	77	0.36	242	85	49		2.27	-8.1
LIMA D+	2nd Half		107	6	26	1	13	1	243			$1	336	327	663	12	74	0.54	218	63	25		4.02	-3.3
Risk Very High	03	Proj	250	27	70	7	35	3	280			$7	338	427	765	8	80	0.44	260	99	44		5.23	6.6

First full year in Wrigley, he went splat. Oddities... sudden spike in bb%, steep drop in ct% and marked trend towards ground balls. This was not the same player as '02, but alleged back pain could be the culprit.

Buchanan,Brian	Yr	Tm	AB	R	H	HR	RBI	SB	Avg	vLH	vRH	R$	OB	Slg	OPS	bb%	ct%	Eye	xBA	PX	SX	G/F	RC/G	RAR
Pos RF	98	aaa	500	59	124	14	66	12	248			$12	289	392	681	5	84	0.37	279	95	99		4.04	-15.6
Age 29 Past Peak	99	aaa	391	48	99	7	43	8	253			$6	291	368	660	5	83	0.31	264	78	88		3.82	-14.9
Bats R	00	MIN	•446	73	116	21	87	4	260	303	184	$13	320	455	775	8	82	0.49	283	112	73	1.75	5.17	2.0
Pwr No change	01	MIN	197	28	54	10	32	1	274	284	268	$7	338	487	825	9	71	0.33	240	130	39	1.11	5.99	5.6
Spd No change	02	2TM	227	31	61	11	28	2	269	225	304	$6	314	467	781	6	74	0.25	251	119	71	1.46	5.15	-0.8
BAvg --	1st Half		128	19	33	5	15	2	258			$2	291	422	713	4	75	0.19	244	96	107		4.26	-3.8
LIMA C+	2nd Half		99	12	28	6	13	0	283			$3	343	525	868	8	73	0.33	259	149	24		6.41	3.5
Risk Moderate	03	Proj	300	41	81	14	43	2	270			$9	324	474	798	7	75	0.32	264	124	64		5.47	2.0

Outwardly, the numbers don't look half bad and cry out for more playing time (he's been hitting HRs at a 25+ per season pace), but the BPIs don't support a big HR future.

Burks,Ellis	Yr	Tm	AB	R	H	HR	RBI	SB	Avg	vLH	vRH	R$	OB	Slg	OPS	bb%	ct%	Eye	xBA	PX	SX	G/F	RC/G	RAR
Pos DH	98	2NL	504	76	147	21	76	11	292	324	279	$22	365	496	861	10	78	0.52	277	131	114	1.65	6.63	19.8
Age 38 Decline	99	SF	390	73	110	31	96	7	282	345	255	$22	390	569	959	15	78	0.80	289	164	54	0.89	8.26	38.8
Bats R	00	SF	393	74	135	24	96	5	344	360	338	$27	425	606	1031	12	88	1.14	325	147	106	1.25	10.63	69.8
Pwr ---	01	CLE	439	83	123	28	74	5	280	245	292	$19	369	542	911	12	81	0.73	293	156	73	1.11	7.58	32.1
Spd No change	02	CLE	518	92	156	32	91	2	301	316	296	$26	356	541	896	8	79	0.41	287	150	48	1.34	7.16	24.4
BAvg --	1st Half		258	38	70	14	41	1	271			$10	336	477	812	9	80	0.48	275	127	40		5.73	0.8
LIMA A	2nd Half		260	54	86	18	50	1	331			$16	376	604	980	7	78	0.34	298	172	57		8.82	25.4
Risk Moderate	03	Proj	400	74	112	25	75	1	280			$17	353	531	884	10	81	0.58	294	151	59		6.88	17.6

In his 16 year career, how many times has he amassed 500 AB? This year was only the 6th time, which is why the pct play was to bet against. And certainly now, one year closer to MY age, we won't be projecting 500 again.

Burnitz,Jeromy	Yr	Tm	AB	R	H	HR	RBI	SB	Avg	vLH	vRH	R$	OB	Slg	OPS	bb%	ct%	Eye	xBA	PX	SX	G/F	RC/G	RAR
Pos RF	98	MIL	609	92	160	38	125	7	263	271	259	$28	339	499	838	10	74	0.44	267	147	64	0.87	6.10	21.4
Age 34 Decline	99	MIL	467	87	126	33	103	7	270	247	282	$22	389	561	950	16	73	0.73	277	173	77	0.79	8.22	49.8
Bats L	00	MIL	564	91	131	31	98	6	232	238	230	$14	347	456	803	15	79	0.82	281	129	68	0.92	5.69	8.3
Pwr +	01	MIL	562	104	141	34	100	0	251	224	262	$18	344	504	848	12	73	0.53	267	146	67	0.79	6.16	9.0
Spd +	02	NYM	479	65	103	19	54	10	215	174	229	$6	300	365	665	11	72	0.43	228	87	68	0.83	3.73	-25.8
BAvg +++	1st Half		261	30	56	9	27	4	215			$2	307	341	648	12	74	0.52	227	72	48		3.53	-15.8
LIMA A	2nd Half		218	35	47	10	27	6	216			$4	290	394	685	10	69	0.34	228	105	88		3.96	-10.0
Risk Low	03	Proj	450	71	104	23	67	6	231			$11	323	432	755	10	73	0.50	249	117	74		4.88	-0.2

Southpaws have progressively given him fits, and with his decline in plate patience and power, what's left is a mess. Does he rebound at all? Yes, but not if he stays in NY.

Burrell,Pat	Yr	Tm	AB	R	H	HR	RBI	SB	Avg	vLH	vRH	R$	OB	Slg	OPS	bb%	ct%	Eye	xBA	PX	SX	G/F	RC/G	RAR
Pos LF	98		0	0	0	0	0	0	0								0							
Age 26 Pre-Peak	99	a/a	450	72	134	24	77	2	298			$18	392	538	930	13	79	0.74	284	142	68		7.94	41.3
Bats R	00	PHI	•551	82	146	21	99	1	265	282	254	$15	368	465	833	14	69	0.53	245	126	51	0.97	6.45	20.6
Pwr No change	01	PHI	539	70	139	27	89	2	258	265	256	$16	343	469	813	11	70	0.43	244	125	56	0.84	5.91	1.8
Spd No change	02	PHI	586	96	165	37	116	1	282	311	274	$27	376	544	921	13	74	0.58	266	157	52	0.76	7.81	25.0
BAvg --	1st Half		281	46	79	19	58	0	281			$14	373	555	928	13	75	0.58	270	158	56		7.84	12.2
LIMA A	2nd Half		305	50	86	18	58	1	282			$14	380	534	914	14	73	0.59	261	155	39		7.78	12.8
Risk Moderate	03	Proj	575	88	153	40	106	1	266			$23	361	545	906	13	73	0.54	269	164	42		7.28	47.8

With an increasing PX trend and decreasing G/F ratio, this power display was for real and will likely continue. BA might drop a bit, but otherwise expect another solid season.

Burroughs,Sean	Yr	Tm	AB	R	H	HR	RBI	SB	Avg	vLH	vRH	R$	OB	Slg	OPS	bb%	ct%	Eye	xBA	PX	SX	G/F	RC/G	RAR
Pos 3B	98		0	0	0	0	0	0	0								0							
Age 22 Growth	99		0	0	0	0	0	0	0								0							
Bats L	00	aa	392	39	103	2	35	5	263			$4	339	360	698	10	91	1.25	285	70	66		4.14	-3.9
Pwr No change	01	aaa	394	58	125	8	53	9	317			$16	370	454	824	8	89	0.73	289	94	84		6.61	24.9
Spd ++	02	SD	•371	44	102	3	32	3	275	218	292	$6	331	364	695	8	88	0.70	267	64	78	2.09	4.54	-1.7
BAvg No change	1st Half		137	12	29	1	7	1	212			($2)	250	270	520	5	84	0.32	239	36	77		2.32	-9.7
LIMA A+	2nd Half		234	32	73	2	25	2	312			$7	376	419	795	9	91	1.09	283	80	69		6.27	11.7
Risk Very High	03	Proj	550	69	158	7	57	8	287			$13	345	396	740	8	89	0.77	279	76	83		5.12	9.8

1-11-.271 in 192 AB at SD. Solid 2nd half salvaged his season and generated some exciting BPIs. They say that his power will come, but for now, there is no sign of it -- especially with that G/F ratio.

Bush,Homer	Yr	Tm	AB	R	H	HR	RBI	SB	Avg	vLH	vRH	R$	OB	Slg	OPS	bb%	ct%	Eye	xBA	PX	SX	G/F	RC/G	RAR
Pos 2B	98	NYY	71	17	27	1	5	6	380	294	407	$5	421	465	886	7	73	0.26	224	58	106	4.43	7.75	7.9
Age 30 Past Peak	99	TOR	485	69	155	5	55	32	320	368	311	$23	348	421	768	4	83	0.26	265	68	137	2.19	5.66	23.3
Bats R	00	TOR	297	38	64	1	18	9	215	317	199	($1)	260	253	513	6	80	0.30	222	27	94	2.80	2.25	-15.3
Pwr No change	01	TOR	•303	40	90	3	30	13	297	283	313	$10	322	376	698	4	82	0.20	245	55	100	1.74	4.49	1.8
Spd -	02	2TM	132	16	30	1	7	4	227	196	244	($0)	239	265	504	1	81	0.08	223	25	97	2.00	2.15	-8.3
BAvg -	1st Half		100	11	23	1	4	3	230			($1)	252	280	532	3	84	0.19	235	34	83		2.41	-5.6
LIMA D	2nd Half		32	5	7	0	3	1	219			($1)	194	219	412	3	72	0.11	187	0	132		1.43	-2.5
Risk Very High	03	Proj	150	19	35	1	11	6	233			$1	266	290	555	4	82	0.24	241	41	94		2.66	-7.0

Zero plate patience means zero value.

Butler,Brent

		Yr	Tm	AB	R	H	HR	RBI	SB	Avg	vLH	vRH	R$	OB	Slg	OPS	bb%	ct%	Eye	xBA	PX	SX	G/F	RC/G	RAR
Pos	2B 3B	98		0	0	0	0	0	0	0								0							
Age	25 Pre-Peak	99	aa	528	61	133	12	48	0	252			$4	284	362	646	4	92	0.59	284	69	35		3.49	-10.7
Bats	R	00	aaa	438	55	126	7	40	1	288			$7	339	420	759	7	93	1.13	307	93	42		5.16	12.9
Pwr	No change	01	COL	* 391	52	113	7	40	4	289	205	263	$10	320	422	742	4	94	0.75	306	88	87	1.46	4.82	10.3
Spd	No change	02	COL	* 449	68	121	11	53	2	269	237	265	$10	292	423	715	3	90	0.30	293	97	99	1.09	4.14	-4.8
BAvg	- -	1st Half		198	28	59	5	23	2	298			$7	325	475	800	4	90	0.42	307	113	114		5.54	6.1
LIMA	C+	2nd Half		251	40	62	6	30	0	247			$3	265	382	647	2	89	0.21	283	85	92		3.21	-9.5
Risk	High	03	Proj	350	49	102	7	38	2	291			$9	321	433	753	4	91	0.50	297	92	80		4.89	8.3

9-42-.259 in 344 AB at COL, but over .300 as late as July 14. That's what we would have expected; the .231 he hit the rest of the way might have been an adjustment period. High contact rate fits Coors very well.

Byrnes,Eric

		Yr	Tm	AB	R	H	HR	RBI	SB	Avg	vLH	vRH	R$	OB	Slg	OPS	bb%	ct%	Eye	xBA	PX	SX	G/F	RC/G	RAR
Pos	LF RF	98		0	0	0	0	0	0	0								0							
Age	27 Peak	99	aa	164	16	31	1	15	4	189			($2)	240	274	514	6	87	0.50	269	67	74		2.02	-15.7
Bats	R	00	a/a	502	83	138	11	67	26	275			$18	351	430	781	11	89	1.07	304	105	103	0.40	5.13	-2.0
Pwr	- -	01	aaa	453	72	112	19	45	21	247			$15	294	424	718	6	87	0.50	293	105	117	1.08	4.45	-11.2
Spd	+ + + + +	02	OAK	* 213	36	48	6	23	7	225	279	216	$5	257	376	632	4	87	0.32	285	98	158	0.88	3.33	-10.1
BAvg	No change	1st Half		157	24	35	4	17	4	223			$3	252	369	621	4	89	0.33	291	100	130		3.14	-8.4
LIMA	C	2nd Half		56	12	13	2	6	3	232			$2	271	393	664	5	82	0.30	267	91	207		3.91	-1.7
Risk	X HIGH	03	Proj	150	25	35	5	16	6	233			$4	280	384	664	6	86	0.46	283	94	135		3.72	-6.4

3-11-.245 in 94 AB at OAK. His BPIs have tailed ever since he left AA ball. He has little value in the majors, but at 27, the clock is striking 12 and his coach may be turning into a pumpkin. (Sorry, Thad Bosley.)

Cabrera,Jolbert

		Yr	Tm	AB	R	H	HR	RBI	SB	Avg	vLH	vRH	R$	OB	Slg	OPS	bb%	ct%	Eye	xBA	PX	SX	G/F	RC/G	RAR
Pos	CF	98	aaa	494	75	139	8	36	19	281			$14	352	383	735	10	88	0.89	276	71	88		4.89	4.1
Age	30 Past Peak	99	aaa	279	35	66	0	22	16	237			$4	290	297	587	7	86	0.54	260	43	140	2.14	3.15	-12.5
Bats	R	00	CLE	* 249	43	68	5	25	8	273	210	274	$6	307	386	692	5	91	0.55	284	66	126	1.22	4.07	-5.1
Pwr	No change	01	CLE	287	50	75	1	38	10	261	257	264	$6	300	348	649	5	86	0.39	266	63	139	1.30	3.71	-10.8
Spd	-	02	2TM	* 277	33	58	1	20	5	209	256	44	($2)	268	264	531	7	87	0.59	248	44	71	1.00	2.24	-22.9
BAvg	+ + + + +	1st Half		135	16	23	0	11	4	170			($3)	233	207	440	8	85	0.55	238	33	92		1.55	-14.1
LIMA	C	2nd Half		142	17	35	1	9	1	246			($1)	301	317	618	7	88	0.65	257	55	52		3.05	-8.2
Risk	Very High	03	Proj	250	36	60	2	23	7	240			$2	290	312	602	7	87	0.55	265	53	99		3.03	-12.9

0-8-.143 in 84 AB at CLE and LA. His BPIs have TAILed, which I suppose is fitting for someone recovering from a posterior injury. He was an END-gamer before, BUTT now he's BEHIND even that. BUMmer.

Cabrera,Orlando

		Yr	Tm	AB	R	H	HR	RBI	SB	Avg	vLH	vRH	R$	OB	Slg	OPS	bb%	ct%	Eye	xBA	PX	SX	G/F	RC/G	RAR
Pos	SS	98	MON	* 533	68	130	3	42	21	244	308	273	$8	298	338	636	7	91	0.85	290	67	149	1.75	3.58	-1.6
Age	28 Peak	99	MON	382	48	97	8	39	2	254	333	228	$4	288	403	691	5	90	0.47	299	96	97	1.28	4.01	4.7
Bats	R	00	MON	422	47	100	13	55	4	237	286	221	$6	280	393	673	6	93	0.89	314	98	60	1.23	3.70	2.1
Pwr	+	01	MON	626	64	173	14	96	19	276	268	279	$22	323	428	751	6	91	0.80	306	98	109	1.20	5.01	26.3
Spd	+ +	02	MON	563	64	148	7	56	25	263	264	263	$15	321	380	701	8	91	0.91	290	87	96	1.26	4.48	8.7
BAvg	+ + +	1st Half		296	29	77	4	30	4	260			$5	313	382	695	7	90	0.77	285	91	47		3.98	0.0
LIMA	A	2nd Half		267	35	71	3	26	21	266			$10	329	378	707	9	91	1.09	293	82	127		5.07	9.1
Risk	Moderate	03	Proj	575	65	167	10	67	22	290			$21	340	422	762	7	91	0.87	298	90	101		5.41	29.4

Despite the drop in HRs, there isn't much difference between 2001 and 2002; in fact, there's been improvement in some areas. xBA says that a run at .300 could be possible, so be prepared to go an extra buck.

Cairo,Miguel

		Yr	Tm	AB	R	H	HR	RBI	SB	Avg	vLH	vRH	R$	OB	Slg	OPS	bb%	ct%	Eye	xBA	PX	SX	G/F	RC/G	RAR
Pos	LF	98	TAM	515	49	138	5	46	19	268	328	249	$11	301	367	668	4	91	0.55	287	67	111	1.65	3.88	-19.5
Age	28 Peak	99	TAM	465	61	137	3	36	22	295	384	274	$14	329	368	697	5	90	0.52	272	46	132	1.35	4.52	-9.0
Bats	R	00	TAM	375	49	98	1	34	28	261	270	259	$11	314	328	642	7	91	0.85	271	49	128	1.19	3.87	-15.3
Pwr	- - -	01	2TM	* 279	43	77	5	27	5	276	409	250	$6	336	394	730	8	88	0.74	277	76	91	1.55	4.61	-5.7
Spd	No change	02	STL	184	28	46	2	23	1	250	273	237	$2	299	353	653	7	80	0.36	249	68	106	1.30	3.72	-15.7
BAvg	-	1st Half		87	10	21	1	11	0	241			$1	275	356	631	4	80	0.24	251	67	138		3.22	-8.6
LIMA	D+	2nd Half		97	18	25	1	12	1	258			$1	321	351	671	8	80	0.47	246	69	75		4.19	-7.0
Risk	Moderate	03	Proj	150	22	39	2	16	3	260			$3	312	353	665	7	85	0.50	262	63	103		3.93	-3.8

Has been a reasonable bench bat in the past, but his declining BPIs have filtered out any residual value. Could rebound, but not worth the risk at the draft table.

Cameron,Mike

		Yr	Tm	AB	R	H	HR	RBI	SB	Avg	vLH	vRH	R$	OB	Slg	OPS	bb%	ct%	Eye	xBA	PX	SX	G/F	RC/G	RAR
Pos	CF	98	CHW	396	53	83	8	43	27	210	218	207	$8	277	336	613	9	74	0.37	244	77	161	1.06	3.10	-21.6
Age	30 Past Peak	99	CIN	542	93	139	21	66	38	256	292	246	$22	352	469	821	13	73	0.55	261	128	171	1.17	6.02	28.9
Bats	R	00	SEA	543	96	145	19	78	24	267	273	266	$19	359	438	797	13	76	0.59	256	100	128	0.86	5.93	20.9
Pwr	No change	01	SEA	540	99	144	25	110	34	267	301	255	$29	350	480	829	11	71	0.45	253	126	147	0.64	6.40	25.2
Spd	No change	02	SEA	545	84	130	25	80	31	239	239	238	$24	335	442	777	13	68	0.45	237	127	146	0.80	5.39	9.2
BAvg	No change	1st Half		274	48	59	13	45	11	215			$9	313	442	755	12	68	0.45	247	141	178		5.01	1.2
LIMA	A	2nd Half		271	36	71	12	35	20	262			$15	357	443	800	13	67	0.45	226	112	106		5.80	8.2
Risk	Very Low	03	Proj	550	89	143	33	86	33	260			$29	350	509	859	12	70	0.47	259	146	139		6.55	29.5

Whatever happened to his BA only lasted for 3 months as his 2nd half was just fine. He's plateaued as a .260ish hitter with speed, but a 30-y/o with these PX trends might have one last power spike left.

Canizaro,Jay

		Yr	Tm	AB	R	H	HR	RBI	SB	Avg	vLH	vRH	R$	OB	Slg	OPS	bb%	ct%	Eye	xBA	PX	SX	G/F	RC/G	RAR
Pos	2B	98	a/a	387	54	73	14	36	4	189			($0)	290	336	626	12	84	0.92	275	88	81		3.37	-9.9
Age	29 Past Peak	99	aaa	364	55	83	19	56	11	228			$10	296	434	730	9	82	0.53	284	119	92	0.83	4.31	1.5
Bats	R	00	MIN	* 447	59	126	12	65	7	282	269	269	$12	337	438	775	8	84	0.53	282	99	83	1.05	5.44	20.8
Pwr	No change	01	MIN	0	0	0	0	0	0	0								0							
Spd	No change	02	MIN	* 359	42	80	9	36	4	223	205	219	$4	283	357	639	8	83	0.50	265	89	79	1.21	3.34	-8.7
BAvg	+ + + + +	1st Half		159	19	37	1	15	1	233			$1	282	333	616	6	84	0.42	260	80	82		3.23	-4.3
LIMA	C	2nd Half		200	23	43	8	21	3	215			$3	283	375	658	9	83	0.56	268	97	74		3.42	-4.4
Risk	High	03	Proj	150	19	38	5	18	2	253			$3	316	408	724	8	83	0.55	272	96	82		4.51	1.4

0-11-.214 in 112 AB at MIN. There are some interesting skills he owns that we may or may not ever get to see. At 29, and after 2002's struggles, odds are against.

Carroll,Jamey

		Yr	Tm	AB	R	H	HR	RBI	SB	Avg	vLH	vRH	R$	OB	Slg	OPS	bb%	ct%	Eye	xBA	PX	SX	G/F	RC/G	RAR
Pos	3B	98	aa	261	36	60	0	16	9	230			$1	323	295	618	12	90	1.38	273	48	121		3.51	-8.6
Age	29 Past Peak	99	aa	561	63	143	4	51	17	255			$8	302	346	648	6	91	0.73	283	65	100		3.62	-14.8
Bats	R	00	a/a	518	65	133	2	35	12	257			$5	308	324	632	7	92	0.97	276	46	103		3.56	-14.0
Pwr	-	01	aaa	267	23	57	0	14	5	213			($2)	255	258	514	5	85	0.38	242	32	89		2.13	-19.6
Spd	+ + +	02	MON	* 501	62	127	8	45	6	253	400	295	$6	302	363	666	7	91	0.76	280	71	84	2.38	3.66	-15.7
BAvg	+ + +	1st Half		191	33	61	4	26	2	319			$8	381	435	816	9	90	1.00	277	73	73		6.13	8.7
LIMA	D+	2nd Half		310	29	66	4	19	4	213			($2)	252	319	571	5	91	0.59	282	70	91		2.50	-20.3
Risk	X HIGH	03	Proj	100	12	25	1	8	2	250			$1	300	337	637	7	90	0.68	272	57	96		3.42	-3.5

1-6-.310 in 71 AB at MON. With a 90% contact rate, a .300 BA is possible, but he does not have the history of being able to maintain that level. Low OB, advanced age will relegate him to intermittent roster filler.

Casanova,Raul

		Yr	Tm	AB	R	H	HR	RBI	SB	Avg	vLH	vRH	R$	OB	Slg	OPS	bb%	ct%	Eye	xBA	PX	SX	G/F	RC/G	RAR
Pos	CA	98	DET	* 213	19	46	8	27	0	216	200	135	$1	304	371	675	11	82	0.69	259	94		3.33	4.00	-0.7
Age	30 Past Peak	99	aaa	160	14	26	5	16	0	163			($3)	188	300	488	3	85	0.21	271	85	33		1.76	-11.0
Bats	S	00	MIL	* 304	28	75	9	45	1	247	246	247	$5	316	405	721	9	82	0.55	273	95	61	1.88	4.45	3.6
Pwr	+ + +	01	MIL	192	21	50	11	33	0	260	333	254	$6	304	484	788	6	85	0.41	296	131		0.81	5.25	9.7
Spd	No change	02	2TM	131	5	26	1	14	0	198	154	194	($2)	271	260	530	9	79	0.48	224	46	4	1.46	2.46	-6.1
BAvg	+ + + + +	1st Half		87	3	16	1	8	0	184			($2)	268	230	498	10	79	0.56	213	28	0		2.18	-4.9
LIMA	D	2nd Half		44	2	10	0	6	0	227			($1)	277	318	595	6	80	0.33	244	81	10		3.07	-1.2
Risk	X HIGH	03	Proj	150	12	36	5	19	0	240			$1	303	372	675	8	82	0.50	260	82	17		3.98	0.2

Spotted performance and injury history makes him virtually impossible to project, but that's okay. He's way too high of a risk to contemplate drafting anyway.

Casey,Sean

		Yr	Tm	AB	R	H	HR	RBI	SB	Avg	vLH	vRH	R$	OB	Slg	OPS	bb%	ct%	Eye	xBA	PX	SX	G/F	RC/G	RAR
Pos	1B	98	CIN	* 397	57	111	8	64	1	280	222	280	$11	369	423	792	12	86	1.04	290	106	58	1.65	5.96	7.4
Age	28 Peak	99	CIN	594	103	197	25	99	0	332	271	356	$27	394	539	933	9	85	0.69	298	130	47	1.76	8.39	55.8
Bats	L	00	CIN	480	69	151	20	85	1	315	250	332	$21	382	517	898	10	83	0.65	295	124	51	1.57	7.75	34.9
Pwr	+ +	01	CIN	533	69	165	13	89	3	310	276	324	$20	361	458	819	7	88	0.68	293	101	50	1.77	6.38	-0.1
Spd	No change	02	CIN	433	58	115	7	44	2	266	231	275	$7	333	372	705	9	89	0.94	273	75	50	1.62	4.59	-15.3
BAvg	+ + +	1st Half		269	44	79	5	33	2	294			$8	369	413	781	11	89	1.10	279	83	56		5.87	1.4
LIMA	A+	2nd Half		164	14	36	2	11	0	220			($1)	273	305	578	7	89	0.67	262	61	23		2.89	-14.2
Risk	Low	03	Proj	500	64	145	14	65	2	290			$15	351	445	796	9	88	0.77	288	101	48		5.90	8.3

One of Mat Olkin's prime examples of how G/F might set the ceiling for power potential. His high rates have never described a true HR hitter, which might mean 1999 was the fluke here.

Castilla,Vinny

		Yr	Tm	AB	R	H	HR	RBI	SB	Avg	vLH	vRH	R$	OB	Slg	OPS	bb%	ct%	Eye	xBA	PX	SX	G/F	RC/G	RAR
Pos	3B	98	COL	645	108	206	46	144	5	319	320	319	$42	359	589	948	6	86	0.45	320	163	69	1.39	7.74	63.4
Age	35 Decline	99	COL	615	83	169	33	102	2	275	225	294	$21	332	478	810	8	88	0.71	300	117	39	1.25	5.75	24.8
Bats	R	00	TAM	331	22	73	6	42	1	221	203	225	$0	252	308	560	4	88	0.34	257	52	38	1.76	2.57	-19.0
Pwr	No change	01	2TM	538	69	140	25	91	1	260	253	261	$16	305	467	772	6	80	0.32	274	126	39	1.36	4.93	6.0
Spd	No change	02	ATL	543	56	126	12	61	4	232	224	233	$5	262	348	610	4	87	0.32	270	74	75	1.05	3.12	-25.2
BAvg	No change	1st Half		292	31	72	9	45	2	247			$6	269	397	666	3	86	0.21	275	91	78		3.66	-8.8
LIMA	C	2nd Half		251	25	54	3	16	2	215			($2)	254	291	545	5	89	0.48	262	53	60		2.54	-16.1
Risk	Very High	03	Proj	400	43	100	12	52	2	250			$7	287	391	678	5	86	0.36	274	87	54		3.89	-7.9

- G/F trend might indicate a deliberate attempt to reclaim his lost power skills. It didn't work.
- Since leaving COL, he's posted nearly identical stats to his road numbers in COL.
- xBA variances are interesting.

Castillo,Luis

		Yr	Tm	AB	R	H	HR	RBI	SB	Avg	vLH	vRH	R$	OB	Slg	OPS	bb%	ct%	Eye	xBA	PX	SX	G/F	RC/G	RAR
Pos	2B	98	FLA	* 534	78	124	1	21	34	232	200	204	$8	332	272	604	13	84	0.94	247	29	124	5.86	3.55	-11.5
Age	27 Peak	99	FLA	487	76	147	0	28	50	302	310	300	$22	386	366	752	12	83	0.79	252	48	130	4.88	5.62	21.0
Bats	S	00	FLA	539	101	180	2	17	62	334	291	350	$32	418	388	806	13	84	0.91	250	37	126	4.74	6.69	39.5
Pwr	- - -	01	FLA	537	76	141	2	45	33	263	281	257	$15	344	341	685	11	83	0.74	252	47	166	2.59	4.28	5.9
Spd	- - - - -	02	FLA	606	86	185	2	39	48	305	329	297	$28	363	361	724	8	87	0.72	256	38	132	3.39	5.14	12.1
BAvg	- -	1st Half		310	45	102	2	18	26	329			$18	386	384	770	9	86	0.67	249	32	132		5.92	13.8
LIMA	A	2nd Half		296	41	83	0	21	22	280			$11	339	338	676	8	89	0.79	263	44	128		4.40	-0.9
Risk	Low	03	Proj	600	90	175	2	38	50	292			$25	363	352	715	10	86	0.78	254	40	140		4.97	16.6

One of the interesting questions with xBA is its consistent de-valuing of these no-power SB guys. Does it indicate an elevated risk level for their ability to maintain BA? Is it a flaw in the formula? Don't know yet.

Castro,Juan

		Yr	Tm	AB	R	H	HR	RBI	SB	Avg	vLH	vRH	R$	OB	Slg	OPS	bb%	ct%	Eye	xBA	PX	SX	G/F	RC/G	RAR
Pos	SS	98	LA	220	25	43	2	14	0	195	217	188	($3)	247	255	501	6	83	0.41	248	45	42	1.30	2.13	-10.4
Age	30 Past Peak	99	aaa	423	36	88	5	35	2	208			($3)	249	298	547	5	86	0.40	263	61	57		2.40	-19.4
Bats	R	00	CIN	* 284	27	71	6	31	0	250	244	240	$3	306	394	701	7	85	0.55	283	91	60	1.70	4.13	5.3
Pwr	+	01	CIN	242	27	54	3	13	0	223	246	216	($1)	263	302	564	5	79	0.26	236	54	38	1.11	2.72	-6.6
Spd	No change	02	CIN	* 99	7	21	2	13	0	212	222	217	($0)	271	303	574	7	80	0.40	232	57	13	1.46	2.84	-3.5
BAvg	+ + +	1st Half		35	2	4	0	4	0	114			($2)	184	143	327	8	89	0.75	240	25	26		0.88	-3.4
LIMA	D	2nd Half		64	5	17	2	9	0	266			$1	319	391	709	7	75	0.31	226	75	9		4.55	1.1
Risk	Very High	03	Proj	150	14	36	3	15	0	240			$1	289	353	642	6	81	0.36	250	70	56		3.54	-1.0

No offensive value... but makes a wonderful decorative doorstop for the holidays!

Castro,Ramon

		Yr	Tm	AB	R	H	HR	RBI	SB	Avg	vLH	vRH	R$	OB	Slg	OPS	bb%	ct%	Eye	xBA	PX	SX	G/F	RC/G	RAR
Pos	CA	98	aa	256	28	55	8	28	0	215			$1	261	340	601	6	83	0.37	261	78	34		2.96	-8.4
Age	27 Peak	99	FLA	* 416	36	86	12	49	0	207	167	182	($0)	257	346	603	6	85	0.45	275	90		0.64	3.00	-13.2
Bats	R	00	FLA	* 356	43	96	12	48	0	270	200	248	$8	323	435	758	7	81	0.42	277	105	24	0.65	5.14	11.7
Pwr	No change	01	aaa	401	56	110	18	63	1	274			$13	322	479	800	7	86	0.49	296	128	41	0.43	5.57	22.1
Spd	No change	02	FLA	101	11	24	6	18	0	238	160	263	$3	330	455	786	12	76	0.58	255	125	10	0.74	5.43	4.1
BAvg	+ + +	1st Half		35	5	9	4	9	0	257			$2	395	600	995	19	71	0.80	261	174	-0		8.95	5.8
LIMA	D	2nd Half		66	6	15	2	9	0	227			$1	292	379	670	8	79	0.43	251	99	17		3.87	-0.7
Risk	X HIGH	03	Proj	150	16	36	5	20	0	240			$2	294	402	696	7	82	0.44	270	103	29		4.16	0.8

Can't hit lefties AT ALL -- .194 BA over last 4 years. But he's the protypical $1 catcher that doesn't get enough AB to hurt you and provides those three extra HRs that will put your team over the top.

Catalanotto,Frank

		Yr	Tm	AB	R	H	HR	RBI	SB	Avg	vLH	vRH	R$	OB	Slg	OPS	bb%	ct%	Eye	xBA	PX	SX	G/F	RC/G	RAR
Pos	LF 2B	98	DET	* 318	42	93	10	52	3	292	364	277	$11	348	478	826	8	81	0.45	282	113	111	1.00	6.17	10.1
Age	28 Peak	99	DET	286	41	79	11	35	3	276	269	277	$8	312	458	770	5	83	0.31	282	114	59	1.00	4.93	-2.1
Bats	L	00	TEX	282	55	82	10	42	6	291	263	293	$10	365	457	823	10	87	0.92	292	96	108	1.21	6.37	10.6
Pwr	+ +	01	TEX	463	77	153	11	54	15	330	326	331	$22	382	490	873	8	88	0.71	295	103	118	1.47	7.39	38.2
Spd	+ + + + +	02	TEX	228	43	59	3	25	9	259	231	274	$6	335	430	764	10	88	0.93	302	114	215	1.37	5.05	0.9
BAvg	+ + +	1st Half		126	25	31	2	15	7	246			$4	336	452	788	12	88	1.13	319	136	258		5.33	1.6
LIMA	A	2nd Half		102	18	28	1	10	2	275			$2	333	402	735	8	87	0.69	280	88	153		4.70	-0.7
Risk	Low	03	Proj	500	89	153	15	80	10	306			$21	368	499	867	9	87	0.77	304	121	139		6.81	26.3

The mark of a talented player is one who, despite a myriad of injuries, manages to maintain -- or improve -- his BPIs. If healthy, there could be a huge comeback in store for 2003.

Cedeno,Roger

		Yr	Tm	AB	R	H	HR	RBI	SB	Avg	vLH	vRH	R$	OB	Slg	OPS	bb%	ct%	Eye	xBA	PX	SX	G/F	RC/G	RAR
Pos	LF	98	LA	240	33	58	2	17	8	242	186	265	$3	318	321	639	10	76	0.47	237	60	103	2.17	3.80	-8.4
Age	28 Peak	99	NYM	453	90	142	4	36	66	313	194	334	$31	394	408	802	12	78	0.60	248	66	155	2.23	6.59	21.1
Bats	S	00	HOU	259	54	73	6	26	25	282	313	275	$13	384	398	782	14	82	0.91	256	58	179	2.25	5.72	3.5
Pwr	No change	01	DET	523	79	153	6	48	55	293	282	297	$28	338	396	734	6	84	0.43	266	59	188	2.52	5.05	5.3
Spd	- - - - -	02	NYM	511	65	133	7	41	25	260	231	273	$13	316	346	663	8	82	0.46	248	56	115	2.03	4.15	-37.4
BAvg	- -	1st Half		273	34	67	3	22	11	245			$4	297	341	638	7	81	0.39	251	64	119		3.57	-24.6
LIMA	A+	2nd Half		238	31	66	4	19	14	277			$9	338	353	691	8	83	0.54	244	47	99		4.87	-12.2
Risk	High	03	Proj	500	75	133	7	43	33	266			$17	325	359	684	8	82	0.48	253	57	146		4.33	-6.5

BPIs dropped pretty much across the board, although there was some sign of life in the 2nd half. Can't blame Shea, because he conquered it before. But after two sub-.350 OB seasons, the ceiling is lower.

Cepicky,Matt

		Yr	Tm	AB	R	H	HR	RBI	SB	Avg	vLH	vRH	R$	OB	Slg	OPS	bb%	ct%	Eye	xBA	PX	SX	G/F	RC/G	RAR
Pos	LF	98		0	0	0	0	0	0	0								0							
Age	25 Pre-Peak	99		0	0	0	0	0	0	0								0							
Bats	L	00		0	0	0	0	0	0	0								0							
Pwr	-	01	aa	459	49	109	16	65	4	237			$8	265	414	679	4	81	0.19	270	103	97		3.28	-27.0
Spd	- - - -	02	MON	* 493	48	117	15	73	6	237	182	222	$9	280	387	667	6	80	0.29	258	96	70	2.29	3.79	-40.6
BAvg	-	1st Half		316	32	80	10	44	4	253			$7	296	424	720	6	83	0.36	277	111	69		4.44	-19.9
LIMA	D+	2nd Half		177	16	37	5	29	2	209			$1	251	322	573	5	74	0.22	224	67	52		2.78	-20.0
Risk	Moderate	03	Proj	200	20	46	6	30	2	230			$3	266	380	647	5	79	0.24	256	91	70		3.31	-8.6

3-15-.216 in 74 AB at MON. Bad signs...
- Sub-.300 OB
- Poor 2nd half
- Only real asset is a little bit of power, but with a 2.29 G/F ratio, any upside is limited.

Chavez,Endy

		Yr	Tm	AB	R	H	HR	RBI	SB	Avg	vLH	vRH	R$	OB	Slg	OPS	bb%	ct%	Eye	xBA	PX	SX	G/F	RC/G	RAR
Pos	CF	98		0	0	0	0	0	0	0								0							
Age	25 Pre-Peak	99		0	0	0	0	0	0	0								0							
Bats	L	00		0	0	0	0	0	0	0								0							
Pwr	-	01	KC	* 349	40	95	1	18	12	272	286	200	$6	302	324	626	4	92	0.56	263	39	80	2.25	3.13	-18.9
Spd	+ + + + +	02	MON	* 530	79	169	5	45	21	319	316	292	$22	359	447	806	6	91	0.69	296	88	134	2.20	5.59	10.1
BAvg	- -	1st Half		255	38	80	3	24	11	314			$11	357	424	780	6	91	0.77	288	79	96		5.30	2.5
LIMA	A	2nd Half		275	41	89	2	21	10	324			$11	361	469	830	5	91	0.62	303	96	168		5.88	7.5
Risk	High	03	Proj	450	61	135	3	32	20	300			$15	336	400	736	5	91	0.63	288	70	122		4.56	2.3

1-9-3-.296 in 125 AB at MON. Nice growth year. 90%+ contact rates mean the .300 BA is for real. SB growth can ride on the back of his improving OB avg. Tuck this one away.

Chavez,Eric

		Tm	AB	R	H	HR	RBI	SB	Avg	vLH	vRH	R$	OB	Slg	OPS	bb%	ct%	Eye	xBA	PX	SX	G/F	RC/G	RAR
Pos	3B	98 OAK	* 574	92	182	26	111	13	317	333	310	$30	368	545	913	7	89	0.70	325	146	88	1.92	7.66	55.2
Age	25 Pre-Peak	99 OAK	356	47	88	13	50	1	247	184	257	$6	333	427	760	11	84	0.82	284	110	59	1.21	5.16	7.4
Bats	L	00 OAK	501	89	139	26	86	2	277	197	303	$16	357	495	852	11	81	0.66	286	121	82	0.92	6.57	33.4
Pwr	-	01 OAK	552	91	159	32	114	8	288	257	304	$27	337	540	877	7	82	0.41	298	155	72	1.18	6.74	38.8
Spd	+ + +	02 OAK	585	87	161	34	109	8	275	209	301	$27	348	513	861	10	80	0.55	289	148	85	0.74	6.58	37.5
BAvg	-	1st Half	281	46	77	20	58	2	274			$14	346	559	905	10	77	0.48	294	174	80		6.99	21.6
LIMA	A	2nd Half	304	41	84	14	51	6	276			$13	349	470	820	10	82	0.63	283	123	79		6.19	15.7
Risk	Moderate	03 Proj	575	90	156	31	107	7	271			$24	339	501	840	9	81	0.55	292	140	80		6.23	29.6

Minor growth in some BPIs, but two warning signs as well:
1. BA vsLH in three of the last four years
2. Sore hammy-induced 2nd half fade.
Growth is coming, but not in '03.

Cintron,Alex

		Tm	AB	R	H	HR	RBI	SB	Avg	vLH	vRH	R$	OB	Slg	OPS	bb%	ct%	Eye	xBA	PX	SX	G/F	RC/G	RAR
Pos	2B	98	0	0	0	0	0	0	0								0							
Age	24 Growth	99	0	0	0	0	0	0	0								0							
Bats	S	00 aa	522	65	142	3	46	7	272			$7	303	358	661	4	92	0.53	282	60	86		3.62	-8.9
Pwr	+	01 aaa	432	44	120	2	29	7	278			$7	299	359	658	3	92	0.37	278	59	83	0.50	3.67	-5.7
Spd	+	02 ARI	* 426	51	119	3	24	7	279	182	226	$7	312	371	683	4	91	0.54	279	68	82	2.24	4.05	-5.7
BAvg	-	1st Half	265	37	78	3	21	5	294			$7	325	419	744	4	91	0.52	294	89	97		4.76	2.0
LIMA	D	2nd Half	161	14	41	0	3	2	255			($0)	290	292	582	5	91	0.57	255	32	52		3.00	-7.3
Risk	High	03 Proj	150	16	41	1	9	2	273			$2	302	354	656	4	92	0.49	278	59	82		3.70	-1.8

0-4-.213 in 75 AB at ARI but .273 before the break and .129 after. This 3-year consistency is nice, but signs of growth are better. Ct% says he'll rarely have a BA that will hurt you, which is worth a buck by itself.

Cirillo,Jeff

		Tm	AB	R	H	HR	RBI	SB	Avg	vLH	vRH	R$	OB	Slg	OPS	bb%	ct%	Eye	xBA	PX	SX	G/F	RC/G	RAR
Pos	3B	98 MIL	604	97	194	14	68	10	321	299	330	$24	400	445	845	12	85	0.90	278	88	73	1.48	7.15	51.7
Age	33 Decline	99 MIL	607	98	198	15	88	7	326	323	327	$24	400	461	862	11	86	0.90	282	90	62	1.03	7.38	57.1
Bats	R	00 COL	598	111	195	11	115	3	326	379	311	$24	394	477	871	10	88	0.93	301	106	64	1.55	7.39	56.7
Pwr	+	01 COL	528	72	165	17	83	12	313	264	327	$25	364	473	838	8	88	0.68	294	97	105	1.20	6.74	33.6
Spd	- - - - -	02 SEA	485	51	121	6	54	8	249	304	226	$8	295	328	622	6	86	0.46	253	58	67	0.99	3.40	-17.0
BAvg	-	1st Half	266	29	68	6	38	8	256			$8	303	357	660	6	88	0.56	265	68	74		3.85	-5.8
LIMA	B+	2nd Half	219	22	53	0	16	0	242			$0	284	292	577	6	84	0.37	237	46	37		2.88	-11.1
Risk	Very Low	03 Proj	450	58	123	8	59	6	273			$11	328	384	712	8	87	0.61	269	77	73		4.62	0.3

Let me offer up a theory here... COL hitters learn that success at Coors requires a more uppercut swing, though thin air still induces ground balls. A player leaving COL with that swing might hit more flies, make more outs. Just a theory, now.

Clark,Brady

		Tm	AB	R	H	HR	RBI	SB	Avg	vLH	vRH	R$	OB	Slg	OPS	bb%	ct%	Eye	xBA	PX	SX	G/F	RC/G	RAR
Pos	LF	98 aa	222	29	48	2	12	8	216			$1	290	302	592	9	87	0.79	271	63	104		3.08	-13.6
Age	30 Past Peak	99 aa	506	73	130	12	53	17	257			$11	344	399	743	12	89	1.24	294	92	90		4.65	-8.3
Bats	R	00 aaa	487	66	127	12	57	9	261			$10	335	427	762	10	92	1.35	315	107	88	6.00	4.94	-4.9
Pwr	- -	01 CIN	* 296	40	72	8	32	9	243	279	256	$6	325	358	683	11	90	1.20	279	67	90	0.86	4.26	-14.7
Spd	- -	02 2NL	* 187	21	42	1	22	1	225	143	220	($0)	260	294	554	5	90	0.47	264	55	56	1.63	2.37	-23.2
BAvg	+ + +	1st Half	97	10	25	1	15	1	258			$2	287	361	648	4	90	0.40	278	78	55		3.20	-9.6
LIMA	D+	2nd Half	90	11	17	0	7	0	189			($2)	232	222	454	5	90	0.56	251	29	64		1.62	-13.3
Risk	X HIGH	03 Proj	150	19	38	2	16	2	253			$2	311	342	653	8	90	0.84	273	62	60		3.67	-5.0

0-10-.192 in 78 AB at CIN and NYM. This was the critical year, and he blew it. After solid BPIs and promise in '00 and '01, he tanked. Thirtysomething first-timers don't usually get second chances.

Clark,Howie

		Tm	AB	R	H	HR	RBI	SB	Avg	vLH	vRH	R$	OB	Slg	OPS	bb%	ct%	Eye	xBA	PX	SX	G/F	RC/G	RAR
Pos	DH	98 a/a	370	46	94	12	49	2	254			$8	317	405	722	8	86	0.68	284	98	51		4.52	-10.1
Age	29 Past Peak	99 a/a	405	42	103	7	33	3	254			$3	314	373	686	8	92	1.03	291	77	70		4.19	-13.9
Bats	L	00 a/a	242	32	63	4	26	3	260			$3	332	364	696	10	92	1.37	289	70	59		4.48	-5.4
Pwr	+ + +	01 MEX	493	68	164	5	64	5	333			$18	380	477	857	7	92	1.03	308	101	101		7.07	26.2
Spd	No change	02 BAL	* 471	50	126	6	39	3	268		320	$7	320	367	687	7	93	1.09	282	72	63	1.25	4.15	-21.6
BAvg	+ + +	1st Half	315	38	89	6	29	3	283			$7	327	406	734	6	94	1.17	296	84	85		4.79	-8.2
LIMA	C	2nd Half	156	12	37	0	10	0	237			($0)	304	288	593	9	90	1.00	256	47	25		3.01	-12.8
Risk	Very High	03 Proj	100	11	29	1	10	1	290			$2	347	404	750	8	92	1.06	287	80	76		5.16	-1.1

0-4-.302 in 53 AB at BAL. A few burritos juiced up his sagging career, but it was the same old thing upon his return. Contact rate and batting eye say that a .300 BA is for real, but the opportunity likely won't be there.

Clark,Tony

		Tm	AB	R	H	HR	RBI	SB	Avg	vLH	vRH	R$	OB	Slg	OPS	bb%	ct%	Eye	xBA	PX	SX	G/F	RC/G	RAR
Pos	1B	98 DET	602	84	175	34	103	3	291	331	274	$25	358	522	879	9	79	0.49	280	139	37	1.47	6.96	22.9
Age	30 Past Peak	99 DET	536	74	150	31	99	2	280	262	284	$20	357	507	864	11	75	0.48	263	133	37	1.17	6.78	15.0
Bats	S	00 DET	208	32	57	13	37	0	274	308	266	$7	349	529	878	10	75	0.47	279	148	25	1.36	6.85	5.2
Pwr	+ +	01 DET	428	67	123	16	75	0	287	321	271	$14	378	481	859	13	75	0.57	252	121	56	2.04	6.95	9.5
Spd	No change	02 BOS	275	25	57	3	29	0	207	159	228	($0)	264	291	554	7	79	0.37	233	61	42	1.40	2.63	-28.3
BAvg	+ + +	1st Half	174	19	36	2	20	0	207			($0)	254	299	553	6	83	0.37	248	66	61		2.58	-18.0
LIMA	C	2nd Half	101	6	21	1	9	0	208			($0)	279	277	557	9	73	0.37	210	53	11		2.72	-10.3
Risk	Moderate	03 Proj	400	46	103	12	55	0	258			$8	329	407	736	10	76	0.45	246	97	37		4.90	-9.5

No formal reports that an injury caused this debacle, but recall that he was coming off of an injury-filled '01 campaign. Odds are he was hiding something all year; cliff drops don't happen without a reason.

Clayton,Royce

		Tm	AB	R	H	HR	RBI	SB	Avg	vLH	vRH	R$	OB	Slg	OPS	bb%	ct%	Eye	xBA	PX	SX	G/F	RC/G	RAR
Pos	SS	98 2TM	541	89	136	9	53	24	251	311	232	$13	318	366	684	9	85	0.64	275	81	115	1.84	4.12	4.7
Age	33 Decline	99 TEX	465	69	134	14	52	8	288	306	283	$13	343	445	788	8	78	0.39	261	93	110	2.03	5.55	18.7
Bats	R	00 TEX	513	70	124	14	54	11	242	196	254	$7	299	384	683	8	82	0.46	266	82	115	1.53	3.94	-9.0
Pwr	- -	01 CHW	433	62	114	9	60	10	263	333	242	$11	315	393	708	7	83	0.46	265	81	106	2.04	4.32	-1.9
Spd	- - -	02 CHW	342	51	86	7	35	5	251	238	257	$6	293	365	658	6	80	0.30	249	76	109	1.96	3.82	-8.8
BAvg	- -	1st Half	229	38	51	6	24	3	223			$3	267	354	621	6	80	0.31	253	83	131		3.30	-9.5
LIMA	D+	2nd Half	113	13	35	1	11	2	310			$3	345	389	734	5	81	0.27	239	63	57		5.06	1.3
Risk	Low	03 Proj	150	21	40	3	17	3	267			$3	314	385	699	6	82	0.37	255	78	97		4.31	2.3

BA	1H	2H
1999	243	316
2000	239	245
2001	179	325
2002	223	310

Someone will grab him - but not until July if they're smart.

Colbrunn,Greg

		Tm	AB	R	H	HR	RBI	SB	Avg	vLH	vRH	R$	OB	Slg	OPS	bb%	ct%	Eye	xBA	PX	SX	G/F	RC/G	RAR
Pos	1B	98 2NL	166	18	51	3	23	4	307	291	339	$7	347	452	798	6	80	0.29	268	103	106	1.06	5.67	1.4
Age	33 Decline	99 ARI	135	20	44	5	24	1	326	361	237	$6	381	519	899	8	83	0.52	283	108	125	0.75	7.64	9.4
Bats	R	00 ARI	329	48	103	15	57	0	313	285	333	$14	392	523	915	12	86	0.96	307	127	34	1.07	8.02	27.3
Pwr	No change	01 ARI	97	12	28	4	18	0	289	235	317	$4	349	495	844	8	86	0.64	301	133	21	1.14	6.49	0.3
Spd	No change	02 ARI	* 196	35	64	12	32	0	327	368	259	$11	374	628	1002	7	89	0.71	341	186	71	1.12	9.18	20.9
BAvg	- -	1st Half	109	18	32	5	20	0	294			$5	358	523	881	9	89	0.92	314	149	33		7.10	4.8
LIMA	B+	2nd Half	87	17	32	7	12	0	368			$7	396	759	1154	4	90	0.44	374	232	121		12.30	17.1
Risk	Very High	03 Proj	300	48	95	16	49	1	317			$15	371	576	947	8	87	0.65	320	157	93		8.19	26.2

Check out the PX trend, his xBA, his strong ct%. Now, if he re-signs with ARI, Durazo is dealt and Grace struggles again, then he could get 500 AB. That would mean 25+ HRs and his already solid .300 BA.

Conine,Jeff

		Tm	AB	R	H	HR	RBI	SB	Avg	vLH	vRH	R$	OB	Slg	OPS	bb%	ct%	Eye	xBA	PX	SX	G/F	RC/G	RAR
Pos	1B	98 KC	309	30	79	8	43	3	256	241	261	$6	313	417	731	8	78	0.38	263	112	49	0.62	4.77	-9.4
Age	36 Decline	99 2AL	444	54	129	13	75	0	291	280	293	$12	335	453	788	6	91	0.75	300	105	32	0.98	5.51	-5.3
Bats	R	00 BAL	409	53	116	13	46	4	284	333	263	$10	342	438	779	8	87	0.68	285	91	69	1.01	5.49	-7.3
Pwr	- -	01 BAL	524	75	163	14	97	12	311	376	291	$24	386	443	829	11	86	0.85	268	82	72	1.05	6.56	4.9
Spd	- -	02 BAL	451	44	123	15	63	8	273	292	266	$15	311	448	759	5	85	0.38	289	115	104	0.95	5.14	-11.4
BAvg	- -	1st Half	256	27	67	10	45	5	262			$9	295	441	736	4	84	0.29	284	117	84		4.72	-9.6
LIMA	A	2nd Half	195	17	56	5	18	3	287			$6	332	456	788	6	88	0.54	295	112	107		5.72	-1.6
Risk	Low	03 Proj	400	45	106	12	57	6	265			$11	320	424	744	7	86	0.57	284	102	90		4.92	-9.0

His highest HR output since '97, but supported by the softest skills set. Support is what matters most when you're getting on in years - You can ask my grandfather...

Conti,Jason

	Tm	AB	R	H	HR	RBI	SB	Avg	vLH	vRH	R$	OB	Slg	OPS	bb%	ct%	Eye	xBA	PX	SX	G/F	RC/G	RAR
Pos RF CF LF	98 aa	530	107	154	14	57	16	291			$19	357	462	820	9	84	0.65	292	107	170		5.97	14.9
Age 28 Peak	99 aaa	520	77	136	7	44	17	262			$9	314	369	684	7	88	0.63	278	67	134		4.05	-16.5
Bats L	00 ARI	* 474	69	126	9	59	11	266	250	229	$11	303	395	697	5	85	0.34	275	79	133	1.15	4.25	-14.2
Pwr --	01 aaa	523	72	148	10	53	4	283			$11	326	415	740	6	87	0.47	278	87	77		4.76	-9.8
Spd No change	02 TAM	222	26	57	3	21	4	257	367	240	$4	313	383	695	8	75	0.33	242	93	105	0.94	4.26	-5.9
BAvg --	1st Half	97	10	19	1	9	1	196			($0)	278	309	587	10	73	0.42	234	93	54		2.89	-6.9
LIMA C+	2nd Half	125	16	38	2	12	3	304			$4	341	440	781	5	77	0.24	248	92	136		5.64	2.0
Risk Very High	03 Proj	250	33	67	4	25	4	268			$5	317	401	718	7	81	0.37	261	90	116		4.52	-5.6

Marginal skills set took a step back in '02. Not enough offense here to justify full-time work.

Coomer,Ron

	Tm	AB	R	H	HR	RBI	SB	Avg	vLH	vRH	R$	OB	Slg	OPS	bb%	ct%	Eye	xBA	PX	SX	G/F	RC/G	RAR
Pos 3B	98 MIN	529	54	146	15	72	2	276	281	274	$12	300	406	706	3	86	0.25	271	81	44	1.57	4.33	-3.4
Age 36 Decline	99 MIN	467	53	123	16	65	2	263	278	259	$10	308	424	732	6	85	0.43	279	99	51	1.22	4.68	2.4
Bats R	00 MIN	544	64	147	16	82	2	270	256	274	$11	316	415	731	6	91	0.72	295	89	54	1.37	4.79	5.0
Pwr ---	01 2TM	349	25	91	8	53	0	261	292	249	$7	317	390	707	8	80	0.41	249	84	20	1.15	4.50	-0.7
Spd No change	02 NYY	148	14	39	3	17	0	264	288	235	$3	292	372	664	4	84	0.26	258	76	24	1.54	3.87	-3.0
BAvg --	1st Half	61	8	21	3	8	0	344			$3	365	541	906	3	84	0.20	286	125	22		7.80	5.8
LIMA F	2nd Half	87	6	18	0	9	0	207			($1)	242	253	495	4	85	0.31	237	42	25		2.06	-6.5
Risk High	03 Proj	150	14	40	3	20	0	267			$3	306	383	688	5	84	0.36	259	78	25		4.22	-1.7

No power, no speed, no plate patience, can't get on base, can't hit RHers, poor 2nd half... a virtual cornucopia of valuable skills. And... 36 years old. Pass.

Cora,Alex

	Tm	AB	R	H	HR	RBI	SB	Avg	vLH	vRH	R$	OB	Slg	OPS	bb%	ct%	Eye	xBA	PX	SX	G/F	RC/G	RAR
Pos SS 2B	98 aaa	299	32	64	3	35	8	214			$2	242	308	550	4	90	0.38	283	64	121	2.80	2.38	-13.0
Age 27 Peak	99 aaa	302	40	79	3	29	7	262			$4	283	348	631	3	91	0.32	278	52	124	1.11	3.26	-5.9
Bats L	00 LA	* 463	53	119	4	48	8	257	226	241	$6	304	371	675	6	87	0.51	280	74	127	1.52	3.95	6.0
Pwr -	01 LA	405	38	88	4	29	0	217	293	209	($3)	273	306	579	7	86	0.53	260	59	56	1.47	2.83	-9.9
Spd No change	02 LA	258	37	75	5	28	7	291	318	288	$9	356	434	790	9	85	0.68	278	90	134	1.61	5.88	15.4
BAvg --	1st Half	80	13	25	2	10	1	313			$3	337	550	887	4	80	0.19	298	136	269		7.09	7.4
LIMA C+	2nd Half	178	24	50	3	18	6	281			$6	363	382	745	11	88	1.05	268	69	71		5.34	7.8
Risk Very High	03 Proj	250	31	66	4	25	4	264			$5	318	392	710	7	86	0.55	277	81	126		4.49	5.7

There's little to back up a .291 BA, so that will likely fall back in '03... which will reduce his SB opportunities... which pretty much takes away any remaining value.

Cordero,Wil

	Tm	AB	R	H	HR	RBI	SB	Avg	vLH	vRH	R$	OB	Slg	OPS	bb%	ct%	Eye	xBA	PX	SX	G/F	RC/G	RAR
Pos LF	98 CHW	341	58	91	13	49	2	267	265	268	$9	311	446	757	6	81	0.33	275	109	89	0.84	4.98	-1.8
Age 31 Past Peak	99 CLE	194	35	58	8	32	2	299	255	317	$7	349	500	849	7	81	0.41	284	128	69	1.31	6.68	9.0
Bats R	00 2TM	496	64	137	16	68	1	276	323	260	$11	320	464	784	6	85	0.42	295	116	75	1.02	5.34	1.2
Pwr +	01 CLE	268	30	67	4	21	0	250	298	228	$2	307	343	650	8	81	0.44	239	61	41	1.11	3.80	-7.6
Spd No change	02 2TM	161	22	43	6	30	2	267	258	279	$5	337	435	772	10	82	0.59	271	109	56	0.94	5.50	-1.1
BAvg -	1st Half	74	7	17	0	10	1	230			($1)	278	284	562	6	80	0.33	229	48	55		2.84	-6.5
LIMA C	2nd Half	87	15	26	6	20	1	299			$4	384	563	947	12	84	0.86	307	160	47		8.45	7.7
Risk Very High	03 Proj	200	27	54	7	30	1	270			$5	332	435	766	8	82	0.52	277	104	70		5.34	-0.8

Hard to believe this once-hot prospect is only 31, and already a journeyman. BPIs were actually better in '02 than '01, but the ABs weren't there. Spotty injury and attitude history are not in his favor.

Cordova,Marty

	Tm	AB	R	H	HR	RBI	SB	Avg	vLH	vRH	R$	OB	Slg	OPS	bb%	ct%	Eye	xBA	PX	SX	G/F	RC/G	RAR
Pos LF DH	98 MIN	438	52	111	10	69	3	253	330	233	$8	330	377	707	10	76	0.49	240	78	56	1.82	4.37	-10.9
Age 33 Decline	99 MIN	425	62	121	14	70	13	285	206	310	$16	357	464	821	10	77	0.50	268	111	108	1.58	6.25	14.5
Bats R	00 2AL	200	23	49	4	18	3	245	212	261	$2	307	340	647	8	83	0.51	247	59	56	1.38	3.69	-9.4
Pwr No change	01 CLE	409	61	123	20	69	0	301	333	289	$17	338	506	844	5	80	0.28	269	121	48	1.39	6.22	18.5
Spd No change	02 BAL	458	55	116	18	64	1	253	274	245	$11	323	434	757	9	76	0.42	256	118	45	1.15	4.82	-1.5
BAvg -	1st Half	238	32	63	9	36	1	265			$7	327	441	768	8	75	0.37	252	115	59		4.94	0.0
LIMA B+	2nd Half	220	23	53	9	28	0	241			$4	318	427	746	10	77	0.49	261	121	40		4.70	-1.6
Risk High	03 Proj	450	57	115	17	63	2	256			$11	318	429	747	8	78	0.42	260	108	56		4.74	-5.4

We told you that 2001's BA was a fluke and he obliged our projections. This is about the best you can hope for right now, your basic $10 outfielder.

Counsell,Craig

	Tm	AB	R	H	HR	RBI	SB	Avg	vLH	vRH	R$	OB	Slg	OPS	bb%	ct%	Eye	xBA	PX	SX	G/F	RC/G	RAR
Pos 3B SS	98 FLA	335	43	84	4	40	3	251	239	254	$4	350	373	723	13	86	1.09	282	87	112	1.64	4.97	5.2
Age 32 Past Peak	99 2NL	174	24	38	0	11	1	218	250	312	($2)	277	259	535	7	86	0.58	253	35	62	1.41	2.55	-10.2
Bats L	00 ARI	152	23	48	2	11	3	316	267	321	$5	395	421	816	12	88	1.11	281	70	78	1.50	6.37	9.7
Pwr --	01 ARI	458	76	126	4	38	6	275	337	258	$8	360	362	723	12	83	0.80	255	60	87	1.65	4.78	1.6
Spd --	02 ARI	436	63	123	2	51	7	282	269	289	$10	349	351	700	9	88	0.87	260	53	75	1.82	4.57	-1.5
BAvg No change	1st Half	300	45	86	1	39	6	287			$8	359	363	723	10	88	0.92	264	60	81		4.91	2.2
LIMA B	2nd Half	136	18	37	1	12	1	272			$2	327	324	650	7	89	0.73	251	37	52		3.86	-3.4
Risk High	03 Proj	400	59	111	3	37	5	278			$7	350	355	705	10	87	0.85	261	55	79		4.60	0.7

Solid BPIs for getting on base, but no pop or speed to speak of. Expect more of the same.

Cox,Steve

	Tm	AB	R	H	HR	RBI	SB	Avg	vLH	vRH	R$	OB	Slg	OPS	bb%	ct%	Eye	xBA	PX	SX	G/F	RC/G	RAR
Pos 1B DH	98 aaa	431	54	104	12	57	3	241			$7	313	381	694	9	81	0.55	264	92	57		4.20	-18.6
Age 28 Peak	99 aaa	534	76	154	18	89	2	288			$16	345	478	822	8	90	0.84	311	124	53	0.86	6.01	6.0
Bats L	00 TAM	318	44	90	11	35	1	283	245	291	$7	374	453	826	13	85	0.98	286	103	44	1.57	6.39	3.3
Pwr +	01 TAM	342	37	88	12	51	2	257	232	264	$8	306	427	733	7	78	0.32	255	109	38	1.65	4.59	-17.6
Spd No change	02 TAM	560	65	142	16	72	5	254	197	275	$13	326	396	722	10	79	0.52	256	97	69	1.19	4.77	-21.4
BAvg No change	1st Half	295	31	85	9	37	3	288			$10	338	437	775	7	79	0.35	255	99	64		5.59	-3.6
LIMA A	2nd Half	265	34	57	7	35	2	215			$3	314	351	664	13	80	0.72	257	95	54		3.99	-17.2
Risk Moderate	03 Proj	500	60	133	16	67	3	266			$12	337	421	758	10	81	0.55	264	102	55		5.23	-6.7

His first F/T season but the results were underwhelming. Troubling signs...
- Tailed badly in the 2nd half
- BA vsLH trend
- Power decline at a time when you'd expect more growth.

Crawford,Carl

	Tm	AB	R	H	HR	RBI	SB	Avg	vLH	vRH	R$	OB	Slg	OPS	bb%	ct%	Eye	xBA	PX	SX	G/F	RC/G	RAR
Pos LF	98	0	0	0	0	0	0	0								0							
Age 21 Growth	99	0	0	0	0	0	0	0								0							
Bats L	00	0	0	0	0	0	0	0								0							
Pwr ---	01 aa	537	64	149	4	51	36	277			$19	324	358	682	6	85	0.46	258	56	111		3.92	-22.1
Spd +++++	02 TAM	* 612	79	176	9	80	34	288	200	276	$26	319	430	748	4	84	0.29	274	92	195	2.00	4.81	-2.2
BAvg --	1st Half	297	50	97	6	42	21	327			$18	359	505	864	5	84	0.32	289	113	227		6.54	14.4
LIMA A+	2nd Half	315	29	79	3	38	13	251			$8	280	359	639	4	84	0.27	260	71	158		3.46	-13.8
Risk High	03 Proj	500	61	136	6	58	29	272			$18	310	386	696	5	85	0.35	267	75	156		4.07	-16.0

2-30-9-.259 in 259 AB at TAM, a reasonable debut. This is your next SB stud. Give him two years to develop his OB skills, then start counting the 50-SB seasons.

Crede,Joe

	Tm	AB	R	H	HR	RBI	SB	Avg	vLH	vRH	R$	OB	Slg	OPS	bb%	ct%	Eye	xBA	PX	SX	G/F	RC/G	RAR
Pos 3B	98	0	0	0	0	0	0	0								0							
Age 24 Growth	99 aa	291	34	68	4	38	2	234			$1	283	330	613	6	86	0.48	264	65	60		3.00	-13.1
Bats R	00 aa	533	78	158	22	87	3	296			$19	360	482	842	9	81	0.52	279	113	42	0.29	6.47	33.9
Pwr --	01 aaa	513	62	134	18	66	3	261			$12	322	439	761	8	82	0.51	277	112	63	0.94	5.13	8.9
Spd No change	02 CHW	* 559	78	164	36	92	0	293	259	295	$26	333	538	871	6	85	0.40	309	152	21	0.74	6.50	32.8
BAvg --	1st Half	280	36	82	19	45	0	293			$13	338	557	895	6	88	0.54	327	166	20		6.90	20.0
LIMA A	2nd Half	279	42	82	17	47	0	294			$13	328	520	847	5	83	0.29	292	138	33		6.11	13.0
Risk Very High	03 Proj	550	74	154	27	84	2	280			$19	329	483	812	7	84	0.45	287	125	42		5.70	18.6

12-85-.285 in 200 AB at CHW, a 30+ HR pace in 550 AB... which is exactly what he did in '02. He's here, he's ready and BPIs looks good for him to become a major power source.

Crisp,Covelli

	Yr	Tm	AB	R	H	HR	RBI	SB	Avg	vLH	vRH	R$	OB	Slg	OPS	bb%	ct%	Eye	xBA	PX	SX	G/F	RC/G	RAR
Pos CF	98		0	0	0	0	0	0	0								0							
Age 23 Growth	99		0	0	0	0	0	0	0								0							
Bats S	00		0	0	0	0	0	0	0								0							
Pwr No change	01		0	0	0	0	0	0	0								0							
Spd +	02	CLE	* 461	79	135	9	52	33	293	270	256	$23	347	406	752	8	85	0.56	266	80	120	1.05	5.16	4.1
BAvg - -	1st Half		233	33	59	4	24	12	253			$7	320	356	677	9	85	0.68	261	71	108		3.93	-6.9
LIMA C+	2nd Half		228	46	76	5	28	21	333			$16	374	456	831	6	85	0.44	271	88	123		6.71	12.7
Risk Moderate	03	Proj	200	36	56	4	23	15	280			$9	333	390	723	7	85	0.53	267	76	113		4.71	-1.2

1-9-4-.260 in 127 AB at CLE. There are the beginnings of some legitimate talent here. His game is speed, and as a top of the order hitter, his early OB avgs are promising. Last piece of the puzzle is opportunity.

Cruz,Deivi

	Yr	Tm	AB	R	H	HR	RBI	SB	Avg	vLH	vRH	R$	OB	Slg	OPS	bb%	ct%	Eye	xBA	PX	SX	G/F	RC/G	RAR
Pos SS	98	DET	454	52	118	5	45	3	260	340	236	$5	281	355	635	3	88	0.24	270	65	77	1.57	3.38	-8.2
Age 30 Past Peak	99	DET	518	64	147	13	58	1	284	290	282	$10	300	427	727	2	89	0.21	288	95	39	1.58	4.47	3.3
Bats R	00	DET	583	68	176	10	82	1	302	345	288	$14	317	449	767	2	93	0.30	308	98	65	1.27	5.12	10.4
Pwr + +	01	DET	414	39	106	7	52	4	256	223	268	$7	285	379	665	4	89	0.37	280	86	62	1.33	3.82	-7.9
Spd No change	02	SD	514	49	135	7	47	2	263	242	272	$6	293	366	659	4	89	0.38	270	71	53	1.49	3.74	-3.7
BAvg - -	1st Half		264	24	66	4	26	1	250			$2	288	352	640	5	89	0.48	270	69	49		3.48	-4.0
LIMA C	2nd Half		250	25	69	3	21	1	276			$4	298	380	678	3	88	0.28	271	74	57		4.03	0.4
Risk Low	03	Proj	450	46	121	7	49	2	269			$7	295	386	680	4	89	0.34	282	81	61		3.99	3.2

Has never shown any offensive value, and that continued in SD. Nothing in the numbers points to any change in potential output.

Cruz,Jacob

	Yr	Tm	AB	R	H	HR	RBI	SB	Avg	vLH	vRH	R$	OB	Slg	OPS	bb%	ct%	Eye	xBA	PX	SX	G/F	RC/G	RAR
Pos DH	98	aaa	511	73	139	23	78	11	272			$19	335	468	802	9	86	0.68	300	121	89	1.04	5.57	2.8
Age 30 Past Peak	99	CLE	* 290	38	77	9	42	3	266	315	280	$7	317	414	731	7	83	0.46	271	88	82	2.56	4.69	-5.4
Bats L	00	CLE	29	3	7	0	5	1	241	400	208	$0	353	345	698	15	86	1.25	278	87	52	1.44	4.84	-0.3
Pwr + + +	01	2TM	* 230	30	55	9	34	1	239	300	209	$4	289	409	697	7	71	0.24	234	100	64	1.53	3.83	-10.6
Spd No change	02	DET	* 131	17	30	2	10	4	229	400	256	$2	327	336	663	13	75	0.58	227	67	138	1.19	4.08	-6.7
BAvg + + +	1st Half		131	17	30	2	10	4	229			$2	327	336	663	13	75	0.58	227	67	138		4.08	-6.7
LIMA C+	2nd Half		0	0	0	0	0	0	0			($0)					0							-0.0
Risk X HIGH	03	Proj	250	33	63	8	32	4	252			$6	319	398	717	9	79	0.46	254	89	95		4.50	-7.8

2-6-3-.273 in 88 AB at DET. He kills LH pitching, but they never give him any ABs vs LHers. But the bottom line...
Apr 10: Back stiffness
May 16: Knee inflammation
Jun 29: Bone chips in elbow

Cruz,Jose

	Yr	Tm	AB	R	H	HR	RBI	SB	Avg	vLH	vRH	R$	OB	Slg	OPS	bb%	ct%	Eye	xBA	PX	SX	G/F	RC/G	RAR
Pos LF RF CF	98	TOR	* 493	82	130	17	63	18	264	289	240	$16	374	440	814	15	74	0.67	254	109	116	1.04	6.26	18.4
Age 29 Past Peak	99	TOR	* 452	80	103	17	59	19	228	275	230	$11	358	407	766	17	75	0.82	259	105	131	1.14	5.52	5.5
Bats S	00	TOR	603	91	146	31	76	15	242	290	224	$15	322	466	788	11	79	0.55	283	127	116	1.09	5.33	2.7
Pwr + + +	01	TOR	577	92	158	34	88	32	274	290	269	$31	326	530	857	7	76	0.33	282	152	131	1.01	6.40	29.9
Spd - -	02	TOR	466	64	114	18	70	7	245	225	253	$13	319	438	757	10	77	0.48	268	124	120	0.96	5.06	1.9
BAvg No change	1st Half		292	36	67	11	40	6	229			$7	310	401	711	10	76	0.49	256	111	85		4.46	-4.4
LIMA A+	2nd Half		174	28	47	7	30	1	270			$6	335	500	835	9	79	0.46	287	145	154		6.19	6.8
Risk Moderate	03	Proj	500	76	133	23	75	11	266			$18	338	485	823	10	77	0.48	276	133	129		6.03	14.3

Poor 1st half derailed his season, more than his decent 2nd half could offset. Declining BPIs are a concern for a 29-year-old, but he should rebound a bit in '03.

Damon,Johnny

	Yr	Tm	AB	R	H	HR	RBI	SB	Avg	vLH	vRH	R$	OB	Slg	OPS	bb%	ct%	Eye	xBA	PX	SX	G/F	RC/G	RAR
Pos CF	98	KC	642	104	178	18	66	26	277	245	291	$21	337	439	776	8	87	0.69	296	97	148	1.16	5.32	9.5
Age 29 Past Peak	99	KC	583	101	179	14	77	36	307	329	300	$29	378	477	855	10	91	1.34	320	106	161	1.39	7.21	44.8
Bats L	00	KC	655	136	214	16	88	46	327	357	316	$37	388	495	882	9	91	1.08	313	102	173	1.49	7.75	61.8
Pwr +	01	OAK	644	108	165	9	49	27	256	265	252	$14	321	363	684	9	89	0.87	280	72	118	1.15	4.16	-15.9
Spd + + + + +	02	BOS	623	118	178	14	63	31	286	306	279	$25	353	443	796	9	89	0.93	296	103	181	1.29	6.02	22.5
BAvg No change	1st Half		306	60	94	5	38	17	307			$15	363	448	811	8	91	0.93	295	93	184		6.34	14.0
LIMA A	2nd Half		317	58	84	9	25	14	265			$11	344	438	782	11	87	0.93	296	113	167		5.73	8.7
Risk Moderate	03	Proj	625	115	190	16	62	37	304			$30	369	468	837	9	89	0.94	301	104	161		6.75	36.3

Was posting a terrific rebound season until he hurt his knee. If healthy, he should get back into $30 territory.

Daubach,Brian

	Yr	Tm	AB	R	H	HR	RBI	SB	Avg	vLH	vRH	R$	OB	Slg	OPS	bb%	ct%	Eye	xBA	PX	SX	G/F	RC/G	RAR
Pos 1B LF DH	98	aaa	512	72	127	23	90	7	248			$15	326	465	791	10	81	0.61	293	140	89	0.40	5.46	-1.9
Age 31 Past Peak	99	BOS	* 412	64	121	22	78	0	294	273	297	$16	358	553	911	9	76	0.41	283	159	61	0.96	7.41	19.5
Bats L	00	BOS	495	55	123	21	76	1	248	216	257	$9	310	448	758	8	74	0.34	257	120	49	1.06	4.93	-17.6
Pwr + +	01	BOS	407	54	107	22	71	1	263	169	279	$13	348	509	856	12	73	0.49	262	148	63	0.89	6.54	3.6
Spd No change	02	BOS	444	62	118	20	78	2	266	242	270	$15	341	464	805	10	72	0.40	248	127	66	1.02	5.83	-2.1
BAvg - -	1st Half		199	24	49	10	33	0	246			$6	327	467	795	11	67	0.36	240	146	23		5.41	-3.6
LIMA B+	2nd Half		245	38	69	10	45	2	282			$10	353	461	814	10	76	0.45	253	111	93		6.19	1.6
Risk Moderate	03	Proj	450	61	117	20	73	1	260			$13	336	463	799	10	73	0.43	254	127	54		5.68	0.4

Fairly consistent performer, but small signs of impending decline. Looks good for 2003, though.

Davis,Ben

	Yr	Tm	AB	R	H	HR	RBI	SB	Avg	vLH	vRH	R$	OB	Slg	OPS	bb%	ct%	Eye	xBA	PX	SX	G/F	RC/G	RAR
Pos CA	98	aa	434	51	108	12	59	3	249			$8	299	392	691	7	89	0.66	293	96	59		4.11	0.9
Age 26 Pre-Peak	99	SD	* 467	49	117	11	62	5	251	239	246	$7	312	392	704	8	78	0.42	258	94	68	1.70	4.39	5.1
Bats S	00	SD	* 351	45	81	9	49	5	231	194	234	$4	318	370	689	11	79	0.60	260	89	69	0.97	4.19	1.3
Pwr No change	01	SD	448	56	107	11	57	4	239	241	238	$6	337	357	694	13	75	0.59	235	75	46	1.20	4.36	11.2
Spd No change	02	SEA	228	24	59	7	43	1	259	235	266	$7	313	404	717	7	75	0.31	239	94	56	1.03	4.50	5.7
BAvg - -	1st Half		121	9	28	1	16	1	231			$1	295	281	576	8	78	0.41	213	36	37		3.03	-2.5
LIMA D+	2nd Half		107	15	31	6	27	0	290			$5	333	542	875	6	71	0.23	264	160	81		6.43	8.9
Risk High	03	Proj	350	41	93	11	59	2	266			$10	334	416	750	9	76	0.42	245	97	54		5.03	10.5

BA shows improvement, but xBA says no. Promising sign is his 2nd half surge, in which he posted some of his best BPIs, albeit in only 107 AB. As we've been waiting for him to emerge, this does bode well for 2003.

Delgado,Carlos

	Yr	Tm	AB	R	H	HR	RBI	SB	Avg	vLH	vRH	R$	OB	Slg	OPS	bb%	ct%	Eye	xBA	PX	SX	G/F	RC/G	RAR
Pos 1B	98	TOR	530	94	155	38	115	3	292	303	288	$27	378	592	971	12	74	0.53	287	181	62	0.74	8.60	49.1
Age 30 Past Peak	99	TOR	573	113	156	44	134	1	272	309	259	$26	367	571	938	13	75	0.61	287	173	43	0.79	7.81	35.9
Bats L	00	TOR	569	115	196	41	137	0	344	319	357	$36	461	664	1125	18	82	1.18	331	191	30	1.33	12.85	134.0
Pwr No change	01	TOR	574	102	160	39	102	3	279	246	293	$25	396	540	936	16	76	0.82	273	151	55	1.12	8.30	39.6
Spd No change	02	TOR	505	103	140	33	108	1	277	238	297	$24	399	549	947	17	75	0.81	285	171	64	0.77	8.47	43.2
BAvg No change	1st Half		278	48	71	17	59	1	255			$11	382	511	893	17	73	0.76	272	162	58		7.41	13.6
LIMA A	2nd Half		227	55	69	16	49	0	304			$13	419	595	1014	17	78	0.88	302	183	61		9.92	30.6
Risk Very Low	03	Proj	500	100	146	39	105	1	292			$27	408	602	1010	16	77	0.84	299	186	50		9.59	67.4

Is there another 40-HR, .300 season left in him? 2nd half surge - despite a sore back - is strong evidence that the talent is still there. At 30, he might still do it, but the key might be his BA vsLH.

Dellucci,David

	Yr	Tm	AB	R	H	HR	RBI	SB	Avg	vLH	vRH	R$	OB	Slg	OPS	bb%	ct%	Eye	xBA	PX	SX	G/F	RC/G	RAR
Pos RF LF	98	ARI	419	43	108	5	51	3	258			$6	312	396	708	7	75	0.32	251	89	171	1.77	4.46	-7.0
Age 29 Past Peak	99	ARI	109	27	43	1	15	2	394	250	419	$6	450	505	955	9	78	0.46	251	78	110	3.13	10.24	17.6
Bats L	00	ARI	* 172	13	39	2	14	3	227		300	$0	285	331	616	8	88	0.67	278	67	92	6.20	3.40	-9.8
Pwr + + +	01	ARI	217	28	60	10	40	2	276	231	283	$8	343	479	822	9	76	0.42	263	117	86	1.83	6.06	2.7
Spd No change	02	ARI	* 244	35	58	7	30	2	238	111	262	$3	319	389	708	11	76	0.50	246	93	86	2.16	4.23	-9.2
BAvg + + +	1st Half		74	10	15	2	8	0	203			($0)	272	338	609	9	82	0.54	260	88	53		2.96	-5.7
LIMA C	2nd Half		170	25	43	5	22	2	253			$4	339	412	750	11	74	0.49	240	96	105		4.86	-3.0
Risk X HIGH	03	Proj	250	33	63	7	33	2	252			$5	323	402	724	9	78	0.48	255	92	85		4.59	-2.4

Seasonal trends are erratic, but that will happen with such small data sets. He could do just about anytning in '03, but within the limits of his history, the results won't likely be worth all that much.

DeRosa,Mark

	Yr	Tm	AB	R	H	HR	RBI	SB	Avg	vLH	vRH	R$	OB	Slg	OPS	bb%	ct%	Eye	xBA	PX	SX	G/F	RC/G	RAR
Pos 2B	98	aa	461	51	105	6	37	5	228			$1	301	321	622	9	90	1.07	280	66	77	1.00	3.48	-9.8
Age 28 Peak	99	aaa	364	35	90	1	34	6	247			$2	283	308	590	5	88	0.43	262	45	76		2.87	-14.2
Bats R	00	aaa	370	52	98	2	30	11	265			$6	325	346	671	8	92	1.10	282	58	101	1.25	4.10	-1.2
Pwr --	01	ATL	* 350	54	97	5	35	8	277	417	250	$9	331	389	719	7	89	0.72	284	80	83	2.08	4.68	8.0
Spd +	02	ATL	* 267	32	75	5	28	4	281	293	299	$7	322	397	719	6	90	0.62	280	74	85	1.70	4.56	0.5
BAvg -	1st Half		65	7	22	0	7	0	338			$2	368	431	798	4	92	0.60	281	67	77		6.27	3.4
LIMA A	2nd Half		202	25	53	5	21	4	262			$5	307	386	693	6	90	0.62	279	76	82		4.10	-2.5
Risk Very High	03	Proj	400	51	122	5	39	7	305			$12	350	408	758	7	90	0.72	281	71	81		5.35	15.3

xBA says that this is a .280 hitter, but contact rates suggest that .300 might not be far off. Was batting .345 before getting hurt, and .279 the rest of the way. Not much production otherwise, but still a good pick.

Deshields,Delino

	Yr	Tm	AB	R	H	HR	RBI	SB	Avg	vLH	vRH	R$	OB	Slg	OPS	bb%	ct%	Eye	xBA	PX	SX	G/F	RC/G	RAR
Pos 2B	98	STL	420	74	122	7	44	26	290	267	298	$18	374	429	803	12	85	0.92	286	92	171	1.84	6.08	25.6
Age 34 Decline	99	BAL	330	46	87	6	34	11	264	171	277	$7	338	364	702	10	84	0.71	258	61	96	1.55	4.35	3.1
Bats L	00	BAL	561	84	166	10	86	37	296	344	278	$26	373	444	817	11	85	0.84	288	98	132	1.51	6.44	44.8
Pwr ---	01	2TM	351	55	82	5	37	23	234	183	249	$9	344	353	697	14	78	0.77	252	75	162	1.63	4.83	8.3
Spd --	02	CHC	146	20	28	3	10	10	192	105	205	$1	293	308	602	13	74	0.55	233	73	133	2.40	3.43	-5.1
BAvg +++++	1st Half		131	18	25	3	8	7	191			$0	269	313	582	10	76	0.45	242	75	137		3.12	-5.7
LIMA C+	2nd Half		15	2	3	0	2	3	200			$1	455	267	721	32	53	1.00	159	58	74		5.92	0.9
Risk Very High	03	Proj	250	37	62	5	26	14	248			$7	332	380	712	11	81	0.67	264	84	145		4.76	5.3

Major skills erosion, but probably still enough there to help some team off the bench. You always hate to see major speed sources go in this roto game.

Diaz,Einar

	Yr	Tm	AB	R	H	HR	RBI	SB	Avg	vLH	vRH	R$	OB	Slg	OPS	bb%	ct%	Eye	xBA	PX	SX	G/F	RC/G	RAR
Pos CA	98	CLE	* 463	66	134	9	68	3	289	188	250	$12	322	406	728	5	92	0.63	291	76	76	1.86	4.82	10.2
Age 30 Past Peak	99	CLE	392	43	110	3	32	11	281	213	302	$8	320	362	683	6	90	0.56	272	59	85	1.25	4.26	1.3
Bats R	00	CLE	250	29	68	4	25	4	272	263	275	$4	303	392	695	4	88	0.38	281	77	94	1.24	4.21	-0.2
Pwr No change	01	CLE	437	54	121	4	56	1	277	196	305	$8	304	387	691	4	90	0.39	280	83	51	1.17	4.18	3.1
Spd No change	02	CLE	320	34	66	2	16	0	206	225	201	($3)	246	284	531	5	92	0.63	272	65	44	1.48	2.32	-13.2
BAvg +++++	1st Half		208	24	45	2	12	0	216			($1)	266	313	578	6	91	0.74	279	78	45		2.79	-5.7
LIMA D+	2nd Half		112	10	21	0	4	0	187			($2)	209	232	441	3	93	0.38	259	41	43		1.57	-7.0
Risk Moderate	03	Proj	350	39	93	3	38	2	266			$5	296	355	651	4	91	0.47	275	68	60		3.73	-3.6

A .206 BA is a complete fluke, given his contact rate, eye ratio and xBA. He will rebound, and possibly close to pre-2002 levels.

DiFelice,Mike

	Yr	Tm	AB	R	H	HR	RBI	SB	Avg	vLH	vRH	R$	OB	Slg	OPS	bb%	ct%	Eye	xBA	PX	SX	G/F	RC/G	RAR
Pos CA	98	TAM	248	17	57	3	23	0	230	279	214	($0)	274	339	612	6	77	0.27	239	71	64	2.78	3.21	-6.6
Age 33 Decline	99	TAM	179	21	55	6	27	0	307	286	315	$6	337	469	806	4	87	0.35	284	103	23	1.25	5.96	9.7
Bats R	00	TAM	204	23	49	6	19	0	240	225	244	$1	282	402	684	6	80	0.30	268	100	49	1.11	3.95	-1.7
Pwr -	01	2TM	* 196	19	39	3	12	1	199	151	205	($2)	238	281	518	5	72	0.18	212	49	72	0.91	2.19	-9.3
Spd No change	02	STL	174	17	40	4	19	0	230	216	236	$1	298	362	660	9	76	0.40	237	90	21	0.93	3.83	-2.0
BAvg No change	1st Half		84	11	20	3	8	0	238			$1	264	381	645	3	77	0.16	242	85	40		3.45	-1.8
LIMA D	2nd Half		90	6	20	1	11	0	222			($0)	327	344	671	13	74	0.61	234	94	9		4.13	-0.2
Risk High	03	Proj	150	14	34	3	15	0	227			$0	284	343	627	7	76	0.34	237	78	31		3.40	-2.7

We talk about the phenomenon of late career power spikes for catchers. This would seem an unlikely candidate until you take a look at his G/F trend. If he hits 10 HRs in '03, you read it here first. If he doesn't, I was lying.

Donnels,Chris

	Yr	Tm	AB	R	H	HR	RBI	SB	Avg	vLH	vRH	R$	OB	Slg	OPS	bb%	ct%	Eye	xBA	PX	SX	G/F	RC/G	RAR
Pos 3B	98	JPN	160	21	47	6	26	1	294			$6	405	488	893	16	71	0.65	249	133	33		7.89	18.3
Age 37 Decline	99	JPN	0	0	0	0	0	0	0								0							
Bats L	00	LA	* 366	64	94	23	68	5	257		333	$14	349	514	863	12	85	0.95	316	149	76	1.56	6.61	26.4
Pwr --	01	LA	* 225	20	38	8	25	0	169	333	165	($2)	255	302	557	10	80	0.57	248	76	22	1.88	2.55	-15.3
Spd No change	02	ARI	* 90	7	22	3	16	0	244	222	239	$2	327	422	749	11	82	0.69	270	108	51	1.86	5.01	0.9
BAvg +++	1st Half		53	3	13	2	10	0	245			$1	322	453	775	10	83	0.67	283	123	72		5.25	1.0
LIMA C	2nd Half		37	4	9	1	6	0	243			$1	333	378	712	12	81	0.71	253	88	19		4.64	-0.0
Risk X HIGH	03	Proj	100	12	24	5	17	1	240			$2	330	458	789	12	81	0.72	285	130	72		5.46	2.9

Was named the Florida State League MVP in 1989 after hitting 17 HRs, 78 RBIs and batting .313.

Drew,J.D.

	Yr	Tm	AB	R	H	HR	RBI	SB	Avg	vLH	vRH	R$	OB	Slg	OPS	bb%	ct%	Eye	xBA	PX	SX	G/F	RC/G	RAR
Pos RF	98	STL	* 182	37	57	11	33	3	313	400	423	$11	421	593	1015	16	79	0.89	304	181	107	0.50	9.98	30.8
Age 27 Peak	99	STL	* 455	82	113	15	52	24	248	264	233	$14	332	424	756	11	79	0.60	270	104	166	0.88	5.26	2.4
Bats L	00	STL	407	73	120	18	57	17	295	257	303	$19	395	479	874	14	76	0.68	259	106	97	1.19	7.16	25.9
Pwr +	01	STL	375	80	121	27	73	13	323	289	332	$27	412	613	1025	13	80	0.76	305	161	145	1.18	10.11	54.8
Spd ----	02	STL	424	61	107	18	56	8	252	262	250	$12	341	429	770	12	75	0.55	249	105	79	1.07	5.41	0.0
BAvg No change	1st Half		261	42	69	11	34	8	264			$9	354	452	806	12	75	0.55	254	114	98		6.08	5.7
LIMA A	2nd Half		163	19	38	7	22	0	233			$2	321	393	713	11	76	0.54	239	92	24		4.43	-5.1
Risk High	03	Proj	450	75	124	23	68	5	276			$17	367	485	852	13	77	0.63	266	121	83		6.61	25.2

The quest for 500 AB continues. BPIs took a big step back, and at 27, we may have to reassess his true ceiling. The monster year may still come, but with his history and knee problem, you cannot bid like it's imminent.

Dunn,Adam

	Yr	Tm	AB	R	H	HR	RBI	SB	Avg	vLH	vRH	R$	OB	Slg	OPS	bb%	ct%	Eye	xBA	PX	SX	G/F	RC/G	RAR
Pos LF 1B	98		0	0	0	0	0	0	0								0							
Age 23 Growth	99		0	0	0	0	0	0	0								0							
Bats L	00		0	0	0	0	0	0	0								0							
Pwr +	01	CIN	* 594	120	184	49	118	14	310	282	254	$40	405	630	1035	14	78	0.71	305	185	78	0.80	9.74	77.4
Spd +++++	02	CIN	535	84	133	26	71	19	249	254	246	$19	394	454	848	19	68	0.75	233	122	86	1.01	6.75	4.4
BAvg +++	1st Half		262	45	80	15	48	7	305			$16	445	538	983	20	67	0.77	235	133	94		9.72	30.1
LIMA A	2nd Half		273	39	53	11	23	12	194			$3	343	374	717	19	69	0.74	231	112	73		4.57	-18.7
Risk Moderate	03	Proj	550	96	144	29	80	21	262			$23	388	482	871	17	72	0.74	254	133	86		7.05	43.6

What can explain the complete 2nd half collapse? Did the league finally catch up to him? Few clues, but xBA does say his 1st half was no better. Hmm. Odds are he will rebound, but the risk has just doubled.

Dunston,Shawon

	Yr	Tm	AB	R	H	HR	RBI	SB	Avg	vLH	vRH	R$	OB	Slg	OPS	bb%	ct%	Eye	xBA	PX	SX	G/F	RC/G	RAR
Pos RF	98	2TM	207	36	46	6	20	9	222	202	234	$4	244	401	645	3	86	0.21	307	116	188	0.78	3.11	-12.0
Age 40 Decline	99	2NL	243	35	78	5	41	10	321	340	309	$12	327	453	779	1	84	0.05	274	82	133	1.16	5.42	2.2
Bats R	00	STL	216	28	54	12	43	3	250	226	273	$7	270	486	756	3	78	0.13	283	134	104	0.88	4.50	-4.8
Pwr No change	01	SF	186	26	52	9	25	3	280	318	245	$7	287	511	798	1	83	0.06	299	133	141	0.89	5.17	-2.7
Spd No change	02	SF	147	7	34	1	9	1	231	229	232	($1)	247	286	532	2	78	0.09	218	40	31	0.80	2.41	-12.8
BAvg --	1st Half		79	3	17	1	5	0	215			($1)	215	278	494	0	77	0.00	216	41	6		1.95	-7.8
LIMA F	2nd Half		68	4	17	0	4	1	250			$0	282	294	576	4	78	0.20	220	38	40		3.00	-4.9
Risk Low	03	Proj	150	14	36	2	16	0	240			$1	256	336	593	2	80	0.11	244	65	68		2.89	-8.8

Plate patience? Nah. Taking pitches is for sissies. Real men get up there and swing the bat. The Law of Averages states that eventually you'll hit something. Like monkeys in a room full of typewriters.

Durazo,Erubiel

	Yr	Tm	AB	R	H	HR	RBI	SB	Avg	vLH	vRH	R$	OB	Slg	OPS	bb%	ct%	Eye	xBA	PX	SX	G/F	RC/G	RAR
Pos 1B	98	MEX	420	84	147	19	98	4	350			$27	431	571	1003	13	81	0.75	294	145	80		10.29	64.8
Age 29 Past Peak	99	ARI	* 499	92	176	28	93	3	353	222	343	$30	428	589	1017	12	84	0.80	298	138	75	0.85	10.42	80.9
Bats L	00	ARI	196	35	52	8	33	1	265	318	259	$5	374	444	818	15	78	0.79	268	109	48	1.28	6.38	6.1
Pwr ++	01	ARI	175	34	47	12	38	0	269	188	287	$8	369	537	907	14	72	0.57	266	157	34	1.10	7.45	6.2
Spd No change	02	ARI	* 258	53	69	18	55	0	267	167	292	$12	390	562	952	17	76	0.84	283	170	88	0.97	8.24	22.3
BAvg +++	1st Half		106	22	28	10	26	0	264			$6	376	594	970	15	72	0.63	270	184	38		8.07	8.4
LIMA A	2nd Half		152	31	41	8	29	0	270			$6	400	539	939	18	79	1.03	292	160	117		8.32	13.8
Risk High	03	Proj	500	99	138	31	103	0	276			$22	387	539	926	15	76	0.75	277	154	62		7.92	43.1

We all want to see him get his shot. His BPIs are poised to produce big numbers. It would have been nice to see more experience vs LHers, who he struggles with. But he only has 86 AB vs LHers the past 2 years.

Durham,Ray

	Yr	Tm	AB	R	H	HR	RBI	SB	Avg	vLH	vRH	R$	OB	Slg	OPS	bb%	ct%	Eye	xBA	PX	SX	G/F	RC/G	RAR
Pos 2B DH	98	CHW	635	126	181	19	67	36	285	281	287	$26	359	455	814	10	83	0.70	290	104	159	1.45	6.23	43.0
Age 31 Past Peak	99	CHW	612	109	181	13	60	34	296	301	294	$24	371	435	805	11	83	0.70	276	85	152	1.76	6.19	42.0
Bats S	00	CHW	614	121	172	17	75	25	280	248	289	$21	358	450	808	11	83	0.71	283	100	155	1.57	5.87	38.0
Pwr +	01	CHW	611	104	163	20	65	23	267	259	269	$20	336	466	803	9	82	0.58	290	123	152	1.09	5.61	25.5
Spd - -	02	2AL	564	114	163	15	70	26	289	255	301	$25	370	450	821	11	84	0.78	281	108	150	1.22	6.44	42.2
BAvg -	1st Half		267	53	74	4	36	17	277			$12	375	363	739	14	81	0.81	240	62	110		5.56	12.7
LIMA A	2nd Half		297	61	89	11	34	9	300			$13	366	529	894	9	86	0.76	318	150	173		7.22	29.1
Risk Very Low	03	Proj	600	115	170	17	70	26	283			$24	360	459	818	11	83	0.71	286	112	153		6.17	37.8

Note how he got a bit more aggressive at the plate in '01, registered career high power numbers and 2nd worst career BA, then returned to his old approach in '02. He is what he is, and that's pretty darn good.

Dye,Jermaine

	Yr	Tm	AB	R	H	HR	RBI	SB	Avg	vLH	vRH	R$	OB	Slg	OPS	bb%	ct%	Eye	xBA	PX	SX	G/F	RC/G	RAR
Pos RF	98	KC	* 371	49	94	15	54	8	253	256	228	$10	304	410	714	7	81	0.39	265	90	80	1.60	4.35	-9.1
Age 29 Past Peak	99	KC	608	96	179	27	119	2	294	267	300	$23	356	526	882	9	80	0.49	293	139	96	1.23	6.97	36.2
Bats R	00	KC	601	107	193	33	118	0	321	323	321	$28	391	561	952	10	84	0.70	305	140	44	1.15	8.62	69.0
Pwr No change	01	2AL	599	91	169	26	106	9	282	293	278	$24	345	467	812	9	81	0.51	272	112	78	1.23	6.08	18.7
Spd - -	02	OAK	504	76	125	24	87	2	248	212	262	$15	320	452	772	10	78	0.49	274	132	64	0.91	5.22	1.6
BAvg -	1st Half		217	27	51	6	33	0	235			$3	317	392	709	11	79	0.58	264	113	28		4.47	-4.5
LIMA A	2nd Half		287	49	74	18	54	2	258			$12	322	498	820	9	78	0.42	281	146	79		5.82	6.2
Risk Moderate	03	Proj	500	78	135	30	104	4	270			$21	337	509	846	9	80	0.51	289	145	65		6.32	16.8

An off year, but his BPIs were not horrible by any means. Remember, a true .280 hitter can hit anywhere from .245 to .315 in any given year and still be within the range of statistical likelihood. He'll rebound in '03.

Easley,Damion

	Yr	Tm	AB	R	H	HR	RBI	SB	Avg	vLH	vRH	R$	OB	Slg	OPS	bb%	ct%	Eye	xBA	PX	SX	G/F	RC/G	RAR
Pos 2B	98	DET	594	84	161	27	100	15	271	290	265	$23	316	478	794	6	81	0.35	288	128	94	1.65	5.42	23.8
Age 33 Decline	99	DET	549	83	146	20	65	11	266	291	261	$14	328	434	762	9	77	0.41	260	103	88	1.28	5.22	20.0
Bats R	00	DET	464	76	120	14	58	13	259	280	251	$11	337	416	753	11	83	0.70	278	96	104	1.18	5.17	18.2
Pwr No change	01	DET	585	77	146	11	65	10	250	236	254	$9	311	376	687	8	85	0.58	269	79	111	1.45	4.15	-2.5
Spd - -	02	DET	* 330	33	71	8	30	1	215	313	198	$2	285	339	624	9	87	0.74	271	84	43	0.97	3.16	-9.9
BAvg + + + + +	1st Half		119	9	20	3	7	1	168			($1)	250	269	519	10	87	0.87	255	56	68		2.13	-7.5
LIMA B	2nd Half		211	24	51	5	23	0	242			$3	304	379	683	8	87	0.68	280	100	32		3.87	-1.6
Risk Low	03	Proj	400	49	101	10	42	2	253			$6	318	386	705	9	85	0.65	269	86	57		4.28	1.0

A .271 xBA, 87% contact rate and 0.74 batting eye ratio are not the skills of a .215 hitter. Given health and opportunity, he should rebound.

Echevarria,Angel

	Yr	Tm	AB	R	H	HR	RBI	SB	Avg	vLH	vRH	R$	OB	Slg	OPS	bb%	ct%	Eye	xBA	PX	SX	G/F	RC/G	RAR
Pos RF	98	aaa	301	29	83	11	35	0	276			$7	294	449	743	3	90	0.26	302	112	34	1.22	4.65	-3.8
Age 31 Past Peak	99	COL	191	28	56	11	35	1	293	286	301	$8	351	503	854	8	82	0.50	282	120	38	1.26	6.55	8.6
Bats R	00	2TM	* 335	33	91	7	37	1	272	196	282	$5	320	403	723	7	87	0.55	282	86	43	1.50	4.69	-4.6
Pwr + + +	01	MIL	133	12	34	5	13	0	256	341	213	$2	298	451	749	6	78	0.28	272	127	23	0.93	4.60	-4.3
Spd No change	02	CHC	* 315	39	79	11	50	0	251	408	204	$7	293	419	712	6	82	0.34	268	103	56	1.54	4.34	-10.2
BAvg - -	1st Half		224	27	52	8	31	0	232			$3	268	402	670	5	82	0.27	266	101	69		3.69	-11.5
LIMA D	2nd Half		91	12	27	3	19	0	297			$4	354	462	815	8	84	0.53	271	107	25		6.21	2.3
Risk X HIGH	03	Proj	150	17	40	5	22	0	267			$4	313	436	749	6	83	0.39	275	110	30		4.89	-0.1

3-21-.306 in 98 AB at CHC, but an MLE .230 at AAA. Roster filler with a little bit of pop, an end-gamer at most.

Eckstein,David

	Yr	Tm	AB	R	H	HR	RBI	SB	Avg	vLH	vRH	R$	OB	Slg	OPS	bb%	ct%	Eye	xBA	PX	SX	G/F	RC/G	RAR
Pos SS	98		0	0	0	0	0	0	0								0							
Age 28 Peak	99	aa	483	88	135	5	43	26	280			$14	372	371	742	13	91	1.61	283	60	120		5.15	19.4
Bats R	00	aaa	474	81	116	3	34	14	245			$4	326	321	646	11	92	1.43	280	57	85		3.64	-5.8
Pwr + +	01	ANA	582	82	166	4	41	29	285	303	278	$17	334	357	692	7	90	0.72	268	52	111	1.58	4.67	3.7
Spd + + + + +	02	ANA	608	107	178	8	63	21	293	302	289	$20	342	388	730	7	93	1.02	279	64	130	1.26	4.79	2.1
BAvg No change	1st Half		280	52	77	4	39	13	275			$10	334	389	724	8	94	1.39	293	79	142		4.62	-0.4
LIMA A	2nd Half		328	55	101	4	24	8	308			$10	348	387	735	6	92	0.77	267	51	114		4.93	2.6
Risk High	03	Proj	600	100	180	6	52	31	300			$23	356	386	742	8	92	1.04	276	59	124		5.23	26.7

Slight improvement over his rookie year. There is a .300 BA in his near future, and with it, a boost in SBs. Watch...

Edmonds,Jim

	Yr	Tm	AB	R	H	HR	RBI	SB	Avg	vLH	vRH	R$	OB	Slg	OPS	bb%	ct%	Eye	xBA	PX	SX	G/F	RC/G	RAR
Pos CF	98	ANA	599	115	184	25	91	7	307	272	324	$24	367	506	873	9	81	0.50	284	126	76	1.32	7.02	40.7
Age 32 Past Peak	99	ANA	204	34	51	5	23	5	250	190	277	$4	341	426	767	12	78	0.62	273	116	115	1.21	5.09	1.9
Bats L	00	STL	525	129	155	42	108	10	295	270	306	$31	411	583	994	16	68	0.62	258	160	79	0.73	9.38	89.2
Pwr - -	01	STL	500	95	152	30	110	5	304	246	323	$28	413	564	977	16	73	0.68	271	157	60	1.07	9.03	86.4
Spd No change	02	STL	476	96	148	28	83	4	311	262	329	$26	416	561	977	15	72	0.64	257	150	73	0.98	9.23	68.4
BAvg - -	1st Half		205	40	66	14	38	2	322			$13	433	610	1042	16	74	0.75	276	176	47		10.65	39.8
LIMA A	2nd Half		271	56	82	14	45	2	303			$13	404	524	928	15	70	0.57	243	130	89		8.23	29.5
Risk Moderate	03	Proj	500	102	152	30	93	3	304			$25	409	556	965	15	72	0.64	262	151	64		8.82	74.5

Small signs of possible decline in '03... xBAs consistently lower than his BA, PX is on a slow descent, and, um... that's it. Like I said, small signs, but probably not enough to make a difference.

Ellis,Mark

	Yr	Tm	AB	R	H	HR	RBI	SB	Avg	vLH	vRH	R$	OB	Slg	OPS	bb%	ct%	Eye	xBA	PX	SX	G/F	RC/G	RAR
Pos 2B	98		0	0	0	0	0	0	0								0							
Age 25 Pre-Peak	99		0	0	0	0	0	0	0								0							
Bats R	00	aa	22	3	6	0	3	1	273			$1	385	318	703	15	73	0.67	211	38	58		5.25	0.8
Pwr - -	01	aaa	472	56	111	8	42	17	235			$7	299	364	663	8	87	0.69	277	84	81		3.63	-7.2
Spd + + + + +	02	OAK	* 429	68	115	6	39	7	268	296	268	$9	342	389	731	10	85	0.75	269	85	124	0.73	4.99	11.8
BAvg No change	1st Half		168	30	44	1	12	3	262			$2	299	363	663	5	85	0.35	262	76	141		3.89	-1.2
LIMA B	2nd Half		261	38	71	5	27	4	272			$6	367	406	773	13	85	1.03	274	91	107		5.73	13.8
Risk Very High	03	Proj	400	57	102	6	36	10	255			$7	324	375	699	9	86	0.72	273	83	107		4.40	2.5

His BPIs may be adequate enough for OAK, but for fantasy purposes, pay a buck for the handful of HRs, maybe $2 for the speed potential and a final dollar for a BA that won't drag you down. Too much.

Encarnacion,Juan

	Yr	Tm	AB	R	H	HR	RBI	SB	Avg	vLH	vRH	R$	OB	Slg	OPS	bb%	ct%	Eye	xBA	PX	SX	G/F	RC/G	RAR
Pos RF CF	98	DET	* 520	86	155	15	63	31	298	250	346	$25	347	462	809	7	78	0.35	270	99	156	1.38	5.91	12.2
Age 27 Peak	99	DET	509	62	130	19	74	33	255	263	254	$21	275	450	725	3	78	0.12	277	116	159	1.32	4.11	-14.3
Bats R	00	DET	547	75	158	14	72	16	289	314	280	$18	325	433	758	5	84	0.32	273	85	131	1.67	5.21	3.2
Pwr + +	01	DET	417	52	101	12	52	9	242	259	236	$8	285	408	693	6	78	0.27	260	98	138	1.11	3.94	-14.4
Spd - - - - -	02	2NL	584	77	158	24	85	21	271	233	282	$24	324	449	772	7	81	0.41	268	103	115	1.19	5.17	-4.3
BAvg - -	1st Half		294	41	81	16	44	9	276			$14	326	490	816	7	80	0.37	274	121	102		5.68	2.5
LIMA A	2nd Half		290	36	77	8	41	12	266			$11	322	407	729	8	81	0.44	261	84	122		4.67	-6.7
Risk Moderate	03	Proj	550	72	151	23	75	19	275			$22	321	466	787	6	80	0.34	274	110	125		5.31	6.9

Follow the baby steps he took in improving his plate patience. Little gains can net out bigger outcomes. If he can continue this path, and work on his BA vs LH, there could be more growth. He's entering his peak now.

Ensberg,Morgan

	Yr	Tm	AB	R	H	HR	RBI	SB	Avg	vLH	vRH	R$	OB	Slg	OPS	bb%	ct%	Eye	xBA	PX	SX	G/F	RC/G	RAR
Pos 3B	98		0	0	0	0	0	0	0								0							
Age 27 Peak	99		0	0	0	0	0	0	0								0							
Bats R	00		0	0	0	0	0	0	0								0							
Pwr + +	01	aaa	316	53	90	20	50	5	285			$15	360	535	895	10	83	0.69	299	147	59		7.09	25.5
Spd + + + + +	02	HOU	* 424	56	109	10	50	10	257	320	224	$10	349	394	743	12	82	0.77	261	83	113	1.00	5.07	5.4
BAvg No change	1st Half		233	25	59	7	29	7	253			$6	331	412	743	10	81	0.60	264	90	133		4.99	2.3
LIMA C+	2nd Half		191	31	50	3	21	3	262			$4	371	372	742	15	83	1.00	256	74	78		5.13	2.9
Risk High	03	Proj	250	38	67	10	33	5	268			$8	356	451	807	12	82	0.77	279	110	93		5.89	10.9

3-19-.242 in 132 AB at HOU. Took a step back in '02, and in some ways it is significant enough for us to question his future potential. Loss of power is concerning. Improved eye might temper the concern.

Erstad,Darin

Erstad,Darin		Tm	AB	R	H	HR	RBI	SB	Avg	vLH	vRH	R$	OB	Slg	OPS	bb%	ct%	Eye	xBA	PX	SX	G/F	RC/G	RAR
Pos	CF	98 ANA	537	84	159	19	82	20	296	263	311	$24	348	486	834	7	86	0.56	303	122	111	1.29	6.34	24.7
Age	28 Peak	99 ANA	585	84	148	13	53	13	253	274	245	$9	309	374	683	7	83	0.47	263	73	114	1.65	4.07	-13.3
Bats	L	00 ANA	676	121	240	25	100	28	355	338	363	$41	411	541	952	9	88	0.78	305	110	123	1.61	9.12	92.5
Pwr	- -	01 ANA	631	89	163	9	63	24	258	204	283	$14	325	360	684	9	82	0.55	254	71	91	1.67	4.23	-14.2
Spd	+ + + +	02 ANA	625	99	177	10	73	23	283	280	285	$21	313	389	702	4	89	0.40	275	73	138	1.51	4.57	-5.7
BAvg	- -	1st Half	307	49	96	6	47	14	313			$15	345	427	771	5	91	0.52	281	77	128		5.76	8.2
LIMA	A+	2nd Half	318	50	81	4	26	9	255			$6	282	352	634	4	88	0.32	269	70	134		3.58	-12.2
Risk	High	03 Proj	625	98	168	10	72	23	269			$18	315	382	698	6	87	0.51	273	77	127		4.42	-9.1

As confounding a player as they come. He gets on base, he doesn't. He has power, then it's gone. Can he hit LHers? Who knows? Even his seemingly consistent speed output is put into question by SX. I hate him.

Escalona,Felix

Escalona,Felix		Tm	AB	R	H	HR	RBI	SB	Avg	vLH	vRH	R$	OB	Slg	OPS	bb%	ct%	Eye	xBA	PX	SX	G/F	RC/G	RAR
Pos	SS 2B	98	0	0	0	0	0	0	0								0							
Age	24 Growth	99	0	0	0	0	0	0	0								0							
Bats	R	00	0	0	0	0	0	0	0								0							
Pwr	No change	01	0	0	0	0	0	0	0								0							
Spd	No change	02 TAM	157	17	34	0	9	7	217	172	227	$1	231	293	524	2	72	0.07	215	59	167	1.19	2.25	-11.1
BAvg	-	1st Half	68	8	17	0	6	3	250			$1	271	338	610	3	75	0.12	229	68	157		2.93	-3.5
LIMA	D+	2nd Half	89	9	17	0	3	4	191			($0)	200	258	458	1	70	0.04	204	52	167		1.79	-7.4
Risk	Low	03 Proj	150	16	36	0	8	7	240			$2	254	320	574	2	72	0.07	219	59	158		2.79	-4.4

Another Rule 5 bonanza. Only asset here is speed, but with a .231 OB avg, we'll never see those SBs. If even TAM can't figure out what to do with him, odds are he won't have a future anywhere.

Estalella,Bobby

Estalella,Bobby		Tm	AB	R	H	HR	RBI	SB	Avg	vLH	vRH	R$	OB	Slg	OPS	bb%	ct%	Eye	xBA	PX	SX	G/F	RC/G	RAR
Pos	CA	98 PHI	* 407	54	93	21	58	0	229	130	210	$8	333	442	776	14	78	0.73	276	135	42	0.98	5.32	17.8
Age	28 Peak	99 aaa	386	46	80	13	49	3	207			$2	290	368	658	10	77	0.52	257	100	63	1.00	3.71	-4.7
Bats	R	00 SF	299	45	70	14	53	3	234	250	229	$7	357	468	825	16	69	0.62	254	141	100	0.72	6.21	21.7
Pwr	No change	01 2TM	* 290	33	60	11	39	0	207	222	190	$2	274	386	661	9	76	0.38	251	108	58	0.64	3.45	-2.8
Spd	No change	02 COL	* 191	26	43	13	37	0	225	136	222	$5	302	508	810	10	76	0.46	279	172	29	0.46	5.21	6.1
BAvg	No change	1st Half	181	25	42	12	33	0	232			$5	312	514	826	10	77	0.51	284	173	29		5.50	7.5
LIMA	C+	2nd Half	10	1	1	1	4	0	100			$0	100	400	500	0	50	0.00		152			1.13	-0.9
Risk	X HIGH	03 Proj	200	27	45	10	32	0	225			$3	317	448	765	12	75	0.54	264	136	54		4.96	6.3

Coming off rotator cuff surgery. His power potential in Coors is alluring, but those BAs are harmful and might not improve much. Still, any COL batter is worth a buck, on speculation alone.

Everett,Adam

Everett,Adam		Tm	AB	R	H	HR	RBI	SB	Avg	vLH	vRH	R$	OB	Slg	OPS	bb%	ct%	Eye	xBA	PX	SX	G/F	RC/G	RAR
Pos	SS	98	0	0	0	0	0	0	0								0							
Age	26 Pre-Peak	99 aa	338	48	83	8	38	18	246			$9	316	349	665	9	83	0.63	259	64	93		4.00	0.8
Bats	R	00 aaa	453	71	105	5	32	11	232			$2	327	329	656	12	81	0.73	252	67	100		3.96	-0.8
Pwr	- - -	01 aaa	444	59	103	5	34	21	232			$7	285	338	623	7	85	0.51	270	67	152		3.39	-8.9
Spd	+ +	02 HOU	* 433	56	108	2	26	14	249	261	169	$5	303	339	642	7	83	0.45	257	59	155	0.70	3.75	-3.0
BAvg	-	1st Half	248	30	58	0	17	7	234			$1	291	302	593	7	86	0.57	257	45	143		3.16	-6.3
LIMA	C	2nd Half	185	26	50	2	9	7	270			$4	318	389	707	7	79	0.34	255	77	157		4.64	3.7
Risk	High	03 Proj	150	21	37	2	10	6	247			$2	307	350	657	8	83	0.51	260	67	138		3.91	0.8

0-4-3-.198 in 88 AB at HOU. The company line in March was, We have enough offense to offset his shortcomings. He's our SS." Noise. Good speed, but poor skills set otherwise.

Everett,Carl

Everett,Carl		Tm	AB	R	H	HR	RBI	SB	Avg	vLH	vRH	R$	OB	Slg	OPS	bb%	ct%	Eye	xBA	PX	SX	G/F	RC/G	RAR
Pos	RF CF	98 HOU	467	72	138	15	76	14	296	268	301	$21	356	482	838	9	78	0.43	276	129	109	1.10	6.06	15.5
Age	32 Past Peak	99 HOU	464	86	151	25	108	27	325	325	326	$34	391	571	962	10	80	0.53	292	150	120	1.00	8.78	54.1
Bats	S	00 BOS	496	82	149	34	108	11	300	348	283	$27	367	587	953	9	77	0.46	299	161	107	0.88	8.10	48.3
Pwr	No change	01 BOS	409	61	105	14	58	9	257	197	285	$11	303	438	740	6	75	0.26	255	111	124	1.13	4.74	-4.3
Spd	- - - - -	02 TEX	374	47	100	16	62	2	267	220	283	$12	327	439	765	8	79	0.43	263	109	39	1.01	5.11	-0.2
BAvg	- -	1st Half	145	13	29	5	18	0	200			$1	247	331	578	6	79	0.30	245	81	21		2.73	-10.5
LIMA	B+	2nd Half	229	34	71	11	44	2	310			$12	375	507	882	9	79	0.51	274	126	43		7.10	14.3
Risk	Low	03 Proj	400	57	109	13	58	1	273			$11	330	431	761	8	78	0.39	255	101	62		5.08	-2.1

Excellent 2nd half, but what can we expect as a follow-up? His plummeting PX ans SX levels alone point to a further descent.

Fabregas,Jorge

Fabregas,Jorge		Tm	AB	R	H	HR	RBI	SB	Avg	vLH	vRH	R$	OB	Slg	OPS	bb%	ct%	Eye	xBA	PX	SX	G/F	RC/G	RAR
Pos	CA	98 2NL	183	11	36	2	20	0	197	217	194	($2)	254	251	505	7	83	0.44	241	38		1.44	2.19	-10.2
Age	33 Decline	99 2TM	231	20	46	3	21	0	199	300	190	($3)	280	299	579	10	88	0.96	271	65	51	0.92	2.93	-8.6
Bats	L	00 KC	* 271	19	70	4	31	2	258	308	279	$3	302	343	645	6	93	0.94	275	52	47	1.68	3.71	-4.3
Pwr	- -	01 ANA	148	9	33	2	16	0	223	143	227	($0)	238	318	556	2	90	0.20	264	56	60	1.08	2.53	-6.1
Spd	No change	02 2TM	155	13	28	3	22	0	181	188	180	($2)	221	265	485	5	92	0.62	265	53	28	1.21	1.91	-9.5
BAvg	+ + + + +	1st Half	55	6	12	0	4	0	218			($2)	283	236	520	8	91	1.00	239	16	35		2.40	-2.6
LIMA	D	2nd Half	100	7	16	3	18	0	160			($2)	184	280	464	3	92	0.38	279	74	22		1.61	-6.9
Risk	Very High	03 Proj	150	11	36	2	18	0	240			$1	277	327	604	5	91	0.56	272	54	47		3.16	-3.5

You look at these 90%+ contact rates and you have to wonder, if he's getting wood on the ball so often, how come he's not getting on base more?" His PX levels hold the answer: He's not getting the ball out of the infield.

Febles,Carlos

Febles,Carlos		Tm	AB	R	H	HR	RBI	SB	Avg	vLH	vRH	R$	OB	Slg	OPS	bb%	ct%	Eye	xBA	PX	SX	G/F	RC/G	RAR
Pos	2B	98 aa	457	87	134	10	41	40	293			$24	378	453	831	12	88	1.13	304	102	182	9.00	6.53	35.3
Age	26 Pre-Peak	99 KC	453	71	116	10	53	20	256	278	250	$12	326	411	737	9	80	0.52	273	91	182	2.54	4.96	13.0
Bats	R	00 KC	339	59	87	2	29	17	257	272	251	$7	328	316	644	10	86	0.75	249	41	116	2.85	3.86	-0.9
Pwr	No change	01 KC	* 390	63	100	10	32	10	256	226	241	$8	308	390	698	7	82	0.42	263	81	115	1.92	4.26	-0.3
Spd	+ + + + +	02 KC	* 405	52	97	5	30	18	240	229	250	$8	314	346	660	10	83	0.66	257	72	141	2.44	3.93	-2.5
BAvg	+ + +	1st Half	209	22	47	2	15	12	225			$4	316	340	656	12	83	0.78	261	82	144		3.97	-1.0
LIMA	B	2nd Half	196	30	50	3	15	6	255			$4	311	352	663	8	84	0.52	252	62	127		3.88	-1.5
Risk	Moderate	03 Proj	400	60	101	6	32	16	253			$9	319	363	682	9	84	0.60	261	72	133		4.19	-0.1

BPIs describe a player who will never display much power, have trouble getting on base, and as a result, be unable to maximize the value of his solid speed skills. Low ceiling.

Feliz,Pedro

Feliz,Pedro		Tm	AB	R	H	HR	RBI	SB	Avg	vLH	vRH	R$	OB	Slg	OPS	bb%	ct%	Eye	xBA	PX	SX	G/F	RC/G	RAR
Pos	3B	98 aa	371	35	89	11	46	0	240			$5	258	394	651	2	85	0.16	281	103	38		3.41	-12.1
Age	25 Pre-Peak	99 aa	491	49	115	12	73	4	234			$6	261	373	634	4	81	0.20	264	84	95		3.29	-17.2
Bats	R	00 aaa	503	64	129	24	80	1	256			$12	288	463	751	4	86	0.31	303	123	48		4.65	3.0
Pwr	+	01 SF	220	23	50	7	22	2	227	397	167	$2	261	373	634	4	77	0.20	250	87	74	1.12	3.28	-9.2
Spd	No change	02 SF	146	14	37	2	13	0	253	184	289	$1	283	336	619	4	82	0.22	237	51	53	1.14	3.35	-5.8
BAvg	- -	1st Half	87	9	24	2	8	0	276			$2	292	368	660	2	80	0.12	234	55	27		3.85	-2.1
LIMA	D	2nd Half	59	5	13	0	5	0	220			($1)	270	288	558	6	83	0.40	242	44	91		2.70	-3.6
Risk	Very High	03 Proj	150	15	36	3	16	0	240			$1	273	361	634	4	82	0.25	255	74	66		3.40	-5.1

Things he's never seen:
- .300 OB average
- 0.40 batting eye ratio
- One of his hits fall safely at Pro Player Stadium
- Catalina at sunset

Fick,Robert

Fick,Robert		Tm	AB	R	H	HR	RBI	SB	Avg	vLH	vRH	R$	OB	Slg	OPS	bb%	ct%	Eye	xBA	PX	SX	G/F	RC/G	RAR
Pos	RF	98 aa	515	77	137	15	87	6	266			$15	341	445	786	10	86	0.81	300	121	93	1.75	5.57	8.1
Age	29 Past Peak	99 DET	* 89	16	22	4	16	1	247			$2	350	382	732	14	85	1.08	261	67	56	0.58	4.86	-0.6
Bats	L	00 DET	* 231	22	50	4	28	3	216	194	265	$0	298	338	636	10	79	0.56	251	76	86	0.79	3.57	-10.6
Pwr	-	01 DET	401	62	109	19	61	0	272	237	280	$12	336	476	813	9	85	0.63	284	121	48	0.97	5.73	8.2
Spd	No change	02 DET	556	66	150	17	63	0	270	281	265	$13	326	433	759	8	84	0.51	280	112	40	0.94	5.13	0.2
BAvg	-	1st Half	283	41	83	10	34	0	293			$9	353	484	837	8	85	0.60	296	132	47		6.37	11.1
LIMA	A	2nd Half	273	25	67	7	29	0	245			$4	297	381	678	7	83	0.43	263	92	33		4.01	-9.3
Risk	Very High	03 Proj	550	68	143	23	71	0	260			$13	323	455	778	9	83	0.56	285	122	46		5.25	0.1

His increase in power has followed along with a decrease in his walk rate, decrease in his G/F ratio, and increase in his ability to hit LHers. It's working for him, for now.

Finley,Steve			Tm	AB	R	H	HR	RBI	SB	Avg	vLH	vRH	R$	OB	Slg	OPS	bb%	ct%	Eye	xBA	PX	SX	G/F	RC/G	RAR
Pos	CF	98	SD	619	92	154	14	67	12	249	188	277	$12	300	401	700	7	83	0.44	284	107	129	1.15	4.28	-2.3
Age	37 Decline	99	ARI	590	100	156	34	103	8	264	259	267	$21	335	525	861	10	84	0.67	309	150	131	1.04	6.34	36.1
Bats	L	00	ARI	539	100	151	35	96	12	280	274	283	$25	358	544	901	11	84	0.75	311	147	111	1.03	7.11	46.6
Pwr	--	01	ARI	495	66	136	14	73	11	275	235	285	$16	338	430	768	9	86	0.70	287	96	99	1.06	5.22	20.1
Spd	---	02	ARI	505	82	145	25	89	16	287	297	282	$26	368	499	867	11	86	0.89	296	123	112	1.13	7.02	33.4
BAvg	No change	1st Half		247	40	70	13	41	9	283			$13	375	494	868	13	86	1.03	293	119	105		7.01	16.5
LIMA	A	2nd Half		258	42	75	12	48	7	291			$13	362	504	866	10	85	0.76	297	128	108		7.02	16.8
Risk	High	03	Proj	500	79	140	22	83	10	280			$20	353	478	831	10	85	0.77	294	118	101		6.25	29.5

2002 looks like a rebound year, but that's deceptive because '01 was driven down by an aberrant 1st half. In truth, 2002 was a point along a slowly declining trend. That trend will continue to edge downward in 2003.

Flaherty,John			Tm	AB	R	H	HR	RBI	SB	Avg	vLH	vRH	R$	OB	Slg	OPS	bb%	ct%	Eye	xBA	PX	SX	G/F	RC/G	RAR
Pos	CA	98	TAM	304	21	63	3	24	0	207	234	200	($3)	261	273	534	7	85	0.48	239	46		1.00	2.26	-17.1
Age	35 Decline	99	TAM	446	53	124	14	71	0	278	175	301	$11	308	415	722	4	86	0.30	268	83	28	1.11	4.53	5.1
Bats	R	00	TAM	394	36	103	10	39	0	261	270	259	$4	297	376	673	5	86	0.35	260	69		0.89	3.99	-2.9
Pwr	---	01	TAM	248	20	59	4	29	1	238	286	230	$2	267	363	630	4	87	0.30	272	87	50	0.83	3.36	-4.3
Spd	No change	02	TAM	281	27	73	4	33	2	260	250	262	$5	297	374	671	5	82	0.30	259	89	46	0.63	3.88	1.6
BAvg	--	1st Half		133	13	33	3	18	1	248			$2	306	383	689	8	81	0.44	262	99	41		4.10	1.7
LIMA	D	2nd Half		148	14	40	1	15	1	270			$2	289	365	654	3	83	0.16	257	80	48		3.68	-0.1
Risk	Low	03	Proj	250	23	63	6	28	1	252			$4	286	389	676	5	84	0.30	270	95	37		3.86	-1.6

On 9/23, Flaherty announced that he had played his last home game at Tropicana Field. We'll see about that. He may have managed to survive 5 years in Tampa, but will he be able to survive... the COMFY CHAIR??!!

Fletcher,Darrin			Tm	AB	R	H	HR	RBI	SB	Avg	vLH	vRH	R$	OB	Slg	OPS	bb%	ct%	Eye	xBA	PX	SX	G/F	RC/G	RAR
Pos	CA	98	TOR	407	37	115	9	52	0	283	203	296	$9	324	410	734	6	90	0.64	284	85	25	0.82	4.91	10.1
Age	36 Decline	99	TOR	412	48	120	18	80	0	291	228	306	$15	333	485	819	6	89	0.55	297	119		0.70	6.02	23.4
Bats	L	00	TOR	416	43	133	20	58	1	320	342	315	$17	351	514	865	5	89	0.44	304	111	35	1.16	6.95	33.8
Pwr	---	01	TOR	416	36	94	11	56	0	226	162	240	$3	268	353	622	5	90	0.56	273	82	21	0.92	3.22	-9.1
Spd	No change	02	TOR	127	8	28	3	22	0	220	375	198	$2	244	339	583	3	90	0.31	277	82	12	0.66	2.77	-3.4
BAvg	No change	1st Half		116	8	26	3	22	0	224			$2	250	353	603	3	91	0.36	285	90	14		2.98	-2.4
LIMA	F	2nd Half		11	0	2	0	0	0	182			($0)	182	182	364	0	82	0.00	200	0	0		1.03	-0.8
Risk	Moderate	03	Proj	0	0	0	0	0	0	0			$0					0			0	0			0.0

Retired, just two years removed from a 20-HR, .320 BA season. While there was certainly some skills erosion since '00, it's tough to look at someone who makes contact 90% of the time and consider him 'done.'

Floyd,Cliff			Tm	AB	R	H	HR	RBI	SB	Avg	vLH	vRH	R$	OB	Slg	OPS	bb%	ct%	Eye	xBA	PX	SX	G/F	RC/G	RAR
Pos	RF LF DH	98	FLA	588	85	166	22	90	27	282	325	267	$29	335	481	817	7	81	0.42	290	138	110	0.95	5.67	12.1
Age	30 Past Peak	99	FLA	251	37	76	11	49	5	303	305	302	$12	377	518	895	11	81	0.64	288	137	66	1.44	7.04	15.6
Bats	L	00	FLA	420	75	126	22	91	24	300	333	286	$27	374	529	903	11	80	0.61	294	139	100	0.90	7.82	34.6
Pwr	No change	01	FLA	555	123	176	31	103	18	317	311	319	$35	383	578	961	10	82	0.58	310	158	136	0.91	8.72	53.5
Spd	-----	02	2TM	520	86	150	28	79	15	288	247	306	$25	379	533	912	13	80	0.72	293	159	77	1.18	7.68	41.1
BAvg	-	1st Half		273	45	79	17	53	9	289			$15	405	538	943	16	76	0.80	275	153	65		8.37	28.9
LIMA	C+	2nd Half		247	41	71	11	26	6	287			$9	348	526	874	9	84	0.58	312	164	83		6.90	12.6
Risk	Moderate	03	Proj	550	99	169	33	112	12	307			$32	382	575	957	11	81	0.64	310	167	80		8.40	55.4

Some will look at '02 as a step down from '01, but there were lots of good things here. Increases in plate patience and power skills indicate that there are still be some big seasons remaining in that bat.

Fordyce,Brook			Tm	AB	R	H	HR	RBI	SB	Avg	vLH	vRH	R$	OB	Slg	OPS	bb%	ct%	Eye	xBA	PX	SX	G/F	RC/G	RAR
Pos	CA	98	CIN	146	8	37	3	14	0	253	302	217	$2	306	377	682	7	81	0.39	262	91		1.21	4.02	0.1
Age	32 Past Peak	99	2TM	333	36	99	9	49	2	297	333	283	$10	339	459	798	6	86	0.44	288	108	54	1.45	5.89	18.2
Bats	R	00	2AL	302	41	91	14	49	0	301	347	287	$11	339	507	845	5	83	0.34	291	120	39	0.85	6.44	20.1
Pwr	No change	01	BAL	292	30	61	5	19	1	209	282	186	($2)	262	322	584	7	81	0.38	248	79	42	1.21	2.80	-10.2
Spd	No change	02	BAL	130	7	30	1	8	1	231	103	267	$0	281	315	596	6	85	0.47	256	69	31	2.07	3.14	-2.2
BAvg	No change	1st Half		77	5	16	1	4	1	208			($0)	265	312	577	7	84	0.50	261	81	40		2.89	-1.9
LIMA	D	2nd Half		53	2	14	0	4	0	264			$0	304	321	624	5	87	0.43	248	52	5		3.53	-0.3
Risk	Moderate	03	Proj	150	12	37	2	13	1	247			$1	293	355	649	6	84	0.41	258	79	30		3.68	-1.8

A fairly good model of the type of end-game $1 catcher that you DON'T draft just so that you can fill out the last spot on your roster and get another beer.

Fox,Andy			Tm	AB	R	H	HR	RBI	SB	Avg	vLH	vRH	R$	OB	Slg	OPS	bb%	ct%	Eye	xBA	PX	SX	G/F	RC/G	RAR
Pos	SS	98	ARI	502	67	139	9	44	14	277	333	264	$13	334	396	730	8	81	0.44	262	80	124	1.44	4.81	17.6
Age	32 Past Peak	99	ARI	274	34	70	6	33	4	255	152	276	$4	336	380	715	11	78	0.54	249	78	85	1.26	4.74	10.0
Bats	L	00	2NL	250	29	58	4	20	10	232	250	230	$3	294	328	622	8	79	0.42	245	58	112	1.62	3.38	-1.2
Pwr	No change	01	FLA	* 123	14	29	4	12	2	236		195	$2	329	382	711	12	85	0.89	270	77	111	1.57	4.53	3.6
Spd	+++++	02	FLA	435	55	109	4	41	31	251	148	277	$13	326	333	660	10	78	0.52	238	52	148	1.43	4.15	2.4
BAvg	No change	1st Half		206	26	51	1	22	13	248			$5	311	320	631	8	78	0.42	235	50	138		3.73	-1.6
LIMA	B	2nd Half		229	29	58	3	19	18	253			$8	340	345	685	12	79	0.61	240	54	149		4.54	4.2
Risk	Very High	03	Proj	350	43	86	5	33	17	246			$8	324	341	665	10	80	0.58	246	57	132		4.10	3.9

Could we have foreseen 31 SBs? Not likely. However, we DID know that FLA was going to be running more in '02 and that he had good speed skills. You might have ventured an extra $1 on the off chance he'd luck into some PT.

Franco,Julio			Tm	AB	R	H	HR	RBI	SB	Avg	vLH	vRH	R$	OB	Slg	OPS	bb%	ct%	Eye	xBA	PX	SX	G/F	RC/G	RAR
Pos	1B	98	JPN	487	78	141	18	77	7	290			$19	377	464	841	12	78	0.64	266	112	77		6.66	17.2
Age	41 Decline	99	MEX	326	91	138	14	77	0	423			$26	537	656	1193	20	87	1.82	313	139	104		17.10	132.8
Bats	R	00	KOR	477	80	156	22	110	0	327			$24	408	518	926	12	77	0.59	264	112	26		8.55	43.2
Pwr	--	01	MEX	497	103	205	21	101	15	412	400	262	$43	476	636	1112	11	85	0.79	305	138	113		13.50	114.3
Spd	-----	02	ATL	338	51	96	6	30	5	284	382	256	$8	358	382	740	10	78	0.52	235	63	81	2.64	5.29	-4.6
BAvg	--	1st Half		172	25	46	3	13	3	267			$3	340	378	718	10	79	0.53	245	72	89		4.81	-4.9
LIMA	C+	2nd Half		166	26	50	3	17	2	301			$5	376	386	762	11	77	0.51	225	54	59		5.81	0.5
Risk	X HIGH	03	Proj	250	44	68	5	33	4	272			$6	355	387	742	11	80	0.63	252	76	89		5.23	-1.1

Globetrotter's real skills came to Earth in Peachtree City. The BPIs tell most of the story. His age tells the rest.

Franco,Matt			Tm	AB	R	H	HR	RBI	SB	Avg	vLH	vRH	R$	OB	Slg	OPS	bb%	ct%	Eye	xBA	PX	SX	G/F	RC/G	RAR
Pos	1B	98	NYM	161	20	44	1	13	0	273	333	268	$2	364	360	724	13	84	0.88	261	63	77	2.19	4.96	-2.3
Age	33 Decline	99	NYM	132	18	31	4	21	0	235		248	$1	369	364	732	18	84	1.33	267	79	21	1.68	5.15	-1.2
Bats	L	00	NYM	* 185	11	38	2	15	0	205	200	242	($2)	293	265	558	11	83	0.74	246	39		1.12	2.80	-15.8
Pwr	No change	01	aaa	433	41	89	6	39	5	206			($1)	276	303	578	9	82	0.54	250	67	66		2.89	-46.6
Spd	No change	02	ATL	* 378	44	106	11	53	2	280	333	317	$11	346	452	799	9	87	0.78	289	108	83	1.61	5.90	2.3
BAvg	-	1st Half		213	24	56	8	30	2	263			$6	311	427	739	7	88	0.58	284	102	49		4.85	-5.6
LIMA	C+	2nd Half		165	20	50	3	23	0	303			$5	388	485	873	12	86	1.00	294	117	110		7.40	9.1
Risk	Very High	03	Proj	250	26	63	5	29	1	252			$3	330	384	714	10	85	0.76	271	86	67		4.66	-5.7

6-30-.317 in 205 AB at ATL. Mini-power display will be a nice addition to the back of his next baseball card, but the odds of it being a predictor of future outbursts is slim.

Fryman,Travis			Tm	AB	R	H	HR	RBI	SB	Avg	vLH	vRH	R$	OB	Slg	OPS	bb%	ct%	Eye	xBA	PX	SX	G/F	RC/G	RAR
Pos	3B	98	CLE	557	74	160	28	96	10	287	309	280	$24	339	504	844	7	78	0.35	275	131	71	0.93	6.11	26.8
Age	34 Decline	99	CLE	322	45	82	10	48	2	255	273	250	$6	308	410	718	7	82	0.44	271	94	81	0.82	4.51	0.0
Bats	R	00	CLE	574	93	184	22	106	1	321	297	327	$23	397	516	913	11	81	0.66	281	117	65	1.11	8.14	67.5
Pwr	No change	01	CLE	* 386	44	107	6	47	2	277	257	265	$8	337	370	708	8	81	0.47	239	64	39	1.12	4.62	2.1
Spd	No change	02	CLE	397	42	86	11	55	0	217	281	186	$4	288	350	638	9	79	0.49	248	84	56	1.35	3.53	-12.8
BAvg	+++	1st Half		249	24	53	7	36	0	213			$2	290	349	639	10	81	0.57	253	82	69		3.55	-8.0
LIMA	F	2nd Half		148	18	33	4	19	0	223			$2	286	351	637	8	76	0.37	240	87	33		3.51	-4.8
Risk	High	03	Proj	0	0	0	0	0	0	0			$0					0			0	0			0.0

Two retirees on one page, and both hang up their cleats just two years removed from a great season. Odd coincidence, though I've heard that Fletcher and Fryman have never been photographed together.

Fullmer,Brad

		Tm	AB	R	H	HR	RBI	SB	Avg	vLH	vRH	R$	OB	Slg	OPS	bb%	ct%	Eye	xBA	PX	SX	G/F	RC/G	RAR
Pos 1B	98	MON	505	58	138	13	73	6	273	244	280	$15	325	446	771	7	86	0.56	301	127	67	1.06	5.12	-4.2
Age 28 Peak	99	MON	* 489	65	138	18	75	4	282	240	283	$15	328	489	816	6	90	0.67	319	137	62	1.18	5.69	4.1
Bats L	00	TOR	482	76	142	32	104	3	295	226	311	$23	336	558	894	6	86	0.44	321	149	63	0.93	6.95	12.9
Pwr No change	01	TOR	522	71	143	18	83	5	274	202	295	$16	323	444	768	7	83	0.43	275	107	72	0.87	5.23	-16.6
Spd + + + + +	02	ANA	429	75	124	19	59	10	289	222	301	$19	338	531	870	7	90	0.73	337	160	144	0.70	6.64	8.6
BAvg -	1st Half		227	39	61	10	30	7	269			$9	320	529	848	7	88	0.61	339	173	168		6.17	1.3
LIMA C+	2nd Half		202	36	63	9	29	3	312			$10	359	535	894	7	92	0.94	333	145	106		7.19	7.5
Risk Moderate	03	Proj	**500**	**84**	**154**	**32**	**108**	**12**	**308**			**$31**	**354**	**588**	**942**	**7**	**88**	**0.58**	**337**	**171**	**113**		**7.89**	**34.3**

Was 2000 a fluke? BPIs say we could see that again, and more. PX and G/F confirm the power potential. Ct% and xBA confirm the BA upside. And SX spike shows some SB upside. Signs are here for a major breakout.

Furcal,Rafael

		Tm	AB	R	H	HR	RBI	SB	Avg	vLH	vRH	R$	OB	Slg	OPS	bb%	ct%	Eye	xBA	PX	SX	G/F	RC/G	RAR
Pos SS	98		0	0	0	0	0	0	0								0							
Age 24 Growth	99		0	0	0	0	0	0	0								0							
Bats S	00	ATL	455	87	134	4	37	40	295	250	306	$21	392	382	774	14	82	0.91	257	58	137	2.24	5.95	36.5
Pwr No change	01	ATL	324	39	89	4	30	22	275	349	249	$12	325	370	695	7	83	0.43	259	69	100	1.82	4.48	8.4
Spd + + + + +	02	ATL	636	95	175	8	47	27	275	288	272	$17	321	387	708	6	82	0.38	260	72	144	1.76	4.34	7.1
BAvg - -	1st Half		329	52	94	4	23	15	286			$10	334	398	732	7	83	0.42	261	71	149		4.50	5.2
LIMA A+	2nd Half		307	43	81	4	24	12	264			$7	307	375	681	6	81	0.33	257	74	136		4.18	1.9
Risk High	03	Proj	**600**	**87**	**156**	**7**	**49**	**25**	**260**			**$13**	**317**	**361**	**678**	**8**	**82**	**0.47**	**258**	**69**	**119**		**4.02**	**5.0**

He's been getting less and less selective at the plate. The potential fallout is further downside to his BA and OB, which in turn will eat into his SB output. Buy him on sale only.

Galarraga,Andres

		Tm	AB	R	H	HR	RBI	SB	Avg	vLH	vRH	R$	OB	Slg	OPS	bb%	ct%	Eye	xBA	PX	SX	G/F	RC/G	RAR
Pos 1B	98	ATL	555	103	169	44	121	7	305	328	297	$36	375	595	970	10	74	0.43	279	177	66	1.30	8.33	51.9
Age 41 Decline	99	ATL	0	0	0	0	0	0	0								0							
Bats R	00	ATL	494	67	149	28	100	3	302	347	287	$24	349	526	875	7	74	0.29	266	129	44	1.41	6.70	18.9
Pwr -	01	2TM	399	50	102	17	69	1	256	268	251	$11	309	459	768	7	71	0.26	243	127	45	1.00	4.92	-17.2
Spd No change	02	MON	292	30	76	9	40	2	260	294	246	$7	329	394	723	9	72	0.37	224	82	35	1.45	4.68	-9.5
BAvg - -	1st Half		77	6	20	1	11	1	260			$1	337	351	688	10	73	0.43	217	65	34		4.50	-3.0
LIMA D+	2nd Half		215	24	56	8	29	1	260			$5	326	409	736	9	72	0.35	226	89	32		4.73	-6.6
Risk X HIGH	03	Proj	**200**	**24**	**49**	**8**	**33**	**1**	**245**			**$5**	**310**	**418**	**728**	**9**	**72**	**0.34**	**239**	**105**	**41**		**4.52**	**-5.3**

All trends are pretty evident that he's about reached the end of the line.

Gant,Ron

		Tm	AB	R	H	HR	RBI	SB	Avg	vLH	vRH	R$	OB	Slg	OPS	bb%	ct%	Eye	xBA	PX	SX	G/F	RC/G	RAR
Pos LF	98	STL	383	60	92	26	67	8	240	286	223	$15	329	493	823	12	76	0.55	279	155	89	1.00	5.96	13.1
Age 38 Decline	99	PHI	516	107	134	17	77	13	260	300	246	$14	364	430	795	14	78	0.76	266	104	128	0.92	5.97	14.1
Bats R	00	2TM	425	69	106	26	54	6	249	315	223	$12	337	492	829	12	79	0.62	285	134	86	0.84	5.77	7.0
Pwr -	01	2TM	252	46	65	10	35	5	258	270	250	$7	348	452	801	12	68	0.44	237	115	134	1.00	5.88	5.1
Spd No change	02	SD	309	58	81	18	59	4	262	294	245	$13	339	489	828	10	81	0.61	280	131	77	0.71	5.70	-8.1
BAvg No change	1st Half		116	21	27	6	22	0	233			$3	336	431	767	13	78	0.72	261	116	47		4.59	-7.4
LIMA C+	2nd Half		193	37	54	12	37	4	280			$10	341	523	865	9	82	0.53	292	139	99		6.47	-0.3
Risk Moderate	03	Proj	**250**	**45**	**64**	**10**	**41**	**3**	**256**			**$7**	**341**	**443**	**784**	**11**	**77**	**0.56**	**261**	**111**	**98**		**5.34**	**4.8**

Perhaps his last hurrah. NIce little performance spike, but many of his underlying gauges still show soft support. Expecting another double-digit R$ season is a bad percentage play.

Garciaparra,Nomar

		Tm	AB	R	H	HR	RBI	SB	Avg	vLH	vRH	R$	OB	Slg	OPS	bb%	ct%	Eye	xBA	PX	SX	G/F	RC/G	RAR
Pos SS	98	BOS	604	111	195	35	122	12	323	320	324	$35	358	584	942	5	90	0.53	340	153	127	1.23	7.88	70.6
Age 29 Past Peak	99	BOS	532	103	190	27	104	14	357	400	346	$35	413	603	1017	9	93	1.31	347	150	112	1.16	10.31	100.9
Bats R	00	BOS	529	104	197	21	96	5	372	383	369	$31	437	599	1037	10	91	1.22	336	143	83	1.17	11.11	111.4
Pwr No change	01	BOS	* 99	16	31	5	11	0	313	313	284	$4	364	515	880	7	89	0.73	297	120	36	0.87	6.97	7.7
Spd No change	02	BOS	635	101	197	24	120	5	310	305	311	$29	352	528	880	6	90	0.65	329	150	95	0.71	7.05	45.8
BAvg - -	1st Half		298	50	94	10	60	3	315			$14	361	534	894	7	91	0.81	334	150	114		7.28	23.8
LIMA C+	2nd Half		337	51	103	14	60	2	306			$15	345	522	867	6	89	0.54	323	149	69		6.84	22.1
Risk Moderate	03	Proj	**625**	**110**	**204**	**30**	**118**	**3**	**326**			**$31**	**377**	**564**	**941**	**7**	**90**	**0.85**	**332**	**152**	**79**		**8.24**	**85.7**

Nice return to form, in every aspect of his game except power. But guess what? PX, G/F and 2nd half surge might mean a return to the 30-HR plateau is just around the corner.

Garcia,Jesse

		Tm	AB	R	H	HR	RBI	SB	Avg	vLH	vRH	R$	OB	Slg	OPS	bb%	ct%	Eye	xBA	PX	SX	G/F	RC/G	RAR
Pos 2B	98	a/a	418	59	108	2	34	17	258			$8	317	325	643	8	86	0.62	261	49	118		3.74	-5.3
Age 29 Past Peak	99	aaa	220	21	48	2	19	8	218			$1	249	295	544	4	91	0.45	276	53	94	1.75	2.22	-12.8
Bats R	00	aaa	372	37	77	1	20	8	207			($3)	255	247	502	6	85	0.42	241	29	85		2.14	-23.3
Pwr No change	01	aaa	375	42	87	2	19	15	232			$3	269	312	581	5	86	0.37	263	59	111	1.00	2.82	-14.6
Spd - - - - -	02	ATL	* 291	30	70	5	19	7	241	154	229	$3	273	337	610	4	85	0.29	255	62	82	1.67	2.99	-13.1
BAvg -	1st Half		151	11	37	2	11	4	245			$2	269	331	600	3	88	0.28	262	55	82		2.91	-7.1
LIMA D	2nd Half		140	19	33	3	8	3	236			$1	277	343	620	5	81	0.30	247	70	77		3.07	-6.0
Risk X HIGH	03	Proj	**100**	**11**	**23**	**1**	**6**	**3**	**230**			**$0**	**268**	**305**	**573**	**5**	**85**	**0.35**	**254**	**52**	**75**		**2.69**	**-4.2**

0-5-.197 in 61 AB at ATL. Triple-A lifer has a bit of speed, but has been unable to find a way to steal first base, thus negating his value.

Garcia,Karim

		Tm	AB	R	H	HR	RBI	SB	Avg	vLH	vRH	R$	OB	Slg	OPS	bb%	ct%	Eye	xBA	PX	SX	G/F	RC/G	RAR
Pos RF	98	ARI	* 439	54	103	16	63	9	235			$10	281	419	700	6	79	0.30	271	109	173	1.47	4.04	-12.8
Age 27 Peak	99	DET	288	38	69	14	32	2	240			$5	289	441	730	6	77	0.30	264	111	98		4.41	-5.8
Bats L	00	aaa	458	56	110	19	73	4	240			$9	296	421	717	7	81	0.41	276	106	65		4.22	-12.9
Pwr - -	01	aaa	507	71	129	34	83	4	254			$18	311	503	814	8	79	0.40	282	137	70	1.15	5.44	1.1
Spd No change	02	CLE	* 581	83	167	31	115	1	287	278	308	$26	325	511	836	5	83	0.32	293	139	58	1.14	5.71	10.4
BAvg - -	1st Half		293	36	68	10	39	1	232			$5	272	396	668	5	86	0.39	284	106	72		3.36	-15.5
LIMA A+	2nd Half		288	47	99	21	76	0	344			$21	378	628	1007	5	79	0.27	301	172	57		9.06	34.2
Risk Very High	03	Proj	**500**	**70**	**131**	**26**	**87**	**3**	**262**			**$17**	**308**	**478**	**786**	**6**	**81**	**0.35**	**281**	**127**	**76**		**5.04**	**-3.2**

16-52-.297 in 202 AB at CLE. Broke out in AAA in '01. Oddly, BAL dealt him to CLE in the middle of that breakout, further showing their fine judgment of talent. Is he for real? Yes, but there are still some soft BPIs.

Giambi,Jason

		Tm	AB	R	H	HR	RBI	SB	Avg	vLH	vRH	R$	OB	Slg	OPS	bb%	ct%	Eye	xBA	PX	SX	G/F	RC/G	RAR
Pos 1B DH	98	OAK	562	92	166	27	110	2	295	257	317	$23	384	489	873	13	82	0.79	277	116	39	0.75	7.25	27.6
Age 32 Past Peak	99	OAK	575	115	181	33	123	1	315	282	330	$28	421	553	974	15	82	0.99	292	141	46	0.84	9.36	67.2
Bats L	00	OAK	510	108	170	43	137	2	333	324	349	$35	474	647	1122	21	81	1.43	318	173	49	0.71	13.05	129.1
Pwr No change	01	OAK	520	109	178	38	120	2	342	333	347	$36	473	660	1133	20	84	1.55	324	192	55	0.74	13.32	130.7
Spd No change	02	NYY	560	120	176	41	122	2	314	299	320	$34	426	598	1024	16	80	0.97	306	176	52	0.70	10.18	80.3
BAvg - -	1st Half		294	53	93	21	64	1	316			$18	424	599	1023	16	80	0.95	308	178	32		10.03	40.4
LIMA C+	2nd Half		266	67	83	20	58	1	312			$16	428	598	1026	17	80	1.00	305	174	72		10.35	40.0
Risk Low	03	Proj	**550**	**118**	**168**	**40**	**125**	**2**	**305**			**$32**	**429**	**594**	**1023**	**18**	**81**	**1.16**	**310**	**174**	**53**		**10.22**	**87.4**

Minor skills drop-off, but for the most part, insignificant. Ride him.

Giambi,Jeremy

		Tm	AB	R	H	HR	RBI	SB	Avg	vLH	vRH	R$	OB	Slg	OPS	bb%	ct%	Eye	xBA	PX	SX	G/F	RC/G	RAR
Pos LF 1B	98	KC	* 383	66	126	19	66	7	329	143	235	$21	419	551	969	13	84	0.97	301	134	79	0.95	9.29	52.3
Age 28 Peak	99	KC	* 415	60	122	13	57	1	294	292	283	$11	390	441	831	14	78	0.72	251	88	54	1.50	6.74	21.5
Bats L	00	OAK	260	42	66	10	50	0	254	266	250	$6	336	423	759	11	77	0.52	253	95	69	1.06	5.22	0.2
Pwr No change	01	OAK	* 398	65	113	12	58	0	284	250	291	$11	383	442	825	14	78	0.73	251	104	29	1.08	6.54	24.1
Spd No change	02	2TM	313	58	81	20	45	0	259	286	251	$9	408	505	913	20	70	0.84	249	149	26	0.89	7.93	24.7
BAvg + + +	1st Half		223	41	62	15	32	0	278			$8	415	534	948	19	73	0.85	261	154	26		8.57	22.4
LIMA A+	2nd Half		90	17	19	5	13	0	211			$0	393	433	826	23	63	0.82	220	137	27		6.50	2.6
Risk Very High	03	Proj	**550**	**96**	**153**	**26**	**84**	**0**	**278**			**$18**	**404**	**481**	**884**	**17**	**73**	**0.77**	**253**	**124**	**34**		**7.59**	**40.2**

All the fans' ire about his limited PT is completely justified. Geez, how can you even think about sitting a .400 OB hitter? And trends are rising as well. I'm giving him 550 AB for '03 whether they like it or not.

Gibbons,Jay

	Yr	Tm	AB	R	H	HR	RBI	SB	Avg	vLH	vRH	R$	OB	Slg	OPS	bb%	ct%	Eye	xBA	PX	SX	G/F	RC/G	RAR
Pos RF 1B	98		0	0	0	0	0	0	0								0							
Age 26 Pre-Peak	99		0	0	0	0	0	0	0								0							
Bats L	00	aa	474	64	134	15	57	2	283			$11	346	458	804	9	89	0.87	306	113	52		5.92	11.7
Pwr + +	01	BAL	225	27	53	15	36	0	236	370	217	$6	289	480	769	7	83	0.44	285	139	22	0.99	4.72	-2.5
Spd No change	02	BAL	490	71	121	28	69	1	247	235	250	$15	310	482	792	8	87	0.68	313	149	45	0.92	5.18	1.0
BAvg + + +	1st Half		248	41	62	12	34	1	250			$7	331	460	791	11	83	0.73	295	138	51		5.46	2.7
LIMA A	2nd Half		242	30	59	16	35	0	244			$8	288	504	792	6	90	0.60	332	160	43		4.86	-1.9
Risk Moderate	03	Proj	**550**	**73**	**156**	**32**	**80**	**1**	**284**			**$21**	**339**	**516**	**855**	**8**	**86**	**0.59**	**305**	**141**	**32**		**6.37**	**19.0**

A nice growth year, and an xBA that makes his prospects all that more intriguing. A .300 hitter? Hard to imagine, but the seeds are there and the trends are favorable.

Giles,Brian

	Yr	Tm	AB	R	H	HR	RBI	SB	Avg	vLH	vRH	R$	OB	Slg	OPS	bb%	ct%	Eye	xBA	PX	SX	G/F	RC/G	RAR
Pos LF	98	CLE	* 396	61	104	18	72	10	263	229	275	$15	384	452	836	16	79	0.93	269	115	61	0.98	6.56	19.0
Age 32 Past Peak	99	PIT	521	109	164	39	115	6	315	299	323	$32	420	614	1035	15	85	1.19	321	175	81	0.81	10.31	90.8
Bats L	00	PIT	559	111	176	35	123	6	315	293	323	$32	431	594	1025	17	88	1.65	333	160	110	0.99	10.46	98.9
Pwr No change	01	PIT	576	116	178	37	95	13	309	267	322	$33	402	590	993	14	88	1.34	336	162	123	0.88	9.19	64.3
Spd No change	02	PIT	497	95	148	38	103	15	298	231	325	$34	448	622	1070	21	85	1.82	330	189	104	0.58	11.08	82.4
BAvg + + + + +	1st Half		259	46	79	19	47	9	305			$18	416	606	1022	16	86	1.36	325	175	98		9.86	29.5
LIMA C+	2nd Half		238	49	69	19	56	6	290			$16	478	639	1117	27	84	2.26	334	205	103		12.34	54.0
Risk Low	03	Proj	**550**	**108**	**176**	**44**	**121**	**13**	**320**			**$40**	**449**	**650**	**1100**	**19**	**86**	**1.66**	**337**	**191**	**105**		**11.82**	**137.1**

Keeps falling short of the elusive 40-HR club, but it was only a lack of AB in '02 that kept him away. His BA vsLH gives us slight pause, but otherwise, all the pieces are in place for the career year in 2003.

Giles,Marcus

	Yr	Tm	AB	R	H	HR	RBI	SB	Avg	vLH	vRH	R$	OB	Slg	OPS	bb%	ct%	Eye	xBA	PX	SX	G/F	RC/G	RAR
Pos 2B	98		0	0	0	0	0	0	0								0							
Age 24 Growth	99		0	0	0	0	0	0	0								0							
Bats R	00	aa	458	60	120	14	51	20	262			$14	347	413	760	12	87	1.03	290	93	89		5.35	17.1
Pwr -	01	ATL	* 496	79	143	14	70	14	288	286	256	$19	351	442	793	9	84	0.60	279	96	101	1.56	5.53	24.8
Spd -	02	ATL	* 328	49	83	11	37	4	253	158	246	$7	327	409	735	10	84	0.67	270	96	78	1.08	4.89	4.0
BAvg + + +	1st Half		160	17	37	5	13	1	231			$1	309	375	684	10	79	0.53	248	85	63		4.07	-2.2
LIMA A	2nd Half		168	32	46	6	24	3	274			$6	344	440	785	10	88	0.90	291	106	81		5.77	6.7
Risk High	03	Proj	**450**	**69**	**126**	**14**	**56**	**10**	**280**			**$15**	**350**	**437**	**787**	**10**	**85**	**0.70**	**279**	**98**	**91**		**5.66**	**22.2**

8-23-.230 in 213 AB at ATL. This was supposed to be a better season. The near daily littany of injuries and family crises affected his play at the plate and on the field. He needs to write it off and start again.

Gil,Benji

	Yr	Tm	AB	R	H	HR	RBI	SB	Avg	vLH	vRH	R$	OB	Slg	OPS	bb%	ct%	Eye	xBA	PX	SX	G/F	RC/G	RAR
Pos 2B	98	aaa	460	63	94	10	54	9	204			$2	255	330	585	6	83	0.41	272	81	126		2.83	-18.5
Age 30 Past Peak	99	aaa	412	50	87	11	43	12	211			$3	246	352	598	4	80	0.23	262	91	103		2.83	-16.6
Bats R	00	ANA	301	28	72	6	23	10	239	301	202	$4	308	352	660	9	80	0.51	251	71	77	1.51	3.75	-1.9
Pwr No change	01	ANA	260	33	77	8	39	3	296	294	299	$9	332	477	809	5	78	0.25	264	110	109	1.45	5.59	10.2
Spd No change	02	ANA	* 154	14	45	5	25	2	292	310	233	$6	319	500	819	4	77	0.17	276	142	99	1.23	5.28	5.3
BAvg - - -	1st Half		87	7	28	3	15	2	322			$5	330	540	870	1	83	0.07	303	151	95		5.55	3.6
LIMA C	2nd Half		67	7	17	2	10	0	254			$1	306	448	753	7	69	0.24	241	131	94		4.88	1.6
Risk Very High	03	Proj	**150**	**16**	**40**	**4**	**21**	**2**	**267**			**$4**	**307**	**447**	**754**	**6**	**77**	**0.25**	**264**	**116**	**107**		**4.65**	**2.1**

This free-swinger found some groove in '02, nailing nearly half of his hits for extra bases. With these BPIs, the odds of that happening again are slim.

Gil,Geronimo

	Yr	Tm	AB	R	H	HR	RBI	SB	Avg	vLH	vRH	R$	OB	Slg	OPS	bb%	ct%	Eye	xBA	PX	SX	G/F	RC/G	RAR
Pos CA	98	aa	241	21	56	4	22	2	232			$1	269	357	626	5	85	0.34	277	86	78		3.27	-5.6
Age 27 Peak	99	aa	343	36	80	11	46	2	233			$4	306	397	703	9	86	0.75	287	104	53		4.34	2.7
Bats R	00	a/a	402	41	100	10	63	2	249			$6	301	378	679	7	85	0.48	271	81	44		3.91	-3.0
Pwr No change	01	BAL	* 421	37	101	8	46	0	240	571	255	$3	269	344	614	4	83	0.24	247	68	33	1.53	3.17	-9.6
Spd No change	02	BAL	422	33	98	12	45	2	232	239	230	$6	269	363	631	5	79	0.24	249	87	33	1.50	3.30	-5.0
BAvg No change	1st Half		200	12	49	8	30	1	245			$5	271	400	671	3	81	0.18	258	97	19		3.76	0.4
LIMA D+	2nd Half		222	21	49	4	15	1	221			$1	267	329	596	6	78	0.29	240	79	42		2.91	-5.3
Risk Very High	03	Proj	**350**	**31**	**83**	**9**	**39**	**1**	**237**			**$4**	**277**	**364**	**641**	**5**	**82**	**0.30**	**255**	**84**	**45**		**3.44**	**-6.6**

Those 12 HRs are going to self-perpetuate his empty value in the eyes of the O's. Yes, he's a good defensive backstop, but the perception is that he's also helping the offense. 422 AB of these BPIs is a killer.

Ginter,Keith

	Yr	Tm	AB	R	H	HR	RBI	SB	Avg	vLH	vRH	R$	OB	Slg	OPS	bb%	ct%	Eye	xBA	PX	SX	G/F	RC/G	RAR
Pos 3B	98		0	0	0	0	0	0	0								0							
Age 26 Pre-Peak	99		0	0	0	0	0	0	0								0							
Bats R	00	aa	462	92	143	25	79	21	310			$27	400	548	948	13	73	0.57	269	138	113	0.25	8.28	58.2
Pwr No change	01	aaa	458	63	115	15	58	7	251			$10	325	434	759	10	72	0.39	248	115	97		4.89	4.7
Spd -	02	2NL	* 516	67	127	13	55	3	246	154	250	$7	330	395	726	11	80	0.62	258	100	52	0.88	4.67	-0.2
BAvg + + +	1st Half		243	34	59	5	24	2	243			$2	326	370	696	11	76	0.51	239	88	52		4.25	-3.4
LIMA B	2nd Half		273	33	68	8	31	1	249			$4	334	418	752	11	83	0.76	275	111	51		5.07	3.4
Risk High	03	Proj	**350**	**50**	**88**	**9**	**41**	**2**	**251**			**$6**	**334**	**412**	**746**	**11**	**76**	**0.53**	**254**	**105**	**70**		**4.84**	**3.3**

1-8-.235 in 81 AB at HOU and MIL. There has been a slight erosion of skills each time he rises a level, which makes his MLB potential questionable. BPI levels now are not encouraging.

Gipson,Charles

	Yr	Tm	AB	R	H	HR	RBI	SB	Avg	vLH	vRH	R$	OB	Slg	OPS	bb%	ct%	Eye	xBA	PX	SX	G/F	RC/G	RAR
Pos LF	98	SEA	* 329	45	72	0	12	14	219			$0	282	277	559	8	83	0.51	248	48	117	1.91	2.88	-23.2
Age 30 Past Peak	99	SEA	* 272	41	59	0	28	20	217	280	200	$4	273	283	556	7	84	0.49	259	44	181	1.50	2.78	-20.0
Bats R	00	SEA	* 243	32	56	1	24	17	230	267	357	$5	325	313	638	12	79	0.68	239	47	176	6.00	3.69	-11.9
Pwr -	01	SEA	64	16	14	0	5	1	219	143	310	($0)	265	313	577	6	69	0.20	223	54	256	6.40	2.70	-3.9
Spd No change	02	SEA	72	22	17	0	8	4	236	175	313	$2	321	361	682	11	81	0.64	264	90	262	4.00	4.53	-0.9
BAvg + + +	1st Half		39	9	11	0	5	2	282			$1	364	462	825	11	85	0.83	297	118	299		6.74	2.3
LIMA C	2nd Half		33	13	6	0	3	2	182			$0	270	242	513	11	76	0.50	226	56	205		2.57	-2.5
Risk High	03	Proj	**100**	**14**	**22**	**0**	**7**	**6**	**220**			**$1**	**293**	**284**	**577**	**9**	**82**	**0.57**	**241**	**47**	**137**		**3.04**	**-6.6**

He's a specialist, that's all. One of the few players you'll see with more runs scored than hits. All those pinch-running runs are what is artificially inflating his SX levels.

Girardi,Joe

	Yr	Tm	AB	R	H	HR	RBI	SB	Avg	vLH	vRH	R$	OB	Slg	OPS	bb%	ct%	Eye	xBA	PX	SX	G/F	RC/G	RAR
Pos CA	98	NYY	254	31	70	3	31	2	276	239	284	$4	313	386	699	5	85	0.37	267	69	106	2.34	4.16	0.5
Age 38 Decline	99	NYY	209	23	50	2	27	3	239	184	256	$2	274	354	628	5	88	0.38	282	84	86	2.04	3.36	-5.0
Bats R	00	CHC	363	47	101	6	40	1	278	202	313	$6	337	375	711	8	83	0.52	260	62	53	2.52	4.75	7.6
Pwr No change	01	CHC	229	22	58	3	25	0	253	263	250	$2	316	345	661	8	78	0.42	237	61	43	2.06	3.91	2.3
Spd No change	02	CHC	234	19	53	1	13	1	226	172	247	($2)	276	291	567	6	85	0.46	246	47	56	2.27	2.83	-9.8
BAvg No change	1st Half		129	9	30	0	4	0	233			($2)	267	287	553	4	86	0.33	245	40	50		2.65	-6.0
LIMA D	2nd Half		105	10	23	1	9	1	219			($0)	287	295	582	9	84	0.59	246	56	46		3.04	-3.8
Risk Moderate	03	Proj	**150**	**15**	**36**	**1**	**13**	**1**	**240**			**$0**	**296**	**329**	**625**	**7**	**83**	**0.47**	**252**	**61**	**65**		**3.46**	**-2.4**

No longer draftable.

Glanville,Doug

	Yr	Tm	AB	R	H	HR	RBI	SB	Avg	vLH	vRH	R$	OB	Slg	OPS	bb%	ct%	Eye	xBA	PX	SX	G/F	RC/G	RAR
Pos CF	98	PHI	678	106	189	8	49	23	279	259	285	$17	321	376	697	6	87	0.47	276	68	140	1.60	4.47	1.5
Age 32 Past Peak	99	PHI	628	101	204	11	73	34	325	250	346	$30	373	457	830	7	87	0.59	287	88	138	1.45	7.02	50.6
Bats R	00	PHI	637	89	175	8	52	31	275	237	285	$18	308	374	682	5	88	0.41	278	63	136	1.52	4.22	-3.7
Pwr No change	01	PHI	634	74	166	14	55	28	262	290	254	$18	283	375	659	3	86	0.21	270	70	121	1.17	3.80	-2.5
Spd -	02	PHI	422	49	105	6	29	19	249	250	248	$8	291	344	634	6	86	0.44	265	61	127	1.10	3.69	-16.3
BAvg -	1st Half		222	24	49	2	14	7	221			$0	276	288	564	7	85	0.50	249	49	84		2.87	-14.3
LIMA B	2nd Half		200	25	56	4	15	12	280			$8	308	405	713	4	89	0.35	282	74	156		4.76	-1.3
Risk Low	03	Proj	**350**	**44**	**90**	**6**	**27**	**16**	**257**			**$9**	**292**	**364**	**656**	**5**	**87**	**0.37**	**273**	**67**	**134**		**3.89**	**-5.3**

Skills erosion has left him with very little value, other than speed. But there are hundreds of minor leaguers that can outrun a train but can't find first base with a telescope. His skills set is no different now.

Glaus,Troy

	Yr	Tm	AB	R	H	HR	RBI	SB	Avg	vLH	vRH	R$	OB	Slg	OPS	bb%	ct%	Eye	xBA	PX	SX	G/F	RC/G	RAR
Pos 3B	98	ANA	* 572	85	148	31	96	6	259	281	203	$19	330	483	813	10	77	0.47	276	134	68	0.75	5.77	22.1
Age 26 Pre-Peak	99	ANA	551	85	132	29	79	5	240	316	246	$12	326	450	776	11	74	0.50	257	124	63	0.83	5.31	14.1
Bats R	00	ANA	563	120	160	47	102	14	284	369	259	$30	403	604	1007	17	71	0.69	283	179	76	0.76	8.96	86.3
Pwr +	01	ANA	588	100	147	41	108	10	250	252	249	$24	365	531	896	15	73	0.68	271	165	78	0.76	7.16	53.7
Spd + + + + +	02	ANA	569	99	142	30	111	10	250	298	230	$23	350	453	804	13	75	0.61	258	126	85	0.94	5.86	24.5
BAvg + + +	1st Half		288	55	72	15	58	6	250			$12	347	465	813	13	75	0.60	266	135	97		5.92	12.9
LIMA A	2nd Half		281	44	70	15	53	4	249			$11	353	441	794	14	74	0.63	251	116	60		5.80	11.5
Risk High	03	Proj	**575**	**101**	**146**	**35**	**107**	**10**	**254**			**$23**	**360**	**495**	**854**	**14**	**74**	**0.63**	**267**	**144**	**77**		**6.55**	**37.3**

There are some warning signs that this decline might not be temporary...
- Declining PX and rising G/F
- Increasing trouble vs LHers

His contact rate is still rising, which provides some hope.

Gomez,Chris

	Yr	Tm	AB	R	H	HR	RBI	SB	Avg	vLH	vRH	R$	OB	Slg	OPS	bb%	ct%	Eye	xBA	PX	SX	G/F	RC/G	RAR
Pos SS	98	SD	449	55	120	4	39	1	267	283	261	$5	342	379	721	10	81	0.59	262	88	61	1.47	4.74	15.2
Age 31 Past Peak	99	SD	234	20	59	1	15	1	252	294	235	$0	330	308	637	10	79	0.55	234	40	44	1.70	3.69	0.7
Bats R	00	SD	54	4	12	0	3	0	222	227	219	($1)	311	222	534	11	91	1.40	244			1.40	2.61	-1.6
Pwr + +	01	2TM	* 434	53	110	12	60	6	253	243	264	$10	297	399	696	6	89	0.57	290	93	78	1.05	4.24	2.6
Spd No change	02	TAM	461	51	122	10	46	1	265	172	286	$8	297	410	707	4	87	0.36	286	103	62	1.01	4.22	-6.2
BAvg - -	1st Half		244	27	63	5	20	0	258			$3	298	406	704	5	87	0.44	288	109	49		4.16	-3.8
LIMA D+	2nd Half		217	24	59	5	26	1	272			$5	295	415	709	3	88	0.27	285	97	81		4.30	-2.4
Risk Very High	03	Proj	**350**	**39**	**90**	**7**	**37**	**0**	**257**			**$5**	**303**	**387**	**690**	**6**	**86**	**0.47**	**273**	**89**	**55**		**4.10**	**3.2**

Despite the apparent power surge the past two years, these have been supported by some of the worst BPIs in his career. There is no more offensive value here.

Gonzalez,Alex

	Yr	Tm	AB	R	H	HR	RBI	SB	Avg	vLH	vRH	R$	OB	Slg	OPS	bb%	ct%	Eye	xBA	PX	SX	G/F	RC/G	RAR
Pos SS	98	FLA	* 508	70	123	11	50	3	242	43	190	$6	288	380	668	6	83	0.38	274	89	127	1.37	3.84	2.5
Age 26 Pre-Peak	99	FLA	560	81	155	14	59	3	277	254	283	$11	296	430	726	3	80	0.13	265	94	111	0.97	4.40	13.1
Bats R	00	FLA	385	35	77	7	42	7	200	245	185	($0)	226	319	546	3	80	0.17	257	74	119	0.83	2.40	-12.8
Pwr + +	01	FLA	515	57	129	9	48	2	250	235	255	$5	292	377	668	6	79	0.28	256	88	55	0.87	3.84	3.3
Spd No change	02	FLA	151	15	34	2	18	3	225	200	231	$1	282	325	607	7	79	0.38	241	66	89	0.63	3.20	-3.6
BAvg No change	1st Half		151	15	34	2	18	3	225			$1	282	325	607	7	79	0.38	241	66	89		3.20	-3.6
LIMA B	2nd Half		0	0	0	0	0	0	0			($0)					0							-0.0
Risk High	03	Proj	**450**	**50**	**115**	**8**	**48**	**6**	**256**			**$7**	**294**	**378**	**672**	**5**	**80**	**0.27**	**254**	**79**	**100**		**3.93**	**2.4**

Dislocated shoulder put an end to another season of useless BPIs. There are only minor signs of growth (bb%, eye) and a G/F ratio that suggests possible power potential. But 26 is when you'd expect to see results.

Gonzalez,Alex S.

	Yr	Tm	AB	R	H	HR	RBI	SB	Avg	vLH	vRH	R$	OB	Slg	OPS	bb%	ct%	Eye	xBA	PX	SX	G/F	RC/G	RAR
Pos SS	98	TOR	568	70	136	13	51	21	239	272	229	$10	275	361	636	5	79	0.23	253	79	103	1.27	3.44	-9.5
Age 30 Past Peak	99	TOR	154	22	45	2	12	4	292	268	301	$4	359	416	774	9	85	0.70	277	91	69	1.19	5.60	6.6
Bats R	00	TOR	527	68	133	15	69	4	252	228	259	$8	309	404	713	8	79	0.38	259	94	69	1.37	4.37	-2.2
Pwr +	01	TOR	636	79	161	17	76	18	253	336	233	$15	300	388	689	6	77	0.29	244	81	105	1.52	3.99	-9.1
Spd - -	02	CHC	513	58	127	18	61	5	248	237	251	$10	309	425	734	8	73	0.34	245	107	95	1.18	4.64	10.5
BAvg -	1st Half		228	27	54	9	30	1	237			$4	298	425	724	8	72	0.31	241	113	80		4.32	2.4
LIMA A+	2nd Half		285	31	73	9	31	4	256			$6	318	425	743	8	75	0.36	247	103	101		4.90	8.2
Risk High	03	Proj	**500**	**60**	**126**	**19**	**58**	**8**	**252**			**$12**	**309**	**434**	**743**	**8**	**76**	**0.34**	**257**	**110**	**96**		**4.68**	**14.4**

Came into 2002 on a 3-year skills decline, and managed to stall the trend ever so slightly. Other than some possible power improvement, he'll remain a mid-level roto pick but a marginal player in any other venue.

Gonzalez,Juan

	Yr	Tm	AB	R	H	HR	RBI	SB	Avg	vLH	vRH	R$	OB	Slg	OPS	bb%	ct%	Eye	xBA	PX	SX	G/F	RC/G	RAR
Pos RF	98	TEX	606	110	193	45	157	2	318	355	306	$38	367	630	997	7	79	0.37	312	187	62	0.77	8.88	69.5
Age 33 Decline	99	TEX	562	114	183	39	128	3	326	342	321	$33	382	601	983	8	81	0.49	304	160	63	0.70	8.88	66.6
Bats R	00	DET	461	69	133	22	67	1	289	360	265	$14	335	505	840	6	82	0.38	291	128	58	0.94	6.18	16.4
Pwr +	01	CLE	532	97	173	35	140	1	325	368	313	$34	373	590	964	7	82	0.44	297	157	51	0.89	8.63	58.1
Spd No change	02	TEX	277	38	78	8	35	2	282	358	250	$8	323	451	774	6	80	0.30	272	120	75	0.95	5.40	2.4
BAvg - -	1st Half		174	23	52	4	20	2	299			$6	351	443	794	7	80	0.40	263	106	57		5.99	4.7
LIMA A	2nd Half		103	15	26	4	15	0	252			$2	274	466	740	3	80	0.14	286	143	87		4.42	-2.1
Risk Moderate	03	Proj	**450**	**71**	**132**	**21**	**80**	**2**	**293**			**$18**	**335**	**514**	**850**	**6**	**81**	**0.33**	**289**	**141**	**71**		**6.41**	**15.9**

As of this writing, I don't know whether he will have surgery on his hand and what the prognosis will be. This projection is for a mid-level rebound, but he could bounce back to '01 levels as well. Stay tuned.

Gonzalez,Luis

	Yr	Tm	AB	R	H	HR	RBI	SB	Avg	vLH	vRH	R$	OB	Slg	OPS	bb%	ct%	Eye	xBA	PX	SX	G/F	RC/G	RAR
Pos LF	98	DET	547	84	146	23	71	12	267	278	263	$17	336	475	811	9	89	0.92	316	127	105	1.02	5.70	9.5
Age 35 Decline	99	ARI	614	112	206	26	111	9	336	327	339	$32	400	549	949	10	90	1.05	318	134	86	1.11	8.70	69.0
Bats L	00	ARI	618	106	192	31	114	2	311	254	333	$28	388	544	932	11	86	0.92	315	142	49	0.86	8.10	55.2
Pwr + +	01	ARI	609	128	198	57	142	1	325	312	331	$43	420	688	1108	14	86	1.20	349	201	84	0.78	11.55	116.3
Spd No change	02	ARI	524	90	151	28	103	9	288	272	297	$27	399	496	896	16	85	1.28	290	118	88	0.97	7.81	23.0
BAvg + + +	1st Half		288	47	83	16	57	4	288			$15	402	514	916	16	87	1.45	300	130	80		8.13	15.8
LIMA A	2nd Half		236	43	68	12	46	5	288			$12	396	475	870	15	84	1.11	276	103	83		7.43	7.2
Risk High	03	Proj	**550**	**100**	**166**	**31**	**110**	**7**	**302**			**$29**	**399**	**534**	**933**	**14**	**86**	**1.16**	**304**	**134**	**89**		**8.35**	**65.8**

Natural letdown after 2001's explosion. At 35, he will probably plateau at this power level, but a return to the .300 club is very likely.

Gonzalez,Raul

	Yr	Tm	AB	R	H	HR	RBI	SB	Avg	vLH	vRH	R$	OB	Slg	OPS	bb%	ct%	Eye	xBA	PX	SX	G/F	RC/G	RAR
Pos CF	98	aa	455	60	123	11	61	9	270			$12	329	404	734	8	92	1.05	300	92	74		4.76	2.0
Age 29 Past Peak	99	aa	505	62	143	13	80	9	283			$15	335	432	766	7	86	0.57	286	95	87		5.35	11.7
Bats R	00	aaa	241	29	54	3	27	4	224			$1	275	315	591	7	93	0.94	285	60	79		2.75	-13.5
Pwr -	01	aaa	539	69	143	9	51	5	265			$9	329	386	715	9	89	0.86	281	84	53	2.00	4.42	-0.3
Spd + + + + +	02	2NL	* 536	79	149	13	62	11	278	273	254	$16	338	405	743	8	87	0.71	274	82	74	3.67	4.82	-2.5
BAvg -	1st Half		318	47	87	8	38	7	274			$9	336	406	742	9	88	0.77	278	85	82		4.88	-0.8
LIMA C	2nd Half		218	32	62	5	24	4	284			$7	342	404	745	8	86	0.63	268	79	61		4.73	-1.6
Risk Very High	03	Proj	**200**	**27**	**54**	**4**	**22**	**3**	**270**			**$5**	**329**	**386**	**715**	**8**	**88**	**0.76**	**279**	**79**	**60**		**4.40**	**0.1**

3-12-4-.260 in 104 AB at CIN and NYM. PX and G/F ratios indicate that he'll probably never hit for much power. SX doesn't equate to double-digit SB output. He looks like a solid .270-.280 hitter with little else.

Gonzalez,Wiki

	Yr	Tm	AB	R	H	HR	RBI	SB	Avg	vLH	vRH	R$	OB	Slg	OPS	bb%	ct%	Eye	xBA	PX	SX	G/F	RC/G	RAR
Pos CA	98	aa	67	18	24	3	23	0	358			$5	456	612	1068	15	91	2.00	348	179	47		11.92	17.8
Age 28 Peak	99	SD	* 400	46	108	16	58	0	270	150	349	$10	315	450	765	6	91	0.70	306	109	38	1.48	5.13	13.3
Bats R	00	SD	284	25	66	5	30	1	232	277	214	$1	306	345	651	10	89	0.97	285	74	40	1.45	3.69	-3.5
Pwr +	01	SD	160	16	44	8	27	2	275	345	235	$6	322	463	784	6	83	0.39	277	107	41	1.43	5.51	9.4
Spd No change	02	SD	164	16	36	1	20	0	220	310	189	($1)	330	299	629	14	85	1.13	251	57	43	2.47	3.68	-2.8
BAvg + + + + +	1st Half		81	12	22	1	14	0	272			$2	404	383	787	18	81	1.20	252	83	26		6.23	5.8
LIMA C+	2nd Half		83	4	14	0	6	0	169			($3)	250	217	467	10	89	1.00	249	31	54		1.88	-6.1
Risk Very High	03	Proj	**350**	**33**	**92**	**8**	**45**	**1**	**263**			**$6**	**340**	**385**	**725**	**10**	**86**	**0.84**	**270**	**77**	**52**		**4.88**	**10.1**

Fractured hand, pulled hamstring, strained hip flexor, sore elbow... There are small signs of something valuable here, but he's not shown enough consistency or health to project anything with certainty.

Goodwin,Tom

	Yr	Tm	AB	R	H	HR	RBI	SB	Avg	vLH	vRH	R$	OB	Slg	OPS	bb%	ct%	Eye	xBA	PX	SX	G/F	RC/G	RAR
Pos LF CF	98	TEX	520	102	151	2	33	38	290	300	289	$19	378	338	716	12	83	0.81	240	33	123	2.73	4.84	-5.2
Age 34 Decline	99	TEX	405	63	105	3	33	39	259	262	259	$15	326	341	667	9	85	0.66	263	49	173	1.89	4.16	-12.8
Bats L	00	2NL	528	94	139	6	58	55	263	340	244	$24	347	352	700	11	78	0.58	239	49	188	1.81	4.91	-7.1
Pwr - -	01	LA	286	51	66	4	22	22	231	250	228	$8	288	336	624	7	80	0.40	251	60	203	1.71	3.33	-21.9
Spd - - - - -	02	SF	* 216	32	52	1	22	19	241	53	289	$7	305	319	625	8	85	0.61	259	51	171	1.79	3.68	-19.1
BAvg + + +	1st Half		86	10	16	0	10	6	186			$0	271	244	515	10	84	0.71	247	40	140		2.24	-11.7
LIMA C	2nd Half		130	22	36	1	12	13	277			$6	329	369	698	7	85	0.53	266	58	182		4.95	-6.3
Risk High	03	Proj	**150**	**24**	**37**	**1**	**14**	**13**	**247**			**$5**	**314**	**331**	**645**	**9**	**82**	**0.55**	**253**	**53**	**168**		**3.87**	**-4.1**

BPIs appear to have plateaued at this level the past two years, and at 34, lend little hope for any improvement. I should keep a count of all these single-skill speedsters that can't get on base. Seems like a lot this year.

Grace,Mark

Grace,Mark	Yr	Tm	AB	R	H	HR	RBI	SB	Avg	vLH	vRH	R$	OB	Slg	OPS	bb%	ct%	Eye	xBA	PX	SX	G/F	RC/G	RAR
Pos 1B	98	CHC	595	92	184	17	89	4	309	271	329	$23	403	471	873	14	91	1.66	308	113	56	1.47	7.33	38.2
Age 38 Decline	99	CHC	593	107	183	16	91	3	309	307	310	$20	393	481	874	12	93	1.89	316	113	74	1.07	7.36	37.6
Bats L	00	CHC	510	75	143	11	82	1	280	305	272	$12	393	429	823	16	95	3.39	320	102	37	1.19	6.58	19.5
Pwr - -	01	ARI	476	66	142	15	78	1	298	295	300	$17	385	466	851	12	92	1.86	310	107	51	1.15	7.05	10.4
Spd No change	02	ARI	298	43	75	7	48	2	252	321	226	$6	352	386	738	13	90	1.53	286	91	53	1.31	5.15	-5.5
BAvg + + + + +	1st Half		181	27	47	5	33	2	260			$5	356	425	781	13	91	1.59	302	114	56		5.76	0.3
LIMA C+	2nd Half		117	16	28	2	15	0	239			$1	346	325	670	14	89	1.46	259	56	29		4.25	-5.7
Risk Moderate	03	Proj	250	36	68	6	39	1	272			$6	371	418	788	14	91	1.78	297	96	54		5.94	4.7

With his plate patience, contact rate and batting eye, he might still have another 40-50 points of batting average in that bat, but it's clear the skills set is on the wane.

Graffanino,Tony

Graffanino,Tony	Yr	Tm	AB	R	H	HR	RBI	SB	Avg	vLH	vRH	R$	OB	Slg	OPS	bb%	ct%	Eye	xBA	PX	SX	G/F	RC/G	RAR
Pos 2B 3B	98	ATL	289	32	61	5	22	1	211	199	222	($1)	272	318	590	8	76	0.35	244	77	57	1.00	2.81	-12.4
Age 30 Past Peak	99	TAM	* 475	76	142	11	69	17	299	367	300	$18	352	472	824	8	87	0.65	305	108	147	0.88	5.96	28.0
Bats R	00	2AL	168	33	46	2	17	7	274	224	300	$4	358	357	715	12	84	0.81	251	52	115	1.17	4.73	4.3
Pwr -	01	CHW	145	23	44	2	15	4	303	319	296	$5	373	407	780	10	80	0.55	246	75	70	1.67	5.98	7.8
Spd No change	02	CHW	229	35	60	6	31	2	262	261	263	$6	327	428	755	9	83	0.58	278	107	131	1.20	5.07	6.8
BAvg No change	1st Half		148	24	43	4	27	2	291			$6	356	466	822	9	81	0.54	277	119	119		6.22	9.8
LIMA B	2nd Half		81	11	17	2	4	0	210			($0)	273	358	631	8	88	0.70	278	85	135		3.35	-1.9
Risk Very High	03	Proj	300	47	84	9	36	5	280			$9	346	444	790	9	83	0.61	277	100	121		5.68	14.0

Torn ACL ended his season, but by the looks of his 2nd half slide, he may have been hurting for awhile. 1st half was more in line with his history, and if healthy, should be the level he'll rebound to in 2003.

Greene,Todd

Greene,Todd	Yr	Tm	AB	R	H	HR	RBI	SB	Avg	vLH	vRH	R$	OB	Slg	OPS	bb%	ct%	Eye	xBA	PX	SX	G/F	RC/G	RAR
Pos CA	98	ANA	* 179	15	42	6	22	1	235	133	341	$2	279	413	692	6	79	0.30	269	119	33	0.91	4.02	-0.4
Age 31 Past Peak	99	ANA	* 395	47	95	19	57	1	241	253	239	$7	263	451	714	3	81	0.16	281	128	41	0.82	3.86	-3.4
Bats R	00	TOR	* 176	23	45	11	22	1	256	260	200	$4	296	472	767	5	82	0.32	284	115	43	0.93	4.96	3.8
Pwr +	01	NYY	* 227	22	48	6	24	3	211	250	200	$1	232	335	567	3	83	0.15	256	78	61	0.79	2.49	-9.7
Spd No change	02	TEX	* 389	48	103	22	68	2	265	271	266	$15	283	491	774	3	84	0.16	300	144	52	0.67	4.91	14.0
BAvg - -	1st Half		188	24	47	10	35	0	250			$6	262	463	725	2	85	0.10	297	135	35		4.16	2.5
LIMA D+	2nd Half		201	24	56	12	33	2	279			$9	303	517	820	3	83	0.21	303	152	50		5.69	11.9
Risk X HIGH	03	Proj	250	29	62	11	36	2	248			$6	272	434	706	3	83	0.20	280	116	52		4.07	-0.0

10-19-.268 in 112 AB at TEX. Looks like he finally learned how to hit, but that's deceptive. Hacked his way to big power numbers, but a .283 OB avg helped nobody. I would not invest draft $ on a follow-up.

Green,Shawn

Green,Shawn	Yr	Tm	AB	R	H	HR	RBI	SB	Avg	vLH	vRH	R$	OB	Slg	OPS	bb%	ct%	Eye	xBA	PX	SX	G/F	RC/G	RAR
Pos RF	98	TOR	630	106	175	35	100	35	278	221	299	$33	331	510	840	7	77	0.35	284	135	128	1.39	6.02	17.0
Age 30 Past Peak	99	TOR	614	134	190	42	123	20	309	280	320	$37	376	588	964	10	81	0.56	310	165	97	1.55	8.42	65.0
Bats L	00	LA	610	98	164	24	99	24	269	259	273	$24	363	472	835	13	80	0.74	286	126	114	1.34	6.51	25.4
Pwr -	01	LA	619	121	184	49	125	20	297	298	297	$41	370	598	968	10	83	0.67	317	167	120	1.27	8.45	55.0
Spd - - - - -	02	LA	582	110	166	42	114	8	285	270	291	$32	384	558	942	14	81	0.83	293	157	68	1.78	8.05	51.0
BAvg No change	1st Half		288	60	81	25	63	4	281			$18	377	601	977	13	78	0.70	296	180	82		8.54	29.7
LIMA C+	2nd Half		294	50	85	17	51	4	289			$14	391	517	908	14	83	1.00	288	135	49		7.57	21.2
Risk Low	03	Proj	600	111	177	40	113	15	295			$35	382	558	940	12	81	0.75	298	153	90		8.12	63.0

Somewhat of an anomaly. A big power hitter with a ground ball tendency. Look at his pct of fly balls hit for extra bases:

'00	31%	| Bonds	31%
'01	31%	| ARod	28%
'02	35%	| MLB avg	23%

Greer,Rusty

Greer,Rusty	Yr	Tm	AB	R	H	HR	RBI	SB	Avg	vLH	vRH	R$	OB	Slg	OPS	bb%	ct%	Eye	xBA	PX	SX	G/F	RC/G	RAR
Pos LF DH	98	TEX	598	107	183	16	108	2	306	337	293	$21	388	455	843	12	84	0.86	276	93	74	1.25	6.83	32.6
Age 34 Decline	99	TEX	556	107	167	20	101	2	300	282	306	$20	403	493	896	15	88	1.43	305	121	67	1.39	7.83	49.6
Bats L	00	TEX	394	65	117	8	65	4	297	245	314	$12	378	459	837	11	85	0.84	290	108	93	1.47	6.76	19.9
Pwr - -	01	TEX	245	38	67	7	29	1	273	233	286	$6	346	453	799	10	87	0.84	294	125	45	1.41	5.68	7.5
Spd No change	02	TEX	* 216	27	64	1	18	1	296	293	298	$4	364	375	739	10	90	1.10	266	59	77	1.81	5.34	2.8
BAvg No change	1st Half		198	24	59	1	17	1	298			$4	359	379	738	9	91	1.12	269	59	80		5.31	2.3
LIMA C+	2nd Half		18	3	5	0	1	0	278			$0	409	333	742	18	78	1.00	223	51	33		5.65	0.5
Risk Moderate	03	Proj	200	31	59	4	27	1	295			$6	372	436	808	11	88	0.99	285	98	67		6.25	7.2

Neck surgery to fuse two vertebrae together, hip surgery... these are not things that make us feel all warm and fuzzy about his future prospects. Some skill still remains but he's only for the high risk-takers.

Grieve,Ben

Grieve,Ben	Yr	Tm	AB	R	H	HR	RBI	SB	Avg	vLH	vRH	R$	OB	Slg	OPS	bb%	ct%	Eye	xBA	PX	SX	G/F	RC/G	RAR
Pos RF	98	OAK	583	94	168	18	89	2	288	253	309	$17	379	458	837	13	79	0.69	266	111	56	2.08	6.67	28.9
Age 26 Pre-Peak	99	OAK	486	80	129	28	86	4	265	156	297	$16	350	481	831	11	78	0.58	270	123	62	1.42	6.31	19.4
Bats L	00	OAK	594	92	166	27	104	3	279	268	285	$19	358	487	845	11	78	0.56	276	124	62	1.51	6.61	30.3
Pwr + + + +	01	TAM	542	72	143	11	72	7	264	293	253	$12	366	387	753	14	71	0.55	222	82	76	2.13	5.48	7.3
Spd No change	02	TAM	482	62	121	19	64	8	251	221	262	$14	345	432	776	13	75	0.57	256	121	64	2.08	5.52	6.2
BAvg No change	1st Half		263	31	67	9	37	3	255			$7	333	433	767	11	76	0.48	261	125	54		5.36	2.0
LIMA A+	2nd Half		219	31	54	10	27	5	247			$7	358	429	787	15	74	0.67	249	116	60		5.69	4.2
Risk Low	03	Proj	500	69	130	18	71	7	260			$14	355	433	788	13	75	0.58	250	111	70		5.78	8.7

As long as he continues with his strong ground ball tendency, those big power numbers are not coming back. All other indicators are fairly stable.

Griffey Jr.,Ken

Griffey Jr.,Ken	Yr	Tm	AB	R	H	HR	RBI	SB	Avg	vLH	vRH	R$	OB	Slg	OPS	bb%	ct%	Eye	xBA	PX	SX	G/F	RC/G	RAR
Pos CF	98	SEA	633	120	180	56	146	20	284	299	279	$41	361	611	972	11	81	0.63	322	184	105	0.71	8.22	68.3
Age 33 Decline	99	SEA	606	123	173	48	134	24	285	229	307	$38	379	576	955	13	82	0.84	313	159	111	0.77	8.23	68.3
Bats L	00	CIN	520	100	141	40	118	6	271	263	274	$26	383	556	939	15	78	0.80	291	156	79	0.69	7.93	61.7
Pwr No change	01	CIN	364	57	104	22	65	2	286	254	303	$16	363	533	896	11	80	0.61	291	143	72	0.92	7.35	39.8
Spd No change	02	CIN	197	17	52	8	23	1	264	217	285	$5	356	426	782	12	80	0.72	254	97	19	0.92	5.52	3.5
BAvg No change	1st Half		74	6	18	2	4	0	243			$0	333	378	712	12	82	0.77	257	88	19		4.40	-1.4
LIMA A	2nd Half		123	11	34	6	19	1	276			$5	369	455	824	13	79	0.69	253	102	21		6.27	5.2
Risk Low	03	Proj	450	59	122	25	71	4	271			$17	362	485	847	12	80	0.71	275	124	49		6.48	30.7

You can still see glimmers of that old skill set, hiding behind his achy knee, quad, hamstring and attitude. All need fixing. This projection is a reasonable upside if he's healthy.

Grissom,Marquis

Grissom,Marquis	Yr	Tm	AB	R	H	HR	RBI	SB	Avg	vLH	vRH	R$	OB	Slg	OPS	bb%	ct%	Eye	xBA	PX	SX	G/F	RC/G	RAR
Pos CF LF	98	MIL	542	57	147	10	60	13	271	253	278	$14	302	382	684	4	86	0.31	275	80	76	1.55	4.01	-6.3
Age 36 Decline	99	MIL	603	92	161	20	83	24	267	322	245	$20	322	415	737	8	82	0.45	270	91	100	1.29	4.90	9.3
Bats R	00	MIL	595	67	145	14	62	20	244	304	228	$11	290	351	641	6	83	0.39	262	64	90	1.48	3.49	-16.7
Pwr + + +	01	LA	448	56	99	21	60	7	221	254	207	$9	248	404	652	3	76	0.15	257	105	86	1.31	3.22	-9.4
Spd - -	02	LA	343	57	95	17	60	5	277	293	267	$15	321	510	831	6	80	0.32	286	139	127	1.14	5.97	10.4
BAvg - -	1st Half		151	25	40	10	30	3	265			$7	319	517	836	7	79	0.39	283	147	73		6.06	5.1
LIMA B	2nd Half		192	32	55	7	30	2	286			$7	322	505	827	5	81	0.27	288	132	155		5.89	5.3
Risk High	03	Proj	350	50	90	15	52	4	257			$10	297	449	746	5	80	0.28	273	113	100		4.61	2.3

First positive RAR in 3 seasons and a rising power trend (in LA!) from a 36-y/o. Will the wonders never cease? Quite likely they will. Bid $10 -- anything else is gravy.

Grudzielanek,Mark

Grudzielanek,Mark	Yr	Tm	AB	R	H	HR	RBI	SB	Avg	vLH	vRH	R$	OB	Slg	OPS	bb%	ct%	Eye	xBA	PX	SX	G/F	RC/G	RAR
Pos 2B	98	2NL	589	62	160	10	62	18	272	264	274	$16	302	362	664	4	88	0.36	273	63	88	1.65	3.96	-4.2
Age 32 Past Peak	99	LA	488	72	159	7	46	6	326	389	299	$15	366	436	803	6	87	0.48	275	72	92	1.66	6.05	25.9
Bats R	00	LA	617	101	172	7	49	12	279	250	290	$11	328	389	717	7	87	0.56	280	73	124	1.81	4.75	5.6
Pwr - - -	01	LA	539	83	146	13	55	4	271	295	264	$11	307	393	700	5	85	0.34	267	74	88	1.49	4.26	5.2
Spd No change	02	LA	536	56	145	9	50	4	271	257	274	$9	299	364	663	4	83	0.25	250	63	57	1.39	3.92	-9.2
BAvg - -	1st Half		261	28	64	4	27	1	245			$2	278	345	623	4	82	0.26	250	70	48		3.37	-8.8
LIMA C	2nd Half		275	28	81	5	23	3	295			$7	319	382	701	4	84	0.23	249	56	52		4.51	0.0
Risk Low	03	Proj	525	67	140	9	49	3	267			$8	301	372	673	5	85	0.32	261	68	69		3.97	-2.1

Since 1999, it's been a 3-year decline in most of his BPIs, and he's once again dropped below replacement value. The good news is his future is now easy to project. The bad news is you don't want it on your team.

Guerrero,Vladimir		Tm	AB	R	H	HR	RBI	SB	Avg	vLH	vRH	R$	OB	Slg	OPS	bb%	ct%	Eye	xBA	PX	SX	G/F	RC/G	RAR
Pos RF	98	MON	623	108	202	38	109	11	324	339	321	$39	367	589	956	6	85	0.44	318	166	112	1.36	8.04	57.8
Age 27 Peak	99	MON	610	102	193	42	131	14	316	287	324	$38	373	600	973	8	90	0.89	336	165	96	1.17	8.45	63.6
Bats R	00	MON	571	101	197	44	123	9	345	376	336	$41	405	664	1069	9	87	0.78	338	173	123	1.29	10.31	91.1
Pwr No change	01	MON	599	107	184	34	108	37	307	319	304	$42	370	566	936	9	85	0.68	321	155	127	1.39	7.65	37.3
Spd -----	02	MON	614	106	206	39	111	40	336	290	347	$52	415	593	1008	12	89	1.20	321	152	95	1.13	9.37	79.0
BAvg -	1st Half		306	48	101	18	55	17	330			$24	404	562	966	11	91	1.31	317	135	86		8.59	31.3
LIMA C+	2nd Half		308	58	105	21	56	23	341			$29	427	623	1050	13	87	1.12	324	168	99		10.18	48.2
Risk Very Low	03	Proj	600	106	197	42	112	32	328			$47	399	613	1012	11	87	0.92	329	166	108		9.19	82.1

The best player in the game right now, and at 27, still many years to cruise at or near this level. It's almost scary. Note 2nd half PX bumps up his HR projection a bit; SX takes a bite out of his SB total.

Guerrero,Wilton		Tm	AB	R	H	HR	RBI	SB	Avg	vLH	vRH	R$	OB	Slg	OPS	bb%	ct%	Eye	xBA	PX	SX	G/F	RC/G	RAR
Pos 2B	98	2NL	*523	60	142	3	34	16	272	325	273	$10	298	358	656	4	86	0.28	270	56	160	1.62	3.86	-5.2
Age 28 Peak	99	MON	315	42	92	2	31	7	292	330	275	$7	320	403	723	4	88	0.34	282	71	146	3.06	4.50	1.9
Bats R	00	MON	288	30	77	2	23	8	267	292	253	$5	313	326	639	6	86	0.46	254	37	99	2.98	3.84	-5.4
Pwr No change	01	CIN	369	34	110	1	30	15	298	250	383	$12	322	369	691	3	89	0.31	267	53	96	2.88	4.23	3.2
Spd +++++	02	2NL	140	12	31	0	5	7	221	136	260	$0	259	250	509	5	77	0.22	214	19	116	2.07	2.36	-9.0
BAvg No change	1st Half		75	9	17	0	3	2	227			($0)	284	253	537	7	83	0.46	227	12	123		2.54	-4.6
LIMA D	2nd Half		65	3	14	0	2	5	215			$1	227	246	473	2	71	0.05	198	27	83		2.14	-4.4
Risk Very High	03	Proj	150	13	37	0	9	7	247			$2	278	294	572	4	82	0.23	235	32	107		2.95	-5.2

Batting average finally caught up with his BPI levels. Even with those 30% of hackers that manage to maintain their BA, the risk of falling is much higher than for those with better skills.

Guiel,Aaron		Tm	AB	R	H	HR	RBI	SB	Avg	vLH	vRH	R$	OB	Slg	OPS	bb%	ct%	Eye	xBA	PX	SX	G/F	RC/G	RAR
Pos RF	98	aaa	183	23	46	4	22	4	251			$4	322	399	721	9	78	0.48	262	99	111		4.68	-2.3
Age 30 Past Peak	99	aaa	257	36	50	9	31	4	195			$1	286	385	671	11	66	0.38	231	124	83		3.55	-12.7
Bats L	00	aaa	258	34	64	10	30	5	248			$5	314	422	737	9	83	0.57	282	103	86		4.88	-2.0
Pwr No change	01	aaa	442	56	99	15	53	5	224			$6	281	387	668	7	83	0.46	273	100	77		3.62	-23.9
Spd --	02	KC	*455	62	120	11	75	7	264	169	254	$13	323	389	712	8	80	0.44	252	86	73	1.40	4.44	-9.6
BAvg --	1st Half		238	39	74	8	47	6	311			$12	376	471	847	10	85	0.69	280	105	91		6.89	13.3
LIMA D	2nd Half		217	23	46	3	28	1	212			$1	263	300	562	6	75	0.27	222	65	48		2.49	-17.5
Risk Very High	03	Proj	100	13	24	3	14	1	240			$2	301	374	675	8	80	0.43	253	88	58		3.89	-4.2

4-38-.233 in 240 AB at KC. Batted .438 in his first 10 games after callup, but just .202 in his remaining 208 AB. Guess it's back to Omaha.

Guillen,Carlos		Tm	AB	R	H	HR	RBI	SB	Avg	vLH	vRH	R$	OB	Slg	OPS	bb%	ct%	Eye	xBA	PX	SX	G/F	RC/G	RAR
Pos SS	98	SEA	*505	73	132	12	52	5	261	286	344	$8	313	388	701	7	84	0.47	268	77	100	0.77	4.42	6.6
Age 27 Peak	99	SEA	0	0	0	0	0	0	0								0					1.17		
Bats S	00	SEA	*375	64	98	9	53	5	261	320	244	$7	333	400	733	10	81	0.56	263	84	103	1.24	4.78	3.2
Pwr +++	01	SEA	456	72	118	5	53	4	259	295	243	$6	336	355	691	10	80	0.60	246	64	98	1.30	4.47	0.1
Spd No change	02	SEA	475	73	124	9	56	4	261	221	275	$9	326	394	720	9	81	0.51	258	89	112	1.06	4.56	-1.7
BAvg No change	1st Half		229	46	68	7	36	3	297			$9	374	485	858	11	83	0.70	285	122	140		6.74	15.2
LIMA B	2nd Half		246	27	56	2	20	1	228			$0	280	309	589	7	79	0.35	233	58	81		2.94	-13.1
Risk Moderate	03	Proj	450	69	116	12	52	4	258			$9	325	405	730	9	81	0.52	263	92	105		4.71	12.9

Stable BPIs are showing little growth. Warning signs in '02... Struggles vs LHers and 2nd half dive, although the latter was impacted by a knee bruise, a strained thigh muscle and a twisted ankle. I think that's all.

Guillen,Jose		Tm	AB	R	H	HR	RBI	SB	Avg	vLH	vRH	R$	OB	Slg	OPS	bb%	ct%	Eye	xBA	PX	SX	G/F	RC/G	RAR
Pos RF	98	PIT	573	60	153	14	84	3	267	275	265	$14	293	414	707	4	83	0.21	277	105	55	2.02	4.17	-14.2
Age 26 Pre-Peak	99	2TM	*454	73	127	11	60	1	280	256	240	$10	327	412	739	7	82	0.40	265	88	49	1.55	4.90	-2.5
Bats R	00	TAM	*394	55	110	17	64	3	279	195	275	$12	321	497	818	6	81	0.33	292	125	116	1.37	5.74	8.6
Pwr --	01	TAM	*254	30	70	9	37	2	276	375	252	$7	300	437	737	3	80	0.18	259	101	45	1.88	4.51	-4.3
Spd No change	02	CIN	*286	30	71	10	40	4	248	252	226	$7	286	399	684	5	83	0.31	264	93	50	1.95	3.68	-14.9
BAvg -	1st Half		121	12	28	4	15	3	231			$2	268	355	623	5	82	0.27	250	72	60		2.86	-9.2
LIMA D	2nd Half		165	18	43	6	25	1	261			$4	299	430	729	5	84	0.33	273	108	41		4.36	-5.2
Risk Very High	03	Proj	150	17	39	5	22	2	260			$4	295	419	714	5	82	0.28	269	100	50		4.15	-3.4

Not likely to gain much power with these G/F ratios. Not likely to gain much playing time with this OB avg trend.

Gutierrez,Ricky		Tm	AB	R	H	HR	RBI	SB	Avg	vLH	vRH	R$	OB	Slg	OPS	bb%	ct%	Eye	xBA	PX	SX	G/F	RC/G	RAR
Pos 2B	98	HOU	491	55	128	2	46	13	261	287	252	$8	334	334	668	10	83	0.64	257	58	92	2.85	4.09	-1.7
Age 32 Past Peak	99	HOU	268	33	70	1	25	2	261	379	223	$2	351	336	687	12	83	0.82	251	45	105	2.91	4.23	-0.6
Bats R	00	CHC	449	73	124	11	56	8	276	356	256	$12	369	401	770	13	87	1.14	281	76	87	2.17	5.73	18.8
Pwr ----	01	CHC	528	76	153	10	66	4	290	258	300	$14	340	402	741	7	89	0.71	280	71	79	2.13	5.07	18.3
Spd No change	02	CLE	353	38	97	4	38	0	275	371	242	$6	314	346	659	5	86	0.42	248	52	30	2.14	3.93	-2.1
BAvg --	1st Half		226	18	56	2	9	0	248			$0	280	301	581	4	86	0.32	238	39	22		2.96	-7.8
LIMA C	2nd Half		127	20	41	2	29	0	323			$5	372	425	797	7	87	0.59	265	76	43		6.05	7.6
Risk Moderate	03	Proj	450	61	122	10	61	1	271			$9	329	384	712	8	87	0.66	266	74	46		4.56	5.1

Recovering from neck surgery, so any projection now is only speculative.
Allegedly moving to 3B in 2003.

Guzman,Cristian		Tm	AB	R	H	HR	RBI	SB	Avg	vLH	vRH	R$	OB	Slg	OPS	bb%	ct%	Eye	xBA	PX	SX	G/F	RC/G	RAR
Pos SS	98	aa	566	69	162	1	41	23	286			$14	312	359	670	4	81	0.20	251	57	116		3.94	1.6
Age 25 Pre-Peak	99	MIN	420	47	95	1	26	9	226	296	200	($1)	265	276	541	5	79	0.24	227	34	105	3.15	2.42	-23.2
Bats S	00	MIN	631	89	156	8	54	28	247	209	261	$11	298	388	687	7	84	0.46	277	78	224	1.99	4.05	-8.9
Pwr ---	01	MIN	493	80	149	10	51	25	302	312	299	$21	331	477	807	4	84	0.27	295	104	205	1.65	5.79	19.5
Spd -----	02	MIN	623	80	170	9	59	12	273	257	281	$14	292	385	677	3	87	0.22	271	78	111	2.04	3.73	-17.3
BAvg --	1st Half		324	36	83	4	30	6	256			$6	270	343	612	2	89	0.17	263	60	92		2.86	-17.1
LIMA A+	2nd Half		299	44	87	5	29	6	291			$9	316	431	748	4	86	0.26	280	98	132		4.83	1.4
Risk Moderate	03	Proj	600	84	166	9	56	24	277			$18	305	407	712	4	85	0.27	276	84	167		4.35	9.8

Battled a knee inflammation at the onset of the season, and you can bet that affected his numbers all year. Still, he did improve his contact rate, which he needs to do to fuel any future growth.

Hairston Jr.,Jerry		Tm	AB	R	H	HR	RBI	SB	Avg	vLH	vRH	R$	OB	Slg	OPS	bb%	ct%	Eye	xBA	PX	SX	G/F	RC/G	RAR
Pos 2B	98	aa	228	41	67	5	34	6	294			$9	346	425	771	7	89	0.72	292	86	114		5.33	8.3
Age 26 Pre-Peak	99	BAL	*588	86	158	11	61	27	269	333	257	$17	313	396	709	6	88	0.53	287	83	122	1.42	4.29	4.3
Bats R	00	BAL	*381	66	99	9	38	13	260	244	259	$8	343	383	726	11	87	0.94	275	76	94	1.44	4.66	8.8
Pwr ++	01	BAL	532	63	124	8	47	29	233	290	216	$11	292	344	636	8	86	0.60	272	72	125	1.06	3.48	-13.4
Spd ++	02	BAL	426	55	114	5	32	21	268	263	269	$13	322	376	697	7	87	0.62	272	80	124	0.96	4.45	4.3
BAvg No change	1st Half		166	18	40	1	13	9	241			$4	288	307	595	6	84	0.41	244	54	95		3.23	-4.5
LIMA A+	2nd Half		260	37	74	4	19	12	285			$9	343	419	762	8	89	0.82	290	96	134		5.35	9.9
Risk High	03	Proj	500	68	139	10	44	30	278			$19	336	401	737	8	87	0.66	278	83	120		5.00	12.4

His PX and G/F trends are interesting, and might boost his HR output. After three stagnant seasons, 2nd half surge might indicate some growth in 2003.

Hall,Toby		Tm	AB	R	H	HR	RBI	SB	Avg	vLH	vRH	R$	OB	Slg	OPS	bb%	ct%	Eye	xBA	PX	SX	G/F	RC/G	RAR
Pos CA	98		0	0	0	0	0	0	0								0							
Age 27 Peak	99	aa	173	15	38	8	27	1	220			$2	233	399	632	2	95	0.38	317	105	37		3.00	-5.5
Bats R	00	a/a	455	46	133	13	66	2	292			$13	316	437	754	3	93	0.48	305	92	36	1.00	5.02	11.6
Pwr --	01	TAM	*561	80	174	22	93	3	310	298	298	$23	345	510	855	5	94	0.86	320	129	48	0.96	6.47	42.7
Spd No change	02	TAM	*422	48	114	8	58	0	270	200	272	$9	303	386	689	5	91	0.56	285	83	41	1.03	4.18	6.1
BAvg -	1st Half		247	24	59	4	33	0	239			$3	268	336	605	4	91	0.45	274	71	29		3.12	-4.2
LIMA B+	2nd Half		175	24	55	4	25	0	314			$6	351	457	808	5	92	0.71	299	100	57		6.02	12.3
Risk X HIGH	03	Proj	450	54	132	13	67	0	293			$14	324	446	771	4	93	0.63	302	102	36		5.24	15.8

6-42-.258 in 330 AB at TAM, but that was .187 before his wake-up call and a robust .309 after. There's a definite .300 hitter here, and some nice pop potential. Look at '01 as an upside, but probably not in '03.

Halter,Shane

	Tm	AB	R	H	HR	RBI	SB	Avg	vLH	vRH	R$	OB	Slg	OPS	bb%	ct%	Eye	xBA	PX	SX	G/F	RC/G	RAR
Pos SS 3B	98 KC	* 301	28	69	3	23	5	229	320	163	$1	268	322	590	5	83	0.31	254	67	70	1.22	2.77	-11.1
Age 33 Decline	99 aaa	474	52	94	4	24	13	198			($3)	262	266	528	8	80	0.43	238	46	87		2.11	-26.7
Bats R	00 DET	238	26	62	3	27	5	261	286	245	$4	302	366	667	6	79	0.29	247	68	102	1.29	3.92	-4.2
Pwr +	01 DET	450	53	128	12	65	3	284	291	282	$13	339	467	805	8	78	0.37	265	115	102	1.07	5.77	18.3
Spd No change	02 DET	410	46	98	10	39	0	239	243	238	$4	305	395	700	9	78	0.42	255	102	87	1.22	4.11	-7.2
BAvg No change	1st Half	190	20	45	3	18	0	237			$1	296	353	649	8	77	0.36	238	79	77		3.54	-6.7
LIMA B	2nd Half	220	26	53	7	21	0	241			$3	313	432	745	9	78	0.48	270	123	107		4.64	-0.2
Risk Very High	03 Proj	300	34	75	7	32	2	250			$4	308	400	708	8	78	0.39	257	97	98		4.26	4.3

Soft skills set does not merit all the playing time they've been giving him. After his '02 season, 400 AB is going to become a distant memory.

Hammonds,Jeffrey

	Tm	AB	R	H	HR	RBI	SB	Avg	vLH	vRH	R$	OB	Slg	OPS	bb%	ct%	Eye	xBA	PX	SX	G/F	RC/G	RAR
Pos CF RF	98 2TM	257	50	72	6	39	8	280	262	280	$9	375	428	803	13	78	0.70	264	100	117	0.94	6.15	12.9
Age 32 Past Peak	99 CIN	262	43	73	17	41	3	279	300	254	$11	346	523	869	9	76	0.42	270	142	47	0.95	6.19	14.8
Bats R	00 COL	454	94	152	20	106	14	335	378	323	$29	394	529	922	9	82	0.53	285	114	102	0.94	8.10	52.5
Pwr ++	01 MIL	174	20	43	6	21	5	247	237	250	$5	303	425	728	7	76	0.33	260	111	94	0.98	4.39	2.4
Spd No change	02 MIL	448	47	115	9	41	4	257	298	247	$6	334	397	731	10	81	0.60	259	91	84	0.99	4.73	-3.4
BAvg No change	1st Half	254	27	70	5	26	2	276			$5	343	417	760	9	80	0.52	258	91	82		4.99	0.2
LIMA B	2nd Half	194	20	45	4	15	2	232			$1	323	371	694	12	81	0.72	261	89	87		4.41	-3.5
Risk Moderate	03 Proj	400	47	101	10	50	2	253			$7	325	399	725	10	79	0.52	259	94	68		4.54	1.9

Check out the power trend. Gaze over at the speed trend. Make note of the 2nd half fade. Remember the injury history. Assess the risk level. Consult your draft budget. ...and pass.

Hansen,Dave

	Tm	AB	R	H	HR	RBI	SB	Avg	vLH	vRH	R$	OB	Slg	OPS	bb%	ct%	Eye	xBA	PX	SX	G/F	RC/G	RAR
Pos 1B	98 JPN	400	42	101	11	55	0	253			$7	324	373	696	10	78	0.47	242	75	30		4.41	-14.6
Age 34 Decline	99 LA	107	14	27	2	17	0	252	267	250	$1	398	402	800	20	81	1.30	271	102	53	1.17	6.32	3.5
Bats L	00 LA	121	18	35	8	26	0	289		310	$6	415	570	985	18	74	0.81	276	155	93	1.57	9.06	15.2
Pwr --	01 LA	140	13	33	2	20	0	236	100	246	$1	378	350	728	19	79	1.10	250	83		1.28	5.04	-6.6
Spd No change	02 LA	120	15	35	2	17	1	292	125	304	$4	366	392	757	10	82	0.64	246	69	43	1.34	5.61	-0.4
BAvg --	1st Half	63	6	15	1	13	1	238			$1	304	349	654	9	81	0.50	250	79	46		3.89	-3.6
LIMA D	2nd Half	57	9	20	1	4	0	351			$2	431	439	869	12	82	0.80	241	57	27		8.04	4.3
Risk Low	03 Proj	150	19	42	2	22	0	280			$3	384	366	750	14	80	0.83	241	63	32		5.53	0.8

This is the type of guy that NEVER gets drafted, but ultimately ALWAYS ends up on someone's roster because he poses no threat to a team's BA. Note that there is some BPI decline now, so be cautious.

Harris,Lenny

	Tm	AB	R	H	HR	RBI	SB	Avg	vLH	vRH	R$	OB	Slg	OPS	bb%	ct%	Eye	xBA	PX	SX	G/F	RC/G	RAR
Pos LF	98 2NL	290	30	75	6	27	6	259	263	258	$6	300	372	672	6	93	0.81	299	82	60	1.82	3.80	-9.7
Age 38 Decline	99 2NL	187	17	58	1	20	2	310	412	300	$5	332	396	727	3	96	0.86	301	69	44	1.72	4.90	-1.4
Bats L	00 2NL	223	31	58	4	26	13	260	158	270	$7	321	381	702	8	90	0.91	288	69	161	2.04	4.72	-4.2
Pwr ++	01 NYM	135	12	30	0	9	3	222		226	($0)	266	274	540	6	93	0.89	272	38	91	2.15	2.44	-13.8
Spd No change	02 MIL	197	23	60	3	17	4	305	467	291	$6	351	411	762	7	91	0.82	281	67	97	1.83	5.54	-5.8
BAvg -	1st Half	66	6	15	1	3	1	227			($0)	261	318	579	4	88	0.38	263	62	56		2.69	-7.5
LIMA C+	2nd Half	131	17	45	2	14	3	344			$7	394	458	852	8	93	1.22	289	70	112		7.53	4.1
Risk X HIGH	03 Proj	200	22	54	2	17	5	270			$4	316	365	681	6	92	0.82	282	61	103		4.21	-3.3

Ditto the above on almost all counts, but this surprising 2nd half at age 38 sure put the brakes on his descent into retirement. Might even be worth drafting now.

Harris,Willie

	Tm	AB	R	H	HR	RBI	SB	Avg	vLH	vRH	R$	OB	Slg	OPS	bb%	ct%	Eye	xBA	PX	SX	G/F	RC/G	RAR
Pos 2B	98	0	0	0	0	0	0	0								0							
Age 24 Growth	99	0	0	0	0	0	0	0								0							
Bats L	00	0	0	0	0	0	0	0								0							
Pwr ---	01 aa	549	76	145	8	43	48	264			$22	316	361	677	7	87	0.57	269	63	129		4.07	-0.7
Spd ++	02 CHW	* 523	62	133	7	41	36	254	237	232	$18	307	342	650	7	85	0.53	254	60	122	1.55	3.68	-7.1
BAvg No change	1st Half	287	36	75	4	20	21	261			$10	318	362	681	8	83	0.50	253	68	139		3.92	-1.8
LIMA B+	2nd Half	236	26	58	3	21	15	246			$7	294	318	611	6	88	0.57	255	52	98		3.38	-5.3
Risk High	03 Proj	350	44	90	5	28	26	257			$12	309	347	656	7	86	0.55	261	60	123		3.80	-4.3

2-12-8-.233 in 163 AB at CHW. Another one with phenomenal speed but first base an elusive concept. History does show some potential, but imagine how many SBs he could get with even a .350 OB avg!

Haselman,Bill

	Tm	AB	R	H	HR	RBI	SB	Avg	vLH	vRH	R$	OB	Slg	OPS	bb%	ct%	Eye	xBA	PX	SX	G/F	RC/G	RAR
Pos CA	98 TEX	105	11	33	6	17	0	314	405	264	$5	333	543	876	3	84	0.18	291	136		1.18	6.82	8.4
Age 36 Decline	99 DET	143	13	39	4	14	2	273	308	260	$3	320	413	733	7	82	0.38	262	90	44	1.59	4.92	3.4
Bats R	00 TEX	193	23	53	6	26	0	275	286	272	$4	327	461	788	7	81	0.42	285	123	30	1.30	5.41	7.0
Pwr --	01 TEX	* 158	14	41	3	26	0	259	318	267	$3	299	354	654	5	77	0.25	225	62	24	1.52	3.70	-1.1
Spd No change	02 TEX	179	16	44	3	18	0	246	362	205	$2	289	335	625	6	86	0.44	254	63	22	1.19	3.44	-1.4
BAvg -	1st Half	144	13	35	3	16	0	243			$2	292	347	639	6	88	0.59	266	72	21		3.60	-0.4
LIMA D	2nd Half	35	3	9	0	2	0	257			$0	278	286	563	3	77	0.13	206	26	28		2.80	-0.9
Risk High	03 Proj	150	15	40	4	20	0	267			$3	311	410	721	6	83	0.38	266	97	29		4.58	2.3

He used to be a good $1 end-game catcher because:
1. He had decent BPIs
2. Behind I-Rod, he'd never get enough AB to hurt you.
But now, no more on both counts.

Hatteberg,Scott

	Tm	AB	R	H	HR	RBI	SB	Avg	vLH	vRH	R$	OB	Slg	OPS	bb%	ct%	Eye	xBA	PX	SX	G/F	RC/G	RAR
Pos 1B DH	98 BOS	359	46	99	12	43	0	276	234	282	$8	353	446	799	11	84	0.74	279	109	33	1.60	5.93	2.1
Age 33 Decline	99 BOS	* 114	15	28	1	14	0	246	267	277	$0	363	333	696	16	83	1.11	250	66	27	1.38	4.68	-4.7
Bats L	00 BOS	230	21	61	8	36	0	265	189	280	$5	369	435	804	14	83	0.97	277	105		1.36	6.03	-0.3
Pwr +++	01 BOS	278	34	68	3	25	1	245	176	260	$1	325	345	670	11	91	1.27	275	76	40	1.55	4.08	-19.4
Spd No change	02 OAK	492	58	138	15	61	0	280	233	291	$13	368	433	801	12	89	1.21	286	98	49	1.24	6.11	2.1
BAvg +++++	1st Half	252	28	70	11	34	0	278			$8	366	464	830	12	89	1.25	296	111	58		6.46	4.0
LIMA B	2nd Half	240	30	68	4	27	0	283			$5	370	400	770	12	88	1.18	276	85	40		5.74	-1.9
Risk Very High	03 Proj	400	47	113	10	53	0	283			$10	370	421	791	12	88	1.13	280	93	43		5.98	4.3

With great BPIs and a chance for more P/T, we expected big things. For half a season he obliged, then the power tanked. Note that he's never really solved LHers, and that limits any further upside.

Helms,Wes

	Tm	AB	R	H	HR	RBI	SB	Avg	vLH	vRH	R$	OB	Slg	OPS	bb%	ct%	Eye	xBA	PX	SX	G/F	RC/G	RAR
Pos 1B 3B	98 aaa	451	50	118	11	67	5	262			$11	312	395	707	7	82	0.40	266	91	65	1.00	4.43	-15.7
Age 26 Pre-Peak	99 aa	113	12	29	6	20	1	257			$3	294	469	763	5	74	0.21	257	126	37		4.92	-2.5
Bats R	00 aaa	539	63	142	16	75	0	263			$10	294	417	711	4	86	0.30	282	91	59	1.00	4.10	-26.7
Pwr ---	01 ATL	216	28	48	10	36	1	222	203	234	$4	291	435	726	9	74	0.38	260	121	109	0.65	4.33	-13.9
Spd No change	02 ATL	210	20	51	6	22	1	243	167	269	$2	281	405	685	5	73	0.19	239	110	39	0.81	3.89	-11.5
BAvg --	1st Half	144	14	35	4	12	1	243			$1	278	396	674	5	76	0.20	245	102	44		3.86	-8.0
LIMA D+	2nd Half	66	6	16	2	10	0	242			$1	286	424	710	6	67	0.18	225	125	33		3.94	-3.5
Risk Very High	03 Proj	200	22	51	7	28	1	255			$4	300	434	734	6	74	0.25	251	113	57		4.49	-5.4

Could have stepped up and claimed the 1B job, but the skills are just not there. Poor eye, low OB avg, but they love those guys with a little power. HRs put fans in the seats, but OB avg puts up wins in the standings.

Helton,Todd

	Tm	AB	R	H	HR	RBI	SB	Avg	vLH	vRH	R$	OB	Slg	OPS	bb%	ct%	Eye	xBA	PX	SX	G/F	RC/G	RAR
Pos 1B	98 COL	530	78	167	25	98	3	315	304	318	$27	377	530	908	9	90	0.98	322	144	48	1.46	7.68	38.2
Age 29 Past Peak	99 COL	578	114	185	35	113	7	320	245	349	$32	392	587	978	11	87	0.88	321	159	91	0.96	8.80	62.7
Bats L	00 COL	580	138	216	42	147	5	372	329	387	$46	467	698	1165	15	89	1.69	361	197	69	1.08	13.96	166.1
Pwr No change	01 COL	587	132	197	49	146	7	336	290	354	$45	431	685	1115	14	82	0.94	336	207	76	0.96	11.78	105.7
Spd -	02 COL	553	107	182	30	109	5	329	327	331	$34	431	577	1008	15	84	1.09	301	150	88	1.02	10.22	84.1
BAvg --	1st Half	289	55	99	16	60	4	343			$21	440	612	1052	15	84	1.06	311	162	117		11.33	54.4
LIMA C+	2nd Half	264	52	83	14	49	1	314			$14	422	538	960	16	83	1.11	288	136	42		9.10	30.3
Risk Very Low	03 Proj	575	119	192	37	124	5	334			$38	430	617	1047	14	85	1.10	319	171	77		10.78	104.0

An off year by his standards, but only because he set the bar so darn high. The skills set is still superb and he still plays half his games in COL, so a rebound is always possible.

Henderson,Rickey

			Tm	AB	R	H	HR	RBI	SB	Avg	vLH	vRH	R$	OB	Slg	OPS	bb%	ct%	Eye	xBA	PX	SX	G/F	RC/G	RAR
Pos	LF	98	OAK	542	101	128	14	57	66	236	256	228	$26	373	347	720	18	79	1.04	249	66	122	1.09	5.33	3.5
Age	44 Decline	99	NYM	438	89	138	12	42	37	315	343	306	$25	423	466	889	16	81	1.00	273	102	96	1.12	7.87	40.4
Bats	R	00	2TM	420	75	98	4	32	36	233	200	242	$11	366	305	671	17	82	1.17	246	46	122	1.07	4.47	-11.4
Pwr	- - - - -	01	SD	* 419	74	95	8	44	26	227	210	235	$11	353	346	699	16	78	0.88	250	76	134	1.13	4.70	-15.9
Spd	- -	02	BOS	179	40	40	5	16	8	223	200	245	$4	359	352	711	18	74	0.81	231	81	127	1.41	4.88	-0.3
BAvg	+ + + + +	1st Half		115	24	27	3	13	5	235			$3	338	365	704	14	73	0.58	230	82	142		4.67	-1.0
LIMA	C+	2nd Half		64	16	13	2	3	3	203			$1	393	328	721	24	75	1.25	233	79	87		5.19	0.6
Risk	High	03	Proj	**200**	**41**	**45**	**5**	**17**	**7**	**225**			**$3**	**368**	**345**	**713**	**18**	**77**	**0.98**	**241**	**77**	**106**		**4.81**	**-2.2**

His consistently great batting eye keeps him valuable despite the low BA. Speed skills are not gone either -- projecting a full season at his current pace, he'd still swipe over 30. SX backs that up.

Hermansen,Chad

			Tm	AB	R	H	HR	RBI	SB	Avg	vLH	vRH	R$	OB	Slg	OPS	bb%	ct%	Eye	xBA	PX	SX	G/F	RC/G	RAR
Pos	CF	98	aaa	458	67	117	24	65	18	255			$19	319	487	806	9	77	0.40	281	144	121		5.66	14.8
Age	25 Pre-Peak	99	PIT	* 556	72	134	26	74	16	241	278	214	$15	285	441	725	6	80	0.30	277	120	88	1.25	4.07	-5.5
Bats	R	00	PIT	* 402	49	78	11	38	13	194	188	183	$1	241	323	565	6	72	0.23	234	77	116	0.81	2.55	-22.7
Pwr	No change	01	PIT	* 502	65	107	16	55	18	213	167	162	$8	262	367	628	6	72	0.23	238	91	136	0.68	3.18	-11.4
Spd	-	02	2NL	* 293	34	59	11	25	8	201	178	214	$2	273	375	649	9	66	0.29	219	107	90	0.64	3.35	-14.9
BAvg	+ + +	1st Half		213	26	43	9	21	8	202			$3	270	385	655	9	67	0.29	225	109	107		3.47	-10.0
LIMA	D+	2nd Half		80	8	16	2	4	0	200			($1)	281	350	631	10	63	0.30	202	103	38		3.03	-4.9
Risk	X HIGH	03	Proj	**150**	**18**	**31**	**5**	**14**	**4**	**207**			**$1**	**270**	**372**	**642**	**8**	**69**	**0.28**	**230**	**102**	**103**		**3.25**	**-5.3**

Shall we rename it the Hermanson Line? He's giving Mario Mendoza a run for his money. PIT finally gave up on him, but then came the Cubs, thinking they could find what the Pirates could not. Silly.

Hernandez,Jose

			Tm	AB	R	H	HR	RBI	SB	Avg	vLH	vRH	R$	OB	Slg	OPS	bb%	ct%	Eye	xBA	PX	SX	G/F	RC/G	RAR
Pos	SS	98	CHC	488	76	124	23	75	4	254	255	254	$15	311	471	782	8	71	0.29	255	135	124	1.66	5.00	19.9
Age	33 Decline	99	2NL	508	79	135	19	62	11	266	292	253	$14	334	425	759	9	71	0.36	237	95	94	1.50	5.24	26.3
Bats	R	00	MIL	446	51	109	11	59	3	244	212	255	$6	308	372	680	8	72	0.33	234	81	48	1.99	3.88	4.9
Pwr	No change	01	MIL	542	67	135	25	78	5	249	339	226	$14	299	443	742	7	66	0.21	225	114	72	1.43	4.59	15.9
Spd	No change	02	MIL	525	72	151	24	73	3	288	253	296	$20	352	478	830	9	64	0.28	213	112	57	1.68	6.14	35.7
BAvg	- -	1st Half		266	37	77	13	40	2	289			$11	357	496	853	10	62	0.27	209	120	81		6.47	20.9
LIMA	C+	2nd Half		259	35	74	11	33	1	286			$9	346	459	806	8	67	0.28	217	105	36		5.82	14.9
Risk	Low	03	Proj	**500**	**66**	**124**	**20**	**64**	**2**	**248**			**$10**	**310**	**422**	**732**	**8**	**67**	**0.27**	**221**	**104**	**57**		**4.51**	**11.8**

Check out his xBA trend. Despite his peaking power skills, there is a huge downside. His run at the strikeout record was not an isolated feat, more likely symptomatic of a larger problem. Expect a decline in '03.

Hernandez,Ramon

			Tm	AB	R	H	HR	RBI	SB	Avg	vLH	vRH	R$	OB	Slg	OPS	bb%	ct%	Eye	xBA	PX	SX	G/F	RC/G	RAR
Pos	CA	98	aa	479	64	127	11	75	3	265			$11	324	384	709	8	91	0.93	287	80	55		4.46	6.1
Age	26 Pre-Peak	99	OAK	* 427	46	109	14	68	2	255	357	245	$8	315	405	720	8	90	0.88	289	89	53	1.24	4.54	5.2
Bats	R	00	OAK	419	52	101	14	62	1	241	243	240	$5	304	387	691	8	85	0.59	273	87	42	1.26	4.20	-0.4
Pwr	-	01	OAK	453	55	115	15	60	1	254	241	261	$9	310	408	719	8	85	0.54	271	98	36	1.45	4.52	8.2
Spd	No change	02	OAK	403	51	94	7	42	0	233	257	224	$3	307	335	642	10	84	0.67	255	74	33	1.45	3.71	0.2
BAvg	+ + + + +	1st Half		204	21	45	4	22	0	221			$1	274	324	598	7	85	0.50	258	72	29		3.07	-3.9
LIMA	B	2nd Half		199	30	49	3	20	0	246			$2	339	347	686	12	83	0.82	253	75	37		4.40	4.6
Risk	Low	03	Proj	**400**	**51**	**107**	**14**	**54**	**1**	**268**			**$10**	**334**	**421**	**755**	**9**	**85**	**0.66**	**274**	**98**	**33**		**5.18**	**13.9**

His added plate patience did not help his power skills any, but with stable BPIs everywhere else, and the nagging injuries he had, this was probably an isolated aberration.

Hidalgo,Richard

			Tm	AB	R	H	HR	RBI	SB	Avg	vLH	vRH	R$	OB	Slg	OPS	bb%	ct%	Eye	xBA	PX	SX	G/F	RC/G	RAR
Pos	RF	98	HOU	211	31	64	7	35	3	303	313	298	$9	355	474	829	7	82	0.46	284	121	57	1.15	6.16	7.6
Age	27 Peak	99	HOU	383	49	87	15	56	8	227	224	228	$7	326	420	746	13	81	0.77	280	121	78	0.79	4.79	-3.9
Bats	R	00	HOU	558	118	175	44	122	13	314	333	308	$37	376	636	1012	9	80	0.51	319	186	104	0.58	9.04	66.5
Pwr	-	01	HOU	512	70	141	19	80	3	275	286	273	$16	345	455	800	10	79	0.50	268	109	66	0.72	5.66	-0.2
Spd	No change	02	HOU	388	54	91	15	48	6	235	263	228	$7	311	415	726	10	78	0.51	261	106	112	0.76	4.58	-10.2
BAvg	+ + +	1st Half		271	46	73	13	41	5	269			$10	344	483	828	10	79	0.54	274	124	121		6.19	6.8
LIMA	A+	2nd Half		117	8	18	2	7	1	154			($3)	233	256	489	9	76	0.43	230	63	75		1.93	-12.8
Risk	Moderate	03	Proj	**500**	**67**	**136**	**22**	**73**	**6**	**272**			**$17**	**342**	**470**	**812**	**10**	**79**	**0.50**	**270**	**118**	**88**		**5.84**	**14.8**

You can write him off if you want, but the 1st half shows that his skills are still there. A July sprained wrist began the downward spiral from which he never recovered. A new venue (Coors?) could do wonders.

Higginson,Bobby

			Tm	AB	R	H	HR	RBI	SB	Avg	vLH	vRH	R$	OB	Slg	OPS	bb%	ct%	Eye	xBA	PX	SX	G/F	RC/G	RAR
Pos	LF	98	DET	612	92	174	25	85	3	284	277	288	$19	351	480	832	9	83	0.62	289	120	70	1.00	6.25	21.3
Age	32 Past Peak	99	DET	377	51	90	12	46	4	239	265	231	$5	349	382	731	15	82	0.97	263	88	43	0.74	4.75	-5.3
Bats	L	00	DET	597	104	179	30	102	15	300	264	316	$27	377	538	915	11	83	0.75	309	141	110	0.69	7.85	51.0
Pwr	- -	01	DET	541	84	150	17	71	20	277	293	271	$20	370	445	816	13	88	1.23	293	102	110	0.74	6.05	23.5
Spd	- - - -	02	DET	444	50	125	10	63	12	282	241	299	$16	342	417	759	8	90	0.91	288	93	94	0.82	5.27	4.8
BAvg	No change	1st Half		208	24	60	5	30	7	288			$8	359	452	811	10	93	1.53	311	110	120		6.18	8.2
LIMA	A+	2nd Half		236	26	65	5	33	5	275			$7	327	386	712	7	87	0.60	268	77	60		4.54	-2.9
Risk	Low	03	Proj	**500**	**68**	**140**	**15**	**71**	**13**	**280**			**$18**	**354**	**439**	**792**	**10**	**88**	**0.92**	**290**	**102**	**92**		**5.74**	**9.7**

He became more aggressive at the plate and it did him no good. OB avg and power dropped, especially in the 2nd half. He needs to go back to his game. He's got great skills if he uses then properly.

Hillenbrand,Shea

			Tm	AB	R	H	HR	RBI	SB	Avg	vLH	vRH	R$	OB	Slg	OPS	bb%	ct%	Eye	xBA	PX	SX	G/F	RC/G	RAR
Pos	3B	98		0	0	0	0	0	0	0								0							
Age	27 Peak	99	aa	282	33	65	6	29	5	230			$2	259	344	603	4	91	0.46	289	75	69		2.80	-14.1
Bats	R	00	aa	529	60	147	7	62	3	278			$9	297	384	680	3	93	0.37	293	72	64		4.01	-6.7
Pwr	+ + + +	01	BOS	468	52	123	12	49	3	263	227	277	$8	283	391	674	3	87	0.21	270	80	61	1.55	3.77	-9.4
Spd	No change	02	BOS	634	94	186	18	83	4	293	269	299	$20	320	459	779	4	85	0.26	287	114	91	1.50	5.38	15.5
BAvg	- -	1st Half		309	44	94	13	49	2	304			$13	328	511	839	3	83	0.20	292	137	82		6.21	15.1
LIMA	B	2nd Half		325	50	92	5	34	2	283			$7	313	409	722	4	87	0.34	281	93	91		4.65	0.9
Risk	High	03	Proj	**600**	**79**	**171**	**14**	**70**	**4**	**285**			**$15**	**309**	**424**	**733**	**3**	**88**	**0.28**	**283**	**93**	**76**		**4.67**	**1.3**

A sabermetric nightmare, but xBA says there is enough contact, power and speed to support his numbers. Power tanked in the 2nd half which tempers our expectations for growth in '03.

Hill,Bobby

			Tm	AB	R	H	HR	RBI	SB	Avg	vLH	vRH	R$	OB	Slg	OPS	bb%	ct%	Eye	xBA	PX	SX	G/F	RC/G	RAR
Pos	2B	98		0	0	0	0	0	0	0								0							
Age	25 Pre-Peak	99		0	0	0	0	0	0	0								0							
Bats	S	00		0	0	0	0	0	0	0								0							
Pwr	+ +	01	aa	209	25	54	2	17	16	258			$7	340	330	671	11	83	0.74	247	47	102		3.95	-1.1
Spd	+ + + + +	02	CHC	* 544	82	131	10	47	26	241	327	225	$12	307	358	666	9	84	0.58	265	76	133	1.83	3.95	-9.4
BAvg	+ + +	1st Half		251	38	55	3	17	13	219			$2	297	303	600	10	82	0.61	247	53	135		3.25	-10.0
LIMA	A+	2nd Half		293	44	76	7	30	13	259			$9	315	406	722	8	85	0.56	281	96	124		4.61	1.0
Risk	High	03	Proj	**500**	**69**	**124**	**8**	**43**	**25**	**248**			**$11**	**320**	**348**	**668**	**10**	**84**	**0.65**	**259**	**65**	**113**		**3.90**	**-3.2**

4-20-6-.253 in 190 AB at CHC. The Cubs' future 2Bman has an intriguing skills set. He could surely develop into a major speed source and on base skills are coming, but the road will have bumps. Be careful in '03.

Hinch,A.J.

			Tm	AB	R	H	HR	RBI	SB	Avg	vLH	vRH	R$	OB	Slg	OPS	bb%	ct%	Eye	xBA	PX	SX	G/F	RC/G	RAR
Pos	CA	98	OAK	337	34	78	9	35	3	231			$3	294	341	636	8	74	0.34	223	66	45	1.12	3.51	-6.1
Age	28 Peak	99	OAK	* 266	33	64	8	29	6	241	224	212	$4	276	361	637	5	79	0.23	246	67	93	1.12	3.44	-5.6
Bats	R	00	aaa	417	58	99	6	42	5	237			$2	304	333	637	9	85	0.63	262	64	72	4.00	3.52	-8.3
Pwr	No change	01	KC	* 289	31	67	14	40	2	232	194	141	$6	272	429	701	5	82	0.31	273	118	42	1.02	3.97	0.3
Spd	No change	02	KC	197	25	49	7	27	3	249	276	231	$5	312	401	713	8	82	0.51	265	95	77	0.94	4.28	3.6
BAvg	No change	1st Half		110	13	26	5	19	1	236			$3	300	409	709	8	85	0.63	278	99	80		4.04	1.2
LIMA	D	2nd Half		87	12	23	2	8	2	264			$2	326	391	717	8	78	0.42	248	90	67		4.60	2.5
Risk	Very High	03	Proj	**150**	**19**	**37**	**5**	**18**	**2**	**247**			**$3**	**303**	**393**	**696**	**7**	**81**	**0.43**	**261**	**93**	**56**		**4.12**	**0.2**

There are worse skills sets, but between intermittent play, assorted injuries and bouncing around from team to team, he's never gotten the stable environment he needs to develop.

Hinske,Eric

	Yr	Tm	AB	R	H	HR	RBI	SB	Avg	vLH	vRH	R$	OB	Slg	OPS	bb%	ct%	Eye	xBA	PX	SX	G/F	RC/G	RAR
Pos 3B	98		0	0	0	0	0	0	0								0							
Age 25 Pre-Peak	99	aaa	15	3	4	1	2	0	267			$0	313	600	913	6	73	0.25	294	158	353		6.71	1.0
Bats L	00	aa	436	70	100	17	67	13	229			$10	338	418	756	14	69	0.54	240	106	141		5.10	9.5
Pwr No change	01	aaa	436	56	106	20	62	16	243			$15	311	438	749	9	79	0.48	271	117	84		4.63	0.9
Spd +++++	02	TOR	566	99	158	24	84	13	279	202	301	$23	365	481	846	12	76	0.56	267	134	106	1.04	6.78	40.8
BAvg -	1st Half		259	48	76	14	44	5	293			$13	386	544	930	13	75	0.60	283	166	93		8.27	31.6
LIMA A	2nd Half		307	51	82	10	40	8	267			$10	348	427	775	11	76	0.52	253	107	101		5.64	10.7
Risk Very High	03	Proj	550	86	147	21	80	18	267			$21	350	453	803	11	76	0.53	262	117	108		5.89	22.8

Prognosis for sophomore year: Subject exceeded expectations in 1st half based on historical trends. 2nd half performance tailed as league adjusted. Area of concern: BA vsLH. Net result and projection still very positive.

Hocking,Denny

	Yr	Tm	AB	R	H	HR	RBI	SB	Avg	vLH	vRH	R$	OB	Slg	OPS	bb%	ct%	Eye	xBA	PX	SX	G/F	RC/G	RAR
Pos 2B SS	98	MIN	198	32	40	3	15	2	202	158	220	($1)	262	288	550	7	78	0.36	235	54	102	1.71	2.56	-9.4
Age 33 Decline	99	MIN	386	47	103	7	41	11	267	242	279	$8	306	378	685	5	86	0.41	270	71	95	1.27	4.00	-0.5
Bats S	00	MIN	373	52	111	4	47	7	298	278	305	$10	378	416	793	11	79	0.62	254	78	103	1.40	5.98	24.5
Pwr --	01	MIN	327	34	82	3	25	6	251	222	260	$3	312	339	651	8	80	0.43	240	62	87	1.34	3.90	-4.0
Spd No change	02	MIN	260	28	65	2	25	0	250	342	212	$2	313	323	636	8	83	0.55	242	59	31	1.35	3.58	-4.4
BAvg No change	1st Half		163	17	40	2	19	0	245			$2	320	319	639	10	82	0.60	235	54	29		3.67	-2.3
LIMA D	2nd Half		97	11	25	0	6	0	258			$0	301	330	631	6	86	0.43	255	67	45		3.41	-2.1
Risk Low	03	Proj	250	29	64	2	22	0	256			$2	317	344	661	8	82	0.49	246	66	51		3.86	-2.7

Peaked in 2000. No indication that there will be any further draft value.

Hollandsworth,Todd

	Yr	Tm	AB	R	H	HR	RBI	SB	Avg	vLH	vRH	R$	OB	Slg	OPS	bb%	ct%	Eye	xBA	PX	SX	G/F	RC/G	RAR
Pos LF RF	98	LA	175	23	47	3	20	4	269	286	264	$4	304	400	704	5	76	0.21	249	82	170	1.97	4.17	-3.8
Age 30 Past Peak	99	LA	261	39	74	9	32	5	284	310	280	$8	344	448	792	8	77	0.39	256	100	96	1.68	5.72	4.6
Bats L	00	2NL	428	81	115	19	47	18	269	250	272	$16	333	449	781	9	77	0.41	264	106	99	1.35	5.37	0.6
Pwr +++	01	COL	117	21	43	6	19	5	368	158	408	$9	408	667	1075	6	83	0.40	334	194	121	1.68	11.62	20.8
Spd -----	02	2TM	430	55	122	16	67	8	284	228	292	$16	345	463	807	9	77	0.41	260	117	65	1.71	5.65	-1.0
BAvg --	1st Half		228	30	67	9	38	5	294			$9	351	487	838	8	75	0.36	260	129	55		5.82	0.7
LIMA A	2nd Half		202	25	55	7	29	3	272			$5	338	436	773	9	79	0.48	260	103	75		5.44	-1.8
Risk Very High	03	Proj	450	68	120	13	65	8	267			$12	325	437	761	8	79	0.40	272	113	90		5.03	-6.2

Always had a soft skill set, but drafters stayed with him for years after his ROY season. 117 AB in COL gave rise to that misplaced fascination again. No longer hits LHers. Won't bat .300. Can't be owned without great injury risk.

Houston,Tyler

	Yr	Tm	AB	R	H	HR	RBI	SB	Avg	vLH	vRH	R$	OB	Slg	OPS	bb%	ct%	Eye	xBA	PX	SX	G/F	RC/G	RAR
Pos 3B	98	CHC	255	26	65	9	33	2	255	263	254	$6	291	396	687	5	79	0.25	257	87	58	1.40	3.97	-4.1
Age 32 Past Peak	99	CLE	276	28	62	10	30	1	225	333	125	$2	303	377	680	10	72	0.40	229	88	47	1.26	4.00	-4.5
Bats L	00	MIL	284	30	71	18	43	2	250	182	256	$8	292	493	785	6	75	0.24	271	139	34	1.04	5.01	5.2
Pwr --	01	MIL	235	36	68	12	38	0	289	280	290	$9	340	472	812	7	74	0.29	244	102	31	1.25	6.00	9.6
Spd No change	02	2NL	320	34	90	7	40	1	281	259	283	$8	315	428	744	5	81	0.26	261	96	77	1.32	4.96	2.6
BAvg --	1st Half		196	23	67	7	32	1	342			$11	371	541	912	4	84	0.29	288	125	76		7.98	19.3
LIMA D+	2nd Half		124	11	23	0	8	0	185			($3)	229	250	479	5	75	0.23	219	49	70		1.90	-10.4
Risk Low	03	Proj	250	29	64	8	32	1	256			$5	300	411	711	6	76	0.27	249	95	55		4.38	-1.3

Hit .464 in June, boosting his trade value, then could not hit a lick once dealt to LA. Soft skills and erratic playing time will likely prevent him from getting into many grooves again.

Hubbard,Trenidad

	Yr	Tm	AB	R	H	HR	RBI	SB	Avg	vLH	vRH	R$	OB	Slg	OPS	bb%	ct%	Eye	xBA	PX	SX	G/F	RC/G	RAR
Pos RF	98	LA	* 238	32	68	9	20	10	286	366	254	$10	341	445	786	8	79	0.40	265	101	94	1.05	5.46	3.4
Age 36 Decline	99	LA	* 228	42	67	4	32	17	294	278	353	$11	364	408	772	10	80	0.56	258	77	117	1.29	5.52	3.1
Bats R	00	2TM	108	18	20	1	6	4	185	244	149	($1)	261	269	529	9	79	0.48	237	45	177	1.50	2.34	-9.5
Pwr ---	01	aaa	358	54	90	12	42	18	251			$12	337	422	758	11	85	0.87	287	101	126	2.00	4.87	-5.8
Spd -----	02	SD	* 158	23	36	3	12	11	228	204	213	$4	299	329	628	9	80	0.52	247	67	100	3.05	3.07	-11.6
BAvg +++	1st Half		91	14	20	3	7	8	220			$3	304	352	656	11	81	0.65	257	79	104		3.51	-5.5
LIMA C	2nd Half		67	9	16	0	5	3	239			$1	292	299	590	7	79	0.36	234	52	89		2.50	-6.0
Risk X HIGH	03	Proj	150	22	35	3	13	8	233			$3	305	351	656	9	81	0.55	258	75	120		3.46	-6.8

Follow his very marked G/F trend, which might indicate a sharp erosion of power skills, yet there is not a strong correlation in his PX scan. There's something here, but we haven't put our finger on it yet.

Huckaby,Ken

	Yr	Tm	AB	R	H	HR	RBI	SB	Avg	vLH	vRH	R$	OB	Slg	OPS	bb%	ct%	Eye	xBA	PX	SX	G/F	RC/G	RAR
Pos CA	98	aaa	150	14	27	1	9	0	180			($3)	250	247	497	9	86	0.67	255	47	62		1.97	-9.7
Age 32 Past Peak	99	aaa	355	30	84	1	28	0	237			($2)	253	296	549	2	92	0.29	270	46	38		2.55	-16.0
Bats R	00	aaa	243	22	55	3	23	2	226			($0)	248	309	557	3	90	0.29	272	53	67		2.51	-11.8
Pwr ----	01	a/a	367	32	91	3	33	1	248			$2	262	322	584	2	82	0.10	240	52	46		2.75	-10.8
Spd No change	02	TOR	* 354	34	85	3	28	0	240	274	237	$1	263	294	557	3	84	0.19	231	37	45	2.52	2.59	-11.5
BAvg --	1st Half		145	11	35	0	12	0	241			$0	281	262	543	5	80	0.28	209	19	29		2.45	-5.4
LIMA F	2nd Half		209	23	50	3	16	0	239			$1	250	316	566	1	87	0.11	248	50	59		2.68	-6.1
Risk X HIGH	03	Proj	150	14	36	1	12	0	240			$0	262	299	562	3	85	0.20	239	43	41		2.61	-6.4

No power, no speed, no plate patience, hits everything on the ground, doesn't get on base, and nowhere is he ever referred to as a "defensive specialist." He is employed for what reason, exactly?

Hudson,Orlando

	Yr	Tm	AB	R	H	HR	RBI	SB	Avg	vLH	vRH	R$	OB	Slg	OPS	bb%	ct%	Eye	xBA	PX	SX	G/F	RC/G	RAR
Pos 2B	98		0	0	0	0	0	0	0								0							
Age 25 Pre-Peak	99		0	0	0	0	0	0	0								0							
Bats S	00	aa	134	13	29	2	12	2	216			($0)	276	321	597	8	90	0.79	276	60	105		2.93	-5.3
Pwr ---	01	a/a	500	70	144	7	67	16	288			$17	353	438	791	9	87	0.79	294	99	144		5.74	25.5
Spd ----	02	TOR	* 609	70	168	12	53	6	276	184	308	$13	319	419	738	6	89	0.56	288	99	94	1.25	4.71	11.0
BAvg -	1st Half		348	45	100	8	28	6	287			$10	333	417	750	6	91	0.73	288	90	73		4.98	9.1
LIMA A+	2nd Half		261	25	68	4	25	0	261			$3	301	421	722	5	86	0.41	288	110	115		4.37	2.0
Risk Very High	03	Proj	500	59	144	11	53	8	288			$14	340	449	789	7	88	0.65	294	104	116		5.53	20.4

4-23-.276 in 192 AB at TOR. BPIs took a slight step back at these higher levels, but there's the beginnings of something intriguing here. Could bat .300 one day, and if he's allowed to run, he might pile up some SBs.

Huff,Aubrey

	Yr	Tm	AB	R	H	HR	RBI	SB	Avg	vLH	vRH	R$	OB	Slg	OPS	bb%	ct%	Eye	xBA	PX	SX	G/F	RC/G	RAR
Pos 1B	98		0	0	0	0	0	0	0								0							
Age 26 Pre-Peak	99	aa	491	70	136	19	64	2	277			$13	345	479	824	9	87	0.81	305	129	55		6.03	5.8
Bats L	00	TAM	* 530	66	148	19	70	1	279	250	291	$12	333	470	803	8	87	0.61	302	119	43	1.54	5.62	-7.3
Pwr ++++	01	TAM	* 477	54	120	11	54	1	252	172	269	$6	292	390	682	5	84	0.35	264	93	43	2.04	3.92	-33.9
Spd No change	02	TAM	* 580	83	180	26	76	4	310	307	315	$25	362	503	865	7	89	0.71	306	127	55	1.31	7.02	18.6
BAvg --	1st Half		243	34	74	10	34	2	305			$10	357	486	843	8	91	0.87	307	120	49		6.59	4.6
LIMA A	2nd Half		337	49	106	16	42	2	315			$15	365	516	882	7	87	0.63	304	131	49		7.34	14.2
Risk High	03	Proj	500	66	154	24	73	2	308			$21	358	518	876	7	87	0.59	304	133	46		7.01	20.9

23-59-.313 in 454 AB at TAM. For real? Quite possibly. Contact rate and OB growth provide a solid foundation, power skills have always been there, and he's put 2001 out of his mind.

Hundley,Todd

	Yr	Tm	AB	R	H	HR	RBI	SB	Avg	vLH	vRH	R$	OB	Slg	OPS	bb%	ct%	Eye	xBA	PX	SX	G/F	RC/G	RAR
Pos CA	98	NYM	124	8	20	3	12	1	161	59	178	($2)	257	266	523	11	56	0.29	174	70	30	0.71	2.29	-6.8
Age 33 Decline	99	LA	376	49	78	24	55	3	207	105	226	$6	290	436	727	10	70	0.39	245	130	50	0.88	4.40	4.3
Bats S	00	LA	299	49	85	24	70	0	284	237	300	$15	378	579	957	13	77	0.65	293	165	21	0.83	8.21	40.7
Pwr +++	01	CHC	* 309	29	57	14	38	0	184	292	176	$0	254	362	617	9	63	0.25	207	104		0.93	3.08	-4.9
Spd No change	02	CHC	275	33	58	17	38	0	211	217	209	$4	295	425	721	11	71	0.41	234	119	17	0.78	4.36	1.4
BAvg +++	1st Half		123	15	26	8	21	0	211			$2	287	431	718	10	67	0.33	224	120	19		4.25	0.2
LIMA D+	2nd Half		152	18	32	9	17	0	211			$1	302	421	723	12	73	0.49	242	118	16		4.45	1.2
Risk High	03	Proj	200	24	45	12	29	0	225			$4	307	436	743	11	69	0.38	233	119	22		4.70	4.6

Has batted .197 over the past two years and still has a job. But the true feat is this... It's tough to hit nearly 20 HRs and have a negative impact on your team's success.

Hunter,Brian L.

Pos CF
Age 32 Past Peak
Bats R
Pwr - -
Spd + +
BAvg - -
LIMA C+
Risk Very High

	Tm	AB	R	H	HR	RBI	SB	Avg	vLH	vRH	R$	OB	Slg	OPS	bb%	ct%	Eye	xBA	PX	SX	G/F	RC/G	RAR
98	DET	595	67	151	4	36	42	254	264	251	$15	296	333	629	6	84	0.38	259	57	123	2.08	3.55	-23.4
99	SEA	539	79	125	4	34	44	232	186	243	$12	281	301	582	6	83	0.41	252	41	171	1.86	3.14	-27.3
00	2NL	240	47	64	1	14	20	267	223	295	$8	341	308	649	10	83	0.68	243	27	136	2.64	4.29	-0.9
01	PHI	145	22	40	2	16	14	276	232	303	$7	348	359	706	10	83	0.64	252	56	109	1.39	4.93	4.6
02	HOU	201	32	54	3	20	5	269	241	301	$5	323	423	745	7	81	0.41	272	105	150	1.55	5.13	1.0
1st Half		83	12	24	1	5	5	289			$3	306	422	728	2	77	0.11	255	91	156		5.04	0.2
2nd Half		118	20	30	2	15	0	254			$1	333	424	757	11	83	0.70	282	114	109		5.18	0.8
03	Proj	200	32	53	2	19	11	265			$6	327	377	703	8	82	0.50	262	75	145		4.69	1.9

I say, if you're not going to make use of his speed skills, which are still obviously good, then why bother? He provides little else on offense, though he does hit RHers well, but he's not getting any younger, you know.

Hunter,Torii

Pos CF
Age 27 Peak
Bats R
Pwr No change
Spd + + + +
BAvg - -
LIMA A
Risk Moderate

	Tm	AB	R	H	HR	RBI	SB	Avg	vLH	vRH	R$	OB	Slg	OPS	bb%	ct%	Eye	xBA	PX	SX	G/F	RC/G	RAR
98	a/a	417	51	116	9	48	12	278			$13	311	427	738	5	82	0.26	276	106	93	3.50	4.48	-1.8
99	MIN	384	52	98	9	35	10	255	295	239	$7	302	380	683	6	81	0.36	259	77	100	1.64	3.97	-9.7
00	MIN	* 545	89	164	19	91	13	301	241	292	$22	333	490	823	5	83	0.29	290	109	142	1.44	5.91	18.9
01	MIN	564	82	147	27	92	9	261	256	262	$19	297	479	776	5	78	0.23	273	129	106	1.36	4.88	-1.2
02	MIN	561	89	162	29	94	23	289	296	286	$31	331	524	855	6	79	0.30	290	151	128	1.50	6.26	23.6
1st Half		315	53	96	18	56	14	305			$20	350	562	912	7	78	0.31	293	163	138		7.35	23.8
2nd Half		246	36	66	11	38	9	268			$11	305	476	781	5	80	0.27	286	136	108		5.02	1.1
03	Proj	550	83	153	34	102	17	278			$28	316	542	858	5	80	0.28	300	159	114		6.01	18.4

Power growth is exciting, and at 27, can still go further. Lack of plate patience, however, will keep his ceiling lower than that of the elite sluggers. In other words, 30-35 HRs is doable; a '50-HR season is unlikely.

Hyzdu,Adam

Pos CF
Age 31 Past Peak
Bats R
Pwr + + +
Spd No change
BAvg + + +
LIMA D
Risk X HIGH

	Tm	AB	R	H	HR	RBI	SB	Avg	vLH	vRH	R$	OB	Slg	OPS	bb%	ct%	Eye	xBA	PX	SX	G/F	RC/G	RAR
98	aaa	100	14	29	3	10	0	290			$3	355	460	815	9	84	0.63	285	111	74		5.95	4.2
99	a/a	424	53	103	23	70	6	243			$12	299	469	768	7	80	0.41	285	133	74		4.81	2.7
00	aa	514	66	110	22	73	2	214			$5	301	409	710	11	77	0.55	269	116	51	1.00	4.12	-7.7
01	PIT	* 333	34	77	13	37	1	231	167	229	$4	269	402	671	5	77	0.22	255	102	46	0.92	3.45	-4.8
02	PIT	* 398	48	85	18	71	1	214	204	245	$6	290	399	690	10	76	0.45	251	112	35	0.60	3.95	-12.9
1st Half		239	23	48	7	37	1	201			$1	265	347	613	8	79	0.42	252	95	38		3.03	-14.4
2nd Half		159	25	37	11	34	0	233			$5	326	478	804	12	72	0.49	247	138	27		5.57	3.1
03	Proj	150	19	36	7	24	0	240			$3	309	428	736	9	76	0.42	255	112	35		4.55	0.8

11-34-.232 in 155 AB at PIT, but that was .389 in the first 52 of those AB, and .149 in the remaining 103 AB. That pretty much rules out any real future here.

Ibanez,Raul

Pos LF 1B DH
Age 30 Past Peak
Bats L
Pwr + + + +
Spd No change
BAvg - -
LIMA A
Risk X HIGH

	Tm	AB	R	H	HR	RBI	SB	Avg	vLH	vRH	R$	OB	Slg	OPS	bb%	ct%	Eye	xBA	PX	SX	G/F	RC/G	RAR
98	SEA	* 288	31	61	7	32	1	212	182	264	$0	275	351	625	8	77	0.37	248	88	72	1.18	3.33	-16.2
99	SEA	* 240	28	64	12	31	6	267	238	261	$0	318	450	768	7	84	0.46	279	103	64	1.13	5.24	0.5
00	SEA	* 180	24	41	2	21	2	228	333	221	$0	287	328	615	8	84	0.54	263	72	69	0.86	3.37	-10.2
01	KC	* 306	46	82	15	58	0	268	200	286	$10	339	487	826	10	81	0.56	278	122	92	1.03	5.93	11.7
02	KC	497	70	146	24	103	5	294	274	300	$24	346	537	884	7	85	0.53	315	158	104	1.06	6.87	29.8
1st Half		182	24	50	6	36	1	275			$6	327	500	827	7	86	0.56	319	155	111		5.86	5.2
2nd Half		315	46	96	18	67	4	305			$17	358	559	916	8	84	0.51	312	160	94		7.51	25.1
03	Proj	550	76	167	30	114	4	304			$27	360	550	909	8	83	0.52	305	149	90		7.45	39.7

Here's the thing... Given his history, 2001 looked more like a peak than an interim step. In retrospect, you can clearly see how the seeds for 2002 were planted. The peak is closer now; he could bat .300 in '03.

Inge,Brandon

Pos CA
Age 25 Pre-Peak
Bats S
Pwr + + + +
Spd No change
BAvg + + +
LIMA C
Risk Very High

	Tm	AB	R	H	HR	RBI	SB	Avg	vLH	vRH	R$	OB	Slg	OPS	bb%	ct%	Eye	xBA	PX	SX	G/F	RC/G	RAR
98		0	0	0	0	0	0	0								0							
99		0	0	0	0	0	0	0								0							
00	a/a	488	51	108	7	59	10	221			$3	271	344	615	6	81	0.36	264	83	98		3.14	-15.1
01	DET	* 279	22	58	1	27	2	208	218	164	($2)	248	305	553	5	79	0.25	242	77	58	1.18	2.39	-13.0
02	DET	* 386	36	82	9	36	2	212	229	195	$2	276	368	644	8	70	0.30	230	97	132	1.01	3.27	-5.0
1st Half		194	25	52	8	24	2	268			$6	336	510	847	9	74	0.40	271	143	208		5.72	12.4
2nd Half		192	11	30	1	12	0	156			($4)	214	224	438	7	67	0.22	192	52	52		1.52	-12.8
03	Proj	250	22	55	3	24	2	220			$0	272	344	616	7	75	0.28	237	85	94		3.06	-7.8

I know that overall offensive levels declined in '02, but I can't remember ever seeing so many Mendoza Line hitters getting so many AB. But my bottom line is: If he can't get on base at least 30% of the time, I'm not looking.

Izturis,Cesar

Pos SS
Age 23 Growth
Bats S
Pwr - -
Spd - - -
BAvg No change
LIMA B
Risk High

	Tm	AB	R	H	HR	RBI	SB	Avg	vLH	vRH	R$	OB	Slg	OPS	bb%	ct%	Eye	xBA	PX	SX	G/F	RC/G	RAR
98		0	0	0	0	0	0	0								0							
99		0	0	0	0	0	0	0								0							
00	aaa	435	51	100	0	25	20	230			$3	260	294	555	4	93	0.60	278	45	135		2.37	-21.3
01	TOR	* 476	49	138	4	42	30	290	200	288	$18	306	382	688	2	93	0.35	288	64	117	1.58	4.11	-4.9
02	LA	439	43	102	1	31	7	232	306	195	($0)	256	303	559	3	91	0.36	271	55	85	1.99	2.50	-19.1
1st Half		290	29	67	0	20	4	231			($1)	262	303	565	4	90	0.40	269	60	76		2.51	-12.7
2nd Half		149	14	35	1	11	3	235			$0	245	302	547	1	94	0.22	275	45	95		2.49	-6.4
03	Proj	450	46	123	2	34	13	273			$9	300	348	648	4	93	0.52	280	54	95		3.57	-2.4

With a 90%+ contact rate, you'd think that at least a few more scribblers would find their way through the infield. xBA clearly thinks so. And his speed game could surely use the lift. It should get better in '03.

Jackson,Damian

Pos 2B
Age 29 Past Peak
Bats R
Pwr + +
Spd - - - - -
BAvg No change
LIMA C+
Risk High

	Tm	AB	R	H	HR	RBI	SB	Avg	vLH	vRH	R$	OB	Slg	OPS	bb%	ct%	Eye	xBA	PX	SX	G/F	RC/G	RAR
98	CIN	* 555	92	135	5	50	23	243	273	333	$10	319	371	690	10	79	0.53	266	96	166	0.71	4.34	2.4
99	SD	388	56	87	9	39	34	224	188	240	$12	317	356	673	12	73	0.50	239	85	126	0.56	4.10	-2.6
00	SD	470	68	120	6	37	28	255	223	266	$12	342	377	719	12	77	0.57	251	79	149	0.99	4.92	7.1
01	SD	440	67	106	4	38	23	241	319	214	$9	310	343	653	9	71	0.34	225	66	172	0.94	3.89	-0.7
02	DET	245	31	63	1	25	12	257	217	270	$6	316	359	675	8	85	0.58	270	86	113	1.09	4.18	0.5
1st Half		138	19	36	1	19	6	261			$4	325	384	709	9	83	0.54	273	105	93		4.68	2.4
2nd Half		107	12	27	0	6	6	252			$2	304	327	631	7	89	0.67	264	60	124		3.59	-1.8
03	Proj	250	34	62	2	22	13	248			$6	315	350	665	9	80	0.49	252	75	130		4.06	-1.1

Consistent mediocrity. Worth a few bucks to roto players for his speed. For sim players, he's roster filler fodder.

Jenkins,Geoff

Pos LF
Age 28 Peak
Bats L
Pwr + +
Spd No change
BAvg -
LIMA A
Risk Low

	Tm	AB	R	H	HR	RBI	SB	Avg	vLH	vRH	R$	OB	Slg	OPS	bb%	ct%	Eye	xBA	PX	SX	G/F	RC/G	RAR
98	MIL	* 477	66	127	15	73	2	266	200	235	$13	314	423	737	6	80	0.35	269	103	82	1.48	4.71	-2.8
99	MIL	447	70	140	21	82	5	313	259	326	$21	363	564	927	7	81	0.40	299	162	88	1.28	7.88	37.6
00	MIL	512	100	155	34	94	11	303	283	309	$28	345	588	933	6	74	0.24	283	165	130	1.21	7.71	37.1
01	MIL	397	60	105	20	63	4	264	316	244	$14	326	474	799	8	70	0.30	244	123	73	1.10	5.55	-3.2
02	MIL	243	35	59	10	29	1	243	200	258	$4	306	444	750	8	75	0.37	258	127	66	1.44	4.67	-14.0
1st Half		243	35	59	10	29	1	243			$4	306	444	750	8	75	0.37	258	127	66		4.67	-14.0
2nd Half		0	0	0	0	0	0	0			($0)					0							-0.0
03	Proj	450	72	120	24	65	0	267			$14	321	505	826	7	75	0.32	269	145	58		5.76	14.0

Dislocated his ankle in June, ending what appeared NOT to be a rebound season from '01. At 28, there should still be something left. Batting eye was always weak, but he still owns those power skills.

Jeter,Derek

Pos SS
Age 28 Peak
Bats R
Pwr No change
Spd - -
BAvg - -
LIMA A
Risk Very Low

	Tm	AB	R	H	HR	RBI	SB	Avg	vLH	vRH	R$	OB	Slg	OPS	bb%	ct%	Eye	xBA	PX	SX	G/F	RC/G	RAR
98	NYY	626	127	203	19	84	30	324	345	318	$33	381	481	862	8	81	0.48	274	92	157	2.46	7.33	64.9
99	NYY	627	134	219	24	102	19	349	282	366	$36	432	552	984	13	81	0.78	291	120	141	1.63	9.79	113.6
00	NYY	593	119	201	15	73	22	339	395	321	$29	407	481	888	10	83	0.69	273	86	125	2.10	8.11	68.0
01	NYY	614	110	191	21	74	27	311	333	305	$30	369	480	849	8	84	0.57	282	105	118	1.96	7.05	49.7
02	NYY	644	124	191	18	75	32	297	315	292	$30	368	421	789	10	82	0.64	259	82	115	2.23	6.24	32.1
1st Half		335	58	103	11	39	19	307			$18	375	445	819	10	82	0.61	263	89	107		6.85	23.1
2nd Half		309	66	88	7	36	13	285			$12	361	395	756	11	82	0.67	254	75	112		5.63	9.4
03	Proj	600	107	174	17	73	27	290			$25	360	431	791	10	83	0.63	268	90	118		6.09	43.6

G/F and PX indicate perhaps that this is the best we're going to see from his power output. xBA suggests that there is some real downside to his BA. Don't be surprised to see some more decline in '03.

Jimenez,D'Angelo	Yr	Tm	AB	R	H	HR	RBI	SB	Avg	vLH	vRH	R$	OB	Slg	OPS	bb%	ct%	Eye	xBA	PX	SX	G/F	RC/G	RAR
Pos 2B 3B	98	a/a	496	78	139	10	74	12	280			$16	370	413	784	13	86	1.01	282	88	105		5.67	24.7
Age 25 Pre-Peak	99	aaa	526	83	164	12	75	22	312			$23	372	452	824	9	90	0.93	296	92	95	1.50	5.90	28.4
Bats S	00	aaa	73	10	16	1	4	1	219			($0)	278	288	566	8	81	0.43	238	43	67		2.70	-3.4
Pwr ++	01	SD	* 522	73	137	8	49	6	262	241	290	$8	338	368	706	10	82	0.64	256	72	61	1.51	4.37	7.2
Spd +++++	02	2TM	* 586	82	149	10	60	11	254	261	247	$10	337	375	712	11	85	0.85	268	77	124	1.65	4.65	6.4
BAvg +++	1st Half		296	37	70	2	29	4	236			$1	313	321	634	10	80	0.55	238	56	118		3.63	-6.4
LIMA A	2nd Half		290	45	79	8	31	7	272			$8	361	431	792	12	91	1.54	300	99	121		5.82	14.3
Risk X HIGH	03	Proj	450	66	126	9	50	10	280			$12	358	406	763	11	86	0.85	278	82	98		5.32	15.7

4-44-6-.252 in 429 AB at SD and CHW, but that was .240 in SD and .287 in his last 108 AB at CHW. Late surge is a good sign, and BPIs show promise. View 1999 as his upside, 2-3 years out.

Johnson,Charles	Yr	Tm	AB	R	H	HR	RBI	SB	Avg	vLH	vRH	R$	OB	Slg	OPS	bb%	ct%	Eye	xBA	PX	SX	G/F	RC/G	RAR
Pos CA	98	2NL	459	44	100	19	58	0	218	265	207	$5	288	381	669	9	72	0.35	238	105		0.71	3.74	-3.7
Age 31 Past Peak	99	BAL	426	58	107	16	54	0	251	355	234	$7	337	413	750	11	75	0.51	242	96	36	1.19	5.12	13.4
Bats R	00	2AL	421	76	128	31	91	2	304	252	324	$22	381	582	962	11	75	0.49	283	155	50	1.21	8.60	59.0
Pwr ++	01	FLA	451	51	117	18	75	0	259	245	261	$12	317	450	767	8	71	0.29	242	121	21	0.94	5.15	21.8
Spd No change	02	FLA	244	18	53	6	36	0	217	275	202	$1	305	369	674	11	75	0.51	241	105	10	1.25	4.00	-1.6
BAvg +++++	1st Half		139	11	31	3	17	0	223			$0	329	360	689	14	78	0.71	245	95	10		4.33	0.6
LIMA D+	2nd Half		105	7	22	3	19	0	210			$1	272	381	653	8	71	0.30	235	118	8		3.54	-2.1
Risk Moderate	03	Proj	300	31	72	11	50	0	240			$6	314	424	738	10	73	0.40	247	118	22		4.76	7.4

On 9/25, Mgr Jeff Torborg announced that CJ would be limited to 80 or 90 games in '03. He played in 83 this year, so that was a stretch. With these declining skills, minimizing the damage could be a good thing.

Johnson,Mark L.	Yr	Tm	AB	R	H	HR	RBI	SB	Avg	vLH	vRH	R$	OB	Slg	OPS	bb%	ct%	Eye	xBA	PX	SX	G/F	RC/G	RAR
Pos CA	98	aa	382	55	93	7	49	0	243			$4	381	348	729	18	84	1.39	260	69	45	0.56	5.17	15.0
Age 27 Peak	99	CHW	207	27	47	4	16	3	227	250	222	$0	342	338	680	15	72	0.62	224	74	55	1.18	4.32	1.2
Bats L	00	CHW	213	29	48	3	23	3	225	174	232	$0	313	319	632	11	81	0.68	248	64	65	0.90	3.63	-4.2
Pwr No change	01	CHW	* 369	42	92	9	39	4	249	179	262	$6	337	369	706	12	83	0.78	253	70	76	0.77	4.58	7.7
Spd No change	02	CHW	263	31	55	4	18	0	209	95	219	($1)	290	293	583	10	80	0.58	233	56	48	1.09	3.02	-5.7
BAvg +++++	1st Half		145	23	30	2	9	0	207			($1)	286	276	562	10	81	0.59	231	48	51		2.80	-4.1
LIMA D+	2nd Half		118	8	25	2	9	0	212			($0)	295	314	609	11	79	0.56	235	66	46		3.29	-1.5
Risk High	03	Proj	250	29	60	6	22	0	240			$2	327	362	689	11	81	0.67	248	76	46		4.31	1.9

Batted .311 in August, if you can believe it. But odds are that no team still had him on their roster to enjoy it. BPIs don't support a .209 BA, so that will rise, but probably not enough to make him much more valuable.

Johnson,Nick	Yr	Tm	AB	R	H	HR	RBI	SB	Avg	vLH	vRH	R$	OB	Slg	OPS	bb%	ct%	Eye	xBA	PX	SX	G/F	RC/G	RAR
Pos 1B	98		0	0	0	0	0	0	0								0							
Age 24 Growth	99	aa	420	100	132	12	77	7	314			$18	454	488	942	20	81	1.35	278	113	88		9.00	50.3
Bats L	00	NYY	0	0	0	0	0	0	0								0							
Pwr ----	01	NYY	* 426	64	99	19	50	8	232			$9	349	413	762	15	76	0.74	250	108	64		5.34	-13.3
Spd No change	02	NYY	389	57	93	15	58	1	239	175	257	$9	324	393	718	11	74	0.49	239	98	39	1.23	4.50	-18.5
BAvg No change	1st Half		238	32	56	11	40	1	235			$6	300	416	716	8	75	0.37	250	113	45		4.34	-12.2
LIMA C+	2nd Half		151	25	37	4	18	0	245			$2	360	358	717	15	73	0.66	221	73	39		4.67	-6.7
Risk Moderate	03	Proj	350	58	87	13	48	1	249			$7	359	406	765	15	76	0.71	244	98	41		5.34	-3.7

Probably not developing in the way the Yankees would have hoped. Fact is, he's proven nothing above AA ball. Great season in '99, since then, nada. He's not doing it at the MLB level, maybe a year in AAA?

Johnson,Russ	Yr	Tm	AB	R	H	HR	RBI	SB	Avg	vLH	vRH	R$	OB	Slg	OPS	bb%	ct%	Eye	xBA	PX	SX	G/F	RC/G	RAR
Pos 3B	98	aaa	466	72	118	5	38	9	253			$6	343	343	687	12	87	1.08	272	67	74		4.23	-4.5
Age 30 Past Peak	99	HOU	* 233	37	67	6	32	3	288	283	281	$7	374	429	803	12	82	0.76	270	96	48	1.21	5.72	9.6
Bats R	00	2TM	230	32	55	2	20	5	239	264	224	$1	319	300	619	11	83	0.68	243	42	72	1.15	3.53	-6.8
Pwr --	01	TAM	248	32	73	4	33	2	294	261	307	$7	379	435	815	12	77	0.60	249	98	72	0.99	6.32	15.1
Spd No change	02	TAM	* 187	28	40	3	18	7	214	208	218	$3	303	321	624	11	82	0.71	253	75	114	0.90	3.51	-6.3
BAvg +++++	1st Half		122	21	28	2	15	6	230			$3	333	336	669	13	82	0.86	255	79	97		4.30	-1.1
LIMA C	2nd Half		65	7	12	1	3	1	185			($0)	243	292	535	7	82	0.42	247	67	129		2.25	-4.6
Risk Very High	03	Proj	150	20	36	2	14	3	240			$2	321	352	673	11	81	0.63	253	77	93		4.05	-2.7

1-12-5-.216 in 111 AB at TAM. Decent plate patience, and has shown signs of some good on base ability, but it's been intermittent and inconsistent. He's not a .214 hitter, but he's not much more valuable at .250.

Jones,Andruw	Yr	Tm	AB	R	H	HR	RBI	SB	Avg	vLH	vRH	R$	OB	Slg	OPS	bb%	ct%	Eye	xBA	PX	SX	G/F	RC/G	RAR
Pos CF	98	ATL	582	89	158	31	90	27	271	312	259	$30	318	515	834	6	78	0.31	289	153	164	1.29	6.03	28.9
Age 26 Pre-Peak	99	ATL	592	97	163	26	84	24	275	271	277	$24	358	483	841	11	83	0.74	290	126	112	1.05	6.25	35.4
Bats R	00	ATL	656	122	199	36	104	21	303	313	301	$34	361	541	902	8	85	0.59	309	136	126	1.25	7.40	61.0
Pwr ++++	01	ATL	625	104	157	34	104	11	251	252	251	$22	313	461	774	8	77	0.39	269	119	98	1.11	5.11	23.0
Spd ---	02	ATL	560	91	148	35	94	8	264	228	270	$23	359	513	872	13	76	0.61	270	148	63	1.06	6.81	33.9
BAvg No change	1st Half		302	48	82	19	54	5	272			$14	371	517	888	14	77	0.69	272	144	63		7.37	24.0
LIMA A	2nd Half		258	43	66	16	40	3	256			$9	345	508	852	12	75	0.54	267	151	54		6.20	10.3
Risk High	03	Proj	600	100	170	42	122	2	283			$29	359	554	913	11	78	0.53	284	156	51		7.27	55.1

Signs of the impending breakout:
1. Marked improvement in plate patience.
2. Highest PX level since 1998
3. Speed game is no more, but that may mean improved focus.
4. He's 26. It's time.

Jones,Chipper	Yr	Tm	AB	R	H	HR	RBI	SB	Avg	vLH	vRH	R$	OB	Slg	OPS	bb%	ct%	Eye	xBA	PX	SX	G/F	RC/G	RAR
Pos LF	98	ATL	601	123	188	34	107	16	313	298	319	$36	407	547	955	14	85	1.03	307	146	113	1.44	8.79	77.5
Age 31 Past Peak	99	ATL	567	116	181	45	110	25	319	352	308	$41	443	633	1076	18	83	1.34	322	186	89	1.24	11.64	128.5
Bats S	00	ATL	579	118	180	36	111	14	311	415	281	$33	408	566	975	14	89	1.48	331	150	78	1.09	8.99	70.6
Pwr No change	01	ATL	572	113	189	38	102	9	330	376	320	$36	428	605	1033	15	86	1.20	320	157	89	1.26	10.09	81.9
Spd -----	02	ATL	548	90	179	26	100	8	327	320	328	$32	437	536	973	16	84	1.20	288	129	65	1.15	9.71	59.9
BAvg -	1st Half		295	48	94	9	51	5	319			$15	402	471	873	12	82	0.79	267	96	78		7.67	11.1
LIMA C+	2nd Half		253	42	85	17	49	3	336			$18	473	613	1086	21	85	1.78	312	167	39		12.33	53.0
Risk Moderate	03	Proj	575	105	187	34	106	7	325			$34	434	573	1008	16	85	1.31	308	148	65		10.03	103.5

Poor first half, by his standards, but was right back in business in the 2nd half. Expect him to come out for a full season in 2003.

Jones,Jacque	Yr	Tm	AB	R	H	HR	RBI	SB	Avg	vLH	vRH	R$	OB	Slg	OPS	bb%	ct%	Eye	xBA	PX	SX	G/F	RC/G	RAR
Pos LF	98	aa	518	73	147	20	80	16	284			$22	328	485	812	6	74	0.25	263	133	103		5.51	7.7
Age 28 Peak	99	MIN	* 520	81	147	12	66	10	283	222	297	$14	314	433	747	4	82	0.26	275	99	106	1.54	4.83	-5.4
Bats L	00	MIN	523	66	149	19	76	7	285	230	294	$16	319	463	781	5	79	0.23	267	103	99	2.07	5.26	1.0
Pwr +++	01	MIN	475	57	131	14	49	12	276	182	288	$14	331	417	748	8	81	0.42	256	90	60	2.12	4.85	1.9
Spd No change	02	MIN	577	96	173	27	85	6	300	213	333	$25	342	511	853	6	78	0.29	276	138	77	1.86	6.31	24.2
BAvg ---	1st Half		319	48	92	11	52	5	288			$13	332	470	803	6	80	0.32	274	122	94		5.59	6.4
LIMA A	2nd Half		258	48	81	16	33	1	314			$13	354	562	916	6	75	0.25	277	157	52		7.27	18.3
Risk Low	03	Proj	575	86	163	34	96	5	283			$24	327	526	853	6	78	0.30	283	147	63		6.01	15.4

Opened up his swing and pumped up the power, but still managed to improve his OB avg. He's not likely a .300 hitter long-term, especially since he hasn't yet solved LHers, but 30+ HRs is easy to project.

Jordan,Brian	Yr	Tm	AB	R	H	HR	RBI	SB	Avg	vLH	vRH	R$	OB	Slg	OPS	bb%	ct%	Eye	xBA	PX	SX	G/F	RC/G	RAR
Pos LF	98	STL	564	100	178	25	91	17	316	351	303	$32	361	534	895	7	88	0.61	319	141	138	1.23	7.37	42.5
Age 36 Decline	99	ATL	576	100	163	23	115	13	283	331	270	$24	341	465	807	8	86	0.63	293	110	102	1.16	5.73	10.4
Bats R	00	ATL	489	71	129	17	77	10	264	402	223	$14	317	421	738	7	84	0.48	281	97	80	1.15	4.88	-6.7
Pwr --	01	ATL	560	82	165	25	97	3	295	292	295	$23	332	496	828	5	84	0.35	293	121	75	1.05	6.06	4.3
Spd No change	02	LA	471	65	134	18	80	2	285	303	279	$17	333	469	802	7	82	0.40	273	113	70	1.17	5.71	-11.6
BAvg --	1st Half		252	44	72	12	40	1	286			$10	338	516	854	7	84	0.49	296	138	102		6.40	-0.9
LIMA B	2nd Half		219	21	62	6	40	1	283			$8	326	416	742	6	79	0.31	247	85	32		4.94	-10.5
Risk High	03	Proj	350	49	98	12	60	0	280			$11	326	452	778	6	83	0.40	276	106	58		5.32	6.1

Mar 22: Sore hamstring
May 3: Tendinitis in knee
May 14: Strained ribcage muscle
Jun 6: Chronic knee pain
Jul 4: Cramps from dehydration
Aug 9: Protruding disc in back
Sep 4: Lower back strain

Justice,David

	Yr	Tm	AB	R	H	HR	RBI	SB	Avg	vLH	vRH	R$	OB	Slg	OPS	bb%	ct%	Eye	xBA	PX	SX	G/F	RC/G	RAR
Pos LF DH RF	98	CLE	540	94	151	21	88	9	280	232	299	$19	369	476	844	12	82	0.78	288	125	87	1.12	6.66	26.5
Age 37 Decline	99	CLE	429	75	123	21	88	1	287	248	299	$16	415	476	890	18	79	1.04	262	109	29	1.36	7.73	38.3
Bats L	00	2AL	524	89	150	41	118	2	286	306	279	$25	378	584	962	13	83	0.85	319	166	48	0.95	8.36	54.4
Pwr No change	01	NYY	381	58	92	18	51	1	241	214	253	$8	336	430	766	12	78	0.65	257	110	47	1.20	5.18	5.7
Spd No change	02	OAK	398	54	106	11	49	4	266	257	270	$10	376	410	786	15	83	1.06	268	93	82	1.00	5.96	13.8
BAvg + + +	1st Half		149	25	40	4	18	2	268			$4	398	396	794	18	85	1.45	265	81	81		6.36	7.4
LIMA A	2nd Half		249	29	66	7	31	2	265			$6	362	418	780	13	82	0.86	269	101	72		5.72	6.4
Risk Moderate	03	Proj	400	60	106	17	59	3	265			$12	369	448	816	14	82	0.90	275	112	67		6.24	14.8

Power skills may have faded, but his solid plate patience continues to make him valuable. Note how his '00 power surge correlated with a big drop in G/F. There's gotta be something to that.

Kapler,Gabe

	Yr	Tm	AB	R	H	HR	RBI	SB	Avg	vLH	vRH	R$	OB	Slg	OPS	bb%	ct%	Eye	xBA	PX	SX	G/F	RC/G	RAR
Pos LF RF CF	98	aa	572	91	155	23	113	7	271			$21	336	479	815	9	85	0.67	307	135	103	0.38	5.88	15.3
Age 27 Peak	99	DET	*470	70	118	21	62	11	251	280	238	$12	324	468	792	10	82	0.61	296	127	125	1.15	5.33	2.3
Bats R	00	TEX	444	59	134	14	66	8	302	286	306	$16	362	473	835	9	87	0.74	298	108	70	1.22	6.47	17.7
Pwr +	01	TEX	483	77	129	17	72	23	267	269	266	$20	349	437	786	11	86	0.87	286	107	97	1.01	5.72	15.6
Spd + + + +	02	2TM	*332	42	95	3	38	12	286	250	293	$10	323	392	714	5	83	0.33	260	74	134	1.23	4.64	-10.8
BAvg - -	1st Half		171	21	45	0	14	5	263			$2	296	339	635	4	85	0.32	258	63	106		3.56	-11.1
LIMA A	2nd Half		161	21	50	3	24	7	311			$7	351	447	798	6	81	0.33	262	85	155		5.99	1.3
Risk Moderate	03	Proj	400	56	124	14	55	9	310			$17	364	490	854	8	84	0.54	291	112	95		6.72	15.4

While this power outage was striking, note that it was not an unreasonable point on his PX trend. Of course, a lingering wrist injury contributed as well. This is a plum. Expectations are low and he's hitting in COL.

Karros,Eric

	Yr	Tm	AB	R	H	HR	RBI	SB	Avg	vLH	vRH	R$	OB	Slg	OPS	bb%	ct%	Eye	xBA	PX	SX	G/F	RC/G	RAR
Pos 1B	98	LA	507	59	150	23	87	7	296	297	296	$23	356	475	831	8	82	0.51	278	113	61	0.87	6.42	16.3
Age 35 Decline	99	LA	578	74	176	34	112	8	304	308	303	$29	363	550	913	8	79	0.45	287	150	46	0.88	7.47	37.2
Bats R	00	LA	584	84	146	31	106	4	250	286	239	$17	323	459	782	10	79	0.52	278	121	48	0.66	5.27	-3.3
Pwr No change	01	LA	438	42	103	15	63	3	235	255	230	$7	301	388	689	9	77	0.41	251	95	43	0.95	4.13	-30.8
Spd No change	02	LA	524	52	142	13	73	4	271	317	260	$13	319	399	718	7	86	0.50	268	82	53	1.36	4.62	-17.5
BAvg -	1st Half		282	28	84	8	38	3	298			$10	331	429	760	5	87	0.39	271	83	43		5.22	-4.2
LIMA B	2nd Half		242	24	58	5	35	1	240			$3	306	364	669	9	84	0.61	263	82	53		4.00	-12.9
Risk Moderate	03	Proj	450	48	121	15	68	3	269			$13	328	425	753	8	82	0.48	267	97	52		5.09	-3.9

Another one with a declining power trend and correlating increase in G/F ratio. In Dodger Stadium, that might be a deadly combination. It will be interesting to see what he might do in a new venue. This proj will change.

Kearns,Austin

	Yr	Tm	AB	R	H	HR	RBI	SB	Avg	vLH	vRH	R$	OB	Slg	OPS	bb%	ct%	Eye	xBA	PX	SX	G/F	RC/G	RAR
Pos RF	98		0	0	0	0	0	0	0								0							
Age 22 Growth	99		0	0	0	0	0	0	0								0							
Bats R	00		0	0	0	0	0	0	0								0							
Pwr + + +	01	aa	205	24	51	5	29	6	249			$5	319	385	704	9	84	0.64	270	87	80		4.08	-8.4
Spd + + +	02	CIN	*417	76	130	17	68	7	312	330	310	$21	401	516	916	13	79	0.70	273	126	97	1.37	8.15	37.5
BAvg - -	1st Half		236	42	67	12	41	3	284			$11	379	500	879	13	74	0.58	254	129	79		7.25	14.3
LIMA A	2nd Half		181	34	63	5	27	4	348			$11	430	536	966	13	86	1.00	296	123	107		9.45	23.9
Risk High	03	Proj	550	86	161	23	94	12	293			$25	374	495	868	11	82	0.72	285	124	93		6.83	34.2

HRs make it look like his power plummeted in the 2nd half but it really didn't. He got extra base hits in 15% of his balls in play in the 1st half; 14% in the 2nd half. There is great talent here.

Kendall,Jason

	Yr	Tm	AB	R	H	HR	RBI	SB	Avg	vLH	vRH	R$	OB	Slg	OPS	bb%	ct%	Eye	xBA	PX	SX	G/F	RC/G	RAR
Pos CA	98	PIT	535	95	175	12	75	26	327	327	313	$30	386	473	859	9	90	1.00	307	105	122	1.32	7.37	56.4
Age 28 Peak	99	PIT	280	61	93	8	41	22	332	271	348	$19	412	511	923	12	89	1.19	307	115	146	1.47	8.88	43.9
Bats R	00	PIT	579	112	185	14	58	22	320	331	316	$25	401	470	871	12	86	1.00	289	93	120	1.34	7.31	60.9
Pwr -	01	PIT	606	84	161	10	53	13	266	279	263	$12	315	358	673	7	92	0.92	281	59	83	1.20	3.84	4.6
Spd + + + + +	02	PIT	545	59	154	3	44	15	283	275	284	$13	342	356	698	8	95	1.69	281	53	87	1.72	4.50	5.2
BAvg + + + + +	1st Half		262	25	74	2	26	9	282			$7	338	359	697	8	97	2.44	287	55	77		4.42	1.8
LIMA A+	2nd Half		283	34	80	1	18	6	283			$5	345	353	699	9	93	1.35	275	51	89		4.57	3.3
Risk Low	03	Proj	500	69	144	11	45	13	288			$15	350	417	767	9	92	1.21	294	81	91		5.33	21.2

Incredible contact hitter with an excellent batting eye, but is not hitting with any authority. He will deny it (though his manager doesn't) but his surgically-repaired thumb is the culprit. We'll see if a winter of rest helps.

Kennedy,Adam

	Yr	Tm	AB	R	H	HR	RBI	SB	Avg	vLH	vRH	R$	OB	Slg	OPS	bb%	ct%	Eye	xBA	PX	SX	G/F	RC/G	RAR
Pos 2B	98	a/a	510	60	140	8	55	18	275			$14	298	406	704	3	90	0.35	301	92	126		4.33	2.7
Age 27 Peak	99	STL	*469	72	136	9	71	17	290	250	256	$17	331	429	760	6	91	0.73	304	94	110	0.83	5.17	12.4
Bats L	00	ANA	598	82	159	9	72	22	266	275	263	$14	299	403	702	4	88	0.38	289	84	166	0.91	4.24	5.2
Pwr + + +	01	ANA	478	48	129	6	40	12	270	242	277	$9	309	372	681	5	85	0.38	262	70	86	0.84	4.04	-3.6
Spd + +	02	ANA	474	65	148	7	52	17	312	275	319	$19	339	449	788	4	83	0.24	272	98	145	0.83	5.79	23.6
BAvg - - -	1st Half		230	34	69	2	23	7	300			$7	329	448	777	4	86	0.31	289	106	172		5.38	8.6
LIMA A+	2nd Half		244	31	79	5	29	10	324			$12	348	451	799	4	80	0.19	257	90	106		6.21	15.1
Risk Very High	03	Proj	500	63	141	8	54	17	282			$15	313	407	720	4	85	0.30	273	86	127		4.63	6.4

He will not likely be among the 30% of hitters with sub-0.50 batting eyes who manage to maintain a .300 BA.

Kent,Jeff

	Yr	Tm	AB	R	H	HR	RBI	SB	Avg	vLH	vRH	R$	OB	Slg	OPS	bb%	ct%	Eye	xBA	PX	SX	G/F	RC/G	RAR
Pos 2B	98	SF	526	94	156	31	128	9	297	254	310	$32	355	555	911	8	79	0.44	297	168	100	0.70	7.34	51.6
Age 35 Decline	99	SF	511	86	148	23	101	13	290	273	296	$23	365	511	876	11	78	0.54	280	141	89	0.78	6.96	43.4
Bats R	00	SF	587	114	196	33	125	12	334	324	335	$37	422	596	1019	13	82	0.84	307	153	109	0.73	9.90	105.4
Pwr + +	01	SF	607	84	181	22	106	7	298	295	299	$25	366	507	873	10	84	0.68	300	132	91	0.94	6.93	57.3
Spd - - - - -	02	SF	623	102	195	37	108	5	313	366	297	$34	366	565	931	8	84	0.51	301	151	74	0.80	7.97	67.0
BAvg - -	1st Half		307	46	97	13	52	3	316			$16	371	508	879	8	85	0.57	285	121	54		7.32	26.9
LIMA C+	2nd Half		316	56	98	24	56	2	310			$19	361	620	981	7	83	0.46	315	181	81		8.59	39.8
Risk Very Low	03	Proj	600	99	186	32	111	7	310			$32	374	557	930	9	83	0.60	302	150	87		7.94	72.5

Is there a 40-HR season still in his future? Probably not. This power surge was driven by a 14-HR August. That's not a streak you can count on happening very often.

Kielty,Bobby

	Yr	Tm	AB	R	H	HR	RBI	SB	Avg	vLH	vRH	R$	OB	Slg	OPS	bb%	ct%	Eye	xBA	PX	SX	G/F	RC/G	RAR
Pos RF CF	98		0	0	0	0	0	0	0								0							
Age 26 Pre-Peak	99		0	0	0	0	0	0	0								0							
Bats S	00	a/a	484	71	117	11	55	5	242			$5	355	386	741	15	80	0.88	266	95	67		5.02	-1.8
Pwr + + +	01	aaa	341	45	88	9	39	4	258			$7	338	413	751	11	82	0.68	273	103	73	0.94	5.23	-1.6
Spd No change	02	MIN	296	49	87	12	46	4	294	264	303	$12	401	486	888	15	77	0.79	266	122	102	0.93	7.73	26.0
BAvg - -	1st Half		142	26	47	5	26	3	331			$8	441	535	976	16	77	0.88	278	141	90		9.81	22.8
LIMA B	2nd Half		154	23	40	7	20	1	260			$5	363	442	805	14	77	0.71	255	103	99		6.09	5.0
Risk High	03	Proj	350	52	95	12	46	4	271			$10	370	440	810	14	80	0.76	266	108	81		6.24	11.4

The good things:
- Excellent base skills
- Rising trends
- .401 OB avg!!

The bad things:
- 2nd half fade
- Crowded MIN outfield

Kingsale,Gene

	Yr	Tm	AB	R	H	HR	RBI	SB	Avg	vLH	vRH	R$	OB	Slg	OPS	bb%	ct%	Eye	xBA	PX	SX	G/F	RC/G	RAR
Pos RF LF	98	aaa	484	70	121	1	35	32	250			$11	319	298	616	9	83	0.61	246	33	134		3.46	-24.5
Age 26 Pre-Peak	99	BAL	*544	77	134	5	47	23	246	250	247	$9	306	322	628	8	85	0.59	257	50	107	1.67	3.16	-32.2
Bats S	00	BAL	*109	20	29	1	15	3	266	190	257	$2	298	358	656	4	87	0.36	267	59	132	1.95	3.50	-5.0
Pwr + +	01	aaa	478	56	102	2	35	27	213			$5	264	291	555	6	86	0.48	262	55	138	4.50	2.67	-39.5
Spd + +	02	2TM	*407	48	105	7	50	18	258	293	281	$11	314	393	707	8	82	0.45	266	91	140	1.51	4.47	-10.0
BAvg -	1st Half		214	24	53	5	24	8	248			$4	288	393	680	5	82	0.31	267	95	118		3.72	-10.0
LIMA B+	2nd Half		193	24	52	2	26	10	269			$6	341	394	735	10	82	0.60	264	86	154		5.35	0.5
Risk X HIGH	03	Proj	350	46	92	4	38	19	263			$10	325	369	694	8	84	0.57	269	72	139		4.42	-9.1

2-28-9-.283 in 210 AB at SD. Overall okay, but 2nd half was very promising. Combine blazing speed and a .350 OB, and you really have something. And I thought he was destined to become Charles Gipson.

Kinkade,Mike			Tm	AB	R	H	HR	RBI	SB	Avg	vLH	vRH	R$	OB	Slg	OPS	bb%	ct%	Eye	xBA	PX	SX	G/F	RC/G	RAR
Pos	1B	98	aaa	416	56	109	6	52	13	262			$10	313	385	698	7	84	0.47	277	86	126		4.41	-14.8
Age	29 Past Peak	99	NYM	* 358	46	91	8	46	7	254	211	185	$7	294	385	679	5	90	0.54	292	85	94	2.10	4.01	-15.1
Bats	R	00	aa	399	61	109	11	62	13	273			$13	336	419	755	9	84	0.59	277	89	100	2.50	5.05	-8.9
Pwr	+	01	BAL	160	19	44	4	16	2	275	284	264	$4	333	381	715	8	81	0.45	240	65	47	1.16	4.69	-7.9
Spd	No change	02	LA	* 337	48	93	9	44	5	276	400	350	$10	322	436	758	6	85	0.46	282	102	102	1.31	5.04	-6.9
BAvg	- -	1st Half		231	33	56	5	24	3	242			$3	289	377	665	6	86	0.47	276	85	103		3.66	-14.4
LIMA	C	2nd Half		106	15	37	4	20	2	349			$7	395	566	961	7	83	0.44	293	139	92		9.21	11.4
Risk	X HIGH	03	Proj	150	21	43	4	21	3	287			$5	338	444	782	7	84	0.48	277	100	89		5.56	0.9

2-11-.380 in 50 AB at LA. It is a rare occasion when I'll say that a .380 hitter is undraftable, but this is it.

Oh okay, go a buck.

Klesko,Ryan			Tm	AB	R	H	HR	RBI	SB	Avg	vLH	vRH	R$	OB	Slg	OPS	bb%	ct%	Eye	xBA	PX	SX	G/F	RC/G	RAR
Pos	1B RF	98	ATL	427	69	117	18	70	5	274	213	284	$16	358	473	831	12	85	0.85	299	135	69	1.13	6.28	12.3
Age	31 Past Peak	99	ATL	404	55	120	21	80	5	297	102	324	$19	379	532	911	12	83	0.77	298	144	66	1.02	7.72	30.2
Bats	L	00	SD	494	88	140	26	92	23	283	256	292	$26	395	516	911	16	84	1.12	305	139	98	1.20	7.86	40.2
Pwr	-	01	SD	538	105	154	30	113	23	286	256	299	$32	387	539	926	14	83	0.99	310	148	143	0.97	8.12	31.1
Spd	- - - - -	02	SD	540	90	162	29	95	6	300	287	305	$27	386	537	923	12	84	0.88	298	146	67	1.02	8.04	41.0
BAvg	-	1st Half		256	43	77	14	42	1	301			$12	399	520	919	14	86	1.17	293	131	35		7.99	19.4
LIMA	A	2nd Half		284	47	85	15	53	5	299			$15	374	553	927	11	82	0.68	302	160	85		8.08	21.5
Risk	Low	03	Proj	550	96	161	29	103	14	293			$29	385	535	920	13	84	0.92	304	147	99		7.96	46.9

Early nagging injuries shut down his SB game and he was never comfortable enough to let loose much after that. Will he steal again in '03? If healthy, he might.

Knoblauch,Chuck			Tm	AB	R	H	HR	RBI	SB	Avg	vLH	vRH	R$	OB	Slg	OPS	bb%	ct%	Eye	xBA	PX	SX	G/F	RC/G	RAR
Pos	LF	98	NYY	603	117	160	17	64	31	265	252	269	$20	348	405	752	11	88	1.09	291	85	127	1.04	5.17	0.5
Age	34 Decline	99	NYY	603	120	176	18	68	28	292	272	297	$24	378	454	832	12	91	1.46	308	101	124	0.84	6.61	28.2
Bats	R	00	NYY	400	75	113	5	26	15	283	210	307	$9	357	385	742	10	89	1.02	277	68	113	1.20	5.14	-0.7
Pwr	No change	01	NYY	521	66	130	9	44	38	250	253	249	$16	325	351	676	10	86	0.79	265	64	117	1.20	4.29	-7.1
Spd	+ + + +	02	KC	316	43	67	6	22	20	212	231	203	$7	284	301	585	9	89	0.89	263	60	114	1.22	3.17	-17.5
BAvg	+ + + + +	1st Half		150	20	25	3	14	12	167			$3	238	253	491	9	90	0.93	266	57	132		2.32	-12.2
LIMA	A	2nd Half		166	23	42	3	8	8	253			$4	326	343	669	10	87	0.86	260	63	87		4.10	-4.4
Risk	High	03	Proj	400	59	102	7	30	24	255			$12	329	356	684	10	88	0.91	269	67	111		4.40	-9.3

xBA says his .212 BA was a fluke, and his 2nd half rebound bears that out. Still, his value has declined to the point where you're only buying his SBs.

Konerko,Paul			Tm	AB	R	H	HR	RBI	SB	Avg	vLH	vRH	R$	OB	Slg	OPS	bb%	ct%	Eye	xBA	PX	SX	G/F	RC/G	RAR
Pos	1B	98	2NL	* 454	60	129	20	90	1	284	288	185	$19	349	467	816	9	86	0.69	294	120	33	1.06	6.08	9.8
Age	27 Peak	99	CHW	513	71	151	24	81	1	294	319	287	$18	351	511	862	8	87	0.66	305	128	67	1.23	6.79	14.1
Bats	R	00	CHW	524	84	156	21	97	1	298	302	297	$18	356	481	836	8	86	0.65	294	110	54	1.13	6.52	7.4
Pwr	- -	01	CHW	582	92	164	32	99	1	282	297	278	$22	343	507	850	8	85	0.61	292	135	41	1.10	6.47	3.7
Spd	No change	02	CHW	570	81	173	27	104	0	304	279	310	$25	353	498	852	7	87	0.61	299	125	26	1.17	6.71	12.7
BAvg	- -	1st Half		307	46	103	20	70	0	336			$20	378	583	961	6	88	0.57	320	153	22		8.72	25.6
LIMA	B+	2nd Half		263	35	70	7	34	0	266			$6	325	399	724	8	87	0.66	275	92	32		4.77	-9.9
Risk	Very Low	03	Proj	575	85	167	26	99	1	290			$22	347	482	829	8	86	0.63	293	120	36		6.28	11.3

Solid season, driven by a 12-HR, .340 BA in June. Without that display, this would have been an off power year. Hit no more than 4 HRs in any other month. This could filter into '03.

Koskie,Corey			Tm	AB	R	H	HR	RBI	SB	Avg	vLH	vRH	R$	OB	Slg	OPS	bb%	ct%	Eye	xBA	PX	SX	G/F	RC/G	RAR
Pos	3B	98	aaa	534	76	140	22	86	12	262			$19	317	455	772	7	81	0.42	283	121	105	0.89	5.09	9.4
Age	29 Past Peak	99	MIN	342	42	106	11	58	4	310	267	316	$13	382	468	850	10	79	0.56	259	100	42	1.22	6.81	25.1
Bats	L	00	MIN	474	79	142	9	65	5	300	333	292	$13	397	441	838	14	78	0.74	257	91	90	1.48	6.86	37.3
Pwr	- -	01	MIN	562	100	155	26	103	27	276	242	290	$28	354	488	842	11	79	0.58	278	130	110	1.16	6.50	36.9
Spd	- - - - -	02	MIN	490	71	131	15	69	10	267	253	274	$16	361	447	808	13	74	0.57	256	125	87	1.06	5.72	18.6
BAvg	-	1st Half		235	39	62	8	36	6	264			$8	364	447	811	14	76	0.66	262	122	106		5.83	9.9
LIMA	A+	2nd Half		255	32	69	7	33	4	271			$7	359	447	806	12	72	0.49	250	128	66		5.62	8.8
Risk	Low	03	Proj	500	77	138	17	76	13	276			$18	363	459	823	12	76	0.58	264	121	95		6.11	24.5

Should we be concerned about: The slow decline in contact rate? The slow decline in batting avg? The slow decline in BA vsRH? The comparable PX rating to '01 that generated 11 fewer HRs? Lots of negative stuff here.

Kotsay,Mark			Tm	AB	R	H	HR	RBI	SB	Avg	vLH	vRH	R$	OB	Slg	OPS	bb%	ct%	Eye	xBA	PX	SX	G/F	RC/G	RAR
Pos	CF	98	FLA	578	72	161	11	68	10	279	261	284	$16	319	403	722	6	89	0.56	291	83	114	1.40	4.63	4.1
Age	27 Peak	99	FLA	495	57	134	8	50	7	271	272	271	$8	311	402	713	6	90	0.58	292	81	118	1.09	4.38	-0.4
Bats	L	00	FLA	530	87	158	12	57	19	298	308	296	$19	350	443	793	7	91	0.91	305	92	120	1.52	5.72	21.3
Pwr	- -	01	SD	406	67	118	10	58	13	291	215	318	$16	366	441	807	11	86	0.83	287	100	95	1.33	6.12	28.4
Spd	No change	02	SD	578	82	169	17	61	11	292	324	277	$20	358	452	809	9	85	0.66	277	96	108	1.11	5.92	17.2
BAvg	- -	1st Half		298	42	91	6	33	7	305			$11	384	450	834	11	88	1.03	284	92	107		6.38	13.6
LIMA	A	2nd Half		280	40	78	11	28	4	279			$9	329	454	782	7	81	0.40	268	100	106		5.42	3.9
Risk	Low	03	Proj	575	86	166	20	71	14	289			$21	351	462	813	9	86	0.68	290	106	105		5.94	28.0

Three years of comparable BPIs, but where does he go from here? The leading indicators don't tell us anything. It could be as simple as age-related development that helps him take the next step. We'll surmise...

Kreuter,Chad			Tm	AB	R	H	HR	RBI	SB	Avg	vLH	vRH	R$	OB	Slg	OPS	bb%	ct%	Eye	xBA	PX	SX	G/F	RC/G	RAR
Pos	CA	98	2AL	252	27	63	2	33	1	250	261	248	$2	337	321	658	12	81	0.67	236	50	53	1.28	4.09	0.0
Age	38 Decline	99	KC	324	31	73	5	35	0	225	279	217	($0)	299	318	617	9	80	0.52	237	63	22	1.54	3.40	-7.7
Bats	S	00	LA	212	32	56	6	28	1	264	288	255	$4	414	410	824	20	77	1.13	258	94	35	1.36	6.87	21.2
Pwr	- - -	01	LA	191	21	41	6	17	0	215	192	223	$0	353	377	730	18	73	0.79	241	101	39	1.15	4.97	9.1
Spd	No change	02	LA	95	8	25	2	12	1	263	462	188	$2	333	379	712	10	67	0.32	206	78	34	1.14	4.75	1.7
BAvg	- -	1st Half		58	5	15	1	9	1	259			$1	358	379	738	13	71	0.53	221	86	36		5.28	2.1
LIMA	D	2nd Half		37	3	10	1	3	0	270			$1	289	378	668	3	62	0.07	184	65	15		3.90	-0.3
Risk	High	03	Proj	100	11	25	2	13	1	250			$1	365	375	740	15	75	0.73	238	85	32		5.29	4.4

His last few seasons weren't half bad (look at that .353 OB with the .215 BA last year), but trend is evident.

Lamb,Mike			Tm	AB	R	H	HR	RBI	SB	Avg	vLH	vRH	R$	OB	Slg	OPS	bb%	ct%	Eye	xBA	PX	SX	G/F	RC/G	RAR
Pos	1B DH	98		0	0	0	0	0	0	0								0							
Age	27 Peak	99	a/a	546	80	161	17	81	3	295			$17	346	487	834	7	90	0.80	315	126	71		6.16	8.5
Bats	L	00	TEX	* 548	72	150	8	51	2	274	286	276	$7	321	383	704	6	88	0.58	274	72	66	1.41	4.44	-27.3
Pwr	-	01	TEX	* 557	70	161	12	68	2	289	300	308	$14	320	424	743	4	90	0.47	286	90	54	1.45	4.89	-22.9
Spd	No change	02	TEX	* 342	56	99	9	36	0	289	211	293	$9	354	409	763	9	85	0.67	263	80	38	1.18	5.52	-4.9
BAvg	-	1st Half		194	24	59	4	19	0	304			$5	348	412	760	6	86	0.46	261	76	28		5.48	-3.0
LIMA	B	2nd Half		148	32	40	5	17	0	270			$4	361	405	766	12	84	0.91	265	86	52		5.58	-1.9
Risk	High	03	Proj	400	62	114	10	45	0	285			$9	341	417	759	8	87	0.67	276	88	50		5.29	-4.5

This is not a bad skills set, even without the pop or speed. It would be acceptable for a middle infielder, but not for a cornerman or DH. Therein lies the rub.

Lampkin,Tom			Tm	AB	R	H	HR	RBI	SB	Avg	vLH	vRH	R$	OB	Slg	OPS	bb%	ct%	Eye	xBA	PX	SX	G/F	RC/G	RAR
Pos	CA	98	STL	216	25	50	6	28	3	231	79	264	$3	308	380	688	10	85	0.75	285	102	71	1.26	4.09	0.6
Age	39 Decline	99	SEA	206	29	60	9	34	1	291	296	291	$7	333	495	828	6	84	0.41	293	119	80	1.06	5.79	10.3
Bats	L	00	SEA	103	15	26	7	23	0	252	100	269	$3	313	534	846	8	83	0.53	317	156	65	1.00	5.93	5.4
Pwr	No change	01	SEA	204	28	46	5	22	1	225	130	238	$1	288	348	636	8	80	0.44	247	80	53	1.12	3.55	-2.5
Spd	No change	02	SD	281	32	61	10	37	4	217	167	227	$3	310	367	677	12	79	0.64	251	88	67	1.06	4.02	-1.7
BAvg	+ + + + +	1st Half		150	12	27	4	15	1	180			($2)	281	307	587	12	79	0.66	242	75	58		2.94	-6.1
LIMA	C	2nd Half		131	20	34	6	22	3	260			$5	345	435	780	11	79	0.63	259	103	63		5.54	5.7
Risk	High	03	Proj	150	20	35	6	22	2	233			$3	310	410	720	10	81	0.57	269	105	78		4.49	2.4

This was the most ABs he's ever gotten in a single major league season... at age 39. They gave him 281 AB of .217 and it wasn't until August 15 that he crossed the Mendoza Line for good. Also the most HRs he's ever hit.

Lane,Jason

	Yr	Tm	AB	R	H	HR	RBI	SB	Avg	vLH	vRH	R$	OB	Slg	OPS	bb%	ct%	Eye	xBA	PX	SX	G/F	RC/G	RAR
Pos RF	98		0	0	0	0	0	0	0								0							
Age 26 Pre-Peak	99		0	0	0	0	0	0	0								0							
Bats R	00		0	0	0	0	0	0	0								0							
Pwr +	01	aa	526	81	149	33	98	11	283			$26	343	544	887	8	83	0.55	307	154	90		6.95	25.9
Spd + + +	02	HOU	* 495	68	131	19	82	12	265	349	192	$18	316	471	786	7	81	0.39	284	132	106	0.50	5.32	-1.4
BAvg - -	1st Half		301	42	80	9	48	10	266			$11	320	449	769	7	81	0.41	278	126	87		5.18	-2.1
LIMA B+	2nd Half		194	26	51	10	34	2	263			$7	309	505	814	6	81	0.36	291	141	117		5.52	0.7
Risk High	03	Proj	350	50	91	18	62	7	260			$13	315	492	807	7	82	0.45	295	141	98		5.53	6.8

4-10-.290 in 69 AB at HOU. As an older prospect, you have to discount his numbers a bit. Note that he didn't make the jump from AA unscathed. Big power, but OB and eye need work, and at 26, the future is now.

Lankford,Ray

	Yr	Tm	AB	R	H	HR	RBI	SB	Avg	vLH	vRH	R$	OB	Slg	OPS	bb%	ct%	Eye	xBA	PX	SX	G/F	RC/G	RAR
Pos LF	98	STL	533	94	156	31	105	26	293	264	303	$35	391	540	931	14	72	0.57	267	162	100	0.94	8.28	59.7
Age 35 Decline	99	STL	422	77	129	15	63	14	306	237	331	$19	378	493	871	10	74	0.45	257	123	95	1.07	7.23	28.0
Bats L	00	STL	392	73	99	26	65	5	253	135	280	$14	366	508	873	15	62	0.47	228	140	94	0.66	6.61	17.0
Pwr + +	01	2NL	389	58	98	19	58	10	252	194	263	$13	355	491	846	14	63	0.43	231	144	132	0.80	6.47	8.6
Spd - - - - -	02	SD	205	20	46	6	26	2	224	194	230	$2	323	356	680	13	70	0.49	218	78	59	1.07	4.08	-16.3
BAvg + + +	1st Half		179	18	43	5	23	2	240			$3	346	369	715	14	70	0.55	218	76	61		4.64	-11.2
LIMA C	2nd Half		26	2	3	1	3	0	115			($1)	148	269	417	4	69	0.13	218	92	32		1.19	-4.1
Risk Low	03	Proj	250	38	60	5	38	1	240			$3	344	374	718	14	67	0.49	217	85	84		4.63	-1.0

Injuries have eroded his skills set to the point where he no longer has any value, and hope for a return to form is fraught with too much risk. His BA and xBA trends tell you all you need to know.

Larkin,Barry

	Yr	Tm	AB	R	H	HR	RBI	SB	Avg	vLH	vRH	R$	OB	Slg	OPS	bb%	ct%	Eye	xBA	PX	SX	G/F	RC/G	RAR
Pos SS	98	CIN	538	93	166	17	72	26	309	285	316	$29	397	504	901	13	87	1.14	310	128	167	1.61	8.14	78.6
Age 39 Decline	99	CIN	583	108	171	12	75	30	293	259	305	$24	391	420	811	14	90	1.63	294	82	116	1.47	6.55	56.9
Bats R	00	CIN	396	71	124	11	41	14	313	307	315	$17	387	487	875	11	92	1.55	318	108	125	1.22	7.30	47.8
Pwr No change	01	CIN	156	29	40	2	17	3	256	333	231	$3	366	372	738	15	84	1.08	271	85	72	1.42	5.11	7.7
Spd +	02	CIN	507	72	124	7	47	13	245	189	262	$7	305	367	672	8	89	0.77	285	88	105	1.18	4.00	0.4
BAvg + + +	1st Half		264	36	60	4	23	6	227			$2	282	341	623	7	88	0.65	278	76	113		3.34	-5.1
LIMA B	2nd Half		243	36	64	3	24	7	263			$5	330	395	725	9	89	0.92	293	101	85		4.80	6.3
Risk Moderate	03	Proj	350	57	91	6	36	7	260			$6	340	396	736	11	88	1.02	290	95	97		4.92	13.1

Thought we'd never see 500 AB again, but this was not the same player. Most of his vital skills are gone. That's what you have to look forward to when you're pushing 40.

LaRocca,Greg

	Yr	Tm	AB	R	H	HR	RBI	SB	Avg	vLH	vRH	R$	OB	Slg	OPS	bb%	ct%	Eye	xBA	PX	SX	G/F	RC/G	RAR
Pos 3B	98	aaa	304	39	76	6	28	5	250			$4	278	385	663	4	88	0.32	289	91	111		3.64	-8.0
Age 30 Past Peak	99	aaa	51	3	13	0	2	2	255			$0	283	294	577	4	78	0.18	225	34	57		2.33	-3.3
Bats R	00	aaa	482	73	118	7	65	10	245			$7	304	382	686	8	87	0.67	291	92	122	1.44	4.07	-5.7
Pwr No change	01	a/a	320	46	89	13	47	2	278			$10	330	466	796	7	87	0.58	293	115	58		5.49	9.1
Spd + + + + +	02	CLE	* 434	70	112	6	39	16	258	333	235	$11	329	373	702	10	87	0.84	277	86	118	1.64	4.57	0.2
BAvg + + +	1st Half		229	31	61	4	23	10	266			$7	341	402	743	10	85	0.76	279	101	101		5.02	3.3
LIMA C	2nd Half		205	39	51	2	16	6	249			$3	316	341	657	9	90	0.95	274	70	126		4.09	-3.0
Risk X HIGH	03	Proj	100	16	26	2	11	2	260			$2	320	402	722	8	87	0.70	286	95	113		4.66	0.2

0-4-.269 in 52 AB at CLE. While there are major leaguers with skills far worse than this, teams don't invest in players at age 30. Some talent will fall through the cracks, but you can't fault a decision with a long-term view.

Larson,Brandon

	Yr	Tm	AB	R	H	HR	RBI	SB	Avg	vLH	vRH	R$	OB	Slg	OPS	bb%	ct%	Eye	xBA	PX	SX	G/F	RC/G	RAR
Pos LF	98		0	0	0	0	0	0	0								0							
Age 26 Pre-Peak	99	aa	172	22	43	10	33	3	248			$6	284	474	758	5	75	0.21	267	134	58		4.06	-5.7
Bats R	00	a/a	490	56	122	18	53	12	249			$11	290	427	716	5	79	0.27	270	109	81		4.22	-15.4
Pwr + + + +	01	aaa	457	51	103	12	46	4	225			$4	261	359	620	5	76	0.20	242	85	62		2.99	-31.1
Spd No change	02	CIN	* 348	44	103	24	65	2	296	308	240	$19	340	566	906	6	82	0.36	294	157	48	0.94	7.13	6.5
BAvg - - -	1st Half		261	31	79	16	43	1	303			$13	343	559	902	6	82	0.35	294	153	44		7.13	4.8
LIMA B	2nd Half		87	13	24	8	22	1	276			$6	330	586	916	7	79	0.39	291	170	41		7.12	1.6
Risk Very High	03	Proj	350	44	92	20	59	4	263			$13	306	493	799	6	79	0.29	277	134	63		5.22	4.9

4-13-.275 in 51 AB at CIN. He's starting his ascent up the peak, and the question is whether he will post his career years in AAA or in the majors. BPIs say he'd probably hold his own in CIN.

LaRue,Jason

	Yr	Tm	AB	R	H	HR	RBI	SB	Avg	vLH	vRH	R$	OB	Slg	OPS	bb%	ct%	Eye	xBA	PX	SX	G/F	RC/G	RAR
Pos CA	98	aa	437	57	131	10	66	3	300			$14	352	487	839	7	87	0.63	310	131	97		6.37	31.4
Age 29 Past Peak	99	CIN	* 353	43	76	12	38	4	215	162	245	$2	263	374	637	6	80	0.33	267	99	71	1.47	3.21	-8.9
Bats R	00	CIN	* 405	53	93	16	48	2	230	300	218	$5	269	412	682	5	86	0.38	296	111	63	1.23	3.73	-4.2
Pwr - -	01	CIN	364	39	86	12	43	3	236	267	227	$5	289	404	693	7	71	0.25	238	104	73	0.96	3.97	4.3
Spd No change	02	CIN	353	42	88	12	52	1	249	207	264	$7	303	405	708	7	67	0.23	214	96	51	1.23	4.28	0.9
BAvg -	1st Half		173	15	41	2	18	1	237			$1	286	312	599	6	65	0.20	190	53	40		3.19	-5.3
LIMA D+	2nd Half		180	27	47	10	34	0	261			$6	318	494	812	8	68	0.26	239	137	65		5.40	6.7
Risk Moderate	03	Proj	350	42	89	13	48	1	254			$7	305	422	727	7	73	0.26	240	104	47		4.47	5.3

Nice save in the 2nd half, but the net result was only marginally better than 2001. Contact rate has been horrible, leading to brutal xBAs. Too much downside, even with the little bit of pop.

Lawrence,Joe

	Yr	Tm	AB	R	H	HR	RBI	SB	Avg	vLH	vRH	R$	OB	Slg	OPS	bb%	ct%	Eye	xBA	PX	SX	G/F	RC/G	RAR
Pos 2B	98		0	0	0	0	0	0	0								0							
Age 26 Pre-Peak	99	aa	250	40	58	5	18	5	232			$1	345	360	705	15	85	1.16	275	86	75		4.27	0.8
Bats R	00	aa	133	16	30	0	7	5	226			$0	335	293	629	14	84	1.05	257	57	73		3.82	-1.7
Pwr No change	01	aaa	318	23	65	1	22	5	204			($2)	273	267	540	9	84	0.59	244	43	77		2.26	-18.5
Spd No change	02	TOR	* 258	26	43	4	24	4	167	171	183	($2)	246	252	498	9	78	0.48	230	57	86	1.02	2.12	-16.3
BAvg + + + + +	1st Half		110	10	22	2	10	2	200			$0	279	273	551	10	73	0.40	206	46	52		2.65	-5.1
LIMA F	2nd Half		148	16	21	2	14	2	142			($2)	221	236	457	9	82	0.58	248	65	102		1.77	-10.9
Risk X HIGH	03	Proj	100	10	19	1	8	1	190			($1)	275	261	537	11	81	0.63	236	52	49		2.42	-5.7

2-15-.180 in 150 AB at TOR. The Peter Principle at work... Batted .232 and .226 in AA, so he got promoted to AAA where he batted .204. This, of course, merited a call-up to TOR where he batted .180.

Lawton,Matt

	Yr	Tm	AB	R	H	HR	RBI	SB	Avg	vLH	vRH	R$	OB	Slg	OPS	bb%	ct%	Eye	xBA	PX	SX	G/F	RC/G	RAR
Pos RF LF	98	MIN	557	91	155	21	77	16	278	275	279	$20	375	478	852	13	89	1.34	314	123	111	1.51	6.69	28.2
Age 31 Past Peak	99	MIN	406	58	105	7	54	26	259	290	248	$14	350	355	705	12	90	1.36	277	64	100	1.77	4.92	-2.0
Bats L	00	MIN	561	84	171	13	88	23	305	294	309	$24	402	460	862	14	89	1.44	300	102	93	1.74	7.38	43.9
Pwr + + +	01	2TM	559	95	155	13	64	29	277	244	287	$21	373	415	788	13	86	1.06	280	92	101	1.81	6.00	11.5
Spd + + + + +	02	CLE	426	72	98	15	57	8	230	178	258	$10	326	390	716	13	92	1.74	301	102	88	1.42	4.34	-10.9
BAvg + + + + +	1st Half		266	51	64	8	29	5	241			$6	342	402	744	13	94	2.56	313	108	100		4.68	-3.8
LIMA A	2nd Half		160	21	34	7	28	3	212			$4	300	369	669	11	88	1.05	282	94	60		3.78	-6.9
Risk High	03	Proj	550	87	155	17	77	18	282			$21	373	435	808	13	89	1.31	292	99	90		6.12	15.7

bb%, ct%, Eye and xBA tell a far different story from what he's actually put up on the board. The percentage play is to go with an expectation of a big rebound. He'll likely go far under value anyway.

LeCroy,Matt

	Yr	Tm	AB	R	H	HR	RBI	SB	Avg	vLH	vRH	R$	OB	Slg	OPS	bb%	ct%	Eye	xBA	PX	SX	G/F	RC/G	RAR
Pos DH	98		0	0	0	0	0	0	0								0							
Age 27 Peak	99	aaa	119	17	32	7	23	0	269			$4	293	496	788	3	86	0.24	300	125	73		4.95	-1.2
Bats R	00	MIN	* 427	59	99	18	62	0	232	169	176	$5	305	426	731	10	82	0.59	284	117	40	0.67	4.59	-8.0
Pwr + + + +	01	MIN	* 436	48	134	18	74	0	307			$18	349	479	828	6	81	0.34	257	104		1.27	6.20	11.4
Spd No change	02	MIN	* 355	45	99	15	63	1	279	289	231	$13	326	468	794	7	82	0.38	278	120	59	0.88	5.49	-1.6
BAvg - -	1st Half		206	29	69	8	37	1	335			$11	380	544	924	8	84	0.45	299	139	77		7.92	14.4
LIMA C+	2nd Half		149	16	30	7	26	0	201			$2	252	362	614	6	79	0.31	250	94	25		3.05	-11.8
Risk High	03	Proj	350	43	94	16	60	0	269			$11	316	453	770	7	81	0.38	272	112	40		5.10	-4.2

7-27-.260 in 181 AB at MIN. At 550 AB, he projects out to 25 HRs and 100 RBIs, but they'll never give him that. BPIs are major league caliber; he just needs the ABs.

Ledee,Ricky

	Yr	Tm	AB	R	H	HR	RBI	SB	Avg	vLH	vRH	R$	OB	Slg	OPS	bb%	ct%	Eye	xBA	PX	SX	G/F	RC/G	RAR
Pos CF	98	NYY	* 439	75	114	18	48	9	260	167	254	$11	341	453	794	11	72	0.44	253	118	109	1.06	5.67	11.5
Age 29 Past Peak	99	NYY	* 365	60	96	12	53	7	263	282	275	$9	339	447	786	10	73	0.43	256	108	145	1.00	5.40	7.0
Bats L	00	2AL	467	59	110	13	77	13	236	241	234	$9	321	381	702	11	79	0.60	257	84	116	1.10	4.36	-5.9
Pwr +	01	TEX	242	33	56	2	36	3	231	267	226	$2	298	351	649	9	76	0.40	244	91	80	1.12	3.58	-10.4
Spd No change	02	PHI	203	33	46	8	23	1	227	80	247	$2	340	419	759	15	75	0.70	255	120	68	0.86	5.04	0.5
BAvg +++++	1st Half		86	10	16	2	9	0	186			($1)	247	314	561	8	77	0.35	241	86	50		2.45	-6.7
LIMA C+	2nd Half		117	23	30	6	14	1	256			$3	400	496	896	19	74	0.93	265	145	87		7.50	10.5
Risk High	03	Proj	**250**	**38**	**63**	**9**	**33**	**1**	**252**			**$5**	**345**	**446**	**791**	**12**	**76**	**0.59**	**260**	**120**	**75**		**5.47**	**8.8**

All things considered, he had an excellent 2nd half. .400 OB, 0.93 eye, 145 PX... but can he keep those levels up for more than 117 AB? As much as we'd like to see him take that next step up, you have to bet against.

Lee,Carlos

	Yr	Tm	AB	R	H	HR	RBI	SB	Avg	vLH	vRH	R$	OB	Slg	OPS	bb%	ct%	Eye	xBA	PX	SX	G/F	RC/G	RAR
Pos LF	98	aa	549	65	147	16	90	9	268			$17	309	415	725	6	92	0.73	304	97	79		4.58	-7.4
Age 26 Pre-Peak	99	CHW	* 586	79	173	19	101	6	295	301	291	$20	318	461	779	3	86	0.24	288	104	78	0.98	5.35	3.1
Bats R	00	CHW	572	107	172	24	92	13	301	327	295	$24	344	484	829	6	84	0.40	287	107	107	1.30	6.26	18.6
Pwr +	01	CHW	558	75	150	24	84	17	269	243	275	$21	315	468	783	6	85	0.45	291	121	97	0.98	5.22	8.5
Spd +	02	CHW	492	82	130	26	80	1	264	295	255	$17	362	484	845	13	85	1.03	301	138	50	0.67	6.37	23.4
BAvg +++++	1st Half		251	35	66	12	38	1	263			$8	337	474	811	10	85	0.76	301	136	54		5.70	6.1
LIMA A	2nd Half		241	47	64	14	42	0	266			$9	385	494	879	16	85	1.31	302	140	52		7.07	17.6
Risk Low	03	Proj	**500**	**85**	**146**	**29**	**96**	**2**	**292**			**$22**	**375**	**525**	**900**	**12**	**86**	**0.96**	**307**	**141**	**51**		**7.33**	**35.6**

Suddenly discovered plate patience, and with his soaring PX trend, he's now a legitimate threat. 30-100-.300 is back within reach.

Lee,Derrek

	Yr	Tm	AB	R	H	HR	RBI	SB	Avg	vLH	vRH	R$	OB	Slg	OPS	bb%	ct%	Eye	xBA	PX	SX	G/F	RC/G	RAR
Pos 1B	98	FLA	454	62	106	17	74	5	233	217	240	$10	305	414	719	9	74	0.39	256	123	74	1.01	4.45	-13.4
Age 27 Peak	99	FLA	* 557	65	125	18	74	4	224	234	199	$5	276	375	652	7	75	0.29	248	93	63	1.31	3.46	-33.2
Bats R	00	FLA	477	70	134	28	70	0	281	228	295	$17	365	507	872	12	74	0.51	263	125	46	1.07	6.84	21.4
Pwr ++	01	FLA	561	83	158	21	75	4	282	310	274	$18	340	474	815	8	78	0.40	269	119	89	0.98	5.97	-7.2
Spd +++++	02	FLA	581	95	157	27	86	19	270	264	272	$25	376	494	870	14	72	0.60	254	133	131	0.83	6.88	22.6
BAvg -	1st Half		301	49	77	16	44	5	256			$10	341	515	856	11	73	0.49	270	153	139		6.18	4.5
LIMA A	2nd Half		280	46	80	11	42	14	286			$14	410	471	881	17	70	0.70	237	112	110		7.60	18.3
Risk Low	03	Proj	**575**	**88**	**153**	**29**	**93**	**12**	**266**			**$22**	**356**	**494**	**850**	**12**	**74**	**0.53**	**262**	**135**	**106**		**6.43**	**19.9**

Interesting how his speed index (SX) jumped up in the 1st half, even before he went on his SB tear. Solid skills, although xBA says he's batting a little over his head. Declining G/F might mean big power is coming.

Lee,Travis

	Yr	Tm	AB	R	H	HR	RBI	SB	Avg	vLH	vRH	R$	OB	Slg	OPS	bb%	ct%	Eye	xBA	PX	SX	G/F	RC/G	RAR
Pos 1B	98	ARI	562	71	151	22	72	8	269	239	283	$18	347	429	775	11	78	0.54	261	101	79	1.68	5.61	3.9
Age 27 Peak	99	ARI	375	57	89	9	50	17	237	216	245	$9	339	363	702	13	87	1.16	280	79	108	1.42	4.69	-8.9
Bats L	00	2NL	404	53	95	9	54	8	235	205	242	$6	341	366	707	14	80	0.82	265	86	79	1.49	4.71	-9.9
Pwr --	01	PHI	555	75	143	20	90	3	258	265	255	$14	342	434	776	11	80	0.65	272	110	56	1.22	5.37	-18.1
Spd No change	02	PHI	536	55	142	13	70	5	265	282	259	$12	332	394	726	9	81	0.52	252	82	60	1.30	4.78	-15.7
BAvg No change	1st Half		271	28	66	6	28	4	244			$4	326	358	684	11	78	0.55	239	72	68		4.30	-12.3
LIMA B	2nd Half		265	27	76	7	42	1	287			$9	339	430	769	7	83	0.48	265	93	44		5.32	-3.2
Risk High	03	Proj	**400**	**47**	**104**	**11**	**57**	**5**	**260**			**$9**	**338**	**401**	**739**	**11**	**81**	**0.62**	**261**	**90**	**61**		**4.98**	**-4.9**

Still no signs of life. PX and G/F hold little hope for any power growth. Plate patience has been on the wane. Contact rate has been exactly at league average for 3 years, and going nowhere. Time to pull the plug.

Leon,Jose

	Yr	Tm	AB	R	H	HR	RBI	SB	Avg	vLH	vRH	R$	OB	Slg	OPS	bb%	ct%	Eye	xBA	PX	SX	G/F	RC/G	RAR
Pos 1B	98		0	0	0	0	0	0	0								0							
Age 26 Pre-Peak	99	aa	335	33	73	16	48	3	218			$5	268	409	677	6	71	0.23	239	113	41		3.61	-20.9
Bats R	00	aa	365	42	85	14	41	6	233			$5	269	397	666	5	80	0.24	265	94	89		3.59	-23.7
Pwr ---	01	a/a	511	66	137	15	67	7	268			$13	310	417	727	6	79	0.29	256	91	88		4.59	-26.9
Spd No change	02	BAL	* 401	42	100	10	45	1	249	290	148	$6	283	369	652	5	83	0.28	256	79	52	2.12	3.68	-27.6
BAvg -	1st Half		269	36	72	8	32	0	268			$6	299	409	708	4	84	0.29	269	93	52		4.38	-12.9
LIMA D	2nd Half		132	6	28	2	13	1	212			$0	252	288	540	5	80	0.26	228	52	26		2.49	-13.9
Risk Very High	03	Proj	**100**	**10**	**24**	**3**	**12**	**1**	**240**			**$1**	**279**	**365**	**644**	**5**	**79**	**0.26**	**246**	**80**	**45**		**3.53**	**-6.4**

3-10-.247 in 89 AB at BAL. Poor batting eye, declining PX trend, unacceptable OB avg, plays for BAL... need I go on?

Lewis,Darren

	Yr	Tm	AB	R	H	HR	RBI	SB	Avg	vLH	vRH	R$	OB	Slg	OPS	bb%	ct%	Eye	xBA	PX	SX	G/F	RC/G	RAR
Pos LF	98	BOS	585	95	157	8	63	29	268	313	251	$17	347	362	709	11	84	0.74	261	62	113	2.48	4.67	-9.1
Age 35 Decline	99	BOS	470	63	113	2	40	16	240	229	245	$4	307	309	615	9	89	0.87	266	43	129	1.80	3.30	-27.6
Bats R	00	BOS	270	44	65	2	17	10	241	277	215	$2	298	307	605	8	87	0.65	258	48	100	1.49	3.20	-16.6
Pwr ----	01	BOS	164	18	46	1	12	5	280	309	253	$3	314	366	680	5	85	0.32	256	62	86	1.24	3.82	-4.4
Spd No change	02	2NL	79	7	19	0	7	1	241	264	192	$0	302	304	606	8	86	0.64	251	44	94	1.20	2.85	-9.0
BAvg +++	1st Half		62	5	16	0	7	1	258			$1	303	339	642	6	90	0.67	272	56	104		3.52	-5.6
LIMA F	2nd Half		17	2	3	0	0	0	176			($1)	300	176	476	15	71	0.60	183	0	64		1.20	-3.0
Risk High	03	Proj	**0**	**0**	**0**	**0**	**0**	**0**	**0**			**$0**					**0**			**0**	**0**			**0.0**

Don't you hate it when the roto news services say things like, "Retired. Take him off your draft list?" It's like the instructions on shampoo bottles, "Apply to hair. Rinse." What did they think I was going to do, drink it?

Lieberthal,Mike

	Yr	Tm	AB	R	H	HR	RBI	SB	Avg	vLH	vRH	R$	OB	Slg	OPS	bb%	ct%	Eye	xBA	PX	SX	G/F	RC/G	RAR
Pos CA	98	PHI	313	39	80	8	45	2	256	308	242	$7	294	399	693	5	86	0.39	285	96	92	0.83	4.14	1.3
Age 31 Past Peak	99	PHI	510	84	153	31	96	0	300	377	276	$23	356	551	907	8	83	0.51	301	151	36	0.94	7.43	53.6
Bats R	00	PHI	389	55	108	15	71	2	278	350	259	$12	345	470	815	9	86	0.75	305	123	49	0.90	6.09	24.7
Pwr +++++	01	PHI	121	21	28	2	11	0	231	417	186	$0	301	347	648	9	83	0.57	263	82	54	0.68	3.72	0.5
Spd No change	02	PHI	476	46	133	15	52	0	279	346	260	$12	333	443	776	7	88	0.66	284	104	32	0.88	5.42	17.9
BAvg -	1st Half		235	23	62	6	24	0	264			$4	313	409	722	7	86	0.50	272	98	19		4.64	3.2
LIMA B+	2nd Half		241	23	71	9	28	0	295			$8	351	477	828	8	90	0.88	297	111	45		6.24	15.3
Risk Moderate	03	Proj	**450**	**57**	**126**	**18**	**55**	**0**	**280**			**$13**	**338**	**467**	**805**	**8**	**86**	**0.64**	**292**	**118**	**39**		**5.84**	**26.0**

Well, it's not 1999, but given the dearth of offensive catching talent, you can't complain too much. Stable BPIs for the most part, but there are small hints of a little more power coming...

Liefer,Jeff

	Yr	Tm	AB	R	H	HR	RBI	SB	Avg	vLH	vRH	R$	OB	Slg	OPS	bb%	ct%	Eye	xBA	PX	SX	G/F	RC/G	RAR
Pos LF 1B	98	aa	502	69	122	16	80	1	243			$9	310	418	729	9	76	0.42	262	113	83		4.57	-7.1
Age 28 Peak	99	CHW	* 284	35	77	7	40	4	271	124	257	$7	328	440	768	8	83	0.49	284	112	86	1.96	5.23	0.5
Bats L	00	aaa	445	56	110	27	69	2	247			$12	311	490	801	8	81	0.48	294	139	41	1.00	5.23	-0.4
Pwr No change	01	CHW	* 373	56	96	24	57	3	257	105	268	$13	318	504	822	8	71	0.31	250	144	50	0.86	5.66	11.0
Spd No change	02	CHW	204	28	47	7	26	0	230	300	227	$3	296	373	669	9	71	0.32	224	92	36	1.40	3.89	-6.6
BAvg No change	1st Half		68	9	13	1	3	0	191			($1)	225	250	475	4	74	0.17	203	37	58		1.86	-6.2
LIMA D+	2nd Half		136	19	34	6	23	0	250			$4	329	434	763	11	69	0.38	234	119	28		5.19	1.1
Risk Very High	03	Proj	**350**	**48**	**89**	**15**	**48**	**1**	**254**			**$9**	**315**	**435**	**751**	**8**	**73**	**0.33**	**245**	**112**	**43**		**4.90**	**-2.5**

Forget the 1st half. You can't produce when you spend all day on the bench. 2nd half shows the continued promise of prior years. He just needs some consistent playing time.

Little,Mark

	Yr	Tm	AB	R	H	HR	RBI	SB	Avg	vLH	vRH	R$	OB	Slg	OPS	bb%	ct%	Eye	xBA	PX	SX	G/F	RC/G	RAR
Pos RF LF	98	aaa	337	54	87	7	42	8	258			$8	296	412	708	5	82	0.30	280	100	156	3.00	3.99	-11.0
Age 30 Past Peak	99	aaa	196	28	46	2	15	8	235			$2	261	342	603	3	79	0.17	254	68	163		2.84	-13.0
Bats R	00	aaa	424	51	99	12	47	16	233			$8	300	399	698	9	80	0.47	270	100	124		3.89	-16.5
Pwr --	01	COL	* 125	22	42	3	16	5	336	326	357	$7	352	472	824	2	78	0.11	257	91	91	1.89	5.65	-0.1
Spd No change	02	2NL	* 194	33	45	2	14	4	232	187	236	$1	290	345	636	8	77	0.36	244	69	175	0.80	3.39	-12.1
BAvg No change	1st Half		77	16	16	0	5	2	208			($1)	307	312	619	13	73	0.52	234	68	210		3.58	-4.6
LIMA C	2nd Half		117	17	29	2	9	2	248			$1	279	368	646	4	79	0.21	251	70	147		3.23	-7.6
Risk X HIGH	03	Proj	**150**	**24**	**38**	**3**	**14**	**4**	**253**			**$3**	**300**	**384**	**684**	**6**	**78**	**0.30**	**254**	**83**	**144**		**3.81**	**-5.0**

0-7-.208 in 130 AB at COL and NYM. These small data sets are tossing BPIs all over the place. One year up, next year down. But whether good or bad, he's 30 and not going anywhere.

Lockhart,Keith

		Tm	AB	R	H	HR	RBI	SB	Avg	vLH	vRH	R$	OB	Slg	OPS	bb%	ct%	Eye	xBA	PX	SX	G/F	RC/G	RAR
Pos 2B	98	ATL	366	50	94	9	37	2	257	189	264	$6	311	388	699	7	90	0.78	295	94	53	0.81	4.29	1.0
Age 38 Decline	99	ATL	161	20	42	1	21	3	261	83	275	$2	339	311	649	11	87	0.90	254	31	79	1.24	4.00	-1.5
Bats L	00	ATL	275	32	73	2	32	4	265	375	251	$4	336	353	688	10	89	0.94	275	57	96	1.20	4.45	-0.0
Pwr --	01	ATL	178	17	39	3	12	1	219	111	225	($0)	284	303	587	8	88	0.73	261	54	40	0.93	2.90	-5.8
Spd No change	02	ATL	296	34	64	5	32	0	216	67	224	($1)	282	331	613	8	83	0.54	256	73	74	0.91	3.20	-12.0
BAvg +++++	1st Half		131	18	25	4	14	0	191			($1)	254	351	605	8	85	0.55	276	99	74		2.98	-6.2
LIMA D+	2nd Half		165	16	39	1	18	0	236			$0	304	315	619	9	82	0.53	241	51	77		3.36	-5.9
Risk X HIGH	03	Proj	150	17	34	2	15	1	227			$0	293	324	617	9	86	0.65	261	63	69		3.31	-3.7

Don't you think that ATL's reliance on players like these eventually comes back to haunt them when they need to win the most? When does the loss of offense offset the gains of defensive specialization?

LoDuca,Paul

		Tm	AB	R	H	HR	RBI	SB	Avg	vLH	vRH	R$	OB	Slg	OPS	bb%	ct%	Eye	xBA	PX	SX	G/F	RC/G	RAR
Pos CA	98	aaa	465	53	117	6	44	14	252			$8	314	346	660	8	93	1.24	290	69	85	0.83	3.93	-1.6
Age 31 Past Peak	99	LA	* 171	24	45	4	17	2	263	278	171	$3	333	380	713	10	94	1.80	299	77	51	1.14	4.44	2.1
Bats R	00	LA	* 344	43	99	5	51	6	288	240	250	$10	348	413	761	9	94	1.60	310	86	72	1.25	5.06	10.6
Pwr ++	01	LA	460	71	147	25	90	2	320	411	290	$25	373	543	916	8	93	1.30	331	134	37	1.08	7.66	58.1
Spd No change	02	LA	580	74	163	10	64	3	281	307	273	$13	321	402	723	6	95	1.10	298	85	62	1.37	4.74	9.5
BAvg +++	1st Half		277	35	88	4	36	3	318			$11	366	444	810	7	96	1.75	306	91	70		6.42	18.9
LIMA A+	2nd Half		303	39	75	6	28	0	248			$2	278	363	642	4	94	0.68	289	79	44		3.48	-6.5
Risk Very High	03	Proj	500	67	148	13	67	2	296			$16	344	441	785	7	94	1.23	306	95	46		5.57	24.3

There are few catchers who are put behind the plate for 85% of a team's games anymore. This is simply a question of stamina -- he batted .221 in Sept. of his breakout year, and faded even earlier when overworked in '03.

Lofton,Kenny

		Tm	AB	R	H	HR	RBI	SB	Avg	vLH	vRH	R$	OB	Slg	OPS	bb%	ct%	Eye	xBA	PX	SX	G/F	RC/G	RAR
Pos CF	98	CLE	600	101	169	12	64	54	282	293	277	$29	373	413	786	13	87	1.09	287	84	146	1.38	6.18	26.2
Age 35 Decline	99	CLE	465	110	140	7	39	25	301	224	327	$17	403	432	835	15	82	0.94	274	85	161	1.24	7.07	35.4
Bats L	00	CLE	543	107	151	15	73	30	278	260	283	$21	370	422	792	13	87	1.10	284	84	142	1.17	6.08	23.6
Pwr No change	01	CLE	517	91	135	14	66	16	261	246	266	$15	323	398	721	8	87	0.68	278	83	117	1.12	4.57	-6.1
Spd +++++	02	2TM	532	98	139	11	51	29	261	248	265	$17	349	414	763	12	86	0.99	287	98	170	1.14	5.30	6.6
BAvg +++	1st Half		277	54	70	3	33	21	253			$9	349	383	732	13	84	0.95	275	85	200		5.04	1.1
LIMA A+	2nd Half		255	44	69	8	18	8	271			$6	350	447	797	11	88	1.03	299	112	126		5.60	5.5
Risk Low	03	Proj	500	92	134	10	53	19	268			$14	350	403	753	11	86	0.93	286	86	139		5.18	7.5

A slight uptick in some of his BPIs, but still very similar to the skills he's displayed for the past three years. Don't count on a 13-SB April again, so his speed output should return to Earth.

Lombard,George

		Tm	AB	R	H	HR	RBI	SB	Avg	vLH	vRH	R$	OB	Slg	OPS	bb%	ct%	Eye	xBA	PX	SX	G/F	RC/G	RAR
Pos CF LF	98	aa	422	65	111	16	49	27	263			$18	351	441	791	12	73	0.50	254	111	132	1.00	5.96	18.2
Age 27 Peak	99	aaa	233	21	43	6	24	18	185			$4	275	322	597	11	64	0.35	211	83	129		2.95	-12.3
Bats L	00	aaa	424	60	106	8	41	27	250			$12	326	384	711	10	74	0.44	243	84	148		4.50	-1.2
Pwr --	01	aaa	44	6	13	3	7	3	295			$3	367	591	958	10	73	0.42	279	162	172		7.28	4.0
Spd No change	02	2TM	* 305	44	73	8	21	16	239	152	255	$7	303	390	693	8	69	0.29	227	94	170	1.24	4.36	-5.3
BAvg -	1st Half		88	12	20	3	9	3	227			$1	299	443	742	9	74	0.39	266	135	181		4.58	-1.0
LIMA B+	2nd Half		217	32	53	5	12	13	244			$5	305	369	674	8	67	0.26	212	77	155		4.26	-4.4
Risk X HIGH	03	Proj	350	48	87	9	31	21	249			$10	321	398	720	10	70	0.36	237	93	150		4.68	-0.5

5-13-13-.241 in 241 AB at DET. Has shown occasional signs of developing into a serviceable hitter, but has yet to really put it all together. Only consistently positive skill is speed, but that's wasted on a near-.300 OB avg.

Long,Terrence

		Tm	AB	R	H	HR	RBI	SB	Avg	vLH	vRH	R$	OB	Slg	OPS	bb%	ct%	Eye	xBA	PX	SX	G/F	RC/G	RAR
Pos CF	98	aa	455	62	125	14	52	21	275			$17	353	442	795	11	79	0.57	269	100	151		5.66	15.0
Age 27 Peak	99	aaa	458	48	123	7	58	18	269			$12	311	384	695	6	87	0.47	278	76	104		4.01	-8.2
Bats L	00	OAK	* 644	114	190	21	94	5	295	263	298	$19	343	467	810	7	87	0.58	298	105	93	1.32	5.97	24.0
Pwr ++	01	OAK	629	90	178	12	85	9	283	278	286	$17	338	412	750	8	84	0.50	267	85	93	1.34	5.19	4.7
Spd --	02	OAK	587	71	141	16	67	3	240	250	237	$9	298	390	688	8	84	0.50	273	101	71	1.17	3.95	-16.7
BAvg +++	1st Half		294	40	72	7	41	2	245			$5	313	398	711	9	81	0.53	270	108	80		4.32	-5.1
LIMA A+	2nd Half		293	31	69	9	26	1	235			$4	282	382	664	6	86	0.46	276	94	63		3.59	-11.4
Risk High	03	Proj	550	73	144	14	67	6	262			$12	316	409	725	7	84	0.51	275	95	88		4.57	-5.6

xBA gives his season a more optimistic spin, but the declining trends are still evident. Those 16 HRs are not nearly enough to offset the other empty offense he provides.

Lopez,Felipe

		Tm	AB	R	H	HR	RBI	SB	Avg	vLH	vRH	R$	OB	Slg	OPS	bb%	ct%	Eye	xBA	PX	SX	G/F	RC/G	RAR
Pos SS	98		0	0	0	0	0	0	0								0							
Age 22 Growth	99		0	0	0	0	0	0	0								0							
Bats S	00	aa	463	42	112	7	34	9	242			$3	281	339	620	5	83	0.32	255	61	77		2.96	-14.7
Pwr ---	01	TOR	* 607	93	166	23	68	19	273	293	244	$21	327	470	796	7	79	0.38	274	113	148	1.24	5.26	15.0
Spd ----	02	TOR	* 455	64	117	10	48	16	257	303	204	$13	327	400	727	9	74	0.40	242	98	131	1.52	4.81	2.0
BAvg --	1st Half		234	32	55	8	30	4	235			$5	301	415	715	9	70	0.31	238	114	131		4.33	-2.5
LIMA A	2nd Half		221	32	62	2	18	12	281			$8	354	385	738	10	78	0.52	245	81	116		5.35	4.7
Risk Very High	03	Proj	400	55	101	10	40	17	253			$11	313	400	714	8	78	0.40	256	95	133		4.43	7.8

8-34-5-.227 in 282 AB at TOR. In looking at power and speed, which will he be more likely to develop into? 30-15? 15-30? 15-15? 30-30? I'd put my money on 15-30. And a .260-.270 BA. But not in 2003.

Lopez,Javy

		Tm	AB	R	H	HR	RBI	SB	Avg	vLH	vRH	R$	OB	Slg	OPS	bb%	ct%	Eye	xBA	PX	SX	G/F	RC/G	RAR
Pos CA	98	ATL	489	73	139	34	106	5	284	275	287	$27	326	540	866	6	83	0.35	303	156	64	1.56	6.34	34.7
Age 32 Past Peak	99	ATL	246	34	78	11	45	0	317	340	311	$11	368	533	901	8	83	0.49	294	136	39	1.78	7.25	24.4
Bats R	00	ATL	481	60	138	24	89	0	287	277	289	$18	335	484	820	7	83	0.44	288	113	28	1.47	6.03	28.9
Pwr -	01	ATL	438	45	117	17	66	1	267	212	280	$12	311	425	736	6	81	0.34	264	92	41	1.39	4.79	16.0
Spd No change	02	ATL	347	31	81	11	52	0	233	255	230	$5	287	372	659	7	82	0.41	254	86	19	1.67	3.68	-5.5
BAvg No change	1st Half		209	17	50	6	28	0	239			$3	274	368	642	5	85	0.31	260	81	21		3.42	-4.9
LIMA D+	2nd Half		138	14	31	5	24	0	225			$2	305	377	682	10	78	0.52	244	93	17		4.08	-0.5
Risk Very High	03	Proj	350	37	89	12	58	0	254			$8	308	399	707	7	81	0.42	259	88	27		4.39	4.4

The rigors of catching have worn him down, which is obvious from a look at many of his BPIs over this 5-year scan. The odds are he might be able to slow or halt the skid temporarily, but as for turning it around, it's unlikely.

Lopez,Luis M.

		Tm	AB	R	H	HR	RBI	SB	Avg	vLH	vRH	R$	OB	Slg	OPS	bb%	ct%	Eye	xBA	PX	SX	G/F	RC/G	RAR
Pos SS	98	NYM	266	37	67	2	22	2	252	241	257	$2	304	338	643	7	77	0.33	243	65	92	1.76	3.63	-0.4
Age 32 Past Peak	99	NYM	104	11	22	2	13	1	212	174	222	($0)	293	308	601	10	68	0.36	211	63	44	0.81	3.11	-1.6
Bats S	00	MIL	201	24	53	6	27	1	264	255	266	$4	295	423	718	4	83	0.26	281	104	45	1.06	4.27	4.4
Pwr +	01	MIL	222	22	60	4	18	0	270	184	288	$3	314	387	701	6	80	0.32	250	70	81	1.36	4.34	4.8
Spd No change	02	2TM	* 207	22	46	5	16	1	222	208	194	($0)	251	348	599	4	83	0.22	259	86	53	1.08	2.97	-8.3
BAvg No change	1st Half		77	14	22	3	9	0	286			$1	321	455	776	5	84	0.33	278	108	51		5.36	2.4
LIMA D	2nd Half		130	8	24	2	7	1	185			($3)	209	285	494	3	82	0.17	248	72	43		1.94	-9.1
Risk High	03	Proj	150	16	36	3	14	1	240			$1	277	375	652	5	81	0.27	264	88	71		3.57	-2.7

2-10-.197 in 117 AB at MIL and BAL. Strained quad muscle suppressed his stats in '02, but it's really tough to tell when the levels are this low to begin with.

Loretta,Mark

		Tm	AB	R	H	HR	RBI	SB	Avg	vLH	vRH	R$	OB	Slg	OPS	bb%	ct%	Eye	xBA	PX	SX	G/F	RC/G	RAR
Pos 3B	98	MIL	434	55	137	6	54	9	316	347	300	$17	376	424	800	9	89	0.89	289	85	60	1.44	6.11	21.8
Age 31 Past Peak	99	MIL	587	93	170	5	67	4	290	300	286	$11	347	390	738	8	90	0.88	285	71	93	1.03	5.16	13.0
Bats R	00	MIL	352	49	99	7	40	0	281	333	266	$7	350	406	756	10	89	0.97	291	83	39	1.68	5.20	8.8
Pwr +++	01	MIL	384	40	111	2	29	1	289	313	281	$6	337	352	689	7	88	0.61	257	44	53	1.19	4.40	-3.3
Spd No change	02	2NL	283	33	86	4	27	1	304	309	302	$8	375	410	784	10	87	0.86	266	77	34	1.03	5.97	11.6
BAvg -	1st Half		92	5	22	0	7	0	239			($0)	320	315	636	11	85	0.79	251	66	9		3.72	-2.8
LIMA B+	2nd Half		191	28	64	4	20	1	335			$8	401	455	856	10	88	0.91	273	82	41		7.34	16.1
Risk Moderate	03	Proj	450	52	133	8	53	1	296			$12	360	413	773	9	88	0.81	275	80	35		5.61	15.0

Sometimes all it takes is a change of scenery. Got out of MIL and had a big party in HOU, batting .424 with a 1.057 OPS, until a hamstring injury forced him out. If healthy, could have a nice run in HOU.

Lowell,Mike		Tm	AB	R	H	HR	RBI	SB	Avg	vLH	vRH	R$	OB	Slg	OPS	bb%	ct%	Eye	xBA	PX	SX	G/F	RC/G	RAR
Pos 3B	98	aaa	525	69	147	22	85	3	280			$18	320	472	793	6	86	0.43	300	123	70	0.86	5.56	16.5
Age 29 Past Peak	99	FLA	*391	40	100	13	54	0	256	250	254	$7	312	399	711	8	79	0.39	254	89		0.69	4.49	0.5
Bats R	00	FLA	508	73	137	22	91	4	270	257	273	$16	340	474	814	10	85	0.72	304	128	59	0.67	6.01	25.7
Pwr ++	01	FLA	551	65	156	18	100	1	283	283	283	$18	335	448	783	7	86	0.54	286	107	31	0.65	5.51	14.1
Spd No change	02	FLA	597	88	165	24	92	4	276	255	283	$20	347	471	818	10	85	0.71	287	125	51	0.61	6.03	25.5
BAvg -	1st Half		313	47	99	13	53	1	316			$15	378	540	918	9	86	0.70	303	149	35		7.70	29.7
LIMA A	2nd Half		284	41	66	11	39	3	232			$5	314	394	709	11	83	0.71	269	99	64		4.50	-1.6
Risk Moderate	03	Proj	600	82	176	29	112	3	293			$26	357	505	862	9	85	0.64	294	131	45		6.79	42.1

Bruised his hip at the beginning of July and you can be darn sure that had something to do with his 2nd half swan dive. Given the pace he was on, if healthy, he could have his career year in 2003.

Lugo,Julio		Tm	AB	R	H	HR	RBI	SB	Avg	vLH	vRH	R$	OB	Slg	OPS	bb%	ct%	Eye	xBA	PX	SX	G/F	RC/G	RAR
Pos SS	98		0	0	0	0	0	0	0								0							
Age 27 Peak	99	aa	445	67	124	8	37	22	279			$13	334	409	743	8	88	0.67	287	83	131		4.85	12.8
Bats R	00	HOU	*521	97	150	13	50	32	288	239	300	$22	346	436	781	8	79	0.41	262	89	150	1.52	5.30	28.7
Pwr +	01	HOU	513	93	135	10	37	12	263	299	254	$10	324	372	696	8	77	0.40	243	68	112	1.20	4.17	8.6
Spd -----	02	HOU	322	45	84	8	35	9	261	270	258	$8	320	388	708	8	77	0.38	243	81	94	1.46	4.51	5.4
BAvg --	1st Half		191	24	51	4	19	5	267			$5	327	377	704	8	74	0.34	227	68	89		4.40	2.5
LIMA A	2nd Half		131	21	33	4	16	4	252			$3	310	405	714	8	82	0.46	267	99	89		4.67	2.8
Risk Moderate	03	Proj	500	81	133	11	49	12	266			$12	325	391	716	8	79	0.42	253	80	107		4.50	11.6

Broken forearm ended his season early. BPIs have been in a holding pattern, leaving little indication that it's going to get any better than this.

Mabry,John		Tm	AB	R	H	HR	RBI	SB	Avg	vLH	vRH	R$	OB	Slg	OPS	bb%	ct%	Eye	xBA	PX	SX	G/F	RC/G	RAR
Pos 1B LF RF	98	STL	377	41	94	9	46	0	249	218	258	$5	305	379	684	7	80	0.39	261	94	26	1.49	4.04	-15.6
Age 32 Past Peak	99	SEA	262	34	64	9	33	2	244	250	244	$4	298	401	699	7	77	0.33	252	97	55	1.09	4.20	-13.7
Bats L	00	2TM	226	35	53	8	32	0	235		264	$3	282	398	680	6	69	0.22	233	101	51	1.19	3.83	-13.3
Pwr No change	01	2NL	154	14	32	6	20	1	208	214	207	$1	269	370	640	8	70	0.28	230	98	36	1.02	3.43	-14.1
Spd No change	02	2TM	214	28	59	11	43	1	276	192	287	$8	323	500	823	7	80	0.36	283	139	60	1.00	5.81	-0.3
BAvg --	1st Half		70	10	24	2	14	0	343			$3	361	514	875	3	80	0.14	270	122	32		7.31	3.0
LIMA D+	2nd Half		144	18	35	9	29	1	243			$4	306	493	799	8	81	0.46	289	148	69		5.20	-2.9
Risk High	03	Proj	200	25	51	8	33	1	255			$5	305	437	742	7	76	0.30	259	113	41		4.71	-7.5

Sometimes things just fall together. He's had many chances before and shown no signs of this type of power. At 32, it's unlikely that there's any further upside from here.

Machado,Robert		Tm	AB	R	H	HR	RBI	SB	Avg	vLH	vRH	R$	OB	Slg	OPS	bb%	ct%	Eye	xBA	PX	SX	G/F	RC/G	RAR
Pos CA	98	aaa	239	24	53	3	21	2	222			($0)	271	326	597	6	89	0.59	282	80	52	1.32	2.97	-7.9
Age 29 Past Peak	99	aaa	129	9	25	2	9	0	194			($2)	212	302	514	2	82	0.13	257	77	34	0.50	1.98	-8.0
Bats R	00	aaa	330	38	86	8	54	1	261			$6	318	385	703	8	86	0.60	273	79	32	0.33	4.20	0.5
Pwr No change	01	CHC	*315	29	72	8	37	0	229	278	185	$2	264	362	626	5	81	0.25	259	87	24	1.27	3.26	-3.1
Spd No change	02	MIL	211	19	55	3	22	0	261	226	290	$2	316	379	695	7	81	0.41	250	83	38	1.10	4.36	1.0
BAvg --	1st Half		100	10	26	2	13	0	260			$2	308	430	738	7	77	0.30	259	117	64		4.76	1.7
LIMA D	2nd Half		111	9	29	1	9	0	261			$1	322	333	656	8	84	0.56	242	53	17		3.97	-0.8
Risk X HIGH	03	Proj	200	19	49	4	22	0	245			$2	295	359	654	7	82	0.39	257	79	29		3.71	-1.7

A safe $1 catcher? Safer than some, not as safe as others. Your team can withstand 200 AB of a .260 BA. It probably could not withstand 200 AB of a .229 BA. And he is just as likely to do either.

Macias,Jose		Tm	AB	R	H	HR	RBI	SB	Avg	vLH	vRH	R$	OB	Slg	OPS	bb%	ct%	Eye	xBA	PX	SX	G/F	RC/G	RAR
Pos CF 3B 2B	98	aa	511	63	129	10	54	5	252			$7	310	384	694	8	92	1.08	299	84	98		4.10	-8.4
Age 29 Past Peak	99	aaa	438	34	89	2	28	8	203			($4)	253	279	531	6	88	0.57	267	48	107	1.00	2.30	-30.6
Bats S	00	DET	*303	40	71	2	30	4	234	350	226	$0	305	314	619	9	88	0.86	260	46	124	1.23	3.38	-13.1
Pwr ++	01	DET	488	62	131	8	51	21	268	238	279	$14	313	392	705	6	89	0.59	285	78	131	1.62	4.46	-7.3
Spd -----	02	2TM	338	43	84	7	39	8	249	250	248	$6	292	379	671	6	83	0.37	266	91	86	1.35	3.62	-13.4
BAvg -	1st Half		194	23	47	3	18	7	242			$3	286	340	627	6	88	0.52	269	70	85		3.36	-9.2
LIMA B	2nd Half		144	20	37	4	21	1	257			$2	301	431	731	6	76	0.26	260	118	88		3.96	-4.2
Risk Very High	03	Proj	350	44	88	10	44	8	251			$8	301	410	711	7	85	0.47	287	100	103		4.13	-6.3

Aside from the big drop in SX, there has only been minor movement in his other BPIs. PX might indicate a power surge into double-digits. Contact rate might indicate further erosion of his BA. Consider a utility player.

Mackowiak,Rob		Tm	AB	R	H	HR	RBI	SB	Avg	vLH	vRH	R$	OB	Slg	OPS	bb%	ct%	Eye	xBA	PX	SX	G/F	RC/G	RAR
Pos RF CF 3B	98		0	0	0	0	0	0	0								0							
Age 26 Pre-Peak	99	aa	195	17	47	3	22	0	241			$1	267	385	652	3	84	0.23	279	99	69		3.36	-9.9
Bats L	00	aa	526	67	136	11	71	15	259			$12	283	390	673	3	82	0.19	269	84	112		3.81	-20.5
Pwr ++++	01	PIT	*332	41	85	7	32	5	256	167	269	$6	300	392	692	6	75	0.25	245	89	92	1.26	4.05	-16.3
Spd -	02	PIT	385	57	94	16	48	9	244	302	237	$10	319	426	744	10	69	0.35	230	113	78	1.11	4.85	-6.8
BAvg -	1st Half		199	29	51	10	26	4	256			$6	305	472	778	7	69	0.23	241	133	71		5.01	-2.4
LIMA B	2nd Half		186	28	43	6	22	5	231			$3	332	376	708	13	68	0.47	219	91	75		4.63	-4.8
Risk High	03	Proj	400	53	99	13	47	6	248			$8	306	409	715	8	74	0.32	246	103	77		4.36	-6.7

Odd phenomenon... He's being more selective at the plate, but making less contact with those pitches he does choose to swing at, and those pitches he does make contact with are travelling further distances.

Magee,Wendell		Tm	AB	R	H	HR	RBI	SB	Avg	vLH	vRH	R$	OB	Slg	OPS	bb%	ct%	Eye	xBA	PX	SX	G/F	RC/G	RAR
Pos CF	98	PHI	*582	73	148	19	64	5	254	258	318	$12	303	430	733	7	84	0.43	289	118	97	0.93	4.66	4.6
Age 30 Past Peak	99	aaa	566	69	133	15	58	7	235			$5	287	371	658	7	79	0.35	257	87	65		3.55	-18.3
Bats R	00	DET	186	31	51	7	31	1	274	273	278	$5	311	430	741	5	85	0.36	274	82	104	1.10	4.89	0.8
Pwr ---	01	DET	207	26	44	5	17	3	213	237	191	$1	291	377	668	10	79	0.52	264	99	138	1.40	3.90	-6.9
Spd No change	02	DET	347	34	94	6	35	2	271	236	283	$7	291	383	675	3	82	0.16	253	81	54	1.62	3.80	-11.0
BAvg --	1st Half		258	27	71	5	26	1	275			$5	300	407	707	3	84	0.22	270	96	54		4.10	-5.9
LIMA D+	2nd Half		89	7	23	1	9	1	258			$1	267	315	581	1	74	0.04	206	39	47		2.97	-4.9
Risk High	03	Proj	250	28	63	5	27	2	252			$4	290	378	668	5	80	0.26	250	80	89		3.85	-7.9

I have this strong suspicion that we are going to see a huge turnover of players this year. Teams will cut all of these low skills guys and we'll never hear from them again Then lots of new faces will appear in 2003.

Magruder,Chris		Tm	AB	R	H	HR	RBI	SB	Avg	vLH	vRH	R$	OB	Slg	OPS	bb%	ct%	Eye	xBA	PX	SX	G/F	RC/G	RAR
Pos LF RF CF	98		0	0	0	0	0	0	0								0							
Age 26 Pre-Peak	99	aa	476	74	113	6	57	16	237			$7	330	330	660	12	82	0.77	254	61	102		3.79	-21.2
Bats S	00	aa	496	79	129	4	36	16	260			$7	339	355	694	11	86	0.83	269	68	97		4.30	-15.3
Pwr ---	01	a/a	519	76	140	16	53	8	270			$13	332	435	767	8	85	0.62	284	100	106	1.38	5.12	-2.4
Spd --	02	CLE	*449	60	105	11	44	5	234	275	186	$6	295	372	667	8	81	0.45	260	95	89	1.02	3.85	-15.0
BAvg No change	1st Half		211	26	51	6	21	2	242			$3	310	398	708	9	83	0.58	273	103	89		4.30	-4.2
LIMA C	2nd Half		238	34	54	5	23	3	227			$3	281	349	630	7	79	0.35	249	88	80		3.48	-10.6
Risk Very High	03	Proj	150	22	37	3	15	3	247			$2	314	380	693	9	82	0.56	264	88	93		4.19	-4.4

6-29-.217 in 258 AB at CLE. Was starting to make some minor progress, when along came 2002. His performance in CLE will likely push him further down the depth chart. Only 26, but chances may have run out.

Marrero,Eli		Tm	AB	R	H	HR	RBI	SB	Avg	vLH	vRH	R$	OB	Slg	OPS	bb%	ct%	Eye	xBA	PX	SX	G/F	RC/G	RAR
Pos RF CA CF	98	STL	*384	46	89	10	37	10	232	293	216	$6	303	375	678	9	84	0.64	282	101	87	0.98	4.03	-11.7
Age 29 Past Peak	99	STL	317	32	61	6	34	11	192	203	189	$0	236	297	532	5	82	0.32	260	67	102	1.22	2.37	-26.1
Bats R	00	STL	102	21	23	5	17	5	225	200	232	$3	288	422	710	8	84	0.56	291	106	155	1.28	4.46	-2.5
Pwr +++	01	STL	203	37	54	6	23	6	266	256	269	$6	317	438	755	7	82	0.42	281	104	156	1.61	4.88	-4.9
Spd -----	02	STL	397	63	104	18	66	14	262	227	273	$17	330	451	780	9	82	0.56	276	113	104	0.83	5.52	1.5
BAvg No change	1st Half		186	26	49	7	30	10	263			$8	332	430	762	9	83	0.59	273	99	115		5.57	0.9
LIMA B+	2nd Half		211	37	55	11	36	4	261			$8	328	469	797	9	81	0.53	277	124	75		5.48	0.5
Risk High	03	Proj	350	59	97	17	61	7	277			$15	337	483	820	8	82	0.51	285	121	100		5.96	11.6

17 of his 18 HRs were hit off RHers, and given his BAs vs LHers in three of the last four years, it seems a straight platoon is his best chance to be productive. And he CAN be, if used correctly.

Martinez,Edgar

	Yr	Tm	AB	R	H	HR	RBI	SB	Avg	vLH	vRH	R$	OB	Slg	OPS	bb%	ct%	Eye	xBA	PX	SX	G/F	RC/G	RAR
Pos DH	98	SEA	556	86	179	29	102	1	322	311	324	$27	431	567	997	16	83	1.10	302	154	33	1.06	9.93	85.7
Age 40 Decline	99	SEA	502	86	169	24	86	7	337	358	331	$26	444	554	998	16	80	0.98	285	133	65	1.40	10.29	85.5
Bats R	00	SEA	556	100	180	37	145	3	324	359	317	$33	423	579	1002	15	83	1.01	306	144	49	0.95	10.01	89.7
Pwr - - -	01	SEA	470	80	144	23	116	4	306	246	328	$25	421	543	964	17	81	1.03	288	150	57	0.95	9.19	62.0
Spd No change	02	SEA	328	42	91	15	59	1	277	306	267	$12	400	485	885	17	79	0.97	279	139	25	0.86	7.54	21.4
BAvg No change	1st Half		59	8	15	2	12	0	254			$2	343	424	767	12	71	0.47	240	117	39		5.04	-1.2
LIMA A	2nd Half		269	34	76	13	47	1	283			$11	412	498	910	18	81	1.13	288	143	27		8.15	23.5
Risk Very Low	03	Proj	400	60	117	18	85	0	293			$17	404	503	907	16	79	0.90	278	136	24		7.93	33.0

After years of decline in his OB avg, it's finally come to rest at... .400?? Although it's doubtful that he'll hit .300 again, it would no surprise me if he did. Solid BPIs all around, still. Does DHing prolong a player's career?

Martinez,Ramon

	Yr	Tm	AB	R	H	HR	RBI	SB	Avg	vLH	vRH	R$	OB	Slg	OPS	bb%	ct%	Eye	xBA	PX	SX	G/F	RC/G	RAR
Pos SS	98	aaa	383	46	98	10	44	0	256			$6	313	386	700	8	90	0.86	289	86	37	1.40	4.28	5.3
Age 30 Past Peak	99	SF	*258	31	70	6	32	3	271	259	267	$5	329	395	724	8	88	0.73	283	80	63	0.98	4.71	8.9
Bats R	00	SF	189	30	57	6	25	3	302	297	304	$7	353	487	840	7	88	0.68	308	115	101	1.01	6.36	16.5
Pwr - -	01	SF	391	48	99	5	37	1	253	293	243	$3	319	353	672	9	87	0.73	267	65	69	1.16	4.05	5.2
Spd No change	02	SF	181	26	49	4	25	2	271	254	279	$5	323	414	737	7	86	0.54	277	91	105	0.72	4.97	5.5
BAvg -	1st Half		96	15	27	2	11	0	281			$2	330	385	716	7	86	0.54	259	59	79		4.74	2.2
LIMA C+	2nd Half		85	11	22	2	14	2	259			$2	315	447	762	8	85	0.54	295	128	113		5.21	3.2
Risk Very High	03	Proj	200	27	56	4	26	2	280			$5	336	425	761	8	87	0.62	284	93	94		5.30	9.6

Serviceable end game pick. Won't make or break your team. Won't require damage control. Won't require replacing. Won't make you sleep on the couch if you're out all night with the guys.

Martinez,Tino

	Yr	Tm	AB	R	H	HR	RBI	SB	Avg	vLH	vRH	R$	OB	Slg	OPS	bb%	ct%	Eye	xBA	PX	SX	G/F	RC/G	RAR
Pos 1B	98	NYY	531	92	149	28	123	2	281	268	287	$22	355	505	859	10	84	0.73	300	136	57	0.95	6.70	16.0
Age 35 Decline	99	NYY	589	95	155	28	105	3	263	261	264	$17	340	458	799	10	85	0.80	290	113	60	1.08	5.64	-5.0
Bats L	00	NYY	569	69	147	16	91	4	258	281	249	$11	320	422	742	8	87	0.70	293	101	81	0.90	4.91	-20.5
Pwr +	01	NYY	589	89	165	34	113	1	280	257	290	$24	328	501	829	7	85	0.47	288	126	48	1.14	5.96	-5.6
Spd No change	02	STL	511	63	134	21	75	3	262	207	278	$14	337	438	776	10	86	0.82	282	107	49	1.05	5.41	-5.0
BAvg + + +	1st Half		248	23	60	9	37	0	242			$4	343	387	730	13	85	1.06	265	87	12		4.77	-7.7
LIMA A	2nd Half		263	40	74	12	38	3	281			$10	332	487	819	7	87	0.57	297	125	80		6.04	2.6
Risk Very Low	03	Proj	550	75	158	28	96	3	287			$23	350	496	846	9	86	0.68	295	123	57		6.47	19.0

Was tentative at the plate in the 1st half as he learned NL pitchers, then found a groove in the 2nd half. If that is any indication, he could have a surprisingly good year in 2003.

Mateo,Ruben

	Yr	Tm	AB	R	H	HR	RBI	SB	Avg	vLH	vRH	R$	OB	Slg	OPS	bb%	ct%	Eye	xBA	PX	SX	G/F	RC/G	RAR
Pos RF	98	aa	433	74	132	18	69	17	305			$23	347	513	860	6	89	0.61	322	135	119		6.54	19.3
Age 25 Pre-Peak	99	TEX	*375	61	109	21	71	8	291	350	216	$17	320	517	837	4	85	0.28	303	131	93	0.79	5.98	10.2
Bats R	00	TEX	206	32	60	7	19	6	291	318	284	$7	324	447	771	5	83	0.29	277	94	90	1.24	5.53	3.2
Pwr + +	01	TEX	*431	49	101	4	40	3	234	412	189	$1	270	339	609	5	84	0.30	259	70	100	1.47	3.12	-25.3
Spd No change	02	CIN	*295	40	79	9	25	5	268	161	309	$7	301	427	728	5	83	0.29	275	105	74	0.65	4.56	-7.5
BAvg - -	1st Half		197	29	57	8	18	1	289			$6	327	482	809	5	84	0.34	283	123	50		5.73	1.9
LIMA D+	2nd Half		98	11	22	1	7	4	224			$1	248	316	564	3	83	0.18	255	69	95		2.66	-7.9
Risk Very High	03	Proj	150	20	39	4	14	3	260			$3	292	404	696	4	84	0.28	275	93	103		4.17	-3.3

2-7-.256 in 86 AB at CIN. Hadn't done much of anything since AA ball, but put up an intriguing 1st half before fading. Talent is here, but it's been severely sidetracked by injury and circumstance. VHigh risk pick.

Matheny,Mike

	Yr	Tm	AB	R	H	HR	RBI	SB	Avg	vLH	vRH	R$	OB	Slg	OPS	bb%	ct%	Eye	xBA	PX	SX	G/F	RC/G	RAR
Pos CA	98	MIL	320	24	76	6	27	1	238	252	230	$2	263	334	597	3	80	0.17	251	69	34	1.19	3.03	-9.2
Age 32 Past Peak	99	TOR	163	16	35	3	17	0	215	164	241	($1)	269	307	575	7	77	0.32	228	59	27	1.30	2.84	-6.5
Bats R	00	STL	417	43	109	6	47	0	261	250	265	$4	314	362	676	7	77	0.33	243	68	33	1.54	4.14	0.9
Pwr -	01	STL	381	40	83	7	42	0	218	184	226	$0	271	304	576	7	80	0.37	238	55	33	1.12	2.83	-8.9
Spd No change	02	STL	315	31	77	3	35	1	244	265	239	$2	314	317	632	9	84	0.65	245	50	43	1.48	3.52	-6.7
BAvg + + +	1st Half		149	16	35	3	17	1	235			$1	305	349	654	9	85	0.65	260	77	43		3.74	-2.1
LIMA D+	2nd Half		166	15	42	0	18	0	253			$1	322	289	612	9	84	0.65	232	26	49		3.30	-4.7
Risk Moderate	03	Proj	350	35	89	4	38	1	254			$3	313	335	648	8	82	0.47	242	54	40		3.75	-2.5

xBA shows that, despite the wild swings in his BA, this is very much the same batter every year. Spike in batting eye might presage some BA improvement, but not likely enough to get excited about.

Matos,Julius

	Yr	Tm	AB	R	H	HR	RBI	SB	Avg	vLH	vRH	R$	OB	Slg	OPS	bb%	ct%	Eye	xBA	PX	SX	G/F	RC/G	RAR
Pos 2B	98		0	0	0	0	0	0	0								0							
Age 28 Peak	99	aa	425	40	103	4	30	4	242			$1	260	327	587	2	93	0.36	284	53	98		2.89	-16.0
Bats R	00	aa	546	43	111	4	25	8	203			($6)	233	267	500	4	90	0.40	267	46	58		1.92	-36.9
Pwr + +	01	a/a	450	47	113	6	31	6	251			$4	272	331	603	3	88	0.25	261	53	63		2.83	-17.0
Spd No change	02	SD	*371	36	93	5	41	2	251	200	264	$4	284	337	620	4	86	0.33	255	60	43	1.59	3.26	-13.7
BAvg - -	1st Half		254	27	68	5	33	1	268			$5	293	390	683	3	87	0.26	270	85	41		3.87	-4.8
LIMA F	2nd Half		117	9	25	0	8	1	214			($1)	264	222	486	6	85	0.44	222	7	44		2.09	-8.6
Risk X HIGH	03	Proj	150	14	35	1	12	1	233			$0	265	295	559	4	88	0.35	255	43	51		2.58	-6.8

2-19-.238 in 185 AB at SD. Swings at a lot of pitches, makes contact very often, ball goes nowhere. No batta, No batta!

Matthews Jr.,Gary

	Yr	Tm	AB	R	H	HR	RBI	SB	Avg	vLH	vRH	R$	OB	Slg	OPS	bb%	ct%	Eye	xBA	PX	SX	G/F	RC/G	RAR
Pos RF	98	aa	254	47	65	6	38	9	256			$8	355	390	745	13	83	0.93	275	87	124		5.37	2.5
Age 28 Peak	99	aaa	422	49	93	8	44	15	220			$4	299	329	628	10	77	0.48	242	70	97	3.60	3.42	-22.3
Bats S	00	CHC	*369	47	74	8	33	8	201	250	169	($0)	261	314	575	8	83	0.48	262	65	128	1.60	2.85	-27.4
Pwr + + + +	01	2NL	405	63	92	14	44	8	227	241	222	$6	327	378	705	13	75	0.60	246	88	93	1.44	4.38	-17.1
Spd + + + + +	02	2TM	345	54	95	7	38	15	275	239	292	$11	356	426	782	11	80	0.62	267	105	126	1.96	5.69	4.7
BAvg -	1st Half		174	32	50	3	15	7	287			$5	358	466	823	10	79	0.51	276	125	164		6.01	4.1
LIMA A	2nd Half		171	22	45	4	23	8	263			$5	354	386	740	12	81	0.75	256	84	80		5.35	0.5
Risk Very High	03	Proj	400	59	106	15	59	14	265			$14	347	443	791	11	79	0.61	274	109	111		5.70	5.8

Ah, the deception of statistics... It looks like his power skills declined in '02, but they actually improved. How? He hit 15 doubles and 2 triples in '01, but 25 and 3 in '02... all told, 4 more extra base hits in 60 fewer ABs.

Mayne,Brent

	Yr	Tm	AB	R	H	HR	RBI	SB	Avg	vLH	vRH	R$	OB	Slg	OPS	bb%	ct%	Eye	xBA	PX	SX	G/F	RC/G	RAR
Pos CA	98	SF	275	26	75	3	32	2	273	306	268	$5	359	360	719	12	83	0.79	259	69	37	1.65	4.95	8.5
Age 35 Decline	99	SF	322	39	97	2	39	2	301	286	305	$7	384	419	803	12	80	0.66	263	96	38	1.41	6.25	23.1
Bats L	00	COL	335	36	101	6	64	1	301	196	318	$11	387	418	805	12	86	0.98	277	80	22	1.31	6.24	23.6
Pwr +	01	2TM	326	28	93	2	40	1	285	206	295	$6	338	344	682	7	87	0.63	249	41	37	1.99	4.30	5.4
Spd No change	02	KC	330	35	78	4	31	4	236	162	256	$3	310	309	619	10	84	0.65	239	48	74	1.46	3.37	-3.4
BAvg + + +	1st Half		129	13	28	0	8	2	217			($0)	308	256	564	12	85	0.89	231	29	81		2.80	-3.7
LIMA D+	2nd Half		201	22	50	4	23	2	249			$3	311	343	654	8	83	0.51	243	60	67		3.75	0.4
Risk Moderate	03	Proj	350	35	89	4	41	3	254			$5	327	330	657	10	85	0.70	246	53	51		3.89	-1.9

One of the few late-round catching picks with a skills set that always warranted at least a token bid. That would've hurt in '02, but he might bounce back just a tad. Struggles vs LHers will limit his upside.

McCarty,Dave

	Yr	Tm	AB	R	H	HR	RBI	SB	Avg	vLH	vRH	R$	OB	Slg	OPS	bb%	ct%	Eye	xBA	PX	SX	G/F	RC/G	RAR
Pos LF	98	aaa	398	57	104	9	40	7	261			$8	339	402	741	11	77	0.51	255	99	73	8.00	4.87	-2.0
Age 33 Decline	99	aaa	466	54	89	22	49	4	191			$1	264	376	639	9	76	0.41	255	105	64		3.17	-29.1
Bats R	00	KC	270	34	75	12	53	0	278	365	223	$8	332	478	810	8	75	0.32	258	115	55	1.19	5.85	5.5
Pwr + +	01	KC	200	26	50	7	26	0	250	202	314	$3	330	405	735	11	78	0.53	244	96	24	1.65	4.90	1.1
Spd No change	02	TAM	*180	25	41	8	21	0	228	188	88	$3	294	411	706	9	72	0.33	240	113	66	1.56	4.13	-4.5
BAvg No change	1st Half		150	23	36	7	20	0	240			$3	301	440	741	8	71	0.30	246	125	78		4.53	-1.9
LIMA D	2nd Half		30	2	5	1	1	0	167			($0)	265	267	531	12	73	0.50	210	54	6		2.44	-2.4
Risk High	03	Proj	100	14	25	4	14	0	250			$2	316	424	741	9	75	0.38	248	109	41		4.74	-1.2

2-4-.136 in 66 AB at TAM. There's still some pop in this bat, but he's just not making contact anymore. Unless he can once more pull out a rabbit at AAA to merit a callup, his career is probably done.

McCracken,Quinton	Yr	Tm	AB	R	H	HR	RBI	SB	Avg	vLH	vRH	R$	OB	Slg	OPS	bb%	ct%	Eye	xBA	PX	SX	G/F	RC/G	RAR
Pos RF CF	98	TAM	614	77	179	7	59	19	292			$17	336	410	746	6	83	0.38	269	81	122	1.54	5.08	-1.4
Age 33 Decline	99	TAM	148	20	37	1	18	6	250	257	248	$3	315	324	639	9	84	0.61	255	50	110	2.39	3.74	-6.2
Bats S	00	aaa	334	35	68	2	18	8	204			($3)	255	269	524	6	86	0.50	257	47	84		2.17	-30.2
Pwr -	01	MIN	* 425	45	115	3	35	5	271	143	240	$6	302	374	676	4	86	0.32	265	72	88	1.69	3.62	-18.5
Spd -	02	ARI	349	60	108	3	40	5	309	306	312	$11	367	458	826	8	81	0.47	271	100	160	1.09	6.35	10.3
BAvg - - -	1st Half		125	22	45	1	9	3	360			$6	398	552	950	6	80	0.32	288	123	232		8.66	12.4
LIMA C+	2nd Half		224	38	63	2	31	2	281			$5	351	406	757	10	81	0.56	261	87	116		5.27	-1.0
Risk X HIGH	03	Proj	**250**	**35**	**68**	**2**	**24**	**3**	**272**			**$4**	**322**	**392**	**714**	**7**	**83**	**0.44**	**268**	**81**	**125**		**4.37**	**-4.1**

This .309 BA was done with smoke and mirrors. Plate patience only improved slightly but contact rate went down. His power surge lasted for 125 AB, then returned to reality... which is what 2003 will look like.

McDonald,John	Yr	Tm	AB	R	H	HR	RBI	SB	Avg	vLH	vRH	R$	OB	Slg	OPS	bb%	ct%	Eye	xBA	PX	SX	G/F	RC/G	RAR
Pos 2B SS	98	aa	514	59	106	2	37	14	206			($1)	260	259	518	7	89	0.63	262	41	97		2.32	-28.8
Age 28 Peak	99	a/a	463	48	126	1	41	10	273			$7	308	330	639	5	91	0.55	269	46	74		3.60	-8.0
Bats R	00	aaa	286	31	70	1	30	3	244			$1	288	315	603	6	91	0.71	276	54	68		3.12	-9.4
Pwr No change	01	aaa	410	44	89	2	28	14	218			$1	267	273	540	6	84	0.43	245	41	90		2.37	-21.8
Spd + + + + +	02	CLE	264	35	66	1	12	3	250	232	256	$1	277	326	603	4	81	0.20	238	55	126	1.38	3.22	-7.0
BAvg -	1st Half		83	9	21	0	7	1	253			$1	279	361	641	3	71	0.13	219	67	224		3.59	-1.3
LIMA D+	2nd Half		181	26	45	1	5	2	249			$1	277	309	586	4	86	0.27	246	50	81		3.05	-5.7
Risk X HIGH	03	Proj	**200**	**24**	**48**	**1**	**13**	**4**	**240**			**$1**	**277**	**311**	**588**	**5**	**84**	**0.31**	**246**	**50**	**112**		**2.97**	**-7.4**

Nearly all his trends have been heading south for awhile. If he hurries, he might beat them to Akron before nightfall.

McEwing,Joe	Yr	Tm	AB	R	H	HR	RBI	SB	Avg	vLH	vRH	R$	OB	Slg	OPS	bb%	ct%	Eye	xBA	PX	SX	G/F	RC/G	RAR
Pos RF SS 1B	98	a/a	572	79	165	11	71	11	288			$17	328	449	778	6	91	0.67	315	114	105	2.67	5.14	1.1
Age 30 Past Peak	99	STL	513	65	141	9	44	7	275	292	267	$9	329	398	726	7	83	0.47	268	81	88	1.77	4.76	-5.4
Bats R	00	NYM	* 324	44	73	6	34	9	225	163	250	$3	266	364	630	5	82	0.31	274	93	117	0.96	3.24	-19.6
Pwr + +	01	NYM	283	41	80	8	30	8	283	250	298	$9	323	449	772	6	80	0.30	271	103	125	1.01	5.10	-4.9
Spd - -	02	NYM	201	22	39	3	26	4	194	204	194	($1)	229	289	517	4	75	0.18	227	62	102	0.93	2.01	-20.4
BAvg + + +	1st Half		104	11	20	3	15	2	192			$0	229	327	556	5	68	0.15	216	77	118		2.15	-10.1
LIMA D+	2nd Half		97	11	19	0	11	2	196			($1)	228	247	475	4	81	0.22	237	45	86		1.83	-10.3
Risk High	03	Proj	**200**	**25**	**46**	**3**	**23**	**4**	**230**			**$2**	**268**	**347**	**616**	**5**	**79**	**0.25**	**251**	**78**	**94**		**3.03**	**-11.2**

A very poor season, by any measure. All his vitals took a dive out of the gate, and there were only minor signs of life in the 2nd half. Could he rebound? Sure. Is it worth investing in? Probably not.

McGriff,Fred	Yr	Tm	AB	R	H	HR	RBI	SB	Avg	vLH	vRH	R$	OB	Slg	OPS	bb%	ct%	Eye	xBA	PX	SX	G/F	RC/G	RAR
Pos 1B	98	TAM	564	73	160	19	81	7	284	274	288	$17	372	443	815	12	79	0.67	262	102	55	1.67	6.35	11.0
Age 39 Decline	99	TAM	529	75	164	32	104	1	310	236	339	$25	407	552	958	14	80	0.80	284	140	35	1.28	8.94	53.5
Bats L	00	TAM	566	82	157	27	106	2	277	273	279	$18	377	452	830	14	79	0.76	260	96	41	1.15	6.61	10.1
Pwr - - -	01	2TM	513	67	157	31	102	1	306	295	310	$26	385	544	929	11	79	0.62	278	136	36	1.30	8.07	28.8
Spd No change	02	CHC	523	67	143	30	103	1	273	213	296	$22	352	505	856	11	81	0.64	279	135	40	0.89	6.53	13.6
BAvg No change	1st Half		278	33	73	14	51	1	263			$10	349	471	820	12	83	0.80	281	123	40		5.96	2.2
LIMA A	2nd Half		245	34	70	16	52	0	286			$12	354	543	897	10	78	0.49	277	149	36		7.21	11.6
Risk Moderate	03	Proj	**500**	**67**	**143**	**28**	**98**	**1**	**286**			**$22**	**368**	**512**	**880**	**11**	**80**	**0.64**	**278**	**131**	**44**		**7.12**	**28.2**

Many were writing him off in the late 90s after several off power years, but he's now strung together four solid seasons. There is some erosion of skills, but he should be able to maintain pretty well in 2003.

McLemore,Mark	Yr	Tm	AB	R	H	HR	RBI	SB	Avg	vLH	vRH	R$	OB	Slg	OPS	bb%	ct%	Eye	xBA	PX	SX	G/F	RC/G	RAR
Pos LF	98	TEX	461	79	114	5	53	12	247	259	242	$7	369	317	686	16	86	1.39	254	47	86	1.55	4.61	-8.5
Age 38 Decline	99	TEX	566	105	155	6	45	16	274	163	299	$10	367	366	732	13	86	1.05	266	57	131	1.27	5.11	-1.1
Bats S	00	SEA	481	72	118	3	46	30	245	293	236	$10	354	316	670	14	84	1.04	249	51	100	1.54	4.20	-15.9
Pwr +	01	SEA	409	78	117	5	57	39	286	169	311	$22	389	406	795	14	79	0.82	258	71	192	1.27	6.52	24.6
Spd - - - - -	02	SEA	337	54	91	7	41	18	270	152	283	$13	382	395	777	15	81	0.97	257	86	107	1.12	5.62	7.9
BAvg No change	1st Half		209	32	57	6	31	13	273			$10	372	411	783	14	81	0.85	260	91	104		5.57	4.4
LIMA B	2nd Half		128	22	34	1	10	5	266			$3	397	367	765	18	81	1.17	252	78	104		5.66	3.2
Risk Low	03	Proj	**350**	**60**	**95**	**5**	**39**	**11**	**271**			**$9**	**383**	**377**	**760**	**15**	**82**	**0.99**	**253**	**71**	**105**		**5.43**	**3.5**

Injuries dogged him in the 2nd half, which becomes more commonplace at his age, but skills are still sharp. Expect good numbers in fewer at bats from now on.

Meluskey,Mitch	Yr	Tm	AB	R	H	HR	RBI	SB	Avg	vLH	vRH	R$	OB	Slg	OPS	bb%	ct%	Eye	xBA	PX	SX	G/F	RC/G	RAR
Pos CA	98	aaa	405	57	118	11	52	2	291			$12	384	464	848	13	87	1.15	301	125	45	1.00	6.99	39.3
Age 29 Past Peak	99	HOU	33	4	7	1	3	1	212			$0	316	333	649	13	82	0.83	258	73	51	1.00	3.97	-0.1
Bats S	00	HOU	337	47	101	14	69	1	300	193	321	$14	398	487	885	14	78	0.74	271	115	32	0.86	7.69	40.5
Pwr No change	01	DET	0	0	0	0	0	0	0								0							
Spd No change	02	DET	27	3	6	0	1	0	222	143	250	($0)	344	222	566	16	89	1.67	219	0	25	1.50	3.05	-0.6
BAvg + + + + +	1st Half		27	3	6	0	1	0	222			($0)	344	222	566	16	89	1.67	219	0	25		3.05	-0.6
LIMA C	2nd Half		0	0	0	0	0	0	0			($0)					0							-0.0
Risk High	03	Proj	**100**	**14**	**25**	**4**	**17**	**0**	**250**			**$2**	**352**	**427**	**780**	**14**	**82**	**0.86**	**276**	**118**	**36**		**5.64**	**5.2**

Not sure why I included him this year. I could've used this slot for another player. Sorry.

Mench,Kevin	Yr	Tm	AB	R	H	HR	RBI	SB	Avg	vLH	vRH	R$	OB	Slg	OPS	bb%	ct%	Eye	xBA	PX	SX	G/F	RC/G	RAR
Pos RF LF	98		0	0	0	0	0	0	0								0							
Age 25 Pre-Peak	99		0	0	0	0	0	0	0								0							
Bats R	00		0	0	0	0	0	0	0								0							
Pwr - - -	01	aa	475	63	114	23	67	3	240			$11	282	457	739	6	87	0.46	305	133	56		4.20	-16.9
Spd No change	02	TEX	* 464	65	113	20	71	1	244	269	256	$12	309	440	749	9	77	0.41	266	127	62	0.79	4.80	-4.6
BAvg No change	1st Half		206	35	51	13	36	1	248			$7	335	510	844	12	78	0.59	292	165	71		6.08	6.4
LIMA B+	2nd Half		258	30	62	7	35	0	240			$4	287	384	671	6	76	0.28	246	97	48		3.87	-9.9
Risk Moderate	03	Proj	**400**	**54**	**102**	**18**	**59**	**1**	**255**			**$11**	**310**	**456**	**766**	**7**	**81**	**0.42**	**280**	**127**	**52**		**4.92**	**-4.0**

15-60-.260 in 366 AB at TEX. Free-swinger with good power, he needs to work the count more. A HR hitter with a .350 OB avg is far more valuable than one with a .300 OB avg. 1st half does show potential to do that.

Menechino,Frank	Yr	Tm	AB	R	H	HR	RBI	SB	Avg	vLH	vRH	R$	OB	Slg	OPS	bb%	ct%	Eye	xBA	PX	SX	G/F	RC/G	RAR
Pos 2B	98	aaa	378	56	88	7	32	7	233			$3	326	341	667	12	82	0.75	256	65	113		3.76	-4.8
Age 32 Past Peak	99	aaa	501	81	125	11	70	3	250			$7	325	385	710	10	81	0.58	262	85	93	4.00	4.42	3.9
Bats R	00	OAK	* 183	38	48	8	28	2	262	224	271	$5	351	464	815	12	73	0.51	257	119	92	0.93	5.63	10.0
Pwr - -	01	OAK	471	82	114	12	60	2	242	317	203	$6	351	374	725	14	79	0.81	248	83	64	1.02	4.83	8.6
Spd No change	02	OAK	* 446	55	86	7	48	6	193	185	218	$1	276	276	551	10	82	0.64	241	58	69	0.95	2.61	-21.4
BAvg + + + + +	1st Half		259	34	49	4	25	3	189			($0)	283	278	561	12	80	0.65	238	64	68		2.79	-11.2
LIMA C+	2nd Half		187	21	37	3	23	3	198			$1	265	273	537	8	85	0.61	244	51	65		2.37	-10.2
Risk X HIGH	03	Proj	**350**	**53**	**87**	**9**	**43**	**4**	**249**			**$6**	**334**	**371**	**706**	**11**	**80**	**0.66**	**250**	**78**	**68**		**4.43**	**2.6**

3-15-.205 in 132 AB at OAK, at which point he was demoted and stunk up the joint even more. His BPIs don't warrant that fate. He played well in '01, got hurt in the 2nd half but maintained his BPIs. There's more here.

Merced,Orlando	Yr	Tm	AB	R	H	HR	RBI	SB	Avg	vLH	vRH	R$	OB	Slg	OPS	bb%	ct%	Eye	xBA	PX	SX	G/F	RC/G	RAR
Pos RF LF	98	2TM	223	24	62	6	40	1	278			$7	337	413	750	8	85	0.59	273	91	30	1.36	4.85	-1.6
Age 36 Decline	99	MON	194	25	52	8	26	2	268	300	266	$5	355	464	818	12	86	0.96	297	122	60	1.13	6.10	6.3
Bats S	00	JPN	202	20	45	2	30	2	223			$1	270	287	557	6	84	0.41	246	40	72		2.67	-15.1
Pwr - - - -	01	HOU	137	19	36	6	29	5	263	600	250	$6	331	453	784	9	77	0.44	262	110	108	1.35	5.54	-0.6
Spd No change	02	HOU	251	35	72	6	30	4	287	231	297	$8	354	434	788	9	80	0.52	261	92	115	1.61	5.94	4.2
BAvg - -	1st Half		81	16	26	4	14	1	321			$5	396	519	914	11	81	0.67	273	118	58		8.28	7.5
LIMA C+	2nd Half		170	19	46	2	16	3	271			$3	333	394	727	9	79	0.46	253	79	131		4.98	-2.2
Risk High	03	Proj	**250**	**34**	**67**	**7**	**38**	**3**	**268**			**$7**	**334**	**420**	**754**	**9**	**80**	**0.51**	**263**	**93**	**88**		**5.17**	**2.2**

Strong 1st half, mediocre 2nd half, but that's they way to do it. By time they realize you're having a mediocre 2nd half, the season is already over.

Merloni,Lou

	Tm	AB	R	H	HR	RBI	SB	Avg	vLH	vRH	R$	OB	Slg	OPS	bb%	ct%	Eye	xBA	PX	SX	G/F	RC/G	RAR
Pos 2B	98 BOS	* 184	24	57	7	33	3	310	265	290	$8	380	484	864	10	82	0.64	275	105	70	1.30	7.19	18.1
Age 32 Past Peak	99 BOS	* 355	56	93	7	44	1	262	184	299	$5	325	389	713	9	86	0.69	276	85	64	1.71	4.59	6.0
Bats R	00 BOS	* 222	20	61	1	21	1	275	294	330	$2	309	374	683	5	83	0.30	259	71	74	2.42	4.23	1.9
Pwr +	01 BOS	* 341	44	82	6	28	4	240	303	257	$3	277	355	631	5	81	0.26	252	80	71	1.27	3.42	-8.9
Spd No change	02 BOS	* 219	29	53	4	20	1	242	321	217	$2	308	379	687	9	83	0.55	268	97	86	0.87	4.05	-0.5
BAvg +++	1st Half	116	15	29	1	8	0	250			$1	326	345	670	10	80	0.57	242	70	75		4.00	-0.5
LIMA D+	2nd Half	103	14	24	3	12	1	233			$2	288	417	706	7	85	0.53	298	128	101		4.06	-0.2
Risk X HIGH	03 Proj	150	19	37	3	15	1	247			$2	300	382	682	7	83	0.44	268	94	80		4.01	-0.9

Sharp increase in plate patience, sharp decline in G/F ratio... if we didn't know better, we'd think there might be a power surge coming. But lots of freaky things happen in these small data sets.

Michaels,Jason

	Tm	AB	R	H	HR	RBI	SB	Avg	vLH	vRH	R$	OB	Slg	OPS	bb%	ct%	Eye	xBA	PX	SX	G/F	RC/G	RAR
Pos CF	98	0	0	0	0	0	0	0								0							
Age 26 Pre-Peak	99	0	0	0	0	0	0	0								0							
Bats R	00 aa	437	55	114	7	57	6	261			$7	298	394	691	5	81	0.28	269	89	93		4.04	-7.1
Pwr ++	01 aaa	418	53	105	15	63	10	251			$12	311	426	736	8	69	0.28	233	106	107		4.72	3.7
Spd +++++	02 PHI	* 137	19	36	2	17	2	263	242	302	$3	344	438	782	11	73	0.46	253	117	152	0.87	5.06	0.4
BAvg --	1st Half	93	15	28	2	16	2	301			$4	356	516	873	8	80	0.42	290	135	200		5.99	2.9
LIMA C	2nd Half	44	4	8	0	1	0	182			($1)	321	273	593	17	59	0.50	181	79	20		3.26	-2.6
Risk Very High	03 Proj	150	21	41	3	23	3	273			$4	323	442	765	7	78	0.33	265	110	121		4.86	2.1

He could stand to make a little better contact with the ball, but other than that, these are not a bad set of BPIs. He'd be a decent late draft pickup if there was any playing time to be had.

Mientkiewicz,Doug

	Tm	AB	R	H	HR	RBI	SB	Avg	vLH	vRH	R$	OB	Slg	OPS	bb%	ct%	Eye	xBA	PX	SX	G/F	RC/G	RAR
Pos 1B	98 aa	502	88	151	15	81	10	301			$21	404	476	880	15	88	1.43	306	125	69	0.64	7.61	34.4
Age 28 Peak	99 MIN	327	34	75	2	32	1	229	256	226	($1)	319	330	649	12	84	0.84	263	72	71	0.89	3.82	-22.0
Bats L	00 aaa	485	72	143	14	72	7	295			$16	355	449	804	8	89	0.83	297	97	74	1.50	5.87	1.7
Pwr +	01 MIN	543	77	166	15	74	2	306	322	300	$18	382	464	846	11	83	0.73	269	106	36	1.08	6.70	7.5
Spd No change	02 MIN	467	60	122	10	64	1	261	257	263	$9	362	392	754	14	85	1.07	272	94	40	0.86	5.34	-9.8
BAvg +++++	1st Half	244	34	63	3	34	1	258			$4	391	369	759	18	86	1.61	270	84	53		5.66	-2.7
LIMA A+	2nd Half	223	26	59	7	30	0	265			$5	328	417	745	9	84	0.58	274	105	27		4.93	-7.3
Risk High	03 Proj	500	67	139	12	69	1	278			$12	362	423	785	12	85	0.89	276	99	34		5.69	0.6

This is a hitter with good base skills, but one critical flaw... ain't got no pop in that bat. Without the raw strength behind his swings, the drop in G/F ratio just means more fly outs, and hence the fall in batting average.

Millar,Kevin

	Tm	AB	R	H	HR	RBI	SB	Avg	vLH	vRH	R$	OB	Slg	OPS	bb%	ct%	Eye	xBA	PX	SX	G/F	RC/G	RAR
Pos LF RF	98 FLA	2	1	1	0	0	0	500			$0	667	500	1167	33	50	1.00	136		53		21.42	1.4
Age 31 Past Peak	99 FLA	* 494	66	136	14	86	2	275	290	283	$13	339	433	773	9	84	0.62	280	98	84	0.72	5.50	5.4
Bats R	00 FLA	259	36	67	14	42	0	259	254	261	$7	349	498	847	12	82	0.77	297	136	66	0.77	6.42	9.2
Pwr ---	01 FLA	449	62	141	20	85	0	314	351	304	$21	369	557	926	8	84	0.56	311	151	68	0.70	7.94	29.8
Spd No change	02 FLA	* 450	59	135	17	58	0	300	317	302	$16	357	504	862	8	82	0.50	282	136	23	0.71	6.74	3.2
BAvg --	1st Half	180	20	44	6	16	0	244			$2	310	428	737	9	76	0.39	253	123	22		4.73	-10.1
LIMA A+	2nd Half	270	39	91	11	42	0	337			$14	389	556	945	8	87	0.64	303	145	26		8.40	15.8
Risk High	03 Proj	500	67	147	20	77	0	294			$18	356	509	865	9	83	0.57	292	137	50		6.81	32.3

Salvaged his season with a great August and Sept in which he hit .378 in 196 AB with nearly half of his season's HR output and 30 of his 58 RBI. That's why we buy these players for six months of production.

Miller,Corky

	Tm	AB	R	H	HR	RBI	SB	Avg	vLH	vRH	R$	OB	Slg	OPS	bb%	ct%	Eye	xBA	PX	SX	G/F	RC/G	RAR
Pos CA	98	0	0	0	0	0	0	0								0							
Age 27 Peak	99 aa	104	16	20	3	13	0	192			($1)	257	365	622	8	76	0.36	260	118	51		3.14	-3.1
Bats R	00 aa	317	30	65	7	33	4	205			($0)	278	322	600	9	87	0.76	275	75	43		2.77	-13.8
Pwr No change	01 a/a	363	49	98	17	62	3	270			$13	331	477	807	8	85	0.59	292	128	48	0.71	5.70	21.9
Spd No change	02 CIN	* 248	20	56	8	31	1	226	412	227	$2	286	383	669	8	86	0.60	276	101	26	0.97	3.70	-3.8
BAvg +++++	1st Half	113	11	32	4	17	0	283			$4	325	469	794	6	83	0.37	279	123	26		5.19	3.4
LIMA D+	2nd Half	135	9	24	4	14	1	178			($2)	255	311	566	9	88	0.88	273	84	29		2.70	-6.4
Risk X HIGH	03 Proj	350	36	92	10	46	0	263			$7	324	410	734	8	85	0.59	274	97	20		4.67	7.6

3-15-.254 in 114 AB at CIN. That was .323 in Apr/May, then .152 in Jun/July, but he got sent down more because of a roster crunch. Didn't get much better in AAA. He showed more promise in 2001. It will return.

Miller,Damian

	Tm	AB	R	H	HR	RBI	SB	Avg	vLH	vRH	R$	OB	Slg	OPS	bb%	ct%	Eye	xBA	PX	SX	G/F	RC/G	RAR
Pos CA	98 ARI	* 231	25	64	3	20	1	277	299	277	$4	324	424	748	6	78	0.32	267	110	95	2.03	5.08	7.6
Age 33 Decline	99 ARI	296	35	80	11	47	0	270	320	244	$7	314	446	760	6	74	0.24	249	113	23	1.15	5.08	9.4
Bats R	00 ARI	324	43	89	10	44	2	275	269	277	$8	347	441	789	10	77	0.49	265	109	42	1.09	5.64	16.1
Pwr +++	01 ARI	380	45	103	13	47	0	271	301	264	$9	333	424	756	8	79	0.44	257	94	24	1.11	5.15	18.5
Spd No change	02 ARI	306	41	77	11	42	0	252	275	238	$6	334	435	769	11	71	0.43	236	120	26	1.87	5.32	11.0
BAvg -	1st Half	211	31	58	9	36	0	275			$7	346	488	834	10	71	0.37	244	139	28		6.29	14.0
LIMA C+	2nd Half	95	10	19	2	6	0	200			($1)	309	316	625	14	72	0.56	218	78	22		3.52	-2.1
Risk Moderate	03 Proj	350	43	93	18	41	0	266			$9	342	480	822	10	75	0.45	258	131	24		6.02	22.8

Back problems put him on the shelf in July, and you can see how well he did upon his return. Was en route to a career power year at that point, but faded. If healthy, he could make that run at 20 HRs again.

Minor,Damon

	Tm	AB	R	H	HR	RBI	SB	Avg	vLH	vRH	R$	OB	Slg	OPS	bb%	ct%	Eye	xBA	PX	SX	G/F	RC/G	RAR
Pos 1B	98 aa	289	32	59	11	43	1	204			$2	270	360	630	8	83	0.54	273	95	55		3.33	-20.2
Age 28 Peak	99 aa	473	65	108	17	70	1	228			$5	327	408	735	13	73	0.53	247	111	68		4.82	-12.9
Bats L	00 aaa	491	65	120	23	84	0	244			$10	330	436	766	11	85	0.84	290	110	30		5.23	-8.4
Pwr ++++	01 aaa	451	56	109	16	53	1	242			$7	293	399	693	7	84	0.46	271	94	57	0.82	4.10	-30.8
Spd No change	02 SF	* 202	28	54	10	29	0	267	250	233	$6	357	485	842	12	81	0.74	278	131	42	0.91	6.47	5.0
BAvg No change	1st Half	116	17	36	5	17	0	310			$5	398	543	942	13	84	0.94	300	148	55		8.56	10.8
LIMA C+	2nd Half	86	11	18	5	12	0	209			$1	299	407	706	11	77	0.55	249	108	22		4.24	-4.1
Risk X HIGH	03 Proj	350	46	85	16	49	0	243			$7	322	431	753	10	81	0.63	273	111	42		5.00	-4.1

An excellent 1st half, but far above anything he had ever done before. 2nd half brought him back down to Earth, but erratic playing time could have caused that. At 28, we might have just seen his career year.

Mirabelli,Doug

	Tm	AB	R	H	HR	RBI	SB	Avg	vLH	vRH	R$	OB	Slg	OPS	bb%	ct%	Eye	xBA	PX	SX	G/F	RC/G	RAR
Pos CA	98 aaa	282	32	54	10	39	2	191			$1	285	344	629	12	80	0.67	264	94	63	0.67	3.43	-5.6
Age 32 Past Peak	99 SF	* 407	58	107	11	49	6	263	240	258	$8	338	415	753	10	83	0.67	278	101	73	0.79	5.18	14.8
Bats R	00 SF	230	23	53	6	28	1	230	229	231	$2	335	370	704	14	75	0.63	246	83	67	0.91	4.57	3.8
Pwr ---	01 BOS	190	20	43	11	29	0	226	283	204	$4	323	453	775	12	70	0.47	236	133		0.85	5.21	7.8
Spd No change	02 BOS	151	17	34	7	25	0	225	364	168	$3	304	411	714	10	78	0.52	263	118	19	0.94	4.39	3.4
BAvg +++	1st Half	70	7	16	3	7	0	229			$1	280	400	680	7	80	0.36	264	109	18		3.87	0.4
LIMA D	2nd Half	81	10	18	4	18	0	222			$2	323	420	742	13	77	0.63	262	125	20		4.85	3.1
Risk High	03 Proj	150	17	35	7	23	0	233			$3	322	415	736	12	76	0.54	252	111	24		4.80	3.5

Given the dynamics within the categories of Rotisserie baseball, a .225 BA in 150 AB often can more than cancel out any gains realized from 7 HRs.

Moeller,Chad

	Tm	AB	R	H	HR	RBI	SB	Avg	vLH	vRH	R$	OB	Slg	OPS	bb%	ct%	Eye	xBA	PX	SX	G/F	RC/G	RAR
Pos CA	98 aa	187	19	42	6	21	2	225			$2	306	374	681	11	78	0.52	255	99	43		4.04	-0.0
Age 28 Peak	99 aa	250	24	56	3	20	0	224			($1)	273	316	589	6	84	0.41	254	60	56		3.00	-8.4
Bats R	00 MIN	* 295	36	70	5	24	1	237	200	217	$0	277	353	629	5	77	0.24	241	73	80	1.96	3.35	-7.8
Pwr ++++	01 ARI	* 330	39	79	7	29	1	239	77	279	$2	293	364	657	7	83	0.45	265	81	52	2.90	3.53	-0.6
Spd No change	02 ARI	* 316	37	88	10	50	1	278	120	338	$10	354	449	803	10	81	0.63	268	106	69	1.21	5.95	17.7
BAvg -	1st Half	180	23	51	7	31	1	283			$7	342	444	786	8	82	0.48	261	93	63		5.72	8.5
LIMA D+	2nd Half	136	14	37	3	19	0	272			$3	369	456	825	13	81	0.81	276	123	79		6.25	9.2
Risk X HIGH	03 Proj	150	17	38	4	18	0	253			$2	321	400	721	9	81	0.53	264	95	62		4.56	2.8

2-16-.286 in 105 AB at ARI. Baseball skills will peak and wane along the bell curve, whether they are in the majors, or AAA or hawking burgers. This season is not a sign of value, but a sign of value passing.

Mohr,Dustan

		Yr	Tm	AB	R	H	HR	RBI	SB	Avg	vLH	vRH	R$	OB	Slg	OPS	bb%	ct%	Eye	xBA	PX	SX	G/F	RC/G	RAR
Pos	RF LF	98		0	0	0	0	0	0	0								0							
Age	26 Pre-Peak	99	aa	42	3	6	0	2	0	143			($2)	217	214	432	9	81	0.50	241	41	116		1.55	-4.7
Bats	R	00	a	0	0	0	0	0	0	0								0							
Pwr	No change	01	aa	569	87	170	21	86	9	299			$23	353	489	843	8	76	0.35	260	121	81	0.92	6.26	15.6
Spd	+	02	MIN	383	55	103	12	45	6	269	203	304	$11	324	433	757	7	78	0.36	260	111	93	1.13	5.05	-0.8
BAvg	- -	1st Half		213	37	63	7	26	4	296			$8	342	474	816	7	75	0.28	259	122	103		6.10	6.4
LIMA	C+	2nd Half		170	18	40	5	19	2	235			$3	301	382	683	9	81	0.48	260	96	72		3.94	-6.3
Risk	Very High	03	Proj	350	50	90	9	46	5	257			$8	315	405	720	8	77	0.37	254	99	91		4.47	-8.5

Had a solid 1st half, but then the league caught up to him. Batted just .190 from July 27 on. His inability to adjust, plus his struggles vs LHers puts his short-term potential into doubt.

Molina,Ben

		Yr	Tm	AB	R	H	HR	RBI	SB	Avg	vLH	vRH	R$	OB	Slg	OPS	bb%	ct%	Eye	xBA	PX	SX	G/F	RC/G	RAR
Pos	CA	98	a/a	339	37	99	9	55	1	292			$11	326	422	748	5	94	0.85	300	85	43		4.99	9.6
Age	28 Peak	99	ANA	* 342	38	93	8	54	1	272	143	314	$7	316	401	717	6	93	0.88	292	85	34	1.28	4.46	3.2
Bats	R	00	ANA	473	59	133	14	71	1	281	293	277	$11	315	421	735	5	93	0.70	297	82	58	0.94	4.85	8.7
Pwr	No change	01	ANA	325	31	85	6	40	0	262	218	281	$5	296	351	647	5	84	0.31	243	57	24	1.13	3.67	-2.7
Spd	No change	02	ANA	428	34	105	5	47	0	245	248	244	$4	271	322	593	3	92	0.44	267	58	22	1.22	3.03	-8.3
BAvg	-	1st Half		253	22	67	1	34	0	265			$3	285	328	613	3	93	0.39	267	54	27		3.31	-2.8
LIMA	D+	2nd Half		175	12	38	4	13	0	217			$0	251	314	566	4	91	0.50	268	63	14		2.67	-5.3
Risk	Very High	03	Proj	400	37	107	7	47	0	268			$6	299	358	656	4	90	0.46	266	62	27		3.82	-3.0

Looked like he might rebound from 2001 in the 1st half, but battled hamstring problems from July on, which negated all the gains. Power has disappeared in any case, but will probably come back when he's 34.

Molina,Jose

		Yr	Tm	AB	R	H	HR	RBI	SB	Avg	vLH	vRH	R$	OB	Slg	OPS	bb%	ct%	Eye	xBA	PX	SX	G/F	RC/G	RAR
Pos	CA	98	aa	320	25	62	2	21	1	194			($5)	252	247	499	7	81	0.40	233	38	45		2.01	-20.0
Age	27 Peak	99	a/a	275	22	63	4	26	0	229			($1)	279	327	606	6	77	0.31	237	66	36	3.33	3.13	-8.1
Bats	R	00	aaa	248	18	50	1	14	1	202			($4)	258	246	504	7	79	0.36	224	33	31		2.00	-16.4
Pwr	No change	01	aaa	213	21	55	4	23	1	258			$3	295	371	666	5	83	0.30	255	73	56	2.60	3.75	-0.1
Spd	No change	02	ANA	* 360	27	94	3	36	0	261	100	340	$4	289	331	619	4	83	0.23	237	52	29	1.00	3.14	-5.9
BAvg	- -	1st Half		252	20	67	2	27	0	266			$3	288	341	630	3	85	0.21	246	57	39		3.25	-3.3
LIMA	F	2nd Half		108	7	27	1	9	0	250			$1	289	306	595	5	79	0.26	218	41	23		2.89	-2.6
Risk	X HIGH	03	Proj	150	12	37	2	13	0	247			$1	286	319	605	5	81	0.29	233	52	30		3.01	-4.8

0-5-.271 in 70 AB at ANA. He's 10 months younger than his brother, but from these BPIs, you'd swear they were twins. Identical soft skills, these perhaps a bit softer, but both sub-0 RARs... it's spooky.

Mondesi,Raul

		Yr	Tm	AB	R	H	HR	RBI	SB	Avg	vLH	vRH	R$	OB	Slg	OPS	bb%	ct%	Eye	xBA	PX	SX	G/F	RC/G	RAR
Pos	RF	98	LA	580	85	162	30	90	16	279	241	289	$27	315	497	811	5	81	0.27	288	135	115	1.08	5.41	7.1
Age	32 Past Peak	99	LA	601	98	152	33	99	36	253	273	247	$28	332	483	814	11	78	0.53	277	133	132	1.06	5.80	13.5
Bats	R	00	TOR	388	78	105	24	67	22	271	311	261	$20	326	523	849	8	81	0.44	304	142	140	1.24	6.13	13.4
Pwr	+ + +	01	TOR	572	88	144	27	84	30	252	299	241	$24	336	453	789	11	78	0.57	267	117	115	1.00	5.45	6.8
Spd	- -	02	2AL	569	90	132	26	88	15	232	244	228	$18	304	432	736	9	82	0.57	287	131	98	0.95	4.56	-10.0
BAvg	+ + +	1st Half		299	51	67	15	45	9	224			$10	297	435	732	9	81	0.54	286	134	113		4.53	-5.6
LIMA	A	2nd Half		270	39	65	11	43	6	241			$8	312	430	742	9	83	0.61	288	127	73		4.61	-4.4
Risk	Low	03	Proj	575	93	150	28	90	17	261			$23	331	469	800	9	81	0.54	283	128	97		5.51	4.7

Given his BPIs, there's no way he should have batted .232. His contact rate improved from '01, and xBA adds 50 points to that BA. His 3-year decline may scare off some bidders, but if it stops under $20, grab him.

Mora,Melvin

		Yr	Tm	AB	R	H	HR	RBI	SB	Avg	vLH	vRH	R$	OB	Slg	OPS	bb%	ct%	Eye	xBA	PX	SX	G/F	RC/G	RAR
Pos	LF SS CF	98	aaa	28	5	5	0	2	0	179			($1)	281	214	496	13	71	0.50	204	32	59		2.20	-2.6
Age	31 Past Peak	99	NYM	* 335	48	80	5	29	16	239	118	214	$6	313	331	644	10	83	0.62	258	62	98	2.50	3.58	-16.6
Bats	R	00	2TM	* 441	66	122	8	53	14	277	280	274	$12	340	408	748	9	81	0.51	265	82	121	0.98	4.85	-5.6
Pwr	+ + + + +	01	BAL	436	49	109	7	48	11	250	308	231	$8	314	362	677	9	79	0.45	246	80	69	0.79	4.11	-8.3
Spd	+ + + + +	02	BAL	557	86	130	19	64	16	233	240	231	$14	319	404	723	11	81	0.65	271	111	113	0.75	4.45	-8.7
BAvg	+ + + + +	1st Half		277	48	72	11	34	13	260			$11	343	440	783	11	82	0.70	281	121	94		5.39	4.1
LIMA	A+	2nd Half		280	38	58	8	30	3	207			$2	295	368	663	11	79	0.60	261	102	118		3.62	-11.8
Risk	X HIGH	03	Proj	500	70	121	12	55	14	242			$11	318	382	700	10	80	0.57	261	92	102		4.24	-14.2

Second year in a row that he's had a solid 1st half and crashed after the break (.292/.200 in '01). This begs the question of stamina, but also, with a .231 BA vsRH, whether he would be better off in a platoon.

Mordecai,Mike

		Yr	Tm	AB	R	H	HR	RBI	SB	Avg	vLH	vRH	R$	OB	Slg	OPS	bb%	ct%	Eye	xBA	PX	SX	G/F	RC/G	RAR
Pos	3B SS	98	MON	119	12	24	3	10	1	202	167	221	($0)	258	345	602	7	83	0.45	274	89	115	1.39	3.04	-5.4
Age	35 Decline	99	MON	226	29	53	5	25	2	235	254	226	$2	297	363	660	8	86	0.65	278	80	81	1.18	3.49	-6.7
Bats	S	00	MON	169	20	48	4	16	2	284	309	267	$4	331	450	781	7	80	0.35	278	116	49	1.21	5.33	4.8
Pwr	- -	01	MON	254	28	71	3	32	2	280	313	252	$6	330	398	727	7	79	0.36	254	82	79	1.14	4.75	0.6
Spd	No change	02	2NL	151	19	37	0	11	2	245	282	205	$0	305	298	603	8	82	0.48	238	46	62	1.92	3.18	-7.0
BAvg	-	1st Half		70	9	15	0	4	1	214			($1)	295	271	566	10	81	0.62	238	50	64		2.77	-4.3
LIMA	D	2nd Half		81	10	22	0	7	1	272			$1	314	321	635	6	83	0.36	237	43	59		3.57	-2.7
Risk	Very High	03	Proj	150	18	39	1	14	2	260			$2	314	347	661	7	81	0.42	249	65	55		3.84	-3.3

Important Facts:
- Batted .309 while playing SS but just .227 as a 3Bman.
-Has not gotten a hit in Bank One Ballpark in over two years and has gone 0 for 22 against Schilling and Johnson.

Mueller,Bill

		Yr	Tm	AB	R	H	HR	RBI	SB	Avg	vLH	vRH	R$	OB	Slg	OPS	bb%	ct%	Eye	xBA	PX	SX	G/F	RC/G	RAR
Pos	3B	98	SF	534	93	157	9	59	3	294	298	293	$14	385	395	780	13	84	0.95	268	75	52	1.48	5.95	25.3
Age	32 Past Peak	99	SF	414	61	120	2	36	4	290	248	306	$7	386	362	749	14	87	1.25	268	58	53	1.50	5.56	15.2
Bats	S	00	SF	560	97	150	10	55	4	268	306	259	$8	330	388	718	8	89	0.84	287	77	94	1.28	4.70	5.2
Pwr	- -	01	CHC	210	38	62	6	23	1	295	391	268	$6	401	448	848	15	91	1.95	300	96	64	1.48	7.07	16.9
Spd	No change	02	2NL	382	52	101	8	42	0	264	221	272	$6	356	401	756	12	89	1.26	281	86	66	1.30	5.34	8.1
BAvg	+ + + + +	1st Half		178	19	43	3	22	0	242			$1	318	354	672	10	92	1.43	282	74	48		4.00	-3.8
LIMA	A	2nd Half		204	33	58	5	20	0	284			$5	387	441	828	14	86	1.17	279	97	85		6.67	13.5
Risk	High	03	Proj	450	71	135	10	48	0	300			$12	389	436	825	13	89	1.30	285	87	65		6.64	30.8

BPIs continue to scream ".300 HITTER!" but just a little bit softer in '02. Perhaps the return to SF, and some consistent health and playing time will help.

Murray,Calvin

		Yr	Tm	AB	R	H	HR	RBI	SB	Avg	vLH	vRH	R$	OB	Slg	OPS	bb%	ct%	Eye	xBA	PX	SX	G/F	RC/G	RAR
Pos	CF	98	a/a	427	58	98	8	32	27	230			$10	313	351	664	11	86	0.88	281	80	129		3.75	-12.0
Age	31 Past Peak	99	aaa	548	81	136	16	49	28	248			$14	291	389	680	6	85	0.40	279	85	120	2.00	3.70	-14.9
Bats	R	00	SF	194	35	47	2	22	9	242	270	203	$4	341	345	686	13	83	0.88	266	72	114	0.81	4.41	-0.0
Pwr	- -	01	SF	* 464	66	108	9	33	10	233	238	248	$4	294	345	638	8	82	0.48	257	70	101	1.22	3.28	-9.3
Spd	+ + + + +	02	2TM	* 228	31	43	2	11	7	189	190	132	($3)	236	276	512	6	85	0.41	259	61	147	1.06	2.28	-18.3
BAvg	+ + + + +	1st Half		155	26	27	1	5	6	174			($3)	234	277	511	7	85	0.50	267	74	182		2.29	-12.6
LIMA	D+	2nd Half		73	5	16	1	6	1	219			($1)	240	274	514	3	86	0.20	238	34	45		2.26	-5.7
Risk	Very High	03	Proj	100	13	23	1	7	2	230			$0	285	333	617	7	84	0.49	264	66	109		3.24	-4.5

0-1-4-.146 in 89 AB at SF and TEX. It was bad, but it shouldn't have been this bad. Fractured kneecap ended his season early, but he's probably not worth even a reserve pick right now.

Myers,Greg

		Yr	Tm	AB	R	H	HR	RBI	SB	Avg	vLH	vRH	R$	OB	Slg	OPS	bb%	ct%	Eye	xBA	PX	SX	G/F	RC/G	RAR
Pos	CA	98	SD	171	19	42	4	20	0	246	105	263	$2	314	374	688	9	79	0.47	258	93	30	1.30	4.14	0.8
Age	37 Decline	99	2NL	200	19	53	5	24	0	265	241	269	$3	350	370	720	12	85	0.87	261	64		1.33	4.90	5.5
Bats	L	00	BAL	125	9	28	3	12	0	224		239	($0)	271	344	615	6	77	0.28	237	75		1.79	3.21	-3.9
Pwr	- -	01	OAK	161	24	36	11	31	0	224	316	211	$4	313	447	760	12	76	0.55	253	120	24	1.18	4.95	5.2
Spd	No change	02	OAK	144	15	32	6	21	0	222	200	227	$2	341	382	723	15	75	0.72	242	99	12	2.10	4.80	5.4
BAvg	+ + + + +	1st Half		82	8	20	5	16	0	244			$3	340	463	804	13	73	0.55	254	132	4		5.76	5.5
LIMA	D	2nd Half		62	7	12	1	5	0	194			($0)	342	274	616	18	77	1.00	224	56	21		3.60	-0.2
Risk	Moderate	03	Proj	150	17	33	6	21	0	220			$2	322	374	696	13	77	0.65	243	92	19		4.34	1.3

Another one whose periodic power is not worth the batting average damage, and at 37, it's not going to get any better.

Nevin,Phil

Pos 3B 1B | Age 32 Past Peak | Bats R | Pwr + | Spd No change | BAvg - - | LIMA A | Risk Moderate

	Tm	AB	R	H	HR	RBI	SB	Avg	vLH	vRH	R$	OB	Slg	OPS	bb%	ct%	Eye	xBA	PX	SX	G/F	RC/G	RAR
98	ANA	237	27	54	8	27	0	228	242	219	$2	280	371	651	7	72	0.25	227	84	46	1.67	3.60	-6.9
99	2TM	383	52	103	24	85	1	269	270	268	$15	355	527	882	12	79	0.62	287	156	30	0.95	6.97	30.9
00	SD	538	87	163	31	107	2	303	342	288	$25	372	543	915	10	78	0.49	283	141	54	1.48	7.80	57.9
01	SD	546	97	167	41	126	4	306	329	297	$33	386	588	974	12	73	0.48	273	161	46	1.23	8.62	69.5
02	SD	407	53	116	12	57	4	285	337	268	$13	346	413	759	9	79	0.44	244	79	60	1.39	5.46	9.8
1st Half		147	17	43	5	21	2	293			$6	354	449	803	9	84	0.61	272	99	47		6.14	6.7
2nd Half		260	36	73	7	36	2	281			$8	342	392	734	8	75	0.38	228	68	54		5.09	3.3
03	Proj	550	80	159	36	106	4	289			$27	357	534	891	10	77	0.46	273	142	50		7.19	45.9

Single-handedly killed my title defense in LABR. The muscles from his May arm injury never regained their strength during the rest of the season. But he should be healthy and back in form in '03.

Nieves,Jose

Pos 2B | Age 27 Peak | Bats R | Pwr + + | Spd No change | BAvg - - | LIMA C | Risk X HIGH

	Tm	AB	R	H	HR	RBI	SB	Avg	vLH	vRH	R$	OB	Slg	OPS	bb%	ct%	Eye	xBA	PX	SX	G/F	RC/G	RAR
98	a/a	390	37	96	7	33	14	246			$7	274	382	656	4	87	0.29	290	96	108		3.44	-8.2
99	CHC	* 573	55	135	11	60	8	236	311	228	$5	268	356	624	4	87	0.35	281	80	72	1.08	3.06	-21.1
00	CHC	* 237	25	54	8	32	2	228	213	212	$3	268	401	669	5	80	0.28	271	97	116	1.45	3.64	-5.8
01	aaa	311	42	87	11	30	6	280			$9	298	463	761	3	85	0.17	289	109	115	1.15	4.33	2.0
02	ANA	* 160	26	43	3	16	3	269	353	217	$4	291	369	660	3	89	0.28	267	65	112	1.65	3.70	-2.0
1st Half		88	14	26	0	6	1	295			$2	311	318	629	2	85	0.15	226	21	76		3.53	-1.5
2nd Half		72	12	17	3	10	2	236			$2	267	431	697	4	93	0.60	320	119	150		3.79	-0.7
03	Proj	150	21	39	4	16	3	260			$4	286	411	697	3	87	0.27	283	91	125		3.91	-1.3

0-6-.289 in 97 AB at ANA. His BPIs have improved slightly since his CHC days, but he's yet to crack a .300 OB avg, which means his offensive value to anyone is nil.

Nieves,Wilbert

Pos CA | Age 25 Pre-Peak | Bats R | Pwr - - | Spd No change | BAvg - - | LIMA F | Risk Very High

	Tm	AB	R	H	HR	RBI	SB	Avg	vLH	vRH	R$	OB	Slg	OPS	bb%	ct%	Eye	xBA	PX	SX	G/F	RC/G	RAR
98		0	0	0	0	0	0	0								0							
99		0	0	0	0	0	0	0								0							
00	a/a	215	15	50	3	25	1	233			$1	273	288	561	5	91	0.63	259	32	30		2.71	-9.4
01	aa	330	25	86	3	36	1	262			$4	294	351	646	4	87	0.36	263	68	32		3.71	-0.5
02	SD	* 309	23	77	6	28	1	249	188	175	$3	268	388	656	3	83	0.16	267	94	59	1.71	3.61	-5.3
1st Half		167	19	52	6	20	0	311			$6	324	521	844	2	83	0.11	288	133	70		6.30	10.2
2nd Half		142	4	25	0	8	1	176			($4)	204	232	436	3	84	0.22	241	49	29		1.55	-11.1
03	Proj	100	7	24	1	10	0	240			$0	268	337	605	4	86	0.28	264	71	29		3.13	-2.5

0-3-.181 in 72 AB at SD. Another strong argument in support of reducing the fantasy roster requirement to just one catcher.

Nixon,Trot

Pos RF | Age 29 Past Peak | Bats L | Pwr - - | Spd - - | BAvg No change | LIMA A | Risk Low

	Tm	AB	R	H	HR	RBI	SB	Avg	vLH	vRH	R$	OB	Slg	OPS	bb%	ct%	Eye	xBA	PX	SX	G/F	RC/G	RAR
98	aaa	536	86	158	19	63	22	295			$24	371	465	836	11	87	0.92	296	108	102	1.43	6.41	23.0
99	BOS	381	67	103	15	52	3	270	116	290	$10	359	472	832	12	80	0.71	283	119	114	1.07	6.38	16.2
00	BOS	427	66	118	12	60	8	276	264	278	$11	369	461	831	13	80	0.74	279	110	150	1.02	6.57	21.8
01	BOS	535	100	150	27	88	7	280	210	298	$21	373	505	878	13	79	0.70	277	133	92	0.89	7.07	34.9
02	BOS	532	81	136	24	94	4	256	233	262	$18	337	470	807	11	80	0.60	284	141	82	0.85	5.74	10.6
1st Half		249	32	63	8	28	4	253			$6	329	414	742	10	79	0.54	261	104	96		4.98	-1.1
2nd Half		283	49	73	16	66	0	258			$11	344	519	863	12	80	0.65	304	173	53		6.45	12.1
03	Proj	525	86	146	33	103	3	278			$23	363	547	910	12	80	0.66	299	163	78		7.36	35.9

Recipe for a power breakout:
1. Rising PX trend
2. Declining G/F ratio trend
3. Stable contact rate
4. Second half power surge
5. Age 29
30 HRs could be a no-brainer.

Norton,Greg

Pos 3B | Age 30 Past Peak | Bats S | Pwr No change | Spd No change | BAvg + + + | LIMA C | Risk Very High

	Tm	AB	R	H	HR	RBI	SB	Avg	vLH	vRH	R$	OB	Slg	OPS	bb%	ct%	Eye	xBA	PX	SX	G/F	RC/G	RAR
98	CHW	299	38	71	9	36	3	237	231	238	$4	298	398	696	8	74	0.34	248	101	83	0.86	4.07	-4.5
99	CHW	436	62	111	16	50	4	255	203	265	$8	356	424	781	14	79	0.74	261	106	46	1.49	5.54	14.8
00	CHW	* 298	39	74	10	41	2	248	125	254	$5	347	389	736	13	78	0.69	248	80	60	1.80	5.08	5.8
01	COL	225	30	60	13	40	1	267	271	265	$8	324	516	839	8	71	0.29	259	144	83	1.02	6.08	9.7
02	COL	180	20	38	7	37	2	211	167	232	$3	311	383	694	13	69	0.47	227	102	67	1.14	4.00	-4.0
1st Half		91	11	16	5	20	2	176			$1	272	363	634	12	69	0.43	225	103	57		3.27	-4.2
2nd Half		89	9	22	2	17	0	247			$2	350	404	754	14	70	0.52	228	102	78		4.84	0.4
03	Proj	250	30	67	10	45	2	268			$8	352	454	806	11	72	0.46	242	110	72		5.79	10.0

We'll attribute this to a thigh bruise and strained hamstring. Otherwise, this would be the first case in recorded history where a batter experienced his worst career offensive year in COL. (Expect a rebound.)

Nunez,Abraham

Pos 2B SS | Age 27 Peak | Bats S | Pwr + + | Spd No change | BAvg + + + + + | LIMA C | Risk High

	Tm	AB	R	H	HR	RBI	SB	Avg	vLH	vRH	R$	OB	Slg	OPS	bb%	ct%	Eye	xBA	PX	SX	G/F	RC/G	RAR
98	PIT	* 418	47	96	3	28	17	230		233	$4	305	297	601	10	83	0.65	255	50	103	1.78	3.28	-12.2
99	PIT	* 317	34	73	0	19	10	230	235	213	$0	301	256	556	9	81	0.53	233	22	80	3.08	2.93	-13.6
00	PIT	* 442	49	105	3	31	16	238	200	222	$4	295	287	582	8	88	0.68	259	33	88	1.95	3.01	-19.7
01	PIT	301	30	79	1	21	8	262	297	258	$4	325	336	661	9	82	0.53	247	48	122	2.81	4.09	1.4
02	PIT	253	28	59	2	15	3	233	176	242	($0)	307	320	627	10	83	0.61	249	63	67	2.33	3.38	-9.0
1st Half		139	16	32	0	9	3	230			($0)	291	302	594	8	86	0.63	260	62	69		2.94	-6.7
2nd Half		114	12	27	2	6	0	237			($0)	326	342	668	12	78	0.60	236	65	64		3.95	-2.0
03	Proj	250	27	65	2	16	5	260			$3	329	338	667	9	83	0.59	249	53	89		4.05	-0.4

There has been improvement in his plate patience and contact rate, which should begin filtering down into his BA. But he has zero power and the speed skills are probably rusty, so the overall package still ain't much.

O'Leary,Troy

Pos LF | Age 33 Decline | Bats L | Pwr No change | Spd No change | BAvg - | LIMA C+ | Risk Moderate

	Tm	AB	R	H	HR	RBI	SB	Avg	vLH	vRH	R$	OB	Slg	OPS	bb%	ct%	Eye	xBA	PX	SX	G/F	RC/G	RAR
98	BOS	611	95	165	23	83	2	270	284	263	$15	311	468	779	6	82	0.33	289	120	105	1.13	5.19	0.7
99	BOS	596	84	167	28	103	1	280	346	257	$19	342	495	837	9	85	0.62	297	127	59	1.10	6.22	19.5
00	BOS	513	68	134	13	70	0	261	252	265	$7	320	411	731	8	85	0.58	279	93	61	0.96	4.70	-7.8
01	BOS	341	50	82	13	50	1	240	154	261	$6	292	437	729	7	79	0.34	269	114	116	1.17	4.31	-4.2
02	MON	* 359	36	103	6	50	1	287	351	275	$10	357	396	752	10	83	0.64	252	71	46	1.45	5.25	-14.4
1st Half		203	21	61	5	31	1	300			$7	349	443	792	7	82	0.42	262	93	51		5.68	-5.2
2nd Half		156	15	42	1	19	0	269			$2	367	333	700	13	84	0.96	240	43	45		4.66	-9.5
03	Proj	350	42	94	9	49	1	269			$8	335	408	742	9	82	0.57	264	87	65		4.93	2.0

3-37-.286 in 273 AB at MON. Add a little plate patience as he tried to salvage his career, and he ends up with his highest OB avg since 1997. Power may be gone, but could make a safe late round pick.

Ochoa,Alex

Pos RF LF | Age 31 Past Peak | Bats R | Pwr + + + | Spd - - - | BAvg + + + | LIMA B+ | Risk High

	Tm	AB	R	H	HR	RBI	SB	Avg	vLH	vRH	R$	OB	Slg	OPS	bb%	ct%	Eye	xBA	PX	SX	G/F	RC/G	RAR
98	MIN	249	35	64	2	25	6	257	245	266	$4	286	353	639	4	86	0.29	271	68	116	2.31	3.48	-12.3
99	2TM	277	47	83	8	40	6	300	319	281	$10	398	466	863	14	84	1.05	285	103	102	1.35	7.13	18.8
00	CIN	244	50	77	13	58	8	316	300	325	$16	377	586	963	9	89	0.89	340	163	130	1.07	8.28	23.2
01	2NL	536	73	148	8	52	17	276	308	267	$15	332	403	735	8	86	0.59	278	82	128	1.62	4.66	-16.8
02	2TM	280	40	73	8	31	10	261	272	253	$8	337	404	740	10	88	0.91	283	96	76	1.56	4.74	-4.7
1st Half		156	22	39	4	13	5	250			$2	350	372	722	13	87	1.14	269	80	68		4.73	-2.7
2nd Half		124	18	34	4	18	5	274			$4	318	444	762	6	89	0.57	300	116	84		4.66	-2.3
03	Proj	300	46	88	9	40	10	293			$12	355	455	810	9	87	0.75	297	105	100		5.80	5.2

Pro-rate his 2002 season to full-time and suddenly he's a 15-HR, 20-SB guy. Not that he'll get that opportunity, but that's exactly what we've been waiting for since 1999. Still some talent hidden here. Take a flyer.

Offerman,Jose

Pos 1B DH | Age 34 Decline | Bats S | Pwr - | Spd + + + + + | BAvg + + + + + | LIMA C+ | Risk Low

	Tm	AB	R	H	HR	RBI	SB	Avg	vLH	vRH	R$	OB	Slg	OPS	bb%	ct%	Eye	xBA	PX	SX	G/F	RC/G	RAR
98	KC	607	102	191	7	66	45	315	338	303	$30	402	438	841	13	84	0.93	278	76	177	1.58	7.17	28.2
99	BOS	586	107	172	8	69	18	294	268	301	$17	393	435	828	14	87	1.22	291	90	147	1.39	6.50	11.7
00	BOS	451	73	115	9	41	0	255	291	240	$3	355	359	714	13	84	1.00	255	61	54	1.48	4.54	-22.8
01	BOS	524	76	140	9	49	5	267	217	284	$9	344	374	718	10	81	0.63	249	69	80	1.17	4.82	-24.2
02	SEA	284	48	66	5	31	9	232	216	238	$5	321	335	655	12	87	0.97	264	71	102	1.61	3.76	-20.4
1st Half		184	28	40	4	21	7	217			$4	318	326	644	13	88	1.23	271	75	86		3.72	-13.6
2nd Half		100	20	26	1	10	2	260			$2	327	350	677	9	84	0.63	251	62	126		3.84	-6.7
03	Proj	250	42	64	4	25	5	256			$5	340	360	700	11	84	0.82	258	67	103		4.38	-10.2

Still maintains a decent batting eye and is getting wood on the ball, but the holes are getting bigger. OB avg decline and troubles vsLHers likely won't turn around. He's nearly done.

Ojeda,Augie

	Yr	Tm	AB	R	H	HR	RBI	SB	Avg	vLH	vRH	R$	OB	Slg	OPS	bb%	ct%	Eye	xBA	PX	SX	G/F	RC/G	RAR
Pos SS	98	aa	254	32	58	1	17	0	228			($2)	315	283	598	11	89	1.10	258	42	48		3.13	-5.8
Age 28 Peak	99	a/a	461	63	108	9	51	5	234			$3	304	338	642	9	91	1.07	281	63	88		3.67	-3.6
Bats S	00	CHC	* 473	57	114	8	44	14	241	250	208	$6	297	349	646	7	93	1.19	297	70	91	1.04	3.57	0.5
Pwr +	01	CHC	144	16	29	1	12	1	201	205	200	($1)	263	271	534	8	86	0.60	255	46	83	1.38	2.48	-5.1
Spd No change	02	CHC	* 361	40	65	1	22	4	180	130	213	($8)	235	252	487	7	93	0.96	276	55	91	1.39	1.91	-22.9
BAvg +++++	1st Half		140	12	25	0	10	2	179			($3)	223	243	466	5	94	1.00	278	50	92		1.84	-9.1
LIMA D	2nd Half		221	28	40	1	12	2	181			($5)	243	258	501	8	91	0.95	274	58	87		1.95	-13.8
Risk X HIGH	03	Proj	**100**	**11**	**20**	**1**	**7**	**1**	**200**			**($1)**	**259**	**290**	**550**	**7**	**91**	**0.87**	**279**	**62**	**99**		**2.52**	**-3.8**

0-4-.186 in 70 AB at CHC. Weak contact hitter who doesn't much get the ball out of the infield. BPIs declining as he enters his peak offensive years. But, then again, offense is the not reason he is employed.

Olerud,John

	Yr	Tm	AB	R	H	HR	RBI	SB	Avg	vLH	vRH	R$	OB	Slg	OPS	bb%	ct%	Eye	xBA	PX	SX	G/F	RC/G	RAR
Pos 1B	98	NYM	557	91	197	22	93	2	354	375	346	$32	449	551	1000	15	87	1.32	306	132	61	1.35	10.45	94.5
Age 34 Decline	99	NYM	581	107	173	19	96	3	298	247	318	$20	422	463	885	18	89	1.89	299	109	52	1.44	8.00	52.1
Bats L	00	SEA	565	84	161	14	103	0	285	242	297	$14	394	439	833	15	83	1.06	277	103	23	1.44	6.75	13.0
Pwr No change	01	SEA	572	91	173	21	95	3	302	246	321	$22	401	472	873	14	88	1.34	286	106	51	1.21	7.54	24.1
Spd No change	02	SEA	553	85	166	22	102	0	300	287	306	$22	406	490	896	15	88	1.48	305	129	23	1.16	7.92	36.1
BAvg +++	1st Half		279	50	88	12	45	0	315			$12	428	534	962	16	86	1.45	314	152	27		9.33	32.0
LIMA A	2nd Half		274	35	78	10	57	0	285			$10	382	445	827	14	90	1.54	294	106	19		6.61	5.7
Risk Very Low	03	Proj	**550**	**84**	**164**	**20**	**99**	**0**	**298**			**$20**	**402**	**472**	**874**	**15**	**87**	**1.38**	**292**	**114**	**29**		**7.53**	**34.7**

About as consistent as they come, even in his intra-season 1H/2H BA performance...

1999 .309 .288
2000 .308 .261
2001 .319 .287
2002 .315 .285

Ordaz,Luis

	Yr	Tm	AB	R	H	HR	RBI	SB	Avg	vLH	vRH	R$	OB	Slg	OPS	bb%	ct%	Eye	xBA	PX	SX	G/F	RC/G	RAR
Pos 2B	98	STL	* 367	33	86	5	37	4	234	115	248	$3	283	319	602	6	90	0.71	280	61	65	2.06	3.19	-11.4
Age 27 Peak	99	aaa	362	24	91	1	35	2	251			$1	289	331	620	5	92	0.63	279	61	47	6.00	3.21	-10.5
Bats R	00	KC	104	17	23	0	11	4	221	172	240	$0	257	240	497	5	90	0.50	244	16	111	2.23	2.08	-5.8
Pwr +	01	KC	* 108	12	29	1	7	2	269	313	225	$2	301	333	634	4	85	0.31	244	46	60	4.71	3.72	-1.8
Spd +++++	02	KC	* 424	47	105	2	30	9	248	200	232	$5	290	323	613	6	90	0.57	264	58	100	1.96	3.21	-11.7
BAvg No change	1st Half		194	14	42	1	10	4	216			$0	240	273	513	3	92	0.38	260	46	64		2.10	-11.6
LIMA D	2nd Half		230	33	63	1	20	5	274			$5	329	365	695	8	88	0.68	266	67	124		4.36	1.7
Risk Very High	03	Proj	**100**	**12**	**25**	**1**	**8**	**2**	**250**			**$1**	**290**	**306**	**596**	**5**	**89**	**0.49**	**253**	**44**	**69**		**3.11**	**-3.3**

0-4-2-.223 in 94 AB at KC. Another weak contact hitter, but with some of the most marked G/F ratios around. Prior to 2002, refused to hit a fly ball. Teammates used to kid him, place bets on where he'd hit it.

Ordonez,Magglio

	Yr	Tm	AB	R	H	HR	RBI	SB	Avg	vLH	vRH	R$	OB	Slg	OPS	bb%	ct%	Eye	xBA	PX	SX	G/F	RC/G	RAR
Pos RF	98	CHW	535	70	151	14	65	9	282	267	287	$15	318	415	733	5	90	0.53	289	84	78	1.61	4.66	-7.9
Age 29 Past Peak	99	CHW	624	100	188	30	117	13	301	320	298	$29	350	510	860	7	90	0.73	315	122	93	1.57	6.63	30.0
Bats R	00	CHW	588	102	185	32	126	18	315	337	310	$33	378	546	924	9	89	0.94	324	132	105	1.26	8.06	56.4
Pwr ++++	01	CHW	593	97	181	31	113	25	305	325	300	$35	379	533	911	11	88	1.00	313	139	88	1.37	7.78	51.1
Spd ----	02	CHW	590	116	189	38	135	7	320	288	329	$37	376	597	973	8	87	0.69	336	179	76	1.12	8.55	63.0
BAvg --	1st Half		298	57	94	13	60	6	315			$16	374	544	918	9	84	0.60	312	157	91		7.65	23.6
LIMA C+	2nd Half		292	59	95	25	75	1	325			$21	379	651	1029	8	90	0.83	361	202	49		9.53	39.9
Risk Very Low	03	Proj	**600**	**108**	**188**	**46**	**138**	**8**	**313**			**$38**	**373**	**615**	**988**	**9**	**88**	**0.81**	**343**	**182**	**68**		**8.66**	**64.1**

Last year's projection in this book read, "34-135-.323" with an upside of going 40-40. While he's decided the speed isn't necessary, the power upside remains. PX and G/F trends are in perfect alignment for a spike.

Ordonez,Rey

	Yr	Tm	AB	R	H	HR	RBI	SB	Avg	vLH	vRH	R$	OB	Slg	OPS	bb%	ct%	Eye	xBA	PX	SX	G/F	RC/G	RAR
Pos SS	98	NYM	505	46	124	1	42	3	246	255	242	$2	278	299	577	4	88	0.38	263	44	57	1.89	2.79	-13.4
Age 32 Past Peak	99	NYM	520	49	134	1	60	8	258	231	267	$5	322	317	639	9	89	0.83	267	47	68	1.78	3.74	2.3
Bats S	00	NYM	133	10	25	0	9	0	188	192	187	($3)	280	226	506	11	88	1.06	256	32	19	1.41	2.28	-5.4
Pwr ---	01	NYM	461	31	114	3	44	3	247	264	244	$3	299	336	635	7	91	0.79	277	62	67	2.15	3.56	-0.9
Spd No change	02	NYM	460	53	117	1	42	2	254	193	276	$3	291	324	615	5	90	0.52	266	54	68	2.23	3.32	-9.1
BAvg No change	1st Half		232	27	55	1	26	2	237			$1	266	315	580	4	89	0.36	268	59	82		2.86	-7.7
LIMA C	2nd Half		228	26	62	0	16	0	272			$2	317	333	650	6	91	0.71	264	49	51		3.82	-1.1
Risk Moderate	03	Proj	**450**	**43**	**110**	**1**	**39**	**2**	**244**			**$1**	**295**	**310**	**606**	**7**	**90**	**0.71**	**266**	**50**	**58**		**3.24**	**-7.0**

And yet ANOTHER weak contact hitter, but this one with a full-time job. It's all in who you know.

Ortiz,David

	Yr	Tm	AB	R	H	HR	RBI	SB	Avg	vLH	vRH	R$	OB	Slg	OPS	bb%	ct%	Eye	xBA	PX	SX	G/F	RC/G	RAR
Pos DH	98	MIN	* 315	51	85	11	50	1	270	245	284	$8	354	448	802	12	75	0.52	255	116	47	1.00	5.97	5.8
Age 27 Peak	99	aaa	496	65	135	22	83	2	272			$15	358	480	837	12	81	0.71	283	128	50		6.37	17.2
Bats L	00	MIN	415	59	117	10	63	1	282	423	249	$9	369	446	814	12	80	0.70	274	110	51	1.16	6.32	15.3
Pwr ++	01	MIN	303	46	71	18	48	1	234	221	240	$8	324	475	799	12	78	0.59	272	141	54	0.74	5.51	1.7
Spd No change	02	MIN	412	52	112	20	75	1	272	203	299	$15	341	500	841	9	79	0.49	287	152	40	0.73	6.18	7.0
BAvg --	1st Half		170	20	40	4	30	0	235			$3	312	394	706	10	80	0.56	268	114	51		4.41	-6.7
LIMA A	2nd Half		242	32	72	16	45	1	298			$12	361	574	935	9	78	0.45	300	179	29		7.64	15.2
Risk Moderate	03	Proj	**400**	**55**	**106**	**25**	**68**	**1**	**265**			**$15**	**343**	**528**	**871**	**11**	**79**	**0.56**	**293**	**163**	**43**		**6.60**	**14.1**

We continue to wait for his first injury-free season, but now it's not something we would bet on. BA vsLH creates a huge downside, but growth in power skills do point to a possible spike in HRs.

Ortiz,Jose

	Yr	Tm	AB	R	H	HR	RBI	SB	Avg	vLH	vRH	R$	OB	Slg	OPS	bb%	ct%	Eye	xBA	PX	SX	G/F	RC/G	RAR
Pos 2B	98	aa	354	54	87	5	42	17	246			$9	314	356	670	9	87	0.76	282	81	111		4.01	-1.6
Age 25 Pre-Peak	99	aaa	377	62	104	8	43	13	276			$11	323	419	742	6	89	0.63	299	99	106		4.94	8.8
Bats R	00	aaa	518	99	169	22	100	20	326			$31	378	529	907	8	88	0.72	313	120	118	1.00	7.56	53.9
Pwr --	01	2TM	* 502	74	119	19	69	10	237	225	246	$11	289	410	700	7	84	0.46	281	102	110	1.19	4.03	-1.3
Spd ----	02	COL	* 303	37	82	6	24	3	271	233	255	$5	314	393	706	6	87	0.50	274	79	83	1.43	4.48	-0.2
BAvg -	1st Half		160	18	39	1	9	2	244			$0	301	306	607	8	86	0.59	249	42	82		3.38	-5.5
LIMA B	2nd Half		143	19	43	5	15	1	301			$5	329	490	818	4	89	0.38	301	120	75		5.86	5.8
Risk X HIGH	03	Proj	**350**	**50**	**96**	**9**	**41**	**7**	**274**			**$10**	**321**	**419**	**740**	**6**	**87**	**0.52**	**284**	**92**	**96**		**4.84**	**7.9**

1-12-.250 in 192 AB at COL. Big disappointment, but SHOULD have done better, especially in COL. Fact is, BPIs are mediocre and trends are heading south, but you have to take that extra $1 risk because of COL.

Osik,Keith

	Yr	Tm	AB	R	H	HR	RBI	SB	Avg	vLH	vRH	R$	OB	Slg	OPS	bb%	ct%	Eye	xBA	PX	SX	G/F	RC/G	RAR
Pos CA	98	PIT	98	8	21	0	7	1	214	273	197	($1)	306	255	561	12	84	0.81	246	38	39	1.20	2.69	-4.2
Age 34 Decline	99	PIT	167	12	31	2	13	0	186	213	170	($3)	236	251	487	6	82	0.37	242	39	42	0.98	1.98	-10.5
Bats R	00	PIT	123	11	36	4	22	3	293	371	261	$5	365	455	820	10	91	1.27	306	97	73	1.76	6.55	9.7
Pwr No change	01	PIT	120	9	25	2	13	1	208	119	256	($0)	286	292	577	10	80	0.54	238	54	35	0.98	2.98	-2.3
Spd No change	02	PIT	100	6	16	2	11	0	160	91	179	($2)	208	250	458	6	75	0.24	218	56	15	1.26	1.67	-7.6
BAvg +++++	1st Half		60	4	11	1	6	0	183			($1)	210	283	493	3	73	0.13	219	69	22		1.91	-4.0
LIMA D	2nd Half		40	2	5	1	5	0	125			($1)	205	200	405	9	78	0.44	215	38	6		1.35	-3.6
Risk Moderate	03	Proj	**100**	**8**	**22**	**2**	**13**	**1**	**220**			**$1**	**279**	**325**	**603**	**8**	**82**	**0.46**	**251**	**67**	**37**		**3.20**	**-2.4**

In my valiant efforts to always find something positive to write about everyone, I present to you the following important fact... In 2002, he batted over .200 against the following clubs: ATL, CHC, FLA, LA, PHI, SF and STL.

Owens,Eric

	Yr	Tm	AB	R	H	HR	RBI	SB	Avg	vLH	vRH	R$	OB	Slg	OPS	bb%	ct%	Eye	xBA	PX	SX	G/F	RC/G	RAR
Pos LF RF CF	98	aaa	294	37	73	5	31	14	248			$7	309	357	667	8	90	0.87	285	70	123		3.89	-10.4
Age 32 Past Peak	99	SD	440	55	117	9	61	33	266	231	281	$18	324	391	715	8	89	0.76	288	81	122	2.04	4.76	-5.3
Bats R	00	SD	583	87	171	6	51	29	293	307	287	$19	344	381	725	7	89	0.71	275	53	132	2.82	4.79	-9.6
Pwr +	01	FLA	400	51	101	5	28	8	253	274	244	$5	303	335	638	7	85	0.49	258	55	82	2.53	3.52	-28.1
Spd +++++	02	FLA	385	44	104	4	37	26	270	266	271	$14	325	366	691	7	91	0.94	282	61	139	2.74	4.33	-26.0
BAvg No change	1st Half		226	31	65	3	26	18	288			$11	353	398	752	9	91	1.15	287	70	145		5.39	-8.0
LIMA A	2nd Half		159	13	39	1	11	8	245			$3	281	321	602	5	92	0.62	273	48	120		3.03	-16.6
Risk High	03	Proj	**400**	**48**	**106**	**4**	**35**	**24**	**265**			**$12**	**316**	**356**	**671**	**7**	**89**	**0.70**	**275**	**58**	**130**		**4.05**	**-8.6**

Has proven that he can fare well with regular playing time. When FLA acquired Encarnacion, he was the most impacted, and his BPIs suffered. Adjust your expectations based on his role in 2003.

Palmeiro,Orlando		Tm	AB	R	H	HR	RBI	SB	Avg	vLH	vRH	R$	OB	Slg	OPS	bb%	ct%	Eye	xBA	PX	SX	G/F	RC/G	RAR
Pos RF LF	98	ANA	* 305	43	85	1	41	7	279	231	329	$7	345	370	716	9	93	1.41	290	65	113	1.38	4.67	-4.6
Age 34 Decline	99	ANA	317	46	88	1	23	5	278	200	287	$4	357	331	688	11	91	1.30	260	40	71	1.49	4.40	-6.8
Bats L	00	ANA	243	38	73	0	25	4	300	258	307	$5	395	399	794	14	92	1.90	291	76	93	1.35	6.36	10.8
Pwr --	01	ANA	230	29	56	2	23	6	243	67	256	$3	318	322	639	10	90	1.04	265	55	78	1.43	3.48	-11.6
Spd +	02	ANA	263	35	79	0	31	7	300	412	284	$8	372	354	726	10	92	1.36	261	46	87	1.25	5.23	0.9
BAvg +++	1st Half		112	20	34	0	10	1	304			$2	361	375	736	8	91	1.00	268	58	99		5.32	0.7
LIMA C+	2nd Half		151	15	45	0	21	6	298			$5	380	338	718	12	92	1.67	254	37	64		5.16	0.2
Risk Very High	03	Proj	250	34	71	1	28	6	284			$6	360	351	712	11	91	1.35	268	54	81		4.83	-3.4

This is why research is an ongoing process. bb%, ct% and eye support his return to the .300 level. xBA says '01's BA was more in line with his skills and '02 is the anomaly. The quest continues...

Palmeiro,Rafael		Tm	AB	R	H	HR	RBI	SB	Avg	vLH	vRH	R$	OB	Slg	OPS	bb%	ct%	Eye	xBA	PX	SX	G/F	RC/G	RAR
Pos 1B DH	98	BAL	619	98	183	43	121	11	296	317	283	$33	375	565	941	11	85	0.87	318	157	62	0.71	7.91	43.1
Age 38 Decline	99	TEX	565	96	183	47	148	2	324	274	341	$37	423	630	1053	15	88	1.41	332	171	31	0.61	10.53	87.5
Bats L	00	TEX	565	102	163	39	120	2	288	326	276	$25	398	558	956	15	86	1.34	322	148	62	0.69	8.61	48.4
Pwr --	01	TEX	600	98	164	47	123	1	273	272	274	$28	378	563	941	14	85	1.12	309	166	27	0.64	8.02	35.0
Spd No change	02	TEX	546	99	149	43	105	2	273	220	295	$27	389	571	961	16	83	1.11	322	185	45	0.48	8.50	46.8
BAvg +++	1st Half		260	41	68	17	45	0	262			$10	368	523	891	14	83	1.02	312	166	22		7.21	10.7
LIMA A	2nd Half		286	58	81	26	60	2	283			$17	408	615	1023	17	82	1.18	331	202	49		9.77	37.4
Risk Very Low	03	Proj	550	97	154	43	112	2	280			$28	390	576	966	15	84	1.15	321	175	48		8.59	54.6

At age 38, believe it or not...
- PX level still trending up
- Walk rate still trending up
- xBAs still indicate BA upside

He could hit 50 HRs in 2003, though BA vsLH might be the first crack in the armor.

Palmer,Dean		Tm	AB	R	H	HR	RBI	SB	Avg	vLH	vRH	R$	OB	Slg	OPS	bb%	ct%	Eye	xBA	PX	SX	G/F	RC/G	RAR
Pos DH	98	KC	572	84	159	34	119	8	278	317	266	$26	334	510	844	8	77	0.36	274	134	80	0.95	6.27	15.4
Age 34 Decline	99	DET	560	92	147	38	100	3	263	390	235	$20	331	518	848	9	73	0.37	263	143	66	0.84	6.12	14.4
Bats R	00	DET	524	73	134	29	102	4	256	228	264	$16	339	471	810	11	72	0.45	252	119	66	0.82	5.81	10.5
Pwr +	01	DET	216	34	48	11	40	4	222	340	184	$6	309	426	735	11	73	0.46	247	121	68	0.76	4.65	-4.8
Spd No change	02	DET	12	0	0	0	0	0	0			($1)	77	0	77	8	58	0.20	143	0	-10	2.00	0.04	-2.1
BAvg +++++	1st Half		12	0	0	0	0	0	0			($1)	77	0	77	8	58	0.20	143	0	-10		0.04	-2.1
LIMA C	2nd Half		0	0	0	0	0	0	0			($0)					0							-0.0
Risk Low	03	Proj	250	39	63	12	47	1	252			$7	327	449	776	10	73	0.41	250	120	62		5.24	-2.1

Neck and shoulder injuries continue to put 2003 at risk, but DET does need a 3Bman.

Paquette,Craig		Tm	AB	R	H	HR	RBI	SB	Avg	vLH	vRH	R$	OB	Slg	OPS	bb%	ct%	Eye	xBA	PX	SX	G/F	RC/G	RAR
Pos 3B	98	aaa	80	13	20	2	12	2	250			$2	259	363	622	1	74	0.05	234	73	99	5.00	3.34	-2.7
Age 34 Decline	99	STL	* 440	56	115	23	84	4	261	204	330	$15	286	484	770	3	82	0.19	290	133	80	1.29	4.91	6.0
Bats R	00	STL	384	47	94	15	61	4	245	221	255	$8	294	435	729	7	78	0.33	273	116	76	0.88	4.40	-0.1
Pwr --	01	STL	340	47	96	15	64	3	282	312	271	$14	318	465	783	5	80	0.27	271	109	59	1.26	5.40	7.3
Spd No change	02	DET	252	20	49	4	20	1	194	271	171	($1)	225	306	531	4	79	0.19	245	81	62	1.39	2.27	-17.2
BAvg +++	1st Half		170	13	35	4	18	1	206			$1	250	347	597	6	81	0.30	261	98	63		2.93	-8.4
LIMA D	2nd Half		82	7	14	0	2	0	171			($2)	171	220	390	0	76	0.00	213	45	54		1.15	-8.0
Risk High	03	Proj	150	16	34	4	18	1	227			$1	256	360	616	4	79	0.18	250	89	51		3.12	-6.6

And the reason that DET needs a 3Bman. This was not an off-year. This was a poor-skilled player to begin with, coming over to a new league in a pitcher's ballpark. Expect no rebound.

Patterson,Corey		Tm	AB	R	H	HR	RBI	SB	Avg	vLH	vRH	R$	OB	Slg	OPS	bb%	ct%	Eye	xBA	PX	SX	G/F	RC/G	RAR
Pos CF	98		0	0	0	0	0	0	0								0							
Age 23 Growth	99		0	0	0	0	0	0	0								0							
Bats L	00	CHC	* 486	78	113	21	80	27	233		194	$17	299	428	727	9	74	0.37	259	113	136	1.30	4.12	-4.4
Pwr No change	01	CHC	* 498	83	114	10	42	21	229	267	208	$9	275	343	619	6	83	0.37	263	73	134	0.91	3.19	-11.2
Spd -	02	CHC	592	71	150	14	54	18	253	188	275	$13	277	392	668	3	76	0.13	247	87	134	1.54	3.83	-19.8
BAvg --	1st Half		298	40	83	7	31	15	279			$11	315	426	741	5	81	0.28	266	91	157		5.12	1.4
LIMA A+	2nd Half		294	31	67	7	23	3	228			$1	236	357	593	1	71	0.04	226	83	84		2.74	-18.9
Risk Moderate	03	Proj	600	85	153	17	59	22	255			$16	291	403	694	5	78	0.22	255	91	126		4.05	-6.1

He got nearly 600 AB, but how much REAL improvement was there? Batted .333 in April, .239 the rest of the way. Had a .236 OB avg in the 2nd half (2 BB in 3 months). No growth in PX or SX. This was NOT a good year.

Paul,Josh		Tm	AB	R	H	HR	RBI	SB	Avg	vLH	vRH	R$	OB	Slg	OPS	bb%	ct%	Eye	xBA	PX	SX	G/F	RC/G	RAR
Pos CA	98		0	0	0	0	0	0	0								0							
Age 27 Peak	99	aa	337	43	84	4	38	6	249			$4	301	353	654	7	80	0.37	252	72	89	2.00	3.60	-5.1
Bats R	00	CHW	* 239	37	56	5	23	6	234	333	260	$2	280	351	631	6	81	0.33	253	66	144	4.29	3.41	-6.0
Pwr ---	01	CHW	* 214	30	56	7	31	6	262	209	292	$7	325	430	755	9	81	0.49	269	110	72	1.34	5.06	7.5
Spd ++	02	CHW	* 335	26	80	0	25	11	239	250	233	$4	290	296	585	7	81	0.38	233	50	85	0.86	3.04	-6.6
BAvg -	1st Half		172	14	42	0	12	8	244			$3	301	308	609	8	80	0.40	234	59	79		3.41	-1.5
LIMA D+	2nd Half		163	12	38	0	13	3	233			$1	277	282	560	6	82	0.34	230	40	78		2.68	-5.0
Risk Very High	03	Proj	250	27	61	3	25	5	244			$3	297	342	638	7	81	0.39	247	69	81		3.53	-4.2

0-11-.240 in 104 AB at CHW. BPIs took a step back in '02, which now adds him to the long list of $1 catchers to avoid.

Payton,Jay		Tm	AB	R	H	HR	RBI	SB	Avg	vLH	vRH	R$	OB	Slg	OPS	bb%	ct%	Eye	xBA	PX	SX	G/F	RC/G	RAR
Pos CF LF	98	aaa	344	38	80	6	24	10	233			$4	277	340	617	6	86	0.45	273	70	109	2.75	3.14	-15.5
Age 30 Past Peak	99	aaa	152	22	48	6	27	3	316			$7	354	526	880	6	91	0.64	323	134	83	0.67	6.89	10.6
Bats R	00	NYM	488	63	142	17	62	5	291	365	271	$15	332	447	779	6	88	0.50	292	94	50	1.32	5.07	9.7
Pwr +++++	01	NYM	361	44	92	8	34	4	255	261	253	$6	290	371	661	5	86	0.35	269	74	73	1.59	3.73	-2.2
Spd +++	02	2NL	445	69	135	16	59	7	303	252	326	$19	346	488	834	6	88	0.54	296	107	127	1.52	6.26	17.4
BAvg --	1st Half		201	25	52	5	19	4	259			$4	307	383	690	7	86	0.50	268	68	124		4.25	-4.4
LIMA A+	2nd Half		244	44	83	11	40	3	340			$15	378	574	952	6	89	0.58	319	140	122		8.30	24.6
Risk X HIGH	03	Proj	500	71	145	20	62	7	290			$18	330	478	809	6	87	0.48	297	111	99		5.66	19.2

A new COL superstar? Here is some perception versus reality...
1. He batted .374 in his 1st month in COL, but had batted .351 in the month prior.
2. He batted just .270 after that 1st month in COL.

Pellow,Kit		Tm	AB	R	H	HR	RBI	SB	Avg	vLH	vRH	R$	OB	Slg	OPS	bb%	ct%	Eye	xBA	PX	SX	G/F	RC/G	RAR
Pos 3B	98	a/a	428	59	94	22	60	5	220			$8	256	437	693	5	78	0.23	280	134	96		3.73	-10.3
Age 29 Past Peak	99	aaa	475	66	117	28	74	5	246			$13	268	488	756	3	81	0.15	291	138	97		4.27	-3.0
Bats R	00	aaa	421	46	92	17	56	5	219			$5	267	385	652	6	83	0.39	276	94	71		3.36	-13.9
Pwr ++++	01	aaa	484	60	122	15	60	3	252			$9	290	372	662	5	83	0.32	254	70	49		3.70	-12.5
Spd No change	02	KC	* 465	54	112	22	61	4	241	225	261	$12	278	439	717	5	80	0.26	277	124	72	0.68	4.14	-5.9
BAvg -	1st Half		265	25	57	11	31	1	215			$4	244	392	636	4	82	0.21	274	112	55		3.14	-11.2
LIMA D+	2nd Half		200	29	55	11	30	3	275			$8	322	500	822	7	79	0.33	280	140	83		5.71	7.1
Risk Very High	03	Proj	150	19	37	7	20	1	247			$4	287	432	719	5	81	0.30	272	110	79		4.21	-1.7

1-5-.238 in 63 AB at KC. Opened up his swing, tapped into some power, and almost made himself look like Randa's replacement. But he's yet to see a .300 OB, so he's fooling nobody. At least not me.

Pena,Carlos		Tm	AB	R	H	HR	RBI	SB	Avg	vLH	vRH	R$	OB	Slg	OPS	bb%	ct%	Eye	xBA	PX	SX	G/F	RC/G	RAR
Pos 1B	98		0	0	0	0	0	0	0								0							
Age 24 Growth	99		0	0	0	0	0	0	0								0							
Bats L	00	aa	529	103	151	27	92	11	285			$22	391	512	904	15	83	1.03	302	134	100		7.94	38.6
Pwr ---	01	aaa	431	59	117	21	62	9	271			$16	372	513	885	14	77	0.69	281	151	80	1.43	7.17	12.1
Spd +++	02	2AL	* 572	65	131	26	76	4	229	265	230	$13	301	427	728	9	74	0.40	255	122	87	0.85	4.48	-27.0
BAvg No change	1st Half		274	30	55	13	36	2	201			$4	280	387	666	10	76	0.45	255	117	46		3.74	-19.5
LIMA A+	2nd Half		298	35	76	13	40	2	255			$8	321	463	784	9	73	0.36	255	126	118		5.26	-6.8
Risk Very High	03	Proj	550	74	140	23	79	7	255			$15	331	456	788	10	76	0.49	267	127	91		5.49	-2.9

19-52-.242 in 397 AB at OAK and DET. Or more accurately, .218 in OAK and .253 in DET. Or even more accurately, .293, .245 and .225 in his three months in DET. So he's not there yet.

Perez,Eddie

	Yr	Tm	AB	R	H	HR	RBI	SB	Avg	vLH	vRH	R$	OB	Slg	OPS	bb%	ct%	Eye	xBA	PX	SX	G/F	RC/G	RAR
Pos CA	98	ATL	149	18	50	6	32	1	336			$9	396	537	933	9	81	0.54	289	141	33		8.62	21.6
Age 34 Decline	99	ATL	309	30	77	7	30	0	249			$2	288	372	661	5	87	0.43	279	83	22		3.78	-2.4
Bats R	00	ATL	22	0	4	0	3	0	182			($0)	182	227	409	0	91	0.00	268	39			1.29	-1.8
Pwr +	01	ATL	* 48	6	15	3	5	0	313			$2	313	542	854	0	75	0.00	261	130		1.33	6.28	3.7
Spd No change	02	CLE	117	6	25	0	4	0	214	222	208	($1)	246	291	536	4	79	0.20	236	71	16	1.28	2.41	-4.5
BAvg +++	1st Half		56	4	14	0	3	0	250			$0	263	339	602	2	75	0.07	232	82	24		3.08	-1.0
LIMA F	2nd Half		61	2	11	0	1	0	180			($1)	231	246	477	6	82	0.36	239	61	7		1.89	-3.3
Risk X HIGH	03	Proj	150	11	36	2	12	0	240			$1	281	349	630	5	82	0.32	254	81	24		3.44	-2.9

Has drawn 5 walks in the past three years.

Perez,Eduardo

	Yr	Tm	AB	R	H	HR	RBI	SB	Avg	vLH	vRH	R$	OB	Slg	OPS	bb%	ct%	Eye	xBA	PX	SX	G/F	RC/G	RAR
Pos RF	98	CIN	172	20	41	4	30	0	238	205	266	$3	321	331	653	11	74	0.47	226	60	29	1.86	3.81	-6.5
Age 33 Decline	99	aaa	416	42	94	12	52	5	226			$4	276	365	642	7	79	0.33	255	89	47	1.63	3.24	-23.5
Bats R	00	STL	* 368	54	98	19	62	9	266	200	344	$14	341	473	814	10	84	0.72	294	116	85	1.46	5.79	6.4
Pwr No change	01	JPN	167	20	37	3	19	3	222			$1	309	341	650	11	71	0.44	226	84	61		3.78	-8.6
Spd No change	02	STL	154	22	31	10	26	0	201	271	143	$2	281	455	735	10	77	0.47	270	149	30	0.90	4.33	-5.3
BAvg +++++	1st Half		67	6	10	3	9	0	149			($1)	219	299	518	8	76	0.38	234	81	19		2.11	-6.9
LIMA D+	2nd Half		87	16	21	7	17	0	241			$3	327	575	901	11	77	0.55	298	202	35		6.67	3.5
Risk Very High	03	Proj	150	20	33	7	23	1	220			$3	300	424	724	10	76	0.48	263	125	51		4.40	-2.4

In July, compiled a slick .344 BA (and 1.213 OPS), but hit just .164 in the other 5 months. His July surge helped raise his BA from .149 to .212, but it became a race against the clock to see if he'd finish above Mendoza.

Perez,Neifi

	Yr	Tm	AB	R	H	HR	RBI	SB	Avg	vLH	vRH	R$	OB	Slg	OPS	bb%	ct%	Eye	xBA	PX	SX	G/F	RC/G	RAR
Pos SS	98	COL	647	80	177	9	59	5	274	302	259	$11	314	382	696	6	89	0.54	284	72	103	0.98	4.24	11.0
Age 29 Past Peak	99	COL	690	108	193	12	70	13	280	230	301	$15	308	403	711	4	92	0.52	297	75	139	1.09	4.46	17.7
Bats S	00	COL	651	92	187	10	71	3	287	357	266	$13	319	427	746	4	90	0.48	299	88	107	0.98	4.83	25.3
Pwr ++	01	2TM	581	83	162	8	59	9	279	266	284	$13	310	396	706	4	88	0.38	280	73	130	0.83	4.34	5.2
Spd -----	02	KC	554	65	131	3	37	8	236	227	240	$3	263	303	566	3	90	0.38	260	49	99	1.05	2.59	-34.2
BAvg -	1st Half		314	40	70	2	24	5	223			$1	245	303	547	3	90	0.28	264	54	140		2.51	-19.9
LIMA B	2nd Half		240	25	61	1	13	3	254			$2	287	304	591	4	91	0.52	255	41	54		2.69	-14.2
Risk Low	03	Proj	450	57	118	4	37	6	262			$6	292	356	649	4	90	0.43	272	63	105		3.51	-3.8

Does xBA give him more credit than he's worth? He does make good contact and has good speed. A .236 BA is probably at least a little low, but with such a poor bb%, there's no wiggle room for an acceptable OB avg.

Perez,Timo

	Yr	Tm	AB	R	H	HR	RBI	SB	Avg	vLH	vRH	R$	OB	Slg	OPS	bb%	ct%	Eye	xBA	PX	SX	G/F	RC/G	RAR
Pos CF LF	98	JPN	230	22	68	5	35	4	296			$8	352	404	756	8	91	0.95	283	70	62		5.36	5.3
Age 28 Peak	99	JPN	23	2	4	0	2	0	174			($1)	269	174	443	12	87	1.00	227		25		1.73	-2.1
Bats L	00	NYM	* 340	50	108	6	35	12	318	125	317	$14	348	453	801	4	92	0.59	304	86	118	1.06	5.62	12.3
Pwr +++	01	NYM	* 431	61	124	10	40	15	288	154	258	$15	324	415	739	5	90	0.53	289	79	112	1.14	4.78	11.0
Spd -	02	NYM	444	52	131	8	47	10	295	156	318	$15	330	437	767	5	92	0.64	299	92	115	1.06	5.20	3.1
BAvg --	1st Half		175	20	57	5	20	2	326			$8	337	491	829	2	91	0.20	303	113	47		5.77	4.1
LIMA A	2nd Half		269	32	74	3	27	8	275			$7	325	401	727	7	92	0.95	296	78	155		4.84	-1.1
Risk High	03	Proj	400	50	114	8	43	11	285			$12	322	419	741	5	91	0.63	296	86	109		4.78	4.8

Contact hitter with decent speed, but as long as they let him face LHers, his numbers will suffer. Case in point is 2nd half when he started playing regularly. He is a .300+ hitter when he faces RHers.

Perez,Tomas

	Yr	Tm	AB	R	H	HR	RBI	SB	Avg	vLH	vRH	R$	OB	Slg	OPS	bb%	ct%	Eye	xBA	PX	SX	G/F	RC/G	RAR
Pos 2B	98	aaa	404	40	101	3	37	4	250			$3	282	332	614	4	83	0.26	253	56	87		3.07	-13.0
Age 29 Past Peak	99	aaa	296	24	67	3	32	2	226			($0)	266	314	580	5	88	0.44	268	62	54		2.81	-12.1
Bats R	00	PHI	* 419	53	107	8	59	4	255	304	205	$7	297	387	684	6	83	0.34	272	85	89	1.50	4.06	-5.0
Pwr +	01	PHI	135	11	41	3	19	0	304	354	276	$4	338	437	775	5	84	0.32	268	84	48	1.10	5.40	5.9
Spd No change	02	PHI	221	24	56	5	21	1	253	250	250	$3	318	389	707	9	81	0.51	258	89	58	1.05	4.52	0.1
BAvg No change	1st Half		92	7	24	2	11	0	261			$1	299	402	701	5	80	0.28	256	99	13		4.29	-0.6
LIMA D	2nd Half		129	17	32	3	10	1	248			$1	331	380	711	11	82	0.70	259	82	78		4.67	0.7
Risk Very High	03	Proj	150	15	40	3	17	1	267			$3	318	395	713	7	83	0.43	263	83	63		4.53	2.0

Just signed a 2-year $1.3 million contract with a $100,000 signing bonus. And my kids' school has to hold a bake sale so they can buy textbooks.

Perry,Herbert

	Yr	Tm	AB	R	H	HR	RBI	SB	Avg	vLH	vRH	R$	OB	Slg	OPS	bb%	ct%	Eye	xBA	PX	SX	G/F	RC/G	RAR
Pos 3B	98	aaa	17	1	5	0	1	0	294			$0	294	529	824	0	88	0.00	353	213			5.63	0.5
Age 33 Decline	99	TAM	* 312	47	83	11	49	0	266	242	259	$7	312	436	748	6	81	0.36	269	105	51	1.53	4.92	3.9
Bats R	00	2AL	411	71	124	12	62	4	302	296	303	$13	340	467	807	6	82	0.32	278	106	85	1.35	5.99	18.7
Pwr ++++	01	CHW	285	38	73	7	32	2	256	256	256	$5	312	411	722	7	81	0.42	264	104	64	1.35	4.51	0.5
Spd No change	02	TEX	450	64	124	22	77	4	276	260	282	$18	326	480	806	7	85	0.52	297	130	66	1.26	5.69	15.6
BAvg -	1st Half		191	31	55	9	37	3	288			$9	343	487	830	8	86	0.62	298	124	91		6.35	10.6
LIMA B	2nd Half		259	33	69	13	40	1	266			$9	314	475	789	6	85	0.45	296	135	38		5.22	5.3
Risk X HIGH	03	Proj	350	51	98	13	53	3	280			$11	329	464	793	7	83	0.44	284	118	67		5.57	10.4

Health and opportunity finally yielded the season that many were waiting for... but Hank Blalock is poised to snatch that away in '03.

Petrick,Ben

	Yr	Tm	AB	R	H	HR	RBI	SB	Avg	vLH	vRH	R$	OB	Slg	OPS	bb%	ct%	Eye	xBA	PX	SX	G/F	RC/G	RAR
Pos LF	98	aa	349	43	87	19	42	6	249			$10	337	490	827	12	81	0.68	294	148	82		5.69	7.5
Age 26 Pre-Peak	99	COL	* 412	66	128	25	74	10	311	333	320	$23	383	573	955	10	85	0.79	312	152	104	1.29	8.17	39.7
Bats R	00	COL	* 394	59	120	11	53	6	305	354	306	$14	373	480	853	10	85	0.72	294	113	87	1.12	6.78	18.3
Pwr ++	01	COL	* 308	48	73	12	45	4	237	213	250	$7	325	429	753	11	74	0.49	255	114	108	0.97	4.89	-9.1
Spd ----	02	COL	* 360	43	97	18	46	6	269	250	163	$13	334	494	829	9	78	0.44	272	131	92	1.35	5.55	-10.8
BAvg --	1st Half		203	24	52	9	27	5	256			$6	326	468	794	9	76	0.44	264	119	140		5.11	-9.0
LIMA C+	2nd Half		157	19	45	9	19	1	287			$6	345	529	874	8	80	0.45	282	148	31		6.16	-1.7
Risk High	03	Proj	200	27	51	9	27	3	255			$6	328	472	800	10	79	0.51	277	130	94		5.29	3.4

5-11-.211 in 95 AB at COL. You can see '01's big drop in batting eye, which did not improve in '02. While his power continues to develop, his on base ability has taken the hit. There's a fundamental flaw somewhere.

Phelps,Josh

	Yr	Tm	AB	R	H	HR	RBI	SB	Avg	vLH	vRH	R$	OB	Slg	OPS	bb%	ct%	Eye	xBA	PX	SX	G/F	RC/G	RAR
Pos DH	98		0	0	0	0	0	0	0								0							
Age 24 Growth	99		0	0	0	0	0	0	0								0							
Bats R	00	aa	184	18	38	7	22	1	207			$1	251	380	632	6	73	0.22	248	102	66		3.22	-11.0
Pwr ++	01	aa	498	82	130	26	82	4	261			$17	349	492	841	12	77	0.59	275	141	62		6.24	14.6
Spd No change	02	TOR	* 522	81	150	34	109	0	287	286	315	$25	344	567	911	8	72	0.30	276	179	46	0.97	7.25	26.1
BAvg --	1st Half		257	40	68	19	51	0	265			$12	332	572	904	9	74	0.39	295	195	44		6.89	10.1
LIMA A	2nd Half		265	41	82	15	58	0	309			$14	356	562	918	7	69	0.23	258	165	48		7.63	16.1
Risk High	03	Proj	550	82	147	31	100	2	267			$20	333	513	845	9	74	0.37	270	153	62		6.20	12.0

15-58-.309 in 265 AB at TOR. Prototypical power hitter with big swing and below avg contact rate. A .309 BA is probably not going to happen again, but 30 HRs in the majors is a good bet. Set to play 1B in 2003.

Piatt,Adam

	Yr	Tm	AB	R	H	HR	RBI	SB	Avg	vLH	vRH	R$	OB	Slg	OPS	bb%	ct%	Eye	xBA	PX	SX	G/F	RC/G	RAR
Pos LF	98		0	0	0	0	0	0	0								0							
Age 27 Peak	99	a/a	494	101	147	29	108	6	298			$24	390	569	959	13	84	0.96	318	167	79		8.45	53.5
Bats R	00	OAK	* 411	57	113	12	62	3	275	369	219	$10	349	433	782	10	76	0.48	252	92	99	1.10	5.57	4.9
Pwr ++++	01	OAK	* 204	20	44	1	18	2	216	245	167	($1)	292	304	596	10	77	0.47	233	67	69	1.24	3.20	-9.8
Spd No change	02	OAK	* 371	51	88	11	50	5	237	233	234	$8	306	383	689	9	85	0.66	276	100	63	1.18	4.02	-10.7
BAvg +++	1st Half		257	36	63	8	32	3	245			$6	310	393	703	9	84	0.60	275	101	63		4.28	-5.2
LIMA B	2nd Half		114	15	25	3	18	2	219			$2	299	360	659	10	86	0.81	279	99	63		3.47	-5.3
Risk Very High	03	Proj	350	47	92	11	54	4	263			$10	337	423	760	10	82	0.62	270	105	64		5.10	-0.3

5-18-.234 in 137 AB at OAK. His productivity is slowly starting to return, but he's still not back to where he was in 2000, and certainly not anywhere near '99. At 27, time is running out.

Piazza,Mike

		Tm	AB	R	H	HR	RBI	SB	Avg	vLH	vRH	R$	OB	Slg	OPS	bb%	ct%	Eye	xBA	PX	SX	G/F	RC/G	RAR
Pos CA	98	2NL	561	88	184	32	111	1	328	323	329	$33	391	570	961	9	86	0.73	314	159	43	1.53	8.87	86.2
Age 34 Decline	99	NYM	534	100	162	40	124	2	303	298	305	$30	364	575	939	9	87	0.73	317	155	45	1.07	7.90	64.5
Bats R	00	NYM	482	90	156	38	113	4	324	354	318	$32	396	614	1010	11	86	0.84	326	163	51	0.99	9.56	84.6
Pwr - -	01	NYM	503	81	151	36	94	0	300	323	295	$26	382	573	955	12	83	0.77	303	157		1.06	8.34	77.3
Spd No change	02	NYM	478	69	134	33	98	0	280	286	278	$23	357	544	901	11	83	0.70	293	150	34	1.03	7.10	44.3
BAvg -	1st Half		243	33	68	15	46	0	280			$11	371	523	893	13	85	0.97	296	140	34		7.12	23.2
LIMA B+	2nd Half		235	36	66	18	52	0	281			$13	342	566	908	9	80	0.48	291	161	45		7.04	20.9
Risk Very Low	03	Proj	**450**	**71**	**130**	**30**	**97**	**0**	**289**			**$23**	**364**	**546**	**910**	**11**	**83**	**0.71**	**299**	**148**	**34**		**7.40**	**49.1**

Declining trends in OB, ct%, xBA and PX all show the slow erosion of his skill set. He's still the pace-setter for CA offense but his lead will begin to dwindle.

Pierre,Juan

		Tm	AB	R	H	HR	RBI	SB	Avg	vLH	vRH	R$	OB	Slg	OPS	bb%	ct%	Eye	xBA	PX	SX	G/F	RC/G	RAR
Pos CF	98		0	0	0	0	0	0	0								0							
Age 25 Pre-Peak	99		0	0	0	0	0	0	0								0							
Bats L	00	COL	* 656	83	215	0	49	48	328	500	284	$31	368	367	736	6	94	1.14	275	29	111	3.03	5.20	15.7
Pwr -	01	COL	617	108	202	2	55	46	327	289	337	$33	369	415	784	6	95	1.41	296	56	173	2.77	5.89	36.9
Spd - - - - -	02	COL	592	90	170	1	35	47	287	294	285	$23	323	343	666	5	91	0.60	269	39	149	3.20	4.20	-13.7
BAvg - -	1st Half		334	45	90	0	16	24	269			$10	303	308	611	5	90	0.50	259	29	132		3.39	-15.8
LIMA A	2nd Half		258	45	80	1	19	23	310			$14	348	388	736	5	92	0.75	282	53	163		5.41	3.4
Risk Moderate	03	Proj	**600**	**96**	**186**	**1**	**44**	**47**	**310**			**$28**	**349**	**377**	**726**	**6**	**93**	**0.89**	**281**	**45**	**153**		**5.06**	**12.1**

What an incredible fuss was made over his off year. Yes, some of his BPIs were down, but the key underlying indicators hardly budged. A .422 BA Sept boosted his 2nd half, and puts momentum back in his corner.

Pierzynski,A.J.

		Tm	AB	R	H	HR	RBI	SB	Avg	vLH	vRH	R$	OB	Slg	OPS	bb%	ct%	Eye	xBA	PX	SX	G/F	RC/G	RAR
Pos CA	98	a/a	420	58	121	10	46	3	288			$11	319	417	736	4	90	0.46	291	85	73	0.75	4.78	9.3
Age 26 Pre-Peak	99	aaa	228	23	56	1	20	0	246			($0)	286	298	585	5	91	0.62	262	41	30	5.00	3.03	-7.3
Bats L	00	MIN	* 471	61	139	8	60	2	295		321	$10	318	437	756	3	89	0.32	296	94	84	1.77	5.11	12.3
Pwr - -	01	MIN	381	51	110	7	55	1	289	167	312	$10	317	441	758	4	85	0.28	279	107	58	1.20	4.75	9.2
Spd No change	02	MIN	440	54	132	6	49	1	300	270	308	$11	320	439	759	3	86	0.21	281	100	95	1.64	5.11	18.4
BAvg - - -	1st Half		226	36	73	5	31	1	323			$9	352	509	861	4	85	0.29	298	130	124		6.80	20.9
LIMA C	2nd Half		214	18	59	1	18	0	276			$3	286	364	650	1	87	0.11	263	68	65		3.62	-0.4
Risk High	03	Proj	**450**	**55**	**126**	**8**	**53**	**1**	**280**			**$9**	**304**	**425**	**729**	**3**	**87**	**0.26**	**285**	**101**	**75**		**4.52**	**6.0**

A legitimate .300 hitter? Hardly. Near zero plate patience and only above average contact does not make for high BA potential. 2nd straight season he hit .300+ in 1st half and faded down the stretch.

Polanco,Placido

		Tm	AB	R	H	HR	RBI	SB	Avg	vLH	vRH	R$	OB	Slg	OPS	bb%	ct%	Eye	xBA	PX	SX	G/F	RC/G	RAR
Pos 3B	98	STL	* 360	39	91	2	28	7	253	188	280	$4	288	344	633	5	94	0.86	300	72	105	1.86	3.52	-10.5
Age 27 Peak	99	STL	* 340	40	91	1	28	3	268	346	237	$3	304	338	643	5	90	0.53	273	48	93	1.67	3.63	-8.4
Bats R	00	STL	323	50	102	5	39	4	316	333	309	$11	348	418	766	5	92	0.62	288	63	93	2.04	5.38	9.5
Pwr + + + +	01	STL	564	87	173	3	38	12	307	350	292	$15	336	383	719	4	92	0.58	281	54	117	2.31	4.90	3.7
Spd - - - - -	02	2NL	548	75	158	9	49	5	288	338	270	$13	321	403	724	5	93	0.63	289	79	77	1.86	4.71	0.5
BAvg -	1st Half		244	25	66	4	21	2	270			$4	294	365	658	3	92	0.42	276	60	65		3.80	-6.3
LIMA B	2nd Half		304	50	92	5	28	3	303			$9	342	434	776	6	93	0.82	299	93	80		5.52	7.7
Risk Moderate	03	Proj	**500**	**71**	**142**	**6**	**44**	**4**	**284**			**$9**	**317**	**385**	**702**	**5**	**92**	**0.63**	**287**	**69**	**82**		**4.39**	**-2.4**

High contact rate will keep his BA in acceptable territory, but decline in OB avg and RC/G show how his overall value is waning. Despite his roto value history, I can never get myself to spend even $10 on these types.

Posada,Jorge

		Tm	AB	R	H	HR	RBI	SB	Avg	vLH	vRH	R$	OB	Slg	OPS	bb%	ct%	Eye	xBA	PX	SX	G/F	RC/G	RAR
Pos CA	98	NYY	358	56	96	17	63	0	268	357	228	$11	353	475	828	12	74	0.51	257	128	30	1.24	6.19	24.4
Age 31 Past Peak	99	NYY	379	50	93	12	57	1	245	303	225	$6	338	401	739	12	76	0.58	248	95	62	1.61	5.01	10.6
Bats S	00	NYY	505	92	145	28	86	2	287	321	272	$18	412	527	938	17	70	0.71	256	141	48	1.20	8.48	74.3
Pwr + + + +	01	NYY	484	59	134	22	95	2	277	272	279	$18	359	475	834	11	73	0.47	242	121	32	1.12	6.16	34.6
Spd No change	02	NYY	511	79	137	20	99	1	268	326	247	$17	368	468	836	14	72	0.57	254	137	50	1.14	6.54	48.2
BAvg -	1st Half		267	45	69	13	50	1	258			$9	351	487	838	12	72	0.51	264	151	67		6.34	23.1
LIMA A+	2nd Half		244	34	68	7	49	0	279			$8	387	447	833	15	72	0.62	244	122	23		6.73	25.0
Risk Low	03	Proj	**500**	**74**	**132**	**21**	**94**	**1**	**264**			**$16**	**365**	**464**	**829**	**14**	**72**	**0.57**	**250**	**129**	**43**		**6.31**	**37.1**

BPIs are stable, but his xBA scan is interesting. While his BA had surged a bit in 2000-01, his xBAs have remained consistent for all 5 years. Was he a better hitter in '00-'01? His '02 BA says maybe not.

Pratt,Todd

		Tm	AB	R	H	HR	RBI	SB	Avg	vLH	vRH	R$	OB	Slg	OPS	bb%	ct%	Eye	xBA	PX	SX	G/F	RC/G	RAR
Pos CA	98	NYM	* 187	20	49	7	39	2	262	267	282	$7	307	455	761	6	78	0.29	275	131	72	1.28	5.05	6.0
Age 36 Decline	99	NYM	140	18	41	3	21	2	293	279	299	$4	361	386	747	10	77	0.47	237	58	50	0.93	5.48	6.4
Bats R	00	NYM	160	33	44	8	25	0	275	256	282	$5	363	463	825	12	81	0.71	275	106	43	1.39	6.36	11.9
Pwr + + +	01	2NL	173	18	32	4	11	1	185	250	165	($2)	319	301	619	16	65	0.56	202	74	36	0.98	3.54	-0.3
Spd No change	02	PHI	106	14	33	3	16	2	311	417	280	$5	438	500	938	18	74	0.86	253	133	44	0.91	9.23	18.7
BAvg - -	1st Half		54	6	20	0	6	1	370			$3	469	519	987	16	72	0.67	246	129	38		10.94	12.3
LIMA C	2nd Half		52	8	13	3	10	1	250			$2	409	481	890	21	75	1.08	260	138	39		7.80	6.8
Risk Very High	03	Proj	**150**	**21**	**40**	**5**	**21**	**2**	**267**			**$4**	**387**	**434**	**821**	**16**	**73**	**0.73**	**243**	**109**	**45**		**6.61**	**13.5**

Is he a .311 hitter? Is he a .185 hitter? BPIs indicate that .311 is closer to his true profile, but the small data sets wreak havoc. And check out that bb% trend -- as long as he keeps doing that, he'll maintain some value.

Prince,Tom

		Tm	AB	R	H	HR	RBI	SB	Avg	vLH	vRH	R$	OB	Slg	OPS	bb%	ct%	Eye	xBA	PX	SX	G/F	RC/G	RAR
Pos CA	98	LA	81	7	15	0	5	0	185	316	145	($2)	250	272	522	8	70	0.29	222	69	85	0.81	2.30	-4.3
Age 38 Decline	99	aaa	28	3	3	1	1	0	107			($1)	194	214	408	10	75	0.43	224	54	39		1.34	-2.4
Bats R	00	PHI	122	14	29	2	16	1	238	208	245	$1	311	361	672	10	75	0.42	245	87	46	1.00	4.09	0.0
Pwr + +	01	MIN	196	19	43	7	23	3	219	203	230	$2	264	357	622	6	80	0.31	248	76	71	0.86	3.21	-4.3
Spd No change	02	MIN	125	14	28	4	16	1	224	224	224	$2	302	392	694	10	79	0.54	265	111	77	0.74	3.80	0.4
BAvg + + + + +	1st Half		71	12	19	4	14	0	268			$3	325	521	846	8	77	0.38	287	156	117		5.44	3.8
LIMA D	2nd Half		54	2	9	0	2	1	167			($1)	274	222	496	13	81	0.80	233	51	34		2.09	-2.8
Risk X HIGH	03	Proj	**100**	**10**	**22**	**3**	**11**	**1**	**220**			**$1**	**290**	**349**	**639**	**9**	**79**	**0.47**	**249**	**85**	**44**		**3.41**	**-2.1**

He batted .274 at home, .261 in day games, .268 on turf, .271 in domed venues, .368 in April, .444 when he swung a the first pitch, .274 when he batted 8th, .310 w/runners in scoring pos... but just .224 overall.

Pujols,Albert

		Tm	AB	R	H	HR	RBI	SB	Avg	vLH	vRH	R$	OB	Slg	OPS	bb%	ct%	Eye	xBA	PX	SX	G/F	RC/G	RAR
Pos LF 3B 1B	98		0	0	0	0	0	0	0								0							
Age 23 Growth	99		0	0	0	0	0	0	0								0							
Bats R	00		0	0	0	0	0	0	0								0							
Pwr - - - -	01	STL	590	112	194	37	130	1	329	279	342	$36	399	610	1009	10	84	0.74	320	168	64	1.09	9.54	70.3
Spd No change	02	STL	590	118	185	34	127	2	314	309	315	$34	388	561	949	11	88	1.04	314	149	59	1.27	8.36	34.9
BAvg -	1st Half		286	57	81	16	54	1	283			$13	369	531	901	12	88	1.15	316	155	52		7.37	8.0
LIMA C+	2nd Half		304	61	104	18	73	1	342			$22	407	589	995	10	88	0.94	313	144	68		9.40	27.7
Risk Low	03	Proj	**575**	**113**	**185**	**34**	**126**	**2**	**322**			**$34**	**394**	**583**	**977**	**11**	**87**	**0.89**	**318**	**157**	**62**		**8.89**	**76.2**

I projected that his numbers would drop off a bit in '02, and he obliged, but not enough to be statistically significant. I surrender. He's good. He's damn good. (But I'll bet $100 that he's at least 26...)

Quinn,Mark

		Tm	AB	R	H	HR	RBI	SB	Avg	vLH	vRH	R$	OB	Slg	OPS	bb%	ct%	Eye	xBA	PX	SX	G/F	RC/G	RAR
Pos RF	98	aa	372	58	109	11	60	3	293			$13	344	468	812	7	90	0.74	309	112	110		6.04	11.1
Age 28 Peak	99	KC	* 488	67	161	26	89	7	330	333	333	$26	365	553	918	5	87	0.42	306	132	55	1.00	7.40	34.3
Bats R	00	KC	500	76	147	20	78	5	294	259	277	$17	340	488	828	7	82	0.38	286	117	80	1.40	6.18	17.8
Pwr No change	01	KC	* 496	60	129	19	62	9	260	288	262	$14	278	448	725	2	85	0.16	287	117	85	1.55	4.22	-12.5
Spd + + + + +	02	KC	* 123	12	25	2	14	2	203	348	189	$1	252	325	577	6	82	0.36	260	86	97	1.29	2.71	-9.0
BAvg + + +	1st Half		123	12	25	2	14	2	203			$1	252	325	577	6	83	0.38	262	86	97		2.71	-9.0
LIMA A	2nd Half		0	0	0	0	0	0	0			($0)					0							-0.0
Risk Very High	03	Proj	**500**	**64**	**138**	**17**	**71**	**5**	**276**			**$15**	**316**	**450**	**766**	**5**	**84**	**0.37**	**284**	**113**	**79**		**5.04**	**-3.2**

2-11-.237 in 76 AB at KC.
The Bizarre Chronicles...
Feb 26: Cracked rib from Kung Fu fighting
Jun 7: Strained hamstring
Jul 21: Sprained ankle, but not reported to media until Aug 4.

Raines,Tim

Info	Yr	Tm	AB	R	H	HR	RBI	SB	Avg	vLH	vRH	R$	OB	Slg	OPS	bb%	ct%	Eye	xBA	PX	SX	G/F	RC/G	RAR
Pos LF	98	NYY	321	53	93	5	47	8	290			$10	394	383	777	15	85	1.12	259	62	81	1.66	6.02	9.4
Age 43 Decline	99	OAK	135	20	29	4	17	4	215	234	197	$2	342	341	682	16	87	1.53	274	76	68	1.21	4.38	-3.6
Bats S	00		0	0	0	0	0	0	0									0						
Pwr No change	01	2TM *	96	15	28	1	9	1	292	278	310	$2	409	438	846	17	90	1.90	299	105	82	1.18	7.27	6.6
Spd No change	02	FLA	89	9	17	1	7	0	191	333	169	($2)	351	258	610	20	79	1.16	223	46	17	1.03	3.57	-9.3
BAvg +++++	1st Half		49	5	10	1	5	0	204			($0)	361	306	667	20	84	1.50	248	66	14		4.27	-3.9
LIMA F	2nd Half		40	4	7	0	2	0	175			($1)	340	200	540	20	73	0.91	195	22	20		2.78	-5.3
Risk High	03	Proj	0	0	0	0	0	0	0			$0						0		0	0			0.0

Maintained a 1.0-plus batting eye ratio right up until the end.

Ramirez,Aramis

Info	Yr	Tm	AB	R	H	HR	RBI	SB	Avg	vLH	vRH	R$	OB	Slg	OPS	bb%	ct%	Eye	xBA	PX	SX	G/F	RC/G	RAR
Pos 3B	98	PIT	* 419	40	107	11	40	0	255	255	230	$6	320	389	709	9	78	0.44	255	92	28	1.17	4.49	-0.1
Age 24 Growth	99	PIT	* 516	72	146	17	63	4	283	200	174	$14	361	459	820	11	90	1.19	306	115	59	0.95	6.21	29.2
Bats R	00	PIT	* 421	44	120	9	57	2	285	238	262	$10	317	425	743	5	85	0.31	280	90	65	1.16	4.88	6.0
Pwr No change	01	PIT	603	83	181	34	112	5	300	297	301	$30	344	536	879	6	83	0.40	300	142	49	0.88	6.79	38.7
Spd No change	02	PIT	522	51	122	18	71	2	234	260	226	$8	274	387	661	5	82	0.31	261	96	44	0.80	3.68	-15.8
BAvg No change	1st Half		204	17	46	4	25	2	225			$1	272	333	605	6	78	0.30	239	72	48		3.18	-9.3
LIMA B+	2nd Half		318	34	76	14	46	0	239			$6	275	421	697	5	84	0.31	274	111	22		4.01	-6.4
Risk Very High	03	Proj	600	66	167	32	97	3	278			$23	321	501	821	6	83	0.36	289	132	44		5.82	23.1

The minor drops in bb%, ct% and eye can't explain a 66 pt. hit in BA. xBA lessens the blow, and attributes the drop to his power game. Lingering injuries sapped his power, but it returned in the 2nd half. So... expect a rebound.

Ramirez,Manny

Info	Yr	Tm	AB	R	H	HR	RBI	SB	Avg	vLH	vRH	R$	OB	Slg	OPS	bb%	ct%	Eye	xBA	PX	SX	G/F	RC/G	RAR
Pos LF DH	98	CLE	571	108	168	45	145	5	294	340	278	$33	377	599	976	12	79	0.63	305	176	70	0.79	8.52	62.4
Age 30 Past Peak	99	CLE	522	131	174	44	165	2	333	383	319	$38	437	663	1100	16	75	0.73	296	186	73	0.80	11.60	113.5
Bats R	00	CLE	439	92	154	38	122	1	351	396	339	$32	457	697	1154	16	73	0.74	301	195	55	0.89	13.35	122.3
Pwr No change	01	BOS	529	93	162	41	125	0	306	342	296	$31	398	609	1007	13	72	0.55	268	175	39	0.87	9.43	82.1
Spd No change	02	BOS	* 466	86	155	34	109	0	333	438	331	$31	429	620	1050	14	80	0.84	308	181	23	1.49	10.90	92.9
BAvg --	1st Half		162	29	49	10	39	0	302			$9	429	537	966	18	81	1.20	292	145	22		9.33	24.9
LIMA C+	2nd Half		304	57	106	24	70	0	349			$22	429	664	1094	12	79	0.67	316	200	24		11.79	68.0
Risk Low	03	Proj	550	104	179	44	136	0	325			$36	424	637	1061	15	77	0.73	298	186	32		10.85	105.3

Returned from his finger injury with a vengeance, and put to rest any question about 2001 being an off year. At 30, he's far from done, and all you can do is pay the money and enjoy the show.

Randa,Joe

Info	Yr	Tm	AB	R	H	HR	RBI	SB	Avg	vLH	vRH	R$	OB	Slg	OPS	bb%	ct%	Eye	xBA	PX	SX	G/F	RC/G	RAR
Pos 3B	98	DET	460	56	117	9	50	8	254	254	255	$7	315	367	683	8	85	0.59	265	73	76	1.35	4.04	-7.4
Age 33 Decline	99	KC	628	92	197	16	84	5	314	356	306	$21	364	473	837	7	87	0.63	292	98	101	1.08	6.57	39.9
Bats R	00	KC	612	88	186	15	106	6	304	310	302	$20	343	438	781	6	89	0.55	286	81	87	1.24	5.63	21.2
Pwr +++	01	KC	581	59	147	13	83	3	253	261	250	$10	303	386	689	7	86	0.53	271	88	53	1.27	4.15	-5.3
Spd No change	02	KC	549	63	155	11	80	2	282	321	270	$15	338	426	764	8	87	0.67	286	101	77	1.28	5.36	13.6
BAvg -	1st Half		250	34	75	8	52	2	300			$11	366	484	850	9	86	0.74	299	129	63		6.76	17.4
LIMA A+	2nd Half		299	29	80	3	28	0	268			$4	313	378	691	6	89	0.59	274	78	73		4.31	-2.2
Risk Low	03	Proj	550	64	154	15	79	3	280			$15	331	432	763	7	87	0.60	286	99	72		5.25	11.0

In 1999, he went for $10 and earned $20. In '00, he went for $15 and earned $20. Slipped in '01, but then went for $10 in '02 and earned $15. In '03, they'll see a declining HR trend and bid $10 again. Just watch.

Redmond,Mike

Info	Yr	Tm	AB	R	H	HR	RBI	SB	Avg	vLH	vRH	R$	OB	Slg	OPS	bb%	ct%	Eye	xBA	PX	SX	G/F	RC/G	RAR
Pos CA	98	FLA	* 204	17	56	4	21	0	275	413	236	$4	299	397	696	3	90	0.33	291	92		1.18	4.26	1.6
Age 31 Past Peak	99	FLA	242	22	73	1	27	0	302	304	300	$5	369	351	721	10	86	0.76	251	39		1.61	5.11	8.2
Bats R	00	FLA	210	17	53	0	15	0	252	321	209	($0)	296	300	596	6	91	0.68	268	36	38	1.54	3.19	-5.6
Pwr ---	01	FLA	141	19	44	4	14	0	312	375	271	$5	370	426	796	8	91	1.00	278	67	26	1.68	6.17	11.3
Spd No change	02	FLA	256	19	78	2	28	0	305	286	312	$7	357	387	744	8	87	0.62	255	63	14	2.25	5.18	7.8
BAvg --	1st Half		124	14	41	1	15	0	331			$5	385	419	805	8	90	0.85	268	68	28		6.10	7.3
LIMA D	2nd Half		132	5	37	1	13	0	280			$2	331	356	687	7	84	0.48	243	58	1		4.41	0.9
Risk Moderate	03	Proj	250	22	74	3	25	0	296			$5	348	380	729	7	88	0.68	264	60	19		4.99	7.8

xBA calls his .300 flirtations a fluke, but he's done it thrice in the past 5 years. Provides no other asset to your team, but a .300 hitting catcher for a buck or two -- heck, even a .270 hitting CA -- is a worthy investment.

Reese,Pokey

Info	Yr	Tm	AB	R	H	HR	RBI	SB	Avg	vLH	vRH	R$	OB	Slg	OPS	bb%	ct%	Eye	xBA	PX	SX	G/F	RC/G	RAR
Pos 2B	98	CIN	133	20	34	1	16	3	256	133	291	$2	327	323	650	10	79	0.50	238	40	132	1.13	3.81	-1.6
Age 29 Past Peak	99	CIN	585	85	167	10	52	38	285	295	282	$22	326	417	743	6	86	0.43	285	89	138	1.07	5.15	15.0
Bats R	00	CIN	518	76	132	12	46	29	255	257	254	$15	314	386	700	8	83	0.52	271	77	152	0.90	4.59	2.3
Pwr No change	01	CIN	428	50	96	9	40	25	224	226	224	$10	281	343	625	7	81	0.41	259	76	127	0.86	3.49	-5.9
Spd -----	02	PIT	421	46	111	4	50	12	264	282	259	$10	329	352	681	9	81	0.51	246	66	81	1.16	4.42	-1.1
BAvg No change	1st Half		183	13	44	1	20	6	240			$2	302	306	608	8	79	0.42	232	51	67		3.50	-5.7
LIMA B	2nd Half		238	33	67	3	30	6	282			$7	350	387	736	10	82	0.58	255	77	76		5.21	5.3
Risk Moderate	03	Proj	450	55	114	7	48	14	253			$9	315	358	673	8	81	0.48	255	71	102		4.17	1.0

This apparent BA rebound is discounted by xBA, and along with his drop in SBs, makes '02 a lot less valuable. Follow the trends in PX, SX, ct%, xBA... and pass when his name comes up.

Relaford,Desi

Info	Yr	Tm	AB	R	H	HR	RBI	SB	Avg	vLH	vRH	R$	OB	Slg	OPS	bb%	ct%	Eye	xBA	PX	SX	G/F	RC/G	RAR
Pos SS 3B LF	98	PHI	494	45	121	5	41	9	245	242	246	$5	292	338	630	6	82	0.38	260	70	86	1.38	3.44	-3.6
Age 29 Past Peak	99	PHI	211	31	51	1	26	4	242	250	240	$2	304	327	631	8	84	0.56	262	61	107	1.16	3.46	-0.9
Bats S	00	2NL	410	55	88	5	46	13	215	194	221	$3	336	300	636	15	83	1.06	255	53	113	1.25	3.97	6.1
Pwr No change	01	NYM	301	43	91	8	36	13	302	240	315	$14	360	472	832	8	78	0.42	271	117	86	1.01	6.37	25.6
Spd +++++	02	SEA	329	55	88	6	43	10	267	202	292	$10	334	374	708	9	84	0.65	258	72	117	1.00	4.66	-0.1
BAvg No change	1st Half		160	28	43	2	24	5	269			$5	361	331	692	13	85	0.96	237	37	103		4.50	-0.9
LIMA B	2nd Half		169	27	45	4	19	5	266			$5	307	414	721	6	84	0.37	278	104	121		4.75	0.4
Risk High	03	Proj	300	45	79	6	36	11	263			$8	333	380	713	9	83	0.60	260	80	102		4.72	8.7

Marginally interesting. Trends are erratic, as has been his playing time, so it's tough to see where he's headed. But he is better than many other end-game infield fillers, so a few dollar investment should pay off.

Renteria,Edgar

Info	Yr	Tm	AB	R	H	HR	RBI	SB	Avg	vLH	vRH	R$	OB	Slg	OPS	bb%	ct%	Eye	xBA	PX	SX	G/F	RC/G	RAR
Pos SS	98	FLA	517	79	146	3	31	41	282	227	297	$20	343	342	686	8	85	0.62	258	46	118	2.17	4.16	7.8
Age 27 Peak	99	STL	585	92	161	11	63	37	275	250	283	$21	335	400	735	8	86	0.65	281	85	118	1.16	5.09	27.1
Bats R	00	STL	562	94	156	16	76	21	278	259	284	$20	350	423	774	10	86	0.82	288	92	89	1.38	5.32	32.0
Pwr ++++	01	STL	493	54	128	10	57	17	260	327	243	$13	314	371	685	7	85	0.53	267	69	106	1.37	4.28	9.8
Spd --	02	STL	544	77	166	11	83	22	305	288	310	$26	363	439	802	8	90	0.86	289	91	100	1.56	6.11	36.2
BAvg --	1st Half		261	31	73	3	33	10	280			$9	338	402	740	8	91	1.00	293	87	105		5.00	8.3
LIMA A	2nd Half		283	46	93	8	50	12	329			$18	385	473	859	8	88	0.76	285	95	87		7.29	29.3
Risk Low	03	Proj	550	77	164	15	75	25	298			$26	357	442	799	8	87	0.72	287	93	101		5.98	38.3

Nailed a .300 BA for the first time since his rookie year ('96), and it's a good possibility that he'll be able to maintain it. Most other BPIs are stable at a time when you'd expect more growth, but that growth still may come.

Richard,Chris

Info	Yr	Tm	AB	R	H	HR	RBI	SB	Avg	vLH	vRH	R$	OB	Slg	OPS	bb%	ct%	Eye	xBA	PX	SX	G/F	RC/G	RAR
Pos DH	98	aa	89	6	17	1	16	0	191			($0)	258	292	550	8	88	0.73	273	69	67		2.43	-8.2
Age 28 Peak	99	a/a	459	65	119	25	78	6	259			$15	313	486	799	7	86	0.55	304	133	70		5.12	-2.5
Bats L	00	2TM	* 590	96	151	29	104	15	256	237	286	$20	328	468	796	10	83	0.61	293	124	93	0.93	5.40	4.0
Pwr +++	01	BAL	483	74	128	15	61	11	265	208	281	$13	328	435	762	9	79	0.45	265	108	94	1.19	4.95	-5.9
Spd ----	02	BAL	* 214	23	50	8	35	0	234	250	230	$4	290	421	711	7	79	0.37	272	129	29	0.89	3.99	-10.9
BAvg No change	1st Half		0	0	0	0	0	0	0			($0)						0		0				-0.0
LIMA A	2nd Half		214	23	50	8	35	0	234			$4	290	421	711	7	79	0.37	272	129	29		3.99	-10.9
Risk Very High	03	Proj	450	63	118	19	73	7	262			$15	324	460	784	8	81	0.49	281	126	69		5.16	-4.8

Batted .284 in his first month back, then .132 the rest of the way, lending suspicion that he might not be completely healed. Sharp drop in many BPIs adds to the suspicion. But I'm a suspicious person by nature.

Rios,Armando

	Yr	Tm	AB	R	H	HR	RBI	SB	Avg	vLH	vRH	R$	OB	Slg	OPS	bb%	ct%	Eye	xBA	PX	SX	G/F	RC/G	RAR
Pos RF	98	aaa	452	61	107	19	73	12	237			$13	300	407	707	8	86	0.63	289	104	88	1.00	4.29	-11.1
Age 31 Past Peak	99	SF	* 259	50	74	10	45	9	286	269	339	$11	364	448	812	11	80	0.62	267	99	81	1.30	6.01	7.6
Bats L	00	SF	233	38	62	10	50	3	266	167	288	$8	352	502	854	12	82	0.72	298	137	142	1.04	6.43	9.0
Pwr ++	01	2NL	319	38	83	14	50	3	260	326	249	$10	335	464	799	10	77	0.49	267	120	85	0.94	5.61	-0.6
Spd No change	02	PIT	* 262	24	65	1	28	2	248	300	258	$2	301	309	611	7	81	0.41	235	49	42	0.89	3.23	-17.5
BAvg -	1st Half		111	14	28	0	9	0	252			$0	325	315	641	10	79	0.52	232	55	41		3.67	-6.1
LIMA B	2nd Half		151	10	37	1	19	2	245			$2	283	305	588	5	83	0.31	237	45	42		2.92	-11.3
Risk Very High	03	Proj	350	41	94	13	50	4	269			$10	333	445	777	9	80	0.49	269	107	68		5.29	4.3

Why he's worth a token bid:
- Current perceived value is nil
- He's been draftable before.
- Has never reached potential.
- BPIs are not half bad.
- At age 31, a healthy season could be a peak season.

Rivas,Luis

	Yr	Tm	AB	R	H	HR	RBI	SB	Avg	vLH	vRH	R$	OB	Slg	OPS	bb%	ct%	Eye	xBA	PX	SX	G/F	RC/G	RAR
Pos 2B	98		0	0	0	0	0	0	0								0							
Age 23 Growth	99	aa	527	70	133	6	44	28	252			$11	303	370	673	7	85	0.49	278	80	136		3.71	-7.5
Bats R	00	MIN	* 543	82	142	5	60	17	262	316	308	$10	316	389	704	7	90	0.77	295	86	138	1.65	4.32	6.2
Pwr --	01	MIN	563	70	150	7	47	31	266	241	275	$16	315	362	677	7	82	0.40	254	60	130	1.86	4.12	-3.0
Spd +	02	MIN	316	46	81	4	35	9	256	234	268	$7	299	392	691	6	84	0.37	276	99	144	1.42	4.09	-0.3
BAvg --	1st Half		83	17	22	0	11	3	265			$2	307	361	668	6	84	0.38	269	89	117		4.21	0.2
LIMA A+	2nd Half		233	29	59	4	24	6	253			$5	296	403	699	6	84	0.37	278	103	146		4.03	-0.6
Risk High	03	Proj	550	80	143	6	57	21	260			$13	306	380	686	6	85	0.43	273	85	140		4.11	-1.6

Despite the disappearance of his SBs, note that his speed skills actually improved. So a rebound is possible, except... as long as his OB avg is hovering close to .300, his ceiling is limited.

Rivera,Mike

	Yr	Tm	AB	R	H	HR	RBI	SB	Avg	vLH	vRH	R$	OB	Slg	OPS	bb%	ct%	Eye	xBA	PX	SX	G/F	RC/G	RAR
Pos CA	98		0	0	0	0	0	0	0								0							
Age 26 Pre-Peak	99	aa	23	3	4	2	6	0	174			$0	240	478	718	8	78	0.40	292	169	21		3.71	-0.3
Bats R	00	a/a	163	8	29	1	8	0	178			($4)	207	276	483	4	85	0.25	267	71	38		1.83	-11.2
Pwr No change	01	aa	427	60	101	21	78	2	237			$11	291	433	725	7	80	0.39	270	115	59		4.34	7.6
Spd No change	02	DET	* 397	49	86	16	59	0	217	273	212	$6	283	393	676	9	77	0.40	256	112	54	1.23	3.81	1.4
BAvg +++	1st Half		206	28	51	10	33	0	248			$6	295	447	742	6	77	0.29	263	123	53		4.65	6.0
LIMA D+	2nd Half		191	21	35	6	26	0	183			$0	271	335	606	11	77	0.52	249	99	55		3.03	-4.1
Risk X HIGH	03	Proj	250	29	61	9	36	0	244			$5	301	412	713	8	79	0.40	261	104	50		4.35	2.2

1-11-.227 in 132 AB at DET. His power is intriguing but his OB skills are not. And Comerica is certainly not going to help either of those.

Rivera,Ruben

	Yr	Tm	AB	R	H	HR	RBI	SB	Avg	vLH	vRH	R$	OB	Slg	OPS	bb%	ct%	Eye	xBA	PX	SX	G/F	RC/G	RAR
Pos CF	98	SD	172	31	36	6	29	5	209	268	133	$3	320	378	698	14	70	0.54	238	106	143	1.36	4.39	-0.1
Age 29 Past Peak	99	SD	411	65	80	23	48	18	195	200	192	$8	290	406	696	12	65	0.38	227	122	104	1.05	3.95	-6.0
Bats R	00	SD	423	62	88	17	57	8	208	188	219	$5	283	400	682	9	68	0.32	234	108	145	0.97	3.81	-8.1
Pwr No change	01	CIN	263	37	67	10	34	6	255	241	261	$7	310	426	736	7	68	0.25	230	103	93	1.34	4.62	5.6
Spd +++++	02	TEX	* 461	57	104	16	60	8	226	200	214	$9	292	390	682	9	76	0.39	251	102	115	0.87	3.88	-14.4
BAvg No change	1st Half		285	42	73	12	46	3	256			$9	316	481	797	8	81	0.47	293	139	147		5.27	3.5
LIMA C	2nd Half		176	15	31	4	14	5	176			$0	253	244	497	9	68	0.32	189	42	37		2.11	-15.3
Risk High	03	Proj	150	19	33	6	18	3	220			$3	290	399	689	9	71	0.34	237	107	98		3.94	-4.5

4-14-4-.209 in 158 AB at TEX. Improved contact rate and production in AAA earned him a call-up, but flailed away like usual once he got a whiff of those major league hot dogs. Always good enough to trade.

Roberts,Brian

	Yr	Tm	AB	R	H	HR	RBI	SB	Avg	vLH	vRH	R$	OB	Slg	OPS	bb%	ct%	Eye	xBA	PX	SX	G/F	RC/G	RAR
Pos 2B	98		0	0	0	0	0	0	0								0							
Age 25 Pre-Peak	99		0	0	0	0	0	0	0								0							
Bats S	00		0	0	0	0	0	0	0								0							
Pwr --	01	BAL	* 515	68	130	4	34	42	252	247	255	$15	316	332	648	9	87	0.72	265	54	136	1.26	4.09	-3.2
Spd +++++	02	BAL	* 441	61	106	4	37	28	240	146	264	$12	316	322	638	10	86	0.79	253	54	151	0.80	3.85	-3.8
BAvg +++	1st Half		260	44	68	4	23	19	262			$10	351	362	713	12	86	1.00	262	67	138		4.98	7.2
LIMA C+	2nd Half		181	17	38	0	14	9	210			$2	263	265	528	7	86	0.50	240	36	155		2.49	-9.0
Risk Moderate	03	Proj	250	32	65	2	19	22	260			$9	325	337	662	9	86	0.71	257	50	152		4.34	1.1

1-11-9-.227 in 128 AB at BAL. 1st half shows the promise that could make him a monster SB machine. Not the SBs, mind you, the OB avg! If he can bring that with him to the bigs, he becomes a roto-god.

Roberts,Dave

	Yr	Tm	AB	R	H	HR	RBI	SB	Avg	vLH	vRH	R$	OB	Slg	OPS	bb%	ct%	Eye	xBA	PX	SX	G/F	RC/G	RAR
Pos CF	98	aa	521	97	145	9	62	41	278			$24	364	397	761	12	81	0.71	265	78	153		5.40	13.1
Age 30 Past Peak	99	CLE	* 493	76	114	2	41	41	231			$12	292	305	597	8	87	0.65	269	48	176		3.36	-22.0
Bats L	00	aaa	472	76	120	11	45	33	254			$16	324	363	687	9	87	0.78	270	63	121		4.28	-4.5
Pwr +	01	a/a	317	38	79	0	22	17	249			$6	300	317	617	7	84	0.45	253	51	126		3.36	-10.5
Spd +++++	02	LA	422	63	117	3	34	45	277	400	270	$21	351	365	716	10	88	0.94	271	54	175	2.10	5.07	1.3
BAvg No change	1st Half		201	32	59	2	16	19	294			$10	360	378	738	9	87	0.78	264	54	145		5.35	2.4
LIMA A	2nd Half		221	31	58	1	18	26	262			$10	343	353	696	11	89	1.13	277	54	194		4.82	-1.0
Risk X HIGH	03	Proj	500	73	140	4	41	53	280			$25	347	366	713	9	86	0.75	267	55	159		5.01	9.7

Just like THIS GUY, see?? The concept is SO simple...
1: Get on base 2: Steal base
His trends show that OB ability can be learned. It takes plate patience, eye and contact. This is a success story.

Robinson,Kerry

	Yr	Tm	AB	R	H	HR	RBI	SB	Avg	vLH	vRH	R$	OB	Slg	OPS	bb%	ct%	Eye	xBA	PX	SX	G/F	RC/G	RAR
Pos LF	98	a/a	551	62	139	3	46	39	252			$16	308	316	623	7	90	0.79	270	41	133		3.38	-27.9
Age 29 Past Peak	99	aaa	464	72	117	1	45	41	252			$15	279	323	602	4	87	0.28	269	46	186		3.20	-26.9
Bats L	00	aaa	437	52	118	0	24	28	270			$11	317	330	646	6	92	0.91	272	39	135		3.39	-24.9
Pwr ++	01	STL	* 226	37	63	1	17	14	279	267	287	$7	324	332	656	6	87	0.52	256	37	130	2.15	4.12	-11.6
Spd +++	02	STL	181	27	47	1	15	7	260	222	262	$3	302	359	661	6	84	0.38	263	61	177	2.00	3.72	-15.4
BAvg --	1st Half		88	20	23	1	6	6	261			$3	330	375	705	9	83	0.60	266	67	209		4.31	-6.1
LIMA C+	2nd Half		93	7	24	0	9	1	258			$1	274	344	618	2	85	0.14	258	56	127		3.17	-9.1
Risk High	03	Proj	200	28	53	1	16	15	265			$6	306	341	648	6	87	0.44	264	49	164		3.78	-5.9

This could have been a success story but he was never given enough opportunity to hone the needed skills. A .330 OB shows promise and he has excellent contact rates. And still owns that speed.

Rodriguez,Alex

	Yr	Tm	AB	R	H	HR	RBI	SB	Avg	vLH	vRH	R$	OB	Slg	OPS	bb%	ct%	Eye	xBA	PX	SX	G/F	RC/G	RAR
Pos SS	98	SEA	686	123	213	42	124	46	310	313	310	$48	353	560	913	6	82	0.37	307	144	136	1.42	7.38	70.6
Age 27 Peak	99	SEA	502	110	143	42	111	21	285	277	287	$32	357	586	942	10	78	0.51	302	168	102	0.98	7.66	54.3
Bats R	00	SEA	554	134	175	41	132	15	316	366	306	$36	420	606	1027	15	78	0.83	303	163	104	1.01	10.20	106.4
Pwr ++++	01	TEX	632	133	201	52	135	18	318	295	324	$45	390	622	1012	11	79	0.57	300	173	93	1.00	9.57	103.2
Spd ---	02	TEX	624	125	187	57	142	9	300	239	320	$43	385	623	1009	12	80	0.71	318	190	81	0.92	9.14	90.8
BAvg --	1st Half		305	63	92	24	65	5	302			$19	395	593	988	13	79	0.72	302	176	79		8.93	42.8
LIMA C+	2nd Half		319	62	95	33	77	4	298			$23	376	652	1028	11	82	0.70	334	205	73		9.33	47.7
Risk Very Low	03	Proj	625	130	191	61	140	10	306			$43	388	652	1040	12	80	0.67	321	198	82		9.65	118.5

Is there a 60+ HR season in his future? Unless the balance of power shifts to the pitching side, 60 is the next logical step in this trend.

Rodriguez,Ivan

	Yr	Tm	AB	R	H	HR	RBI	SB	Avg	vLH	vRH	R$	OB	Slg	OPS	bb%	ct%	Eye	xBA	PX	SX	G/F	RC/G	RAR
Pos CA	98	TEX	579	88	186	21	91	9	321	317	323	$26	357	513	870	5	85	0.36	299	121	106	1.72	7.18	53.9
Age 31 Past Peak	99	TEX	600	116	199	35	113	25	332	325	333	$39	357	558	916	4	89	0.38	320	130	105	1.96	7.40	57.9
Bats R	00	TEX	363	66	126	27	83	5	347	342	349	$25	380	667	1046	5	87	0.40	349	180	103	1.42	9.64	59.0
Pwr ++++	01	TEX	442	70	136	25	65	10	308	289	312	$23	342	541	883	5	83	0.32	295	137	92	1.19	6.93	39.7
Spd -----	02	TEX	408	67	128	19	60	5	314	306	317	$19	353	542	895	6	83	0.35	303	152	85	1.08	7.11	42.3
BAvg ---	1st Half		131	14	36	3	15	2	275			$4	317	412	729	6	83	0.36	270	100	55		4.85	4.6
LIMA B+	2nd Half		277	53	92	16	45	3	332			$16	371	603	974	6	82	0.35	317	177	94		8.34	39.0
Risk Low	03	Proj	475	77	150	25	76	8	316			$24	352	554	906	5	84	0.35	307	148	95		7.29	46.2

A terrific 2nd half, but his durability will always be a question. The percentage play is to NOT give him even 500 AB. That's what you pay for. Anything he gives you above that is gravy.

Rolen,Scott			Tm	AB	R	H	HR	RBI	SB	Avg	vLH	vRH	R$	OB	Slg	OPS	bb%	ct%	Eye	xBA	PX	SX	G/F	RC/G	RAR
Pos	3B	98	PHI	601	120	174	31	110	14	290	280	292	$31	385	532	917	13	77	0.66	285	161	108	0.94	7.74	64.2
Age	28 Peak	99	PHI	421	74	113	26	77	12	268	330	252	$19	369	525	894	14	73	0.59	268	155	88	0.64	7.34	40.3
Bats	R	00	PHI	483	88	144	26	89	8	298	283	302	$23	365	551	916	10	80	0.52	295	147	129	0.79	7.72	50.6
Pwr	++	01	PHI	554	96	160	25	107	16	289	283	290	$28	373	498	871	12	77	0.58	274	130	92	0.68	7.07	43.0
Spd	+++++	02	2NL	580	89	154	31	110	8	266	288	260	$24	347	503	850	11	82	0.71	292	137	118	0.84	6.36	31.2
BAvg	No change	1st Half		282	37	69	11	48	3	245			$7	332	433	765	12	80	0.67	271	115	81		5.22	4.9
LIMA	A	2nd Half		298	52	85	20	62	5	285			$17	360	570	931	11	84	0.74	313	157	144		7.54	27.2
Risk	Very Low	03	Proj	**575**	**97**	**166**	**32**	**110**	**11**	**289**			**$29**	**369**	**538**	**907**	**11**	**80**	**0.63**	**291**	**146**	**115**		**7.47**	**54.0**

Was he happy to leave Philly? Batted .259 with an .830 OPS before the trade, .278/.915 after, so I suppose he was. That late surge also helps his trends going into '03. Solid.

Rollins,Jimmy			Tm	AB	R	H	HR	RBI	SB	Avg	vLH	vRH	R$	OB	Slg	OPS	bb%	ct%	Eye	xBA	PX	SX	G/F	RC/G	RAR
Pos	SS	98		0	0	0	0	0	0	0								0							
Age	24 Growth	99	a/a	545	73	149	10	51	22	273			$15	332	398	730	8	93	1.30	300	77	120		4.52	10.0
Bats	S	00	PHI	* 523	59	137	9	61	23	262	333	317	$14	319	413	732	8	89	0.79	300	94	150	1.19	4.73	19.4
Pwr	-	01	PHI	656	97	180	14	54	46	274	318	262	$27	324	419	743	7	84	0.44	277	86	189	1.06	5.13	30.1
Spd	-	02	PHI	637	82	156	11	60	31	245	243	246	$15	304	380	684	8	84	0.52	273	85	156	1.19	4.01	0.6
BAvg	+++	1st Half		329	43	88	7	30	14	267			$10	315	429	744	7	84	0.45	284	101	157		4.69	7.1
LIMA	A	2nd Half		308	39	68	4	30	17	221			$5	292	328	620	9	83	0.60	261	68	148		3.35	-6.0
Risk	Low	03	Proj	**625**	**82**	**164**	**11**	**59**	**36**	**262**			**$20**	**319**	**398**	**717**	**8**	**85**	**0.58**	**280**	**84**	**159**		**4.59**	**16.2**

A 30-point drop in BA, however:
- Batting eye improved
- bb% and ct% remained stable
- xBA was virtually unchanged.

There were more notable drops during the 2nd half, so we can't project a complete rebound.

Rolls,Damian			Tm	AB	R	H	HR	RBI	SB	Avg	vLH	vRH	R$	OB	Slg	OPS	bb%	ct%	Eye	xBA	PX	SX	G/F	RC/G	RAR
Pos	RF	98	aa	160	14	29	1	7	2	181			($3)	206	231	437	3	86	0.23	251	38	70		1.58	-16.5
Age	25 Pre-Peak	99		0	0	0	0	0	0	0								0							
Bats	R	00	aa	51	5	11	0	2	0	216			($1)	298	294	592	11	86	0.86	267	66	41		2.89	-3.6
Pwr	+	01	TAM	237	33	62	2	12	12	262	225	280	$5	291	342	633	4	80	0.21	243	57	115	1.04	3.52	-11.0
Spd	+++++	02	TAM	* 340	49	87	5	35	14	256	500	260	$9	299	365	664	6	84	0.38	256	70	157	3.15	3.80	-13.6
BAvg	--	1st Half		186	30	46	4	22	13	247			$7	310	376	687	8	84	0.59	264	74	204		4.59	-3.1
LIMA	D+	2nd Half		154	19	41	1	13	1	266			$2	285	351	635	3	82	0.15	246	64	86		2.94	-9.9
Risk	Very High	03	Proj	**150**	**20**	**37**	**2**	**11**	**10**	**247**			**$4**	**279**	**330**	**610**	**4**	**83**	**0.26**	**249**	**57**	**136**		**3.28**	**-8.8**

0-6-.292 in 89 AB at TAM. There is some growth here, but not enough to make him truly valuable. Good speed, but low OB avg (yet again) limits his upside.

Rowand,Aaron			Tm	AB	R	H	HR	RBI	SB	Avg	vLH	vRH	R$	OB	Slg	OPS	bb%	ct%	Eye	xBA	PX	SX	G/F	RC/G	RAR
Pos	CF LF	98		0	0	0	0	0	0	0								0							
Age	25 Pre-Peak	99		0	0	0	0	0	0	0								0							
Bats	R	00	aa	532	72	129	20	88	19	242			$16	289	415	705	6	79	0.32	269	100	122		4.13	-7.3
Pwr	---	01	CHW	* 452	70	129	21	64	12	285	309	279	$19	337	493	830	7	85	0.50	293	130	80	2.13	6.16	16.9
Spd	-	02	CHW	302	41	78	7	29	0	258	265	255	$5	287	394	681	4	82	0.22	263	92	72	1.65	3.92	-8.5
BAvg	--	1st Half		78	6	17	1	5	0	218			($0)	228	346	574	1	79	0.06	260	104	45		2.41	-5.6
LIMA	A	2nd Half		224	35	61	6	24	0	272			$5	306	411	717	5	83	0.29	263	89	82		4.55	-2.2
Risk	High	03	Proj	**500**	**68**	**131**	**16**	**60**	**7**	**262**			**$13**	**300**	**427**	**727**	**5**	**82**	**0.31**	**276**	**108**	**89**		**4.51**	**-5.8**

Had a solid season in 2001, which lends hope that there's room to grow from 2002. Don't see that happening right away, but he's not far off.

Rushford,Jim			Tm	AB	R	H	HR	RBI	SB	Avg	vLH	vRH	R$	OB	Slg	OPS	bb%	ct%	Eye	xBA	PX	SX	G/F	RC/G	RAR
Pos	RF	98		0	0	0	0	0	0	0								0							
Age	29 Past Peak	99		0	0	0	0	0	0	0								0							
Bats	L	00		0	0	0	0	0	0	0								0							
Pwr	No change	01	aa	187	27	51	6	23	2	273			$5	333	449	783	8	87	0.71	295	113	74		5.35	-0.2
Spd	No change	02	MIL	* 501	51	116	7	59	1	232	182	136	$2	291	339	630	8	89	0.75	272	75	49	1.04	3.43	-30.6
BAvg	+++++	1st Half		240	25	60	1	30	1	250			$2	313	350	663	8	89	0.85	277	79	58		4.00	-10.5
LIMA	D	2nd Half		261	26	56	6	29	0	215			($0)	270	330	600	7	89	0.67	269	71	43		2.96	-19.7
Risk	High	03	Proj	**100**	**12**	**25**	**1**	**12**	**0**	**250**			**$1**	**309**	**346**	**655**	**8**	**88**	**0.73**	**271**	**70**	**39**		**3.76**	**-3.5**

1-6-.143 in 77 AB at MIL. Fared well at AAA this year, earning the call-up, but his age-adjusted MLEs tell the real story. No future.

Sadler,Donnie			Tm	AB	R	H	HR	RBI	SB	Avg	vLH	vRH	R$	OB	Slg	OPS	bb%	ct%	Eye	xBA	PX	SX	G/F	RC/G	RAR
Pos	CF	98	BOS	* 255	44	57	5	24	14	224	310	200	$5	303	357	660	10	81	0.59	269	77	187	1.38	3.92	-7.5
Age	27 Peak	99	BOS	* 279	38	78	1	18	5	280	172	321	$4	323	380	703	6	82	0.36	261	70	127	1.87	4.43	-3.1
Bats	R	00	BOS	* 412	53	82	5	30	12	199	80	270	($1)	275	282	556	9	83	0.61	247	48	132	1.33	2.77	-25.7
Pwr	+	01	KC	185	28	30	1	5	7	162	88	195	($3)	236	211	447	9	80	0.49	230	36	105	1.36	1.64	-19.2
Spd	+++++	02	TEX	* 162	26	30	0	10	7	185	71	200	($0)	246	241	486	7	84	0.50	238	40	164	1.32	1.74	-15.7
BAvg	+++++	1st Half		68	10	13	0	5	3	191			$0	236	235	471	6	82	0.33	226	27	171		1.88	-6.2
LIMA	D	2nd Half		94	16	17	0	5	4	181			($0)	252	245	497	9	85	0.64	247	49	157		1.64	-9.5
Risk	X HIGH	03	Proj	**100**	**15**	**19**	**0**	**6**	**4**	**190**			**($0)**	**256**	**253**	**509**	**8**	**83**	**0.51**	**240**	**42**	**140**		**2.07**	**-8.8**

0-7-5-.163 in 98 AB at TEX. Has not seen the Mendoza line this entire millennium. Nor has he even batted .100 vs LHers. A .300 OB avg is a distant, far off land. But he can run.

Saenz,Olmedo			Tm	AB	R	H	HR	RBI	SB	Avg	vLH	vRH	R$	OB	Slg	OPS	bb%	ct%	Eye	xBA	PX	SX	G/F	RC/G	RAR
Pos	1B	98	aaa	466	64	111	19	74	2	238			$10	287	410	697	6	90	0.71	304	109	52		4.05	-21.6
Age	32 Past Peak	99	OAK	255	41	70	11	41	1	275	297	257	$7	332	475	807	8	82	0.47	283	125	51	1.09	5.73	-1.3
Bats	R	00	OAK	214	40	67	9	33	1	313	319	308	$8	385	514	899	10	81	0.63	284	116	90	1.06	7.81	11.9
Pwr	++++	01	OAK	305	33	67	9	32	0	220	237	205	$1	265	384	649	6	79	0.30	258	107	44	0.97	3.41	-26.4
Spd	No change	02	OAK	156	15	43	6	18	1	276	317	247	$5	331	468	799	8	80	0.42	277	127	58	0.93	5.60	-1.8
BAvg	--	1st Half		90	7	27	3	10	1	300			$3	357	478	835	8	80	0.44	270	115	74		6.59	1.7
LIMA	C	2nd Half		66	8	16	3	8	0	242			$1	296	455	750	7	80	0.38	287	143	40		4.41	-3.2
Risk	High	03	Proj	**150**	**18**	**39**	**6**	**19**	**1**	**260**			**$3**	**316**	**455**	**770**	**8**	**81**	**0.42**	**279**	**125**	**65**		**5.07**	**-2.7**

Good 1st half. Bad 2nd half. Net gain over 2001. Net loss over 2000. Marginal end-gamer.

Salmon,Tim			Tm	AB	R	H	HR	RBI	SB	Avg	vLH	vRH	R$	OB	Slg	OPS	bb%	ct%	Eye	xBA	PX	SX	G/F	RC/G	RAR
Pos	RF DH	98	ANA	463	84	139	26	88	0	300	273	310	$20	414	533	948	16	78	0.90	278	140	34	0.91	8.75	56.8
Age	34 Decline	99	ANA	353	60	94	17	69	4	266	301	257	$12	377	490	867	15	77	0.77	276	135	83	0.81	7.04	23.4
Bats	R	00	ANA	568	108	165	34	97	0	290	226	315	$21	400	540	941	15	76	0.75	278	144	43	0.96	8.36	64.1
Pwr	+++	01	ANA	475	63	108	17	49	9	227	232	226	$7	357	383	740	17	75	0.79	239	94	66	0.73	5.13	0.9
Spd	--	02	ANA	483	84	138	22	88	6	286	299	280	$21	377	503	880	13	79	0.70	285	146	73	0.76	7.21	33.0
BAvg	-	1st Half		275	50	78	13	51	5	284			$13	373	520	893	12	80	0.70	298	164	69		7.21	18.7
LIMA	A	2nd Half		208	34	60	9	37	1	288			$8	383	481	864	13	78	0.70	267	123	65		7.19	14.2
Risk	High	03	Proj	**500**	**82**	**146**	**31**	**101**	**5**	**292**			**$25**	**395**	**543**	**938**	**15**	**77**	**0.74**	**282**	**153**	**60**		**8.31**	**51.1**

Solid rebound season, in some ways even better than 2000 (ct%, PX, xBA). Might leverage those gains into some big numbers in 2003.

Sanchez,Alex			Tm	AB	R	H	HR	RBI	SB	Avg	vLH	vRH	R$	OB	Slg	OPS	bb%	ct%	Eye	xBA	PX	SX	G/F	RC/G	RAR
Pos	CF	98		0	0	0	0	0	0	0								0							
Age	26 Pre-Peak	99	aa	510	54	114	2	22	37	224			$7	253	267	519	4	87	0.30	252	30	114		1.82	-42.1
Bats	L	00	a/a	532	69	138	2	29	42	259			$15	291	318	609	4	89	0.39	261	40	125		2.79	-28.5
Pwr	--	01	MIL	* 403	50	108	1	25	28	268	200	206	$12	308	340	647	5	88	0.48	267	48	151	2.42	3.70	-2.8
Spd	+++++	02	MIL	394	55	114	1	33	37	289	267	292	$19	341	358	699	7	84	0.50	253	41	174	2.40	4.50	-5.7
BAvg	--	1st Half		212	30	64	0	18	19	302			$11	362	354	716	9	83	0.56	241	29	169		4.73	-1.6
LIMA	A+	2nd Half		182	25	50	1	15	18	275			$8	316	363	679	6	86	0.42	265	56	176		4.22	-4.1
Risk	High	03	Proj	**500**	**65**	**136**	**1**	**35**	**32**	**272**			**$15**	**314**	**336**	**650**	**6**	**86**	**0.45**	**258**	**42**	**149**		**3.56**	**-12.6**

Excellent 1st half, supported by fine BPIs. OB avg dropped nearly 50 points in 2nd half as pitchers adjusted. Despite that, he managed to maintain his SB output. However, it will become more difficult in 2003.

Sanchez,Rey

			Tm	AB	R	H	HR	RBI	SB	Avg	vLH	vRH	R$	OB	Slg	OPS	bb%	ct%	Eye	xBA	PX	SX	G/F	RC/G	RAR
Pos	2B	98	SF	316	44	90	2	30	0	285	377	259	$5	319	361	680	5	85	0.34	262	58	64	1.59	4.26	0.5
Age	35 Decline	99	KC	479	66	141	2	56	11	294	326	286	$11	325	370	695	4	90	0.46	272	49	125	2.34	4.42	5.3
Bats	R	00	KC	509	68	139	1	38	7	273	290	267	$5	311	322	633	5	89	0.51	253	36	89	3.35	3.65	-4.5
Pwr	+	01	2TM	544	56	153	0	37	11	281	256	290	$9	301	336	637	3	91	0.31	266	38	118	2.81	3.74	-5.9
Spd	- - - - -	02	BOS	357	46	102	1	38	2	286	273	289	$7	318	345	663	5	91	0.55	258	43	85	1.84	3.99	-1.4
BAvg	- -	1st Half		154	22	49	1	19	1	318			$5	340	416	755	3	92	0.42	277	64	126		5.28	5.3
LIMA	D+	2nd Half		203	24	53	0	19	1	261			$2	302	291	593	6	91	0.63	243	27	52		3.15	-6.0
Risk	Moderate	03	Proj	**350**	**43**	**99**	**1**	**32**	**4**	**283**			**$6**	**313**	**341**	**654**	**4**	**91**	**0.47**	**259**	**41**	**95**		**3.90**	**-3.1**

He's had these occasional half season spurts when he bats .300, then always comes back down to Earth. Net effect is a decent BA with empty stats behind it, and the promise of yet another season of 400-500 AB.

Sandberg,Jared

			Tm	AB	R	H	HR	RBI	SB	Avg	vLH	vRH	R$	OB	Slg	OPS	bb%	ct%	Eye	xBA	PX	SX	G/F	RC/G	RAR
Pos	3B	98		0	0	0	0	0	0	0								0							
Age	25 Pre-Peak	99		0	0	0	0	0	0	0								0							
Bats	R	00	a/a	259	26	65	6	35	4	251			$4	322	398	719	9	83	0.60	275	96	62		4.44	-0.0
Pwr	- -	01	TAM	* 486	53	109	17	65	1	224	195	211	$6	298	381	679	9	74	0.40	234	98	31	1.88	3.97	-7.4
Spd	No change	02	TAM	* 472	72	112	21	72	4	237	209	235	$12	312	439	750	10	63	0.29	220	132	76	1.28	4.82	3.9
BAvg	-	1st Half		228	33	56	10	34	1	246			$6	304	439	742	8	64	0.23	223	128	51		4.66	0.7
LIMA	B	2nd Half		244	39	56	11	38	3	230			$6	319	439	757	12	61	0.34	217	137	90		4.97	3.2
Risk	Very High	03	Proj	**500**	**65**	**117**	**19**	**72**	**4**	**234**			**$10**	**309**	**412**	**721**	**10**	**69**	**0.35**	**234**	**114**	**62**		**4.47**	**-2.1**

18-54-.229 in 358 AB at TAM. There is growth in power, and minor growth in plate patience. But the total product is barely replacement level. Buy those HRs, but make sure Suzuki is also on the shopping list.

Sanders,Reggie

			Tm	AB	R	H	HR	RBI	SB	Avg	vLH	vRH	R$	OB	Slg	OPS	bb%	ct%	Eye	xBA	PX	SX	G/F	RC/G	RAR
Pos	RF	98	CIN	481	83	129	14	59	20	268	248	274	$18	338	418	756	10	72	0.37	239	94	152	2.03	5.10	1.5
Age	35 Decline	99	SD	478	92	136	26	72	36	285	303	277	$28	370	527	897	12	77	0.60	281	140	160	1.12	7.15	31.9
Bats	R	00	ATL	340	43	79	11	37	21	232	264	224	$10	298	403	701	9	77	0.41	266	108	112	1.24	4.32	-9.8
Pwr	+ +	01	ARI	441	84	116	33	90	14	263	256	266	$24	333	549	881	9	71	0.37	270	159	121	0.95	6.21	7.5
Spd	+	02	SF	505	75	126	23	85	18	250	289	237	$19	313	455	769	9	76	0.39	263	119	142	0.91	5.04	-5.8
BAvg	-	1st Half		257	40	64	8	44	12	249			$10	313	416	730	9	77	0.40	257	101	148		4.62	-6.3
LIMA	A	2nd Half		248	35	62	15	41	6	250			$10	314	496	810	8	75	0.38	269	137	124		5.49	0.6
Risk	Very High	03	Proj	**450**	**71**	**114**	**23**	**74**	**13**	**253**			**$17**	**320**	**476**	**797**	**9**	**75**	**0.39**	**265**	**129**	**120**		**5.30**	**5.7**

There are signs of skills erosion, but a guy who can put up a 15-HR half season still has something left. However, the big news flash is this was his first 500 AB season EVER. At age 35. EVER!

Santiago,Benito

			Tm	AB	R	H	HR	RBI	SB	Avg	vLH	vRH	R$	OB	Slg	OPS	bb%	ct%	Eye	xBA	PX	SX	G/F	RC/G	RAR
Pos	CA	98	TOR	29	3	9	0	4	0	310			$1	333	483	816	3	79	0.17	287	150	27	0.64	6.06	1.7
Age	38 Decline	99	CHC	350	28	87	7	36	1	249	250	248	$3	312	377	689	8	80	0.45	257	83	57	1.16	4.20	1.8
Bats	R	00	CIN	252	22	66	8	45	2	262	268	259	$6	314	409	722	7	82	0.42	270	88	47	1.11	4.53	3.5
Pwr	+ +	01	SF	477	39	125	6	45	5	262	256	264	$7	296	369	665	5	84	0.29	262	71	80	1.37	3.81	3.1
Spd	No change	02	SF	478	56	133	16	74	4	278	276	279	$16	317	450	767	5	85	0.37	280	103	92	1.41	5.15	13.8
BAvg	- -	1st Half		245	28	67	7	38	1	273			$7	315	457	773	6	85	0.41	287	114	102		5.17	7.2
LIMA	C	2nd Half		233	28	66	9	36	3	283			$9	318	442	760	5	85	0.33	271	92	71		5.14	6.6
Risk	Very High	03	Proj	**400**	**40**	**108**	**11**	**55**	**3**	**270**			**$10**	**311**	**414**	**726**	**6**	**84**	**0.37**	**269**	**89**	**69**		**4.59**	**7.4**

The magic of skills ownership... For four years his power was MIA, likely reducing expectations at the draft table. But if you're going to risk an extra $1, do it on the player who hit 30 HRs six years ago. Ah, retrospect...

Santiago,Ramon

			Tm	AB	R	H	HR	RBI	SB	Avg	vLH	vRH	R$	OB	Slg	OPS	bb%	ct%	Eye	xBA	PX	SX	G/F	RC/G	RAR
Pos	SS	98		0	0	0	0	0	0	0								0							
Age	21 Growth	99		0	0	0	0	0	0	0								0							
Bats	S	00		0	0	0	0	0	0	0								0							
Pwr	No change	01		0	0	0	0	0	0	0								0							
Spd	+	02	DET	* 325	48	84	6	31	13	258	222	250	$9	297	375	673	5	81	0.30	248	67	185	1.74	3.80	-8.6
BAvg	- -	1st Half		247	42	68	6	24	10	275			$9	317	421	738	6	81	0.33	258	80	214		4.58	-0.7
LIMA	D+	2nd Half		78	6	16	0	7	3	205			$0	235	231	465	4	81	0.20	216	24	78		1.83	-6.6
Risk	Moderate	03	Proj	**350**	**40**	**77**	**2**	**32**	**9**	**220**			**$2**	**255**	**286**	**542**	**5**	**81**	**0.25**	**234**	**41**	**127**		**2.38**	**-14.9**

4-20-8-.243 in 222 AB at DET. The Tigers' next SS? Maybe. But his 2nd half .205 BA says that he's far from ready, at least not at the plate. What's the rush?

Schneider,Brian

			Tm	AB	R	H	HR	RBI	SB	Avg	vLH	vRH	R$	OB	Slg	OPS	bb%	ct%	Eye	xBA	PX	SX	G/F	RC/G	RAR
Pos	CA	98		0	0	0	0	0	0	0								0							
Age	26 Pre-Peak	99	aa	421	41	101	13	56	2	240			$5	286	380	666	6	89	0.57	284	86	45		3.74	-4.5
Bats	L	00	MON	* 353	25	82	4	38	1	232	364	204	$0	273	306	579	5	83	0.33	249	46	50	1.59	2.89	-12.7
Pwr	+ +	01	MON	41	4	13	1	6	0	317			$2	404	463	868	13	93	2.00	303	99		0.93	7.57	5.3
Spd	No change	02	MON	207	21	57	5	29	1	275	280	275	$5	342	459	801	9	80	0.51	274	125	71	1.31	5.65	9.4
BAvg	-	1st Half		93	7	22	1	14	1	237			$1	290	387	677	7	82	0.41	273	110	85		3.62	-1.7
LIMA	C	2nd Half		114	14	35	4	15	0	307			$4	383	518	900	11	79	0.58	274	137	54		7.74	13.0
Risk	High	03	Proj	**200**	**18**	**57**	**9**	**35**	**1**	**285**			**$8**	**339**	**494**	**833**	**8**	**82**	**0.46**	**284**	**126**	**41**		**6.09**	**13.1**

Pretty good choice for an end-game backstop. Gets on base, good power growth and 2nd half surge are all solid signs. And at 26, a mini-breakout within his 200 AB allotment is not out of the question.

Segui,David

			Tm	AB	R	H	HR	RBI	SB	Avg	vLH	vRH	R$	OB	Slg	OPS	bb%	ct%	Eye	xBA	PX	SX	G/F	RC/G	RAR
Pos	DH	98	SEA	522	79	159	19	84	3	305	297	307	$19	364	487	851	9	85	0.61	290	117	59	1.45	6.81	23.1
Age	36 Decline	99	2AL	440	57	131	14	52	1	298	271	303	$12	356	468	824	8	86	0.67	288	106	58	1.13	6.26	13.2
Bats	S	00	2AL	574	93	192	19	103	0	334	310	344	$24	391	510	901	8	85	0.63	291	111	38	1.62	7.95	49.4
Pwr	- - -	01	BAL	292	48	88	10	46	1	301	338	288	$11	402	473	874	14	79	0.80	259	108	50	1.21	7.50	21.1
Spd	No change	02	BAL	95	10	25	2	16	0	263	192	290	$2	340	368	708	10	77	0.50	232	73	20	1.19	4.68	-2.9
BAvg	No change	1st Half		95	10	25	2	16	0	263			$2	340	368	708	10	77	0.50	232	73	20		4.68	-2.9
LIMA	C+	2nd Half		0	0	0	0	0	0	0			($0)					0							-0.0
Risk	High	03	Proj	**350**	**49**	**97**	**10**	**56**	**0**	**277**			**$10**	**351**	**432**	**784**	**10**	**82**	**0.62**	**267**	**102**	**42**		**5.68**	**2.1**

Would return from wrist surgery into BAL's 1B/DH logjam, so AB may be at a premium unless someone is moved. He's the vet with the declning BPIs, so expectations must be tempered.

Selby,Bill

			Tm	AB	R	H	HR	RBI	SB	Avg	vLH	vRH	R$	OB	Slg	OPS	bb%	ct%	Eye	xBA	PX	SX	G/F	RC/G	RAR
Pos	3B	98	a/a	411	44	94	12	46	3	229			$4	283	389	672	7	85	0.51	288	110	65		3.86	-8.4
Age	32 Past Peak	99	aaa	447	53	102	14	61	2	228			$4	293	387	680	8	85	0.63	283	100	60		3.92	-7.8
Bats	L	00	CLE	* 430	62	101	17	72	1	235		262	$6	297	416	713	8	85	0.58	286	103	84	1.17	4.32	-2.3
Pwr	+ + + +	01	CIN	* 422	41	92	13	53	1	218		231	$3	260	372	632	5	87	0.44	286	95	58	1.06	3.29	-17.7
Spd	No change	02	CLE	* 343	38	82	11	39	4	239	160	224	$7	302	411	713	8	82	0.51	277	114	90	1.24	4.35	-2.2
BAvg	+ + +	1st Half		198	20	50	4	17	4	253			$4	315	399	714	8	81	0.47	268	107	82		4.55	-0.0
LIMA	C	2nd Half		145	18	32	7	22	0	221			$3	285	428	712	8	84	0.57	289	123	90		4.07	-2.2
Risk	Very High	03	Proj	**150**	**17**	**34**	**5**	**20**	**1**	**227**			**$2**	**285**	**399**	**683**	**7**	**84**	**0.52**	**282**	**108**	**70**		**3.90**	**-3.2**

6-21-.214 in 159 AB at CLE, but managed to crack a .300 OB, at least in the 1st half. Too bad he never mastered the art of first base acquisition, because his power skills would have made a nice little package.

Sexson,Richie

			Tm	AB	R	H	HR	RBI	SB	Avg	vLH	vRH	R$	OB	Slg	OPS	bb%	ct%	Eye	xBA	PX	SX	G/F	RC/G	RAR
Pos	1B	98	CLE	* 518	84	153	30	106	2	295	241	345	$24	363	546	909	10	79	0.51	291	152	61	1.45	7.51	28.8
Age	28 Peak	99	CLE	479	72	122	31	116	3	255	277	246	$18	304	514	818	7	76	0.29	278	139	117	1.26	5.42	-7.1
Bats	R	00	2TM	537	89	146	30	91	2	272	220	286	$18	344	499	843	10	70	0.37	253	131	61	1.27	6.38	10.5
Pwr	- - -	01	MIL	598	94	162	45	125	2	271	295	264	$28	337	547	884	9	70	0.34	259	152	61	1.15	6.60	4.1
Spd	No change	02	MIL	570	86	159	29	102	0	279	238	288	$22	358	504	861	11	76	0.51	263	137	41	1.33	6.78	19.4
BAvg	-	1st Half		296	53	84	18	57	0	284			$13	348	530	878	9	76	0.41	269	145	51		6.88	10.8
LIMA	B+	2nd Half		274	33	75	11	45	0	274			$9	368	474	843	13	76	0.62	257	127	32		6.64	8.3
Risk	Low	03	Proj	**575**	**87**	**158**	**33**	**108**	**0**	**275**			**$23**	**350**	**512**	**861**	**10**	**74**	**0.44**	**261**	**140**	**42**		**6.60**	**22.6**

Odd that he had better plate patience, made 6% more contact, but saw a decline in his power. The 45 HRs of 2001 was a bit over his head, but he should consistently be in the 30-35 range each year.

Sheets,Andy

		Tm	AB	R	H	HR	RBI	SB	Avg	vLH	vRH	R$	OB	Slg	OPS	bb%	ct%	Eye	xBA	PX	SX	G/F	RC/G	RAR
Pos	2B	98 SD	194	31	47	7	29	7	242			$6	316	407	723	10	68	0.34	230	98	164	1.06	4.63	2.6
Age	31 Past Peak	99 ANA	* 289	27	58	3	32	1	201	214	190	($3)	240	266	507	5	75	0.21	216	45	48	1.18	2.12	-16.8
Bats	R	00 aaa	281	31	57	6	30	4	203			($0)	280	310	589	10	84	0.67	259	62	86		2.99	-10.8
Pwr	No change	01 TAM	* 378	33	84	5	32	8	222	163	209	$2	283	328	611	8	79	0.41	245	73	82	1.11	3.23	-12.4
Spd	+ +	02 TAM	* 523	61	131	15	76	7	250	268	241	$13	296	407	703	6	79	0.31	259	103	103	1.37	4.16	0.6
BAvg	- -	1st Half	312	37	78	8	46	5	250			$8	291	423	714	5	81	0.30	275	115	139		4.35	2.2
LIMA	C	2nd Half	211	24	53	7	30	2	251			$5	304	384	688	7	76	0.31	237	84	45		3.89	-1.5
Risk	X HIGH	**03 Proj**	**250**	**27**	**63**	**6**	**31**	**4**	**252**			**$5**	**307**	**384**	**691**	**7**	**78**	**0.37**	**249**	**84**	**88**		**4.13**	**-0.5**

4-22-.248 in 149 AB at TAM. This perceived power spike was about 3 months long and mostly driven by his newfound playing time. Only marginal gains for the rest of his skills, but he's 31 after all.

Sheffield,Gary

		Tm	AB	R	H	HR	RBI	SB	Avg	vLH	vRH	R$	OB	Slg	OPS	bb%	ct%	Eye	xBA	PX	SX	G/F	RC/G	RAR
Pos	RF	98 2NL	437	73	132	22	85	22	302	312	300	$28	427	524	951	18	89	2.07	323	145	94	0.95	8.96	60.2
Age	34 Decline	99 LA	549	103	165	34	101	11	301	336	288	$28	409	523	932	16	88	1.58	308	126	62	0.81	8.40	61.2
Bats	R	00 LA	501	105	163	43	109	4	325	285	339	$33	439	643	1081	17	86	1.42	332	174	62	0.84	11.13	101.2
Pwr	+	01 LA	515	98	160	36	100	10	311	374	294	$32	417	583	1000	15	87	1.40	324	155	81	0.91	9.61	68.6
Spd	- -	02 ATL	492	82	151	25	84	12	307	293	310	$28	395	512	908	13	89	1.36	304	123	75	1.04	8.07	42.9
BAvg	No change	1st Half	250	37	67	13	40	8	268			$11	353	460	813	12	87	1.00	289	110	78		6.29	7.1
LIMA	A	2nd Half	242	45	84	12	44	4	347			$17	438	566	1004	14	92	1.95	319	136	56		10.24	38.8
Risk	Low	**03 Proj**	**500**	**91**	**157**	**29**	**93**	**10**	**314**			**$29**	**414**	**544**	**958**	**15**	**88**	**1.47**	**313**	**135**	**74**		**8.98**	**68.2**

BPIs are still superb all around, but these may be early signs of an impending decline. Despite HR drop, note his PX was the same as '99 when he hit 9 more HRs. In '02, it was more doubles instead. Stay with him.

Shinjo,Tsuyoshi

		Tm	AB	R	H	HR	RBI	SB	Avg	vLH	vRH	R$	OB	Slg	OPS	bb%	ct%	Eye	xBA	PX	SX	G/F	RC/G	RAR
Pos	CF	98 JPN	414	39	92	6	27	1	222			($1)	267	331	597	6	84	0.38	266	75	69		3.04	-19.9
Age	31 Past Peak	99 JPN	471	53	120	14	58	8	255			$9	289	418	708	5	85	0.32	284	96	125		4.27	-4.6
Bats	R	00 JPN	511	71	142	28	85	15	278			$22	320	491	812	6	82	0.34	288	121	82		5.52	14.6
Pwr	No change	01 NYM	400	46	107	10	56	4	268	305	258	$10	311	405	716	6	83	0.36	267	89	60	1.03	4.36	5.2
Spd	No change	02 SF	369	42	86	9	37	5	233	291	214	$4	282	363	645	6	87	0.53	276	79	102	1.42	3.63	-15.0
BAvg	+ + +	1st Half	246	26	57	5	23	4	232			$2	276	337	613	6	89	0.56	272	66	84		3.31	-12.4
LIMA	C+	2nd Half	123	16	29	4	14	1	236			$2	293	415	708	8	84	0.50	280	106	117		4.31	-2.5
Risk	Moderate	**03 Proj**	**350**	**42**	**87**	**8**	**43**	**5**	**249**			**$6**	**296**	**380**	**676**	**6**	**84**	**0.43**	**271**	**83**	**98**		**3.96**	**-4.6**

Despite 35 point drop in BA, the last two seasons were not all that different from a skills perspective. Consider those the outer edges of the range of expectation for 2003.

Shumpert,Terry

		Tm	AB	R	H	HR	RBI	SB	Avg	vLH	vRH	R$	OB	Slg	OPS	bb%	ct%	Eye	xBA	PX	SX	G/F	RC/G	RAR
Pos	2B	98 aaa	402	37	92	9	28	6	229			$3	265	376	641	5	87	0.39	291	96	98	1.80	3.11	-12.6
Age	36 Decline	99 COL	* 341	68	119	15	48	16	349	395	324	$22	408	601	1009	9	87	0.74	324	162	141	0.61	10.30	64.3
Bats	R	00 COL	263	52	68	9	40	8	259	277	249	$8	330	456	786	10	85	0.70	295	109	192	0.87	5.32	7.3
Pwr	- -	01 COL	242	37	70	4	24	14	289	233	322	$10	331	438	769	6	82	0.34	275	92	190	1.17	5.45	11.1
Spd	- - - - -	02 COL	234	30	55	6	21	4	235	294	201	$2	298	372	670	8	82	0.51	263	87	86	1.05	3.94	-4.1
BAvg	+ + +	1st Half	130	17	33	3	12	4	254			$3	331	377	708	10	84	0.71	263	82	70		4.64	0.6
LIMA	C+	2nd Half	104	13	22	3	9	0	212			($0)	255	365	620	5	81	0.30	260	94	79		3.13	-4.3
Risk	Moderate	**03 Proj**	**200**	**29**	**51**	**4**	**21**	**2**	**255**			**$3**	**310**	**403**	**712**	**7**	**83**	**0.46**	**273**	**92**	**118**		**4.37**	**1.7**

Looking from the outside, a poor season, but he still batted .321 in Coors (.160 on the road). So they should just save on his traveling expenses, pay him for half a season, and let him get a second job during road trips.

Sierra,Ruben

		Tm	AB	R	H	HR	RBI	SB	Avg	vLH	vRH	R$	OB	Slg	OPS	bb%	ct%	Eye	xBA	PX	SX	G/F	RC/G	RAR
Pos	LF DH	98 CHW	* 182	17	36	6	24	4	198			$1	247	346	594	6	84	0.40	271	88	83	1.12	2.79	-13.1
Age	37 Decline	99 ind	422	76	124	28	82	3	294			$20	380	555	935	12	85	0.94	311	149	70		8.10	40.4
Bats	S	00 TEX	* 499	57	134	16	68	5	269	400	178	$11	330	419	749	8	87	0.73	284	89	67	1.05	5.07	-1.9
Pwr	- -	01 TEX	* 438	66	121	26	76	4	276	321	281	$18	318	518	837	6	85	0.42	303	141	80	0.96	6.04	17.6
Spd	No change	02 SEA	419	47	113	13	60	4	270	266	272	$12	320	418	738	7	84	0.47	274	101	58	1.39	4.94	0.1
BAvg	- -	1st Half	272	35	84	10	50	2	309			$12	356	489	845	7	84	0.47	289	124	49		6.73	15.0
LIMA	C+	2nd Half	147	12	29	3	10	2	197			($0)	253	286	539	7	84	0.48	247	58	52		2.51	-10.9
Risk	Very High	**03 Proj**	**350**	**42**	**93**	**11**	**48**	**2**	**266**			**$9**	**318**	**417**	**735**	**7**	**85**	**0.51**	**275**	**96**	**56**		**4.83**	**-3.2**

A nagging strained quad was at least partially to blame for his 2nd half fade. At 37, stuff like this is apt to happen more frequently.

Simon,Randall

		Tm	AB	R	H	HR	RBI	SB	Avg	vLH	vRH	R$	OB	Slg	OPS	bb%	ct%	Eye	xBA	PX	SX	G/F	RC/G	RAR
Pos	1B	98 aaa	484	44	112	10	60	3	231			$4	263	335	598	4	89	0.40	276	68	52	1.80	2.96	-37.7
Age	27 Peak	99 ATL	* 277	34	83	6	32	2	300	222	325	$7	345	433	778	6	90	0.68	294	93	41	2.38	5.45	0.4
Bats	L	00 aaa	432	44	103	15	65	5	238			$8	283	403	686	6	92	0.79	307	96	71		3.78	-26.0
Pwr	- -	01 DET	* 478	50	145	13	62	0	303	233	319	$15	346	450	796	6	91	0.70	285	94	29	2.12	5.70	-8.2
Spd	No change	02 DET	482	51	145	19	82	0	301	255	320	$19	319	459	778	3	94	0.43	302	98	28	1.81	5.37	-8.6
BAvg	- -	1st Half	261	26	74	10	45	0	284			$9	297	441	738	2	95	0.36	306	101	24		4.63	-10.3
LIMA	B	2nd Half	221	25	71	9	37	0	321			$10	345	480	825	3	93	0.50	297	95	36		6.34	2.3
Risk	Very High	**03 Proj**	**400**	**42**	**121**	**14**	**61**	**0**	**303**			**$14**	**333**	**452**	**785**	**4**	**92**	**0.59**	**294**	**93**	**32**		**5.52**	**-1.6**

Extreme contact hitter is a legitimate .300 threat. Pushing 20 HRs with barely league average power skills is a bit of a stretch, however. Expect HRs to drop a bit, and possibly his playing time as a result.

Singleton,Chris

		Tm	AB	R	H	HR	RBI	SB	Avg	vLH	vRH	R$	OB	Slg	OPS	bb%	ct%	Eye	xBA	PX	SX	G/F	RC/G	RAR
Pos	CF	98 aaa	413	45	91	5	36	8	220			$1	260	327	587	5	84	0.33	267	67	143		2.87	-21.8
Age	31 Past Peak	99 CHW	496	72	149	17	72	20	300	408	281	$22	330	490	820	4	91	0.49	321	115	139	1.36	6.02	18.0
Bats	L	00 CHW	511	83	130	11	62	22	254	206	262	$13	302	382	684	6	83	0.41	268	76	147	1.29	4.10	-10.1
Pwr	+ + +	01 CHW	392	57	117	7	45	12	298	300	298	$14	333	431	764	5	84	0.33	272	84	120	1.33	4.92	-0.4
Spd	+ +	02 BAL	466	67	122	9	50	20	262	208	272	$15	294	410	704	4	82	0.25	273	103	168	1.33	4.41	-6.4
BAvg	- -	1st Half	235	34	60	4	27	8	255			$6	289	413	701	4	80	0.23	268	106	190		4.20	-4.7
LIMA	A	2nd Half	231	33	62	5	23	12	268			$8	299	407	706	4	85	0.29	278	99	132		4.64	-1.6
Risk	Moderate	**03 Proj**	**400**	**58**	**108**	**8**	**45**	**16**	**270**			**$12**	**305**	**412**	**717**	**5**	**84**	**0.31**	**276**	**93**	**148**		**4.50**	**-4.7**

Marginal skills set would not likely ever appear on one of my rosters, even with the SB potential. Declining bb%, ct%, eye are fundamental flaws that will filter into everything else.

Smith,Bobby

		Tm	AB	R	H	HR	RBI	SB	Avg	vLH	vRH	R$	OB	Slg	OPS	bb%	ct%	Eye	xBA	PX	SX	G/F	RC/G	RAR
Pos	3B	98 TAM	370	44	102	11	55	5	276	269	279	$10	337	422	758	8	70	0.31	228	87	89	2.06	5.19	7.4
Age	29 Past Peak	99 TAM	* 424	62	107	16	59	15	252	167	185	$12	314	422	736	8	73	0.33	247	99	116	2.68	4.58	0.9
Bats	R	00 TAM	* 436	56	107	19	68	13	245	250	228	$12	296	440	736	7	76	0.30	266	116	92	0.98	4.50	0.1
Pwr	- -	01 aaa	415	58	109	19	60	9	263			$14	329	467	796	9	77	0.44	269	123	93	1.83	5.63	13.8
Spd	- -	02 2TM	* 356	26	72	8	32	9	202	154	180	$1	251	329	579	6	78	0.29	246	88	70	1.00	2.79	-19.8
BAvg	+ + +	1st Half	171	12	32	2	14	5	187			($2)	253	275	528	8	75	0.36	227	66	69		2.48	-11.4
LIMA	D	2nd Half	185	14	40	6	18	4	216			$1	249	378	627	4	79	0.21	263	109	58		3.07	-8.6
Risk	High	**03 Proj**	**100**	**10**	**23**	**3**	**12**	**2**	**230**			**$1**	**284**	**390**	**674**	**7**	**77**	**0.32**	**259**	**104**	**61**		**3.83**	**-2.3**

1-6-.175 in 63 AB at TAM, but was released soon after and spent most of '02 in the MIL system. Poor season, especially after showing glimmers of skill in '01. But there are few 2nd, 3rd or 6th chances for 29-y/o's.

Smith,Jason

		Tm	AB	R	H	HR	RBI	SB	Avg	vLH	vRH	R$	OB	Slg	OPS	bb%	ct%	Eye	xBA	PX	SX	G/F	RC/G	RAR
Pos	3B	98	0	0	0	0	0	0	0								0							
Age	25 Pre-Peak	99	0	0	0	0	0	0	0								0							
Bats	L	00 aa	481	50	101	11	56	15	210			$4	242	339	580	4	73	0.15	235	76	129		2.52	-27.6
Pwr	+ + +	01 aaa	271	28	54	3	15	5	199			($2)	228	292	519	4	74	0.14	226	55	141		2.12	-19.6
Spd	+ + +	02 TAM	* 271	34	65	4	30	7	240		217	$5	267	358	625	4	77	0.16	240	78	158	1.27	3.35	-9.7
BAvg	- -	1st Half	140	18	35	4	16	4	250			$4	276	407	683	3	77	0.16	253	99	147		3.91	-2.7
LIMA	D+	2nd Half	131	16	30	0	14	3	229			$1	257	305	563	4	76	0.16	226	56	154		2.78	-6.9
Risk	Very High	**03 Proj**	**150**	**17**	**33**	**2**	**14**	**4**	**220**			**$1**	**248**	**326**	**574**	**4**	**75**	**0.15**	**233**	**68**	**139**		**2.70**	**-8.5**

1-6-3-.200 in 65 AB at TAM. Offensively, this skills set is quite offensive. Horrible. Ick. Yes, he's got some speed, but so does this kid down on the corner and you don't see me putting him on my team.

Snow,J.T.			Tm	AB	R	H	HR	RBI	SB	Avg	vLH	vRH	R$	OB	Slg	OPS	bb%	ct%	Eye	xBA	PX	SX	G/F	RC/G	RAR
Pos	1B	98	SF	435	65	108	15	79	1	248	164	265	$11	337	423	760	12	81	0.69	278	121	49	0.86	5.15	-3.4
Age	35 Decline	99	SF	570	93	156	24	98	0	274	231	292	$17	369	451	820	13	79	0.71	264	106	37	0.83	6.18	14.5
Bats	L	00	SF	536	82	152	19	96	1	284	256	292	$17	362	459	821	11	76	0.51	261	108	49	0.95	6.21	12.9
Pwr	- -	01	SF	285	43	70	8	34	0	246	306	233	$4	368	379	747	16	72	0.68	227	81	44	1.09	5.33	-10.2
Spd	No change	02	SF	422	47	104	6	53	0	246	229	250	$4	339	360	699	12	79	0.66	243	79	42	1.30	4.55	-16.0
BAvg	+ + +	1st Half		223	24	50	3	31	0	224			$0	305	323	628	10	81	0.62	245	71	26		3.54	-15.4
LIMA	C+	2nd Half		199	23	54	3	22	0	271			$3	375	402	777	14	76	0.69	240	88	62		5.84	0.9
Risk	Low	03	Proj	350	46	90	8	47	0	257			$6	356	396	752	13	76	0.65	245	90	53		5.30	-0.8

While his batting eye BPIs have remained fairly stable, note how his power decline correlates with an increased tendency toward the ground ball. Pac Bell has been a killer; his Slg there the past two years: .289 and .311.

Snyder,Earl			Tm	AB	R	H	HR	RBI	SB	Avg	vLH	vRH	R$	OB	Slg	OPS	bb%	ct%	Eye	xBA	PX	SX	G/F	RC/G	RAR
Pos	1B	98		0	0	0	0	0	0	0								0							
Age	26 Pre-Peak	99		0	0	0	0	0	0	0								0							
Bats	R	00		0	0	0	0	0	0	0								0							
Pwr	- -	01	a/a	424	64	111	17	68	4	262			$12	342	472	814	11	75	0.50	265	136	65		5.85	-6.5
Spd	No change	02	CLE	*455	66	109	19	63	0	240	192	207	$10	307	433	740	9	75	0.39	260	128	45	0.56	4.62	-19.4
BAvg	-	1st Half		243	38	63	13	38	0	259			$8	328	490	818	9	74	0.39	267	151	37		5.74	-1.8
LIMA	C+	2nd Half		212	28	46	6	25	0	217			$2	281	368	649	8	77	0.39	251	102	63		3.51	-16.3
Risk	High	03	Proj	250	36	61	10	36	0	244			$5	317	442	758	10	75	0.43	262	129	59		4.91	-5.9

1-4-.200 in 55 AB at CLE. BPIs took a step back from '01, and his debut performance was underwhelming. Good power, marginal skills otherwise. His type come a dime a dozen.

Soriano,Alfonso			Tm	AB	R	H	HR	RBI	SB	Avg	vLH	vRH	R$	OB	Slg	OPS	bb%	ct%	Eye	xBA	PX	SX	G/F	RC/G	RAR
Pos	2B	98		0	0	0	0	0	0	0								0							
Age	25 Pre-Peak	99	a/a	443	56	116	14	68	21	262			$16	312	424	736	7	85	0.47	285	100	103	1.50	4.06	-1.6
Bats	R	00	NYY	*509	79	129	13	57	14	253	150	200	$10	284	409	693	4	85	0.29	285	97	127	0.76	3.87	-1.1
Pwr	- -	01	NYY	574	77	154	18	73	43	268	255	271	$27	303	432	736	5	78	0.23	263	103	126	0.97	4.58	4.9
Spd	-	02	NYY	696	128	209	39	102	41	300	316	297	$44	323	547	870	3	77	0.15	291	161	137	0.78	6.34	45.7
BAvg	- - -	1st Half		343	60	111	19	48	23	324			$25	346	589	935	3	76	0.15	295	176	143		7.67	36.0
LIMA	C+	2nd Half		353	68	98	20	54	18	278			$20	299	507	807	3	79	0.15	287	146	126		5.22	11.4
Risk	Low	03	Proj	650	105	187	36	100	42	288			$39	317	527	844	4	80	0.21	293	148	131		5.84	31.9

xBA paints a brighter picture for his BA than bb%, ct% and eye do, but you have to wonder why pitchers would throw him anything close to the zone. PX and SX are huge, OB is soft, and he did tail off in the 2nd half.

Sosa,Sammy			Tm	AB	R	H	HR	RBI	SB	Avg	vLH	vRH	R$	OB	Slg	OPS	bb%	ct%	Eye	xBA	PX	SX	G/F	RC/G	RAR
Pos	RF	98	CHC	643	134	198	66	158	18	308	287	315	$54	378	647	1025	10	73	0.43	288	197	78	1.02	9.13	84.5
Age	34 Decline	99	CHC	625	114	180	63	141	7	288	313	279	$39	367	635	1002	11	73	0.46	281	190	60	0.90	8.43	66.8
Bats	R	00	CHC	604	106	193	50	138	7	320	347	313	$40	409	634	1043	13	72	0.54	282	178	56	1.01	10.16	97.5
Pwr	- -	01	CHC	577	146	189	64	160	0	328	387	316	$47	440	737	1177	17	73	0.76	309	225	75	0.92	13.01	145.4
Spd	No change	02	CHC	556	122	160	49	108	2	288	366	270	$32	399	594	993	16	74	0.72	273	167	70	1.12	9.20	71.3
BAvg	-	1st Half		291	61	91	27	53	2	313			$20	425	649	1075	16	77	0.84	293	186	80		11.11	56.7
LIMA	C+	2nd Half		265	61	69	22	55	0	260			$12	370	532	902	15	71	0.61	251	146	43		7.36	17.3
Risk	Very Low	03	Proj	550	121	160	50	114	1	291			$32	397	612	1009	15	73	0.66	278	178	56		9.30	81.3

2nd half fade was partly due to a strained back. With strong BPIs otherwise, that bodes well for a rebound. However, at 34, these naggy injuries might become more frequent.

Spencer,Shane			Tm	AB	R	H	HR	RBI	SB	Avg	vLH	vRH	R$	OB	Slg	OPS	bb%	ct%	Eye	xBA	PX	SX	G/F	RC/G	RAR
Pos	RF LF	98	NYY	*409	74	123	25	83	1	301	465	208	$19	362	567	929	9	84	0.59	315	163	55	0.53	7.75	33.3
Age	31 Past Peak	99	NYY	*255	40	65	10	29	0	255	289	197	$4	324	412	736	9	77	0.45	248	92	38	0.71	4.55	-4.2
Bats	R	00	NYY	248	33	70	9	40	1	282	312	269	$7	333	460	793	7	82	0.42	275	100	88	0.78	5.51	3.8
Pwr	No change	01	NYY	*456	53	107	13	57	7	235	313	242	$7	295	382	677	8	83	0.50	267	91	88	1.03	3.97	-15.7
Spd	No change	02	NYY	288	32	71	6	34	0	247	267	239	$4	320	375	695	10	78	0.50	248	88	55	1.01	4.17	-8.6
BAvg	No change	1st Half		182	26	45	5	24	0	247			$3	328	390	719	11	76	0.50	244	95	62		4.48	-3.7
LIMA	D+	2nd Half		106	6	26	1	10	0	245			$1	304	349	653	8	83	0.50	254	76	54		3.66	-4.8
Risk	Very High	03	Proj	300	33	76	8	38	0	253			$5	316	394	711	8	81	0.49	259	91	55		4.37	-8.2

Hamstring woes cut his season short, but in some ways it was merciful. Never reached the expectations that most had for him, and BPIs continue to decline.

Spiezio,Scott			Tm	AB	R	H	HR	RBI	SB	Avg	vLH	vRH	R$	OB	Slg	OPS	bb%	ct%	Eye	xBA	PX	SX	G/F	RC/G	RAR
Pos	1B 3B	98	OAK	406	54	105	9	50	1	259	264	256	$6	331	377	708	10	86	0.79	268	76	45	0.87	4.49	-16.2
Age	30 Past Peak	99	OAK	*352	55	99	13	57	0	281	229	249	$10	358	486	844	11	86	0.86	302	133	42	0.65	6.56	7.4
Bats	S	00	ANA	297	47	72	17	49	1	242	250	241	$7	332	465	797	12	81	0.71	285	120	68	0.78	5.46	-5.8
Pwr	No change	01	ANA	457	57	124	13	54	5	271	239	282	$11	322	438	759	7	86	0.52	285	106	88	0.65	5.11	-16.2
Spd	-	02	ANA	491	80	140	12	82	6	285	368	248	$17	371	436	807	12	89	1.29	296	107	73	0.69	5.99	0.1
BAvg	+ + +	1st Half		227	32	63	4	39	2	278			$7	374	405	779	13	86	1.09	277	98	45		5.66	-2.4
LIMA	A+	2nd Half		264	48	77	8	43	4	292			$10	368	462	830	11	92	1.60	313	115	94		6.27	2.5
Risk	High	03	Proj	500	76	137	16	76	5	274			$15	350	442	792	11	87	0.91	292	109	77		5.65	0.0

Excellent batting eye and on base skills, his xBA says his BA should have been closer to .300. That's the good news. The bad news is his league average power is weak for a 1Bman. He's barely replacement level.

Spivey,Junior			Tm	AB	R	H	HR	RBI	SB	Avg	vLH	vRH	R$	OB	Slg	OPS	bb%	ct%	Eye	xBA	PX	SX	G/F	RC/G	RAR
Pos	2B	98	aa	119	22	34	3	14	7	286			$5	406	454	859	17	82	1.09	283	116	113		6.91	11.3
Age	28 Peak	99	aa	164	29	42	2	14	10	256			$4	354	396	751	13	87	1.19	292	87	174		4.36	1.0
Bats	R	00	a/a	136	20	37	3	14	2	272			$3	313	471	783	6	88	0.47	315	126	150		5.23	4.2
Pwr	+ + + +	01	ARI	*357	52	81	9	41	10	227	323	214	$6	310	353	663	11	80	0.59	253	74	113	1.56	3.75	-2.1
Spd	No change	02	ARI	538	103	162	16	78	11	301	324	291	$23	376	476	852	11	81	0.65	275	110	124	1.22	6.82	39.9
BAvg	- -	1st Half		240	53	78	9	43	8	325			$15	407	563	969	12	83	0.83	307	144	189		9.17	36.4
LIMA	A+	2nd Half		298	50	84	7	35	3	282			$8	352	406	758	10	80	0.53	250	82	59		5.20	6.5
Risk	X HIGH	03	Proj	550	94	151	12	69	9	275			$14	350	427	777	10	82	0.65	273	97	118		5.36	22.1

2002 might have been his career year. His BPIs don't support a .300 BA, but more than that, his 2nd half fade was significant. Use that as your benchmark projecting forward.

Stairs,Matt			Tm	AB	R	H	HR	RBI	SB	Avg	vLH	vRH	R$	OB	Slg	OPS	bb%	ct%	Eye	xBA	PX	SX	G/F	RC/G	RAR
Pos	RF LF	98	OAK	523	88	154	26	106	8	294	280	301	$24	366	511	876	10	82	0.63	292	132	75	1.09	7.09	32.2
Age	35 Decline	99	OAK	531	94	137	38	102	2	258	236	268	$19	365	533	897	14	77	0.72	283	154	58	0.87	6.90	32.4
Bats	L	00	OAK	476	74	108	21	81	5	227	202	235	$8	336	414	750	14	74	0.64	254	110	61	0.95	5.03	0.2
Pwr	+ +	01	CHC	340	48	85	17	61	2	250	172	257	$10	349	462	811	13	78	0.68	272	128	38	0.93	5.80	1.4
Spd	No change	02	MIL	270	41	66	16	41	2	244	154	249	$8	333	478	811	12	81	0.72	284	138	51	0.99	5.81	3.5
BAvg	+ + +	1st Half		67	13	16	4	13	1	239			$2	311	507	818	9	84	0.64	310	168	76		5.65	0.5
LIMA	B	2nd Half		203	28	50	12	28	1	246			$5	341	468	808	12	81	0.74	274	128	37		5.85	2.9
Risk	Moderate	03	Proj	300	47	74	16	51	3	247			$9	340	471	811	12	79	0.68	279	135	52		5.80	8.8

A strict platoon player now, but his BAs vs RHers don't exactly elicit fear. Power is his game, however, and those skills have actually been on a late career upswing. A good late-rounder if you have BA help elsewhere.

Stevens,Lee			Tm	AB	R	H	HR	RBI	SB	Avg	vLH	vRH	R$	OB	Slg	OPS	bb%	ct%	Eye	xBA	PX	SX	G/F	RC/G	RAR
Pos	1B	98	TEX	344	52	91	20	59	0	265	167	274	$11	325	512	837	8	73	0.33	265	141	83	1.42	5.89	1.5
Age	35 Decline	99	TEX	517	76	146	24	81	2	282	304	277	$16	348	485	833	9	74	0.39	257	122	48	1.41	6.21	5.0
Bats	L	00	MON	449	60	119	22	75	0	265	281	260	$13	336	481	817	10	77	0.46	273	128	41	1.22	5.93	6.8
Pwr	- -	01	MON	542	77	133	25	95	2	245	243	246	$14	336	452	788	12	71	0.47	248	126	53	1.46	5.52	-15.2
Spd	No change	02	2TM	358	50	73	15	57	1	204	137	221	$3	308	377	685	13	75	0.61	246	103	69	1.17	4.12	-20.3
BAvg	+ + + + +	1st Half		209	28	39	10	31	1	187			$1	315	368	683	16	72	0.66	236	105	63		4.14	-12.1
LIMA	C+	2nd Half		149	22	34	5	26	0	228			$1	299	389	688	9	80	0.50	260	101	67		4.10	-8.2
Risk	Low	03	Proj	300	42	70	13	50	1	233			$6	320	421	741	11	75	0.51	257	114	54		4.82	-10.7

The output was a lot worse than his BPIs would indicate. Got off to a horrible start and never really came around. Batted just .129 in Jacobs Field, which is not going to win him any friends.

Stewart,Shannon

		Yr	Tm	AB	R	H	HR	RBI	SB	Avg	vLH	vRH	R$	OB	Slg	OPS	bb%	ct%	Eye	xBA	PX	SX	G/F	RC/G	RAR
Pos	LF DH	98	TOR	516	90	144	12	55	51	279	296	273	$27	362	417	779	11	85	0.87	283	89	132	1.60	5.60	7.6
Age	29 Past Peak	99	TOR	608	102	185	11	67	37	304	369	291	$27	366	411	777	9	86	0.71	272	69	113	1.77	5.73	10.6
Bats	R	00	TOR	583	107	186	21	69	20	319	309	322	$26	360	518	878	6	86	0.47	309	122	133	1.34	7.18	35.2
Pwr	No change	01	TOR	640	103	202	12	60	27	316	333	312	$26	362	463	824	7	89	0.64	295	97	127	1.56	6.36	32.1
Spd	No change	02	TOR	577	103	175	10	45	14	303	302	304	$18	363	442	805	9	90	0.90	293	98	136	1.52	6.27	24.2
BAvg	-	1st Half		255	38	72	4	19	3	282			$5	332	420	752	7	92	0.90	303	105	87		5.25	2.5
LIMA	A	2nd Half		322	65	103	6	26	11	320			$13	387	460	846	10	88	0.90	285	93	157		7.16	22.7
Risk	Very Low	03	Proj	600	105	185	13	55	25	308			$24	363	456	819	8	88	0.75	295	99	137		6.43	24.3

An off year? Not really. Batting eye improved, other BPIs remained stable, and speed, well, that also improved thanks to his 2nd half surge. Odds are he'll be undervalued at the draft; if he stops under $20, grab him.

Stinnett,Kelly

		Yr	Tm	AB	R	H	HR	RBI	SB	Avg	vLH	vRH	R$	OB	Slg	OPS	bb%	ct%	Eye	xBA	PX	SX	G/F	RC/G	RAR
Pos	CA	98	ARI	274	35	71	11	34	0	259	253	262	$6	343	438	781	11	73	0.47	249	117	41	1.13	5.48	13.1
Age	33 Decline	99	ARI	284	36	66	14	38	2	232	303	211	$5	292	426	718	8	71	0.29	241	115	47	1.02	4.32	2.4
Bats	R	00	ARI	240	22	52	8	33	0	217	250	208	$1	274	346	620	7	77	0.34	245	74	22	1.09	3.21	-6.4
Pwr	+ +	01	CIN	187	27	48	9	25	2	257	325	238	$5	319	460	779	8	67	0.28	234	123	55	0.84	5.11	8.8
Spd	No change	02	CIN	* 179	15	35	3	17	2	196	286	208	($2)	265	302	567	9	75	0.39	231	74	50	0.83	2.79	-7.9
BAvg	+ + +	1st Half		54	3	9	0	2	0	167			($2)	196	259	456	4	78	0.17	239	80	24		1.62	-4.1
LIMA	D	2nd Half		125	12	26	3	15	2	208			$0	293	320	613	11	74	0.47	226	71	50		3.39	-3.2
Risk	High	03	Proj	250	26	59	7	28	2	236			$3	298	378	676	8	73	0.33	237	92	44		3.97	-0.1

3-13-.226 in 93 AB at CIN. Groin injury laid waste to his 1st half, and I'm willing to bet the pain lingered into the 2nd half as well. Should rebound back to his previously mediocre levels.

Stynes,Chris

		Yr	Tm	AB	R	H	HR	RBI	SB	Avg	vLH	vRH	R$	OB	Slg	OPS	bb%	ct%	Eye	xBA	PX	SX	G/F	RC/G	RAR
Pos	3B 2B	98	CIN	347	52	88	6	27	15	254	277	241	$8	317	340	657	8	90	0.89	278	58	115	2.30	4.13	-4.0
Age	30 Past Peak	99	CIN	113	18	27	2	14	5	239	292	225	$2	312	301	613	10	88	0.92	261	35	85	1.58	3.41	-3.7
Bats	R	00	CIN	380	71	127	12	40	5	334	398	315	$16	386	497	883	8	86	0.59	292	103	79	1.57	7.62	37.8
Pwr	+	01	BOS	361	52	101	8	33	4	280	349	251	$8	318	410	728	5	84	0.36	267	84	78	1.99	4.55	1.1
Spd	No change	02	CHC	195	25	47	5	26	1	241	240	242	$3	315	374	689	10	85	0.72	267	83	65	0.87	4.19	-3.0
BAvg	+ + +	1st Half		105	19	24	4	14	1	229			$1	341	390	732	15	90	1.64	290	99	59		4.97	1.0
LIMA	C	2nd Half		90	6	23	1	12	0	256			$1	280	356	635	3	80	0.17	242	65	70		3.30	-3.7
Risk	High	03	Proj	250	34	67	6	29	3	268			$5	323	393	716	7	85	0.53	269	80	73		4.55	-0.0

Odd season. Struggled at the plate when he was making better contact. Added 27 points to his BA in the 2nd half when he was hacking away. Given his BPIs, his BA should have been higher so expect a rebound.

Surhoff,B.J.

		Yr	Tm	AB	R	H	HR	RBI	SB	Avg	vLH	vRH	R$	OB	Slg	OPS	bb%	ct%	Eye	xBA	PX	SX	G/F	RC/G	RAR
Pos	1B	98	BAL	573	79	160	22	92	9	279	254	290	$20	336	457	793	8	86	0.60	291	111	66	1.07	5.51	-4.3
Age	38 Decline	99	BAL	673	104	207	28	107	5	308	327	302	$26	349	492	841	6	88	0.55	301	112	70	1.01	6.55	13.2
Bats	L	00	2TM	539	69	157	14	68	10	291	395	290	$16	341	443	785	7	89	0.71	300	98	85	0.98	5.72	-0.7
Pwr	- - -	01	ATL	484	68	131	10	58	9	271	219	280	$12	324	405	729	7	90	0.79	295	91	87	1.10	4.80	-23.6
Spd	- - - - -	02	ATL	75	5	22	0	9	1	293		284	$2	369	360	729	11	93	1.80	274	58	32	1.43	4.53	-2.8
BAvg	+ + + + +	1st Half		75	5	22	0	9	1	293			$2	369	360	729	11	93	1.80	274	58	32		4.53	-2.8
LIMA	A+	2nd Half		0	0	0	0	0	0	0			($0)					0							-0.0
Risk	Moderate	03	Proj	500	59	145	10	66	8	290			$15	348	420	768	8	90	0.90	290	89	58		5.29	-1.3

Torn ACL ended his season before it really began. BPIs remain fine, though at 38, his productivity may be gone. ATL could sure use a 1Bman, but there's probably not enough left to justify giving him the job.

Suzuki,Ichiro

		Yr	Tm	AB	R	H	HR	RBI	SB	Avg	vLH	vRH	R$	OB	Slg	OPS	bb%	ct%	Eye	xBA	PX	SX	G/F	RC/G	RAR
Pos	RF	98	JPN	506	79	181	13	71	11	358			$28	408	518	926	8	93	1.23	318	110	93		8.73	57.3
Age	29 Past Peak	99	JPN	411	80	141	21	68	12	343			$25	408	572	980	10	89	0.98	320	138	95		9.31	55.0
Bats	L	00	JPN	395	73	153	12	73	21	387			$31	461	539	1000	12	91	1.50	303	94	90		10.76	72.2
Pwr	No change	01	SEA	692	127	242	8	69	56	350	318	362	$43	377	457	833	4	92	0.57	293	70	151	2.63	6.93	38.2
Spd	- - - -	02	SEA	647	111	208	8	51	31	321	356	308	$28	386	425	811	10	90	1.10	276	70	137	2.48	6.33	24.7
BAvg	- -	1st Half		323	62	116	2	28	21	359			$19	430	467	897	11	92	1.48	285	76	163		8.33	33.3
LIMA	C+	2nd Half		324	49	92	6	23	10	284			$9	341	383	724	8	89	0.80	267	64	102		4.67	-4.5
Risk	Low	03	Proj	650	114	219	10	69	34	337			$33	393	448	841	8	91	1.01	285	74	128		6.97	34.8

Superb 1st half, displaying the BPIs that he had shown in JPN. But he couldn't keep it up. It could be burnout -- he amassed as many plate appearances in the past two years as in his last THREE years in Japan.

Sweeney,Mark

		Yr	Tm	AB	R	H	HR	RBI	SB	Avg	vLH	vRH	R$	OB	Slg	OPS	bb%	ct%	Eye	xBA	PX	SX	G/F	RC/G	RAR
Pos	1B	98	SD	192	17	45	2	15	1	234		247	$0	326	339	664	12	81	0.70	256	71	92	1.38	3.92	-9.2
Age	33 Decline	99	aaa	342	47	81	10	39	2	237			$3	320	377	698	11	77	0.54	249	87	59	2.00	4.31	-14.8
Bats	L	00	MIL	73	9	16	1	6	0	219		222	($0)	329	342	672	14	75	0.67	249	90	26	0.83	4.14	-3.2
Pwr	- - - - -	01	MIL	* 493	57	118	8	61	4	239	200	262	$5	313	359	672	10	83	0.62	265	82	71	0.92	4.04	-36.5
Spd	No change	02	SD	66	3	12	1	4	0	182	89	189	($1)	229	273	501	6	71	0.21	209	62	7	0.71	2.06	-7.3
BAvg	+ + + + +	1st Half		61	3	10	1	4	0	164			($2)	215	262	478	6	69	0.21	205	68	10		1.84	-7.2
LIMA	F	2nd Half		5	0	2	0	0	0	400			$0	400	400	800	0	100	0.00	251	0	-10		6.80	0.2
Risk	Very High	03	Proj	100	10	22	2	10	0	220			($0)	294	330	624	9	76	0.44	236	74	37		3.39	-6.3

Was released on July 13.

Sweeney,Mike

		Yr	Tm	AB	R	H	HR	RBI	SB	Avg	vLH	vRH	R$	OB	Slg	OPS	bb%	ct%	Eye	xBA	PX	SX	G/F	RC/G	RAR
Pos	1B DH	98	KC	282	32	73	8	35	2	259	302	247	$5	317	408	725	8	87	0.63	282	99	41	1.15	4.52	-10.8
Age	29 Past Peak	99	KC	575	101	185	22	102	6	322	350	316	$25	380	520	900	9	92	1.13	323	125	84	1.45	7.80	34.2
Bats	R	00	KC	618	105	206	29	144	8	333	374	322	$34	402	523	925	10	89	1.06	304	109	63	1.15	8.45	46.8
Pwr	No change	01	KC	559	97	170	29	99	10	304	268	317	$28	376	542	918	10	89	1.00	318	150	70	1.24	7.84	27.9
Spd	-	02	KC	483	83	163	25	89	9	337	357	334	$30	413	563	976	11	90	1.29	325	147	67	1.21	9.13	49.1
BAvg	-	1st Half		285	53	103	15	45	3	361			$18	433	604	1037	11	91	1.38	339	163	47		10.41	40.7
LIMA	C+	2nd Half		198	30	60	10	44	6	303			$12	384	505	889	12	89	1.18	306	124	85		7.51	9.8
Risk	Very Low	03	Proj	550	91	180	33	116	10	327			$34	399	574	973	11	89	1.11	327	152	68		8.99	58.7

Phenomenal 1st half. 2nd half was curtailed by back and hip ailments, but there are a few thousand healthy players that would kill for those numbers. Expect a huge season in 2003.

Tarasco,Tony

		Yr	Tm	AB	R	H	HR	RBI	SB	Avg	vLH	vRH	R$	OB	Slg	OPS	bb%	ct%	Eye	xBA	PX	SX	G/F	RC/G	RAR
Pos	LF	98	aaa	343	41	84	12	35	2	245			$5	313	408	721	9	87	0.79	292	105	53	4.33	4.51	-5.6
Age	32 Past Peak	99	aaa	377	53	82	12	44	7	218			$3	284	366	650	8	89	0.85	293	94	73	0.77	3.48	-19.7
Bats	L	00	JPN	380	40	91	19	57	1	239			$7	309	429	738	9	77	0.45	260	105	37		4.67	-7.0
Pwr	- - -	01	aaa	366	44	90	5	48	12	246			$8	320	377	697	10	87	0.85	285	91	102		4.17	-12.7
Spd	No change	02	NYM	* 249	32	59	7	29	6	237	333	241	$4	280	369	650	6	88	0.52	279	81	92	1.12	3.45	-23.1
BAvg	+ + +	1st Half		185	22	42	3	19	5	227			$2	263	324	587	5	90	0.47	273	62	101		2.81	-20.6
LIMA	C	2nd Half		64	10	17	4	10	1	266			$3	329	500	829	9	84	0.60	293	136	57		5.69	-1.6
Risk	High	03	Proj	150	19	37	5	20	3	247			$4	309	422	731	8	85	0.62	287	107	87		4.47	-1.3

6-15-.250 in 96 AB at NYM. This power spurt (34 HR pace!) was a poorly veiled attempt to land a 2003 contract with the team. Shame on him for disguising his real skill level. Did he think we wouldn't know the truth?

Tatis,Fernando

		Yr	Tm	AB	R	H	HR	RBI	SB	Avg	vLH	vRH	R$	OB	Slg	OPS	bb%	ct%	Eye	xBA	PX	SX	G/F	RC/G	RAR
Pos	3B	98	2TM	532	69	147	11	58	13	276	287	273	$14	322	415	738	6	77	0.29	256	96	110	1.00	4.86	5.4
Age	28 Peak	99	STL	537	104	160	34	107	21	298	290	301	$32	391	553	944	13	76	0.64	278	150	95	0.80	8.19	66.1
Bats	S	00	STL	324	59	82	18	64	2	253	261	250	$10	365	491	856	15	71	0.61	259	141	60	0.66	6.50	22.8
Pwr	+ + + +	01	MON	145	20	37	2	11	0	255	235	261	$1	329	359	688	10	70	0.37	219	74	35	1.24	4.37	-1.4
Spd	No change	02	MON	381	43	87	15	55	2	228	230	228	$6	293	399	692	8	76	0.39	248	103	52	1.21	4.03	-7.8
BAvg	No change	1st Half		175	23	47	9	26	1	269			$6	319	497	816	7	77	0.33	270	138	68		5.78	5.9
LIMA	B	2nd Half		206	20	40	6	29	1	194			($0)	272	316	587	10	76	0.44	230	74	36		2.85	-12.0
Risk	Moderate	03	Proj	400	53	97	14	54	2	243			$7	319	408	726	10	74	0.43	245	103	53		4.60	0.6

There are still drafters that look at his 1999 season and it becomes a reflex reaction to cough up that extra buck. I've got a bottle of Robitussin I'd like to share with them.

Taylor,Reggie

			Tm	AB	R	H	HR	RBI	SB	Avg	vLH	vRH	R$	OB	Slg	OPS	bb%	ct%	Eye	xBA	PX	SX	G/F	RC/G	RAR
Pos	CF LF	98	aa	337	41	85	4	18	18	252			$7	274	353	627	3	82	0.16	260	67	149		3.22	-13.9
Age	26 Pre-Peak	99	aa	526	61	129	13	50	31	245			$14	266	378	645	3	87	0.22	283	77	143		2.91	-26.1
Bats	L	00	aaa	422	49	106	11	35	19	251			$10	282	389	670	4	82	0.23	262	75	149		3.45	-14.2
Pwr	- -	01	aaa	464	52	120	6	46	29	259			$15	294	386	679	5	80	0.24	260	79	171		3.70	-10.4
Spd	- - - -	02	CIN	287	41	73	9	38	11	254	184	265	$9	289	429	718	5	72	0.18	246	105	156	1.11	3.99	-8.4
BAvg	- -	1st Half		102	12	26	3	19	8	255			$5	269	412	681	2	76	0.08	253	87	188		3.25	-5.1
LIMA	B	2nd Half		185	29	47	6	19	3	254			$4	299	438	737	6	70	0.22	240	115	126		4.40	-3.2
Risk	Very High	03	Proj	300	38	76	7	34	15	253			$9	286	407	693	4	77	0.20	256	92	164		3.71	-6.1

Finally made it to the majors and had to make an impression. So he abandoned what little plate patience he had to pump up those power numbers. Chicks dig the longball, but so do GMs. (But RAR tells the true story.)

Tejada,Miguel

			Tm	AB	R	H	HR	RBI	SB	Avg	vLH	vRH	R$	OB	Slg	OPS	bb%	ct%	Eye	xBA	PX	SX	G/F	RC/G	RAR
Pos	SS	98	OAK	365	53	85	11	45	5	233	210	242	$5	288	384	671	7	76	0.33	252	96	79	1.35	3.64	-4.1
Age	26 Pre-Peak	99	OAK	593	93	149	21	84	8	251	271	245	$13	317	427	744	9	84	0.61	286	106	94	1.35	4.71	8.5
Bats	R	00	OAK	607	105	167	30	115	6	275	220	296	$21	346	479	826	10	83	0.65	291	118	83	1.10	6.25	33.4
Pwr	- -	01	OAK	622	107	166	31	113	11	267	273	264	$24	314	476	790	6	86	0.48	296	123	98	1.00	5.31	16.1
Spd	- - - - -	02	OAK	662	108	204	34	131	7	308	285	314	$34	346	508	853	5	87	0.45	301	125	72	1.25	6.64	39.4
BAvg	- - -	1st Half		331	54	99	15	59	2	299			$15	333	489	823	5	88	0.43	302	123	60		6.06	13.8
LIMA	C+	2nd Half		331	54	105	19	72	5	317			$20	358	526	884	6	87	0.48	300	126	69		7.26	26.0
Risk	Low	03	Proj	650	108	192	37	122	8	295			$32	342	518	860	7	86	0.49	302	133	77		6.59	55.5

Here is a case where xBA accurately projected his eventual rise in BA. Not much plate patience, but makes good contact and has still-developing power skills. Has not reached his ceiling yet.

Thomas,Frank

			Tm	AB	R	H	HR	RBI	SB	Avg	vLH	vRH	R$	OB	Slg	OPS	bb%	ct%	Eye	xBA	PX	SX	G/F	RC/G	RAR
Pos	DH	98	CHW	585	109	155	29	109	7	265	226	277	$20	381	480	862	16	84	1.18	299	130	86	0.69	7.08	33.4
Age	34 Decline	99	CHW	486	74	148	15	77	3	305	253	314	$16	410	471	881	15	86	1.32	288	109	40	0.88	7.67	38.7
Bats	R	00	CHW	582	115	191	43	143	1	328	407	314	$35	437	625	1062	16	84	1.19	326	171	28	0.79	11.01	115.5
Pwr	No change	01	CHW	68	8	15	4	10	0	221	313	192	$1	321	441	762	13	82	0.83	274	127		0.59	5.03	-0.7
Spd	No change	02	CHW	523	77	132	28	92	3	252	214	264	$18	360	472	832	14	78	0.77	277	139	58	0.40	6.37	12.8
BAvg	+ + +	1st Half		281	41	70	14	54	2	249			$10	343	459	802	12	79	0.67	276	133	66		5.82	1.6
LIMA	A	2nd Half		242	36	62	14	38	1	256			$8	379	488	867	17	77	0.87	278	147	35		7.04	11.6
Risk	Low	03	Proj	525	86	147	29	99	3	280			$22	391	515	905	15	81	0.97	292	146	52		7.75	39.9

Batting eye trend tells a lot. It took a .359 BA in Sept just to get him up over .250; that shows there is still SOME skill left. But with only one vintage-Thomas season in the past five, it's time to redefine our expectations.

Thome,Jim

			Tm	AB	R	H	HR	RBI	SB	Avg	vLH	vRH	R$	OB	Slg	OPS	bb%	ct%	Eye	xBA	PX	SX	G/F	RC/G	RAR
Pos	1B	98	CLE	440	89	129	30	85	1	293	289	295	$21	412	584	996	17	68	0.63	262	175	64	1.06	9.48	56.4
Age	32 Past Peak	99	CLE	494	101	137	33	108	0	277	239	292	$20	425	540	966	20	65	0.74	238	150	48	1.23	9.11	57.0
Bats	L	00	CLE	557	106	150	37	106	1	269	250	277	$20	397	531	928	17	69	0.69	258	148	49	1.00	8.14	40.0
Pwr	+ + + +	01	CLE	526	101	153	49	124	0	291	232	313	$31	414	624	1038	17	65	0.60	244	186	29	0.97	10.05	68.7
Spd	No change	02	CLE	480	101	146	52	118	1	304	245	333	$35	445	677	1122	20	71	0.88	294	215	47	0.78	11.98	103.2
BAvg	-	1st Half		262	43	74	24	57	0	282			$15	418	599	1017	19	71	0.79	274	183	32		9.55	33.0
LIMA	C+	2nd Half		218	58	72	28	61	1	330			$20	477	771	1247	22	72	0.98	318	254	66		15.35	74.7
Risk	Very Low	03	Proj	500	105	149	56	133	1	298			$36	433	693	1126	19	69	0.76	287	222	48		11.80	108.8

All his BPIs and trends support the damage he's been inflicting. At 32, this could be his peak, but the way he finished 2002, this might still be a step along the trend.

Thompson,Ryan

			Tm	AB	R	H	HR	RBI	SB	Avg	vLH	vRH	R$	OB	Slg	OPS	bb%	ct%	Eye	xBA	PX	SX	G/F	RC/G	RAR
Pos	LF	98	JPN	107	10	29	2	16	1	271			$3	345	393	737	10	70	0.38	225	89	35		4.95	-0.2
Age	35 Decline	99	aaa	424	44	94	11	46	3	222			$2	270	354	624	6	76	0.28	244	82	61	1.00	3.02	-27.6
Bats	R	00	aaa	376	44	89	21	66	7	237			$11	283	471	753	6	81	0.33	292	134	83	0.78	4.46	-9.1
Pwr	+ +	01	aaa	416	43	88	13	51	3	212			$3	234	373	606	3	81	0.15	269	105	55	1.13	2.68	-31.6
Spd	No change	02	MIL	* 410	46	102	19	56	1	249	300	218	$9	277	454	731	4	80	0.19	269	119	74	0.76	4.17	-28.5
BAvg	- -	1st Half		301	34	78	12	38	0	259			$7	281	442	723	3	83	0.18	274	107	69		4.07	-21.6
LIMA	D+	2nd Half		109	12	24	7	18	1	220			$3	267	486	753	6	70	0.21	252	153	86		4.44	-6.9
Risk	Very High	03	Proj	150	16	35	7	22	1	233			$3	270	437	707	5	77	0.22	266	121	75		3.91	-3.8

8-24-.248 in 137 AB at MIL. Just celebrated his 10th anniversary of being traded with Jeff Kent to the Mets for David Cone. (Mets fans remember that stuff and the anguish that deal caused.)

Torrealba,Yorvit

			Tm	AB	R	H	HR	RBI	SB	Avg	vLH	vRH	R$	OB	Slg	OPS	bb%	ct%	Eye	xBA	PX	SX	G/F	RC/G	RAR
Pos	CA	98	aa	207	18	45	0	13	0	217			($2)	280	251	531	8	86	0.60	241	31	29		2.28	-11.3
Age	24 Growth	99	a/a	280	30	64	5	25	0	229			($0)	259	334	593	4	86	0.30	267	67	51		2.79	-10.9
Bats	R	00	aa	398	47	108	4	30	2	271			$4	324	357	681	7	87	0.61	266	59	52		4.17	0.2
Pwr	+ +	01	aaa	398	42	94	6	29	1	236			$1	262	347	609	3	88	0.30	273	73	68		2.97	-9.3
Spd	No change	02	SF	136	17	38	2	14	0	279	385	255	$2	347	397	744	9	85	0.70	266	86	28	2.07	5.20	4.3
BAvg	-	1st Half		59	8	17	1	5	0	288			$1	344	390	734	8	81	0.45	245	70	32		5.07	1.6
LIMA	D	2nd Half		77	9	21	1	9	0	273			$1	349	403	751	10	88	1.00	282	99	25		5.30	2.7
Risk	X HIGH	03	Proj	150	17	42	5	23	0	280			$5	333	440	773	7	86	0.58	284	103	30		5.32	6.2

Amidst the small data sets and the bouncing between levels, there's actually a bit of skills growth going on here. He won't ever be a 30-HR hitter, but with some PT, he could grow into a 10-15 HR, .280 type of guy.

Torres,Andres

			Tm	AB	R	H	HR	RBI	SB	Avg	vLH	vRH	R$	OB	Slg	OPS	bb%	ct%	Eye	xBA	PX	SX	G/F	RC/G	RAR
Pos	CF	98		0	0	0	0	0	0	0								0							
Age	25 Pre-Peak	99		0	0	0	0	0	0	0								0							
Bats	S	00	aa	54	3	7	0	0	2	130			($2)	203	130	333	8	72	0.33	189		63		0.93	-6.2
Pwr	- - - -	01	aa	252	44	67	1	18	16	266			$7	342	357	699	10	85	0.74	265	68	127		4.03	-3.3
Spd	+ + + + +	02	DET	* 532	79	129	3	41	40	242	235	189	$16	315	327	642	10	78	0.49	232	54	191	2.00	3.69	-19.8
BAvg	No change	1st Half		285	38	59	2	24	20	207			$6	276	288	563	9	79	0.45	230	47	201		2.80	-18.5
LIMA	B+	2nd Half		247	41	70	1	17	20	283			$10	359	372	731	11	78	0.53	235	63	173		4.91	0.3
Risk	Very High	03	Proj	350	56	90	2	26	25	257			$10	331	346	677	10	81	0.58	247	61	160		3.98	-10.2

0-3-2-.200 in 70 AB at DET. Despite mixed success in '02, there is promise here. Pair his 2nd half OB avg with his blazing speed and you have something very exciting. He could be an impact player very soon.

Trammell,Bubba

			Tm	AB	R	H	HR	RBI	SB	Avg	vLH	vRH	R$	OB	Slg	OPS	bb%	ct%	Eye	xBA	PX	SX	G/F	RC/G	RAR
Pos	RF LF	98	TAM	* 416	67	113	26	75	5	272	324	264	$17	347	531	878	10	80	0.57	297	156	67	0.92	6.70	20.5
Age	31 Past Peak	99	TAM	* 469	70	129	21	65	0	275	227	309	$12	351	475	827	10	86	0.83	294	123	27	0.66	6.15	16.1
Bats	R	00	2TM	245	28	65	10	45	4	265	305	245	$8	343	457	800	11	80	0.59	277	112	87	0.80	5.91	6.1
Pwr	- -	01	SD	490	66	128	25	92	2	261	279	255	$17	327	467	794	9	84	0.62	289	117	65	0.84	5.49	-2.7
Spd	No change	02	SD	403	54	98	17	56	1	243	305	213	$8	331	414	746	12	82	0.75	266	101	41	0.90	4.87	-7.0
BAvg	+ + +	1st Half		213	29	50	7	25	1	235			$2	337	366	704	13	84	0.97	259	78	40		4.51	-6.3
LIMA	A	2nd Half		190	25	48	10	31	0	253			$5	324	468	792	10	81	0.54	273	126	49		5.24	-1.0
Risk	Moderate	03	Proj	400	53	106	19	65	1	265			$12	342	460	801	10	82	0.66	278	114	51		5.69	10.1

Poor 1st half and BA vsRHers brought down a season that was not all that different from '01. He tried to make up ground in the 2nd half - and did VERY well - but the depressed stats of slow starts are tough to overcome.

Truby,Chris

			Tm	AB	R	H	HR	RBI	SB	Avg	vLH	vRH	R$	OB	Slg	OPS	bb%	ct%	Eye	xBA	PX	SX	G/F	RC/G	RAR
Pos	3B	98	aa	325	39	78	11	48	7	240			$8	274	422	695	4	86	0.32	298	115	125		3.96	-5.5
Age	29 Past Peak	99	aa	465	65	107	21	72	16	230			$12	275	422	697	6	79	0.30	273	111	116		3.82	-9.2
Bats	R	00	HOU	* 526	55	139	13	85	7	264	355	220	$13	298	411	708	5	84	0.30	279	89	102	0.72	4.32	-1.3
Pwr	- -	01	HOU	* 457	54	118	18	80	9	258	265	186	$15	307	468	775	7	79	0.33	279	127	118	0.80	4.84	2.3
Spd	No change	02	2TM	394	37	86	5	23	2	218	206	217	($2)	241	332	574	3	75	0.12	233	75	119	0.91	2.63	-23.1
BAvg	-	1st Half		224	18	52	3	12	2	232			($1)	252	348	600	3	77	0.12	240	73	124		2.88	-11.5
LIMA	C	2nd Half		170	19	34	2	11	0	200			($3)	227	312	539	3	72	0.13	223	76	99		2.32	-11.5
Risk	High	03	Proj	250	27	59	6	28	3	236			$2	270	383	653	4	77	0.20	258	93	109		3.47	-8.2

Batted .257 in MON, but was eaten up by the AL. Batted .199 after the trade to DET, .219 in tough Comerica with 0 HRs, 3 BB and 26 K. Even went 1 for 18 vs TEX pitching, a team with a 5.15 ERA. Yeesh.

Tucker,Michael

Tucker,Michael			Tm	AB	R	H	HR	RBI	SB	Avg	vLH	vRH	R$	OB	Slg	OPS	bb%	ct%	Eye	xBA	PX	SX	G/F	RC/G	RAR
Pos	RF LF DH	98	ATL	414	54	101	13	46	8	244	263	242	$9	324	418	742	11	73	0.44	253	119	101	1.01	4.87	-1.8
Age	31 Past Peak	99	CIN	296	55	75	11	44	11	253	154	268	$9	336	426	762	11	73	0.46	244	95	162	1.17	5.20	0.9
Bats	L	00	CIN	270	55	72	15	36	13	267	167	276	$12	369	511	881	14	76	0.69	278	136	153	0.88	6.84	14.3
Pwr	+ +	01	2NL	436	62	110	12	61	16	252	211	263	$13	324	415	739	10	77	0.45	258	94	164	1.31	4.72	-13.1
Spd	- - - -	02	KC	475	65	118	12	56	23	248	208	256	$16	328	406	734	11	78	0.53	259	105	146	1.14	4.75	-5.6
BAvg	No change	1st Half		202	30	48	3	20	12	238			$6	339	361	700	13	79	0.74	251	83	156		4.54	-3.9
LIMA	A+	2nd Half		273	35	70	9	36	11	256			$10	319	440	758	8	77	0.40	265	121	130		4.90	-1.9
Risk	High	03	Proj	500	75	126	16	64	22	252			$16	333	427	759	11	77	0.52	261	108	148		5.06	-3.1

He is still getting 80-90 AB each year vsLHers, which is 80-90 AB too many. Without them, he'd be a very valuable platoon player instead of a moderately valuable full-timer. Speed is on the rise, but at 31, is probably at peak.

Tyner,Jason

Tyner,Jason			Tm	AB	R	H	HR	RBI	SB	Avg	vLH	vRH	R$	OB	Slg	OPS	bb%	ct%	Eye	xBA	PX	SX	G/F	RC/G	RAR
Pos	LF	98		0	0	0	0	0	0	0								0							
Age	26 Pre-Peak	99	a/a	526	78	147	0	28	42	279			$17	345	327	672	9	92	1.20	270	34	126		4.19	-16.0
Bats	L	00	2TM	* 451	49	119	0	34	31	264	150	240	$12	305	288	594	6	91	0.69	254	19	97	2.71	2.92	-31.9
Pwr	+	01	TAM	* 553	73	157	0	32	41	284	321	270	$18	318	324	642	5	91	0.55	259	25	139	2.69	3.86	-14.2
Spd	+ + + + +	02	TAM	* 519	67	131	0	32	24	252	189	221	$10	301	299	600	6	92	0.84	255	34	134	2.56	3.23	-26.9
BAvg	+ + +	1st Half		296	38	64	0	17	15	216			$3	268	260	528	7	91	0.78	251	31	148		2.53	-21.7
LIMA	C	2nd Half		223	29	67	0	15	9	300			$7	345	350	694	6	93	0.94	259	37	111		4.35	-3.9
Risk	High	03	Proj	150	19	41	0	9	14	273			$6	318	313	632	6	92	0.79	257	30	129		3.78	-6.2

0-9-7-.214 in 168 AB at TAM but he can do better than that. High contact hitter has shown occasional glimmers of on base ability, the only thing standing in the way of 50-SB seasons. But it's a BIG thing.

Uribe,Juan

Uribe,Juan			Tm	AB	R	H	HR	RBI	SB	Avg	vLH	vRH	R$	OB	Slg	OPS	bb%	ct%	Eye	xBA	PX	SX	G/F	RC/G	RAR
Pos	SS	98		0	0	0	0	0	0	0								0							
Age	23 Growth	99		0	0	0	0	0	0	0								0							
Bats	R	00		0	0	0	0	0	0	0								0							
Pwr	+	01	COL	* 567	65	173	15	92	12	305	311	298	$24	325	517	842	3	85	0.20	306	129	177	1.00	5.96	38.8
Spd	- - - -	02	COL	566	69	136	6	49	9	240	241	240	$4	283	341	624	6	79	0.28	244	65	132	1.34	3.41	-9.7
BAvg	-	1st Half		312	45	78	2	24	5	250			$2	299	346	646	7	80	0.35	248	63	146		3.74	-2.3
LIMA	A+	2nd Half		254	24	58	4	25	4	228			$1	263	335	598	5	78	0.21	239	68	98		3.03	-7.2
Risk	Moderate	03	Proj	550	63	145	10	65	10	264			$12	296	409	706	4	81	0.24	268	91	145		4.25	8.2

A disappointment, but perhaps I should have known better. Coors clouded my vision, discounting his age and poor batting eye. In past years, it didn't matter; in '02 it did. In '03, he'll need to make it on his own.

Valentin,John

Valentin,John			Tm	AB	R	H	HR	RBI	SB	Avg	vLH	vRH	R$	OB	Slg	OPS	bb%	ct%	Eye	xBA	PX	SX	G/F	RC/G	RAR
Pos	SS 1B	98	BOS	588	113	145	23	73	4	247	250	245	$11	334	442	776	12	86	0.94	301	126	70	0.82	5.24	23.6
Age	36 Decline	99	BOS	450	58	114	12	70	0	253	277	247	$7	314	398	712	8	85	0.59	273	93	40	0.83	4.47	3.1
Bats	R	00	BOS	35	6	9	2	2	0	257	400	233	$1	297	457	754	5	86	0.40	292	108	66	0.79	4.22	-0.3
Pwr	No change	01	BOS	* 109	14	21	3	8	0	193	176	209	($1)	290	312	602	12	86	1.00	259	73	30	1.21	3.19	-4.5
Spd	No change	02	NYM	208	18	50	3	30	0	240	178	274	$2	313	356	669	10	82	0.59	254	84	17	0.82	4.03	0.3
BAvg	+ + +	1st Half		100	10	23	3	16	0	230			$1	306	380	686	10	81	0.58	257	98	19		4.14	0.5
LIMA	D	2nd Half		108	8	27	0	14	0	250			$1	319	333	653	9	83	0.61	251	72	17		3.91	-0.2
Risk	Very High	03	Proj	150	17	38	3	19	0	253			$2	329	376	705	10	84	0.71	265	83	29		4.54	3.8

He's clinging on to his last remaining skills, but there is little left worth chasing at the draft table, and at 36, little reason to hope for much more.

Valentin,Jose

Valentin,Jose			Tm	AB	R	H	HR	RBI	SB	Avg	vLH	vRH	R$	OB	Slg	OPS	bb%	ct%	Eye	xBA	PX	SX	G/F	RC/G	RAR
Pos	3B SS	98	MIL	428	65	96	16	49	10	224	229	223	$8	324	393	716	13	75	0.60	258	114	71	0.74	4.41	-1.2
Age	33 Decline	99	MIL	256	45	58	10	38	3	227	253	215	$4	349	418	767	16	80	0.92	272	107	134	0.56	5.28	7.2
Bats	S	00	CHW	568	107	155	25	92	19	273	215	282	$22	341	491	833	9	81	0.56	296	128	150	0.69	6.32	32.8
Pwr	- -	01	CHW	438	74	113	28	68	9	258	203	267	$17	334	509	843	10	74	0.44	265	144	87	0.74	5.97	21.1
Spd	- -	02	CHW	474	70	118	25	75	3	249	152	259	$15	311	479	790	8	79	0.43	285	144	89	0.79	5.20	9.5
BAvg	-	1st Half		249	31	60	10	39	2	241			$6	300	434	734	8	78	0.38	266	120	102		4.47	-0.7
LIMA	A+	2nd Half		225	39	58	15	36	1	258			$9	324	529	853	9	81	0.51	307	169	72		6.08	10.7
Risk	Low	03	Proj	500	82	127	27	78	2	254			$15	326	489	815	10	78	0.49	281	142	83		5.60	15.9

Slightly more aggressive at the plate in '02, which didn't do anything for his productivity, but took a bite out of his OB avg, which he could ill afford. Was a bit better in the 2nd half, but has probably already hit his ceiling.

Vander Wal,John

Vander Wal,John			Tm	AB	R	H	HR	RBI	SB	Avg	vLH	vRH	R$	OB	Slg	OPS	bb%	ct%	Eye	xBA	PX	SX	G/F	RC/G	RAR
Pos	RF	98	2NL	129	21	36	5	20	0	279	167	285	$4	384	512	896	15	74	0.65	274	165	63	1.41	7.55	11.0
Age	37 Decline	99	SD	246	26	67	6	41	2	272	111	285	$6	367	419	786	13	76	0.63	252	101	35	1.64	5.86	6.1
Bats	L	00	PIT	384	74	115	24	94	11	299	200	314	$23	410	563	973	16	76	0.78	286	157	75	0.89	9.18	51.2
Pwr	No change	01	2NL	452	58	122	14	70	8	270	296	266	$14	365	442	808	13	73	0.56	248	107	94	0.94	5.96	4.3
Spd	No change	02	NYY	219	30	57	6	20	1	260	238	263	$4	331	429	760	10	74	0.40	251	120	67	0.94	5.13	0.1
BAvg	- -	1st Half		144	19	40	3	15	1	278			$3	346	444	790	9	74	0.41	256	123	78		5.64	2.4
LIMA	C	2nd Half		75	11	17	3	5	0	227			$1	301	400	701	10	72	0.38	241	114	36		4.25	-2.1
Risk	Very High	03	Proj	200	29	51	6	26	0	255			$4	343	429	773	12	74	0.51	249	116	57		5.34	0.6

The decline is in full swing, further expedited by erratic playing time. It's tough to staty in a groove when you spend so much time on the bench, especially for a 37-year-old.

Varitek,Jason

Varitek,Jason			Tm	AB	R	H	HR	RBI	SB	Avg	vLH	vRH	R$	OB	Slg	OPS	bb%	ct%	Eye	xBA	PX	SX	G/F	RC/G	RAR
Pos	CA	98	BOS	221	31	56	7	33	2	253	278	216	$5	307	407	714	7	80	0.38	262	99	56	1.34	4.35	1.8
Age	31 Past Peak	99	BOS	483	70	130	20	76	1	269	282	266	$12	333	482	815	9	82	0.54	292	134	55	1.07	5.80	24.9
Bats	S	00	BOS	448	55	111	10	65	1	248	254	245	$5	337	388	725	12	81	0.71	265	92	44	1.20	4.80	8.2
Pwr	- -	01	BOS	174	19	51	7	25	0	293	283	298	$6	369	489	858	11	80	0.60	267	121	35	1.48	6.92	16.6
Spd	No change	02	BOS	467	58	124	10	61	4	266	263	266	$11	325	392	717	8	80	0.43	253	90	63	1.20	4.60	13.2
BAvg	- -	1st Half		228	28	61	6	28	2	268			$6	321	404	725	7	82	0.43	262	95	52		4.70	7.1
LIMA	B+	2nd Half		239	30	63	4	33	2	264			$5	328	381	709	9	78	0.43	244	85	68		4.50	6.1
Risk	High	03	Proj	450	55	121	12	63	2	269			$11	337	418	755	9	80	0.52	260	100	51		5.17	15.6

His 1999 power still resides somewhere in his skills set. It's been dormant for three years and may never appear again. But if you have to take a chance on someone who MIGHT provide that extra HR, go with the history.

Vaughn,Greg

Vaughn,Greg			Tm	AB	R	H	HR	RBI	SB	Avg	vLH	vRH	R$	OB	Slg	OPS	bb%	ct%	Eye	xBA	PX	SX	G/F	RC/G	RAR
Pos	LF	98	SD	573	112	156	50	119	11	272	267	275	$34	360	597	957	12	79	0.65	310	195	106	0.80	7.90	55.9
Age	37 Decline	99	CIN	550	104	135	45	118	15	245	262	240	$26	346	535	881	13	75	0.62	279	160	100	0.84	6.80	29.9
Bats	R	00	TAM	461	83	117	28	74	8	254	264	251	$15	364	499	863	15	72	0.63	266	140	85	1.12	6.83	25.3
Pwr	- - -	01	TAM	485	74	113	24	82	11	233	192	244	$14	331	433	764	13	73	0.55	248	120	68	1.00	5.10	6.0
Spd	+ + + + +	02	TAM	251	28	41	8	29	3	163	80	184	($0)	281	315	596	14	67	0.50	218	96	92	0.78	3.01	-16.1
BAvg	+ + + + +	1st Half		251	28	41	8	29	3	163			($0)	281	315	596	14	67	0.50	218	96	92		3.01	-16.1
LIMA	C	2nd Half		0	0	0	0	0	0	0			($0)					0							-0.0
Risk	Low	03	Proj	200	31	48	6	32	2	240			$4	344	387	731	14	72	0.57	232	92	75		4.88	-1.7

How much does TAM value him? He was activated from the DL on 9/1 and rode the bench all of Sept. With one $8 million year left on his contract, you have to wonder what team would assume that much risk.

Vaughn,Mo

Vaughn,Mo			Tm	AB	R	H	HR	RBI	SB	Avg	vLH	vRH	R$	OB	Slg	OPS	bb%	ct%	Eye	xBA	PX	SX	G/F	RC/G	RAR
Pos	1B	98	BOS	609	107	205	40	115	0	337	333	338	$35	397	591	988	9	76	0.42	276	147	41	1.19	9.42	70.2
Age	35 Decline	99	ANA	524	63	147	33	108	0	281	336	258	$21	348	508	855	9	76	0.43	258	127		1.10	6.59	11.3
Bats	L	00	ANA	614	93	167	36	117	2	272	204	303	$21	355	498	853	11	71	0.44	251	128	44	0.96	6.63	11.2
Pwr	No change	01	ANA	0	0	0	0	0	0	0								0							
Spd	No change	02	NYM	487	67	126	26	72	0	259	272	254	$14	339	456	795	11	70	0.41	231	113	23	1.02	5.63	-1.2
BAvg	-	1st Half		232	25	58	9	31	0	250			$4	326	405	731	10	72	0.39	225	93	20		4.72	-7.3
LIMA	B	2nd Half		255	42	68	17	41	0	267			$10	351	502	853	11	69	0.42	235	132	27		6.53	6.7
Risk	High	03	Proj	500	72	137	30	96	0	274			$20	351	497	848	11	72	0.42	247	128	28		6.50	18.0

Considering the one year layoff and playing half his games in Shea (.251 home, .267 road), this was not a bad season. His 2nd half surge was very encouraging and might set the stage for a solid year in '03.

Vazquez,Ramon

	Yr	Tm	AB	R	H	HR	RBI	SB	Avg	vLH	vRH	R$	OB	Slg	OPS	bb%	ct%	Eye	xBA	PX	SX	G/F	RC/G	RAR
Pos 2B SS 3B	98		0	0	0	0	0	0	0								0							
Age 26 Pre-Peak	99	aa	438	56	96	5	44	8	219			$0	314	317	630	12	81	0.74	255	68	91		3.67	-7.2
Bats L	00	aa	405	55	103	7	56	1	253			$5	339	371	709	11	79	0.61	251	76	61		4.43	3.1
Pwr - - -	01	aaa	501	79	130	8	72	8	259			$11	349	360	710	12	84	0.85	257	68	70		4.58	7.5
Spd + + + + +	02	SD	423	50	116	2	32	7	274	157	297	$7	344	362	706	10	81	0.57	248	61	112	2.17	4.72	2.9
BAvg -	1st Half		159	15	38	1	11	1	239			($0)	320	302	622	11	78	0.54	223	37	88		3.52	-5.0
LIMA B+	2nd Half		264	35	78	1	21	6	295			$7	359	398	756	9	83	0.59	262	75	116		5.56	8.8
Risk High	03	Proj	**500**	**66**	**131**	**5**	**52**	**11**	**262**			**$9**	**342**	**358**	**699**	**11**	**81**	**0.65**	**253**	**65**	**104**		**4.57**	**7.5**

Serviceable player, won't likely ever light up the scoreboard, but at least he gets on base almost 35% of the time. Might crack double digits in SBs, but not likely in roto value on Draft Day.

Velarde,Randy

	Yr	Tm	AB	R	H	HR	RBI	SB	Avg	vLH	vRH	R$	OB	Slg	OPS	bb%	ct%	Eye	xBA	PX	SX	G/F	RC/G	RAR
Pos 2B	98	ANA	188	29	49	4	26	7	261	303	252	$5	374	404	778	15	78	0.81	259	97	96	1.66	5.84	11.0
Age 40 Decline	99	2AL	631	105	200	16	76	24	317	348	308	$27	385	455	840	10	84	0.71	276	81	129	1.55	6.90	57.0
Bats R	00	OAK	485	82	135	12	41	9	278	262	285	$10	351	400	751	10	80	0.57	254	76	80	1.46	5.30	20.9
Pwr No change	01	2AL	* 363	53	100	9	35	6	275	297	271	$9	339	416	755	9	75	0.38	240	90	89	1.24	5.25	10.9
Spd - - - - -	02	OAK	150	24	36	3	11	4	240	162	250	$2	313	373	687	10	77	0.47	252	100	90	1.49	4.36	1.1
BAvg No change	1st Half		116	19	32	3	9	4	276			$4	328	448	776	7	78	0.36	274	129	93		5.62	5.3
LIMA F	2nd Half		34	5	4	0	2	0	118			($1)	268	118	386	17	74	0.78	182	0	48		1.33	-3.3
Risk Very High	03	Proj	**0**	**0**	**0**	**0**	**0**	**0**	**0**			**$0**					**0**			**0**	**0**			**0.0**

For the sake of argument, his BPIs still indicate potential for 10-15 HRs, 10-15 SB and a .250-.260 BA should some team decide to lure him away from retirement plans with a promise of a full-time job. Tampa?

Ventura,Robin

	Yr	Tm	AB	R	H	HR	RBI	SB	Avg	vLH	vRH	R$	OB	Slg	OPS	bb%	ct%	Eye	xBA	PX	SX	G/F	RC/G	RAR
Pos 3B	98	CHW	590	84	155	21	91	1	263	277	257	$14	350	436	785	12	81	0.71	271	106	62	0.99	5.66	21.3
Age 35 Decline	99	NYM	588	88	177	32	120	1	301	271	314	$26	379	529	908	11	81	0.68	289	140	30	0.83	7.73	62.1
Bats L	00	NYM	469	61	109	24	84	3	232	225	234	$11	338	439	777	14	81	0.82	282	120	41	1.07	5.22	12.7
Pwr No change	01	NYM	456	70	108	21	61	2	237	271	228	$9	360	419	779	16	78	0.87	260	107	34	0.95	5.45	12.0
Spd No change	02	NYY	465	68	115	27	93	3	247	218	255	$17	369	458	827	16	78	0.89	270	128	43	0.86	6.35	28.5
BAvg + + + + +	1st Half		242	40	62	19	58	2	256			$12	371	521	891	15	79	0.85	287	154	45		7.27	22.2
LIMA A	2nd Half		223	28	53	8	35	1	238			$5	368	390	758	17	78	0.94	252	99	31		5.40	6.5
Risk Low	03	Proj	**450**	**64**	**115**	**25**	**88**	**1**	**256**			**$15**	**371**	**464**	**835**	**16**	**79**	**0.87**	**269**	**125**	**27**		**6.38**	**27.1**

GOOD THINGS
- Batting eye BPIs still solid.
- 1st half power surge
- xBA indicates some BA upside

BAD THINGS
- BA vs LHers
- 2nd half fade

Vidro,Jose

	Yr	Tm	AB	R	H	HR	RBI	SB	Avg	vLH	vRH	R$	OB	Slg	OPS	bb%	ct%	Eye	xBA	PX	SX	G/F	RC/G	RAR
Pos 2B	98	MON	* 440	52	107	1	43	6	243	125	237	$3	316	316	632	10	88	0.90	274	61	81	1.65	3.63	-7.9
Age 28 Peak	99	MON	494	67	150	12	59	0	304	260	315	$13	342	476	818	6	90	0.57	308	120	41	1.36	5.95	24.6
Bats S	00	MON	606	101	200	24	97	5	330	373	315	$28	380	540	920	7	89	0.71	319	133	66	1.74	7.96	65.7
Pwr + +	01	MON	486	82	155	15	59	4	319	348	308	$19	360	486	845	6	90	0.63	305	108	77	1.44	6.76	41.7
Spd No change	02	MON	604	103	190	19	96	2	315	297	321	$26	377	490	867	9	88	0.86	296	114	70	1.67	7.20	51.3
BAvg - -	1st Half		311	54	104	8	55	2	334			$16	389	495	885	8	88	0.78	293	109	68		7.69	30.9
LIMA A	2nd Half		293	49	86	11	41	0	294			$10	363	485	848	10	88	0.94	298	119	60		6.72	20.6
Risk Moderate	03	Proj	**600**	**99**	**187**	**23**	**86**	**3**	**312**			**$25**	**367**	**504**	**871**	**8**	**89**	**0.78**	**306**	**123**	**67**		**7.11**	**56.2**

He still owns 2000's power skills, so despite the recent plateau, that level remains an upside possibility. And at 28, we might see those stats sooner rather than later.

Vina,Fernando

	Yr	Tm	AB	R	H	HR	RBI	SB	Avg	vLH	vRH	R$	OB	Slg	OPS	bb%	ct%	Eye	xBA	PX	SX	G/F	RC/G	RAR
Pos 2B	98	MIL	637	101	198	7	45	22	311	324	305	$22	365	427	792	8	93	1.17	304	86	120	1.50	5.69	29.5
Age 34 Decline	99	MIL	154	17	41	1	16	5	266	333	236	$3	327	331	659	8	96	2.33	291	50	66	1.53	4.00	-1.4
Bats L	00	STL	487	81	146	4	31	10	300	267	311	$11	348	398	746	7	93	1.00	292	65	116	1.38	5.07	9.2
Pwr -	01	STL	631	95	191	9	56	17	303	315	299	$20	336	418	755	5	94	0.91	301	73	133	1.43	5.23	24.4
Spd - - -	02	STL	622	75	168	1	54	17	270	238	280	$11	318	338	656	7	94	1.22	280	50	103	1.55	3.81	-13.1
BAvg + + + + +	1st Half		315	38	90	1	33	11	286			$9	326	368	695	6	93	0.90	284	63	100		4.25	-2.4
LIMA A+	2nd Half		307	37	78	0	21	6	254			$2	310	306	616	8	95	1.67	274	37	101		3.38	-10.6
Risk Low	03	Proj	**625**	**85**	**182**	**2**	**51**	**16**	**291**			**$15**	**337**	**366**	**703**	**6**	**94**	**1.18**	**285**	**53**	**110**		**4.51**	**7.9**

Extreme contact hitter with a good batting eye, a .300 BA will always be close within reach. His brief flirtation with some power and speed seems to have dissipated, you'll have to settle for just the BA.

Vizcaino,Jose

	Yr	Tm	AB	R	H	HR	RBI	SB	Avg	vLH	vRH	R$	OB	Slg	OPS	bb%	ct%	Eye	xBA	PX	SX	G/F	RC/G	RAR
Pos SS 3B 2B	98	LA	237	30	62	3	29	7	262	380	230	$6	311	338	649	7	85	0.49	262	56	78	1.67	3.77	0.7
Age 35 Decline	99	LA	266	27	67	1	29	2	252	329	224	$1	304	297	601	7	91	0.87	268	35	47	2.69	3.27	-2.7
Bats S	00	2TM	267	32	67	0	14	6	251	233	258	$1	308	303	611	8	84	0.51	245	38	93	1.57	3.14	-7.2
Pwr + + +	01	HOU	256	38	71	1	14	3	277	250	282	$3	317	344	661	6	87	0.45	258	43	114	1.51	3.95	2.5
Spd No change	02	HOU	406	53	123	5	37	3	303	337	292	$11	342	397	738	6	90	0.60	271	64	65	1.11	4.94	11.8
BAvg - -	1st Half		156	20	47	1	12	3	301			$4	339	353	692	5	89	0.53	253	38	61		4.31	1.6
LIMA D+	2nd Half		250	33	76	4	25	0	304			$7	343	424	767	6	91	0.65	283	80	62		5.35	10.4
Risk Moderate	03	Proj	**350**	**46**	**99**	**3**	**27**	**4**	**283**			**$6**	**326**	**358**	**684**	**6**	**88**	**0.54**	**264**	**52**	**80**		**4.17**	**4.5**

A Minute-Made man, his stat surge was a product of the ex-Enron factor. Batted .347 at home, .261 on the road. Hit 4 of 5 HRs at home. Had a 1.0 eye ratio at home, 0.3 on the road. Micro-managers take note.

Vizquel,Omar

	Yr	Tm	AB	R	H	HR	RBI	SB	Avg	vLH	vRH	R$	OB	Slg	OPS	bb%	ct%	Eye	xBA	PX	SX	G/F	RC/G	RAR
Pos SS	98	CLE	576	86	166	2	50	37	288	274	294	$20	357	372	729	10	89	0.97	277	60	135	1.06	5.10	20.1
Age 36 Decline	99	CLE	574	112	191	5	66	42	333	333	333	$31	401	436	836	10	91	1.30	293	73	137	0.99	7.26	55.0
Bats S	00	CLE	613	101	176	7	66	22	287	218	311	$17	376	375	751	12	88	1.21	267	58	102	1.23	5.44	18.7
Pwr + + +	01	CLE	611	84	156	2	50	13	255	228	266	$7	323	334	657	9	88	0.85	265	53	115	1.27	3.85	-11.6
Spd - - - -	02	CLE	582	85	160	14	72	18	275	281	273	$20	339	418	756	9	89	0.88	289	96	114	0.85	5.09	7.5
BAvg No change	1st Half		285	43	84	10	45	11	295			$14	378	484	862	12	91	1.46	313	121	122		6.53	17.1
LIMA A+	2nd Half		297	42	76	4	27	7	256			$6	298	354	652	6	87	0.47	266	71	105		3.84	-7.5
Risk Moderate	03	Proj	**550**	**82**	**151**	**8**	**58**	**18**	**275**			**$15**	**342**	**384**	**726**	**9**	**89**	**0.90**	**277**	**74**	**117**		**4.83**	**17.8**

Through July 31, he had posted 13-57-13-.304, the last four weeks accomplished with a torn labrum. He then went 0 for 27 and hobbled to the finish. But good skilled players are more apt to provide surprises like this.

Walbeck,Matt

	Yr	Tm	AB	R	H	HR	RBI	SB	Avg	vLH	vRH	R$	OB	Slg	OPS	bb%	ct%	Eye	xBA	PX	SX	G/F	RC/G	RAR
Pos CA	98	ANA	338	41	87	6	46	1	257	354	241	$5	318	367	685	8	80	0.44	247	71	64	1.17	4.22	1.4
Age 33 Decline	99	ANA	288	26	69	3	22	2	240	266	232	$0	303	306	608	8	84	0.57	241	42	51	1.38	3.22	-8.3
Bats S	00	ANA	146	17	29	6	12	0	199	276	179	($1)	235	356	591	5	85	0.32	275	89	45	1.55	2.66	-6.9
Pwr - - -	01	aaa	339	32	78	4	39	1	230			$1	293	322	614	8	85	0.58	255	66	34		3.27	-5.2
Spd No change	02	DET	* 160	8	33	1	8	0	206	286	219	($1)	240	256	496	4	85	0.29	234	39	13	1.42	2.06	-7.8
BAvg + + +	1st Half		108	6	18	1	6	0	167			($2)	211	231	442	5	89	0.50	252	49	18		1.58	-6.9
LIMA F	2nd Half		52	2	15	0	2	0	288			$1	302	308	610	2	77	0.08	199	18	6		3.38	-0.5
Risk X HIGH	03	Proj	**100**	**7**	**23**	**1**	**7**	**0**	**230**			**($0)**	**270**	**307**	**577**	**5**	**83**	**0.32**	**240**	**55**	**27**		**2.84**	**-3.7**

0-3-.235 in 85 AB at DET.
No value.

Walker,Larry

	Yr	Tm	AB	R	H	HR	RBI	SB	Avg	vLH	vRH	R$	OB	Slg	OPS	bb%	ct%	Eye	xBA	PX	SX	G/F	RC/G	RAR
Pos RF	98	COL	454	113	165	23	67	14	363	321	381	$33	442	630	1072	12	87	1.05	335	184	120	1.73	11.72	99.4
Age 36 Decline	99	COL	438	108	166	37	115	11	379	345	395	$40	451	710	1161	12	88	1.10	343	189	111	1.40	13.55	119.5
Bats L	00	COL	314	64	97	9	51	5	309	341	297	$13	397	506	904	13	87	1.15	308	119	145	1.54	7.64	24.6
Pwr - - - -	01	COL	497	107	174	38	123	14	350	378	338	$42	442	662	1104	14	79	0.80	310	180	103	1.61	12.05	105.6
Spd - - - - -	02	COL	477	95	161	26	104	6	338	337	338	$33	417	602	1019	12	85	0.89	312	163	92	1.46	9.94	70.3
BAvg - -	1st Half		251	55	86	17	58	4	343			$20	421	625	1047	12	86	0.97	319	165	98		10.62	42.4
LIMA B+	2nd Half		226	40	75	9	46	2	332			$14	412	575	988	12	83	0.82	305	160	83		9.23	28.1
Risk Moderate	03	Proj	**450**	**93**	**145**	**25**	**96**	**3**	**322**			**$27**	**408**	**587**	**995**	**13**	**84**	**0.90**	**312**	**161**	**85**		**9.26**	**64.1**

One of the few COL players who remains productive on the road. Hardly a blemish in his BPIs, but at 36, you'd expect to start seeing some skills erosion.

Walker,Todd

			Tm	AB	R	H	HR	RBI	SB	Avg	vLH	vRH	R$	OB	Slg	OPS	bb%	ct%	Eye	xBA	PX	SX	G/F	RC/G	RAR
Pos	2B	98	MIN	528	85	167	12	62	19	316	271	326	$22	372	473	846	8	88	0.72	300	107	106	1.42	6.79	44.2
Age	29 Past Peak	99	MIN	531	62	148	6	46	18	279	178	302	$12	343	397	740	9	84	0.63	273	83	102	1.75	4.95	14.9
Bats	L	00	2TM	* 497	78	148	11	70	13	298	357	286	$17	362	433	795	9	90	0.98	292	82	114	1.39	5.97	27.6
Pwr	No change	01	2NL	551	93	163	17	75	1	296	269	302	$18	355	459	815	8	85	0.62	284	104	52	1.15	5.88	33.3
Spd	No change	02	CIN	612	79	183	11	64	8	299	278	306	$19	352	431	783	8	87	0.62	278	91	78	1.25	5.69	22.5
BAvg	- -	1st Half		286	35	78	4	27	0	273			$4	329	378	707	8	86	0.60	262	73	44		4.47	-0.2
LIMA	A	2nd Half		326	44	105	7	37	8	322			$15	372	479	851	7	87	0.63	291	107	92		6.91	24.2
Risk	Moderate	03	Proj	600	87	180	16	71	9	300			$21	357	456	813	8	87	0.67	288	102	81		6.06	36.5

Solid 2nd half might ordinarily indicate that he could be ready to take the next step up, but he's had a .300-plus half season in each of the past three years. We'll give him a slight uptick, but no more.

Ward,Daryle

			Tm	AB	R	H	HR	RBI	SB	Avg	vLH	vRH	R$	OB	Slg	OPS	bb%	ct%	Eye	xBA	PX	SX	G/F	RC/G	RAR
Pos	LF	98	aaa	466	60	120	15	73	2	258			$11	302	418	721	6	86	0.46	289	107	62		4.54	-6.8
Age	27 Peak	99	HOU	* 391	54	113	27	80	1	289	250	275	$18	333	552	886	6	83	0.39	302	152	41	0.96	6.75	19.1
Bats	L	00	HOU	264	36	68	20	47	0	258	304	253	$10	297	538	835	5	77	0.25	286	152	54	0.78	5.65	2.6
Pwr	+ +	01	HOU	213	21	56	9	39	0	263	308	257	$6	323	460	783	8	77	0.40	266	124		1.09	5.41	-2.7
Spd	No change	02	HOU	453	41	125	12	72	1	276	204	286	$13	325	424	749	7	82	0.40	262	100	22	0.88	4.94	-21.8
BAvg	- -	1st Half		254	16	70	3	30	0	276			$4	311	390	701	5	81	0.27	250	86	14		4.26	-17.2
LIMA	B	2nd Half		199	25	55	9	42	1	276			$8	342	467	810	9	83	0.61	277	117	36		5.87	-4.1
Risk	Moderate	03	Proj	450	49	126	19	80	1	280			$16	332	475	807	7	81	0.40	274	121	34		5.76	14.0

There is one small clue to his power outage... His Slg on the road the past four years has been .513, .421, .395, .394. Have our power expectations been driven by Minute Maid/ Enron/Astros Field inflation?

Wells,Vernon

			Tm	AB	R	H	HR	RBI	SB	Avg	vLH	vRH	R$	OB	Slg	OPS	bb%	ct%	Eye	xBA	PX	SX	G/F	RC/G	RAR
Pos	CF	98		0	0	0	0	0	0	0								0							
Age	24 Growth	99	TOR	* 323	41	98	7	41	11	303	412	225	$12	352	443	794	7	86	0.53	283	91	97	1.04	5.79	9.8
Bats	R	00	aaa	493	69	122	15	59	21	247			$13	308	432	740	8	87	0.67	305	113	141		4.72	2.1
Pwr	No change	01	TOR	* 509	64	144	13	52	19	283	372	264	$17	323	442	765	6	87	0.44	288	105	96	1.30	4.89	-0.9
Spd	No change	02	TOR	608	87	167	23	100	9	275	260	280	$22	306	457	763	4	86	0.32	294	119	104	1.13	4.97	1.7
BAvg	- -	1st Half		274	37	70	9	36	5	255			$8	301	409	710	6	85	0.43	278	104	72		4.28	-5.0
LIMA	A	2nd Half		334	50	97	14	64	4	290			$15	309	497	806	3	87	0.21	307	131	121		5.59	7.0
Risk	Moderate	03	Proj	600	82	166	24	89	11	277			$22	315	477	792	5	86	0.41	302	126	100		5.26	6.5

Further evidence that TOR's running game was suppressed. SB down, speed skills (SX) up. Good power growth, but he's become a hacker; that .306 OB is nothing to be proud of. But there's 30-30 potential here.

White,Rondell

			Tm	AB	R	H	HR	RBI	SB	Avg	vLH	vRH	R$	OB	Slg	OPS	bb%	ct%	Eye	xBA	PX	SX	G/F	RC/G	RAR
Pos	LF	98	MON	357	54	107	17	58	16	300	347	287	$21	354	513	867	8	84	0.53	301	138	106	1.70	6.64	19.2
Age	31 Past Peak	99	MON	539	83	168	22	64	10	312	374	293	$22	350	505	855	6	84	0.38	290	114	108	1.48	6.56	23.0
Bats	R	00	2NL	357	59	111	13	61	5	311	338	304	$16	369	493	862	8	78	0.42	272	116	62	2.25	6.93	17.9
Pwr	- -	01	CHC	323	43	99	17	50	1	307	268	317	$15	358	529	888	7	83	0.46	292	132	48	1.47	7.27	14.5
Spd	No change	02	NYY	455	59	109	14	62	1	240	286	226	$8	279	378	657	5	81	0.29	258	92	48	1.57	3.61	-18.2
BAvg	-	1st Half		244	30	62	9	34	0	254			$6	303	393	696	7	79	0.33	247	86	28		4.26	-5.0
LIMA	B+	2nd Half		211	29	47	5	28	1	223			$2	251	360	611	4	83	0.23	271	100	69		2.92	-12.6
Risk	Moderate	03	Proj	450	63	122	17	66	3	271			$13	317	444	760	6	82	0.36	273	110	64		5.02	-1.5

Huge 2nd half slump, going 0 for 27 at one point. From a BPI perspective, the whole season was a downer. But he's still only 31; his injury history depresses our expectations but the skills are still there.

Widger,Chris

			Tm	AB	R	H	HR	RBI	SB	Avg	vLH	vRH	R$	OB	Slg	OPS	bb%	ct%	Eye	xBA	PX	SX	G/F	RC/G	RAR
Pos	CA	98	MON	417	36	97	15	53	6	233	250	228	$8	283	388	671	7	80	0.34	266	102	65	1.13	3.84	-2.0
Age	31 Past Peak	99	MON	383	42	101	14	56	1	264	350	233	$9	314	441	755	7	78	0.33	263	113	37	1.16	4.79	8.9
Bats	R	00	2TM	292	32	68	13	35	1	233	260	223	$4	304	438	743	9	78	0.48	275	121	58	1.14	4.59	4.0
Pwr	No change	01	SEA	0	0	0	0	0	0	0								0							
Spd	No change	02	NYY	* 281	23	61	7	33	0	217	294	298	$2	257	356	613	5	87	0.41	279	96	37	1.00	2.88	-6.9
BAvg	+ + +	1st Half		217	19	42	7	28	0	194			$1	239	350	589	6	87	0.46	285	103	48		2.51	-7.8
LIMA	D	2nd Half		64	4	19	0	5	0	297			$1	318	375	693	3	86	0.22	259	72	14		4.42	1.4
Risk	Moderate	03	Proj	150	13	39	5	27	0	260			$4	305	420	725	6	82	0.37	270	105	26		4.46	1.8

0-5-.297 in 64 AB at NYY. Family crises have set his career back and you can see how rusty his skills have become. But his short stint in NY was promising, and his history bodes well for '03. Take a flyer.

Wigginton,Ty

			Tm	AB	R	H	HR	RBI	SB	Avg	vLH	vRH	R$	OB	Slg	OPS	bb%	ct%	Eye	xBA	PX	SX	G/F	RC/G	RAR
Pos	3B	98		0	0	0	0	0	0	0								0							
Age	25 Pre-Peak	99		0	0	0	0	0	0	0								0							
Bats	R	00	aa	453	53	113	16	64	4	249			$9	280	417	697	4	78	0.19	263	101	69		3.86	-8.0
Pwr	+ + +	01	a/a	288	30	66	6	21	4	229			$2	297	340	638	9	77	0.42	238	73	52		3.50	-9.6
Spd	+ + + + +	02	NYM	* 499	62	139	11	61	6	279	314	296	$13	339	417	756	8	87	0.71	279	93	71	1.07	5.19	7.9
BAvg	-	1st Half		250	30	74	4	33	4	296			$8	353	404	757	8	87	0.67	267	73	71		5.39	5.5
LIMA	C	2nd Half		249	32	65	7	28	2	261			$5	326	430	756	9	87	0.75	290	112	64		4.99	2.4
Risk	X HIGH	03	Proj	200	23	56	7	26	2	280			$6	338	453	790	8	82	0.49	275	108	66		5.53	6.1

6-18-.302 in 116 AB at NYM, a rather productive cup of tea. Not on the NYM depth chart radar right now, but BPIs show good growth. Keep him on your radar.

Wilkerson,Brad

			Tm	AB	R	H	HR	RBI	SB	Avg	vLH	vRH	R$	OB	Slg	OPS	bb%	ct%	Eye	xBA	PX	SX	G/F	RC/G	RAR
Pos	CF LF 1B	98		0	0	0	0	0	0	0								0							
Age	25 Pre-Peak	99	aa	422	56	91	6	42	3	216			($1)	333	315	648	15	80	0.88	247	67	59		3.73	-12.3
Bats	L	00	a/a	441	80	121	17	68	11	274			$15	377	501	879	14	80	0.85	300	147	89		6.85	33.4
Pwr	+ +	01	MON	* 350	50	84	13	49	13	240			$10	367	411	778	17	70	0.67	237	102	98		5.58	19.8
Spd	+ + + + +	02	MON	507	92	135	20	59	7	266	230	274	$14	367	469	837	14	68	0.50	236	120	137	1.00	6.24	21.3
BAvg	-	1st Half		249	41	70	6	23	2	281			$6	365	426	791	12	72	0.48	233	85	122		5.66	5.5
LIMA	A+	2nd Half		258	51	65	14	36	5	252			$8	369	512	881	16	64	0.52	238	153	150		6.78	15.8
Risk	Very High	03	Proj	500	84	127	24	64	8	254			$14	365	477	842	15	71	0.61	253	133	102		6.22	30.7

Found his power groove in the 2nd half but this is not yet a fait accompli. His 64% contact rate shows no skill other than being able to swing a bat hard. OB and bb% show promise but he was a better hitter 2 years ago.

Williams,Bernie

			Tm	AB	R	H	HR	RBI	SB	Avg	vLH	vRH	R$	OB	Slg	OPS	bb%	ct%	Eye	xBA	PX	SX	G/F	RC/G	RAR
Pos	CF	98	NYY	499	101	169	26	97	15	339	350	333	$32	424	575	999	13	84	0.91	307	140	112	1.82	9.65	78.5
Age	34 Decline	99	NYY	591	116	202	25	115	9	342	297	359	$32	437	536	973	14	84	1.05	289	112	94	1.78	9.39	90.6
Bats	S	00	NYY	537	108	165	30	121	13	307	289	315	$29	388	566	954	12	84	0.85	319	149	126	1.83	8.46	64.5
Pwr	- -	01	NYY	540	102	166	26	94	11	307	311	306	$27	395	522	917	13	88	1.16	305	134	69	1.33	8.01	54.1
Spd	- - - -	02	NYY	612	102	204	19	102	8	333	354	326	$30	413	493	906	12	84	0.86	280	109	74	1.87	8.26	67.2
BAvg	- -	1st Half		302	56	92	10	40	3	305			$12	403	464	867	14	82	0.94	272	105	68		7.31	24.5
LIMA	A	2nd Half		310	46	112	9	62	5	361			$19	423	523	945	10	86	0.75	288	112	73		9.32	43.5
Risk	Very Low	03	Proj	600	107	191	18	110	6	318			$26	400	485	885	12	85	0.92	285	110	75		7.63	53.2

For years we had been waiting for the eventual power surge, but he's had just one 30 HR season. His consistently elevated G/F ratio may hold the key; this could be the best we can expect from now on.

Williams,Matt

			Tm	AB	R	H	HR	RBI	SB	Avg	vLH	vRH	R$	OB	Slg	OPS	bb%	ct%	Eye	xBA	PX	SX	G/F	RC/G	RAR
Pos	3B	98	ARI	510	72	136	20	71	5	267	300	255	$16	324	439	763	8	80	0.42	273	114	73	1.27	5.20	11.1
Age	37 Decline	99	ARI	627	98	190	35	142	2	303	333	291	$30	346	536	882	6	85	0.44	304	140	60	1.02	7.02	49.0
Bats	R	00	ARI	371	43	102	12	47	1	275	311	260	$9	312	431	743	5	86	0.39	288	94	54	1.19	4.79	4.2
Pwr	- - -	01	ARI	408	58	112	16	65	1	275	313	259	$13	312	466	777	5	83	0.31	287	122	50	0.85	5.27	7.2
Spd	No change	02	ARI	226	30	57	13	41	3	252	289	242	$8	316	473	789	9	82	0.51	280	122	90	1.10	5.33	4.6
BAvg	No change	1st Half		0	0	0	0	0	0	0			($0)					0			0				-0.0
LIMA	B+	2nd Half		226	30	57	13	41	3	252			$8	316	473	789	9	82	0.51	280	122	90		5.33	4.6
Risk	Very High	03	Proj	350	47	93	16	58	2	266			$11	314	465	779	7	83	0.43	286	118	74		5.24	7.4

Given his age and injury history, it is a credit to him that he was able to post nearly identical BPIs to last year. But, given his age and injury history, he is a high risk pick for 2003.

Wilson,Craig

		Yr	Tm	AB	R	H	HR	RBI	SB	Avg	vLH	vRH	R$	OB	Slg	OPS	bb%	ct%	Eye	xBA	PX	SX	G/F	RC/G	RAR
Pos	RF 1B	98	aa	148	15	44	4	16	3	297			$5	346	446	792	7	84	0.46	279	104	51		5.81	3.3
Age	26 Pre-Peak	99	aa	362	49	91	18	59	1	251			$9	316	470	785	9	75	0.37	263	130	58		5.14	0.7
Bats	R	00	aaa	396	66	100	27	68	1	253			$12	312	520	832	8	74	0.33	278	152	57		5.66	6.5
Pwr	+ +	01	PIT	* 203	30	61	14	34	3	300	378	283	$11	355	552	906	8	68	0.27	245	133	104	1.23	7.36	10.6
Spd	No change	02	PIT	368	48	97	16	57	2	264	313	242	$11	323	443	765	8	68	0.28	224	106	54	0.98	5.05	-4.1
BAvg	- -	1st Half		185	25	53	6	32	1	286			$7	327	438	764	6	69	0.19	220	96	46		5.08	-1.8
LIMA	B	2nd Half		183	23	44	10	25	1	240			$4	319	448	767	10	68	0.36	229	116	63		5.03	-2.2
Risk	Very High	03	Proj	350	48	89	19	55	1	254			$10	315	471	786	8	70	0.30	243	124	62		5.19	3.1

His greatest accomplishment occurred on August 4 when he played his 5th game at catcher, thereby qualifying at that postion in many leagues. Still just a hacker with power, his value will be limited in 2003.

Wilson,Dan

		Yr	Tm	AB	R	H	HR	RBI	SB	Avg	vLH	vRH	R$	OB	Slg	OPS	bb%	ct%	Eye	xBA	PX	SX	G/F	RC/G	RAR
Pos	CA	98	SEA	325	39	82	9	44	2	252	317	237	$5	304	394	698	7	83	0.43	267	90	60	0.99	4.25	1.6
Age	34 Decline	99	SEA	414	46	110	7	38	5	266	255	269	$6	314	382	695	7	80	0.35	253	77	85	0.95	4.43	3.5
Bats	R	00	SEA	268	31	63	5	27	1	235	234	235	$1	293	336	629	8	81	0.43	246	65	43	1.12	3.39	-7.0
Pwr	No change	01	SEA	377	44	100	10	42	3	265	290	252	$8	302	403	705	5	82	0.29	258	88	60	0.83	4.31	4.2
Spd	No change	02	SEA	359	35	106	6	44	1	295	288	298	$9	329	396	724	5	77	0.22	234	71	48	0.96	4.88	12.8
BAvg	- - -	1st Half		169	16	53	3	23	1	314			$6	341	414	755	4	78	0.18	232	67	62		5.42	8.7
LIMA	D+	2nd Half		190	19	53	3	21	0	279			$4	318	379	697	5	77	0.26	235	74	24		4.44	4.3
Risk	Moderate	03	Proj	350	37	91	6	40	1	260			$5	301	366	666	6	79	0.28	242	72	48		3.91	-1.7

This near-.300 season is deceptive as his batting eye continued to decline. 2nd half fade will likely foretell a decline in 2003, and if xBA has any say, even worse.

Wilson,Enrique

		Yr	Tm	AB	R	H	HR	RBI	SB	Avg	vLH	vRH	R$	OB	Slg	OPS	bb%	ct%	Eye	xBA	PX	SX	G/F	RC/G	RAR
Pos	3B	98	CLE	* 311	51	90	6	34	10	289	388	244	$10	336	412	748	7	91	0.79	294	85	86	1.86	4.97	4.0
Age	29 Past Peak	99	CLE	332	41	87	2	24	5	262	255	266	$3	314	352	666	7	88	0.61	271	68	75	1.52	3.91	-6.2
Bats	S	00	2TM	239	27	70	5	27	2	293	349	273	$6	342	427	769	7	90	0.75	294	87	57	1.62	5.38	6.8
Pwr	No change	01	2TM	228	17	48	2	20	0	211	188	217	($2)	241	281	521	4	84	0.24	243	47	46	2.10	2.01	-17.3
Spd	No change	02	NYY	105	17	19	2	11	1	181	105	224	($0)	239	295	534	7	79	0.36	240	66	169	1.06	2.27	-7.4
BAvg	+ + + + +	1st Half		54	10	10	2	8	0	185			$0	254	296	551	8	83	0.56	246	60	83		2.33	-3.8
LIMA	D+	2nd Half		51	7	9	0	3	1	176			($1)	222	294	516	6	75	0.23	234	72	265		2.20	-3.6
Risk	High	03	Proj	150	19	33	2	14	1	220			$0	267	322	589	6	82	0.37	251	63	116		2.83	-8.1

Fell off the cliff in 2001, and has been unable to climb back up. Part of the reason was that he was 28 last year, but only 25 the year before. Plus, some stuff about a nerve problem in his fingers. Or something.

Wilson,Jack

		Yr	Tm	AB	R	H	HR	RBI	SB	Avg	vLH	vRH	R$	OB	Slg	OPS	bb%	ct%	Eye	xBA	PX	SX	G/F	RC/G	RAR
Pos	SS	98		0	0	0	0	0	0	0								0							
Age	25 Pre-Peak	99		0	0	0	0	0	0	0								0							
Bats	R	00	aa	482	74	126	7	45	3	261			$5	330	392	722	9	85	0.70	277	81	112		4.52	7.6
Pwr	- -	01	PIT	* 493	60	121	4	30	3	245	220	224	$1	279	325	604	4	84	0.28	252	56	73	1.23	3.05	-8.5
Spd	No change	02	PIT	527	77	133	4	47	5	252	360	223	$4	301	332	633	7	86	0.50	258	54	103	1.16	3.59	-6.2
BAvg	No change	1st Half		250	31	65	0	15	4	260			$2	307	316	623	6	86	0.49	250	42	98		3.49	-3.7
LIMA	B	2nd Half		277	46	68	4	32	1	245			$2	296	347	643	7	86	0.51	263	66	95		3.68	-2.5
Risk	Moderate	03	Proj	500	70	130	5	41	6	260			$6	306	350	656	6	85	0.45	261	61	100		3.82	1.0

Slight improvement in his BPIs, mostly due to him figuring out LHers. But 75% of his AB are vs RHers, and those guys still have his number. Went undrafted and unFAABed for four months in LABR, a feat for a F/T player.

Wilson,Preston

		Yr	Tm	AB	R	H	HR	RBI	SB	Avg	vLH	vRH	R$	OB	Slg	OPS	bb%	ct%	Eye	xBA	PX	SX	G/F	RC/G	RAR
Pos	CF	98	2NL	* 480	68	107	19	69	12	223	80	231	$11	274	410	685	7	73	0.26	255	123	121	4.20	3.82	-8.5
Age	28 Peak	99	FLA	482	67	135	26	71	11	280	285	279	$19	343	502	845	9	68	0.29	238	128	104	1.13	6.32	29.0
Bats	R	00	FLA	605	94	160	31	121	36	264	250	269	$32	326	486	812	8	69	0.29	248	130	120	1.27	5.53	21.1
Pwr	No change	01	FLA	468	70	128	23	71	20	274	208	293	$22	325	494	819	7	77	0.34	277	132	111	0.99	5.69	25.3
Spd	+	02	FLA	510	80	124	23	65	20	243	242	244	$17	320	429	750	10	73	0.41	244	109	105	1.40	4.73	-3.9
BAvg	No change	1st Half		287	51	69	13	39	18	240			$12	331	443	774	12	70	0.45	243	120	136		5.14	1.6
LIMA	A	2nd Half		223	29	55	10	26	2	247			$5	306	413	718	8	76	0.35	242	95	46		4.20	-5.3
Risk	Low	03	Proj	500	75	130	26	72	29	260			$24	324	471	795	9	73	0.35	257	124	115		5.41	16.0

Hurt his wrist crashing into the Wrigley Field wall on 7/13, then his hamstring, and his power and speed went MIA the rest of the way. Odds are he will be undervalued, so if healthy, grab him if bidding stops under $20.

Wilson,Tom

		Yr	Tm	AB	R	H	HR	RBI	SB	Avg	vLH	vRH	R$	OB	Slg	OPS	bb%	ct%	Eye	xBA	PX	SX	G/F	RC/G	RAR
Pos	CA	98	aaa	370	39	88	7	35	2	238			$3	284	343	628	6	84	0.40	261	69	68		3.41	-7.2
Age	32 Past Peak	99	a/a	319	34	66	15	42	0	208			$2	299	398	697	12	73	0.49	244	114			4.07	-0.2
Bats	R	00	aaa	330	45	75	15	50	2	226			$5	331	416	748	14	71	0.54	244	111	39		4.91	8.3
Pwr	+	01	aaa	280	35	61	7	38	0	218			$1	307	343	650	11	79	0.61	245	78	46	0.40	3.71	-0.5
Spd	No change	02	TOR	265	33	68	8	37	0	257	337	220	$6	328	385	713	10	70	0.35	218	84	26	0.96	4.63	7.9
BAvg	- -	1st Half		144	21	35	5	19	0	243			$3	339	382	721	13	70	0.49	220	88	30		4.80	5.2
LIMA	D+	2nd Half		121	12	33	3	18	0	273			$3	312	388	701	5	70	0.19	215	78	21		4.42	2.7
Risk	Very High	03	Proj	250	30	65	11	40	0	260			$7	335	429	763	10	73	0.42	239	103	26		5.24	9.3

Drafters might go an extra buck based on the promise of power displayed several years ago. That's not a bad pct play in '03. Older CA's tend to have late power spikes and he does own those skills.

Wilson,Vance

		Yr	Tm	AB	R	H	HR	RBI	SB	Avg	vLH	vRH	R$	OB	Slg	OPS	bb%	ct%	Eye	xBA	PX	SX	G/F	RC/G	RAR
Pos	CA	98	aaa	154	15	35	3	13	0	227			$0	261	305	566	4	84	0.28	247	48	36		2.56	-6.8
Age	30 Past Peak	99	aaa	53	9	12	2	4	1	226			$1	268	377	645	5	83	0.33	272	90	87		3.23	-1.4
Bats	R	00	aaa	404	38	88	12	49	9	218			$4	253	361	614	4	84	0.30	276	88	75		2.90	-15.1
Pwr	+ +	01	NYM	* 285	23	65	5	33	0	228	286	300	$1	259	333	593	4	82	0.24	254	72	26	1.31	2.85	-6.3
Spd	No change	02	NYM	163	19	40	5	26	0	245	125	275	$3	268	380	648	3	80	0.16	250	84	41	1.04	3.41	-3.8
BAvg	- -	1st Half		84	9	21	2	14	0	250			$1	259	381	640	1	86	0.08	268	88	34		3.38	-2.0
LIMA	F	2nd Half		79	10	19	3	12	0	241			$1	277	380	657	5	75	0.20	231	80	45		3.44	-1.8
Risk	X HIGH	03	Proj	150	16	38	4	20	0	253			$2	282	374	656	4	81	0.21	252	75	33		3.54	-2.0

Stable skill set, which is not a good thing at this level. BPIs are poor and not likely going anywhere as he enters his 30something years.

Winn,Randy

		Yr	Tm	AB	R	H	HR	RBI	SB	Avg	vLH	vRH	R$	OB	Slg	OPS	bb%	ct%	Eye	xBA	PX	SX	G/F	RC/G	RAR
Pos	CF	98	TAM	* 461	73	127	2	31	35	275	289	274	$15	336	367	703	8	80	0.47	255	54	197	2.89	4.43	-6.0
Age	28 Peak	99	TAM	* 510	77	150	5	50	17	294	238	278	$14	333	416	749	6	83	0.35	273	83	129	2.65	4.75	-0.8
Bats	S	00	TAM	* 462	77	128	6	46	19	277	256	250	$12	363	387	750	12	86	0.98	273	73	108	1.73	5.09	5.1
Pwr	+ + + +	01	TAM	429	54	117	6	50	12	273	306	259	$11	332	401	733	8	81	0.47	261	84	118	1.91	4.63	-4.3
Spd	+ + + +	02	TAM	607	87	181	14	75	27	298	347	283	$27	356	461	818	8	82	0.50	277	110	153	1.46	6.24	25.8
BAvg	- -	1st Half		313	46	96	6	39	15	307			$15	348	473	821	6	85	0.43	291	114	172		6.25	13.1
LIMA	A	2nd Half		294	41	85	8	36	12	289			$12	365	449	814	11	79	0.56	262	107	124		6.22	12.6
Risk	Moderate	03	Proj	600	96	167	19	78	34	278			$27	343	459	802	9	82	0.55	284	114	154		5.75	16.0

Hints of this breakout were scattered across the past few years. Legitimate? Somewhat. BA will drop a bit, but at 28, there could still be a 20-40 year out there. I'd be more confident if he wasn't in Safeco, though.

Wise,DeWayne

		Yr	Tm	AB	R	H	HR	RBI	SB	Avg	vLH	vRH	R$	OB	Slg	OPS	bb%	ct%	Eye	xBA	PX	SX	G/F	RC/G	RAR
Pos	RF	98		0	0	0	0	0	0	0								0							
Age	25 Pre-Peak	99		0	0	0	0	0	0	0								0							
Bats	L	00		0	0	0	0	0	0	0								0							
Pwr	+ + + +	01	a/a	386	41	84	7	37	12	218			$4	254	332	586	5	85	0.32	266	68	130		2.72	-30.7
Spd	No change	02	TOR	* 452	58	106	11	49	16	235	136	189	$11	276	374	650	5	88	0.47	284	94	118	1.45	3.37	-24.0
BAvg	No change	1st Half		278	42	77	7	37	9	277			$10	323	424	748	6	85	0.45	277	97	127		4.76	-3.0
LIMA	C	2nd Half		174	16	29	4	12	7	167			$0	199	293	492	4	93	0.54	296	90	102		1.71	-17.7
Risk	High	03	Proj	150	17	38	4	14	6	253			$4	289	398	688	5	87	0.41	284	91	104		3.88	-6.2

3-13-5-.179 in 112 AB at TOR. 1st half showed some signs of growth. He needs to maintain that level at a minimum if there's any hope of sticking in the bigs.

Womack,Tony		Yr	Tm	AB	R	H	HR	RBI	SB	Avg	vLH	vRH	R$	OB	Slg	OPS	bb%	ct%	Eye	xBA	PX	SX	G/F	RC/G	RAR
Pos	SS	98	PIT	655	85	185	3	45	58	282	244	295	$28	322	357	679	5	86	0.40	267	55	159	1.82	4.54	16.9
Age	33 Decline	99	ARI	614	111	170	4	41	72	277	290	272	$29	333	370	703	8	89	0.76	281	60	186	1.31	4.87	24.1
Bats	L	00	ARI	617	95	167	7	57	45	271	276	269	$22	304	384	689	5	88	0.41	280	65	199	1.52	4.26	13.6
Pwr	+	01	ARI	481	66	128	3	30	28	266	188	286	$13	300	345	645	5	89	0.43	271	52	151	1.66	3.78	2.1
Spd	-----	02	ARI	590	90	160	5	57	29	271	214	297	$18	324	353	676	7	86	0.58	262	54	132	1.58	4.14	2.9
BAvg	-	1st Half		301	43	76	1	27	11	252			$5	306	322	628	7	84	0.47	251	48	134		3.60	-3.5
LIMA	A+	2nd Half		289	47	84	4	30	18	291			$13	343	384	727	7	89	0.74	273	60	125		4.73	6.7
Risk	High	03	Proj	600	90	159	5	51	27	265			$15	310	353	663	6	88	0.53	270	56	144		3.88	2.4

Speed skills are in decline, and struggles vsLHers continue, but he still maintains his roto value, in a one-dimensional sort of way. 2nd half surge shows he can still step it up, but 1st half levels will become more prevalent at 33.

Woodward,Chris		Yr	Tm	AB	R	H	HR	RBI	SB	Avg	vLH	vRH	R$	OB	Slg	OPS	bb%	ct%	Eye	xBA	PX	SX	G/F	RC/G	RAR
Pos	SS	98	a/a	338	42	78	4	30	4	231			$1	297	322	620	9	83	0.55	257	69	58		3.26	-6.1
Age	26 Pre-Peak	99	aaa	281	38	74	1	16	3	263			$1	337	359	696	10	86	0.78	271	73	85	1.33	4.52	5.3
Bats	R	00	TOR	* 247	35	62	7	35	3	251	235	172	$4	305	433	738	7	79	0.37	277	116	105	0.93	4.76	2.0
Pwr	++	01	TOR	* 256	34	67	12	31	0	262	77	220	$6	300	500	800	5	82	0.30	292	142	93	1.18	5.23	6.0
Spd	No change	02	TOR	312	48	86	13	45	3	276	149	315	$11	331	468	799	8	77	0.36	263	118	123	0.82	5.77	10.6
BAvg	--	1st Half		58	11	16	3	5	1	276			$2	333	621	954	8	76	0.36	314	195	387		7.65	5.4
LIMA	A	2nd Half		254	37	70	10	40	2	276			$9	331	433	764	8	77	0.36	251	100	58		5.34	5.3
Risk	High	03	Proj	450	67	115	17	55	4	256			$10	309	463	772	7	79	0.37	280	126	151		5.13	18.4

Played full time in the 2nd half, but would have been a .315 hitter had he not been forced to face LHers. So any effort to keep him as a full-timer will depress his overall output.

Wooten,Shawn		Yr	Tm	AB	R	H	HR	RBI	SB	Avg	vLH	vRH	R$	OB	Slg	OPS	bb%	ct%	Eye	xBA	PX	SX	G/F	RC/G	RAR
Pos	DH	98	aa	28	2	8	1	5	0	286			$1	333	500	833	7	82	0.40	296	153			6.17	0.7
Age	30 Past Peak	99	aa	518	55	119	15	69	2	230			$5	285	361	646	7	77	0.34	246	80	50		3.58	-27.4
Bats	R	00	a/a	443	61	128	18	63	4	289			$14	333	494	827	6	86	0.47	305	123	93		6.10	12.2
Pwr	No change	01	ANA	221	24	69	8	32	2	312	304	321	$9	327	466	793	2	81	0.12	257	90	61	0.67	5.79	2.9
Spd	No change	02	ANA	* 155	15	42	3	24	2	271	282	310	$4	298	394	692	4	79	0.18	250	91	54	0.89	4.28	-6.3
BAvg	--	1st Half		17	1	4	0	3	0	235			$0	235	294	529	0	82	0.00	237	54	22		2.31	-1.6
LIMA	D+	2nd Half		138	14	38	3	21	2	275			$4	306	406	711	4	78	0.20	251	95	55		4.57	-4.4
Risk	X HIGH	03	Proj	350	41	93	9	41	1	266			$7	302	414	716	5	81	0.28	265	97	69		4.49	-10.7

Attracted attention by hacking his way to decent BAs in '00 and '01, but his recent xBA shows h is true baseline. 2000 was his only notable year, but bidders will recall it with fondness. You look at the big picture.

Young,Dmitri		Yr	Tm	AB	R	H	HR	RBI	SB	Avg	vLH	vRH	R$	OB	Slg	OPS	bb%	ct%	Eye	xBA	PX	SX	G/F	RC/G	RAR
Pos	DH	98	CIN	536	81	166	14	83	2	310	320	306	$20	365	481	847	8	82	0.50	288	128	50	1.51	6.63	20.5
Age	29 Past Peak	99	CIN	373	63	112	14	56	3	300	266	314	$13	352	504	856	7	81	0.42	286	132	82	1.80	6.72	16.4
Bats	S	00	CIN	548	68	166	18	88	0	303	333	292	$19	346	491	837	6	85	0.45	298	116	61	1.85	6.28	18.2
Pwr	++	01	CIN	540	68	163	21	69	8	302	280	311	$22	347	481	828	6	86	0.48	290	108	79	1.61	6.18	13.8
Spd	-----	02	DET	201	25	57	7	27	2	284	296	279	$7	324	458	782	6	81	0.31	274	121	55	1.79	5.52	-0.8
BAvg	--	1st Half		187	23	52	5	23	2	278			$5	318	433	751	6	80	0.30	268	112	58		5.10	-3.0
LIMA	A	2nd Half		14	2	5	2	4	0	357			$1	400	786	1186	7	86	0.50	362	231	-10		12.76	3.1
Risk	Low	03	Proj	500	67	139	16	70	1	278			$13	324	453	777	6	83	0.40	280	116	53		5.30	-3.0

Early results look like his stats were negatively impacted by Comerica, but there's not enough data to decide for sure. After his slow recovery, expect there to be some drop-off from previous years, though.

Young,Eric		Yr	Tm	AB	R	H	HR	RBI	SB	Avg	vLH	vRH	R$	OB	Slg	OPS	bb%	ct%	Eye	xBA	PX	SX	G/F	RC/G	RAR
Pos	2B	98	LA	452	78	129	8	43	42	285	258	292	$24	350	396	746	9	93	1.41	302	81	125	1.52	5.23	14.6
Age	35 Decline	99	LA	456	73	128	2	41	51	281	295	275	$22	368	355	723	12	94	2.42	292	56	118	1.29	4.86	8.3
Bats	R	00	CHC	607	98	180	6	47	54	297	341	284	$28	363	399	761	9	94	1.62	301	74	126	1.40	5.93	28.3
Pwr	----	01	CHC	603	98	168	6	42	31	279	308	271	$18	326	393	719	7	93	0.93	301	82	132	1.27	4.56	11.4
Spd	----	02	MIL	496	57	139	3	28	31	280	292	278	$16	333	369	702	7	92	1.03	284	65	114	1.43	4.53	0.4
BAvg	+++	1st Half		260	30	62	2	17	13	238			$4	300	335	635	8	93	1.28	289	68	115		3.48	-8.3
LIMA	A+	2nd Half		236	27	77	1	11	18	326			$12	369	407	776	6	92	0.80	279	62	106		5.95	10.4
Risk	Low	03	Proj	500	69	139	3	33	29	278			$15	333	370	703	8	93	1.12	290	68	119		4.51	6.3

2nd half surge put him back on track and net result was only slightly off from '01. MIL sat him down the stretch because they needed to look at younger guys, but even at 35, his skill set is better than anyone they have.

Young,Kevin		Yr	Tm	AB	R	H	HR	RBI	SB	Avg	vLH	vRH	R$	OB	Slg	OPS	bb%	ct%	Eye	xBA	PX	SX	G/F	RC/G	RAR
Pos	1B	98	PIT	592	88	160	27	108	15	270	248	277	$26	321	481	802	7	79	0.35	282	141	96	0.95	5.47	1.5
Age	33 Decline	99	PIT	584	103	174	26	106	22	298	308	294	$29	378	522	900	11	79	0.60	283	138	122	0.86	7.40	37.4
Bats	R	00	PIT	496	77	128	20	88	8	258	264	256	$15	303	433	736	6	81	0.33	276	106	79	0.73	4.65	-12.2
Pwr	-	01	PIT	449	53	104	14	65	15	232	270	224	$11	297	399	696	9	73	0.35	250	110	77	0.67	3.89	-34.9
Spd	-----	02	PIT	468	60	115	16	51	4	246	283	235	$8	319	408	727	10	78	0.50	255	102	55	0.60	4.49	-18.1
BAvg	-	1st Half		225	29	54	8	20	2	240			$3	308	422	730	9	76	0.40	254	120	49		4.32	-9.8
LIMA	B	2nd Half		243	31	61	8	31	2	251			$5	328	395	723	10	81	0.61	255	86	62		4.64	-8.3
Risk	Very Low	03	Proj	450	60	109	14	57	3	242			$7	309	399	709	9	78	0.44	256	101	56		4.19	-16.7

The business of baseball... He made too much money to sit on the bench, but not too much to have a negative impact at a key offensive position for a team that was 15th in the NL in scoring.

Young,Mike		Yr	Tm	AB	R	H	HR	RBI	SB	Avg	vLH	vRH	R$	OB	Slg	OPS	bb%	ct%	Eye	xBA	PX	SX	G/F	RC/G	RAR
Pos	2B	98		0	0	0	0	0	0	0								0							
Age	26 Pre-Peak	99		0	0	0	0	0	0	0								0							
Bats	R	00	aa	533	60	133	6	58	18	250			$9	301	373	674	7	85	0.49	277	82	128		3.85	-5.7
Pwr	--	01	TEX	* 575	80	147	18	72	6	256	255	247	$12	307	409	716	7	79	0.36	257	93	87	1.44	4.43	2.5
Spd	+++++	02	TEX	573	77	150	9	62	6	262	290	251	$11	311	382	693	7	80	0.37	252	80	118	1.64	4.14	0.3
BAvg	--	1st Half		257	32	67	7	36	6	261			$8	314	409	723	7	78	0.36	253	94	120		4.54	3.3
LIMA	B	2nd Half		316	45	83	2	26	0	263			$3	309	361	669	6	82	0.38	249	69	106		3.81	-2.9
Risk	Moderate	03	Proj	450	60	116	7	51	6	258			$8	308	376	684	7	81	0.38	254	78	109		4.04	-2.2

You can't justify giving this guy full time ABs either. BPIs are way too soft for a 3Bman... oh, but wait. He's 26 with two years of experience. In that case, I'll project 30 HRs and a .325 BA. (It's near the end. I'm giddy.)

Zaun,Gregg		Yr	Tm	AB	R	H	HR	RBI	SB	Avg	vLH	vRH	R$	OB	Slg	OPS	bb%	ct%	Eye	xBA	PX	SX	G/F	RC/G	RAR
Pos	CA	98	FLA	298	19	56	5	29	5	188	87	206	($1)	273	292	565	11	83	0.67	261	71	73	1.16	2.76	-11.8
Age	31 Past Peak	99	TEX	93	12	23	1	12	1	247	211	257	$1	320	323	643	10	92	1.43	271	44	90	1.62	3.87	-0.8
Bats	S	00	2AL	234	36	64	7	33	7	274	324	265	$7	386	410	797	16	85	1.26	274	83	66	1.08	6.13	15.0
Pwr	---	01	KC	125	15	40	6	18	1	320	264	361	$6	380	536	916	9	87	0.75	299	135	30	1.20	7.56	14.2
Spd	No change	02	HOU	185	18	41	3	24	1	222	316	197	$1	269	319	588	6	81	0.33	242	62	67	1.11	2.98	-6.8
BAvg	No change	1st Half		115	13	27	2	17	1	235			$1	302	348	649	9	83	0.55	255	72	82		3.79	-1.5
LIMA	D	2nd Half		70	5	14	1	7	0	200			($1)	211	271	483	1	77	0.06	220	46	26		1.85	-4.8
Risk	Very High	03	Proj	150	16	42	4	19	1	280			$4	337	404	742	8	83	0.50	259	80	40		5.03	4.9

One of my prime $1 sleepers went pbffft. But then the news on 10/14 that he had surgery for a torn elbow tendon, and it all came into focus. If these players really think they can hide injuries, they're idiots.

Zeile,Todd		Yr	Tm	AB	R	H	HR	RBI	SB	Avg	vLH	vRH	R$	OB	Slg	OPS	bb%	ct%	Eye	xBA	PX	SX	G/F	RC/G	RAR
Pos	3B	98	2TM	572	85	155	19	94	4	271	279	269	$17	349	437	787	11	84	0.77	284	108	69	1.02	5.61	19.9
Age	37 Decline	99	TEX	588	80	172	24	98	1	293	291	293	$19	354	488	842	9	84	0.60	288	122	38	1.18	6.47	36.0
Bats	R	00	NYM	544	67	146	22	79	3	268	248	274	$14	356	467	823	12	84	0.87	297	121	53	1.22	6.09	29.8
Pwr	+++	01	NYM	531	66	141	10	62	1	266	288	260	$9	354	373	727	12	81	0.72	250	70	45	1.38	5.04	6.2
Spd	No change	02	COL	506	61	138	18	87	1	273	274	272	$16	357	425	782	12	82	0.72	259	93	29	1.79	5.71	16.7
BAvg	No change	1st Half		268	34	77	13	49	0	287			$11	368	481	849	11	84	0.77	275	116	17		6.76	18.0
LIMA	A	2nd Half		238	27	61	5	38	1	256			$5	344	361	706	12	80	0.67	240	68	35		4.63	-0.4
Risk	Moderate	03	Proj	500	62	145	20	86	1	290			$19	372	465	838	12	82	0.73	271	106	37		6.63	33.6

En route to a Coors-inflated breakout, he ran into a .145 BA in July. Rebounded to hit over .300 the rest of the way, but without the power. Net result lost the Coors edge. It's still there, though, lying in wait for 2003.

The Pitchers

QUALIFICATION: All pitchers who accumulated at least 40 IP in the majors in 2002 are included. Some select players with fewer than 40 IP are included if we believe they will have an impact in 2003. Remember that low IP totals raise the risk of any analysis or projection, so be cautious when reviewing any pitcher with fewer than 50 IP in 2002.

This book is designed to be an historical analysis, so players who will likely have a vital role in 2003, but spent the better part of 2002 on the sidelines or in the minors, are not included. We cover some of them briefly on page 146 and others in the Top Prospects section. All of these players will appear on BaseballHQ.com over the winter as their 2003 roles and projected impacts become clearer.

THROWS: The side from which he throws — right (RH) or left (LH).

ROLE: Pitchers are classified as Starters (20 or more batters faced per game projected for 2003) or Relievers (under 20 BF/G).

AGE: Each pitcher's current age is shown, along with a description of the associated stage in his career.

TYPE evaluates the extent to which a pitcher allows the ball to be put into play. CONTACT represents those pitchers who allow the ball to be put into play a great deal. POWER represents those with high strikeout and/or walk totals who keep the ball out of play.

(BURN)OUT POTENTIAL evaluates a pitcher's workload level and trend over the past five years. Each incidence of a high-risk season is noted. Based on the number and severity of incidences, the potential for future burnout is rated as None, Low, Moderate, High and Very High.

ERA POTENTIAL: This looks at a pitcher's 2002 ERA to XERA variance, his BPV level and his strand rate in determining the likely direction for his 2003 ERA. It is the same as the ERA Potential (EP) gauge used during the season on Baseball HQ to project in-season changes in ERA. A pitcher's potential change in performance from 2002 is expressed on a graphical +/- scale. The scale runs from "- - - - -" representing high potential for decline to "+ + + + +" representing high potential for improvement. Plusses are always good and minuses are always bad, so there is no confusion. Also note that this is *not* the *amount* of performance change; it represents the *probability* of change.

Each pitcher's 2003 projection may or may not reflect these indicators. We evaluate every projection and often overrule the BPIs if we feel the situation warrants it.

SUPPORT: The average number of runs (per 9 innings pitched) scored by the offense during the time he is the pitcher of record.

LIMA GRADE: Rating that evaluates how well that pitcher would be a good fit for a team employing the LIMA Plan. Best grades will go to pitchers who have excellent base skills (BPV) and had a 2002 Rotisserie value under $20. Lowest grades will go to poor skills and values over $20.

FORECAST RISK: Refer to the description in the Forecaster's Toolbox.

PLAYER STAT LINES: The past five year's statistics represent the total accumulated in the majors as well as in Triple-A and Double-A ball during each year. All minor league stats used have been converted to their equivalent major league performance level. Levels below Double-A are not included. See the note in the Foundation Philosophies section for the rationale behind using minor league statistics in this manner.

TEAM DESIGNATIONS: An asterisk (*) appearing with a team name means that major league equivalent Triple-A and/or Double-A numbers are included in that year's stat line. A designation of "a/a" means the stats were accumulated at both Triple-A and Double-A levels that year. "JPN" means Japan, "MEX" means Mexico, "TWN" means Taiwan, "KOR" means Korea and "ind" means independent league.

The designation "2TM" appears whenever a player was on more than one major league team, crossing leagues, in a season. "2AL" and "2NL" represent more than one team in the same league. Complete season stats are presented for players who crossed leagues during the season.

SABERMETRIC CATEGORIES: Descriptions of all the sabermetric categories appear in the glossary. The decimal point has been suppressed on several categories to conserve space.

New categories for 2003...

vLH / vRH: Complete 5-year scan of each pitcher's opposition batting average versus left-handed and right-handed hitters. Data shown is at the major league level only.

G/F: Ground ball to fly ball ratio. Data shown is at the major league level only. A "G" or an "F" at the bottom of the column indicates that the pitcher exhibited a strong tendency one way or the other in 2002.

2003 FORECASTS: It is far too early to be making definitive projections for 2003, especially on playing time. Focus on the skill levels and trends, then consult Baseball HQ for playing time revisions as players change teams and roles become finalized. A free projections update will also be available online at BaseballForecaster.com in the spring.

Forecasts are computed from a player's trends over the past five years. Adjustments were made for leading indicators and variances between skill and output. After reviewing the leading indicators, you might opt to make further adjustments.

Although each year's numbers include all playing time at the Double-A level or above, the 2003 forecast only represents potential playing time at the major league level, and again is highly preliminary.

CAPSULE COMMENTARIES: For each player, a brief analysis of their BPIs and the potential impact on performance in 2003 is provided. For those who played only a portion of 2002 at the major league level, and whose isolated MLB stats are significantly different from their full-season total, their MLB stats are listed here. Note that these commentaries look at performance related issues only. Playing time expectations may impact these analyses, so you will have to adjust accordingly, especially as we get closer to Opening Day. Upside (UP) and downside (DN) statistical potential appears for some players. These are less grounded in hard data and more speculative of longer-term potential.

Abbott,Paul

Abbott,Paul	Yr	Tm	W	L	Sv	IP	ERA	Br/IP	R$	BF/G	OBA	vLH	vRH	H%	xERA	RAR	Ctl	Dom	Cmd	hr/9	G/F	S%	BPV	BPX
RH Starter	98	SEA *	4	1	0	39	2.98	1.30	$6	23.6	235	228	297	31%	3.18	14.0	3.9	9.2	2.4	0.5	2.11	78%	99	211
AGE 35 Decl	99	SEA *	7	3	0	86	3.98	1.29	$10	13.4	236	159	231	28%	3.73	21.8	3.8	8.1	2.1	1.0	1.10	72%	70	175
TYPE Power	00	SEA	9	7	0	179	4.22	1.36	$13	21.9	245	259	222	26%	4.12	40.5	4.0	5.0	1.3	1.2	0.90	72%	28	72
BURN none	01	SEA	17	4	0	163	4.25	1.42	$13	25.3	240	243	232	27%	4.23	26.9	4.8	6.5	1.4	1.2	0.76	73%	40	80
ERA Potl ++	02	SEA *	1	4	0	34	11.05	2.31	($10)	19.9	367	383	315	42%	9.22 +	-27.2	6.1	7.6	1.3	2.1	0.87	52%	-9	-18
Support 3.76	1st Half		1	4	0	34	11.05	2.31	($10)	19.9	367			42%	9.22 +	-27.2	6.1	7.6	1.3	2.1		52%	-9	-18
LIMA D	2nd Half		0	0	0	0	0.00	0.00																
Risk X HIGH	03	Proj	8	7	0	120	5.40	1.56	($0)	19.9	268			30%	5.07	-0.5	4.7	7.0	1.5	1.4	--	68%	34	69

Between the death of his father in April and his injuries, this was a lost season. However, with his soft skills set and advancing age, expectations for a rebound should be tempered.

Acevedo,Juan

Acevedo,Juan	Yr	Tm	W	L	Sv	IP	ERA	Br/IP	R$	BF/G	OBA	vLH	vRH	H%	xERA	RAR	Ctl	Dom	Cmd	hr/9	G/F	S%	BPV	BPX
RH Reliever	98	STL	8	3	15	98	2.57	1.14	$23	8.0	231	269	203	26%	2.93	35.0	2.7	5.1	1.9	0.6	1.15	80%	61	110
AGE 32 Past	99	STL	6	8	4	102	5.91	1.60	$0	9.2	286	275	301	29%	5.58	-5.0	4.2	4.6	1.1	1.5	1.14	66%	3	7
TYPE	00	MIL	3	7	0	82	3.83	1.31	$5	5.6	249	287	220	27%	4.12	19.8	3.4	5.6	1.6	1.2	0.98	75%	37	82
BURN none	01	2NL	2	5	0	60	4.19	1.71	($2)	4.8	286	319	264	34%	5.35 -	9.4	5.2	7.0	1.3	0.9	1.28	77%	41	76
ERA Potl -	02	DET	1	5	28	74	2.68	1.23	$18	4.7	246	264	228	28%	3.10	24.1	2.8	5.2	1.9	0.5	1.32	79%	62	117
Support 1.45	1st Half		1	4	12	42	3.21	1.14	$9	5.5	233			29%	2.44 +	10.6	2.6	6.6	2.6	0.2		70%	96	182
LIMA D	2nd Half		0	1	16	32	1.97	1.34	$9	4.0	262			27%	3.95 -	13.4	3.1	3.4	1.1	0.8		90%	20	39
Risk Moderate	03	Proj	2	5	26	75	3.24	1.40	$17	5.0	262			29%	4.11 -	21.4	3.6	5.4	1.5	0.8	--	80%	41	84

BPIs were closer-worthy in the 1st half, but despite a 1.97 ERA after the break, his skills took a tumble. Net result was a season that was not at the level we'd expect for a dominant closer. Bid with caution.

Adams,Terry

Adams,Terry	Yr	Tm	W	L	Sv	IP	ERA	Br/IP	R$	BF/G	OBA	vLH	vRH	H%	xERA	RAR	Ctl	Dom	Cmd	hr/9	G/F	S%	BPV	BPX
RH Reliever	98	CHC	7	7	1	72	4.36	1.57	$4	5.1	261	223	280	33%	4.58	8.4	5.1	9.1	1.8	0.9	2.82	74%	69	124
AGE 30 Peak	99	CHC	6	3	13	65	4.02	1.35	$14	5.3	247	184	289	29%	4.16	13.3	3.9	7.9	2.0	1.2	2.41	75%	58	127
TYPE Power	00	LA	6	9	2	84	3.53	1.41	$9	5.5	252	220	268	29%	3.88	23.6	4.2	6.0	1.4	0.6	2.68	76%	51	113
BURN none	01	LA	12	8	0	166	4.33	1.36	$10	16.5	269	232	295	33%	3.81 +	22.9	2.9	7.6	2.6	0.5	2.29	67%	87	162
ERA Potl No chg	02	PHI	7	9	0	136	4.37	1.40	$5	12.8	256	246	263	30%	3.90	19.9	3.8	6.4	1.7	0.6	2.70	69%	59	121
Support 4.02	1st Half		4	5	0	86	3.86	1.38	$4	24.7	264			30%	4.09	18.4	3.3	6.2	1.8	0.7		73%	56	115
LIMA B	2nd Half		3	4	0	50	5.24	1.43	$0	7.0	243			29%	3.57 +	1.5	4.7	6.7	1.4	0.4		61%	66	135
Risk Moderate	03	Proj	5	6	0	80	4.39	1.41	$4	5.9	257			31%	3.88 +	11.4	3.9	6.9	1.7	0.6	G	69%	65	130

Posted a 5.00 ERA as a starter, but 2.38 from the pen. Odd, because his BPIs were starting to come into their own in '01 as a starter. At their present level, his BPIs are only worth a marginal bid.

Affeldt,Jeremy

Affeldt,Jeremy	Yr	Tm	W	L	Sv	IP	ERA	Br/IP	R$	BF/G	OBA	vLH	vRH	H%	xERA	RAR	Ctl	Dom	Cmd	hr/9	G/F	S%	BPV	BPX
LH Starter	98		0	0	0	0	0.00	0.00																
AGE 23 Growth	99		0	0	0	0	0.00	0.00																
TYPE Power	00		0	0	0	0	0.00	0.00																
BURN none	01	aa	10	6	0	145	4.53	1.47	$5	25.5	295			35%	4.61	17.3	2.6	6.6	2.5	0.6		69%	70	134
ERA Potl -	02	KC	3	4	0	83	4.45	1.52	($1)	10.0	269	283	271	32%	4.47	7.3	4.3	7.5	1.7	0.9	1.24	72%	56	107
Support 5.45	1st Half		1	4	0	50	4.49	1.60	($2)	16.2	280			34%	4.69	4.1	4.5	7.7	1.7	0.7		72%	60	113
LIMA D+	2nd Half		2	0	0	33	4.38	1.40	$1	6.2	250			29%	4.13	3.2	4.1	7.1	1.7	1.1		71%	51	97
Risk High	03	Proj	4	6	0	120	4.50	1.48	$1	20.3	276			33%	4.47	14.0	3.6	7.1	2.0	0.8	--	70%	58	119

5.46 ERA as a starter, 4.03 as a reliever with slightly better BPIs, but slated for a rotation spot. AA season showed some potential, but jumping AAA may delay him from reaching it.

Alfonseca,Antonio

Alfonseca,Antonio	Yr	Tm	W	L	Sv	IP	ERA	Br/IP	R$	BF/G	OBA	vLH	vRH	H%	xERA	RAR	Ctl	Dom	Cmd	hr/9	G/F	S%	BPV	BPX
RH Reliever	98	FLA	4	6	8	70	4.10	1.54	$6	5.4	275	330	251	30%	5.11 -	10.6	4.2	5.9	1.4	1.3	1.44	78%	26	47
AGE 31 Peak	99	FLA	4	5	21	77	3.27	1.40	$18	4.6	267	270	278	30%	3.84 -	23.5	3.4	5.4	1.6	0.5	1.59	77%	53	116
TYPE Power	00	FLA	5	6	45	70	4.24	1.51	$30	4.6	293	277	303	33%	4.96 -	13.0	3.1	6.0	2.0	0.9	1.91	74%	47	103
BURN none	01	FLA	4	4	28	61	3.09	1.36	$22	4.5	283	302	259	32%	4.39 -	18.7	2.2	5.9	2.7	0.9	2.02	81%	63	117
ERA Potl No chg	02	CHC	2	5	19	74	4.01	1.47	$13	4.9	259	304	220	32%	4.13	14.3	4.4	7.4	1.7	0.6	2.23	73%	65	133
Support 1.82	1st Half		1	1	11	36	2.50	1.31	$11	4.8	234			30%	3.04 -	14.3	4.0	7.5	1.9	0.3		80%	85	175
LIMA C	2nd Half		1	4	8	38	5.45	1.63	$3	5.1	282			33%	5.17	0.1	4.7	7.3	1.6	0.9		67%	47	96
Risk Very Low	03	Proj	3	6	22	75	4.32	1.47	$15	4.8	274			32%	4.41	11.4	3.6	6.6	1.8	0.7	G	71%	57	114

Threw harder in '02, but with less command. LHers have hit him hard for two years now. Still, his ability to keep the ball on the ground may help him salvage a closer's role somewhere. Expect limited success, though.

Almanza,Armando

Almanza,Armando	Yr	Tm	W	L	Sv	IP	ERA	Br/IP	R$	BF/G	OBA	vLH	vRH	H%	xERA	RAR	Ctl	Dom	Cmd	hr/9	G/F	S%	BPV	BPX
LH Reliever	98	a/a	7	2	9	68	3.71	1.62	$10	5.2	273			37%	4.42 -	15.7	5.0	10.1	2.0	0.4		77%	91	177
AGE 30 Peak	99	FLA *	2	4	3	44	6.14	1.68	($1)	5.2	262	63	194	36%	4.94 +	-3.5	6.1	11.3	1.8	1.0	0.64	64%	78	169
TYPE Power	00	FLA	4	2	0	46	4.88	1.76	$0	3.2	226	191	253	29%	4.33 +	4.6	8.4	9.0	1.1	0.6	0.63	72%	69	151
BURN none	01	FLA	2	2	0	41	4.83	1.46	$0	3.5	227	210	244	27%	4.70	2.9	5.7	9.9	1.7	1.8	0.51	73%	52	97
ERA Potl +	02	FLA	3	2	2	45	4.40	1.31	$4	3.7	221	255	208	29%	4.12	6.4	4.6	11.4	2.5	1.6	0.61	73%	83	171
Support 4.73	1st Half		2	2	0	16	2.80	1.30	$3	4.0	223			27%	4.21 -	5.7	4.5	10.6	2.4	1.7		89%	74	151
LIMA B+	2nd Half		1	0	2	29	5.29	1.31	$1	3.6	220			29%	4.08 +	0.6	4.7	11.8	2.5	1.6		64%	88	181
Risk Low	03	Proj	3	2	2	50	4.32	1.38	$4	3.6	230			29%	4.23	7.6	4.9	10.6	2.2	1.4	F	74%	76	152

Volatile ERA was driven by swings in strand rate, but the underlying skills were good. Trouble with the HR ball will limit his upside, but he's a decent end-game pick in deep leagues.

Alvarez,Juan

Alvarez,Juan	Yr	Tm	W	L	Sv	IP	ERA	Br/IP	R$	BF/G	OBA	vLH	vRH	H%	xERA	RAR	Ctl	Dom	Cmd	hr/9	G/F	S%	BPV	BPX
LH Reliever	98	a/a	4	5	12	60	5.70	1.58	$6	4.7	274			31%	5.00 +	-2.2	4.7	6.8	1.5	1.1		65%	40	77
AGE 29 Peak	99	a/a	1	5	4	59	3.51	1.25	$7	4.9	265			30%	4.03 -	17.3	2.1	6.1	2.9	1.1		76%	67	154
TYPE Power	00	aaa	3	1	0	38	3.79	1.45	$3	3.8	251	471	462	27%	4.24	10.0	4.5	5.2	1.2	0.9	0.85	76%	32	76
BURN none	01	aaa	2	2	0	67	5.91	1.60	($4)	6.3	297			30%	6.30	-4.4	3.6	4.7	1.3	2.0		68%	-10	-18
ERA Potl --	02	TEX *	0	4	1	58	4.97	1.64	($4)	3.8	278	233	250	31%	5.27	1.1	5.0	6.1	1.2	1.2	0.84	72%	24	45
Support 2.27	1st Half		0	0	1	30	4.19	1.73	($1)	4.2	292			33%	5.10 -	3.7	5.1	5.1	1.0	0.6		76%	30	57
LIMA F	2nd Half		0	4	0	28	5.81	1.54	($2)	3.5	262			28%	5.45	-2.6	4.8	7.1	1.5	1.9		68%	18	34
Risk Very High	03	Proj	1	3	0	50	5.04	1.56	($2)	4.3	277			30%	5.29	2.2	4.3	5.8	1.3	1.4	--	71%	19	39

Showed some skill in 1999, but nothing since. Not enough command of his pitches to have value.

Alvarez,Wilson

Alvarez,Wilson	Yr	Tm	W	L	Sv	IP	ERA	Br/IP	R$	BF/G	OBA	vLH	vRH	H%	xERA	RAR	Ctl	Dom	Cmd	hr/9	G/F	S%	BPV	BPX
LH Reliever	98	TAM	6	14	0	143	4.72	1.38	$5	24.6	244			27%	4.16 +	17.9	4.3	6.7	1.6	1.1		68%	46	98
AGE 32 Past	99	TAM	9	9	0	160	4.22	1.49	$9	25.2	261			30%	4.73 -	35.4	4.4	7.2	1.6	1.2		75%	43	108
TYPE Power	00	TAM	0	0	0	0	0.00	0.00																
BURN none	01	a/a	2	4	0	38	4.26	1.32	$2	17.9	251			32%	3.01 +	5.9	3.3	7.6	2.3	0.0		64%	98	188
ERA Potl -	02	TAM *	3	3	1	83	4.88	1.52	($1)	14.7	273	299	263	30%	5.05	2.5	4.1	6.6	1.6	1.4	0.55	72%	31	59
Support 4.92	1st Half		3	2	0	50	3.94	1.47	$2	22.1	269			29%	4.74 -	7.8	3.9	6.1	1.5	1.3		78%	33	62
LIMA D+	2nd Half		0	1	1	33	6.31	1.59	($3)	9.9	280			31%	5.53 +	-5.3	4.4	7.4	1.7	1.6		63%	29	56
Risk High	03	Proj	3	5	0	80	4.95	1.46	($0)	15.9	264			31%	4.45 +	4.5	4.1	7.1	1.8	1.0	F	68%	51	104

2-3, 5.28 ERA in 75 IP at TAM. It has been a long road back, but his BPIs had already eroded four years ago. There was a brief glimmer of hope in '01, but that was in AA. He's not draftable at the MLB level.

Anderson,Brian

Anderson,Brian	Yr	Tm	W	L	Sv	IP	ERA	Br/IP	R$	BF/G	OBA	vLH	vRH	H%	xERA	RAR	Ctl	Dom	Cmd	hr/9	G/F	S%	BPV	BPX
LH Starter	98	ARI	12	13	0	208	4.33	1.18	$14	26.6	274	291	271	27%	4.59	25.3	1.0	4.1	4.0	1.7	0.88	70%	57	104
AGE 31 Peak	99	ARI	8	2	1	130	4.57	1.32	$9	17.8	282	295	275	30%	4.59	17.0	1.9	5.2	2.7	1.2	1.02	69%	49	106
TYPE Contact	00	ARI	11	7	0	213	4.05	1.24	$17	26.9	273	266	278	27%	4.66 -	44.9	1.6	4.4	2.7	1.6	1.02	74%	35	76
BURN none	01	ARI	4	9	0	133	5.21	1.40	($1)	19.8	294	272	304	29%	5.44	2.8	2.0	3.7	1.8	1.7	0.96	68%	6	12
ERA Potl -	02	ARI	6	11	0	156	4.79	1.32	$4	18.9	283	302	278	30%	4.80	14.0	1.8	4.7	2.5	1.3	1.18	67%	40	81
Support 4.33	1st Half		3	7	0	81	5.33	1.37	($0)	16.6	300			31%	5.28	1.4	1.4	4.3	3.0	1.4		64%	41	83
LIMA C+	2nd Half		3	4	0	75	4.21	1.27	$4	22.4	265			28%	4.28	12.6	2.3	5.0	2.2	1.2		71%	43	88
Risk Moderate	03	Proj	7	9	0	160	4.67	1.31	$6	20.5	282			29%	4.85	16.8	1.9	4.4	2.4	1.5	--	69%	32	64

Another season of pinpoint control, zero dominance, and gopheritis. He's not walking anybody because batters don't feel the need to wait on him. The pitches are fat, juicy, and headed over the fence.

Anderson,Jimmy		Tm	W	L	Sv	IP	ERA	Br/IP	R$	BF/G	OBA	vLH	vRH	H%	xERA	RAR	Ctl	Dom	Cmd	hr/9	G/F	S%	BPV	BPX
LH Starter	98	aaa	9	10	0	123	5.34	1.77	($3)	16.5	302			33%	5.47	1.5	5.0	4.3	0.9	0.6		69%	21	41
AGE 27 Growth	99	PIT	* 13	3	0	162	4.28	1.54	$9	21.3	297	231	235	34%	4.56	27.5	3.2	5.3	1.7	0.4	2.76	71%	51	111
TYPE Contact	00	PIT	* 6	11	0	166	4.93	1.57	($1)	24.8	296	303	292	32%	4.96	15.5	3.4	4.6	1.3	0.7	2.96	68%	30	66
BURN none	01	PIT	9	17	0	206	5.11	1.53	($2)	27.0	285	324	279	31%	4.67	7.1	3.6	3.9	1.1	0.7	2.53	66%	24	45
ERA Potl - -	02	PIT	8	13	0	140	5.46	1.64	($5)	22.8	297	273	306	30%	5.79	-0.1	4.1	3.0	0.7	1.3	2.66	69%	-9	-19
Support 5.05	1st Half		6	8	0	94	4.40	1.43	$4	25.6	253			25%	4.60	13.4	4.3	3.1	0.7	1.2		73%	0	1
LIMA F	2nd Half		2	5	0	46	7.65	2.07	($10)	19.1	373			38%	8.24 -	-13.4	3.5	2.9	0.8	1.4		64%	-26	-53
Risk High	03	Proj	5	9	0	100	5.22	1.69	($4)	22.0	311			32%	5.80 -	3.1	3.8	3.6	1.0	1.0	G	70%	5	10

At 27, he's supposed to be in a growth stage, but his BPIs are doing anything but. Terrible skills and getting worse. NOT worth an end-game pick. NOT worth a flyer. NOT worth a plug nickel.

Appier,Kevin		Tm	W	L	Sv	IP	ERA	Br/IP	R$	BF/G	OBA	vLH	vRH	H%	xERA	RAR	Ctl	Dom	Cmd	hr/9	G/F	S%	BPV	BPX
RH Starter	98	KC	* 4	5	0	53	9.00	1.98	($8)	26.0	363	294	393	37%	8.38 +	-23.7	3.4	4.4	1.3	2.0	1.35	56%	-25	-53
AGE 35 Decl	99	2AL	16	14	0	209	5.17	1.50	$9	27.2	281	297	262	31%	5.00	19.7	3.6	5.6	1.6	1.2	1.25	68%	31	77
TYPE	00	OAK	15	11	0	195	4.52	1.55	$11	28.1	267	296	224	30%	4.78	36.3	4.7	6.0	1.3	1.1	0.93	73%	32	83
BURN none	01	NYM	11	10	0	206	3.58	1.19	$18	25.7	237	242	233	28%	3.41	49.4	2.8	7.5	2.7	1.0	1.19	73%	80	149
ERA Potl -	02	ANA	14	12	0	188	3.93	1.36	$12	25.1	265	250	286	30%	4.24	29.7	3.1	6.3	2.1	1.1	0.83	75%	50	95
Support 4.59	1st Half		6	6	0	87	4.54	1.50	$2	24.1	299			34%	5.04 -	6.6	2.7	6.3	2.3	1.0		72%	51	97
LIMA D+	2nd Half		8	6	0	101	3.39	1.23	$10	26.1	232			26%	3.55	23.1	3.4	6.3	1.9	1.2		77%	51	96
Risk Moderate	03	Proj	13	13	0	200	4.23	1.38	$11	26.0	263			29%	4.32	30.5	3.3	6.4	1.9	1.1	--	72%	48	97

Managed to keep his ERA under 4.00, but according to xERA, that won't last. Skills were off from '01, but remain barely acceptable. At 35, whatever you pay may be more than what you get back.

Armas Jr.,Tony		Tm	W	L	Sv	IP	ERA	Br/IP	R$	BF/G	OBA	vLH	vRH	H%	xERA	RAR	Ctl	Dom	Cmd	hr/9	G/F	S%	BPV	BPX
RH Starter	98		0	0	0	0	0.00	0.00																
AGE 25 Growth	99	aa	9	7	0	149	3.38	1.28	$16	26.0	246	250	353	28%	3.39	46.2	3.2	5.6	1.8	0.6	0.43	74%	58	135
TYPE Power	00	MON	* 8	11	0	114	4.42	1.35	$8	23.2	237	266	183	25%	3.97	18.4	4.3	5.4	1.3	1.1	1.30	70%	34	75
BURN none	01	MON	9	14	0	196	4.04	1.38	$8	24.8	245	275	225	30%	3.87	34.9	4.2	8.1	1.9	0.8	1.04	72%	70	130
ERA Potl -	02	MON	12	12	0	164	4.45	1.38	$9	24.3	244	309	190	28%	4.27	22.3	4.3	7.2	1.7	1.2	1.42	71%	48	99
Support 4.66	1st Half		8	7	0	102	3.79	1.24	$11	25.0	226			25%	3.71	22.8	3.8	7.2	1.9	1.2		74%	56	115
LIMA C+	2nd Half		4	5	0	62	5.52	1.62	($2)	23.4	271			31%	5.19	-0.5	5.1	7.1	1.4	1.2		67%	38	78
Risk High	03	Proj	13	15	0	200	3.96	1.38	$13	23.9	248			29%	4.12	40.0	4.1	7.7	1.9	1.0	--	74%	60	121

If not for July and August, would have had an ERA under 4.00. Has not yet crossed the 2.0 cmd threshold or roped in those lefty hitters to take the next step up, but he's close.

Arrojo,Rolando		Tm	W	L	Sv	IP	ERA	Br/IP	R$	BF/G	OBA	vLH	vRH	H%	xERA	RAR	Ctl	Dom	Cmd	hr/9	G/F	S%	BPV	BPX
RH Reliever	98	TAM	14	12	0	202	3.56	1.29	$20	26.6	255	301	205	29%	3.87	56.6	2.9	6.8	2.3	0.9	1.73	75%	66	140
AGE 34 Decl	99	TAM	7	12	0	140	5.21	1.59	$1	26.3	291	315	272	33%	5.64	12.5	3.9	6.9	1.8	1.5	1.31	71%	31	78
TYPE	00	2TM	10	11	0	172	5.64	1.48	$3	23.7	278	298	256	31%	4.96 +	2.7	3.6	6.5	1.8	1.3	1.36	64%	39	92
BURN none	01	BOS	5	4	5	103	3.49	1.19	$12	10.3	232	238	221	27%	3.12	27.5	3.1	6.8	2.2	0.7	1.72	72%	75	151
ERA Potl + +	02	BOS	4	3	1	81	5.00	1.36	$2	11.9	267	313	221	30%	3.97 +	1.2	3.0	5.7	1.9	0.8	1.34	63%	52	98
Support 4.09	1st Half		4	2	1	61	4.12	1.26	$4	12.8	248			29%	3.15 +	8.1	2.9	5.9	2.0	0.4		66%	69	131
LIMA C+	2nd Half		0	1	0	20	7.73	1.67	($3)	10.1	318			33%	6.50 +	-6.9	3.2	5.0	1.6	1.8		55%	-0	-0
Risk Moderate	03	Proj	3	4	1	80	4.39	1.39	$2	12.3	274			30%	4.51	10.5	2.9	6.1	2.1	1.1	--	71%	47	95

Back injury derailed his 2nd half and casts a pall on his short-term future. BPIs are marginal, but they are better as a starter. He'll likely pitch out of the pen.

Asencio,Miguel		Tm	W	L	Sv	IP	ERA	Br/IP	R$	BF/G	OBA	vLH	vRH	H%	xERA	RAR	Ctl	Dom	Cmd	hr/9	G/F	S%	BPV	BPX
RH Starter	98		0	0	0	0	0.00	0.00																
AGE 22 Growth	99		0	0	0	0	0.00	0.00																
TYPE	00		0	0	0	0	0.00	0.00																
BURN none	01		0	0	0	0	0.00	0.00																
ERA Potl - - -	02	KC	4	7	0	123	5.12	1.63	($5)	18.0	282	264	302	29%	5.31	-0.3	4.7	4.2	0.9	1.2	1.41	71%	6	11
Support 4.23	1st Half		1	1	0	41	6.33	1.53	($3)	11.5	246			22%	5.27 +	-6.8	5.5	3.3	0.6	2.0		63%	-21	-40
LIMA F	2nd Half		3	6	0	82	4.51	1.67	($2)	25.1	298			32%	5.33 -	6.5	4.3	4.7	1.1	0.9		74%	21	39
Risk Low	03	Proj	3	4	0	80	5.29	1.61	($3)	22.7	278			28%	5.37	0.9	4.7	4.2	0.9	1.4	--	70%	2	5

Posted a 4.51 ERA as a starter, versus 11 IP, 14 ER from the pen. But his BPIs are awful and the only place he SHOULD be pitching is in Double-A.

Ashby,Andy		Tm	W	L	Sv	IP	ERA	Br/IP	R$	BF/G	OBA	vLH	vRH	H%	xERA	RAR	Ctl	Dom	Cmd	hr/9	G/F	S%	BPV	BPX
RH Starter	98	SD	17	9	0	226	3.34	1.24	$23	28.5	259	251	268	29%	3.80	57.3	2.3	6.0	2.6	0.9	2.18	76%	66	120
AGE 35 Decl	99	SD	14	10	0	206	3.80	1.25	$20	27.7	260	281	240	28%	4.00	48.2	2.4	5.8	2.4	1.1	2.01	74%	55	119
TYPE Contact	00	2NL	12	13	0	199	4.93	1.39	$9	27.7	278	312	251	29%	4.82	18.7	2.8	4.8	1.7	1.3	1.55	68%	25	56
BURN High	01	LA	2	0	0	11	4.02	1.34	$2	23.9	307	188	344	33%	5.40 -	2.0	0.8	5.6	7.0	1.6	2.60	77%	126	234
ERA Potl -	02	LA	9	13	0	181	3.93	1.35	$10	25.8	260	285	233	28%	4.21	37.1	3.2	5.3	1.6	1.0	1.49	74%	40	82
Support 4.21	1st Half		7	6	0	104	3.37	1.15	$13	26.5	229			25%	3.27	29.1	2.9	5.9	2.1	1.0		74%	59	122
LIMA D+	2nd Half		2	7	0	77	4.68	1.61	($3)	24.9	298			32%	5.49 -	8.0	3.7	4.6	1.2	1.1		73%	17	34
Risk Very High	03	Proj	9	11	0	160	4.22	1.38	$8	26.4	270			29%	4.46	26.5	3.0	5.2	1.8	1.1	--	72%	37	75

A pretty good season, save for a stretch in July and his blister-shortened Sept. But those two months knocked off his BPIs and now he's staring at a declining trend at age 35. Bid cautiously.

Astacio,Pedro		Tm	W	L	Sv	IP	ERA	Br/IP	R$	BF/G	OBA	vLH	vRH	H%	xERA	RAR	Ctl	Dom	Cmd	hr/9	G/F	S%	BPV	BPX
RH Starter	98	COL	13	14	0	209	6.24	1.53	($5)	26.6	294	258	330	33%	5.72 +	-28.2	3.2	7.3	2.3	1.7	1.43	62%	38	69
AGE 33 Past	99	COL	17	11	0	232	5.04	1.44	$11	29.7	283	306	268	33%	5.07	15.7	2.9	8.1	2.8	1.5	1.26	69%	62	135
TYPE Power	00	COL	12	9	0	196	5.28	1.50	$4	27.1	282	290	274	34%	5.26	9.2	3.5	8.9	2.5	1.5	1.63	68%	60	133
BURN none	01	2NL	8	14	0	169	5.11	1.39	$2	28.0	275	286	268	32%	4.62	5.9	2.9	7.7	2.7	1.2	1.18	65%	67	124
ERA Potl No chg	02	NYM	12	11	0	191	4.81	1.34	$8	26.2	263	237	283	29%	4.69	16.7	3.0	7.2	2.4	1.5	1.03	69%	51	104
Support 4.37	1st Half		7	3	0	101	2.93	1.14	$15	27.4	232			27%	3.19	34.2	2.6	7.1	2.8	0.9		78%	83	169
LIMA C	2nd Half		5	8	0	90	6.92	1.56	($6)	25.1	295			32%	6.37 +	-17.5	3.4	7.2	2.1	2.2		60%	18	36
Risk Very Low	03	Proj	12	10	0	180	4.05	1.31	$14	26.2	254			28%	4.46	33.8	3.1	7.1	2.3	1.5	--	75%	50	100

Last spring, I wrote that he could have a sub-3.00 ERA, and I was right... for 4 months. The bottom fell out in August, which he claims was NOT due to injury, but a healthy arm's ERA doesn't suddenly jump 4 runs.

Bacsik,Mike		Tm	W	L	Sv	IP	ERA	Br/IP	R$	BF/G	OBA	vLH	vRH	H%	xERA	RAR	Ctl	Dom	Cmd	hr/9	G/F	S%	BPV	BPX
LH Starter	98	0	0	0	0	0	0.00	0.00																
AGE 25 Growth	99	aa	11	11	0	149	5.62	1.57	$2	25.7	308			32%	5.95	1.6	2.8	4.4	1.6	1.6		68%	5	12
TYPE Contact	00	a/a	7	4	0	100	4.50	1.28	$9	26.3	275			29%	4.28	16.9	1.9	4.1	2.1	1.1		67%	37	87
BURN none	01	a/a	13	6	0	158	4.27	1.30	$12	23.8	282			30%	4.45	24.3	1.8	5.1	2.9	1.1	1.13	70%	58	111
ERA Potl - - -	02	NYM	* 8	7	0	163	4.47	1.60	($1)	20.5	320	216	304	35%	5.89 -	21.6	2.5	5.1	2.1	1.2	1.35	75%	31	63
Support 5.98	1st Half		5	4	0	93	4.06	1.57	$1	19.0	323			36%	5.59 -	17.4	2.0	5.6	2.8	0.9		76%	56	115
LIMA C+	2nd Half		3	3	0	70	5.01	1.64	($3)	22.8	315			33%	6.29 -	4.2	3.1	4.5	1.5	1.5		74%	3	7
Risk ****	03	Proj	7	5	0	120	4.65	1.48	$3	23.0	303			32%	5.35 -	12.9	2.3	4.8	2.1	1.2	--	72%	31	62

3-2, 4.42 ERA in 55 IP at NYM. Soft-tosser with decent command, but gives up a ton of hits, and HRs. More time in Shea could help, but probably not nearly enough.

Baez,Danys		Tm	W	L	Sv	IP	ERA	Br/IP	R$	BF/G	OBA	vLH	vRH	H%	xERA	RAR	Ctl	Dom	Cmd	hr/9	G/F	S%	BPV	BPX
RH Reliever	98		0	0	0	0	0.00	0.00																
AGE 25 Growth	99		0	0	0	0	0.00	0.00																
TYPE Power	00	aa	4	9	0	102	4.68	1.45	$3	24.8	287			33%	4.43	14.8	2.8	5.6	2.0	0.6		67%	55	130
BURN High	01	CLE	5	3	0	50	2.51	1.08	$9	4.7	194	188	193	25%	2.53	19.9	3.6	9.3	2.6	0.9	0.82	82%	100	200
ERA Potl -	02	CLE	10	11	6	165	4.42	1.47	$7	18.6	256	278	233	30%	4.07	15.2	4.5	7.1	1.6	0.8	1.06	71%	57	107
Support 4.46	1st Half		6	6	0	90	4.40	1.51	$2	24.9	249			30%	3.93	8.5	5.2	7.3	1.4	0.6		71%	61	114
LIMA B	2nd Half		4	5	6	75	4.44	1.41	$5	14.1	264			31%	4.24	6.7	3.6	6.8	1.9	1.0		70%	54	103
Risk X HIGH	03	Proj	6	5	22	80	3.83	1.33	$18	5.1	242			29%	3.59	16.5	3.8	7.7	2.0	0.8	--	73%	71	144

Has displayed closer-worthy BPIs in the past, but not this year. His conversion to closer was just 13 games, 11 IP with a 3.97 ERA and a poor 1.3 Cmd. While he might still grow into the role, don't bet the bank.

Bailey,Cory		Tm	W	L	Sv	IP	ERA	Br/IP	R$	BF/G	OBA	vLH	vRH	H%	xERA	RAR	Ctl	Dom	Cmd	hr/9	G/F	S%	BPV	BPX
RH Reliever	98	aaa	7	2	10	94	2.59	1.12	$20	6.7	247			29%	2.83	35.8	1.7	6.1	**3.6**	0.4		77%	106	205
AGE 32 Peak	99	aaa	2	1	18	46	3.52	1.52	$13	4.8	290			34%	5.33 -	13.4	3.3	8.0	**2.4**	1.4		83%	55	127
TYPE Power	00	aaa	2	4	12	72	4.25	1.82	$5	6.2	309			36%	5.35 -	14.6	5.0	6.0	**1.2**	0.3		75%	47	111
BURN none	01	KC *	2	1	1	77	3.04	1.27	$6	5.6	214	164	297	27%	2.75	25.2	4.6	7.7	**1.7**	0.4	3.05	76%	84	167
ERA Potl ----	02	KC *	4	4	10	65	3.59	1.70	$5	5.5	273	282	324	30%	4.85 -	13.3	5.8	5.1	**0.9**	0.7	2.59	80%	29	55
Support 3.91	1st Half		3	4	1	45	3.79	1.75	$1	5.9	286			31%	5.46 -	7.9	5.6	4.6	**0.8**	1.0		81%	13	24
LIMA D+	2nd Half		1	0	9	20	3.13	1.59	$5	4.8	241			30%	3.48	5.3	6.3	6.3	**1.0**	0.0		78%	65	124
Risk Very High	03	Proj	**3**	**2**	**0**	**75**	**4.56**	**1.61**	**($1)**	**5.5**	**269**			**32%**	**4.30**	**8.1**	**5.2**	**6.4**	**1.2**	**0.4**	**G**	**70%**	**54**	**111**

3-4, 4.11 ERA in 46 IP at KC. An elevated strand rate has made his ERA acceptable, but his Cmd ratio and xERA trend tells a more accurate story. He won't be anywhere near a 4.00 ERA in 2003.

Baldwin,James		Tm	W	L	Sv	IP	ERA	Br/IP	R$	BF/G	OBA	vLH	vRH	H%	xERA	RAR	Ctl	Dom	Cmd	hr/9	G/F	S%	BPV	BPX
RH Reliever	98	CHW	13	6	0	159	5.32	1.48	$6	18.9	282	291	262	32%	4.83	7.1	3.4	6.1	**1.8**	1.0	1.09	65%	43	91
AGE 31 Peak	99	CHW	12	13	0	199	5.11	1.51	$6	25.2	281	272	285	30%	5.37	20.3	3.7	5.6	**1.5**	1.5	1.21	70%	18	45
TYPE Contact	00	CHW	14	7	0	178	4.65	1.37	$15	26.3	269	279	264	28%	4.99	30.0	3.0	5.9	**2.0**	1.7	1.18	72%	26	68
BURN none	01	2TM	10	11	0	175	4.42	1.45	$5	26.4	279	260	299	29%	4.97 -	23.4	3.2	4.9	**1.5**	1.3	1.10	73%	22	41
ERA Potl --	02	SEA	7	10	0	150	5.28	1.52	($2)	22.2	297	323	274	31%	5.56	-3.5	2.9	5.3	**1.8**	1.6	0.87	69%	18	34
Support 5.40	1st Half		6	6	0	97	4.55	1.45	$2	26.5	285			30%	4.97	7.3	3.0	5.3	**1.8**	1.3		72%	28	53
LIMA F	2nd Half		1	4	0	53	6.62	1.64	($5)	17.3	319			33%	6.66	-10.8	2.9	5.3	**1.8**	2.0		64%	-0	-0
Risk Low	03	Proj	**4**	**5**	**0**	**80**	**5.06**	**1.50**	**($0)**	**11.4**	**292**			**31%**	**5.49**	**3.3**	**3.0**	**5.3**	**1.7**	**1.6**	**--**	**71%**	**18**	**36**

He did use Safeco to his advantage (4.21 ERA), but the road was long and hard (6.61). With mediocre BPIs and the likelihood that he will pitch on the visiting team from time to time, this is one arm to avoid.

Banks,Willie		Tm	W	L	Sv	IP	ERA	Br/IP	R$	BF/G	OBA	vLH	vRH	H%	xERA	RAR	Ctl	Dom	Cmd	hr/9	G/F	S%	BPV	BPX
RH Reliever	98	2TM	2	3	1	58	4.81	1.57	($0)	6.2	248			28%	4.49	4.8	5.7	6.2	**1.1**	0.9		71%	37	73
AGE 34 Past	99	JPN	7	4	1	69	3.52	1.55	$7	13.4	245			30%	4.21 -	20.1	5.7	8.0	**1.4**	0.8		79%	59	138
TYPE	00	aaa	2	4	0	51	6.18	1.78	($4)	26.7	311			32%	5.92	-2.8	4.6	2.8	**0.6**	0.9		65%	-4	-9
BURN none	01	aaa	10	5	0	170	3.92	1.54	$5	24.5	294	200		34%	4.94 -	34.2	3.3	6.2	**1.9**	0.8	0.56	76%	50	95
ERA Potl +	02	BOS *	3	3	2	65	4.29	1.22	$4	7.7	234	246	200	25%	3.36 +	7.1	3.2	5.3	**1.7**	1.0	1.44	67%	45	86
Support 6.23	1st Half		2	2	1	35	5.63	1.39	$0	9.5	255			26%	4.38 +	-2.4	3.8	4.6	**1.2**	1.3		61%	18	35
LIMA C+	2nd Half		1	1	1	30	2.72	1.01	$4	6.2	207			24%	2.16 +	9.5	2.4	6.0	**2.5**	0.6		75%	84	159
Risk X HIGH	03	Proj	**3**	**3**	**0**	**60**	**4.50**	**1.40**	**$2**	**10.8**	**262**			**29%**	**4.17**	**7.0**	**3.6**	**5.4**	**1.5**	**0.9**	**--**	**69%**	**40**	**80**

2-1, 3.23 ERA in 39 IP at BOS. He has a history of putting up decent BPIs for short stretches, but you never know when they will occur, and for how long, so it's tough to keep paying attention.

Batista,Miguel		Tm	W	L	Sv	IP	ERA	Br/IP	R$	BF/G	OBA	vLH	vRH	H%	xERA	RAR	Ctl	Dom	Cmd	hr/9	G/F	S%	BPV	BPX
RH Starter	98	MON	3	5	0	135	3.80	1.53	($0)	10.7	270	310	246	31%	4.56 -	25.9	4.3	6.1	**1.4**	0.8	2.09	77%	43	78
AGE 32 Peak	99	MON	8	7	1	134	4.90	1.52	$4	15.3	279	339	230	32%	4.50	11.6	3.9	6.4	**1.6**	0.7	1.40	68%	52	113
TYPE	00	KC *	4	9	3	93	8.03	1.83	($9)	12.3	321	298	333	33%	7.67	-26.4	4.5	5.7	**1.3**	2.5	1.11	60%	-23	-61
BURN none	01	ARI	11	8	0	139	3.36	1.24	$15	12.1	224	218	232	25%	3.28	37.3	3.9	5.8	**1.5**	0.8	1.35	76%	51	95
ERA Potl +	02	ARI	8	9	0	184	4.30	1.32	$8	21.6	249	269	223	28%	3.60 +	28.5	3.4	5.5	**1.6**	0.6	1.74	67%	54	111
Support 4.68	1st Half		4	5	0	82	5.04	1.43	$0	18.8	266			30%	4.17 +	4.6	3.6	5.8	**1.6**	0.7		64%	51	104
LIMA C	2nd Half		4	4	0	102	3.71	1.23	$8	24.9	234			26%	3.14 +	23.9	3.3	5.2	**1.6**	0.5		70%	57	117
Risk High	03	Proj	**9**	**10**	**0**	**180**	**4.35**	**1.39**	**$7**	**22.2**	**256**			**28%**	**4.19**	**26.6**	**3.8**	**5.7**	**1.5**	**1.0**	**G**	**71%**	**41**	**82**

Got off to a slow start and apparently surged down the stretch, but his BPIs say that each half was identical in its mediocrity. The net result of the season is what you need to benchmark for 2003 bids.

Bauer,Rick		Tm	W	L	Sv	IP	ERA	Br/IP	R$	BF/G	OBA	vLH	vRH	H%	xERA	RAR	Ctl	Dom	Cmd	hr/9	G/F	S%	BPV	BPX
RH Reliever	98		0	0	0	0	0.00	0.00																
AGE 26 Growth	99		0	0	0	0	0.00	0.00																
TYPE Contact	00	aa	6	8	1	129	6.84	1.75	($8)	23.2	337			36%	6.72	-18.6	2.9	5.3	**1.9**	1.4		62%	16	39
BURN Low	01	BAL *	12	15	0	207	4.87	1.40	$6	26.3	292	274	254	31%	5.05	17.1	2.1	5.3	**2.5**	1.3	1.54	68%	42	85
ERA Potl ---	02	BAL	6	8	1	87	4.24	1.46	$4	6.7	266	288	253	27%	4.86 -	10.1	3.9	4.8	**1.2**	1.4	1.67	76%	12	23
Support 3.44	1st Half		3	5	1	41	5.46	1.75	($1)	5.7	301			32%	6.17 -	-2.0	4.8	5.0	**1.0**	1.5		72%	1	2
LIMA C	2nd Half		3	3	0	46	3.14	1.20	$4	8.2	232			23%	3.69 -	12.0	3.1	4.5	**1.4**	1.4		81%	25	47
Risk Very High	03	Proj	**5**	**6**	**0**	**80**	**4.73**	**1.46**	**$2**	**11.0**	**285**			**30%**	**5.09**	**6.9**	**3.0**	**5.1**	**1.7**	**1.4**	**G**	**71%**	**23**	**46**

Despite being a soft-tosser, his BPIs fared better when he was able to air it out over longer stretches. xERA shows how he should have been closer to a 5.00 ERA, and that's what you should expect in 2003.

Beckett,Josh		Tm	W	L	Sv	IP	ERA	Br/IP	R$	BF/G	OBA	vLH	vRH	H%	xERA	RAR	Ctl	Dom	Cmd	hr/9	G/F	S%	BPV	BPX
RH Starter	98		0	0	0	0	0.00	0.00																
AGE 22 Growth	99		0	0	0	0	0.00	0.00																
TYPE Power	00		0	0	0	0	0.00	0.00																
BURN none	01	FLA *	10	3	0	98	2.20	1.08	$19	23.1	211	231	104	28%	2.92 -	41.5	2.9	10.4	**3.5**	1.1	0.60	87%	116	215
ERA Potl +	02	FLA	6	7	0	107	4.12	1.28	$7	19.5	236	246	218	30%	3.77	19.2	3.7	9.5	**2.6**	1.1	0.82	71%	86	176
Support 4.93	1st Half		2	3	0	53	3.89	1.17	$4	21.7	219			26%	3.36 +	11.2	3.4	8.8	**2.6**	1.2		71%	83	170
LIMA A	2nd Half		4	4	0	54	4.35	1.39	$3	17.9	252			33%	4.18	8.0	4.0	10.2	**2.5**	1.0		71%	89	183
Risk Moderate	03	Proj	**12**	**8**	**0**	**160**	**3.38**	**1.21**	**$19**	**24.5**	**228**			**29%**	**3.44**	**44.6**	**3.4**	**9.9**	**2.9**	**1.1**	**--**	**77%**	**97**	**196**

BPIs remain superb for this youngster, but after three DL trips, we're hoping for some blister-free baseball in 2003. And a home team environment that fosters further growth.

Beimel,Joe		Tm	W	L	Sv	IP	ERA	Br/IP	R$	BF/G	OBA	vLH	vRH	H%	xERA	RAR	Ctl	Dom	Cmd	hr/9	G/F	S%	BPV	BPX
LH Reliever	98		0	0	0	0	0.00	0.00																
AGE 26 Growth	99		0	0	0	0	0.00	0.00																
TYPE	00	aa	1	6	0	62	5.23	1.74	($3)	28.9	327			33%	6.46 -	4.4	3.3	3.3	**1.0**	1.3		73%	-9	-20
BURN Low	01	PIT	7	11	0	115	5.24	1.56	($1)	12.3	288	268	298	31%	5.05	2.0	3.8	4.5	**1.2**	0.9	1.67	67%	21	40
ERA Potl -	02	PIT	2	5	0	85	4.66	1.56	($3)	7.2	269	262	269	30%	4.84	9.1	4.8	5.6	**1.2**	1.0	1.77	72%	31	64
Support 4.85	1st Half		1	2	0	47	2.67	1.31	$4	7.7	235			26%	3.58 -	17.6	4.0	5.5	**1.4**	0.8		83%	47	97
LIMA F	2nd Half		1	3	0	38	7.14	1.88	($7)	6.7	306			34%	6.40 +	-8.5	5.7	5.7	**1.0**	1.2		62%	13	27
Risk Very High	03	Proj	**1**	**3**	**0**	**40**	**5.40**	**1.63**	**($2)**	**9.6**	**290**			**31%**	**5.43**	**0.3**	**4.3**	**5.0**	**1.2**	**1.1**	**G**	**68%**	**17**	**35**

Deceptive 1st half performance (poor BPIs, 83% strand rate) netted him more opportunities to fail, and he didn't disappoint. Well, I suppose they WERE a bit disappointed he couldn't keep the magic going...

Beirne,Kevin		Tm	W	L	Sv	IP	ERA	Br/IP	R$	BF/G	OBA	vLH	vRH	H%	xERA	RAR	Ctl	Dom	Cmd	hr/9	G/F	S%	BPV	BPX
RH Reliever	98	aa	13	9	0	175	4.01	1.50	$9	27.6	261			31%	4.18	33.3	4.5	6.8	**1.5**	0.6		74%	57	110
AGE 29 Pre-Peak	99	aaa	5	5	0	113	5.73	1.56	($2)	25.3	310			33%	5.44	-0.6	2.6	4.3	**1.6**	1.0		64%	22	51
TYPE	00	CHW *	2	5	0	82	5.69	1.47	($1)	10.0	288	283	245	33%	5.22	2.5	3.0	7.2	**2.4**	1.4	0.62	64%	49	128
BURN High	01	TOR	0	0	0	7	12.86	2.71	($3)	7.9	397			45%	10.17 +	-6.9	7.7	6.4	**0.8**	1.3	0.54	50%	-7	-14
ERA Potl --	02	LA *	12	3	0	154	3.91	1.42	$11	19.7	273	208	276	30%	4.46 -	32.0	3.3	5.2	**1.6**	0.9	0.97	75%	39	79
Support 6.21	1st Half		7	2	0	93	4.06	1.37	$7	23.4	276			31%	4.28	17.4	2.6	5.2	**2.0**	0.8		71%	50	102
LIMA C+	2nd Half		5	1	0	61	3.68	1.50	$4	15.9	267			29%	4.74 -	14.6	4.3	5.1	**1.2**	1.0		79%	27	55
Risk X HIGH	03	Proj	**4**	**2**	**0**	**60**	**4.65**	**1.48**	**$2**	**7.3**	**281**			**31%**	**4.86**	**6.5**	**3.5**	**5.7**	**1.7**	**1.1**	**--**	**71%**	**36**	**73**

2-0, 3.41 in 29 IP at LA, which was way over his head. BPIs are nowhere near a sub-4.00 ERA level yet (check out his xERA), and at 29, it's a longshot to expect that they ever will be.

Bell,Rob		Tm	W	L	Sv	IP	ERA	Br/IP	R$	BF/G	OBA	vLH	vRH	H%	xERA	RAR	Ctl	Dom	Cmd	hr/9	G/F	S%	BPV	BPX
RH Starter	98		0	0	0	0	0.00	0.00																
AGE 26 Growth	99	aa	3	6	0	72	3.63	1.40	$5	25.9	293			35%	4.72 -	20.0	2.1	7.8	**3.6**	1.0		77%	90	208
TYPE	00	CIN *	11	8	0	181	4.87	1.40	$8	24.5	249	226	257	27%	5.01	18.4	4.2	7.7	**1.8**	1.9	0.86	73%	31	69
BURN none	01	2TM *	7	12	0	176	6.34	1.60	($10)	24.8	300	308	290	32%	6.21	-21.7	3.5	6.1	**1.8**	1.9	0.84	64%	12	23
ERA Potl -	02	TEX *	10	3	0	177	5.54	1.48	($1)	26.0	288	307	282	31%	5.19	-10.3	3.0	6.0	**2.0**	1.4	1.14	65%	33	62
Support 6.32	1st Half		8	3	0	109	4.86	1.38	$4	26.1	272			31%	4.29 +	3.6	3.0	6.5	**2.2**	1.0		66%	56	106
LIMA F	2nd Half		2	0	0	68	6.64	1.64	($6)	25.7	313			32%	6.63	-13.9	3.2	5.3	**1.7**	2.1		64%	-4	-8
Risk Very High	03	Proj	**4**	**3**	**0**	**80**	**5.63**	**1.51**	**($1)**	**25.3**	**290**			**31%**	**5.58**	**-2.7**	**3.3**	**6.3**	**1.9**	**1.7**	**--**	**67%**	**25**	**50**

4-3, 6.22 in 94 IP at TEX. There's some hint of skill and some evidence of growth, but he still gives up a ton of hits, and usually at the wrong time. There's no hint that this tendency will end soon. Avoid.

Benes,Alan

	Yr	Tm	W	L	Sv	IP	ERA	Br/IP	R$	BF/G	OBA	vLH	vRH	H%	xERA	RAR	Ctl	Dom	Cmd	hr/9	G/F	S%	BPV	BPX
RH Reliever	98	STL	0	0	0	0	0.00	0.00														—		
AGE 31 Peak	99	a/a	0	1	0	12	4.50	1.75	($1)	8.0	334			33%	6.78 -	1.9	3.0	3.0	1.0	1.5	2.00	79%	-18	-41
TYPE	00	STL	• 3	4	0	85	6.35	1.80	($7)	10.3	309	276	300	32%	6.67	-8.2	4.9	5.1	1.0	1.7	1.03	68%	-5	-11
BURN none	01	aaa	9	6	0	156	4.67	1.80	($4)	21.7	326	184	389	36%	6.45 -	15.6	3.9	5.3	1.4	1.2	0.81	77%	15	30
ERA Potl -	02	CHC	• 12	11	0	152	5.63	1.67	($4)	19.9	306	239	306	34%	5.87	-3.4	3.8	5.9	1.5	1.2	0.58	68%	26	54
Support 5.03	1st Half		5	6	0	64	8.28	2.00	($12)	17.5	349			38%	7.75 +	-24.2	4.4	5.8	1.3	1.5		59%	1	2
LIMA F	2nd Half		7	5	0	88	3.69	1.43	$7	22.5	271			31%	4.50 -	20.9	3.5	6.0	1.7	0.9		77%	46	94
Risk Very High	03	Proj	5	5	0	80	5.40	1.74	($3)	17.7	313			34%	6.18 -	0.6	4.1	5.6	1.4	1.2	F	71%	18	36

2-2-, 4.38 ERA in 39 IP at CHC. Looked slightly better in the 2nd half, but batters are still getting good wood on his pitches. At 31, there will be no surprises.

Benes,Andy

	Yr	Tm	W	L	Sv	IP	ERA	Br/IP	R$	BF/G	OBA	vLH	vRH	H%	xERA	RAR	Ctl	Dom	Cmd	hr/9	G/F	S%	BPV	BPX
RH Starter	98	ARI	14	13	0	231	3.97	1.28	$15	28.5	253	259	243	29%	3.86	39.1	2.9	6.4	2.2	1.0	1.21	71%	60	108
AGE 35 Decl	99	ARI	13	12	0	198	4.82	1.51	$7	26.6	279	273	273	30%	5.28	19.3	3.7	6.4	1.7	1.5	1.20	73%	27	60
TYPE Power	00	STL	12	9	0	166	4.88	1.46	$8	24.2	271	268	280	30%	5.16	16.7	3.7	7.4	2.0	1.6	0.86	72%	39	86
BURN none	01	STL	7	7	0	107	7.39	1.71	($9)	18.4	288	286	286	29%	6.89 +	-29.1	5.1	6.6	1.3	2.5	0.90	62%	-12	-22
ERA Potl ----	02	STL	• 6	5	0	114	2.92	1.37	$10	22.2	239	245	214	26%	3.94 -	38.8	4.3	5.6	1.3	0.9	0.81	83%	40	81
Support 5.10	1st Half		0	3	0	21	6.86	2.10	($5)	17.6	329			34%	7.82 -	-3.9	6.4	4.3	0.7	1.7		70%	-22	-46
LIMA C+	2nd Half		6	2	0	93	2.03	1.20	$15	24.0	215			24%	3.06 -	42.8	3.9	5.9	1.5	0.8		88%	56	115
Risk Moderate	03	Proj	7	9	0	140	4.69	1.53	$1	24.9	265			29%	4.97	14.3	4.6	6.0	1.3	1.3	--	73%	27	55

GUARANTEED that his 2nd half will generate interest in March, but you stay far away because:
1. His BPIs were still mediocre
2. 88% strand rate = ERA spike
3. Down history is not on the side of a 35-year-old.

Benitez,Armando

	Yr	Tm	W	L	Sv	IP	ERA	Br/IP	R$	BF/G	OBA	vLH	vRH	H%	xERA	RAR	Ctl	Dom	Cmd	hr/9	G/F	S%	BPV	BPX
RH Reliever	98	BAL	5	6	22	68	3.83	1.28	$19	4.0	200	181	211	27%	3.47	16.6	5.2	11.5	2.2	1.3	0.66	75%	91	195
AGE 30 Peak	99	NYM	4	3	22	78	1.85	1.04	$26	4.0	154	177	127	28%	1.46	38.7	4.7	14.8	3.1	0.5	0.43	84%	165	358
TYPE Power	00	NYM	4	4	41	76	2.61	1.01	$36	3.9	154	136	159	21%	2.15	30.8	4.5	12.6	2.8	1.2	0.66	82%	123	270
BURN none	01	NYM	6	4	43	76	3.78	1.30	$32	4.4	216	212	215	28%	3.81	16.1	4.7	11.0	2.3	1.4	0.74	77%	84	156
ERA Potl No chg	02	NYM	1	0	33	67	2.28	1.06	$31	4.3	196	160	220	26%	2.70	28.5	3.4	10.6	3.2	1.1	0.65	86%	114	233
Support 1.07	1st Half		0	0	19	31	2.60	1.12	$16	4.2	221			29%	2.98	12.0	2.9	9.5	3.3	0.9		81%	111	228
LIMA C	2nd Half		1	0	14	36	2.01	1.01	$15	4.4	172			23%	2.46	16.5	3.8	11.6	3.1	1.3		90%	117	239
Risk Low	03	Proj	3	2	37	75	2.76	1.12	$32	4.3	191			25%	2.88	27.1	4.1	11.3	2.8	1.2	F	82%	106	214

Nothing speaks louder than results, and he has converted over 90% of his save opps over the past three years, including 89% in '02. BPIs are still solid, making him one of the safest closer bets in either league.

Benoit,Joaquin

	Yr	Tm	W	L	Sv	IP	ERA	Br/IP	R$	BF/G	OBA	vLH	vRH	H%	xERA	RAR	Ctl	Dom	Cmd	hr/9	G/F	S%	BPV	BPX
RH Starter	98		0	0	0	0	0.00	0.00																
AGE 23 Growth	99		0	0	0	0	0.00	0.00																
TYPE Power	00	aa	4	4	0	82	5.16	1.43	$2	22.3	273			32%	4.40 +	6.6	3.3	7.0	2.1	0.9		64%	61	144
BURN none	01	a/a	10	5	0	153	5.12	1.53	$1	24.3	268			33%	4.82	6.2	4.5	8.7	1.9	1.1	0.78	68%	61	117
ERA Potl +	02	TEX	• 12	9	1	182	4.64	1.46	$5	24.2	252	275	268	30%	3.93 +	11.3	4.6	7.3	1.6	0.7	0.90	68%	61	116
Support 4.25	1st Half		8	3	0	94	3.83	1.26	$8	24.6	229			27%	3.21 +	16.1	3.8	7.4	1.9	0.8		71%	71	134
LIMA D+	2nd Half		4	6	1	88	5.52	1.67	($4)	23.8	274			33%	4.69 +	-4.8	5.4	7.3	1.3	0.6		66%	53	101
Risk High	03	Proj	6	9	0	140	5.01	1.50	($0)	23.8	263			32%	4.36 +	6.6	4.4	7.8	1.8	0.8	--	67%	61	124

4-5, 5.36 ERA in 84 IP at TEX. BPIs have eroded at each level he's been promoted to. With a 1.0 Cmd ratio in the majors, there's still a long way to go before he is draftworthy.

Benson,Kris

	Yr	Tm	W	L	Sv	IP	ERA	Br/IP	R$	BF/G	OBA	vLH	vRH	H%	xERA	RAR	Ctl	Dom	Cmd	hr/9	G/F	S%	BPV	BPX
RH Starter	98	aaa	8	10	0	156	6.00	1.46	($2)	24.4	288			32%	5.35 +	-11.9	2.8	6.6	2.3	1.6		62%	40	77
AGE 28 Pre-Peak	99	PIT	11	14	0	196	4.09	1.36	$13	27.1	250	279	225	29%	3.75	38.3	3.8	6.4	1.7	0.7	1.64	71%	56	123
TYPE Power	00	PIT	10	12	0	217	3.85	1.34	$14	28.9	252	276	225	30%	4.01	51.6	3.6	7.6	2.1	1.0	1.76	74%	66	144
BURN High	01	PIT	0	0	0	0	0.00	0.00																
ERA Potl --	02	PIT	• 10	8	0	154	4.32	1.48	$6	22.6	280	313	281	31%	4.98 -	23.5	3.4	6.0	1.7	1.2	1.05	74%	36	74
Support 4.97	1st Half		3	6	0	71	4.82	1.58	($2)	21.3	293			33%	5.28	6.1	3.7	6.2	1.7	1.0		71%	39	79
LIMA C	2nd Half		7	2	0	83	3.89	1.39	$7	23.9	268			29%	4.73 -	17.4	3.2	5.7	1.8	1.3		77%	34	70
Risk Very High	03	Proj	12	11	0	200	4.19	1.42	$9	24.8	268			30%	4.59	34.0	3.5	6.5	1.9	1.1	--	74%	46	92

9-6, 4.71 ERA in 130 IP at PIT. BPIs are not back to his pre-injury level, and there was no improvement during the season -- not a good sign. With his current BPIs, he's a late round pick, but keep an eye on him.

Bere,Jason

	Yr	Tm	W	L	Sv	IP	ERA	Br/IP	R$	BF/G	OBA	vLH	vRH	H%	xERA	RAR	Ctl	Dom	Cmd	hr/9	G/F	S%	BPV	BPX
RH Starter	98	2TM	6	9	0	127	5.66	1.69	($6)	21.7	277	311	238	30%	5.45	-4.0	5.5	5.9	1.1	1.2	0.72	68%	22	43
AGE 31 Peak	99	2NL	• 7	3	0	110	6.05	1.85	($6)	19.5	294	267	336	34%	5.85	-7.5	6.1	6.4	1.0	1.0	1.00	68%	27	59
TYPE Power	00	2TM	12	10	0	169	5.48	1.59	$3	24.6	274	267	281	32%	5.24	6.3	4.7	7.6	1.6	1.3	1.14	68%	39	93
BURN none	01	CHC	11	11	0	188	4.31	1.32	$10	24.9	244	289	209	29%	3.99	26.6	3.7	8.4	2.3	1.1	0.96	71%	70	129
ERA Potl +	02	CHC	2	10	0	90	5.50	1.46	($4)	23.2	283	326	264	32%	5.08	-0.5	3.1	6.8	2.2	1.3	1.07	64%	46	95
Support 3.78	1st Half		1	9	0	81	5.21	1.44	($3)	23.6	284			32%	4.99	2.7	2.9	6.9	2.4	1.2		66%	53	108
LIMA D+	2nd Half		1	1	0	9	8.18	1.59	($1)	19.8	266			27%	5.89 +	-3.2	5.1	6.1	1.2	2.0		50%	2	5
Risk Moderate	03	Proj	6	9	0	120	5.25	1.46	$0	22.8	274			32%	4.84	3.3	3.5	7.2	2.0	1.2	--	66%	50	101

It's easier to figure out what went right in '01 than what has gone wrong in every other year. He ruled RHers in '01, lucked out with a 29% hit rate and 71% strand. That's the thing -- skill lasts but luck always runs out.

Bernero,Adam

	Yr	Tm	W	L	Sv	IP	ERA	Br/IP	R$	BF/G	OBA	vLH	vRH	H%	xERA	RAR	Ctl	Dom	Cmd	hr/9	G/F	S%	BPV	BPX
RH Reliever	98		0	0	0	0	0.00	0.00																
AGE 26 Growth	99		0	0	0	0	0.00	0.00																
TYPE	00	DET	• 5	7	0	142	3.35	1.22	$15	20.3	245	242	300	28%	3.38	48.8	2.8	5.8	2.1	0.8	1.59	75%	61	159
BURN none	01	DET	• 6	11	0	152	6.10	1.70	($10)	22.7	325	185	348	36%	5.99	-12.5	3.1	5.4	1.7	0.9	1.58	64%	31	62
ERA Potl No chg	02	DET	• 6	9	0	158	4.67	1.42	$1	18.6	290	321	295	33%	4.75	9.2	2.4	6.4	2.6	1.1	1.18	69%	58	110
Support 4.25	1st Half		4	5	0	101	3.20	1.23	$7	26.2	250			30%	3.09	25.7	2.6	6.3	2.4	0.4		74%	81	153
LIMA C+	2nd Half		2	4	0	57	7.28	1.78	($7)	12.7	352			38%	7.70	-16.5	2.2	6.6	3.0	2.2		63%	21	40
Risk Moderate	03	Proj	3	5	0	80	4.95	1.44	$0	17.4	287			32%	4.94	4.5	2.7	6.1	2.3	1.2	--	68%	44	90

4-7, 6.24 ERA in 101 IP at DET. Good skills foundation, and pitched lights-out in Toledo in the 1st half, but still lots of holes, mostly due to a lack of movement on his pitches. Had a 9.00 ERA in 44 IP at Comerica.

Biddle,Rocky

	Yr	Tm	W	L	Sv	IP	ERA	Br/IP	R$	BF/G	OBA	vLH	vRH	H%	xERA	RAR	Ctl	Dom	Cmd	hr/9	G/F	S%	BPV	BPX
RH Reliever	98		0	0	0	0	0.00	0.00																
AGE 26 Growth	99		0	0	0	0	0.00	0.00																
TYPE Power	00	aa	11	6	0	146	4.68	1.66	$4	29.1	305	333	321	35%	5.57 -	21.0	3.8	6.1	1.6	1.0	0.97	73%	35	83
BURN Low	01	CHW	7	8	0	128	5.41	1.47	($0)	18.8	275	270	274	30%	4.81 +	1.4	3.7	6.0	1.6	1.1	1.19	65%	36	73
ERA Potl --	02	CHW	3	4	1	84	3.86	1.39	$3	7.9	245	287	205	28%	4.33	14.1	4.3	7.7	1.8	1.4	1.67	78%	48	91
Support 3.24	1st Half		1	1	1	30	3.60	1.40	$1	5.6	255			28%	4.59 -	6.1	3.9	6.6	1.7	1.5		81%	34	64
LIMA B	2nd Half		2	3	0	54	4.00	1.39	$1	10.1	240			28%	4.18	8.0	4.5	8.3	1.9	1.3		76%	56	106
Risk Moderate	03	Proj	4	4	0	80	4.39	1.40	$3	8.4	254			29%	4.37	10.5	3.9	7.4	1.9	1.2	G	72%	51	104

Threw harder, struck out more batters, walked more batters. Net result was some very minor growth. Keeping his ERA under 4.00 in 2003 will be more of a challenge.

Boehringer,Brian

	Yr	Tm	W	L	Sv	IP	ERA	Br/IP	R$	BF/G	OBA	vLH	vRH	H%	xERA	RAR	Ctl	Dom	Cmd	hr/9	G/F	S%	BPV	BPX
RH Reliever	98	SD	5	2	0	76	4.38	1.58	$1	6.1	259	263	253	31%	4.89 -	8.7	5.3	7.9	1.5	1.2	0.90	75%	46	84
AGE 33 Past	99	SD	6	5	0	94	3.26	1.40	$8	12.3	268	223	298	30%	4.32 -	28.8	3.4	6.1	1.8	1.0	1.21	80%	48	104
TYPE Power	00	SD	0	3	0	16	5.63	1.75	($2)	10.7	285	280	289	28%	6.71 -	0.0	5.6	5.1	0.9	2.3	1.60	75%	-20	-45
BURN none	01	2TM	0	4	2	69	3.65	1.39	$2	5.8	256	316	208	31%	4.12	16.4	3.8	7.8	2.1	0.9	0.87	76%	67	128
ERA Potl +	02	PIT	4	4	1	79	3.42	1.24	$8	4.7	226	250	218	28%	3.08	21.6	3.8	7.4	2.0	0.6	0.69	73%	79	161
Support 3.73	1st Half		1	2	0	41	2.84	1.12	$5	4.6	205			27%	1.98 +	14.5	3.5	7.4	2.1	0.0		72%	103	212
LIMA B	2nd Half		3	2	1	38	4.05	1.38	$3	4.8	247			28%	4.28	7.1	4.0	7.4	1.8	1.2		74%	52	108
Risk Moderate	03	Proj	3	4	0	75	3.72	1.35	$4	5.6	246			29%	3.82	17.4	3.8	7.6	2.0	0.8	F	74%	67	135

Slightly depressed hit rate kept his OBA low, and in turn, his ERA. That's not to say he doesn't deserve it. BPIs are solid, and few at the draft table will know that he's had a sub-4.00 ERA in 3 of the last 4 years.

Borbon,Pedro

	Yr	Tm	W	L	Sv	IP	ERA	Br/IP	R$	BF/G	OBA	vLH	vRH	H%	xERA	RAR	Ctl	Dom	Cmd	hr/9	G/F	S%	BPV	BPX
LH Reliever	98	a/a	0	3	0	43	6.49	1.95	($7)	5.8	335			37%	6.49	-6.1	4.8	4.4	0.9	0.6		65%	15	29
AGE 35 Decl	99	LA	4	3	1	50	4.14	1.36	$5	3.1	217	156	258	24%	3.48 +	9.4	5.2	5.9	1.1	0.9	0.74	71%	44	96
TYPE Power	00	TOR	1	1	1	41	6.55	2.01	($5)	3.4	279	209	360	31%	6.16	-3.5	8.3	6.3	0.8	1.1	0.85	68%	20	53
BURN none	01	TOR	2	4	0	53	3.73	1.13	$5	3.0	243	182	306	28%	3.70	12.5	2.0	7.6	3.8	1.4	1.06	73%	90	181
ERA Potl -	02	2TM	4	4	1	50	5.40	1.56	$1	3.1	273	240	324	32%	5.57	-0.9	4.5	9.0	2.0	1.8	0.57	71%	42	83
Support 4.47	1st Half		2	3	0	29	5.59	1.52	$1	3.7	268			31%	5.46	-1.2	4.3	8.7	2.0	1.9		68%	40	78
LIMA C+	2nd Half		2	1	1	21	5.14	1.62	$2	2.6	280			34%	5.73 -	0.4	4.7	9.4	2.0	1.7		73%	46	91
Risk Low	03	Proj	3	3	0	50	5.04	1.54	$1	3.1	269			31%	5.15	2.5	4.5	7.9	1.8	1.4	F	71%	42	86

Effective vs LHers only, but as his HR rate grows dangerously high, any value is now at risk. Can be useful if micro-managed outside of Minute Maid Park, but probably not worth the effort.

Borowski,Joe

	Yr	Tm	W	L	Sv	IP	ERA	Br/IP	R$	BF/G	OBA	vLH	vRH	H%	xERA	RAR	Ctl	Dom	Cmd	hr/9	G/F	S%	BPV	BPX
RH Reliever	98	aaa	4	3	4	83	4.12	1.61	$3	7.1	278			32%	5.05 -	14.6	4.8	6.6	1.4	1.0		77%	39	76
AGE 31 Peak	99	aaa	6	2	4	89	6.38	1.73	($1)	7.1	306			35%	5.57 +	-8.1	4.4	5.7	1.3	0.8		62%	32	74
TYPE Power	00	ind	10	5	1	80	4.28	1.38	$11	8.6	250			32%	3.94	15.9	3.9	9.3	2.4	0.9		71%	84	199
BURN none	01	aaa	8	8	1	112	3.62	1.26	$11	11.7	258			32%	3.79	27.1	2.5	8.2	3.3	0.9	3.00	74%	95	183
ERA Potl No chg	02	CHC	4	4	2	95	2.75	1.19	$12	5.3	239	209	260	30%	3.45 -	34.5	2.7	9.2	3.3	0.9	1.02	82%	104	214
Support 1.98	1st Half		2	4	2	45	3.40	1.22	$6	5.0	244			29%	4.04 -	12.4	2.8	8.4	3.0	1.4		79%	78	159
LIMA B	2nd Half		2	0	0	50	2.16	1.16	$7	5.7	234			32%	2.92 -	22.1	2.7	9.9	3.7	0.5		84%	128	264
Risk High	03	Proj	5	4	1	85	3.39	1.28	$9	6.9	250			31%	3.71	23.5	3.1	8.7	2.8	0.8	--	76%	91	183

Excellent BPIs and growth, but his 2.75 ERA was boosted at least a little by an 84% 2nd half strand rate. Despite the great skills, is not likely closer material due to a low 69% relief effectiveness ratio.

Bottalico,Ricky

	Yr	Tm	W	L	Sv	IP	ERA	Br/IP	R$	BF/G	OBA	vLH	vRH	H%	xERA	RAR	Ctl	Dom	Cmd	hr/9	G/F	S%	BPV	BPX
RH Reliever	98	PHI *	1	6	7	55	6.03	1.79	($3)	5.3	291	375	257	31%	6.03	-5.9	5.7	4.9	0.9	1.3	0.81	68%	5	9
AGE 33 Past	99	STL	3	7	20	73	4.93	1.81	$8	5.1	287	310	268	35%	5.62 -	6.0	6.0	8.1	1.3	1.0	1.20	74%	45	98
TYPE Power	00	KC	9	6	16	72	4.86	1.47	$17	5.1	242	241	237	26%	4.64	10.2	5.1	7.0	1.4	1.5	1.06	71%	32	84
BURN none	01	PHI	3	4	3	67	3.90	1.24	$6	4.2	235	282	218	26%	3.99	13.2	3.4	7.7	2.3	1.5	0.83	75%	58	107
ERA Potl --	02	PHI	0	3	0	27	4.67	1.70	($2)	4.2	302	311	292	37%	5.70 -	2.9	4.3	8.0	1.8	1.0	1.36	74%	51	105
Support 2.30	1st Half		0	3	0	27	4.65	1.70	($2)	4.2	302			36%	5.67 -	2.9	4.3	8.0	1.8	1.0		74%	51	105
LIMA D	2nd Half		0	0	0	-0	0.00	0.00																
Risk Moderate	03	Proj	2	4	1	40	4.73	1.58	$0	4.6	271			31%	5.23 -	3.9	4.7	7.4	1.6	1.4	--	74%	38	76

Torn labrum ended his 2002 season and puts 2003 into doubt. Skills have been middling and at 33, upside is limited.

Bradford,Chad

	Yr	Tm	W	L	Sv	IP	ERA	Br/IP	R$	BF/G	OBA	vLH	vRH	H%	xERA	RAR	Ctl	Dom	Cmd	hr/9	G/F	S%	BPV	BPX
RH Reliever	98	CHW *	7	3	2	99	2.64	1.22	$15	6.0	256			28%	3.30 -	40.0	2.3	4.2	1.8	0.5		79%	54	115
AGE 28 Pre-Peak	99	aaa	9	3	5	74	2.07	1.09	$20	6.3	243			29%	2.56 -	36.0	1.7	5.8	3.4	0.2		81%	106	246
TYPE Contact	00	aaa	3	4	10	53	1.87	1.06	$15	3.8	227	474	125	27%	2.36 -	27.6	2.0	6.1	3.0	0.3	17.00	83%	99	235
BURN none	01	OAK *	2	1	3	59	1.83	1.12	$10	5.1	258	300	274	32%	3.47 -	28.9	1.2	8.2	6.8	0.9	3.13	90%	167	334
ERA Potl ++	02	OAK	4	2	2	75	3.12	1.16	$8	4.1	257	267	247	31%	2.82	20.0	1.7	6.7	4.0	0.2	3.28	72%	121	228
Support 3.23	1st Half		3	2	1	40	1.80	0.90	$8	4.3	215			27%	1.60	17.8	1.1	7.4	6.6	0.2		80%	188	356
LIMA A	2nd Half		1	0	1	35	4.64	1.46	$0	3.9	299			35%	4.21	2.2	2.3	5.9	2.6	0.3		66%	77	145
Risk X HIGH	03	Proj	4	2	4	75	3.00	1.19	$10	4.4	257			30%	3.16	23.8	1.9	6.5	3.4	0.5	G	75%	99	202

Superb BPIs and good growth, but note the 2nd half fade in his first full season in the majors. That will depress short-term expectations a tad. Closer-worthy? Skills say yes. REff% of 86% is encouraging as well.

Brock,Chris

	Yr	Tm	W	L	Sv	IP	ERA	Br/IP	R$	BF/G	OBA	vLH	vRH	H%	xERA	RAR	Ctl	Dom	Cmd	hr/9	G/F	S%	BPV	BPX
RH Reliever	98	SF *	11	3	0	142	3.86	1.42	$9	20.6	285	277	281	33%	4.65 -	26.2	2.7	7.0	2.6	0.9	0.68	75%	66	119
AGE 33 Past	99	SF	6	8	0	106	5.52	1.56	($0)	25.0	293	318	261	32%	5.60	0.4	3.5	6.5	1.9	1.5	0.74	68%	28	61
TYPE Contact	00	PHI	7	8	1	93	4.35	1.35	$8	6.3	245	224	247	25%	4.93 -	15.9	4.0	6.7	1.7	2.0	1.08	77%	21	45
BURN none	01	PHI *	9	2	0	110	5.15	1.57	$1	13.4	306	373	211	34%	5.77 -	3.1	2.9	5.9	2.0	1.4	1.20	71%	29	54
ERA Potl ---	02	BAL	2	1	0	49	4.59	1.51	($0)	9.4	303	253	337	31%	5.55 -	3.4	2.6	4.2	1.6	1.5	1.10	74%	10	19
Support 6.55	1st Half		1	0	0	17	5.82	1.94	($1)	9.2	343			36%	7.39 -	-1.6	4.2	4.8	1.1	1.6		73%	-9	-17
LIMA F	2nd Half		1	1	0	32	3.94	1.28	$1	9.6	279			28%	4.57 -	5.0	1.7	3.9	2.3	1.4		75%	30	56
Risk Very High	03	Proj	3	2	0	50	4.68	1.52	$1	10.1	295			31%	5.46 -	4.6	3.1	5.2	1.7	1.4	--	74%	20	41

Consistently poor xERAs say that he's been pitching over his head for years, and several other BPIs corroborate. That's not good news for someone with an ERA that flirts with 5.00.

Brower,Jim

	Yr	Tm	W	L	Sv	IP	ERA	Br/IP	R$	BF/G	OBA	vLH	vRH	H%	xERA	RAR	Ctl	Dom	Cmd	hr/9	G/F	S%	BPV	BPX
RH Reliever	98	aa	13	5	0	155	4.12	1.41	$11	29.2	288			31%	4.40	27.2	2.4	4.4	1.8	0.6		71%	42	81
AGE 30 Peak	99	CLE *	14	12	0	185	5.25	1.49	$8	22.7	285	286	259	29%	5.33	15.3	3.3	4.1	1.2	1.5	0.82	68%	5	12
TYPE	00	CLE *	11	7	0	163	4.86	1.54	$7	22.0	299	292	324	32%	5.27	23.1	3.0	5.0	1.6	1.1	1.32	71%	26	68
BURN none	01	CIN *	8	10	1	140	4.05	1.40	$7	12.6	253	273	227	28%	4.34	24.7	4.0	6.6	1.7	1.2	1.40	75%	44	82
ERA Potl +	02	2NL	3	2	0	80	4.39	1.36	$2	6.6	254	254	251	30%	3.76 +	11.5	3.6	6.4	1.8	0.6	1.86	67%	63	129
Support 3.92	1st Half		3	0	0	50	3.95	1.28	$4	7.5	250			31%	2.95 +	10.1	3.1	6.5	2.1	0.0		66%	88	181
LIMA C+	2nd Half		0	2	0	30	5.12	1.50	($2)	5.5	262			28%	5.11	1.4	4.5	6.3	1.4	1.5		70%	25	51
Risk X HIGH	03	Proj	3	3	0	60	4.50	1.43	$2	6.7	265			29%	4.51	7.7	3.8	6.0	1.6	1.1	G	71%	40	81

Improvement in Cmd carried over into '02, but hit a brick wall at mid-season when he was traded to MON. At 24, this is a minor setback; at 30, teams are far less forgiving.

Brown,Kevin

	Yr	Tm	W	L	Sv	IP	ERA	Br/IP	R$	BF/G	OBA	vLH	vRH	H%	xERA	RAR	Ctl	Dom	Cmd	hr/9	G/F	S%	BPV	BPX
RH Reliever	98	SD	18	7	0	257	2.38	1.07	$37	28.5	237	245	225	32%	2.44	98.2	1.7	9.0	5.2	0.3	3.02	77%	163	295
AGE 38 Decl	99	LA	18	9	0	252	3.00	1.07	$37	28.7	228	255	189	28%	2.66	86.0	2.1	7.9	3.7	0.7	2.20	74%	115	250
TYPE Power	00	LA	13	6	0	230	2.58	0.99	$36	27.3	218	221	206	27%	2.52	93.8	1.8	8.5	4.6	0.8	2.11	78%	134	295
BURN none	01	LA	10	4	0	115	2.66	1.15	$17	23.4	224	263	184	28%	2.81	41.8	3.0	8.1	2.7	0.6	2.57	79%	98	181
ERA Potl No chg	02	LA	4	4	0	73	4.44	1.37	$3	16.5	264	245	296	31%	4.41	10.0	3.2	7.9	2.5	1.1	1.53	70%	68	139
Support 4.52	1st Half		2	3	0	44	4.08	1.27	$3	20.5	266			32%	4.10	8.1	2.2	7.8	3.5	1.0		71%	90	185
LIMA B+	2nd Half		2	1	0	29	4.98	1.52	$0	12.8	262			31%	4.90	1.8	4.7	8.1	1.7	1.2		70%	50	103
Risk Moderate	03	Proj	8	5	0	120	3.98	1.34	$9	18.9	254			30%	3.97	23.8	3.5	7.7	2.2	0.9	G	72%	71	142

Time to come to grips with reality, folks. There is no guarantee that he'll be 100% in '03, he is now a significant injury risk, and possibly more than any other factor, he's now 38.

Buddie,Mike

	Yr	Tm	W	L	Sv	IP	ERA	Br/IP	R$	BF/G	OBA	vLH	vRH	H%	xERA	RAR	Ctl	Dom	Cmd	hr/9	G/F	S%	BPV	BPX
RH Reliever	98	NYY *	9	1	4	84	4.61	1.39	$10	7.2	271			30%	4.00 +	11.8	3.1	4.7	1.5	0.5		66%	45	96
AGE 32 Peak	99	aaa	9	2	0	78	3.12	1.44	$11	6.9	290			35%	4.06 -	27.0	2.5	6.1	2.4	0.2		77%	77	179
TYPE	00	aaa	8	5	2	88	4.81	1.52	$6	10.9	257	252	353	27%	4.68	11.2	4.9	4.5	0.9	1.1	1.50	71%	16	38
BURN none	01	MIL *	4	2	5	87	3.52	1.40	$7	6.5	241	185	256	27%	3.70	21.5	4.6	4.8	1.0	0.6	1.92	76%	39	72
ERA Potl -	02	2NL *	5	6	2	81	5.11	1.64	($1)	6.8	278	319	271	30%	5.01	3.8	5.0	4.7	0.9	0.8	2.45	69%	24	49
Support 5.67	1st Half		1	3	0	45	5.60	1.73	($4)	7.0	291			33%	5.62	-0.8	5.2	6.4	1.2	1.0		68%	31	64
LIMA C+	2nd Half		4	3	2	36	4.50	1.53	$3	6.7	262			27%	4.26	4.6	4.7	2.5	0.5	0.5		70%	14	28
Risk X HIGH	03	Proj	4	6	1	75	4.44	1.53	$2	7.1	264			29%	4.46	10.2	4.7	4.4	0.9	0.7	G	72%	27	55

1-2, 4.62 ERA in 39 IP at MIL and MON. Soft-tosser with poor control and no sign of any growth. But they'll keep trying because there's still a chance he could recapture the 78 IP of AAA magic from 1999.

Buehrle,Mark

	Yr	Tm	W	L	Sv	IP	ERA	Br/IP	R$	BF/G	OBA	vLH	vRH	H%	xERA	RAR	Ctl	Dom	Cmd	hr/9	G/F	S%	BPV	BPX
LH Starter	98		0	0	0	0	0.00	0.00																
AGE 24 Growth	99		0	0	0	0	0.00	0.00																
TYPE Contact	00	CHW *	12	5	0	169	3.56	1.25	$21	16.0	267	260	279	29%	3.89	53.3	2.0	5.2	2.6	0.9	1.15	74%	60	157
BURN Moderate	01	CHW	16	8	0	221	3.30	1.07	$28	27.6	232	208	236	25%	3.07	64.8	2.0	5.1	2.6	1.0	1.10	73%	65	131
ERA Potl -	02	CHW	19	12	0	239	3.58	1.24	$21	29.3	259	228	271	28%	3.74	48.9	2.3	5.0	2.2	0.9	1.50	74%	51	97
Support 6.55	1st Half		11	6	0	121	3.64	1.25	$12	28.1	248			27%	3.57	23.8	2.9	5.2	1.8	0.9		74%	47	90
LIMA F	2nd Half		8	6	0	118	3.51	1.23	$10	30.6	270			29%	3.91	25.1	1.7	4.9	2.9	1.0		75%	62	116
Risk Moderate	03	Proj	16	11	0	225	3.72	1.27	$19	26.2	265			29%	3.95	49.7	2.3	5.0	2.2	1.0	G	74%	50	101

Superb run support nearly made him a 20-game winner on a .500 ballclub. His BPIs were not as magical as '01, and he's still essentially a soft-tosser, so bidding him into the mid-$20s is a high risk exercise.

Burba,Dave

		Tm	W	L	Sv	IP	ERA	Br/IP	R$	BF/G	OBA	vLH	vRH	H%	xERA	RAR	Ctl	Dom	Cmd	hr/9	G/F	S%	BPV	BPX
RH Starter	98	CLE	15	10	0	203	4.12	1.37	$16	27.3	268	253	286	29%	4.65 -	41.8	3.1	5.8	**1.9**	1.3	1.12	75%	37	79
AGE 36 Decl	99	CLE	15	9	0	220	4.25	1.40	$17	27.9	254	224	279	29%	4.40	47.6	3.9	7.1	**1.8**	1.2	1.04	73%	48	121
TYPE Power	00	CLE	16	6	0	191	4.47	1.52	$13	26.5	270	259	274	33%	4.56	36.8	4.3	8.5	**2.0**	0.9	1.40	72%	67	173
BURN none	01	CLE	10	10	0	150	6.23	1.61	($5)	21.3	307	359	255	36%	5.47 +	-15.0	3.2	7.1	**2.2**	1.0	1.11	61%	53	106
ERA Potl No chg	02	2AL	5	5	0	149	5.07	1.44	($2)	18.1	272	247	293	30%	4.43 +	0.8	3.5	5.8	**1.7**	1.0	0.97	66%	41	78
Support 5.33	1st Half		4	4	0	96	5.06	1.40	$0	24.4	274			30%	4.40 +	0.6	3.0	5.9	**2.0**	1.0		65%	46	87
LIMA D	2nd Half		1	1	0	53	5.08	1.52	($2)	12.4	268			30%	4.47 +	0.2	4.4	5.6	**1.3**	0.8		67%	36	68
Risk Low	03	Proj	**6**	**5**	**0**	**120**	**4.80**	**1.48**	**$1**	**23.0**	**279**			**32%**	**4.68**	**9.1**	**3.5**	**6.5**	**1.9**	**1.0**	**--**	**69%**	**48**	**98**

Despite an ERA over 5.00, his BPIs and xERA reflect a return to pre-2001 levels. Of course, nobody else but you and I know that. Is he a $1 sleeper for a 4.50 ERA and few wins? At 36, it's probably a 50-50 shot.

Burkett,John

		Tm	W	L	Sv	IP	ERA	Br/IP	R$	BF/G	OBA	vLH	vRH	H%	xERA	RAR	Ctl	Dom	Cmd	hr/9	G/F	S%	BPV	BPX
RH Starter	98	TEX	9	13	0	195	5.68	1.42	$1	26.4	295	276	308	33%	4.72 +	-0.5	2.1	6.0	**2.8**	0.9	1.35	60%	66	141
AGE 38 Decl	99	TEX	9	8	0	147	5.63	1.56	$1	22.0	307	279	337	34%	5.50	4.7	2.8	5.9	**2.1**	1.1	1.59	65%	40	99
TYPE	00	ATL	10	6	0	134	4.90	1.59	$4	19.5	300	294	309	36%	5.21	13.1	3.4	7.4	**2.2**	0.9	1.53	70%	58	129
BURN none	01	ATL	12	12	0	219	3.04	1.17	$22	26.4	232	223	235	28%	3.06	68.3	2.9	7.7	**2.7**	0.7	1.19	76%	90	166
ERA Potl -	02	BOS	13	8	0	173	4.53	1.44	$7	26.0	290	278	296	32%	4.99	13.4	2.6	6.5	**2.5**	1.3	1.20	72%	49	92
Support 6.45	1st Half		7	3	0	78	3.92	1.43	$5	26.2	292			33%	4.99 -	12.4	2.4	6.6	**2.7**	1.3		77%	55	104
LIMA C+	2nd Half		6	5	0	95	5.03	1.44	$1	25.9	288			32%	5.00	1.0	2.8	6.4	**2.3**	1.3		68%	44	84
Risk High	03	Proj	**9**	**7**	**0**	**140**	**4.37**	**1.40**	**$6**	**24.2**	**279**			**32%**	**4.52**	**18.7**	**2.8**	**6.8**	**2.5**	**1.0**	**--**	**71%**	**61**	**124**

BPIs were very similar to 2001, but his hit rate jumped 4% and he got snakebit by the longball, allowing 8 more HRs in 46 fewer IP. If he was 10 years younger, I'd project a return to a sub-4 ERA, but he's not so I can't.

Burnett,A.J.

		Tm	W	L	Sv	IP	ERA	Br/IP	R$	BF/G	OBA	vLH	vRH	H%	xERA	RAR	Ctl	Dom	Cmd	hr/9	G/F	S%	BPV	BPX
RH Starter	98		0	0	0	0	0.00	0.00																
AGE 26 Growth	99	FLA	* 10	14	0	161	5.53	1.71	($3)	22.6	286	269	221	34%	5.34	0.3	5.3	7.8	**1.5**	1.0	1.78	68%	47	103
TYPE Power	00	FLA	3	7	0	82	4.82	1.51	$0	28.0	257	302	219	29%	4.40	8.9	4.8	6.2	**1.3**	0.9	1.17	69%	42	93
BURN Low	01	FLA	11	12	0	173	4.06	1.32	$11	27.2	229	247	213	26%	3.71	30.4	4.3	6.7	**1.5**	1.0	1.13	72%	50	93
ERA Potl + +	02	FLA	12	9	0	204	3.31	1.19	$22	27.1	210	242	177	27%	2.71 +	58.7	4.0	9.0	**2.3**	0.5	1.10	73%	98	201
Support 3.74	1st Half		8	5	0	127	3.26	1.23	$14	29.3	218			28%	3.00	37.5	4.0	8.5	**2.1**	0.6		75%	88	181
LIMA C	2nd Half		4	4	0	77	3.39	1.13	$9	24.0	196			27%	2.22 +	21.3	4.0	9.7	**2.4**	0.4		69%	115	235
Risk Moderate	03	Proj	**11**	**12**	**0**	**200**	**3.96**	**1.29**	**$14**	**26.3**	**228**			**29%**	**3.33 +**	**40.0**	**4.1**	**8.5**	**2.1**	**0.7**	**--**	**70%**	**82**	**165**

Took a huge step up in '02, nearly doubling his BPV. For real? Despite the trends not preparing us for such a leap, it's tough to discount a good performance by a young arm that is backed up by his BPIs.

Byrd,Paul

		Tm	W	L	Sv	IP	ERA	Br/IP	R$	BF/G	OBA	vLH	vRH	H%	xERA	RAR	Ctl	Dom	Cmd	hr/9	G/F	S%	BPV	BPX
RH Starter	98	2NL	* 10	7	0	159	3.85	1.30	$11	25.8	253	214	213	29%	3.81	29.6	3.1	6.3	**2.0**	0.8	0.95	72%	59	106
AGE 32 Peak	99	PHI	15	11	0	199	4.61	1.38	$13	26.8	268	303	230	27%	4.82	24.9	3.2	4.8	**1.5**	1.5	1.07	72%	16	35
TYPE Contact	00	PHI	2	9	0	83	6.51	1.49	($4)	21.6	275	333	222	28%	5.54 +	-9.8	3.8	5.7	**1.5**	1.8	0.89	60%	11	24
BURN High	01	2TM	* 7	10	0	140	4.76	1.44	$2	25.4	296	352	236	32%	5.06	12.5	2.3	5.2	**2.3**	1.2	0.99	69%	41	79
ERA Potl No chg	02	KC	17	11	0	228	3.91	1.15	$20	28.1	258	269	241	27%	3.94	36.6	1.5	5.1	**3.4**	1.4	0.80	72%	63	118
Support 4.73	1st Half		10	5	0	103	4.10	1.14	$11	26.2	256			26%	4.03	13.9	1.6	5.3	**3.4**	1.6		71%	60	113
LIMA F	2nd Half		7	6	0	125	3.75	1.15	$10	29.9	261			27%	3.87	22.7	1.4	4.9	**3.4**	1.3		73%	65	122
Risk X HIGH	03	Proj	**12**	**13**	**0**	**200**	**4.55**	**1.30**	**$11**	**26.3**	**271**			**29%**	**4.51**	**22.1**	**2.2**	**5.3**	**2.4**	**1.4**	**--**	**69%**	**41**	**83**

Why there will be a huge drop-off in 2003...
- 27% hit rate won't last in KC
- Dominance is getting worse
- Homer prone
- Heaviest workload ever and 88 IP increase from 2001.

Cabrera,Jose

		Tm	W	L	Sv	IP	ERA	Br/IP	R$	BF/G	OBA	vLH	vRH	H%	xERA	RAR	Ctl	Dom	Cmd	hr/9	G/F	S%	BPV	BPX
RH Reliever	98	HOU	* 0	0	0	9	7.00	1.33	($1)	4.8	262	714	182	33%	3.20 +	-2.1	3.0	7.0	**2.3**	0.0	0.63	42%	94	169
AGE 31 Peak	99	HOU	* 7	1	7	80	2.48	0.94	$21	5.4	196	143	241	23%	1.85 +	32.9	2.3	7.0	**3.1**	0.6	0.61	76%	106	230
TYPE	00	HOU	* 2	4	6	74	5.58	1.54	$1	5.2	305	314	304	34%	5.49	0.5	2.7	6.2	**2.3**	1.2	0.74	65%	43	95
BURN High	01	ATL	7	4	2	59	2.89	1.30	$10	4.5	238	247	233	28%	3.52 -	19.6	3.8	6.5	**1.7**	0.8	0.67	81%	60	111
ERA Potl -	02	MIL	6	10	0	103	6.82	1.62	($8)	9.4	311	276	343	32%	6.60	-18.7	3.1	5.3	**1.7**	2.0	0.74	62%	0	0
Support 4.62	1st Half		4	5	0	57	4.88	1.38	$2	7.5	281			28%	5.72 -	4.5	2.5	5.8	**2.3**	2.2		74%	16	33
LIMA D	2nd Half		2	5	0	46	9.24	1.92	($11)	13.0	345			36%	7.71 +	-23.2	3.9	4.7	**1.2**	1.8		52%	-14	-28
Risk X HIGH	03	Proj	**6**	**6**	**0**	**80**	**4.95**	**1.50**	**$2**	**6.7**	**287**			**31%**	**5.29**	**5.4**	**3.3**	**5.9**	**1.8**	**1.4**	**F**	**70%**	**30**	**60**

2001 was over his head, but we still didn't anticipate this type of implosion. Nearly all BPIs fell, some more than others; high hit rate and low strand rate didn't help. But it's an odd-numbered year, so he'll have a 2.75 ERA.

Callaway,Mickey

		Tm	W	L	Sv	IP	ERA	Br/IP	R$	BF/G	OBA	vLH	vRH	H%	xERA	RAR	Ctl	Dom	Cmd	hr/9	G/F	S%	BPV	BPX
RH Starter	98	a/a	10	9	0	137	5.72	1.74	($4)	23.6	315			33%	6.15	-5.2	3.9	4.1	**1.0**	1.2		69%	3	5
AGE 27 Pre-Peak	99	a/a	9	4	0	110	5.24	1.65	$2	22.9	311			35%	5.41	6.8	3.4	5.2	**1.5**	0.7		68%	34	79
TYPE Contact	00	aaa	11	6	0	117	5.54	1.76	$1	21.1	328			35%	6.08 -	3.5	3.5	4.2	**1.2**	0.8		69%	14	34
BURN none	01	aaa	11	7	0	134	4.16	1.41	$9	18.7	300			33%	4.79 -	22.6	1.8	4.7	**2.6**	0.9	1.00	72%	51	99
ERA Potl - - -	02	ANA	* 11	3	0	125	2.59	1.23	$15	22.6	257	215	254	29%	3.59 -	42.2	2.3	6.0	**2.6**	0.9	3.00	83%	69	131
Support 6.55	1st Half		7	0	0	62	1.74	1.19	$11	21.3	245			28%	3.07 -	28.1	2.5	5.5	**2.2**	0.6		89%	69	130
LIMA C	2nd Half		4	3	0	63	3.43	1.27	$5	24.0	268			30%	4.11 -	14.1	2.1	6.6	**3.1**	1.1		78%	71	134
Risk Moderate	03	Proj	**10**	**5**	**0**	**120**	**3.83**	**1.41**	**$9**	**21.6**	**287**			**32%**	**4.55 -**	**24.8**	**2.5**	**5.3**	**2.2**	**0.9**	**G**	**75%**	**48**	**97**

2-1, 4.24 ERA in 34 IP at ANA. Nicely developing skill set. A sub-3.00 ERA won't last, but mid-3's is possible if he continues these trends.

Carpenter,Chris

		Tm	W	L	Sv	IP	ERA	Br/IP	R$	BF/G	OBA	vLH	vRH	H%	xERA	RAR	Ctl	Dom	Cmd	hr/9	G/F	S%	BPV	BPX
RH Starter	98	TOR	12	7	0	175	4.37	1.36	$12	22.7	264	267	264	31%	4.17	30.1	3.1	7.0	**2.2**	0.9	1.72	70%	63	135
AGE 28 Pre-Peak	99	TOR	9	8	0	150	4.38	1.50	$8	27.6	295	299	290	34%	5.01 -	30.0	2.9	6.4	**2.2**	1.0	1.36	73%	52	130
TYPE	00	TOR	10	12	0	175	6.27	1.64	($3)	23.5	292	294	287	31%	5.83	-8.4	4.3	5.8	**1.4**	1.5	1.35	64%	14	36
BURN none	01	TOR	11	11	0	215	4.10	1.41	$9	27.4	274	287	262	31%	4.72 -	39.9	3.1	6.6	**2.1**	1.2	1.65	75%	47	94
ERA Potl - -	02	TOR	* 4	7	0	97	6.39	1.76	($8)	23.9	327	329	276	35%	6.73	-16.7	3.5	5.2	**1.5**	1.7	1.18	67%	2	3
Support 4.79	1st Half		1	3	0	40	8.96	2.16	($9)	20.4	375			37%	9.99 -	-20.7	4.3	5.1	**1.2**	3.1		64%	-58	******
LIMA F	2nd Half		3	4	0	57	4.58	1.47	$1	27.8	288			32%	4.44	4.0	3.0	5.2	**1.7**	0.6		69%	46	87
Risk Low	03	Proj	**1**	**1**	**0**	**20**	**5.40**	**1.65**	**($1)**	**22.9**	**307**			**34%**	**5.88**	**-0.1**	**3.6**	**5.9**	**1.6**	**1.4**	**--**	**70%**	**22**	**45**

Best case scenario, he's back by the All Star break after having surgery to repair a torn labrum. Better case scenario is that we don't anticipate ANY value in '03 so there's no temptation to take a flyer.

Carrara,Giovanni

		Tm	W	L	Sv	IP	ERA	Br/IP	R$	BF/G	OBA	vLH	vRH	H%	xERA	RAR	Ctl	Dom	Cmd	hr/9	G/F	S%	BPV	BPX
RH Reliever	98	JPN	3	2	1	81	4.89	1.44	$1	9.6	250			29%	4.16 +	5.9	4.6	6.4	**1.4**	0.9		67%	47	91
AGE 35 Decl	99	aaa	12	7	0	158	4.04	1.41	$13	17.5	269			29%	4.59 -	35.0	3.3	5.6	**1.7**	1.2		75%	35	81
TYPE	00	aaa	7	2	0	96	4.59	1.51	$5	23.6	294	280	412	34%	5.33 -	15.0	3.0	7.0	**2.3**	1.3	1.06	73%	48	114
BURN none	01	LA	* 7	3	0	114	3.24	1.17	$12	8.8	239	259	207	28%	3.66	32.5	2.5	7.8	**3.1**	1.3	1.09	79%	81	151
ERA Potl - - -	02	LA	6	3	1	90	3.30	1.28	$10	6.0	246	248	240	26%	4.23 -	26.0	3.2	5.6	**1.8**	1.4	0.93	81%	34	70
Support 4.76	1st Half		5	2	1	45	3.99	1.35	$6	5.2	266			27%	4.69 -	8.9	3.0	4.8	**1.6**	1.4		76%	22	46
LIMA D+	2nd Half		1	1	0	45	2.61	1.20	$5	7.1	226			24%	3.78 -	17.2	3.4	6.4	**1.9**	1.4		87%	46	94
Risk Very High	03	Proj	**3**	**4**	**0**	**80**	**4.05**	**1.30**	**$4**	**8.2**	**252**			**27%**	**4.28**	**15.0**	**3.2**	**6.0**	**1.9**	**1.4**	**--**	**74%**	**40**	**80**

Thanks to a 26% hit rate and 81% strand rate, his ERA didn't reflect the significant drop in skills this year. That's good news because you know somebody else will waste a roster spot on him.

Cassidy,Scott

		Tm	W	L	Sv	IP	ERA	Br/IP	R$	BF/G	OBA	vLH	vRH	H%	xERA	RAR	Ctl	Dom	Cmd	hr/9	G/F	S%	BPV	BPX
RH Reliever	98		0	0	0	0	0.00	0.00																
AGE 27 Pre-Peak	99		0	0	0	0	0.00	0.00																
TYPE	00	aa	2	2	0	42	7.71	1.79	($5)	24.7	333			37%	7.01 +	-11.0	3.4	6.4	**1.9**	1.7		58%	15	36
BURN none	01	a/a	9	9	0	160	4.39	1.48	$4	26.1	284			31%	5.01 -	22.2	3.3	5.6	**1.7**	1.2		74%	32	61
ERA Potl + + +	02	TOR	* 2	4	0	75	5.64	1.24	($0)	5.1	224	242	209	23%	3.95 +	-5.4	3.8	6.1	**1.6**	1.7	0.80	58%	30	57
Support 4.23	1st Half		1	1	0	45	4.60	1.09	$2	5.3	196			21%	2.79 +	3.1	3.6	6.2	**1.7**	1.2		60%	53	100
LIMA F	2nd Half		1	3	0	30	7.20	1.47	($2)	4.9	262			25%	5.70 +	-8.4	4.2	6.0	**1.4**	2.4		56%	-3	-6
Risk Very High	03	Proj	**2**	**4**	**0**	**60**	**5.10**	**1.43**	**($0)**	**8.4**	**268**			**28%**	**5.04**	**2.2**	**3.6**	**6.0**	**1.7**	**1.7**	**F**	**69%**	**23**	**47**

Lots of bad news here... Any gains his ERA makes due to his 58% strand will be offset by the losses incurred from his 23% hit rate. Fly ball pitcher with acute gopheritis. Has done better as a starter but destined for the pen.

Castillo,Frank	Tm	W	L	Sv	IP	ERA	Br/IP	R$	BF/G	OBA	vLH	vRH	H%	xERA	RAR	Ctl	Dom	Cmd	hr/9	G/F	S%	BPV	BPX
RH Starter	98 DET	3	9	1	116	6.83	1.67	($9)	19.7	314	278	351	35%	6.08 +	-18.2	3.4	6.3	**1.8**	1.3	1.18	60%	29	62
AGE 34 Past	99 aaa	7	5	0	119	5.82	1.70	($3)	28.9	332			36%	6.38 -	-2.0	2.6	5.4	**2.0**	1.3		68%	25	57
TYPE	00 TOR	10	5	0	138	3.59	1.22	$18	22.8	223	225	216	25%	3.48	43.0	3.7	6.8	**1.9**	1.2	0.77	75%	55	142
BURN none	01 BOS	10	9	0	136	4.23	1.27	$11	22.0	264	251	268	30%	3.96	22.9	2.3	5.9	**2.5**	0.9	1.12	69%	63	126
ERA Potl No chg	02 BOS	6	15	1	163	5.08	1.42	($1)	19.7	275	281	269	31%	4.50 +	0.6	3.2	6.2	**1.9**	1.0	1.16	66%	46	87
Support 3.97	1st Half	5	8	0	94	4.69	1.28	$3	24.7	249			28%	3.69 +	5.3	3.1	5.9	**1.9**	1.0		65%	53	100
LIMA D	2nd Half	1	7	1	69	5.62	1.63	($4)	15.7	307			35%	5.60	-4.7	3.4	6.5	**1.9**	1.2		67%	38	72
Risk Low	03 Proj	**6**	**9**	**0**	**120**	**4.88**	**1.42**	**$2**	**24.8**	**276**			**31%**	**4.55**	**7.9**	**3.1**	**6.2**	**2.0**	**1.1**	**--**	**67%**	**48**	**98**

Had nearly identical BPIs in 2000 and finished with an ERA a run and a half lower. Strand and hit rates can turn bums into heroes and vice versa. Not saying '02 was wonderful, but it wasn't as bad as it seemed.

Chacon,Shawn	Tm	W	L	Sv	IP	ERA	Br/IP	R$	BF/G	OBA	vLH	vRH	H%	xERA	RAR	Ctl	Dom	Cmd	hr/9	G/F	S%	BPV	BPX
RH Starter	98	0	0	0	0	0.00	0.00																
AGE 25 Growth	99	0	0	0	0	0.00	0.00																
TYPE Power	00 aa	10	10	0	173	5.36	1.73	($2)	29.8	295			35%	5.63	9.3	5.0	7.9	**1.6**	1.0		70%	46	108
BURN Low	01 COL	* 8	10	0	184	4.79	1.48	$0	26.1	255	261	259	29%	4.90	14.1	4.6	7.8	**1.7**	1.5	1.20	72%	41	75
ERA Potl --	02 COL	* 7	11	0	139	5.75	1.56	($5)	24.9	274	319	220	28%	5.77	-5.5	4.5	5.2	**1.2**	1.9	1.18	68%	-1	-1
Support 3.54	1st Half	4	5	0	71	4.80	1.40	$2	23.7	247			25%	4.78	6.3	4.3	5.7	**1.3**	1.6		71%	18	37
LIMA F	2nd Half	3	6	0	68	6.76	1.72	($8)	26.3	300			30%	6.80	-11.8	4.6	4.6	**1.0**	2.1		65%	-20	-41
Risk High	03 Proj	**6**	**8**	**0**	**120**	**5.48**	**1.58**	**($3)**	**25.7**	**274**			**30%**	**5.56**	**-0.3**	**4.6**	**6.5**	**1.4**	**1.7**	**--**	**69%**	**19**	**38**

Management of a pitching staff in COL is an exercise in futility. Those with good skills have to be micro-managed, those with skills potential get the spoils, and those with no skills put their careers on the line each night.

Chen,Bruce	Tm	W	L	Sv	IP	ERA	Br/IP	R$	BF/G	OBA	vLH	vRH	H%	xERA	RAR	Ctl	Dom	Cmd	hr/9	G/F	S%	BPV	BPX
LH Reliever	98 ATL	* 17	8	0	183	3.24	1.20	$23	23.6	225	364	275	30%	2.99	48.9	3.4	9.6	**2.8**	0.7	0.68	75%	107	193
AGE 25 Growth	99 ATL	* 8	5	0	129	4.88	1.35	$7	18.4	250	222	203	30%	4.38 +	11.5	3.7	8.9	**2.4**	1.5	0.52	68%	65	140
TYPE Power	00 2NL	7	4	0	134	3.29	1.21	$15	15.0	235	223	235	27%	3.66	42.0	3.1	7.5	**2.4**	1.2	0.60	78%	68	150
BURN none	01 2NL	* 9	7	0	171	4.68	1.36	$5	23.6	257	278	256	29%	4.72	15.6	3.4	7.6	**2.2**	1.6	0.62	71%	47	86
ERA Potl +	02 2NL	2	5	0	77	5.61	1.66	($6)	6.4	281	252	287	36%	5.10 +	-1.6	5.0	9.4	**1.9**	0.8	0.74	66%	69	142
Support 5.68	1st Half	2	4	0	48	6.74	1.89	($7)	11.0	314			42%	5.92 +	-8.2	5.4	10.1	**1.9**	0.6		63%	75	154
LIMA D+	2nd Half	0	1	0	29	3.74	1.28	$1	3.6	220			26%	3.74	6.7	4.4	8.1	**1.9**	1.2		76%	61	126
Risk Very High	03 Proj	**3**	**4**	**0**	**80**	**4.50**	**1.41**	**$1**	**7.9**	**254**			**30%**	**4.47**	**10.2**	**4.1**	**8.4**	**2.1**	**1.2**	**F**	**72%**	**61**	**123**

Had a few good stretches out of the pen, which CIN is using to justify putting him back in the rotation. But his Cmd trend tells the true story of a difficult student whose good skills are being worn down. Too risky.

Clemens,Roger	Tm	W	L	Sv	IP	ERA	Br/IP	R$	BF/G	OBA	vLH	vRH	H%	xERA	RAR	Ctl	Dom	Cmd	hr/9	G/F	S%	BPV	BPX
RH Starter	98 TOR	20	6	0	234	2.65	1.10	$38	28.5	204	197	198	29%	2.23	94.2	3.4	10.4	**3.1**	0.4	1.86	76%	129	275
AGE 40 Decl	99 NYY	14	10	0	187	4.62	1.47	$12	27.4	260	263	259	31%	4.41	31.3	4.3	7.8	**1.8**	1.0	1.37	70%	59	149
TYPE Power	00 NYY	13	8	0	204	3.70	1.31	$21	27.0	242	206	267	29%	3.92	60.3	3.7	8.3	**2.2**	1.1	1.08	76%	69	179
BURN none	01 NYY	20	3	0	220	3.52	1.26	$25	27.9	248	235	258	31%	3.55	58.0	2.9	8.7	**3.0**	0.8	1.48	74%	96	193
ERA Potl ++	02 NYY	13	7	0	187	4.24	1.29	$11	26.3	253	220	283	33%	3.67 +	21.8	3.0	9.5	**3.1**	0.9	1.26	69%	101	191
Support 5.10	1st Half	8	3	0	108	4.16	1.29	$7	26.8	247			33%	3.39 +	13.7	3.3	10.0	**3.0**	0.7		68%	109	205
LIMA C+	2nd Half	5	4	0	79	4.34	1.29	$4	25.5	262			32%	4.06	8.1	2.6	8.8	**3.3**	1.1		70%	91	173
Risk Low	03 Proj	**10**	**7**	**0**	**160**	**4.22**	**1.32**	**$10**	**27.1**	**250**			**31%**	**3.87**	**24.6**	**3.4**	**8.7**	**2.5**	**1.0**	**--**	**70%**	**80**	**162**

Takes a fair amount of bad luck to have an ERA over 4.00 with a BPV over 100. xERA shows what his ERA should have been, and now remember that he's 40. Amazing, but the descent has to begin eventually.

Clement,Matt	Tm	W	L	Sv	IP	ERA	Br/IP	R$	BF/G	OBA	vLH	vRH	H%	xERA	RAR	Ctl	Dom	Cmd	hr/9	G/F	S%	BPV	BPX
RH Starter	98 aaa	12	9	0	185	3.89	1.40	$12	25.8	251	294	278	30%	3.73	38.1	4.1	7.0	**1.7**	0.5	1.75	72%	67	130
AGE 28 Pre-Peak	99 SD	10	12	0	180	4.50	1.53	$5	25.9	272	319	235	32%	4.65	25.2	4.3	6.8	**1.6**	0.9	1.92	72%	47	102
TYPE Power	00 SD	13	17	0	205	5.14	1.56	$4	27.0	251	267	227	30%	4.52 +	13.5	5.5	7.5	**1.4**	1.0	2.06	68%	49	108
BURN none	01 FLA	9	10	0	169	5.06	1.52	($0)	24.2	265	286	248	31%	4.46 +	7.0	4.5	7.1	**1.6**	0.8	1.36	67%	54	100
ERA Potl ++	02 CHC	12	11	0	205	3.60	1.20	$20	26.4	219	219	212	28%	3.09 +	51.0	3.7	9.4	**2.5**	0.8	1.62	72%	97	200
Support 5.31	1st Half	6	5	0	104	3.71	1.15	$11	26.5	216			28%	2.99 +	24.4	3.4	9.2	**2.7**	0.9		70%	99	203
LIMA C+	2nd Half	6	6	0	101	3.48	1.26	$10	26.3	222			29%	3.19	26.7	4.1	9.6	**2.3**	0.7		74%	96	198
Risk Low	03 Proj	**12**	**12**	**0**	**200**	**3.96**	**1.32**	**$14**	**25.7**	**236**			**30%**	**3.58**	**40.0**	**4.1**	**8.8**	**2.2**	**0.8**	**G**	**72%**	**82**	**164**

Exhibited the best control of his career and took a huge step up. Pretty much maintatined those levels all year, which bodes well for a good follow-up in '03.

Coggin,Dave	Tm	W	L	Sv	IP	ERA	Br/IP	R$	BF/G	OBA	vLH	vRH	H%	xERA	RAR	Ctl	Dom	Cmd	hr/9	G/F	S%	BPV	BPX
RH Reliever	98 aa	4	8	0	108	5.08	1.71	($5)	25.0	286			31%	5.23	5.0	5.3	4.7	**0.9**	0.8		70%	22	43
AGE 26 Growth	99 aa	2	5	0	42	9.00	2.00	($8)	23.0	347			35%	8.02 +	-18.6	4.5	4.1	**0.9**	1.9		56%	-29	-67
TYPE Power	00 PHI	* 8	5	0	122	5.23	1.61	$1	25.2	280	341	299	32%	4.86	6.5	4.6	5.5	**1.2**	0.7	1.48	67%	35	77
BURN none	01 PHI	* 11	12	0	192	4.22	1.49	$5	26.5	281	275	270	31%	4.52	29.5	3.5	5.2	**1.5**	0.7	1.96	72%	41	76
ERA Potl +	02 PHI	2	5	0	77	4.68	1.51	($1)	9.0	230	287	189	28%	3.71 +	8.1	6.0	7.5	**1.3**	0.5	1.82	68%	66	136
Support 3.74	1st Half	0	2	0	42	6.43	1.71	($6)	10.8	252			29%	4.89 +	-5.5	6.9	6.6	**1.0**	0.9		62%	39	80
LIMA D+	2nd Half	2	3	0	35	2.57	1.26	$4	7.3	202			28%	2.29	13.5	4.9	8.5	**1.7**	0.0		77%	102	209
Risk X HIGH	03 Proj	**3**	**5**	**0**	**75**	**4.56**	**1.52**	**($0)**	**9.3**	**257**			**30%**	**4.19**	**9.0**	**4.9**	**6.5**	**1.3**	**0.6**	**G**	**70%**	**52**	**105**

An 8.13 ERA as a starter, 2.31 from the pen. However... his bulpen work resulted in a 1.3 Cmd ratio, which was depressed by a horrible 6.4 walk rate. Others might take a flyer on his "fine" pen ERA, but you don't.

Colome,Jesus	Tm	W	L	Sv	IP	ERA	Br/IP	R$	BF/G	OBA	vLH	vRH	H%	xERA	RAR	Ctl	Dom	Cmd	hr/9	G/F	S%	BPV	BPX
RH Reliever	98	0	0	0	0	0.00	0.00																
AGE 22 Growth	99	0	0	0	0	0.00	0.00																
TYPE Power	00 aa	10	6	0	125	3.67	1.34	$14	23.1	249			29%	3.70	35.0	3.6	6.5	**1.8**	0.7		74%	60	143
BURN none	01 TAM	* 2	6	0	65	4.43	1.40	$1	6.5	250	186	222	28%	4.38	9.2	4.2	6.8	**1.6**	1.2	1.37	72%	43	85
ERA Potl +	02 TAM	* 4	9	1	70	6.04	1.76	($4)	6.5	281	414	287	33%	5.27 +	-8.8	5.9	7.5	**1.3**	0.9	1.15	66%	43	81
Support 3.48	1st Half	2	5	0	39	6.21	1.89	($4)	7.0	303			39%	5.53 +	-5.8	6.0	8.5	**1.4**	0.5		65%	62	116
LIMA C+	2nd Half	2	4	1	31	5.83	1.59	($0)	6.1	250			27%	4.95 +	-3.0	5.8	6.1	**1.1**	1.5		66%	20	38
Risk Very High	03 Proj	**3**	**5**	**0**	**50**	**4.86**	**1.54**	**$0**	**7.2**	**262**			**30%**	**4.68**	**3.4**	**4.9**	**6.8**	**1.4**	**1.1**	**--**	**70%**	**41**	**83**

2-7, 8.34 ERA in 41 IP at TAM. His BPIs are nothing to write home about, but in his defense, his horrible '02 was driven by two bad outings...
Apr 11 @BAL: 1/3 IP 7 ER
May 14 @NYY: 2/3 IP 6 ER

Colon,Bartolo	Tm	W	L	Sv	IP	ERA	Br/IP	R$	BF/G	OBA	vLH	vRH	H%	xERA	RAR	Ctl	Dom	Cmd	hr/9	G/F	S%	BPV	BPX
RH Starter	98 CLE	14	9	0	204	3.71	1.39	$16	28.4	263	271	248	31%	3.98	53.3	3.5	7.0	**2.0**	0.7	1.52	74%	66	142
AGE 29 Peak	99 CLE	18	5	0	205	3.95	1.27	$24	26.9	242	255	229	28%	3.78	52.7	3.3	7.1	**2.1**	1.1	1.52	72%	62	155
TYPE	00 CLE	15	8	0	188	3.88	1.39	$19	27.0	235	242	225	31%	3.86	51.2	4.7	10.1	**2.2**	1.0	1.13	75%	84	218
BURN none	01 CLE	14	12	0	222	4.09	1.40	$12	28.2	260	278	242	31%	4.32	41.4	3.6	8.1	**2.2**	1.1	1.15	74%	67	134
ERA Potl -	02 2TM	20	8	0	233	2.94	1.24	$29	29.4	250	242	261	28%	3.51 -	72.9	2.7	5.8	**2.1**	0.8	1.37	79%	61	120
Support 5.17	1st Half	10	4	0	116	2.56	1.16	$18	29.6	241			27%	3.28 -	42.2	2.4	5.8	**2.4**	0.9		82%	67	131
LIMA D	2nd Half	10	4	0	117	3.31	1.32	$13	29.1	259			29%	3.75	30.7	3.0	5.7	**1.9**	0.7		77%	57	111
Risk Very Low	03 Proj	**18**	**9**	**0**	**225**	**3.48**	**1.29**	**$23**	**28.7**	**251**			**29%**	**3.77**	**58.3**	**3.1**	**6.7**	**2.2**	**0.9**	**--**	**76%**	**64**	**130**

Ironically, this big breakout year was accomplished with the least impressive BPIs since his rookie year. Was pitching more deliberately, improved his control but was less dominant. xERA adds some perspective.

Cordero,Francisco		W	L	Sv	IP	ERA	Br/IP	R$	BF/G	OBA	vLH	vRH	H%	xERA	RAR	Ctl	Dom	Cmd	hr/9	G/F	S%	BPV	BPX
RH Reliever	98	0	0	0	0	0.00	0.00																
AGE 25 Growth	99 DET	* 6	3	27	71	2.03	1.38	$27	4.6	225	133	405	29%	3.41 -	36.5	5.1	9.3	**1.8**	0.6	1.12	88%	85	213
TYPE Power	00 TEX	1	2	0	77	5.37	1.75	($4)	6.4	286	310	271	31%	5.78	5.6	5.6	5.7	**1.0**	1.3	0.79	72%	15	39
BURN none	01 TEX	0	1	0	2	4.29	2.38	($0)	3.7	336			38%	7.01 -	0.3	8.6	4.3	**0.5**	0.0	0.75	80%	24	48
ERA Potl +	02 TEX	* 2	2	12	57	2.84	1.23	$10	4.7	237	189	216	31%	3.07	17.4	3.2	9.1	**2.9**	0.6	1.00	79%	104	197
Support 5.16	1st Half	0	2	4	29	3.10	1.34	$2	5.6	248			33%	3.50	7.8	3.7	9.3	**2.5**	0.6		78%	95	180
LIMA C	2nd Half	2	0	8	28	2.56	1.10	$8	4.0	225			29%	2.62	9.6	2.6	9.0	**3.5**	0.6		79%	118	223
Risk High	03 Proj	**3**	**2**	**33**	**75**	**3.48**	**1.28**	**$22**	**8.3**	**238**			**30%**	**3.46**	**19.0**	**3.6**	**8.5**	**2.4**	**0.8**	**--**	**75%**	**83**	**169**

2-0, 1.80 ERA, 10 saves in 45 IP at TEX. BPIs are clearly closer-worthy, but after two down years with injuries, one has to question his durability. If healthy, there is definitely a future bullpen stud here.

Cormier,Rheal

	Tm	W	L	Sv	IP	ERA	Br/IP	R$	BF/G	OBA	vLH	vRH	H%	xERA	RAR	Ctl	Dom	Cmd	hr/9	G/F	S%	BPV	BPX
LH Reliever	98 aa	0	0	0	10	7.20	1.90	($2)	16.1	362			34%	9.63 -	-2.4	2.7	4.5	1.7	3.6		73%	-63	******
AGE 36 Decl	99 BOS	2	0	0	63	3.71	1.25	$5	4.4	256	198	276	29%	3.47	18.2	2.6	5.6	2.2	0.6	1.61	71%	66	165
TYPE Power	00 BOS	3	3	0	68	4.63	1.34	$4	4.5	278	264	280	31%	4.28	11.7	2.2	5.7	2.5	0.9	1.49	67%	59	153
BURN none	01 PHI	5	6	1	51	4.23	1.29	$5	3.6	254	294	223	29%	3.82	7.8	3.0	6.5	2.2	0.9	2.05	69%	63	116
ERA Potl +	02 PHI	5	6	0	60	5.25	1.55	$0	5.0	265	291	253	31%	4.68 +	1.7	4.8	7.4	1.5	0.9	2.63	67%	51	105
Support 4.65	1st Half	3	4	0	29	5.59	1.48	$1	4.0	248			29%	4.32 +	-0.5	5.0	7.1	1.4	0.9		63%	50	103
LIMA B	2nd Half	2	2	0	31	4.94	1.61	($0)	6.4	280			34%	5.03	2.2	4.6	7.5	1.6	0.9		70%	52	107
Risk Low	03 Proj	4	5	0	60	4.65	1.43	$2	4.5	265			31%	4.36	6.5	3.8	6.8	1.8	0.9	G	69%	53	107

Over past 2-3 years, has been throwing harder, getting more strikeouts, walking more and inducing more ground balls. This would not be a bad trend if it worked, but his Cmd and ERA have suffered.

Cornejo,Nate

	Tm	W	L	Sv	IP	ERA	Br/IP	R$	BF/G	OBA	vLH	vRH	H%	xERA	RAR	Ctl	Dom	Cmd	hr/9	G/F	S%	BPV	BPX
RH Starter	98	0	0	0	0	0.00	0.00																
AGE 23 Growth	99	0	0	0	0	0.00	0.00																
TYPE Contact	00 aa	5	7	0	91	5.34	1.54	$1	25.4	282			32%	4.47 +	5.1	3.9	5.0	1.3	0.5		64%	41	98
BURN none	01 a/a	16	3	0	154	2.98	1.23	$22	27.8	253	302	381	29%	3.50 -	50.3	2.5	6.3	2.5	0.7	1.79	78%	74	142
ERA Potl -	02 DET *	10	13	0	182	5.34	1.64	($4)	27.7	328	273	337	36%	5.63	-5.6	2.3	5.0	2.1	0.8	2.23	67%	41	77
Support 3.60	1st Half	5	7	0	99	4.82	1.63	($2)	26.5	318			35%	5.62 -	3.8	2.8	5.3	1.9	1.0		72%	32	61
LIMA B	2nd Half	5	6	0	83	5.96	1.65	($3)	29.2	341			38%	5.64	-9.5	1.7	4.7	2.7	0.5		62%	55	104
Risk Very High	03 Proj	6	9	0	120	4.58	1.48	$2	27.8	299			34%	4.70	12.8	2.6	5.4	2.1	0.7	G	69%	52	106

1-5, 5.04 ERA in 50 IP at DET. Poster boy for the effects of random hit rates. His BPIs show some promise, but there's a ways to go before he puts the pieces together. Decent option in a deep Ultra league.

Creek,Doug

	Tm	W	L	Sv	IP	ERA	Br/IP	R$	BF/G	OBA	vLH	vRH	H%	xERA	RAR	Ctl	Dom	Cmd	hr/9	G/F	S%	BPV	BPX
LH Reliever	98 JPN	0	4	0	29	5.59	1.66	($2)	19.0	220			25%	4.62 +	-0.6	7.8	7.4	1.0	1.2		68%	39	75
AGE 34 Past	99 aaa	7	3	1	130	5.12	1.65	$0	23.7	285	143	313	32%	6.03 -	10.0	4.7	8.0	1.7	1.9	0.09	75%	25	58
TYPE Power	00 TAM *	1	3	1	78	4.02	1.43	$3	6.2	214	170	260	28%	3.94	19.8	6.0	10.6	1.8	1.3	0.51	76%	75	195
BURN none	01 TAM	2	5	0	62	4.34	1.61	($1)	4.3	225	198	250	29%	4.34	9.5	7.1	9.5	1.3	1.0	0.68	75%	65	130
ERA Potl ++++	02 SEA	3	2	0	55	5.89	1.67	($3)	4.9	269	239	277	36%	4.34 +	-5.8	5.7	9.2	1.6	0.3	0.93	62%	80	151
Support 5.01	1st Half	2	0	0	27	6.29	1.76	($2)	4.9	281			34%	5.99	-4.3	6.0	9.3	1.6	1.7		67%	37	71
LIMA C	2nd Half	1	2	0	28	5.50	1.58	($1)	4.8	256			37%	2.72 +	-1.5	5.5	9.1	1.6	-1.0		57%	122	230
Risk High	03 Proj	2	2	0	50	4.14	1.54	$0	5.2	242			32%	4.05	8.2	5.8	9.4	1.6	0.7	–	74%	75	153

His major downfall is the BB, but there are other good things. Throws hard, keeps the ball in the park and posted an unduly inflated ERA in '02 due to H% and S%. That will rebound, making him a marginal pick.

Cressend,Jack

	Tm	W	L	Sv	IP	ERA	Br/IP	R$	BF/G	OBA	vLH	vRH	H%	xERA	RAR	Ctl	Dom	Cmd	hr/9	G/F	S%	BPV	BPX
RH Reliever	98 aa	10	11	0	149	6.04	1.77	($7)	24.1	329			38%	6.23	-12.2	3.5	6.6	1.9	1.0		66%	40	78
AGE 27 Pre-Peak	99 aa	8	10	0	160	6.02	1.68	($5)	26.3	313			36%	5.54	-6.9	3.5	6.5	1.9	0.8		63%	47	109
TYPE Power	00 MIN *	4	4	8	100	4.32	1.63	$6	7.0	297	350	371	36%	4.84 -	21.3	4.0	7.1	1.8	0.5	1.83	73%	63	162
BURN none	01 MIN *	5	4	1	74	3.77	1.30	$7	5.6	259	294	198	29%	4.00	17.0	2.8	5.8	2.1	1.0	1.56	74%	53	106
ERA Potl - - -	02 MIN	0	1	0	32	5.91	1.84	($4)	6.6	307	355	261	33%	6.64 -	-3.4	5.3	6.2	1.2	1.7	0.79	72%	4	8
Support 5.63	1st Half	0	1	0	32	5.91	1.84	($4)	6.6	307			33%	6.64 -	-3.4	5.3	6.2	1.2	1.7		72%	4	8
LIMA D	2nd Half	0	0	0	0	0.00	0.00																
Risk Very High	03 Proj	1	1	0	20	4.95	1.65	($0)	7.6	299			34%	5.32	1.1	4.1	6.3	1.6	0.9	F	71%	39	79

Had surgery in Sept for a torn labrum and will provide little value in 2003.

Crudale,Mike

	Tm	W	L	Sv	IP	ERA	Br/IP	R$	BF/G	OBA	vLH	vRH	H%	xERA	RAR	Ctl	Dom	Cmd	hr/9	G/F	S%	BPV	BPX
RH Reliever	98	0	0	0	0	0.00	0.00																
AGE 26 Growth	99	0	0	0	0	0.00	0.00																
TYPE Power	00	0	0	0	0	0.00	0.00																
BURN none	01 aa	4	9	9	80	4.61	1.51	$6	5.7	299			37%	5.12 -	8.7	2.8	8.4	3.0	1.0		71%	79	151
ERA Potl No chg	02 STL *	4	0	7	66	2.04	1.10	$16	4.3	224	247	216	29%	2.68 -	30.3	2.6	8.4	3.3	0.5	0.66	84%	113	232
Support 4.96	1st Half	1	0	7	30	2.09	1.06	$9	4.8	227			30%	2.37	13.6	2.1	8.6	4.1	0.3		81%	140	286
LIMA A	2nd Half	3	0	0	36	2.00	1.14	$7	3.9	222			28%	2.94 -	16.7	3.0	8.2	2.8	0.7		87%	95	196
Risk Moderate	03 Proj	3	3	2	60	3.30	1.27	$7	4.7	255			32%	3.65	17.3	2.7	8.4	3.1	0.8	F	76%	97	195

3-0, 1.90 ERA in 52 IP at STL. Excellent BPIs for two years now, little fanfare and no set role, making him a terrific LIMA pick. 84% strand rate means his ERA is heading up, but another run won't hurt him.

Cruz,Juan

	Tm	W	L	Sv	IP	ERA	Br/IP	R$	BF/G	OBA	vLH	vRH	H%	xERA	RAR	Ctl	Dom	Cmd	hr/9	G/F	S%	BPV	BPX
RH Reliever	98	0	0	0	0	0.00	0.00																
AGE 24 Growth	99	0	0	0	0	0.00	0.00																
TYPE Power	00	0	0	0	0	0.00	0.00																
BURN High	01 CHC *	12	7	0	166	3.90	1.34	$12	22.8	243			31%	3.51	32.5	4.0	8.8	2.2	0.6		71%	88	164
ERA Potl -	02 CHC	3	11	1	97	3.99	1.47	$2	9.5	235	250	234	27%	4.20	19.1	5.5	7.5	1.4	1.0	1.16	76%	51	105
Support 3.14	1st Half	1	10	0	64	4.49	1.61	($3)	13.8	249			28%	4.83	8.3	6.0	7.0	1.2	1.1		75%	38	78
LIMA B+	2nd Half	2	1	1	33	3.01	1.22	$5	5.7	206			25%	2.99	10.8	4.4	8.5	1.9	0.8		78%	81	166
Risk Very High	03 Proj	5	7	0	100	3.78	1.36	$6	10.4	232			29%	3.64	22.4	4.6	8.3	1.8	0.8	–	74%	72	145

Took a step back in '02, and now looks slightly better suited for the bullpen, at least in the short term.

	ERA	OBA	Cmd
Starter	3.75	.267	1.0
Reliever	4.18	.217	1.8

Cruz,Nelson

	Tm	W	L	Sv	IP	ERA	Br/IP	R$	BF/G	OBA	vLH	vRH	H%	xERA	RAR	Ctl	Dom	Cmd	hr/9	G/F	S%	BPV	BPX
RH Reliever	98 aaa	10	6	0	126	6.07	1.71	($4)	16.7	333			37%	6.30	-10.8	2.7	5.9	2.2	1.1		65%	36	69
AGE 30 Peak	99 DET *	9	6	0	128	4.71	1.37	$9	14.1	265	299	265	29%	4.46	19.9	3.2	5.9	1.9	1.2	1.31	68%	41	102
TYPE Power	00 DET *	7	6	0	93	4.35	1.35	$9	10.5	272	236	268	31%	4.45	19.5	2.7	6.5	2.4	1.2	1.32	71%	55	143
BURN none	01 HOU	3	3	2	82	4.17	1.17	$6	5.1	237	273	209	28%	3.58 +	13.2	2.6	8.2	3.1	1.2	0.82	68%	86	160
ERA Potl - -	02 HOU *	2	7	1	86	4.81	1.50	($1)	7.8	284	299	272	32%	5.46 -	7.4	3.5	7.0	2.0	1.6	1.02	73%	36	74
Support 4.37	1st Half	0	5	1	42	5.34	1.59	($3)	7.3	296			31%	6.22 -	0.6	3.6	6.2	1.7	1.9		72%	11	23
LIMA B	2nd Half	2	2	0	44	4.31	1.41	$1	8.3	271			32%	4.73	6.8	3.3	7.8	2.4	1.2		73%	61	124
Risk Very High	03 Proj	3	5	1	75	4.56	1.40	$2	7.5	272			31%	4.77	9.0	3.1	7.2	2.3	1.3	–	71%	53	106

Decent skill set, but trouble with the gopherball makes him a risk to implode at any time. His xERA in '02 is fair warning. High risk,. moderate reward.

D'Amico,Jeff

	Tm	W	L	Sv	IP	ERA	Br/IP	R$	BF/G	OBA	vLH	vRH	H%	xERA	RAR	Ctl	Dom	Cmd	hr/9	G/F	S%	BPV	BPX
RH Starter	98 MIL	0	0	0	0	0.00	0.00																
AGE 27 Growth	99 MIL *	0	0	0	6	19.50	2.67	($4)	11.2	434			48%	11.02 +	-11.2	4.5	6.0	1.3	1.5	1.00	20%	-13	-28
TYPE	00 MIL *	13	8	0	193	2.75	1.16	$27	27.2	237	242	234	26%	3.28 -	74.5	2.6	5.5	2.1	0.9	1.03	81%	58	129
BURN High	01 MIL	2	4	0	47	6.11	1.61	($3)	21.4	311	333	289	33%	6.62 -	-4.7	3.1	6.1	2.0	2.1	0.60	68%	8	16
ERA Potl +	02 NYM	6	10	0	145	4.97	1.30	$3	21.1	271	249	283	30%	4.48	9.6	2.3	6.3	2.7	1.2	0.82	64%	58	120
Support 3.52	1st Half	4	7	0	98	4.59	1.14	$6	24.9	246			27%	3.68 +	11.4	2.0	6.4	3.2	1.2		63%	75	155
LIMA C+	2nd Half	2	3	0	47	5.74	1.64	($3)	16.5	319			35%	6.14	-1.8	2.9	5.9	2.1	1.3		67%	30	62
Risk X HIGH	03 Proj	6	8	0	120	5.03	1.46	$1	21.0	291			32%	5.38	6.9	2.7	6.0	2.2	1.5	–	70%	34	69

Good skills are worthless if you can't count on him being on the mound. The injury risk, and any performance fallout as a result, far outweighs the possible gain. No more than a token bid, and only for the brave.

Daal,Omar

	Tm	W	L	Sv	IP	ERA	Br/IP	R$	BF/G	OBA	vLH	vRH	H%	xERA	RAR	Ctl	Dom	Cmd	hr/9	G/F	S%	BPV	BPX
LH Starter	98 ARI	8	12	0	162	2.89	1.21	$15	20.3	242	283	237	29%	3.26	51.0	2.8	7.3	2.6	0.7	1.68	78%	85	153
AGE 31 Peak	99 ARI	16	9	0	214	3.66	1.25	$23	27.9	238	204	242	27%	3.44	54.1	3.3	6.2	1.9	0.9	1.26	73%	58	125
TYPE	00 2NL	4	19	0	167	6.14	1.68	($11)	24.0	306	298	307	33%	6.05	-11.5	3.9	5.2	1.3	1.4	1.33	65%	11	24
BURN none	01 PHI	13	7	0	185	4.47	1.38	$9	24.9	276	214	286	29%	4.71	22.2	2.7	5.2	1.9	1.3	1.17	71%	33	62
ERA Potl -	02 LA	11	9	0	161	3.91	1.22	$15	17.1	238	243	237	26%	3.71	33.3	3.0	5.9	1.9	1.1	1.08	72%	50	102
Support 4.41	1st Half	6	3	0	69	3.65	1.06	$11	12.5	217			25%	3.07 +	16.8	2.5	7.4	3.0	1.2		70%	84	172
LIMA D	2nd Half	5	6	0	92	4.11	1.34	$5	23.0	253			27%	4.19	16.6	3.4	4.7	1.4	1.1		72%	29	59
Risk Moderate	03 Proj	11	9	0	160	4.16	1.31	$12	24.2	259			28%	4.21	27.7	2.9	5.6	1.9	1.1	–	72%	44	88

His 3.39 home ERA (4.48 road) with .233 OBA and 2.3 Cmd make him great for micro-managers. Another split of note:

	ERA	OBA	Cmd
Starter	4.55	.256	1.8
Reliever	1.50	.155	2.9

Darensbourg,Vic	Tm	W	L	Sv	IP	ERA	Br/IP	R$	BF/G	OBA	vLH	vRH	H%	xERA	RAR	Ctl	Dom	Cmd	hr/9	G/F	S%	BPV	BPX
LH Reliever	98 FLA	0	7	1	71	3.68	1.15	$3	4.9	206	168	236	27%	2.61 +	14.8	3.8	9.4	2.5	0.6	0.76	69%	103	185
AGE 32 Peak	99 FLA	* 0	1	1	45	8.00	1.87	($8)	3.3	332	264	413	38%	6.13 +	-14.8	4.2	5.4	1.3	0.6	0.82	54%	30	65
TYPE	00 FLA	5	3	0	62	4.06	1.44	$5	4.8	259	190	295	32%	4.35	13.0	4.1	8.6	2.1	1.0	0.70	74%	68	151
BURN none	01 FLA	1	2	1	48	4.29	1.29	$2	3.5	277	294	262	32%	4.00	6.9	1.9	6.2	3.3	0.7	1.03	67%	84	155
ERA Potl ---	02 FLA	1	2	0	48	6.19	1.81	($6)	5.4	311	254	331	33%	6.95 -	-4.7	4.9	6.2	1.3	1.9	0.99	70%	0	1
Support 5.21	1st Half	1	2	0	31	4.06	1.61	($0)	5.0	268			28%	5.69 -	5.8	5.2	6.1	1.2	1.7		82%	10	21
LIMA D+	2nd Half	0	0	0	17	10.06	2.18	($6)	6.2	377			41%	9.25 +	-10.5	4.2	6.4	1.5	2.1		55%	-14	-29
Risk Moderate	03 Proj	1	2	0	50	4.32	1.40	$0	4.4	277			32%	4.62	7.6	2.9	6.7	2.3	1.1	--	72%	56	112

He faced 200 batters in '02, and 133 of them were... RHers! This is the result. What was Torborg thinking? He does fine vs LHers, and did so again in 2002.

Davis,Doug	Tm	W	L	Sv	IP	ERA	Br/IP	R$	BF/G	OBA	vLH	vRH	H%	xERA	RAR	Ctl	Dom	Cmd	hr/9	G/F	S%	BPV	BPX
LH Starter	98	0	0	0	0	0.00	0.00																
AGE 27 Pre-Peak	99 a/a	11	4	0	152	3.43	1.45	$14	26.6	279	400	800	33%	4.60 -	46.1	3.3	7.6	2.3	0.9	0.75	80%	66	153
TYPE	00 TEX	* 15	9	0	167	4.62	1.62	$9	18.1	277	314	280	30%	5.34 -	28.9	4.9	6.1	1.2	1.3	1.22	75%	23	61
BURN none	01 TEX	* 13	10	0	201	4.39	1.52	$6	27.9	290	307	291	33%	4.72	29.5	3.3	5.7	1.8	0.7	1.25	71%	48	96
ERA Potl +	02 TEX	* 7	8	0	120	5.47	1.51	($1)	28.0	304	243	312	33%	5.16	-5.9	2.5	5.1	2.1	1.0	0.95	65%	37	69
Support 4.98	1st Half	6	6	0	91	5.61	1.54	($1)	27.2	305			32%	5.57	-6.2	2.8	4.6	1.7	1.4		66%	16	30
LIMA B	2nd Half	1	2	0	29	5.02	1.39	($0)	31.0	302			37%	3.84 +	0.3	1.6	6.6	4.2	0.0		60%	122	231
Risk Moderate	03 Proj	7	7	0	120	4.50	1.50	$3	26.5	294			34%	4.74	14.0	2.9	6.0	2.1	0.8	--	71%	53	107

3-5, 5.03 ERA in 59 IP at TEX. His first four starts generated PQS scores of 5,4,4,3, but then the bottom dropped out. Got hurt in AAA and lost most of the 2nd half. Strong AAA BPIs bode well for a return to the majors.

Day,Zach	Tm	W	L	Sv	IP	ERA	Br/IP	R$	BF/G	OBA	vLH	vRH	H%	xERA	RAR	Ctl	Dom	Cmd	hr/9	G/F	S%	BPV	BPX
RH Reliever	98	0	0	0	0	0.00	0.00																
AGE 24 Growth	99	0	0	0	0	0.00	0.00																
TYPE	00 aa	4	2	0	46	4.30	1.39	$4	24.8	253			32%	3.39 +	9.0	3.9	7.2	1.9	0.2		67%	81	191
BURN none	01 a/a	12	12	0	169	4.74	1.47	$5	25.6	287			32%	4.52	15.4	3.0	5.0	1.7	0.6		67%	44	84
ERA Potl +	02 MON	* 9	7	1	127	4.32	1.31	$9	14.9	249	158	244	29%	3.65 +	19.3	3.4	5.9	1.7	0.6	3.14	67%	58	118
Support 7.23	1st Half	6	6	0	79	5.11	1.29	$4	19.6	249			28%	3.62 +	3.7	3.2	5.6	1.8	0.7		59%	55	113
LIMA C+	2nd Half	3	1	1	48	3.01	1.36	$5	10.8	250			29%	3.70 -	15.7	3.8	6.4	1.7	0.6		79%	62	127
Risk Very High	03 Proj	7	5	0	100	4.23	1.35	$7	17.1	264			30%	3.81	16.4	3.1	5.9	1.9	0.5	G	68%	61	123

4-1, 3.65 ERA in 37 IP at MON. Signs of promise, but marginal growth from '01. There is something potentially very good here, but Cmd and strand rate currently stand in his way

de los Santos,Valerio		W	L	Sv	IP	ERA	Br/IP	R$	BF/G	OBA	vLH	vRH	H%	xERA	RAR	Ctl	Dom	Cmd	hr/9	G/F	S%	BPV	BPX
LH Reliever	98 MIL	* 6	2	10	92	3.60	1.32	$12	6.5	273	167	145	33%	3.88	20.2	2.3	7.2	3.1	0.6	0.88	73%	91	164
AGE 27 Pre-Peak	99 MIL	0	1	0	8	6.75	2.38	($2)	6.1	347	286	357	39%	8.17 -	-1.3	7.9	5.6	0.7	1.1	0.43	72%	1	1
TYPE Power	00 MIL	2	3	0	73	5.16	1.43	($0)	4.8	259	273	243	29%	5.12	4.6	4.1	8.6	2.1	1.8	0.73	71%	44	97
BURN none	01 MIL	0	0	0	1	9.00	2.00	($0)	4.9	262			35%	4.86 +	-0.5	9.0	9.0	1.0	0.0		50%	78	144
ERA Potl -	02 MIL	2	3	0	57	3.16	1.19	$6	4.6	207	219	207	24%	2.80	17.6	4.1	6.0	1.5	0.6	0.57	75%	61	126
Support 3.28	1st Half	1	2	0	19	3.28	1.04	$3	5.4	156			20%	1.24 +	5.6	4.7	7.0	1.5	0.0		65%	98	200
LIMA C+	2nd Half	1	1	0	38	3.10	1.27	$3	4.3	231			25%	3.59 -	12.0	3.8	5.5	1.4	1.0		80%	43	89
Risk High	03 Proj	2	2	1	50	3.96	1.28	$4	4.9	234			27%	3.73	10.0	3.8	7.2	1.9	1.1	F	72%	59	119

Opposing batters are not hitting him, however... his low hit rate and mediocre BPIs say that his 3.16 ERA was a fluke. Skills are not yet back to where they were pre-injury, and 2nd half fade puts durability into question.

DeJean,Mike	Tm	W	L	Sv	IP	ERA	Br/IP	R$	BF/G	OBA	vLH	vRH	H%	xERA	RAR	Ctl	Dom	Cmd	hr/9	G/F	S%	BPV	BPX
RH Reliever	98 COL	3	1	2	74	3.04	1.38	$6	5.4	272	283	286	29%	3.94 -	21.8	2.9	3.3	1.1	0.5	1.59	79%	29	53
AGE 32 Past	99 COL	2	4	0	61	8.41	1.89	($10)	5.2	325	376	310	33%	7.32 +	-23.4	4.7	4.6	1.0	1.9	1.42	57%	-20	-43
TYPE Power	00 COL	4	4	0	53	4.92	1.58	$1	4.4	265	293	254	28%	5.31	5.1	5.1	5.8	1.1	1.5	1.10	73%	15	32
BURN none	01 MIL	4	2	2	84	2.78	1.36	$8	4.8	240	227	242	30%	3.37 -	29.1	4.2	7.3	1.7	0.4	1.41	80%	74	138
ERA Potl ---	02 MIL	1	5	27	75	3.12	1.40	$21	4.8	238	259	213	29%	3.88 -	23.5	4.7	7.8	1.7	0.8	1.71	81%	64	131
Support 0.84	1st Half	0	3	14	41	3.29	1.34	$11	4.9	232			29%	3.49	11.9	4.4	7.9	1.8	0.7		77%	74	152
LIMA D	2nd Half	1	2	13	34	2.91	1.47	$10	4.7	244			29%	4.35 -	11.6	5.0	7.7	1.5	1.1		85%	52	108
Risk Low	03 Proj	3	4	24	75	3.48	1.44	$18	4.7	251			30%	4.24 -	19.8	4.4	7.8	1.8	1.0	G	79%	60	120

Closer-worthy? BPIs say "no." But he did convert 90% of his save opps, which means the job got done, in 2002 at least. Long-term, I'd be surprised if he ever saw a 30-save season.

Dempster,Ryan	Tm	W	L	Sv	IP	ERA	Br/IP	R$	BF/G	OBA	vLH	vRH	H%	xERA	RAR	Ctl	Dom	Cmd	hr/9	G/F	S%	BPV	BPX
RH Starter	98 FLA	* 8	9	0	132	4.76	1.51	$1	22.6	270	394	287	30%	4.79	8.4	4.2	6.0	1.4	1.1	1.86	71%	34	61
AGE 25 Growth	99 FLA	* 8	9	0	177	4.78	1.58	$1	26.5	262	282	243	30%	4.99	18.2	5.2	7.7	1.5	1.3	1.15	73%	41	88
TYPE Power	00 FLA	14	10	0	226	3.66	1.36	$19	29.3	248	249	239	30%	4.18 -	59.5	3.9	8.3	2.2	1.2	1.08	78%	65	143
BURN Moderate	01 FLA	15	12	0	211	4.95	1.56	$3	27.8	268	270	269	32%	4.70	11.9	4.8	7.3	1.5	0.9	1.22	69%	50	93
ERA Potl +	02 2NL	10	13	0	209	5.38	1.54	($4)	28.2	279	332	248	33%	4.65 +	2.1	4.0	6.6	1.6	0.7	1.10	64%	53	108
Support 5.64	1st Half	5	7	0	114	4.81	1.49	($0)	29.6	270			31%	4.65	9.9	4.0	6.5	1.6	0.9		69%	46	94
LIMA D+	2nd Half	5	6	0	95	6.07	1.59	($5)	26.8	289			35%	4.66 +	-7.8	4.0	6.6	1.7	0.4		59%	61	124
Risk Moderate	03 Proj	11	12	0	200	4.82	1.49	$3	27.6	270			32%	4.50	17.1	4.0	6.9	1.7	0.8	--	68%	55	110

Posted a 4.79 ERA while with FLA, then folded in CIN to the tune of a 6.19 mark. In his defense, a 35% hit rate and 59% strand rate killed his ERA in the 2nd half, but the skills are still just marginal.

Dessens,Elmer	Tm	W	L	Sv	IP	ERA	Br/IP	R$	BF/G	OBA	vLH	vRH	H%	xERA	RAR	Ctl	Dom	Cmd	hr/9	G/F	S%	BPV	BPX
RH Starter	98 PIT	* 5	7	0	104	5.18	1.52	($2)	9.4	302	298	301	33%	5.24	0.7	2.7	4.8	1.8	1.0	1.91	67%	29	53
AGE 31 Peak	99 JPN	0	1	0	16	3.94	1.75	($1)	9.3	347			36%	6.64 -	3.8	2.3	3.4	1.5	1.1		81%	4	8
TYPE Contact	00 CIN	* 13	5	1	169	4.20	1.46	$12	16.8	292	328	269	33%	4.51	32.4	2.7	5.2	1.9	0.6	1.84	71%	51	112
BURN none	01 CIN	10	14	0	205	4.48	1.35	$7	26.8	277	325	230	30%	4.79	24.4	2.5	5.6	2.3	1.4	1.27	71%	39	73
ERA Potl ----	02 CIN	7	8	0	178	3.03	1.25	$16	24.7	256	244	268	27%	4.12 -	57.8	2.5	4.7	1.9	1.2	1.48	82%	35	73
Support 4.10	1st Half	5	4	0	101	2.58	1.28	$11	24.9	264			28%	4.08 -	38.9	2.4	4.3	1.8	1.0		85%	36	74
LIMA D	2nd Half	2	4	0	77	3.62	1.21	$5	24.4	246			25%	4.17 -	18.9	2.6	5.3	2.0	1.5		78%	35	71
Risk High	03 Proj	9	10	0	200	4.10	1.33	$10	20.2	270			29%	4.48	36.4	2.5	5.0	2.0	1.2	--	73%	35	71

High strand rate and low hit rate masked this soft-tosser's mediocre skill set. In some ways, his '01 season showed more, but at minimum, his xERA tells the true tale. Don't expect a sub-4.00 ERA in 2003.

Donnelly,Brendan	Tm	W	L	Sv	IP	ERA	Br/IP	R$	BF/G	OBA	vLH	vRH	H%	xERA	RAR	Ctl	Dom	Cmd	hr/9	G/F	S%	BPV	BPX
RH Reliever	98 a/a	6	6	13	83	3.25	1.51	$13	6.4	266			32%	4.51 -	24.2	4.3	7.8	1.8	0.9		81%	60	117
AGE 31 Peak	99 a/a	5	6	3	74	3.89	1.38	$8	7.2	270			31%	4.19	17.9	3.0	6.8	2.2	0.9		74%	63	147
TYPE Power	00 aaa	4	9	1	59	8.24	2.12	($9)	6.5	351			38%	8.00	-19.6	5.3	5.6	1.1	1.5		62%	-5	-12
BURN none	01 a/a	9	2	13	70	3.34	1.51	$15	5.5	291			34%	5.16 -	19.5	3.2	7.7	2.4	1.2		82%	59	113
ERA Potl +	02 ANA	* 5	1	7	82	2.96	1.13	$12	4.7	214	242	148	28%	2.66	23.7	3.3	9.6	2.9	0.8	0.98	77%	109	205
Support 3.62	1st Half	4	0	6	35	4.84	1.22	$6	5.4	237			30%	3.42 +	1.2	3.1	9.2	3.0	1.0		62%	95	180
LIMA B	2nd Half	1	1	1	47	1.54	1.07	$6	4.2	195			27%	2.09 -	22.4	3.5	10.0	2.9	0.6		89%	119	226
Risk Moderate	03 Proj	5	3	1	60	3.90	1.40	$5	5.3	262			32%	4.28	11.8	3.6	8.4	2.3	1.1	--	75%	71	144

1-1, 2.20 ERA in 49 IP at ANA. Any pitcher who manages a 100+ BPV over a full season is someone worth keeping an eye on. Growth is there as well, but at 31, we are likely witnessing his peak performance.

Dotel,Octavio	Tm	W	L	Sv	IP	ERA	Br/IP	R$	BF/G	OBA	vLH	vRH	H%	xERA	RAR	Ctl	Dom	Cmd	hr/9	G/F	S%	BPV	BPX
RH Reliever	98 a/a	12	8	0	168	3.27	1.20	$19	25.6	222			29%	2.97	48.7	3.5	9.2	2.6	0.7		74%	100	194
AGE 29 Pre-Peak	99 NYM	* 13	5	0	155	4.94	1.34	$11	20.6	224	210	240	28%	3.79 +	12.7	4.8	9.3	2.0	1.2	0.80	66%	71	154
TYPE Power	00 HOU	3	7	16	125	5.40	1.50	$7	11.1	265	282	250	32%	5.39	3.8	4.4	10.2	2.3	1.9	0.51	70%	56	124
BURN High	01 HOU	7	5	2	105	2.66	1.20	$14	7.1	211	238	178	33%	2.55	38.1	4.0	12.4	3.1	0.4	0.79	79%	139	259
ERA Potl No chg	02 HOU	6	4	6	97	1.86	0.88	$25	4.4	175	190	159	25%	1.60	46.8	2.5	10.9	4.4	0.6	0.53	83%	158	324
Support 3.42	1st Half	4	3	2	50	2.69	1.04	$11	4.8	199			26%	2.85	18.5	3.1	11.0	3.6	1.3		82%	119	243
LIMA C+	2nd Half	2	1	4	47	0.96	0.70	$15	4.0	148			23%	0.27 +	28.3	1.9	10.9	5.7	0.0		85%	211	432
Risk Moderate	03 Proj	6	4	6	100	2.70	1.04	$19	6.0	201			28%	2.35	36.9	3.0	10.8	3.6	0.7	F	77%	134	270

Continued his journey from thrower to pitcher, knocking 1.5 BBs off his control, 1.5 Ks off his dominance, and IMPROVING his command. Posted a 1.53 ERA at his tough home ballpark.

Douglass,Sean	Tm	W	L	Sv	IP	ERA	Br/IP	R$	BF/G	OBA	vLH	vRH	H%	xERA	RAR	Ctl	Dom	Cmd	hr/9	G/F	S%	BPV	BPX
RH Starter	98	0	0	0	0	0.00	0.00																
AGE 24 Growth	99	0	0	0	0	0.00	0.00																
TYPE Power	00 aa	9	8	0	160	5.06	1.48	$5	26.0	285			32%	4.94	15.0	3.2	6.0	**1.9**	1.1		68%	40	94
BURN none	01 aaa	10	10	0	182	4.40	1.49	$4	25.9	281	209	316	34%	4.71	24.9	3.5	8.1	**2.3**	0.9	1.09	72%	69	133
ERA Potl No chg	02 BAL	* 4	11	0	119	5.81	1.69	($8)	19.0	282	269	297	34%	5.28 +	-11.3	5.3	7.9	**1.5**	1.1	1.20	66%	45	85
Support 4.56	1st Half	1	2	0	47	5.34	1.65	($3)	18.0	265			31%	4.84 +	-1.5	5.7	7.2	**1.3**	1.0		68%	43	82
LIMA D+	2nd Half	3	9	0	72	6.12	1.72	($5)	19.7	293			35%	5.56 +	-9.8	5.0	8.2	**1.7**	1.1		65%	47	89
Risk Very High	03 Proj	**4**	**6**	**0**	**80**	**5.06**	**1.60**	**($1)**	**21.3**	**283**			**34%**	**5.06**	**3.3**	**4.4**	**7.7**	**1.7**	**1.0**	**–**	**70%**	**51**	**103**

0-5, 6.11 ERA in 53 IP at BAL. Is there something we're missing?

	ERA	OBA	Cmd
Starter	7.43	.312	1.3
Reliever	2.03	.188	1.1

Cmd says maybe we shouldn't jump to judge so quickly.

Drese,Ryan	Tm	W	L	Sv	IP	ERA	Br/IP	R$	BF/G	OBA	vLH	vRH	H%	xERA	RAR	Ctl	Dom	Cmd	hr/9	G/F	S%	BPV	BPX
RH Starter	98	0	0	0	0	0.00	0.00																
AGE 27 Growth	99	0	0	0	0	0.00	0.00																
TYPE	00	0	0	0	0	0.00	0.00																
BURN none	01 a/a	11	10	0	184	4.70	1.36	$7	23.2	266	205	288	30%	4.13 +	17.9	3.1	6.2	**2.0**	0.8	2.64	66%	56	107
ERA Potl +	02 CLE	* 11	9	0	159	5.94	1.65	($4)	25.0	304	333	297	35%	5.36 +	-17.8	3.7	6.6	**1.8**	0.9	1.25	64%	43	82
Support 6.36	1st Half	7	6	0	84	5.88	1.62	($1)	25.5	294			35%	4.98 +	-8.7	4.0	6.9	**1.8**	0.7		63%	52	99
LIMA B	2nd Half	4	3	0	75	6.02	1.68	($4)	24.6	315			35%	5.80	-9.1	3.5	6.1	**1.8**	1.1		65%	33	63
Risk Low	03 Proj	**6**	**8**	**0**	**120**	**4.95**	**1.48**	**$1**	**24.0**	**284**			**32%**	**4.68**	**6.7**	**3.3**	**6.4**	**1.9**	**0.9**	**–**	**67%**	**50**	**102**

10-9, 6.57 ERA in 137 IP at CLE. BPIs were not all that different from '01, but the ERA results were, thanks to a 35% hit rate and 64% strand rate. Those should improve, but he still may be over a year away.

Driskill,Travis	Tm	W	L	Sv	IP	ERA	Br/IP	R$	BF/G	OBA	vLH	vRH	H%	xERA	RAR	Ctl	Dom	Cmd	hr/9	G/F	S%	BPV	BPX
RH Starter	98 aa	3	0	0	32	6.47	1.78	($2)	25.1	347			37%	6.74	-4.4	2.5	4.5	**1.8**	1.1		64%	16	31
AGE 31 Peak	99 aaa	9	8	0	132	6.68	1.67	($5)	19.6	332			35%	6.78	-17.4	2.5	5.0	**2.0**	1.8		63%	8	18
TYPE Contact	00 aaa	12	11	0	179	5.93	1.78	($5)	30.0	344			37%	6.64 -	-4.1	2.7	4.4	**1.7**	1.1		68%	14	34
BURN none	01 aaa	11	5	0	178	5.51	1.51	($0)	28.2	314			34%	5.86	-2.1	2.0	5.7	**2.9**	1.5		67%	42	80
ERA Potl -	02 BAL	* 10	10	0	154	4.56	1.42	$5	20.3	281	289	277	30%	4.82	11.3	2.9	5.3	**1.8**	1.3	1.48	72%	30	57
Support 4.55	1st Half	7	3	0	76	3.54	1.26	$8	19.9	259			26%	4.34 -	16.0	2.5	4.8	**2.0**	1.5		80%	27	52
LIMA D	2nd Half	3	7	0	78	5.55	1.58	($3)	20.6	302			34%	5.30	-4.6	3.2	5.7	**1.8**	1.0		66%	34	64
Risk X HIGH	03 Proj	**4**	**5**	**0**	**80**	**5.29**	**1.54**	**($1)**	**23.8**	**307**			**33%**	**5.61**	**0.9**	**2.6**	**5.3**	**2.0**	**1.4**	**–**	**68%**	**28**	**56**

8-8, 4.98 ERA in 132 IP at BAL, which is quite a feat for a 31-y/o pitcher with marginal skills. There are dozens of old arms with these BPIs in the minors, but most get passed up for pitchers with more of a future.

Duckworth,Brandon		W	L	Sv	IP	ERA	Br/IP	R$	BF/G	OBA	vLH	vRH	H%	xERA	RAR	Ctl	Dom	Cmd	hr/9	G/F	S%	BPV	BPX
RH Starter	98	0	0	0	0	0.00	0.00																
AGE 27 Growth	99	0	0	0	0	0.00	0.00																
TYPE Power	00 aa	13	7	0	165	3.98	1.41	$15	26.4	271			33%	4.40	39.3	3.2	8.4	**2.6**	1.0		74%	77	181
BURN none	01 PHI	* 16	4	0	216	3.63	1.29	$19	27.6	255	256	221	30%	3.70	50.4	3.0	7.3	**2.5**	0.8	1.75	74%	77	143
ERA Potl +	02 PHI	8	9	0	163	5.41	1.45	($1)	23.7	266	248	273	33%	4.93	1.0	3.8	9.2	**2.4**	1.4	0.85	66%	65	133
Support 5.36	1st Half	4	5	0	85	4.65	1.45	$1	24.8	257			33%	4.53	9.2	4.2	9.7	**2.3**	1.2		71%	75	155
LIMA C	2nd Half	4	4	0	78	6.24	1.45	($3)	22.7	277			32%	5.37 +	-8.1	3.4	8.7	**2.6**	1.7		60%	54	111
Risk Low	03 Proj	**11**	**7**	**0**	**180**	**4.50**	**1.36**	**$9**	**24.9**	**260**			**32%**	**4.33**	**23.0**	**3.4**	**8.6**	**2.6**	**1.2**	**–**	**70%**	**74**	**149**

There's a lot to like about this skill set, but his ERA was hurt by a low S%, high H% and his gopheritis. His 48/31 DOM/DIS split shows emerging talent with lots of inconsistency. That's curable, though.

Durocher,Jayson	Tm	W	L	Sv	IP	ERA	Br/IP	R$	BF/G	OBA	vLH	vRH	H%	xERA	RAR	Ctl	Dom	Cmd	hr/9	G/F	S%	BPV	BPX
RH Reliever	98	0	0	0	0	0.00	0.00																
AGE 28 Pre-Peak	99 a/a	2	6	8	87	3.31	1.32	$11	8.0	222			24%	3.32	27.8	4.7	5.2	**1.1**	0.7		77%	43	100
TYPE Power	00 a/a	4	6	21	70	4.37	1.77	$12	5.7	296			35%	5.62 -	13.0	5.3	7.6	**1.4**	0.9		77%	45	106
BURN none	01 a/a	4	1	6	43	6.70	1.74	$1	5.9	275			34%	5.78 +	-7.3	6.1	9.2	**1.5**	1.5		63%	43	83
ERA Potl -	02 MIL	* 2	1	2	74	2.67	1.20	$9	5.2	199	187	144	25%	2.90	27.7	4.5	9.1	**2.0**	0.9	0.96	82%	87	178
Support 5.25	1st Half	1	0	2	36	3.47	1.46	$2	6.1	238			31%	4.39 -	9.7	5.2	10.4	**2.0**	1.2		81%	75	153
LIMA B	2nd Half	1	1	0	38	1.90	0.95	$7	4.4	158			20%	1.48	18.0	3.8	7.9	**2.1**	0.5		82%	100	204
Risk Moderate	03 Proj	**2**	**3**	**6**	**60**	**3.45**	**1.35**	**$7**	**5.5**	**239**			**30%**	**3.78**	**16.1**	**4.2**	**8.9**	**2.1**	**0.9**	**–**	**77%**	**78**	**156**

1-1, 1.88 ERA in 48 IP at MIL. Showing improvement in his biggest Achilles Heel -- allowing BBs. If he can keep that up, everything else will fall into place and he becomes much more draftable.

Eaton,Adam	Tm	W	L	Sv	IP	ERA	Br/IP	R$	BF/G	OBA	vLH	vRH	H%	xERA	RAR	Ctl	Dom	Cmd	hr/9	G/F	S%	BPV	BPX
RH Starter	98	0	0	0	0	0.00	0.00																
AGE 25 Growth	99 a/a	6	5	0	98	3.21	1.14	$13	26.5	224			26%	3.07	32.6	2.9	6.9	**2.3**	0.9		75%	73	169
TYPE Power	00 SD	* 11	5	0	192	3.70	1.36	$15	25.7	253	302	215	29%	3.89	49.5	3.7	6.4	**1.8**	0.8	1.31	75%	56	123
BURN Low	01 SD	8	5	0	116	4.34	1.27	$8	28.7	248	260	220	29%	4.30	16.0	3.1	8.4	**2.7**	1.5	0.98	72%	67	124
ERA Potl -	02 SD	2	2	0	45	4.99	1.29	$1	23.7	230	333	162	24%	4.22 +	2.8	4.0	6.0	**1.5**	1.6	0.83	66%	29	58
Support 3.78	1st Half	0	0	0	0	0.00	0.00																
LIMA B	2nd Half	2	2	0	45	4.99	1.29	$1	23.7	230			24%	4.23 +	2.8	4.0	6.0	**1.5**	1.6		66%	29	58
Risk High	03 Proj	**7**	**5**	**0**	**120**	**4.13**	**1.28**	**$8**	**20.2**	**240**			**27%**	**3.94**	**21.4**	**3.5**	**6.8**	**1.9**	**1.2**	**–**	**72%**	**52**	**104**

BPIs show that he's not quite healed yet. Dominance and control pale compared to '01, and his poise with runners on base was far off from his history. Expect more healing in '03, but don't expect miracles.

Eischen,Joey	Tm	W	L	Sv	IP	ERA	Br/IP	R$	BF/G	OBA	vLH	vRH	H%	xERA	RAR	Ctl	Dom	Cmd	hr/9	G/F	S%	BPV	BPX
LH Reliever	98 aaa	2	5	2	73	5.18	1.56	($1)	5.4	292			33%	5.26	2.5	3.6	6.2	**1.7**	1.1		69%	36	71
AGE 32 Past	99 aaa	1	3	1	41	10.98	2.49	($13)	8.2	397			44%	9.80 +	-29.0	5.7	5.7	**1.0**	1.5		55%	-15	-35
TYPE Power	00 aaa	0	4	0	60	5.70	1.72	($5)	25.3	313			31%	6.48 -	0.5	3.9	3.8	**1.0**	1.7		71%	-14	-34
BURN none	01 MON	* 2	4	7	81	3.78	1.37	$6	6.0	264	231	270	30%	4.58 -	17.2	3.2	6.9	**2.1**	1.3	1.89	78%	48	90
ERA Potl - -	02 MON	* 7	1	6	67	1.07	1.12	$20	3.9	222	173	261	30%	2.31 -	39.3	2.8	8.5	**3.0**	0.1	3.64	91%	120	247
Support 4.86	1st Half	2	1	4	36	1.00	1.14	$10	4.6	239			31%	2.67 -	21.6	2.2	8.2	**3.7**	0.2		93%	126	259
LIMA B	2nd Half	5	0	2	31	1.17	1.10	$11	3.3	202			28%	1.88 -	17.8	3.5	8.7	**2.5**	0.0		88%	120	245
Risk X HIGH	03 Proj	**4**	**4**	**2**	**70**	**3.21**	**1.36**	**$7**	**5.2**	**259**			**31%**	**3.96 -**	**21.0**	**3.3**	**7.2**	**2.2**	**0.8**	**G**	**79%**	**68**	**138**

Obvious reasons why he'll never see this ERA again:
- Allowed 1 HR in 67 IP.
- 91% strand rate
- MON will be less stable in '03
- If Bob Gibson couldn't do it, he won't either.

Embree,Alan	Tm	W	L	Sv	IP	ERA	Br/IP	R$	BF/G	OBA	vLH	vRH	H%	xERA	RAR	Ctl	Dom	Cmd	hr/9	G/F	S%	BPV	BPX
LH Reliever	98 ARI	4	2	1	53	4.23	1.48	$3	4.3	272	260	275	31%	4.83 -	7.2	3.9	7.3	**1.9**	1.2	1.10	75%	48	87
AGE 33 Past	99 SF	3	2	0	58	3.41	1.17	$7	3.5	204	200	200	25%	2.87 +	16.6	4.0	8.2	**2.0**	0.9	0.56	74%	78	170
TYPE Power	00 SF	3	5	2	60	4.95	1.45	$3	4.2	268	286	267	33%	4.14 +	5.5	3.8	7.4	**2.0**	0.6	0.74	65%	69	151
BURN none	01 2TM	1	4	0	54	7.33	1.52	($6)	3.9	299	180	299	35%	6.37 +	-13.8	2.8	9.8	**3.5**	2.3	0.85	56%	57	110
ERA Potl -	02 2TM	4	6	2	62	2.03	1.08	$12	3.6	212	156	244	30%	2.66 -	26.9	2.9	11.8	**4.1**	0.9	1.45	87%	142	279
Support 3.63	1st Half	3	4	0	30	0.89	1.16	$7	3.2	212			32%	2.59 -	17.8	3.6	12.2	**3.4**	0.6		97%	140	274
LIMA B+	2nd Half	1	2	2	32	3.12	1.01	$5	4.3	212			29%	2.73	9.1	2.3	11.4	**5.0**	1.1		75%	152	298
Risk Very Low	03 Proj	**5**	**3**	**1**	**60**	**3.75**	**1.25**	**$7**	**3.8**	**245**			**32%**	**3.85**	**13.4**	**3.0**	**10.2**	**3.4**	**1.2**	**–**	**75%**	**103**	**208**

Those who heeded our big BUY signals after '01's 7.03 ERA were duly rewarded. Pitched 21.1 scoreless IP in SD before getting dealt to BOS. Expect a letdown, but not all that much.

Erickson,Scott	Tm	W	L	Sv	IP	ERA	Br/IP	R$	BF/G	OBA	vLH	vRH	H%	xERA	RAR	Ctl	Dom	Cmd	hr/9	G/F	S%	BPV	BPX
RH Starter	98 BAL	16	13	0	251	4.01	1.41	$16	30.2	286	309	244	33%	4.51 -	55.2	2.5	6.7	**2.7**	0.8	2.85	73%	70	149
AGE 35 Decline	99 BAL	15	12	0	230	4.81	1.49	$11	29.8	273	270	289	29%	4.78	32.6	3.9	4.1	**1.1**	1.1	2.80	70%	16	40
TYPE Contact	00 BAL	5	8	0	92	7.91	1.90	($10)	27.8	328	390	270	34%	6.90 +	-24.6	4.7	4.0	**0.9**	1.4	2.02	58%	-10	-25
BURN High	01 BAL	0	0	0	0	0.00	0.00																
ERA Potl - -	02 BAL	5	12	0	160	5.57	1.63	($8)	25.1	299	304	302	31%	5.45	-9.9	3.8	4.2	**1.1**	1.1	2.31	67%	9	18
Support 4.59	1st Half	3	7	0	104	4.67	1.50	($2)	27.1	276			29%	4.64	6.1	3.8	4.3	**1.1**	1.0		70%	21	40
LIMA F	2nd Half	2	5	0	56	7.24	1.86	($7)	22.3	337			35%	6.96	-16.0	3.9	3.9	**1.0**	1.4		62%	-12	-22
Risk High	03 Proj	**3**	**9**	**0**	**100**	**5.76**	**1.70**	**($6)**	**25.7**	**309**			**33%**	**5.88**	**-5.2**	**4.0**	**4.3**	**1.1**	**1.2**	**G**	**68%**	**7**	**14**

Putting him out there on pace for 200 IP after a near-2 year layoff was unconscionable. Some teams still don't get it.

Escobar,Kelvim	Tm	W	L	Sv	IP	ERA	Br/IP	R$	BF/G	OBA	vLH	vRH	H%	xERA	RAR	Ctl	Dom	Cmd	hr/9	G/F	S%	BPV	BPX
RH Reliever	98 TOR *	9	5	1	138	4.16	1.37	$10	17.0	250	238	237	31%	3.92	27.7	3.9	8.5	2.2	0.8	0.94	71%	77	164
AGE 27 Growth	99 TOR	14	11	0	174	5.69	1.63	$3	24.0	293	279	306	34%	5.32	4.2	4.2	6.7	1.6	1.0	1.11	66%	40	101
TYPE Power	00 TOR	10	15	2	180	5.35	1.51	$6	18.5	268	282	253	30%	4.91	13.5	4.3	7.1	1.7	1.3	1.04	67%	40	104
BURN none	01 TOR	6	8	0	126	3.50	1.15	$12	8.7	207	203	206	27%	2.57 +	33.5	3.7	8.6	2.3	0.6	1.36	70%	97	194
ERA Potl -	02 TOR	5	7	38	78	4.27	1.53	$20	4.6	254	245	246	33%	4.54	8.7	5.1	9.8	1.9	1.2	1.03	75%	69	130
Support 1.15	1st Half	4	4	14	39	4.59	1.56	$8	5.0	256			34%	4.41	2.7	5.3	10.1	1.9	0.9		72%	77	146
LIMA C	2nd Half	1	3	24	39	3.94	1.49	$12	4.2	253			31%	4.66 -	6.0	4.9	9.5	2.0	1.4		79%	61	115
Risk High	03 Proj	4	6	29	75	4.32	1.41	$18	4.6	246			30%	4.13	10.5	4.4	8.9	2.0	1.1	--	72%	69	140

Put up far more closer-worthy BPIs in '01 when he was a starter, but he did close out 83% of his save opps this year. Still some weaknesses, however... High walk rate, 2nd half HR rate, .275 OBA in his 1st 15 pitches...

Estes,Shawn	Tm	W	L	Sv	IP	ERA	Br/IP	R$	BF/G	OBA	vLH	vRH	H%	xERA	RAR	Ctl	Dom	Cmd	hr/9	G/F	S%	BPV	BPX
LH Starter	98 SF	7	12	0	149	5.07	1.54	($2)	26.6	263	247	274	32%	4.53 +	3.3	4.8	8.2	1.7	0.8	2.02	68%	62	112
AGE 30 Peak	99 SF	11	11	0	203	4.92	1.58	$2	28.6	267	270	267	31%	4.72	17.0	5.0	7.0	1.4	0.9	1.53	70%	46	99
TYPE Power	00 SF	15	6	0	190	4.26	1.59	$10	28.6	266	216	285	31%	4.39	34.8	5.1	6.4	1.3	0.5	2.06	73%	51	113
BURN none	01 SF	9	8	0	159	4.02	1.43	$7	25.6	252	227	262	29%	3.91	28.7	4.4	6.2	1.4	0.6	1.64	72%	53	98
ERA Potl -	02 2NL	5	12	0	160	5.12	1.59	($6)	24.9	275	302	276	32%	4.77	7.3	4.7	6.1	1.3	0.7	1.72	68%	42	87
Support 3.30	1st Half	3	5	0	89	4.24	1.52	$0	26.3	272			33%	4.43	14.5	4.1	7.0	1.7	0.6		72%	60	122
LIMA D	2nd Half	2	7	0	71	6.22	1.68	($7)	23.3	278			30%	5.20 +	-7.2	5.3	5.1	1.0	0.9		63%	23	48
Risk Very Low	03 Proj	7	10	0	160	4.56	1.56	($0)	25.6	268			31%	4.58	19.2	4.8	6.2	1.3	0.7	G	71%	44	88

No surprises from this skill set as it's remained remarkably consistent for many years. But he clearly did not like it in CIN, where he posted a 7.71 ERA after pitching to a 4.55 mark with the Mets.

Eyre,Scott	Tm	W	L	Sv	IP	ERA	Br/IP	R$	BF/G	OBA	vLH	vRH	H%	xERA	RAR	Ctl	Dom	Cmd	hr/9	G/F	S%	BPV	BPX
LH Reliever	98 CHW	3	8	0	107	5.38	1.66	($5)	14.9	274			28%	6.11 -	3.9	5.4	6.1	1.1	2.0		74%	0	1
AGE 30 Peak	99 CHW *	7	5	0	93	5.13	1.71	$1	13.0	317			37%	5.80 -	9.3	3.6	6.6	1.8	0.9		71%	43	109
TYPE Power	00 CHW *	4	3	12	67	4.57	1.54	$10	5.0	268			33%	4.26	12.1	4.6	7.3	1.6	0.5		70%	62	162
BURN none	01 TOR *	5	8	2	95	4.17	1.44	$4	5.2	274	323	192	34%	4.61	16.7	3.4	8.6	2.5	1.0	0.58	74%	74	148
ERA Potl No chg	02 2TM	2	4	0	74	4.50	1.57	($1)	4.7	277	233	317	34%	4.43	7.6	4.4	7.1	1.6	0.5	1.35	71%	61	120
Support 3.98	1st Half	2	3	0	54	5.15	1.59	($1)	6.8	279			34%	4.51 +	0.9	4.5	7.0	1.6	0.5		66%	59	116
LIMA D+	2nd Half	0	1	0	20	2.73	1.52	$1	2.6	273			33%	4.21 -	6.7	4.1	7.3	1.8	0.5		83%	68	133
Risk Very High	03 Proj	3	5	0	75	4.08	1.53	$1	4.3	277			33%	4.57	13.4	4.1	7.4	1.8	0.7	--	74%	61	124

Made some gains in '01, but gave it all back in '02. Has historically fared better vs LHers, but they've been using him equally against both sides the past 2 years. A situational role could improve his stats.

Farnsworth,Jeff	Tm	W	L	Sv	IP	ERA	Br/IP	R$	BF/G	OBA	vLH	vRH	H%	xERA	RAR	Ctl	Dom	Cmd	hr/9	G/F	S%	BPV	BPX
RH Reliever	98	0	0	0	0	0.00	0.00																
AGE 27 Pre-Peak	99	0	0	0	0	0.00	0.00																
TYPE Contact	00 aa	9	3	2	101	5.14	1.51	$6	11.5	298			33%	4.81	8.4	2.8	5.0	1.8	0.7		65%	43	102
BURN none	01 aa	11	10	0	155	5.94	1.89	($10)	27.6	351			39%	6.65 -	-10.7	3.3	5.1	1.6	0.7		68%	29	55
ERA Potl --	02 DET	2	3	0	70	5.79	1.84	($7)	7.6	336	367	315	36%	6.28 -	-6.4	3.7	3.6	1.0	0.8	1.53	68%	6	12
Support 3.09	1st Half	1	1	0	30	4.77	1.59	($1)	7.2	303			32%	5.21	1.4	3.3	3.9	1.2	0.9		71%	16	30
LIMA F	2nd Half	1	2	0	40	6.56	2.04	($6)	7.9	360			38%	7.09 -	-7.7	4.1	3.4	0.8	0.7		67%	1	1
Risk Very High	03 Proj	3	2	0	50	5.22	1.72	($2)	10.5	322			35%	5.72 -	1.0	3.4	4.3	1.3	0.7	G	70%	21	44

If hit rates are supposed to be random, then someone better let him know, because these elevated levels are killing his ERA. Not that he's got the BPIs to support better, but you take the help wherever you can get it.

Farnsworth,Kyle	Tm	W	L	Sv	IP	ERA	Br/IP	R$	BF/G	OBA	vLH	vRH	H%	xERA	RAR	Ctl	Dom	Cmd	hr/9	G/F	S%	BPV	BPX
RH Reliever	98 a/a	13	11	0	184	5.48	1.45	$4	25.9	290			33%	5.04	-1.2	2.6	6.7	2.5	1.2		64%	54	105
AGE 27 Growth	99 CHC *	7	11	0	169	4.63	1.42	$5	22.2	274	277	267	28%	5.21 -	20.7	3.2	5.1	1.6	1.8	0.91	74%	12	25
TYPE Power	00 CHC *	2	11	10	102	5.73	1.79	($2)	7.1	287	258	314	34%	5.94	-1.4	5.9	8.2	1.4	1.3	1.03	70%	36	80
BURN none	01 CHC	4	6	2	82	2.74	1.15	$11	4.4	219	223	207	31%	2.96	28.8	3.2	11.7	3.7	0.9	0.74	80%	133	246
ERA Potl ++	02 CHC	4	7	1	49	7.35	1.63	($3)	4.7	288	392	216	34%	6.09 +	-12.4	4.4	8.8	2.0	1.8	0.85	57%	37	76
Support 7.52	1st Half	2	2	0	15	5.40	1.20	$2	4.1	221			28%	3.49 +	0.1	3.6	9.6	2.7	1.2		56%	88	181
LIMA D+	2nd Half	2	5	1	34	8.21	1.82	($5)	5.0	315			36%	7.24 +	-12.5	4.8	8.5	1.8	2.1		57%	17	34
Risk High	03 Proj	5	8	2	70	5.01	1.49	$3	5.3	267			33%	4.99	4.1	4.1	9.3	2.3	1.4	--	70%	62	125

If he had a league average H% and S%, he would have allowed 7 fewer hits, 11 fewer ER, and an ERA of 5.33. Still not great, but at least on the same planet. WHY this all happened? Nobody seems to know. Neither do I.

Fassero,Jeff	Tm	W	L	Sv	IP	ERA	Br/IP	R$	BF/G	OBA	vLH	vRH	H%	xERA	RAR	Ctl	Dom	Cmd	hr/9	G/F	S%	BPV	BPX
LH Reliever	98 SEA	13	12	0	224	3.97	1.29	$18	29.5	261	288	251	29%	4.32	50.5	2.6	7.1	2.7	1.3	1.00	74%	62	131
AGE 40 Decline	99 2AL	5	14	0	156	7.21	1.87	($16)	20.2	321	271	330	35%	7.33	-28.0	4.8	6.6	1.4	2.0	1.27	65%	-1	-4
TYPE Power	00 BOS	8	8	0	130	4.78	1.56	$5	15.3	294	255	307	34%	5.25	19.8	3.5	6.7	1.9	1.1	1.68	72%	44	114
BURN none	01 CHC	4	4	12	73	3.44	1.22	$14	3.7	242	247	228	32%	3.31	18.9	2.8	9.7	3.4	0.7	1.49	73%	115	213
ERA Potl ++	02 2NL	8	6	0	69	5.35	1.57	$2	4.2	294	318	275	36%	4.78 +	1.0	3.5	7.3	2.1	0.5	2.32	64%	68	139
Support 7.30	1st Half	2	5	0	32	6.15	1.52	($1)	4.1	290			33%	5.18 +	-3.0	3.4	6.7	2.0	1.1		60%	46	94
LIMA B	2nd Half	6	1	0	37	4.65	1.60	$3	4.4	298			38%	4.44	4.0	3.7	7.8	2.1	0.0		68%	87	179
Risk Very High	03 Proj	5	4	0	60	4.80	1.52	$2	5.1	281			33%	4.65	5.3	3.8	7.1	1.9	0.8	G	69%	58	117

If he had a league average H% and S%, he would have allowed 17 fewer hits, 11 fewer ER, and an ERA of 3.91. Theoretically, this means '03 should be better, but at age 40, it's tough to count on anything.

Fernandez,Jared	Tm	W	L	Sv	IP	ERA	Br/IP	R$	BF/G	OBA	vLH	vRH	H%	xERA	RAR	Ctl	Dom	Cmd	hr/9	G/F	S%	BPV	BPX
RH Reliever	98 a/a	4	8	1	143	7.17	1.83	($17)	16.6	330			35%	6.47 +	-33.4	4.0	4.3	1.1	1.0		60%	7	14
AGE 31 Peak	99 a/a	15	9	1	182	5.49	1.57	$6	24.0	312			32%	5.74	5.1	2.6	3.5	1.3	1.3		67%	3	7
TYPE Contact	00 aaa	10	4	4	113	4.30	1.51	$11	16.2	291			31%	4.91 -	22.1	3.2	4.0	1.3	0.9		73%	21	49
BURN none	01 aaa	10	10	0	208	5.63	1.72	($10)	29.2	332	250	276	35%	6.61	-5.7	2.8	4.4	1.6	1.4	1.33	70%	5	9
ERA Potl ---	02 CIN *	13	8	1	178	4.70	1.66	$1	20.4	324	191	346	35%	6.08 -	18.1	2.8	4.9	1.7	1.1	1.63	74%	23	46
Support 5.86	1st Half	11	5	1	113	5.09	1.68	$1	22.6	334			35%	6.53 -	5.5	2.4	4.2	1.8	1.4		73%	10	21
LIMA F	2nd Half	2	3	0	65	4.02	1.63	($1)	17.4	306			35%	5.32 -	12.6	3.5	6.0	1.7	0.7		76%	45	92
Risk X HIGH	03 Proj	2	2	0	40	4.95	1.65	($1)	6.3	320			34%	5.96 -	2.7	2.9	4.7	1.6	1.1	G	72%	20	39

1-3, 4.50 ERA in 50 IP at CIN. It's been proven that strikeout artists have more longevity. So the odds of a soft-tosser breaking through at age 31 and offering a team any sort of long-term upside is miniscule.

Fetters,Mike	Tm	W	L	Sv	IP	ERA	Br/IP	R$	BF/G	OBA	vLH	vRH	H%	xERA	RAR	Ctl	Dom	Cmd	hr/9	G/F	S%	BPV	BPX
RH Reliever	98 2AL	2	8	5	58	4.33	1.49	$4	4.3	274	292	246	32%	4.51	10.3	3.9	6.6	1.7	0.8	1.85	72%	53	113
AGE 38 Decline	99 BAL	1	0	0	31	5.81	1.84	($2)	5.5	286	296	264	31%	6.19	0.3	6.4	6.4	1.0	1.5	1.97	71%	14	34
TYPE Power	00 LA	6	2	5	50	3.24	1.20	$12	4.0	199	189	224	22%	3.24	16.0	4.5	7.2	1.6	1.3	2.81	79%	54	119
BURN none	01 2NL	3	2	9	47	5.54	1.59	$4	3.9	269	247	269	30%	5.22	-1.1	5.0	7.1	1.4	1.3	1.02	68%	33	62
ERA Potl -	02 2NL	3	3	0	55	4.09	1.64	$0	3.9	255	306	230	32%	4.52	10.1	6.1	8.7	1.4	0.7	2.12	76%	67	137
Support 3.76	1st Half	0	0	0	28	3.19	1.49	$0	4.1	239			30%	4.23 -	8.6	5.4	8.6	1.6	1.0		82%	63	130
LIMA B	2nd Half	3	3	0	27	5.04	1.79	($0)	3.6	270			35%	4.82	1.5	6.7	8.7	1.3	0.3		70%	71	145
Risk High	03 Proj	4	3	0	50	5.04	1.66	($0)	4.0	254			31%	4.77	2.8	6.3	7.9	1.3	0.9	G	71%	51	103

Declining trends that signal the beginning of the end...
- Baserunners per inning
- BA vs LHers
- Control ratio
- Command ratio

Figueroa,Nelson	Tm	W	L	Sv	IP	ERA	Br/IP	R$	BF/G	OBA	vLH	vRH	H%	xERA	RAR	Ctl	Dom	Cmd	hr/9	G/F	S%	BPV	BPX
RH Starter	98 a/a	14	5	0	165	4.85	1.50	$7	26.1	295			32%	5.45 -	12.7	2.9	6.2	2.1	1.4		72%	35	68
AGE 28 Pre-Peak	99 aaa	11	6	0	128	4.22	1.36	$12	22.8	277			31%	4.44	25.4	2.5	6.0	2.4	1.1		72%	54	126
TYPE	00 ARI *	13	8	0	178	3.89	1.29	$18	26.7	271	310	258	30%	4.13	41.4	2.1	5.1	2.4	1.0	1.20	72%	53	117
BURN none	01 PHI *	8	7	0	176	3.78	1.41	$7	23.8	277	333	241	32%	4.34 -	37.3	3.0	6.4	2.1	0.8	1.43	75%	59	110
ERA Potl --	02 MIL *	6	7	0	132	5.11	1.50	($1)	16.2	283	273	269	29%	5.33	6.3	3.5	4.8	1.4	1.4	0.95	69%	14	28
Support 4.35	1st Half	1	5	0	63	5.00	1.29	$0	16.6	249			23%	5.00	3.9	3.1	4.6	1.5	2.1		70%	-1	-2
LIMA C+	2nd Half	5	2	0	69	5.20	1.69	($2)	16.0	311			34%	5.63	2.4	3.8	5.1	1.3	0.8		69%	28	58
Risk High	03 Proj	6	6	0	120	4.43	1.43	$3	23.7	279			31%	4.78	16.5	3.1	6.0	2.0	1.1	--	72%	42	85

1-7, 5.03 ERA in 93 IP at MIL. When a player's BPIs take a sudden turn for the worse, with no explanation, I always do a scan of the DL log. He sprained his ankle on May 8 and I'll bet it affected his numbers all year.

Fikac,Jeremy	Tm	W	L	Sv	IP	ERA	Br/IP	R$	BF/G	OBA	vLH	vRH	H%	xERA	RAR	Ctl	Dom	Cmd	hr/9	G/F	S%	BPV	BPX
RH Reliever	98	0	0	0	0	0.00	0.00																
AGE 28 Pre-Peak	99	0	0	0	0	0.00	0.00																
TYPE Power	00	0	0	0	0	0.00	0.00																
BURN none	01 SD *	8	0	18	98	2.30	1.16	$26	5.2	237		234	29%	2.88 -	40.3	2.6	7.0	**2.7**	0.5	1.46	82%	93	172
ERA Potl -	02 SD	5	7	1	72	5.38	1.60	($1)	4.8	285	274	263	33%	5.76	0.8	4.3	8.3	**1.9**	1.6	1.08	71%	39	81
Support 4.83	1st Half	4	5	1	40	4.93	1.64	$1	5.1	289			32%	6.10 -	2.9	4.5	6.9	**1.6**	1.8		76%	18	36
LIMA C	2nd Half	1	2	0	32	5.94	1.54	($2)	4.4	281			35%	5.34 +	-2.1	4.0	9.9	**2.5**	1.4		64%	68	140
Risk Low	03 Proj	**5**	**4**	**2**	**75**	**3.96**	**1.41**	**$6**	**4.9**	**267**			**32%**	**4.50 -**	**15.0**	**3.5**	**8.0**	**2.3**	**1.1**	**--**	**75%**	**66**	**133**

Inauspicious follow-up to his promising 2001 campaign. The HR-ball did him in, and RHers hit 10 of the 13 he allowed. Control was worse than '01 as well. 2nd half brought some improvement, but still a ways from '01 levels.

Finley,Chuck	Tm	W	L	Sv	IP	ERA	Br/IP	R$	BF/G	OBA	vLH	vRH	H%	xERA	RAR	Ctl	Dom	Cmd	hr/9	G/F	S%	BPV	BPX
LH Starter	98 ANA	11	9	0	223	3.39	1.43	$15	28.5	250	263	242	31%	4.03 -	67.7	4.4	8.6	**1.9**	0.8	1.39	79%	73	156
AGE 40 Decline	99 ANA	12	11	0	213	4.44	1.37	$14	27.7	247	234	249	30%	3.98	40.9	4.0	8.5	**2.1**	1.0	1.37	69%	72	180
TYPE Power	00 CLE	16	11	0	218	4.17	1.43	$18	27.9	256	240	260	31%	4.21	50.9	4.2	7.8	**1.9**	0.9	1.80	73%	62	160
BURN High	01 CLE	8	7	0	113	5.57	1.47	$1	22.6	291	250	299	34%	5.00 +	-1.2	2.8	7.6	**2.7**	1.1	1.38	63%	67	134
ERA Potl + +	02 2TM	11	15	0	190	4.17	1.37	$9	25.5	255	174	272	32%	3.74	28.1	3.7	8.2	**2.2**	0.6	1.77	70%	82	161
Support 4.48	1st Half	4	10	0	95	3.88	1.47	$3	26.1	270			34%	4.07	17.6	3.9	7.9	**2.0**	0.5		73%	77	150
LIMA B	2nd Half	7	5	0	95	4.45	1.27	$7	24.9	239			30%	3.41 +	10.4	3.5	8.6	**2.5**	0.8		65%	88	173
Risk High	03 Proj	**10**	**10**	**0**	**160**	**4.39**	**1.39**	**$8**	**25.6**	**262**			**32%**	**4.11**	**22.0**	**3.5**	**8.1**	**2.3**	**0.8**	**G**	**70%**	**74**	**150**

Those who saw '01 as an anomaly and took a flyer on a 39-year-old were rewarded. LHers coming over to the NL tend to have an early edge and his BPIs bore that out as well. At 40, he's stilll worth that flyer.

Fiore,Tony	Tm	W	L	Sv	IP	ERA	Br/IP	R$	BF/G	OBA	vLH	vRH	H%	xERA	RAR	Ctl	Dom	Cmd	hr/9	G/F	S%	BPV	BPX
RH Reliever	98 aaa	4	7	1	94	5.07	1.66	($2)	10.5	282			33%	4.68	4.5	5.0	5.6	**1.1**	0.4		68%	44	85
AGE 31 Peak	99 aaa	2	1	19	67	5.24	1.93	$6	6.1	313			36%	5.56	4.1	5.8	5.5	**1.0**	0.1		70%	41	96
TYPE	00 aaa	9	6	8	90	3.50	1.53	$14	6.3	266	400	289	29%	4.24 -	27.2	4.6	3.9	**0.8**	0.5	1.88	77%	28	66
BURN High	01 aaa	6	1	4	111	3.97	1.49	$6	9.1	285			32%	4.25	21.5	3.2	4.9	**1.5**	0.3	2.25	72%	50	96
ERA Potl - -	02 MIN *	12	3	0	104	3.38	1.32	$12	8.8	239	247	203	26%	3.75	24.1	3.9	5.2	**1.3**	1.0	0.70	78%	35	67
Support 4.25	1st Half	8	2	0	63	3.56	1.27	$8	11.0	236			26%	3.27	13.1	3.6	5.0	**1.4**	0.7		73%	46	87
LIMA C+	2nd Half	4	1	0	41	3.09	1.40	$4	6.8	243			25%	4.48 -	11.0	4.4	5.5	**1.3**	1.5		86%	19	37
Risk X HIGH	03 Proj	**5**	**4**	**0**	**80**	**4.28**	**1.49**	**$3**	**7.8**	**269**			**30%**	**4.39**	**11.7**	**4.1**	**5.1**	**1.3**	**0.8**	**F**	**72%**	**34**	**70**

Less a product of skill than of his environment. BPIs were poor, but was heped by 26% hit rate and 86% 2nd half strand rate. Odds of yet another sub-4.00 ERA are slim.

Flores,Randy	Tm	W	L	Sv	IP	ERA	Br/IP	R$	BF/G	OBA	vLH	vRH	H%	xERA	RAR	Ctl	Dom	Cmd	hr/9	G/F	S%	BPV	BPX
LH Reliever	98	0	0	0	0	0.00	0.00																
AGE 27 Pre-Peak	99	0	0	0	0	0.00	0.00																
TYPE	00 a/a	11	11	1	164	4.61	1.75	$2	21.9	321			36%	5.91 -	25.3	3.7	5.1	**1.4**	0.8		75%	25	60
BURN none	01 a/a	14	7	0	164	4.23	1.75	$3	27.4	315			34%	6.20 -	26.3	4.1	5.1	**1.3**	1.2		79%	13	24
ERA Potl -	02 2TM *	3	5	2	85	5.93	1.72	($5)	7.9	311	326	351	34%	5.87	-7.5	4.0	5.3	**1.3**	1.1	1.79	66%	21	40
Support 3.41	1st Half	0	1	2	27	6.64	1.51	($1)	4.0	302			35%	4.83 +	-5.0	2.7	6.0	**2.3**	0.7		54%	58	114
LIMA F	2nd Half	3	4	0	58	5.60	1.81	($3)	13.7	315			34%	6.35 -	-2.5	4.7	5.0	**1.1**	1.2		71%	7	14
Risk Moderate	03 Proj	**1**	**3**	**0**	**40**	**5.18**	**1.70**	**($2)**	**10.9**	**311**			**34%**	**5.91 -**	**1.3**	**3.8**	**5.2**	**1.4**	**1.1**	**G**	**71%**	**18**	**37**

0-2, 7.45 ERA in 29 IP at TEX and COL. Historically high hit rates and low dominance are killer weaknesses anywhere, but worse in COL. Pass, then pass again. And when you're done, pass one more time.

Fogg,Josh	Tm	W	L	Sv	IP	ERA	Br/IP	R$	BF/G	OBA	vLH	vRH	H%	xERA	RAR	Ctl	Dom	Cmd	hr/9	G/F	S%	BPV	BPX
RH Starter	98	0	0	0	0	0.00	0.00																
AGE 26 Growth	99 aa	3	2	0	55	7.53	1.75	($5)	25.7	335			36%	6.72 +	-13.5	2.9	5.6	**1.9**	1.5		57%	17	39
TYPE	00 aa	11	7	0	192	3.82	1.53	$11	31.7	311			35%	4.87 -	50.0	2.3	5.5	**2.4**	0.5		75%	60	143
BURN Low	01 aaa	4	7	5	127	6.31	1.61	($6)	14.0	321	206	214	35%	6.63	-15.1	2.5	6.8	**2.7**	2.0	1.27	65%	30	57
ERA Potl - -	02 PIT	12	12	0	194	4.36	1.38	$9	25.3	267	292	243	28%	4.68	28.5	3.2	5.2	**1.6**	1.3	1.32	73%	29	59
Support 3.70	1st Half	8	6	0	97	3.70	1.14	$13	24.7	243			24%	3.93	22.9	2.1	4.6	**2.2**	1.5		75%	35	73
LIMA C	2nd Half	4	6	0	97	5.02	1.62	($3)	25.9	289			32%	5.43	5.7	4.3	5.9	**1.4**	1.1		71%	28	57
Risk X HIGH	03 Proj	**10**	**11**	**0**	**200**	**4.91**	**1.52**	**$1**	**26.9**	**297**			**32%**	**5.48 -**	**14.7**	**3.0**	**5.8**	**1.9**	**1.4**	**--**	**71%**	**30**	**61**

Play close heed to that 2nd half. Opposing batters figured him out, and he was unable to adjust. Other owners will bid an extra buck in hopes that he returns to those 1st half levels; that won't happen in 2003.

Fossum,Casey	Tm	W	L	Sv	IP	ERA	Br/IP	R$	BF/G	OBA	vLH	vRH	H%	xERA	RAR	Ctl	Dom	Cmd	hr/9	G/F	S%	BPV	BPX
LH Reliever	98	0	0	0	0	0.00	0.00																
AGE 25 Growth	99	0	0	0	0	0.00	0.00																
TYPE Power	00	0	0	0	0	0.00	0.00																
BURN none	01 BOS *	6	9	0	161	4.02	1.35	$6	20.9	270	188	275	33%	3.84	31.5	2.8	7.3	**2.6**	0.5	1.21	70%	85	170
ERA Potl No chg	02 BOS *	5	7	1	131	3.78	1.44	$4	11.9	292	277	265	36%	4.60 -	23.3	2.5	8.6	**3.5**	0.9	1.14	76%	94	178
Support 4.89	1st Half	2	1	1	36	2.75	1.19	$4	4.8	245			28%	3.24	11.4	2.5	6.5	**2.6**	0.8		80%	77	146
LIMA B	2nd Half	3	6	0	95	4.17	1.53	($0)	24.8	308			39%	5.12 -	11.9	2.5	9.4	**3.8**	0.9		75%	101	192
Risk Moderate	03 Proj	**10**	**6**	**0**	**180**	**3.75**	**1.37**	**$10**	**11.9**	**278**			**34%**	**4.11**	**39.0**	**2.6**	**7.9**	**3.0**	**0.7**	**--**	**74%**	**89**	**181**

5-4, 3.48 ERA in 106 IP at BOS. Excellent skill set, his ERA even overcame an elevated hit rate. There have been few LHers who've excelled in Fenway, but this one has the makings of the next Bruce Hurst or Bob Ojeda.

Foulke,Keith	Tm	W	L	Sv	IP	ERA	Br/IP	R$	BF/G	OBA	vLH	vRH	H%	xERA	RAR	Ctl	Dom	Cmd	hr/9	G/F	S%	BPV	BPX
RH Starter	98 CHW	3	2	1	65	4.15	1.09	$7	4.8	217	270	173	25%	3.18 +	13.2	2.8	7.9	**2.9**	1.2	0.79	66%	81	174
AGE 30 Peak	99 CHW	3	3	9	105	2.23	0.89	$24	6.0	196	182	193	26%	2.09	51.2	1.8	10.5	**5.9**	0.9	0.72	82%	174	436
TYPE Power	00 CHW	3	1	34	88	2.97	1.00	$33	4.8	210	221	192	27%	2.50	34.7	2.3	9.3	**4.1**	0.9	0.63	75%	128	332
BURN none	01 CHW	4	9	42	81	2.33	0.98	$36	4.4	200	212	183	26%	1.82 +	34.2	2.4	8.3	**3.4**	0.3	0.66	76%	127	254
ERA Potl + +	02 CHW	2	4	11	77	2.92	1.01	$12	4.7	230	266	185	27%	2.65	22.5	1.5	6.8	**4.5**	0.8	1.04	75%	119	225
Support 4.64	1st Half	1	4	9	38	4.26	1.18	$6	4.7	246			28%	3.62 +	4.3	2.4	7.3	**3.1**	1.2		68%	79	150
LIMA B+	2nd Half	1	0	2	39	1.62	0.85	$7	4.6	214			25%	1.70	18.2	0.7	6.2	**9.0**	0.5		84%	225	425
Risk Very Low	03 Proj	**9**	**7**	**0**	**140**	**3.34**	**1.16**	**$15**	**26.0**	**239**			**29%**	**3.07**	**38.0**	**2.5**	**7.7**	**3.1**	**0.7**	**--**	**73%**	**97**	**197**

Apr 3: 2/3 IP, 4 ER @ SEA
May 29: 1 1/3, 5 ER vs NYY
July 4: 0 IP, 3 ER vs DET
...and the rest of the season he was untouchable, allowing runs in only 10 of his other 63 games. Where's the problem?

Fox,Chad	Tm	W	L	Sv	IP	ERA	Br/IP	R$	BF/G	OBA	vLH	vRH	H%	xERA	RAR	Ctl	Dom	Cmd	hr/9	G/F	S%	BPV	BPX
RH Reliever	98 MIL	1	4	0	57	3.95	1.33	$1	4.9	258	241	273	35%	3.72	9.8	3.2	10.1	**3.2**	0.6	1.07	71%	112	202
AGE 32 Past	99 MIL	0	0	0	7	10.29	2.14	($2)	5.9	358	222	409	56%	7.83 +	-4.4	5.1	15.4	**3.0**	1.3	0.78	50%	100	218
TYPE Power	00 MIL	0	0	0	0	0.00	0.00																
BURN none	01 MIL *	8	2	2	72	1.88	1.21	$15	4.3	191	158	197	27%	2.67 -	33.7	4.9	10.9	**2.2**	0.8	0.95	89%	106	197
ERA Potl - - - -	02 MIL *	1	1	0	9	2.97	2.20	($0)	7.8	336	182	500	42%	6.56 -	3.0	6.9	7.9	**1.1**	0.0	0.88	85%	59	121
Support 5.79	1st Half	1	1	0	9	2.97	2.20	($0)	7.8	336			42%	6.56 -	3.0	6.9	7.9	**1.1**	0.0		85%	59	121
LIMA A	2nd Half	0	0	0	0	0.00	0.00																
Risk High	03 Proj	**3**	**2**	**1**	**40**	**3.38**	**1.40**	**$4**	**4.7**	**221**			**29%**	**3.47**	**11.1**	**5.4**	**9.5**	**1.8**	**0.7**	**--**	**77%**	**84**	**169**

Solid talent that can't stay off the DL. Only has value if you can tuck him away on a deep reserve list.

Franklin,Ryan	Tm	W	L	Sv	IP	ERA	Br/IP	R$	BF/G	OBA	vLH	vRH	H%	xERA	RAR	Ctl	Dom	Cmd	hr/9	G/F	S%	BPV	BPX
RH Reliever	98 aaa	5	6	1	127	5.74	1.64	($5)	17.0	326			35%	6.41 -	-5.3	2.5	5.7	**2.3**	1.6		68%	25	49
AGE 30 Peak	99 aaa	6	9	2	135	6.47	1.56	($3)	20.9	314			34%	5.91 +	-13.9	2.5	5.3	**2.2**	1.5		60%	26	59
TYPE Contact	00 aaa	11	5	0	164	5.32	1.36	$8	22.6	284			31%	5.26	9.6	2.2	6.7	**3.1**	1.8		66%	48	114
BURN none	01 SEA	5	1	0	78	3.57	1.28	$7	8.6	257	276	232	28%	4.41 -	20.0	2.8	6.9	**2.5**	1.5	0.62	79%	53	106
ERA Potl +	02 SEA	7	5	0	118	4.04	1.18	$8	11.8	260	265	247	28%	3.71	16.8	1.7	5.0	**3.0**	1.1	0.82	69%	63	119
Support 4.10	1st Half	4	1	0	44	3.46	1.00	$6	7.5	224			23%	2.92 +	9.7	1.6	5.3	**3.3**	1.2		71%	74	139
LIMA C+	2nd Half	3	4	0	74	4.39	1.29	$2	17.2	280			30%	4.18	7.1	1.7	4.8	**2.8**	1.0		68%	57	107
Risk High	03 Proj	**7**	**4**	**0**	**120**	**3.98**	**1.23**	**$9**	**11.8**	**260**			**28%**	**4.13**	**22.4**	**2.1**	**5.8**	**2.8**	**1.4**	**--**	**73%**	**55**	**112**

Became more precise with his pitches and it served him well. Has at least a 50-50 shot at getting his ERA back down under 4.00.

Fultz,Aaron

		Tm	W	L	Sv	IP	ERA	Br/IP	R$	BF/G	OBA	vLH	vRH	H%	xERA	RAR	Ctl	Dom	Cmd	hr/9	G/F	S%	BPV	BPX
LH Reliever	98	aa	5	7	15	78	5.08	1.67	$7	5.6	304			36%	5.30	3.7	3.9	7.2	1.8	0.7		69%	55	106
AGE 29 Peak	99	aaa	9	8	0	137	5.06	1.47	$5	16.3	281			32%	5.64 -	11.7	3.4	8.4	2.5	2.0		73%	43	99
TYPE Power	00	SF	5	2	1	69	4.69	1.37	$5	5.1	256	221	284	31%	4.19 +	8.7	3.6	8.1	2.2	1.0	1.57	68%	68	149
BURN none	01	SF	3	1	1	71	4.56	1.28	$3	4.5	259	237	276	31%	4.09	7.6	2.7	8.5	3.2	1.1	1.12	67%	87	161
ERA Potl -	02	SF •	3	5	3	63	4.56	1.58	$1	4.7	279	302	284	33%	4.79	7.6	4.4	6.8	1.5	0.7	1.04	72%	51	105
Support 4.35	1st Half		2	2	0	29	5.59	1.72	($2)	4.8	300			34%	5.96	-0.5	4.7	6.5	1.4	1.2		70%	26	54
LIMA B	2nd Half		1	3	3	34	3.68	1.46	$3	4.7	261			32%	3.81	8.1	4.2	7.1	1.7	0.3		73%	73	150
Risk High	03	Proj	3	3	1	60	4.05	1.42	$3	4.9	262			31%	4.27	11.3	3.8	7.5	2.0	0.9	--	73%	63	126

2-2, 4.83 ERA in 41 IP at SF. Had an 11.17 ERA in April, a killer for a reliever because you carry that with you longer than anyone else, no matter how good the rest of the year was. And it WAS good (2.84 ERA).

Fyhrie,Mike

		Tm	W	L	Sv	IP	ERA	Br/IP	R$	BF/G	OBA	vLH	vRH	H%	xERA	RAR	Ctl	Dom	Cmd	hr/9	G/F	S%	BPV	BPX
RH Reliever	98	aaa	3	7	0	100	8.10	1.85	($16)	19.9	327			35%	6.61 +	-35.7	4.3	4.2	1.0	1.2		55%	0	1
AGE 33 Past	99	ANA •	9	9	0	165	5.18	1.47	$5	20.7	273	256	307	32%	4.62 +	15.2	3.7	6.8	1.9	1.0	0.80	66%	51	128
TYPE	00	ANA •	2	1	1	67	2.54	1.31	$8	6.9	243	222	300	29%	3.47 -	30.5	3.6	6.8	1.9	0.7	1.14	83%	67	174
BURN High	01	2TM •	1	2	2	35	3.86	1.43	$2	4.9	251	205	310	30%	3.78	7.3	4.4	6.4	1.5	0.5	1.47	73%	59	113
ERA Potl +	02	OAK	9	6	0	125	3.24	1.23	$12	17.9	241	203	278	28%	2.98	31.3	3.0	6.0	2.0	0.4	0.94	74%	72	136
Support 4.44	1st Half		4	4	0	56	3.69	1.35	$4	16.0	247			28%	3.43	10.6	3.9	5.1	1.3	0.5		73%	50	94
LIMA C	2nd Half		5	2	0	69	2.87	1.13	$8	20.0	236			29%	2.61	20.7	2.3	6.8	2.9	0.4		75%	97	184
Risk X HIGH	03	Proj	5	5	0	100	3.60	1.33	$6	9.4	250			29%	3.49	23.7	3.5	6.2	1.8	0.5	--	73%	63	129

Excellent 2nd half, all but 9 innings of it accomplished at AAA, however.

	G	IP	ERA	Cmd
Starter	4	23	6.65	1.8
Reliever	12	26	2.46	1.2

Inconclusive.

Gagne,Eric

		Tm	W	L	Sv	IP	ERA	Br/IP	R$	BF/G	OBA	vLH	vRH	H%	xERA	RAR	Ctl	Dom	Cmd	hr/9	G/F	S%	BPV	BPX
RH Reliever	98		0	0	0	0	0.00	0.00																
AGE 27 Growth	99	LA •	13	5	0	197	2.56	1.11	$30	25.6	207	196	154	26%	2.59	78.8	3.3	8.5	2.5	0.8	0.88	81%	94	205
TYPE Power	00	LA •	9	7	0	156	4.72	1.52	$4	23.9	271	263	276	31%	5.26 -	19.0	4.3	7.4	1.7	1.6	0.70	74%	35	78
BURN none	01	LA •	9	7	0	174	4.34	1.22	$11	19.5	245	256	247	28%	3.93	23.8	2.7	8.1	3.0	1.3	0.72	69%	77	142
ERA Potl No chg	02	LA	4	1	52	82	1.98	0.87	$51	4.0	192	213	163	29%	1.76	38.3	1.8	12.5	7.1	0.7	0.80	82%	222	454
Support 1.75	1st Half		0	0	29	41	1.31	0.66	$29	3.9	165			26%	0.93	22.9	0.9	12.9	14.8	0.7		88%	389	799
LIMA C	2nd Half		4	1	23	41	2.65	1.08	$23	4.2	218			33%	2.61	15.4	2.6	12.1	4.6	0.7		78%	161	330
Risk High	03	Proj	5	2	45	80	3.15	1.10	$39	4.3	224			29%	3.05	24.7	2.6	10.2	4.0	1.0	--	76%	124	250

Could this have been foreseen? No. However, the skills potential had been evident for awhile. Those who looked beyond the 4.00-plus ERAs to the terrific Cmd ratios, grabbed a bargain. I got him for $3 in LABR on 3/2.

Garcia,Freddy

		Tm	W	L	Sv	IP	ERA	Br/IP	R$	BF/G	OBA	vLH	vRH	H%	xERA	RAR	Ctl	Dom	Cmd	hr/9	G/F	S%	BPV	BPX
RH Starter	98	a/a	10	8	0	166	4.07	1.40	$9	27.6	250			30%	4.16	30.3	4.1	7.8	1.9	1.0		74%	61	118
AGE 26 Growth	99	SEA	17	8	0	201	4.07	1.47	$17	26.7	266	255	273	32%	4.34	48.4	4.0	7.6	1.9	0.8	1.40	74%	63	158
TYPE Power	00	SEA	9	5	0	124	3.92	1.42	$11	25.6	242	272	205	26%	4.42	33.2	4.6	5.7	1.2	1.2	1.15	76%	32	83
BURN Low	01	SEA	18	6	0	238	3.06	1.13	$31	28.3	229	242	205	26%	2.82	77.3	2.6	6.2	2.4	0.6	1.45	74%	78	156
ERA Potl +	02	SEA	16	10	0	223	4.40	1.30	$13	27.7	265	255	265	31%	4.20	21.1	2.5	7.3	2.9	1.2	1.13	70%	70	132
Support 6.00	1st Half		11	5	0	121	3.57	1.07	$15	26.9	233			27%	3.25	25.0	1.9	7.5	3.9	1.3		73%	97	183
LIMA C	2nd Half		5	5	0	102	5.39	1.57	($3)	28.6	300			35%	5.32	-3.8	3.3	7.1	2.2	1.1		67%	48	92
Risk Low	03	Proj	13	11	0	225	4.08	1.32	$13	27.3	257			30%	4.00	38.8	3.1	6.8	2.2	1.0	--	72%	60	122

In '03, he will be overvalued in roto leagues because of his 16 wins, but that was driven by high run support. Faded in the 2nd half, and all these innings may finally be catching up to him. Despite BPI growth, be careful.

Garland,Jon

		Tm	W	L	Sv	IP	ERA	Br/IP	R$	BF/G	OBA	vLH	vRH	H%	xERA	RAR	Ctl	Dom	Cmd	hr/9	G/F	S%	BPV	BPX
RH Starter	98		0	0	0	0	0.00	0.00																
AGE 23 Growth	99	aa	3	1	0	39	5.31	1.56	$1	25.0	286			32%	4.98	2.0	3.9	5.5	1.4	0.9		67%	33	77
TYPE	00	CHW •	13	10	0	178	4.09	1.52	$13	24.7	283	304	278	32%	4.62 -	43.6	3.6	5.4	1.5	0.7	1.40	74%	41	106
BURN Very High	01	CHW •	6	10	1	150	3.66	1.50	$5	16.6	273	276	278	30%	4.76 -	36.7	4.0	5.1	1.3	1.0	1.49	79%	27	55
ERA Potl -	02	CHW	12	12	0	192	4.59	1.41	$6	25.2	258	287	220	28%	4.27	13.2	3.9	5.3	1.3	1.1	1.14	70%	31	59
Support 5.00	1st Half		7	5	0	97	4.54	1.44	$3	24.9	265			28%	4.49	7.4	3.8	4.4	1.2	1.1		71%	20	38
LIMA C	2nd Half		5	7	0	95	4.65	1.38	$2	25.5	250			28%	4.05 +	5.8	4.0	6.1	1.5	1.0		68%	42	80
Risk X HIGH	03	Proj	12	12	0	200	4.91	1.48	$4	25.9	270			30%	4.56	12.4	3.9	5.4	1.4	1.0	--	68%	32	66

Non-descript soft-tosser who doesn't have any notable strengths, and whose growth trend is essentially flat. On the good side, he's only 23. On the bad side, he's thrown a lot of innings for 23.

Ginter,Matt

		Tm	W	L	Sv	IP	ERA	Br/IP	R$	BF/G	OBA	vLH	vRH	H%	xERA	RAR	Ctl	Dom	Cmd	hr/9	G/F	S%	BPV	BPX
RH Reliever	98		0	0	0	0	0.00	0.00																
AGE 25 Growth	99		0	0	0	0	0.00	0.00																
TYPE	00	aa	11	8	0	179	3.27	1.43	$16	28.8	275	345	533	32%	4.04 -	59.7	3.3	5.6	1.7	0.5	0.82	77%	56	132
BURN Low	01	CHW •	3	3	0	116	4.19	1.29	$4	11.6	252	533	345	30%	3.41 +	20.1	3.1	6.4	2.1	0.5	1.02	67%	73	146
ERA Potl ---	02	CHW •	2	0	1	70	4.63	1.64	($2)	6.9	296	342	208	32%	5.59 -	4.5	4.1	5.8	1.4	1.3	0.79	75%	21	41
Support 5.63	1st Half		2	0	1	38	3.53	1.57	$1	7.1	281			30%	5.30 -	8.0	4.2	5.7	1.3	1.4		83%	18	35
LIMA D	2nd Half		0	0	0	32	5.94	1.73	($3)	6.7	314			35%	5.94	-3.6	4.0	5.9	1.5	1.1		67%	25	48
Risk X HIGH	03	Proj	2	1	0	60	4.50	1.50	($0)	9.1	281			32%	4.68	7.0	3.6	6.0	1.7	0.9	F	71%	43	87

1-0, 4.50 ERA in 54 IP at CHW. Note how his G/F tendency shifted to flyballs in '02, and with it zoomed his HR rate, xERA and everything else. And please, keep him away from LHed hitters. Please.

Glavine,Tom

		Tm	W	L	Sv	IP	ERA	Br/IP	R$	BF/G	OBA	vLH	vRH	H%	xERA	RAR	Ctl	Dom	Cmd	hr/9	G/F	S%	BPV	BPX
LH Starter	98	ATL	20	6	0	229	2.47	1.20	$32	28.6	238	244	235	28%	3.05 -	84.7	2.9	6.2	2.1	0.5	1.62	81%	74	133
AGE 37 Decline	99	ATL	14	11	0	234	4.12	1.46	$12	29.3	282	267	292	32%	4.42	44.9	3.2	5.3	1.7	0.7	1.74	73%	45	97
TYPE Contact	00	ATL	21	9	0	241	3.40	1.19	$33	28.3	246	242	245	27%	3.48	72.0	2.4	5.7	2.3	0.9	1.45	75%	62	137
BURN none	01	ATL	16	7	0	219	3.57	1.41	$16	27.1	256	251	263	27%	4.28 -	52.6	4.0	4.8	1.2	1.0	1.15	78%	28	52
ERA Potl ---	02	ATL	18	11	0	224	2.97	1.29	$27	26.2	250	244	254	27%	3.78 -	74.6	3.1	5.1	1.6	0.8	1.06	80%	45	91
Support 5.01	1st Half		11	3	0	123	1.75	1.06	$26	27.2	220			25%	2.57 -	61.1	2.3	5.3	2.3	0.6		87%	73	151
LIMA F	2nd Half		7	8	0	101	4.46	1.57	$2	25.1	283			30%	5.25 -	13.4	4.1	4.8	1.2	1.2		74%	17	35
Risk Low	03	Proj	14	10	0	200	3.92	1.38	$14	26.8	262			29%	4.19	41.2	3.4	5.1	1.5	0.9	--	74%	38	77

Continues to succeed in spite of mediocre BPIs. In '02, he got help from ATL's pen (80% strand). More weaknesses... Note his declining G/F ratio, which had helped him for so long, & 2nd half fall. One day...

Glover,Gary

		Tm	W	L	Sv	IP	ERA	Br/IP	R$	BF/G	OBA	vLH	vRH	H%	xERA	RAR	Ctl	Dom	Cmd	hr/9	G/F	S%	BPV	BPX
RH Reliever	98	aa	0	5	0	37	7.30	1.92	($7)	22.4	297			31%	5.68 +	-9.2	6.6	2.9	0.4	0.5		59%	8	15
AGE 26 Growth	99	a/a	12	8	0	162	4.56	1.40	$11	25.9	271			32%	4.14	24.8	3.1	6.8	2.2	0.7		68%	66	153
TYPE Contact	00	aaa	9	9	0	166	6.13	1.61	($3)	27.8	307			33%	5.77	-8.1	3.3	5.5	1.7	1.3		63%	23	54
BURN none	01	CHW •	7	6	0	138	4.30	1.17	$10	10.8	242	237	269	26%	3.75 +	21.8	2.4	5.8	2.4	1.3	1.15	67%	53	106
ERA Potl +	02	CHW	7	8	1	138	5.22	1.36	$2	14.4	259	280	219	26%	4.44 +	-2.0	3.4	4.6	1.3	1.4	0.86	65%	18	34
Support 6.05	1st Half		3	3	1	57	4.89	1.54	$0	11.1	271			29%	4.67	1.7	4.4	4.7	1.1	0.9		70%	23	44
LIMA C+	2nd Half		4	5	0	81	5.45	1.24	$2	18.7	250			24%	4.29 +	-3.7	2.7	4.4	1.7	1.7		60%	17	32
Risk High	03	Proj	4	5	0	80	5.18	1.38	$1	6.5	264			28%	4.46 +	2.1	3.3	5.1	1.6	1.2	--	65%	28	57

	G	IP	ERA	Cmd
Starter	22	116	5.97	1.3
Reliever	19	22	1.21	1.8

Not much of a sample size, but a tendency is a tendency.

Gordon,Tom

		Tm	W	L	Sv	IP	ERA	Br/IP	R$	BF/G	OBA	vLH	vRH	H%	xERA	RAR	Ctl	Dom	Cmd	hr/9	G/F	S%	BPV	BPX
RH Reliever	98	BOS	7	4	46	79	2.73	1.01	$40	4.3	198	189	193	27%	1.78 +	30.9	2.8	8.9	3.1	0.2	1.50	72%	127	272
AGE 35 Decline	99	BOS	0	2	11	18	5.50	1.61	$5	3.9	251	300	205	36%	4.64 +	0.9	6.0	12.0	2.0	1.0	0.56	67%	89	223
TYPE Power	00	BOS	0	0	0	0	0.00	0.00																
BURN none	01	CHC	1	2	27	45	3.39	1.06	$20	3.8	201	188	188	32%	2.44 +	11.9	3.2	13.4	4.2	0.8	1.05	70%	159	295
ERA Potl ++	02	HOU	1	3	1	43	3.96	1.44	$1	5.2	261	269	255	36%	3.86	8.7	4.0	10.0	2.5	0.4	0.86	72%	103	212
Support 3.59	1st Half		0	0	1	1	22.50	3.33	($1)	3.8	228			23%	7.92 +	-2.7	22.5	0.0	0.0	0.0		25%	9	19
LIMA A+	2nd Half		1	3	0	42	3.43	1.38	$2	5.3	262			36%	3.74	11.4	3.4	10.3	3.0	0.4		75%	115	235
Risk Moderate	03	Proj	2	3	9	50	3.60	1.28	$9	4.6	242			34%	3.13	12.4	3.4	10.1	2.9	0.4	--	71%	118	238

Is he ready to return to a stopper role? BPIs are marginal for success, but his trend, injury history and age are working against him. A terrific LIMA or speculative pick, but definitely do not pay closer prices.

Graves,Danny

Graves,Danny		Tm	W	L	Sv	IP	ERA	Br/IP	R$	BF/G	OBA	vLH	vRH	H%	xERA	RAR	Ctl	Dom	Cmd	hr/9	G/F	S%	BPV	BPX
RH Starter	98	CIN	* 3	1	8	95	3.22	1.31	$10	5.4	260	256	249	29%	3.67	25.7	2.9	5.1	1.7	0.6	2.55	76%	53	96
AGE 29 Peak	99	CIN	8	7	27	111	3.08	1.25	$29	6.2	223	220	233	25%	3.21	36.7	4.0	5.6	1.4	0.8	2.32	78%	49	107
TYPE Contact	00	CIN	10	5	30	91	2.57	1.35	$32	5.9	240	261	226	26%	3.70 -	37.3	4.1	5.2	1.3	0.8	2.21	84%	41	91
BURN High	01	CIN	6	5	32	80	4.16	1.26	$25	5.1	269	301	243	30%	3.87	13.0	2.0	5.5	2.7	0.8	1.99	68%	68	126
ERA Potl -	02	CIN	7	3	32	98	3.21	1.27	$32	6.0	264	272	259	30%	3.73 -	29.5	2.3	5.3	2.3	0.6	2.20	76%	64	131
Support 2.10	1st Half		3	1	24	46	2.73	1.21	$22	4.9	261			31%	3.31 -	16.9	1.9	6.0	3.1	0.4		78%	92	190
LIMA F	2nd Half		4	2	8	52	3.65	1.31	$10	7.6	266			29%	4.10	12.6	2.6	4.7	1.8	0.9		75%	42	85
Risk Low	03	Proj	12	7	0	160	3.94	1.34	$13	26.2	271			30%	4.08	32.5	2.6	5.3	2.0	0.7	G	72%	53	106

+/- On Becoming a Starter...
+ Good BPIs
+ GB tendency will help ERA
-- Not terribly dominant
-- LHers can hit him
-- Untested with a heavy workload

Greisinger,Seth

Greisinger,Seth		Tm	W	L	Sv	IP	ERA	Br/IP	R$	BF/G	OBA	vLH	vRH	H%	xERA	RAR	Ctl	Dom	Cmd	hr/9	G/F	S%	BPV	BPX
RH Starter	98	DET	* 9	13	0	188	4.74	1.44	$5	26.5	274	313	250	29%	4.70	23.1	3.4	4.9	1.4	1.1	1.23	69%	27	57
AGE 27 Pre-Peak	99	DET	0	0	0	0	0.00	0.00																
TYPE Contact	00	DET	0	0	0	0	0.00	0.00																
BURN none	01	DET	0	0	0	0	0.00	0.00																
ERA Potl -	02	DET	* 5	3	0	73	4.92	1.50	$1	21.6	280	333	275	31%	4.38 +	1.8	3.7	4.8	1.3	0.6	1.00	67%	37	69
Support 5.02	1st Half		4	3	0	64	5.05	1.43	$1	21.5	279			31%	4.27 +	0.5	3.1	4.8	1.5	0.7		64%	39	74
LIMA C+	2nd Half		1	0	0	9	4.04	2.02	($0)	22.0	285			33%	5.18 -	1.3	8.1	5.1	0.6	0.0		78%	41	78
Risk Low	03	Proj	2	2	0	40	4.95	1.43	$1	24.8	276			30%	4.44 +	2.2	3.2	4.7	1.5	0.9	--	66%	33	66

2-2, 6.32 ERA in 37 IP at DET. Would be an interesting case study in the development of a pitcher who's missed the core growth years, but he can't stay healthy long enough for us to observe.

Grimsley,Jason

Grimsley,Jason		Tm	W	L	Sv	IP	ERA	Br/IP	R$	BF/G	OBA	vLH	vRH	H%	xERA	RAR	Ctl	Dom	Cmd	hr/9	G/F	S%	BPV	BPX
RH Reliever	98	aaa	6	3	0	88	4.50	1.67	$1	7.8	262			29%	5.12 -	11.0	6.0	5.7	0.9	1.1		76%	23	45
AGE 35 Decline	99	NYY	7	2	1	75	3.60	1.41	$9	5.9	238	165	275	27%	3.88	22.8	4.8	5.9	1.2	0.8	2.17	77%	43	108
TYPE Power	00	NYY	3	2	1	96	5.06	1.48	$2	6.7	270	228	299	29%	4.54 +	11.0	3.9	5.0	1.3	0.9	1.82	67%	29	76
BURN none	01	KC	1	5	0	80	3.03	1.24	$5	4.6	239	261	218	28%	3.50	26.3	3.1	6.9	2.2	0.9	3.30	79%	67	134
ERA Potl No chg	02	KC	4	7	1	72	4.00	1.43	$3	4.4	243	248	225	30%	3.55	10.7	4.8	7.4	1.6	0.5	3.27	72%	68	129
Support 3.28	1st Half		3	4	0	30	5.68	1.63	($0)	4.4	241			29%	3.86 +	-2.3	6.6	6.0	0.9	0.3		63%	53	100
LIMA B+	2nd Half		1	3	1	42	2.79	1.29	$3	4.4	243			31%	3.33 -	13.0	3.4	8.4	2.4	0.6		80%	88	167
Risk Moderate	03	Proj	3	6	1	80	3.60	1.30	$5	4.8	242			29%	3.43	18.9	3.6	7.1	2.0	0.7	G	73%	70	143

Assorted injuries in the 1st half affected his control more than anything else. Once that was corrected, he soared. Should follow up well in 2003.

Groom,Buddy

Groom,Buddy		Tm	W	L	Sv	IP	ERA	Br/IP	R$	BF/G	OBA	vLH	vRH	H%	xERA	RAR	Ctl	Dom	Cmd	hr/9	G/F	S%	BPV	BPX
LH Reliever	98	OAK	3	1	0	57	4.26	1.44	$3	3.3	278	243	304	32%	4.29	10.7	3.2	5.7	1.8	0.6	1.42	71%	52	112
AGE 37 Decline	99	OAK	3	2	0	46	5.09	1.43	$2	2.6	270	245	315	32%	3.76 +	4.8	3.5	6.3	1.8	0.2	2.34	62%	70	176
TYPE	00	BAL	6	3	4	59	4.87	1.42	$8	3.7	274	193	326	32%	4.28 +	8.2	3.2	6.7	2.1	0.8	1.52	66%	61	160
BURN none	01	BAL	1	4	11	66	3.55	1.11	$11	3.8	256	194	291	31%	3.06	17.1	1.2	7.4	6.0	0.5	1.70	68%	158	316
ERA Potl No chg	02	BAL	3	2	2	62	1.60	0.90	$11	3.4	201	181	208	24%	1.79	29.1	1.7	7.0	4.0	0.6	1.54	87%	123	233
Support 2.90	1st Half		2	2	1	31	2.03	0.90	$6	3.4	186			22%	1.62	12.8	2.3	6.4	2.8	0.6		81%	96	182
LIMA B+	2nd Half		1	0	1	31	1.16	0.90	$6	3.4	215			26%	1.95 -	16.4	1.2	7.5	6.5	0.6		92%	176	333
Risk Low	03	Proj	3	2	4	60	2.85	1.08	$9	3.5	235			28%	2.72	20.2	2.0	7.1	3.6	0.6	G	75%	108	220

The big difference in 2002 was that he tied up the 136 RHers he faced, something he had never done before. A sub-2.00 ERA won't happen again, but he could well be worth over $10 for a single digit bid.

Gryboski,Kevin

Gryboski,Kevin		Tm	W	L	Sv	IP	ERA	Br/IP	R$	BF/G	OBA	vLH	vRH	H%	xERA	RAR	Ctl	Dom	Cmd	hr/9	G/F	S%	BPV	BPX
RH Reliever	98	aa	0	0	0	5	9.00	1.80	($1)	11.8	362			37%	9.35	-2.4	1.8	7.2	4.0	3.6		57%	2	4
AGE 29 Pre-Peak	99	aa	2	5	10	62	4.21	1.81	$4	6.2	335			36%	6.45 -	12.4	3.5	4.8	1.4	1.0		79%	15	35
TYPE Power	00	a/a	3	3	11	59	5.95	1.98	$1	6.2	322			39%	6.15	-1.5	5.8	6.9	1.2	0.5		68%	43	102
BURN none	01	aaa	2	5	22	60	4.80	1.60	$11	4.7	307			35%	5.67 -	5.0	3.2	6.5	2.0	1.2		73%	39	75
ERA Potl - - - -	02	ATL	* 3	1	3	58	3.26	1.67	$3	4.2	265	169	306	30%	5.04 -	17.1	5.9	5.7	1.0	0.9	2.09	84%	29	59
Support 2.26	1st Half		2	1	2	36	1.75	1.44	$6	4.5	222			26%	3.72 -	17.9	5.8	6.8	1.2	0.8		92%	53	109
LIMA D	2nd Half		1	0	1	22	5.73	2.05	($2)	3.8	326			34%	7.19 -	-0.8	6.1	4.1	0.7	1.2		74%	-8	-17
Risk High	03	Proj	2	2	0	50	4.86	1.78	($3)	4.6	302			34%	5.79 -	4.0	5.0	5.8	1.1	0.9	G	74%	26	53

2-1, 3.53 ERA in 51 IP at ATL. Rode the momentum of the ATL bullpen, but did not have the skills to back it up. Check out his xERAs and 2nd half line, and see if this is an arm you'd venture even $1 on.

Guardado,Eddie

Guardado,Eddie		Tm	W	L	Sv	IP	ERA	Br/IP	R$	BF/G	OBA	vLH	vRH	H%	xERA	RAR	Ctl	Dom	Cmd	hr/9	G/F	S%	BPV	BPX
LH Reliever	98	MIN	3	1	0	65	4.56	1.44	$2	3.6	264	206	325	30%	4.80	9.6	3.9	7.3	1.9	1.4	0.73	73%	44	95
AGE 31 Peak	99	MIN	2	5	2	48	4.69	1.29	$4	3.2	215	176	258	27%	3.52 +	7.6	4.7	9.4	2.0	1.1	0.55	66%	77	192
TYPE Power	00	MIN	7	4	9	61	3.97	1.31	$14	3.7	242	287	208	25%	4.76 -	15.9	3.7	7.6	2.1	2.1	0.46	80%	34	89
BURN none	01	MIN	7	1	12	66	3.53	1.06	$17	3.9	201	167	216	26%	2.36 +	17.3	3.1	9.1	2.9	0.7	0.64	68%	110	221
ERA Potl +	02	MIN	1	3	45	67	2.96	1.06	$27	3.9	219	263	200	27%	2.97	19.3	2.4	9.4	3.9	1.2	0.61	79%	113	214
Support 0.93	1st Half		1	1	24	38	2.59	0.97	$16	4.0	200			26%	2.26	12.9	2.4	9.7	4.1	0.9		79%	131	247
LIMA C+	2nd Half		0	2	21	29	3.44	1.18	$11	3.8	242			29%	3.90	6.4	2.5	9.1	3.6	1.6		79%	90	170
Risk Low	03	Proj	4	3	39	70	3.47	1.10	$28	3.8	224			28%	3.12	17.8	2.6	9.5	3.7	1.2	F	74%	110	224

Joins Billy Wagner as the only LH frontline closer in the bigs. The role is rare for a port-sider, but these BPIs have been closer-worthy for awhile. He's for real; bid full value.

Guthrie,Mark

Guthrie,Mark		Tm	W	L	Sv	IP	ERA	Br/IP	R$	BF/G	OBA	vLH	vRH	H%	xERA	RAR	Ctl	Dom	Cmd	hr/9	G/F	S%	BPV	BPX
LH Reliever	98	LA	2	1	0	54	3.50	1.48	$1	4.5	269	256	274	33%	4.14 -	12.5	4.0	7.5	1.9	0.5	1.42	77%	71	127
AGE 37 Decline	99	CHC	1	3	2	58	5.43	1.40	$0	4.4	258	182	167	28%	4.72 +	0.9	3.7	7.0	1.9	1.6	1.12	65%	38	83
TYPE Power	00	TOR	3	6	0	71	4.68	1.50	$2	4.1	259	265	261	31%	4.50	11.7	4.7	8.0	1.7	1.0	1.25	71%	56	147
BURN none	01	OAK	6	2	1	52	4.49	1.32	$6	4.1	250	259	241	31%	4.14	6.9	3.5	9.0	2.6	1.2	1.05	69%	77	155
ERA Potl -	02	NYM	5	3	1	48	2.44	1.13	$10	2.9	205	187	223	26%	2.52	19.4	3.6	8.3	2.3	0.6	2.28	80%	95	195
Support 10.13	1st Half		2	0	1	20	1.80	0.95	$6	2.3	175			23%	1.63	9.8	3.2	9.0	2.9	0.5		83%	120	247
LIMA C+	2nd Half		3	3	0	28	2.89	1.25	$5	3.3	226			28%	3.16	9.6	3.9	7.7	2.0	0.6		79%	79	162
Risk Moderate	03	Proj	4	3	1	50	3.96	1.28	$5	3.4	234			28%	3.55	10.0	3.8	7.7	2.0	0.9	G	71%	71	142

Ctl, Dom and Cmd are not all that different from last year, but just about everything else looks like a completely different player. Shea helped a little, the LH coming to the NL helped a little. The odds of it recurring are nil.

Hackman,Luther

Hackman,Luther		Tm	W	L	Sv	IP	ERA	Br/IP	R$	BF/G	OBA	vLH	vRH	H%	xERA	RAR	Ctl	Dom	Cmd	hr/9	G/F	S%	BPV	BPX
RH Reliever	98	aa	3	12	0	139	9.00	2.07	($30)	24.8	369			38%	8.87	-66.4	3.8	4.8	1.3	2.2		59%	-30	-58
AGE 28 Pre-Peak	99	a/a	11	9	0	163	5.52	1.65	$0	28.7	301			34%	5.48	3.8	3.9	6.5	1.6	1.0		67%	38	89
TYPE	00	aaa	8	9	0	119	5.45	1.59	$1	25.5	312	1000	333	34%	5.44	5.0	2.8	4.5	1.6	0.9	0.75	66%	27	63
BURN none	01	STL	* 1	4	1	62	4.06	1.19	$3	4.7	249	308	172	26%	3.92	10.8	2.3	5.5	2.4	1.3	0.79	71%	49	91
ERA Potl - - -	02	STL	5	4	0	81	4.11	1.59	$1	8.5	283	298	279	31%	4.95 -	14.6	4.3	5.1	1.2	0.8	1.11	75%	31	63
Support 5.11	1st Half		1	3	0	34	3.43	1.44	$1	6.5	238			26%	3.72	9.3	5.0	4.2	0.8	0.5		77%	35	71
LIMA C+	2nd Half		4	1	0	47	4.61	1.71	($0)	10.8	312			35%	5.85 -	5.4	3.8	5.8	1.5	1.0		75%	30	61
Risk X HIGH	03	Proj	4	5	0	80	4.73	1.51	$0	7.9	285			31%	4.97	7.8	3.5	5.2	1.5	1.0	--	71%	30	60

2001 was the only year when he displayed any marginal talent and the difference was in his ability to handle RHed batters. With that lost again in '02 and no growth anywhere else, he becomes undraftable in '03.

Halama,John

Halama,John		Tm	W	L	Sv	IP	ERA	Br/IP	R$	BF/G	OBA	vLH	vRH	H%	xERA	RAR	Ctl	Dom	Cmd	hr/9	G/F	S%	BPV	BPX
LH Reliever	98	HOU	* 13	4	0	153	4.41	1.35	$10	28.4	290	261	304	33%	4.27	16.9	1.8	5.3	2.9	0.6	1.20	67%	70	127
AGE 31 Peak	99	SEA	11	10	0	179	4.22	1.39	$13	20.3	277	286	280	30%	4.52	39.5	2.8	5.3	1.9	1.0	1.31	72%	41	102
TYPE Contact	00	SEA	14	9	0	166	5.09	1.58	$8	24.9	305	343	297	33%	5.40	18.3	3.0	4.7	1.6	1.0	1.18	69%	24	62
BURN none	01	SEA	* 12	7	0	129	4.12	1.31	$12	16.0	282	354	273	30%	4.61	23.6	1.8	4.7	2.6	1.3	1.29	73%	42	84
ERA Potl -	02	SEA	* 6	6	0	115	4.14	1.48	$2	15.3	295	246	298	34%	4.61	14.9	2.7	6.0	2.3	0.7	1.42	73%	59	111
Support 4.19	1st Half		3	2	0	54	2.32	1.20	$6	13.1	243			29%	2.98 -	20.2	2.7	6.8	2.6	0.5		82%	86	163
LIMA C+	2nd Half		3	4	0	61	5.75	1.72	($4)	17.7	336			37%	6.06	-5.3	2.7	5.3	2.0	0.9		67%	35	66
Risk Moderate	03	Proj	7	5	0	100	4.41	1.45	$4	17.5	295			33%	4.78	12.8	2.4	5.4	2.2	0.9	--	71%	48	98

Displayed the best dominance of his career in the 1st half, but could not keep it up. And despite his most fervent desires:

	G	IP	ERA	Cmd
Starter	10	50	4.83	1.8
Reliever	21	51	2.31	2.4

Halladay,Roy

	Yr	Tm	W	L	Sv	IP	ERA	Br/IP	R$	BF/G	OBA	vLH	vRH	H%	xERA	RAR	Ctl	Dom	Cmd	hr/9	G/F	S%	BPV	BPX
RH Starter	98	aaa	10	5	0	130	4.71	1.45	$6	24.7	265	226	100	29%	4.60	12.6	3.9	5.6	1.4	1.1	0.80	70%	32	63
AGE 25 Growth	99	TOR	8	7	1	149	3.93	1.58	$7	18.6	271	274	266	29%	5.04 -	38.8	4.8	5.0	1.0	1.1	1.36	79%	18	45
TYPE	00	TOR	* 5	8	0	111	8.59	1.92	($15)	21.5	340	364	350	36%	7.38 +	-39.9	4.2	4.9	1.2	1.6	1.41	55%	-8	-21
BURN High	01	TOR	* 8	4	0	153	3.12	1.12	$17	25.8	246	228	255	31%	2.90	48.5	1.8	7.7	4.2	0.5	2.56	73%	127	253
ERA Potl +	02	TOR	19	7	0	239	2.94	1.19	$26	28.9	249	259	228	30%	2.93	69.4	2.3	6.3	2.7	0.4	2.75	75%	89	168
Support 5.94	1st Half		9	4	0	120	3.15	1.15	$13	28.7	249			30%	2.81	31.4	2.0	7.1	3.6	0.4		72%	112	212
LIMA D+	2nd Half		10	3	0	119	2.72	1.24	$14	29.1	249			29%	3.04	38.0	2.7	5.6	2.1	0.4		78%	71	134
Risk X HIGH	03	Proj	15	8	0	225	3.56	1.32	$18	25.8	265			31%	3.61	54.5	2.7	6.3	2.3	0.5	G	73%	74	150

Even the best young rising stars are not without SOME risk. Most notably, his 86 IP workload increase from '01 is high, and might have contributed to 2nd half fade, especially in his Dom level. If bidding hits $20, hold.

Hamilton,Joey

	Yr	Tm	W	L	Sv	IP	ERA	Br/IP	R$	BF/G	OBA	vLH	vRH	H%	xERA	RAR	Ctl	Dom	Cmd	hr/9	G/F	S%	BPV	BPX
RH Reliever	98	SD	13	13	0	217	4.27	1.50	$6	28.2	264	282	253	31%	4.25	28.1	4.4	6.1	1.4	0.6	1.77	72%	49	89
AGE 32 Past	99	TOR	7	8	0	98	6.52	1.60	($1)	20.1	299	348	243	32%	5.56 +	-8.5	3.6	5.1	1.4	1.2	1.30	60%	20	51
TYPE	00	TOR	2	1	0	33	3.55	1.21	$4	22.7	231	247	213	24%	3.25	10.5	3.3	4.1	1.3	0.8	1.05	73%	35	91
BURN none	01	2TM	6	10	0	139	5.95	1.70	($9)	24.7	330	348	327	37%	6.38	-9.8	2.8	5.9	2.1	1.3	1.51	67%	30	57
ERA Potl -	02	CIN	* 5	10	1	138	5.02	1.47	($1)	14.4	276	303	258	31%	4.60	8.1	3.6	6.1	1.7	0.8	1.98	66%	46	95
Support 3.68	1st Half		3	5	0	77	4.67	1.57	($1)	24.7	281			32%	4.79	8.2	4.2	5.7	1.4	0.7		70%	41	83
LIMA C+	2nd Half		2	5	1	61	5.47	1.35	$0	9.3	268			30%	4.35 +	-0.1	2.8	6.5	2.3	1.0		60%	58	119
Risk Very High	03	Proj	4	5	0	80	4.50	1.40	$2	9.6	274			31%	4.52	10.2	3.0	6.0	2.0	1.0	G	70%	47	94

	G	IP	ERA	Cmd
Starter	17	91	5.56	1.4
Reliever	22	34	4.50	2.9

Given that there has been no growth in his skills, this first attempt at bullpen work should be taken as a positive sign.

Hammond,Chris

	Yr	Tm	W	L	Sv	IP	ERA	Br/IP	R$	BF/G	OBA	vLH	vRH	H%	xERA	RAR	Ctl	Dom	Cmd	hr/9	G/F	S%	BPV	BPX
LH Reliever	98	CIN	* 1	5	0	42	5.57	1.88	($5)	25.2	321			36%	6.68 -	-1.9	4.9	6.2	1.3	1.3		73%	16	29
AGE 37 Decline	99		0	0	0	0	0.00	0.00																
TYPE Power	00		0	0	0	0	0.00	0.00																
BURN none	01	aaa	10	4	1	82	4.04	1.60	$7	7.6	313			38%	5.27 -	15.2	2.9	7.6	2.6	0.7		76%	73	139
ERA Potl --	02	ATL	7	2	0	76	0.95	1.11	$18	4.9	198	174	206	26%	1.98 -	45.9	3.7	7.5	2.0	0.1	1.67	92%	99	204
Support 4.50	1st Half		6	2	0	41	1.75	1.17	$10	5.3	189			25%	2.12	20.4	4.6	7.9	1.7	0.2		85%	94	193
LIMA C	2nd Half		1	0	0	35	0.00	1.03	$8	4.4	209			27%	1.81 -	25.5	2.6	7.0	2.7	0.0		100%	112	229
Risk High	03	Proj	5	3	0	60	3.30	1.38	$6	6.5	262			32%	3.77	17.3	3.5	7.2	2.1	0.5	G	76%	76	153

A different pitcher came back to baseball in 2001, one with an improved skill set. But it was a LUCKY pitcher that came to ATL in 2002. 92% strand and 26% hit rates are pure luck, and won't happen again for a 37 y/o.

Hampton,Mike

	Yr	Tm	W	L	Sv	IP	ERA	Br/IP	R$	BF/G	OBA	vLH	vRH	H%	xERA	RAR	Ctl	Dom	Cmd	hr/9	G/F	S%	BPV	BPX
LH Starter	98	HOU	11	7	0	211	3.37	1.46	$10	28.9	276	277	278	31%	4.45 -	52.8	3.5	5.8	1.7	0.8	2.70	79%	47	85
AGE 30 Peak	99	HOU	22	4	0	239	2.90	1.28	$33	29.6	234	149	259	28%	3.08	84.7	3.8	6.7	1.8	0.5	2.56	78%	71	155
TYPE	00	NYM	15	10	0	217	3.15	1.35	$23	28.1	241	257	237	29%	3.35	72.1	4.1	6.3	1.5	0.4	2.51	77%	64	141
BURN Moderate	01	COL	14	13	0	203	5.41	1.58	($1)	28.6	292	346	284	31%	5.56	-1.2	3.8	5.4	1.4	1.4	1.75	69%	18	33
ERA Potl --	02	COL	7	15	0	178	6.17	1.79	($17)	28.0	312	376	293	32%	6.33	-16.9	4.6	3.7	0.8	1.2	1.67	67%	-4	-9
Support 5.44	1st Half		4	9	0	98	6.88	1.95	($15)	28.1	328			36%	6.60	-18.7	5.1	4.7	0.9	0.8		64%	12	24
LIMA F	2nd Half		3	6	0	80	5.29	1.60	($4)	27.8	292			28%	6.00 -	1.8	3.9	2.6	0.7	1.7		72%	-25	-51
Risk Low	03	Proj	9	11	0	160	4.95	1.60	($1)	27.8	289			31%	5.35	10.8	4.1	4.6	1.1	1.1	G	71%	15	30

If not for his contract, he'd be an easy sell... Save Mike Hampton from COL! Extract him from hell and let him rediscover his skills! One problem: His skills deserted him long ago. Stay far away, no matter where he ends up.

Haney,Chris

	Yr	Tm	W	L	Sv	IP	ERA	Br/IP	R$	BF/G	OBA	vLH	vRH	H%	xERA	RAR	Ctl	Dom	Cmd	hr/9	G/F	S%	BPV	BPX
LH Reliever	98	2TM	6	6	0	102	7.06	1.62	($6)	12.2	308			32%	6.27 +	-22.2	3.3	4.9	1.5	1.8		59%	1	2
AGE 34 Past	99	CLE	* 2	7	0	98	4.50	1.46	$2	16.5	273			30%	4.31	18.0	3.6	4.8	1.3	0.6		69%	38	95
TYPE	00	aaa	8	3	0	92	3.33	1.36	$11	26.2	292		333	32%	4.70 -	30.0	1.8	5.6	3.2	1.1	0.50	80%	64	152
BURN none	01	JPN	2	4	0	31	5.81	1.48	($0)	19.5	280			27%	5.77	-1.6	3.5	4.6	1.3	2.0		67%	-6	-12
ERA Potl No chg	02	BOS	* 2	0	5	59	3.97	1.46	$3	5.3	281	286	265	33%	4.12	9.0	3.2	6.1	1.9	0.5	1.72	72%	62	117
Support 1.50	1st Half		2	0	5	37	3.15	1.37	$5	5.1	272			33%	3.80 -	9.7	2.9	6.8	2.3	0.5		78%	76	143
LIMA C+	2nd Half		0	0	0	22	5.34	1.60	($2)	5.5	296			33%	4.67 +	-0.7	3.7	4.9	1.3	0.4		65%	41	78
Risk X HIGH	03	Proj	2	2	0	40	4.73	1.48	$0	5.7	285			32%	4.69	3.4	3.2	5.4	1.7	0.9	G	69%	39	80

0-0, 4.20 ERA in 30 IP at BOS. Pitched well in Pawtucket this year, but made no impact in Fenway. Skill are marginal on a good day, but bad days come far too often.

Harang,Aaron

	Yr	Tm	W	L	Sv	IP	ERA	Br/IP	R$	BF/G	OBA	vLH	vRH	H%	xERA	RAR	Ctl	Dom	Cmd	hr/9	G/F	S%	BPV	BPX
RH Starter	98		0	0	0	0	0.00	0.00																
AGE 24 Growth	99		0	0	0	0	0.00	0.00																
TYPE Power	00		0	0	0	0	0.00	0.00																
BURN none	01	aa	10	8	0	150	4.56	1.52	$4	24.7	312			36%	4.94	17.3	2.2	5.6	2.6	0.5		69%	64	123
ERA Potl +	02	OAK	* 10	7	0	133	4.06	1.48	$6	21.7	267	237	287	33%	4.05	18.7	4.1	7.6	1.9	0.5	0.67	72%	71	134
Support 4.48	1st Half		8	4	0	87	1.86	1.24	$13	22.7	236			31%	2.69 -	38.0	3.3	8.1	2.5	0.2		85%	102	194
LIMA B	2nd Half		2	3	0	46	8.25	1.94	($7)	20.2	321			37%	6.63 +	-19.3	5.5	6.7	1.2	1.2		57%	21	40
Risk Moderate	03	Proj	8	7	0	120	4.80	1.58	$1	22.5	297			35%	4.89	9.1	3.5	7.0	2.0	0.7	F	69%	60	121

5-4, 4.85 ERA in 78 IP at OAK. Had a 2.02 ERA after his first 6 MLB starts, then 7.17 the rest of the way. Had a 3.05 ERA at home, 6.81 on the road. Talent is here, consistency is not. That will come, but it may be a wait.

Harper,Travis

	Yr	Tm	W	L	Sv	IP	ERA	Br/IP	R$	BF/G	OBA	vLH	vRH	H%	xERA	RAR	Ctl	Dom	Cmd	hr/9	G/F	S%	BPV	BPX
RH Reliever	98		0	0	0	0	0.00	0.00																
AGE 26 Growth	99	aa	6	3	0	72	6.50	1.51	$0	22.8	290			33%	5.32 +	-7.7	3.3	7.1	2.2	1.4		58%	45	103
TYPE	00	TAM	* 11	7	0	187	4.09	1.27	$18	24.5	264	234	254	28%	3.97	45.7	2.4	4.1	1.7	1.0	0.72	70%	34	89
BURN none	01	TAM	* 12	8	0	162	4.94	1.38	$7	25.8	285			29%	5.48 -	11.7	2.3	5.6	2.5	1.9	1.00	71%	25	50
ERA Potl No chg	02	TAM	* 6	11	1	104	6.22	1.61	($4)	11.5	320	301	280	35%	6.30	-15.6	2.6	6.4	2.5	1.7	1.15	65%	29	56
Support 3.36	1st Half		4	5	1	61	4.99	1.37	$2	13.1	294			32%	5.31	0.9	1.8	6.9	3.9	1.8		69%	67	127
LIMA C+	2nd Half		2	6	0	43	7.99	1.96	($7)	10.0	354			38%	7.72	-16.5	3.8	5.7	1.5	1.7		61%	-1	-1
Risk High	03	Proj	5	6	0	80	4.95	1.43	$2	14.5	285			30%	5.20	4.5	2.7	5.9	2.2	1.6	--	70%	31	64

	G	IP	ERA	Cmd
Starter	7	31	8.33	1.5
Reliever	30	54	3.81	2.7

Clearly better out of the bullpen. Adjust your expectations based on his role.

Hasegawa,Shigetoshi

	Yr	Tm	W	L	Sv	IP	ERA	Br/IP	R$	BF/G	OBA	vLH	vRH	H%	xERA	RAR	Ctl	Dom	Cmd	hr/9	G/F	S%	BPV	BPX
RH Reliever	98	ANA	8	3	5	97	3.15	1.22	$16	6.6	239	212	261	26%	3.82 -	32.6	3.0	6.8	2.3	1.3	0.94	81%	57	121
AGE 34 Decline	99	ANA	4	6	2	77	4.91	1.48	$4	5.3	269	274	277	28%	5.23	9.9	4.0	5.1	1.3	1.6	0.74	72%	10	25
TYPE	00	ANA	10	6	9	95	3.59	1.45	$17	6.3	271	246	291	30%	4.58 -	29.6	3.6	5.6	1.6	1.0	1.28	79%	36	92
BURN none	01	ANA	5	6	0	55	4.08	1.30	$5	5.1	250	221	270	29%	3.75	10.4	3.3	6.7	2.1	0.8	1.29	70%	64	127
ERA Potl -	02	SEA	8	3	1	70	3.21	1.29	$9	5.6	233	284	199	26%	3.10	17.7	3.9	5.0	1.3	0.5	1.10	76%	50	95
Support 5.12	1st Half		4	1	1	34	1.05	0.96	$8	5.1	186			21%	1.49	18.6	2.9	5.0	1.7	0.3		91%	76	144
LIMA C	2nd Half		4	2	0	36	5.28	1.59	$1	6.0	273			30%	4.64 +	-0.8	4.8	5.0	1.1	0.8		67%	30	57
Risk Moderate	03	Proj	8	5	2	80	4.28	1.41	$7	5.7	259			29%	4.06	11.7	3.8	5.3	1.4	0.8	--	71%	40	82

Despite lower ERA, his BPIs were off. Allowed more balls in play (lower Dom) and lucked out with a 26% hit rate on those balls. 2nd half drop-off should be a warning sign.

Hawkins,LaTroy

	Yr	Tm	W	L	Sv	IP	ERA	Br/IP	R$	BF/G	OBA	vLH	vRH	H%	xERA	RAR	Ctl	Dom	Cmd	hr/9	G/F	S%	BPV	BPX
RH Reliever	98	MIN	7	14	0	190	5.26	1.51	($1)	25.5	297	296	302	32%	5.40	10.2	2.9	5.0	1.7	1.3	1.13	68%	23	49
AGE 30 Peak	99	MIN	10	14	0	174	6.67	1.71	($7)	24.4	327	310	335	35%	6.56	-18.7	3.1	5.3	1.7	1.5	1.10	63%	13	32
TYPE	00	MIN	2	5	14	87	3.41	1.34	$15	5.6	257	238	267	29%	3.81	29.3	3.3	6.1	1.8	0.7	1.32	76%	57	149
BURN none	01	MIN	1	5	28	51	5.99	1.92	$9	4.0	290	276	305	34%	5.59	-3.4	6.9	6.3	0.9	0.5	1.17	67%	38	77
ERA Potl No chg	02	MIN	6	0	0	80	2.14	0.98	$13	4.8	218	225	211	26%	2.16	31.8	1.7	7.1	4.2	0.6	1.34	81%	125	237
Support 5.49	1st Half		3	0	0	48	1.68	0.85	$9	5.5	200			24%	1.79	22.1	1.3	7.7	5.9	0.7		86%	162	305
LIMA C+	2nd Half		3	0	0	32	2.83	1.16	$4	4.1	244			29%	2.71	9.7	2.3	6.2	2.8	0.3		75%	93	175
Risk High	03	Proj	4	3	3	80	3.49	1.26	$8	4.8	250			30%	3.33	20.2	2.9	6.9	2.3	0.6	--	73%	79	160

Nearly got cut after a horrible spring. Then made some minor adjustments (changed arm angle, worked faster, pitched around the plate more) and became unhittable. Most (not all) of this is for real.

Haynes,Jimmy		Tm	W	L	Sv	IP	ERA	Br/IP	R$	BF/G	OBA	vLH	vRH	H%	xERA	RAR	Ctl	Dom	Cmd	hr/9	G/F	S%	BPV	BPX
RH Starter	98	OAK	11	9	0	194	5.10	1.63	($0)	26.8	295	308	288	33%	5.53	14.4	4.1	6.2	1.5	1.2	1.07	71%	30	65
AGE 30 Peak	99	OAK	7	12	0	142	6.34	1.68	($5)	21.8	283	283	280	31%	5.63 +	-8.9	5.1	5.9	1.2	1.3	0.90	64%	18	46
TYPE	00	MIL	12	13	0	199	5.33	1.65	($1)	27.6	289	319	276	30%	5.29	7.9	4.5	4.0	0.9	0.9	1.29	68%	11	24
BURN none	01	MIL	8	17	0	172	4.86	1.51	($0)	24.6	273	259	291	30%	4.79	11.7	4.1	5.9	1.4	1.0	1.70	70%	34	64
ERA Potl - -	02	CIN	15	10	0	196	4.13	1.48	$10	25.4	275	280	276	31%	4.74 -	34.8	3.7	5.8	1.6	1.0	1.34	74%	38	79
Support 4.71	1st Half		8	6	0	91	4.45	1.45	$5	24.9	278			30%	5.00 -	12.3	3.3	5.6	1.7	1.3		73%	31	63
LIMA D+	2nd Half		7	4	0	105	3.86	1.51	$5	25.9	273			31%	4.51 -	22.5	4.1	5.9	1.4	0.7		75%	46	93
Risk Moderate	03	Proj	13	13	0	200	4.64	1.54	$4	25.5	278			31%	4.90	21.9	4.1	5.6	1.4	1.0	--	72%	32	65

Made minor gains in Ctl in the 1st half, but it was short-term. Bullpen helped keep his ERA down, but xERA tells the real story. This is the prototypical inning-eater, always there every 5th day to take one for the team.

Helling,Rick		Tm	W	L	Sv	IP	ERA	Br/IP	R$	BF/G	OBA	vLH	vRH	H%	xERA	RAR	Ctl	Dom	Cmd	hr/9	G/F	S%	BPV	BPX
RH Starter	98	TEX	20	7	0	216	4.41	1.33	$20	27.8	255	253	252	29%	4.16	35.9	3.2	6.8	2.1	1.1	0.61	70%	55	118
AGE 32 Peak	99	TEX	13	11	0	219	4.85	1.43	$11	27.2	270	263	281	28%	5.15	30.0	3.5	5.4	1.5	1.7	0.72	72%	15	38
TYPE	00	TEX	16	13	0	217	4.48	1.43	$16	27.0	257	238	267	28%	4.49	41.6	4.1	6.1	1.5	1.2	0.56	72%	35	90
BURN none	01	TEX	12	11	0	215	5.19	1.48	$2	27.9	297	296	298	32%	5.58	8.6	2.6	6.4	2.4	1.6	0.81	69%	38	76
ERA Potl -	02	ARI	11	12	0	182	4.40	1.28	$11	24.7	264	283	249	28%	4.60	25.8	2.4	6.2	2.6	1.5	0.71	71%	48	98
Support 5.69	1st Half		7	5	0	97	4.36	1.20	$9	25.0	251			26%	4.37	14.3	2.3	5.9	2.6	1.7		71%	44	90
LIMA D+	2nd Half		4	7	0	85	4.45	1.37	$3	24.3	278			31%	4.86	11.4	2.5	6.6	2.6	1.4		72%	52	106
Risk Low	03	Proj	11	11	0	180	4.45	1.35	$9	25.6	268			29%	4.72	24.2	2.9	6.3	2.2	1.5	F	72%	42	85

BPIs are peaking, but the HR ball has obscured any growth. If you were ever to take a longshot bet on a player having an unexpected breakout year if he could correct one flaw, this would be a good candidate.

Hendrickson,Mark		Tm	W	L	Sv	IP	ERA	Br/IP	R$	BF/G	OBA	vLH	vRH	H%	xERA	RAR	Ctl	Dom	Cmd	hr/9	G/F	S%	BPV	BPX
LH Starter	98		0	0	0	0	0.00	0.00																
AGE 28 Pre-Peak	99	aa	2	7	0	55	7.53	1.87	($7)	22.0	346			39%	6.47 +	-13.5	3.4	5.2	1.5	0.7		58%	30	69
TYPE Contact	00	aa	3	1	0	39	4.85	1.36	$3	27.8	267			28%	4.63	4.8	3.0	5.1	1.7	1.4		68%	26	62
BURN none	01	aaa	2	9	0	73	6.29	1.60	($6)	8.7	323			31%	6.68	-8.5	2.3	3.3	1.4	2.0		65%	-19	-36
ERA Potl -	02	TOR *	10	5	0	128	3.87	1.32	$9	15.5	271	194	204	30%	4.13	21.2	2.5	5.3	2.2	1.0	1.25	74%	49	93
Support 5.40	1st Half		4	4	0	78	4.83	1.51	($0)	26.6	308			33%	5.53 -	2.9	2.3	5.4	2.4	1.4		72%	34	64
LIMA C+	2nd Half		6	1	0	50	2.35	1.02	$9	8.9	204			23%	1.94	18.4	2.7	5.2	1.9	0.4		78%	75	143
Risk X HIGH	03	Proj	8	8	0	120	4.73	1.40	$5	24.7	282			30%	4.68	10.3	2.6	4.8	1.8	1.1	--	69%	32	65

3-0, 2.50 ERA in 36 IP at TOR. Was dominating in 4 late starts, but 3 of them were vs BAL and TAM. Skills show some promise, but at 28, he's late in the development curve due to his stint in the NBA.

Hentgen,Pat		Tm	W	L	Sv	IP	ERA	Br/IP	R$	BF/G	OBA	vLH	vRH	H%	xERA	RAR	Ctl	Dom	Cmd	hr/9	G/F	S%	BPV	BPX
RH Starter	98	TOR	12	11	0	177	5.18	1.56	$3	27.4	294	288	299	31%	5.60	11.3	3.5	4.8	1.4	1.4	1.21	70%	11	23
AGE 34 Past	99	TOR	11	12	0	199	4.79	1.46	$8	25.6	286	300	265	30%	5.24	28.7	2.9	5.3	1.8	1.4	1.14	71%	24	61
TYPE Contact	00	STL	15	12	0	194	4.73	1.50	$10	26.0	270	252	295	29%	4.78	23.4	4.1	5.5	1.3	1.1	1.32	71%	28	63
BURN none	01	BAL	2	3	0	62	3.48	1.13	$5	27.9	226	178	275	24%	3.19	16.7	2.8	4.8	1.7	1.0	1.15	73%	45	89
ERA Potl - - -	02	BAL *	0	4	0	28	6.43	1.79	($4)	26.4	325	333	341	32%	7.33 -	-5.0	3.9	4.5	1.2	2.3	1.00	70%	-26	-49
Support 2.45	1st Half		0	0	0	0	0.00	0.00																
LIMA F	2nd Half		0	4	0	28	6.43	1.79	($4)	26.3	325			32%	7.33 -	-5.0	3.9	4.5	1.2	2.3		70%	-26	-49
Risk Moderate	03	Proj	8	17	0	200	5.04	1.51	($1)	26.8	284			30%	5.36	8.8	3.5	5.0	1.4	1.5	--	71%	12	24

Given what they did with Scott Erickson, it's conceivable that BAL will put him on the mound for 200 IP and drive a stake through whatever is left of his career. Stay far, far away, like in Pomona or somewhere.

Heredia,Felix		Tm	W	L	Sv	IP	ERA	Br/IP	R$	BF/G	OBA	vLH	vRH	H%	xERA	RAR	Ctl	Dom	Cmd	hr/9	G/F	S%	BPV	BPX
LH Reliever	98	2NL	3	3	2	58	5.10	1.63	($1)	3.7	258	202	299	33%	4.18 +	1.0	5.9	8.4	1.4	0.3	1.10	67%	74	134
AGE 27 Pre-Peak	99	CHC	3	1	1	52	4.85	1.56	$1	3.4	276	247	292	34%	5.04	4.9	4.3	8.7	2.0	1.2	0.85	72%	57	125
TYPE Power	00	CHC	7	3	2	58	4.79	1.36	$7	3.4	219	195	236	26%	3.56 +	6.5	5.1	8.0	1.6	0.9	1.11	66%	65	143
BURN none	01	CHC	2	2	0	35	6.17	1.74	($3)	3.4	313	288	338	36%	6.44	-3.8	4.1	7.2	1.8	1.5	0.82	67%	26	48
ERA Potl - -	02	TOR	1	2	0	52	3.63	1.48	$0	4.3	258	224	281	28%	4.25 -	10.2	4.5	5.4	1.2	0.9	1.16	78%	35	66
Support 4.64	1st Half		0	1	0	30	4.50	1.83	($3)	5.3	299			32%	6.03 -	2.4	5.7	5.4	0.9	1.2		78%	12	22
LIMA C+	2nd Half		1	1	0	22	2.45	1.00	$3	3.3	195			22%	1.81 +	7.8	2.9	5.3	1.9	0.4		76%	75	141
Risk Low	03	Proj	3	2	0	50	4.32	1.46	$2	3.7	258			30%	4.26	7.0	4.3	6.5	1.5	0.9	--	72%	47	95

Ridiculous 22% hit rate held down his ERA in the 2nd half, but that won't happen again. BPIs are mediocre, but he's had intermittent success vs LHers, which is why he's employed. Still, not a great risk.

Herges,Matt		Tm	W	L	Sv	IP	ERA	Br/IP	R$	BF/G	OBA	vLH	vRH	H%	xERA	RAR	Ctl	Dom	Cmd	hr/9	G/F	S%	BPV	BPX
RH Reliever	98	aaa	3	5	0	94	5.65	1.78	($7)	11.9	329			37%	6.07	-2.7	3.5	5.7	1.6	0.8		68%	35	68
AGE 33 Past	99	LA *	8	5	0	155	4.47	1.35	$8	17.4	269	250	259	29%	4.30	22.3	2.8	5.3	1.9	1.0	0.65	69%	41	90
TYPE Power	00	LA	11	3	1	110	3.19	1.27	$17	7.8	243	268	235	28%	3.34	36.1	3.3	6.1	1.9	0.6	2.04	76%	65	144
BURN none	01	LA	9	8	1	99	3.45	1.44	$9	5.8	258	280	243	30%	4.10 -	25.4	4.2	6.9	1.7	0.7	1.58	78%	58	107
ERA Potl - - - -	02	MON	2	5	6	64	4.08	1.66	$3	4.7	307	315	300	35%	6.05 -	11.8	3.7	7.0	1.9	1.4	1.43	80%	34	70
Support 4.04	1st Half		2	2	6	38	3.08	1.76	$4	4.4	322			38%	5.91 -	12.1	3.8	6.9	1.8	0.7		84%	48	99
LIMA C+	2nd Half		0	3	0	26	5.54	1.50	($2)	5.2	283			30%	6.25 -	-0.3	3.5	7.3	2.1	2.4		72%	13	27
Risk High	03	Proj	2	4	2	70	4.76	1.50	$0	5.7	281			32%	5.12	6.5	3.6	6.8	1.9	1.3	--	72%	41	82

It takes an incredible amount of good luck to have an ERA nearly two full runs lower than an xERA. And if your ERA is already over 4, then it was a really bad season. 35% hit rate hurt, but BPIs didn't help much.

Hermanson,Dustin			W	L	Sv	IP	ERA	Br/IP	R$	BF/G	OBA	vLH	vRH	H%	xERA	RAR	Ctl	Dom	Cmd	hr/9	G/F	S%	BPV	BPX
RH Starter	98	MON	14	11	0	187	3.13	1.17	$22	23.9	236	237	231	28%	3.40	52.8	2.7	7.4	2.8	1.0	1.38	78%	80	144
AGE 30 Peak	99	MON	9	14	0	216	4.21	1.36	$10	27.2	270	272	271	31%	4.12	38.7	2.9	6.0	2.1	0.8	0.94	70%	56	123
TYPE	00	MON	12	14	4	198	4.77	1.52	$8	23.1	288	317	272	30%	5.18	22.7	3.4	4.3	1.3	1.2	1.40	71%	14	31
BURN none	01	STL	14	13	0	192	4.45	1.40	$10	25.1	265	276	255	28%	4.90	23.6	3.4	5.8	1.7	1.6	1.14	74%	24	45
ERA Potl +	02	BOS *	1	2	0	35	6.14	1.73	($3)	9.6	317	325	373	35%	5.66	-4.9	3.8	5.4	1.4	0.8	0.90	64%	30	57
Support 9.82	1st Half		0	0	0	0	0.00	0.00																
LIMA C+	2nd Half		1	2	0	35	6.14	1.73	($3)	9.6	317			35%	5.66	-4.9	3.8	5.4	1.4	0.8		64%	30	57
Risk Moderate	03	Proj	7	9	0	140	4.89	1.50	$1	22.1	285			31%	4.93	9.0	3.4	5.5	1.6	1.1	--	69%	32	65

1-1, 7.77 ERA in 22 IP at BOS. Injury troubles and declining BPIs make him a high risk pick, especially if he lands a rotation slot.

Hernandez,Carlos		Tm	W	L	Sv	IP	ERA	Br/IP	R$	BF/G	OBA	vLH	vRH	H%	xERA	RAR	Ctl	Dom	Cmd	hr/9	G/F	S%	BPV	BPX
LH Starter	98		0	0	0	0	0.00	0.00																
AGE 23 Growth	99		0	0	0	0	0.00	0.00																
TYPE Power	00		0	0	0	0	0.00	0.00																
BURN none	01	aa	13	3	0	156	4.27	1.44	$9	25.2	249	156	235	32%	4.10	24.1	4.6	9.2	2.0	0.9	0.72	72%	77	148
ERA Potl -	02	HOU *	7	5	0	122	4.35	1.51	$3	20.8	255	262	261	30%	4.42	18.2	4.9	7.6	1.6	0.9	1.32	73%	56	114
Support 4.62	1st Half		5	3	0	81	4.44	1.49	$2	22.4	262			30%	4.69	11.1	4.4	7.2	1.6	1.1		73%	47	96
LIMA B	2nd Half		2	2	0	41	4.16	1.53	$1	18.3	242			31%	3.89	7.1	5.7	8.3	1.5	0.4		72%	74	152
Risk High	03	Proj	9	5	0	140	3.99	1.43	$8	25.4	249			31%	4.00	27.5	4.4	8.4	1.9	0.8	--	73%	72	146

A work-in-progress here. There are signs that he could develop into a good pitcher, but he needs to focus on getting that walk rate down. Any growth will have to travel by way of the ol' base on balls.

Hernandez,Livan		Tm	W	L	Sv	IP	ERA	Br/IP	R$	BF/G	OBA	vLH	vRH	H%	xERA	RAR	Ctl	Dom	Cmd	hr/9	G/F	S%	BPV	BPX
RH Starter	98	FLA	10	12	0	234	4.73	1.58	($3)	31.9	286	277	299	31%	5.51 -	15.9	4.0	6.2	1.6	1.4	1.08	74%	25	45
AGE 28 Pre-Peak	99	SF	8	12	0	199	4.66	1.52	$2	29.5	288	292	280	33%	4.98	23.7	3.4	6.5	1.9	1.0	1.21	71%	45	98
TYPE	00	SF	17	11	0	240	3.75	1.36	$21	31.1	273	273	272	31%	4.21	60.4	2.7	6.2	2.3	0.8	1.44	74%	60	133
BURN Very High	01	SF	13	15	0	226	5.25	1.55	($1)	29.8	294	299	296	33%	5.13	3.5	3.4	5.5	1.6	1.0	1.29	67%	35	64
ERA Potl -	02	SF	12	16	0	216	4.38	1.41	($8)	28.3	277	295	273	31%	4.41	31.4	3.0	5.6	1.9	0.8	1.36	70%	49	101
Support 4.67	1st Half		6	9	0	111	4.46	1.45	$3	28.6	285			32%	4.65	14.9	2.9	5.3	1.8	0.8		70%	44	91
LIMA C	2nd Half		6	7	0	105	4.29	1.36	$5	28.1	267			30%	4.14	16.4	3.0	5.8	1.9	0.8		69%	54	111
Risk Moderate	03	Proj	13	15	0	225	4.52	1.45	$7	28.9	281			32%	4.62	28.2	3.1	5.8	1.8	0.9	--	70%	46	92

By 28, many pitchers are beginning their approach to their peak period. But he's already thrown over 1200 IP since age 21 and has become a sub-.500 workhorse. Which is okay if you have low aspirations.

Hernandez,Orlando

Hernandez,Orlando	Yr Tm	W	L	Sv	IP	ERA	Br/IP	R$	BF/G	OBA	vLH	vRH	H%	xERA	RAR	Ctl	Dom	Cmd	hr/9	G/F	S%	BPV	BPX
RH Starter	98 NYY	* 18	4	0	183	3.69	1.29	$22	27.6	243	271	162	31%	3.44	48.3	3.5	8.7	**2.5**	0.6	0.96	72%	91	195
AGE 37 Decline	99 NYY	17	9	0	214	4.12	1.28	$23	27.2	237	273	187	27%	3.68	50.2	3.7	6.6	**1.8**	1.0	0.80	70%	55	138
TYPE	00 NYY	12	13	0	195	4.52	1.21	$18	27.8	253	280	210	27%	4.22	36.4	2.4	6.5	**2.8**	1.6	0.71	68%	55	142
BURN none	01 NYY	4	7	0	94	4.87	1.40	$1	23.9	253	278	213	27%	4.96	7.7	4.0	7.4	**1.8**	1.8	0.65	72%	33	65
ERA Potl +	02 NYY	9	5	1	151	3.57	1.16	$13	24.7	246	224	248	28%	3.41	31.1	2.2	7.0	**3.2**	1.0	0.82	73%	84	158
Support 5.61	1st Half	5	2	1	61	3.08	1.03	$9	24.2	214			24%	2.81	16.6	2.3	7.0	**3.0**	1.2		76%	82	156
LIMA C	2nd Half	4	3	0	90	3.90	1.26	$5	25.0	266			31%	3.81	14.5	2.1	6.9	**3.3**	0.9		71%	85	161
Risk High	03 Proj	7	6	0	120	4.05	1.25	$8	25.0	249			28%	3.95	21.2	2.9	7.1	2.5	1.3	--	72%	61	125

I now know why I did so poorly in the experts leagues in '02. It's all these deviant performances. A 37-year-old posting a 250% performance spike? This is not first we've seen. It's screwing up the entire universal order.

Hernandez,Roberto

Hernandez,Roberto	Yr Tm	W	L	Sv	IP	ERA	Br/IP	R$	BF/G	OBA	vLH	vRH	H%	xERA	RAR	Ctl	Dom	Cmd	hr/9	G/F	S%	BPV	BPX
RH Reliever	98 TAM	2	6	26	71	4.05	1.35	$17	4.5	215	184	242	26%	3.24 +	15.3	5.2	7.0	**1.3**	0.6	1.73	70%	63	134
AGE 38 Decline	99 TAM	2	3	43	73	3.08	1.38	$30	4.4	248	241	248	33%	3.25	27.3	4.1	8.5	**2.1**	0.1	1.95	76%	97	242
TYPE	00 TAM	4	7	32	73	3.20	1.35	$26	4.6	269	328	223	32%	4.36 -	26.5	2.8	7.5	**2.7**	1.1	1.43	81%	69	178
BURN none	01 KC	5	6	28	67	4.15	1.41	$19	4.6	267	299	230	30%	4.37	12.0	3.5	6.2	**1.8**	0.9	1.37	73%	48	95
ERA Potl No chg	02 KC	1	3	26	53	4.25	1.45	$12	4.3	293	282	317	34%	4.81 -	6.1	2.5	6.8	**2.7**	1.0	1.78	73%	63	118
Support 1.56	1st Half	1	0	13	26	2.77	1.15	$9	4.2	239			28%	2.99	8.1	2.4	6.9	**2.9**	0.7		79%	88	166
LIMA C	2nd Half	0	3	13	27	5.67	1.74	$3	4.3	339			38%	6.56 -	-2.0	2.7	6.7	**2.5**	1.3		70%	40	75
Risk Moderate	03 Proj	2	4	23	50	4.14	1.44	$13	4.4	281			33%	4.52	8.2	3.1	6.8	2.2	0.9	G	73%	60	122

A nice little BPI rebound, but I'm not buying any stock, because...
- He's 38
- He's teased us before
- His near-.300 OBA
- No job, but leaving KC is a plus
- It's Roberto Hernandez

Hernandez,Runelvys

Hernandez,Runelvys	Yr Tm	W	L	Sv	IP	ERA	Br/IP	R$	BF/G	OBA	vLH	vRH	H%	xERA	RAR	Ctl	Dom	Cmd	hr/9	G/F	S%	BPV	BPX
RH Starter	98	0	0	0	0	0.00	0.00																
AGE 22 Growth	99	0	0	0	0	0.00	0.00																
TYPE Contact	00	0	0	0	0	0.00	0.00																
BURN none	01	0	0	0	0	0.00	0.00																
ERA Potl +	02 KC	* 12	7	0	181	3.93	1.33	$11	26.5	276	302	236	32%	3.87	28.6	2.3	5.8	**2.5**	0.6	1.78	71%	70	133
Support 6.54	1st Half	7	3	0	84	3.85	1.31	$7	27.4	273			31%	3.60	14.2	2.2	5.5	**2.4**	0.4		70%	71	135
LIMA B	2nd Half	5	4	0	97	3.99	1.35	$4	25.9	279			32%	4.10	14.4	2.3	6.1	**2.6**	0.7		72%	69	131
Risk Moderate	03 Proj	9	10	0	180	4.70	1.42	$4	26.9	287			32%	4.38	16.1	2.6	5.5	2.1	0.7	G	67%	54	110

4-4, 4.72 ERA in 75 IP at KC. Some promise here, but I'm not yet buying stock, because...
- Monthly ERAs in KC were 3.75, 4.08, 4.81
- Could pitch 200 IP at age 22
- The Kansas City Royals

Hiljus,Erik

Hiljus,Erik	Yr Tm	W	L	Sv	IP	ERA	Br/IP	R$	BF/G	OBA	vLH	vRH	H%	xERA	RAR	Ctl	Dom	Cmd	hr/9	G/F	S%	BPV	BPX
RH Reliever	98 aa	2	3	2	65	4.57	1.45	$2	6.8	237			31%	4.17	7.5	5.1	10.4	**2.0**	1.1		71%	79	154
AGE 30 Peak	99 a/a	3	3	5	77	4.21	1.09	$10	7.2	222			30%	2.78 +	15.4	2.6	10.4	**4.0**	0.8		62%	133	309
TYPE Power	00 aaa	5	3	2	70	4.24	1.44	$6	6.6	291	125	571	37%	4.22	14.2	2.6	8.1	**3.2**	0.4	0.43	69%	100	237
BURN none	01 OAK	* 13	5	0	167	3.88	1.25	$16	22.5	255	248	281	30%	4.21	35.9	2.6	8.2	**3.2**	1.4	0.58	75%	78	157
ERA Potl -	02 OAK	* 4	6	0	82	7.34	1.82	($9)	21.7	330	274	299	36%	6.82 +	-24.5	3.9	5.8	**1.5**	1.5	0.48	61%	9	17
Support 6.31	1st Half	3	5	0	72	6.86	1.76	($7)	24.1	320			35%	6.46	-16.9	3.9	6.0	**1.5**	1.5		63%	14	27
LIMA B+	2nd Half	1	1	0	10	10.80	2.30	($2)	13.1	390			41%	9.37 +	-7.6	4.5	4.5	**1.0**	1.8		52%	-29	-55
Risk Very High	03 Proj	2	2	0	40	4.95	1.45	$0	10.9	281			34%	4.75	2.2	3.2	8.1	2.6	1.1	F	68%	68	138

3-3, 6.60 ERA in 45 IP at OAK. A bad, bad, bad year because of...
- Erratic usage
- Messed up mechanics
- Harang footsteps
- Last year's broken ankle wasn't really, really healed.

Hitchcock,Sterling

Hitchcock,Sterling	Yr Tm	W	L	Sv	IP	ERA	Br/IP	R$	BF/G	OBA	vLH	vRH	H%	xERA	RAR	Ctl	Dom	Cmd	hr/9	G/F	S%	BPV	BPX
LH Reliever	98 SD	9	7	1	176	3.94	1.23	$12	18.7	254	258	249	29%	4.22	30.6	2.5	8.1	**3.3**	1.5	1.15	74%	77	139
AGE 32 Peak	99 SD	12	14	0	205	4.13	1.36	$14	26.6	259	253	254	31%	4.35	39.0	3.3	8.5	**2.6**	1.3	0.90	74%	70	152
TYPE	00 SD	1	6	0	65	4.97	1.46	($1)	25.9	273	220	279	32%	5.20	5.8	3.6	8.4	**2.3**	1.7	1.22	71%	51	111
BURN none	01 2TM	* 8	5	0	87	5.48	1.56	$1	24.4	316	375	297	35%	5.27	-0.7	2.4	5.3	**2.2**	0.7	1.00	64%	48	93
ERA Potl --	02 NYY	* 1	2	0	46	7.22	2.10	($8)	10.5	378	316	331	43%	8.04 -	-13.1	3.5	6.6	**1.9**	1.2	0.86	66%	24	45
Support 4.58	1st Half	1	0	0	28	9.86	2.37	($8)	13.6	404			45%	9.62	-18.0	4.1	6.0	**1.5**	1.6		58%	-6	-12
LIMA B	2nd Half	0	2	0	18	3.03	1.69	($1)	7.5	332			41%	5.53 -	4.9	2.5	7.6	**3.0**	0.5		83%	82	155
Risk Very High	03 Proj	4	4	0	70	4.76	1.50	$1	10.3	293			34%	4.98	5.7	3.0	6.9	2.3	1.0	--	70%	56	115

1-2, 5.54 ERA in 39 IP at NYY. Everyone was ready to write him off when, all of a sudden, he started getting it together in the 2nd half out of the bullpen. The sample size is very small, but he ain't dead yet.

Hoffman,Trevor

Hoffman,Trevor	Yr Tm	W	L	Sv	IP	ERA	Br/IP	R$	BF/G	OBA	vLH	vRH	H%	xERA	RAR	Ctl	Dom	Cmd	hr/9	G/F	S%	BPV	BPX
RH Reliever	98 SD	4	2	53	73	1.48	0.85	$44	4.2	166	171	159	25%	1.01	36.7	2.6	10.6	**4.1**	0.2	0.92	83%	164	296
AGE 35 Decline	99 SD	2	3	40	67	2.15	0.94	$34	4.0	203	215	182	27%	2.01	30.5	2.0	9.8	**4.9**	0.7	1.29	81%	155	338
TYPE Power	00 SD	4	7	43	72	3.00	1.00	$37	4.0	231	200	246	31%	2.73	25.4	1.4	10.6	**7.7**	0.9	0.81	74%	209	459
BURN none	01 SD	3	4	43	60	3.44	1.15	$31	3.9	221	214	218	26%	3.58	15.5	3.1	9.4	**3.0**	1.5	0.75	78%	86	159
ERA Potl +	02 SD	2	5	38	59	2.75	1.19	$32	4.0	238	186	275	34%	2.82	21.4	2.7	10.5	**3.8**	0.3	0.83	76%	142	291
Support 0.30	1st Half	1	1	20	31	2.32	1.29	$17	4.2	235			36%	3.01 -	13.1	3.8	11.9	**3.2**	0.3		82%	137	280
LIMA C	2nd Half	1	4	18	28	3.23	1.08	$15	3.7	241			32%	2.61 +	8.3	1.6	9.0	**5.6**	0.3		69%	169	346
Risk Low	03 Proj	3	5	39	60	2.85	1.10	$32	4.0	228			31%	2.86	20.9	2.4	10.1	4.2	0.8	--	77%	135	272

When a player hits 35, it makes sense to start looking for areas of possible weakness, just to assess your risk. Not much here. His .275 BA vsRH might be a concern, but he overcame a 34% hit rate, so I'm not worried.

Holmes,Darren

Holmes,Darren	Yr Tm	W	L	Sv	IP	ERA	Br/IP	R$	BF/G	OBA	vLH	vRH	H%	xERA	RAR	Ctl	Dom	Cmd	hr/9	G/F	S%	BPV	BPX
RH Reliever	98 NYY	0	3	2	51	3.35	1.31	$3	6.4	269			30%	3.93 -	15.7	2.5	5.5	**2.2**	0.7		76%	59	127
AGE 37 Decline	99 ARI	4	3	0	49	3.67	1.53	$4	5.0	266			31%	4.22 -	12.3	4.6	6.4	**1.4**	0.6		76%	53	116
TYPE Power	00 2TM	* 1	2	2	38	7.82	1.76	($4)	5.9	322			36%	6.52 +	-10.5	3.8	6.2	**1.6**	1.4		56%	19	45
BURN none	01	0	0	0	0	0.00	0.00																
ERA Potl No chg	02 ATL	2	2	1	54	1.83	0.98	$11	3.8	212	230	198	27%	2.19	26.2	2.0	7.8	**3.9**	0.5	0.97	84%	127	260
Support 4.28	1st Half	2	1	1	33	1.63	0.93	$8	3.9	204			24%	2.27 -	17.0	1.9	7.0	**3.7**	0.8		89%	110	226
LIMA C+	2nd Half	0	1	0	21	2.16	1.06	$3	3.8	225			31%	2.05	9.2	2.2	9.1	**4.2**	0.0		77%	153	313
Risk High	03 Proj	2	2	1	50	3.78	1.30	$4	4.6	258			31%	3.76	11.2	2.9	7.2	2.5	0.7	--	72%	78	156

What did they put in the drinking water in Atlanta?

And where can I get some?

Holtz,Mike

Holtz,Mike	Yr Tm	W	L	Sv	IP	ERA	Br/IP	R$	BF/G	OBA	vLH	vRH	H%	xERA	RAR	Ctl	Dom	Cmd	hr/9	G/F	S%	BPV	BPX
LH Reliever	98 ANA	* 2	2	3	40	4.03	1.74	$2	3.0	302	308	350	41%	4.99 -	8.8	4.7	9.9	**2.1**	0.2	1.76	75%	91	194
AGE 30 Peak	99 ANA	* 4	4	1	49	5.69	1.61	$1	4.6	270	237	340	33%	5.37	1.2	5.1	9.4	**1.8**	1.5	1.00	68%	51	129
TYPE Power	00 ANA	3	3	0	41	5.05	1.34	$3	2.9	242	213	300	30%	3.73 +	4.7	4.0	8.8	**2.2**	0.9	1.42	63%	80	206
BURN none	01 ANA	1	2	0	37	4.86	1.49	($1)	2.6	277	313	227	35%	4.93	3.1	3.6	9.2	**2.5**	1.2	2.04	70%	72	144
ERA Potl --	02 2TM	* 2	2	0	41	5.26	1.90	($3)	3.5	280	306	284	32%	5.88 -	0.1	7.2	6.4	**0.9**	1.1	1.36	74%	23	45
Support 6.17	1st Half	0	0	0	19	6.09	1.93	($2)	4.2	333			35%	7.09 -	-2.1	4.7	4.7	**1.0**	1.4		71%	-5	-9
LIMA D	2nd Half	2	2	0	22	4.52	1.87	$0	3.1	226			27%	4.82	2.2	9.5	7.8	**0.8**	0.8		77%	49	97
Risk Moderate	03 Proj	1	3	0	40	4.95	1.70	($2)	3.1	271			32%	5.29	2.5	5.9	7.9	1.3	1.1	--	73%	43	86

Second year in a row that LH hitters batted over .300 off him. That pretty much negates any value he has.

Howry,Bob

Howry,Bob	Yr Tm	W	L	Sv	IP	ERA	Br/IP	R$	BF/G	OBA	vLH	vRH	H%	xERA	RAR	Ctl	Dom	Cmd	hr/9	G/F	S%	BPV	BPX
RH Reliever	98 CHW	* 1	5	14	85	3.27	1.07	$16	5.1	208	149	231	24%	2.72 +	27.2	3.0	7.4	**2.5**	0.9	0.70	73%	82	175
AGE 29 Peak	99 CHW	5	3	28	67	3.63	1.43	$22	4.2	235	226	233	31%	4.07	20.1	5.1	10.7	**2.1**	1.1	0.79	78%	84	212
TYPE	00 CHW	2	4	7	71	3.17	1.17	$12	4.5	212	174	256	26%	2.82	26.1	3.7	7.6	**2.1**	0.8	1.05	75%	79	205
BURN none	01 CHW	4	5	5	78	4.72	1.47	$4	5.0	278	306	253	32%	4.97	8.0	3.5	7.4	**2.1**	1.3	0.98	71%	50	101
ERA Potl + +	02 2AL	3	5	0	68	4.24	1.29	$2	4.3	259	239	280	31%	3.22 +	7.9	2.8	6.0	**2.1**	0.3	0.68	65%	76	144
Support 3.41	1st Half	0	1	0	36	3.49	1.25	$1	4.2	239			26%	3.30	7.8	3.2	5.2	**1.6**	0.7		74%	50	95
LIMA B+	2nd Half	3	4	0	32	5.08	1.35	$2	4.4	280			35%	3.13 +	0.1	2.3	6.8	**3.0**	-0.3		57%	111	210
Risk Low	03 Proj	3	5	0	70	3.86	1.31	$4	4.5	256			30%	3.63	14.2	3.1	6.3	2.0	0.6	F	71%	65	133

Decent BPIs, but not the best situational player. His REff% hit a 3-year high of 75% in '02, his OBA with runners on base is .280, and he's become an extreme flyball pitcher. That's why he's not closer material.

Hudson,Tim	Yr	Tm	W	L	Sv	IP	ERA	Br/IP	R$	BF/G	OBA	vLH	vRH	H%	xERA	RAR	Ctl	Dom	Cmd	hr/9	G/F	S%	BPV	BPX
RH Starter	98	aa	10	9	0	134	5.04	1.60	$2	27.5	283			32%	5.00	7.1	4.4	5.8	1.3	0.9		69%	35	67
AGE 27 Pre-Peak	99	OAK *	18	2	0	203	2.84	1.28	$30	26.6	233	234	240	30%	3.08	82.5	3.8	8.7	2.3	0.4	2.27	78%	96	241
TYPE	00	OAK	20	6	0	202	4.14	1.24	$27	26.3	229	231	221	27%	3.50 +	47.9	3.7	7.5	2.1	1.1	2.02	70%	66	170
BURN Low	01	OAK	18	9	0	235	3.37	1.22	$25	27.8	246	255	233	29%	3.43	66.5	2.7	6.9	2.5	0.8	2.26	75%	78	156
ERA Potl -	02	OAK	15	9	0	238	2.99	1.26	$20	29.2	261	283	239	30%	3.58 -	67.5	2.3	5.7	2.5	0.7	2.03	79%	67	127
Support 4.80	1st Half		6	7	0	123	3.58	1.31	$7	29.0	258			29%	3.77	25.2	3.0	6.0	2.0	0.8		75%	57	108
LIMA D+	2nd Half		9	2	0	115	2.35	1.19	$14	29.5	264			30%	3.38 -	42.3	1.6	5.5	3.3	0.6		83%	86	163
Risk Low	03	Proj	17	8	0	225	3.48	1.25	$22	28.5	252			29%	3.53	56.9	2.7	6.4	2.4	0.8	G	74%	70	143

Follow his Ctl and Dom trends since 1999. This is both good and bad news. He is increasing his precision, but soon he'll reach the point where the loss of dominance may have a negative impact on his success.

Irabu,Hideki	Yr	Tm	W	L	Sv	IP	ERA	Br/IP	R$	BF/G	OBA	vLH	vRH	H%	xERA	RAR	Ctl	Dom	Cmd	hr/9	G/F	S%	BPV	BPX
RH Reliever	98	NYY	13	9	0	173	4.06	1.29	$16	25.1	233	218	250	28%	4.05	37.0	4.0	6.6	1.7	1.4	0.95	74%	40	86
AGE 34 Past	99	NYY	11	7	0	169	4.85	1.34	$11	22.5	274	288	242	31%	4.68	23.2	2.4	7.1	2.9	1.4	0.82	68%	62	155
TYPE	00	MON	2	5	0	54	7.31	1.68	($5)	22.7	335	356	328	38%	6.59 +	-12.2	2.3	7.0	3.0	1.5	1.27	57%	48	106
BURN none	01	MON *	1	4	0	38	5.68	1.53	($2)	24.1	314	333	290	37%	5.78	-1.6	2.1	8.3	3.9	1.4	0.96	65%	81	150
ERA Potl - -	02	TEX	3	8	16	47	5.74	1.43	$8	5.4	278	269	289	28%	5.55	-4.0	3.1	5.7	1.9	2.1	1.76	66%	10	19
Support 2.87	1st Half		3	7	14	42	5.79	1.40	$7	5.5	280			27%	5.76	-3.8	2.8	5.6	2.0	2.4		67%	4	7
LIMA C	2nd Half		0	1	2	5	5.40	1.60	$1	4.5	262			33%	3.77 +	-0.2	5.4	7.2	1.3	0.0		63%	74	140
Risk High	03	Proj	3	5	5	50	4.86	1.40	$4	5.7	284			31%	5.32	3.4	2.5	6.8	2.7	1.8	G	72%	42	86

It was a string of 13 games, from April 16 to May 15... 14 IP, 8 H, 1 ER and 9 saves. The rest of the season he went 2-8 with a 7.91 ERA. Blood clots were discovered in his lungs in July and ended his season.

Ishii,Kazuhisa	Yr	Tm	W	L	Sv	IP	ERA	Br/IP	R$	BF/G	OBA	vLH	vRH	H%	xERA	RAR	Ctl	Dom	Cmd	hr/9	G/F	S%	BPV	BPX
LH Starter	98	JPN	14	6	0	196	3.31	1.30	$19	29.5	212			29%	3.25	55.8	4.8	11.1	2.3	0.9		77%	101	196
AGE 29 Peak	99	JPN	8	6	0	133	4.80	1.28	$9	24.3	219			30%	3.26 +	15.9	4.4	11.0	2.5	0.9		63%	103	239
TYPE Power	00	JPN	10	9	0	173	2.76	1.21	$23	24.7	219			31%	3.02	69.6	3.8	10.9	2.9	0.8		81%	114	269
BURN none	01	JPN	12	6	0	175	3.39	1.24	$17	27.0	215			27%	3.21	47.5	4.2	8.9	2.1	0.9		76%	82	157
ERA Potl -	02	LA	14	10	0	154	4.27	1.58	$7	24.7	240	223	245	29%	4.66	24.6	6.2	8.4	1.3	1.2	1.04	76%	50	103
Support 4.56	1st Half		11	4	0	94	3.54	1.58	$8	26.5	249			32%	4.31 -	24.3	5.8	8.9	1.5	0.7		79%	70	145
LIMA C+	2nd Half		3	6	0	60	5.42	1.57	($2)	22.4	225			23%	5.21	0.3	6.8	7.5	1.1	2.0		72%	20	41
Risk Low	03	Proj	11	9	0	160	3.99	1.47	$8	25.1	238			29%	4.34	31.3	5.3	8.7	1.6	1.2	–	77%	59	118

While he's never been a control artist, per se, he really struggled with the MLB strike zone. Year ended when he took a line drive to the head, and although he's okay, we won't know the mental pitching impact until March.

Isringhausen,Jason	Yr	Tm	W	L	Sv	IP	ERA	Br/IP	R$	BF/G	OBA	vLH	vRH	H%	xERA	RAR	Ctl	Dom	Cmd	hr/9	G/F	S%	BPV	BPX
RH Reliever	98	NYM	0	0	0	0	0.00	0.00																
AGE 30 Peak	99	2TM *	4	5	9	115	3.91	1.37	$12	11.0	241	159	280	28%	4.00	27.5	4.2	7.3	1.7	1.1	1.18	75%	54	125
TYPE Power	00	OAK	6	4	33	69	3.78	1.43	$27	4.6	256	242	265	31%	4.07	19.7	4.2	7.4	1.8	0.8	1.42	75%	62	162
BURN none	01	OAK	4	3	34	71	2.66	1.08	$28	4.4	212	240	152	28%	2.51	26.9	2.9	9.4	3.2	0.6	1.07	78%	117	235
ERA Potl + +	02	STL	3	2	32	65	2.49	0.98	$32	4.2	201	247	164	29%	1.57 +	25.8	2.5	9.4	3.8	0.0	1.48	72%	151	309
Support 1.24	1st Half		2	1	17	38	2.61	1.05	$17	4.4	207			29%	1.82 +	14.5	2.8	9.5	3.3	0.0		73%	140	288
LIMA C	2nd Half		1	1	15	27	2.33	0.89	$15	4.0	191			27%	1.22 +	11.3	2.0	9.3	4.7	0.0		71%	171	350
Risk Low	03	Proj	4	3	32	70	3.09	1.10	$29	4.5	215			29%	2.37 +	22.2	3.0	9.1	3.1	0.4	--	72%	120	242

He's grown into the closer's role in a big way and we can officially label him a member of the Elite. However, expect a slight drop-off in '03 as NL batters get a second look at him.

Izquierdo,Hansel	Yr	Tm	W	L	Sv	IP	ERA	Br/IP	R$	BF/G	OBA	vLH	vRH	H%	xERA	RAR	Ctl	Dom	Cmd	hr/9	G/F	S%	BPV	BPX
RH Reliever	98		0	0	0	0	0.00	0.00																
AGE 26 Growth	99		0	0	0	0	0.00	0.00																
TYPE Contact	00		0	0	0	0	0.00	0.00																
BURN none	01	aa	7	2	0	56	5.46	1.27	$5	23.5	272			28%	5.00	-0.3	1.9	5.9	3.1	1.9		63%	43	83
ERA Potl - -	02	FLA *	6	6	0	107	5.13	1.71	($4)	14.6	314	356	246	34%	5.87 -	4.7	3.8	4.5	1.2	0.9	1.96	71%	16	33
Support 4.55	1st Half		4	1	0	54	3.32	1.51	$4	10.0	261			29%	4.34 -	15.5	4.6	5.3	1.1	0.7		79%	39	79
LIMA C+	2nd Half		2	5	0	53	6.99	1.91	($9)	25.5	361			38%	7.44	-10.8	2.9	3.6	1.2	1.2		64%	-6	-11
Risk High	03	Proj	3	4	0	80	4.61	1.36	$2	17.1	281			30%	4.84	9.0	2.4	5.5	2.3	1.4	G	70%	40	81

2-0, 4.66 ERA in 29 IP at FLA. Showed some promise in '01, much less in '02. His year ended with elbow surgery, which begs the question, "exactly how long was that elbow hurting him?" His BPIs might reappear now in BOS

Jackson,Mike	Yr	Tm	W	L	Sv	IP	ERA	Br/IP	R$	BF/G	OBA	vLH	vRH	H%	xERA	RAR	Ctl	Dom	Cmd	hr/9	G/F	S%	BPV	BPX
RH Reliever	98	CLE	1	1	40	64	1.55	0.88	$33	3.5	192	210	182	24%	1.70	35.2	1.8	7.7	4.2	0.6	1.00	87%	135	288
AGE 38 Decline	99	CLE	3	4	39	69	4.04	1.25	$28	4.0	236	238	225	26%	3.98	16.9	3.4	7.2	2.1	1.4	1.52	73%	52	131
TYPE Contact	00	PHI	0	0	0	0	0.00	0.00																
BURN none	01	HOU	5	3	4	69	4.70	1.30	$6	4.4	259	294	231	27%	4.81	6.2	2.9	6.0	2.1	1.8	0.97	71%	28	53
ERA Potl -	02	MIN	2	3	0	55	3.27	1.31	$3	4.0	276	275	288	30%	4.02 -	13.5	2.1	4.7	2.2	0.8	1.03	78%	51	96
Support 4.09	1st Half		2	2	0	34	2.12	1.18	$4	4.0	232			26%	2.59	13.6	2.9	4.5	1.5	0.3		82%	60	114
LIMA C+	2nd Half		0	1	0	21	5.14	1.52	($1)	4.1	336			36%	6.34 -	-0.1	0.9	5.1	6.0	1.7		71%	93	176
Risk Moderate	03	Proj	2	2	1	50	4.68	1.44	$1	4.2	288			30%	4.99	4.6	2.7	4.9	1.8	1.3	–	71%	27	54

Despite his ills and bouncing around teams, he's always maintained an interesting skill set. However, sharply declining Dom rate at his age likely spells the beginning of the end.

James,Delvin	Yr	Tm	W	L	Sv	IP	ERA	Br/IP	R$	BF/G	OBA	vLH	vRH	H%	xERA	RAR	Ctl	Dom	Cmd	hr/9	G/F	S%	BPV	BPX
RH Starter	98		0	0	0	0	0.00	0.00																
AGE 25 Growth	99		0	0	0	0	0.00	0.00																
TYPE Contact	00	aa	1	3	0	37	3.41	1.14	$4	25.0	251			28%	3.24	11.7	1.7	5.6	3.3	0.7		72%	85	202
BURN none	01	a/a	5	7	0	128	4.99	1.45	($0)	14.7	292			32%	4.69	7.4	2.6	5.0	1.9	0.8		66%	44	84
ERA Potl -	02	TAM *	3	6	0	81	5.67	1.53	($3)	20.0	311	299	303	34%	5.59	-6.1	2.3	5.4	2.3	1.3	0.87	65%	35	65
Support 2.36	1st Half		1	4	0	37	5.56	1.40	($1)	20.1	271			29%	4.54 +	-2.3	3.1	5.1	1.6	1.2		62%	29	55
LIMA C+	2nd Half		2	2	0	44	5.75	1.64	($2)	20.0	341			37%	6.47 -	-3.8	1.6	5.8	3.5	1.4		68%	52	98
Risk X HIGH	03	Proj	4	8	0	120	4.95	1.42	$0	21.7	291			32%	4.78	6.7	2.3	5.3	2.3	1.1	–	67%	45	92

0-3, 6.62 ERA in 34 IP at TAM. Soft-tosser with good control but gives up a ton of hits, and at the wrong times. These are correctable flaws on an upwardly mobile club; less so on TAM where everyone is like him.

Jarvis,Kevin	Yr	Tm	W	L	Sv	IP	ERA	Br/IP	R$	BF/G	OBA	vLH	vRH	H%	xERA	RAR	Ctl	Dom	Cmd	hr/9	G/F	S%	BPV	BPX
RH Starter	98	JPN *	2	2	0	23	5.87	1.48	$0	16.9	302			34%	4.53 +	-1.4	2.3	4.7	2.0	0.4		58%	53	103
AGE 33 Past	99	aaa	10	2	0	103	4.63	1.61	$6	27.5	324	355	472	34%	6.14 -	14.7	2.4	4.4	1.9	1.4	0.81	75%	13	31
TYPE	00	COL *	6	6	0	154	4.68	1.34	$6	21.2	269	337	271	27%	4.87	19.7	2.7	4.4	1.7	1.6	1.30	71%	13	30
BURN none	01	SD	12	11	0	193	4.80	1.23	$11	25.1	258	257	252	27%	4.52	14.6	2.3	6.2	2.7	1.7	1.11	67%	46	85
ERA Potl No chg	02	SD	2	4	0	38	4.03	1.26	$3	19.9	262	218	304	29%	4.19	7.3	2.4	6.4	2.7	1.2	0.91	72%	62	128
Support 3.86	1st Half		2	3	0	35	2.83	1.14	$5	20.3	239			29%	2.95	12.3	2.3	6.7	2.9	0.5		76%	93	190
LIMA B	2nd Half		0	1	0	3	17.99	2.67	($2)	16.8	453			35%	18.64 -	-5.0	3.0	3.0	1.0	9.0		40%	******	******
Risk X HIGH	03	Proj	7	6	0	120	3.90	1.26	$10	25.1	259			29%	4.12	25.0	2.5	6.2	2.5	1.2	–	73%	57	116

Had elbow surgery on July 10, ending a valient attempt to break through the 4.00 ERA barrier for the first time ever. I always root for the ground-breakers. If healthy, his BPIs support another run in '03.

Jennings,Jason	Yr	Tm	W	L	Sv	IP	ERA	Br/IP	R$	BF/G	OBA	vLH	vRH	H%	xERA	RAR	Ctl	Dom	Cmd	hr/9	G/F	S%	BPV	BPX
RH Starter	98		0	0	0	0	0.00	0.00																
AGE 24 Growth	99		0	0	0	0	0.00	0.00																
TYPE	00	aa	1	3	0	36	5.97	1.52	($1)	26.8	296			32%	6.01	-1.0	3.0	7.2	2.4	2.0		66%	30	71
BURN none	01	a/a *	13	9	0	196	6.02	1.65	($6)	27.2	315	247	310	37%	5.62	-15.6	3.2	6.6	2.1	0.9	1.59	63%	49	94
ERA Potl -	02	COL	16	8	0	185	4.52	1.46	$10	25.4	278	299	267	31%	5.01	23.2	3.4	6.2	1.8	1.3	1.64	73%	37	75
Support 6.51	1st Half		8	4	0	88	4.80	1.50	$3	24.3	293			33%	5.07	7.8	3.0	6.5	2.2	1.0		70%	51	105
LIMA C	2nd Half		8	4	0	97	4.28	1.44	$6	26.4	264			28%	4.95 -	15.3	3.8	5.9	1.5	1.5		76%	25	51
Risk High	03	Proj	14	10	0	200	4.73	1.44	$8	25.6	275			31%	4.86	19.5	3.3	6.5	1.9	1.3	G	70%	42	84

To give you an idea of the extent of his feat, here are his '02 stats converted to a league average ballpark:
ERA: 3.50 WHIP: 1.34
Cmd: 2.0 Dom: 6.6
HR/9: 0.9 BPV: 50

Jensen,Ryan		Tm	W	L	Sv	IP	ERA	Br/IP	R$	BF/G	OBA	vLH	vRH	H%	xERA	RAR	Ctl	Dom	Cmd	hr/9	G/F	S%	BPV	BPX
RH Starter	98	aaa	0	0	0	6	6.00	1.33	($0)	12.8	191			22%	3.71 +	-0.5	6.0	9.0	1.5	1.5		57%	57	111
AGE 27 Pre-Peak	99	aaa	11	10	0	156	5.08	1.47	$6	25.4	273			33%	4.49 +	13.0	3.8	7.6	2.0	0.9		66%	62	144
TYPE	00	aaa	5	8	0	135	5.73	1.70	($5)	24.0	314			36%	5.83	0.5	3.7	6.3	1.7	1.0		67%	35	83
BURN none	01	SF	* 12	4	0	148	3.71	1.36	$12	21.1	259	338	219	30%	4.05	32.8	3.4	6.3	1.8	0.9	1.20	75%	54	100
ERA Potl -	02	SF	13	8	0	171	4.53	1.46	$8	23.4	275	288	270	30%	4.80	21.4	3.5	5.5	1.6	1.1	0.84	71%	33	68
Support 6.55	1st Half		7	6	0	83	4.55	1.35	$6	22.1	257			28%	4.26	10.1	3.4	5.4	1.6	1.1		69%	37	77
LIMA C	2nd Half		6	2	0	88	4.50	1.56	$2	24.6	291			32%	5.31 -	11.3	3.6	5.6	1.6	1.1		74%	30	61
Risk High	03	Proj	11	7	0	160	4.56	1.48	$6	23.5	278			31%	4.79	19.2	3.5	6.0	1.7	1.0	--	71%	41	82

Likes Pac Bell, posting a 3.66 ERA at home. But other than that, there's not a whole lot here to build hopes on. BPIs are mediocre and not showing any growth.

Jimenez,Jose		Tm	W	L	Sv	IP	ERA	Br/IP	R$	BF/G	OBA	vLH	vRH	H%	xERA	RAR	Ctl	Dom	Cmd	hr/9	G/F	S%	BPV	BPX
RH Reliever	98	STL	* 18	6	0	201	3.40	1.36	$19	28.7	252	316	217	27%	3.71	49.3	3.7	4.2	1.1	0.6	3.29	76%	36	65
AGE 29 Peak	99	STL	* 7	16	0	189	5.57	1.52	($3)	25.4	280	304	249	32%	4.59 +	-0.6	3.8	6.1	1.6	0.8	2.50	63%	47	102
TYPE Contact	00	COL	5	2	24	70	3.21	1.30	$22	4.1	241	245	234	28%	3.32	22.8	3.6	5.6	1.6	0.5	2.88	76%	58	128
BURN none	01	COL	6	1	17	55	4.09	1.42	$15	4.3	265	255	271	30%	4.39	9.4	3.6	6.1	1.7	1.0	3.03	74%	44	82
ERA Potl +	02	COL	2	10	41	73	3.58	1.19	$33	4.1	270	266	264	30%	3.83	18.4	1.4	5.8	4.3	0.9	3.04	73%	100	204
Support 0.98	1st Half		2	4	21	41	2.85	1.27	$18	4.3	271			32%	3.42 -	14.4	2.0	5.7	2.9	0.2		76%	89	183
LIMA D	2nd Half		0	6	20	32	4.51	1.10	$14	3.8	268			28%	4.35	4.0	0.6	5.9	10.5	1.7		66%	207	424
Risk Moderate	03	Proj	4	7	31	75	3.72	1.24	$26	4.5	264			30%	3.82	17.4	2.0	5.8	2.8	0.8	G	72%	71	142

Walked just 2 batters in 32 IP in the 2nd half and continued to keep the ball on the ground more than just about any pitcher in baseball. Could this be the secret to success in COL? We'll see if he can do it again in '03.

Johnson,Jason		Tm	W	L	Sv	IP	ERA	Br/IP	R$	BF/G	OBA	vLH	vRH	H%	xERA	RAR	Ctl	Dom	Cmd	hr/9	G/F	S%	BPV	BPX
RH Starter	98	TAM	* 3	5	0	72	5.37	1.53	($1)	21.4	285	292	324	31%	5.43	2.8	3.6	6.0	1.7	1.5	0.69	68%	24	51
AGE 29 Peak	99	BAL	* 12	9	0	159	5.26	1.54	$6	23.6	264	242	289	29%	4.99	12.9	4.8	6.3	1.3	1.3	0.83	68%	29	72
TYPE	00	BAL	* 4	11	0	162	5.27	1.47	$1	21.6	254	267	288	29%	4.60 +	13.9	4.5	7.2	1.6	1.3	0.92	67%	42	109
BURN none	01	BAL	10	12	0	196	4.09	1.38	$9	26.4	260	263	252	27%	4.53	36.7	3.5	5.2	1.5	1.3	1.09	75%	27	54
ERA Potl -	02	BAL	6	14	0	136	4.43	1.40	$2	25.5	274	261	290	31%	4.62	12.3	3.0	6.8	2.3	1.3	1.18	72%	51	96
Support 3.36	1st Half		4	5	0	60	3.44	1.18	$6	24.6	248			29%	3.10	13.4	2.2	6.6	2.9	0.6		72%	88	167
LIMA C+	2nd Half		2	9	0	76	5.22	1.57	($3)	26.2	294			32%	5.82 -	-1.1	3.6	6.9	1.9	1.8		72%	25	47
Risk High	03	Proj	7	13	0	160	4.33	1.39	$5	24.7	269			30%	4.61	22.2	3.2	6.6	2.1	1.3	--	73%	46	93

Revealed at Baseball HQ... In the starts in which he threw less than 90 pitches, his following outings yielded an ERA of 1.76. In those in which he threw more than 90 pitches, his following outings yielded an ERA of 7.65.

Johnson,Randy		Tm	W	L	Sv	IP	ERA	Br/IP	R$	BF/G	OBA	vLH	vRH	H%	xERA	RAR	Ctl	Dom	Cmd	hr/9	G/F	S%	BPV	BPX
LH Starter	98	2TM	19	11	0	244	3.28	1.18	$29	29.5	228	186	229	33%	3.12	70.3	3.2	12.1	3.8	0.8	1.27	75%	137	267
AGE 38 Decline	99	ARI	17	9	0	271	2.49	1.02	$42	30.5	213	103	219	31%	2.62	110.9	2.3	12.1	5.2	1.0	1.25	82%	164	357
TYPE Power	00	ARI	19	7	0	248	2.65	1.12	$39	28.6	224	226	224	34%	2.89	99.1	2.8	12.6	4.6	0.8	1.18	80%	157	345
BURN Moderate	01	ARI	21	6	0	249	2.49	1.01	$41	28.0	205	196	204	33%	2.24	95.9	2.6	13.4	5.2	0.7	1.19	79%	184	341
ERA Potl No chg	02	ARI	24	5	0	260	2.32	1.03	$49	29.3	212	221	206	30%	2.65	109.3	2.5	11.6	4.7	0.9	1.42	83%	154	316
Support 5.99	1st Half		12	2	0	124	2.39	1.05	$25	29.0	217			30%	2.86	51.0	2.4	11.2	4.7	1.0		84%	147	302
LIMA C	2nd Half		12	3	0	136	2.25	1.02	$27	29.7	207			30%	2.45	58.3	2.5	11.9	4.7	0.8		83%	160	328
Risk Very Low	03	Proj	19	7	0	250	2.81	1.06	$38	29.3	217			31%	2.69	88.6	2.6	11.4	4.5	0.8	--	77%	149	299

Over the past six years, he has averaged 20 wins and 340 strikeouts per season. In the past 4 years, covering 140 starts, he's posted a PQS score of less than 3 only seven times, and only two scores less than 2.

Jones,Bobby J.		Tm	W	L	Sv	IP	ERA	Br/IP	R$	BF/G	OBA	vLH	vRH	H%	xERA	RAR	Ctl	Dom	Cmd	hr/9	G/F	S%	BPV	BPX
RH Starter	98	NYM	9	9	0	195	4.06	1.26	$11	27.2	259	232	290	28%	3.98	30.7	2.4	5.3	2.2	1.1	1.20	71%	49	88
AGE 33 Past	99	NYM	* 6	5	0	82	5.05	1.38	$4	20.7	289	327	272	32%	4.49 +	5.5	2.1	5.3	2.5	0.9	1.36	64%	56	121
TYPE Contact	00	NYM	11	6	0	154	5.08	1.43	$7	24.8	282	264	297	29%	5.11	11.4	2.9	5.0	1.7	1.5	0.85	68%	21	46
BURN none	01	SD	8	19	0	195	5.12	1.48	($2)	26.0	313	281	320	33%	5.93 -	6.4	1.8	5.2	3.0	1.7	1.30	71%	35	65
ERA Potl -	02	SD	7	8	0	108	5.50	1.44	$1	24.8	306	276	322	32%	5.73	-0.6	1.8	5.0	2.9	1.7	0.96	66%	34	70
Support 5.08	1st Half		5	4	0	64	5.34	1.36	$2	24.9	277			28%	5.00	1.0	2.5	4.6	1.8	1.5		64%	20	40
LIMA C+	2nd Half		2	4	0	44	5.73	1.55	($2)	24.6	344			37%	6.80 -	-1.6	0.6	5.5	9.0	1.8		68%	153	314
Risk High	03	Proj	7	9	0	120	5.03	1.42	$3	24.8	300			31%	5.48	6.9	1.9	5.0	2.7	1.6	--	69%	34	69

Case study in how a pitcher with pinpoint control can be unable to get his ERA under 5.00. Note:
- Marginal dominance
- Chronic gopheritis
- BA vs RHers
- Heck, BA vs everybody.

Jones,Todd		Tm	W	L	Sv	IP	ERA	Br/IP	R$	BF/G	OBA	vLH	vRH	H%	xERA	RAR	Ctl	Dom	Cmd	hr/9	G/F	S%	BPV	BPX
RH Reliever	98	DET	1	4	28	63	4.99	1.49	$14	4.3	246	240	259	30%	4.31 +	5.6	5.1	8.1	1.6	1.0	2.02	68%	58	124
AGE 35 Decline	99	DET	4	4	30	66	3.82	1.50	$21	4.5	256	290	224	32%	4.42 -	18.2	4.8	8.7	1.8	1.0	1.41	77%	66	165
TYPE Power	00	DET	2	4	42	64	3.52	1.44	$29	4.2	271	294	256	35%	4.32 -	20.5	3.5	9.4	2.7	0.8	1.94	78%	88	229
BURN none	01	2AL	5	5	13	68	4.24	1.71	$8	4.6	312	325	301	36%	6.00 -	11.4	3.8	7.1	1.9	1.2	2.20	79%	39	78
ERA Potl +	02	COL	1	4	1	82	4.72	1.37	$0	4.4	266	233	301	32%	4.42	8.1	3.1	8.0	2.6	1.1	1.42	68%	72	147
Support 2.84	1st Half		1	1	1	42	4.29	1.38	$1	4.4	248			32%	3.57 +	6.6	4.1	8.8	2.2	0.4		68%	91	186
LIMA B	2nd Half		0	3	0	40	5.17	1.35	($1)	4.5	285			31%	5.31	1.5	2.0	7.2	3.6	1.8		67%	62	127
Risk Low	03	Proj	3	5	1	80	4.39	1.48	$1	4.5	281			34%	4.89 -	11.4	3.4	8.0	2.4	1.1	--	73%	63	126

Went through three stretches of 13,12,12 and 8 games without giving up a run, then would get nailed. Of course, he was activated onto my LABR team always precisely just in time to get nailed.

Julio,Jorge		Tm	W	L	Sv	IP	ERA	Br/IP	R$	BF/G	OBA	vLH	vRH	H%	xERA	RAR	Ctl	Dom	Cmd	hr/9	G/F	S%	BPV	BPX
RH Reliever	98		0	0	0	0	0.00	0.00																
AGE 24 Growth	99		0	0	0	0	0.00	0.00																
TYPE Power	00		0	0	0	0	0.00	0.00																
BURN none	01	a/a	2	3	19	77	3.86	1.39	$13	5.2	259	286	290	33%	4.06	16.1	3.6	9.0	2.5	0.8	1.19	74%	85	163
ERA Potl - -	02	BAL	5	6	25	68	1.99	1.21	$21	4.2	223	213	214	27%	2.89 -	28.4	3.6	7.3	2.0	0.7	0.93	87%	77	146
Support 1.19	1st Half		4	4	16	37	2.67	1.27	$13	4.2	240			28%	3.55 -	12.1	3.4	7.0	2.1	1.0		84%	64	120
LIMA C	2nd Half		1	2	9	31	1.17	1.13	$8	4.2	202			26%	2.10 -	16.3	3.8	7.6	2.0	0.3		91%	93	177
Risk Low	03	Proj	3	5	32	70	2.83	1.24	$23	4.5	236			30%	3.16	23.8	3.3	8.5	2.5	0.6	--	79%	93	189

Closer-worthy skill set? Not quite yet. ERA was impressive and he did convert 81% of his save opps, but he does not yet have the dominance necessary to be a member of the Elite. Could be soon, though.

Karsay,Steve		Tm	W	L	Sv	IP	ERA	Br/IP	R$	BF/G	OBA	vLH	vRH	H%	xERA	RAR	Ctl	Dom	Cmd	hr/9	G/F	S%	BPV	BPX
RH Reliever	98	CLE	* 6	6	0	103	5.41	1.59	($1)	17.2	328	288	333	37%	5.60	3.4	1.9	5.8	3.0	0.8	1.09	66%	63	135
AGE 31 Peak	99	CLE	10	2	1	78	3.00	1.29	$15	6.6	244	209	281	30%	3.51 -	30.0	3.5	7.8	2.3	0.7	2.38	79%	80	201
TYPE Power	00	CLE	5	9	20	76	3.78	1.36	$19	4.5	269	223	304	33%	3.89	21.8	3.0	7.8	2.6	0.6	1.76	73%	86	223
BURN none	01	2TM	3	5	8	88	2.35	1.11	$15	4.8	227	257	203	29%	2.66	36.2	2.6	8.5	3.3	0.5	2.08	81%	115	220
ERA Potl -	02	NYY	6	4	12	88	3.27	1.33	$13	4.8	260	243	269	30%	3.73	21.6	3.1	6.6	2.2	0.7	2.21	77%	67	127
Support 4.48	1st Half		3	3	3	48	2.43	1.12	$7	4.9	223			27%	2.58	17.3	2.8	7.3	2.6	0.6		80%	92	174
LIMA C+	2nd Half		3	1	9	40	4.30	1.58	$5	4.7	300			34%	5.13 -	4.3	3.4	5.9	1.7	0.9		75%	40	75
Risk Low	03	Proj	6	5	8	90	3.30	1.32	$12	5.0	262			31%	3.77	24.9	2.9	7.2	2.5	0.7	G	77%	77	157

It appears that he is not cut out for a full-time closer's job as that is when his BPIs took a tumble. Has converted only 69%, 67% and 75% of save opps the past three years, which is too low.

Kennedy,Joe		Tm	W	L	Sv	IP	ERA	Br/IP	R$	BF/G	OBA	vLH	vRH	H%	xERA	RAR	Ctl	Dom	Cmd	hr/9	G/F	S%	BPV	BPX
LH Starter	98		0	0	0	0	0.00	0.00																
AGE 23 Growth	99		0	0	0	0	0.00	0.00																
TYPE Contact	00		0	0	0	0	0.00	0.00																
BURN none	01	TAM	* 13	8	0	190	3.27	1.21	$20	25.3	255	225	279	29%	3.63	56.4	2.2	6.8	3.1	0.9	0.97	76%	83	166
ERA Potl -	02	TAM	8	11	0	196	4.55	1.32	$5	27.7	270	273	268	29%	4.19	14.7	2.5	5.0	2.0	1.1	0.87	68%	41	78
Support 5.45	1st Half		5	7	0	110	4.17	1.24	$5	28.6	260			28%	3.91	13.8	2.2	5.8	2.6	1.1		70%	59	111
LIMA C+	2nd Half		3	4	0	86	5.03	1.43	($1)	26.7	282			30%	4.54	0.9	2.9	4.0	1.4	0.9		66%	23	43
Risk Moderate	03	Proj	10	10	0	200	4.77	1.39	$5	26.9	280			30%	4.70	16.0	2.7	5.1	1.9	1.2	--	69%	33	68

It is so obvious that this 23-year-old does not have the durability to shoulder 200 IP per year. But he'll hit the glue factory on someone else's watch, so who cares, right?

Kent,Steve

	Yr	Tm	W	L	Sv	IP	ERA	Br/IP	R$	BF/G	OBA	vLH	vRH	H%	xERA	RAR	Ctl	Dom	Cmd	hr/9	G/F	S%	BPV	BPX
LH Reliever	98		0	0	0	0	0.00	0.00																
AGE 24 Growth	99		0	0	0	0	0.00	0.00																
TYPE Power	00		0	0	0	0	0.00	0.00																
BURN none	01		0	0	0	0	0.00	0.00																
ERA Potl -	02	TAM	0	2	1	57	5.68	1.84	($6)	8.0	294	316	283	34%	5.74	-4.4	6.0	6.5	1.1	0.9	1.03	70%	29	55
Support 3.61	1st Half		0	2	1	33	5.17	1.72	($2)	7.7	278			31%	5.09	-0.3	5.7	5.4	1.0	0.8		70%	27	52
LIMA D	2nd Half		0	0	0	24	6.40	2.01	($4)	8.4	315			38%	6.64	-4.1	6.4	7.9	1.2	1.1		69%	31	60
Risk Low	03 Proj		0	1	0	40	5.85	1.90	($5)	8.0	303			35%	6.01	-2.6	6.1	7.0	1.1	0.9	--	69%	33	68

Rule 5 draftee and nothing much here to like. At last report, he was struggling in the AFL as well, which means it's unlikely that we'll be seeing much of him in 2003.

Kile,Darryl

	Yr	Tm	W	L	Sv	IP	ERA	Br/IP	R$	BF/G	OBA	vLH	vRH	H%	xERA	RAR	Ctl	Dom	Cmd	hr/9	G/F	S%	BPV	BPX
RH Reliever	98	COL	13	17	0	230	5.20	1.53	($1)	28.5	284	312	260	32%	5.05	1.0	3.8	6.2	1.6	1.1	1.22	68%	37	67
AGE 34 Past	99	COL	8	13	0	190	6.63	1.76	($14)	27.8	296	318	281	31%	6.19	-27.6	5.2	5.5	1.1	1.6	1.27	64%	4	9
TYPE Contact	00	STL	20	9	0	232	3.92	1.18	$29	28.0	247	230	262	28%	3.80	53.2	2.2	7.4	3.3	1.3	1.23	72%	81	179
BURN none	01	STL	16	11	0	227	3.09	1.29	$22	28.1	263	279	253	31%	3.92 -	69.2	2.6	7.1	2.8	0.9	1.24	79%	77	142
ERA Potl -	02	STL	5	4	0	84	3.75	1.31	$7	25.4	257	246	264	28%	4.05	19.2	3.0	5.4	1.8	1.0	1.06	74%	44	91
Support 4.36	1st Half		5	4	0	84	3.74	1.31	$7	25.4	257			28%	4.03	19.4	3.0	5.3	1.8	1.0		74%	44	91
LIMA D+	2nd Half		0	0	0	-0	0.00	0.00																
Risk Low	03 Proj		0	0	0	0	0.00	0.00													--		0	

Rest in peace.

Kim,Byung-Hyun

	Yr	Tm	W	L	Sv	IP	ERA	Br/IP	R$	BF/G	OBA	vLH	vRH	H%	xERA	RAR	Ctl	Dom	Cmd	hr/9	G/F	S%	BPV	BPX
RH Reliever	98		0	0	0	0	0.00	0.00																
AGE 24 Growth	99	ARI *	7	2	2	78	3.23	1.15	$13	6.9	182	265	180	25%	2.11 +	24.2	4.7	10.0	2.1	0.5	1.41	72%	110	238
TYPE Power	00	ARI	6	6	14	70	4.49	1.40	$14	5.0	208	237	171	33%	3.68 +	10.7	5.9	14.2	2.4	1.2	0.98	71%	115	253
BURN none	01	ARI	5	6	19	98	2.94	1.04	$24	5.0	173	199	151	23%	2.21 +	31.9	4.0	10.4	2.6	0.9	1.07	76%	109	202
ERA Potl No chg	02	ARI	8	3	36	84	2.04	1.07	$41	4.7	213	220	198	29%	2.43	38.5	2.8	9.9	3.5	0.5	1.70	84%	130	266
Support 3.32	1st Half		3	1	20	47	2.48	1.10	$21	5.0	199			30%	2.54	18.8	3.6	12.4	3.4	0.8		81%	139	284
LIMA C	2nd Half		5	2	16	37	1.46	1.03	$21	4.3	230			28%	2.30 -	19.7	1.7	6.6	3.9	0.2		86%	122	251
Risk Low	03 Proj		7	4	35	85	2.65	1.07	$36	4.8	203			28%	2.37	32.0	3.2	10.2	3.2	0.6	G	78%	124	249

Not only was he unaffected by his '01 World Series blowups, he got even better this year. Though it does beg the question... what if the D'backs had lost the Series?

Kim,Sun Woo

	Yr	Tm	W	L	Sv	IP	ERA	Br/IP	R$	BF/G	OBA	vLH	vRH	H%	xERA	RAR	Ctl	Dom	Cmd	hr/9	G/F	S%	BPV	BPX
RH Starter	98		0	0	0	0	0.00	0.00																
AGE 25 Growth	99	aa	9	8	0	149	6.10	1.54	($1)	25.6	306			35%	5.31 +	-8.0	2.7	6.7	2.5	1.0		61%	55	128
TYPE	00	aaa	11	7	0	134	7.86	1.83	($10)	24.5	348			39%	6.92 +	-37.6	2.9	6.4	2.2	1.2		56%	35	82
BURN none	01	BOS *	6	9	0	130	6.51	1.62	($8)	15.1	306	303	321	35%	5.29 +	-17.8	3.3	6.4	1.9	0.8	1.28	58%	49	99
ERA Potl -	02	2TM *	10	2	0	138	3.59	1.27	$13	17.0	248	247	297	27%	3.56	31.1	3.1	5.4	1.8	0.8	1.17	74%	52	101
Support 5.11	1st Half		2	2	0	47	5.94	1.32	$0	11.1	262			29%	4.04 +	-4.2	2.9	5.9	2.1	1.0		54%	53	104
LIMA C+	2nd Half		8	0	0	91	2.37	1.24	$14	23.7	240			27%	3.32 -	35.3	3.2	5.1	1.6	0.7		84%	51	101
Risk High	03 Proj		8	5	0	120	4.58	1.38	$6	23.5	270			30%	4.27	13.5	3.1	5.9	1.9	0.9	--	68%	50	102

3-0, 4.78 ERA in 49 IP at BOS and MON.

	G	IP	ERA	Cmd
Starter	5	27	3.00	1.3
Reliever	14	22	6.85	3.2

All his starts were in the 2nd half and he had a 0.89 ERA in Sept

King,Ray

	Yr	Tm	W	L	Sv	IP	ERA	Br/IP	R$	BF/G	OBA	vLH	vRH	H%	xERA	RAR	Ctl	Dom	Cmd	hr/9	G/F	S%	BPV	BPX
LH Reliever	98	a/a	2	5	5	62	4.06	1.42	$4	4.3	268			31%	4.19	11.3	3.5	6.7	1.9	0.7		72%	60	117
AGE 29 Pre-Peak	99	CHC *	4	4	2	54	3.17	1.46	$6	5.0	236	308	280	29%	3.44	17.2	5.3	6.8	1.3	0.3	2.71	78%	66	143
TYPE Power	00	MIL *	3	5	1	53	2.36	1.24	$8	3.4	230	204	157	27%	2.86 -	23.4	3.5	6.1	1.7	0.3	1.33	81%	71	157
BURN none	01	MIL	0	4	1	55	3.60	1.35	$1	2.9	240	210	276	29%	3.70	13.0	4.1	8.0	2.0	0.8	1.74	75%	72	133
ERA Potl -	02	MIL	3	2	0	66	3.00	1.32	$6	3.6	250	219	280	30%	3.69 -	21.7	3.4	7.0	2.0	0.7	1.90	79%	69	142
Support 4.02	1st Half		2	2	0	31	3.18	1.35	$3	3.4	248			31%	3.65	9.5	3.8	7.8	2.1	0.6		78%	78	161
LIMA B	2nd Half		1	0	0	35	2.84	1.29	$3	3.9	251			29%	3.73 -	12.3	3.1	6.2	2.0	0.8		81%	61	125
Risk Very Low	03 Proj		2	3	1	60	3.15	1.28	$5	3.4	245			29%	3.44	18.5	3.3	7.1	2.1	0.6	G	77%	75	151

Success is... showing some skill, having a job to do (in this case to get LH batters out), and doing that job without fanfare. He'll never save 50 games or hit 50 HRs, but he's no less of a success in his anointed role.

Kinney,Matt

	Yr	Tm	W	L	Sv	IP	ERA	Br/IP	R$	BF/G	OBA	vLH	vRH	H%	xERA	RAR	Ctl	Dom	Cmd	hr/9	G/F	S%	BPV	BPX
RH Starter	98		0	0	0	0	0.00	0.00																
AGE 26 Growth	99	aa	4	7	0	60	9.15	1.98	($10)	21.0	324			37%	7.01 +	-27.7	5.7	6.6	1.2	1.4		53%	14	32
TYPE	00	MIN *	13	6	0	188	4.59	1.49	$11	25.1	263	305	194	31%	4.60	33.2	4.4	7.4	1.7	1.1	0.77	72%	49	128
BURN none	01	aaa	6	11	0	161	6.04	1.71	($11)	25.7	308			35%	6.19	-13.3	4.1	6.9	1.7	1.5		67%	27	52
ERA Potl - -	02	MIN *	4	8	0	97	6.58	1.75	($8)	22.7	325	336	246	34%	7.20 -	-19.2	3.5	6.0	1.7	2.2	0.81	68%	-5	-9
Support 2.59	1st Half		3	8	0	76	5.55	1.73	($5)	22.2	311			33%	6.83 -	-4.5	4.1	6.4	1.5	2.1		75%	-0	-1
LIMA F	2nd Half		1	0	0	21	10.33	1.82	($4)	24.8	373			38%	8.56 +	-14.6	1.3	4.7	3.7	2.6		44%	8	16
Risk X HIGH	03 Proj		4	4	0	80	5.63	1.63	($3)	22.7	305			33%	6.00	-2.7	3.5	6.2	1.8	1.6	--	69%	21	43

2-7, 4.64 ERA in 66 IP at MIN. We could blame this season on the sore shoulder that landed him on the DL for most of the 2nd half, but his numbers were only marginally lower than his history. I'm losing interest.

Kline,Steve

	Yr	Tm	W	L	Sv	IP	ERA	Br/IP	R$	BF/G	OBA	vLH	vRH	H%	xERA	RAR	Ctl	Dom	Cmd	hr/9	G/F	S%	BPV	BPX
LH Reliever	98	MON	3	6	1	71	2.78	1.45	$5	4.0	236	178	253	32%	3.59 -	23.4	5.2	9.6	1.9	0.5	1.89	82%	89	161
AGE 30 Peak	99	MON	7	4	0	69	3.78	1.29	$9	3.5	223	194	232	28%	3.50	16.3	4.3	9.0	2.1	1.0	2.04	74%	77	167
TYPE	00	MON	1	5	14	82	3.51	1.40	$11	4.3	275	243	297	32%	4.38 -	23.3	3.0	7.0	2.4	0.9	2.08	78%	65	144
BURN none	01	2NL	3	3	9	75	1.80	1.09	$16	3.4	200	149	238	24%	2.16	35.8	3.5	6.5	1.9	0.4	1.70	85%	82	152
ERA Potl +	02	STL	2	1	6	60	3.30	1.27	$9	3.7	242	230	266	29%	3.25	17.3	3.3	6.3	1.9	0.5	1.56	74%	71	146
Support 4.32	1st Half		0	0	2	20	4.05	1.15	$2	3.4	252			35%	2.63 +	3.8	1.8	9.5	5.3	0.0		61%	172	352
LIMA B	2nd Half		2	1	4	40	2.92	1.32	$6	3.9	237			26%	3.56 -	13.6	4.0	4.7	1.2	0.7		80%	40	83
Risk Very Low	03 Proj		3	3	4	75	3.60	1.29	$8	3.8	246			29%	3.36	18.6	3.4	6.4	1.9	0.5	G	72%	69	139

Same essential skills as in 2001, but an ERA that more closely approximated reality. Note the gradual decline in his Dom rate, however. That might spell some trouble within a year or two.

Knotts,Gary

	Yr	Tm	W	L	Sv	IP	ERA	Br/IP	R$	BF/G	OBA	vLH	vRH	H%	xERA	RAR	Ctl	Dom	Cmd	hr/9	G/F	S%	BPV	BPX
RH Reliever	98		0	0	0	0	0.00	0.00																
AGE 26 Growth	99	aa	6	3	0	81	4.44	1.51	$5	29.9	280			31%	5.13 -	13.6	3.7	6.3	1.7	1.3		75%	33	77
TYPE Power	00	aa	9	8	0	156	5.77	1.65	($2)	26.4	301			34%	5.36	-0.2	3.9	5.5	1.4	0.9		65%	31	74
BURN Low	01	aaa	6	8	0	124	5.08	1.47	$0	23.7	289			34%	4.81	5.7	2.9	7.2	2.5	0.9	1.17	66%	64	123
ERA Potl -	02	FLA *	8	4	3	83	4.23	1.47	$8	5.2	245	191	194	28%	4.29	13.7	5.0	6.5	1.3	1.0	1.05	73%	43	88
Support 6.46	1st Half		3	1	2	39	5.98	1.61	($0)	5.1	241			24%	5.63	-2.8	6.4	6.0	0.9	2.1		69%	0	0
LIMA C+	2nd Half		5	3	1	44	2.67	1.34	$8	5.3	249			31%	3.10	16.4	3.7	7.0	1.9	0.0		78%	87	178
Risk X HIGH	03 Proj		4	3	1	50	4.50	1.50	$3	6.3	269			31%	4.60	6.4	4.1	6.5	1.6	0.9	--	71%	46	92

3-1, 4.50 ERA in 30 IP at FLA. Despite a mediocre ERA in the majors and marginal overall BPIs, he held batters to a BA under .200 in his 30 IP. Small signs like that are what dreams are made of.

Koch,Billy

	Yr	Tm	W	L	Sv	IP	ERA	Br/IP	R$	BF/G	OBA	vLH	vRH	H%	xERA	RAR	Ctl	Dom	Cmd	hr/9	G/F	S%	BPV	BPX
RH Reliever	98	aaa	0	1	0	6	13.50	2.67	($3)	16.8	371			50%	9.69 +	-6.5	9.0	12.0	1.3	1.5		47%	36	69
AGE 28 Pre-Peak	99	TOR *	3	5	31	88	4.09	1.48	$21	6.3	264	209	261	32%	4.45	21.0	4.2	7.8	1.9	0.9	1.94	74%	60	151
TYPE Power	00	TOR	9	3	33	78	2.65	1.23	$35	4.8	261	255	261	31%	3.54 -	34.2	2.1	6.9	3.3	0.7	1.63	81%	93	243
BURN none	01	TOR	2	5	36	69	4.82	1.48	$19	4.4	262	292	243	31%	4.42	6.2	4.3	7.2	1.7	0.9	1.36	68%	53	107
ERA Potl +	02	OAK	11	4	44	93	3.29	1.28	$33	4.6	218	237	196	28%	3.01	22.6	4.5	9.0	2.0	0.7	1.29	76%	88	166
Support 1.92	1st Half		4	0	19	43	3.55	1.35	$13	4.7	224			30%	3.19	9.0	4.8	9.8	2.0	0.6		75%	93	176
LIMA D	2nd Half		7	4	25	50	3.07	1.22	$20	4.6	213			26%	2.85	13.6	4.1	8.3	2.0	0.7		77%	83	156
Risk High	03 Proj		7	4	37	80	3.60	1.34	$27	4.7	239			29%	3.58	18.9	4.1	8.1	2.0	0.8	--	75%	74	151

Reasons why a $30 bid is risky:
- Has yet to crack a 100 BPV
- Excessive IP for a closer in '02
- Inconsistent; just one season removed from 2001's struggles
- With a more typical win total, his value drops below $30.

Kolb,Danny

	Yr	Tm	W	L	Sv	IP	ERA	Br/IP	R$	BF/G	OBA	vLH	vRH	H%	xERA	RAR	Ctl	Dom	Cmd	hr/9	G/F	S%	BPV	BPX
RH Reliever	98	aa	12	11	0	163	6.40	1.86	($10)	26.9	329			35%	6.29	-21.3	4.3	4.0	0.9	0.8		65%	10	19
AGE 28 Pre-Peak	99	TEX	* 8	6	0	130	5.12	1.72	($0)	17.7	309	280	260	34%	5.47	13.0	4.1	4.2	1.0	0.6	3.09	70%	21	52
TYPE	00	aaa	4	1	4	19	3.79	1.53	$6	6.0	251			30%	4.41 -	5.0	5.2	8.1	1.5	0.9		78%	57	135
BURN none	01	TEX	* 1	1	0	36	3.00	1.28	$3	5.0	228	257	261	27%	3.78 -	12.0	4.0	8.8	2.2	1.3	2.56	83%	70	141
ERA Potl -	02	TEX	3	7	1	40	4.26	1.65	$1	4.7	261	291	172	30%	4.11	4.5	5.8	4.9	0.8	0.2	2.65	72%	43	82
Support 4.78	1st Half		0	0	0	0	0.00	0.00																
LIMA C+	2nd Half		3	7	1	40	4.27	1.65	$1	4.7	261			30%	4.11	4.5	5.8	4.9	0.8	0.2		72%	43	82
Risk Very High	03	Proj	5	7	1	80	4.61	1.63	$1	7.9	283			32%	4.83	8.1	4.6	5.3	1.1	0.7	G	72%	34	69

Came back from a rotator cuff tear but left his skills on the trainer's table. Had been making progress through 2001, but now his short-term future is in doubt.

Komiyama,Satoru

	Yr	Tm	W	L	Sv	IP	ERA	Br/IP	R$	BF/G	OBA	vLH	vRH	H%	xERA	RAR	Ctl	Dom	Cmd	hr/9	G/F	S%	BPV	BPX
RH Reliever	98	JPN	11	12	0	202	3.56	1.24	$17	31.1	282			31%	4.32 -	50.5	1.2	5.6	4.7	1.1		76%	97	188
AGE 37 Decline	99	JPN	7	10	0	142	4.06	1.14	$14	27.5	252			28%	3.52 +	31.2	1.7	6.1	3.6	1.0		67%	85	198
TYPE Contact	00	JPN	8	11	0	161	3.97	1.26	$14	25.9	268			29%	4.35	38.6	2.1	6.0	2.9	1.3		74%	59	139
BURN none	01	JPN	12	9	0	149	3.02	1.21	$19	25.6	263			29%	3.44	47.9	1.8	4.5	2.5	0.5		76%	65	124
ERA Potl No chg	02	NYM	* 3	4	0	87	3.62	1.23	$6	8.6	259	305	298	30%	4.02	21.5	2.2	6.9	3.2	1.1	0.97	75%	78	159
Support 4.36	1st Half		0	3	0	35	4.63	1.34	($0)	7.1	278			31%	4.72	3.9	2.3	6.2	2.7	1.3		69%	54	110
LIMA B+	2nd Half		3	1	0	52	2.94	1.15	$7	10.1	246			29%	3.55 -	17.6	2.1	7.4	3.6	1.0		80%	94	194
Risk High	03	Proj	2	2	0	40	3.60	1.23	$4	7.2	262			30%	3.80	9.9	2.0	6.1	3.0	0.9	--	73%	75	151

0-3, 5.65 ERA in 43 IP at NYM. It's often been said that baseball in Japan is equivalent to AAA in the States. Well, he pitched superbly at Norfolk, comparable to his JPN stats, but had several very bad outiings in the bigs.

Koplove,Mike

	Yr	Tm	W	L	Sv	IP	ERA	Br/IP	R$	BF/G	OBA	vLH	vRH	H%	xERA	RAR	Ctl	Dom	Cmd	hr/9	G/F	S%	BPV	BPX
RH Reliever	98		0	0	0	0	0.00	0.00																
AGE 26 Growth	99		0	0	0	0	0.00	0.00																
TYPE Power	00	aa	4	3	6	46	4.70	1.37	$7	5.6	253			31%	3.52 +	6.6	3.7	7.4	2.0	0.4		64%	79	188
BURN none	01	a/a	7	7	13	76	3.20	1.53	$14	5.6	269	192	250	33%	4.34 -	22.6	4.4	7.9	1.8	0.6	1.71	80%	69	132
ERA Potl + +	02	ARI	* 7	3	3	91	2.66	1.07	$18	4.7	216	174	230	27%	2.29	34.1	2.7	7.0	2.6	0.3	2.38	75%	100	205
Support 3.21	1st Half		1	2	3	40	1.12	0.85	$11	4.5	204			26%	1.49	23.4	1.1	7.2	6.4	0.2		88%	185	379
LIMA B+	2nd Half		6	1	0	51	3.88	1.25	$7	4.8	226			28%	2.92 +	10.8	3.9	6.9	1.8	0.4		68%	78	159
Risk Moderate	03	Proj	5	3	0	60	3.15	1.28	$7	5.1	242			30%	3.25	18.5	3.5	7.4	2.1	0.5	G	76%	82	165

6-1, 3.39 ERA in 61 IP at ARI. Solid BPIs, good growth. His control tailed a little bit in the 2nd half as NL hitters got another look at him. But his BPIs are still within an acceptable range. Good LIMA pick.

Lackey,John

	Yr	Tm	W	L	Sv	IP	ERA	Br/IP	R$	BF/G	OBA	vLH	vRH	H%	xERA	RAR	Ctl	Dom	Cmd	hr/9	G/F	S%	BPV	BPX
RH Starter	98		0	0	0	0	0.00	0.00																
AGE 24 Growth	99		0	0	0	0	0.00	0.00																
TYPE Contact	00	aa	6	1	0	57	4.74	1.42	$5	30.9	309			34%	5.30 -	7.8	1.4	5.8	4.1	1.3		70%	77	182
BURN Moderate	01	a/a	12	11	0	185	5.06	1.31	$8	27.9	277			31%	4.14 +	9.0	2.0	5.7	2.8	0.8		61%	68	131
ERA Potl -	02	ANA	* 17	6	0	209	3.27	1.29	$19	25.9	263	208	317	30%	3.60	51.5	2.5	6.0	2.4	0.6	1.31	76%	68	130
Support 5.98	1st Half		9	3	0	114	2.84	1.21	$13	26.2	251			29%	3.09	34.7	2.4	6.1	2.6	0.5		77%	81	153
LIMA C	2nd Half		8	3	0	95	3.79	1.38	$7	25.5	276			31%	4.22	16.8	2.7	5.9	2.1	0.9		75%	54	103
Risk High	03	Proj	13	11	0	200	3.96	1.35	$13	27.5	277			31%	4.17	37.7	2.4	6.0	2.5	0.8	--	72%	63	128

9-4, 3.67 ERA in 108 IP at ANA. An exciting young player with three critical caveats...
1. Excessive innings for his age
2. RHed hitters teed off on him
3. Post-season heroics will inflate his price on Draft Day.

Lawrence,Brian

	Yr	Tm	W	L	Sv	IP	ERA	Br/IP	R$	BF/G	OBA	vLH	vRH	H%	xERA	RAR	Ctl	Dom	Cmd	hr/9	G/F	S%	BPV	BPX
RH Starter	98		0	0	0	0	0.00	0.00																
AGE 26 Growth	99		0	0	0	0	0.00	0.00																
TYPE Contact	00	a/a	11	6	0	173	2.50	1.14	$27	24.2	249			30%	3.08 -	75.6	1.9	6.7	3.6	0.6		80%	103	245
BURN none	01	SD	* 6	8	1	159	3.68	1.28	$9	18.6	254	281	215	30%	3.67	35.9	2.9	6.7	2.3	0.7	2.42	73%	71	131
ERA Potl +	02	SD	12	12	0	210	3.69	1.34	$15	25.6	280	324	236	33%	4.18 -	49.9	2.2	6.4	2.9	0.7	2.51	74%	77	158
Support 4.93	1st Half		7	4	0	114	3.63	1.28	$10	28.2	275			32%	3.98	27.9	1.9	6.3	3.3	0.7		73%	87	178
LIMA B	2nd Half		5	8	0	96	3.75	1.42	$5	23.1	285			33%	4.42 -	22.0	2.6	6.5	2.5	0.7		74%	69	141
Risk Moderate	03	Proj	10	11	0	200	3.51	1.26	$16	22.0	268			31%	3.76	52.1	2.1	6.3	3.1	0.7	G	73%	84	168

Had already put up nearly 200 IP by the end of August after having never shouldered that level of workload. Is it any wonder he hit a wall? His BPIs remain solid, but you'll have to monitor his durability.

Leiter,Al

	Yr	Tm	W	L	Sv	IP	ERA	Br/IP	R$	BF/G	OBA	vLH	vRH	H%	xERA	RAR	Ctl	Dom	Cmd	hr/9	G/F	S%	BPV	BPX
LH Starter	98	NYM	17	6	0	193	2.47	1.15	$29	28.1	217	261	205	28%	2.50	71.4	3.3	8.1	2.5	0.4	1.69	79%	101	181
AGE 37 Decline	99	NYM	13	12	0	213	4.23	1.42	$12	28.9	258	260	262	30%	4.06	37.7	3.9	6.8	1.7	0.8	1.13	71%	57	124
TYPE Power	00	NYM	16	8	0	208	3.20	1.21	$27	27.7	231	118	248	29%	3.23	67.6	3.3	8.7	2.6	0.8	1.27	76%	91	201
BURN none	01	NYM	11	11	0	187	3.32	1.20	$18	26.6	252	254	251	29%	3.54	51.3	2.2	6.8	3.1	0.9	1.05	75%	84	157
ERA Potl No chg	02	NYM	13	13	0	204	3.49	1.29	$18	26.0	252	221	257	30%	3.96	53.9	3.0	7.6	2.5	1.0	1.18	77%	72	148
Support 4.01	1st Half		8	6	0	106	2.97	1.15	$15	25.4	229			27%	3.07	35.5	2.8	7.3	2.6	0.8		77%	85	174
LIMA C	2nd Half		5	7	0	98	4.05	1.44	$4	26.7	276			32%	4.92 -	18.5	3.3	7.9	2.4	1.3		76%	59	121
Risk Low	03	Proj	13	12	0	200	3.74	1.35	$15	27.5	260			31%	4.10	46.0	3.2	7.6	2.4	0.9	--	75%	70	141

Continues to be a good rotation anchor, but you can see the coming decline at age 37. Be safe and don't bid out of the middle teens.

Levine,Al

	Yr	Tm	W	L	Sv	IP	ERA	Br/IP	R$	BF/G	OBA	vLH	vRH	H%	xERA	RAR	Ctl	Dom	Cmd	hr/9	G/F	S%	BPV	BPX
RH Reliever	98	TEX	* 1	4	1	111	5.75	1.55	($5)	11.8	303	266	314	31%	5.59	-1.4	2.9	3.5	1.2	1.3	1.59	65%	2	3
AGE 34 Decline	99	ANA	1	1	0	85	3.39	1.24	$7	7.1	241	233	255	24%	4.00 -	28.3	3.1	3.9	1.3	1.4	1.37	79%	16	40
TYPE	00	ANA	3	4	2	95	3.88	1.55	$5	8.3	268	261	269	28%	4.70 -	25.9	4.6	4.0	0.9	0.9	1.78	77%	15	39
BURN none	01	ANA	8	10	2	75	2.39	1.32	$13	5.0	251	288	229	27%	3.82 -	31.1	3.4	4.8	1.4	0.8	1.82	86%	38	77
ERA Potl - -	02	ANA	4	4	5	63	4.29	1.51	$4	5.4	256	240	263	28%	4.54	6.9	4.9	5.7	1.2	1.1	1.32	75%	29	54
Support 3.53	1st Half		3	2	4	35	4.11	1.51	$3	4.7	245			27%	4.77 -	4.7	5.4	7.2	1.3	1.5		79%	31	59
LIMA C+	2nd Half		1	2	1	28	4.50	1.50	$0	6.5	269			29%	4.25	2.3	4.2	3.9	0.9	0.6		70%	25	46
Risk Low	03	Proj	4	5	3	70	4.24	1.44	$4	6.0	259			28%	4.37	10.6	4.1	4.8	1.2	1.0	--	73%	25	51

Soft-tosser with marginal Ctl, yet seems to hold his own in the pen. Or does he? REff% the past three years has been 71%, 66%, 76%, and he converted only 71% of his save opps in 2002. Pass.

Lidle,Cory

	Yr	Tm	W	L	Sv	IP	ERA	Br/IP	R$	BF/G	OBA	vLH	vRH	H%	xERA	RAR	Ctl	Dom	Cmd	hr/9	G/F	S%	BPV	BPX
RH Starter	98	aaa	0	0	0	5	0.00	0.80	$1	18.6	124			14%	0.30	3.6	3.6	3.6	1.0	0.0		100%	73	142
AGE 31 Peak	99	TAM	* 1	0	0	11	5.73	1.91	($0)	6.6	354	750	278	42%	7.63 -	0.2	3.3	8.2	2.5	1.6	1.40	74%	37	92
TYPE Contact	00	TAM	* 10	8	0	146	4.19	1.40	$12	15.8	291	295	293	33%	4.69 -	33.8	2.2	6.2	2.8	1.0	2.76	72%	63	162
BURN none	01	OAK	13	6	0	188	3.59	1.15	$20	26.4	243	213	276	26%	3.55	47.7	2.3	5.6	2.5	1.1	1.81	73%	60	120
ERA Potl +	02	OAK	8	10	0	196	3.86	1.20	$11	25.2	259	248	269	29%	3.47	32.8	1.9	5.2	2.7	0.8	1.42	69%	68	129
Support 5.11	1st Half		2	7	0	84	5.46	1.59	($4)	23.7	325			37%	5.51	-4.0	2.1	5.7	2.7	0.9		66%	54	102
LIMA C+	2nd Half		6	3	0	112	2.65	0.90	$15	26.7	200			22%	1.93 +	36.8	1.8	4.9	2.8	0.7		74%	81	153
Risk Very High	03	Proj	12	8	0	200	3.47	1.16	$20	23.3	247			27%	3.35	51.0	2.1	5.7	2.8	0.9	--	73%	71	144

Poor start had owners bailing, but his BPIs tell the true story. Skills were solid - and consistent - all year, but a 37% hit rate and 66% strand rate killed his 1st half ERA. Bidding may be slow, but you take him to the limit.

Lieber,Jon

	Yr	Tm	W	L	Sv	IP	ERA	Br/IP	R$	BF/G	OBA	vLH	vRH	H%	xERA	RAR	Ctl	Dom	Cmd	hr/9	G/F	S%	BPV	BPX
RH Starter	98	PIT	8	14	1	171	4.11	1.30	$9	24.9	274	311	232	32%	4.42	25.9	2.1	7.3	3.5	1.2	1.23	72%	80	144
AGE 33 Past	99	CHC	10	11	0	203	4.08	1.34	$12	27.9	283	333	236	34%	4.62 -	39.9	2.0	8.2	4.0	1.2	1.33	74%	96	208
TYPE Contact	00	CHC	12	11	0	251	4.41	1.20	$18	29.6	259	285	234	29%	4.05	41.0	1.9	6.9	3.6	1.3	1.69	67%	80	177
BURN none	01	CHC	20	6	0	232	3.80	1.15	$27	27.8	257	298	219	28%	3.59	48.7	1.6	5.7	3.6	1.0	1.34	70%	85	157
ERA Potl + +	02	CHC	6	8	0	141	3.70	1.17	$12	27.5	278	308	246	31%	3.98	33.2	0.8	5.6	7.3	1.0	1.23	71%	156	321
Support 3.70	1st Half		6	4	0	105	3.26	1.12	$13	28.3	269			30%	3.57	31.0	0.8	5.2	6.8	0.8		73%	152	311
LIMA B+	2nd Half		0	4	0	36	5.00	1.31	($1)	25.4	302			33%	5.19	2.2	0.7	6.5	8.7	1.5		66%	171	350
Risk Very Low	03	Proj	1	1	0	20	4.05	1.20	$2	27.5	271			30%	4.29	3.8	1.4	6.3	4.7	1.4	--	71%	96	193

Reconstructive elbow surgery will keep him out most of the 2003 season.

Ligtenberg,Kerry	Tm	W	L	Sv	IP	ERA	Br/IP	R$	BF/G	OBA	vLH	vRH	H%	xERA	RAR	Ctl	Dom	Cmd	hr/9	G/F	S%	BPV	BPX
RH Reliever	98 ATL	3	2	30	73	2.71	1.03	$26	3.8	199	176	207	26%	2.30	24.7	3.0	9.7	**3.3**	0.7	1.15	77%	121	218
AGE 31 Peak	99	0	0	0	0	0.00	0.00																
TYPE Power	00 ATL	2	3	12	52	3.63	1.29	$11	3.7	226	206	236	27%	3.73	14.0	4.1	8.8	**2.1**	1.2	0.67	77%	71	156
BURN none	01 ATL	3	3	1	59	3.04	1.35	$5	4.8	230	241	216	29%	3.39	18.4	4.6	8.5	**1.9**	0.6	0.90	79%	81	150
ERA Potl -	02 ATL	3	4	0	66	3.00	1.29	$6	5.3	218	214	212	25%	3.34	21.7	4.5	7.0	**1.5**	0.8	0.72	80%	61	125
Support 4.32	1st Half	1	3	0	33	2.18	1.45	$3	5.8	231			28%	3.90 -	14.6	5.4	7.6	**1.4**	0.8		89%	59	122
LIMA C+	2nd Half	2	1	0	33	3.83	1.12	$4	4.9	206			23%	2.79 +	7.2	3.6	6.3	**1.8**	0.8		68%	64	132
Risk Very Low	03 Proj	**3**	**3**	**2**	**60**	**3.45**	**1.30**	**$6**	**4.7**	**228**			**27%**	**3.40**	**16.1**	**4.2**	**7.1**	**1.7**	**0.8**	**F**	**75%**	**64**	**130**

More magic at Turner Field... Mediocre BPIs yield a 3.00 ERA thanks to a 25% hit rate and 80% strand rate. And for their next trick, Ziegfried and Roy will make a World Series win appear from behind the curtain. Or not.

Lilly,Ted	Tm	W	L	Sv	IP	ERA	Br/IP	R$	BF/G	OBA	vLH	vRH	H%	xERA	RAR	Ctl	Dom	Cmd	hr/9	G/F	S%	BPV	BPX
LH Reliever	98 a/a	11	9	0	182	4.85	1.60	$1	28.4	306			37%	5.43 -	14.2	3.2	7.8	**2.4**	1.0		71%	61	120
AGE 27 Growth	99 MON	* 8	6	0	113	5.26	1.35	$5	19.3	275			32%	4.50 +	4.4	2.5	7.6	**3.0**	1.2		63%	73	159
TYPE	00 aaa	8	11	0	137	4.80	1.61	$3	28.2	311	286	200	36%	5.57 -	17.7	3.0	7.2	**2.4**	1.1	0.90	72%	55	130
BURN Moderate	01 NYY	* 5	6	0	145	5.09	1.41	$0	20.2	262	229	278	31%	4.72	7.7	3.7	8.6	**2.3**	1.4	0.74	67%	60	121
ERA Potl No chg	02 2AL	5	7	0	100	3.69	1.11	$8	18.3	221	154	231	24%	3.27	19.0	2.8	6.9	**2.5**	1.4	0.68	73%	64	121
Support 4.14	1st Half	3	6	0	76	3.43	1.06	$6	19.0	210			23%	2.86 +	17.2	2.8	7.0	**2.5**	1.2		73%	71	134
LIMA C+	2nd Half	2	1	0	24	4.54	1.26	$2	16.6	255			27%	4.60	1.8	2.6	6.8	**2.6**	1.9		72%	42	80
Risk High	03 Proj	**8**	**8**	**0**	**140**	**4.05**	**1.26**	**$10**	**19.5**	**253**			**28%**	**4.16**	**24.7**	**2.7**	**7.1**	**2.6**	**1.4**	**F**	**73%**	**60**	**123**

H% and S% once again come into play as they make him into a draftable commodity. There are still weaknesses, most notably the HR ball and possibly chronic shoulder woes, but the foundation is here for growth.

Lima,Jose	Tm	W	L	Sv	IP	ERA	Br/IP	R$	BF/G	OBA	vLH	vRH	H%	xERA	RAR	Ctl	Dom	Cmd	hr/9	G/F	S%	BPV	BPX
RH Reliever	98 HOU	16	8	0	233	3.71	1.12	$24	28.5	258	266	245	29%	3.85	47.7	1.2	6.5	**5.3**	1.3	1.09	73%	114	206
AGE 30 Peak	99 HOU	21	10	0	246	3.59	1.22	$30	29.1	270	287	248	31%	4.00	64.6	1.6	6.8	**4.3**	1.1	1.33	75%	98	214
TYPE Contact	00 HOU	7	16	0	196	6.65	1.63	($11)	27.0	312	364	272	32%	6.76	-26.9	3.1	5.7	**1.8**	2.2	0.92	64%	-1	-2
BURN none	01 2TM	6	12	0	165	5.56	1.42	($2)	22.4	297	301	298	30%	5.75	-3.0	2.1	4.6	**2.2**	1.9	1.04	67%	12	23
ERA Potl ++	02 DET	4	6	0	68	7.81	1.57	($5)	15.3	310	319	308	32%	5.92 +	-24.6	2.8	4.4	**1.6**	1.6	0.74	51%	5	9
Support 5.14	1st Half	1	4	0	22	11.35	1.76	($5)	11.5	324			30%	7.80 +	-18.6	3.6	3.6	**1.0**	2.8		34%	-52	-98
LIMA F	2nd Half	3	2	0	46	6.09	1.48	($1)	18.3	302			33%	5.02 +	-6.0	2.4	4.7	**2.0**	1.0		59%	35	67
Risk Low	03 Proj	**3**	**5**	**0**	**60**	**5.40**	**1.47**	**($0)**	**13.9**	**296**			**30%**	**5.68**	**-0.3**	**2.6**	**4.8**	**1.9**	**1.8**	**F**	**68%**	**10**	**21**

Interesting correlation... As his G/F ratio goes, so go his BPIs and ERA. When he keeps the ball on the ground more, he fares better... but he's been creating more flies than a zipper factory...

Lincoln,Mike	Tm	W	L	Sv	IP	ERA	Br/IP	R$	BF/G	OBA	vLH	vRH	H%	xERA	RAR	Ctl	Dom	Cmd	hr/9	G/F	S%	BPV	BPX
RH Reliever	98 aa	15	7	0	173	4.68	1.53	$8	29.6	316			34%	5.39 -	17.3	2.0	4.8	**2.4**	0.9		71%	43	83
AGE 28 Pre-Peak	99 MIN	* 8	12	0	135	7.53	1.76	($10)	23.4	334	358	282	35%	6.77 +	-30.0	3.1	4.1	**1.3**	1.5	1.36	58%	-4	-9
TYPE	00 MIN	* 4	4	0	95	5.87	1.55	($1)	21.2	306	378	388	33%	5.00 +	0.5	2.7	4.4	**1.6**	0.7	1.46	61%	33	87
BURN Low	01 PIT	* 7	5	0	131	3.57	1.33	$9	11.4	269	196	240	30%	4.14 -	31.5	2.6	5.7	**2.2**	0.9	1.41	76%	54	101
ERA Potl ----	02 PIT	* 2	4	2	86	2.82	1.46	$5	5.8	285	276	296	33%	4.60 -	30.5	3.0	6.5	**2.1**	0.7	1.82	83%	60	123
Support 3.48	1st Half	0	2	1	41	1.31	1.31	$5	5.8	279			34%	4.05 -	22.9	2.0	7.2	**3.7**	0.7		94%	100	205
LIMA B	2nd Half	2	2	1	45	4.20	1.60	$0	5.8	291			33%	5.10 -	7.6	4.0	5.8	**1.5**	0.8		75%	38	78
Risk X HIGH	03 Proj	**3**	**3**	**1**	**70**	**3.86**	**1.47**	**$3**	**8.3**	**288**			**33%**	**4.68 -**	**15.0**	**3.0**	**6.3**	**2.1**	**0.8**	**G**	**75%**	**57**	**114**

Was sent down in May after 11 games and a 0.54 ERA, raising the ire of fantasy owners. But that ERA was built on a high OBA and 90%+ strand rate. He eventually came back down to Earth. (Still a good LIMA pick.)

Lloyd,Graeme	Tm	W	L	Sv	IP	ERA	Br/IP	R$	BF/G	OBA	vLH	vRH	H%	xERA	RAR	Ctl	Dom	Cmd	hr/9	G/F	S%	BPV	BPX
LH Reliever	98 NYY	3	0	0	38	1.66	0.84	$9	2.9	195	198	182	21%	1.82	20.3	1.4	4.7	**3.3**	0.7	1.35	86%	93	199
AGE 36 Decline	99 TOR	5	3	3	72	3.63	1.26	$10	4.1	251	268	238	27%	4.18 -	21.7	2.9	5.9	**2.0**	1.4	1.38	78%	42	105
TYPE	00 MON	0	0	0	0	0.00	0.00																
BURN none	01 MON	9	5	1	70	4.37	1.36	$8	3.6	272	252	284	31%	4.14	9.4	2.7	5.6	**2.1**	0.8	2.03	69%	55	103
ERA Potl ++	02 2NL	4	5	5	57	5.21	1.51	$3	3.8	294	326	281	35%	4.32 +	1.9	3.0	5.8	**1.9**	0.2	1.57	62%	67	138
Support 5.21	1st Half	2	3	5	27	6.62	1.65	$1	3.3	337			36%	6.79	-4.2	2.0	5.0	**2.5**	1.7		63%	20	42
LIMA B	2nd Half	2	2	0	30	3.93	1.38	$2	4.6	250			34%	2.07 +	6.1	3.9	6.6	**1.7**	-1.2		62%	117	239
Risk Moderate	03 Proj	**3**	**4**	**1**	**50**	**4.50**	**1.44**	**$2**	**3.8**	**281**			**32%**	**4.28**	**6.4**	**3.1**	**5.6**	**1.8**	**0.5**	**G**	**68%**	**54**	**110**

High hit rate and low strand rate inflated his ERA by about a full run. BPIs are starting to erode with age, so it's probably best not to chase what would be a rebound season in '03.

Loaiza,Esteban	Tm	W	L	Sv	IP	ERA	Br/IP	R$	BF/G	OBA	vLH	vRH	H%	xERA	RAR	Ctl	Dom	Cmd	hr/9	G/F	S%	BPV	BPX
RH Starter	98 2TM	9	11	0	171	5.16	1.47	$2	21.4	292	287	303	31%	5.37	6.2	2.7	5.7	**2.1**	1.5	1.53	69%	30	59
AGE 31 Peak	99 TEX	9	5	0	120	4.58	1.40	$9	17.3	274	257	290	31%	4.26	20.8	3.0	5.8	**1.9**	0.8	1.15	68%	53	132
TYPE Contact	00 2AL	10	13	1	199	4.57	1.43	$11	25.5	289	287	289	32%	5.04	35.9	2.6	6.2	**2.4**	1.3	1.18	72%	46	118
BURN none	01 TOR	11	11	0	190	5.02	1.47	$3	23.2	308	329	286	33%	5.45	11.8	1.9	5.2	**2.8**	1.3	1.36	69%	44	88
ERA Potl +	02 TOR	* 11	10	0	169	5.43	1.48	$0	26.6	308	308	311	34%	5.06	-7.2	2.1	5.3	**2.5**	1.0	1.32	64%	50	94
Support 6.24	1st Half	5	4	0	76	4.72	1.43	$2	25.5	304			33%	4.53	4.0	1.8	4.4	**2.5**	0.6		66%	54	103
LIMA C+	2nd Half	6	6	0	93	6.01	1.53	($2)	27.6	311			34%	5.50 +	-11.2	2.3	6.0	**2.6**	1.3		62%	45	86
Risk Moderate	03 Proj	**9**	**11**	**0**	**160**	**4.89**	**1.45**	**$3**	**25.9**	**300**			**33%**	**5.06**	**10.2**	**2.2**	**5.5**	**2.5**	**1.1**	**--**	**68%**	**46**	**94**

H% and S% are supposed to be random and always regressing to the mean, but these trends are scary. Despite decent enough BPIs, external gauges have wreaked havoc with his ERA. A waste of good run suppt.

Lohse,Kyle	Tm	W	L	Sv	IP	ERA	Br/IP	R$	BF/G	OBA	vLH	vRH	H%	xERA	RAR	Ctl	Dom	Cmd	hr/9	G/F	S%	BPV	BPX
RH Starter	98	0	0	0	0	0.00	0.00																
AGE 24 Growth	99 aa	3	4	0	70	7.33	1.77	($7)	29.9	336			36%	6.64 +	-15.3	3.1	4.8	**1.5**	1.3		59%	10	23
TYPE	00 aa	3	18	0	167	8.25	1.77	($22)	28.0	336			37%	6.85 +	-55.6	3.1	5.7	**1.8**	1.5		53%	15	36
BURN Low	01 MIN	* 11	10	0	177	4.78	1.40	$6	23.2	287	348	219	32%	4.98	16.7	2.4	6.7	**2.8**	1.3	0.89	69%	57	114
ERA Potl -	02 MIN	13	8	0	180	4.25	1.39	$9	24.3	263	308	213	29%	4.50	20.6	3.5	6.2	**1.8**	1.3	0.83	74%	38	72
Support 5.98	1st Half	7	5	0	88	5.42	1.51	$1	24.4	291			32%	5.14	-3.7	3.2	5.4	**1.7**	1.2		66%	28	54
LIMA C	2nd Half	6	3	0	92	3.13	1.28	$8	24.2	233			26%	3.88 -	24.3	3.8	6.9	**1.8**	1.4		83%	47	89
Risk Very High	03 Proj	**9**	**9**	**0**	**160**	**4.89**	**1.45**	**$3**	**25.0**	**281**			**31%**	**4.98**	**10.2**	**3.2**	**6.2**	**2.0**	**1.4**	**--**	**70%**	**37**	**75**

Small signs of BPI life, but still too many holes to fix. Might have the makings of a superb RH setup man if anyone ever read these numbers.

Looper,Braden	Tm	W	L	Sv	IP	ERA	Br/IP	R$	BF/G	OBA	vLH	vRH	H%	xERA	RAR	Ctl	Dom	Cmd	hr/9	G/F	S%	BPV	BPX
RH Reliever	98 aaa	2	4	20	43	3.98	1.58	$12	4.4	308	667	125	39%	5.27 -	8.4	2.9	8.8	**3.0**	0.8	2.00	77%	84	163
AGE 28 Pre-Peak	99 FLA	3	3	0	83	3.80	1.53	$2	5.1	291	343	257	33%	4.79 -	19.5	3.4	5.4	**1.6**	0.8	1.89	77%	40	88
TYPE	00 FLA	5	1	2	67	4.43	1.59	$4	4.1	273	359	230	30%	4.42	10.8	4.8	3.9	**0.8**	0.4	3.04	71%	29	63
BURN none	01 FLA	3	3	3	71	3.55	1.31	$6	4.2	239	250	236	27%	3.80	17.3	3.8	6.6	**1.7**	1.0	1.69	76%	53	98
ERA Potl -	02 FLA	2	5	13	86	3.14	1.17	$10	4.5	231	278	191	26%	3.25	26.7	2.9	5.8	**2.0**	0.8	1.25	76%	59	122
Support 2.93	1st Half	0	3	0	42	4.27	1.40	($0)	4.7	261			29%	4.61	6.7	3.6	6.2	**1.7**	1.3		74%	37	77
LIMA D+	2nd Half	2	2	13	44	2.05	0.96	$17	4.4	201			23%	1.93	20.0	2.3	5.3	**2.4**	0.4		80%	84	173
Risk Low	03 Proj	**3**	**4**	**20**	**80**	**3.49**	**1.23**	**$19**	**4.3**	**244**			**28%**	**3.47**	**21.1**	**2.8**	**6.0**	**2.1**	**0.8**	**--**	**74%**	**63**	**126**

Does not have the dominance, or consistent command over LH hitters to be a successful long-term closer. But he could well post a few short runs of saves until either his BPIs catch up to him or he rediscovers 1998.

Lopez,Albie	Tm	W	L	Sv	IP	ERA	Br/IP	R$	BF/G	OBA	vLH	vRH	H%	xERA	RAR	Ctl	Dom	Cmd	hr/9	G/F	S%	BPV	BPX
RH Reliever	98 TAM	7	4	1	79	2.61	1.33	$12	6.2	246	227	262	29%	3.72 -	32.3	3.6	7.0	**1.9**	0.8	1.26	84%	65	138
AGE 31 Peak	99 TAM	3	2	1	64	4.64	1.41	$4	5.4	268	257	267	29%	4.54	10.6	3.4	5.2	**1.5**	1.1	1.79	70%	31	78
TYPE	00 TAM	11	13	2	185	4.13	1.45	$14	18.0	276	306	248	29%	4.79 -	44.1	3.4	4.7	**1.4**	1.2	1.76	75%	22	56
BURN none	01 2TM	9	19	0	205	4.82	1.47	$1	27.3	281	299	267	31%	4.89	16.4	3.3	6.0	**1.8**	1.1	1.27	69%	38	74
ERA Potl --	02 ATL	1	4	0	59	4.42	1.54	($2)	8.5	290	344	268	33%	5.19 -	8.2	3.5	6.4	**1.8**	1.1	1.57	74%	42	86
Support 2.75	1st Half	1	4	0	36	4.99	1.69	($2)	10.4	297			35%	4.90	2.3	4.5	6.0	**1.3**	0.2		68%	52	107
LIMA D	2nd Half	0	0	0	23	3.54	1.31	$1	6.5	279			29%	5.65 -	5.9	2.0	7.1	**3.6**	2.4		88%	46	95
Risk Very High	03 Proj	**3**	**5**	**0**	**80**	**4.28**	**1.45**	**$1**	**8.7**	**281**			**31%**	**5.06 -**	**12.6**	**3.2**	**6.1**	**1.9**	**1.4**	**G**	**75%**	**35**	**71**

Moving to the bullpen did nothing to help his BPIs, though three trips to the DL might have had something to do with that.

Lopez,Rodrigo	Tm	W	L	Sv	IP	ERA	Br/IP	R$	BF/G	OBA	vLH	vRH	H%	xERA	RAR	Ctl	Dom	Cmd	hr/9	G/F	S%	BPV	BPX
RH Starter	98	0	0	0	0	0.00	0.00																
AGE 27 Growth	99 aa	10	8	0	169	4.79	1.54	$5	26.9	298			34%	4.91	20.6	3.1	6.1	2.0	0.7		69%	51	118
TYPE	00 aaa	8	7	0	109	5.28	1.66	$1	25.0	305			36%	5.33	7.0	3.8	6.6	1.7	0.7		68%	48	113
BURN High	01 aaa	2	2	0	52	3.84	1.26	$3	19.8	256			27%	4.10	11.0	2.6	5.1	2.0	1.2		74%	39	75
ERA Potl -	02 BAL	15	9	0	196	3.58	1.19	$18	24.4	237	228	241	26%	3.42	40.0	2.8	6.2	2.2	1.1	1.01	74%	59	112
Support 6.22	1st Half	6	3	0	92	3.12	1.16	$9	22.1	231			26%	2.91	24.5	2.8	5.3	1.9	0.7		75%	59	112
LIMA D+	2nd Half	9	6	0	104	3.99	1.22	$9	26.9	243			27%	3.87	15.5	2.9	7.1	2.5	1.4		73%	60	113
Risk X HIGH	03 Proj	13	10	0	200	3.92	1.31	$14	25.6	260			29%	4.03	38.9	2.8	6.1	2.1	1.0	--	73%	53	109

The O's have the beginnings of a pitching talent here. His 2002 ERA was a bit understated due to a 26% hit rate, so that will rise a bit. But he has a good shot to keep it under the 4.00 level.

Lowe,Derek	Tm	W	L	Sv	IP	ERA	Br/IP	R$	BF/G	OBA	vLH	vRH	H%	xERA	RAR	Ctl	Dom	Cmd	hr/9	G/F	S%	BPV	BPX
RH Reliever	98 BOS	3	9	4	123	4.02	1.37	$7	8.4	266	292	245	31%	3.71	26.9	3.1	5.6	1.8	0.4	4.58	69%	63	135
AGE 29 Peak	99 BOS	6	3	15	109	2.64	1.00	$27	5.8	215	232	188	25%	2.30	47.1	2.1	6.6	3.2	0.6	3.17	75%	102	255
TYPE Contact	00 BOS	4	4	42	91	2.57	1.23	$37	5.1	259	268	247	32%	3.42 -	40.8	2.2	7.8	3.6	0.6	3.45	81%	108	279
BURN High	01 BOS	5	10	24	91	3.55	1.45	$18	5.9	286	317	250	35%	4.47 -	23.6	2.9	8.1	2.8	0.7	3.57	77%	85	170
ERA Potl +	02 BOS	21	8	0	219	2.59	0.98	$35	26.7	212	209	213	24%	2.04 +	73.8	2.0	5.2	2.6	0.5	3.46	75%	85	160
Support 6.84	1st Half	11	4	0	111	2.19	0.90	$21	26.5	191			22%	1.44 +	43.4	2.1	5.8	2.7	0.3		76%	99	187
LIMA D	2nd Half	10	4	0	108	3.00	1.06	$15	26.8	232			25%	2.66	30.4	1.8	4.7	2.5	0.7		74%	70	132
Risk Low	03 Proj	16	11	0	200	3.15	1.16	$25	9.3	244			28%	3.03	59.4	2.3	5.8	2.6	0.6	G	74%	78	158

The Baseball HQ forums buzzed all year with speculation about his hit rate falling from 35% to 24%. Given his drop in Dom, did the BOS defense improve all that much? And what are the odds of a repeat performance?

Lowe,Sean	Tm	W	L	Sv	IP	ERA	Br/IP	R$	BF/G	OBA	vLH	vRH	H%	xERA	RAR	Ctl	Dom	Cmd	hr/9	G/F	S%	BPV	BPX
RH Reliever	98 aaa	12	11	0	158	4.44	1.63	$4	24.8	297	500	364	33%	5.55 -	20.9	4.0	5.5	1.4	1.1	4.67	76%	24	46
AGE 32 Peak	99 CHW	4	1	0	95	3.69	1.43	$6	6.5	251	267	258	28%	4.21 -	27.7	4.4	5.9	1.3	0.9	1.40	77%	40	100
TYPE Power	00 CHW	4	1	0	70	5.51	1.67	($1)	6.4	283	345	241	32%	5.51	3.8	5.0	6.8	1.4	1.3	1.24	69%	29	76
BURN High	01 CHW	* 10	5	3	137	3.88	1.23	$14	12.1	259	281	233	28%	3.67	29.5	2.2	5.1	2.3	0.8	1.45	70%	57	115
ERA Potl +	02 2NL	* 6	4	0	101	6.15	1.78	($8)	8.5	323	348	294	38%	6.05	-9.3	3.9	7.2	1.8	0.8	1.93	65%	48	99
Support 4.54	1st Half	2	2	0	45	6.20	1.87	($5)	7.4	314			38%	6.48	-4.5	5.2	8.4	1.6	1.2		68%	41	83
LIMA B	2nd Half	4	2	0	56	6.11	1.71	($4)	9.6	331			39%	5.71	-4.9	2.9	6.3	2.2	0.5		62%	58	118
Risk X HIGH	03 Proj	3	3	0	60	4.95	1.43	$1	8.4	268			31%	4.41 +	4.1	3.6	6.5	1.8	0.9	G	66%	51	102

5-3, 5.81 ERA in 79 IP at PIT and COL. How bad was it? If he posted league average hit and strand rates, his ERA in 2002 would have been 4.37. So, expect some improvement, but not nearly draftable in COL.

Lyon,Brandon	Tm	W	L	Sv	IP	ERA	Br/IP	R$	BF/G	OBA	vLH	vRH	H%	xERA	RAR	Ctl	Dom	Cmd	hr/9	G/F	S%	BPV	BPX
RH Starter	98	0	0	0	0	0.00	0.00																
AGE 23 Growth	99	0	0	0	0	0.00	0.00																
TYPE Contact	00	0	0	0	0	0.00	0.00																
BURN none	01 TOR	* 15	7	0	190	4.50	1.27	$14	25.7	280	296	232	31%	4.34	25.1	1.6	5.6	3.5	1.1	1.14	67%	73	146
ERA Potl -	02 TOR	* 5	13	0	137	6.23	1.65	($9)	21.6	328	321	289	34%	6.03	-20.7	2.4	3.9	1.6	1.2	1.07	63%	12	22
Support 4.94	1st Half	2	5	0	72	5.73	1.51	($3)	18.8	304			31%	5.83	-6.1	2.5	4.1	1.7	1.7		66%	1	2
LIMA C+	2nd Half	3	8	0	65	6.78	1.80	($6)	25.6	353			38%	6.26 +	-14.6	2.4	3.7	1.6	0.6		60%	24	45
Risk High	03 Proj	4	6	0	80	4.61	1.40	$2	23.0	292			31%	4.72	8.1	2.1	4.6	2.2	1.0	--	69%	39	80

1-4, 6.53 ERA in 62 IP at TOR. Soft-tossing contact pitchers tend to have more erratic paths to success. Slight variations in control can have more profound impact on their command. At 23, there's a long road ahead.

Maddux,Greg	Tm	W	L	Sv	IP	ERA	Br/IP	R$	BF/G	OBA	vLH	vRH	H%	xERA	RAR	Ctl	Dom	Cmd	hr/9	G/F	S%	BPV	BPX
RH Starter	98 ATL	18	9	0	251	2.22	0.98	$40	28.8	221	219	220	27%	2.22	101.2	1.6	7.3	4.5	0.5	3.25	79%	136	245
AGE 37 Decline	99 ATL	19	9	0	219	3.58	1.35	$24	28.3	295	300	288	33%	4.28 -	57.8	1.5	5.6	3.7	0.7	2.22	75%	87	189
TYPE Contact	00 ATL	19	9	0	249	3.00	1.07	$38	28.4	243	269	214	29%	2.92	87.7	1.5	6.9	4.5	0.7	2.66	74%	122	269
BURN none	01 ATL	17	11	0	233	3.05	1.06	$31	27.3	251	264	243	29%	3.09	72.2	1.0	6.7	6.4	0.8	1.84	74%	156	290
ERA Potl - -	02 ATL	16	6	0	199	2.62	1.20	$29	24.1	257	232	276	29%	3.46 -	75.6	2.0	5.3	2.6	0.6	2.23	80%	72	147
Support 4.38	1st Half	7	2	0	89	3.03	1.23	$12	23.1	257			29%	3.43	29.0	2.3	5.2	2.2	0.5		76%	66	135
LIMA D+	2nd Half	9	4	0	110	2.29	1.17	$18	25.0	257			29%	3.49 -	46.6	1.8	5.5	3.0	0.7		84%	78	161
Risk Low	03 Proj	14	9	0	200	3.33	1.22	$22	26.7	259			29%	3.53	56.9	2.1	5.6	2.7	0.7	G	74%	73	147

At first glance, yet another solid season. At second glance, his lowest set of BPIs since... (drumroll, please)... 1-9-9-0. Five or 10 years ago, this would have been written off as a blip on the radar, but at age 37.....

Maduro,Calvin	Tm	W	L	Sv	IP	ERA	Br/IP	R$	BF/G	OBA	vLH	vRH	H%	xERA	RAR	Ctl	Dom	Cmd	hr/9	G/F	S%	BPV	BPX
RH Starter	98 aaa	12	9	0	177	6.41	1.65	($6)	28.9	313			34%	6.06	-23.1	3.3	5.2	1.6	1.4		63%	16	31
AGE 28 Pre-Peak	99 aaa	11	11	0	169	4.85	1.57	$5	26.2	301			33%	5.65 -	19.3	3.2	6.4	2.0	1.4		73%	34	78
TYPE	00 BAL	* 1	0	0	27	8.33	1.85	($4)	6.8	283	286	340	34%	5.69 +	-8.8	6.7	8.0	1.2	1.0	0.49	53%	42	108
BURN Low	01 BAL	* 7	13	0	160	4.78	1.37	$4	20.2	261	261	217	28%	4.46	15.1	3.4	5.2	1.5	1.2	1.05	68%	29	58
ERA Potl - -	02 BAL	2	5	0	56	5.63	1.54	($2)	20.8	288	243	310	29%	5.82	-3.9	3.5	4.7	1.3	1.9	0.89	69%	-5	-9
Support 4.61	1st Half	2	5	0	56	5.60	1.53	($2)	20.8	288			29%	5.79	-3.8	3.5	4.6	1.3	1.9		69%	-5	-9
LIMA F	2nd Half	0	0	0	-0	0.00	0.00																
Risk X HIGH	03 Proj	2	3	0	40	5.40	1.53	($1)	22.2	290			31%	5.52	-0.2	3.4	5.4	1.6	1.6	--	69%	16	32

Three straight years with elbow problems have laid waste to his BPIs and make him an extremely high risk.

Mahomes,Pat	Tm	W	L	Sv	IP	ERA	Br/IP	R$	BF/G	OBA	vLH	vRH	H%	xERA	RAR	Ctl	Dom	Cmd	hr/9	G/F	S%	BPV	BPX
RH Reliever	98 JPN	0	4	0	44	5.93	2.05	($7)	21.8	330			35%	7.20 -	-3.0	5.9	4.9	0.8	1.2		73%	-1	-2
AGE 32 Past	99 NYM	* 12	1	0	101	3.83	1.34	$14	9.6	232	211	189	25%	3.85	23.2	4.4	6.3	1.4	1.2	0.81	75%	42	92
TYPE Power	00 NYM	5	3	0	94	5.46	1.72	($3)	8.2	266	256	268	30%	5.58	2.2	6.3	7.3	1.2	1.4	0.68	71%	27	59
BURN High	01 TEX	7	6	0	107	5.71	1.59	($2)	8.6	276	254	300	29%	5.40	-3.3	4.6	5.1	1.1	1.4	1.00	67%	11	22
ERA Potl -	02 CHC	* 5	6	14	104	3.63	1.28	$17	7.3	248	308	276	28%	4.07	25.5	3.1	7.1	2.3	1.2	0.77	76%	59	122
Support 3.03	1st Half	5	2	1	53	4.41	1.21	$6	8.4	261			30%	3.88 +	7.5	1.9	7.1	3.8	1.0		66%	95	195
LIMA C+	2nd Half	0	4	13	51	2.82	1.35	$11	6.4	234			26%	4.26 -	18.0	4.4	7.1	1.6	1.4		87%	42	86
Risk Very High	03 Proj	2	2	0	40	4.50	1.48	$1	8.0	262			29%	4.85	5.1	4.3	6.5	1.5	1.4	F	74%	33	67

1-1, 3.94 ERA in 32 IP at CHC. Made great strides with his control, for at least half a season anyway. Given his history, we probably won't see that again.

Mairena,Oswaldo	Tm	W	L	Sv	IP	ERA	Br/IP	R$	BF/G	OBA	vLH	vRH	H%	xERA	RAR	Ctl	Dom	Cmd	hr/9	G/F	S%	BPV	BPX
LH Reliever	98	0	0	0	0	0.00	0.00																
AGE 27 Pre-Peak	99 aa	4	3	2	57	3.32	1.47	$6	5.1	258			30%	3.93 -	18.2	4.4	6.2	1.4	0.5		78%	55	128
TYPE	00 a/a	2	6	0	58	3.88	1.48	$2	4.8	288	333	667	32%	4.38 -	14.6	3.1	4.8	1.6	0.5	2.50	73%	45	107
BURN none	01 a/a	7	4	3	74	5.72	1.58	$2	6.3	311			36%	5.35	-2.9	2.8	6.8	2.4	0.9		64%	59	114
ERA Potl - - -	02 FLA	5	3	1	62	5.23	1.71	($1)	5.1	317	315	269	34%	6.26 -	1.9	3.6	5.4	1.5	1.3	0.93	72%	16	32
Support 4.81	1st Half	2	1	0	17	4.19	1.45	$2	4.2	281			29%	4.85 -	2.9	3.1	3.7	1.2	1.0		74%	14	28
LIMA D	2nd Half	3	2	1	45	5.62	1.81	($3)	5.6	329			36%	6.80 -	-1.0	3.8	6.0	1.6	1.4		72%	16	33
Risk Low	03 Proj	5	4	1	60	4.80	1.60	$2	5.2	301			34%	5.33 -	5.3	3.5	5.6	1.6	0.9	--	71%	35	70

Fooled by sub-4.00 ERAs in the minors, MLB personnel continue to throw good money after bad investments. BPIs are marginal, consistency is bad, growth is not apparent.

Mantei,Matt	Tm	W	L	Sv	IP	ERA	Br/IP	R$	BF/G	OBA	vLH	vRH	H%	xERA	RAR	Ctl	Dom	Cmd	hr/9	G/F	S%	BPV	BPX
RH Reliever	98 FLA	* 4	6	12	70	3.58	1.27	$12	5.1	198	200	205	29%	2.55 +	15.5	5.1	10.9	2.1	0.4	0.55	71%	114	205
AGE 29 Peak	99 2NL	1	3	32	65	2.77	1.35	$23	4.3	194	159	217	32%	2.92	24.2	6.1	13.7	2.3	0.7	0.63	82%	125	272
TYPE Power	00 ARI	1	1	17	45	4.59	1.46	$10	4.2	196	183	200	27%	3.41 +	6.3	7.0	10.6	1.5	0.8	0.47	69%	87	192
BURN none	01 ARI	0	0	2	7	2.57	1.43	$1	3.8	233	455	63	34%	5.39 -	2.6	5.1	15.4	3.0	2.6	0.33	100%	87	161
ERA Potl -	02 ARI	* 3	3	0	40	3.38	1.53	$3	4.0	276	250	260	34%	4.56 -	11.2	4.1	8.1	2.0	0.7	0.61	79%	70	144
Support 4.39	1st Half	1	1	0	15	0.60	1.39	$3	4.6	260			32%	3.38 -	9.8	3.6	6.6	1.8	0.0		95%	81	166
LIMA B+	2nd Half	2	2	0	25	5.06	1.61	($0)	3.8	285			36%	5.27	1.3	4.3	9.0	2.1	1.1		70%	63	130
Risk Moderate	03 Proj	3	4	6	60	3.60	1.47	$7	4.2	239			32%	3.78	14.9	5.3	9.8	1.9	0.6	F	76%	87	175

2-2, 4.85 ERA in 26 IP at ARI. Dominance is nowhere near it once was and it appears his overall skills have dropped down a notch. This may be temporary as he builds himself back, but we're a long ways from 1999.

Maroth,Mike

	Tm	W	L	Sv	IP	ERA	Br/IP	R$	BF/G	OBA	vLH	vRH	H%	xERA	RAR	Ctl	Dom	Cmd	hr/9	G/F	S%	BPV	BPX
LH Starter	98	0	0	0	0	0.00	0.00																
AGE 25 Growth	99	0	0	0	0	0.00	0.00																
TYPE Contact	00 aa	9	14	0	164	4.72	1.56	$4	27.2	304			33%	5.02	22.9	3.0	3.8	**1.3**	0.7		70%	25	59
BURN none	01 aaa	7	10	0	131	5.43	1.69	($5)	25.2	324			35%	5.72	-0.1	3.1	3.7	**1.2**	0.7		67%	17	33
ERA Potl +	02 DET	* 14	11	0	201	4.12	1.27	$13	26.3	259	252	284	29%	3.46 +	26.6	2.6	4.7	**1.8**	0.6	1.64	67%	52	98
Support 3.85	1st Half	9	3	0	102	3.52	1.19	$11	26.3	244			27%	3.10	21.7	2.6	4.7	**1.8**	0.6		71%	54	102
LIMA C+	2nd Half	5	8	0	99	4.74	1.35	$2	26.3	274			30%	3.83 +	4.9	2.6	4.6	**1.8**	0.5		64%	50	95
Risk High	03 Proj	**11**	**13**	**0**	**180**	**4.75**	**1.47**	**$5**	**26.3**	**291**			**32%**	**4.53**	**14.9**	**2.8**	**4.2**	**1.5**	**0.7**	**G**	**67%**	**34**	**69**

6-10, 4.50 ERA in 128 IP at DET. Extreme soft-tosser improved slightly in '02. Might see some limited success for two reasons: 1. He keeps the ball on the ground, and 2. He pitches in Comerica Park.

Marquis,Jason

	Tm	W	L	Sv	IP	ERA	Br/IP	R$	BF/G	OBA	vLH	vRH	H%	xERA	RAR	Ctl	Dom	Cmd	hr/9	G/F	S%	BPV	BPX
RH Reliever	98	0	0	0	0	0.00	0.00																
AGE 24 Growth	99 aa	3	4	0	55	5.07	1.51	$1	20.3	265			28%	4.76	4.6	4.4	5.1	**1.1**	1.1		68%	22	51
TYPE Power	00 ATL	* 5	5	0	111	5.59	1.58	($2)	15.6	292	226	281	32%	5.48	0.6	3.8	6.2	**1.6**	1.3	1.48	67%	29	63
BURN none	01 ATL	5	6	0	129	3.49	1.33	$7	14.4	237	220	243	27%	3.78	32.5	4.1	6.8	**1.7**	1.0	1.39	77%	54	101
ERA Potl -	02 ATL	8	10	0	119	4.99	1.54	$1	23.1	284	292	276	32%	5.43	7.5	3.8	6.7	**1.8**	1.4	1.10	71%	33	67
Support 5.67	1st Half	6	5	0	71	4.17	1.36	$6	25.4	259			29%	4.59	12.3	3.4	7.1	**2.1**	1.4		74%	48	98
LIMA C+	2nd Half	2	5	0	48	6.21	1.80	($5)	20.5	319			35%	6.69	-4.8	4.3	6.2	**1.4**	1.5		68%	14	28
Risk High	03 Proj	**9**	**8**	**0**	**140**	**4.44**	**1.50**	**$4**	**18.2**	**278**			**32%**	**4.95 -**	**19.1**	**3.7**	**7.0**	**1.9**	**1.2**	**--**	**73%**	**46**	**93**

Had a 3.23 ERA and 2.0 Cmd in May-July but struggled the rest of the year. HR/9 and G/F ratios show he was getting the ball up in the zone too much. Talent is here; 36/41 DOM/DIS show that consistency is the problem.

Marte,Damaso

	Tm	W	L	Sv	IP	ERA	Br/IP	R$	BF/G	OBA	vLH	vRH	H%	xERA	RAR	Ctl	Dom	Cmd	hr/9	G/F	S%	BPV	BPX
LH Reliever	98 aa	7	6	0	121	6.32	1.69	($7)	25.4	312			35%	5.98	-14.4	3.7	6.5	**1.8**	1.2		63%	33	64
AGE 28 Pre-Peak	99 aaa	3	3	0	73	6.78	1.88	($7)	11.3	313			33%	7.17	-10.6	5.3	6.3	**1.2**	2.0		68%	-4	-10
TYPE Power	00 aa	0	0	0	6	3.00	1.67	$0	6.9	293			30%	5.90 -	2.2	4.5	4.5	**1.0**	1.5		89%	-1	-1
BURN none	01 PIT	* 3	2	1	77	4.68	1.23	$3	6.4	257	310	223	30%	4.19	7.1	2.3	8.2	**3.5**	1.4	0.71	66%	84	156
ERA Potl +	02 CHW	1	1	10	60	2.85	1.03	$10	3.5	206	149	252	29%	2.30 +	18.1	2.7	10.8	**4.0**	0.8	1.27	75%	140	265
Support 4.03	1st Half	1	0	0	31	3.48	1.19	$2	3.4	222			30%	3.02	6.7	3.5	10.2	**2.9**	0.9		74%	107	202
LIMA A	2nd Half	0	1	10	29	2.17	0.86	$8	3.5	189			28%	1.53 +	11.4	1.9	11.5	**6.2**	0.6		78%	197	373
Risk X HIGH	03 Proj	**2**	**2**	**16**	**60**	**3.60**	**1.22**	**$12**	**5.2**	**245**			**33%**	**3.58**	**14.2**	**2.7**	**10.7**	**3.9**	**1.1**	**--**	**74%**	**121**	**247**

Excellent BPIs and ascent from the depths of 1999. He's got the talent and opportunity to close, and converted 83% of his opps, so guile may be okay too. But as a LHer, there is the risk of moving back to a situational role.

Martinez,Pedro

	Tm	W	L	Sv	IP	ERA	Br/IP	R$	BF/G	OBA	vLH	vRH	H%	xERA	RAR	Ctl	Dom	Cmd	hr/9	G/F	S%	BPV	BPX
RH Starter	98 BOS	19	7	0	233	2.89	1.09	$36	28.4	222	225	209	28%	3.00	86.2	2.6	9.7	**3.7**	1.0	1.08	79%	117	250
AGE 31 Peak	99 BOS	23	4	0	213	2.07	0.92	$50	26.4	210	221	187	34%	1.81	108.4	1.6	13.2	**8.5**	0.4	1.30	79%	259	648
TYPE Power	00 BOS	18	6	0	217	1.74	0.74	$54	27.4	173	150	184	25%	1.19 +	121.2	1.3	11.8	**8.9**	0.7	1.25	83%	256	665
BURN High	01 BOS	7	3	0	116	2.40	0.94	$20	24.9	204	216	176	32%	1.78 +	48.0	1.9	12.6	**6.5**	0.4	1.44	75%	215	431
ERA Potl +	02 BOS	20	4	0	199	2.26	0.92	$36	25.5	204	203	191	29%	1.85	75.8	1.8	10.8	**6.0**	0.6	1.16	78%	187	353
Support 6.23	1st Half	9	2	0	102	3.08	0.99	$15	25.0	217			30%	2.36 +	27.7	1.8	10.5	**5.7**	0.8		72%	170	321
LIMA C	2nd Half	11	2	0	97	1.39	0.86	$22	26.1	190			28%	1.31	48.1	1.8	11.2	**6.3**	0.4		86%	205	388
Risk Moderate	03 Proj	**18**	**5**	**0**	**200**	**2.61**	**0.99**	**$34**	**26.1**	**216**			**30%**	**2.23**	**73.9**	**1.9**	**10.6**	**5.5**	**0.6**	**--**	**76%**	**172**	**350**

You can keep bidding $35 if you want, but the trends are evident that $30 may be more prudent. Dom and Cmd are declining, but he could still well earn $40 -- it's just that the risk of not getting fair return on your $$ is greater.

Matthews,Mike

	Tm	W	L	Sv	IP	ERA	Br/IP	R$	BF/G	OBA	vLH	vRH	H%	xERA	RAR	Ctl	Dom	Cmd	hr/9	G/F	S%	BPV	BPX
LH Reliever	98 aaa	9	6	0	130	5.26	1.68	($2)	24.9	293			31%	5.72	2.9	4.6	5.2	**1.1**	1.2		71%	14	27
AGE 29 Peak	99 a/a	3	7	0	71	7.99	1.85	($9)	9.4	303			31%	6.51 +	-21.8	5.6	4.7	**0.8**	1.5		57%	-5	-13
TYPE Power	00 aaa	3	1	0	52	3.63	1.38	$5	24.9	206	227	476	25%	3.24	14.8	5.9	7.8	**1.3**	0.7	0.86	75%	68	160
BURN none	01 STL	3	4	1	89	3.24	1.20	$8	7.2	228	133	268	26%	3.46	25.4	3.3	7.3	**2.2**	1.1	0.77	78%	66	122
ERA Potl - -	02 MIL	2	1	0	45	4.00	1.60	$0	4.3	253	208	292	29%	4.75 -	8.8	5.8	6.8	**1.2**	1.0	1.00	78%	40	82
Support 4.53	1st Half	1	0	0	23	3.12	1.30	$2	3.6	226			25%	3.80 -	7.2	4.3	6.6	**1.5**	1.2		81%	47	96
LIMA C+	2nd Half	1	1	0	22	4.93	1.92	($2)	5.3	280			33%	5.75 -	1.5	7.4	7.0	**0.9**	0.8		75%	36	74
Risk X HIGH	03 Proj	**2**	**2**	**0**	**50**	**4.14**	**1.48**	**$1**	**6.1**	**250**			**29%**	**4.45**	**8.8**	**4.9**	**7.0**	**1.4**	**1.1**	**--**	**75%**	**45**	**91**

Just a few problems...
- Walks far too many batters
- Dominance is declining
- RHed batters kill him
- 2nd half fade
- Plays for Milwaukee

Mays,Joe

	Tm	W	L	Sv	IP	ERA	Br/IP	R$	BF/G	OBA	vLH	vRH	H%	xERA	RAR	Ctl	Dom	Cmd	hr/9	G/F	S%	BPV	BPX
RH Starter	98 aa	5	3	0	57	7.26	1.81	($4)	24.5	330			38%	6.17 +	-14.0	3.8	6.0	**1.6**	0.8		58%	35	67
AGE 27 Growth	99 MIN	6	11	0	171	4.37	1.44	$7	15.2	271	255	284	30%	4.79	34.4	3.5	6.1	**1.7**	1.3	1.54	73%	35	89
TYPE Contact	00 MIN	* 9	15	0	175	5.29	1.60	$2	23.3	299	300	298	34%	5.34	14.6	3.5	6.0	**1.7**	1.0	1.56	68%	36	93
BURN none	01 MIN	17	13	0	233	3.16	1.15	$28	27.9	238	237	233	25%	3.36	72.5	2.5	4.7	**1.9**	1.0	1.28	77%	47	95
ERA Potl - -	02 MIN	5	8	0	102	5.12	1.38	$1	24.4	286	275	315	29%	4.84	-0.2	2.3	3.6	**1.6**	1.3	1.18	66%	13	25
Support 4.34	1st Half	0	2	0	11	12.05	2.59	($4)	20.6	411			39%	11.89	-10.4	5.6	2.4	**0.4**	3.2		56%	******	******
LIMA C+	2nd Half	5	6	0	91	4.26	1.23	$5	25.1	266			27%	3.97	10.3	1.9	3.8	**2.0**	1.1		68%	34	64
Risk High	03 Proj	**10**	**12**	**0**	**180**	**4.60**	**1.34**	**$8**	**22.5**	**271**			**29%**	**4.30**	**18.5**	**2.6**	**4.6**	**1.8**	**1.1**	**--**	**68%**	**34**	**69**

Dominance trend points to a pitcher on the short path out the door. Returned well from elbow inflammation in the 2nd half, but 3.8 K/9 is not going to cut it. Consider him cheap roster filler with limited upside.

May,Darrell

	Tm	W	L	Sv	IP	ERA	Br/IP	R$	BF/G	OBA	vLH	vRH	H%	xERA	RAR	Ctl	Dom	Cmd	hr/9	G/F	S%	BPV	BPX
LH Starter	98 JPN	5	11	0	147	3.73	1.35	$7	24.1	254			29%	3.94	33.4	3.5	6.4	**1.8**	0.9		74%	56	109
AGE 30 Peak	99 JPN	7	7	0	122	3.91	1.19	$13	25.1	234			29%	3.59	29.2	3.0	9.2	**3.1**	1.3		72%	92	212
TYPE	00 JPN	12	7	0	159	2.89	1.04	$27	25.2	218			28%	2.87	61.2	2.3	9.6	**4.1**	1.1		78%	123	292
BURN none	01 JPN	10	8	0	159	4.13	1.29	$11	25.7	263			33%	4.36	27.5	2.5	9.5	**3.7**	1.4		73%	97	186
ERA Potl - -	02 KC	* 5	10	0	147	5.02	1.45	($2)	19.5	281	288	273	30%	5.27	1.8	3.1	6.4	**2.1**	1.7	0.78	71%	29	55
Support 4.25	1st Half	3	4	0	65	4.13	1.49	$1	20.5	278			31%	4.89 -	8.5	3.6	6.1	**1.7**	1.2		76%	34	64
LIMA C+	2nd Half	2	6	0	82	5.72	1.42	($3)	18.7	283			30%	5.58	-6.7	2.8	6.7	**2.4**	2.1		66%	27	51
Risk Low	03 Proj	**7**	**8**	**0**	**140**	**4.69**	**1.39**	**$4**	**22.3**	**271**			**30%**	**4.80**	**12.7**	**3.0**	**6.9**	**2.3**	**1.5**	**F**	**71%**	**45**	**93**

30-year-old globetrotter is not going to have a high ceiling, but his current BPIs show small signs of short-term success. Biggest problem is his HR rate, but as a flyball pitcher, that might not be correctable.

Meadows,Brian

	Tm	W	L	Sv	IP	ERA	Br/IP	R$	BF/G	OBA	vLH	vRH	H%	xERA	RAR	Ctl	Dom	Cmd	hr/9	G/F	S%	BPV	BPX
RH Starter	98 FLA	11	13	0	174	5.22	1.54	($0)	25.0	311	351	281	33%	5.45	0.3	2.4	4.5	**1.9**	1.0	1.32	67%	29	53
AGE 27 Growth	99 FLA	11	15	0	178	5.61	1.52	$1	25.5	299	313	291	30%	5.67	-1.6	2.9	3.6	**1.3**	1.6	1.09	67%	-3	-7
TYPE Contact	00 2TM	13	10	0	196	5.14	1.52	$6	26.4	297	309	287	30%	5.58	16.3	2.9	3.6	**1.2**	1.5	1.22	70%	-1	-2
BURN none	01 KC	* 7	11	0	155	7.32	1.73	($15)	25.7	352	350	352	36%	7.54	-38.0	1.8	4.7	**2.6**	2.0	1.03	61%	7	14
ERA Potl No chg	02 PIT	* 10	14	0	188	4.88	1.37	$5	23.7	291	267	248	32%	4.78	14.6	1.9	5.4	**2.8**	1.1	1.16	66%	56	115
Support 2.87	1st Half	5	6	0	85	5.49	1.46	($0)	21.9	300			34%	5.31	-0.4	2.2	6.7	**3.0**	1.3		64%	60	123
LIMA C+	2nd Half	5	8	0	103	4.37	1.30	$5	25.6	284			30%	4.33	15.0	1.7	4.3	**2.6**	0.9		68%	52	106
Risk Moderate	03 Proj	**8**	**10**	**0**	**140**	**4.56**	**1.33**	**$7**	**23.8**	**285**			**31%**	**4.52**	**16.7**	**1.9**	**5.1**	**2.7**	**1.0**	**--**	**68%**	**55**	**110**

1-6, 3.88 ERA in 62 IP at PIT. Has become stingier with the base on balls and is gaining a bit more dominance, yielding a nice little growth spurt. Others' expectations will be low so you might be able to nab him for $1.

Mecir,Jim

	Tm	W	L	Sv	IP	ERA	Br/IP	R$	BF/G	OBA	vLH	vRH	H%	xERA	RAR	Ctl	Dom	Cmd	hr/9	G/F	S%	BPV	BPX
RH Reliever	98 TAM	7	2	0	84	3.11	1.20	$12	5.1	223	227	224	28%	2.96	28.7	3.5	8.3	**2.3**	0.6	2.03	76%	90	191
AGE 33 Past	99 TAM	0	1	0	20	2.70	1.45	$1	5.1	210	214	200	27%	2.83	8.5	6.3	6.8	**1.1**	0.0	1.45	79%	76	191
TYPE Power	00 2AL	10	3	5	85	2.96	1.25	$19	5.6	226	204	245	28%	2.87	33.5	3.8	7.4	**1.9**	0.4	1.68	76%	82	214
BURN none	01 OAK	2	8	3	63	3.43	1.27	$6	4.9	233	195	267	30%	3.18	17.3	3.7	8.7	**2.3**	0.6	1.56	74%	93	186
ERA Potl No chg	02 OAK	6	4	1	67	4.30	1.45	$4	4.8	265	204	297	32%	4.06	7.2	3.9	7.1	**1.8**	0.7	1.53	71%	63	119
Support 6.12	1st Half	2	1	0	36	4.72	1.33	$1	4.7	233			27%	3.63 +	1.9	4.2	7.2	**1.7**	1.0		66%	58	109
LIMA B+	2nd Half	4	3	1	31	3.80	1.59	$3	5.0	299			36%	4.56 -	5.4	3.5	7.0	**2.0**	0.3		75%	71	133
Risk Low	03 Proj	**5**	**5**	**2**	**65**	**3.74**	**1.37**	**$6**	**5.0**	**253**			**31%**	**3.62**	**14.2**	**3.7**	**7.6**	**2.0**	**0.6**	**G**	**73%**	**76**	**155**

He's been having a tougher time with RHed batters and that has taken its toll on his other BPIs. Good guy to have around when you're down by 3 runs and the bases are loaded, but that's just not enough.

Mendoza,Ramiro

Mendoza,Ramiro	Yr	Tm	W	L	Sv	IP	ERA	Br/IP	R$	BF/G	OBA	vLH	vRH	H%	xERA	RAR	Ctl	Dom	Cmd	hr/9	G/F	S%	BPV	BPX
RH Reliever	98	NYY	10	2	1	130	3.25	1.24	$17	13.2	263	289	236	28%	3.59	41.9	2.1	3.9	1.9	0.6	2.13	75%	46	99
AGE 30 Peak	99	NYY	9	9	3	123	4.32	1.37	$12	9.9	289	283	285	32%	4.58	25.6	2.0	5.9	3.0	1.0	2.11	70%	66	166
TYPE Contact	00	NYY	7	4	0	65	4.28	1.32	$8	19.7	264	299	220	27%	4.36	14.3	2.8	4.1	1.5	1.2	1.21	71%	21	55
BURN none	01	NYY	8	4	6	100	3.77	1.12	$15	7.2	240	248	236	27%	3.13 +	23.0	2.1	6.3	3.0	0.8	1.71	68%	84	169
ERA Potl +	02	NYY	8	4	4	91	3.46	1.30	$10	6.2	284	261	286	32%	4.08 -	20.0	1.6	6.0	3.8	0.8	2.04	75%	91	171
Support 5.30	1st Half		5	2	1	50	3.24	1.30	$6	6.8	295			34%	4.51 -	12.5	1.1	6.7	6.2	1.1		80%	133	252
LIMA C+	2nd Half		3	2	3	41	3.73	1.29	$5	5.6	271			31%	3.55	7.5	2.2	5.3	2.4	0.4		71%	70	132
Risk Moderate	03	Proj	9	5	4	100	3.69	1.25	$13	7.4	268			30%	3.79	22.5	2.0	5.6	2.8	0.8	G	72%	70	142

Lots of good things...
- Solid BPIs and trends
- Keeps the ball on the ground
- Great team environment

Two bad things...
- Opposition BA spike
- 2nd half fade.

Mercado,Hector

Mercado,Hector	Yr	Tm	W	L	Sv	IP	ERA	Br/IP	R$	BF/G	OBA	vLH	vRH	H%	xERA	RAR	Ctl	Dom	Cmd	hr/9	G/F	S%	BPV	BPX
LH Reliever	98	NYM	0	0	0	0	0.00	0.00																
AGE 29 Pre-Peak	99	aaa	0	0	0	6	1.50	1.00	$1	11.8	191			21%	1.49	3.4	3.0	3.0	1.0	0.0		83%	56	129
TYPE Power	00	aaa	1	5	2	77	3.62	1.64	$2	7.5	267	252	233	33%	4.23 -	22.0	5.5	6.8	1.2	0.2	1.21	77%	61	145
BURN none	01	CIN	* 4	2	1	66	3.68	1.61	$2	4.4	273	287	252	36%	4.79 -	14.9	4.9	9.5	1.9	0.8	1.02	79%	74	137
ERA Potl +	02	PHI	* 5	3	3	72	3.50	1.36	$8	5.4	225	125	252	30%	3.28	19.0	4.9	9.5	1.9	0.5	1.45	74%	93	191
Support 2.77	1st Half		2	2	1	27	5.96	1.54	($0)	4.5	274			36%	4.56 +	-1.8	4.3	9.3	2.2	0.7		60%	81	166
LIMA A	2nd Half		3	1	2	45	2.00	1.25	$8	6.2	192			26%	2.50 -	20.8	5.2	9.6	1.8	0.4		85%	101	208
Risk High	03	Proj	2	2	0	40	3.83	1.45	$2	5.1	252			32%	4.00	8.7	4.5	9.0	2.0	0.7	--	75%	80	162

2-2, 4.62 ERA in 39 IP at PHI. Fared well in the minors but has been unable to take those sub-4.00 ERAs to the bigs. Posted a 3.55 in 3 starts (only 12.2 IP), with 2.1 Cmd. Could advance if he cut down on BBs.

Mercker,Kent

Mercker,Kent	Yr	Tm	W	L	Sv	IP	ERA	Br/IP	R$	BF/G	OBA	vLH	vRH	H%	xERA	RAR	Ctl	Dom	Cmd	hr/9	G/F	S%	BPV	BPX
LH Reliever	98	STL	11	11	0	161	5.08	1.56	$0	23.3	304	324	308	33%	5.01	3.3	3.0	4.0	1.4	0.6	1.17	67%	28	51
AGE 35 Decline	99	2TM	8	5	0	129	4.81	1.64	$2	19.6	289	304	213	32%	5.41 -	15.3	4.5	5.7	1.3	1.1	1.11	73%	24	56
TYPE Power	00	ANA	1	3	0	48	6.55	1.79	($4)	10.8	296	235	324	30%	6.92	-4.1	5.4	5.6	1.0	2.2	0.69	69%	-16	-42
BURN none	01		0	0	0	0	0.00	0.00																
ERA Potl ---	02	COL	3	1	0	45	6.97	1.81	($5)	3.6	313	209	350	32%	8.02 -	-9.1	4.8	7.4	1.5	3.0	0.97	70%	-21	-42
Support 5.11	1st Half		1	0	0	24	4.13	1.46	$1	3.3	262			33%	4.25	4.3	4.1	9.0	2.2	0.8		73%	80	164
LIMA F	2nd Half		2	1	0	21	10.19	2.22	($6)	3.9	363			31%	12.28 -	-13.4	5.5	5.5	1.0	5.5		68%	************	
Risk High	03	Proj	2	2	0	40	6.08	1.68	($3)	5.6	290			30%	7.02 -	-3.3	4.7	7.2	1.5	2.7	--	73%	-9	-18

Had a 3.64 ERA on Aug 16, then posted an 11.30 mark over 19 games down the stretch, which might have been the remnants of his hand injury. Still, it's a marginal skills pitcher in COL. End of story.

Mesa,Jose

Mesa,Jose	Yr	Tm	W	L	Sv	IP	ERA	Br/IP	R$	BF/G	OBA	vLH	vRH	H%	xERA	RAR	Ctl	Dom	Cmd	hr/9	G/F	S%	BPV	BPX
RH Reliever	98	2TM	8	7	1	84	4.60	1.53	$5	4.9	277	338	223	32%	4.72	9.4	4.1	6.7	1.7	0.9	1.74	71%	49	96
AGE 36 Decline	99	SEA	3	6	33	68	5.03	1.82	$16	4.7	305	331	271	33%	6.44 -	7.7	5.3	5.6	1.1	1.5	1.17	76%	6	15
TYPE Power	00	SEA	4	6	1	80	5.39	1.62	$0	5.5	282	257	300	35%	5.32	5.6	4.6	9.4	2.0	1.2	0.88	69%	61	159
BURN none	01	PHI	3	3	42	69	2.34	1.23	$32	4.0	250	236	255	31%	3.26 -	28.0	2.6	7.7	3.0	0.5	1.30	83%	97	181
ERA Potl No chg	02	PHI	4	6	45	75	3.00	1.39	$36	4.4	235	225	237	29%	3.59 -	24.7	4.7	7.7	1.6	0.6	1.06	80%	71	145
Support 1.31	1st Half		2	4	20	38	2.36	1.20	$19	4.1	218			28%	2.79	15.9	3.8	8.0	2.1	0.5		82%	90	185
LIMA F	2nd Half		2	2	25	37	3.67	1.58	$17	4.6	252			30%	4.42 -	8.8	5.6	7.3	1.3	0.7		78%	54	111
Risk Moderate	03	Proj	4	5	34	70	3.47	1.46	$25	4.5	253			30%	4.14 -	18.6	4.5	7.3	1.6	0.8	--	78%	59	119

A troubling season. Walks were up and he posted his lowest G/F ratio since the '00 disaster. His saves conversions dropped from 90% to 83%. Note also that the higher his BF/G, the worse he does. Warning signs here.

Middlebrook,Jason

Middlebrook,Jason	Yr	Tm	W	L	Sv	IP	ERA	Br/IP	R$	BF/G	OBA	vLH	vRH	H%	xERA	RAR	Ctl	Dom	Cmd	hr/9	G/F	S%	BPV	BPX
RH Reliever	98		0	0	0	0	0.00	0.00																
AGE 27 Pre-Peak	99	aa	4	6	0	63	9.14	1.87	($9)	23.2	329			35%	6.78 +	-29.1	4.4	4.4	1.0	1.3		50%	-2	-4
TYPE	00	a/a	5	14	0	120	7.58	1.78	($12)	22.6	320			34%	6.33 +	-29.2	4.1	4.3	1.0	1.2		57%	2	6
BURN none	01	aaa	12	5	0	162	3.50	1.34	$14	23.8	271	205	310	30%	4.04 -	41.7	2.6	5.3	2.0	0.7	1.12	75%	53	102
ERA Potl ++++	02	2NL	* 6	9	0	111	5.27	1.32	$2	15.7	260	235	237	31%	3.81 +	2.9	3.0	7.0	2.3	0.6	1.48	59%	74	152
Support 3.33	1st Half		3	7	0	68	5.67	1.47	($2)	15.7	275			33%	4.39 +	-2.0	3.6	6.9	1.9	0.7		60%	62	127
LIMA B	2nd Half		3	2	0	43	4.62	1.10	$4	15.7	234			28%	2.88 +	4.8	2.1	7.1	3.4	0.6		57%	103	212
Risk X HIGH	03	Proj	8	7	0	120	4.35	1.36	$7	18.3	268			32%	4.01	17.7	2.9	7.0	2.4	0.7	--	68%	73	147

2-3, 4.76 in 51 IP at SD and NYM. Between BPI growth, new home at Shea and ungodly 59% strand rate, this is one pitcher who could take a big step up. However, fared better in the pen than as a starter, so be careful.

Miller,Justin

Miller,Justin	Yr	Tm	W	L	Sv	IP	ERA	Br/IP	R$	BF/G	OBA	vLH	vRH	H%	xERA	RAR	Ctl	Dom	Cmd	hr/9	G/F	S%	BPV	BPX
RH Starter	98		0	0	0	0	0.00	0.00																
AGE 25 Growth	99		0	0	0	0	0.00	0.00																
TYPE Power	00	a/a	9	5	0	142	3.99	1.24	$14	21.9	238			28%	3.29 +	33.6	3.2	6.3	2.0	0.7		68%	66	156
BURN none	01	aaa	7	10	0	165	5.07	1.50	($1)	25.2	287			32%	5.27	7.7	3.3	6.3	1.9	1.4		70%	34	65
ERA Potl -	02	TOR	* 12	7	0	146	4.43	1.53	$5	19.7	255	296	240	29%	4.19	13.2	5.0	5.7	1.1	0.7	1.34	72%	40	76
Support 5.72	1st Half		4	5	0	64	5.74	1.79	($4)	17.8	273			31%	5.19 +	-5.4	6.6	6.3	1.0	0.8		68%	33	63
LIMA C+	2nd Half		8	2	0	82	3.41	1.32	$8	21.7	240			27%	3.41	18.6	3.8	5.3	1.4	0.7		75%	48	90
Risk Moderate	03	Proj	7	9	0	140	4.56	1.46	$3	21.9	263			29%	4.41	15.1	4.1	6.0	1.5	1.0	--	71%	40	81

9-5, 5.56 ERA in 102 IP at TOR. His performance has eroded at each level he's risen to. Plus, look at these brutal ERA splits:

Day - 3.59 Night - 7.24
Home - 3.97 Away - 7.49
Turf - 4.63 Grass - 7.71

Miller,Wade

Miller,Wade	Yr	Tm	W	L	Sv	IP	ERA	Br/IP	R$	BF/G	OBA	vLH	vRH	H%	xERA	RAR	Ctl	Dom	Cmd	hr/9	G/F	S%	BPV	BPX
RH Starter	98	aa	5	0	0	62	2.32	1.24	$9	25.8	226			25%	3.33 -	25.8	3.8	5.7	1.5	0.9		86%	49	96
AGE 26 Growth	99	aaa	11	9	0	162	4.94	1.46	$7	27.3	272			31%	4.43 +	16.3	3.7	6.4	1.7	0.8		67%	50	117
TYPE Power	00	HOU	* 10	11	0	210	5.01	1.43	$5	28.6	269	309	222	31%	4.43 +	17.4	3.6	6.8	1.9	0.9	1.39	66%	54	119
BURN Low	01	HOU	16	8	0	212	3.40	1.22	$22	27.4	234	216	250	27%	3.78	55.9	3.2	7.8	2.4	1.3	1.37	79%	66	122
ERA Potl +	02	HOU	* 15	4	0	172	3.30	1.31	$20	26.0	252	254	245	31%	3.74	49.8	3.3	8.0	2.4	0.7	1.24	77%	81	166
Support 6.12	1st Half		3	3	0	58	5.28	1.50	($1)	23.3	288			33%	5.20	1.4	3.3	7.4	2.3	1.2		67%	53	109
LIMA C	2nd Half		12	1	0	114	2.29	1.22	$21	27.8	232			29%	3.00 -	48.4	3.3	8.2	2.5	0.5		83%	96	196
Risk Moderate	03	Proj	19	7	0	200	3.02	1.25	$28	26.1	242			30%	3.49	65.3	3.2	8.2	2.6	0.8	--	79%	86	173

An incredible 2nd half, posting a 67/0 DOM/DIS split, and even fared well in Minute Maid. He's at a good point in his career to take another step up.

Millwood,Kevin

Millwood,Kevin	Yr	Tm	W	L	Sv	IP	ERA	Br/IP	R$	BF/G	OBA	vLH	vRH	H%	xERA	RAR	Ctl	Dom	Cmd	hr/9	G/F	S%	BPV	BPX
RH Starter	98	ATL	17	8	0	174	4.08	1.33	$16	23.9	263	277	243	32%	4.06	26.8	2.9	8.4	2.9	0.9	1.08	71%	86	155
AGE 28 Pre-Peak	99	ATL	18	7	0	228	2.68	1.00	$39	27.1	207	230	175	25%	2.47	87.4	2.3	8.1	3.5	0.9	0.88	78%	107	232
TYPE	00	ATL	10	13	0	212	4.67	1.30	$11	24.9	263	289	235	30%	4.15 +	27.4	2.6	7.1	2.7	1.1	0.71	66%	69	152
BURN Very High	01	ATL	7	7	0	121	4.31	1.33	$6	24.5	262	282	244	28%	4.60	17.1	3.0	6.2	2.1	1.5	0.88	73%	40	73
ERA Potl +	02	ATL	18	8	0	217	3.24	1.16	$30	25.3	233	246	215	28%	3.05	64.6	2.7	7.4	2.7	0.7	1.22	74%	90	185
Support 5.23	1st Half		5	5	0	105	3.85	1.22	$8	24.2	254			30%	3.66	22.7	2.3	6.9	3.0	0.9		70%	83	171
LIMA C	2nd Half		13	3	0	112	2.66	1.10	$23	26.4	212			27%	2.47	42.0	3.1	7.8	2.6	0.5		77%	98	202
Risk High	03	Proj	19	7	0	200	3.06	1.14	$31	24.6	234			28%	3.02	64.1	2.5	7.4	3.0	0.7	--	75%	94	190

The difference in 2002... He cut his HR rate in half, thanks to keeping the ball on the ground more. This is another one who will likely join the ranks of the Elite in 2003. Maddux, who?

Milton,Eric

Milton,Eric	Yr	Tm	W	L	Sv	IP	ERA	Br/IP	R$	BF/G	OBA	vLH	vRH	H%	xERA	RAR	Ctl	Dom	Cmd	hr/9	G/F	S%	BPV	BPX
LH Starter	98	MIN	8	14	0	172	5.65	1.54	($2)	24.0	287	361	259	31%	5.32	0.2	3.7	5.6	1.5	1.3	0.52	65%	24	52
AGE 27 Pre-Peak	99	MIN	7	11	0	206	4.50	1.23	$13	25.1	246	253	240	28%	3.88 +	37.8	2.8	7.1	2.6	1.2	0.58	67%	66	166
TYPE	00	MIN	13	10	0	200	4.86	1.25	$17	25.2	267	242	265	30%	4.49	28.2	2.0	7.2	3.6	1.6	0.62	66%	74	192
BURN Low	01	MIN	15	7	0	220	4.33	1.29	$15	26.5	263	246	259	29%	4.46	34.0	2.5	6.4	2.6	1.4	0.59	71%	52	104
ERA Potl +++	02	MIN	13	9	0	171	4.84	1.19	$11	24.2	264	306	249	29%	3.95 +	6.1	1.6	6.4	4.0	1.3	0.67	62%	87	165
Support 4.68	1st Half		9	6	0	106	5.34	1.27	$5	24.7	277			30%	4.29 +	-3.3	1.7	5.8	3.4	1.2		60%	70	132
LIMA B	2nd Half		4	3	0	65	4.03	1.05	$6	23.4	241			27%	3.41 +	9.4	1.4	7.4	5.3	1.4		67%	121	228
Risk Low	03	Proj	13	9	0	200	4.14	1.21	$16	25.0	261			29%	4.03	32.9	1.9	7.0	3.7	1.3	F	70%	84	171

Assemble 1999's OppBA, 1999's hit rate, 2002's control, 2000's Dom, 1999's HR rate and 2001's strand rate... and you'd get a perennial All Star. The pieces are there for a major step up. It could come in 2003.

Mlicki,Dave		Tm	W	L	Sv	IP	ERA	Br/IP	R$	BF/G	OBA	vLH	vRH	H%	xERA	RAR	Ctl	Dom	Cmd	hr/9	G/F	S%	BPV	BPX
RH Reliever	98	2NL	8	7	0	181	4.57	1.39	$4	26.0	269	297	238	30%	4.52	16.1	3.1	5.8	1.9	1.1	1.29	70%	41	74
AGE 34 Decline	99	DET	14	13	0	199	4.61	1.46	$12	26.4	281	271	280	31%	4.87	33.5	3.3	5.4	1.7	1.1	1.15	71%	33	82
TYPE	00	DET	6	11	0	119	5.59	1.57	$0	22.3	299	281	301	31%	5.53	5.1	3.3	4.3	1.3	1.3	1.46	66%	10	25
BURN none	01	2TM	11	11	0	167	6.19	1.66	($7)	22.5	301	321	291	31%	6.47	-17.2	4.0	5.2	1.3	2.0	0.98	68%	-6	-12
ERA Potl -	02	HOU *	5	11	0	98	5.05	1.54	($1)	17.5	292	351	245	33%	5.17	5.4	3.4	5.9	1.7	1.0	1.05	69%	38	78
Support 4.08	1st Half		3	6	0	55	3.92	1.36	$3	23.6	265			28%	4.46 -	11.4	3.1	5.2	1.7	1.1		75%	34	71
LIMA F	2nd Half		2	5	0	43	6.50	1.77	($5)	13.4	324			38%	6.08	-6.0	3.8	6.7	1.8	0.8		63%	43	87
Risk High	03	Proj	4	7	0	80	5.63	1.60	($3)	15.1	299			33%	5.60	-1.8	3.6	5.6	1.6	1.2	--	67%	25	50

4-10, 5.34 ERA in 86 IP at HOU. If you were to look hard enough for positive signs, you will find a few small ones. But since he will never be a 20-game winner or have an ERA under 4.00, it's not worth the effort to look.

Moehler,Brian		Tm	W	L	Sv	IP	ERA	Br/IP	R$	BF/G	OBA	vLH	vRH	H%	xERA	RAR	Ctl	Dom	Cmd	hr/9	G/F	S%	BPV	BPX
RH Starter	98	DET	14	13	0	221	3.91	1.25	$20	27.9	261	267	252	28%	4.14	51.8	2.3	5.0	2.2	1.2	1.64	73%	42	90
AGE 31 Peak	99	DET	10	16	0	196	5.05	1.47	$6	26.9	293	293	294	32%	4.96	21.5	2.7	4.9	1.8	1.0	1.58	67%	33	83
TYPE Contact	00	DET	12	9	0	178	4.50	1.47	$11	27.0	307	285	324	34%	5.14 -	33.7	2.0	5.2	2.6	1.0	1.79	71%	49	126
BURN none	01	DET *	0	2	0	18	5.00	1.28	($0)	25.2	283			29%	4.33 +	1.2	1.5	3.5	2.3	1.0	1.20	62%	38	77
ERA Potl - -	02	2TM *	5	6	0	87	5.38	1.49	$0	22.6	317	296	308	32%	5.79	-1.3	1.7	3.7	2.3	1.4	1.29	67%	18	35
Support 6.14	1st Half		2	1	0	24	6.75	1.63	($0)	27.3	347			34%	6.34	-4.8	1.1	1.9	1.7	1.1		58%	-2	-4
LIMA D	2nd Half		3	5	0	63	4.86	1.44	$1	21.2	305			31%	5.58 -	3.5	1.9	4.4	2.4	1.6		71%	23	46
Risk Moderate	03	Proj	5	8	0	120	5.10	1.48	($0)	22.0	309			32%	5.38	5.1	2.0	4.2	2.2	1.2	--	68%	28	56

3-5, 4.86 ERA in 63 IP at DET and CIN. Serves 'em up straight over the plate. Batters don't bother waiting on the ball because they know the hits will be plentiful. Anything positive coming out of this is a fluke.

Morgan,Mike		Tm	W	L	Sv	IP	ERA	Br/IP	R$	BF/G	OBA	vLH	vRH	H%	xERA	RAR	Ctl	Dom	Cmd	hr/9	G/F	S%	BPV	BPX
RH Reliever	98	CHC	4	3	0	120	4.19	1.47	$1	23.0	289	286	353	30%	5.45 -	16.8	2.9	4.5	1.5	1.6	2.20	78%	9	17
AGE 43 Decline	99	TEX	13	10	0	140	6.24	1.66	$1	18.8	318	318	329	32%	6.39	-6.8	3.1	3.9	1.3	1.6	2.19	65%	-7	-16
TYPE Contact	00	ARI	5	5	5	101	4.89	1.61	$3	7.6	301	273	331	33%	5.32	10.0	3.6	5.0	1.4	0.9	2.56	71%	27	60
BURN none	01	ARI	1	0	0	38	4.26	1.63	($1)	5.6	296	208	354	34%	4.90 -	5.6	4.0	5.7	1.4	0.5	2.06	73%	45	84
ERA Potl - - -	02	ARI	1	1	0	37	4.86	1.43	($0)	5.2	297	328	262	29%	5.64 -	2.9	2.2	3.6	1.7	1.7	1.45	72%	1	3
Support 3.97	1st Half		1	1	0	32	5.59	1.46	($1)	5.0	295			28%	5.92	-0.6	2.5	3.4	1.3	2.0		68%	-15	-30
LIMA F	2nd Half		0	0	0	5	0.00	1.25	$1	6.7	307			36%	3.72 -	3.5	0.0	5.6		0.0		100%	27	56
Risk High	03	Proj	2	1	0	35	5.14	1.54	($0)	5.0	299			31%	5.51	1.5	3.1	4.4	1.4	1.3	--	69%	13	26

In retrospect, many players find that there's really nothing wrong with retirement. The millions saved tend to get spent a bit slower, the food is better, and you don't have to shower with naked men all the time.

Morris,Matt		Tm	W	L	Sv	IP	ERA	Br/IP	R$	BF/G	OBA	vLH	vRH	H%	xERA	RAR	Ctl	Dom	Cmd	hr/9	G/F	S%	BPV	BPX
RH Starter	98	STL *	8	5	1	131	2.74	1.29	$14	25.1	250	234	251	30%	3.50 -	43.8	3.2	6.8	2.2	0.6	1.62	81%	73	131
AGE 28 Pre-Peak	99		0	0	0	0	0.00	0.00																
TYPE	00	STL	3	3	4	53	3.57	1.32	$7	7.3	262	255	266	30%	3.65	14.6	2.9	5.8	2.0	0.5	1.31	73%	64	141
BURN none	01	STL	22	8	0	216	3.17	1.26	$28	26.6	263	237	286	33%	3.54	63.7	2.2	7.7	3.4	0.5	2.01	76%	104	193
ERA Potl +	02	STL	17	9	0	210	3.43	1.30	$22	27.7	262	267	255	32%	3.82	57.1	2.7	7.3	2.7	0.7	1.65	75%	82	169
Support 5.31	1st Half		10	5	0	121	3.27	1.26	$15	28.1	245			30%	3.46	35.4	3.0	7.9	2.6	0.7		76%	87	179
LIMA C	2nd Half		7	4	0	89	3.64	1.37	$8	27.3	283			33%	4.31 -	21.7	2.3	6.6	2.8	0.7		75%	76	156
Risk Moderate	03	Proj	16	9	0	200	3.33	1.29	$22	27.2	265			32%	3.74	56.9	2.5	7.0	2.8	0.6	G	75%	85	171

Not quite as dominant as 2001, but those were lofty levels to maintain. Still, these are solid BPIs with many good years yet ahead.

Moss,Damian		Tm	W	L	Sv	IP	ERA	Br/IP	R$	BF/G	OBA	vLH	vRH	H%	xERA	RAR	Ctl	Dom	Cmd	hr/9	G/F	S%	BPV	BPX
LH Starter	98		0	0	0	0	0.00	0.00																
AGE 26 Growth	99	aa	1	3	0	32	9.78	2.33	($9)	24.1	377			41%	9.15 +	-17.6	5.6	5.3	1.0	1.7		58%	-19	-44
TYPE Power	00	aaa	9	6	0	160	3.82	1.59	$8	24.9	248			28%	4.43 -	41.6	5.9	6.1	1.0	0.8		78%	38	90
BURN none	01	a/a	5	5	0	107	4.12	1.42	$4	18.6	254			30%	4.58	18.6	4.1	8.2	2.0	1.3	0.91	76%	54	104
ERA Potl - -	02	ATL	12	6	0	179	3.42	1.28	$18	22.8	217	165	232	23%	3.50	48.9	4.5	5.6	1.2	1.0	1.02	77%	41	84
Support 4.88	1st Half		4	2	0	80	3.15	1.20	$9	22.0	193			22%	2.80	24.7	4.7	6.2	1.3	0.8		76%	57	118
LIMA D	2nd Half		8	4	0	99	3.64	1.34	$9	23.4	235			25%	4.06	24.2	4.3	5.1	1.2	1.2		78%	28	57
Risk Very High	03	Proj	11	11	0	180	4.30	1.41	$8	25.1	245			27%	4.28	27.8	4.5	6.3	1.4	1.2	--	73%	38	77

Smoke and mirrors. With poor command and a 23% hit rate that's headed north, he will be hard-pressed to post an ERA much below 4.00 in 2003.

Mota,Guillermo		Tm	W	L	Sv	IP	ERA	Br/IP	R$	BF/G	OBA	vLH	vRH	H%	xERA	RAR	Ctl	Dom	Cmd	hr/9	G/F	S%	BPV	BPX
RH Reliever	98		0	0	0	0	0.00	0.00																
AGE 29 Peak	99	MON *	4	4	5	74	2.80	1.39	$10	4.9	259	250	262	29%	3.85 -	27.3	3.6	5.1	1.4	0.6	1.33	82%	45	98
TYPE Power	00	MON *	5	6	7	93	3.87	1.38	$11	6.2	243	244	246	27%	3.79	21.9	4.3	5.1	1.2	0.8	0.86	73%	39	87
BURN High	01	MON	1	3	0	49	5.30	1.40	($1)	4.0	269	310	248	28%	5.03	0.4	3.3	5.7	1.7	1.6	0.98	67%	22	41
ERA Potl + +	02	LA *	2	6	1	96	3.74	1.21	$6	6.3	230	188	213	28%	2.95 +	22.1	3.3	7.4	2.3	0.5	0.96	68%	87	178
Support 3.56	1st Half		2	1	1	47	2.86	1.10	$7	7.0	231			30%	2.43	16.4	2.3	8.2	3.6	0.2		73%	128	262
LIMA B+	2nd Half		0	5	0	49	4.59	1.31	($0)	5.8	229			27%	3.44 +	5.7	4.2	6.6	1.6	0.7		65%	60	123
Risk X HIGH	03	Proj	2	4	1	60	3.90	1.25	$4	5.2	239			28%	3.55	12.5	3.3	7.1	2.1	0.9	--	71%	67	136

1-3, 4.20 ERA in 60 IP at LA. Likes LA, posting a home ERA 1.50 runs lower than on the road. Still, his BPIs do support a sub-4.00 ERA. There are some good things here, but Chavez Ravine does help.

Moyer,Jamie		Tm	W	L	Sv	IP	ERA	Br/IP	R$	BF/G	OBA	vLH	vRH	H%	xERA	RAR	Ctl	Dom	Cmd	hr/9	G/F	S%	BPV	BPX
LH Starter	98	SEA	15	9	0	234	3.54	1.18	$26	28.2	262	258	255	30%	3.65	66.4	1.6	6.1	3.8	0.9	1.34	73%	92	196
AGE 40 Decline	99	SEA	14	8	0	228	3.87	1.24	$23	29.6	268	234	278	30%	3.92	61.2	1.9	5.4	2.9	0.9	1.07	71%	67	167
TYPE Contact	00	SEA	13	10	0	154	5.49	1.47	$8	26.0	285	290	278	31%	5.05	8.6	3.1	5.7	1.8	1.3	1.16	65%	33	85
BURN none	01	SEA	20	6	0	209	3.44	1.10	$29	25.5	241	255	234	26%	3.33	57.2	1.9	5.1	2.7	1.0	0.90	73%	63	127
ERA Potl +	02	SEA	13	8	0	230	3.33	1.08	$22	27.0	234	276	206	25%	3.13	54.8	2.0	5.8	2.9	1.1	0.84	74%	72	135
Support 4.80	1st Half		7	3	0	113	3.26	1.05	$12	26.4	226			24%	2.98	27.9	2.1	5.0	2.4	1.1		74%	57	109
LIMA F	2nd Half		6	5	0	117	3.39	1.10	$10	27.7	242			27%	3.27	26.9	1.8	6.5	3.5	1.1		74%	87	164
Risk Moderate	03	Proj	12	10	0	200	4.01	1.20	$16	26.5	252			26%	3.82	36.5	2.2	5.0	2.3	1.2	--	71%	46	93

Another anomaly. Skills are supposed to erode as one gets older. Stamina is supposed to decline. Heck, I know I can't go 200 innings anymore. And yet, there I go, projecting another 200 IP season, fool that I am.

Mulder,Mark		Tm	W	L	Sv	IP	ERA	Br/IP	R$	BF/G	OBA	vLH	vRH	H%	xERA	RAR	Ctl	Dom	Cmd	hr/9	G/F	S%	BPV	BPX
LH Starter	98		0	0	0	0	0.00	0.00																
AGE 25 Growth	99	aaa	6	7	0	128	4.92	1.55	$2	26.0	319			35%	5.44 -	13.3	2.0	5.0	2.4	0.9		69%	45	105
TYPE	00	OAK	9	10	0	154	5.44	1.69	($0)	26.3	305	368	288	33%	5.92	9.8	4.0	5.1	1.3	1.3	1.68	70%	13	34
BURN Low	01	OAK	21	8	0	229	3.46	1.16	$29	27.5	[illegible]	[illegible]	[illegible]	[illegible]	[illegible]	[illegible]	[illegible]	[illegible]	3.0	0.6	1.93	71%	85	171
ERA Potl +	02	OAK	19	7	0	207	3.48	1.14	$24	28.0	238	244	228	27%	3.16	45.1	2.4	6.9	2.9	0.9	1.58	73%	82	156
Support 5.47	1st Half		9	4	0	81	4.22	1.38	$7	26.8	273			32%	4.12	9.7	2.9	6.3	2.2	0.8		70%	61	115
LIMA C	2nd Half		10	3	0	126	3.00	0.99	$17	29.0	213			24%	2.55	35.5	2.1	7.3	3.5	1.0		75%	100	189
Risk Low	03	Proj	19	9	0	225	3.32	1.16	$27	27.0	242			28%	3.27	61.7	2.3	7.0	3.0	0.9	G	74%	86	175

Nice recovery in the 2nd half, netting him out with a near-identical season to 2001 (as per xERA). There is growth in many of the BPIs and he could be poised to take it up a tick.

Mulholland,Terry		Tm	W	L	Sv	IP	ERA	Br/IP	R$	BF/G	OBA	vLH	vRH	H%	xERA	RAR	Ctl	Dom	Cmd	hr/9	G/F	S%	BPV	BPX
LH Reliever	98	CHC	6	5	3	112	2.89	1.24	$12	6.7	240	256	227	28%	3.22	35.1	3.1	5.8	1.8	0.6	2.09	78%	64	115
AGE 40 Decline	99	2NL	10	8	1	170	4.39	1.45	$9	17.7	295	290	299	31%	4.99 -	26.2	2.4	4.4	1.8	1.1	1.65	72%	28	60
TYPE Contact	00	ATL	9	9	1	156	5.13	1.53	$3	12.9	310	294	312	32%	5.73 -	10.5	2.4	4.5	1.9	1.4	1.95	70%	18	41
BURN none	01	2NL	1	1	0	65	4.69	1.46	($1)	7.0	298	266	308	32%	5.60 -	5.9	2.3	5.8	2.5	1.7	1.62	73%	32	60
ERA Potl - -	02	2TM	3	2	0	79	5.70	1.54	($3)	9.5	312	312	315	32%	6.07	-4.5	2.4	4.3	1.8	1.7	1.31	67%	5	10
Support 5.35	1st Half		0	0	0	21	8.92	1.84	($4)	6.7	363			33%	9.67 -	-10.3	2.1	4.2	2.0	3.8		60%	-65	******
LIMA F	2nd Half		3	2	0	58	4.52	1.44	$2	11.4	291			31%	4.75	5.8	2.5	4.4	1.8	0.9		70%	32	62
Risk Very High	03	Proj	1	1	0	40	5.40	1.53	($1)	8.9	307			31%	6.04 -	0.1	2.5	4.7	1.9	1.8	--	70%	8	16

No other page in this book has three 40-somethings on it. In fact, we've NEVER hit this trifecta before. It's a first in Forecaster history. Rejoice! The geezers rule the planet!

Mullen,Scott

Mullen,Scott	Tm	W	L	Sv	IP	ERA	Br/IP	R$	BF/G	OBA	vLH	vRH	H%	xERA	RAR	Ctl	Dom	Cmd	hr/9	G/F	S%	BPV	BPX
LH Reliever	98 aa	8	2	0	70	4.24	1.30	$8	24.6	259			28%	3.83	11.1	2.8	4.5	1.6	0.8		68%	40	79
AGE 28 Pre-Peak	99 a/a	10	10	0	169	6.60	1.71	($8)	27.0	318			34%	6.42	-20.5	3.6	5.3	1.5	1.5		63%	8	18
TYPE Contact	00 a/a	5	3	7	94	4.02	1.39	$11	8.3	268	143	350	31%	4.05	21.9	3.3	6.2	1.9	0.7	1.07	72%	59	139
BURN none	01 aaa	5	4	5	63	7.43	1.92	($4)	4.7	336	250	389	36%	7.09	-16.9	4.4	4.9	1.1	1.3	1.17	62%	0	0
ERA Potl - -	02 KC	* 5	7	0	71	3.30	1.42	$5	4.9	283	263	270	31%	4.24 -	17.2	2.8	4.7	1.7	0.6	1.48	78%	43	81
Support 5.63	1st Half	1	4	0	39	3.22	1.48	$1	5.9	299			34%	4.04 -	9.9	2.5	4.6	1.8	0.0		76%	61	115
LIMA C+	2nd Half	4	3	0	32	3.39	1.35	$4	4.0	262			27%	4.49 -	7.4	3.1	4.8	1.5	1.4		82%	21	41
Risk X HIGH	03 Proj	4	4	0	50	4.14	1.40	$3	5.3	273			30%	4.34	8.2	3.1	4.9	1.6	0.9	--	72%	36	73

4-5, 3.15 ERA in 40 IP at KC. Where did this sub-4.00 ERA come from? He got help from a 78% strand rate, low HR rate, and keeping the ball on the ground more. But xERA says it won't happen again.

Munro,Peter

Munro,Peter	Tm	W	L	Sv	IP	ERA	Br/IP	R$	BF/G	OBA	vLH	vRH	H%	xERA	RAR	Ctl	Dom	Cmd	hr/9	G/F	S%	BPV	BPX
RH Starter	98 aaa	7	9	0	151	7.33	1.81	($16)	27.5	328			37%	6.64 +	-38.4	3.9	6.2	1.6	1.3		60%	21	41
AGE 27 Pre-Peak	99 aaa	6	1	0	69	3.64	1.59	$5	17.3	286			35%	4.88 -	19.1	4.2	7.7	1.8	0.8		79%	59	137
TYPE Contact	00 aaa	5	5	0	93	3.90	1.39	$7	26.8	257			29%	3.73	23.2	3.7	4.9	1.3	0.5		72%	46	109
BURN High	01 aaa	8	6	0	88	6.10	1.69	($2)	12.3	301			33%	6.17	-8.0	4.3	6.4	1.5	1.6		67%	17	33
ERA Potl +	02 HOU	* 12	6	0	174	3.57	1.24	$18	19.1	264	328	255	30%	3.50	44.1	2.1	5.4	2.6	0.5	1.63	71%	76	156
Support 4.35	1st Half	7	1	0	96	3.56	1.11	$13	19.4	245			29%	2.84 +	24.5	1.8	5.7	3.2	0.4		67%	96	198
LIMA C	2nd Half	5	5	0	78	3.58	1.40	$6	18.7	286			32%	4.31 -	19.7	2.4	5.1	2.1	0.6		75%	55	113
Risk X HIGH	03 Proj	9	6	0	120	3.98	1.28	$11	20.2	265			30%	3.93	23.8	2.4	5.7	2.4	0.8	G	71%	61	123

5-5, 3.60 ERA in 80 IP at HOU. Cut his walk rate in half, kept the ball in the park, and took a big step up. The obstacle now is convincing the big club that a 27-year-old has an upside worth investing a rotation spot on.

Mussina,Mike

Mussina,Mike	Tm	W	L	Sv	IP	ERA	Br/IP	R$	BF/G	OBA	vLH	vRH	H%	xERA	RAR	Ctl	Dom	Cmd	hr/9	G/F	S%	BPV	BPX
RH Starter	98 BAL	13	10	0	206	3.49	1.12	$25	28.7	245	245	240	29%	3.33	59.7	1.8	7.6	4.3	1.0	1.46	72%	113	240
AGE 34 Past	99 BAL	18	7	0	203	3.50	1.28	$27	27.5	266	268	268	32%	3.77	64.4	2.3	7.6	3.3	0.7	1.55	74%	96	240
TYPE	00 BAL	11	15	0	237	3.79	1.19	$24	28.7	261	223	281	31%	3.77	67.3	1.7	8.0	4.6	1.1	1.49	72%	115	298
BURN none	01 NYY	17	11	0	228	3.16	1.07	$30	26.8	239	240	234	30%	2.96	71.2	1.7	8.4	5.1	0.8	1.02	73%	141	283
ERA Potl + +	02 NYY	18	10	0	215	4.06	1.19	$19	26.8	255	257	248	30%	3.71	30.1	2.0	7.6	3.8	1.1	1.08	69%	95	180
Support 6.30	1st Half	11	3	0	108	4.74	1.16	$10	26.0	252			28%	3.95 +	5.3	1.9	7.5	3.9	1.5		64%	87	164
LIMA B	2nd Half	7	7	0	107	3.37	1.22	$9	27.6	259			31%	3.47	24.8	2.1	7.8	3.7	0.8		74%	104	197
Risk Very Low	03 Proj	16	11	0	225	3.56	1.19	$22	27.2	257			31%	3.61	54.5	2.0	7.8	4.0	1.0	--	73%	105	214

His 1st half ERA was a fluke, inflated by a 64% strand rate. BPIs are solid, he's as good as ever, and if your league-mates are hesitant to bid a pitcher with a 4-plus ERA into the mid-$20s, be ready to snatch up a bargain.

Myers,Brett

Myers,Brett	Tm	W	L	Sv	IP	ERA	Br/IP	R$	BF/G	OBA	vLH	vRH	H%	xERA	RAR	Ctl	Dom	Cmd	hr/9	G/F	S%	BPV	BPX
RH Starter	98	0	0	0	0	0.00	0.00																
AGE 22 Growth	99	0	0	0	0	0.00	0.00																
TYPE Contact	00	0	0	0	0	0.00	0.00																
BURN none	01 aa	13	4	0	156	4.56	1.42	$8	26.1	286			33%	4.91	18.0	2.7	6.8	2.6	1.2		71%	56	108
ERA Potl +	02 PHI	* 13	11	0	200	4.19	1.27	$15	27.0	266	225	314	30%	4.03	34.1	2.2	5.7	2.6	0.9	1.72	69%	62	128
Support 5.63	1st Half	7	6	0	105	4.45	1.21	$8	27.1	267			31%	3.65 +	14.2	1.6	6.3	3.9	0.7		63%	101	207
LIMA C	2nd Half	6	5	0	95	3.89	1.33	$7	26.9	264			28%	4.45 -	19.9	2.8	5.0	1.8	1.2		75%	32	67
Risk High	03 Proj	8	8	0	140	4.56	1.34	$7	27.1	274			30%	4.44	16.7	2.4	5.5	2.3	1.1	G	68%	48	97

4-5, 4.25 ERA in 72 IP at PHI. This one may not be able to handle the abuse of 200 IP at age 21. Significant 2nd half fade is the key. BPIs are terrific, but the risk of a breakdown is great.

Myers,Mike

Myers,Mike	Tm	W	L	Sv	IP	ERA	Br/IP	R$	BF/G	OBA	vLH	vRH	H%	xERA	RAR	Ctl	Dom	Cmd	hr/9	G/F	S%	BPV	BPX
LH Reliever	98 MIL	2	2	1	50	2.70	1.32	$5	3.0	238	162	303	28%	3.69 -	17.0	4.0	7.2	1.8	0.9	1.37	84%	62	111
AGE 33 Past	99 MIL	2	1	0	41	5.27	1.44	$0	2.5	285	190	392	33%	5.17	1.5	2.9	7.7	2.7	1.5	1.48	67%	55	119
TYPE Power	00 COL	0	1	1	45	2.00	1.06	$6	2.3	159	120	224	20%	1.64	21.9	4.8	8.2	1.7	0.4	1.41	83%	96	212
BURN none	01 COL	2	3	0	40	3.60	1.40	$2	2.4	221	231	216	28%	3.25	9.5	5.4	8.1	1.5	0.5	1.96	74%	77	144
ERA Potl No chg	02 ARI	4	3	4	37	4.38	1.51	$5	2.4	272	241	317	34%	4.30	5.4	4.1	7.5	1.8	0.5	2.73	70%	70	143
Support 4.38	1st Half	3	3	2	19	4.22	1.30	$4	2.5	260			35%	3.56 +	3.2	2.8	9.4	3.3	0.5		67%	115	236
LIMA B	2nd Half	1	0	2	18	4.55	1.74	$1	2.2	285			33%	5.10 -	2.2	5.6	5.6	1.0	0.5		73%	37	76
Risk Very Low	03 Proj	2	3	2	40	3.83	1.45	$3	2.4	247			31%	3.73	8.7	4.7	7.7	1.6	0.5	G	73%	72	145

Allowed runs in only 11 of his 69 outings, and more than 1 run only 5 times. Pitchers who rack up small innings in many games should be avoided because one bad outing can ruin an entire season's ERA.

Myette,Aaron

Myette,Aaron	Tm	W	L	Sv	IP	ERA	Br/IP	R$	BF/G	OBA	vLH	vRH	H%	xERA	RAR	Ctl	Dom	Cmd	hr/9	G/F	S%	BPV	BPX
RH Starter	98	0	0	0	0	0.00	0.00																
AGE 25 Growth	99 aa	12	7	0	164	4.72	1.46	$9	25.7	259			29%	4.56	21.5	4.3	6.3	1.5	1.2		70%	37	87
TYPE Power	00 a/a	7	5	0	127	5.53	1.58	$0	26.0	274			29%	5.64	4.0	4.7	6.7	1.4	1.8	0.20	70%	17	40
BURN none	01 TEX	* 9	8	0	156	5.88	1.55	($3)	21.8	283	316	265	34%	5.03 +	-8.4	3.9	7.8	2.0	1.0	0.97	63%	56	111
ERA Potl + +	02 TEX	* 9	9	0	154	5.55	1.56	($3)	22.3	268	396	257	33%	4.64 +	-9.2	4.8	8.1	1.7	0.9	0.61	65%	58	109
Support 6.14	1st Half	5	4	0	92	3.91	1.33	$5	26.0	249			30%	3.45	14.7	3.5	7.3	2.1	0.6		71%	75	143
LIMA D	2nd Half	4	5	0	62	7.98	1.92	($8)	18.8	295			36%	6.39 +	-23.9	6.7	9.3	1.4	1.5		59%	38	71
Risk Moderate	03 Proj	5	9	0	120	5.25	1.61	($3)	21.7	276			33%	5.15	1.9	4.8	7.8	1.6	1.2	F	69%	45	91

2-5, 10.06 ERA in 48 IP at TEX. Lots of problems here...
- Falls apart with men on base.
- Allows too many fly balls.
- LHers kill him.
- Can't cut it in the majors...

7.89 lifetime ERA over 147 IP.

Nagy,Charles

Nagy,Charles	Tm	W	L	Sv	IP	ERA	Br/IP	R$	BF/G	OBA	vLH	vRH	H%	xERA	RAR	Ctl	Dom	Cmd	hr/9	G/F	S%	BPV	BPX
RH Reliever	98 CLE	15	10	0	210	5.23	1.50	$6	28.2	297	270	323	31%	5.52	12.1	2.8	5.1	1.8	1.5	1.91	69%	21	45
AGE 36 Decline	99 CLE	17	11	0	202	4.95	1.47	$13	26.9	295	323	263	32%	5.12	25.1	2.6	5.6	2.1	1.2	1.77	69%	40	100
TYPE Contact	00 CLE	2	7	0	57	8.21	1.61	($5)	23.5	306	303	295	32%	6.75 +	-17.5	3.3	6.5	2.0	2.4	1.30	52%	3	7
BURN none	01 CLE	* 10	7	0	108	5.42	1.67	$0	23.6	331	293	391	35%	5.92 -	1.0	2.4	3.6	1.5	0.8	1.81	68%	16	33
ERA Potl -	02 CLE	* 2	6	0	84	7.16	1.67	($9)	16.1	343	415	290	35%	7.05	-23.2	1.8	4.0	2.2	1.9	1.32	60%	-2	-4
Support 3.70	1st Half	0	3	0	38	8.22	1.64	($6)	13.4	329			32%	6.92 +	-16.0	2.3	3.8	1.6	2.1		52%	-18	-34
LIMA F	2nd Half	2	3	0	46	6.27	1.70	($3)	19.3	354			36%	7.16 -	-7.2	1.4	4.1	3.0	1.8		67%	19	36
Risk Very High	03 Proj	2	4	0	50	5.76	1.66	($3)	19.1	332			34%	6.58 -	-2.6	2.3	4.3	1.8	1.6	--	69%	5	10

1-4, 9.00 ERA in 48 IP at CLE. A walking injury time bomb. Risk is far too great and potential gain is far too small.

Neagle,Denny

Neagle,Denny	Tm	W	L	Sv	IP	ERA	Br/IP	R$	BF/G	OBA	vLH	vRH	H%	xERA	RAR	Ctl	Dom	Cmd	hr/9	G/F	S%	BPV	BPX
LH Starter	98 ATL	16	11	0	210	3.56	1.22	$21	27.2	249	255	248	29%	3.74	47.2	2.6	7.1	2.8	1.1	0.86	75%	73	132
AGE 34 Decline	99 CIN	* 11	5	0	128	4.36	1.16	$15	22.7	229	198	237	23%	3.95	20.4	3.0	5.9	2.0	1.8	0.59	70%	34	74
TYPE	00 2TM	15	9	0	209	4.52	1.39	$15	26.5	263	295	249	29%	4.60	34.7	3.5	6.3	1.8	1.3	0.75	72%	38	90
BURN none	01 COL	9	8	0	170	5.39	1.48	($1)	25.0	286	300	279	32%	5.35	-0.6	3.2	7.4	2.3	1.5	0.60	67%	45	83
ERA Potl -	02 COL	8	11	0	164	5.27	1.42	$0	20.3	269	315	251	29%	4.92	4.2	3.5	6.1	1.8	1.4	1.08	66%	32	66
Support 3.94	1st Half	4	5	0	91	5.23	1.35	$1	24.3	259			27%	4.75	2.8	3.3	5.9	1.8	1.6		65%	29	61
LIMA C+	2nd Half	4	6	0	73	5.32	1.51	($1)	17.0	280			31%	5.13	1.4	3.7	6.3	1.7	1.2		67%	35	73
Risk Moderate	03 Proj	9	9	0	160	5.06	1.43	$3	21.7	271			30%	4.91	8.4	3.4	6.5	1.9	1.4	--	68%	38	77

BPIs have been mediocre for four years now and COL just exacerbates the damage even more. Most troubling is that in his two years in COL, he's posted just as horrible an ERA on the road as at home.

Nelson,Jeff

Nelson,Jeff	Tm	W	L	Sv	IP	ERA	Br/IP	R$	BF/G	OBA	vLH	vRH	H%	xERA	RAR	Ctl	Dom	Cmd	hr/9	G/F	S%	BPV	BPX
RH Reliever	98 NYY	5	3	3	40	3.82	1.65	$5	4.1	280	295	268	36%	4.45 -	9.9	4.9	7.9	1.6	0.2	1.29	75%	73	155
AGE 36 Decline	99 NYY	2	1	1	30	4.20	1.63	$2	3.5	242	229	253	34%	4.22	6.7	6.6	10.5	1.6	0.6	1.82	74%	85	213
TYPE Power	00 NYY	8	4	0	69	2.47	1.29	$13	4.0	184	232	157	25%	2.30	31.9	5.9	9.2	1.6	0.3	0.89	80%	99	257
BURN none	01 SEA	4	3	4	65	2.76	1.14	$11	3.8	140	167	119	22%	1.62 +	23.7	6.1	12.2	2.0	0.4	0.97	76%	129	259
ERA Potl + +	02 SEA	3	2	2	45	4.00	1.40	$3	4.7	221	224	218	31%	3.45 +	6.7	5.4	11.0	2.0	0.8	0.50	73%	96	181
Support 6.31	1st Half	1	0	0	12	4.43	1.80	($0)	4.4	289			38%	5.34 -	1.1	5.9	9.6	1.6	0.7		76%	67	126
LIMA A	2nd Half	2	2	2	33	3.84	1.25	$3	4.9	192			27%	2.74 +	5.6	5.2	11.5	2.2	0.8		71%	107	203
Risk High	03 Proj	5	3	1	60	3.90	1.50	$4	4.3	235			32%	3.88	11.8	5.7	10.5	1.8	0.8	F	75%	87	177

Hard thrower with some warning signs...
- Walks far too many batters.
- Increasing flyball tendency
- Age 36

Nen,Robb		Tm	W	L	Sv	IP	ERA	Br/IP	R$	BF/G	OBA	vLH	vRH	H%	xERA	RAR	Ctl	Dom	Cmd	hr/9	G/F	S%	BPV	BPX
RH Reliever	98	SF	7	7	40	88	1.53	0.95	$40	4.4	192	234	125	28%	1.70	43.8	2.6	11.2	**4.4**	0.4	1.17	86%	164	296
AGE 33 Past	99	SF	3	8	37	72	4.00	1.47	$24	4.4	280	354	210	36%	4.67 -	14.9	3.4	9.6	**2.9**	1.0	1.14	76%	87	188
TYPE Power	00	SF	4	3	41	66	1.50	0.85	$39	3.7	166	188	135	26%	1.26	36.5	2.6	12.5	**4.8**	0.5	1.16	87%	182	402
BURN none	01	SF	4	5	45	77	3.03	1.04	$37	3.9	210	240	162	29%	2.41 +	24.1	2.6	10.8	**4.2**	0.7	1.08	73%	146	270
ERA Potl No chg	02	SF	6	2	43	73	2.22	1.15	$41	4.4	237	224	242	33%	2.67	31.7	2.5	10.0	**4.1**	0.2	1.32	80%	145	298
Support 1.83	1st Half		3	0	21	36	1.75	0.78	$24	4.0	185			25%	1.34	17.9	1.3	9.3	**7.4**	0.5		81%	214	439
LIMA C	2nd Half		3	2	22	37	2.68	1.51	$18	4.7	282			40%	3.96 -	13.8	3.6	10.7	**2.9**	0.0		80%	124	255
Risk Very Low	03	Proj	**5**	**4**	**44**	**75**	**2.40**	**1.12**	**$39**	**4.2**	**227**			**32%**	**2.64**	**30.7**	**2.6**	**10.7**	**4.0**	**0.5**	**--**	**80%**	**144**	**290**

As reliable as they come, and no signs of a letup.

Neugebauer,Nick		Tm	W	L	Sv	IP	ERA	Br/IP	R$	BF/G	OBA	vLH	vRH	H%	xERA	RAR	Ctl	Dom	Cmd	hr/9	G/F	S%	BPV	BPX
RH Starter	98		0	0	0	0	0.00	0.00																
AGE 22 Growth	99		0	0	0	0	0.00	0.00																
TYPE Power	00	aa	1	3	0	50	4.14	1.60	$0	22.6	208			28%	3.48 +	10.9	7.7	9.2	**1.2**	0.4		73%	83	196
BURN none	01	a/a	8	8	0	137	3.81	1.34	$9	21.6	237			34%	3.39	29.6	4.1	11.2	**2.7**	0.6	0.50	72%	114	218
ERA Potl - - - -	02	MIL	* 1	10	0	74	5.22	1.81	($8)	20.6	274	318	226	30%	6.33 -	2.3	6.7	7.7	**1.1**	1.8	1.49	76%	15	32
Support 3.42	1st Half		1	4	0	35	5.13	1.65	($2)	22.9	244			27%	5.50	1.6	6.7	7.9	**1.2**	1.8		75%	25	51
LIMA D	2nd Half		0	6	0	39	5.31	1.95	($6)	19.0	299			33%	7.08 -	0.8	6.7	7.4	**1.1**	1.8		78%	7	15
Risk X HIGH	03	Proj	**5**	**10**	**0**	**120**	**4.58**	**1.62**	**($2)**	**25.9**	**254**			**30%**	**4.94**	**14.1**	**5.9**	**8.3**	**1.4**	**1.2**	**--**	**75%**	**48**	**96**

1-7, 4.75 ERA in 55 IP at MIL. The promising pitcher from 2001 did not show up in 2002 and battled a shoulder injury. This is a setback, but on another team, he'd spend '03 in AAA, which is where a 22-year-old belongs.

Nichting,Chris		Tm	W	L	Sv	IP	ERA	Br/IP	R$	BF/G	OBA	vLH	vRH	H%	xERA	RAR	Ctl	Dom	Cmd	hr/9	G/F	S%	BPV	BPX
RH Reliever	98	aaa	8	6	1	96	5.25	1.66	$1	10.2	309			37%	5.49	2.3	3.6	7.6	**2.1**	0.8		69%	58	113
AGE 37 Decline	99	aaa	8	5	0	127	5.67	1.53	$1	22.6	292			32%	5.44	0.5	3.3	6.3	**1.9**	1.4		66%	32	75
TYPE Power	00	aa	2	3	26	66	6.14	1.61	$12	6.4	321	308	360	36%	5.79	-3.3	2.5	5.9	**2.4**	1.1	2.14	62%	43	103
BURN none	01	2NL	* 2	4	18	75	4.32	1.37	$12	4.6	284	408	248	34%	5.17 -	10.5	2.3	9.4	**4.1**	1.7	1.10	75%	90	167
ERA Potl -	02	COL	* 2	5	1	68	8.34	1.90	($13)	6.4	349	167	361	36%	8.29	-26.2	3.4	5.7	**1.7**	2.4	1.04	59%	-17	-36
Support 7.93	1st Half		1	1	1	35	3.57	1.19	$3	4.8	276			31%	4.29 -	8.9	1.0	6.6	**6.5**	1.3		76%	138	283
LIMA F	2nd Half		1	4	0	33	13.49	2.66	($18)	8.7	413			41%	12.60 +	-35.2	6.1	4.7	**0.8**	3.6		51%	-91	
Risk X HIGH	03	Proj	**1**	**3**	**0**	**40**	**7.20**	**1.80**	**($6)**	**6.5**	**336**			**37%**	**7.43**	**-9.4**	**3.4**	**6.8**	**2.0**	**2.0**	**--**	**63%**	**10**	**19**

1-1, 4.50 ERA in 36 IP at COL. The Bizarro World of NIchting:
- Platoon split trends
- Consistently elevated hit rates
- Wild swings in strand rates
- 2001's strikeout performance
- 1H to 2H BPV swing

Nomo,Hideo		Tm	W	L	Sv	IP	ERA	Br/IP	R$	BF/G	OBA	vLH	vRH	H%	xERA	RAR	Ctl	Dom	Cmd	hr/9	G/F	S%	BPV	BPX
RH Starter	98	2NL	6	12	0	157	4.93	1.43	($0)	23.5	227	210	240	29%	3.97 +	6.5	5.4	9.6	**1.8**	1.1	1.09	67%	72	129
AGE 34 Decline	99	MIL	* 14	9	0	200	4.32	1.40	$13	27.0	253	280	235	30%	4.37	32.9	4.0	8.2	**2.1**	1.3	0.83	73%	59	129
TYPE Power	00	DET	8	12	0	190	4.74	1.47	$6	26.1	263	241	284	31%	4.90	29.9	4.2	8.6	**2.0**	1.5	0.88	72%	53	136
BURN none	01	BOS	13	10	0	198	4.50	1.35	$10	25.6	234	221	242	30%	3.96 +	26.1	4.4	10.0	**2.3**	1.2	1.08	70%	81	162
ERA Potl -	02	LA	16	6	0	220	3.40	1.32	$21	27.4	234	218	253	28%	3.83	60.8	4.1	7.9	**1.9**	1.1	0.95	78%	64	131
Support 4.70	1st Half		8	5	0	99	3.55	1.42	$8	26.9	231			27%	4.02	25.4	5.2	7.1	**1.4**	1.0		78%	50	103
LIMA D+	2nd Half		8	1	0	121	3.27	1.23	$14	27.9	235			28%	3.68	35.4	3.3	8.6	**2.6**	1.1		78%	81	165
Risk Low	03	Proj	**13**	**8**	**0**	**200**	**3.96**	**1.36**	**$14**	**26.7**	**239**			**29%**	**4.05**	**40.0**	**4.2**	**8.6**	**2.0**	**1.2**	**--**	**75%**	**67**	**134**

While his ERA harkened back to his LA glory days, his BPIs did not, at least not in the 1st half. Re-acclimated to the NL in the 2nd half, he shone. At 34, his odds of a repeat are about 50-50.

Nunez,Vladimir		Tm	W	L	Sv	IP	ERA	Br/IP	R$	BF/G	OBA	vLH	vRH	H%	xERA	RAR	Ctl	Dom	Cmd	hr/9	G/F	S%	BPV	BPX
RH Reliever	98	aaa	4	4	2	100	5.40	1.48	($0)	12.6	290	200	353	32%	4.91	0.4	3.0	5.8	**1.9**	1.0	1.57	64%	43	83
AGE 28 Pre-Peak	99	2NL	7	10	1	108	4.08	1.38	$8	10.6	238	268	226	28%	3.80	21.2	4.5	7.2	**1.6**	0.9	0.97	72%	56	123
TYPE Power	00	FLA	* 6	13	0	157	5.78	1.61	($5)	22.3	292	339	305	34%	5.39	-3.2	4.0	7.3	**1.8**	1.1	1.07	65%	45	98
BURN High	01	FLA	4	5	0	92	2.74	1.18	$10	7.3	233	213	253	26%	3.28 -	32.4	2.9	6.3	**2.1**	0.9	1.03	81%	64	119
ERA Potl No chg	02	FLA	6	5	20	97	3.43	1.21	$24	5.2	226	191	251	26%	3.17	26.3	3.4	6.8	**2.0**	0.7	0.93	73%	70	143
Support 2.58	1st Half		4	3	18	47	3.06	1.19	$19	5.1	236			27%	3.28	15.1	2.9	6.1	**2.1**	0.8		77%	66	136
LIMA D+	2nd Half		2	2	2	50	3.78	1.22	$5	5.3	217			26%	3.05 +	11.2	4.0	7.4	**1.9**	0.7		70%	73	151
Risk Very High	03	Proj	**4**	**5**	**2**	**85**	**3.81**	**1.26**	**$7**	**7.0**	**241**			**28%**	**3.55**	**18.7**	**3.3**	**6.8**	**2.1**	**0.8**	**--**	**72%**	**65**	**132**

Closer-caliber BPIs? Marginally. But the bottom line was that he was converting only 71% of his save opps, and that's too low. Solid role pitcher, which means he could be a serviceable pickup at the end of your draft.

Ohka,Tomokazu		Tm	W	L	Sv	IP	ERA	Br/IP	R$	BF/G	OBA	vLH	vRH	H%	xERA	RAR	Ctl	Dom	Cmd	hr/9	G/F	S%	BPV	BPX
RH Starter	98	JPN	0	0	0	2	9.00	2.00	($0)	4.9	262			30%	4.91 +	-1.0	9.0	4.5	**0.5**	0.0		50%	40	78
AGE 27 Growth	99	a/a	15	0	0	140	2.83	1.26	$23	24.4	262			30%	3.89 -	53.8	2.3	6.5	**2.8**	1.0		82%	72	166
TYPE Contact	00	BOS	* 12	12	0	199	3.61	1.26	$22	26.1	264	277	243	28%	4.02	61.4	2.3	4.7	**2.1**	1.0	1.36	75%	44	113
BURN none	01	2TM	* 5	14	0	149	5.92	1.59	($8)	22.4	321	329	290	36%	5.89	-9.9	2.3	5.7	**2.5**	1.2	1.48	64%	41	79
ERA Potl -	02	MON	13	8	0	192	3.19	1.24	$21	25.0	264	218	298	29%	3.91 -	58.4	2.1	5.5	**2.6**	0.9	1.36	78%	64	131
Support 4.48	1st Half		7	4	0	98	3.30	1.29	$10	24.3	271			30%	4.08 -	28.3	2.2	5.7	**2.6**	0.8		77%	64	132
LIMA D+	2nd Half		6	4	0	94	3.07	1.19	$12	25.7	256			28%	3.73 -	30.1	2.0	5.4	**2.7**	1.0		78%	63	130
Risk X HIGH	03	Proj	**12**	**11**	**0**	**200**	**3.92**	**1.26**	**$16**	**23.9**	**268**			**30%**	**4.06**	**41.2**	**2.0**	**5.7**	**2.9**	**1.0**	**--**	**72%**	**66**	**132**

Despite 2001's near-6 ERA, his BPIs predicted 2002 all along. Nice skills set, keeps the ball on the ground, but has trouble vs RHers. That could become a huge problem if not corrected.

Oliver,Darren		Tm	W	L	Sv	IP	ERA	Br/IP	R$	BF/G	OBA	vLH	vRH	H%	xERA	RAR	Ctl	Dom	Cmd	hr/9	G/F	S%	BPV	BPX
LH Starter	98	2TM	10	11	0	160	5.73	1.69	($5)	25.4	311	277	318	34%	5.79	-6.5	3.7	4.9	**1.3**	1.0	1.51	67%	19	38
AGE 32 Past	99	STL	9	9	0	196	4.27	1.38	$9	28.1	263	320	254	29%	3.99	33.5	3.4	5.5	**1.6**	0.7	1.44	70%	47	102
TYPE Power	00	TEX	2	9	0	108	7.42	1.79	($12)	24.2	331	376	326	35%	6.65 +	-21.8	3.5	4.1	**1.2**	1.3	1.01	59%	-2	-6
BURN none	01	TEX	11	11	0	154	6.02	1.65	($4)	25.1	303	311	304	33%	5.88	-11.0	3.8	6.1	**1.6**	1.3	1.24	65%	24	48
ERA Potl - -	02	BOS	* 4	7	0	74	5.84	1.84	($5)	18.5	304	462	272	33%	5.91	-7.2	5.5	4.9	**0.9**	1.0	1.41	69%	13	24
Support 6.98	1st Half		4	5	0	58	4.66	1.67	($0)	19.0	300			32%	5.54 -	3.5	4.2	5.0	**1.2**	1.1		74%	17	32
LIMA F	2nd Half		0	2	0	16	10.12	2.44	($5)	17.1	318			35%	7.26 +	-10.8	10.1	4.5	**0.4**	0.6		55%	11	21
Risk High	03	Proj	**3**	**7**	**0**	**80**	**5.96**	**1.90**	**($8)**	**20.3**	**309**			**34%**	**6.24**	**-6.4**	**5.7**	**5.0**	**0.9**	**1.0**	**--**	**69%**	**11**	**22**

Players like this astound me. He draws a major league paycheck but has NEVER posted a set of BPIs worth noting. Why does he keep finding takers? Was he a tools guy that all the scouts fawned over? No other reason.

Olsen,Kevin		Tm	W	L	Sv	IP	ERA	Br/IP	R$	BF/G	OBA	vLH	vRH	H%	xERA	RAR	Ctl	Dom	Cmd	hr/9	G/F	S%	BPV	BPX
RH Reliever	98		0	0	0	0	0.00	0.00																
AGE 26 Growth	99		0	0	0	0	0.00	0.00																
TYPE	00	aa	3	4	0	54	0.17	1.61	($1)	27.2	296			33%	5.63 +	-2.9	3.8	6.5	**1.7**	1.3		63%	30	72
BURN none	01	aa	10	[illegible]	0	[illegible]	[illegible]	[illegible]	[illegible]	25.2	209			31%	3.69	37.1	1.5	6.7	**4.5**	0.8	1.13	70%	113	217
ERA Potl -	02	FLA	* 2	10	0	104	4.24	1.42	$0	18.1	262	292	248	29%	4.31	17.0	3.8	5.1	**1.3**	0.9	0.73	72%	35	73
Support 3.07	1st Half		0	5	0	54	4.65	1.59	($3)	15.3	268			31%	4.77	5.9	5.0	6.1	**1.2**	0.8		72%	39	80
LIMA B	2nd Half		2	5	0	50	3.80	1.24	$4	23.0	255			27%	3.81	11.1	2.5	4.0	**1.6**	0.9		72%	34	69
Risk Very High	03	Proj	**3**	**5**	**0**	**80**	**4.28**	**1.35**	**$3**	**16.3**	**269**			**30%**	**4.22**	**12.6**	**2.8**	**5.7**	**2.0**	**0.9**	**F**	**70%**	**51**	**104**

0-5, 4.58 ERA in 55 IP at FLA. Has not successfully made the jump from AA ball, which means he should spend all of '03 in AAA. But that will never happen.

Orosco,Jesse		Tm	W	L	Sv	IP	ERA	Br/IP	R$	BF/G	OBA	vLH	vRH	H%	xERA	RAR	Ctl	Dom	Cmd	hr/9	G/F	S%	BPV	BPX
LH Reliever	98	BAL	4	1	7	57	3.16	1.30	$10	3.5	223			27%	3.48	19.1	4.4	7.9	**1.8**	0.9		79%	67	143
AGE 46 Decline	99	BAL	0	2	1	32	5.34	1.50	($0)	2.2	237			29%	4.58 +	2.3	5.6	9.8	**1.8**	1.4		67%	61	154
TYPE Power	00	STL	* 0	1	0	3	3.00	2.33	($0)	2.0	321			40%	9.37 -	1.1	9.0	12.0	**1.3**	3.0		100%	1	2
BURN none	01	LA	* 1	1	0	23	2.74	1.30	$2	2.2	245	300	275	34%	3.95 -	8.1	3.5	11.7	**3.3**	1.2	1.23	85%	111	206
ERA Potl - - -	02	LA	1	2	1	27	3.00	1.33	$3	2.1	240	238	214	27%	4.21 -	8.9	4.0	7.3	**1.8**	1.3	0.74	84%	50	102
Support 7.00	1st Half		1	1	1	12	3.69	1.80	$1	2.3	304			32%	6.45 -	2.9	5.2	5.2	**1.0**	1.5		85%	2	4
LIMA C+	2nd Half		0	1	0	15	2.43	0.95	$2	1.8	177			21%	2.36	6.0	3.0	9.1	**3.0**	1.2		83%	101	207
Risk Very High	03	Proj	**1**	**1**	**0**	**30**	**3.90**	**1.57**	**$0**	**2.6**	**262**			**29%**	**4.95 -**	**6.2**	**5.1**	**6.0**	**1.2**	**1.2**	**F**	**79%**	**27**	**55**

I believe he is the last remaining active player who is older than me. If you haven't reached that point in your baseball fandom, it's a sobering experience. Guess I should give up hope of playing shortstop for the Mets.

Ortiz,Ramon

	Yr	Tm	W	L	Sv	IP	ERA	Br/IP	R$	BF/G	OBA	vLH	vRH	H%	xERA	RAR	Ctl	Dom	Cmd	hr/9	G/F	S%	BPV	BPX
RH Starter	98	aa	2	1	0	47	5.74	1.45	($1)	29.3	286			34%	5.43	-2.0	2.9	8.8	3.1	1.7		64%	63	123
AGE 30 Peak	99	ANA	* 16	10	0	203	4.57	1.43	$15	26.8	263	293	233	31%	4.58	35.5	3.9	7.8	2.0	1.2	1.67	71%	55	139
TYPE	00	ANA	* 14	12	0	200	5.31	1.36	$12	25.9	243	250	219	27%	4.08 +	16.2	4.1	6.3	1.5	1.2	1.30	63%	41	106
BURN none	01	ANA	13	11	0	208	4.37	1.44	$8	28.3	275	285	263	30%	4.68	31.2	3.3	5.8	1.8	1.1	1.31	72%	40	80
ERA Potl - -	02	ANA	15	9	0	217	3.77	1.18	$18	27.8	235	218	243	25%	3.92	38.7	2.8	6.7	2.4	1.7	1.04	76%	49	92
Support 6.67	1st Half		8	5	0	109	3.47	1.07	$12	29.0	219			22%	3.75	23.9	2.6	6.8	2.6	2.0		81%	48	91
LIMA D	2nd Half		7	4	0	108	4.08	1.29	$6	26.7	251			28%	4.09	14.8	3.1	6.7	2.2	1.3		73%	50	95
Risk Low	03	Proj	13	9	0	200	4.32	1.30	$13	27.2	252			28%	4.23	28.1	3.1	6.6	2.1	1.4	--	71%	47	95

Has been making gains, but some are more real than others. GOOD: Improved control and command
BAD: Opposition BA artificially depressed by 25% hit rate
UGLY: Rising home run rate

Ortiz,Russ

	Yr	Tm	W	L	Sv	IP	ERA	Br/IP	R$	BF/G	OBA	vLH	vRH	H%	xERA	RAR	Ctl	Dom	Cmd	hr/9	G/F	S%	BPV	BPX
RH Starter	98	SF	* 7	5	0	138	3.84	1.42	$6	18.7	247	283	252	30%	4.06	25.8	4.4	8.3	1.9	0.9	1.11	75%	67	121
AGE 28 Pre-Peak	99	SF	18	9	0	207	3.83	1.52	$16	27.8	245	251	238	28%	4.36 -	47.7	5.4	7.1	1.3	1.0	1.23	78%	45	98
TYPE Power	00	SF	14	12	0	195	5.03	1.56	$6	26.5	259	267	255	30%	4.92	15.8	5.2	7.7	1.5	1.3	1.27	71%	42	93
BURN none	01	SF	17	9	0	218	3.30	1.27	$22	27.7	233	275	191	28%	3.17	60.4	3.8	7.0	1.9	0.5	1.21	75%	73	136
ERA Potl -	02	SF	14	10	0	214	3.62	1.33	$17	27.6	240	247	235	27%	3.57	52.8	4.0	5.8	1.5	0.6	1.24	74%	53	109
Support 5.37	1st Half		6	5	0	104	3.80	1.38	$6	26.4	246			28%	3.91	23.1	4.1	6.0	1.4	0.8		74%	48	99
LIMA D+	2nd Half		8	5	0	110	3.44	1.28	$11	28.9	235			27%	3.24	29.7	3.8	5.6	1.5	0.5		73%	58	119
Risk Low	03	Proj	14	9	0	200	3.96	1.37	$14	26.8	243			28%	3.75	40.0	4.2	6.1	1.5	0.7	--	72%	52	104

Despite sharp drop in his strikeout rate, managed to hold the line on the rest of his numbers. That might become tougher to do with his particular skill set. Expect an ERA closer to 4.00 in 2003.

Osuna,Antonio

	Yr	Tm	W	L	Sv	IP	ERA	Br/IP	R$	BF/G	OBA	vLH	vRH	H%	xERA	RAR	Ctl	Dom	Cmd	hr/9	G/F	S%	BPV	BPX
RH Reliever	98	LA	7	1	6	64	3.08	1.28	$12	5.0	216	173	243	28%	3.49	18.5	4.5	10.1	2.3	1.1	0.89	81%	86	155
AGE 30 Peak	99	LA	0	0	0	5	7.20	1.40	($0)	4.3	221		333	31%	2.76 +	-1.1	5.4	9.0	1.7	0.0	0.80	43%	100	217
TYPE Power	00	LA	3	6	0	67	3.76	1.37	$4	6.3	231	229	229	30%	3.75	16.8	4.7	9.4	2.0	0.9	0.58	75%	79	174
BURN none	01	CHW	0	0	0	4	21.95	2.44	($3)	5.5	409			47%	14.64 +	-9.0	4.4	13.2	3.0	6.6	0.38	0%	-82	
ERA Potl + +	02	CHW	8	2	11	67	3.90	1.37	$12	4.9	253	250	250	34%	3.19 +	10.9	3.8	8.9	2.4	0.1	0.89	69%	103	195
Support 6.38	1st Half		4	1	4	38	4.26	1.37	$5	5.3	246			31%	2.97 +	4.3	4.0	7.3	1.8	0.0		65%	88	167
LIMA B+	2nd Half		4	1	7	29	3.41	1.38	$7	4.5	262			37%	3.47	6.6	3.4	10.9	3.2	0.3		74%	125	237
Risk High	03	Proj	5	3	7	65	3.46	1.32	$10	5.2	240			32%	3.32	16.6	3.9	9.6	2.5	0.6	--	74%	99	202

Solid rebound season, excellent BPI levels, and with that strand rate he has some ERA upside. Converted 79% of his save opps which makes him marginally closer-worthy.

Oswalt,Roy

	Yr	Tm	W	L	Sv	IP	ERA	Br/IP	R$	BF/G	OBA	vLH	vRH	H%	xERA	RAR	Ctl	Dom	Cmd	hr/9	G/F	S%	BPV	BPX
RH Starter	98		0	0	0	0	0.00	0.00																
AGE 25 Growth	99		0	0	0	0	0.00	0.00																
TYPE Power	00	aa	11	4	0	129	2.79	1.23	$20	28.2	269			34%	3.48 -	51.3	1.7	8.2	4.7	0.5		78%	134	317
BURN Low	01	HOU	* 16	6	0	172	3.30	1.13	$24	21.1	253	241	228	32%	3.42	47.7	1.6	9.1	5.8	0.9	1.46	74%	152	281
ERA Potl +	02	HOU	19	9	0	233	3.01	1.19	$32	27.4	247	251	244	31%	3.29	76.3	2.4	8.0	3.4	0.7	1.41	77%	105	215
Support 5.52	1st Half		8	5	0	116	3.25	1.25	$13	28.5	261			32%	3.68	34.3	2.2	8.1	3.6	0.7		76%	107	219
LIMA C	2nd Half		11	4	0	117	2.77	1.13	$20	26.3	231			29%	2.90	42.0	2.5	7.9	3.1	0.6		77%	103	212
Risk High	03	Proj	20	8	0	225	2.96	1.17	$33	27.1	250			31%	3.32	75.2	2.0	8.2	4.0	0.7	--	77%	117	235

Slight drop-off in command, but that's okay. If he's learning that he does not have to pitch as hard to get the same results, this is a good thing for his career longevity.

Padilla,Vicente

	Yr	Tm	W	L	Sv	IP	ERA	Br/IP	R$	BF/G	OBA	vLH	vRH	H%	xERA	RAR	Ctl	Dom	Cmd	hr/9	G/F	S%	BPV	BPX
RH Starter	98		0	0	0	0	0.00	0.00																
AGE 25 Growth	99	aaa	3	4	0	93	3.87	1.40	$8	22.3	295	500	455	33%	4.39 -	22.8	1.9	4.7	2.5	0.6	0.50	73%	58	135
TYPE Contact	00	2NL	* 4	8	3	87	4.02	1.61	$4	5.7	295	337	252	36%	4.85 -	18.9	3.9	7.4	1.9	0.5	2.31	75%	65	143
BURN High	01	PHI	* 10	1	0	115	3.60	1.21	$13	12.2	260	308	258	31%	3.59	27.2	2.0	7.6	3.9	0.8	2.50	72%	107	198
ERA Potl No chg	02	PHI	14	11	0	206	3.28	1.22	$23	26.6	254	272	236	29%	3.53	60.2	2.3	5.6	2.4	0.7	1.98	75%	67	138
Support 4.81	1st Half		10	5	0	113	3.26	1.17	$16	27.3	244			28%	3.14	33.3	2.4	6.2	2.6	0.6		73%	81	167
LIMA D+	2nd Half		4	6	0	93	3.30	1.27	$8	25.9	266			29%	4.00 -	26.9	2.2	4.8	2.2	0.9		77%	50	103
Risk X HIGH	03	Proj	13	10	0	200	3.74	1.30	$17	27.2	268			31%	3.90	46.0	2.4	5.9	2.4	0.7	G	73%	67	135

As good as this is, there are warning signs to be aware of...
- Sharp increase in workload
- Decline in dominance
- Drop in groundball tendency

These make it less likely that he'll take another step up in '03.

Paniagua,Jose

	Yr	Tm	W	L	Sv	IP	ERA	Br/IP	R$	BF/G	OBA	vLH	vRH	H%	xERA	RAR	Ctl	Dom	Cmd	hr/9	G/F	S%	BPV	BPX
RH Reliever	98	SEA	* 5	1	6	90	3.00	1.32	$12	6.2	262	211	189	32%	3.64 -	32.1	2.9	7.0	2.4	0.5	1.30	78%	80	172
AGE 29 Peak	99	SEA	6	11	3	77	4.09	1.65	$6	6.0	257	273	256	33%	4.46	18.4	6.1	8.6	1.4	0.6	1.53	75%	68	170
TYPE Power	00	SEA	3	0	5	80	3.48	1.32	$10	4.9	231	208	253	29%	3.36	26.1	4.3	8.0	1.9	0.7	0.87	75%	76	196
BURN none	01	SEA	4	3	3	66	4.36	1.47	$4	4.8	241	257	216	27%	4.17	9.9	5.2	6.3	1.2	1.0	0.66	72%	41	83
ERA Potl - -	02	DET	* 2	1	2	56	4.64	1.46	$1	4.6	284	276	309	31%	5.39 -	3.5	3.0	7.2	2.4	1.8	0.63	75%	38	72
Support 2.59	1st Half		0	1	0	32	4.50	1.28	($0)	4.6	250			28%	4.38	2.6	3.1	7.6	2.5	1.7		71%	52	98
LIMA D	2nd Half		2	0	2	24	4.83	1.69	$1	4.7	326			36%	6.72 -	0.9	3.0	6.7	2.3	1.9		78%	21	41
Risk Low	03	Proj	1	2	0	40	4.73	1.53	($1)	4.9	281			31%	5.37 -	3.4	3.8	7.0	1.8	1.6	F	74%	32	65

0-1, 5.93 ERA in 41 IP at DET. Follow his 5-year home run rate and associated G/F ratio to tell you all you need to know.

Park,Chan Ho

	Yr	Tm	W	L	Sv	IP	ERA	Br/IP	R$	BF/G	OBA	vLH	vRH	H%	xERA	RAR	Ctl	Dom	Cmd	hr/9	G/F	S%	BPV	BPX
RH Starter	98	LA	15	9	0	220	3.72	1.34	$16	27.6	243	252	235	30%	3.58	44.7	4.0	7.8	2.0	0.7	1.48	73%	75	135
AGE 29 Peak	99	LA	13	11	0	194	5.24	1.59	$2	26.5	275	358	207	32%	5.32	7.9	4.6	8.1	1.7	1.4	1.17	70%	42	91
TYPE Power	00	LA	18	10	0	226	3.27	1.31	$26	28.1	213	229	199	27%	3.29	71.5	4.9	8.6	1.8	0.8	1.22	78%	76	167
BURN none	01	LA	15	11	0	234	3.50	1.17	$23	26.6	217	230	204	27%	3.03	58.5	3.5	8.4	2.4	0.9	1.00	73%	86	159
ERA Potl +	02	TEX	9	9	0	148	6.32	1.66	($7)	26.1	283	287	254	33%	5.37 +	-24.1	4.9	7.5	1.5	1.2	1.10	63%	39	74
Support 6.43	1st Half		3	4	0	51	8.12	1.61	($5)	23.1	277			30%	5.49 +	-20.6	4.8	6.9	1.4	1.6		49%	24	45
LIMA D+	2nd Half		6	5	0	97	5.38	1.69	($3)	28.0	287			34%	5.30	-3.6	5.0	7.9	1.6	1.0		69%	47	90
Risk Low	03	Proj	13	11	0	200	4.95	1.57	$2	27.2	274			33%	4.90	11.2	4.5	7.9	1.8	1.1	--	70%	52	106

His previous success was in part driven by Dodger Stadium, where he had a home ERA over a run lower than on the road. Moving to a hitters league and ballpark wreaked havoc, and might not fully recover.

Paronto,Chad

	Yr	Tm	W	L	Sv	IP	ERA	Br/IP	R$	BF/G	OBA	vLH	vRH	H%	xERA	RAR	Ctl	Dom	Cmd	hr/9	G/F	S%	BPV	BPX
RH Reliever	98	aa	1	3	1	35	7.71	2.00	($6)	21.5	313			37%	5.89 +	-10.7	6.4	6.2	1.0	0.3		58%	42	81
AGE 27 Pre-Peak	99	aa	0	4	0	41	10.10	2.54	($14)	14.9	377			41%	8.72 +	-24.2	7.5	4.6	0.6	0.7		57%	0	1
TYPE Contact	00	a/a	5	3	0	83	5.31	1.42	$3	18.0	264			28%	4.27 +	5.0	3.7	4.6	1.2	0.9		63%	29	70
BURN none	01	BAL	* 4	6	1	70	5.66	1.77	($3)	5.8	306	186	352	34%	6.29 -	-1.6	4.8	6.4	1.4	1.4	2.04	71%	18	37
ERA Potl -	02	CLE	* 0	2	1	48	3.18	1.29	$2	5.3	265	226	262	30%	3.58	12.4	2.4	5.2	2.2	0.6	1.88	76%	62	117
Support 3.79	1st Half		0	2	1	35	3.85	1.31	$1	5.5	277			30%	4.00	5.9	2.1	4.9	2.4	0.8		72%	56	105
LIMA C+	2nd Half		0	0	0	13	1.38	1.23	$1	4.9	231			28%	2.44 -	6.5	3.5	6.2	1.8	0.0		88%	84	159
Risk X HIGH	03	Proj	1	3	0	40	4.05	1.38	$1	8.2	276			31%	4.31	7.1	2.7	5.4	2.0	0.9	G	73%	47	96

0-2, 4.11 ERA in 35 IP at CLE. Growth season was cut short by elbow tendinitis. A marginal end-game flyer if healthy.

Parris,Steve

	Yr	Tm	W	L	Sv	IP	ERA	Br/IP	R$	BF/G	OBA	vLH	vRH	H%	xERA	RAR	Ctl	Dom	Cmd	hr/9	G/F	S%	BPV	BPX
RH Starter	98	CIN	* 12	6	0	183	4.47	1.33	$9	25.1	263	291	188	32%	4.08	18.7	2.9	8.0	2.7	0.9	1.40	68%	79	142
AGE 35 Decline	99	CIN	* 11	6	0	163	3.70	1.39	$13	25.1	265	301	228	30%	4.42 -	40.3	3.3	6.3	1.9	1.2	1.16	78%	45	97
TYPE	00	CIN	12	17	0	192	4.82	1.55	$5	26.0	295	309	279	32%	5.56 -	20.7	3.3	5.5	1.6	1.4	1.07	73%	21	47
BURN none	01	TOR	* 4	6	0	116	4.66	1.55	($1)	23.6	294	361	224	30%	5.62 -	12.9	3.4	4.4	1.3	1.5	1.11	75%	6	12
ERA Potl - -	02	TOR	* 6	6	0	95	5.31	1.64	($2)	25.5	304	341	282	33%	5.67	-2.5	3.7	5.3	1.4	1.2	0.92	70%	19	36
Support 7.88	1st Half		1	2	0	34	3.42	1.37	$1	24.5	272			30%	4.10 -	7.7	2.9	5.3	1.8	0.8		77%	47	88
LIMA F	2nd Half		5	4	0	61	6.37	1.79	($3)	26.0	321			34%	6.55	-10.2	4.1	5.3	1.3	1.5		67%	5	10
Risk High	03	Proj	3	4	0	60	4.95	1.57	($0)	24.5	296			32%	5.50 -	3.4	3.5	5.3	1.5	1.4	--	72%	19	38

5-5, 6.00 ERA in 75 IP at TOR. Reasons why he's undraftable:
- Declining command
- LHers kill him
- xERA shows a consistency that's tough to take a liking to.
- And he's 35, goshdarnit.

Pavano,Carl

	Yr	Tm	W	L	Sv	IP	ERA	Br/IP	R$	BF/G	OBA	vLH	vRH	H%	xERA	RAR	Ctl	Dom	Cmd	hr/9	G/F	S%	BPV	BPX
RH Starter	98	MON	* 7	9	0	152	4.07	1.26	$8	23.6	248	260	244	27%	3.90	23.7	3.0	5.7	1.9	1.1	1.42	71%	47	84
AGE 27 Growth	99	MON	6	8	0	104	5.63	1.46	$1	24.0	285	290	279	33%	4.46 +	-1.1	3.0	6.1	2.0	0.7	1.74	60%	56	121
TYPE	00	MON	8	4	0	97	3.06	1.27	$13	27.1	245	312	188	28%	3.52	33.3	3.2	5.9	1.9	0.7	1.58	78%	59	130
BURN High	01	MON	* 3	7	0	69	5.74	1.62	($4)	26.1	319	384	295	36%	6.25 -	-3.4	2.7	6.8	2.5	1.6	1.26	68%	37	69
ERA Potl - -	02	2NL	* 9	10	0	156	5.02	1.60	($2)	17.6	315	357	276	35%	5.73 -	9.3	2.7	5.8	2.1	1.1	1.49	70%	39	79
Support 4.37	1st Half		5	8	0	87	5.88	1.72	($6)	23.8	324			35%	6.63 -	-5.0	3.3	5.7	1.7	1.5		69%	14	28
LIMA C+	2nd Half		4	2	0	69	3.92	1.44	$3	13.1	302			35%	4.60 -	14.2	2.0	5.9	3.0	0.5		73%	77	158
Risk Very High	03	Proj	9	8	0	140	4.76	1.51	$3	26.9	300			34%	5.19	13.1	2.7	5.9	2.2	1.0	--	70%	46	92

6-10, 5.16 ERA in 136 IP at MON and FLA, though that's not quite as accurate as this:

	MON	FLA	Start	Pen
ERA	6.30	3.80	5.42	3.80
CMD	1.6	2.9	1.9	3.0

Adjust expectations accordingly.

Peavy,Jake

	Yr	Tm	W	L	Sv	IP	ERA	Br/IP	R$	BF/G	OBA	vLH	vRH	H%	xERA	RAR	Ctl	Dom	Cmd	hr/9	G/F	S%	BPV	BPX
RH Starter	98		0	0	0	0	0.00	0.00																
AGE 21 Green	99		0	0	0	0	0.00	0.00																
TYPE Power	00		0	0	0	0	0.00	0.00																
BURN High	01	aa	2	1	0	28	3.21	1.18	$3	23.0	210			30%	3.01	8.3	3.9	11.9	3.1	1.0		77%	120	231
ERA Potl +	02	SD	* 10	12	0	177	4.01	1.37	$10	24.5	264	321	225	33%	4.08	34.3	3.3	8.4	2.6	0.8	1.26	72%	84	172
Support 5.25	1st Half		4	7	0	89	3.54	1.34	$6	23.7	248			32%	3.54	23.0	3.6	8.3	2.3	0.5		74%	88	180
LIMA B+	2nd Half		6	5	0	88	4.50	1.41	$4	25.4	279			34%	4.63	11.3	2.9	8.5	3.0	1.0		70%	82	168
Risk X HIGH	03	Proj	9	10	0	160	4.11	1.38	$8	24.5	267			33%	4.17	28.9	3.2	8.4	2.7	0.8	--	72%	83	166

6-7, 4.55 ERA in 97 IP at SD. His DOM/DIS split was 59/24, which indicates great talent but problems with consistency. That will improve as he matures, but at 21, let's hope SD allows him to do it at a reasonable pace.

Penny,Brad

	Yr	Tm	W	L	Sv	IP	ERA	Br/IP	R$	BF/G	OBA	vLH	vRH	H%	xERA	RAR	Ctl	Dom	Cmd	hr/9	G/F	S%	BPV	BPX
RH Starter	98		0	0	0	0	0.00	0.00																
AGE 24 Growth	99	aa	3	7	0	122	4.94	1.48	$0	23.3	298			37%	4.80	12.3	2.5	8.3	3.3	0.8		67%	90	208
TYPE	00	FLA	* 10	7	0	134	4.49	1.48	$8	22.7	253	249	274	29%	4.32	20.4	4.7	6.3	1.3	0.9	1.27	71%	42	93
BURN Low	01	FLA	10	10	0	205	3.69	1.16	$17	27.0	240	236	244	28%	3.09 +	46.1	2.4	6.8	2.9	0.7	1.50	69%	88	162
ERA Potl - -	02	FLA	8	7	0	129	4.67	1.53	$2	23.9	289	294	284	32%	5.34 -	13.6	3.5	6.5	1.9	1.3	1.31	73%	37	77
Support 4.87	1st Half		3	3	0	41	4.81	1.77	($1)	24.2	313			33%	6.38 -	3.6	4.4	4.4	1.0	1.3		76%	0	0
LIMA B	2nd Half		5	4	0	88	4.61	1.42	$2	23.8	277			32%	4.85	10.0	3.1	7.5	2.4	1.2		71%	59	120
Risk Very High	03	Proj	11	11	0	200	4.14	1.42	$9	24.1	275			31%	4.59	35.2	3.1	6.6	2.1	1.0	--	73%	53	106

BPIs show that his elbow woes likely impacted all his 1st half starts. 2nd half was more encouraging, though he did have some problems with the longball. He looks good to go for 2003.

Percival,Troy

	Yr	Tm	W	L	Sv	IP	ERA	Br/IP	R$	BF/G	OBA	vLH	vRH	H%	xERA	RAR	Ctl	Dom	Cmd	hr/9	G/F	S%	BPV	BPX
RH Reliever	98	ANA	2	7	42	66	3.67	1.24	$28	4.1	194	206	164	29%	2.70 +	17.6	5.0	11.8	2.4	0.7	0.58	71%	116	248
AGE 33 Past	99	ANA	4	6	31	57	3.79	1.05	$26	3.8	191	214	152	22%	2.92 +	15.9	3.5	9.2	2.6	1.4	0.55	71%	84	212
TYPE Power	00	ANA	5	5	32	50	4.50	1.44	$23	4.0	230	237	220	28%	4.17	9.5	5.4	8.8	1.6	1.3	0.65	72%	59	152
BURN none	01	ANA	4	2	39	57	2.67	1.00	$31	3.9	195	176	202	29%	1.91 +	21.5	2.8	11.2	3.9	0.5	0.81	74%	152	304
ERA Potl -	02	ANA	4	1	40	56	1.93	1.13	$27	3.9	194	247	138	27%	2.44 -	23.8	4.0	10.9	2.7	0.8	0.53	88%	115	217
Support 1.76	1st Half		2	1	19	24	2.24	1.29	$12	3.8	218			32%	3.07 -	9.2	4.5	12.0	2.7	0.7		86%	117	220
LIMA C+	2nd Half		2	0	21	32	1.69	1.00	$15	4.0	174			23%	1.96	14.6	3.7	10.2	2.8	0.8		90%	114	215
Risk Very Low	03	Proj	4	3	41	60	2.70	1.13	$29	3.9	199			27%	2.51	21.4	3.9	10.7	2.7	0.8	F	79%	114	232

Walked a few more batters in '02, allowed a few more fly balls, but otherwise still remains a solid pick. However, with an 88% strand rate, his ERA is headed back up over 2.00, and likely closer to 3.00, for sure.

Perez,Odalis

	Yr	Tm	W	L	Sv	IP	ERA	Br/IP	R$	BF/G	OBA	vLH	vRH	H%	xERA	RAR	Ctl	Dom	Cmd	hr/9	G/F	S%	BPV	BPX
LH Starter	98	ATL	* 7	8	3	167	3.99	1.32	$9	15.4	258	500	182	33%	3.97	27.9	3.1	9.2	3.0	0.9	3.14	72%	93	168
AGE 24 Growth	99	ATL	4	6	0	93	6.00	1.65	($4)	23.6	276	333	266	33%	5.21 +	-5.6	5.1	7.9	1.5	1.2	2.14	65%	45	98
TYPE	00	ATL	0	0	0	0	0.00	0.00																
BURN Very High	01	ATL	* 8	8	0	118	4.65	1.49	$3	18.0	289	342	278	34%	4.56	11.3	3.1	6.9	2.2	0.6	1.60	68%	66	123
ERA Potl + +	02	LA	15	10	0	222	3.00	0.99	$34	27.1	225	223	226	25%	2.72	73.1	1.5	6.3	4.1	0.9	1.36	73%	108	221
Support 4.94	1st Half		9	4	0	123	2.56	0.88	$25	27.5	208			24%	2.04 +	47.7	1.2	6.1	4.9	0.7		74%	133	272
LIMA D+	2nd Half		6	6	0	99	3.55	1.13	$12	26.7	246			28%	3.56	25.4	1.9	6.5	3.4	1.1		73%	84	173
Risk X HIGH	03	Proj	12	11	0	200	3.60	1.17	$20	24.8	246			29%	3.40	49.7	2.3	7.0	3.1	0.9	--	72%	88	177

Buy him, keep him, but be aware of two risks...
- Huge workload increase could lead to burnout. Note '02 signs within 1H/2H splits already.
- 25% hit rate means his ERA will likely rise into the mid-3's.

Perez,Oliver

	Yr	Tm	W	L	Sv	IP	ERA	Br/IP	R$	BF/G	OBA	vLH	vRH	H%	xERA	RAR	Ctl	Dom	Cmd	hr/9	G/F	S%	BPV	BPX
LH Starter	98		0	0	0	0	0.00	0.00																
AGE 21 Green	99		0	0	0	0	0.00	0.00																
TYPE Power	00		0	0	0	0	0.00	0.00																
BURN none	01		0	0	0	0	0.00	0.00																
ERA Potl -	02	SD	* 5	5	0	113	3.11	1.30	$10	23.8	207	294	191	26%	3.48	35.6	5.1	9.8	1.9	1.1	0.80	81%	79	163
Support 3.90	1st Half		3	0	0	41	1.97	1.29	$6	24.8	189			25%	2.61 -	19.3	5.7	9.2	1.6	0.4		86%	93	191
LIMA B+	2nd Half		2	5	0	72	3.76	1.31	$3	23.4	217			27%	3.99	16.3	4.8	10.2	2.1	1.5		78%	72	148
Risk Moderate	03	Proj	6	6	0	140	4.31	1.44	$3	24.4	236			30%	4.16	21.5	5.1	9.5	1.8	1.1	F	73%	70	141

4-5, 3.50 ERA in 90 IP at SD. A good future investment, but temper your '03 expectations:
- He hasn't solved LHers yet.
- He still walks a lot of batters.
- Keeps ball up = HR problems
- He's only 21.

Person,Robert

	Yr	Tm	W	L	Sv	IP	ERA	Br/IP	R$	BF/G	OBA	vLH	vRH	H%	xERA	RAR	Ctl	Dom	Cmd	hr/9	G/F	S%	BPV	BPX
RH Starter	98	TOR	* 6	4	12	97	4.82	1.57	$8	9.3	260	311	278	27%	5.59 -	10.9	5.2	6.9	1.3	1.9	0.80	76%	14	29
AGE 33 Past	99	2TM	10	7	2	148	4.68	1.51	$7	15.6	250	280	229	29%	4.82	20.1	5.2	8.5	1.6	1.5	0.76	74%	46	107
TYPE Power	00	PHI	9	7	0	173	3.64	1.38	$13	26.6	228	178	272	29%	3.49	46.1	4.9	8.5	1.7	0.7	0.69	75%	77	169
BURN none	01	PHI	15	7	0	208	4.20	1.24	$16	26.3	234	235	233	26%	3.98	32.6	3.5	7.9	2.3	1.5	0.59	72%	60	111
ERA Potl -	02	PHI	* 4	6	0	95	5.49	1.47	($2)	23.2	247	243	239	27%	4.74 +	-0.4	4.9	6.3	1.3	1.4	0.56	66%	28	58
Support 5.44	1st Half		3	5	0	77	5.02	1.36	$1	23.6	238			26%	4.22 +	4.5	4.3	6.5	1.5	1.3		66%	40	82
LIMA C+	2nd Half		1	1	0	18	7.50	1.94	($3)	21.9	283			29%	6.98 +	-4.9	7.5	5.5	0.7	2.0		65%	-13	-27
Risk High	03	Proj	7	6	0	120	4.65	1.41	$4	20.8	244			26%	4.58	12.9	4.5	6.2	1.4	1.5	F	72%	28	56

Recovery from his late season shoulder surgery will cut into his 2003 innings. Given his short-term track record of acceptable BPIs, expectations for future productivity should be low.

Pettitte,Andy

	Yr	Tm	W	L	Sv	IP	ERA	Br/IP	R$	BF/G	OBA	vLH	vRH	H%	xERA	RAR	Ctl	Dom	Cmd	hr/9	G/F	S%	BPV	BPX
LH Starter	98	NYY	16	11	0	216	4.25	1.45	$14	28.6	271	281	271	31%	4.40	40.8	3.6	6.1	1.7	0.8	2.22	72%	48	102
AGE 30 Peak	99	NYY	14	11	0	191	4.71	1.60	$8	27.8	286	275	293	32%	5.11	29.7	4.2	5.7	1.4	0.9	2.08	72%	32	81
TYPE	00	NYY	19	9	0	204	4.36	1.46	$18	28.0	276	256	275	31%	4.40	42.3	3.5	5.5	1.6	0.7	1.70	71%	19	110
BURN none	01	NYY	15	10	0	200	4.00	1.32	$15	27.4	284	251	289	34%	4.08	39.8	1.8	7.4	4.0	0.6	1.50	70%	108	215
ERA Potl +	02	NYY	* 13	5	0	140	3.21	1.28	$15	25.6	271	255	276	32%	3.46	35.5	2.1	6.4	3.1	0.4	1.34	75%	93	177
Support 5.21	1st Half		2	2	0	40	3.35	1.44	$2	22.0	275			31%	4.19 -	9.5	3.3	5.4	1.6	0.7		78%	46	87
LIMA C	2nd Half		11	3	0	100	3.16	1.21	$13	27.5	270			33%	3.16	26.1	1.5	6.9	4.5	0.3		73%	128	242
Risk Low	03	Proj	17	9	0	200	3.74	1.33	$18	25.8	276			32%	3.89	43.7	2.3	6.4	2.8	0.6	--	72%	79	161

Do players step up their game in their free agent year? The evidence here says yes, but the odds are really about 50-50. In this case, his ERA has caught up to his BPIs. Coincidence that it happened now.

Phelps,Travis

	Yr	Tm	W	L	Sv	IP	ERA	Br/IP	R$	BF/G	OBA	vLH	vRH	H%	xERA	RAR	Ctl	Dom	Cmd	hr/9	G/F	S%	BPV	BPX
RH Reliever	98		0	0	0	0	0.00	0.00																
AGE 25 Growth	99		0	0	0	0	0.00	0.00																
TYPE Power	00	a/a	10	9	0	138	3.78	1.33	$14	21.7	243			29%	3.58	36.6	3.8	7.2	1.9	0.7		73%	68	161
BURN none	01	TAM	* 4	2	5	77	2.81	1.18	$12	5.4	233	223	227	28%	3.10	27.6	2.9	7.5	2.6	0.7	1.00	79%	86	172
ERA Potl +	02	TAM	* 4	4	8	68	5.16	1.54	$3	5.7	250	267	187	30%	4.58 +	-0.5	5.4	8.6	1.6	1.2	0.52	69%	54	102
Support 4.06	1st Half		3	2	8	36	5.50	1.56	$4	4.9	272			33%	4.73 +	-1.9	4.5	8.3	1.8	1.0		65%	59	111
LIMA B+	2nd Half		1	2	0	32	4.78	1.53	($1)	7.1	224			27%	4.40	1.4	6.5	9.0	1.4	1.4		73%	51	97
Risk High	03	Proj	2	4	1	60	4.05	1.38	$2	6.5	239			29%	3.79	10.6	4.5	8.1	1.8	0.9	F	73%	67	136

1-2, 4.86 ERA in 37 IP at TAM. His pitches were up in the zone this year, and you can see the result. More walks, more hits, more HRs, lower strand rate and higher ERA. It's a fundamental flaw that needs to be corrected.

Phillips,Jason		Tm	W	L	Sv	IP	ERA	Br/IP	R$	BF/G	OBA	vLH	vRH	H%	xERA	RAR	Ctl	Dom	Cmd	hr/9	G/F	S%	BPV	BPX
RH Starter	98	a/a	9	13	0	182	4.75	1.53	$1	27.0	296			34%	5.00	16.7	3.1	5.9	**1.9**	0.8		70%	46	90
AGE 29 Pre-Peak	99	PIT	* 0	0	0	10	12.60	2.80	($5)	8.2	376			48%	10.35 +	-9.4	9.9	10.8	**1.1**	1.8		54%	13	29
TYPE Contact	00	aaa	2	4	0	30	5.70	1.77	($1)	23.4	287			30%	5.78	0.2	5.7	4.5	**0.8**	1.2		69%	5	12
BURN none	01	a/a	4	4	0	68	6.88	1.72	($6)	13.1	310			34%	5.77 +	-13.3	4.1	4.9	**1.2**	0.9		59%	20	38
ERA Potl -	02	CLE	* 8	7	0	139	4.85	1.36	$3	24.8	277	247	277	30%	4.48	4.7	2.5	5.3	**2.1**	1.2	1.55	67%	41	77
Support 5.40	1st Half		6	4	0	86	4.39	1.24	$5	25.6	273			30%	3.82 +	8.3	1.7	5.5	**3.3**	0.8		66%	78	148
LIMA C+	2nd Half		2	3	0	53	5.60	1.55	($2)	23.7	283			29%	5.55	-3.5	3.9	4.9	**1.3**	1.7		68%	3	7
Risk X HIGH	**03**	**Proj**	**3**	**4**	**0**	**60**	**4.95**	**1.43**	**$1**	**20.1**	**281**			**30%**	**4.81**	**3.4**	**3.0**	**5.1**	**1.7**	**1.2**	**G**	**68%**	**29**	**59**

1-3, 5.05 ERA in 41 IP at CLE, which was a sharp drop-off from the more promising numbers he posted in AAA. At 29, the future was yesterday, so with his Sept. elbow surgery, he'll have to be good AND healthy to stick.

Pickford,Kevin		Tm	W	L	Sv	IP	ERA	Br/IP	R$	BF/G	OBA	vLH	vRH	H%	xERA	RAR	Ctl	Dom	Cmd	hr/9	G/F	S%	BPV	BPX
LH Reliever	98	a/a	11	2	0	138	3.98	1.29	$13	22.3	270			30%	4.08	26.8	2.2	5.9	**2.7**	0.9		71%	65	127
AGE 28 Pre-Peak	99		0	0	0	0	0.00	0.00																
TYPE	00	aa	0	5	0	22	10.64	2.55	($8)	12.0	392			41%	9.60 +	-14.4	6.5	3.3	**0.5**	1.2		57%	-30	
BURN none	01	ind	3	5	0	38	8.29	1.95	($6)	20.6	322			33%	7.46 +	-14.6	5.4	4.5	**0.8**	1.9		59%	-22	
ERA Potl +	02	SD	* 4	9	1	99	6.80	1.83	($12)	13.1	316	375	291	34%	6.02 +	-17.9	4.8	4.5	**0.9**	0.7	1.70	61%	17	35
Support 2.40	1st Half		3	6	0	71	4.18	1.45	$2	15.5	253			28%	4.04	12.2	4.4	5.2	**1.2**	0.6		71%	41	84
LIMA F	2nd Half		1	3	1	28	13.45	2.81	($15)	10.1	435			45%	11.03 +	-30.1	5.8	2.9	**0.5**	1.0		49%	-33	-68
Risk X HIGH	**03**	**Proj**	**2**	**4**	**0**	**40**	**5.85**	**1.78**	**($3)**	**9.9**	**303**			**32%**	**6.01**	**-2.1**	**5.0**	**4.3**	**0.9**	**1.1**	**G**	**68%**	**4**	**9**

0-2, 6.00 ERA in 30 IP at SD.
Quest for something good:
- HR rate is improving.
- OBA was good in the 1st half.
- Had a great season in 1998.

Everything else is bad, very bad, or downright awful.

Pineda,Luis		Tm	W	L	Sv	IP	ERA	Br/IP	R$	BF/G	OBA	vLH	vRH	H%	xERA	RAR	Ctl	Dom	Cmd	hr/9	G/F	S%	BPV	BPX
RH Reliever	98		0	0	0	0	0.00	0.00																
AGE 28 Pre-Peak	99		0	0	0	0	0.00	0.00																
TYPE Power	00		0	0	0	0	0.00	0.00																
BURN none	01	a/a	7	3	0	112	3.54	1.21	$11	13.6	233	135	367	28%	3.17	28.3	3.1	7.7	**2.5**	0.7	0.61	72%	85	163
ERA Potl No chg	02	CIN	* 1	4	0	44	4.48	1.45	($0)	6.7	224	250	200	27%	3.99	5.8	5.7	8.3	**1.5**	1.0	0.76	71%	60	124
Support 3.62	1st Half		1	4	0	44	4.47	1.44	($0)	6.7	224			27%	3.98 +	5.9	5.7	8.3	**1.5**	1.0		71%	61	124
LIMA B+	2nd Half		0	0	0	-0	0.00	0.00																
Risk Moderate	**03**	**Proj**	**1**	**1**	**0**	**15**	**4.20**	**1.33**	**$1**	**6.4**	**221**			**27%**	**3.24 +**	**2.5**	**4.8**	**7.8**	**1.6**	**0.6**	**F**	**68%**	**74**	**148**

September rotator cuff surgery will likely cost him most, if not all of the 2003 season.

Pineiro,Joel		Tm	W	L	Sv	IP	ERA	Br/IP	R$	BF/G	OBA	vLH	vRH	H%	xERA	RAR	Ctl	Dom	Cmd	hr/9	G/F	S%	BPV	BPX
RH Starter	98	aa	1	0	0	5	7.20	2.20	($0)	25.6	362			37%	8.70 -	-1.2	5.4	3.6	**0.7**	1.8		70%	-36	
AGE 24 Growth	99	aa	10	15	0	166	6.23	1.69	($5)	27.3	325			36%	6.21	-11.9	3.0	5.6	**1.8**	1.2		64%	25	57
TYPE	00	SEA	* 10	2	0	132	4.64	1.42	$10	21.2	270	357	294	31%	4.29	22.5	3.4	5.9	**1.7**	0.8	1.03	68%	48	124
BURN none	01	SEA	* 12	5	0	152	3.08	1.18	$19	17.8	226	230	150	27%	2.92	49.0	3.3	6.8	**2.1**	0.6	1.00	75%	76	152
ERA Potl -	02	SEA	14	7	0	194	3.25	1.25	$17	21.9	257	270	240	29%	3.88 -	48.3	2.5	6.3	**2.5**	1.1	1.28	79%	61	115
Support 5.60	1st Half		8	3	0	92	2.93	1.28	$10	18.4	251			29%	3.75 -	26.8	3.0	6.6	**2.2**	1.0		81%	60	114
LIMA C	2nd Half		6	4	0	102	3.53	1.23	$8	26.4	262			29%	4.00	21.5	2.0	6.1	**3.0**	1.2		77%	65	123
Risk Very High	**03**	**Proj**	**14**	**8**	**0**	**200**	**3.51**	**1.25**	**$19**	**20.9**	**259**			**30%**	**3.78**	**49.8**	**2.4**	**6.5**	**2.7**	**0.9**	**--**	**75%**	**71**	**144**

Solid BPIs and good trends. There's a lot to like here.

Plesac,Dan		Tm	W	L	Sv	IP	ERA	Br/IP	R$	BF/G	OBA	vLH	vRH	H%	xERA	RAR	Ctl	Dom	Cmd	hr/9	G/F	S%	BPV	BPX
LH Reliever	98	TOR	4	3	4	50	3.78	1.14	$9	2.6	225	198	264	30%	2.88 +	12.6	2.9	9.9	**3.4**	0.7	0.96	68%	120	256
AGE 41 Decline	99	2TM	2	4	1	44	5.93	1.52	($0)	3.1	287	192	364	38%	5.32 +	-1.4	3.5	10.8	**3.1**	1.4	0.84	63%	85	197
TYPE Power	00	ARI	5	1	0	40	3.15	1.50	$6	2.9	232	260	194	31%	4.03 -	13.3	5.9	10.1	**1.7**	0.9	1.05	82%	79	174
BURN none	01	TOR	4	5	1	45	3.59	1.29	$5	3.1	211	184	234	34%	3.12	11.4	4.8	13.6	**2.8**	0.8	0.87	74%	130	260
ERA Potl +	02	2TM	3	3	1	36	4.25	1.25	$4	2.5	210	120	300	26%	3.67 +	4.9	4.5	10.3	**2.3**	1.5	0.72	72%	77	152
Support 2.72	1st Half		2	3	1	21	5.09	1.42	$2	2.8	251			33%	4.39 +	0.5	4.2	10.6	**2.5**	1.3		67%	83	163
LIMA B+	2nd Half		1	0	0	15	3.04	1.01	$3	2.2	144			13%	2.65	4.4	4.9	9.7	**2.0**	1.8		83%	72	141
Risk Moderate	**03**	**Proj**	**3**	**4**	**1**	**40**	**4.50**	**1.45**	**$3**	**2.9**	**242**			**31%**	**4.24**	**4.9**	**5.0**	**10.1**	**2.0**	**1.1**	**F**	**72%**	**77**	**155**

He's having a tougher time keeping the ball down ad it's reflected in his HR rate and inability to improve his BB rate. But as long as he's getting those LHers out, he'll have a job somewhere.

Politte,Cliff		Tm	W	L	Sv	IP	ERA	Br/IP	R$	BF/G	OBA	vLH	vRH	H%	xERA	RAR	Ctl	Dom	Cmd	hr/9	G/F	S%	BPV	BPX
RH Reliever	98	STL	* 8	10	0	155	5.86	1.58	($6)	24.9	299	315	293	34%	5.57	-12.9	3.4	6.6	**1.9**	1.3	1.04	65%	37	67
AGE 29 Pre-Peak	99	aa	9	8	5	109	4.62	1.57	$8	13.2	305	269	279	35%	5.56 -	15.7	3.0	6.8	**2.3**	1.2	1.16	74%	45	105
TYPE Power	00	PHI	* 12	7	0	171	3.68	1.36	$16	22.2	250	224	263	30%	3.87	44.7	3.7	7.7	**2.1**	0.8	1.06	75%	69	152
BURN none	01	PHI	2	3	0	26	2.42	1.23	$4	4.7	247	231	257	30%	3.38 -	10.2	2.8	8.0	**2.9**	0.7	1.70	83%	93	173
ERA Potl + + +	02	2TM	3	3	1	73	3.70	1.16	$7	4.4	217	272	159	28%	2.72 +	15.4	3.5	8.9	**2.6**	0.6	0.87	69%	100	197
Support 3.54	1st Half		3	1	0	34	3.70	1.17	$5	4.8	213			27%	2.62 +	7.2	3.7	8.2	**2.2**	0.5		68%	92	181
LIMA B+	2nd Half		0	2	1	39	3.70	1.16	$3	4.1	220			29%	2.81 +	8.2	3.2	9.5	**2.9**	0.7		69%	109	213
Risk X HIGH	**03**	**Proj**	**4**	**4**	**1**	**75**	**3.48**	**1.23**	**$8**	**7.1**	**235**			**29%**	**3.33**	**19.4**	**3.2**	**8.6**	**2.7**	**0.8**	**--**	**74%**	**91**	**184**

Closer-worthy? Base BPIs are solid, but a few warning signs...
- Declining G/F ratio.
- Low strand rate in 2002.
- Sudden trouble vs LHers
- Converted only 1 in 4 save opportunities in 2002.

Ponson,Sidney		Tm	W	L	Sv	IP	ERA	Br/IP	R$	BF/G	OBA	vLH	vRH	H%	xERA	RAR	Ctl	Dom	Cmd	hr/9	G/F	S%	BPV	BPX
RH Starter	98	BAL	8	9	1	135	5.27	1.47	$3	19.1	292	263	323	32%	5.19	7.0	2.8	5.7	**2.0**	1.3	1.14	67%	35	75
AGE 26 Growth	99	BAL	12	12	0	210	4.71	1.46	$10	28.8	277	287	277	29%	5.17	32.6	3.4	4.8	**1.4**	1.5	1.03	72%	13	32
TYPE	00	BAL	9	13	0	222	4.82	1.38	$10	29.8	263	259	258	29%	4.44	32.3	3.4	6.2	**1.8**	1.2	1.13	68%	41	108
BURN Moderate	01	BAL	5	10	0	138	4.95	1.43	$0	26.1	292	321	258	31%	5.20	9.8	2.4	5.5	**2.3**	1.4	1.28	69%	36	72
ERA Potl -	02	BAL	7	9	0	176	4.09	1.34	$5	26.7	257	243	273	28%	4.30	23.9	3.2	6.1	**1.9**	1.3	1.48	74%	40	77
Support 4.09	1st Half		3	4	0	103	4.02	1.35	$2	25.9	254			28%	4.19	15.0	3.5	6.1	**1.8**	1.2		74%	41	77
LIMA C	2nd Half		4	5	0	73	4.19	1.32	$3	28.1	262			28%	4.45	8.9	2.8	6.2	**2.2**	1.5		74%	41	77
Risk Moderate	**03**	**Proj**	**8**	**11**	**0**	**180**	**4.50**	**1.37**	**$5**	**26.6**	**270**			**29%**	**4.64**	**20.9**	**3.0**	**5.9**	**2.0**	**1.4**	**--**	**71%**	**38**	**77**

Had an inconsistent season, but displayed his best command when he came back from the DL in September -- 2.6 versus 1.8 the rest of the year. Is probably still recovering from the effects of his 1999-00 workload abuse.

Porzio,Mike		Tm	W	L	Sv	IP	ERA	Br/IP	R$	BF/G	OBA	vLH	vRH	H%	xERA	RAR	Ctl	Dom	Cmd	hr/9	G/F	S%	BPV	BPX
LH Reliever	98		0	0	0	0	0.00	0.00																
AGE 30 Peak	99	aaa	5	1	0	42	4.71	2.00	$0	5.9	317			34%	7.09 -	5.5	6.2	5.8	**0.9**	1.5		81%	1	2
TYPE Power	00	a/a	7	7	0	147	8.08	1.96	($19)	27.6	351			36%	8.35	-45.7	3.9	5.3	**1.4**	2.3		62%	-24	
BURN none	01	a/a	7	6	0	147	6.73	1.92	($16)	21.6	332			35%	7.26 -	-25.8	4.7	5.1	**1.1**	1.6		67%	-5	
ERA Potl - -	02	CHW	* 8	7	0	118	6.02	1.75	($6)	12.0	310	269	229	34%	6.52 -	-14.4	4.3	6.3	**1.5**	1.8	0.66	70%	9	17
Support 5.23	1st Half		2	4	0	53	8.95	2.25	($12)	15.3	372			39%	9.73 -	-27.4	5.2	6.4	**1.2**	2.7		64%	-36	-68
LIMA F	2nd Half		6	3	0	65	3.61	1.34	$6	9.9	250			28%	3.88	13.0	3.6	6.2	**1.7**	1.0		76%	50	94
Risk High	**03**	**Proj**	**3**	**2**	**0**	**40**	**5.85**	**1.78**	**($2)**	**9.4**	**316**			**34%**	**6.75 -**	**-2.6**	**4.3**	**5.9**	**1.4**	**1.8**	**F**	**71%**	**2**	**4**

2-2, 4.81 ERA in 43 IP at CHW. Must be a tools guy because he certainly ain't no sabermetric darling.

Pote,Lou		Tm	W	L	Sv	IP	ERA	Br/IP	R$	BF/G	OBA	vLH	vRH	H%	xERA	RAR	Ctl	Dom	Cmd	hr/9	G/F	S%	BPV	BPX
RH Reliever	98	aa	8	10	0	154	6.08	1.85	($11)	23.0	343			38%	6.77 -	-13.3	3.4	5.4	**1.6**	1.1		68%	20	40
AGE 31 Peak	99	ANA	* 8	10	3	179	6.03	1.68	($4)	18.7	323	184	239	36%	6.22	-3.9	3.0	6.2	**2.1**	1.3	3.18	66%	32	80
TYPE Power	00	ANA	* 3	2	13	80	3.81	1.42	$13	6.2	268	294	245	33%	4.10	22.6	3.5	7.6	**2.2**	0.7	2.11	74%	73	189
BURN none	01	ANA	2	0	2	86	4.18	1.39	$3	8.4	266	268	250	30%	4.49	15.1	3.3	6.9	**2.1**	1.1	2.24	73%	52	104
ERA Potl +	02	ANA	* 2	3	0	89	4.75	1.30	$0	9.9	244	221	172	28%	3.74 +	4.2	3.5	6.8	**1.9**	1.0	1.88	65%	57	107
Support 4.11	1st Half		0	1	0	40	2.91	1.17	$2	6.3	187			20%	2.60	11.8	4.7	5.6	**1.2**	0.9		79%	49	93
LIMA B	2nd Half		2	2	0	49	6.27	1.41	($2)	17.6	286			34%	4.67 +	-7.6	2.6	7.7	**3.0**	1.1		56%	74	140
Risk High	**03**	**Proj**	**1**	**1**	**0**	**50**	**4.14**	**1.40**	**$1**	**9.4**	**266**			**30%**	**4.38**	**8.2**	**3.4**	**6.8**	**2.0**	**1.1**	**G**	**73%**	**53**	**107**

0-2, 3.24 ERA in 50 IP at ANA. His BPIs are not half bad, but you can definitely see the beginnings of erosion here. Low strand rate puffed up his ERA so that should improve, given the opportunity.

Powell,Brian	Yr	Tm	W	L	Sv	IP	ERA	Br/IP	R$	BF/G	OBA	vLH	vRH	H%	xERA	RAR	Ctl	Dom	Cmd	hr/9	G/F	S%	BPV	BPX
RH Starter	98	DET	*13	10	0	184	4.93	1.43	$8	24.3	277	232	364	29%	4.91	17.9	3.1	4.9	**1.6**	1.3	1.22	69%	22	47
AGE 26 Growth	99	aaa	4	4	0	48	7.31	1.77	($3)	25.0	314			35%	5.94 +	-10.4	4.3	5.4	**1.3**	0.9		58%	23	54
TYPE Contact	00	HOU	*11	5	0	134	6.43	1.60	($1)	22.5	294	295	269	30%	5.62 +	-14.5	3.8	4.2	**1.1**	1.3	0.58	61%	4	10
BURN none	01	aaa	9	9	0	147	4.71	1.59	$1	26.5	310			33%	5.66 -	13.9	2.9	4.8	**1.7**	1.2	0.33	73%	22	43
ERA Potl -	02	DET	*11	8	0	176	5.16	1.56	($1)	23.9	313	293	262	34%	5.34	-1.3	2.5	5.0	**2.0**	1.0	1.03	68%	35	67
Support 3.28	1st Half		9	3	0	94	5.65	1.63	$0	26.7	329			37%	5.59	-6.8	2.2	5.4	**2.4**	0.8		65%	50	94
LIMA F	2nd Half		2	5	0	82	4.60	1.47	($1)	21.2	293			31%	5.06	5.5	2.7	4.5	**1.6**	1.2		72%	22	41
Risk X HIGH	03	Proj	**7**	**11**	**0**	**160**	**5.01**	**1.56**	**($2)**	**23.9**	**305**			**33%**	**5.43**	**7.8**	**2.9**	**4.8**	**1.6**	**1.1**	**--**	**70%**	**23**	**47**

1-5, 4.89 ERA in 57 IP at DET. There is some growth here, but it's painfully slow, and not across the board. With an OBA still over .300 and showing no improvement, his ceiling will be very low.

Powell,Jay	Yr	Tm	W	L	Sv	IP	ERA	Br/IP	R$	BF/G	OBA	vLH	vRH	H%	xERA	RAR	Ctl	Dom	Cmd	hr/9	G/F	S%	BPV	BPX
RH Reliever	98	2NL	7	7	7	70	3.34	1.36	$12	4.8	227	221	228	28%	3.51	17.8	4.8	8.0	**1.7**	0.8	2.04	78%	69	125
AGE 31 Peak	99	HOU	5	4	4	75	4.32	1.63	$4	5.1	279	304	265	37%	4.45	12.3	4.8	9.2	**1.9**	0.4	1.54	72%	84	183
TYPE Power	00	HOU	1	1	0	27	5.67	1.78	($2)	4.4	276	233	297	32%	4.84 +	-0.1	6.3	5.3	**0.8**	0.3	1.23	66%	40	87
BURN none	01	2NL	5	3	7	75	3.24	1.41	$10	4.4	262	296	233	30%	4.42 -	21.4	3.7	6.5	**1.7**	1.1	2.50	81%	46	85
ERA Potl --	02	TEX	*5	2	0	59	5.34	1.68	($1)	4.4	296	222	270	33%	5.62	-1.8	4.4	6.3	**1.4**	1.2	2.07	70%	26	50
Support 7.25	1st Half		3	1	0	16	11.67	2.22	($3)	4.6	380			40%	9.37 +	-14.2	4.4	5.6	**1.3**	2.2		47%	-28	-53
LIMA C+	2nd Half		2	1	0	43	2.94	1.47	$2	4.4	258			30%	4.19 -	12.4	4.4	6.5	**1.5**	0.8		83%	48	91
Risk Moderate	03	Proj	**3**	**3**	**2**	**60**	**4.95**	**1.62**	**$0**	**4.5**	**287**			**33%**	**5.20**	**3.4**	**4.4**	**6.9**	**1.6**	**1.1**	**G**	**71%**	**41**	**83**

3-2, 3.49 ERA in 49 IP at TEX. Command has fallen short of acceptable levels for 5 years now, and with injury history, makes him a very high risk. Add in his home ballpark, and he's pretty much undraftable.

Prior,Mark	Yr	Tm	W	L	Sv	IP	ERA	Br/IP	R$	BF/G	OBA	vLH	vRH	H%	xERA	RAR	Ctl	Dom	Cmd	hr/9	G/F	S%	BPV	BPX
RH Starter	98		0	0	0	0	0.00	0.00																
AGE 22 Growth	99		0	0	0	0	0.00	0.00																
TYPE Power	00		0	0	0	0	0.00	0.00																
BURN none	01		0	0	0	0	0.00	0.00																
ERA Potl +	02	CHC	*11	8	0	167	3.07	1.17	$21	24.4	229	204	242	33%	3.12	53.4	3.0	11.7	**3.9**	0.8	0.81	77%	138	283
Support 4.63	1st Half		7	3	0	96	3.28	1.10	$14	22.7	198			29%	2.52 +	28.1	3.7	12.2	**3.3**	0.7		72%	136	279
LIMA C+	2nd Half		4	5	0	71	2.79	1.26	$8	26.9	267			37%	3.93 -	25.3	2.0	11.0	**5.4**	0.9		82%	155	319
Risk Moderate	03	Proj	**13**	**7**	**0**	**180**	**3.25**	**1.22**	**$21**	**25.7**	**246**			**35%**	**3.44**	**53.1**	**2.7**	**11.5**	**4.3**	**0.8**	**--**	**76%**	**140**	**282**

6-6, 3.34 ERA in 116 IP at CHC. The real deal. This projection gives CHC the benefit of the doubt that they will not overwork him, but sometimes "need" outweighs "smarts" in the good ol' boy decision-making process.

Prokopec,Luke	Yr	Tm	W	L	Sv	IP	ERA	Br/IP	R$	BF/G	OBA	vLH	vRH	H%	xERA	RAR	Ctl	Dom	Cmd	hr/9	G/F	S%	BPV	BPX
RH Reliever	98	aa	3	0	0	26	2.08	1.27	$5	21.8	197			25%	2.54	11.7	5.2	7.6	**1.5**	0.3		84%	82	159
AGE 25 Growth	99	aa	8	12	0	157	5.68	1.41	$3	25.2	289			33%	4.67 +	0.5	2.4	6.2	**2.6**	1.0		60%	60	140
TYPE Contact	00	LA	*8	4	0	149	2.66	1.19	$19	22.7	257	229	296	31%	3.27 -	59.3	1.9	7.1	**3.7**	0.5	0.61	79%	108	237
BURN none	01	LA	8	7	0	138	4.89	1.35	$4	20.3	273	234	296	29%	5.06	8.8	2.6	5.9	**2.3**	1.8	0.72	70%	31	57
ERA Potl -	02	TOR	2	9	0	73	6.66	1.58	($6)	13.7	304	346	250	30%	6.54	-15.2	3.1	5.3	**1.7**	2.3	0.70	64%	-8	-15
Support 3.77	1st Half		2	7	0	63	5.86	1.57	($3)	23.6	302			31%	6.05	-6.3	3.1	5.3	**1.7**	1.9		67%	6	11
LIMA F	2nd Half		0	2	0	10	11.70	1.60	($2)	3.8	316			24%	9.66 +	-8.8	2.7	5.4	**2.0**	5.4		30%	-96	******
Risk X HIGH	03	Proj	**1**	**1**	**0**	**15**	**4.80**	**1.47**	**$0**	**8.2**	**274**			**29%**	**4.80**	**1.1**	**3.6**	**4.8**	**1.3**	**1.2**	**F**	**70%**	**21**	**43**

Is expected to miss most, if not all of the 2003 season following shoulder surgery.

Puffer,Brandon	Yr	Tm	W	L	Sv	IP	ERA	Br/IP	R$	BF/G	OBA	vLH	vRH	H%	xERA	RAR	Ctl	Dom	Cmd	hr/9	G/F	S%	BPV	BPX
RH Reliever	98		0	0	0	0	0.00	0.00																
AGE 27 Pre-Peak	99		0	0	0	0	0.00	0.00																
TYPE Power	00		0	0	0	0	0.00	0.00																
BURN none	01	aa	6	1	8	82	3.07	1.38	$12	6.3	232			28%	3.54	25.8	4.7	7.5	**1.6**	0.7		79%	67	128
ERA Potl -	02	HOU	*5	4	0	84	4.07	1.43	$4	5.5	248	319	234	29%	3.71	15.6	4.5	6.2	**1.4**	0.4	1.92	71%	59	121
Support 5.48	1st Half		2	1	0	38	4.03	1.55	$1	6.1	246			30%	3.82	7.3	5.7	6.9	**1.2**	0.2		72%	65	134
LIMA C+	2nd Half		3	3	0	46	4.11	1.33	$3	5.1	249			28%	3.62	8.3	3.5	5.7	**1.6**	0.6		69%	55	114
Risk Low	03	Proj	**1**	**1**	**0**	**40**	**4.28**	**1.48**	**$0**	**5.9**	**252**			**29%**	**4.09**	**6.3**	**4.7**	**6.1**	**1.3**	**0.7**	**G**	**71%**	**48**	**96**

3-3, 4.43 ERA in 69 IP at HOU. Keeps ball in the park but can't get lefties out. Keeps ball on the ground but is showing no BPI growth. His AA season was unexciting; what makes them think it will get better in the bigs?

Quantrill,Paul	Yr	Tm	W	L	Sv	IP	ERA	Br/IP	R$	BF/G	OBA	vLH	vRH	H%	xERA	RAR	Ctl	Dom	Cmd	hr/9	G/F	S%	BPV	BPX
RH Reliever	98	TOR	3	4	7	80	2.59	1.38	$11	4.2	281	258	305	33%	4.10 -	32.9	2.5	6.6	**2.7**	0.6	2.45	83%	78	167
AGE 34 Decline	99	TOR	3	2	0	48	3.38	1.46	$4	5.1	281	261	294	31%	4.69 -	16.1	3.2	5.3	**1.6**	0.9	2.15	80%	37	92
TYPE	00	TOR	2	5	1	83	4.54	1.50	$2	5.4	299	299	296	33%	4.86	15.2	2.7	5.1	**1.9**	0.8	1.70	70%	42	110
BURN none	01	TOR	11	2	2	83	3.04	1.18	$16	4.3	269	355	232	31%	3.53 -	27.2	1.3	6.3	**4.8**	0.7	2.06	76%	121	242
ERA Potl -	02	LA	5	4	1	76	2.72	1.38	$9	3.8	272	254	275	33%	3.63 -	27.8	3.0	6.3	**2.1**	0.1	2.25	79%	79	163
Support 3.05	1st Half		0	2	0	40	3.36	1.22	$2	3.9	251			31%	3.03	11.3	2.5	6.7	**2.7**	0.2		71%	96	196
LIMA B	2nd Half		5	2	1	36	2.01	1.56	$7	3.7	294			35%	4.30 -	16.5	3.5	5.8	**1.6**	0.0		86%	65	134
Risk Moderate	03	Proj	**7**	**4**	**2**	**80**	**3.04**	**1.38**	**$10**	**4.1**	**278**			**32%**	**3.99 -**	**25.9**	**2.6**	**6.0**	**2.3**	**0.5**	**G**	**78%**	**70**	**141**

Control was not quite as good as 2001, but his overall BPIs were more than serviceable. Consistently outperforms his stats, which will only be helped by Dodger Stadium. Solid end-game pick.

Quevedo,Ruben	Yr	Tm	W	L	Sv	IP	ERA	Br/IP	R$	BF/G	OBA	vLH	vRH	H%	xERA	RAR	Ctl	Dom	Cmd	hr/9	G/F	S%	BPV	BPX
RH Starter	98		0	0	0	0	0.00	0.00																
AGE 24 Growth	99	aaa	9	6	0	150	4.92	1.27	$10	22.4	253			30%	4.16 +	15.6	2.8	8.8	**3.1**	1.4		65%	82	189
TYPE Power	00	CHC	*10	12	0	162	6.16	1.56	($2)	21.4	270	245	289	30%	5.28 +	-11.5	4.7	7.3	**1.6**	1.5	0.71	63%	32	72
BURN none	01	MIL	*13	10	0	197	3.56	1.32	$16	26.1	250	275	241	31%	3.84	47.6	3.4	8.9	**2.6**	0.9	0.59	76%	86	159
ERA Potl --	02	MIL	6	11	0	141	5.68	1.62	($7)	23.7	287	271	302	30%	6.03	-4.2	4.4	6.1	**1.4**	1.8	0.60	70%	10	20
Support 4.92	1st Half		3	6	0	92	4.30	1.48	$1	23.8	268			29%	4.89 -	14.4	4.0	6.2	**1.6**	1.3		75%	34	69
LIMA D	2nd Half		3	5	0	49	8.30	1.91	($9)	23.5	321			32%	8.19	-18.6	5.2	5.9	**1.1**	2.8		62%	-33	-67
Risk Very High	03	Proj	**7**	**10**	**0**	**140**	**4.89**	**1.46**	**$1**	**23.6**	**266**			**30%**	**4.88**	**10.7**	**4.0**	**6.9**	**1.7**	**1.4**	**F**	**70%**	**39**	**78**

Solid BPIs coming into '02, but struggled early. Posted 5,5,5,5 PQS scores in May, then tanked again. He finished with a horrible 28/52 DOM/DIS split. There is talent here, but it will be tough to mine. High risk.

Radke,Brad	Yr	Tm	W	L	Sv	IP	ERA	Br/IP	R$	BF/G	OBA	vLH	vRH	H%	xERA	RAR	Ctl	Dom	Cmd	hr/9	G/F	S%	BPV	BPX
RH Starter	98	MIN	12	14	0	213	4.31	1.32	$14	28.2	284	324	236	32%	4.39	38.6	1.8	6.2	**3.4**	1.0	1.24	69%	77	165
AGE 30 Peak	99	MIN	12	14	0	218	3.76	1.30	$20	27.9	280	281	278	30%	4.47 -	61.7	1.8	5.0	**2.8**	1.2	1.35	75%	62	131
TYPE Contact	00	MIN	12	16	0	226	4.46	1.38	$14	28.6	290	297	274	32%	4.71	44.1	2.0	5.6	**2.8**	1.1	1.34	70%	66	146
BURN none	01	MIN	15	11	0	226	3.94	1.15	$21	27.9	269	271	271	30%	3.77	46.7	1.0	5.5	**5.3**	1.0	1.11	68%	116	232
ERA Potl ++	02	MIN	9	5	0	118	4.73	1.22	$7	23.3	271	247	300	29%	3.83 +	6.0	1.5	4.7	**3.1**	0.9	1.05	62%	67	126
Support 6.08	1st Half		4	2	0	51	5.27	1.31	$2	21.7	272			29%	4.03 +	-1.1	2.3	4.2	**1.8**	0.9		60%	38	72
LIMA B	2nd Half		5	3	0	67	4.31	1.15	$5	24.7	271			30%	3.67 +	7.1	0.9	5.1	**5.4**	0.9		64%	117	222
Risk Low	03	Proj	**14**	**10**	**0**	**200**	**3.83**	**1.21**	**$18**	**25.0**	**269**			**29%**	**3.83**	**41.3**	**1.5**	**5.1**	**3.5**	**0.9**	**--**	**71%**	**76**	**155**

xERA shows the reality of this season, mucked up by a 62% strand rate. As a soft tosser, his ceiling will be limited, but he's certainly matured to the point where he should be posting better numbers than these.

Reames,Britt	Yr	Tm	W	L	Sv	IP	ERA	Br/IP	R$	BF/G	OBA	vLH	vRH	H%	xERA	RAR	Ctl	Dom	Cmd	hr/9	G/F	S%	BPV	BPX
RH Reliever	98		0	0	0	0	0.00	0.00																
AGE 29 Peak	99		0	0	0	0	0.00	0.00																
TYPE Power	00	STL	*10	6	0	154	4.02	1.33	$13	22.6	249	208	206	31%	3.61	33.2	3.6	8.1	**2.2**	0.6	1.19	70%	82	180
BURN High	01	MON	*8	11	0	149	5.38	1.50	($1)	13.5	277	297	258	32%	5.03	-0.2	3.8	7.0	**1.8**	1.3	1.65	67%	42	78
ERA Potl -	02	MON	*4	6	0	110	4.66	1.49	($1)	9.9	264	342	234	32%	4.59	11.7	4.3	7.9	**1.8**	1.0	1.66	70%	58	119
Support 3.57	1st Half		2	2	0	47	5.36	1.51	($1)	6.9	274			35%	4.57 +	0.6	4.0	8.8	**2.2**	0.8		64%	76	156
LIMA B	2nd Half		2	4	0	63	4.14	1.48	$1	14.6	256			29%	4.60	11.1	4.6	7.1	**1.6**	1.1		75%	45	93
Risk X HIGH	03	Proj	**3**	**4**	**0**	**60**	**4.50**	**1.47**	**$1**	**9.7**	**265**			**31%**	**4.58**	**7.7**	**4.1**	**7.5**	**1.9**	**1.1**	**G**	**72%**	**54**	**109**

1-4, 5.03 ERA in 68 IP at MON.

	G	IP	ERA	Cmd
Starter	6	20	7.53	1.7
Reliever	36	48	3.97	2.2

No question where he belongs.

Redding,Tim		Tm	W	L	Sv	IP	ERA	Br/IP	R$	BF/G	OBA	vLH	vRH	H%	xERA	RAR	Ctl	Dom	Cmd	hr/9	G/F	S%	BPV	BPX
RH Reliever	98		0	0	0	0	0.00	0.00																
AGE 25 Growth	99		0	0	0	0	0.00	0.00																
TYPE Power	00	aa	2	0	0	26	4.50	1.65	$1	23.8	197			22%	4.15	4.4	8.7	6.9	0.8	1.0		75%	43	101
BURN none	01	HOU	* 17	4	0	183	4.28	1.27	$17	23.3	240	247	311	30%	3.80	26.7	3.4	9.2	2.7	1.1	0.98	70%	85	158
ERA Potl + +	02	HOU	* 6	9	0	111	6.00	1.50	($3)	16.9	272	258	290	32%	5.16 +	-8.0	4.0	8.6	2.2	1.5	0.99	62%	54	110
Support 3.44	1st Half		5	5	0	77	4.90	1.37	$3	20.7	259			31%	4.51	5.7	3.5	8.2	2.3	1.3		67%	63	129
LIMA B	2nd Half		1	4	0	34	8.50	1.77	($7)	12.2	300			36%	6.63 +	-13.8	5.0	9.6	1.9	1.9		53%	36	75
Risk X HIGH	03	Proj	8	10	0	140	4.63	1.37	$6	16.7	253			31%	4.39	15.5	3.7	9.1	2.4	1.3	--	70%	71	143

3-6, 5.42 ERA in 73 IP at HOU. While there was a drop-off in his BPIs, it wasn't enough to justify a nearly 2-run ballooning of his ERA. You can thank his strand rate and shoulder problems for that. If healthy, will rebound.

Redman,Mark		Tm	W	L	Sv	IP	ERA	Br/IP	R$	BF/G	OBA	vLH	vRH	H%	xERA	RAR	Ctl	Dom	Cmd	hr/9	G/F	S%	BPV	BPX
LH Starter	98	a/a	10	9	0	147	5.57	1.66	($3)	24.9	304			35%	5.79	-2.8	3.9	7.3	1.9	1.2		68%	41	80
AGE 29 Pre-Peak	99	aaa	9	9	0	133	5.55	1.52	$2	24.6	290	385	273	34%	4.74 +	2.6	3.3	6.8	2.0	0.7	1.29	63%	58	135
TYPE Contact	00	MIN	12	9	0	151	4.77	1.41	$11	20.4	283	282	281	32%	4.88	23.2	2.7	7.0	2.6	1.3	0.75	70%	56	144
BURN High	01	MIN	* 2	7	0	73	5.18	1.55	($2)	21.7	299	333	285	32%	5.47	3.0	3.1	5.3	1.7	1.2	0.93	69%	26	52
ERA Potl No chg	02	DET	8	15	0	203	4.21	1.29	$7	28.5	269	289	261	30%	3.74	24.3	2.3	4.8	2.1	0.7	1.01	68%	55	104
Support 3.68	1st Half		3	8	0	112	3.61	1.31	$4	29.7	270			30%	3.70	22.5	2.4	4.8	2.0	0.6		73%	55	104
LIMA C	2nd Half		5	7	0	91	4.96	1.27	$3	27.2	269			29%	3.79 +	1.8	2.1	4.9	2.3	0.8		61%	56	105
Risk X HIGH	03	Proj	9	15	0	200	4.32	1.32	$9	24.2	270			29%	4.12	28.1	2.4	5.0	2.1	0.9	--	69%	46	94

On a team with a better bullpen, we could safely project an ERA under 4.00. But despite his declining K rate, he could see some short-term success and be wholly draftable... but not in DET. There he is a sub-$10 arm.

Reed,Rick		Tm	W	L	Sv	IP	ERA	Br/IP	R$	BF/G	OBA	vLH	vRH	H%	xERA	RAR	Ctl	Dom	Cmd	hr/9	G/F	S%	BPV	BPX
RH Starter	98	NYM	16	11	0	212	3.48	1.12	$25	27.6	258	249	271	29%	3.81	49.9	1.2	6.5	5.3	1.3	1.37	75%	115	207
AGE 37 Decline	99	NYM	11	5	0	149	4.59	1.41	$9	24.8	280	296	269	31%	4.90	19.1	2.8	6.3	2.2	1.4	1.39	72%	42	90
TYPE Contact	00	NYM	11	5	0	184	4.11	1.23	$16	25.4	270	273	260	29%	4.34	37.5	1.7	5.9	3.6	1.4	1.24	72%	70	155
BURN none	01	2TM	12	12	0	202	4.05	1.20	$16	26.0	270	276	260	30%	4.15	37.1	1.4	6.3	4.6	1.2	1.07	71%	98	188
ERA Potl +	02	MIN	15	7	0	188	3.78	1.16	$18	23.2	266	262	257	28%	4.17	33.3	1.2	5.8	4.7	1.5	0.91	75%	88	167
Support 6.13	1st Half		6	4	0	84	4.82	1.30	$4	22.2	284			29%	5.14	3.3	1.6	5.9	3.7	1.9		70%	53	100
LIMA C	2nd Half		9	3	0	104	2.95	1.05	$14	24.3	251			27%	3.38	30.1	1.0	5.7	6.0	1.2		79%	129	244
Risk Moderate	03	Proj	13	9	0	200	4.10	1.23	$16	25.1	270			29%	4.40	34.1	1.6	5.8	3.6	1.5	--	73%	66	133

He's keeping the ball on the ground more, which helps offset the slight BPI decline. Still solid overall, but at 37, the risk starts to increase.

Reed,Steve		Tm	W	L	Sv	IP	ERA	Br/IP	R$	BF/G	OBA	vLH	vRH	H%	xERA	RAR	Ctl	Dom	Cmd	hr/9	G/F	S%	BPV	BPX
RH Reliever	98	2TM	4	3	1	80	3.15	1.04	$11	4.5	199	228	177	24%	2.49 +	24.5	3.0	8.2	2.7	0.9	1.04	73%	94	183
AGE 37 Decline	99	CLE	3	2	0	61	4.28	1.46	$3	4.2	286	267	295	32%	5.26 -	13.0	3.0	6.5	2.2	1.5	1.33	76%	39	97
TYPE	00	CLE	2	0	0	56	4.34	1.41	$3	4.3	269	271	268	30%	4.52	11.8	3.4	6.3	1.9	1.1	1.61	72%	44	115
BURN none	01	2TM	3	3	1	58	3.56	1.29	$5	3.5	241	514	148	28%	3.69	14.5	3.6	7.1	2.0	0.9	0.87	75%	64	122
ERA Potl No chg	02	2NL	2	5	1	67	2.01	1.04	$11	4.2	229	181	259	28%	2.34	30.9	1.9	6.7	3.6	0.3	1.78	81%	117	239
Support 4.16	1st Half		2	3	0	35	1.79	0.94	$7	4.2	202			25%	1.97	17.2	2.1	7.9	3.9	0.5		84%	128	263
LIMA B	2nd Half		0	2	1	32	2.26	1.16	$4	4.1	256			30%	2.76 -	13.7	1.7	5.4	3.2	0.0		78%	102	210
Risk Moderate	03	Proj	2	3	1	60	3.00	1.18	$7	4.0	242			29%	3.14	19.7	2.6	6.6	2.6	0.6	G	76%	83	166

His highest BPV and first 100+ level since 1995. Ten years ago, he saved 43 games in the minors, and his pen indicators have shown some potential to close. At 37, he won't get that chance, but he's still draftable.

Reichert,Dan		Tm	W	L	Sv	IP	ERA	Br/IP	R$	BF/G	OBA	vLH	vRH	H%	xERA	RAR	Ctl	Dom	Cmd	hr/9	G/F	S%	BPV	BPX
RH Reliever	98	a/a	2	5	0	53	8.83	1.83	($9)	22.9	322			34%	6.81 +	-24.1	4.4	5.1	1.2	1.5		51%	-0	-1
AGE 26 Growth	99	KC	* 11	4	0	147	5.57	1.55	$4	26.3	267	342	311	32%	4.45 +	5.9	4.7	7.5	1.6	0.7	2.03	63%	60	151
TYPE Power	00	KC	8	10	2	153	4.70	1.62	$4	15.8	267	274	268	30%	4.80	24.8	5.3	5.5	1.0	0.9	2.78	72%	30	78
BURN none	01	KC	* 9	13	0	155	6.56	1.71	($10)	19.4	295	309	243	33%	5.63 +	-22.3	4.8	5.9	1.2	1.0	2.40	62%	26	53
ERA Potl +	02	KC	* 3	6	0	82	6.91	1.77	($8)	8.9	314	295	314	34%	6.02 +	-19.9	4.3	5.2	1.2	1.1	2.22	61%	15	29
Support 5.73	1st Half		3	5	0	62	5.21	1.54	($1)	10.3	297			32%	5.37	-0.9	3.2	5.1	1.6	1.3		69%	20	39
LIMA D	2nd Half		0	1	0	20	12.27	2.47	($8)	6.7	364			41%	8.05 +	-19.0	7.7	5.5	0.7	0.5		46%	16	30
Risk Very High	03	Proj	4	7	0	100	5.58	1.69	($5)	10.2	297			33%	5.40	-2.8	4.5	5.6	1.2	0.9	G	67%	28	57

3-5, 5.32 ERA in 66 IP at KC.

	IP	ERA	OBA	Cmd
Starter	35	7.01	.348	1.6
Reliever	31	3.45	.254	1.3

Might have better success in the pen, but poor Cmd will come back to bite him wherever he is.

Reitsma,Chris		Tm	W	L	Sv	IP	ERA	Br/IP	R$	BF/G	OBA	vLH	vRH	H%	xERA	RAR	Ctl	Dom	Cmd	hr/9	G/F	S%	BPV	BPX
RH Starter	98		0	0	0	0	0.00	0.00																
AGE 25 Growth	99		0	0	0	0	0.00	0.00																
TYPE Contact	00	aa	7	2	0	90	3.30	1.26	$12	26.8	266			29%	3.72	29.7	2.1	4.8	2.3	0.7		75%	58	136
BURN none	01	CIN	7	15	0	182	5.29	1.42	($1)	21.9	289	279	296	31%	4.90	1.8	2.4	4.7	2.0	1.1	1.05	64%	33	61
ERA Potl - -	02	CIN	* 8	12	0	159	3.74	1.35	$10	19.4	265	265	268	29%	4.36 -	36.7	2.9	5.4	1.8	1.1	1.46	76%	40	83
Support 3.32	1st Half		3	6	0	90	3.60	1.38	$4	24.2	266			30%	3.91	22.4	3.2	5.0	1.6	0.5		74%	50	102
LIMA C	2nd Half		5	6	0	69	3.91	1.30	$6	15.3	265			27%	4.94 -	14.3	2.6	5.9	2.3	1.8		79%	30	61
Risk High	03	Proj	9	11	0	160	4.22	1.35	$9	23.6	274			29%	4.50	26.5	2.6	5.1	2.0	1.1	--	72%	39	78

xERA shows that it wasn't as good as it seemed. BPIs back that up. Expect a letdown.

Remlinger,Mike		Tm	W	L	Sv	IP	ERA	Br/IP	R$	BF/G	OBA	vLH	vRH	H%	xERA	RAR	Ctl	Dom	Cmd	hr/9	G/F	S%	BPV	BPX
LH Reliever	98	CIN	8	15	0	164	4.83	1.53	($1)	20.9	262	264	267	31%	4.87	9.0	4.8	7.9	1.7	1.3	1.08	71%	47	85
AGE 37 Decline	99	ATL	10	1	1	83	2.39	1.22	$17	4.7	220	205	219	27%	3.21 -	35.1	3.8	8.8	2.3	1.0	1.12	86%	83	180
TYPE Power	00	ATL	5	3	12	72	3.49	1.27	$15	4.3	213	203	209	27%	3.10	20.7	4.6	9.0	1.9	0.7	1.60	74%	85	187
BURN none	01	ATL	3	3	1	75	2.76	1.20	$8	4.2	241	322	194	33%	3.55 -	26.2	2.8	11.2	4.0	1.1	0.91	83%	126	234
ERA Potl No chg	02	ATL	7	3	0	68	1.99	1.12	$14	3.8	200	235	184	27%	2.28	31.6	3.7	9.1	2.5	0.4	1.32	84%	110	225
Support 4.37	1st Half		5	0	0	40	1.57	1.00	$11	3.7	181			25%	1.59	20.9	3.4	9.2	2.7	0.2		85%	125	256
LIMA B	2nd Half		2	3	0	28	2.58	1.29	$4	3.8	226			29%	3.26 -	10.8	4.2	9.0	2.2	0.6		82%	90	184
Risk Low	03	Proj	5	4	1	70	3.34	1.33	$8	4.3	236			30%	3.57	19.8	4.1	9.0	2.2	0.8	--	77%	85	170

Rode the ATL pen's magical mystery tour to another great season. In some ways it was better than 2001, despite his age. Still, law of averages says to expect a drop-off in 2003.

Reyes,Dennys		Tm	W	L	Sv	IP	ERA	Br/IP	R$	BF/G	OBA	vLH	vRH	H%	xERA	RAR	Ctl	Dom	Cmd	hr/9	G/F	S%	BPV	BPX
LH Reliever	98	2NL	* 6	9	0	135	3.39	1.43	$6	19.6	235	236	263	33%	3.60	33.4	5.1	10.8	2.1	0.6	1.16	77%	100	179
AGE 26 Growth	99	CIN	2	2	2	61	3.84	1.51	$3	4.2	236	234	231	32%	3.89	14.0	5.8	10.6	1.8	0.7	2.76	76%	88	192
TYPE Power	00	CIN	2	1	0	43	4.58	1.67	($0)	3.2	261	178	330	31%	5.00	6.0	6.0	7.5	1.2	1.0	1.10	75%	43	94
BURN none	01	CIN	* 6	8	0	87	4.86	1.63	($0)	9.4	271	167	276	33%	4.93	5.9	5.3	8.5	1.6	0.9	1.27	71%	58	107
ERA Potl - -	02	2TM	4	4	0	82	5.38	1.74	($4)	6.6	298	299	299	34%	5.76	-1.2	4.9	6.5	1.3	1.1	1.81	71%	29	57
Support 5.88	1st Half		0	1	0	32	3.09	1.47	$1	4.0	230			29%	3.10	9.3	5.6	7.0	1.3	0.0		77%	77	152
LIMA D	2nd Half		4	3	0	50	6.84	1.92	($4)	10.5	335			36%	7.46 -	-10.5	4.5	6.1	1.4	1.8		67%	-1	-1
Risk High	03	Proj	4	4	0	80	4.95	1.68	($2)	6.0	278			33%	5.22	5.0	5.3	7.5	1.4	1.0	G	72%	44	89

After spending the first part of the season in the COL pitching hell, he must have felt a wave of relief when they told him he'd been traded mid-season. Unfortunately, he went to the 2nd worst pitching hell in TEX.

Reynolds,Shane		Tm	W	L	Sv	IP	ERA	Br/IP	R$	BF/G	OBA	vLH	vRH	H%	xERA	RAR	Ctl	Dom	Cmd	hr/9	G/F	S%	BPV	BPX
RH Starter	98	HOU	19	8	0	233	3.51	1.33	$21	28.3	281	252	308	34%	4.36 -	53.7	2.0	8.1	3.9	1.0	2.02	77%	101	182
AGE 35 Decline	99	HOU	16	14	0	231	3.86	1.24	$23	27.5	277	282	269	33%	3.97	52.3	1.4	7.7	5.3	0.9	1.81	71%	131	284
TYPE	00	HOU	7	8	0	131	5.22	1.49	$2	26.3	289	278	294	32%	5.27	7.1	3.1	6.4	2.1	1.4	1.76	68%	38	83
BURN none	01	HOU	14	11	0	182	4.35	1.34	$12	27.7	288	303	279	31%	4.72	24.9	1.8	5.0	2.8	1.2	1.86	71%	52	96
ERA Potl - -	02	HOU	3	6	0	74	4.86	1.43	$0	24.8	277	257	284	29%	5.22	5.9	3.2	5.7	1.8	1.6	1.80	71%	24	50
Support 4.99	1st Half		3	6	0	74	4.86	1.43	$0	24.8	277			29%	5.22	5.9	3.2	5.7	1.8	1.6		71%	24	50
LIMA C+	2nd Half		0	0	0	0	0.00	0.00																
Risk Moderate	03	Proj	6	6	0	100	4.59	1.49	$2	21.0	282			31%	5.10 -	11.6	3.4	5.9	1.7	1.3	G	73%	32	64

Chronic back woes and declining BPIs make him a high risk pick at this point.

Rhodes,Arthur		Tm	W	L	Sv	IP	ERA	Br/IP	R$	BF/G	OBA	vLH	vRH	H%	xERA	RAR	Ctl	Dom	Cmd	hr/9	G/F	S%	BPV	BPX
LH Reliever	98	BAL	4	4	4	77	3.51	1.29	$9	7.2	230	172	263	30%	3.52	22.2	4.0	9.7	2.4	0.9	1.21	76%	90	193
AGE 33 Past	99	BAL	3	4	3	53	5.43	1.66	$1	5.6	223	206	228	27%	4.93 +	3.1	7.6	10.0	1.3	1.5	0.95	71%	52	131
TYPE Power	00	SEA	5	8	0	69	4.30	1.16	$9	3.9	207	220	193	28%	2.73 +	14.9	3.8	10.0	2.7	0.8	1.17	64%	106	275
BURN none	01	SEA	8	0	3	68	1.72	0.85	$19	3.6	193	200	177	27%	1.72	34.3	1.6	11.0	6.9	0.7	1.22	85%	208	416
ERA Potl ++	02	SEA	10	4	2	69	2.35	0.84	$17	3.9	188	158	215	27%	1.39 +	25.5	1.7	10.6	6.2	0.5	1.40	74%	196	371
Support 7.11	1st Half		4	1	1	27	3.31	1.10	$5	3.4	231			31%	2.40 +	6.5	2.3	9.3	4.0	0.3		69%	139	262
LIMA B	2nd Half		6	3	1	42	1.72	0.67	$12	4.4	157			23%	0.73 +	18.9	1.3	11.4	8.8	0.6		80%	258	488
Risk Low	03	Proj	8	4	2	70	2.70	0.96	$15	4.0	212			29%	2.12 +	25.0	1.8	10.5	5.9	0.6	--	74%	180	366

Many Rotisserie players have a mental block about the value of starters vs relievers. They'll sooner pay $15 for a 200 IP arm with a 3.75 ERA and hopes for anywhere from 10-18 wins... than one Arthur Rhodes.

Riedling,John		Tm	W	L	Sv	IP	ERA	Br/IP	R$	BF/G	OBA	vLH	vRH	H%	xERA	RAR	Ctl	Dom	Cmd	hr/9	G/F	S%	BPV	BPX
RH Reliever	98	aa	3	10	0	102	5.65	1.75	($7)	19.9	300			35%	5.64	-3.0	4.9	6.9	1.4	0.9		68%	39	76
AGE 27 Pre-Peak	99	a/a	10	5	6	77	2.92	1.34	$17	5.1	233			28%	3.13	28.6	4.3	6.9	1.6	0.4		78%	73	169
TYPE Power	00	CIN *	9	4	6	90	2.90	1.33	$17	5.8	246	280	143	30%	3.82 -	32.9	3.7	8.4	2.3	0.9	3.67	82%	77	169
BURN none	01	CIN	1	1	1	33	2.44	1.08	$5	4.6	190	185	188	23%	1.94 +	13.0	3.8	6.2	1.6	0.3	2.25	77%	81	150
ERA Potl -	02	CIN *	4	5	0	63	4.57	1.63	($0)	6.2	277	320	163	33%	4.50	7.5	5.0	5.9	1.2	0.3	3.96	70%	51	104
Support 3.28	1st Half		2	1	0	28	6.70	1.81	($3)	6.7	329			38%	5.78 +	-4.7	3.8	5.7	1.5	0.3		60%	46	94
LIMA B	2nd Half		2	4	0	35	2.84	1.49	$3	5.9	228			27%	3.47 -	12.2	5.9	5.9	1.0	0.3		80%	58	120
Risk Moderate	03	Proj	5	5	0	80	3.71	1.44	$5	5.8	250			30%	3.75	18.7	4.5	6.4	1.4	0.5	G	74%	60	121

2-4, 2.74 ERA in 46 IP at CIN. This is not the same pitcher that was showing promise in 2000. CIN likes these extreme ground ball hurlers, but will that alone overcome such mediocre BPIs?

Riggan,Jerrod		Tm	W	L	Sv	IP	ERA	Br/IP	R$	BF/G	OBA	vLH	vRH	H%	xERA	RAR	Ctl	Dom	Cmd	hr/9	G/F	S%	BPV	BPX
RH Reliever	98		0	0	0	0	0.00	0.00																
AGE 29 Pre-Peak	99		0	0	0	0	0.00	0.00																
TYPE Power	00	aa	2	0	28	65	1.38	1.17	$27	5.1	231		429	30%	2.61 -	38.1	2.9	8.0	2.8	0.3	0.75	89%	107	253
BURN none	01	NYM *	5	3	13	79	3.08	1.29	$15	5.3	249	276	216	30%	3.88 -	24.2	3.2	8.0	2.5	1.0	1.20	81%	75	139
ERA Potl - -	02	CLE *	6	2	3	78	5.19	1.74	($0)	6.5	323	371	375	37%	5.81 -	-0.8	3.6	6.0	1.7	0.8	1.39	71%	37	71
Support 3.82	1st Half		4	1	2	48	4.29	1.64	$2	6.9	299			35%	4.77	5.2	3.9	5.8	1.5	0.4		73%	50	94
LIMA D	2nd Half		2	1	1	30	6.62	1.91	($2)	6.0	358			40%	7.48 -	-6.1	3.0	6.3	2.1	1.5		67%	20	38
Risk High	03	Proj	2	2	0	50	4.86	1.56	($1)	5.7	291			34%	4.99	3.4	3.6	6.5	1.8	0.9	--	70%	46	94

2-1, 7.64 ERA in 33 IP at CLE. The trend is short but clear, and tells us just about all we need to know. At 29, a pitcher should be approaching his peak. I suppose an inverse peak would be, oh, I dunno... an abyss?

Rijo,Jose		Tm	W	L	Sv	IP	ERA	Br/IP	R$	BF/G	OBA	vLH	vRH	H%	xERA	RAR	Ctl	Dom	Cmd	hr/9	G/F	S%	BPV	BPX
RH Reliever	98		0	0	0	0	0.00	0.00																
AGE 38 Decline	99		0	0	0	0	0.00	0.00																
TYPE Contact	00		0	0	0	0	0.00	0.00																
BURN none	01	CIN *	0	0	0	34	3.97	1.68	($2)	7.8	300	143	327	33%	5.62 -	6.4	4.2	5.3	1.3	1.1	0.82	79%	21	40
ERA Potl - -	02	CIN	5	4	0	77	5.14	1.42	$1	10.8	291	284	282	30%	5.33	3.3	2.3	4.4	1.9	1.5	1.17	68%	18	37
Support 5.61	1st Half		4	3	0	48	5.24	1.41	$2	16.0	281			28%	5.34	1.4	2.8	4.1	1.5	1.7		68%	4	8
LIMA C	2nd Half		1	1	0	29	4.98	1.42	($0)	7.0	306			33%	5.31	1.8	1.6	5.0	3.2	1.2		68%	53	110
Risk Moderate	03	Proj	2	2	0	70	4.76	1.53	($1)	8.7	299			32%	5.47 -	6.5	3.0	4.9	1.7	1.3	--	72%	21	42

A great story, but no longer anywhere near the great talent he was in the early 1990s. Posted a 22/56 DOM/DIS split and was only marginally better out of the pen. Undraftable.

Rincon,Juan		Tm	W	L	Sv	IP	ERA	Br/IP	R$	BF/G	OBA	vLH	vRH	H%	xERA	RAR	Ctl	Dom	Cmd	hr/9	G/F	S%	BPV	BPX
RH Starter	98		0	0	0	0	0.00	0.00																
AGE 24 Growth	99		0	0	0	0	0.00	0.00																
TYPE	00	aa	3	9	0	89	6.37	1.76	($7)	27.8	316			36%	6.12	-7.3	4.1	6.8	1.6	1.1		64%	33	79
BURN none	01	aa	14	6	0	158	4.61	1.56	$6	21.5	284			33%	4.85	17.1	4.0	6.7	1.7	0.8	0.40	71%	49	95
ERA Potl -	02	MIN *	7	6	0	129	5.43	1.59	($3)	20.1	309	283	415	34%	5.51	-5.7	3.0	5.9	2.0	1.1	1.22	67%	37	70
Support 3.77	1st Half		4	4	0	85	6.01	1.56	($4)	23.9	306			34%	5.41 +	-10.4	2.8	5.8	2.0	1.2		62%	37	69
LIMA D	2nd Half		3	2	0	44	4.31	1.66	$0	15.5	315			36%	5.69 -	4.7	3.3	6.2	1.9	1.0		76%	37	71
Risk High	03	Proj	3	4	0	60	5.10	1.63	($1)	21.0	304			35%	5.51	2.2	3.6	6.3	1.8	1.1	--	70%	37	76

0-2, 6.43 ERA in 28 IP at MIN, but with a solid 2.3 command ratio. Still, there are too many problems with everything else. Pass.

Rincon,Ricardo		Tm	W	L	Sv	IP	ERA	Br/IP	R$	BF/G	OBA	vLH	vRH	H%	xERA	RAR	Ctl	Dom	Cmd	hr/9	G/F	S%	BPV	BPX
LH Reliever	98	PIT	0	2	14	65	2.91	1.22	$11	4.5	214	131	250	27%	3.05	20.3	4.0	8.9	2.2	0.8	1.40	79%	87	156
AGE 33 Past	99	CLE	2	3	0	44	4.50	1.48	$2	3.3	248	233	261	27%	4.54	8.1	4.9	6.1	1.3	1.2	1.14	73%	32	79
TYPE Power	00	CLE	2	0	0	20	2.70	1.50	$3	2.5	232	216	240	31%	3.59 -	8.6	5.9	9.0	1.5	0.5	0.87	83%	81	212
BURN none	01	CLE	2	1	2	54	2.83	1.20	$6	3.3	224	213	233	29%	2.84	19.2	3.5	8.3	2.4	0.5	1.19	77%	95	191
ERA Potl +++++	02	2AL	1	4	1	56	4.18	1.04	$3	3.1	229	203	267	28%	2.52 +	7.0	1.8	7.9	4.5	0.6	1.07	59%	131	247
Support 2.57	1st Half		0	2	0	29	3.08	1.13	$2	3.2	254			30%	3.05	7.9	1.5	7.1	4.6	0.6		74%	125	236
LIMA A+	2nd Half		1	2	1	27	5.37	0.93	$2	3.0	201			26%	1.93 +	-1.0	2.0	8.7	4.3	0.7		39%	138	261
Risk Moderate	03	Proj	2	3	1	60	2.85	1.07	$7	3.2	225			27%	2.68	20.2	2.3	8.0	3.5	0.8	--	76%	109	223

A huge season derailed by a 59% strand rate. How bad was it? In the 2nd half, 6 out of every 10 baserunners eventually scored. That won't happen again. Expect a sub-3.00 ERA in 2003. Tuck this guy away.

Riske,David		Tm	W	L	Sv	IP	ERA	Br/IP	R$	BF/G	OBA	vLH	vRH	H%	xERA	RAR	Ctl	Dom	Cmd	hr/9	G/F	S%	BPV	BPX
RH Reliever	98	aa	0	0	1	3	0.00	1.33	$1	6.4	191			31%	2.27 -	2.2	6.0	12.0	2.0	0.0		100%	131	254
AGE 26 Growth	99	CLE *	4	1	18	65	3.05	1.05	$21	4.4	186	316	341	25%	1.91 +	24.6	3.6	9.0	2.5	0.4	0.88	71%	112	280
TYPE Power	00	a/a	0	0	1	7	2.57	1.14	$1	5.7	202			18%	3.21 -	3.0	3.9	1.3	0.3	1.3		86%	-9	-22
BURN none	01	CLE *	3	2	16	80	2.70	1.35	$15	5.3	244	143	232	33%	3.62 -	29.8	3.9	10.2	2.6	0.7	0.93	82%	102	204
ERA Potl +	02	CLE *	2	3	4	66	5.17	1.56	($0)	4.6	252	253	259	34%	5.02	-0.5	5.4	11.8	2.2	1.6	0.73	71%	72	137
Support 3.68	1st Half		1	2	1	27	5.96	1.95	($3)	4.0	307			42%	6.81 -	-3.1	6.3	12.2	1.9	1.7		73%	58	110
LIMA A	2nd Half		1	1	3	39	4.62	1.28	$2	5.3	209			27%	3.76 +	2.6	4.8	11.5	2.4	1.6		70%	84	159
Risk Very High	03	Proj	2	2	4	60	3.90	1.40	$4	4.8	239			32%	3.95	11.8	4.7	10.8	2.3	1.1	F	75%	89	182

2-2, 5.29 ERA in 51 IP at CLE. Hard thrower, but struggled with his control and the home run ball in '02. He's done better before and he's young, so he'll improve.

Ritchie,Todd		Tm	W	L	Sv	IP	ERA	Br/IP	R$	BF/G	OBA	vLH	vRH	H%	xERA	RAR	Ctl	Dom	Cmd	hr/9	G/F	S%	BPV	BPX
RH Starter	98	MIN *	1	3	4	84	4.92	1.56	($0)	7.4	277	255	316	34%	4.57	8.3	4.3	7.7	1.8	0.6	1.26	68%	64	137
AGE 31 Peak	99	PIT	15	9	0	172	3.51	1.30	$20	25.9	258	280	243	29%	3.86	47.0	2.8	5.6	2.0	0.9	1.81	76%	52	113
TYPE Contact	00	PIT	9	8	0	187	4.81	1.39	$7	26.0	283	311	258	31%	4.81	20.4	2.5	6.0	2.4	1.3	1.55	68%	48	105
BURN none	01	PIT	11	13	0	207	4.48	1.27	$10	26.3	265	286	238	29%	4.04	24.7	2.3	5.4	2.4	1.0	1.35	67%	54	101
ERA Potl - -	02	CHW	5	15	0	133	6.09	1.71	($9)	23.7	319	349	282	35%	6.08	-17.5	3.5	5.2	1.5	1.2	1.14	66%	17	32
Support 4.78	1st Half		4	10	0	99	5.36	1.57	($3)	26.2	304			33%	5.36	-3.3	3.1	5.1	1.6	1.1		67%	27	50
LIMA D	2nd Half		1	5	0	34	8.23	2.12	($7)	19.0	361			39%	8.18	-14.2	4.8	5.6	1.2	1.6		62%	-7	-13
Risk Low	03	Proj	9	13	0	160	4.84	1.43	$4	26.8	285			31%	4.90	11.4	2.8	5.6	2.0	1.2	--	69%	37	75

Shoulder woes probably dogged him most of the year, whether you read it in the media or not. That and the readjustment to the AL caused this debacle. He'll get better if healthy, though not a whole lot.

Rivera,Mariano		Tm	W	L	Sv	IP	ERA	Br/IP	R$	BF/G	OBA	vLH	vRH	H%	xERA	RAR	Ctl	Dom	Cmd	hr/9	G/F	S%	BPV	BPX
RH Reliever	98	NYY	3	0	36	61	1.91	1.06	$30	4.5	218	235	194	25%	2.39	30.6	2.5	5.3	2.1	0.4	1.60	84%	74	159
AGE 33 Past	99	NYY	4	3	45	69	1.83	0.88	$41	4.0	181	143	219	22%	1.32 +	37.4	2.3	6.8	2.9	0.3	2.05	80%	112	282
TYPE	00	NYY	7	4	36	75	2.87	1.10	$35	4.6	215	210	206	26%	2.43	30.6	3.0	6.9	2.3	0.5	1.47	75%	88	229
BURN none	01	NYY	4	6	50	80	2.34	0.91	$41	4.3	212	187	229	28%	2.01	33.6	1.3	9.3	6.9	0.6	2.13	76%	197	394
ERA Potl ++	02	NYY	1	4	28	46	2.74	1.00	$18	4.0	212	181	225	27%	2.16 +	14.6	2.2	8.0	3.7	0.6	1.41	74%	121	229
Support 0.98	1st Half		1	3	19	28	1.60	0.92	$13	4.0	185			25%	1.38	13.3	2.6	9.3	3.6	0.3		84%	140	265
LIMA B	2nd Half		0	1	9	18	4.55	1.12	$5	4.0	253			28%	3.41 +	1.3	1.5	6.1	4.0	1.0		61%	94	179
Risk Low	03	Proj	3	5	43	75	2.88	1.04	$31	4.2	221			27%	2.43	25.0	2.2	7.7	3.6	0.6	--	74%	114	231

Looked sound after coming off the DL, so should be back to his typical productivity in 2003.

Roa,Joe	Tm	W	L	Sv	IP	ERA	Br/IP	R$	BF/G	OBA	vLH	vRH	H%	xERA	RAR	Ctl	Dom	Cmd	hr/9	G/F	S%	BPV	BPX
RH Starter	98 aaa	12	9	0	162	5.56	1.51	$2	26.6	317			33%	5.80	-2.7	1.8	4.5	**2.5**	1.4		66%	28	55
AGE 31 Peak	99	0	0	0	0	0.00	0.00																
TYPE Contact	00 aa	6	5	0	103	5.59	1.83	($4)	25.8	325			34%	6.34 -	2.3	4.3	3.3	**0.8**	1.0		70%	-3	-6
BURN none	01 a/a	6	8	0	160	5.06	1.56	($3)	27.5	338			36%	6.06 -	7.7	1.1	4.2	**3.9**	1.2		70%	59	113
ERA Potl No chg	02 PHI	• 18	4	0	182	3.02	1.15	$29	23.9	258	328	244	28%	3.44	59.5	1.5	4.9	**3.2**	0.7	0.95	76%	79	161
Support 5.30	1st Half	12	0	0	97	2.32	1.14	$21	26.3	256			30%	2.97 -	40.8	1.6	5.5	**3.5**	0.3		80%	101	208
LIMA C+	2nd Half	6	4	0	85	3.81	1.15	$10	21.6	259			27%	3.99	18.8	1.5	4.3	**2.9**	1.3		72%	53	108
Risk Very High	03 Proj	**11**	**6**	**0**	**160**	**3.94**	**1.24**	**$15**	**23.8**	**274**			**30%**	**4.01**	**32.5**	**1.6**	**4.8**	**3.0**	**0.9**	**--**	**70%**	**66**	**132**

4-4, 4.06 ERA in 71 IP at PHI. There are many ways to do this. You can focus on the Mark Priors and invest in high risk long-term upside. Or you can catch a journeyman at peak for low risk, high, short-term value.

Roberts,Grant	Tm	W	L	Sv	IP	ERA	Br/IP	R$	BF/G	OBA	vLH	vRH	H%	xERA	RAR	Ctl	Dom	Cmd	hr/9	G/F	S%	BPV	BPX
RH Reliever	98	0	0	0	0	0.00	0.00																
AGE 25 Growth	99 a/a	9	7	0	159	5.38	1.48	$3	25.0	285			33%	4.42 +	6.8	3.2	6.3	**2.0**	0.6		62%	60	140
TYPE	00 aaa	7	8	0	157	3.84	1.49	$8	27.7	277	353	333	32%	4.13	40.4	3.7	5.6	**1.5**	0.3	1.63	73%	54	129
BURN none	01 NYM	• 4	5	2	93	5.23	1.56	($1)	9.1	308	324	197	37%	5.00	1.8	2.7	7.3	**2.7**	0.6	1.33	65%	76	140
ERA Potl ---	02 NYM	3	1	0	46	2.15	1.28	$7	5.5	249	261	248	29%	3.51 -	20.4	3.1	6.3	**2.0**	0.6	1.27	86%	67	138
Support 4.60	1st Half	1	0	0	33	1.36	1.36	$4	5.4	249			30%	3.41 -	18.2	3.8	6.5	**1.7**	0.3		91%	72	148
LIMA B	2nd Half	2	1	0	13	4.19	1.09	$3	5.7	248			26%	3.77	2.2	1.4	5.6	**4.0**	1.4		67%	81	166
Risk High	03 Proj	**3**	**2**	**0**	**60**	**3.60**	**1.33**	**$4**	**8.5**	**262**			**31%**	**3.65**	**14.9**	**3.0**	**6.3**	**2.1**	**0.5**	**--**	**73%**	**71**	**143**

86% strand rate will force his ERA back up into a normal range. Decent skills worth backfilling a pitching staff with, but little upside value right now. Not likely to develop into a closer, or anything like that.

Roberts,Willis	Tm	W	L	Sv	IP	ERA	Br/IP	R$	BF/G	OBA	vLH	vRH	H%	xERA	RAR	Ctl	Dom	Cmd	hr/9	G/F	S%	BPV	BPX
RH Reliever	98 a/a	6	4	2	79	4.67	1.71	$1	7.2	301			35%	5.27 -	8.0	4.4	5.8	**1.3**	0.6		72%	40	78
AGE 27 Pre-Peak	99 aaa	5	8	0	92	7.04	1.98	($10)	14.5	323			35%	6.85	-16.6	5.7	4.6	**0.8**	1.2		65%	-0	-1
TYPE Power	00 a/a	11	8	0	156	6.52	1.75	($6)	24.3	317			33%	6.32	-15.8	4.0	4.6	**1.2**	1.3		64%	4	9
BURN none	01 BAL	9	10	6	132	4.91	1.49	$6	12.7	276	264	284	31%	4.77	10.2	3.8	6.5	**1.7**	1.0	1.48	69%	44	89
ERA Potl --	02 BAL	5	4	1	75	3.36	1.48	$4	5.0	272	276	266	32%	4.18 -	17.5	3.8	6.1	**1.6**	0.6	1.61	78%	53	100
Support 3.72	1st Half	5	2	1	45	1.79	1.33	$7	5.2	239			27%	3.36 -	20.1	4.0	5.2	**1.3**	0.6		89%	48	90
LIMA C+	2nd Half	0	2	0	30	5.74	1.71	($3)	4.8	317			39%	5.43	-2.5	3.6	7.6	**2.1**	0.6		65%	63	118
Risk Very High	03 Proj	**4**	**5**	**0**	**75**	**4.44**	**1.55**	**$1**	**7.1**	**282**			**32%**	**4.76**	**9.3**	**4.0**	**6.1**	**1.5**	**0.8**	**G**	**72%**	**43**	**87**

Great 1st half ERA, but poor BPIs. With that foundation, he could have done anything in the 2nd half and the perception would have been that he was still pitching well. And that's exactly what happened.

Rocker,John	Tm	W	L	Sv	IP	ERA	Br/IP	R$	BF/G	OBA	vLH	vRH	H%	xERA	RAR	Ctl	Dom	Cmd	hr/9	G/F	S%	BPV	BPX
LH Reliever	98 ATL	• 2	4	3	57	1.89	1.19	$8	4.2	183	164	178	24%	2.58 -	25.5	5.1	9.8	**1.9**	0.8	1.91	89%	94	170
AGE 28 Pre-Peak	99 ATL	4	5	38	72	2.50	1.17	$32	4.0	188	140	191	30%	2.33	29.4	4.6	13.0	**2.8**	0.6	1.16	81%	136	295
TYPE Power	00 ATL	1	2	24	53	2.89	1.70	$15	4.1	219	243	202	34%	4.30 -	19.5	8.2	13.1	**1.6**	0.8	0.80	86%	98	215
BURN none	01 2TM	5	9	23	66	4.35	1.50	$16	4.3	237	239	233	33%	3.75 +	9.5	5.6	10.7	**1.9**	0.5	1.17	71%	96	185
ERA Potl +++	02 TEX	• 3	4	1	35	6.15	1.60	($0)	4.1	277	364	266	38%	5.14 +	-4.9	4.6	11.5	**2.5**	1.3	1.16	63%	83	157
Support 6.66	1st Half	2	3	1	31	5.73	1.56	($0)	4.1	283			39%	5.27	-2.6	4.0	12.0	**3.0**	1.4		66%	91	171
LIMA A	2nd Half	1	1	0	4	9.73	1.89	$0	3.6	223			29%	4.00 +	-2.3	9.7	7.3	**0.8**	0.0		43%	70	132
Risk High	03 Proj	**2**	**3**	**0**	**40**	**4.28**	**1.58**	**$0**	**4.3**	**252**			**34%**	**4.43**	**5.9**	**5.6**	**10.8**	**1.9**	**0.9**	**--**	**75%**	**83**	**168**

2-3, 6.75 ERA in 24 IP at TEX. This would make a marvelous case study. Was his career destined to be derailed by injuries, or did the media kill the closer? Tune in to tonight's edition of 20/20.

Rodriguez,Felix	Tm	W	L	Sv	IP	ERA	Br/IP	R$	BF/G	OBA	vLH	vRH	H%	xERA	RAR	Ctl	Dom	Cmd	hr/9	G/F	S%	BPV	BPX
RH Reliever	98 ARI	0	2	5	44	6.14	1.66	($2)	4.7	262	268	253	31%	4.98 +	-5.3	5.9	7.4	**1.2**	1.0	1.18	63%	42	76
AGE 30 Peak	99 SF	2	3	0	66	3.82	1.45	$2	6.1	265	223	288	32%	4.25	15.3	4.0	7.5	**1.9**	0.8	0.96	76%	62	135
TYPE Power	00 SF	4	2	3	81	2.66	1.32	$11	4.5	221	160	267	31%	3.11	32.3	4.7	10.5	**2.3**	0.6	0.86	81%	105	231
BURN none	01 SF	9	1	0	80	1.69	1.00	$18	3.9	190	150	213	26%	1.95	39.5	3.0	10.2	**3.4**	0.6	0.65	87%	132	245
ERA Potl +++	02 SF	8	6	0	69	4.17	1.19	$10	4.0	214	234	196	26%	2.88 +	11.9	3.8	7.6	**2.0**	0.7	0.76	65%	80	164
Support 3.78	1st Half	2	4	0	34	5.29	1.53	($1)	4.2	267			33%	4.80 +	0.8	4.5	8.7	**1.9**	1.1		67%	63	129
LIMA B+	2nd Half	6	2	0	35	3.09	0.86	$10	3.8	154			19%	1.01 +	11.1	3.1	6.4	**2.1**	0.3		62%	99	203
Risk Low	03 Proj	**8**	**4**	**0**	**75**	**3.12**	**1.19**	**$12**	**4.2**	**215**			**27%**	**2.80**	**23.4**	**3.7**	**8.5**	**2.3**	**0.6**	**F**	**75%**	**93**	**187**

BPIs were off considerably, but did make a slight rebound in the 2nd half. xERA tells a truer tale and bodes well for better numbers in 2003.

Rogers,Kenny	Tm	W	L	Sv	IP	ERA	Br/IP	R$	BF/G	OBA	vLH	vRH	H%	xERA	RAR	Ctl	Dom	Cmd	hr/9	G/F	S%	BPV	BPX
LH Starter	98 OAK	16	8	0	238	3.17	1.18	$29	28.8	242	226	247	27%	3.26	79.2	2.5	5.2	**2.1**	0.7	1.73	75%	60	127
AGE 38 Decline	99 2TM	10	4	0	195	4.20	1.41	$11	27.2	273	204	264	31%	4.22	39.1	3.2	5.8	**1.8**	0.7	1.86	71%	52	120
TYPE Contact	00 TEX	13	13	0	227	4.56	1.48	$12	29.4	286	314	276	32%	4.63	41.2	3.1	5.0	**1.6**	0.8	1.69	70%	38	100
BURN High	01 TEX	5	7	0	120	6.21	1.66	($8)	27.5	307	323	302	33%	5.96	-11.8	3.7	5.5	**1.5**	1.3	1.47	64%	18	36
ERA Potl -	02 TEX	13	8	0	210	3.86	1.34	$11	27.1	264	193	280	28%	4.02	35.1	3.0	4.6	**1.5**	0.9	2.02	74%	35	66
Support 4.83	1st Half	8	4	0	102	3.26	1.24	$10	26.6	248			26%	3.45	25.3	2.8	4.3	**1.5**	0.8		76%	40	75
LIMA D+	2nd Half	5	4	0	108	4.42	1.44	$2	27.6	278			30%	4.55	9.8	3.2	4.8	**1.5**	1.0		71%	30	58
Risk Very High	03 Proj	**10**	**8**	**0**	**180**	**4.60**	**1.44**	**$5**	**27.1**	**279**			**30%**	**4.62**	**18.5**	**3.2**	**5.0**	**1.6**	**1.0**	**G**	**70%**	**32**	**65**

Another Bizarro Road Show... He puts up solid stats despite:
- Being 37 and getting older
- BPIs as marginal as ever
- Tough home ballpark
- Better TEX pitchers struggled in 2002.

Romero,J.C.	Tm	W	L	Sv	IP	ERA	Br/IP	R$	BF/G	OBA	vLH	vRH	H%	xERA	RAR	Ctl	Dom	Cmd	hr/9	G/F	S%	BPV	BPX
LH Reliever	98 aa	6	3	2	78	3.23	1.40	$8	6.6	214			27%	3.17	23.0	5.7	7.8	**1.4**	0.5		77%	75	145
AGE 26 Growth	99 a/a	8	5	8	73	3.82	1.68	$10	6.6	270			33%	4.97 -	18.3	5.8	8.0	**1.4**	0.9		79%	52	121
TYPE Power	00 MIN	• 6	9	4	122	5.45	1.59	$3	19.0	287	281	322	32%	5.14	7.6	4.0	6.0	**1.5**	1.0	1.79	67%	34	89
BURN none	01 MIN	• 4	7	0	128	5.34	1.53	($4)	21.9	291	286	276	33%	5.05	2.4	3.4	6.0	**1.8**	1.0	1.44	66%	41	83
ERA Potl -	02 MIN	9	2	1	81	1.89	1.21	$14	4.1	213	216	211	28%	2.46 -	34.9	4.0	8.4	**2.1**	0.3	1.84	85%	97	184
Support 5.00	1st Half	3	1	0	46	1.76	1.13	$7	4.1	226			30%	2.46 -	20.7	2.7	9.2	**3.4**	0.4		86%	124	234
LIMA C+	2nd Half	6	1	1	35	2.06	1.32	$7	4.1	196			25%	2.47	14.2	5.7	7.5	**1.3**	0.3		84%	81	152
Risk Very High	03 Proj	**6**	**4**	**2**	**80**	**3.49**	**1.40**	**$7**	**6.5**	**247**			**30%**	**3.74**	**20.2**	**4.3**	**7.3**	**1.7**	**0.7**	**G**	**76%**	**65**	**133**

Nice growth year, but a sub-2.00 ERA is just absurd. xERA provides a more likely level, but with his BPIs, 2003 will probably see an ERA somewhere in the 3.00's... which should still supply some good value.

Rueter,Kirk	Tm	W	L	Sv	IP	ERA	Br/IP	R$	BF/G	OBA	vLH	vRH	H%	xERA	RAR	Ctl	Dom	Cmd	hr/9	G/F	S%	BPV	BPX
RH Starter	98 SF	16	9	0	187	4.38	1.34	$13	24.1	268	238	271	28%	4.53	21.6	2.7	4.9	**1.8**	1.3	1.32	71%	30	53
AGE 32 Peak	99 SF	15	10	0	184	5.43	1.49	$6	24.6	297	236	312	31%	5.35	2.9	2.7	4.6	**1.7**	1.4	0.91	66%	18	39
TYPE Contact	00 SF	11	9	0	184	3.96	1.45	$11	25.1	283	244	301	29%	4.89 -	41.1	3.0	3.5	**1.1**	1.1	1.02	76%	9	21
BURN none	01 SF	14	12	0	195	4.43	1.43	$9	25.0	279	278	284	29%	4.80	24.5	3.0	3.8	**1.3**	1.2	1.02	72%	14	26
ERA Potl ---	02 SF	14	8	0	203	3.24	1.27	$21	25.8	263	244	267	27%	4.06 -	60.4	2.4	3.4	**1.4**	1.0	1.31	78%	23	47
Support 5.26	1st Half	7	5	0	103	3.50	1.33	$9	27.4	269			28%	4.29 -	27.1	2.6	3.4	**1.3**	1.0		77%	20	41
LIMA F	2nd Half	7	3	0	100	2.97	1.21	$13	24.3	256			26%	3.83 -	33.3	2.2	3.3	**1.5**	1.0		80%	26	54
Risk Low	03 Proj	**12**	**10**	**0**	**200**	**4.23**	**1.37**	**$11**	**25.2**	**276**			**28%**	**4.56**	**32.8**	**2.7**	**3.6**	**1.4**	**1.1**	**--**	**72%**	**18**	**36**

There is nothing here that would suggest he'd ever have an ERA under 4.00. As such, in good conscience, I can't project anything better, even though he continues to defy logic, science and universal order.

Rupe,Ryan	Tm	W	L	Sv	IP	ERA	Br/IP	R$	BF/G	OBA	vLH	vRH	H%	xERA	RAR	Ctl	Dom	Cmd	hr/9	G/F	S%	BPV	BPX
RH Starter	98	0	0	0	0	0.00	0.00																
AGE 28 Pre-Peak	99 TAM	• 10	11	0	168	4.39	1.31	$13	24.5	249	261	247	28%	3.88 +	33.3	3.4	6.2	**1.8**	1.0	1.07	68%	52	129
TYPE	00 TAM	• 5	7	0	110	6.87	1.66	($6)	21.9	320	313	330	35%	6.55	-14.1	3.0	6.3	**2.1**	1.8	0.98	61%	19	48
BURN none	01 TAM	5	12	0	143	6.60	1.46	($7)	22.4	285	294	272	32%	5.62 +	-21.4	3.0	7.7	**2.6**	1.9	0.83	58%	42	83
ERA Potl ++++	02 TAM	5	10	0	90	5.60	1.20	$2	24.7	246	246	241	28%	3.59 +	-5.9	2.5	6.7	**2.7**	1.1	1.68	54%	69	131
Support 5.10	1st Half	5	9	0	87	5.57	1.16	$3	25.4	243			28%	3.47 +	-5.5	2.3	6.9	**3.0**	1.1		52%	78	147
LIMA B	2nd Half	0	1	0	3	6.43	2.50	($1)	15.2	336			34%	7.24 -	-0.5	9.6	0.0	**0.0**	0.0		71%	-12	-23
Risk High	03 Proj	**8**	**13**	**0**	**160**	**4.67**	**1.33**	**$6**	**22.6**	**269**			**30%**	**4.39**	**15.0**	**2.6**	**6.8**	**2.6**	**1.2**	**G**	**68%**	**59**	**121**

This is the type of skill set that is just one small tweak away from success. Solid and improving BPIs, but a horrible strand rate. That's partly his fault (but correctable) and partly the fault of the TAM bullpen. Sleeper.

Rusch,Glendon	Yr	Tm	W	L	Sv	IP	ERA	Br/IP	R$	BF/G	OBA	vLH	vRH	H%	xERA	RAR	Ctl	Dom	Cmd	hr/9	G/F	S%	BPV	BPX
LH Starter	98	KC *	7	16	1	168	6.25	1.60	($6)	23.8	311	237	322	34%	5.92	-13.5	3.0	5.7	**1.9**	1.4	1.33	63%	25	53
AGE 28 Pre-Peak	99	aaa	4	7	0	114	5.05	1.67	($2)	26.1	331	375	357	39%	5.88 -	9.8	2.4	6.8	**2.8**	0.9	0.63	70%	62	143
TYPE	00	NYM	11	11	0	190	4.02	1.26	$16	25.7	268	304	256	32%	3.89	40.9	2.1	7.4	**3.6**	0.9	1.09	70%	95	210
BURN none	01	NYM	8	12	0	179	4.63	1.45	$2	23.7	300	300	301	36%	5.11	17.8	2.2	7.8	**3.6**	1.2	1.11	71%	84	155
ERA Potl -	02	MIL	10	16	0	210	4.71	1.44	$3	26.9	277	237	292	30%	4.96	20.9	3.3	6.0	**1.8**	1.3	1.57	71%	36	73
Support 5.00	1st Half		5	6	0	107	4.62	1.37	$3	27.0	279			31%	4.63	12.0	2.5	6.2	**2.5**	1.1		69%	55	114
LIMA B	2nd Half		5	10	0	103	4.81	1.52	($0)	26.9	275			29%	5.30 -	8.9	4.0	5.8	**1.4**	1.5		73%	20	41
Risk High	03	Proj	**10**	**15**	**0**	**200**	**4.23**	**1.38**	**$9**	**25.3**	**279**			**31%**	**4.72 -**	**32.8**	**2.6**	**6.4**	**2.5**	**1.2**	**G**	**73%**	**53**	**107**

His hit rate, which had inflated his ERA, returned to Earth in '02. Ordinarily, this would have improved his ERA. But Ctl and Dom hit the skids, especially in the 2nd half, killing his season. He still owns those skills though.

Ryan,B.J.	Yr	Tm	W	L	Sv	IP	ERA	Br/IP	R$	BF/G	OBA	vLH	vRH	H%	xERA	RAR	Ctl	Dom	Cmd	hr/9	G/F	S%	BPV	BPX
LH Reliever	98	aa	1	0	4	16	3.38	1.44	$3	4.4	250			33%	4.32 -	4.4	4.5	10.7	**2.4**	1.1		81%	85	166
AGE 27 Growth	99	2TM *	4	1	7	85	3.28	1.26	$13	5.0	224	192	190	30%	2.95	27.5	4.0	9.8	**2.4**	0.5	1.50	75%	105	243
TYPE Power	00	BAL *	2	4	0	66	5.96	1.55	($2)	5.3	252	175	252	30%	5.09 +	-0.5	5.4	8.9	**1.7**	1.6	0.92	65%	44	115
BURN none	01	BAL	2	4	2	53	4.25	1.45	$2	3.8	239	198	261	30%	4.14	8.8	5.1	9.2	**1.8**	1.0	1.16	73%	69	139
ERA Potl +	02	BAL	2	1	1	57	4.74	1.47	($0)	3.7	241	192	283	30%	4.19 +	2.8	5.2	8.8	**1.7**	1.1	1.36	70%	62	118
Support 3.90	1st Half		1	0	0	25	7.56	1.96	($4)	3.7	299			37%	6.87 +	-8.2	6.8	10.1	**1.5**	1.8		64%	33	62
LIMA C	2nd Half		1	1	1	32	2.53	1.09	$4	3.8	189			23%	2.10	11.0	3.9	7.9	**2.0**	0.6		79%	90	169
Risk Low	03	Proj	**2**	**2**	**2**	**60**	**4.50**	**1.45**	**$1**	**4.0**	**239**			**30%**	**4.09**	**7.0**	**5.1**	**9.0**	**1.8**	**1.1**	**--**	**71%**	**67**	**136**

Despite some positive signs within some of his BPIs, he is still walking too many batters. After three years of 5+ walk rates, you'd think by now someone would have helped him find his control. This could be his ceiling.

Saarloos,Kirk	Yr	Tm	W	L	Sv	IP	ERA	Br/IP	R$	BF/G	OBA	vLH	vRH	H%	xERA	RAR	Ctl	Dom	Cmd	hr/9	G/F	S%	BPV	BPX
RH Starter	98		0	0	0	0	0.00	0.00																
AGE 23 Growth	99		0	0	0	0	0.00	0.00																
TYPE	00		0	0	0	0	0.00	0.00																
BURN none	01		0	0	0	0	0.00	0.00																
ERA Potl + +	02	HOU *	18	8	0	184	3.86	1.21	$23	22.3	248	301	302	29%	3.43	39.4	2.5	6.9	**2.8**	0.7	2.45	69%	83	170
Support 5.59	1st Half		10	3	0	91	3.25	1.17	$15	23.3	233			29%	2.82	27.0	2.9	7.4	**2.6**	0.4		72%	95	196
LIMA C+	2nd Half		8	5	0	93	4.46	1.24	$9	21.4	262			30%	4.03	12.4	2.1	6.4	**3.0**	1.1		66%	72	148
Risk Moderate	03	Proj	**12**	**10**	**0**	**160**	**4.28**	**1.29**	**$13**	**22.4**	**259**			**30%**	**3.92**	**25.3**	**2.7**	**6.5**	**2.4**	**0.9**	**G**	**68%**	**66**	**133**

6-7, 6.04 ERA in 85 IP at HOU, but it was a 17.65 ERA in his first 3 starts, then after a brief demotion, he hurled 20 IP of 1.77 ERA, then 56 IP of 5.79. Posted 29/41 DOM/DIS. Talent is here, but he's not quite ready.

Sabathia,C.C.	Yr	Tm	W	L	Sv	IP	ERA	Br/IP	R$	BF/G	OBA	vLH	vRH	H%	xERA	RAR	Ctl	Dom	Cmd	hr/9	G/F	S%	BPV	BPX
LH Starter	98		0	0	0	0	0.00	0.00																
AGE 22 Growth	99		0	0	0	0	0.00	0.00																
TYPE Power	00	aa	3	7	0	90	4.20	1.40	$4	22.9	244			30%	3.76	18.8	4.4	8.1	**1.8**	0.7		71%	72	172
BURN Low	01	CLE	17	5	0	180	4.40	1.35	$14	23.3	227	254	223	28%	3.68 +	26.2	4.7	8.5	**1.8**	0.9	0.79	69%	70	141
ERA Potl +	02	CLE	13	11	0	210	4.37	1.36	$9	27.2	251	240	255	29%	3.71 +	20.7	3.8	6.4	**1.7**	0.7	1.22	68%	57	108
Support 5.49	1st Half		6	6	0	97	4.72	1.41	$2	26.3	253			30%	3.62 +	5.0	4.1	6.5	**1.6**	0.5		65%	63	119
LIMA C	2nd Half		7	5	0	113	4.07	1.32	$6	28.1	248			28%	3.79	15.7	3.5	6.3	**1.8**	1.0		72%	52	99
Risk Moderate	03	Proj	**10**	**13**	**0**	**200**	**5.22**	**1.50**	**$0**	**26.0**	**256**			**29%**	**4.45 +**	**4.0**	**4.7**	**6.5**	**1.4**	**1.0**	**--**	**66%**	**40**	**82**

The workload at his age is horrific, and with his svelte physique, this is a walking time bomb. It would not be the least bit surprising to see his stat line implode in 2003. In fact, that's what I'm going to project.

Santana,Johan	Yr	Tm	W	L	Sv	IP	ERA	Br/IP	R$	BF/G	OBA	vLH	vRH	H%	xERA	RAR	Ctl	Dom	Cmd	hr/9	G/F	S%	BPV	BPX
LH Starter	98		0	0	0	0	0.00	0.00																
AGE 24 Growth	99		0	0	0	0	0.00	0.00																
TYPE Power	00	MIN	2	3	0	86	6.49	1.81	($7)	13.6	296	263	317	34%	5.95 +	-6.6	5.7	6.7	**1.2**	1.2	0.88	65%	26	68
BURN High	01	MIN	1	0	0	43	4.79	1.53	($1)	12.8	291	290	293	32%	5.30 -	4.0	3.3	5.8	**1.8**	1.3	1.18	72%	31	62
ERA Potl +	02	MIN *	13	8	1	156	3.11	1.27	$16	17.2	220	195	216	31%	3.11	41.7	4.3	11.6	**2.7**	0.8	0.70	78%	113	213
Support 3.90	1st Half		8	3	0	82	3.07	1.29	$9	20.4	222			32%	3.24	22.5	4.4	11.7	**2.7**	0.9		80%	111	210
LIMA B	2nd Half		5	5	1	74	3.16	1.26	$7	14.7	217			31%	2.97	19.3	4.3	11.4	**2.7**	0.7		77%	115	217
Risk X HIGH	03	Proj	**10**	**5**	**0**	**160**	**3.66**	**1.33**	**$12**	**24.3**	**239**			**32%**	**3.60**	**36.7**	**4.0**	**10.0**	**2.5**	**0.8**	**F**	**75%**	**94**	**191**

8-6, 3.00 ERA in 108 IP at MIN. The next great pitcher is here. BPIs are already solid, but a few more tweaks (reduce walk rate a bit, keep ball down more) and you can expect a breakout season. Big-time sleeper.

Santana,Julio	Yr	Tm	W	L	Sv	IP	ERA	Br/IP	R$	BF/G	OBA	vLH	vRH	H%	xERA	RAR	Ctl	Dom	Cmd	hr/9	G/F	S%	BPV	BPX
RH Reliever	98	TAM	5	6	0	145	4.40	1.47	$3	18.2	269	296	248	28%	4.72	24.4	3.8	3.8	**1.0**	1.1	1.53	73%	11	23
AGE 30 Peak	99	TAM	1	4	0	55	7.36	1.78	($6)	11.8	299	265	331	32%	6.41 +	-11.0	5.2	5.6	**1.1**	1.6	1.35	60%	2	5
TYPE Power	00	MON *	6	8	0	131	5.83	1.50	($1)	12.1	275	327	236	31%	5.02 +	-3.5	3.9	7.1	**1.8**	1.3	1.07	63%	42	93
BURN none	01	aaa	8	8	0	132	6.07	1.69	($6)	24.3	321			35%	6.59 -	-11.4	3.2	6.6	**2.1**	1.7		68%	23	44
ERA Potl - - -	02	DET *	3	6	1	69	2.86	1.37	$5	6.6	247	261	219	27%	4.11 -	20.8	4.0	6.2	**1.5**	1.2	1.12	85%	40	77
Support 3.47	1st Half		3	3	1	42	3.20	1.42	$3	6.5	247			26%	4.53 -	10.8	4.5	6.4	**1.4**	1.5		85%	29	55
LIMA C+	2nd Half		0	3	0	27	2.33	1.30	$1	6.7	247			28%	3.44 -	10.0	3.3	6.0	**1.8**	0.7		85%	59	112
Risk X HIGH	03	Proj	**2**	**5**	**0**	**60**	**4.35**	**1.48**	**$0**	**7.1**	**274**			**31%**	**4.83**	**8.2**	**3.8**	**6.3**	**1.7**	**1.2**	**--**	**74%**	**37**	**76**

His 2.85 ERA will entice at least a few unknowledgable owners in your league to toss in a token buck. His xERA tells his true skill level. So save your dollar for... like maybe the OTHER Santana above.

Santiago,Jose	Yr	Tm	W	L	Sv	IP	ERA	Br/IP	R$	BF/G	OBA	vLH	vRH	H%	xERA	RAR	Ctl	Dom	Cmd	hr/9	G/F	S%	BPV	BPX
RH Reliever	98	aa	3	4	23	82	4.28	1.57	$13	6.4	304	500	400	32%	5.28 -	12.6	3.1	3.3	**1.1**	0.9	3.00	74%	10	20
AGE 28 Pre-Peak	99	KC *	3	5	2	58	3.10	1.24	$8	6.2	262	210	284	26%	4.04 -	21.5	2.2	2.3	**1.1**	1.1	2.78	80%	7	16
TYPE Contact	00	KC *	8	7	6	86	3.87	1.40	$13	6.6	273	230	298	31%	4.37 -	23.5	3.0	5.9	**1.9**	0.9	2.00	75%	48	124
BURN none	01	PHI	4	6	0	91	4.64	1.40	$1	5.4	292	352	252	32%	4.30	8.9	2.2	4.2	**2.0**	0.5	2.94	66%	48	90
ERA Potl No chg	02	PHI *	4	5	7	75	4.80	1.49	$5	5.2	299	304	282	34%	4.99	6.6	2.6	5.8	**2.2**	0.8	2.36	69%	50	104
Support 4.60	1st Half		1	3	0	37	5.09	1.40	($1)	4.7	272			31%	4.48 +	1.8	3.2	6.1	**1.9**	1.0		65%	48	99
LIMA C+	2nd Half		3	2	7	38	4.51	1.58	$5	5.7	323			36%	5.48 -	4.8	2.1	5.5	**2.6**	0.7		72%	55	114
Risk High	03	Proj	**3**	**3**	**0**	**50**	**4.14**	**1.40**	**$3**	**5.5**	**284**			**32%**	**4.40**	**8.8**	**2.5**	**5.0**	**2.0**	**0.7**	**G**	**71%**	**49**	**98**

1-3, 6.70 ERA in 47 IP at PHI. There are some good things hidden here...

- Improving command.
- Extreme gound ball tendency.
- S% and H% have ERA upside. Worth a late round flyer.

Sasaki,Kazuhiro	Yr	Tm	W	L	Sv	IP	ERA	Br/IP	R$	BF/G	OBA	vLH	vRH	H%	xERA	RAR	Ctl	Dom	Cmd	hr/9	G/F	S%	BPV	BPX
RH Reliever	98	JPN	1	1	45	56	0.64	0.80	$36	4.1	168			28%	0.82	35.9	2.1	12.5	**6.0**	0.2		93%	218	424
AGE 35 Decline	99	JPN	1	1	19	23	1.96	1.09	$15	4.0	227			37%	2.39	11.5	2.3	13.3	**5.7**	0.4		83%	197	456
TYPE Power	00	SEA	2	5	37	62	3.18	1.17	$29	4.0	193	198	170	25%	3.22	22.7	4.5	11.3	**2.5**	1.4	0.88	81%	94	243
BURN none	01	SEA	0	4	45	66	3.26	0.89	$31	3.7	205	218	168	25%	2.11 +	19.7	1.5	8.4	**5.6**	0.8	0.76	66%	159	317
ERA Potl No chg	02	SEA	4	5	37	60	2.55	1.07	$26	3.9	206	207	194	28%	2.52	20.5	3.0	11.0	**3.7**	0.9	0.97	81%	129	244
Support 2.08	1st Half		2	2	18	29	0.93	0.97	$14	3.9	189			30%	1.21	16.2	2.8	11.5	**4.1**	0.0		89%	173	326
LIMA C+	2nd Half		2	3	19	31	4.06	1.16	$12	4.0	222			27%	3.75	4.3	3.2	10.5	**3.3**	1.7		73%	90	170
Risk Low	03	Proj	**3**	**5**	**37**	**65**	**3.32**	**1.12**	**$26**	**4.0**	**218**			**28%**	**2.92**	**17.8**	**3.0**	**10.0**	**3.3**	**1.0**	**--**	**74%**	**111**	**226**

After an incredible start, faded and ended up having his 3rd elbow surgery. Might start off a little slow in 2003, but should eventually be back to his expected productivity levels.

Sauerbeck,Scott	Yr	Tm	W	L	Sv	IP	ERA	Br/IP	R$	BF/G	OBA	vLH	vRH	H%	xERA	RAR	Ctl	Dom	Cmd	hr/9	G/F	S%	BPV	BPX
LH Reliever	98	aaa	7	13	0	160	4.67	1.72	($4)	27.5	313			36%	5.37 -	16.3	3.9	5.4	**1.4**	0.5		72%	40	79
AGE 31 Peak	99	PIT	4	1	2	67	2.01	1.36	$10	4.4	219	167	252	26%	3.41 -	31.7	5.1	7.4	**1.4**	0.8	2.27	89%	62	134
TYPE Power	00	PIT	5	4	1	75	4.07	1.82	$1	4.8	264	222	305	36%	4.87 -	15.7	7.3	9.9	**1.4**	0.5	2.39	77%	76	168
BURN none	01	PIT	2	2	2	62	5.64	1.62	($3)	4.0	258	272	248	37%	4.38 +	-2.3	5.8	11.4	**2.0**	0.6	1.40	64%	96	178
ERA Potl No chg	02	PIT	5	4	0	62	2.32	1.24	$10	3.3	222	147	273	30%	3.02 -	26.0	3.9	10.2	**2.6**	0.6	2.02	84%	109	223
Support 5.46	1st Half		2	0	0	30	2.68	1.36	$3	3.4	234			32%	3.20 -	11.2	4.5	9.2	**2.1**	0.3		80%	98	201
LIMA A	2nd Half		3	4	0	32	1.98	1.13	$7	3.2	211			29%	2.85 -	14.8	3.4	11.0	**3.3**	0.8		88%	122	250
Risk Low	03	Proj	**4**	**4**	**0**	**60**	**3.00**	**1.32**	**$6**	**3.8**	**232**			**32%**	**3.31**	**19.7**	**4.2**	**10.5**	**2.5**	**0.6**	**G**	**79%**	**106**	**214**

Great LIMA pick because:

- Excellent and growing BPIs
- Pitches on the Pirates
- LHers get no respect
- Nobody in your league will believe he has any value.
- Guaranteed you get him for $1.

Schilling,Curt

	Tm	W	L	Sv	IP	ERA	Br/IP	R$	BF/G	OBA	vLH	vRH	H%	xERA	RAR	Ctl	Dom	Cmd	hr/9	G/F	S%	BPV	BPX
RH Starter	98 PHI	15	14	0	268	3.26	1.11	$28	30.9	238	249	223	32%	3.01	71.1	2.0	10.1	4.9	0.8	1.65	73%	148	267
AGE 36 Decline	99 PHI	15	6	0	180	3.55	1.13	$25	30.4	239	246	227	27%	3.49	48.1	2.2	7.6	3.5	1.3	1.21	74%	88	191
TYPE Power	00 2NL	11	12	0	210	3.81	1.19	$20	29.7	256	243	268	29%	3.83	51.1	1.9	7.2	3.7	1.2	1.17	72%	91	200
BURN Moderate	01 ARI	22	6	0	256	2.99	1.08	$37	29.3	247	248	242	32%	3.54 -	81.7	1.4	10.3	7.5	1.3	1.10	80%	186	345
ERA Potl ++	02 ARI	23	7	0	259	3.23	0.97	$44	28.0	230	242	208	31%	2.82	77.3	1.1	11.0	9.6	1.0	1.18	71%	246	504
Support 5.93	1st Half	13	3	0	131	3.23	0.89	$26	27.8	220			31%	2.57 +	39.2	0.9	12.0	13.5	1.1		69%	333	683
LIMA C	2nd Half	10	4	0	128	3.24	1.05	$20	28.2	240			31%	3.07	38.1	1.4	9.9	7.1	0.9		73%	187	384
Risk Moderate	03 Proj	20	8	0	250	3.46	1.05	$35	29.2	240			31%	3.21	66.9	1.4	10.3	7.1	1.1	--	72%	186	374

Top SP BPVs of Past 10 Years:

1. P.Martinez 1999 259
2. B. Saberhagen 1994 258
3. P.Martinez 2000 256
4. C.Schilling 2002 246
5. G.Maddux 1997 225
6. G.Maddux 1995 217

Schmidt,Jason

	Tm	W	L	Sv	IP	ERA	Br/IP	R$	BF/G	OBA	vLH	vRH	H%	xERA	RAR	Ctl	Dom	Cmd	hr/9	G/F	S%	BPV	BPX
RH Starter	98 PIT	11	14	0	214	4.08	1.40	$8	28.0	274	283	270	31%	4.48	33.2	3.0	6.6	2.2	1.0	1.26	73%	56	102
AGE 30 Peak	99 PIT	13	11	0	212	4.20	1.43	$12	28.0	268	288	241	30%	4.45	38.2	3.6	6.3	1.7	1.0	1.53	73%	45	98
TYPE Power	00 PIT	2	5	0	63	5.42	1.77	($4)	26.9	285	250	307	34%	5.44	1.8	5.8	7.3	1.2	0.9	1.53	70%	42	93
BURN none	01 2NL	* 14	8	0	166	3.74	1.30	$16	24.1	246	282	217	31%	3.54	36.1	3.4	8.6	2.6	0.7	1.06	72%	90	167
ERA Potl ++	02 SF	* 15	8	0	197	3.47	1.20	$23	26.2	225	259	180	29%	3.05	52.4	3.4	9.4	2.7	0.7	0.77	72%	103	211
Support 4.76	1st Half	6	2	0	90	3.50	1.19	$10	24.7	233			30%	3.22	23.7	3.0	9.5	3.2	0.8		73%	108	221
LIMA C+	2nd Half	9	6	0	107	3.45	1.21	$14	27.6	218			29%	2.89 +	28.7	3.8	9.3	2.4	0.6		72%	101	206
Risk Moderate	03 Proj	14	10	0	200	3.78	1.28	$18	25.5	239			30%	3.48	44.8	3.6	8.8	2.5	0.8	F	72%	89	179

Cracked a 100 level BPV, and at 30, can now be considered in peak mode. Solid numbers all around, though increasing fly ball frequency could become a concern, and injury history is always in the background.

Schoeneweis,Scott

	Tm	W	L	Sv	IP	ERA	Br/IP	R$	BF/G	OBA	vLH	vRH	H%	xERA	RAR	Ctl	Dom	Cmd	hr/9	G/F	S%	BPV	BPX
LH Reliever	98 aaa	11	8	0	180	6.75	1.71	($11)	30.8	320			35%	6.15 +	-31.8	3.4	5.8	1.7	1.2		61%	26	50
AGE 29 Peak	99 ANA	* 3	5	0	74	8.39	2.01	($12)	9.1	367	266	313	40%	7.99	-25.0	3.4	5.7	1.7	1.5	2.03	58%	7	18
TYPE Contact	00 ANA	7	10	0	170	5.45	1.47	$2	27.6	276	294	271	29%	4.79 +	10.4	3.5	4.1	1.2	1.1	2.44	64%	16	41
BURN High	01 ANA	10	11	0	205	5.09	1.48	$1	28.2	282	209	304	30%	4.75	10.8	3.4	4.6	1.4	0.9	1.84	66%	27	54
ERA Potl -	02 ANA	9	8	1	118	4.88	1.42	$4	9.5	263	202	290	28%	4.59	3.6	3.7	5.0	1.3	1.3	1.30	69%	21	40
Support 6.33	1st Half	6	6	0	90	5.39	1.51	($0)	26.6	274			29%	4.87 +	-3.5	4.0	4.4	1.1	1.2		66%	14	26
LIMA C+	2nd Half	3	2	1	28	3.23	1.15	$4	2.9	226			24%	3.68	7.0	2.9	6.8	2.3	1.6		81%	51	96
Risk X HIGH	03 Proj	3	4	0	60	4.35	1.30	$3	7.7	255			27%	4.11	8.2	3.0	5.3	1.8	1.2	--	70%	36	74

Has found a home in the bullpen:

	IP	ERA	OBA	Cmd
Starter	90	5.38	.276	1.1
Reliever	28	3.25	.225	2.3

This is not to say that he's now draftable. Low Dom and high BA vs RHers are still a problem.

Seanez,Rudy

	Tm	W	L	Sv	IP	ERA	Br/IP	R$	BF/G	OBA	vLH	vRH	H%	xERA	RAR	Ctl	Dom	Cmd	hr/9	G/F	S%	BPV	BPX
RH Reliever	98 ATL	* 6	1	9	57	2.21	1.12	$15	4.6	199	286	125	31%	2.27	23.1	3.8	12.3	3.3	0.5	1.38	82%	143	258
AGE 34 Decline	99 ATL	6	1	3	53	3.40	1.28	$10	4.0	239	239	230	29%	3.20	15.3	3.6	7.0	2.0	0.5	1.02	74%	75	162
TYPE Power	00 ATL	2	4	2	21	4.29	1.14	$4	3.7	202	294	114	23%	3.15 +	3.8	3.9	8.6	2.2	1.3	0.67	67%	74	163
BURN none	01 2NL	0	2	1	36	2.75	1.17	$3	3.9	185	151	197	24%	2.73	12.6	4.8	10.3	2.2	1.0	0.83	82%	95	176
ERA Potl +++	02 TEX	1	3	0	37	5.59	1.51	($2)	4.4	235	220	238	31%	4.30 +	-2.4	5.8	10.5	1.8	1.2	0.92	65%	72	136
Support 3.27	1st Half	0	3	0	21	5.55	1.56	($2)	4.3	232			32%	4.44 +	-1.2	6.4	11.9	1.9	1.3		67%	81	153
LIMA C	2nd Half	1	0	0	16	5.66	1.45	($0)	4.6	238			29%	4.11 +	-1.2	5.1	8.5	1.7	1.1		62%	59	112
Risk Moderate	03 Proj	2	2	0	40	4.28	1.55	$0	4.5	247			32%	4.31	5.9	5.6	9.7	1.7	0.9	--	74%	73	148

Between his declining control and constant DL trips, the risk is too high to consider him.

Sedlacek,Shawn

	Tm	W	L	Sv	IP	ERA	Br/IP	R$	BF/G	OBA	vLH	vRH	H%	xERA	RAR	Ctl	Dom	Cmd	hr/9	G/F	S%	BPV	BPX
RH Starter	98	0	0	0	0	0.00	0.00																
AGE 25 Growth	99	0	0	0	0	0.00	0.00																
TYPE Contact	00 aa	15	6	3	140	4.69	1.61	$11	18.1	318			34%	5.48 -	20.0	2.7	4.2	1.5	0.8		71%	26	61
BURN none	01 a/a	11	11	0	168	5.20	1.46	$3	26.3	309			33%	5.41	5.1	1.8	4.7	2.6	1.2		67%	39	75
ERA Potl ++	02 KC	* 11	11	0	182	5.48	1.40	$2	26.2	279	324	279	31%	4.59 +	-9.2	2.8	5.8	2.1	1.1	1.02	62%	44	83
Support 5.44	1st Half	8	6	0	116	4.26	1.20	$8	28.2	258			29%	3.36 +	13.2	1.9	5.8	3.0	0.7		65%	80	152
LIMA D	2nd Half	3	5	0	66	7.65	1.76	($8)	23.7	314			33%	6.75 +	-22.4	4.2	5.7	1.4	1.9		59%	-2	-4
Risk Moderate	03 Proj	6	9	0	120	5.70	1.53	($2)	24.2	303			33%	5.44	-5.3	2.7	5.2	1.9	1.3	--	64%	27	56

3-5, 6.75 ERA in 84 IP at KC. Soft-tosser with decent control and small signs of growth. But not yet posting a level of BPIs that merit draft consideration.

Sele,Aaron

	Tm	W	L	Sv	IP	ERA	Br/IP	R$	BF/G	OBA	vLH	vRH	H%	xERA	RAR	Ctl	Dom	Cmd	hr/9	G/F	S%	BPV	BPX
RH Starter	98 TEX	19	11	0	212	4.24	1.52	$14	28.6	285	295	270	34%	4.57	40.2	2.8	7.1	2.0	0.6	1.45	72%	64	137
AGE 32 Past	99 TEX	18	9	0	205	4.79	1.53	$12	27.7	297	286	299	36%	5.06	29.8	3.1	8.2	2.7	0.9	1.86	70%	73	183
TYPE Contact	00 SEA	17	10	0	211	4.52	1.40	$18	26.8	271	276	265	31%	4.14	39.4	3.2	5.8	1.9	0.7	1.28	68%	53	138
BURN none	01 SEA	15	5	0	215	3.60	1.24	$20	26.3	263	231	296	28%	3.99	54.3	2.1	4.8	2.2	1.0	1.01	75%	47	93
ERA Potl -	02 ANA	8	9	0	160	4.89	1.49	($0)	27.2	296	315	283	31%	5.13	4.6	2.8	4.6	1.7	1.2	1.17	70%	23	44
Support 5.79	1st Half	7	5	0	98	5.05	1.55	$1	27.4	306			32%	5.35	0.8	2.8	4.3	1.6	1.1		69%	20	37
LIMA D	2nd Half	1	4	0	62	4.65	1.41	($1)	26.8	280			30%	4.79	3.8	2.8	5.1	1.8	1.3		71%	29	55
Risk Low	03 Proj	8	8	0	160	4.44	1.40	$5	26.6	281			30%	4.60	19.8	2.7	5.0	1.8	1.1	--	71%	35	71

A scan of his 5-year Dom trend tells the story of a pitcher losing his grip on effectiveness. Add in his rotator cuff problem and he becomes a very high risk to provide much value in 2003.

Sheets,Ben

	Tm	W	L	Sv	IP	ERA	Br/IP	R$	BF/G	OBA	vLH	vRH	H%	xERA	RAR	Ctl	Dom	Cmd	hr/9	G/F	S%	BPV	BPX
RH Starter	98	0	0	0	0	0.00	0.00																
AGE 24 Growth	99	0	0	0	0	0.00	0.00																
TYPE Power	00 a/a	8	8	0	154	2.57	1.26	$19	23.8	248			29%	3.20 -	65.8	3.0	6.0	2.0	0.4		80%	72	170
BURN Low	01 MIL	* 12	11	0	161	4.75	1.45	$6	26.0	286	324	251	31%	5.06	13.3	2.9	5.5	1.9	1.3	1.59	70%	33	62
ERA Potl No chg	02 MIL	11	16	0	216	4.17	1.42	$8	27.6	280	318	247	33%	4.55	37.4	2.9	7.1	2.4	0.9	1.47	72%	66	136
Support 4.28	1st Half	4	9	0	102	4.32	1.57	($0)	27.0	287			34%	4.78	15.7	3.9	6.8	1.8	0.6		73%	57	116
LIMA B	2nd Half	7	7	0	114	4.03	1.29	$8	28.2	274			32%	4.35	21.7	2.1	7.4	3.6	1.1		72%	86	177
Risk High	03 Proj	12	14	0	200	3.96	1.39	$12	26.1	277			33%	4.45	40.0	2.7	7.2	2.6	0.9	--	74%	70	140

Nice growth year. He's still allowing too many hits, however. His high 33% hit rate should come down by itself, but that may not be enough. Could get his ERA down a touch below 4.00 in 2003.

Shields,Scot

	Tm	W	L	Sv	IP	ERA	Br/IP	R$	BF/G	OBA	vLH	vRH	H%	xERA	RAR	Ctl	Dom	Cmd	hr/9	G/F	S%	BPV	BPX
RH Reliever	98	0	0	0	0	0.00	0.00																
AGE 27 Pre-Peak	99 aa	4	4	0	74	4.01	1.35	$6	31.6	254			30%	4.47	16.7	3.5	8.4	2.4	1.5		76%	61	141
TYPE	00 aaa	7	13	0	163	6.68	1.62	($7)	27.4	286			34%	5.23 +	-20.1	4.4	7.4	1.7	1.0		58%	46	109
BURN Very High	01 aaa	6	11	0	148	5.27	1.37	$1	21.9	286	63	292	30%	5.12	3.1	2.2	5.7	2.6	1.6	0.71	66%	40	77
ERA Potl +	02 ANA	* 7	5	1	96	2.81	1.06	$13	6.7	217	184	191	25%	2.63	29.5	2.5	6.7	2.6	0.8	1.92	77%	81	154
Support 4.96	1st Half	2	3	1	58	3.57	1.17	$4	7.0	255			30%	3.47	11.9	1.9	7.1	3.8	0.9		73%	99	188
LIMA B	2nd Half	5	2	0	38	1.66	0.89	$9	6.3	151			16%	1.34	17.6	3.6	5.9	1.7	0.7		87%	74	140
Risk X HIGH	03 Proj	4	4	0	60	3.60	1.22	$6	7.5	255			29%	3.61	14.2	2.3	6.6	2.9	0.9	G	73%	78	159

5-3, 2.20 ERA in 49 IP at ANA. Made nice gains in Dom, HR rate, and G/F ratio, but low 25% hit rate will correct itself and push his ERA back into the mid-3.00s.

Shuey,Paul

	Tm	W	L	Sv	IP	ERA	Br/IP	R$	BF/G	OBA	vLH	vRH	H%	xERA	RAR	Ctl	Dom	Cmd	hr/9	G/F	S%	BPV	BPX
RH Reliever	98 CLE	* 5	4	4	66	3.53	1.45	$8	5.3	249	230	229	33%	4.06 -	18.8	4.6	10.2	2.2	0.8	1.87	78%	88	188
AGE 32 Past	99 CLE	8	5	6	81	3.56	1.33	$14	4.8	229	223	223	32%	3.57	25.1	4.4	11.4	2.6	0.9	2.88	76%	105	264
TYPE Power	00 CLE	4	2	0	63	3.42	1.28	$8	4.7	222	203	235	30%	3.03	21.1	4.3	9.8	2.3	0.6	1.62	74%	101	261
BURN none	01 CLE	5	3	2	54	2.83	1.46	$7	5.0	258	280	225	39%	3.58 -	19.2	4.3	11.6	2.7	0.2	2.47	79%	125	250
ERA Potl +	02 2TM	8	2	1	70	3.34	1.27	$11	4.3	227	226	217	30%	2.91	18.1	4.0	8.5	2.1	0.4	2.64	73%	94	184
Support 6.22	1st Half	2	0	0	29	2.48	1.14	$5	3.8	220			29%	2.40	10.8	3.1	8.7	2.8	0.3		78%	113	221
LIMA B+	2nd Half	6	2	1	41	3.95	1.37	$7	4.6	232			30%	3.26 +	7.2	4.6	8.3	1.8	0.4		70%	83	164
Risk Low	03 Proj	7	3	2	70	3.21	1.34	$10	4.6	236			32%	3.20	20.6	4.2	9.8	2.3	0.4	G	76%	103	209

Did not fare all that well upon his trade to LA, but that was likely just an acclimation period to the new league. He could post VERY nice numbers once he's become settled in the NL.

Silva,Carlos

	Yr	Tm	W	L	Sv	IP	ERA	Br/IP	R$	BF/G	OBA	vLH	vRH	H%	xERA	RAR	Ctl	Dom	Cmd	hr/9	G/F	S%	BPV	BPX
RH Reliever	98		0	0	0	0	0.00	0.00																
AGE 24 Growth	99		0	0	0	0	0.00	0.00																
TYPE Contact	00		0	0	0	0	0.00	0.00																
BURN none	01	aa	15	8	0	180	4.60	1.39	$10	27.7	304			33%	4.94	19.8	1.5	4.6	3.1	1.0		69%	57	110
ERA Potl -	02	PHI	5	0	2	87	3.10	1.26	$10	5.2	264	292	276	29%	3.52	27.4	2.3	4.3	1.9	0.4	2.81	75%	56	115
Support 4.18	1st Half		1	0	0	42	2.14	1.19	$5	4.9	248			29%	3.12 -	18.7	2.4	5.8	2.5	0.4		83%	79	162
LIMA D+	2nd Half		4	0	2	45	4.00	1.33	$6	5.5	279			30%	3.90	8.8	2.2	3.0	1.4	0.4		69%	34	70
Risk High	03	Proj	2	3	0	80	4.05	1.36	$2	5.9	283			30%	4.26	15.0	2.3	3.9	1.8	0.7	G	71%	39	78

Always check out a rookie's 2nd tour of the league because that is the level you can expect for the short term. Here, league caught up to him, so expect some growing pains in 2003.

Simontacchi,Jason

	Yr	Tm	W	L	Sv	IP	ERA	Br/IP	R$	BF/G	OBA	vLH	vRH	H%	xERA	RAR	Ctl	Dom	Cmd	hr/9	G/F	S%	BPV	BPX
RH Starter	98	ind	10	2	0	110	2.95	1.13	$17	27.8	249			29%	3.58 -	36.6	1.7	7.5	4.4	1.1		80%	108	210
AGE 29 Peak	99		0	0	0	0	0.00	0.00																
TYPE Contact	00		0	0	0	0	0.00	0.00																
BURN none	01	aaa	7	13	0	143	6.67	1.76	($12)	20.9	361			38%	7.25 -	-23.9	1.5	4.2	2.8	1.4		64%	23	45
ERA Potl -	02	STL *	16	6	0	185	3.79	1.34	$18	26.3	266	248	257	28%	4.26	41.3	2.9	4.6	1.6	1.0	1.15	75%	34	70
Support 4.71	1st Half		10	2	0	91	2.97	1.25	$15	27.1	268			28%	4.00 -	30.4	2.0	4.3	2.2	0.9		80%	45	93
LIMA C	2nd Half		6	4	0	94	4.59	1.42	$3	25.5	264			28%	4.51	10.9	3.7	5.0	1.3	1.1		70%	29	59
Risk Very High	03	Proj	10	10	0	160	4.39	1.36	$9	23.6	277			29%	4.62	22.9	2.5	4.9	2.0	1.2	--	71%	35	70

11-5, 4.03 in 143 IP at STL. Ditto for the 2nd half here. This is not a high skills pitcher, it is a 29-year-old journeyman with a low ceiling. Great story, but all fairy tales must end.

Smith,Bud

	Yr	Tm	W	L	Sv	IP	ERA	Br/IP	R$	BF/G	OBA	vLH	vRH	H%	xERA	RAR	Ctl	Dom	Cmd	hr/9	G/F	S%	BPV	BPX
LH Reliever	98		0	0	0	0	0.00	0.00																
AGE 23 Growth	99		0	0	0	0	0.00	0.00																
TYPE	00	a/a	17	2	0	163	2.60	1.13	$31	24.5	239			29%	2.89	69.1	2.3	7.3	3.2	0.6		79%	103	244
BURN none	01	STL *	14	8	0	192	3.28	1.27	$19	24.4	264	295	235	30%	3.85 -	53.6	2.3	6.5	2.8	0.8	1.16	77%	76	140
ERA Potl -	02	2NL	4	6	0	103	4.98	1.62	($4)	23.4	302	326	342	35%	4.99	6.7	3.6	5.7	1.6	0.4	1.14	68%	49	100
Support 4.69	1st Half		2	5	0	62	4.77	1.61	($2)	21.7	288			34%	4.72	5.8	4.2	6.1	1.4	0.4		69%	51	105
LIMA D+	2nd Half		2	1	0	41	5.29	1.64	($2)	26.6	323			37%	5.39	0.9	2.6	5.1	1.9	0.4		66%	48	98
Risk High	03	Proj	1	1	0	15	4.20	1.47	$1	13.2	287			33%	4.48	2.5	3.0	6.0	2.0	0.6	--	71%	58	116

Heavy 2001 workload may have been the culprit for his struggles and injuries in 2002. Was diagnosed with a torn labrum at the end of the season, which means he'll likely miss most or all of 2003.

Smith,Dan

	Yr	Tm	W	L	Sv	IP	ERA	Br/IP	R$	BF/G	OBA	vLH	vRH	H%	xERA	RAR	Ctl	Dom	Cmd	hr/9	G/F	S%	BPV	BPX
RH Reliever	98	aa	13	9	0	159	7.75	1.64	($9)	26.9	310			32%	6.61 +	-49.5	3.4	5.4	1.6	2.0		55%	-3	-5
AGE 27 Pre-Peak	99	MON *	9	13	0	161	5.53	1.54	($0)	23.2	284	322	273	32%	5.04 +	0.3	3.8	6.6	1.7	1.1	0.95	65%	41	88
TYPE	00	aaa	7	10	0	124	6.39	1.64	($4)	23.5	315		400	33%	5.86 +	-10.4	3.0	4.1	1.4	1.2	0.43	61%	10	25
BURN none	01	aaa	6	4	0	106	6.03	1.70	($6)	23.3	311			32%	6.63 -	-8.6	3.8	4.8	1.2	1.9		69%	-9	-17
ERA Potl -	02	MON *	6	5	2	129	4.11	1.25	$9	11.5	251	151	239	27%	4.16	23.3	2.8	5.8	2.1	1.3	0.90	72%	43	89
Support 4.24	1st Half		5	4	0	89	4.14	1.28	$6	20.8	270			29%	4.48	15.7	2.1	5.4	2.5	1.3		72%	47	96
LIMA C+	2nd Half		1	1	2	40	4.05	1.20	$4	5.7	205			22%	3.46 +	7.5	4.3	6.7	1.6	1.3		71%	47	97
Risk Very High	03	Proj	2	2	1	50	4.32	1.32	$3	5.7	242			26%	4.28	7.6	3.8	5.9	1.6	1.4	--	72%	32	64

1-1, 3.52 ERA in 46 IP at MON. It would appear that he might be better suited to pen work, but don't go investing just yet. As a reliever, he posted a .210 OBA, 4.0 Ctl, 6,6 Dom and 1.6 Cmd. Improvement, but not a gimme.

Smith,Mike

	Yr	Tm	W	L	Sv	IP	ERA	Br/IP	R$	BF/G	OBA	vLH	vRH	H%	xERA	RAR	Ctl	Dom	Cmd	hr/9	G/F	S%	BPV	BPX
RH Reliever	98		0	0	0	0	0.00	0.00																
AGE 25 Growth	99		0	0	0	0	0.00	0.00																
TYPE Contact	00		0	0	0	0	0.00	0.00																
BURN Low	01	aa	6	2	0	93	3.19	1.34	$8	28.3	272			31%	4.11 -	27.7	2.6	6.1	2.3	0.8		79%	63	121
ERA Potl -	02	TOR *	8	7	0	156	4.72	1.44	$2	20.0	270	378	217	29%	4.21 +	8.0	3.6	4.7	1.3	0.7	1.17	67%	34	64
Support 5.09	1st Half		6	5	0	87	4.64	1.36	$3	23.4	259			29%	3.83 +	5.5	3.4	4.9	1.5	0.7		66%	42	79
LIMA C+	2nd Half		2	2	0	69	4.83	1.54	($2)	17.1	284			31%	4.69	2.5	3.8	4.3	1.1	0.8		69%	24	46
Risk High	03	Proj	2	2	0	50	4.86	1.42	$0	14.5	273			30%	4.21 +	3.4	3.2	5.2	1.6	0.7	--	66%	44	89

0-3, 6.69 ERA in 35 IP at TOR. Performed well in AA, meriting a promotion to AAA. But rather than letting him master AAA, they called him up to the bigs and watched him flounder. Yes, flounder. Like a fish.

Smith,Travis

	Yr	Tm	W	L	Sv	IP	ERA	Br/IP	R$	BF/G	OBA	vLH	vRH	H%	xERA	RAR	Ctl	Dom	Cmd	hr/9	G/F	S%	BPV	BPX
RH Starter	98	aaa	4	6	0	67	6.04	1.66	($3)	25.6	315			33%	5.97	-5.5	3.2	4.2	1.3	1.2		65%	8	15
AGE 30 Peak	99	aa	3	2	0	38	8.05	1.84	($4)	25.9	322			35%	6.06 +	-12.0	4.5	4.3	0.9	0.7		54%	15	34
TYPE Contact	00	a/a	13	8	0	165	5.45	1.53	$5	24.5	305			33%	5.36	6.8	2.7	4.7	1.8	1.1		66%	27	64
BURN none	01	a/a	15	8	1	162	4.67	1.55	$7	24.1	323			34%	5.27 -	16.4	1.8	3.4	1.9	0.6		70%	32	62
ERA Potl -	02	STL *	8	9	0	139	4.72	1.44	$3	21.7	296	273	357	32%	5.18	13.8	2.3	5.4	2.4	1.2	1.58	70%	41	84
Support 5.33	1st Half		4	4	0	93	3.86	1.29	$6	24.5	270			30%	4.16	19.9	2.2	5.7	2.6	1.0		73%	60	123
LIMA F	2nd Half		4	5	0	46	6.46	1.74	($3)	17.9	344			36%	7.22 -	-6.1	2.3	4.7	2.0	1.8		66%	4	7
Risk High	03	Proj	1	1	0	20	5.40	1.55	($1)	22.4	316			33%	5.86	0.1	2.3	4.5	2.0	1.4	G	68%	20	41

4-2, 7.17 ERA in 54 IP at STL. Good job by STL to grab a journeyman minor leaguer right at peak for a short-term hit, but he couldn't cut it in the majors. I'd be surprised if we ever saw him in the bigs again.

Smoltz,John

	Yr	Tm	W	L	Sv	IP	ERA	Br/IP	R$	BF/G	OBA	vLH	vRH	H%	xERA	RAR	Ctl	Dom	Cmd	hr/9	G/F	S%	BPV	BPX
RH Reliever	98	ATL	17	3	0	168	2.89	1.13	$26	26.1	234	248	212	31%	2.79	52.7	2.4	9.3	3.9	0.5	1.56	75%	130	235
AGE 36 Decline	99	ATL	11	8	0	186	3.19	1.12	$24	25.9	243	264	229	29%	2.98	58.6	1.9	7.5	3.9	0.7	1.37	73%	113	246
TYPE Power	00	ATL	0	0	0	0	0.00	0.00																
BURN none	01	ATL	3	3	10	59	3.36	1.07	$13	6.5	242	263	211	30%	3.25	15.9	1.5	8.7	5.7	1.1	1.21	73%	147	272
ERA Potl + + +	02	ATL	3	2	55	80	3.26	1.04	$46	4.2	207	213	199	28%	2.21 +	23.5	2.7	9.6	3.5	0.5	1.28	68%	132	270
Support 0.56	1st Half		0	2	27	43	4.58	1.23	$18	4.6	243			32%	3.29 +	5.1	2.9	9.6	3.3	0.6		62%	114	234
LIMA C	2nd Half		3	0	28	37	1.71	0.82	$28	3.8	162			23%	0.94 +	18.5	2.4	9.5	3.9	0.2		79%	154	317
Risk Moderate	03	Proj	4	2	47	80	2.59	1.04	$41	6.0	218			29%	2.52	30.7	2.3	9.5	4.2	0.7	--	78%	136	274

Fun Facts about his 1st year as a full-time closer:
- Without his 0.2 IP 8 ER outing on Apr 6 vs NYM, his ERA would have been 2.39.
- In 2nd half, converted 96% of his save opportunities.

Soriano,Rafael

	Yr	Tm	W	L	Sv	IP	ERA	Br/IP	R$	BF/G	OBA	vLH	vRH	H%	xERA	RAR	Ctl	Dom	Cmd	hr/9	G/F	S%	BPV	BPX
RH Starter	98		0	0	0	0	0.00	0.00																
AGE 23 Growth	99		0	0	0	0	0.00	0.00																
TYPE Power	00		0	0	0	0	0.00	0.00																
BURN none	01	aa	2	2	0	48	3.94	1.13	$4	24.3	224			28%	3.04 +	9.5	2.8	9.0	3.2	0.9		67%	103	198
ERA Potl -	02	SEA *	2	6	1	93	3.86	1.24	$4	19.4	242	297	179	27%	3.97	15.5	3.1	7.3	2.4	1.4	0.54	75%	57	108
Support 3.04	1st Half		2	6	1	81	3.99	1.23	$3	21.1	239			26%	4.00	12.1	3.1	7.0	2.3	1.6		74%	50	94
LIMA B	2nd Half		0	0	0	12	3.00	1.33	$0	12.8	262			35%	3.77 -	3.4	3.0	9.7	3.3	0.7		80%	107	202
Risk High	03	Proj	7	6	0	120	3.98	1.19	$10	22.4	233			27%	3.60	22.4	3.0	7.8	2.6	1.3	F	71%	71	145

0-3, 4.60 ERA in 47 IP at SEA. The beginnings of something good here. Needs to keep the ball down more, which will improve his HR rate, and get LHed hitters under control. That solved, he'll shine big time.

Sosa,Jorge

	Yr	Tm	W	L	Sv	IP	ERA	Br/IP	R$	BF/G	OBA	vLH	vRH	H%	xERA	RAR	Ctl	Dom	Cmd	hr/9	G/F	S%	BPV	BPX
RH Reliever	98		0	0	0	0	0.00	0.00																
AGE 25 Growth	99		0	0	0	0	0.00	0.00																
TYPE	00		0	0	0	0	0.00	0.00																
BURN none	01		0	0	0	0	0.00	0.00																
ERA Potl -	02	TAM	2	7	0	106	5.18	1.41	($3)	13.9	239	289	183	24%	4.36 +	-1.0	4.7	4.3	0.9	1.4	0.69	67%	9	18
Support 3.99	1st Half		0	1	0	33	5.44	1.51	($2)	8.1	267			28%	4.92 +	-1.5	4.4	4.6	1.1	1.4		67%	11	21
LIMA F	2nd Half		2	6	0	73	5.06	1.36	($1)	20.8	226			22%	4.11 +	0.4	4.8	4.2	0.9	1.5		67%	9	17
Risk Low	03	Proj	1	2	0	40	4.73	1.43	($0)	12.4	242			24%	4.40	3.4	4.7	4.3	0.9	1.4	F	71%	11	22

Most teams that are committed to keeping a Rule 5 pitcher will tuck him in the corner of the pen, give him 40 token innings and pray for improvement next year. On TAM, he gets 106 IP and costs them 7 games.

Sparks,Steve

Sparks,Steve		Tm	W	L	Sv	IP	ERA	Br/IP	R$	BF/G	OBA	vLH	vRH	H%	xERA	RAR	Ctl	Dom	Cmd	hr/9	G/F	S%	BPV	BPX
RH Starter	98	ANA	* 9	12	0	197	5.11	1.51	$1	26.5	281	289	238	32%	4.85	14.5	3.7	6.0	1.6	1.0	1.33	67%	40	85
AGE 37 Decline	99	ANA	5	11	0	148	5.41	1.67	($4)	24.3	283	293	270	29%	5.58	9.1	5.0	4.4	0.9	1.3	1.17	70%	5	13
TYPE Contact	00	DET	* 12	12	1	194	4.17	1.38	$16	23.2	270	269	255	29%	4.04	45.3	3.0	4.2	1.4	0.6	1.40	70%	36	92
BURN none	01	DET	14	9	0	232	3.65	1.33	$17	28.2	272	280	263	29%	4.15 -	57.1	2.5	4.5	1.8	0.9	1.53	75%	40	80
ERA Potl -	02	DET	* 8	16	0	205	6.36	1.72	($14)	22.1	313	299	312	34%	5.88	-34.4	3.9	4.6	1.2	1.1	1.42	63%	13	24
Support 5.05	1st Half		3	8	0	102	7.38	1.83	($13)	20.3	333			35%	6.28 +	-31.2	3.8	3.9	1.0	0.9		58%	7	13
LIMA F	2nd Half		5	8	0	103	5.34	1.61	($3)	24.5	293			32%	5.48	-3.2	3.9	5.4	1.4	1.3		69%	19	35
Risk Very High	03	Proj	7	11	0	160	5.12	1.54	($2)	23.8	292			31%	5.08	5.3	3.4	4.7	1.4	1.0	--	68%	23	46

Knuckleballers can be good inning-eaters, but they have to at least keep their team in the ballgame. He didn't in 2002, and it would be a surprise to see him get close to 200 IP again, even on DET.

Speier,Justin

Speier,Justin		Tm	W	L	Sv	IP	ERA	Br/IP	R$	BF/G	OBA	vLH	vRH	H%	xERA	RAR	Ctl	Dom	Cmd	hr/9	G/F	S%	BPV	BPX
RH Reliever	98	2NL	* 3	6	12	72	6.25	1.57	$2	5.1	288	240	362	31%	6.16	-9.8	3.9	7.5	1.9	2.1	0.65	66%	19	35
AGE 29 Peak	99	ATL	* 2	4	3	69	5.61	1.64	($2)	6.8	291	275	226	33%	5.68	-0.6	4.3	7.3	1.7	1.4	1.00	69%	33	72
TYPE Power	00	CLE	* 5	2	9	81	3.66	1.27	$14	5.7	239	171	274	30%	3.63	24.4	3.4	8.8	2.5	1.0	0.59	74%	83	216
BURN none	01	COL	* 7	3	2	88	4.30	1.26	$8	5.7	253	221	234	29%	4.14	12.6	2.8	7.7	2.8	1.3	0.65	70%	69	128
ERA Potl No chg	02	COL	* 7	1	3	76	4.50	1.28	$9	4.3	259	240	197	29%	4.41	9.8	2.6	6.9	2.6	1.4	0.63	69%	57	117
Support 6.79	1st Half		5	0	3	38	4.03	1.42	$6	4.7	286			34%	4.70 -	7.3	2.6	7.8	3.0	0.9		74%	79	162
LIMA C+	2nd Half		2	1	0	38	4.97	1.13	$2	3.8	230			23%	4.12 +	2.5	2.6	5.9	2.3	1.9		63%	35	73
Risk Moderate	03	Proj	5	2	3	65	4.57	1.29	$7	4.8	256			29%	4.33	7.7	2.9	7.3	2.5	1.4	F	69%	59	119

5-1, 4.35 ERA in 62 IP at COL. A flyball pitcher in COL will tend to have a short life span, but he succeeded in spite of that. For comparison, a hurler with his ERA and BPIs in a neutral park would have an ERA of 3.60.

Spooneybarger,Tim

Spooneybarger,Tim			W	L	Sv	IP	ERA	Br/IP	R$	BF/G	OBA	vLH	vRH	H%	xERA	RAR	Ctl	Dom	Cmd	hr/9	G/F	S%	BPV	BPX
RH Reliever	98		0	0	0	0	0.00	0.00																
AGE 23 Growth	99		0	0	0	0	0.00	0.00																
TYPE Power	00		0	0	0	0	0.00	0.00																
BURN none	01	a/a	4	2	5	76	2.49	1.21	$12	5.1	233			32%	2.70	29.9	3.2	9.4	2.9	0.2	1.75	79%	119	229
ERA Potl --	02	ATL	* 2	0	12	71	2.15	1.21	$16	4.3	206	150	234	24%	2.83 -	31.4	4.3	6.6	1.5	0.6	1.80	85%	66	136
Support 2.10	1st Half		1	0	11	39	2.08	1.26	$12	4.3	214			26%	2.88 -	17.7	4.4	7.2	1.6	0.5		85%	75	155
LIMA B+	2nd Half		1	0	1	32	2.25	1.16	$5	4.2	196			22%	2.78 -	13.8	4.2	5.9	1.4	0.8		85%	55	113
Risk Moderate	03	Proj	2	1	1	60	3.30	1.30	$5	4.7	232			29%	3.16	17.3	4.1	7.5	1.9	0.5	G	75%	79	159

1-0, 2.65 ERA in 51 IP at ATL. Overachieved. His ERA was suppressed by an 85% strand rate and 24% hit rate, and unsupported by a mediocre 1.5 command ratio. It heads up in 2003.

Stanton,Mike

Stanton,Mike		Tm	W	L	Sv	IP	ERA	Br/IP	R$	BF/G	OBA	vLH	vRH	H%	xERA	RAR	Ctl	Dom	Cmd	hr/9	G/F	S%	BPV	BPX
LH Reliever	98	NYY	4	1	6	79	5.47	1.23	$7	4.9	242	253	232	27%	4.05 +	2.0	3.0	7.9	2.7	1.5	1.12	58%	65	139
AGE 35 Decline	99	NYY	2	2	0	62	4.35	1.44	$2	3.7	289	256	308	36%	4.51	12.6	2.6	8.6	3.3	0.7	1.07	70%	96	240
TYPE	00	NYY	2	3	0	68	4.10	1.35	$4	4.2	262	339	199	35%	3.81	16.5	3.2	9.9	3.1	0.7	1.06	70%	108	280
BURN none	01	NYY	9	4	0	80	2.58	1.36	$12	4.5	262	283	251	34%	3.67 -	31.1	3.3	8.8	2.7	0.4	0.96	82%	98	197
ERA Potl -	02	NYY	7	1	6	78	3.00	1.29	$11	4.2	249	268	247	28%	3.28	22.0	3.2	5.1	1.6	0.5	0.96	77%	55	104
Support 7.38	1st Half		3	1	1	42	2.78	1.21	$5	4.6	242			27%	3.15	13.1	2.8	5.3	1.9	0.6		79%	60	113
LIMA C	2nd Half		4	0	5	36	3.26	1.39	$6	3.8	257			29%	3.44	8.9	3.8	4.8	1.3	0.3		76%	51	97
Risk Low	03	Proj	5	3	2	80	3.60	1.38	$6	4.2	264			31%	3.82	18.9	3.3	6.3	1.9	0.6	--	74%	64	130

His dominance plunged in '02, and while it did not damage his ERA all that much, the fallout is yet to come. Bid into double digits at your own risk.

Stark,Dennis

Stark,Dennis		Tm	W	L	Sv	IP	ERA	Br/IP	R$	BF/G	OBA	vLH	vRH	H%	xERA	RAR	Ctl	Dom	Cmd	hr/9	G/F	S%	BPV	BPX
RH Starter	98		0	0	0	0	0.00	0.00																
AGE 28 Pre-Peak	99	aa	9	11	0	147	6.24	1.80	($7)	26.7	317			34%	6.26	-10.8	4.4	5.3	1.2	1.2		66%	13	31
TYPE	00	aa	4	3	0	49	3.31	1.33	$6	26.0	237			29%	3.02	16.1	4.0	6.1	1.5	0.2		73%	70	166
BURN none	01	a/a	16	3	0	172	3.51	1.35	$17	25.4	268	320	342	31%	4.24 -	44.1	2.9	6.5	2.3	0.9	0.59	77%	59	114
ERA Potl ---	02	COL	* 12	6	0	165	4.19	1.37	$11	18.2	242	228	224	24%	4.70 -	28.0	4.2	5.2	1.2	1.7	1.01	77%	12	26
Support 6.52	1st Half		5	3	0	77	3.84	1.49	$4	16.2	248			28%	4.34 -	16.7	5.0	6.2	1.2	0.9		77%	40	83
LIMA C+	2nd Half		7	3	0	88	4.51	1.27	$7	20.5	237			21%	5.01 -	11.2	3.6	4.3	1.2	2.4		76%	-12	-25
Risk Very High	03	Proj	8	8	0	140	4.63	1.47	$3	24.6	270			29%	4.90	15.5	3.9	5.6	1.5	1.3	--	72%	26	53

11-4, 4.01 ERA in 128 IP at COL. Had a 3.21 ERA at Coors with an 84% strand rate and an incredible 19% hit rate. With these BPIs, it's impossible to imagine ever seeing something like this again.

Stechschulte,Gene

Stechschulte,Gene			W	L	Sv	IP	ERA	Br/IP	R$	BF/G	OBA	vLH	vRH	H%	xERA	RAR	Ctl	Dom	Cmd	hr/9	G/F	S%	BPV	BPX
RH Reliever	98		0	0	0	0	0.00	0.00																
AGE 29 Peak	99	a/a	2	6	19	45	4.60	1.69	$11	5.1	287			34%	5.17 -	6.6	5.0	7.4	1.5	0.8		74%	49	114
TYPE Power	00	STL	* 5	1	26	76	4.26	1.46	$20	5.3	254	205	283	26%	4.76 -	13.9	4.5	5.2	1.2	1.4	1.41	76%	17	38
BURN none	01	STL	1	5	6	70	3.86	1.44	$4	4.6	265	275	272	29%	4.73 -	14.1	3.9	6.6	1.7	1.3	1.35	78%	39	72
ERA Potl -	02	STL	* 7	2	5	42	4.07	1.33	$10	4.6	238	263	221	26%	3.76	7.8	4.1	5.6	1.4	0.9	1.45	71%	44	90
Support 5.34	1st Half		6	2	3	36	4.49	1.36	$7	4.7	239			27%	3.96 +	4.7	4.2	6.2	1.5	1.0		69%	46	93
LIMA C+	2nd Half		1	0	2	6	1.53	1.19	$3	4.0	231			24%	2.53 -	3.1	3.1	1.5	0.5	0.0		86%	28	58
Risk Moderate	03	Proj	3	3	0	50	4.32	1.46	$2	4.9	258			28%	4.68	7.6	4.3	6.1	1.4	1.3	--	74%	32	65

6-2, 4.78 ERA in 32 IP at STL. Shoulder and elbow tendinitis ended his season early. But these marginal skill sets are fairly easy to replace.

Stein,Blake

Stein,Blake		Tm	W	L	Sv	IP	ERA	Br/IP	R$	BF/G	OBA	vLH	vRH	H%	xERA	RAR	Ctl	Dom	Cmd	hr/9	G/F	S%	BPV	BPX
RH Reliever	98	OAK	* 8	10	0	140	5.97	1.58	($3)	21.8	263	230	278	30%	5.23 +	-5.9	5.2	7.4	1.4	1.5	0.68	65%	32	69
AGE 29 Peak	99	KC	* 5	4	0	182	4.75	1.41	$5	24.6	250	256	226	29%	4.17 +	27.4	4.3	6.9	1.6	1.0	0.72	68%	51	128
TYPE Power	00	KC	* 11	5	0	128	4.59	1.41	$11	26.3	250	217	272	27%	4.66	22.6	4.2	7.1	1.7	1.6	0.91	73%	36	93
BURN none	01	KC	7	8	1	131	4.74	1.46	$3	15.9	233	229	237	26%	4.42	13.1	5.4	7.8	1.4	1.4	0.93	71%	44	88
ERA Potl +	02	KC	* 0	5	1	56	7.70	2.00	($10)	8.4	325	319	293	38%	6.76 +	-19.5	5.8	7.5	1.3	1.1	0.66	61%	29	55
Support 5.01	1st Half		0	2	1	26	9.27	2.10	($6)	10.1	345			42%	7.60 +	-14.6	5.5	8.6	1.6	1.4		55%	29	55
LIMA D	2nd Half		0	3	0	30	6.32	1.91	($4)	7.2	305			35%	6.02	-4.9	6.0	6.6	1.1	0.9		67%	30	56
Risk X HIGH	03	Proj	1	3	0	40	4.95	1.60	($1)	11.3	262			30%	5.08	2.2	5.4	7.4	1.4	1.4	F	72%	36	72

0-4, 8.02 ERA in 46 IP at KC. BPIs have shown no growth at a stage of his career when he should be thinking about peak numbers. Pass.

Stephenson,Garrett

Stephenson,Garrett			W	L	Sv	IP	ERA	Br/IP	R$	BF/G	OBA	vLH	vRH	H%	xERA	RAR	Ctl	Dom	Cmd	hr/9	G/F	S%	BPV	BPX
RH Reliever	98	PHI	* 1	10	0	96	6.92	1.64	($11)	23.1	312	404	235	33%	6.32 +	-21.8	3.3	5.3	1.6	1.7	1.19	60%	8	15
AGE 31 Peak	99	STL	* 7	4	0	116	4.03	1.38	$8	21.7	273	320	236	30%	4.45	23.5	2.9	6.0	2.1	1.1	0.82	74%	47	103
TYPE	00	STL	16	9	0	200	4.50	1.36	$16	26.8	270	310	231	29%	4.70	30.3	2.8	5.5	2.0	1.4	0.98	71%	33	73
BURN none	01	aaa	0	0	0	2	0.00	1.00	$0	7.8	262			35%	2.34 -	1.5	0.0	9.0		0.0		100%	57	109
ERA Potl +	02	STL	* 2	6	0	57	5.35	1.59	($3)	17.2	284	355	223	34%	4.81 +	0.8	4.2	6.9	1.6	0.6	0.73	66%	55	113
Support 4.80	1st Half		1	4	0	29	6.78	1.71	($4)	19.3	298			36%	5.59 +	-5.2	4.6	8.0	1.7	0.9		60%	52	107
LIMA C+	2nd Half		1	2	0	28	3.86	1.46	$1	15.3	269			31%	3.99	6.0	3.9	5.8	1.5	0.3		73%	58	119
Risk X HIGH	03	Proj	6	9	0	120	4.88	1.43	$2	19.3	270			30%	4.51	9.3	3.5	6.2	1.7	1.0	F	67%	45	91

2-5, 5.40 ERA in 45 IP at STL. Lost most of the past two years to injury, and experienced control problems upon his return. If he can stay healthy, there should be improvement, but that is a huge IF.

Stephens,John

Stephens,John		Tm	W	L	Sv	IP	ERA	Br/IP	R$	BF/G	OBA	vLH	vRH	H%	xERA	RAR	Ctl	Dom	Cmd	hr/9	G/F	S%	BPV	BPX
RH Starter	98		0	0	0	0	0.00	0.00																
AGE 23 Growth	99		0	0	0	0	0.00	0.00																
TYPE	00		0	0	0	0	0.00	0.00																
BURN Moderate	01	a/a	13	9	0	190	3.03	1.07	$25	28.1	234			29%	2.91	60.8	1.8	8.5	4.6	0.8		75%	132	253
ERA Potl ++	02	BAL	* 13	10	0	207	4.26	1.19	$14	25.8	258	268	273	30%	3.63 +	23.6	1.9	7.0	3.7	1.0	0.87	67%	92	174
Support 4.29	1st Half		10	4	0	117	2.77	1.00	$17	27.0	232			28%	2.51	36.7	1.3	7.4	5.6	0.7		75%	151	285
LIMA A	2nd Half		3	6	0	90	6.19	1.44	($4)	24.6	288			32%	5.07 +	-13.1	2.7	6.5	2.4	1.4		59%	45	85
Risk High	03	Proj	7	6	0	120	4.05	1.18	$10	25.9	254			30%	3.56	21.2	2.0	7.5	3.7	1.0	--	68%	98	199

2-5, 6.09 ERA in 65 IP at BAL. Young and raw,but with incredible skills potential. You won't find this level of BB stinginess in many places. Tuck him on reserve and pray for some maturity.

Stewart,Scott

	Yr	Tm	W	L	Sv	IP	ERA	Br/IP	R$	BF/G	OBA	vLH	vRH	H%	xERA	RAR	Ctl	Dom	Cmd	hr/9	G/F	S%	BPV	BPX
LH Reliever	98	a/a	8	11	2	142	5.58	1.56	($1)	19.3	298			31%	5.73	-2.8	3.2	5.2	**1.6**	1.5		68%	15	29
AGE 27 Pre-Peak	99	a/a	7	4	0	105	4.89	1.54	$3	13.0	299			35%	4.96	11.4	3.1	6.7	**2.2**	0.8		69%	58	134
TYPE Power	00	aaa	3	5	5	72	4.00	1.49	$6	6.0	305			36%	4.55 -	17.0	2.3	6.0	**2.7**	0.4		72%	75	177
BURN none	01	MON	3	1	3	47	3.83	1.19	$6	3.1	245	286	215	29%	3.51	9.7	2.5	7.5	**3.0**	1.0	1.07	71%	85	158
ERA Potl + +	02	MON	4	2	17	64	3.09	1.11	$20	3.8	214	159	235	28%	2.57 +	20.3	3.1	9.4	**3.0**	0.6	2.06	73%	116	238
Support 1.83	1st Half		3	1	9	40	1.80	0.97	$15	3.9	193			27%	1.66	19.7	2.7	9.9	**3.7**	0.2		82%	146	299
LIMA C+	2nd Half		1	1	8	24	5.27	1.34	$5	3.8	246			30%	4.10 +	0.6	3.8	8.7	**2.3**	1.1		62%	72	148
Risk X HIGH	**03**	**Proj**	**4**	**3**	**31**	**65**	**3.32**	**1.18**	**$27**	**4.1**	**234**			**29%**	**3.24**	**18.6**	**2.9**	**8.6**	**3.0**	**0.8**	**G**	**75%**	**97**	**195**

There are so few LH closers because managers like to save them for situational work. But this one's got the goods... great BPIs and converted 89% of his save opps. If only they let him keep the role.

Stone,Ricky

	Yr	Tm	W	L	Sv	IP	ERA	Br/IP	R$	BF/G	OBA	vLH	vRH	H%	xERA	RAR	Ctl	Dom	Cmd	hr/9	G/F	S%	BPV	BPX
RH Reliever	98	a/a	12	7	0	187	4.62	1.40	$8	26.0	276			32%	4.29	20.3	2.9	6.2	**2.2**	0.8		67%	59	115
AGE 28 Pre-Peak	99	aaa	6	10	0	167	5.50	1.65	($5)	28.3	311			35%	5.78	4.5	3.4	5.9	**1.7**	1.1		68%	30	70
TYPE Power	00	aaa	9	5	5	120	5.00	1.61	$6	11.3	311			34%	5.18	12.3	3.0	4.7	**1.6**	0.6		68%	36	86
BURN Low	01	aaa	6	3	2	102	4.68	1.57	$2	8.0	308			35%	5.39 -	10.2	2.8	6.1	**2.2**	1.0	2.83	72%	46	88
ERA Potl - -	02	HOU	3	3	1	77	3.62	1.45	$3	4.3	264	288	258	31%	4.58 -	18.9	4.0	7.4	**1.9**	1.1	2.10	79%	54	110
Support 3.38	1st Half		3	2	0	41	2.18	1.38	$5	4.3	237			27%	3.87 -	18.1	4.6	6.3	**1.4**	0.9		89%	48	99
LIMA B	2nd Half		0	1	1	36	5.28	1.54	($2)	4.3	294			36%	5.39	0.9	3.3	8.5	**2.6**	1.3		68%	65	133
Risk High	**03**	**Proj**	**3**	**3**	**1**	**75**	**3.96**	**1.41**	**$3**	**6.0**	**269**			**31%**	**4.43**	**15.0**	**3.4**	**6.7**	**2.0**	**1.0**	**G**	**74%**	**55**	**110**

Rookie 2nd half is deceptive here. ERA got worse but BPIs got better. Might be a cheap reserve rounder who could put up LIMA-caliber numbers.

Strickland,Scott

	Yr	Tm	W	L	Sv	IP	ERA	Br/IP	R$	BF/G	OBA	vLH	vRH	H%	xERA	RAR	Ctl	Dom	Cmd	hr/9	G/F	S%	BPV	BPX
RH Reliever	98		0	0	0	0	0.00	0.00																
AGE 27 Growth	99	MON *	4	2	8	75	3.00	1.35	$12	6.4	246	400	156	34%	3.27	25.6	3.8	10.1	**2.6**	0.4	1.36	78%	111	240
TYPE Power	00	MON	4	3	9	48	3.00	1.13	$13	4.0	219	290	174	29%	2.62	16.9	3.0	9.0	**3.0**	0.6	1.22	75%	111	245
BURN none	01	MON	2	6	9	81	3.22	1.33	$9	4.5	227	274	189	29%	3.65	23.3	4.5	9.4	**2.1**	1.0	0.97	80%	80	148
ERA Potl No chg	02	2NL	6	9	2	68	3.57	1.38	$8	4.2	241	313	188	31%	3.95	17.2	4.4	9.1	**2.1**	0.9	0.89	77%	78	159
Support 3.80	1st Half		6	4	2	36	3.74	1.27	$8	3.9	228			28%	3.80	8.3	4.0	9.2	**2.3**	1.2		76%	76	156
LIMA B+	2nd Half		0	5	0	32	3.39	1.50	($0)	4.7	256			33%	4.12 -	8.9	4.8	9.0	**1.9**	0.6		78%	81	165
Risk Moderate	**03**	**Proj**	**4**	**7**	**1**	**70**	**3.34**	**1.34**	**$6**	**4.5**	**236**			**30%**	**3.60**	**19.8**	**4.2**	**9.3**	**2.2**	**0.8**	**--**	**77%**	**86**	**173**

Hard-thrower who can be a little wild. Kills RHers, struggles vs LHers. Learning to keep the ball on the ground more. Might have been closer-caliber but his saves% topped out at 75%, which is not good enough.

Sturtze,Tanyon

	Yr	Tm	W	L	Sv	IP	ERA	Br/IP	R$	BF/G	OBA	vLH	vRH	H%	xERA	RAR	Ctl	Dom	Cmd	hr/9	G/F	S%	BPV	BPX
RH Starter	98	aaa	4	1	0	37	4.86	1.81	$0	12.5	301			34%	6.12 -	2.8	5.4	6.8	**1.3**	1.2		76%	26	50
AGE 32 Past	99	aaa	9	4	3	104	4.67	1.34	$11	13.4	250	167	500	30%	3.59 +	14.3	3.5	7.1	**2.0**	0.6	0.56	64%	71	165
TYPE	00	2AL	5	2	0	68	4.76	1.48	$4	10.3	273	269	275	30%	4.70	10.5	3.8	5.8	**1.5**	1.1	1.51	70%	35	92
BURN none	01	TAM	11	12	1	195	4.43	1.43	$7	21.8	267	283	261	29%	4.53	27.6	3.6	5.1	**1.4**	1.1	0.95	71%	30	59
ERA Potl - -	02	TAM	4	18	0	224	5.18	1.61	($11)	30.7	300	323	282	32%	5.61	-2.3	3.6	5.5	**1.5**	1.3	0.89	71%	21	39
Support 3.90	1st Half		1	8	0	104	4.93	1.72	($7)	30.2	309			35%	5.50 -	2.5	4.1	5.7	**1.4**	0.8		72%	33	63
LIMA D	2nd Half		3	10	0	120	5.40	1.51	($5)	31.2	293			30%	5.70	-4.8	3.1	5.3	**1.7**	1.8		69%	11	20
Risk Very High	**03**	**Proj**	**9**	**13**	**0**	**200**	**4.91**	**1.54**	**($0)**	**26.2**	**285**			**31%**	**5.14**	**12.4**	**3.7**	**5.6**	**1.5**	**1.2**	**--**	**71%**	**27**	**54**

I suppose when you've got nothing else, you give a pitcher like this 226 IP, let him go 4-18 with lousy BPIs and face 30.7 batters per game. That's tough to justify on any team, but they play a different game in TAM.

Sullivan,Scott

	Yr	Tm	W	L	Sv	IP	ERA	Br/IP	R$	BF/G	OBA	vLH	vRH	H%	xERA	RAR	Ctl	Dom	Cmd	hr/9	G/F	S%	BPV	BPX
RH Reliever	98	CIN	5	5	1	102	5.21	1.31	$2	6.4	254	288	230	29%	4.20 +	0.4	3.2	7.6	**2.4**	1.2	1.03	63%	63	113
AGE 32 Peak	99	CIN	5	4	3	113	3.03	1.19	$14	5.9	216	242	202	24%	2.96	38.1	3.7	6.2	**1.7**	0.8	0.89	78%	60	130
TYPE Power	00	CIN	3	6	3	106	3.48	1.18	$11	5.5	225	214	235	26%	3.43	30.6	3.2	8.1	**2.5**	1.2	0.77	76%	76	168
BURN none	01	CIN	7	1	0	103	3.32	1.26	$10	5.5	244	252	237	29%	3.60	28.3	3.1	7.2	**2.3**	0.9	1.01	77%	71	131
ERA Potl No chg	02	CIN	6	5	1	78	6.12	1.59	($2)	5.0	297	357	253	35%	6.01	-6.9	3.6	9.0	**2.5**	1.7	0.80	65%	50	104
Support 5.15	1st Half		5	2	0	48	4.85	1.35	$4	4.8	257			30%	4.78	3.9	3.4	9.1	**2.7**	1.7		70%	65	134
LIMA D+	2nd Half		1	3	1	30	8.15	1.98	($6)	5.2	354			42%	8.01	-10.8	3.9	8.8	**2.2**	1.8		60%	29	60
Risk Very Low	**03**	**Proj**	**3**	**3**	**0**	**60**	**4.50**	**1.37**	**$2**	**5.1**	**259**			**30%**	**4.52**	**7.7**	**3.5**	**8.1**	**2.3**	**1.4**	**--**	**71%**	**61**	**122**

It would appear that he FINALLY broke down after all those years of excessive usage. However, from a performance perspective, he didn't do badly. H% and S% inflated his ERA. But his new shoulder woes are another story.

Suppan,Jeff

	Yr	Tm	W	L	Sv	IP	ERA	Br/IP	R$	BF/G	OBA	vLH	vRH	H%	xERA	RAR	Ctl	Dom	Cmd	hr/9	G/F	S%	BPV	BPX
RH Starter	98	2TM *	5	10	0	145	4.65	1.40	$2	20.9	288	231	337	33%	4.74	15.2	2.3	6.6	**2.9**	1.1	1.16	69%	65	127
AGE 28 Pre-Peak	99	KC	10	12	0	208	4.54	1.37	$12	27.9	275	259	289	29%	4.62	37.0	2.7	4.5	**1.7**	1.2	1.57	70%	25	64
TYPE Contact	00	KC	10	9	0	217	4.94	1.49	$6	27.4	282	284	283	30%	5.27	28.4	3.5	5.3	**1.5**	1.5	1.39	71%	18	46
BURN Low	01	KC	10	14	0	218	4.37	1.38	$7	27.6	270	235	306	29%	4.46	32.4	3.1	5.0	**1.6**	1.1	1.36	71%	33	65
ERA Potl - -	02	KC	9	16	0	208	5.32	1.43	($1)	27.4	281	276	281	29%	4.93	-6.0	2.9	4.7	**1.6**	1.4	1.30	66%	19	36
Support 5.15	1st Half		7	6	0	114	4.57	1.21	$6	26.2	258			26%	4.32	8.1	2.1	4.7	**2.3**	1.7		68%	29	55
LIMA D	2nd Half		2	10	0	94	6.23	1.69	($8)	28.9	306			33%	5.67 +	-14.1	4.0	4.8	**1.2**	1.1		64%	16	30
Risk Moderate	**03**	**Proj**	**8**	**14**	**0**	**200**	**4.64**	**1.38**	**$4**	**26.9**	**272**			**29%**	**4.61**	**19.6**	**2.9**	**5.0**	**1.7**	**1.3**	**--**	**70%**	**28**	**57**

First half looked like he was finally making some progress, but just went CRASH in the 2nd half. You reach a point as a fantasy leaguer when you have to cut your losses and decide NOT to take a chance anymore.

Swindell,Greg

	Yr	Tm	W	L	Sv	IP	ERA	Br/IP	R$	BF/G	OBA	vLH	vRH	H%	xERA	RAR	Ctl	Dom	Cmd	hr/9	G/F	S%	BPV	BPX
LH Reliever	98	2AL	5	6	2	90	3.60	1.37	$8	4.8	266	265	268	29%	4.57 -	24.9	3.1	6.3	**2.0**	1.3	0.89	79%	43	93
AGE 38 Decline	99	ARI	4	0	1	64	2.53	1.17	$10	4.2	230	215	239	26%	3.38 -	25.8	3.0	7.2	**2.4**	1.1	0.84	85%	69	150
TYPE Contact	00	ARI	2	6	1	76	3.20	1.20	$8	4.9	249	157	300	30%	3.45	24.7	2.4	7.6	**3.2**	0.8	0.71	76%	93	205
BURN none	01	ARI	2	6	2	53	4.57	1.11	$4	3.3	254	259	244	27%	4.43	5.7	1.4	7.1	**5.3**	2.0	0.47	68%	96	178
ERA Potl + +	02	ARI	0	2	0	34	6.09	1.26	($2)	4.1	284	339	234	28%	5.64	-2.9	1.3	6.1	**4.6**	2.4	0.49	59%	60	123
Support 4.09	1st Half		0	0	0	17	5.82	1.12	($0)	4.3	238			18%	5.41	-0.8	2.1	4.2	**2.0**	3.2		62%	-21	-42
LIMA C+	2nd Half		0	2	0	17	6.35	1.41	($1)	3.9	324			38%	5.87	-2.0	0.5	7.9	**15.0**	1.6		57%	305	626
Risk High	**03**	**Proj**	**1**	**3**	**0**	**35**	**4.89**	**1.23**	**$1**	**3.9**	**273**			**29%**	**4.80**	**2.7**	**1.5**	**6.9**	**4.5**	**1.8**	**F**	**67%**	**83**	**166**

Interesting strand rate trend over past 4 years. A decline like this cannot be solely attributed to other pitchers, especially since he is a reliever himself. Is he increasingly losing his nerve with men on base?

Tam,Jeff

	Yr	Tm	W	L	Sv	IP	ERA	Br/IP	R$	BF/G	OBA	vLH	vRH	H%	xERA	RAR	Ctl	Dom	Cmd	hr/9	G/F	S%	BPV	BPX
RH Reliever	98	NYM *	4	4	11	78	3.00	0.95	$17	5.0	223	286	225	25%	2.27 +	23.3	1.3	5.8	**4.5**	0.6	2.08	70%	123	222
AGE 32 Past	99	2TM *	2	3	3	58	3.88	1.47	$4	6.1	297	200	185	32%	4.77 -	14.1	2.5	4.0	**1.6**	0.8	2.11	75%	31	71
TYPE Contact	00	OAK	3	3	3	85	2.64	1.28	$12	5.0	264	360	209	30%	3.37 -	37.3	2.4	4.9	**2.0**	0.3	2.49	79%	64	166
BURN none	01	OAK	2	4	3	74	3.03	1.31	$7	4.5	245	247	251	28%	3.28	24.4	3.5	5.3	**1.5**	0.4	2.08	77%	59	118
ERA Potl +	02	OAK *	2	5	2	69	5.48	1.57	($2)	5.2	316	300	352	35%	5.00	-3.4	2.3	4.6	**1.9**	0.5	2.54	63%	44	84
Support 4.69	1st Half		0	2	1	39	7.83	1.97	($7)	5.8	374			41%	6.99 +	-14.2	2.5	3.9	**1.5**	0.5		57%	22	42
LIMA B	2nd Half		2	3	1	30	2.41	1.04	$5	4.4	222			25%	2.41	10.8	2.1	5.4	**2.6**	0.6		79%	79	150
Risk Moderate	**03**	**Proj**	**2**	**2**	**0**	**40**	**3.83**	**1.33**	**$2**	**4.9**	**271**			**31%**	**3.70**	**8.3**	**2.5**	**5.0**	**2.0**	**0.5**	**G**	**71%**	**59**	**120**

1-2, 5.18 ERA in 40 IP at OAK. Soft-tosser who keeps the ball on the ground and in the park. Gave up a ton of grounders up through the box and into CF in the 1st half, then returned to form. Serviceable reserve pick.

Tankersley,Dennis

	Yr	Tm	W	L	Sv	IP	ERA	Br/IP	R$	BF/G	OBA	vLH	vRH	H%	xERA	RAR	Ctl	Dom	Cmd	hr/9	G/F	S%	BPV	BPX
RH Reliever	98		0	0	0	0	0.00	0.00																
AGE 24 Growth	99		0	0	0	0	0.00	0.00																
TYPE Power	00		0	0	0	0	0.00	0.00																
BURN none	01	a/a	5	3	0	84	3.43	1.19	$8	21.6	220			28%	3.09	22.4	3.5	9.0	**2.5**	0.9		74%	93	178
ERA Potl -	02	SD *	7	11	0	152	5.38	1.66	($7)	19.3	272	363	263	32%	5.14	1.6	5.4	7.7	**1.4**	1.0	0.98	69%	46	95
Support 5.26	1st Half		4	5	0	83	5.40	1.65	($4)	22.4	277			34%	5.07	0.7	5.2	8.0	**1.5**	0.9		68%	54	111
LIMA D+	2nd Half		3	6	0	69	5.36	1.66	($4)	16.6	265			31%	5.22	0.9	5.8	7.3	**1.3**	1.2		70%	37	77
Risk High	**03**	**Proj**	**4**	**5**	**0**	**80**	**4.84**	**1.54**	**($0)**	**19.8**	**264**			**32%**	**4.71**	**6.6**	**4.7**	**8.2**	**1.7**	**1.0**	**--**	**70%**	**58**	**116**

1-4, 8.12 ERA in 51 IP at SD. As we learned at the AFL Symposium, no matter how nice the BPIs might look, he's got some personal demons to exorcise that will keep his ceiling low.

Tavarez,Julian	Tm	W	L	Sv	IP	ERA	Br/IP	R$	BF/G	OBA	vLH	vRH	H%	xERA	RAR	Ctl	Dom	Cmd	hr/9	G/F	S%	BPV	BPX
RH Reliever	98 SF	5	3	1	85	3.81	1.55	$3	6.3	286	331	273	33%	4.60 -	16.3	3.8	5.5	1.4	0.5	2.57	76%	45	82
AGE 29 Peak	99 SF	2	0	0	54	6.00	1.67	($3)	5.3	299	345	265	33%	5.64	-3.3	4.2	5.5	1.3	1.2	2.20	65%	21	45
TYPE	00 COL	11	5	1	120	4.43	1.48	$9	10.3	268	260	273	29%	4.44	19.3	4.0	4.7	1.2	0.8	2.86	71%	29	64
BURN none	01 CHC	10	9	0	161	4.53	1.50	$4	20.9	275	320	249	31%	4.48	18.2	3.9	6.0	1.6	0.7	2.86	70%	47	87
ERA Potl -	02 FLA	10	12	0	153	5.41	1.71	($6)	24.4	303	332	285	33%	5.34	1.0	4.4	3.9	0.9	0.5	1.94	67%	21	43
Support 4.63	1st Half	6	4	0	73	5.67	1.63	($2)	25.6	287			31%	4.97 +	-2.1	4.4	4.2	0.9	0.6		64%	24	49
LIMA D	2nd Half	4	8	0	80	5.17	1.79	($5)	23.5	318			34%	5.68 -	3.0	4.3	3.7	0.9	0.4		70%	18	38
Risk Very High	03 Proj	6	10	0	120	4.95	1.62	($2)	15.6	291			32%	5.01	8.1	4.1	4.7	1.1	0.7	G	69%	29	58

Pete Rose was banned from baseball for betting on games. Even if he did, evidence showed he always bet on his team to win. By putting a guy like this out there for 150+ IP, isn't that like betting on your team to lose?

Tejera,Michael	Tm	W	L	Sv	IP	ERA	Br/IP	R$	BF/G	OBA	vLH	vRH	H%	xERA	RAR	Ctl	Dom	Cmd	hr/9	G/F	S%	BPV	BPX
LH Starter	98	0	0	0	0	0.00	0.00																
AGE 26 Growth	99	0	0	0	0	0.00	0.00																
TYPE	00	0	0	0	0	0.00	0.00																
BURN none	01 aa	9	8	0	141	5.04	1.62	($1)	25.6	313			36%	5.88 -	7.2	3.0	6.9	2.3	1.3		72%	44	84
ERA Potl -	02 FLA	8	8	1	139	4.47	1.47	$4	13.0	269	228	280	30%	4.73	18.5	3.9	6.2	1.6	1.1	1.07	72%	38	79
Support 3.93	1st Half	3	1	1	48	3.18	1.31	$5	7.3	232			26%	3.52	14.7	4.1	5.4	1.3	0.7		78%	46	95
LIMA C+	2nd Half	5	7	0	91	5.15	1.55	($1)	21.4	287			32%	5.37	3.8	3.8	6.5	1.7	1.3		70%	35	71
Risk Low	03 Proj	7	7	0	120	4.65	1.52	$2	21.3	285			32%	5.08	12.9	3.5	6.4	1.8	1.1	--	72%	40	81

Considering that his AA numbers weren't all that great, this jump to the majors wasn't half bad. Did fare better out of the pen than in the rotation, so adjust your expectations based on his projected role.

Thomson,John	Tm	W	L	Sv	IP	ERA	Br/IP	R$	BF/G	OBA	vLH	vRH	H%	xERA	RAR	Ctl	Dom	Cmd	hr/9	G/F	S%	BPV	BPX
RH Starter	98 COL	8	11	0	161	4.81	1.39	$3	26.7	277	303	261	31%	4.66	9.2	2.7	5.9	2.2	1.2	1.29	68%	45	82
AGE 29 Peak	99 COL •	1	12	0	83	8.78	2.04	($18)	21.7	344	278	361	37%	7.74 +	-36.0	5.0	5.3	1.1	1.6	1.44	57%	-8	-18
TYPE Contact	00 COL	0	0	0	0	0.00	0.00																
BURN none	01 COL •	9	8	0	161	4.25	1.35	$8	26.4	282	177	294	31%	4.84 -	24.1	2.2	6.2	2.8	1.4	1.16	73%	54	100
ERA Potl -	02 2NL	9	14	0	181	4.72	1.35	$6	25.8	283	285	264	30%	4.92	17.8	2.2	5.3	2.4	1.4	0.87	69%	40	81
Support 4.56	1st Half	6	7	0	104	5.01	1.26	$5	25.6	274			29%	4.63	6.2	1.7	5.5	3.2	1.5		64%	56	116
LIMA C+	2nd Half	3	7	0	77	4.33	1.48	$1	26.0	293			31%	5.31 -	11.6	2.8	5.0	1.8	1.3		75%	26	52
Risk High	03 Proj	12	8	0	160	3.94	1.33	$13	24.3	276			30%	4.48 -	32.5	2.3	5.9	2.5	1.1	--	74%	54	109

A pitcher to jump on now that his solid BPIs are out of pitching hell and into a great pitchers' park like Shea. His 4.31 ERA in 54 IP with the Mets was underwhelming, but he did have a 3.44 ERA in Shea.

Thurman,Corey	Tm	W	L	Sv	IP	ERA	Br/IP	R$	BF/G	OBA	vLH	vRH	H%	xERA	RAR	Ctl	Dom	Cmd	hr/9	G/F	S%	BPV	BPX
RH Reliever	98	0	0	0	0	0.00	0.00																
AGE 24 Growth	99	0	0	0	0	0.00	0.00																
TYPE Power	00 aa	4	5	0	50	6.11	1.52	$1	24.7	273			29%	5.82	-2.3	4.1	7.0	1.7	2.2		66%	13	32
BURN none	01 a/a	13	5	0	160	4.05	1.25	$15	25.7	234			27%	3.58	29.4	3.5	7.1	2.0	1.0		70%	63	121
ERA Potl --	02 TOR	2	3	0	68	4.37	1.62	($2)	7.2	253	236	259	28%	5.06 -	6.7	6.0	7.4	1.2	1.5	0.69	78%	31	59
Support 4.37	1st Half	1	1	0	37	2.92	1.59	$0	7.3	240			30%	3.70 -	10.8	6.3	6.8	1.1	0.2		81%	63	119
LIMA D	2nd Half	1	2	0	31	6.10	1.65	($2)	7.1	268			27%	6.69 -	-4.1	5.5	8.1	1.5	2.9		73%	-6	-11
Risk X HIGH	03 Proj	7	6	0	120	4.73	1.48	$3	11.0	252			28%	4.84	10.3	4.7	7.4	1.6	1.6	F	73%	34	69

TOR rode his poor BPIs into the 2nd half because of his low 1st half ERA. When ERA and BPIs equalized, it ended up costing them 21 runs. Of course, hindsight is always 20/20, but you coulda seen that coming.

Thurman,Mike	Tm	W	L	Sv	IP	ERA	Br/IP	R$	BF/G	OBA	vLH	vRH	H%	xERA	RAR	Ctl	Dom	Cmd	hr/9	G/F	S%	BPV	BPX
RH Reliever	98 MON •	11	12	0	172	4.23	1.46	$6	22.9	269	208	258	29%	4.63	23.1	3.8	5.3	1.4	1.0	1.45	74%	31	55
AGE 29 Peak	99 MON	7	11	0	146	4.07	1.32	$10	21.3	254	283	223	27%	3.99	28.9	3.2	5.2	1.6	1.0	1.25	72%	39	84
TYPE Contact	00 MON •	4	12	0	108	6.90	1.87	($12)	23.6	320	336	303	35%	6.21 +	-18.4	4.8	5.0	1.0	0.8	1.25	62%	18	39
BURN none	01 MON	9	11	0	147	5.33	1.51	($0)	23.3	293	343	257	32%	5.32	0.8	3.1	5.9	1.9	1.3	1.22	67%	33	62
ERA Potl --	02 NYY •	8	3	0	109	4.53	1.58	$2	20.5	320	361	303	35%	5.45 -	8.4	2.2	5.3	2.4	0.9	1.61	73%	45	85
Support 5.73	1st Half	6	3	0	74	5.71	1.75	($2)	24.7	347			38%	6.64 -	-6.0	2.3	5.2	2.3	1.2		69%	28	53
LIMA B	2nd Half	2	0	0	35	2.05	1.20	$4	14.4	256			30%	2.93 -	14.4	2.1	5.4	2.6	0.3		83%	84	158
Risk Very High	03 Proj	2	2	0	75	4.44	1.39	$1	14.7	284			32%	4.40	9.3	2.4	5.4	2.3	0.8	G	69%	53	107

1-0, 5.18 ERA in 33 IP at NYY. First season his BPIs even marginally justified big league action, but his 35% hit rate was just a killer. Small 2nd half sample shows he CAN be effective. Maybe more pen work?

Timlin,Mike	Tm	W	L	Sv	IP	ERA	Br/IP	R$	BF/G	OBA	vLH	vRH	H%	xERA	RAR	Ctl	Dom	Cmd	hr/9	G/F	S%	BPV	BPX
RH Reliever	98 SEA	3	3	19	79	2.96	1.19	$19	4.6	259	263	264	31%	3.34	28.6	1.8	6.8	3.8	0.6	2.22	76%	106	226
AGE 37 Decline	99 BAL	3	9	27	63	3.57	1.17	$23	4.2	223	198	240	25%	3.50	19.4	3.3	7.1	2.2	1.3	2.30	75%	60	151
TYPE Contact	00 2TM	5	4	12	64	4.21	1.59	$11	4.7	270	311	241	31%	4.99 -	13.4	4.9	7.3	1.5	1.1	1.44	77%	42	100
BURN High	01 STL	4	5	3	72	4.11	1.34	$5	4.6	277	319	257	31%	4.15	12.1	2.4	5.9	2.5	0.7	2.84	70%	64	119
ERA Potl No chg	02 2NL	4	6	0	96	3.00	0.93	$15	5.1	217	208	214	21%	2.99	31.6	1.3	4.7	3.6	1.4	1.83	77%	73	149
Support 4.00	1st Half	1	3	0	46	2.93	0.93	$7	5.4	227			22%	3.28	15.6	1.0	5.1	5.2	1.6		80%	102	210
LIMA D+	2nd Half	3	3	0	50	3.06	0.92	$9	4.9	208			20%	2.73	16.1	1.6	4.3	2.7	1.3		74%	58	118
Risk Very High	03 Proj	4	5	0	80	3.60	1.25	$7	4.9	267			28%	4.16 -	19.9	2.0	4.7	2.3	1.1	G	76%	45	91

Has given up dominace for precision, and it seems to have served him well. Extraordinarily low hit rate will push his ERA back up, but he'll still be a valuable end-game pick.

Tollberg,Brian	Tm	W	L	Sv	IP	ERA	Br/IP	R$	BF/G	OBA	vLH	vRH	H%	xERA	RAR	Ctl	Dom	Cmd	hr/9	G/F	S%	BPV	BPX
RH Starter	98 a/a	9	8	3	151	5.60	1.43	$3	16.8	303			34%	5.39	-3.5	1.8	7.2	3.9	1.4		64%	76	147
AGE 30 Peak	99 aaa	1	2	0	29	6.21	1.62	($1)	26.3	334			37%	5.88	-2.0	1.9	5.6	3.0	0.9		61%	57	132
TYPE Contact	00 SD •	10	5	0	194	3.43	1.29	$17	25.6	272	286	262	31%	4.04 -	57.1	2.1	5.7	2.7	0.8	1.17	76%	67	147
BURN none	01 SD •	11	4	0	137	4.47	1.39	$8	25.7	295	282	290	32%	4.97 -	16.5	1.9	5.1	2.7	1.2	1.34	71%	48	88
ERA Potl ---	02 SD	1	5	0	61	6.20	1.75	($8)	23.8	338	373	317	36%	7.03 -	-6.0	2.8	4.9	1.7	1.6	1.16	68%	4	9
Support 4.38	1st Half	1	5	0	61	6.18	1.75	($8)	23.8	338			36%	7.00 -	-5.9	2.8	4.9	1.7	1.6		68%	5	9
LIMA D	2nd Half	0	0	0	-0	0.00	0.00																
Risk Very High	03 Proj	1	1	0	15	4.80	1.47	$0	21.9	299			32%	5.23	1.3	2.4	5.4	2.3	1.2	--	70%	39	78

I took a bunch of heat on the HQ reader forums for sticking with this guy through his early struggles. When it was revealed that he would need elbow surgery, it answered a lot of questions.

Tomko,Brett	Tm	W	L	Sv	IP	ERA	Br/IP	R$	BF/G	OBA	vLH	vRH	H%	xERA	RAR	Ctl	Dom	Cmd	hr/9	G/F	S%	BPV	BPX
RH Starter	98 CIN	13	12	0	210	4.45	1.25	$13	25.8	250	253	242	29%	3.71 +	22.0	2.7	6.9	2.5	0.9	0.87	66%	71	129
AGE 30 Peak	99 CIN •	7	7	0	184	4.94	1.37	$5	22.6	269	250	275	30%	4.81	15.0	3.0	6.8	2.3	1.6	1.00	69%	44	95
TYPE Contact	00 SEA	7	5	1	92	4.69	1.43	$7	12.5	262	270	260	28%	4.53	15.1	3.9	5.8	1.5	1.2	1.09	70%	33	86
BURN none	01 SEA •	13	7	0	161	5.03	1.44	$6	23.4	294	365	229	33%	5.10	9.8	2.4	6.8	2.8	1.2	0.80	68%	59	118
ERA Potl -	02 SD	10	10	0	204	4.50	1.33	$8	27.1	269	270	264	29%	4.66	26.2	2.6	5.6	2.1	1.4	1.50	71%	38	77
Support 4.67	1st Half	4	5	0	111	3.80	1.29	$6	27.6	260			29%	4.27	24.6	2.8	6.2	2.3	1.2		75%	52	106
LIMA C	2nd Half	6	5	0	93	5.33	1.38	$2	26.6	280			29%	5.11	1.6	2.5	4.8	1.9	1.6		65%	20	42
Risk Very High	03 Proj	11	9	0	180	4.55	1.36	$9	22.0	275			30%	4.70	21.8	2.6	5.9	2.3	1.3	G	70%	45	90

Stamina was always the issue when he struggled with CIN and bounced around roles in SEA. He pitched well in 2002, but stamina remains an issue as he faded notably in the 2nd half. This is not a 200 IP pitcher.

Torres,Salomon	Tm	W	L	Sv	IP	ERA	Br/IP	R$	BF/G	OBA	vLH	vRH	H%	xERA	RAR	Ctl	Dom	Cmd	hr/9	G/F	S%	BPV	BPX
RH Starter	98	0	0	0	0	0.00	0.00																
AGE 31 Peak	99	0	0	0	0	0.00	0.00																
TYPE Contact	00	0	0	0	0	0.00	0.00																
BURN High	01 KOR	0	2	0	5	19.80	5.00	($5)	19.8	515			52%	26.19 -	-9.6	18.0	9.0	0.5	9.0		70%	-99	
ERA Potl -	02 PIT •	10	6	0	192	4.78	1.55	($0)	27.7	311	241	273	35%	5.19	17.5	2.5	5.4	2.1	0.7	1.73	69%	50	102
Support 5.70	1st Half	3	3	0	96	5.44	1.75	($8)	28.0	336			38%	6.15 -	0.3	2.9	5.5	1.9	0.8		69%	38	79
LIMA C+	2nd Half	7	3	0	96	4.12	1.35	$7	27.4	283			32%	4.23	17.2	2.2	5.3	2.5	0.7		70%	63	129
Risk Very High	03 Proj	7	4	0	120	4.05	1.35	$7	27.0	276			31%	4.11	22.6	2.5	5.4	2.2	0.7	G	71%	58	116

2-1, 2.70 ERA in 30 IP at PIT. A remarkable season, given his long layoff. Most fantasy leaguers will not give him much attention, but he's showing some skill and 31 is not too old. An interesting end game pick.

Trachsel,Steve		Tm	W	L	Sv	IP	ERA	Br/IP	R$	BF/G	OBA	vLH	vRH	H%	xERA	RAR	Ctl	Dom	Cmd	hr/9	G/F	S%	BPV	BPX
RH Starter	98	CHC	15	8	0	208	4.46	1.38	$10	27.1	258	240	277	29%	4.38	21.7	3.6	6.4	**1.8**	1.2	1.09	71%	44	80
AGE 32 Past	99	CHC	8	18	0	205	5.58	1.41	$1	26.1	281	285	276	31%	4.95 +	-0.8	2.8	6.5	**2.3**	1.4	1.27	63%	45	97
TYPE	00	2AL	8	15	0	200	4.81	1.53	$4	26.2	291	298	290	31%	5.20	29.5	3.3	4.9	**1.5**	1.2	1.13	71%	23	59
BURN none	01	NYM	* 13	13	0	192	4.45	1.24	$13	25.8	255	232	273	29%	4.11	23.5	2.5	7.2	**2.8**	1.3	1.31	68%	67	125
ERA Potl - -	02	NYM	12	11	0	178	3.29	1.39	$15	24.8	257	233	281	29%	4.12 -	51.8	3.7	5.5	**1.5**	0.8	1.39	79%	43	88
Support 4.77	1st Half		6	7	0	97	3.89	1.43	$5	24.9	259			28%	4.26	20.4	4.0	5.1	**1.3**	0.8		75%	36	73
LIMA C	2nd Half		6	4	0	81	2.56	1.35	$10	24.6	255			29%	3.94 -	31.4	3.5	5.9	**1.7**	0.8		84%	52	107
Risk Low	**03**	**Proj**	**11**	**11**	**0**	**180**	**3.95**	**1.35**	**$12**	**25.6**	**259**			**29%**	**4.03**	**36.3**	**3.3**	**6.0**	**1.8**	**0.9**	**--**	**73%**	**51**	**103**

His 2001 BPIs merited a better ERA, which is what we projected for 2002, and he obliged. However, his 2002 BPIs now do not support a 3.29 ERA. For 2003? Back to 4.00 territory.

Tucker,T.J.		Tm	W	L	Sv	IP	ERA	Br/IP	R$	BF/G	OBA	vLH	vRH	H%	xERA	RAR	Ctl	Dom	Cmd	hr/9	G/F	S%	BPV	BPX
RH Reliever	98		0	0	0	0	0.00	0.00																
AGE 24 Growth	99	aa	8	5	0	116	4.79	1.37	$7	26.2	272			30%	4.28 +	14.1	2.8	5.8	**2.1**	0.9		66%	51	118
TYPE Power	00	aa	2	2	0	52	5.37	1.33	$1	22.1	250			22%	5.16	2.8	3.5	3.8	**1.1**	2.3		68%	-17	-39
BURN none	01	a/a	8	10	0	166	4.34	1.46	$4	27.0	266			28%	4.94 -	24.1	4.0	5.4	**1.4**	1.4		75%	21	40
ERA Potl - -	02	MON	6	3	4	61	4.13	1.64	$5	4.9	286	269	300	33%	5.07 -	10.8	4.6	6.2	**1.4**	0.7	1.77	76%	41	85
Support 3.96	1st Half		4	0	4	41	1.98	1.34	$10	4.7	247			31%	3.08 -	19.1	3.7	6.6	**1.8**	0.0		84%	82	168
LIMA C	2nd Half		2	3	0	20	8.55	2.25	($5)	5.2	355			37%	9.15 -	-8.3	6.3	5.4	**0.9**	2.2		65%	-33	-68
Risk X HIGH	**03**	**Proj**	**4**	**4**	**1**	**60**	**4.65**	**1.65**	**$1**	**8.1**	**290**			**33%**	**5.41 -**	**6.5**	**4.5**	**6.2**	**1.4**	**1.1**	**G**	**74%**	**31**	**63**

Follow the saves. Follow the saves. He was the closer du jour for a brief period, but these are not the BPIs of a closer. His 57% saves conversion rate pretty much ends that possibility. Not even a marginal LIMA pick either.

Urbina,Ugueth		Tm	W	L	Sv	IP	ERA	Br/IP	R$	BF/G	OBA	vLH	vRH	H%	xERA	RAR	Ctl	Dom	Cmd	hr/9	G/F	S%	BPV	BPX
RH Reliever	98	MON	6	3	34	69	1.30	1.01	$33	4.2	160	159	154	26%	1.35	36.4	4.3	12.2	**2.8**	0.3	0.77	88%	149	268
AGE 29 Pre-Peak	99	MON	6	6	41	75	3.72	1.27	$32	4.4	218	198	215	32%	3.04 +	18.4	4.3	12.0	**2.8**	0.7	0.89	72%	120	261
TYPE Power	00	MON	0	1	8	13	4.12	1.22	$5	4.2	229	269	174	40%	3.05 +	2.6	3.4	15.1	**4.4**	0.7	1.00	67%	172	378
BURN none	01	2TM	2	2	24	66	3.67	1.24	$18	4.3	237	278	196	33%	3.73	15.5	3.3	12.1	**3.7**	1.2	0.83	75%	121	233
ERA Potl +	02	BOS	1	6	40	60	3.00	1.07	$24	3.9	206	257	143	27%	2.81	16.9	3.0	10.7	**3.6**	1.2	0.51	79%	116	220
Support 0.60	1st Half		0	3	21	30	2.70	1.20	$12	4.1	228			30%	2.86	9.7	3.3	9.0	**2.7**	0.6		79%	103	194
LIMA C+	2nd Half		1	3	19	30	3.30	0.93	$12	3.7	183			23%	2.75 +	7.3	2.7	12.3	**4.6**	1.8		77%	134	253
Risk Moderate	**03**	**Proj**	**2**	**4**	**38**	**60**	**3.15**	**1.12**	**$25**	**4.1**	**210**			**29%**	**2.87**	**17.8**	**3.3**	**11.6**	**3.5**	**1.1**	**F**	**77%**	**124**	**253**

The Rodney Dangerfield of closers. BPIs are clearly worthy and he has converted 86% and 87% of save opps the past two years, but can't seem to keep a job. Betcha you can grab him cheap.

Valdes,Ismael		Tm	W	L	Sv	IP	ERA	Br/IP	R$	BF/G	OBA	vLH	vRH	H%	xERA	RAR	Ctl	Dom	Cmd	hr/9	G/F	S%	BPV	BPX
RH Starter	98	LA	11	10	0	174	3.98	1.36	$10	27.6	258	250	260	29%	4.06	29.2	3.4	6.3	**1.8**	0.9	0.99	73%	54	97
AGE 29 Peak	99	LA	9	14	0	203	3.99	1.33	$12	27.0	271	271	269	30%	4.62 -	42.3	2.6	6.3	**2.5**	1.4	0.93	76%	48	104
TYPE Contact	00	2NL	2	7	0	107	5.64	1.53	($4)	22.7	291	330	261	31%	5.87	-0.1	3.4	6.2	**1.9**	1.9	0.79	68%	17	38
BURN none	01	ANA	9	13	0	163	4.47	1.39	$6	26.1	278	294	261	30%	4.63	22.2	2.8	5.5	**2.0**	1.1	1.08	71%	41	83
ERA Potl -	02	2AL	8	12	0	196	4.18	1.23	$9	26.2	260	255	259	27%	3.95	24.4	2.2	4.7	**2.2**	1.2	0.93	70%	41	77
Support 4.27	1st Half		5	6	0	93	3.96	1.19	$6	25.5	251			27%	3.35 +	14.3	2.2	4.4	**2.0**	0.8		68%	49	92
LIMA C	2nd Half		3	6	0	103	4.37	1.26	$3	26.9	268			27%	4.50	10.1	2.1	5.0	**2.4**	1.6		71%	34	64
Risk Moderate	**03**	**Proj**	**7**	**12**	**0**	**180**	**4.35**	**1.33**	**$6**	**25.5**	**270**			**29%**	**4.25**	**24.5**	**2.6**	**5.3**	**2.1**	**1.1**	**--**	**70%**	**45**	**91**

Early career workload abuse sidetracked some of his mid-20s years. But has redefined himself as less dominant and has been seeing some success with that approach. Not a sub-4.00 pitcher, but serviceable.

Van Poppel,Todd		Tm	W	L	Sv	IP	ERA	Br/IP	R$	BF/G	OBA	vLH	vRH	H%	xERA	RAR	Ctl	Dom	Cmd	hr/9	G/F	S%	BPV	BPX
RH Reliever	98	2TM	* 7	9	0	157	5.84	1.60	($6)	18.7	302	371	244	33%	5.81	-8.7	3.4	5.9	**1.7**	1.4	0.70	66%	24	46
AGE 31 Peak	99	aaa	10	6	0	163	5.96	1.63	($2)	27.5	305			35%	5.91	-5.8	3.5	7.0	**2.0**	1.4		66%	35	80
TYPE Power	00	CHC	* 7	9	2	126	3.63	1.41	$10	9.0	252	234	261	32%	4.04	33.7	4.1	8.7	**2.1**	0.9	0.97	77%	75	166
BURN none	01	CHC	4	1	0	75	2.52	1.35	$7	5.4	230	281	194	31%	3.79 -	28.6	4.6	10.8	**2.4**	1.1	0.88	87%	91	169
ERA Potl +	02	TEX	3	2	1	72	5.50	1.51	($2)	6.4	283	291	262	36%	5.46	-3.8	3.6	10.6	**2.9**	1.8	0.76	68%	71	135
Support 4.95	1st Half		1	0	1	36	4.50	1.42	$0	6.5	278			32%	4.93	2.9	3.0	8.0	**2.7**	1.5		73%	58	111
LIMA C	2nd Half		2	2	0	36	6.50	1.61	($2)	6.3	288			40%	5.98 +	-6.7	4.2	13.2	**3.1**	2.0		64%	82	156
Risk High	**03**	**Proj**	**4**	**3**	**1**	**75**	**3.96**	**1.35**	**$5**	**6.7**	**243**			**31%**	**4.25**	**14.1**	**4.0**	**10.2**	**2.6**	**1.4**	**F**	**76%**	**78**	**160**

BPIs improved but his numbers tanked. Thank H% and S%, which should regress to the mean and bring his ERA back down. End-game sleeper who could return $5-7 on a $1 investment.

Vazquez,Javier		Tm	W	L	Sv	IP	ERA	Br/IP	R$	BF/G	OBA	vLH	vRH	H%	xERA	RAR	Ctl	Dom	Cmd	hr/9	G/F	S%	BPV	BPX
RH Starter	98	MON	5	15	0	172	6.07	1.53	($10)	23.2	288	276	309	32%	5.60	-19.2	3.6	7.3	**2.0**	1.6	1.19	64%	35	64
AGE 26 Growth	99	MON	* 13	10	0	196	5.28	1.40	$7	25.6	272	234	272	31%	4.65 +	7.0	3.1	7.1	**2.3**	1.3	1.20	65%	53	115
TYPE	00	MON	11	9	0	217	4.06	1.42	$12	28.6	287	279	291	35%	4.70 -	45.6	2.5	8.1	**3.2**	1.0	1.51	74%	84	185
BURN Low	01	MON	16	11	0	223	3.43	1.08	$27	27.9	238	220	246	29%	3.14	58.0	1.8	8.4	**4.7**	1.0	1.28	72%	128	237
ERA Potl +	02	MON	10	13	0	230	3.91	1.27	$14	28.3	273	282	262	31%	4.27	47.6	1.9	7.0	**3.7**	1.1	0.94	73%	86	177
Support 4.30	1st Half		5	4	0	122	3.61	1.17	$11	29.4	260			29%	3.86	30.2	1.6	6.3	**3.9**	1.1		73%	90	185
LIMA B+	2nd Half		5	9	0	108	4.25	1.38	$4	27.3	286			34%	4.73	17.4	2.3	7.8	**3.4**	1.1		72%	84	173
Risk Low	**03**	**Proj**	**15**	**10**	**0**	**225**	**3.72**	**1.21**	**$22**	**27.4**	**261**			**31%**	**3.91**	**52.3**	**2.0**	**7.6**	**3.9**	**1.1**	**--**	**73%**	**98**	**197**

Is plateauing early, perhaps thanks to his early career overuse. Had trouble keeping the ball down in '02, and looks like his pitches lost their movement in the 2nd half. All correctable problems, though.

Venafro,Mike		Tm	W	L	Sv	IP	ERA	Br/IP	R$	BF/G	OBA	vLH	vRH	H%	xERA	RAR	Ctl	Dom	Cmd	hr/9	G/F	S%	BPV	BPX
LH Reliever	98	a/a	3	4	14	69	5.22	1.61	$6	5.3	276			31%	5.32	2.0	4.8	6.7	**1.4**	1.3		70%	30	58
AGE 29 Peak	99	TEX	* 3	2	1	79	3.87	1.32	$7	4.7	269	193	299	30%	3.92	21.1	2.5	4.9	**2.0**	0.7	3.59	71%	51	128
TYPE	00	TEX	3	1	1	56	3.85	1.52	$4	3.2	288	252	351	33%	4.32	15.5	3.4	5.1	**1.5**	0.3	3.32	73%	51	131
BURN none	01	TEX	5	5	4	60	4.80	1.37	$6	3.7	242	258	227	27%	3.33 +	5.5	4.2	4.4	**1.0**	0.3	2.06	63%	45	91
ERA Potl -	02	OAK	* 2	3	0	47	5.35	1.55	($1)	3.8	304	270	337	33%	5.53	-1.5	2.9	5.2	**1.8**	1.3	2.36	68%	23	43
Support 3.16	1st Half		2	1	0	30	3.29	1.43	$2	4.0	274			28%	4.39 -	7.3	3.3	3.3	**1.0**	0.9		80%	14	27
LIMA C+	2nd Half		0	2	0	17	9.00	1.76	($3)	3.6	352			41%	7.57 +	-8.9	2.1	8.5	**4.0**	2.1		50%	56	106
Risk Low	**03**	**Proj**	**2**	**3**	**1**	**40**	**4.73**	**1.40**	**$1**	**3.6**	**271**			**30%**	**4.51**	**3.4**	**3.2**	**5.6**	**1.8**	**1.1**	**G**	**69%**	**38**	**78**

2-2, 4.62 ERA in 37 IP at OAK. Keeps the ball on the ground, which apparently is becoming a highly sought-after skill, without regard to far more important BPIs. But it hasn't been helping him much lately.

Veres,Dave		Tm	W	L	Sv	IP	ERA	Br/IP	R$	BF/G	OBA	vLH	vRH	H%	xERA	RAR	Ctl	Dom	Cmd	hr/9	G/F	S%	BPV	BPX
RH Reliever	98	COL	3	1	8	76	2.84	1.24	$11	5.0	238	239	228	30%	3.28	24.4	3.2	8.8	**2.7**	0.7	1.29	80%	96	173
AGE 36 Decline	99	COL	4	8	31	77	5.14	1.62	$17	4.8	288	328	263	34%	5.78 -	4.2	4.3	8.3	**1.9**	1.6	1.63	73%	38	83
TYPE Power	00	STL	3	5	29	75	2.87	1.20	$26	4.4	235	210	261	29%	3.15	27.8	3.0	8.0	**2.7**	0.7	1.66	79%	91	200
BURN none	01	STL	3	2	13	63	3.75	1.30	$13	5.3	257	257	220	27%	4.00 -	14.0	[illegible]	[illegible]	[illegible]	1.7	1.00	70%	61	101
ERA Potl -	02	STL	5	8	4	82	3.51	1.29	$10	4.9	225	190	246	25%	3.90	21.4	4.3	7.5	**1.7**	1.3	1.13	79%	52	107
Support 5.12	1st Half		3	3	2	43	3.14	1.33	$6	5.2	209			23%	3.54	13.4	5.2	6.5	**1.2**	1.0		81%	47	96
LIMA C	2nd Half		2	5	2	39	3.92	1.26	$4	4.5	241			28%	4.29	8.0	3.2	8.5	**2.6**	1.6		76%	65	133
Risk Low	**03**	**Proj**	**4**	**6**	**2**	**75**	**3.60**	**1.29**	**$7**	**4.5**	**235**			**27%**	**4.00**	**18.6**	**3.8**	**8.0**	**2.1**	**1.3**	**--**	**78%**	**61**	**122**

Was it fair that he lost the closer's job? Well, BPIs have been in decline, he is 36 and his saves conversion pct over the past three years has been 81%, 79%, 50%. However, I still think there are saves left in that arm.

Villafuerte,Brandon			W	L	Sv	IP	ERA	Br/IP	R$	BF/G	OBA	vLH	vRH	H%	xERA	RAR	Ctl	Dom	Cmd	hr/9	G/F	S%	BPV	BPX
RH Reliever	98	a/a	1	2	1	66	5.32	1.86	($6)	7.9	316			38%	5.85 -	1.0	5.0	7.5	**1.5**	0.5		71%	52	100
AGE 27 Growth	99	aa	6	10	5	124	3.77	1.46	$10	14.7	269			32%	4.35 -	31.9	3.8	6.8	**1.8**	0.8		76%	56	130
TYPE Power	00	aa	4	9	4	87	8.17	2.05	($11)	9.4	350	286	222	42%	6.93 +	-28.1	4.8	7.0	**1.5**	0.6	3.00	58%	40	94
BURN none	01	aaa	5	5	10	68	4.50	1.71	$6	7.1	312			38%	5.87 -	8.4	3.8	8.1	**2.1**	1.1	1.09	76%	53	103
ERA Potl - - -	02	SD	* 9	6	2	90	2.00	1.26	$18	4.8	235	286	213	29%	3.08 -	41.7	3.5	7.0	**2.0**	0.4	2.30	85%	80	164
Support 1.97	1st Half		7	4	1	49	2.20	1.24	$12	5.1	224			27%	2.87 -	21.5	3.8	6.8	**1.8**	0.4		83%	77	158
LIMA B	2nd Half		2	2	1	41	1.76	1.27	$6	4.5	248			30%	3.33 -	20.2	3.1	7.3	**2.4**	0.4		88%	85	175
Risk X HIGH	**03**	**Proj**	**4**	**4**	**3**	**60**	**3.90**	**1.35**	**$6**	**5.8**	**249**			**30%**	**3.65**	**12.5**	**3.8**	**7.4**	**2.0**	**0.6**	**G**	**71%**	**73**	**146**

1-2, 1.41 ERA in 32 IP at SD. Decent enough skill set, but his 2002 stats were clearly over his head. This projection represents a more league-normalized view of his skill.

Villone,Ron

Villone,Ron	Yr	Tm	W	L	Sv	IP	ERA	Br/IP	R$	BF/G	OBA	vLH	vRH	H%	xERA	RAR	Ctl	Dom	Cmd	hr/9	G/F	S%	BPV	BPX
LH Reliever	98	CLE	* 2	2	7	49	4.77	1.85	$1	4.9	288	229	333	33%	5.75 -	5.9	6.4	6.8	1.1	0.9	1.73	76%	33	70
AGE 33 Past	99	CIN	* 11	7	3	161	3.91	1.30	$16	14.4	215	253	212	25%	2.92 +	35.2	4.8	6.6	1.4	0.5	1.30	70%	66	143
TYPE	00	CIN	10	10	0	141	5.43	1.65	$0	18.4	279	252	296	29%	5.57	3.8	5.0	4.9	1.0	1.4	1.02	70%	7	16
BURN none	01	2NL	6	10	0	114	5.91	1.63	($5)	9.8	292	250	300	35%	5.69	-8.3	4.2	8.9	2.1	1.4	1.45	66%	52	97
ERA Potl + + +	02	PIT	4	6	0	93	5.81	1.39	($2)	8.9	266	233	289	30%	4.19 +	-4.3	3.3	5.3	1.6	0.8	1.22	57%	44	91
Support 4.06	1st Half		2	6	0	63	5.84	1.41	($2)	12.4	258			30%	4.06 +	-3.2	3.8	6.4	1.7	0.7		57%	55	114
LIMA D	2nd Half		2	0	0	30	5.74	1.34	$0	5.5	282			29%	4.45 +	-1.1	2.1	3.0	1.4	0.9		57%	20	40
Risk High	03	Proj	**4**	**4**	**0**	**80**	**5.63**	**1.49**	**($1)**	**8.6**	**276**			**31%**	**4.77 +**	**-1.8**	**3.7**	**5.9**	**1.6**	**1.0**	**--**	**63%**	**38**	**76**

A 57% strand rate asks -- is it HIS fault or the bullpen's? The play-by-play for his 7 starts (37 IP, 28 ER) show that he left only 4 runners for the pen, and only 2 scored. Lots of big innings that he could not get out of.

Vizcaino,Luis

Vizcaino,Luis	Yr	Tm	W	L	Sv	IP	ERA	Br/IP	R$	BF/G	OBA	vLH	vRH	H%	xERA	RAR	Ctl	Dom	Cmd	hr/9	G/F	S%	BPV	BPX
RH Reliever	98	aa	3	2	0	38	5.21	1.74	($1)	25.3	300			31%	6.58 -	1.1	4.7	5.2	1.1	1.9		76%	-8	-15
AGE 27 Pre-Peak	99	a/a	8	8	0	118	5.34	1.53	$3	16.4	289	286	167	32%	5.21	5.7	3.5	6.4	1.8	1.2	2.33	67%	37	87
TYPE Power	00	OAK	* 6	3	5	67	6.72	1.70	$2	6.9	300	270	333	35%	5.53 +	-7.2	4.4	7.1	1.6	0.9	0.89	60%	43	112
BURN none	01	OAK	* 4	3	8	78	3.46	1.24	$11	5.2	257	241	282	31%	4.30 -	21.1	2.4	9.1	3.8	1.5	1.09	80%	92	185
ERA Potl + +	02	MIL	5	3	5	81	3.00	1.05	$16	4.2	194	225	170	25%	2.29 +	26.7	3.3	8.8	2.6	0.7	0.65	73%	104	214
Support 4.65	1st Half		5	1	1	45	3.39	1.09	$9	4.3	206			27%	2.64 +	12.5	3.2	9.4	2.9	0.8		71%	108	221
LIMA C+	2nd Half		0	2	4	36	2.51	1.00	$7	4.1	179			22%	1.85 +	14.2	3.5	8.0	2.3	0.5		76%	100	206
Risk High	03	Proj	**4**	**3**	**16**	**80**	**3.38**	**1.19**	**$18**	**4.8**	**224**			**28%**	**3.18**	**22.3**	**3.4**	**8.6**	**2.5**	**0.9**	**F**	**75%**	**88**	**177**

Definitely closer-worthy... Solid BPIs and converted 83% of save opps. However, 25% hit rate means his ERA could come up and it's never good to be a fly ball pitcher with the game on the line in the 9th.

Wagner,Billy

Wagner,Billy	Yr	Tm	W	L	Sv	IP	ERA	Br/IP	R$	BF/G	OBA	vLH	vRH	H%	xERA	RAR	Ctl	Dom	Cmd	hr/9	G/F	S%	BPV	BPX
LH Reliever	98	HOU	4	3	30	60	2.70	1.18	$24	4.2	214	302	189	36%	2.97	20.4	3.8	14.6	3.9	0.9	1.10	82%	154	278
AGE 31 Peak	99	HOU	4	1	39	74	1.58	0.78	$39	4.2	144	152	131	26%	0.85 +	39.3	2.8	15.1	5.4	0.6	1.08	85%	212	460
TYPE Power	00	HOU	2	4	6	27	6.29	1.69	$3	4.5	267	321	232	31%	6.02	-2.4	6.0	9.3	1.6	2.0	0.73	68%	30	67
BURN none	01	HOU	2	5	39	62	2.75	1.03	$31	3.8	201	261	182	29%	2.29	21.8	2.9	11.4	4.0	0.7	1.19	76%	145	268
ERA Potl +	02	HOU	4	2	35	75	2.52	0.97	$36	4.2	194	180	201	26%	2.25	29.5	2.6	10.6	4.0	0.8	1.10	79%	138	284
Support 2.40	1st Half		2	1	13	37	2.68	1.14	$14	4.5	217			28%	2.84	13.8	3.2	9.5	3.0	0.7		79%	110	225
LIMA C	2nd Half		2	1	22	38	2.37	0.82	$23	3.8	170			24%	1.67 +	15.7	2.1	11.6	5.4	0.9		78%	176	362
Risk Low	03	Proj	**4**	**3**	**40**	**75**	**2.64**	**1.03**	**$36**	**4.1**	**203**			**28%**	**2.46**	**28.3**	**2.8**	**10.8**	**3.9**	**0.8**	**--**	**79%**	**136**	**274**

BPIs look as solid as ever, but with one small caveat. His saves conversion rate dropped from 95% in 2001 to 85% in 2002. Still within acceptable territory, but perhaps a warning sign in case 2003 is bumpy.

Wakefield,Tim

Wakefield,Tim	Yr	Tm	W	L	Sv	IP	ERA	Br/IP	R$	BF/G	OBA	vLH	vRH	H%	xERA	RAR	Ctl	Dom	Cmd	hr/9	G/F	S%	BPV	BPX
RH Reliever	98	BOS	17	8	0	216	4.58	1.34	$16	25.6	257	286	224	28%	4.35	31.0	3.3	6.1	1.8	1.3	0.94	69%	41	88
AGE 36 Decline	99	BOS	6	11	15	140	5.08	1.56	$10	12.8	270	280	256	30%	5.03	14.9	4.6	6.7	1.4	1.2	0.92	70%	35	87
TYPE Power	00	BOS	6	10	0	159	5.49	1.48	$1	13.7	275	250	289	29%	5.37	9.0	3.7	5.8	1.6	1.8	1.00	68%	15	39
BURN none	01	BOS	9	12	3	168	3.91	1.36	$11	16.0	247	230	261	30%	3.73	35.6	3.9	7.9	2.0	0.7	1.24	72%	75	150
ERA Potl +	02	BOS	11	5	3	163	2.82	1.06	$21	14.4	208	195	213	25%	2.49	50.0	2.8	7.4	2.6	0.8	0.98	77%	88	166
Support 5.57	1st Half		2	3	3	60	2.70	1.10	$7	9.6	195			23%	2.51	19.3	3.8	7.5	2.0	0.9		80%	76	144
LIMA D+	2nd Half		9	2	0	103	2.88	1.03	$15	20.3	216			26%	2.47	30.7	2.3	7.3	3.2	0.8		75%	100	189
Risk Low	03	Proj	**9**	**8**	**1**	**160**	**3.71**	**1.24**	**$13**	**14.8**	**234**			**27%**	**3.43**	**35.5**	**3.4**	**7.2**	**2.1**	**1.0**	**--**	**73%**	**67**	**137**

His first $20 season since 1995. A recap of his usage...

ERA/Cmd	Starter	Reliever
1999	5.86/1.3	3.50/1.7
2000	5.90/1.3	4.82/1.9
2001	4.30/1.6	3.23/3.4
2002	2.39/3.3	3.44/2.1

Walker,Jamie

Walker,Jamie	Yr	Tm	W	L	Sv	IP	ERA	Br/IP	R$	BF/G	OBA	vLH	vRH	H%	xERA	RAR	Ctl	Dom	Cmd	hr/9	G/F	S%	BPV	BPX
LH Reliever	98	KC	* 5	2	0	63	5.14	1.76	($1)	22.7	353	318	404	38%	6.81 -	4.3	2.0	4.6	2.3	1.1	1.33	73%	26	54
AGE 31 Peak	99	aaa	0	1	0	17	5.29	1.65	($1)	19.4	324			37%	5.41	0.9	2.6	5.3	2.0	0.5		67%	48	111
TYPE Contact	00	aaa	3	10	0	101	6.86	1.94	($12)	20.5	375			36%	9.18 -	-14.9	2.2	3.5	1.6	2.8		72%	-49	
BURN none	01	aaa	7	2	2	93	5.61	1.80	($3)	11.5	343			35%	7.20 -	-2.4	2.9	3.9	1.3	1.6		73%	-12	
ERA Potl + +	02	DET	* 1	2	2	56	3.52	0.93	$6	3.2	202	202	194	21%	2.95 +	11.9	1.9	7.7	4.0	1.8	0.73	73%	92	174
Support 2.27	1st Half		1	0	2	29	3.09	1.07	$4	3.6	226			24%	3.69 -	7.8	2.2	7.7	3.6	1.9		84%	75	143
LIMA B	2nd Half		0	2	0	27	3.99	0.77	$2	2.9	173			17%	2.16 +	4.1	1.7	7.6	4.6	1.7		56%	113	214
Risk X HIGH	03	Proj	**2**	**2**	**4**	**50**	**3.78**	**1.12**	**$6**	**5.3**	**242**			**26%**	**3.87**	**10.6**	**2.0**	**6.5**	**3.3**	**1.6**	**F**	**74%**	**66**	**134**

1-1, 3.77 ERA in 43 IP at DET. Reasons to take a cheap flyer:
- As a LHer, there will be a job
- Reasonable to be peaking now
- At 31 and on KC, other owners either won't know about him, think he's for real, or care.

Walker,Pete

Walker,Pete	Yr	Tm	W	L	Sv	IP	ERA	Br/IP	R$	BF/G	OBA	vLH	vRH	H%	xERA	RAR	Ctl	Dom	Cmd	hr/9	G/F	S%	BPV	BPX
RH Starter	98	aaa	1	4	0	33	8.45	1.91	($6)	7.2	321			30%	8.13	-13.4	5.2	3.8	0.7	2.7		60%	-53	
AGE 34 Past	99	aaa	8	4	5	62	6.24	1.77	$3	6.1	319			34%	7.05 -	-4.5	4.1	6.4	1.6	2.0		70%	2	3
TYPE Contact	00	aaa	7	3	5	73	4.32	1.55	$8	5.6	282	615	200	33%	4.60	14.1	3.9	6.3	1.6	0.6	1.83	72%	51	121
BURN none	01	aaa	13	4	0	174	3.98	1.35	$13	26.6	273			30%	4.09	33.5	2.7	4.7	1.7	0.7	2.00	71%	44	84
ERA Potl -	02	2TM	* 10	5	1	149	4.35	1.40	$8	16.1	271	288	254	29%	4.55	18.4	3.1	5.1	1.6	1.1	1.17	72%	32	62
Support 5.52	1st Half		3	0	1	52	3.11	1.25	$6	9.4	258			28%	4.04 -	15.1	2.4	6.0	2.5	1.2		81%	56	110
LIMA C	2nd Half		7	5	0	97	5.02	1.48	$3	25.1	278			29%	4.82	3.3	3.5	4.6	1.3	1.1		68%	22	42
Risk X HIGH	03	Proj	**10**	**8**	**0**	**160**	**4.61**	**1.45**	**$6**	**25.9**	**278**			**30%**	**4.73**	**17.2**	**3.3**	**5.0**	**1.5**	**1.1**	**--**	**70%**	**29**	**58**

His 2001 year, while outwardly acceptable, was not supported by good BPIs and represented a huge jump in workload. That workload appears to have finally caught up to him in the 2nd half. At 34, there is no more upside.

Washburn,Jarrod

Washburn,Jarrod	Yr	Tm	W	L	Sv	IP	ERA	Br/IP	R$	BF/G	OBA	vLH	vRH	H%	xERA	RAR	Ctl	Dom	Cmd	hr/9	G/F	S%	BPV	BPX
LH Starter	98	ANA	* 10	9	0	174	5.01	1.50	$4	25.6	277	276	241	30%	4.91	15.0	3.8	5.7	1.5	1.1	0.65	69%	32	68
AGE 28 Pre-Peak	99	ANA	* 5	10	0	120	6.23	1.43	($0)	19.3	270	216	273	31%	4.53 +	-5.7	3.5	6.5	1.9	1.1	0.90	56%	48	121
TYPE	00	ANA	* 10	2	0	114	3.94	1.35	$13	25.7	244	215	215	25%	4.31	30.2	3.9	5.2	1.3	1.4	0.62	76%	23	59
BURN none	01	ANA	11	10	0	193	3.78	1.29	$14	27.1	265	287	257	29%	4.25	44.2	2.5	5.9	2.3	1.2	0.65	75%	51	103
ERA Potl -	02	ANA	18	6	0	206	3.15	1.17	$24	26.4	240	199	246	27%	3.19	54.1	2.6	6.1	2.4	0.8	0.60	76%	68	129
Support 5.20	1st Half		8	2	0	98	3.48	1.26	$9	25.7	253			29%	3.84	21.4	2.7	7.1	2.6	1.1		77%	69	130
LIMA D	2nd Half		10	4	0	108	2.84	1.09	$15	27.0	226			25%	2.60	32.7	2.4	5.1	2.1	0.6		76%	67	127
Risk Very High	03	Proj	**15**	**8**	**0**	**200**	**3.42**	**1.20**	**$21**	**25.8**	**244**			**27%**	**3.42**	**52.2**	**2.6**	**6.0**	**2.3**	**0.9**	**F**	**75%**	**64**	**130**

Solid BPIs and nice trends as he enters his peak years. Appears to have overcome his early career workload abuse, but do keep that tidbit in your back pocket in case he hits some unexpected bumps.

Weathers,David

Weathers,David	Yr	Tm	W	L	Sv	IP	ERA	Br/IP	R$	BF/G	OBA	vLH	vRH	H%	xERA	RAR	Ctl	Dom	Cmd	hr/9	G/F	S%	BPV	BPX
RH Reliever	98	2NL	6	5	0	110	4.91	1.55	($1)	11.2	295	326	275	36%	4.69	4.8	3.4	7.7	2.3	0.5	1.91	67%	76	136
AGE 33 Past	99	MIL	7	4	2	93	4.65	1.51	$5	6.5	280	290	273	32%	5.11	11.2	3.7	7.2	1.9	1.4	1.49	73%	42	92
TYPE Power	00	MIL	3	5	1	76	3.07	1.38	$7	4.7	254	223	278	29%	3.99 -	26.0	3.8	5.9	1.6	0.8	1.34	81%	48	105
BURN none	01	2NL	4	5	4	86	2.41	1.15	$13	4.4	211	213	218	25%	2.68	34.1	3.6	6.9	1.9	0.6	1.11	82%	76	141
ERA Potl - - -	02	NYM	6	3	0	77	2.92	1.36	$9	4.6	241	267	232	29%	3.71 -	26.2	4.2	7.1	1.7	0.7	1.49	81%	64	131
Support 5.35	1st Half		2	3	0	41	2.63	1.22	$5	4.6	242			28%	3.52 -	15.6	2.8	7.0	2.5	0.9		83%	74	152
LIMA C+	2nd Half		4	0	0	36	3.26	1.53	$4	4.7	240			29%	3.93 -	10.6	5.8	7.3	1.3	0.5		79%	62	127
Risk Low	03	Proj	**5**	**3**	**0**	**75**	**3.12**	**1.35**	**$7**	**4.8**	**241**			**28%**	**3.65 -**	**23.4**	**4.1**	**7.0**	**1.7**	**0.7**	**--**	**79%**	**63**	**126**

Had trouble with his control in the 2nd half, which might be the first sign of some skills erosion. But as long as he keeps the ball on the ground and in the park, and throws with his left hand, he'll continue to be employable.

Weaver,Jeff

Weaver,Jeff	Yr	Tm	W	L	Sv	IP	ERA	Br/IP	R$	BF/G	OBA	vLH	vRH	H%	xERA	RAR	Ctl	Dom	Cmd	hr/9	G/F	S%	BPV	BPX
RH Starter	98		0	0	0	0	0.00	0.00																
AGE 26 Growth	99	DET	9	12	0	163	5.58	1.42	$4	23.6	277	310	236	30%	5.05 +	6.4	3.1	6.3	2.0	1.5	1.20	64%	35	89
TYPE Contact	00	DET	11	15	0	200	4.32	1.29	$17	27.1	267	267	266	29%	4.22	42.6	2.3	6.1	2.6	1.2	1.51	70%	58	151
BURN none	01	DET	13	16	0	229	4.09	1.32	$17	29.5	267	278	253	30%	3.96	42.9	2.7	6.0	2.2	0.7	1.21	70%	62	124
ERA Potl +	02	2AL	11	11	2	199	3.53	1.21	$16	25.7	256	233	268	30%	3.23	42.1	2.2	6.0	2.8	0.5	1.27	71%	81	153
Support 4.33	1st Half		6	8	0	121	3.19	1.20	$10	29.3	247			29%	2.84	31.1	2.5	5.6	2.3	0.3		72%	78	147
LIMA C+	2nd Half		5	3	2	78	4.05	1.23	$6	21.5	270			31%	3.83	11.0	1.7	6.6	3.8	0.9		69%	93	175
Risk Low	03	Proj	**15**	**10**	**0**	**180**	**3.35**	**1.18**	**$21**	**25.5**	**254**			**29%**	**3.47**	**48.7**	**2.0**	**6.2**	**3.1**	**0.9**	**--**	**74%**	**80**	**163**

His BPIs have been solid for awhile, and the trends have been good, but you have to think that this huge change in environment, from DET to NYY, is going to kick-start his stats in a big way.

Weber,Ben

	Yr	Tm	W	L	Sv	IP	ERA	Br/IP	R$	BF/G	OBA	vLH	vRH	H%	xERA	RAR	Ctl	Dom	Cmd	hr/9	G/F	S%	BPV	BPX
RH Reliever	98	TWN	12	7	7	144	3.56	1.40	$17	11.1	270			33%	4.19 -	36.0	3.3	7.6	**2.3**	0.8		76%	74	143
AGE 33 Past	99	aaa	2	4	8	86	3.66	1.36	$9	7.2	266			30%	3.81	23.4	3.0	5.5	**1.8**	0.5		73%	58	134
TYPE Contact	00	2TM •	5	10	7	101	4.08	1.40	$10	7.4	287	250	188	33%	4.46	22.8	2.4	6.5	**2.7**	0.8	2.14	72%	69	164
BURN none	01	ANA	6	2	0	68	3.44	1.42	$6	5.3	256	210	278	29%	3.87	18.7	4.1	5.3	**1.3**	0.5	2.65	76%	47	94
ERA Potl -	02	ANA	7	2	7	78	2.54	1.18	$14	5.1	241	243	253	27%	2.89	26.8	2.5	5.0	**2.0**	0.5	3.66	80%	64	120
Support 5.08	1st Half		4	2	1	40	2.92	1.20	$6	5.5	241			28%	3.12	11.8	2.7	6.1	**2.3**	0.7		78%	70	133
LIMA C	2nd Half		3	0	6	38	2.14	1.16	$8	4.7	241			27%	2.64 -	15.1	2.4	3.8	**1.6**	0.2		81%	56	106
Risk Moderate	03	Proj	**6**	**3**	**4**	**80**	**3.26**	**1.29**	**$10**	**5.6**	**254**			**29%**	**3.47**	**22.6**	**2.9**	**5.3**	**1.8**	**0.6**	**G**	**76%**	**57**	**116**

Extreme groundball pitcher, which helps offset BPIs that are otherwise unnoteworthy. Probably a bit over his head in 2002. Expect a slight letdown.

Wells,Bob

	Yr	Tm	W	L	Sv	IP	ERA	Br/IP	R$	BF/G	OBA	vLH	vRH	H%	xERA	RAR	Ctl	Dom	Cmd	hr/9	G/F	S%	BPV	BPX
RH Reliever	98	SEA	2	2	0	51	6.15	1.37	($0)	7.3	272	361	194	27%	5.43 +	-3.4	2.8	5.1	**1.8**	2.1	0.69	60%	6	13
AGE 36 Decline	99	MIN	8	3	1	87	3.83	1.23	$13	4.8	244	246	243	26%	3.50	23.8	2.9	4.6	**1.6**	0.8	0.70	71%	42	105
TYPE Contact	00	MIN	0	7	10	86	3.66	1.10	$13	4.6	248	233	255	28%	3.76	26.0	1.6	7.9	**5.1**	1.5	0.44	74%	116	300
BURN none	01	MIN	8	5	2	68	5.15	1.32	$7	4.4	272	264	277	30%	4.81	3.1	2.4	6.5	**2.7**	1.6	0.47	65%	49	98
ERA Potl - -	02	MIN	2	2	0	62	5.95	1.63	($4)	5.4	322	355	300	34%	6.00	-7.0	2.6	4.5	**1.7**	1.3	0.92	65%	15	28
Support 3.88	1st Half		0	1	0	33	7.36	1.97	($6)	5.8	371			40%	8.28 -	-10.0	2.7	5.7	**2.1**	1.9		66%	2	4
LIMA F	2nd Half		2	1	0	29	4.34	1.24	$2	5.0	255			27%	3.40 +	3.0	2.5	3.1	**1.3**	0.6		65%	30	57
Risk Moderate	03	Proj	**2**	**3**	**1**	**65**	**4.98**	**1.42**	**$0**	**5.0**	**285**			**30%**	**5.00**	**3.3**	**2.6**	**4.7**	**1.8**	**1.4**	**--**	**68%**	**22**	**45**

BPIs have eroded, and quickly. H% and S% levels are likely to regress to the mean a bit, helping his ERA, but at this age, his draftability is still suspect.

Wells,David

	Yr	Tm	W	L	Sv	IP	ERA	Br/IP	R$	BF/G	OBA	vLH	vRH	H%	xERA	RAR	Ctl	Dom	Cmd	hr/9	G/F	S%	BPV	BPX
LH Starter	98	NYY	18	4	0	214	3.49	1.05	$32	28.3	244	245	237	27%	3.39	62.1	1.2	6.9	**5.6**	1.2	1.12	72%	129	275
AGE 40 Decline	99	TOR	17	10	0	231	4.83	1.33	$17	28.9	274	295	266	31%	4.55	32.2	2.4	6.6	**2.7**	1.2	1.27	67%	60	149
TYPE Contact	00	TOR	20	8	0	229	4.12	1.30	$26	27.6	292	288	289	34%	4.35	54.9	1.2	6.5	**5.4**	0.9	1.19	70%	121	315
BURN High	01	CHW	5	7	0	100	4.49	1.41	$3	27.1	298	206	328	33%	4.95	13.3	1.9	5.3	**2.8**	1.1	1.12	71%	54	108
ERA Potl +	02	NYY	19	7	0	206	3.76	1.24	$20	27.6	266	213	274	30%	3.78	37.2	2.0	6.0	**3.0**	0.9	1.08	72%	74	140
Support 7.46	1st Half		8	5	0	106	3.48	1.23	$10	27.6	252			29%	3.29	23.1	2.5	6.1	**2.4**	0.6		73%	74	139
LIMA D+	2nd Half		11	2	0	100	4.05	1.24	$11	27.7	279			30%	4.30	14.1	1.4	5.9	**4.3**	1.3		72%	88	165
Risk X HIGH	03	Proj	**11**	**9**	**0**	**160**	**4.16**	**1.35**	**$10**	**26.3**	**278**			**31%**	**4.38**	**25.8**	**2.4**	**5.7**	**2.4**	**1.0**	**--**	**72%**	**54**	**109**

Amazing rebound season, but at age 40, the odds of a repeat, or near repeat, or even anything remotely close to a repeat, is remote. Not impossible, but certainly remote. It would be like a 90% pct play to bet against.

Wells,Kip

	Yr	Tm	W	L	Sv	IP	ERA	Br/IP	R$	BF/G	OBA	vLH	vRH	H%	xERA	RAR	Ctl	Dom	Cmd	hr/9	G/F	S%	BPV	BPX
RH Starter	98		0	0	0	0	0.00	0.00																
AGE 26 Growth	99	CHW •	12	3	0	105	3.60	1.25	$17	24.3	227	267	209	26%	3.11 +	31.9	3.8	5.7	**1.5**	0.6	1.32	72%	58	146
TYPE	00	CHW •	12	12	0	167	6.41	1.85	($7)	22.2	314	290	339	34%	6.63	-11.1	5.1	5.9	**1.2**	1.5	1.19	67%	9	22
BURN none	01	CHW •	12	12	0	158	4.84	1.56	$3	16.1	284	267	294	33%	5.01	13.6	4.0	6.8	**1.7**	1.0	1.52	70%	46	92
ERA Potl -	02	PIT	12	14	0	198	3.59	1.35	$15	25.6	261	274	249	29%	4.20 -	49.5	3.2	6.1	**1.9**	1.0	1.98	77%	50	103
Support 4.22	1st Half		9	4	0	96	3.09	1.30	$13	25.3	250			29%	3.63 -	30.4	3.3	5.9	**1.8**	0.7		78%	59	120
LIMA C	2nd Half		3	10	0	102	4.06	1.40	$2	25.9	271			30%	4.72 -	19.1	3.2	6.3	**2.0**	1.2		75%	43	88
Risk Very High	03	Proj	**13**	**15**	**0**	**200**	**4.01**	**1.37**	**$13**	**21.4**	**264**			**30%**	**4.22**	**38.8**	**3.2**	**6.3**	**2.0**	**0.9**	**G**	**73%**	**53**	**107**

NL batters caught up to him a bit in the 2nd half, but he still netted out with a slight growth year. A 3.59 ERA was over his head though. He might finish '03 with a near-4.00 ERA and still be able to show BPI growth.

Westbrook,Jake

	Yr	Tm	W	L	Sv	IP	ERA	Br/IP	R$	BF/G	OBA	vLH	vRH	H%	xERA	RAR	Ctl	Dom	Cmd	hr/9	G/F	S%	BPV	BPX
RH Reliever	98		0	0	0	0	0.00	0.00																
AGE 25 Growth	99	aa	11	5	0	174	4.71	1.53	$6	28.7	294			31%	4.83	23.1	3.2	4.0	**1.2**	0.7		69%	25	57
TYPE Contact	00	aaa	5	7	0	89	5.36	1.57	$1	25.0	293	375	563	34%	4.53 +	4.8	3.6	5.4	**1.5**	0.3	1.09	64%	50	119
BURN Low	01	CLE •	12	5	0	128	5.06	1.52	$4	16.3	294	298	313	34%	4.74	7.2	3.2	6.1	**1.9**	0.6	1.98	66%	55	109
ERA Potl + +	02	CLE •	2	4	0	62	6.39	1.44	($3)	18.0	303	292	300	32%	4.94 +	-10.6	1.9	4.2	**2.2**	1.0	1.83	55%	36	68
Support 4.75	1st Half		0	1	0	15	6.60	1.20	($1)	20.6	287			32%	3.15 +	-3.0	0.6	3.6	**6.0**	0.0		39%	145	275
LIMA B	2nd Half		2	3	0	47	6.32	1.51	($2)	17.4	308			32%	5.51 +	-7.6	2.3	4.4	**1.9**	1.3		59%	20	38
Risk X HIGH	03	Proj	**3**	**3**	**0**	**50**	**4.68**	**1.36**	**$2**	**10.2**	**288**			**32%**	**4.28**	**4.6**	**2.0**	**4.9**	**2.5**	**0.7**	**G**	**66%**	**57**	**115**

1-3, 5.93 ERA in 41 IP at CLE. At a league avg strand rate, he'd have had a 4.50 ERA in '02. That would have been more representative of the moderate BPI growth he exhibited. Expect possible positive value in '03.

White,Gabe

	Yr	Tm	W	L	Sv	IP	ERA	Br/IP	R$	BF/G	OBA	vLH	vRH	H%	xERA	RAR	Ctl	Dom	Cmd	hr/9	G/F	S%	BPV	BPX
LH Reliever	98	CIN	5	5	9	98	4.03	1.15	$12	5.8	237	231	231	26%	3.87	15.8	2.5	7.6	**3.1**	1.6	0.60	72%	71	128
AGE 31 Peak	99	CIN	1	2	0	61	4.43	1.34	$1	5.2	283	355	247	33%	5.26 -	9.2	2.1	9.0	**4.4**	1.9	0.51	75%	86	188
TYPE	00	2NL	11	2	5	84	2.36	0.94	$24	4.8	213	200	217	28%	2.16	36.8	1.6	9.0	**5.6**	0.6	0.62	78%	165	363
BURN none	01	COL	1	7	0	67	6.29	1.43	($4)	4.2	270	269	271	27%	5.82	-8.4	3.5	6.3	**1.8**	2.4	0.62	63%	4	8
ERA Potl + +	02	CIN	6	1	0	54	3.00	1.09	$10	3.5	243	202	267	29%	2.87	17.8	1.7	6.8	**4.1**	0.5	0.64	73%	118	243
Support 4.64	1st Half		3	1	0	41	2.63	0.95	$8	3.7	227			27%	2.26	15.5	1.1	6.1	**5.6**	0.4		73%	151	309
LIMA B+	2nd Half		3	0	0	13	4.15	1.54	$2	3.1	290			37%	4.81 -	2.3	3.5	9.0	**2.6**	0.7		74%	85	174
Risk Moderate	03	Proj	**4**	**3**	**1**	**60**	**3.60**	**1.12**	**$8**	**4.4**	**242**			**28%**	**3.53**	**14.9**	**2.0**	**7.5**	**3.8**	**1.2**	**F**	**73%**	**96**	**194**

Groin injury ended his season prematurely. Superb BPIs, but doesn't like pitching at home:

ERA/Cmd	Home	Away
2000	3.13/4.2	1.42/8.4
2001	7.43/1.1	4.88/3.5
2002	5.14/5.3	0.68/3.3

White,Rick

	Yr	Tm	W	L	Sv	IP	ERA	Br/IP	R$	BF/G	OBA	vLH	vRH	H%	xERA	RAR	Ctl	Dom	Cmd	hr/9	G/F	S%	BPV	BPX
RH Reliever	98	TAM •	6	8	0	121	4.90	1.53	$1	11.5	305	246	259	33%	5.19	12.3	2.7	4.7	**1.8**	0.9	1.56	69%	32	69
AGE 34 Past	99	TAM	5	3	0	108	4.08	1.57	$4	7.7	302	309	301	36%	5.03 -	25.9	3.2	6.8	**2.1**	0.7	1.56	75%	60	150
TYPE	00	2TM	5	9	3	99	3.54	1.22	$12	6.2	229	268	193	26%	3.24	29.5	3.4	6.1	**1.8**	0.8	1.22	73%	58	138
BURN none	01	NYM	4	5	2	69	3.90	1.27	$6	5.3	267	271	249	31%	3.97	13.6	2.2	6.6	**3.0**	0.9	1.60	72%	77	143
ERA Potl +	02	2NL •	5	8	0	67	4.55	1.40	$3	4.4	270	295	245	32%	4.04 +	8.1	3.2	6.2	**1.9**	0.5	1.50	67%	62	128
Support 3.45	1st Half		2	6	0	29	6.16	1.58	($1)	4.7	310			34%	5.75	-2.8	2.8	5.2	**1.9**	1.2		62%	27	56
LIMA B+	2nd Half		3	2	0	38	3.32	1.26	$5	4.2	235			30%	2.73 +	10.9	3.6	6.9	**1.9**	0.0		71%	90	184
Risk Moderate	03	Proj	**4**	**5**	**0**	**70**	**3.73**	**1.34**	**$5**	**5.1**	**265**			**31%**	**3.89**	**16.2**	**3.0**	**6.6**	**2.2**	**0.6**	**--**	**73%**	**69**	**138**

Here's a real stunner:

	ERA	OBA	Cmd
With COL	6.20	.310	1.5
With STL	0.82	.169	4.7

He should be fine in 2003, no matter where he ends up... except COL, um, or TEX, um or..

Wickman,Bob

	Yr	Tm	W	L	Sv	IP	ERA	Br/IP	R$	BF/G	OBA	vLH	vRH	H%	xERA	RAR	Ctl	Dom	Cmd	hr/9	G/F	S%	BPV	BPX
RH Reliever	98	MIL	6	9	25	82	3.73	1.44	$19	5.0	254	270	256	32%	3.87	16.6	4.3	7.8	**1.8**	0.5	2.50	74%	73	131
AGE 34 Past	99	MIL	3	8	37	74	3.41	1.53	$24	4.6	264	197	314	32%	4.35 -	21.2	4.6	7.3	**1.6**	0.7	2.89	79%	57	124
TYPE Power	00	2TM	3	5	30	72	3.12	1.33	$24	4.4	239	258	214	30%	2.99	25.6	4.0	6.9	**1.7**	0.1	2.33	75%	81	191
BURN none	01	CLE	5	0	32	67	2.41	1.12	$28	3.9	244	279	205	32%	2.90	27.7	1.9	8.8	**4.7**	0.5	2.34	80%	142	285
ERA Potl + +	02	CLE	1	3	20	34	4.50	1.53	$9	4.2	305	275	294	39%	4.94	2.8	2.6	9.5	**3.6**	0.8	1.60	71%	100	100
Support 0.79	1st Half		0	2	18	28	4.16	1.60	$7	4.2	312			43%	4.78 -	3.5	2.9	10.6	**3.7**	0.3		73%	123	233
LIMA B	2nd Half		1	1	2	6	6.10	1.19	$2	4.0	265			23%	5.66	-0.8	1.5	4.6	**3.0**	3.1		60%	1	2
Risk Low	03	Proj	**0**	**1**	**0**	**10**	**4.50**	**1.60**	**($0)**	**4.5**	**281**			**34%**	**4.09**	**1.2**	**4.5**	**6.3**	**1.4**	**0.0**	**G**	**69%**	**66**	**134**

Tommy John surgery on his elbow will shelve him for most, if not all, of the 2003 season. Odds are he will not be looking at a closing job once he returns.

Williamson,Scott

	Yr	Tm	W	L	Sv	IP	ERA	Br/IP	R$	BF/G	OBA	vLH	vRH	H%	xERA	RAR	Ctl	Dom	Cmd	hr/9	G/F	S%	BPV	BPX
RH Reliever	98	a/a	4	5	0	121	3.94	1.34	$5	22.4	247			32%	3.42 +	24.1	3.7	8.4	**2.3**	0.4		70%	90	175
AGE 27 Growth	99	CIN	12	7	19	93	2.42	1.04	$32	5.9	171	171	172	23%	1.99	39.0	4.2	10.4	**2.5**	0.8	0.90	81%	112	243
TYPE Power	00	CIN	5	8	6	112	3.29	1.49	$10	10.3	226	251	204	32%	3.61	35.0	6.0	10.9	**1.8**	0.6	1.15	79%	97	213
BURN none	01	CIN	0	0	0	0	0.00	0.00		1.8						0.1	90.0	0.0	**0.0**	0.0	1.00	100%	55	
ERA Potl +	02	CIN	3	4	8	74	2.92	1.11	$14	4.7	181	198	170	25%	2.22 +	25.2	4.4	10.2	**2.3**	0.6	0.86	75%	111	228
Support 4.14	1st Half		2	2	0	31	4.06	1.29	$2	4.8	194			28%	2.53 +	5.8	5.5	10.2	**1.8**	0.3		67%	107	220
LIMA B+	2nd Half		1	2	8	43	2.09	0.98	$12	4.7	171			23%	2.00	19.4	3.6	10.3	**2.9**	0.8		84%	118	242
Risk Low	03	Proj	**4**	**5**	**27**	**75**	**3.36**	**1.28**	**$23**	**4.9**	**212**			**29%**	**2.98**	**21.0**	**4.7**	**10.2**	**2.2**	**0.6**	**--**	**75%**	**102**	**204**

He looks ready to step right into the closer's role, but don't bet the rent just yet. Warning signs:
- Control is slightly high
- Injury history
- Saves conversions in '99, '00, and '02 = 73%, 75% and 67%.

Williams,David

Williams,David	Yr	Tm	W	L	Sv	IP	ERA	Br/IP	R$	BF/G	OBA	vLH	vRH	H%	xERA	RAR	Ctl	Dom	Cmd	hr/9	G/F	S%	BPV	BPX
LH Starter	98		0	0	0	0	0.00	0.00																
AGE 24 Growth	99		0	0	0	0	0.00	0.00																
TYPE Power	00		0	0	0	0	0.00	0.00																
BURN Moderate	01	PIT *	9	10	0	183	3.59	1.23	$14	23.0	239	255	241	24%	3.90	43.5	3.1	4.7	1.5	1.3	1.00	77%	27	50
ERA Potl --	02	PIT	2	5	0	43	5.02	1.44	($0)	20.8	239	86	271	25%	4.99	2.5	5.0	6.9	1.4	1.9	1.24	72%	21	43
Support 2.28	1st Half		2	5	0	43	5.01	1.44	$0	20.9	238			25%	4.97	2.6	5.0	6.9	1.4	1.9		72%	21	43
LIMA F	2nd Half		0	0	0	-0	0.00	0.00																
Risk Moderate	03	Proj	6	11	0	120	4.80	1.53	$0	22.2	271			29%	5.40 -	10.5	4.3	6.0	1.4	1.7	--	74%	17	34

3 Smart Reasons to Draft Him:
- LHers went 3 for 35 vs him.
- Labrum surgery makes him seem more studly
- You're an alumnus of Delaware Tech Community College

Williams,Mike

Williams,Mike	Yr	Tm	W	L	Sv	IP	ERA	Br/IP	R$	BF/G	OBA	vLH	vRH	H%	xERA	RAR	Ctl	Dom	Cmd	hr/9	G/F	S%	BPV	BPX
RH Reliever	98	PIT *	4	4	1	88	4.09	1.28	$5	7.0	248	182	223	30%	4.22	13.5	3.2	8.9	2.8	1.4	1.85	74%	75	135
AGE 33 Past	99	PIT	3	4	23	58	5.12	1.72	$12	4.6	278	253	289	38%	5.62 -	3.3	5.7	11.8	2.1	1.4	1.44	74%	71	155
TYPE Power	00	PIT	3	4	24	72	3.50	1.33	$20	4.3	216	233	208	27%	3.53	20.5	5.0	8.9	1.8	1.0	1.68	77%	72	159
BURN none	01	2NL	6	4	22	64	3.80	1.48	$18	4.3	250	259	231	30%	4.59 -	13.5	4.9	8.3	1.7	1.3	1.40	79%	52	97
ERA Potl -	02	PIT	2	6	46	61	2.95	1.23	$36	4.3	239	281	180	27%	3.52 -	20.5	3.1	6.3	2.0	0.9	1.40	80%	62	127
Support 0.73	1st Half		1	2	23	32	1.96	0.97	$21	4.3	210			23%	2.71 -	15.0	2.0	6.7	3.4	1.1		89%	92	188
LIMA F	2nd Half		1	4	23	29	4.05	1.52	$15	4.3	269			31%	4.43	5.5	4.4	5.9	1.4	0.6		74%	47	95
Risk Low	03	Proj	3	5	35	65	3.32	1.29	$27	4.3	243			28%	3.65	18.6	3.5	6.9	2.0	0.8	--	77%	65	131

It's true that winning teams will generate more save opps, but that's not a smart approach to drafting closers. Stick to TOG, no matter what team he's on. Though BPIs are soft here, he did convert 93% of save opps.

Williams,Woody

Williams,Woody	Yr	Tm	W	L	Sv	IP	ERA	Br/IP	R$	BF/G	OBA	vLH	vRH	H%	xERA	RAR	Ctl	Dom	Cmd	hr/9	G/F	S%	BPV	BPX
RH Starter	98	TOR	10	9	0	209	4.47	1.32	$11	27.7	249	268	220	27%	4.47	33.1	3.5	6.5	1.9	1.5	0.66	72%	37	79
AGE 36 Decline	99	SD	12	12	0	208	4.41	1.38	$12	27.1	266	260	275	29%	4.67	31.6	3.2	5.9	1.9	1.4	0.86	73%	34	74
TYPE	00	SD	10	8	0	168	3.75	1.23	$17	30.3	243	232	245	26%	3.84	42.3	2.9	5.9	2.1	1.2	1.02	74%	48	106
BURN none	01	2NL	15	9	0	220	4.05	1.27	$16	27.1	265	251	281	29%	4.45	38.8	2.3	6.3	2.8	1.4	1.00	74%	55	101
ERA Potl -	02	STL	10	4	0	108	2.50	1.03	$21	23.7	218	182	256	25%	2.70	42.8	2.2	6.8	3.2	0.8	1.07	80%	94	192
Support 4.62	1st Half		5	3	0	63	2.28	1.04	$12	25.1	216			24%	2.87 -	26.9	2.4	6.8	2.8	1.0		85%	82	169
LIMA D+	2nd Half		5	1	0	45	2.81	1.00	$10	22.0	222			26%	2.47	15.9	1.8	6.8	3.8	0.6		74%	113	232
Risk High	03	Proj	10	7	0	140	3.73	1.26	$14	26.6	260			29%	4.04	32.4	2.4	6.5	2.7	1.1	--	74%	66	134

Late career BPI spikes are not common, and are rarely repeated. H% and S% helped his ERA in '02. He'll likely have no such luck in '03.

Wilson,Paul

Wilson,Paul	Yr	Tm	W	L	Sv	IP	ERA	Br/IP	R$	BF/G	OBA	vLH	vRH	H%	xERA	RAR	Ctl	Dom	Cmd	hr/9	G/F	S%	BPV	BPX
RH Starter	98	aaa	4	1	0	38	4.97	1.45	$2	23.7	300			35%	4.50	2.3	2.1	5.9	2.8	0.5		64%	75	145
AGE 30 Peak	99		0	0	0	0	0.00	0.00																
TYPE	00	TAM *	6	9	0	134	3.96	1.24	$12	21.4	252	228	189	29%	3.30 +	35.0	2.6	6.0	2.3	0.5	1.31	68%	72	188
BURN none	01	TAM	8	9	0	151	4.88	1.44	$3	17.8	279	286	270	32%	4.88	12.2	3.1	7.1	2.3	1.3	1.13	69%	52	105
ERA Potl --	02	TAM	6	12	0	193	4.85	1.48	($3)	28.3	287	309	267	30%	5.12	6.6	3.1	5.2	1.7	1.4	1.22	71%	23	43
Support 4.37	1st Half		2	6	0	100	4.23	1.40	$0	28.8	273			29%	4.62	11.8	3.1	5.2	1.7	1.3		74%	30	56
LIMA D	2nd Half		4	6	0	93	5.52	1.57	($3)	27.8	301			32%	5.66	-5.2	3.2	5.1	1.6	1.5		68%	16	30
Risk High	03	Proj	9	11	0	180	4.30	1.44	$5	27.1	283			31%	4.80 -	25.8	3.0	5.6	1.9	1.2	--	73%	37	76

He's been slowly building back his workload over the past three years, but his durability is limited. Hit a wall in Sept., (15 IP, 22 ER), pumping his ERA from 4.14 to 4.85. This is a 160-180 IP pitcher max.

Witasick,Jay

Witasick,Jay	Yr	Tm	W	L	Sv	IP	ERA	Br/IP	R$	BF/G	OBA	vLH	vRH	H%	xERA	RAR	Ctl	Dom	Cmd	hr/9	G/F	S%	BPV	BPX
RH Reliever	98	OAK *	12	10	0	176	4.76	1.36	$10	22.2	265	259	362	30%	4.71	21.2	3.1	7.9	2.5	1.5	1.18	70%	58	123
AGE 30 Peak	99	KC	9	12	0	158	5.58	1.73	($3)	23.0	300	322	286	33%	6.01	6.1	4.7	5.8	1.2	1.3	1.11	70%	16	41
TYPE Power	00	SD	6	10	0	150	5.82	1.67	($6)	20.9	296	287	281	34%	5.90	-3.8	4.4	7.3	1.7	1.4	1.58	68%	31	68
BURN none	01	2TM	8	2	1	79	3.30	1.41	$9	5.4	259	305	271	37%	4.15 -	22.4	3.8	12.1	3.2	0.9	1.42	80%	116	222
ERA Potl +	02	SF	1	0	0	70	2.44	1.16	$7	6.2	230	228	238	28%	2.75	28.3	2.8	7.2	2.5	0.4	1.59	79%	94	193
Support 3.82	1st Half		1	0	0	37	2.18	1.18	$5	6.9	217			27%	2.51	16.3	3.6	7.5	2.1	0.2		81%	93	190
LIMA B+	2nd Half		0	0	0	33	2.74	1.13	$3	5.5	245			29%	3.02	11.9	1.9	6.9	3.6	0.5		77%	106	217
Risk Moderate	03	Proj	3	2	0	75	3.24	1.25	$6	7.1	241			30%	3.51	22.2	3.2	8.4	2.6	0.8	G	77%	87	174

Proof that skills don't cost much. His BPIs rank right up with the best of them, but because he neither racks up wins or saves, he gets overlooked on draft day. But he represents immediate profit to his owners.

Wohlers,Mark

Wohlers,Mark	Yr	Tm	W	L	Sv	IP	ERA	Br/IP	R$	BF/G	OBA	vLH	vRH	H%	xERA	RAR	Ctl	Dom	Cmd	hr/9	G/F	S%	BPV	BPX
RH Reliever	98	ATL *	0	4	8	33	15.18	3.52	($19)	4.9	325	171	297	39%	11.68 +	-44.2	19.5	9.8	0.5	2.2	1.63	56%	-6	
AGE 33 Past	99	ATL *	0	0	0	3	30.00	6.33	($5)	5.6	321			35%	19.43 +	-9.8	45.0	9.0	0.2	3.0		50%	-41	
TYPE	00	CIN *	2	4	0	48	5.60	1.64	($2)	5.9	281	205	183	31%	5.46	0.2	4.9	6.3	1.3	1.3	0.84	68%	25	56
BURN none	01	NYY	4	1	0	67	4.29	1.40	$3	4.8	267	196	267	31%	4.45	10.8	3.3	7.2	2.2	1.1	1.28	72%	58	117
ERA Potl ++	02	CLE	3	4	7	71	4.82	1.37	$4	4.8	262	256	265	30%	3.91 +	2.8	3.3	5.8	1.8	0.8	1.97	65%	52	98
Support 2.02	1st Half		0	1	0	30	6.26	1.62	($3)	5.5	297			36%	4.89 +	-4.7	3.9	7.7	2.0	0.6		60%	66	125
LIMA C+	2nd Half		3	3	7	41	3.75	1.18	$7	4.3	233			25%	3.18 +	7.4	2.9	4.4	1.5	0.9		70%	41	77
Risk Very High	03	Proj	3	4	1	70	4.63	1.46	$1	4.7	273			31%	4.46	6.9	3.6	6.2	1.7	0.9	G	69%	46	95

Got his shot to reclaim a closer's job, but failed. Let's assess:
"T"ALENT: Not nearly closer caliber.
"O"PPORTUNITY: Granted.
"G"UILE: Converted his opps at only 64%.

Wolf,Randy

Wolf,Randy	Yr	Tm	W	L	Sv	IP	ERA	Br/IP	R$	BF/G	OBA	vLH	vRH	H%	xERA	RAR	Ctl	Dom	Cmd	hr/9	G/F	S%	BPV	BPX
LH Starter	98	a/a	11	7	0	173	4.63	1.43	$7	26.9	289			34%	4.67	18.5	2.6	6.9	2.6	0.9		69%	67	131
AGE 26 Growth	99	PHI *	10	14	0	198	4.91	1.51	$3	25.8	268	209	278	32%	4.86	16.9	4.3	8.1	1.9	1.3	0.71	70%	51	111
TYPE Power	00	PHI	11	9	0	206	4.37	1.42	$10	28.0	265	227	276	31%	4.49	34.8	3.6	7.0	1.9	1.1	0.82	72%	52	114
BURN Low	01	PHI	10	11	0	163	3.70	1.23	$14	24.2	246	171	268	30%	3.50	36.4	2.8	8.4	3.0	0.8	0.79	72%	94	174
ERA Potl +	02	PHI	11	9	0	210	3.21	1.12	$24	27.4	225	258	216	26%	3.15	63.1	2.7	7.4	2.7	1.0	0.99	75%	82	168
Support 4.02	1st Half		4	6	0	93	4.35	1.35	$3	26.5	253			28%	4.28	13.8	3.6	6.5	1.8	1.2		71%	46	95
LIMA D+	2nd Half		7	3	0	117	2.31	0.93	$22	28.1	201			24%	2.26	49.3	2.0	8.1	4.0	0.8		81%	123	252
Risk Low	03	Proj	11	10	0	200	3.60	1.22	$18	26.7	241			29%	3.54	49.7	2.9	7.6	2.6	0.9	--	74%	79	158

Pitch Counts

Age	IP	Avg	High	%100+
23	206	110	134	84%
24	163	100	138	52%
25	210	103	126(2)	71%

You have to be at least a little bit concerned.

Wood,Kerry

Wood,Kerry	Yr	Tm	W	L	Sv	IP	ERA	Br/IP	R$	BF/G	OBA	vLH	vRH	H%	xERA	RAR	Ctl	Dom	Cmd	hr/9	G/F	S%	BPV	BPX
RH Starter	98	CHC	13	6	0	166	3.41	1.22	$18	26.4	200	228	169	30%	2.77 +	40.6	4.6	12.6	2.7	0.8	1.02	74%	126	226
AGE 25 Growth	99		0	0	0	0	0.00	0.00																
TYPE Power	00	CHC	8	7	0	137	4.80	1.45	$5	26.0	225	223	229	27%	4.04 +	15.3	5.7	8.7	1.5	1.1	0.98	69%	60	133
BURN Low	01	CHC	12	6	0	174	3.36	1.26	$17	26.0	206	201	203	29%	3.03	46.8	4.8	11.2	2.4	0.8	0.86	76%	106	196
ERA Potl +	02	CHC	12	11	0	213	3.68	1.25	$18	26.9	220	223	219	28%	3.34	50.9	4.1	9.2	2.2	0.9	0.83	73%	85	175
Support 5.85	1st Half		7	5	0	101	4.19	1.30	$8	26.6	204			25%	3.00 +	17.2	5.2	7.6	1.5	0.6		68%	72	147
LIMA B	2nd Half		5	6	0	112	3.21	1.21	$11	27.2	233			31%	3.65	33.7	3.1	10.6	3.4	1.2		79%	107	219
Risk Moderate	03	Proj	12	9	0	200	3.47	1.21	$20	26.6	216			28%	3.17	53.3	3.9	10.1	2.6	0.9	--	75%	98	197

Still has trouble with his control, though he did show some nice improvement in the 2nd half. As well hyped as he has been, he'll probably need to get his Cmd ratio over 3 to move into the true NL Elite. Not likely in '03.

Worrell,Tim

Worrell,Tim	Yr	Tm	W	L	Sv	IP	ERA	Br/IP	R$	BF/G	OBA	vLH	vRH	H%	xERA	RAR	Ctl	Dom	Cmd	hr/9	G/F	S%	BPV	BPX
RH Reliever	98	2AL	2	7	0	103	5.24	1.31	$1	10.1	267	243	277	30%	4.53 +	5.7	2.5	7.2	2.8	1.4	0.97	63%	62	132
AGE 35 Decline	99	OAK	2	2	0	69	4.17	1.49	$2	5.7	262	285	229	32%	4.33	15.7	4.4	8.1	1.8	0.8	0.98	73%	66	165
TYPE Power	00	2TM *	7	6	3	79	3.29	1.46	$11	5.3	268	221	276	30%	4.98 -	26.2	3.9	7.2	1.9	1.5	0.96	84%	39	92
BURN none	01	SF	2	5	0	78	3.46	1.33	$3	4.5	244	248	234	30%	3.38	20.0	3.8	7.3	1.9	0.5	0.94	74%	76	141
ERA Potl -	02	SF	8	2	0	72	2.25	1.18	$14	3.7	213	204	218	26%	2.59	30.9	3.8	6.9	1.8	0.4	0.72	82%	81	166
Support 5.88	1st Half		4	0	0	37	2.19	1.14	$8	3.8	223			28%	2.47	16.2	2.9	7.5	2.6	0.2		80%	103	210
LIMA D+	2nd Half		4	2	0	35	2.31	1.23	$7	3.5	202			24%	2.72	14.7	4.6	6.2	1.3	0.5		83%	64	132
Risk Moderate	03	Proj	4	4	0	75	3.96	1.36	$4	4.4	249			28%	4.13	15.0	3.8	6.7	1.8	1.1	F	74%	50	100

An 82% strand rate and 26% hit rate pushed his ERA under 3.00, but that won't happen again, especially not at age 35. Drop in G/F ratio is a warning sign to his HR rate as well. ERA might actually spike in 2003.

Wright,Danny

	Yr	Tm	W	L	Sv	IP	ERA	Br/IP	R$	BF/G	OBA	vLH	vRH	H%	xERA	RAR	Ctl	Dom	Cmd	hr/9	G/F	S%	BPV	BPX
RH Starter	98		0	0	0	0	0.00	0.00																
AGE 25 Growth	99		0	0	0	0	0.00	0.00																
TYPE	00	aa	2	4	0	43	3.56	1.42	$3	26.7	224			25%	3.70	12.7	5.4	5.7	1.0	0.8		77%	41	97
BURN none	01	CHW *	12	10	0	200	4.37	1.48	$7	26.6	274	264	342	32%	4.58	30.0	3.7	6.6	1.8	0.9	1.62	72%	50	100
ERA Potl -	02	CHW	14	12	0	196	5.19	1.38	$5	25.6	266	257	270	29%	4.66 +	-2.2	3.3	6.2	1.9	1.5	1.13	66%	35	67
Support 5.82	1st Half		5	8	0	94	6.02	1.49	($2)	24.4	283			29%	5.33 +	-11.5	3.3	5.3	1.6	1.6		63%	14	27
LIMA C	2nd Half		9	4	0	102	4.42	1.29	$7	26.8	249			28%	4.05	9.4	3.2	7.2	2.3	1.3		70%	56	105
Risk High	03	Proj	13	12	0	200	4.46	1.37	$10	26.0	262			29%	4.33	24.5	3.3	6.6	2.0	1.2	–	70%	49	100

Some improvement in the 2nd half, which is a good sign, but he'll need to maintain those BPIs for a full year just to become a league average pitcher.

Wright,Jamey

	Yr	Tm	W	L	Sv	IP	ERA	Br/IP	R$	BF/G	OBA	vLH	vRH	H%	xERA	RAR	Ctl	Dom	Cmd	hr/9	G/F	S%	BPV	BPX
RH Starter	98	COL	9	14	0	206	5.68	1.60	($8)	27.4	288	275	311	30%	5.26	-12.2	4.1	3.8	0.9	1.0	1.93	65%	8	14
AGE 28 Pre-Peak	99	COL *	9	10	0	194	6.31	1.79	($13)	27.7	322	331	291	35%	6.45	-19.8	4.1	5.2	1.3	1.3	1.66	66%	10	21
TYPE Power	00	MIL	7	9	0	164	4.11	1.49	$6	27.9	253	266	257	28%	4.11	33.4	4.8	5.3	1.1	0.7	2.15	73%	39	86
BURN Low	01	MIL	11	12	0	194	4.91	1.54	$1	26.2	268	260	282	29%	4.95	11.8	4.5	6.0	1.3	1.2	1.90	71%	29	53
ERA Potl -	02	2NL *	8	14	0	144	5.31	1.60	($3)	25.0	270	271	267	29%	5.04	2.9	5.0	5.4	1.1	1.1	1.70	68%	25	51
Support 2.99	1st Half		2	7	0	58	6.79	1.73	($7)	24.7	302			32%	6.87	-10.4	4.6	6.8	1.5	2.2		66%	1	3
LIMA D	2nd Half		6	7	0	86	4.30	1.50	$3	25.3	246			28%	3.79 +	13.3	5.2	4.5	0.9	0.3		70%	41	85
Risk Moderate	03	Proj	6	9	0	120	4.95	1.58	($1)	25.7	271			30%	4.98	8.1	4.8	5.5	1.1	1.1	G	70%	26	52

Complete record of his PQS-5s:
8/3/99 @CIN 10/1/00 @HOU
6/3/00 vCOL 8/31/01 vHOU
6/19/00 @FLA 5/24/02 vSD
9/4/00 @SD
During the same period, Randy Johnson has had 94 PQS-5s.

Wunsch,Kelly

	Yr	Tm	W	L	Sv	IP	ERA	Br/IP	R$	BF/G	OBA	vLH	vRH	H%	xERA	RAR	Ctl	Dom	Cmd	hr/9	G/F	S%	BPV	BPX
LH Reliever	98	a/a	8	7	0	153	5.59	1.58	($3)	26.5	315			35%	5.49	-3.2	2.5	5.3	2.1	0.9		65%	40	77
AGE 30 Peak	99	a/a	6	2	1	92	3.91	1.55	$6	10.8	292			32%	4.65 -	22.0	3.5	4.5	1.3	0.5		75%	36	83
TYPE Power	00	CHW	6	3	1	61	2.95	1.29	$11	3.1	225	160	275	27%	3.13	24.3	4.3	7.5	1.8	0.6	3.42	79%	74	193
BURN none	01	CHW	2	1	0	22	7.74	1.36	($1)	2.9	252	233	262	27%	4.67 +	-6.7	3.7	6.5	1.8	1.6	2.05	42%	32	64
ERA Potl - - -	02	CHW *	3	1	0	43	3.35	1.60	$2	3.2	266	208	268	31%	4.44 -	10.1	5.2	6.1	1.2	0.6	2.55	80%	44	83
Support 5.40	1st Half		2	0	0	25	3.96	1.64	$1	3.9	291			32%	4.66 -	3.8	4.3	4.0	0.9	0.4		75%	29	55
LIMA B	2nd Half		1	1	0	18	2.50	1.56	$1	2.6	228			28%	4.13 -	6.3	6.5	9.0	1.4	1.0		88%	62	118
Risk Very High	03	Proj	3	3	0	60	4.20	1.50	$1	3.8	259			30%	4.23	9.4	4.7	6.6	1.4	0.8	G	73%	50	102

Came back from rotator cuff surgery with a softer skill set, which is something he could ill afford. A 3.35 ERA will draw some end-game bids, but there are too many holes here to make him draft-worthy.

Yan,Esteban

	Yr	Tm	W	L	Sv	IP	ERA	Br/IP	R$	BF/G	OBA	vLH	vRH	H%	xERA	RAR	Ctl	Dom	Cmd	hr/9	G/F	S%	BPV	BPX
RH Reliever	98	TAM	5	4	1	88	3.88	1.35	$7	5.9	239	222	245	28%	3.98	21.0	4.2	7.9	1.9	1.1	1.38	75%	60	129
AGE 28 Pre-Peak	99	TAM	3	4	0	61	5.90	1.79	($3)	5.7	309	310	342	35%	6.15	-0.2	4.7	6.8	1.4	1.2	1.19	68%	29	72
TYPE Power	00	TAM	7	8	0	137	6.23	1.46	$0	14.0	290	316	258	32%	5.48 +	-5.9	2.8	7.3	2.6	1.7	1.07	60%	45	117
BURN none	01	TAM	4	6	22	62	3.91	1.21	$18	4.7	268	272	252	34%	3.90	13.1	1.6	9.3	5.8	1.0	1.42	71%	149	298
ERA Potl -	02	TAM	7	8	19	69	4.30	1.43	$14	5.5	265	273	246	30%	4.62	7.4	3.8	6.9	1.8	1.3	1.06	74%	43	81
Support 2.22	1st Half		4	3	11	32	5.03	1.58	$7	5.0	290			31%	5.46	0.3	3.9	5.0	1.3	1.4		72%	12	23
LIMA C	2nd Half		3	5	8	37	3.67	1.30	$7	6.0	241			29%	3.88	7.1	3.7	8.6	2.3	1.2		77%	70	133
Risk High	03	Proj	5	7	8	70	4.50	1.44	$7	6.0	270			31%	4.73	8.1	3.6	7.7	2.1	1.3	–	73%	54	109

Failed to follow up on 2001's fine BPIs, which was the first strike against success. Saved only 71% of his opportunities (strike 2) and had an OBA of .280 in first 15 pitches (strike 3). This is not closer worthy.

Yoshii,Masato

	Yr	Tm	W	L	Sv	IP	ERA	Br/IP	R$	BF/G	OBA	vLH	vRH	H%	xERA	RAR	Ctl	Dom	Cmd	hr/9	G/F	S%	BPV	BPX
RH Reliever	98	NYM	6	8	0	171	3.94	1.28	$7	24.8	256	274	240	28%	4.08	29.6	2.8	6.2	2.2	1.2	1.18	73%	52	94
AGE 38 Decline	99	NYM	12	8	0	174	4.40	1.30	$14	23.7	255	278	245	27%	4.20	26.8	3.0	5.4	1.8	1.3	0.86	70%	36	78
TYPE Contact	00	COL	6	15	0	167	5.87	1.52	($4)	25.6	299	282	328	31%	5.85	-5.4	2.9	4.7	1.7	1.7	1.00	65%	7	15
BURN none	01	MON	4	7	0	113	4.78	1.35	$1	11.5	285	278	280	30%	4.95	8.9	2.1	5.0	2.4	1.4	1.16	69%	36	67
ERA Potl -	02	MON	4	9	0	131	4.12	1.34	$4	18.0	279	250	307	30%	4.49	23.5	2.2	5.1	2.3	1.0	1.51	72%	47	97
Support 4.93	1st Half		2	2	0	56	4.16	1.39	$2	13.5	284			31%	4.78 -	9.7	2.4	5.8	2.4	1.1		73%	49	101
LIMA C+	2nd Half		2	7	0	75	4.09	1.30	$3	24.3	275			29%	4.27	13.7	2.0	4.6	2.2	1.0		71%	46	93
Risk High	03	Proj	4	8	0	120	4.58	1.38	$2	17.2	281			30%	4.81	14.1	2.5	4.8	1.9	1.3	G	70%	30	61

Moderate skill set with a few glaring weaknesses. Normally worth an end-game flyer, but not at age 38.

Zambrano,Carlos

	Yr	Tm	W	L	Sv	IP	ERA	Br/IP	R$	BF/G	OBA	vLH	vRH	H%	xERA	RAR	Ctl	Dom	Cmd	hr/9	G/F	S%	BPV	BPX
RH Starter	98		0	0	0	0	0.00	0.00																
AGE 21 Green	99		0	0	0	0	0.00	0.00																
TYPE Power	00	a/a	5	6	6	117	2.62	1.22	$18	11.3	214			26%	2.58	49.3	4.1	6.7	1.6	0.3		78%	78	184
BURN none	01	aaa	11	7	0	157	4.30	1.23	$12	20.4	224			29%	2.91 +	23.6	3.7	9.0	2.4	0.5	1.22	64%	99	191
ERA Potl -	02	CHC	4	8	0	117	3.38	1.40	$6	14.4	225	209	253	28%	3.59	32.5	5.2	8.0	1.5	0.7	2.10	77%	69	142
Support 3.07	1st Half		0	0	0	24	2.24	1.49	$1	5.6	218			30%	3.42 -	10.4	6.3	9.3	1.5	0.4		86%	87	178
LIMA B+	2nd Half		4	8	0	93	3.68	1.38	$5	25.0	227			27%	3.63	22.1	4.9	7.7	1.5	0.8		75%	65	133
Risk X HIGH	03	Proj	8	8	0	160	3.71	1.39	$9	24.6	236			30%	3.47	37.3	4.7	8.3	1.8	0.5	G	73%	80	161

Held his own in AAA at 19 and in the majors at 20, which analysts will tell you is a sure sign of future success. But BPIs did take a step back in '02, so don't be building your team around him just yet.

Zambrano,Victor

	Yr	Tm	W	L	Sv	IP	ERA	Br/IP	R$	BF/G	OBA	vLH	vRH	H%	xERA	RAR	Ctl	Dom	Cmd	hr/9	G/F	S%	BPV	BPX
RH Starter	98		0	0	0	0	0.00	0.00																
AGE 28 Pre-Peak	99	aa	7	2	1	82	5.93	1.84	($2)	9.8	324			39%	6.01	-2.5	4.4	7.1	1.6	0.7		67%	47	110
TYPE Power	00	aaa	0	6	8	62	5.37	1.69	$1	5.4	308			35%	6.00 -	3.2	3.9	6.8	1.7	1.3		71%	32	75
BURN High	01	TAM *	7	4	14	81	3.00	1.26	$18	5.2	237	205	198	30%	3.50 -	27.0	3.4	9.1	2.6	0.9	1.12	80%	91	182
ERA Potl -	02	TAM *	8	9	2	128	5.20	1.59	($0)	11.1	266	292	266	29%	4.93	-1.7	5.1	6.0	1.2	1.2	1.07	69%	27	50
Support 5.29	1st Half		3	4	0	44	5.52	1.55	($1)	6.8	239			26%	4.49 +	-2.5	5.9	6.5	1.1	1.2		66%	33	62
LIMA C+	2nd Half		5	5	2	84	5.04	1.61	($0)	16.5	280			31%	5.16	0.8	4.6	5.7	1.2	1.2		71%	24	45
Risk X HIGH	03	Proj	7	11	0	140	4.76	1.54	$0	22.3	271			31%	4.83	11.5	4.4	7.0	1.6	1.1	–	71%	43	88

	IP	ERA	OBA	Cmd
Starter	65	4.27	.278	1.3
Reliever	49	7.21	.278	0.9

When you come down to it, both choices are equally distasteful... which means, odds are he'll be TAM's Opening Day starter.

Zerbe,Chad

	Yr	Tm	W	L	Sv	IP	ERA	Br/IP	R$	BF/G	OBA	vLH	vRH	H%	xERA	RAR	Ctl	Dom	Cmd	hr/9	G/F	S%	BPV	BPX
LH Reliever	98		0	0	0	0	0.00	0.00																
AGE 31 Peak	99	aa	1	3	0	41	2.85	1.32	$4	24.8	266			28%	3.65 -	15.6	2.6	2.9	1.1	0.4		79%	28	66
TYPE Contact	00	a/a	9	4	0	120	4.80	1.63	$4	21.0	332	222	308	36%	5.52 -	15.4	2.1	4.0	1.9	0.5	6.00	70%	36	87
BURN none	01	SF *	6	4	5	64	3.94	1.44	$8	6.3	288	396	215	32%	4.52 -	12.2	2.7	4.9	1.8	0.7	1.71	74%	45	83
ERA Potl - - -	02	SF *	2	0	0	66	2.59	1.30	$6	5.3	250	247	240	27%	3.42	25.4	3.3	4.1	1.3	0.4	2.00	81%	44	89
Support 3.83	1st Half		2	0	0	43	2.08	1.32	$5	7.0	247			28%	3.24 -	19.5	3.5	4.2	1.2	0.2		84%	49	101
LIMA C+	2nd Half		0	0	0	23	3.54	1.27	$1	3.6	254			27%	3.75	5.9	2.8	3.9	1.4	0.8		74%	34	70
Risk High	03	Proj	2	1	0	50	3.78	1.42	$2	6.2	277			30%	4.19	11.2	3.1	4.0	1.3	0.5	G	74%	34	69

2-0, 3.05 ERA in 56 IP at SF. Even the softest of tossers can succeed for short periods of time. 2nd half fade indicates that NL batters have figured him out. Expect a letdown in '03.

Zito,Barry

	Yr	Tm	W	L	Sv	IP	ERA	Br/IP	R$	BF/G	OBA	vLH	vRH	H%	xERA	RAR	Ctl	Dom	Cmd	hr/9	G/F	S%	BPV	BPX
LH Starter	98		0	0	0	0	0.00	0.00																
AGE 25 Growth	99	a/a	3	1	0	28	4.82	1.57	$2	25.2	269			36%	4.44	3.3	4.8	9.6	2.0	0.6		69%	82	190
TYPE Power	00	OAK *	15	9	0	193	3.44	1.33	$23	25.7	234	194	195	29%	3.28	63.9	4.2	7.3	1.7	0.5	0.82	74%	72	188
BURN Very High	01	OAK	17	8	0	214	3.49	1.23	$23	25.4	234	234	229	29%	3.27	57.2	3.4	8.6	2.6	0.8	0.85	74%	91	182
ERA Potl -	02	OAK	23	5	0	229	2.75	1.14	$32	26.5	220	275	203	25%	2.94	72.2	3.1	7.2	2.3	0.9	0.74	81%	75	141
Support 6.79	1st Half		10	3	0	105	3.59	1.21	$11	25.5	235			27%	3.62	21.3	3.1	8.2	2.7	1.3		76%	75	141
LIMA D	2nd Half		13	2	0	124	2.04	1.07	$21	27.5	207			24%	2.36	50.9	3.1	6.3	2.0	0.7		85%	75	141
Risk High	03	Proj	18	8	0	225	3.48	1.26	$23	26.1	244			29%	3.48	56.9	3.2	7.1	2.2	0.8	F	75%	72	146

Cy Young winner, but he had a little outside help. 25% hit rate and 81% strand artificially lowered his ERA. BPIs were off from 2001. And his workload, well, I wouldn't be signing him to a long term deal, nosireebob.

PQS Pitching Logs:
New Perspectives in PQS

Pure Quality Starts

PQS is the next step in following pitching lines. The old Quality Start method — minimum 6 IP, maximum 3 earned runs — is overly simplistic and does not measure any real skill. Bill James "game score" methodology is better, but is not feasible for quick calculation.

In PQS, we give a starting pitcher credit for exhibiting certain skills in each of his starts. Then by tracking his "PQS Score" over time, we can follow his progress. Here are the criteria...

1. The pitcher must have gone a minimum of 6 innings. This measures stamina. For a 6 IP performance, the pitcher gets 1 point. If he goes less than 5 innings, he automatically gets a total PQS score of zero, no matter what other stats he produces.

2. He must have allowed no more than an equal number of hits to the number of innings pitched. This measures hit prevention and earns him 1 point.

3. His number of strikeouts must be no fewer than two less than his innings pitched (IP minus K must be 2 or less). This measures dominance and earns him 1 point.

4. He must have struck out at least twice as many batters as he walked. This measures command and earns him 1 point.

5. He must have allowed no more than one home run. This measures his ability to keep the ball in the park and earns him 1 point.

At first it may seem like a bit of work, but guaranteed, after a week or so, you'll be able to glance at a pitcher's stat line and immediately determine his PQS score. A perfect PQS score would be 5. Any pitcher who averages 3 or more over the course of the season is probably performing admirably. The nice thing about PQS is it allows you to approach each start as more than an all-or-nothing event.

Note the absence of earned runs. Just as BPV serves as a leading indicator to ERA — without the use of earned runs — so does PQS. No matter how many runs a pitcher allows, if he scores high on the PQS scale, he has hurled a good game in terms of his base skills. The number of runs allowed — a function of not only the pitcher's ability but that of his bullpen and defense — will even out over time.

Embracing Imprecision

Up until now, we've always approached performance measures on an aggregate basis. What is a player's batting average or ERA? What are a player's accumulated BPIs over time? Each individual event that these statistics chronicle gets dumped into a huge pool of data. We then use our formulas to try to sort and slice and manipulate the data into more usable information.

Pure Quality Starts (PQS) take a different approach. It says that the smallest unit of measure should not be the "event" but instead be the "game." Within that game, we can accumulate all the strikeouts, hits and walks, and evaluate that outing as a whole. After all, when a pitcher takes the mound, he is either "on" or "off" his game; he is either dominant or struggling, or somewhere in between.

PQS captures the array of events and slaps an evaluative label on that individual outing. Randy Johnson was a "5" today. Kirk Rueter was a "2." Frank Castillo was a "0." It doesn't matter if a few extra balls got through the infield, or the pitcher was given the hook in the 4th or 6th inning, or the bullpen was able to strand their inherited baserunners. When we look at performance in the aggregate, *those events do matter,* and will affect a pitcher's BPI's and ERA. But with PQS, the minutia is less relevant than the overall performance.

With the addition of Gene McCaffrey's Domination and Disaster percentages, which further sort out the PQS ratings, we've simplified the analysis even more. It's gotten to the point where we know that a PQS-4 or 5 represents the pinnacle of skill, PQS-2 or 3 indicates mid-level skill, and PQS-0 or 1 is a car wreck.

The DOM/DIS percentages allow us to judge not only a pitcher's overall skill in a given game, but also his game-to-game consistency. For starting pitchers, probably more than any other player, the differentiation between skill and consistency is important. When we use traditional gauges to evaluate starters in the aggregate, skill and consistency are lumped together, and we lose the advantage that evaluating the two elements separately provides us.

Is this simplification of performance measurement a good thing? I think it is. We often say that baseball is a game of inches, and have demonstrated proof that the differences in certain established norms of performance are more perception than reality. More to the point, what can be concluded about the differences between the following performances?

IP	H	ER	BB	K	HR
3.1	7	4	2	3	0
4.1	8	7	1	2	2
2.2	6	7	2	1	3
1.2	5	5	2	1	0

All of these performances generated a PQS score of 0. All of them were disasters, separated perhaps only by how much patience the manager had in leaving this pitcher out on the mound. Yet, in figuring Wilson Alvarez's ERA, each line will have a different impact *even though the skills demonstrated in these four starts could be considered identical.*

PQS says that a disaster is a disaster, no matter how long the pitcher goes or how many runs he gives up. Similarly...

IP	H	ER	BB	K	HR
6.0	3	1	1	7	1
8.0	6	0	0	11	1
7.0	5	5	2	8	1
9.0	2	0	3	7	0
7.1	7	3	2	7	1

All of these scored a 5 on the PQS scale. All of them displayed an equally elite level of raw skill. The only differences between these outings were a few extra balls making their way between the fielders, a relief pitcher failing to strand a few acquired baserunners, or the manager deciding to pull the pitcher an inning or two early to get a pinch-hitter into a close game.

But it's enough for us to view all five of Vicente Padilla's performances as equivalent in terms of the level of skill displayed. That's the beauty of PQS.

For our purposes in projecting player performance for fantasy league applications, it is becoming more and more apparent that less is more. If we embrace a certain level of imprecision in our analyses, we open ourselves up to more flexibility in decision-making. We don't get hung up on choosing between a 3.45 ERA and a 3.75 ERA — which, in the grand scheme of things, might represent identical levels of skill — and focus instead on general benchmarks, percentage plays, changes from year to year, and leveraging market perception to our advantage.

Despite all this, we still need to make sure we have a *general* sense of what level of skill each point in the PQS scale is measuring. One of the obstacles we face as fantasy leaguers is the challenge of bringing back all this data to our games. It's nice to know that a pitcher has a 2.3 PQS average, but how will that translate to more Rotisserie points or sim game victories? Do we really know what a PQS-5 is, other than it being something "very good?"

We routinely evaluate each player using our litany of BPIs, but we can do the same to evaluate the evaluators. Exactly what does a typical PQS performance look like?

PQS	5	4	3	2	1	0
%	18%	23%	23%	14%	5%	18%
ERA	1.88	2.82	3.93	5.78	7.11	12.89
xERA	1.54	2.87	4.22	6.38	7.64	11.33
Br/IP	0.88	1.10	1.36	1.67	1.91	2.56
OOB	232	273	317	364	395	467
bb/9	2.0	2.3	3.2	3.6	4.2	5.7
k/9	9.2	6.7	5.2	4.6	3.7	5.9
Cmd	4.6	2.9	1.6	1.3	0.9	1.0
HR/9	0.5	0.8	1.0	1.7	2.0	2.8
BPV	160	94	40	-2	-29	-51

The assumption inherent in the PQS model is that each step along the scale is of equal distance. That turns out to be a fallacy. PQS-4's and 5's still represent the elite performances, but once we drop below a score of 3, the levels plummet, and quickly. In fact, while we typically define a "disaster" performance as a PQS 0 or 1, an argument can be made that any performance of PQS-2 or less could be considered equally disastrous.

We've looked upon a PQS-3 as an average level of play, but it seems that such a stat line is really the absolute *minimum* necessary to describe an acceptable outing. If PQS-3 is to be considered the "floor," do the remaining BPIs reflect the same thing? In some cases, they don't, requiring better performance to reach acceptable levels. We generally consider a strikeout rate of 6.0 as the minimum necessary for success, but a PQS-3 only generates a rate of 5.2. Similarly, we require a minimum command ratio of 2.0, but a PQS-3 only generates 1.6.

Given these facts, we need to push our expectations higher, looking more to PQS-4's and 5's as acceptable levels of play. And that means the DOM/DIS percentages become even more important in evaluating performance.

If we were to re-sort this data into our more familiar DOM/DIS ranges, the difference in performance becomes much more notably delineated...

PQS	DOM	2/3	DIS
%	41%	37%	23%
ERA	2.39	4.58	11.19
xERA	2.26	4.98	10.24
Br/IP	1.00	1.47	2.37
OOB	.255	.335	.448
bb/9	2.1	3.4	5.3
k/9	7.8	5.0	5.2
Cmd	3.6	1.5	1.0
HR/9	0.6	1.3	2.5
BPV	123	25	-44

The first thing we notice is that the percent of starts in each category shows that we've set the bar for DOM/DIS appropriately high. The benchmarks we've been using say that we should target pitchers with at least 50% DOM starts and no more than 20% DIS starts, two levels that seem reasonable given the league averages of 41%/23%.

More importantly, the mid-range now looks much more "average." This further simplification muddies the sharp difference between PQS-2's and 3's. A good thing? I'm not sure. Can we reasonably conclude that a PQS-2 is really all that different from a PQS-3? Or should PQS-2 be lumped in with the rest of the PQS-0 and PQS-1 disasters?

We'd have to play with the numbers a bit more to answer these questions, but I'm not sure that is an effort worth expending. It is enough to categorize levels of skill using broad strokes, and know intuitively that there is going to be some variability within those levels due to nothing more than chance.

But overall, a dominant performance is a dominant performance, whether it's Randy Johnson hurling yet another 8-hit, 14-strikeout "gem" or Dan Reichert throwing a 7-inning 6-hitter for his only PQS-5 of the season. And a disaster is still a disaster, whether the pitcher is given the hook in the first or allowed to "take one for the team."

Skill versus Consistency

DOM/DIS percentages open up a new perspective. What DOM/DIS provides us with is two separate scales of performance, each measuring a different aspect of skill. In tandem, however, they measure something completely different -- *consistency*. This is important because a pitcher might possess incredible skill but be unable to sustain it on a start-by-start basis. His seasonal stat line might be identical to another pitcher who possessed less skill, but was more consistent. ERA's, WHIP's, and even BPI's don't capture that subtle difference.

DOM/DIS *does* capture that difference, and in doing so, helps us identify pitchers who might be better or worse than their stats -- and sabermetrics -- indicate.

Let's start with some basics...

Domination Per Cent (DOM%) measures the portion of a pitcher's starts that scored a 4 or 5 on the PQS scale. DOM% can run from 0% (indicating no dominating starts) to 100% (indicating all dominating starts).

Disaster Per Cent (DIS%) measures the portion of a pitcher's starts that scored a 0 or 1 on the PQS scale. DIS% can run from 0% (indicating no disastrous starts) to 100% (indicating all disastrous starts).

These scales are independent of each other, but can paint interesting, and often bizarre pictures when observed together in light of SKILL and CONSISTENCY. See if you can follow along...

- *The best possible DOM/DIS rating is 100/0.* This represents the pinnacle of skill *and* the pinnacle of consistency.
- *Would the worst possible rating be 0/100?* Not really. This represents the lowest level of skill but a high level of consistency. Consistently bad.
- *Would the worst possible rating be 0/0?* No again. This actually represents a higher level of skill than above, and an equally high level of consistency.
- *How about 50/50?* Um, no. This scenario does represent the pinnacle of *inconsistency,* but the skill level here is moderately high.

The fact is, it is possible to have the highest skill and the best consistency. In fact, *any* rating with a zero on one side might be considered highly consistent. However, it is impossible to have the lowest skill and the worst consistency. A pitcher can be consistently bad, but if he is bad *and* inconsistent, that means he does have some good outings.

Got all that? It's important. Why?

Take my friend, Todd Ritchie. Please.

Back in 1999, he posted a 3.50 ERA along with some moderately good BPIs... 2.0 command, 2.8 bb/9, 0.9 HR rate. These levels indicated growth from prior years, and we projected the trend to continue in 2000.

We, er... I was wrong.

A scan of his PQS log that year revealed very few truly dominating starts, but also very few truly disastrous ones. His DOM/DIS rating was 38/12. Using our 50/20 minimum baseline for success, Ritchie's success that year looks more like it was based on the avoidance of disaster than any display of dominating skill. In the years since then, he has managed to keep his DIS under 20%, but his DOM has yet to crack 50%. And his ERA has yet to come within a run of his 1999 line.

In general, a 3.50 ERA is not an easy feat. In fact, over the past few years, all the other starting pitchers who posted approximately 3.50 ERAs also had markedly different looking DOM/DIS scores...

PITCHER	YR	ERA	DOM%	DIS%
===========	===	====	====	====
Mussina,M	99	3.50	55	13
Schilling,C	99	3.55	71	4
Clemens,R	01	3.52	70	3
Mulder,M	01	3.46	56	15
Park,C	01	3.50	66	11
Zito,B	01	3.49	57	11

Disaster avoidance seems to be common among these 3.50 hurlers. However, unlike Ritchie, all exhibited far more dominance. The difference between these DOM levels and Ritchie's 38% was anywhere from 6 to 12 more dominating starts over the course of the season.

This all leads to the question, "what is the optimal balance between skill and consistency that leads to success?"

Which of these pitchers would you most want to own?

PITCHER	DOM%	DIS%
========	====	====
A	68	27
B	50	13
C	39	6

It's a tough choice. Is it more important to demonstrate a high level of skill or can a pitcher succeed by avoiding disaster? Ritchie may have already answered the question; still, he did post that 3.50 ERA in 1999. The answer...

PITCHER	YR	ERA	DOM%	DIS%
===========	==	====	=====	====
A Wood,K	01	3.36	68	27
B Wolf,R	00	4.37	50	13
C Leiter,A	99	4.23	39	6

Domination wins -- this time -- but only because we might not have a clear picture of consistency. Yet.

One way to measure consistency is to track the variance between DOM and DIS rates. The larger the variance, the higher the consistency of good or bad starts. We can call this the *Consistency Variance* (CVar).

In the previous example, Kerry Wood's CVar was 41%. Randy Wolf's was 37% and Al Leiter's was 33%. So, not only did Wood post the most dominating starts of this trio, he was also the most consistent. Perhaps a pitcher's increased consistency can offset an elevated Disaster rate. Perhaps that is why Wood posted the lowest ERA.

It appears that consistency does matter, but how much? The following grid begins to help us evaluate...

	DOM%				
DIS%	0%	30%	40%	50%	60+%
====	====	====	====	====	====
0%	-A-	4.46	3.89	3.47	3.09
10%	4.55	4.49	4.32	4.23	3.71
20%	4.83	4.70	4.56	4.50	3.95
30%	5.53	5.08	4.92	-B-	-B-
40+%	5.90	-B-	-B-	-B-	-C-

How to use this chart... Increasing domination moves left to right. Increasing disaster moves top to bottom. Increasing positive consistency moves left to right. Increasing negative consistency moves top to bottom. Increasing *inconsistency* moves top left to bottom right.

Note that the spread of ERA's goes pretty much as we'd expect them to. Our 50/20 success baseline equates to a 4.50 ERA, which these days, is probably the minimum level at which we'd consider rostering a pitcher for our fantasy teams.

Also note that there are certain outlying levels of consistency and inconsistency that major league pitchers simply do not reach. "A," "B" and "C" represent those levels; there were no pitchers with DOM/DIS rates in those cells. We can call this phenomenon, and the limits shown above, as the *consistency threshold.*

There were no pitchers with both a DOM% under 30% and a DIS% under 10%. "A" represents the height of consistent mediocrity, those PQS-2's and 3's. On the other end of the scale are the "B" and "C" scenarios, pitchers whose performances swing from domination to disaster with wanton abandon.

"C" represents the pinnacle of inconsistency. These are hurlers with no middle ground, who pitch only at either extreme of the scale. This is theoretical, of course. No pitchers are that schizophrenic.

The magic of this chart... If we were to extrapolate the expected ERA's for each cell outside of the consistency threshold (A, B, C), the ERA for "A" would be nearly identical to the ERA of "C" (and would be around 4.50). It's a graphic display of the old question we've bandied about here over the years... "Which would you rather have, a pitcher with PQS scores of 3,3,3,3 or 5,0,5,0?" Their ERA's, as shown above, would be about the same.

qERA

The DOM/DIS grid above allows us to compare domination and disaster performances, and calculate an expected ERA based entirely on a pitcher's overall game-by-game performance. This is, in fact, an ERA based purely on PQS, and so we can call it the PQS ERA, or *qERA* for short.

We can now look at a pitcher's DOM/DIS percentages, and using the above as a lookup table, figure out at what ERA level he should be performing at. But first, we need to do two things... Replace the missing A/B/C cells with data, and explode the chart so that we can easily get down to the detail of a 57/19 DOM/DIS performance, for instance. We can do this by means of extrapolating the current data. Filling in the blanks gives us this:

	DOM%				
DIS%	0%	30%	40%	50%	60+%
====	====	====	====	====	====
0%	4.50	4.46	3.89	3.47	3.09
10%	4.55	4.49	4.32	4.23	3.71
20%	4.83	4.70	4.56	4.50	3.95
30%	5.53	5.08	4.92	4.71	4.39
40+%	5.90	5.49	5.21	4.96	4.67

The exploded table is huge, needless to say, but you can still get a sense of where pitchers fall from the above.

And we can now go back to the earlier charts and add some more information...

PITCHER	ERA	DOM%	DIS%	qERA
==========	====	=====	====	====
Wood,K	3.36	68	27	3.50
Wolf,R	4.37	50	13	4.23
Leiter,A	4.23	39	6	4.29

The relative ERA's remain the same, but the range in value is now a little closer. Wood overachieved slightly when he posted a 3.36 ERA in 2001. Is this 3.50 qERA more predictive of his ERA in 2002? He finished at 3.68. A single data point, but interesting.

Even more interesting is that Wood's xERA in 2001 was only 3.03. We've been using xERA as a predictive measure, but in this case it failed. Could it be because xERA is just another gauge that looks at performance in the aggregate? Let's fill out this table...

PITCHER	ERA	xERA	qERA
==========	====	====	====
Wood,K	3.36	3.03	3.50
Wolf,R	4.37	4.49	4.23
Leiter,A	4.23	4.06	4.29

Readers have often asked me, when trying to project future ERA, should they look at a pitcher's projected ERA or projected xERA, and I've always told them that reality probably exists somewhere in between. In these cases, it seems that reality rests squarely between xERA and qERA.

But this is a small sample size. Trying to measure overall performance using PQS scores, and then converting it to an aggregate number like an ERA, has its obstacles. But it is intriguing nonetheless. There is more work to be done, but not today.

I leave you with one pitcher's three-year scan, from the accompanying PQS logs. Meet Frank Castillo:

YEAR	ERA	xERA	qERA
==========	====	====	====
2000	3.59	3.48	**4.37**
2001	**4.23**	3.96	**5.08**
2002	**5.08**	4.50	4.40

His qERA in 2000 accurately projected the rise in his 2001 ERA. Then his 2001 qERA *nailed* his 2002 ERA. Just one player, for sure, but enough to open our eyes to the possibilities.

The following pitching logs include:

- Up to three years of data for all pitchers who had at least five starts in 2002.
- Number of starts in that year. (No.)
- Start-by-start listing of PQS scores, separated by half season. These are not time-phased, so any gaps between half seasons do not necessarily represent gaps of time.
- Average pitch counts for all starts (PC)
- Domination and Disaster percentages (DOM, DIS)
- Earned Run Average (ERA)
- Expected Earned Run Average (xERA)
- PQS Earned Run Average (qERA)

PQS PITCHING LOGS

Pitcher	Year	No.	FIRST HALF	SECOND HALF	PC	DOM	DIS	ERA	xERA	qERA
Abbott,Paul	2000	26	3 0 4 0 4 1 4 0 5 4 5	2 3 4 1 3 3 0 4 3 3 4 3 3 2 0	97	35%	27%	4.22	4.12	4.82
	2001	27	0 3 4 5 0 3 2 3 5 2 3 3 4	2 5 3 5 4 3 4 0 2 2 3 3 1 3	100	30%	15%	4.25	4.23	4.60
	2002	5	0 2 3 0 0		91	0%	60%	12.12	8.60	9.02
Acevedo,Jose	2001	18	0 0 5 3	4 0 1 3 0 5 4 0 5 5 0 5 4 4	85	50%	39%	5.07	4.60	4.87
Adams,Terry	2001	22	0 5 2 2 3 5 4	3 5 1 5 0 4 5 3 0 4 5 4 4 3 3	100	50%	18%	4.33	3.81	4.37
	2002	19	3 2 1 3 5 0 5 2 4 3 0 3 5 3 3 3 0	0 1	90	21%	32%	4.37	3.90	5.21
Affeldt,Jeremy	2002	7	0 0 3 3 0 5 0		86	14%	57%	4.45	4.47	7.77
Alvarez,Wilson	2002	10	0 4 0 5 0 3 1 4 0	0	81	30%	60%	4.88	5.05	7.45
Anderson,Brian	2000	32	1 3 2 4 2 3 2 4 4 3 0 4 0 3 4 4 2	5 4 1 3 2 0 0 4 3 0 4 5 4 2 2	93	38%	22%	4.05	4.66	4.64
	2001	22	0 0 3 2 3 5 2 3 4 4 5	4 3 3 0 0 3 2 0 0 3 0	81	23%	32%	5.21	5.44	5.21
	2002	24	0 0 4 2 5 3 2 4 1 3 0 4 3	3 2 5 4 4 1 4 3 3 0 0	87	33%	29%	4.79	4.80	4.90
Anderson,Jimmy	2000	26	0 4 3 0 2 4 0 0 0 3 0 3	3 3 4 4 4 0 3 0 4 2 2 0 0 1	87	23%	42%	4.93	4.96	5.50
	2001	34	3 0 4 5 3 2 3 2 4 1 5 2 3 5 1 3 0 2	4 2 3 0 0 2 3 3 2 0 3 4 2 3 3 3	93	21%	21%	5.11	4.67	4.75
	2002	25	2 3 4 1 0 2 3 1 3 1 0 3 1 3 1 3 0 1	0 3 2 2 3 2 0	86	4%	44%	5.46	5.80	5.90
Appier,Kevin	2000	31	3 3 4 2 3 3 0 5 1 4 4 3 3 2 2 4	2 3 3 5 3 0 2 3 5 4 0 4 2 4 2	108	32%	13%	4.52	4.78	4.49
	2001	33	5 2 2 4 2 3 0 3 4 5 5 5 5 0 5 5 5	5 5 0 3 5 3 2 5 0 4 3 3 4 5 5	100	58%	12%	3.58	3.40	3.97
	2002	32	2 5 5 0 4 4 4 5 4 2 3 0 0 0 5 3 4	5 2 3 4 4 2 3 4 3 5 5 3 0 1 4	99	50%	19%	3.93	4.24	4.37
Armas Jr.,Tony	2000	17	2 3 4 3 5 3 0 0 2 3 0	1 0 3 5 2 0	88	18%	35%	4.42	3.97	5.45
	2001	34	4 2 5 3 3 5 3 4 5 5 3 3 4 4 4 3 0 5 4	5 5 0 4 0 5 4 5 3 5 5 0 1 3 0	99	56%	18%	4.04	3.86	4.10
	2002	29	2 5 3 4 5 5 4 4 1 4 3 3 2 3 0 5 5 2	2 0 4 0 0 0 4 5 4 3 4	94	48%	21%	4.45	4.27	4.53
Arrojo,Rolando	2000	32	2 5 0 0 2 0 4 0 5 2 3 4 4 3 4 3	1 5 4 3 0 3 5 5 3 4 0 5 4 0 4 3	90	44%	25%	5.64	4.95	4.74
	2001	9	2 3 4	5 0 5 5 5 0	83	56%	22%	3.49	3.12	4.23
	2002	8	3 5 5 5 0	2 0 0	70	38%	38%	5.00	3.97	5.13
Arroyo,Bronson	2000	12	1 2 0 2	3 3 4 5 0 3 0 0	81	17%	42%	5.16	4.73	5.60
	2001	13	3 3 0 0 0 1 0 1	3 1 3 0 3	78	0%	62%	4.79	4.64	9.02
	2002	4	0	2 4 3	79	25%	25%	4.00	4.70	4.93
Asencio,Miguel	2002	21	3 3 3 3 1 0 2	3 0 2 0 3 3 1 2 4 3 2 4 2 3	91	10%	24%	5.12	5.31	4.79
Ashby,Andy	2000	32	2 4 2 3 0 2 4 5 0 0 1 3 1 4 3 3	3 0 5 4 0 4 3 0 1 5 0 3 3 5 2 3	92	28%	31%	4.93	4.82	5.13
	2001	2	3 3		85	0%	0%	4.02	5.40	4.50
	2002	30	5 3 2 4 5 2 4 3 5 3 4 2 3 4 0 2 3	1 3 1 3 4 5 3 3 2 0 2 0 0	91	30%	20%	3.93	4.21	4.71
Astacio,Pedro	2000	32	3 0 5 2 2 3 5 3 5 4 1 5 5 1 2 0 4 5	3 3 4 5 5 0 4 3 5 1 2 0 0 0	100	41%	28%	5.28	5.26	4.74
	2001	26	5 4 4 5 4 0 2 0 4 5 3 5 0 3 2 3 2 5	3 5 0 4 3 4 4 5	99	54%	15%	5.11	4.61	4.37
	2002	31	4 4 5 2 4 4 4 5 4 2 3 5 4 5 3 2 0	2 4 5 4 5 2 0 1 4 4 0 0 5 2	97	58%	16%	4.81	4.69	4.10
Bacsik,Mike	2002	9	2	4 0 5 2 3 1 0 2	94	22%	33%	4.42	5.29	5.21
Baez,Danys	2002	26	3 1 0 4 4 3 5 4 3 3 4 5 2 5 3 0 4	5 3 4 0 2 2 3 3 5	104	42%	15%	4.42	4.07	4.44
Baldwin,James	2000	28	3 4 0 2 2 5 3 3 1 5 4 5 4 0 3 3 0	4 0 3 4 5 2 1 3 0 0 0	97	32%	32%	4.65	4.99	5.08
	2001	28	3 0 2 4 3 2 0 4 0 2 3 3 1 0	4 4 4 5 5 5 3 3 4 0 4 2 2 3	98	36%	21%	4.42	4.98	4.64
	2002	23	5 4 0 3 0 2 3 3 2 5 5 0 4 3 3 2 3	4 4 1 5 0 0	88	35%	26%	5.28	5.56	4.82
Batista,Miguel	2000	9	0 1 2 3 2 0 3 2 2		91	0%	33%	8.03	7.67	5.53
	2001	18	1 0 0 0 5 4 1 2	2 2 4 3 4 4 0 5 5 2	87	39%	33%	3.36	3.27	5.00
	2002	29	3 2 3 4 5 3 0 4 2 5 3 2 0 4	3 2 5 4 3 3 5 2 4 0 3 3 3 1 3	92	31%	14%	4.30	3.60	4.49
Beckett,Josh	2001	4		4 5 4 5	87	100%	0%	1.50	2.40	2.00
	2002	21	4 4 4 5 3 2 5 5 0 0	3 5 4 4 3 0 3 0 0 0 3	83	43%	29%	4.12	3.77	4.74
Beimel,Joe	2001	15	3 4 0 1 1 0 2	2 2 2 1 1 0 0 0	77	7%	60%	5.24	5.05	8.72
	2002	8	4 1 4 3 0	5 2 2	82	38%	25%	4.66	4.84	4.82
Bell,Rob	2000	26	5 4 1 0 4 5 0 3 5 0 5 3 0 0 0	3 3 2 0 3 3 3 0 4 3 4	86	31%	35%	4.87	5.01	5.19
	2001	27	3 4 4 0 0 2 5 0 2 0 2 0 4	3 4 1 0 2 3 5 3 0 4 4 1 0 1	89	30%	41%	6.34	6.21	5.29
	2002	15	4 4 1 0 5 5 3 4 1	4 1 2 2 3 0	97	40%	33%	6.22	5.68	4.92
Benes,Alan	2002	7		3 3 0 5 3 0 5	91	29%	29%	4.38	4.24	4.93
Benes,Andy	2000	27	1 3 5 5 5 3 5 4 4 1 3 4 5 4 4 3 5	3 3 0 2 2 3 1 3 3 4	102	44%	15%	4.88	5.16	4.44
	2001	19	0 3 2 2 0 5 1 4 3 0 4 3 5 3 0 0 0	3 5	95	26%	37%	7.39	6.88	5.27
	2002	17	0 0 0	0 0 3 5 3 3 5 2 3 4 1 3 4 2	94	24%	35%	2.78	3.72	5.36
Benoit,Joaquin	2002	14	3 2	3 4 0 5 3 0 4 0 0 2 4 0	97	29%	36%	5.36	5.04	5.27
Benson,Kris	2000	32	4 3 0 4 5 4 3 3 5 3 5 5 4 4 4 4 3 4	0 5 5 4 3 4 2 0 4 3 4 3 5 3	108	59%	9%	3.85	4.02	3.68
	2002	25	0 5 0 0 2 2 0 0 3 3 5	1 1 0 3 2 3 2 4 4 4 1 4 1 1	83	24%	44%	4.32	4.98	5.50
Bere,Jason	2000	31	5 5 1 2 3 0 2 3 3 0 0 0 4 4 5 5 5 3	0 5 4 5 0 0 5 3 0 4 0 0 2	97	39%	35%	5.48	5.23	5.13
	2001	32	3 5 5 5 0 5 0 4 0 3 4 2 3 3 4 5	5 3 5 3 5 5 0 4 0 5 4 0 5 0 2 3	93	50%	22%	4.31	3.99	4.50
	2002	16	5 4 0 0 3 3 2 4 1 3 4 5 5 5 0	0	86	44%	31%	5.72	5.33	4.92
Bernero,Adam	2000	5		4 4 3 0 1	88	40%	40%	3.35	3.38	5.21
	2002	11	4 3 0 3 5 4 3 0 0	2 0	92	27%	36%	6.24	5.84	5.27
Biddle,Rocky	2001	21	3 4 3 2 3 2 3 0 3 5 0 4 4 3 5	3 4 0 1 3 5	91	33%	19%	5.41	4.81	4.60
	2002	7	0 0 0 3 3 3 1		72	0%	57%	4.09	4.62	8.24
Brown,Kevin	2000	33	4 2 3 5 4 5 4 4 4 5 5 4 5 4 5 3 5	3 5 4 4 5 4 0 5 4 5 5 3 3 5 5 3	105	76%	3%	2.58	2.53	2.84
	2001	19	5 3 5 5 5 5 5 0 3 2 3 5 2	4 2 1 3 5 2	93	47%	11%	2.66	2.81	4.28
	2002	10	0 5 0 4 4 5 4 2 0	3	75	50%	30%	4.86	4.94	4.71
Buehrle,Mark	2000	3		5 2 0	95	33%	33%	3.56	3.89	5.08
	2001	32	4 0 2 3 5 3 2 4 4 3 4 4 3 3 3 4	4 5 5 3 4 3 2 3 3 4 4 0 3 3 2 5	103	44%	6%	3.30	3.07	4.11
	2002	34	5 4 3 4 4 0 5 3 4 3 4 5 3 4 2 4 2 2 4	5 3 3 4 2 3 4 5 3 4 1 3 4 2 4	103	53%	6%	3.58	3.74	3.85
Burba,Dave	2000	32	3 0 4 3 5 5 5 0 4 5 4 2 2 3 2 5 2	4 4 3 5 0 4 4 3 3 4 2 5 3 3 0	103	47%	13%	4.47	4.57	4.28
	2001	27	5 0 4 3 3 3 4 0 5 2 2 0 5 0 4 2 0	5 4 4 0 0 4 3 0 0 4	88	41%	33%	6.23	5.47	4.92
	2002	22	3 2 2 5 0 5 4 4 3 2 2 2 0 4 3 2 0	3 2 2 4 2	95	27%	14%	5.21	3.79	4.50
Burkett,John	2000	22	0 0 5 5 4 3 0 5 5 5 2 3	3 0 4 1 5 2 2 3 4 2	92	41%	23%	4.90	5.21	4.56
	2001	34	2 0 4 5 5 4 5 5 5 2 5 5 5 1 5 5 5 5 2	3 5 4 5 5 1 4 5 4 2 0 2 3 2 3	97	62%	12%	3.04	3.05	3.71
	2002	29	2 5 5 4 4 3 3 1 2 3 3 5 2 2	3 4 2 5 0 4 0 3 2 0 3 4 0 5 5	93	38%	17%	4.53	4.99	4.52
Burnett,A.J.	2000	13		5 0 2 4 3 3 5 5 2 4 3 0 4	104	46%	15%	4.82	4.40	4.40
	2001	27	4 4 2 0 3 4 4 5 1 4 0 3	4 2 3 3 3 0 3 4 1 4 4 5 3 5 5	103	48%	19%	4.06	3.70	4.40
	2002	29	5 3 5 4 4 3 3 5 2 3 5 4 4 4 5 3 4 5 5	5 0 5 5 5 3 5 5 4 4	110	72%	3%	3.31	2.71	2.99
Byrd,Paul	2000	15	0 0 5 4 4 0 4 3 0 5 2 5 3	3 0	91	40%	33%	6.51	5.54	4.92
	2001	16	3 2 2 2 3 0	3 1 4 4 2 5 3 0 3 2	90	19%	19%	4.45	4.86	4.65
	2002	33	3 4 4 4 3 4 3 5 4 4 3 0 2 0 2 4 1 1	3 3 5 4 4 2 4 4 4 2 0 1 5 4 2	97	48%	18%	3.91	3.94	4.40
Cabrera,Jose	2002	11	0 4 3 0 4 2	2 3 0 3 3	90	18%	27%	6.82	6.61	5.03
Callaway,Mickey	2002	6		4 5 4 0 0 5	90	67%	33%	4.24	3.62	4.29
Carpenter,Chris	2000	27	3 3 0 4 4 3 3 4 4 1 0 3 3 3 0 0 0 3	2 0 0 0 2 3 4 4 0	96	22%	37%	6.27	5.84	5.36
	2001	34	5 5 3 2 5 3 3 0 4 4 5 3 3 2 0 4 4 3	5 3 0 3 0 0 2 1 5 1 5 2 5 0 3 5	97	38%	24%	4.10	4.72	4.64
	2002	13	0 0 1 3 3 2	5 3 4 3 0 3 3	90	15%	31%	5.30	5.61	5.29

PQS PITCHING LOGS

Pitcher	Year	No.	FIRST HALF	SECOND HALF	PC	DOM	DIS	ERA	xERA	qERA
Castillo,Frank	2000	24	0 5 0 0 3 4 4 5 4 3 3 4 5 3 4 2 4	4 3 5 4 0 3 5	94	54%	17%	3.59	3.48	4.37
	2001	26	2 0 4 1 3 0 1 3 4 5 4 2 3 3 0 0	0 2 5 3 4 3 4 0 2 5	86	31%	31%	4.23	3.96	5.08
	2002	23	4 4 4 0 3 5 3 3 4 4 4 0 2 3 3 3 2	4 0 0 4 4 4	97	48%	17%	5.08	4.50	4.40
Chacon,Shawn	2001	27	2 0 4 3 5 4 1 5 5 3 3 3 2	5 5 2 2 2 0 2 4 3 4 5 3 3 3	101	37%	11%	4.79	4.89	4.41
	2002	21	0 5 3 2 3 4 4 3 3 3 4 0 3	3 3 0 4 0 0 3 2	96	24%	24%	5.75	5.61	4.75
Chen,Bruce	2000	14		4 3 0 5 4 4 3 5 5 3 0 4 2 3	97	50%	14%	3.29	3.66	4.23
	2001	27	2 3 4 4 2 3 0 3 3 5 1 5 0 3 3 0	3 5 4 3 3 3 2 0 5 0 0	91	26%	26%	4.68	4.72	4.93
	2002	6	0 0 3 2 0 0		70	0%	67%	5.61	5.11	9.80
Clemens,Roger	2000	31	3 4 2 5 5 5 5 0 4 0 5 2 0 5 4	3 5 4 3 5 2 3 2 4 4 5 5 4 4 4 0	107	61%	13%	3.70	3.92	3.71
	2001	33	4 4 4 3 4 4 3 5 5 4 3 3 5 5 5 5 4 5	4 1 3 4 5 5 5 3 4 5 3 3 4 4 3	108	70%	3%	3.52	3.55	2.99
	2002	29	0 5 3 5 5 4 5 3 5 5 0 4 5 5 2 0 2 2	4 5 2 4 5 2 5 5 2 4 4	104	62%	10%	4.35	3.73	3.71
Clement,Matt	2000	34	5 3 5 2 4 4 0 3 2 5 4 4 0 3 1 2 4 3 3	5 0 0 4 4 3 3 1 3 4 2 4 4 5 2	104	44%	18%	5.14	4.52	4.44
	2001	31	2 5 2 5 2 0 0 3 5 2 3 0 5 3 1 3 0 0	5 3 0 4 5 3 4 3 4 3 0 5 0	90	32%	29%	5.06	4.46	4.90
	2002	32	3 5 5 3 4 0 3 3 5 5 5 3 3 4 2 5 3	5 5 3 3 5 4 2 4 3 5 5 0 3 5 0	101	50%	9%	3.60	3.09	3.85
Coggin,David	2000	5	4 1 3 4	2	97	40%	20%	5.23	4.86	4.56
	2001	16	0 5	5 2 1 2 4 4 4 4 3 0 4 4 0 2	90	50%	25%	4.22	4.51	4.61
	2002	7	0 2 0 4 0	0 0	69	14%	71%	4.68	3.71	9.84
Colon,Bartolo	2000	30	3 4 0 5 5 0 3 5 4 3 3 5 0 4 5	1 3 2 5 4 5 0 2 5 3 4 5 5 5 5	109	57%	17%	3.88	3.86	4.10
	2001	34	4 3 4 5 4 5 3 2 5 3 3 2 5 5 0 5 0 3	5 4 2 4 5 4 3 4 4 4 1 2 5 5 5 0	108	59%	12%	4.09	4.32	3.97
	2002	33	4 4 0 2 2 5 5 3 3 4 4 4 0 3 4 2 5 3	3 3 2 5 3 4 4 4 3 5 3 5 3 1 3	108	45%	9%	2.94	3.60	3.98
Cruz,Juan	2001	8		5 4 3 4 0 4 2 4	85	63%	13%	3.26	3.59	3.71
	2002	9	0 5 0 3 4 1 0 0 5		89	33%	56%	3.99	4.20	6.91
Cruz,Nelson	2002	5	0 5	0 4 0	70	40%	60%	4.50	5.45	7.05
D'Amico,Jeff	2000	23	3 5 4 3 2 0 4 2	4 3 4 3 4 5 2 4 4 2 3 5 5 2 3	102	48%	4%	2.75	3.28	3.68
	2001	10	3 5 5 0	0 0 0 3 0 2	80	20%	50%	6.11	6.61	6.74
	2002	22	5 5 4 4 2 5 0 5 5 5 0 5 0 3 3 0 2	2 2 3 0 1	94	41%	27%	4.97	4.48	4.74
Daal,Omar	2000	28	4 4 1 3 0 2 2 5 0 3 2 1 0 0 0 0	3 5 4 0 4 2 4 3 3 3 3 3	93	25%	32%	6.14	6.05	5.13
	2001	32	3 2 5 5 2 5 2 1 5 3 3 0 3 0 4 0 2 3	4 2 2 3 4 1 1 2 2 0 0 5 5 4	89	31%	25%	4.47	4.71	4.90
	2002	23	5 5 4 2 0 4 3 2 0	2 3 4 5 4 3 3 3 3 0 0 0 2 5	85	35%	22%	3.91	3.71	4.64
Davis,Doug	2000	13	0 2 0	2 0 3 3 3 2 0 3 2 2	103	0%	31%	4.62	5.34	5.53
	2001	30	0 2 2 0 0 2 0 0 4 5 4 5 3 3 3	4 4 3 4 3 3 4 3 4 3 5 4 0 2 3	102	37%	20%	4.39	4.72	4.64
	2002	10	5 4 4 3 0 1 2 1 2 0		95	30%	40%	5.03	4.93	5.29
Dempster,Ryan	2000	33	3 5 5 4 4 5 5 2 3 1 4 5 2 5 3 4 3 3	2 3 3 4 5 4 5 3 4 5 3 3 5 5 3	109	55%	3%	3.66	4.18	3.38
	2001	34	3 4 3 5 0 4 5 3 0 2 4 5 5 2 4 5 2 3 5	4 5 3 5 4 3 0 2 4 4 4 0 3 0 0	105	50%	18%	4.95	4.70	4.37
	2002	33	5 5 2 4 3 3 4 5 5 1 3 3 0 3 5 5 4 3	0 3 0 3 0 4 3 2 3 4 0 2 5 2 3	101	36%	18%	5.38	4.66	4.52
Dessens,Elmer	2000	16	2	2 1 3 4 5 3 2 0 5 0 3 3 3 3 4	96	25%	19%	4.20	4.51	4.62
	2001	34	4 0 4 1 1 2 2 4 3 5 5 4 2 3 2 3 3 3	3 4 4 4 3 0 3 2 2 2 4 0 3 0 5 2	94	32%	18%	4.48	4.78	4.60
	2002	30	0 4 4 4 3 4 4 3 3 3 0 3 2 3 1 4 3 0	3 4 4 3 0 1 4 3 4 2 3 4	90	37%	20%	3.03	4.13	4.64
Douglass,Sean	2002	8	0 0 3 2	1 4 4 1	92	25%	50%	6.11	6.00	6.56
Dreifort,Darren	2000	33	3 2 2 5 3 1 1 4 0 4 0 0 4 5 3 3 4 3	5 5 5 1 4 1 1 4 4 2 3 4 5 3 4	97	45%	24%	4.17	4.39	4.53
	2001	16	0 3 5 4 5 4 3 5 2 4 5 0 3 3 3 2		95	44%	13%	5.12	4.24	4.32
Drese,Ryan	2001	4		1 2 4 4	98	50%	25%	3.48	3.29	4.61
	2002	26	1 2 0 0 4 2 4 5 3 4 0 4 3 3 0 3 5	0 2 0 1 2 4 0 1 2	94	27%	38%	6.57	5.93	5.27
Driskill,Travis	2002	19	5 4 5 2 5 1 1 3	1 0 3 0 5 4 3 1 1 0 3	97	32%	42%	4.98	5.24	5.29
Duckworth,Brandon	2001	11		4 5 3 5 3 2 3 4 3 3 0	102	36%	9%	3.63	3.69	4.29
	2002	29	5 4 5 0 3 3 5 0 2 3 0 4 5 5 0 4 1	4 4 5 0 4 0 0 5 3 0 5 3	98	48%	31%	5.41	4.94	4.82
Durbin,Chad	2000	16	4 1 4 0 3 3 0 0 0 0 3 0	3 0 1 0	84	13%	63%	6.80	6.06	8.46
	2001	29	0 3 4 3 3 0 5 2 4 0 3 2 0 0	3 5 2 4 0 2 1 4 2 3 3 0 0 5 1	100	24%	34%	4.81	4.90	5.21
Eaton,Adam	2000	22	4 3 3 4 1 3 5 2	4 3 4 4 4 5 3 5 0 0 1 3 1 3	100	41%	23%	3.70	3.89	4.56
	2001	17	2 3 2 4 5 3 3 5 4 3 4 2 5 5 4 4 4		108	59%	0%	4.34	4.30	3.38
	2002	6		0 0 3 5 4 5	90	50%	33%	5.45	4.21	4.71
Elarton,Scott	2000	29	3 0 3 0 4 0 3 2 4 0 0 5 4 5 5	5 0 3 5 4 2 4 3 4 4 3 3 2 0	104	41%	24%	4.82	4.90	4.56
	2001	23	4 0 4 5 4 1 2 2 3 2 3 2 0 3 5 3 1 0	0 2 4 4 0	95	30%	30%	7.08	6.21	5.08
Erickson,Scott	2000	16	3 0 2 2 5 5 2 3 0 1 1 3 2	2 2 0	98	13%	31%	7.91	6.90	5.37
	2002	28	3 4 3 0 2 3 3 0 2 5 0 3 2 1 4 2 4 3	3 5 1 0 0 3 0 0 0 0	94	18%	39%	5.57	5.45	5.45
Estes,Shawn	2000	30	1 3 3 4 0 1 5 3 5 2 3 0 3 2 3	3 3 3 4 4 3 5 0 4 3 5 4 4 1 3	103	33%	20%	4.26	4.39	4.71
	2001	27	0 5 4 3 4 2 5 4 3 3 4 4 1 3 0 0	3 4 4 3 0 0 3 0 5 5 0	93	41%	30%	4.02	3.91	4.92
	2002	29	5 5 1 1 5 3 2 4 4 1 2 2 5 2 4 0 2	2 3 5 3 5 0 2 2 4 1 0 0	94	34%	28%	5.12	4.14	4.90
Fernandez,Jared	2002	8	3	5 2 4 3 0 0 3	93	25%	25%	4.50	5.41	4.93
Figueroa,Nelson	2000	3	3 0	1	83	0%	67%	3.89	4.13	9.80
	2001	13	4 5 3	0 4 3 2 5 2 4 2 2 1	94	38%	15%	3.78	4.34	4.52
	2002	11	2 3 3 3 3 0 0 3 2	2 2	90	0%	18%	5.03	5.24	4.69
Finley,Chuck	2000	34	2 3 5 4 5 2 5 4 3 5 4 3 3 3 2 3 5 3	4 3 3 1 4 0 4 2 0 3 5 3 3 4 5 5	108	44%	9%	4.17	4.21	4.11
	2001	22	3 0 4 3 5 4 5 5 0 4 0 0 0	0 1 2 0 4 5 5 5 1	83	45%	41%	5.57	5.00	5.14
	2002	32	4 0 4 2 4 4 4 2 3 5 5 4 5 3 5 2 3	0 4 4 4 0 5 5 5 5 5 0 4 3 3 5	98	63%	13%	4.17	3.83	3.71
Fogg,Josh	2002	33	5 5 3 3 3 4 5 5 3 0 4 2 2 2 1 4 4	3 0 0 4 2 2 2 3 1 4 0 4 2 4 2 4	89	39%	18%	4.36	4.68	4.52
Fossum,Casey	2001	7		0 1 3 0 3 4 0	87	14%	57%	4.90	4.28	7.77
	2002	13		5 3 5 3 3 4 0 3 5 0 5 2 3	98	38%	15%	3.48	4.23	4.52
Franklin,Ryan	2002	12	3 3	0 1 1 3 5 2 0 5 4 2	86	25%	33%	4.04	3.71	5.13
Garcia,Freddy	2000	20	0 4 2 0 4	5 3 3 5 3 1 1 3 2 5 4 2 3 0 4	99	35%	25%	3.92	4.22	4.82
	2001	34	0 2 5 5 2 4 3 0 4 2 3 3 4 5 5 3 3 4	3 0 3 3 4 4 5 4 3 4 5 5 5 3 3 4	104	50%	[illegible]	[illegible]	[illegible]	[illegible]
	2002	34	2 3 3 0 2 5 5 5 5 3 4 4 4 5 5 5 0 4 5	1 0 4 5 3 2 2 2 3 3 3 4 3 2 3	106	44%	12%	4.40	4.19	4.32
Garland,Jon	2000	13	0	3 0 3 2 0 4 4 3 0 0 4 0	92	23%	46%	4.09	4.62	6.12
	2001	16	0 2 0 4 3	3 2 2 3 4 3 2 0 2 3 4	89	19%	19%	3.66	4.76	4.65
	2002	33	1 0 5 1 2 4 1 1 0 4 4 4 3 0 3 3 2 3	3 0 0 4 5 4 0 1 5 4 2 3 2 2 4	94	33%	33%	4.59	4.27	5.08
George,Chris	2001	13		1 0 0 4 3 2 3 2 2 3 2 0 3	89	8%	31%	4.62	4.60	5.45
	2002	6	2 3 1 1 0 0		81	0%	67%	5.67	5.57	9.80
Glavine,Tom	2000	35	5 5 5 3 5 5 3 3 3 1 4 2 3 5 4 2 2 3 3	4 3 4 3 2 0 5 3 2 4 5 3 5 3 4 4	106	46%	6%	3.40	3.48	3.98
	2001	35	3 2 4 4 1 5 2 2 2 5 3 1 2 0 2 2 3 0 3	3 3 4 3 4 4 3 0 2 5 4 3 3 3 3 4	98	29%	14%	3.57	4.28	4.50
	2002	36	5 3 4 4 5 3 5 2 2 3 4 5 3 5 4 2 5 2 0 0	0 3 1 2 3 3 4 3 3 4 2 4 2 4 1 0	100	39%	17%	2.97	3.78	4.52
Glover,Gary	2001	11		0 0 2 2 5 3 1 4 3 5 0	86	27%	36%	4.30	3.75	5.27
	2002	22	0 0 2 0 1 5 0 0 3 3	2 3 4 4 1 4 0 3 2 0 0 3	88	18%	45%	5.22	4.44	6.25
Greisinger,Seth	2002	8	3 0 3 0 3 4 0 0		80	13%	50%	6.32	5.63	7.08
Hackman,Luther	2002	6	0	0 2 0 0 4	74	17%	67%	4.11	4.95	8.85
Halama,John	2000	30	4 0 2 2 5 0 4 2 2 4 0 2 0 4 0 3	4 2 2 3 2 4 0 4 3 0 0 2 3 2	86	27%	27%	5.09	5.40	4.93

PQS PITCHING LOGS

Pitcher	Year	No.	FIRST HALF	SECOND HALF	PC	DOM	DIS	ERA	xERA	qERA
	2001	17	0 4 5 4 0 4 2 2 0 0 2 0 5 3 0 1	0	77	29%	47%	4.12	4.70	5.98
	2002	10	5 2 4 0 3 1 2 0 0 0		83	20%	50%	3.56	4.40	6.74
Halladay,Roy	2000	13	4 0 0 3 0 1 0 5 0 0	5 0 0	92	23%	69%	8.59	7.38	8.60
	2001	16	4	2 0 5 4 4 3 5 5 4 5 0 5 5 2 5	93	69%	13%	3.12	2.91	3.61
	2002	34	5 5 4 5 0 4 4 5 3 4 4 4 4 4 5 4 4 4	4 3 5 4 4 5 4 3 1 3 2 3 4 4 4 4	103	76%	6%	2.94	2.92	3.13
Hamilton,Joey	2000	6		5 4 3 3 0 0	85	33%	33%	3.55	3.26	5.08
	2001	26	3 3 5 2 2 4 4 4 5 4 0 4 4 3 1 1 0 4	2 4 0 2 0 4 0 2	89	42%	27%	5.95	6.39	4.74
	2002	17	2 4 4 4 3 5 0 0 4 3 1 0 3 4 0 2	0	88	35%	35%	5.30	4.69	5.13
Hampton,Mike	2000	34	2 3 0 4 3 1 1 5 4 5 3 5 3 0 0 3 5 2 5 5	2 4 4 4 2 3 0 3 3 5 5 4 5 4	101	47%	18%	3.15	3.35	4.40
	2001	32	3 2 3 4 3 4 3 2 3 3 5 1 1 4 0 2 2 2	0 1 4 0 3 1 0 5 5 5 3 2 4 3	104	28%	25%	5.41	5.56	4.93
	2002	30	0 2 2 3 0 3 2 4 4 3 0 2 1 1 3 4 2 2	2 1 2 2 1 3 4 3 4 1 3 2	100	17%	27%	6.17	6.33	5.03
Harang,Aaron	2002	15	5 4 3 0 5 5 3 0	2 0 3 3 2 0 0	94	27%	33%	4.85	4.83	5.13
Harper,Travis	2000	5		0 2 3 4 3	97	20%	20%	4.09	3.97	4.75
	2002	7	0 4 4	3 0 0 0	78	29%	57%	5.51	5.43	7.14
Haynes,Jimmy	2000	33	1 2 3 3 3 2 1 3 1 3 3 2 4 2 2 3 3 3	0 0 3 4 4 2 2 3 0 2 1 1 3 2 3	101	9%	24%	5.33	5.29	4.81
	2001	29	0 2 0 3 2 3 4 3 5 4 5 2 2 2 5 4 0 2 5	0 4 3 4 3 4 5 3 0 0	93	38%	21%	4.86	4.79	4.64
	2002	34	0 5 4 3 1 3 1 2 2 4 3 2 4 3 4 4 2 4	5 4 3 2 1 2 2 0 2 5 4 2 3 5 4 3	95	38%	15%	4.13	4.74	4.52
Helling,Rick	2000	35	0 4 5 3 4 4 4 3 2 3 5 2 2 4 3 2 2 3 4	1 5 3 2 4 4 4 4 3 1 0 0 4 3 0 2	108	40%	17%	4.48	4.50	4.44
	2001	34	4 0 0 2 5 4 1 1 1 2 3 5 4 5 2 4 3 3 3	5 3 3 4 0 2 3 3 4 4 4 3 4 1 2	106	38%	21%	5.19	5.58	4.64
	2002	30	3 4 3 2 4 0 5 2 4 2 3 1 4 4 5 4 4 0	0 4 5 5 4 4 0 1 4 3 3 3	93	50%	20%	4.53	4.76	4.50
Hentgen,Pat	2000	32	2 4 3 2 4 3 3 0 3 4 4 1 4 2 0 2 3 2	3 0 4 3 4 3 3 3 3 3 3 5 4 1	99	28%	16%	4.73	4.78	4.62
	2001	9	4 4 5 1 3 2 2 3 3		106	33%	11%	3.48	3.19	4.49
	2002	4		0 0 4 2	94	25%	50%	6.43	7.33	6.56
Hermanson,Dustin	2000	30	3 0 4 4 3 0 0 0 5 3 2 2 2 0	3 5 0 4 1 1 4 3 5 1 4 2 0 4 3 0	98	30%	37%	4.77	5.18	5.19
	2001	33	2 2 0 3 4 3 4 4 3 0 2 0 0 4 0 5 5 4	3 4 5 5 4 3 2 2 1 2 2 3 4 5 0	96	39%	21%	4.45	4.90	4.64
	2002	1		3	83	0%	0%	7.77	7.16	4.50
Hernandez,Carlos	2001	3		5 5 0	92	67%	33%	1.05	1.99	4.29
	2002	21	1 2 5 5 5 3 5 3 4 4 2 0 2 0 0	0 5 0 4 3 1	90	38%	33%	4.35	4.42	5.00
Hernandez,Livan	2000	33	4 0 4 2 4 3 3 3 3 5 5 4 2 2 4 2 4 4	4 5 3 2 4 4 5 3 0 5 2 5 3 2 2	116	48%	6%	3.75	4.21	3.98
	2001	34	5 0 2 2 0 4 4 1 4 2 5 2 4 1 4 2 3 2 4	4 3 2 3 2 5 3 4 0 3 3 3 3 0 3	109	32%	18%	5.25	5.13	4.60
	2002	33	3 4 2 3 4 3 3 3 0 1 5 4 5 2 0 4 0 0	5 4 2 2 3 3 3 5 3 2 4 5 2 0 4	105	36%	18%	4.38	4.41	4.52
Hernandez,Orlando	2000	29	2 5 4 4 3 4 0 4 3 2 5 3 2 0 3 4	1 0 3 2 4 5 5 3 4 3 3 5 4	106	45%	14%	4.52	4.22	4.28
	2001	16	0 4 0 3 2 3 3 5 0	0 5 3 5 4 4 0	99	38%	31%	4.87	4.96	5.00
	2002	22	5 4 5 5 3 4 4 0 5	2 4 5 3 0 2 3 4 4 5 4 4 5	101	68%	9%	3.64	3.33	3.38
Hernandez,Runelvys	2002	12		3 5 2 3 4 3 3 4 4 3 1 3	96	33%	8%	4.72	4.65	4.48
Hiljus,Erik	2001	11	5	3 3 0 2 2 3 3 3 3 0	84	9%	18%	3.88	4.21	4.68
	2002	9	1 2 3 4 4 0 2 0 0		89	22%	44%	6.60	6.32	5.50
Hitchcock,Sterling	2000	11	4 1 4 3 4 5 1 5 4 4 0		103	64%	27%	4.97	5.20	4.17
	2001	12	5	4 2 3 2 0 2 4 4 1 0 5	91	42%	25%	5.48	5.28	4.74
	2002	2	0 0		91	0%	100%	5.54	6.48	15.00
Hudson,Tim	2000	33	5 2 0 0 5 5 2 4 2 4 3 3 5 5 3 4 5 4	0 1 3 4 0 3 0 3 5 3 4 4 5 4 5	98	52%	18%	4.14	3.50	4.37
	2001	35	3 5 0 5 0 3 4 5 4 4 4 5 5 5 4 5 1 5 4	5 5 3 2 4 4 4 0 3 3 4 5 0 3 3 4	103	63%	14%	3.37	3.43	3.71
	2002	34	5 4 4 3 4 4 2 4 1 2 2 4 4 5 5 4 2 3 4	3 1 4 4 3 5 4 4 5 4 4 4 3 4 3	102	65%	6%	2.99	3.58	3.38
Irabu,Hideki	2000	11	0 4 5 2 4 0 5 0 5 3	4	77	55%	27%	7.31	6.59	4.39
	2001	3	3 4 3		96	33%	0%	5.68	5.77	4.46
	2002	2	2 1		89	0%	50%	5.74	5.55	7.46
Ishii,Kazuhisa	2002	28	4 4 4 2 5 4 3 3 2 3 3 4 0 5 4 0 4	3 4 4 0 2 3 4 3 0 4 0	96	46%	18%	4.27	4.66	4.40
James,Delvin	2002	6	4 2 0 4 0	0	73	33%	50%	6.62	5.55	6.37
Jarvis,Kevin	2000	19	3 3 0 2 4 2 4 0 5 3 0 4 0	3 0 0 4 3 1	86	26%	37%	4.68	4.87	5.27
	2001	32	3 0 3 3 5 3 4 4 5 3 5 0 2 2 2 3 5 5	1 4 5 1 2 3 5 3 3 2 4 3 0 2	90	34%	16%	4.80	4.51	4.60
	2002	7	4 3 4 4 4 0 0		79	57%	29%	4.37	4.50	4.39
Jennings,Jason	2001	7		5 4 3 2 0 0 4	90	43%	29%	4.60	4.41	4.74
	2002	32	4 0 2 3 3 0 4 5 0 3 5 3 4 0 1 2 3	1 5 3 3 4 4 3 4 4 0 4 1 2 2 3	94	34%	25%	4.52	5.01	4.90
Jensen,Ryan	2001	7	2	0 1 4 0 4 0	87	29%	57%	3.71	4.05	7.14
	2002	31	4 5 0 3 0 5 3 4 4 1 0 3 3 3 3 2 5	1 5 5 1 4 2 0 3 3 0 0 0 2 4	88	32%	32%	4.53	4.80	5.08
Johnson,Jason	2000	13	3 3 1 0 4 3 2 2 3 3 4 3	2	107	15%	15%	5.27	4.60	4.65
	2001	32	4 0 3 3 0 4 4 0 4 4 4 5 3 0 0 3 3 4	4 5 3 3 3 0 5 2 0 3 2 5 2 2	102	38%	22%	4.09	4.53	4.64
	2002	22	5 1 0 5 3 5 0 5 4 1	4 1 2 4 5 3 3 3 0 3 4 4	96	45%	27%	4.60	4.67	4.67
Johnson,Randy	2000	35	4 5 5 5 5 5 5 5 5 3 5 4 5 5 5 5 5 4 5	5 5 3 5 0 4 5 5 0 5 4 5 5 5 4 0	115	86%	9%	2.65	2.89	2.88
	2001	34	5 2 5 5 5 4 5 5 5 3 4 5 4 5 5 4 5 5 5	5 5 5 5 5 5 4 5 5 5 4 4 5 4 5	117	94%	0%	2.49	2.24	2.39
	2002	35	5 5 5 4 5 5 5 3 5 5 2 4 5 4 5 5 5 4 5	4 4 2 5 5 5 5 5 5 5 3 5 4 5 5 5	113	89%	0%	2.32	2.65	2.54
Jones,Bobby J.	2000	27	0 0 0 4 0 1 1 0 5 2 5 3	5 1 1 5 2 2 4 0 3 3 0 4 2 3 4	92	30%	41%	5.08	5.11	5.29
	2001	33	2 5 3 4 3 5 5 4 5 3 3 2 3 0 2 3 0 4	2 3 4 0 3 2 3 4 3 0 2 0 5 0 0	95	30%	21%	5.12	5.93	4.71
	2002	18	2 2 3 5 3 0 2 4 4 0 3	3 3 4 3 2 3 0	93	22%	17%	5.50	5.74	4.63
Kennedy,Joe	2001	20	3 5 0 4 4 2 4	3 4 2 5 0 3 5 4 4 2 3 2 3	94	45%	10%	3.27	3.63	4.28
	2002	30	2 2 2 3 3 4 4 3 5 1 2 3 4 2 2 4 4	2 0 0 4 3 2 3 3 0 1 2 3 4	103	27%	17%	4.55	4.19	4.62
Kile,Darryl	2000	34	5 3 0 5 5 5 5 2 3 5 4 5 5 2 4 0 2 4 5	0 5 3 4 3 4 4 2 4 4 5 4 4 2 3	104	62%	9%	3.92	3.80	3.50
	2001	34	1 2 3 4 5 4 3 4 4 5 4 5 2 2 4 4 3 5	3 4 4 2 5 4 3 5 3 2 3 4 5 5 4 3	99	59%	3%	3.09	3.92	3.38
	2002	14	4 4 4 4 2 2 2 3 4 4 3 0 0 4		97	50%	14%	3.75	4.05	4.23
Kim,Sun Woo	2001	2		0 4	87	50%	50%	6.51	5.29	5.81
	2002	5	3 0	2 0 4	84	20%	40%	4.78	4.17	5.50
Kinney,Matt	2000	8		3 5 4 3 0 2 2 5	95	38%	13%	4.59	4.60	4.41
	2002	12	3 0 5 4 0 3 4 3 2 0 2 1		90	25%	33%	4.64	6.13	5.13
Lackey,John	2002	18	5 3 3	4 0 4 3 5 5 4 3 2 3 5 0 3 0 2	98	39%	17%	3.67	4.06	4.52
Lawrence,Brian	2001	15	5 5	4 3 0 5 3 3 4 4 3 5 4 5 0	93	60%	13%	3.68	3.66	3.71
	2002	31	2 4 4 5 4 3 4 0 3 4 5 5 5 5 4 2 0 5	4 5 3 4 5 3 4 2 3 4 3 3 3	97	58%	6%	3.69	4.18	3.68
Leiter,Al	2000	31	5 4 2 2 2 5 5 5 5 4 4 3 5 3 2 5 5	2 5 5 5 1 5 2 5 0 3 5 3 3 2	112	55%	6%	3.20	3.24	3.68
	2001	29	5 3 5 0 5 5 3 5 3 5 4 5 3 2	5 5 4 4 0 3 4 5 5 5 3 3 5 5 0	104	62%	10%	3.32	3.54	3.71
	2002	33	5 5 0 5 5 4 0 4 4 3 3 0 3 3 5 5 4 2	4 4 0 5 3 3 4 5 5 0 3 5 5 2 0	103	55%	18%	3.49	3.96	4.10
Lidle,Cory	2000	11	3 4 2 0 3 0 0	3 0 3 4	84	18%	36%	4.19	4.69	5.45
	2001	29	0 4 5 4 2 4 3 2 3 5 5 5 0 2 4	3 1 3 5 4 4 4 3 0 3 4 4 4 5	94	55%	14%	3.59	3.55	3.97
	2002	30	2 4 0 3 5 3 2 3 0 2 0 3 3 3 3	0 4 1 3 5 3 4 5 3 5 4 1 3 3 3	95	27%	20%	3.89	3.51	4.73
Lieber,Jon	2000	35	3 2 3 5 2 5 4 0 4 3 5 5 5 1 3 3 2 3 4	5 3 4 5 2 4 4 0 3 5 2 3 3 3 4 2	105	43%	9%	4.41	4.05	4.11
	2001	34	5 5 5 4 5 4 1 4 4 4 5 4 4 4 4 4 3 3	2 3 4 3 4 4 4 4 4 3 0 4 1 2 5 3	96	68%	9%	3.80	3.59	3.38
	2002	21	2 5 3 4 4 2 4 3 3 4 1 3 4 5 4 2 4	4 3 2 5	93	52%	5%	3.70	3.98	3.85

PQS PITCHING LOGS

Pitcher	Year	No.	FIRST HALF	SECOND HALF	PC	DOM	DIS	ERA	xERA	qERA
Lilly,Ted	2001	21	3 4 0 0 0 4 0 2 5 3 5 0 4	0 0 3 4 3 0 0 4	90	33%	43%	5.09	4.72	5.29
	2002	16	5 5 1 2 5 3 3 0 2 5 0	5 2 0 0 3	87	31%	31%	3.69	2.42	5.08
Lima,Jose	2000	32	3 3 3 2 0 0 4 2 4 0 4 3 1 1 4 0 4	2 3 4 2 1 0 1 3 4 3 4 2 2 0 5	97	28%	31%	6.65	6.76	5.13
	2001	27	0 4 3 0 0 1 5 0 0 2 1 2	0 4 2 3 4 2 3 0 2 0 3 4 3 2 2	87	19%	37%	5.56	5.76	5.45
	2002	12	0 0 5 0	0 5 2 0 2 0 4 0	70	25%	58%	7.81	5.92	7.14
Loaiza,Esteban	2000	31	2 5 2 2 1 0 4 4 4 3 2 0 2 2 4 0	3 3 5 5 1 3 5 0 5 3 5 4 3 3 1	102	35%	23%	4.57	5.04	4.64
	2001	30	4 4 3 4 3 4 2 0 4 3 2 5 4 1 0 4 2 0	3 4 3 3 2 2 2 2 4 0 5 2	96	37%	17%	5.02	5.45	4.52
	2002	25	2 5 3 3 0 0 2 3 0 2 0	5 3 3 3 4 3 0 4 2 1 3 2 0 4	94	20%	28%	5.72	5.32	4.98
Lohse,Kyle	2001	16	4 5 1 5	2 0 0 2 3 4 1 4 3 0 0 0	88	31%	44%	4.78	4.98	5.29
	2002	31	0 0 5 5 3 0 5 2 4 3 2 2 0 0 5 3 0 4	5 3 3 3 3 2 3 5 2 4 3 5 3	96	32%	19%	4.25	4.49	4.60
Lopez,Albie	2000	24	3 3 4 4 4 2 2 4	2 2 3 4 4 3 4 2 3 5 0 0 0 3 5 2	100	38%	13%	4.13	4.79	4.41
	2001	33	5 4 4 5 3 2 2 0 3 1 0 0 2 3 3 1 3 3	4 1 1 5 2 3 5 5 4 5 0 0 2 5 5	97	36%	27%	4.82	4.89	4.82
	2002	4	0 2 3 0		83	0%	50%	4.42	4.43	7.46
Lopez,Rodrigo	2002	28	1 2 3 5 3 5 2 4 4 3 4 1 4 4	3 4 5 5 1 3 3 4 3 3 3 3 0 5	99	43%	14%	3.58	3.42	4.32
Lowe,Derek	2001	3		4 4 5	73	100%	0%	3.55	4.47	2.00
	2002	32	3 3 5 3 4 5 3 4 5 5 3 4 2 5 4 5 2	4 4 5 3 4 5 2 3 3 2 4 4 5 3 4	96	59%	0%	2.59	2.04	3.38
Lyon,Brandon	2001	11		4 0 4 1 5 4 4 0 4 4 5	84	73%	27%	4.50	4.34	3.97
	2002	10	0 3 2 3 4 2 0 3 0 0		89	10%	40%	6.53	6.30	5.70
Maddux,Greg	2000	34	5 3 5 4 4 4 2 4 5 5 5 5 4 4 5 4 0 4	3 4 3 3 5 4 4 5 4 2 4 4 4 4 5 4	92	79%	3%	3.00	2.93	2.84
	2001	34	4 5 5 5 2 5 4 5 3 4 4 4 3 4 4 5 5 4	3 5 4 4 4 3 4 4 3 5 4 3 3 4 4 4	88	76%	0%	3.05	3.09	2.84
	2002	34	4 0 3 0 2 5 4 3 3 3 3 5 3 3 3 4 3 4	4 4 4 4 5 4 4 2 3 3 5 1 0 4 5 4	79	50%	12%	2.62	3.47	4.23
Maduro,Calvin	2000	2	0 3		93	0%	50%	8.33	5.70	7.46
	2001	12		4 3 4 3 0 0 4 0 0 3 4 5	91	42%	33%	4.78	4.46	4.92
	2002	10	0 2 3 3 4 4 2 3 0 0		89	20%	30%	5.63	5.82	5.21
Maroth,Mike	2002	21	3 4 2 0 3 0	5 0 4 0 4 4 2 3 3 2 1 4 4 4 4	95	43%	24%	4.50	3.78	4.56
Marquis,Jason	2001	16	5 2 4 3 5	0 3 5 3 4 0 3 3 4 3 3	98	38%	13%	3.49	3.78	4.41
	2002	22	5 3 1 3 5 1 4 4 0 5 3 4	0 4 3 0 4 0 2 0 0 0	88	36%	41%	5.05	5.50	5.25
Martinez,Pedro	2000	29	5 5 5 5 5 5 5 5 5 5 5 5 4 4	5 5 5 5 5 0 5 5 5 5 5 5 5 4	109	97%	3%	1.74	1.19	2.20
	2001	18	5 5 5 4 5 5 5 5 5 5 5 5 5 4 0	0 5 0	99	83%	17%	2.40	1.78	3.43
	2002	30	0 5 4 5 5 3 0 5 5 5 4 3 4 4 5 4 5 4	5 5 5 5 5 5 4 5 5 4 4 4	103	87%	7%	2.26	1.85	2.88
Mays,Joe	2000	28	4 0 4 0 2 1 4 2 5 0 3 0 5 3 0 3 2 0 2	1 4 5 0 0 0 3 3 4	93	29%	39%	5.29	5.36	5.27
	2001	34	4 4 2 3 3 5 2 5 3 4 3 3 2 2 2 4 4 3	0 3 3 5 4 2 0 5 5 5 4 4 4 5 3 3	100	47%	6%	3.16	3.36	3.98
	2002	17	0 0 0	3 2 3 2 4 4 0 2 1 3 3 4 0 5	89	24%	35%	5.40	5.18	5.36
May,Darrell	2002	22	0 0 0 5 2 2 1 3 4 0 5	4 3 0 0 2 2 3 3 5 3 3	92	23%	32%	5.02	5.27	5.21
Meadows,Brian	2000	32	2 3 2 1 3 4 2 3 0 1 0 0 2 0 0 2 2 1	4 3 3 0 0 3 4 2 3 3 5 3 0 0	89	13%	38%	5.14	5.56	5.54
	2001	10	0 4 3 0 2 0 3 3 0 0		79	10%	50%	7.32	7.54	7.08
	2002	11		3 4 0 4 3 3 4 0 3 4 1	83	36%	27%	3.92	3.96	4.82
Middlebrook,Jason	2002	5	0 0	4 5 3	83	40%	40%	4.76	2.95	5.21
Miller,Justin	2002	18	0 3 0 3 0 3 5 3 0 0	0 2 4 5 5 0 4 2	87	28%	39%	5.56	4.94	5.27
Miller,Wade	2000	16	4	2 5 0 2 2 5 4 0 5 4 2 3 5 5 5	108	56%	13%	5.01	4.43	3.97
	2001	32	5 5 4 4 3 4 3 3 4 4 2 1 3 0 4 3 5 1	3 2 5 5 0 4 5 3 5 5 4 4 5 5	104	59%	13%	3.40	3.78	3.97
	2002	26	0 4 1 0 1 5 5 3 3 1 5	3 3 4 2 4 3 4 5 5 5 4 4 5 4 3	99	54%	19%	3.29	3.67	4.37
Millwood,Kevin	2000	35	0 5 4 2 5 3 3 0 4 0 5 5 0 0 4 5 4 5 4 0	4 5 3 4 2 5 5 4 3 3 5 4 5 5 2	97	60%	17%	4.67	4.15	3.83
	2001	21	4 3 4 2 4 2 0	3 4 4 0 4 3 5 2 5 0 5 4 3 3	88	48%	14%	4.31	4.59	4.28
	2002	35	4 5 4 0 0 3 5 3 4 0 3 5 0 4 4 5 5 4 5	4 5 5 3 5 4 3 5 5 4 3 4 3 2 3 5	95	63%	11%	3.24	3.05	3.71
Milton,Eric	2000	33	2 4 2 2 5 5 2 0 0 5 5 5 0 5 3 3 5 0 3	0 4 5 5 4 4 3 4 3 0 0 3 4 5	98	48%	21%	4.86	4.49	4.53
	2001	34	2 3 5 4 3 2 5 3 0 3 3 5 0 4 1 2 3 5	5 4 0 1 3 4 3 4 3 4 4 4 2 4 4 0	103	44%	18%	4.33	4.46	4.44
	2002	29	4 0 4 4 0 4 3 0 2 4 5 0 3 4 5 0 0 5 3	5 4 5 5 5 0 0 4 4	93	55%	31%	4.84	3.95	4.55
Mlicki,Dave	2000	22	0 4 5 0 3 2 0 3 2 4 0 4 0 0 3	2 1 0 2 4 0 5	83	27%	41%	5.59	5.53	5.40
	2001	29	0 1 4 0 3 5 4 0 0 4 2 4 0 0 0 0	0 4 3 2 3 2 1 2 5 3 3 0 0	91	24%	45%	6.19	6.47	6.12
	2002	16	1 2 5 4 5 0 5 3 0 0	3 0 3 0 0 0	76	25%	50%	5.34	5.41	6.56
Moehler,Brian	2000	29	3 3 3 2 2 3 4 4 4 3 2 1 4	2 4 1 0 5 5 4 4 1 5 3 1 3 0 4 1	93	38%	24%	4.50	5.14	4.64
	2002	12	4	3 3 3 1 2 4 4 0 0 0 0	80	25%	42%	4.86	5.67	5.40
Morris,Matt	2001	34	0 5 4 5 4 5 4 5 5 2 5 2 4 3 2 3 4 0	5 5 4 0 4 4 5 4 2 4 5 0 5 0 5 5	98	68%	15%	3.17	3.53	3.73
	2002	32	5 5 4 3 4 3 3 5 5 3 0 2 3 5 5 4 5 3 1	5 5 5 0 4 5 3 5 2 3 0 4 4	100	56%	13%	3.43	3.82	3.97
Moss,Damian	2002	29	5 4 4 3 4 2 3 3 4 3 0 5 4 2	1 5 3 4 4 1 3 1 2 3 4 0 4 0 5	98	45%	21%	3.42	3.50	4.53
Moyer,Jamie	2000	26	3 4 1 4 4 5 4 4 4 2 5	5 3 3 2 4 0 0 1 2 4 5 4 3 2 0	96	50%	19%	5.49	5.05	4.37
	2001	33	2 2 5 2 3 4 0 2 4 2 3 5 2 4 4 1 3	3 3 4 4 5 3 0 4 5 5 4 4 4 3 4 4	94	52%	9%	3.44	3.34	3.85
	2002	34	5 3 3 1 4 4 1 4 0 4 4 1 4 4 0 5 3 4 3	4 3 5 5 4 4 2 4 5 5 3 0 5 0 4	101	59%	21%	3.33	3.13	4.23
Mulder,Mark	2000	27	4 4 2 0 5 4 3 0 1 0 2 0 4 0 4	3 0 4 2 3 0 3 3 0 2 2 4	92	30%	33%	5.44	5.92	5.08
	2001	34	2 5 5 3 4 5 3 4 4 4 2 0 4 3 2 1 5 5	5 3 1 5 5 4 5 0 0 3 5 5 3 4 2 4	97	56%	15%	3.46	3.19	4.10
	2002	30	5 3 0 0 1 0 4 3 5 3 3 5 3 5	4 5 4 2 5 3 3 4 3 5 3 5 2 5 4 5	100	50%	13%	3.48	3.16	4.23
Munro,Peter	2002	14	0	4 2 5 3 0 3 2 4 1 0 4 0 0	79	29%	43%	3.60	3.53	5.40
Mussina,Mike	2000	34	3 4 3 4 1 4 0 3 2 4 5 5 4 5 4 0 5 4 5	5 3 5 5 1 2 0 5 5 5 4 5 0 5 5	107	65%	18%	3.79	3.78	3.73
	2001	34	4 4 4 0 4 5 3 3 2 5 5 3 3 4 4 2 4 5	0 2 4 5 0 3 4 4 5 5 5 5 4 5 4 0	102	65%	12%	3.16	2.96	3.61
	2002	33	4 4 5 3 2 3 5 4 3 5 3 5 4 1 2 4 2 4	5 4 4 0 3 4 4 3 5 3 5 4 5 5 3	101	61%	6%	4.06	3.71	3.50
Myers,Brett	2002	12		4 0 2 2 3 1 2 2 1 4 0 2	89	17%	33%	4.25	4.09	5.29
Myette,Aaron	2001	15	0 0 0	4 3 4 3 4 3 5 0 0 4 5 0	88	40%	40%	5.88	5.03	5.21
	2002	12	3	1 0 0 0 3 3 3 0 0 0 0	83	0%	67%	10.13	8.05	9.80
Nagy,Charles	2000	11	0 5 2 0 4 0 4 2	0 0 0	91	27%	55%	8.21	6.76	7.14
	2001	13	3 1 2 2 0 3	1 4 3 2 0 1 0	82	8%	46%	5.42	5.92	6.53
	2002	7	0	4 0 0 5 0 0	67	29%	71%	9.00	7.75	8.88
Neagle,Denny	2000	33	5 0 3 3 5 4 4 3 4 3 4 3 2 3 4 5 4 4	3 5 4 4 1 0 3 3 3 2 4 4 0 3 0	105	45%	15%	4.52	4.62	4.40
	2001	30	2 5 3 4 4 4 5 4 3 4 1 2 3 4 0	1 1 2 0 4 2 4 4 3 5 5 5 0 3	99	50%	20%	5.39	5.34	4.50
	2002	28	5 0 3 2 5 5 3 4 5 0 3 2 2 3 3 0 0	5 5 3 1 4 5 3 1 0 0 0	89	32%	32%	5.27	4.92	5.08
Neugebauer,Nick	2001	2		4 0	68	50%	50%	7.50	6.19	5.81
	2002	12	3 0 4 2 4 5 1	0 0 2 0 0	90	25%	50%	4.75	6.06	6.56
Nomo,Hideo	2000	31	4 5 4 2 4 4 0 2 0 4 4 5 3 5 0 4 1 5 4	0 0 2 5 5 4 3 5 0 4 4 3	100	58%	23%	4.74	4.90	4.23
	2001	33	5 4 4 0 4 5 2 0 3 5 4 5 5 2 5 3 4 4	2 3 5 4 0 3 3 4 5 2 3 5 0 4 5	98	58%	12%	4.50	3.96	3.97
	2002	34	0 3 4 4 4 4 2 0 1 5 4 2 3 4 3 4 5 5	4 4 3 3 3 4 3 5 5 5 5 4 4 3 5 5	102	62%	9%	3.40	3.83	3.50
Ohka,Tomo	2000	12		3 2 3 4 2 3 3 4 0 0 4 3	92	25%	17%	3.61	4.02	4.62
	2001	21	0 4 4 3 2 0 2 0 1	4 0 4 0 1 1 2 2 3 5 2 5	81	29%	38%	5.47	5.55	5.27
Ohka,Tomokazu	2002	31	2 5 0 5 5 2 4 2 4 5 4 5 3 3 2 3 5	4 0 3 0 3 1 5 3 3 5 3 0 3 5	91	42%	16%	3.19	3.91	4.44
Oliver,Darren	2000	21	0 3 5 2 3 1 3 3 0 0 1 3 0	2 0 0 3 2 2 3 0	89	5%	43%	7.42	6.65	5.80
	2001	27	3 3 2 4 0 0 0 4 2 3 0 3 1 0	3 4 2 4 0 3 2 3 0 1 4 1 4	90	22%	37%	6.02	5.88	5.36

PQS PITCHING LOGS

Pitcher	Year	No.	FIRST HALF	SECOND HALF	PC	DOM	DIS	ERA	xERA	qERA
	2002	9	3 3 0 4 3 0 2 0 0		84	11%	44%	4.66	5.54	5.70
Olsen,Kevin	2002	8	0 0 3 0 4 5 0 0		83	25%	63%	4.58	4.80	7.72
Ortiz,Ramon	2000	18	2 2 3 3 2 0 4	4 4 2 4 3 0 3 5 4 4 3	96	39%	11%	5.31	4.08	4.41
	2001	32	5 5 2 2 4 2 4 5 2 2 4 5 1 2 2 4 4	4 3 5 3 5 0 3 4 2 2 5 3 0 3 2	99	44%	9%	4.37	4.68	4.11
	2002	32	2 3 2 5 4 4 5 3 2 4 4 3 4 5 3 4 5	0 5 1 3 0 3 1 5 2 4 5 3 5 5 2	101	50%	13%	3.77	3.92	4.23
Ortiz,Russ	2000	32	3 1 1 2 4 5 0 1 3 4 1 1 3 0 5 0 3	3 3 0 5 5 4 3 4 5 4 4 4 5 4 3	106	44%	28%	5.03	4.92	4.74
	2001	33	1 5 5 5 4 2 5 4 5 2 2 2 0 3 4 2 5 4	4 4 2 4 4 4 4 3 3 4 0 4 5 5 4	106	64%	9%	3.30	3.17	3.50
	2002	33	4 2 4 3 3 3 3 4 5 2 1 4 5 0 4 3 2 3	5 3 2 0 5 4 3 3 3 5 3 5 3 3 5	109	39%	9%	3.62	3.57	4.29
Oswalt,Roy	2001	20	5 1 4 5 5 5	5 0 4 4 5 1 5 5 5 5 5 5 0 0	93	75%	25%	3.30	3.42	3.87
	2002	34	5 3 4 5 5 2 5 3 5 4 3 4 1 4 4 5 5 3	5 4 3 5 4 3 4 3 5 5 3 5 4 5 5 0	100	68%	6%	3.01	3.29	3.38
Padilla,Vicente	2002	32	5 3 5 5 4 4 3 5 3 4 3 3 4 3 5 2 0 5	3 3 2 3 4 2 5 5 4 3 1 3 2 0	95	44%	9%	3.28	3.53	4.11
Park,Chan Ho	2000	34	3 5 3 3 1 4 0 5 4 4 4 2 4 4 5 4 4 4 5	3 4 3 2 4 5 5 5 5 4 3 2 5 5 5	109	68%	6%	3.27	3.29	3.38
	2001	35	5 3 5 3 3 5 5 5 5 4 5 4 4 4 5 5 5 4 5	0 5 5 3 3 2 4 2 5 1 4 0 5 3 4 0	105	66%	11%	3.50	3.02	3.61
	2002	25	2 4 3 0 3 0 4 3 4 3 4	4 2 3 3 2 0 4 5 4 3 3 3 0 5	102	36%	16%	5.77	5.09	4.52
Parque,Jim	2000	32	0 0 2 4 2 4 2 0 4 4 2 4 4 3 4 3 4	3 3 3 3 5 0 3 0 4 3 3 4 3 3 0	99	34%	19%	4.28	4.83	4.60
	2001	5	1 0 3 3 0		88	0%	60%	8.04	6.88	9.02
	2002	4		2 0 4 0	74	25%	50%	10.08	9.48	6.56
Parris,Steve	2000	33	4 0 3 0 3 3 4 2 4 4 2 3 3 0 3 1 4 3	0 2 3 3 3 3 2 4 4 3 3 4 2 0 2	100	24%	18%	4.82	5.56	4.63
	2001	19	0 0 1 3 2 0 2 4 3 2 0 3 4 3 3 4	5 3 3	94	21%	26%	4.66	5.62	4.98
	2002	14	1 0 4 2 4	4 2 0 3 4 0 0 1 0	93	29%	50%	6.00	6.36	6.56
Patterson,John	2002	5		5 5 0 5 3	92	0%	0%	3.28	4.30	4.50
Pavano,Carl	2000	15	4 3 4 2 3 4 5 4 4 3 3 0 1 4 3		100	47%	13%	3.06	3.52	4.28
	2001	8		0 0 0 3 5 5 4 3	89	38%	38%	5.74	6.25	5.13
	2002	22	3 4 2 4 2 2 3 0 4 0 3 4 0 0	0 0 4 3 4 5 3 0	84	32%	32%	5.16	5.01	5.08
Peavy,Jake	2002	17	5 0 4	5 4 0 3 4 5 0 5 5 5 0 2 5 3	96	59%	24%	4.55	4.63	4.23
Penny,Brad	2000	23	3 5 4 4 2 4 0 5 0 3 0 0 0 5 3 2 0	2 0 4 5 3 3	91	35%	30%	4.49	4.32	5.00
	2001	31	4 5 2 5 0 4 5 4 5 5 0 3 4 5 5 5 5 3	4 3 3 5 3 5 4 3 4 5 4 3 3	94	65%	6%	3.69	3.08	3.38
	2002	24	3 0 2 2 3 0 4 0 0 0	0 5 0 3 5 5 3 1 5 4 0 5 1 1	87	29%	46%	4.67	5.34	5.98
Perez,Odalis	2001	16	0 3 0 0 3 5 4 4 5 4 3 4 4 3	0 0	92	44%	31%	4.92	4.72	4.92
	2002	32	4 4 4 4 4 4 3 5 3 0 4 4 5 5 4 4 4 3	3 3 2 5 3 2 5 3 4 5 2 3 5 5	94	63%	3%	3.00	2.72	3.29
Perez,Oliver	2002	15	3 3 4 3 5	5 5 3 4 4 4 3 0 0 5	100	53%	13%	3.50	3.92	4.23
Person,Robert	2000	28	3 5 4 3 3 5 3 4 5 3 5 2 5 3	4 4 1 4 5 3 4 4 4 5 5 3 4 0	110	61%	7%	3.64	3.49	3.50
	2001	33	0 5 4 4 0 4 5 3 4 4 3 0 2 0 4 3 4 2	3 4 2 2 0 5 4 4 5 5 3 5 5 1 0	100	52%	21%	4.20	3.97	4.50
	2002	16	2 4 3 4 3 3 3 5 4 0 4 3 3	3 2 0	92	31%	13%	5.48	4.69	4.49
Pettitte,Andy	2000	32	1 4 3 3 0 0 3 4 1 2 1 4 1 4 3 3	0 5 2 3 2 4 4 4 3 4 3 5 5 1 3 0	108	34%	28%	4.36	4.41	4.90
	2001	31	5 3 2 5 3 5 5 4 5 3 3 3 4 0 5 4	3 0 4 4 5 3 4 3 4 3 0 5 5 0 2	101	52%	13%	4.00	4.08	4.23
	2002	22	5 0 0 0 0 2 5 0	4 3 3 5 4 3 5 4 3 4 4 5 5 4	97	55%	23%	3.29	3.63	4.23
Phillips,Jason	2002	6	4	3 3 1 3 1	94	17%	33%	5.05	4.95	5.29
Pineiro,Joel	2000	1		5	97	100%	0%	4.64	4.30	2.00
	2001	11		0 5 5 5 4 0 3 2 4 4 0	85	55%	27%	3.08	2.92	4.39
	2002	28	0 5 2 5 2 0 1 3 4 3 4 3 3	4 2 4 3 2 2 3 5 4 3 5 5 4 2 3	100	39%	11%	3.25	3.88	4.41
Ponson,Sidney	2000	32	2 3 4 2 0 1 3 2 1 3 3 5 3 0 3 4 4 0	4 2 2 4 5 0 3 3 2 4 5 4 4 2	107	34%	19%	4.82	4.44	4.60
	2001	23	4 0 2 0 3 3 4 4 2 2 4 2 4 0	2 0 2 2 4 0 2 3 0	93	26%	26%	4.95	5.20	4.93
	2002	28	3 0 4 4 5 3 4 4 4 5 0 4 3 4 0 2 0 3	2 3 4 4 4 3 4 4 3 5	99	54%	14%	4.09	4.30	4.23
Powell,Brian	2000	5		3 4 0 1 2	79	20%	40%	6.43	5.63	5.50
	2002	9		4 2 0 5 0 0 3 2 3	83	22%	33%	4.89	5.47	5.21
Prior,Mark	2002	19	5 5 0 5 5 2 5 3 5	4 5 4 3 5 5 5 0 5 3	106	68%	11%	3.34	3.39	3.61
Prokopec,Luke	2000	3		0 2 1	82	0%	67%	2.66	3.27	9.80
	2001	22	5 5 4 3 0 4 5 4 3 2 2 2 5 3 1	3 3 4 0 0 2 2	95	36%	18%	4.89	5.05	4.52
	2002	12	0 3 4 4 1 0 3 0 2 5 4 2		89	33%	33%	6.85	6.81	5.08
Quevedo,Ruben	2000	15	3 1	4 3 5 4 0 3 3 0 0 4 0 3 2	100	27%	33%	6.16	5.28	5.13
	2001	10		0 5 5 5 4 5 3 5 2 0	101	60%	20%	3.56	3.84	3.95
	2002	25	0 0 2 4 1 2 0 3 5 5 5 5 1 0 0 4 1 0	3 1 1 4 0 0 2	95	28%	52%	5.76	6.11	6.56
Radke,Brad	2000	34	3 3 4 4 2 4 3 5 3 3 5 3 2 2 5 1 3 5 4	3 5 4 4 2 3 0 4 5 1 4 1 4 3 0	104	44%	15%	4.46	4.71	4.44
	2001	33	4 3 5 4 3 4 4 0 4 0 3 3 4 5 4 2 4 3 4	3 1 4 3 0 3 5 4 3 4 3 0 3 3	96	45%	15%	3.94	3.77	4.40
	2002	21	0 4 3 1 0 1 5 3 0 0	5 4 4 2 2 3 4 4 3 0 5	82	38%	33%	4.73	3.83	5.00
Reames,Britt	2000	7		0 2 4 2 4 5 2	95	43%	14%	4.02	3.61	4.32
	2001	13	4 1 4 3 1 0 3 0 5 5 3 0	4	86	38%	38%	5.38	5.03	5.13
	2002	7	0 0	5 5 0 3 0	62	29%	57%	5.03	4.94	7.14
Redding,Tim	2001	9	2 5 0	3 2 3 0 2 0	93	11%	33%	4.28	3.79	5.37
	2002	14	0 0 5 4 3 5 4 0 0 0 4 3 2	0	86	36%	43%	5.42	5.13	5.25
Redman,Mark	2000	24	4 4 3 4 4 5 4 0 0 3 3 0 4	5 4 4 0 5 4 0 5 0 3 2	94	54%	25%	4.77	4.89	4.61
	2001	11	0 4 3 0 2 1 4 2 4	2 0	94	27%	36%	5.18	5.47	5.27
	2002	30	0 3 5 2 5 4 2 4 2 4 5 3 3 3 3 3 4 2	3 4 5 4 5 4 0 5 3 4 2 0 0	105	47%	13%	4.21	3.74	4.28
Reed,Rick	2000	30	4 5 3 5 2 4 1 5 3 0 3 3 4 0 0	3 5 4 4 2 4 3 4 5 3 4 4 2 5 0	92	50%	17%	4.11	4.34	4.37
	2001	31	4 4 5 4 5 5 3 5 4 4 3 3 5 4 4 0 5	5 0 3 3 2 4 0 4 0 4 3 3 2 0	93	55%	16%	4.05	4.15	4.10
	2002	32	2 3 0 3 4 4 4 0 0 4 0 4 1 2 5 0 3 4	4 3 1 5 3 4 5 5 5 4 4 3 0 1	88	47%	28%	3.78	4.17	4.67
Reichert,Dan	2000	18	0 5 5	0 5 2 4 3 3 3 4 3 1 3 1 0 0 1	100	28%	39%	4.70	4.80	5.27
	2001	19	3 3 3 4 4 2 2 3 4 3 2 1 0 5 4 0 3	3 0	91	26%	21%	6.56	5.63	4.73
	2002	6	5 0 1 2 3 1		95	17%	50%	5.32	5.37	6.90
Reitsma,Chris	2001	29	5 5 3 4 0 2 4 3 2 3 2 4 1 0 3 2 2 2	1 3 0 4 1 0 4 4 4 0 0	92	31%	31%	5.29	4.89	5.08
	2002	21	3 0 3 0 3 3 4 3 5 1 0 3 5 1 4 2 0	3 0 3 0	86	19%	38%	3.65	4.52	5.45
Reyes,Dennys	2001	6		3 0 3 3 0 2	83	0%	33%	4.86	4.93	5.53
	2002	5		0 1 0 3 0	80	0%	80%	5.38	5.76	12.14
Reynolds,Shane	2000	22	4 3 3 3 3 5 3 5 3 4 2 4 4 3 5 0 4 4	0 1 3 0	98	41%	18%	5.22	5.27	4.44
	2001	28	3 0 0 5 4 4 4 3 4 4 4 3 5 4 3	0 1 4 4 4 2 3 5 5 1 3 4 3	91	54%	18%	4.35	4.72	4.37
	2002	13	2 0 2 2 5 4 4 3 4 2 3 0 0		91	31%	23%	4.86	5.22	4.71
Rijo,Jose	2002	9	2 5 1 0 2 4 0 1	0	79	22%	56%	5.14	5.33	7.36
Ritchie,Todd	2000	31	4 3 3 4 2 3 0 3 2 0 4 5 1 4 4 4 0 3	4 0 4 2 4 4 4 4 5 2 2 3 3	91	45%	16%	4.81	4.81	4.40
	2001	33	4 2 2 5 1 2 3 4 1 4 2 3 5 4 4 4 3 3	4 3 0 5 3 3 3 0 3 0 5 4 3 0 4	91	39%	18%	4.48	4.04	4.52
	2002	23	5 2 3 5 5 1 1 1 2 0 0 3 4 3 0 3 3 4 0	3 3 0 2	97	22%	35%	6.09	6.08	5.36
Roa,Joe	2002	11		0 3 3 4 3 4 4 3 4 3 0	88	36%	18%	4.06	4.72	4.52
Rodriguez,Ricardo	2002	7		2 4 0 3 3 0 4	95	29%	29%	5.69	4.43	4.93
Rogers,Kenny	2000	33	3 3 3 1 3 2 3 2 3 3 5 4 4 3 4 5 2 2	4 4 3 0 3 3 4 2 2 3 1 4 4 3 0	107	30%	12%	4.56	4.64	4.49
	2001	20	4 2 3 3 4 2 2 2 1 4 5 4 5 3 2 0 0 4	4 0	98	40%	20%	6.21	5.96	4.56

PQS PITCHING LOGS

Pitcher	Year	No.	FIRST HALF	SECOND HALF	PC	DOM	DIS	ERA	xERA	qERA
	2002	33	3 5 2 4 5 3 0 4 2 3 3 4 1 0 0 4 3 0	3 3 4 0 2 4 3 4 1 2 4 4 2 5 4	101	39%	21%	3.86	4.01	4.64
Rueter,Kirk	2000	31	0 1 4 4 3 3 3 2 1 0 3 3 4 0 2 3	2 3 3 2 2 3 0 0 0 3 1 3 4 2 4	95	16%	29%	3.96	4.89	5.03
	2001	34	0 4 4 0 1 2 0 3 3 2 3 1 3 4 4 1 4 2	3 3 0 3 3 5 2 2 2 3 3 2 1 3 4 3	94	21%	24%	4.43	4.80	4.75
	2002	33	4 3 4 3 2 2 4 1 2 2 4 2 0 3 3 2 2 2	3 2 4 4 1 1 1 4 3 4 4 0 2 3 2	99	27%	18%	3.24	4.06	4.62
Rupe,Ryan	2000	18	3 0 0 3 3 1 0	3 3 2 3 2 3 4 5 1 0 0	87	11%	39%	6.87	6.56	5.54
	2001	26	0 4 1 4 1 3 5 0 5 5 5 0 3 3	0 5 0 3 4 2 2 2 0 4 5 0	91	38%	35%	6.60	5.62	5.13
	2002	15	5 3 3 5 3 5 5 0 3 4 4 2 5 0	0	92	47%	20%	5.60	3.59	4.53
Rusch,Glendon	2000	30	4 3 5 3 5 2 4 5 5 1 4 5 4 3 5	3 4 4 4 0 3 4 4 4 5 4 2 0 5 3	104	63%	10%	4.02	3.89	3.71
	2001	33	0 5 5 0 0 5 2 0 2 0 5 0 0 5 4 3 4 4	5 2 3 4 5 0 0 2 0 4 5 0 3 3 5	93	42%	33%	4.63	5.11	4.92
	2002	34	3 4 4 5 5 5 0 3 4 0 1 4 3 3 4 4 4 0	0 3 4 4 2 3 3 2 2 5 4 3 4 3 0 3	106	44%	18%	4.71	4.96	4.44
Saarloos,Kirk	2002	17	0 0 0	4 4 2 3 3 4 0 5 4 2 0 1 3 0	78	29%	41%	6.04	5.37	5.40
Sabathia,C.C.	2001	33	2 2 3 2 3 4 2 0 0 0 3 5 5 5 0 5 0	5 3 4 4 0 4 4 5 0 5 5 0 1 5 4 4	95	48%	27%	4.40	3.68	4.67
	2002	33	4 3 5 0 0 1 4 2 4 5 0 4 2 4 3 3 2	3 2 2 2 2 5 4 3 4 4 4 4 4 3 3 4	102	45%	12%	4.37	3.71	4.28
Santana,Johan	2000	5	2 0 0	2 0	85	0%	60%	6.49	5.96	9.02
	2001	4	0 2 3 1		78	0%	50%	4.79	5.30	7.46
	2002	14	4 0 5 0 5 5	0 0 5 5 4 4 5 4	99	71%	29%	3.00	2.75	3.97
Schilling,Curt	2000	29	3 4 2 2 0 3 5 2 5 5 5 4 5	2 3 4 4 4 4 3 4 3 4 2 4 5 2 5 4	106	59%	3%	3.81	3.83	3.38
	2001	35	5 5 3 4 3 3 4 3 5 4 5 4 5 4 3 4 4 4 5	3 0 5 2 5 5 5 5 3 5 5 5 2 5 5 4	106	71%	3%	2.99	3.54	2.99
	2002	35	5 5 4 4 5 4 4 5 5 4 5 5 5 5 4 4 4 3 5	5 4 5 5 5 5 5 5 5 4 4 4 5 5 3 4	106	94%	0%	3.23	2.82	2.39
Schmidt,Jason	2000	11	4 4 2 0 4 1 3 4 2 2 1		110	36%	27%	5.42	5.44	4.82
	2001	25	4 4 2 2 5 0 4 0 5 5 3	4 5 5 5 0 3 5 3 4 5 5 4 4 3	100	64%	12%	3.74	3.54	3.71
	2002	29	2 0 0 0 5 0 4 5 5 5 5 3 5 1	4 4 4 5 5 5 4 5 5 4 5 5 3 5 5	104	72%	17%	3.45	3.03	3.63
Schoeneweis,Scott	2000	27	3 3 3 0 4 4 1 1 2 4 2 4 2 0	2 1 2 4 3 3 2 3 5 4 0 0 0	95	26%	30%	5.45	4.79	5.13
	2001	32	3 3 2 4 3 3 2 2 0 4 3 4 5 3 0 0 3	3 1 0 3 4 4 3 0 2 2 4 2 4 2 2	99	25%	19%	5.09	4.75	4.62
	2002	15	4 1 3 0 3 2 3 1 3 5 3 2 0 3 0		91	13%	33%	4.88	4.58	5.37
Sedlacek,Shawn	2002	14	4 3 2 3	4 2 3 0 2 0 5 3 2 0	92	21%	21%	6.75	5.88	4.75
Sele,Aaron	2000	34	3 3 0 1 2 4 4 3 3 4 4 5 3 0 3 5 5 3	3 3 3 3 2 3 3 0 3 0 4 5 3 3 3 2	100	26%	15%	4.52	4.14	4.62
	2001	33	2 4 0 4 2 5 3 2 3 3 3 4 0 0 3 3 2 4	3 5 3 2 1 5 3 4 3 4 0 4 4 5 1	98	36%	18%	3.60	3.99	4.52
	2002	26	1 1 4 2 1 3 3 3 2 2 3 4 2 1 0 4 3	2 4 4 2 5 3 3 2 0	100	23%	23%	4.89	5.13	4.75
Sheets,Ben	2001	25	4 4 4 3 4 3 0 0 4 3 4 2 4 3 4 2	5 0 4 4 1 3 0 2 3	95	44%	20%	4.75	5.05	4.56
	2002	34	4 4 4 0 0 2 5 3 5 5 2 3 2 0 5 3 1 5	5 5 3 1 3 1 5 5 1 5 4 4 4 4 5 5	103	56%	21%	4.17	4.56	4.23
Simontacchi,Jason	2002	24	4 1 4 2 3 2 4 0 3 3	3 3 1 0 0 3 3 5 3 2 4 2 5 3	91	25%	21%	4.03	4.53	4.73
Smith,Bud	2001	14	3	3 4 4 5 3 4 3 2 0 4 5 3 0	91	43%	14%	3.28	3.85	4.32
	2002	10	3 1 0 0 1 0 2 0	4 0	86	10%	70%	6.94	6.35	9.84
Smith,Mike	2002	6	0 0 0 0	0 0	75	0%	100%	6.69	5.97	15.00
Smith,Travis	2002	10	2 5 5 0 3 3	2 0 4 0	77	30%	30%	7.17	6.37	5.08
Smyth,Steve	2002	7		0 3 5 0 0 0 0	62	14%	71%	9.35	7.83	9.84
Soriano,Rafael	2002	8	2 2 4 4 4 1 0 0		86	38%	38%	4.60	4.73	5.13
Sosa,Jorge	2002	14	0 3 3	3 4 3 1 0 0 4 3 1 1 3	90	14%	43%	5.18	4.36	5.70
Sparks,Steve	2000	15	1	2 1 2 4 4 5 4 3 3 5 0 0 4 4	102	47%	27%	4.17	4.04	4.67
	2001	33	0 4 1 3 3 3 0 1 4 2 4 5 2 3 3 4 4	4 3 1 5 0 0 5 5 2 4 3 5 4 3 4 3	107	42%	21%	3.65	4.16	4.56
	2002	30	4 2 3 3 1 3 2 0 3 0 2 0 0 3 2 3	0 2 4 5 4 5 3 2 4 0 2 0 3 2	98	20%	27%	5.52	5.54	4.98
Stark,Denny	2002	20	3 5 2 2 4	4 3 0 3 3 3 3 1 1 0 3 4 2 3 0	89	20%	25%	4.01	4.50	4.98
Stein,Blake	2000	17	2	3 3 2 4 3 1 0 4 4 2 4 0 3 5 3 2	109	29%	18%	4.59	4.67	4.62
	2001	15	0 4 3 5 0 0 3 4 0 4	3 0 3 4 2	89	33%	33%	4.74	4.42	5.08
	2002	2	0 2		78	0%	50%	8.02	6.29	7.46
Stephenson,Garrett	2000	31	5 3 2 2 1 4 1 2 3 5 2 3 3 5 2 0 0	4 4 3 0 4 3 5 2 2 1 3 3 2 2	104	26%	19%	4.50	4.70	4.62
	2002	10	0 5 0 0 3 3 0	0 0 2	78	10%	60%	5.40	4.91	8.46
Stephens,John	2002	10		0 5 5 5 3 1 4 4 4 1	95	60%	30%	6.09	5.19	4.39
Stottlemyre,Todd	2000	18	2 4 1 0 1 5 3 5 4 3 3 4 4 0	0 4 0 0	84	39%	39%	4.92	5.07	5.13
Sturtze,Tanyon	2000	6	1	3 5 3 5 0	90	33%	33%	4.76	4.70	5.08
	2001	27	3 5 0 3 3 4 1 3 4 3 3 4	5 2 1 1 4 3 5 3 4 2 3 1 3 2 4	106	33%	19%	4.43	4.53	4.60
	2002	33	1 2 2 4 4 2 2 4 2 2 2 2 3 5 3 4 1 4	4 2 0 1 2 3 3 4 2 3 3 2 0 5 3	108	27%	15%	5.18	5.60	4.62
Suppan,Jeff	2000	33	3 5 5 4 0 0 3 3 5 3 5 0 3 3 1 3 2 0	4 2 3 2 2 4 2 3 3 3 1 2 0 4 3	106	24%	21%	4.94	5.27	4.75
	2001	34	0 3 4 3 3 4 2 4 0 3 4 2 3 3 4 2 3 2	4 4 4 4 3 3 3 3 2 1 4 2 0 2 2 3	105	29%	12%	4.37	4.46	4.50
	2002	33	2 4 3 4 4 4 0 4 4 5 3 0 2 2 3 3 2 4 4	2 2 3 3 4 3 1 2 1 0 3 2 3 4	104	33%	15%	5.32	4.93	4.60
Tankersley,Dennis	2002	9	3 4 2 4 0 0 0	1 0	81	22%	56%	8.12	7.76	7.36
Tavarez,Julian	2000	12		3 3 3 3 4 2 3 3 0 2 2 4	91	17%	8%	4.43	4.44	4.50
	2001	28	2 4 4 5 2 5 1 4 2 3 3 3 3 3 3 0 0	3 3 4 4 2 0 2 0 0 1 4	93	29%	25%	4.53	4.48	4.93
	2002	27	0 1 2 0 0 3 3 3 3 3 4 1 2 3	0 3 1 2 3 3 2 4 3 3 1 1 4	94	11%	33%	5.41	5.35	5.37
Tejera,Michael	2002	18	0 3 5 3 5 4	4 3 2 3 5 1 4 4 0 0 1 0	99	39%	33%	4.47	4.73	5.00
Thomson,John	2001	14	1 4 2	5 4 3 5 2 4 4 3 3 5 5	99	57%	7%	4.25	4.83	3.68
	2002	30	4 4 4 0 5 5 2 4 3 4 2 0 3 1 2 2 3 4	1 2 3 2 0 4 3 5 1 0 2 5	98	37%	23%	4.72	3.94	4.64
Thurman,Mike	2000	17	2 0 0	5 0 2 2 2 3 3 3 0 4 2 5 2 0	87	18%	29%	6.90	6.21	5.03
	2001	26	0 3 0 4 5 4 0 0 4 0 2 3 1	2 4 0 4 3 2 3 5 3 4 4 2 3	90	35%	27%	5.33	5.31	4.82
	2002	3	3 0	0	90	0%	67%	5.18	5.57	9.80
Tollberg,Brian	2000	19	5 5 2 0	5 4 4 0 3 1 3 4 5 2 5 2 2 1 4	91	47%	21%	3.43	4.04	4.53
	2001	19	4 3 4 3 4 4	0 2 5 5 2 2 2 4 2 3 2 3 2	88	37%	5%	4.47	4.96	4.29
	2002	12	0 3 4 1 0 4 4 3 2 3 2 0		83	25%	33%	6.20	7.04	5.13
Tomko,Brett	2000	8	5 2 4 2 3 0 4 4		93	50%	13%	4.69	4.53	4.23
	2001	4	0 4 0	4	87	50%	50%	5.03	5.10	5.81
	2002	32	3 2 4 5 4 2 4 3 2 0 5 3 4 1 4 2 2 3	4 3 2 0 4 0 4 4 0 4 4 3 0 0	96	41%	22%	4.50	4.66	4.56
Torres,Salomon	2002	5		4 0 3 1 2	83	20%	40%	2.70	2.93	5.50
Towers,Josh	2001	20	2 4 4 3 3 2 3 3	3 3 2 2 2 3 2 3 3 4 2 3	92	15%	0%	4.52	4.69	4.48
	2002	3	1 2 1		96	0%	67%	8.00	9.07	9.80
Trachsel,Steve	2000	34	5 0 0 3 0 4 5 5 2 0 0 1 5 2 3 3 2 1 0	4 1 0 3 3 3 0 2 5 3 3 0 3 3 0	97	21%	38%	4.81	5.20	5.36
	2001	28	1 5 0 3 5 3 4 0 4 4 5 3 4 0	4 4 5 5 5 0 3 5 4 3 4 3 4 5	97	61%	18%	4.45	4.11	3.83
	2002	30	2 1 3 0 0 3 1 3 3 5 3 4 4 3 5 4 0	4 4 1 4 0 3 4 4 3 0 5 3 3	95	37%	27%	3.38	4.13	4.82
Valdes,Ismael	2000	21	0 4 0 4 4 4 2 0 4	3 0 3 0 0 0 5 2 1 0 5 2	85	33%	43%	5.64	5.87	5.29
	2001	27	4 3 2 5 3 3 1 3 5 4 0 4	4 5 1 5 3 3 3 0 0 3 3 2 0 0 3	96	30%	26%	4.47	4.63	4.90
	2002	31	4 0 3 2 5 4 4 2 1 3 4 3 0 3 5 1	3 2 4 4 3 5 3 4 2 2 4 2 5 0 1	95	39%	19%	4.18	3.13	4.52
Van Hekken,Andy	2002	5		3 3 0 3 3	89	0%	20%	3.00	4.92	4.83
Vazquez,Javier	2000	33	4 4 2 3 2 5 1 5 4 3 3 3 3 4 0 4 4	0 3 3 4 3 4 5 4 0 3 5 5 4 4 4 3	107	52%	12%	4.06	4.70	4.23
	2001	32	2 5 0 5 0 0 3 5 5 3 3 5 4 5 3 3 5 2 4	5 5 5 2 5 4 5 5 3 5 5 5 3	106	59%	9%	3.43	3.14	3.68
	2002	34	4 4 3 5 4 5 4 4 5 4 2 3 5 2 2 4 0 2 3	4 5 4 4 0 4 5 0 1 2 3 5 5 3 4	104	59%	12%	3.91	4.27	3.97

PQS PITCHING LOGS

Pitcher	Year	No.	FIRST HALF	SECOND HALF	PC	DOM	DIS	ERA	xERA	qERA
Villone,Ron	2000	23	1 3 0 1 1 2 3 3 2 2 0 0 2 3 0 2 0	3 3 1 2 0 5	98	4%	43%	5.43	5.57	5.90
	2001	12	2 0 0 0 3 3	4 3 0 3 4 0	90	17%	42%	5.91	5.69	5.60
	2002	7	3 3 0 3 0 4 3		90	14%	29%	5.81	4.19	5.08
Wakefield,Tim	2000	17	0 2 0 3 3 4	3 1 3 5 3 0 3 0 1 4 2	94	18%	35%	5.49	5.37	5.45
	2001	17	5 5 5 4 4 5 5 4 4	4 2 0 4 4 1 4 3	101	76%	12%	3.91	3.73	3.41
	2002	16	4 5 3 5	4 4 2 5 4 4 5 5 5 4 3 3	95	75%	0%	2.82	2.48	2.84
Walker,Pete	2002	20	0 4 4 0 2	0 4 1 0 4 3 4 3 4 0 3 1 4 2 3	93	35%	35%	4.37	4.46	5.13
Washburn,Jarrod	2000	13	3 3 4 3 0 5 3 4 0 2	4 3 2	95	31%	15%	3.94	4.31	4.60
	2001	30	2 1 0 2 5 5 2 2 4 3 3 3 3 5 5 4	3 4 3 4 0 5 5 4 4 2 5 3 2 0	102	43%	13%	3.78	4.25	4.32
	2002	32	3 3 0 3 3 3 4 2 5 5 5 2 5 2 4 5 5	3 3 3 3 4 3 4 2 2 4 3 3 4 4 2	105	41%	3%	3.15	3.19	3.89
Wayne,Justin	2002	5		0 3 3 4 0	81	20%	40%	5.43	4.57	5.50
Weaver,Jeff	2000	29	4 2 3 3 4 4 0 4 4 0 4 1 4 2	1 3 4 5 0 2 2 3 5 0 3 3 5 1 4	105	41%	24%	4.32	4.22	4.56
	2001	33	3 3 2 4 2 4 5 2 4 5 4 4 4 3 2 3 1 4	3 3 3 3 4 3 3 3 3 4 4 0 4 5 4	110	45%	6%	4.09	3.96	3.98
	2002	26	2 2 2 1 4 3 4 4 3 5 5 2 0 5 5 4 4 4	4 2 4 3 3 4 4 4	109	58%	8%	3.53	3.23	3.68
Wells,David	2000	35	5 4 0 5 5 3 5 3 4 0 4 5 4 4 3 5 4 3 3	3 0 5 2 4 0 0 5 4 3 0 5 4 5 4 0	93	57%	20%	4.12	4.35	4.23
	2001	16	2 3 1 4 3 3 3 3 2 3 0 0 5 4 3 0		90	19%	25%	4.49	4.95	5.03
	2002	31	3 4 3 4 1 3 3 4 4 0 5 5 3 4 5 5 1	3 4 4 4 0 3 1 3 5 4 4 4 4 4	101	58%	16%	3.76	3.78	4.10
Wells,Kip	2000	19	0 3 3 4 0 3 0 4 0 0 0 5 0 0	4 0 2 1 2	89	21%	53%	6.41	6.63	6.74
	2001	20	3 5 4 4 3 2 5 3 3 4	3 4 0 0 0 0 0 3 0 0	89	30%	35%	4.84	5.02	5.19
	2002	33	2 0 1 5 4 4 3 5 4 3 4 2 4 0 5 3 3 0	4 3 2 5 2 4 2 2 2 5 1 5 2 5 5	94	45%	15%	3.59	4.20	4.40
Williams,David	2001	18	1 3 3	3 4 5 1 0 0 2 3 2 5 0 2 3 4 0	87	22%	33%	3.59	3.90	5.21
	2002	9	5 4 2 5 0 0 0 0 4		85	44%	44%	5.02	4.99	5.21
Williams,Woody	2000	23	5 0 3 4 2 3 3 3	4 4 4 4 3 4 3 4 4 5 3 4 4 5 4	113	61%	4%	3.75	3.84	3.29
	2001	34	2 2 4 3 0 5 3 3 4 5 4 3 2 4 5 2 0 2 5	1 5 1 4 4 0 0 4 2 4 4 3 5 5 4	103	50%	18%	4.05	4.44	4.37
	2002	17	0 5 5 4 2 3 4 4 4 5 5 4	0 5 4 4 0	92	71%	18%	2.53	2.90	3.63
Wilson,Paul	2000	7		5 4 4 0 0 5 5	89	71%	29%	3.96	3.30	3.97
	2001	24	3 4 0 0 3 2 3 3 3 5 0 0	4 4 2 5 1 2 5 3 5 5 4 5	94	42%	21%	4.88	4.88	4.56
	2002	30	3 3 2 2 4 2 3 3 2 4 2 0 4 3 2 4	5 3 4 4 3 4 3 3 2 0 0 3 0 0	104	27%	17%	4.85	5.12	4.62
Wolf,Randy	2000	32	3 4 3 5 5 3 4 5 0 3 5 1 3 4 5 4 5	4 5 3 3 3 0 2 0 3 5 4 2 5 2 5	110	50%	13%	4.37	4.49	4.23
	2001	25	0 2 0 3 3 4 5 5 5 4 0 4 2 0 3	5 4 4 5 3 4 0 5 4 5	100	56%	20%	3.70	3.50	4.23
	2002	31	4 4 3 2 0 4 3 4 2 4 4 2 4 4 3 4	5 5 5 3 5 4 1 5 4 5 4 5 5 5 3	103	68%	6%	3.21	3.16	3.38
Wood,Kerry	2000	22	4 2 0 4 4 4 0 5 4 5 4	1 4 4 0 4 0 5 5 4 0 5	104	68%	27%	4.80	4.04	4.07
	2001	28	4 0 5 4 5 3 5 0 4 5 5 4 3 5 3 3 4 3	4 5 3 3 5 5 5 3 4 5	108	64%	7%	3.36	3.02	3.50
	2002	33	4 5 3 0 2 3 5 4 4 4 2 4 4 0 3 2 4	4 5 4 4 5 5 2 4 5 3 5 4 4 3 5 5	103	67%	6%	3.68	3.35	3.38
Wright,Danny	2001	12		2 3 4 2 0 0 1 1 3 2 3 0	93	8%	42%	4.37	4.58	5.80
	2002	33	3 4 0 1 4 3 0 0 4 4 0 3 3 5 2 3 0 4	3 4 4 4 4 0 3 2 5 3 4 2 5 4 5	95	45%	21%	5.19	4.66	4.53
Wright,Jamey	2000	25	3 4 5 0 3 5 4 3 0	2 2 4 3 3 3 1 1 2 3 5 3 2 4 2 5	105	32%	16%	4.11	4.11	4.60
	2001	33	3 4 0 3 2 4 3 1 2 4 2 0 2 3 2 3 3	4 4 0 0 4 3 1 4 3 5 1 0 0 4 4 2	98	30%	27%	4.91	4.95	4.90
	2002	22	0 5 2 3 3 3 0 3 3 2	2 3 0 2 3 2 3 3 3 3 0 3	96	5%	18%	5.30	4.07	4.68
Wright,Jaret	2000	9	3 4 0 3 3 1 4 0 0		96	22%	44%	4.67	3.87	5.50
	2001	7	3 0 1 4 0 4 0		76	29%	57%	5.95	5.08	7.14
	2002	6		0 0 0 0 3 0	71	0%	83%	15.91	12.73	12.14
Yoshii,Masato	2000	29	3 3 3 1 0 4 2 3 0 3 3 0 4 4 3 3 0	2 1 2 4 4 3 1 1 5 1 2 0	91	21%	34%	5.87	5.85	5.21
	2001	11	0 5 2 4 0 2 0 0	5 3 4	79	36%	36%	4.78	4.94	5.13
	2002	20	4 0 2 0 0 3 3 3	3 3 3 3 4 4 3 4 2 2 0 2	75	20%	20%	4.12	4.49	4.75
Zambrano,Carlos	2001	1		0	70	0%	100%	16.25	10.26	15.00
	2002	16	0 3	3 5 4 0 4 5 0 4 3 4 0 5 4 3	99	50%	25%	3.67	3.91	4.61
Zambrano,Victor	2002	11		5 2 5 4 2 2 2 3 3 3 4	94	36%	0%	5.53	5.16	4.18
Zito,Barry	2000	14		3 4 3 4 3 4 4 4 3 5 4 3 4 5	104	64%	0%	3.44	3.28	3.29
	2001	35	4 3 3 5 5 5 0 0 5 5 5 2 2 3 4 5 3 3 5	4 0 0 5 5 3 2 5 5 3 5 5 4 4 4 3	101	57%	11%	3.49	3.27	3.97
	2002	35	5 5 4 0 5 0 5 4 5 3 4 5 2 4 5 5 0 3 5	3 4 4 3 3 4 5 3 5 3 3 5 5 2 2 5	105	60%	9%	2.75	2.94	3.50

Bullpen Leading Indicators:
Are We Losing the Bullpen Battle?

False Saviors

In 2002, the LABR experts league drafted 28 potential sources of saves at a cost of $617. After only five weeks of the season, there were already six Major League teams (BAL, TEX, CHC, FLA, LA, MON) that had turned over their closer's role, negating much, if not all, of the draft day investment of their fantasy owners.

Of course, there was a flipside to this horror story, names like Eric Gagne, Juan Acevedo, Mike DeJean and Jorge Julio. These were surprise saves sources whose owners are reaping the benefit of being a little bit lucky. But in a game like Rotisserie, where the saves category constitutes 20-25% of a team's score, this type of turnover -- *through no fault or skill of any owner* -- can have a dramatic impact on the final standings.

These experiences have become typical over the past five years. Saves used to be a stable commodity that almost always paid off. In the mid-1990s, your top closers would almost always garner bids in the high $30's. But, as the turnover in roles has increased, the risk of investing even $35 in a closer has skyrocketed. Here's an historical look...

NUMBER OF CLOSERS

YEAR	Drafted	Avg $	Failed	%	New Sources
1996	24	$30	3	13%	2
1997	26	$30	5	19%	8
1998	25	$32	11	44%	9
1999	23	$25	5	22%	7
2000	27	$25	10	37%	9
2001	25	$26	7	28%	7
2002	28	$22	8	29%	12

A bit of explanation here... CLOSERS DRAFTED refers to the number of top saves sources purchased in both AL and NL Rotisserie Leagues each year. For the most part, these only include relievers drafted for at least $15 or so. AVG $ refers to the average 4x4 purchase price of these pitchers. FAILED is the number (and percentage) of CLOSERS DRAFTED that did not return at least 50% of their value that year. The Failures include those that lost their value due to ineffectiveness, injury or managerial decision. NEW SOURCES are the arms that were not drafted for saves (or in some cases, not drafted at all), but finished with enough saves value to rank among the top closers for that year.

The chart shows us that, prior to 1998, about 16% of all drafted closers went belly-up. Since 1998, that rate has almost doubled.

1998 was a critical turning point. Confidence in bullpen investments that year was at its peak, as evidenced by the $32 average closer price. But the near-50% failure rate took its toll. The fallout from that experience was a steep decline in prices the following year, which has persisted in the four seasons since.

Here are the names that have caused extreme anguish, or ecstasy, or both, over the past few years alone...

1998	1999	2000	2001	2002
FAILURES				
Bottalico	Acevedo	Howry	Jones,T	Alfonseca
Brantley	Beck	Jackson	Kohlmeier	Anderson
Eckersely	Gordon	Mantei	Leskanic	Foulke
Hernandz,R	Ligtenberg	Rocker	Lowe	Fox
Jones,D	Taylor,B	Shuey	Mantei	Gordon
Jones,T		Timlin	Rocker	Strickland
Loiselle		Trombley	Veres	Wickman
Mesa		Urbina		Zimmerman
Myers,R		Wagner		
Slocumb		Williamson		
Wohlers				
NEW SOURCES				
Acevedo	Foulke	Dotel	Fassero	Acevedo
Benitez	Graves	Isringhsn	Gordon	Baez
Howry	Koch	Jimenez	Kim	Cordero
Jackson,M	Lowe	Kohlmeir	Mesa	DeJean
Ligtenberg	Rocker	Leskanic	Prinz	Gagne
Mantei	Williamson	Sasaki	Yan	Irabu
Olsen,G	Zimmermn	Strickland	Zimmermn	Julio
Taylor,B		Wells,B		Looper
Wickman		Williams		Marte
				Nunez
				Osuna
				Williamson

Right now, choosing saves correctly is about a 67% percentage play, which is borderline at best. However, the downside in choosing incorrectly is far more damaging than in any other Rotisserie category. Why? Because Saves are the toughest category to replace. If you lose a starting pitcher, you still have other starters contributing. If you lose a hitter, that's still only one of 14 bats racking up stats. The only other category that comes close in scarcity is SBs, but the fleet of foot are far less risky than the bullpen aces, and there are still far more sources of replacement stolen bases than saves.

As such, saves always come at a premium... at the draft table, in trade talks and in the free agent pool. Any guess how many closers have managed to maintain full frontline value for all seven years of this analysis?

Only three... Trevor Hoffman, Robb Nen and Troy Percival. You need to drop down to a 5-year view to add even one more name, Armando Benitez. And that's it. Every other closer has had at least one down year in the last five. So, in all of baseball, only four closers have returned full draft value for five straight years.

Sounds like a pretty strong argument against signing closers to long-term contracts, doesn't it?

So what is an intelligent fantasy leaguer to do?

1. We can discount closers at the draft table (which is what happened at LABR)... but that only softens the blow of overspending; it does not address the risk of losing your investment completely for every third closer you buy.

2. We can pay top dollar for the cream of the crop in hopes of better assuring a return on investment... but Mark Wohlers, Rod Beck, Ricky Bottalico and Todd Jones were all once considered in that "cream" class.

3. We can play it close to the vest and spend prudently, buying only bargains and loading our reserves with contingency plans... but that might yield an even lower return than buying arms at the 33% failure rate.

4. We can punt saves completely and focus on skills, speculative saves and firming up the other categories... but that can put us at a competitive disadvantage.

5. Or we can just assume the risk and pray a lot.

I'm not much of a religious guy, so I hope there's something better to hang our hats on. But the percentage plays are underwhelming, which leaves us being more *reactive than proactive when it comes to* managing our bullpens. It's a heckuva way to run a fantasy team, yet that's what we've been doing.

Prospecting for Opportunity

Projecting saves requires a different process than just about any other aspect of baseball performance forecasting.

Good skill alone doesn't necessarily win jobs, though a lack of skill can sometimes lose a job. Sometimes. Managerial whim varies from ballclub to ballclub. On some teams, three blown saves and you're out; on other teams, a designated closer can go for weeks without a successful save and keep his job. And, still other teams have the dreaded "committee," which is an excuse for managerial indecision or lack of apparent options. Of course, a committee could morph into a primary go-to guy at any time if someone steps up and grabs the job. What does that take? Typically, some super-secret quality we are not made privy to.

What this all means is that, in order for us to project who is going to get the ball with the game on the line in the ninth inning, we have to do some speculating. We can rely on our sabermetric tools and try to be scientific about it, but that alone won't get the job done. It also requires some gut feel. Gut can negate science, however, which makes the process more of an art. Got all that?

We use the Rule of TOG here, which captures the elements as well as anything else. Talent, Opportunity and Guile are the three qualities that are required for saves. But we've been playing with TOG for six years now and still haven't nailed it. Talent is measurable, but Opportunity comes and goes, and HQ bullpen analyst, Doug Dennis, is still out somewhere on his quest for the Holy Guile.

I think we still need to be grounded at least a little bit in science. To aid in this process, we have a terrific tool at HQ, the Bullpen Leading Indicator Charts, which are compiled by Matt Dodge. These charts help focus on many of the statistical and situational factors that might go into a manager's decision to grant any individual pitcher a save opportunity. It's not all-encompassing, but it's a good start. In the following pages, we provide a three-year scan of indicators for all pitchers who posted at least 1 save and/or 3 holds in 2002.

These are the gauges that I look at...

Saves Percentage... which could be the single most important number on the chart, especially for identifying closers who might be in danger of losing their job. What it says is simple... "Who is getting it done?" and that is probably the biggest determining factor for a manager. Bottom line is that, skills or no skills, a pitcher will not keep getting the call if he is not consistently converting his save opportunities. The benchmark I use is 80%. That's where it all begins.

Base Performance Value... The components of BPV are evaluated in a variety of ways. I like to target command ratio first, but what I like doesn't matter. Major league managers tend to look for dominance. If a pitcher can strike out eight or nine batters per 9 IP, he's immediate closer material, sometimes even if he's also walking nearly that many. In using BPV, we can set a benchmark of 75 as the minimum level necessary for success. BPV's over 100 are much better, however.

Situational Performance... is the last piece of the puzzle. Our bullpen chart includes the opposition batting averages for each pitcher versus RH and LH hitters, with runners on base, in his first 15 pitches, etc. which are all good indicators. However, beyond RH/LH performance, I'm not sure how many of these gauges managers really look at. Still, they might provide some clues, and we'll set a benchmark of a .250 BA for these indicators.

The tools are here. Whether or not a major league manager will make a decision reflective of this information remains to be seen. But I do think the data can help us increase our odds of uncovering those elusive saves and minimizing at least some of the risk.

Let's go through a process to identify areas of opportunity for the saves prospector. For the purposes of this book, I'll provide the step-by-step and a preliminary list of names. But be aware that saves are more volatile than any other projection, and any speculations on saves I could provide will be outdated by the time you read this. So you may want to set aside an hour and go through this exercise again, preferably as close to your draft as possible.

The first step involves identifying the *teams* where opportunities might open up. We accomplish this by doing a comprehensive analysis of the current incumbent closer crop.

The Elite: For the purposes of setting the bar, let's define the Elite as any current frontline closer who meets or exceeds *all the benchmarks* listed above. These are pitchers who, barring injury, are not likely in danger of losing their jobs. What's also important is that this identifies teams that would not likely be good sources of hidden saves. In creating this list, start with pitchers who met the criteria in 2002, but give a higher ranking to those who've been able to maintain these levels over multiple years.

The players who meet all the benchmarks are Armando Benitez, Eric Gagne, Trevor Hoffman, Jason Isringhausen,

Byung-Hyun Kim, Billy Koch, Mariano Rivera, Kaz Sasaki and Billy Wagner. Also on this list, but not officially a "frontliner," are Scott Stewart and Luis Vizcaino, two arms that could well succeed if given the Opportunity.

The Near Elite: These are the closers that are doing the job (80% saves pct) but have fallen short in only one or two of the other indicators, or have been inconsistent over time. Looking objectively, these are pitchers who should not lose their jobs unless their areas of vulnerability begin to fester. The teams represented here, and those in the Elite category, should only be marginal sources of new saves.

This list includes Eddie Guardado, Jose Jimenez, Jorge Julio, Damaso Marte, Robb Nen, Troy Percival, John Smoltz and Ugueth Urbina.

A Question of Guile: These pitchers are putting up decent peripheral and situational numbers, but are unable to close the door at the 80% level. For some, this might not be a big deal. For others, this might be a danger sign. In fact, several of these arms have already lost jobs. If the managers of these teams are the types that are impatient, or expect immediate results, these could be bullpens that might provide some hidden saves at some point.

The list: Francsico Cordero, Keith Foulke, Buddy Groom, Roberto Hernandez, Vladimir Nunez, Antonio Osuna, Scott Williamson. Opportunities might be available in Chicago (AL), Cincinnati, Florida, Kansas City and Texas.

Pushing the Envelope: These closers are getting the job done, but have questionable support stats. Given their skills levels, will they be able to maintain that 80% success rate? For some managers, it doesn't matter as long as the games are being saved. For you, these might present moderate opportunities to go prospecting on these teams.

This list contains Mike Dejean, Jose Mesa and Mike Williams. Opportunities might be forthcoming on Milwaukee, Philadelphia and Pittsburgh.

The Problem Children: The final group is composed of closers who really have no business being put on the mound with a game on the line. They are neither getting the job done, nor posting acceptable BPI's or situational numbers. These represent teams where the best potential for new saves sources might be found.

The hit list: Juan Acevedo, Antonio Alfonseca, Danys Baez, Kelvim Escobar, Danny Graves, Braden Looper and Esteban Yan. Teams: Chicago (NL), Cincy again, Cleveland, Detroit, Florida again, Tampa and Toronto.

The Art and Science of Speculating

The next step is to look at all the non-closers who are putting up solid numbers and attempt to identify those that might step into save opportunities at some point.

Two separate lists here... the first contains pitchers on teams identified above as having some potential for hidden saves. The second list contains the high-skilled arms on teams with a solid incumbent. While these latter pitchers will not likely get many saves, they are safe havens for those trying to shore up ERA/WHIP, and if they ever get dealt, you never know what opportunities might lie down the road.

The gauges we'll look at here are similar. Saves percentage, however, is not something that will have meaning for these pitchers. Instead, we'll use Reliever Effectiveness...

Reliever Effectiveness Per Cent (Eff%)... calculated as *(Wins + Saves + Holds) / (Wins + Losses + SaveOpps + Holds).* This is a measure of the effectiveness of relief pitchers in pressure situations. How often does a reliever contribute positively to the outcome of the game? A record of consistent, positive impact on game outcomes breeds managerial confidence, and that confidence could pave the way to Opportunity. For those pitchers that are suddenly thrust into a closer's role, this formula helps gauge their potential to succeed based on past successes in similar roles.

The 80% benchmark still works fine for this new evaluator. You might consider revising some of the other benchmarks in order to cast out a slightly larger net for speculating on this group.

The prime candidates (high skilled pitchers in uncertain bullpens): Brian Boehringer (PIT), Blaine Neal (FLA), Ray King* (MIL), Cliff Politte (TOR), Carl Sadler* (CLE), Scott Sauerbeck* (PIT) and Gabe White* (CIN).

Not a whole lot to choose from, and some of the names likely are longshots. Those names with asterisks are left-handers.

The secondary candidates (high skilled pitchers in pens with a solid frontliner): Chad Bradford (OAK), Mike Crudale (STL), Chris Hammond (ATL), Latroy Hawkins (MIN), Mike Koplove (ARI), Mike Remlinger (ATL), J.C. Romero (MIN), Arthur Rhodes (SEA), Paul Shuey (LA), Jay Witasick (SD) and Tim Worrell (SF).

Some more tips...

- Downgrade the lefthanders on your list. While an Eddie Guardado comes along every so often, MLB mangers still like to reserve their precious left-handers for situational work.

- Remember that every team will have at least some saves. If your analysis concludes that there are no arms worthy in a particular pen, reduce your benchmarks and cast out a wider net. Someone *will* get saves, though probably not all that many.

- Prospect starters. Closers are often created out of failed starters, so keep an eye out for rotation arms that have solid BPI's but...

- are getting squeezed out of a rotation spot (e.g. Gagne)
- have failed or had marginal success as a starter (e.g. Acevedo, Escobar)
- are injury rehabs in need of a lighter workload (e.g. Smoltz)

- Go deeper into each team's system. While minor leaguers are not the best prospecting ground for closers – and especially minor league closers – those with exceptional BPI's do occasionally make the leap.

- Play out some conditional speculations. You can find more situational stats to speculate with on ESPN.com's web site.

Bullpen Indicators

				BPIs			Results		Runners		Pitch Ct		Platoon	
Pitcher			**Tm**	**IP/g**	**bpv**	**S%**	**Sv%**	**Eff%**	**Emp**	**On**	**0-15**	**16-30**	**vLH**	**vRH**
Acevedo,Juan	R	00	MIL	1.3	37	75%	0%	53%	211	297	231	269	287	220
		01	FLA	1.0	28	77%	0%	38%	269	296	303	302	319	264
		02	DET	1.1	66	79%	80%	71%	293	199	263	197	264	228
Adams,Terry	R	00	LA	1.3	51	76%	29%	62%	217	276	275	207	226	262
		01	LA	3.9	91	67%	0%	64%	255	282	250	241	232	295
		02	PHI	3.0	59	69%	0%	66%	235	281	268	179	246	263
Alfonseca,Antonio	R	00	FLA	1.0	24	74%	92%	83%	298	284	281	310	277	303
		01	FLA	1.1	70	81%	82%	76%	313	241	281	278	302	259
		02	CHC	1.1	64	73%	68%	60%	270	245	247	287	304	220
Almanza,Armando	L	00	FLA	0.7	69	72%	0%	74%	186	258	234	200	179	260
		01	FLA	0.8	45	73%	0%	78%	244	212	282	139	210	244
		02	FLA	0.9	80	73%	50%	81%	222	225	198	293	255	208
Alvarez,Juan	L	02	TEX	0.8	26	71%	0%	59%	194	288	229	313	233	250
Anderson,Matt	R	00	DET	1.1	66	68%	100%	87%	217	238	206	274	200	247
		01	DET	0.9	108	61%	92%	92%	242	268	255	271	291	222
Arrojo,Rolando	R	01	BOS	2.5	78	72%	71%	68%	223	238	226	274	238	221
		02	BOS	2.8	56	63%	25%	60%	231	317	239	275	313	221
Baez,Danys	R	01	CLE	1.2	99	82%	0%	83%	176	214	159	273	188	193
		02	CLE	4.2	55	71%	75%	55%	237	282	168	258	278	233
Bailey,Cory	R	01	KC	1.3	82	74%	0%	87%	244	222	228	264	164	297
		02	KC	1.2	7	80%	14%	47%	312	302	385	203	282	324
Banks,Willie	R	02	BOS	1.3	52	78%	100%	75%	190	262	274	93	246	200
Bauer,Rick	R	02	BAL	1.5	19	77%	20%	63%	266	269	239	258	288	253
Beimel,Joe	L	02	PIT	1.6	29	72%	0%	54%	265	268	260	272	262	269
Benitez,Armando	R	00	NYM	1.0	38	82%	89%	83%	132	171	140	171	133	161
		01	NYM	1.0	80	77%	93%	88%	225	198	221	179	212	215
		02	NYM	1.1	114	86%	89%	89%	216	149	202	183	160	220
Benoit,Joaquin	R	02	TEX	5.0	33	69%	100%	50%	299	247	220	327	275	268
Biddle,Rocky	R	02	CHW	1.8	37	78%	33%	57%	220	278	282	182	287	205
Boehringer,Brian	R	01	SF	1.4	67	76%	100%	56%	196	305	245	305	333	202
		02	PIT	1.1	78	73%	17%	79%	220	241	205	291	250	218
Borbon,Pedro	L	00	TOR	0.7	20	68%	100%	93%	177	378	294	263	209	360
		01	TOR	0.8	97	73%	0%	63%	215	278	257	184	182	306
		02	HOU	0.7	41	71%	20%	73%	266	277	282	250	240	324
Borowski,Joe	R	02	CHC	1.3	108	82%	33%	69%	252	220	247	262	209	260
Bottalico,Ricky	R	00	KC	1.2	41	71%	70%	67%	237	241	250	241	241	237
		01	PHI	1.0	59	75%	43%	78%	281	195	223	254	282	218
		02	PHI	0.9	52	74%	0%	79%	319	286	313	259	311	292
Bowie,Micah	L	02	OAK	0.9	31	95%		100%	250	269	297	0	273	250
Boyd,Jason	R	02	SD	1.2	-3	55%	0%	63%	254	353	308	268	235	356
Bradford,Chad	R	01	OAK	1.0	132	88%	25%	64%	293	268	289	237	300	274
		02	OAK	1.0	129	72%	40%	86%	241	269	268	186	267	247
Brohawn,Troy	L	01	ARI	0.8	31	70%	33%	72%	278	305	270	342	386	233
		02	SF	0.5	55	40%		75%	188	333	200	400	250	200
Brower,Jim	R	01	CIN	2.8	41	75%	50%	48%	258	232	234	226	272	228
		02	MON	1.5	64	67%	0%	75%	225	287	252	303	254	251
Bukvich,Ryan	R	02	KC	1.0	36	65%	0%	86%	244	306	293	235	171	358
Cabrera,Jose	R	00	HOU	1.1	43	63%	67%	69%	287	333	316	297	314	304
		01	ATL	1.1	60	81%	25%	60%	179	316	255	206	247	233
		02	MIL	2.1	5	62%	0%	45%	331	292	333	309	276	343
Carrara,Giovanni	R	01	LA	1.8	80	79%	0%	79%	237	207	221	309	259	267
		02	LA	1.4	37	81%	17%	72%	229	267	273	247	248	240
Cassidy,Scott	R	02	TOR	1.1	30	58%	0%	42%	220	224	216	205	242	209
Castillo,Frank	R	02	BOS	4.5	50	66%	50%	30%	234	340	291	301	281	269
Cerda,Jaime	L	02	NYM	0.8	80	81%		100%	170	292	257	174	268	204
Chen,Bruce	L	02	CIN	1.4	67	66%		55%	259	294	291	282	252	287
Colome,Jesus	R	01	TAM	1.6	24	81%		73%	208	208	270	136	188	220
		02	TAM	1.3	9	61%	0%	29%	328	351	420	213	414	287
Condrey,Clayton	R	02	SD	2.9	80	85%		67%	220	212	222	389	250	188
Cook,Dennis	L	00	NYM	0.9	48	69%	25%	67%	248	292	287	236	322	238
		01	PHI	0.7	63	69%	0%	69%	267	226	257	194	215	274
		02	ANA	0.7	42	76%	0%	80%	196	293	250	222	264	206
Cordero,Francisco	R	00	TEX	1.4	15	72%	0%	50%	304	271	315	242	310	271
		02	TEX	1.2	121	84%	83%	87%	181	246	188	226	189	216
Cormier,Rheal	L	00	BOS	1.1	59	67%	0%	71%	276	274	315	176	264	280
		01	PHI	0.9	66	69%	17%	62%	221	282	247	250	294	223
		02	PHI	1.1	49	67%	0%	61%	242	295	275	217	291	253
Creek,Doug	L	00	TAM	1.3	39	72%	33%	44%	207	243	263	164	170	260
		01	TAM	0.9	53	75%	0%	68%	226	233	238	188	198	250
		02	SEA	1.1	75	62%	0%	67%	223	296	234	220	239	277
Crudale,Mike	R	02	STL	1.1	118	85%	0%	90%	242	214	248	220	247	216
Cruz,Juan	R	02	CHC	2.2	45	76%	25%	33%	241	241	281	222	250	234
Darensbourg,Vic	L	00	FLA	1.1	28	74%	0%	67%	305	214	248	253	190	295
		01	FLA	0.8	92	67%	33%	76%	274	280	300	152	294	262
		02	FLA	1.2	0	70%		67%	294	319	348	281	254	331
Day,Zach	R	02	MON	2.0	62	70%	50%	78%	190	232	170	211	158	244
De los Santos,Val	L	00	MIL	1.1	44	70%	0%	73%	241	272	247	238	273	243
		02	MIL	1.1	59	75%		75%	218	200	215	183	219	207
DeJean,Mike	R	00	COL	1.0	15	73%	0%	58%	274	262	255	277	293	254
		01	MIL	1.1	73	80%	50%	78%	258	214	252	198	227	242
		02	MIL	1.1	61	81%	90%	78%	242	230	228	254	259	213
Donnelly,Brendan	R	02	ANA	1.1	125	80%	33%	83%	156	218	189	143	242	148

Bullpen Indicators

				BPIs			Results		Runners		Pitch Ct		Platoon	
Pitcher			**Tm**	**IP/g**	**bpv**	**S%**	**Sv%**	**Eff%**	**Emp**	**On**	**0-15**	**16-30**	**vLH**	**vRH**
Dotel,Octavio	R	00	HOU	2.5	61	70%	70%	58%	269	259	225	222	282	250
		01	HOU	1.7	137	79%	50%	77%	182	236	200	148	238	178
		02	HOU	1.2	161	83%	60%	84%	190	144	179	167	190	159
Drew,Tim	R	02	MON	2.3	145	69%	67%	80%	194	208	192	133	273	158
Durocher,Jayson	R	02	MIL	1.2	95	84%	0%	67%	185	123	165	190	187	144
Eischen,Joey	L	02	MON	0.9	119	88%	67%	90%	212	239	244	151	173	261
Elder,Dave	R	02	CLE	1.5	81	77%		60%	268	171	268	188	243	200
Embree,Alan	L	00	SF	1.0	69	65%	40%	64%	263	283	279	288	286	267
		01	CHW	0.9	62	56%	0%	59%	295	299	320	266	220	352
		02	BOS	0.9	144	87%	29%	69%	188	226	241	96	156	244
Escobar,Kelvim	R	00	TOR	4.2	85	67%	67%	48%	262	273	290	250	282	253
		01	TOR	2.1	96	70%		70%	209	198	192	240	203	206
		02	TOR	1.0	65	75%	83%	74%	258	233	275	145	245	246
Eyre,Scott	L	01	TOR	0.9	90	76%	67%	67%	276	250	238	444	192	323
		02	SF	1.1	61	71%	0%	80%	268	282	266	258	233	317
Farnsworth,Kyle	R	00	CHC	1.7	36	67%	17%	39%	278	303	322	247	258	314
		01	CHC	1.1	134	80%	67%	81%	222	202	204	242	223	207
		02	CHC	1.0	38	57%	14%	48%	240	353	261	349	392	216
Fassero,Jeff	L	00	BOS	3.4	44	72%	0%	62%	294	299	276	241	255	307
		01	CHC	0.9	118	73%	71%	82%	215	258	241	210	247	228
		02	STL	1.0	71	64%	0%	70%	257	333	271	364	318	275
Fetters,Mike	R	00	LA	1.0	54	79%	71%	85%	219	187	210	188	191	221
		01	PIT	0.9	31	68%	75%	84%	218	294	254	250	247	269
		02	ARI	0.9	74	73%	0%	79%	225	278	250	244	306	230
Fikac,Jeremy	R	01	SD	1.1	126	89%	0%	80%	170	158	153	207	0	234
		02	SD	1.1	41	69%	0%	55%	265	270	254	275	274	263
File,Bob	R	01	TOR	1.2	45	74%	0%	69%	192	257	226	205	242	207
Fiore,Tony	R	02	MIN	1.9	38	79%		83%	228	217	231	240	247	203
Flores,Randy	L	02	COL	1.0	-31	65%	50%	50%	327	355	309	400	326	351
Fossum,Casey	L	02	BOS	2.5	97	78%	100%	69%	294	241	275	270	277	265
Foulke,Keith	R	00	CHW	1.2	22	75%	87%	87%	203	212	214	194	221	192
		01	CHW	1.1	131	76%	93%	79%	182	221	213	145	212	183
		02	CHW	1.2	127	75%	79%	75%	211	253	219	198	266	185
Fox,Chad	R	01	MIL	1.0	98	89%	50%	87%	185	176	193	151	158	197
Franklin,Ryan	R	01	SEA	2.1	57	79%	0%	83%	260	236	239	279	276	232
		02	SEA	2.9	71	69%	0%	63%	233	291	244	208	265	247
Fultz,Aaron	L	00	SF	1.2	68	68%	33%	76%	254	274	263	282	221	284
		01	SF	1.1	92	67%	50%	89%	259	259	241	291	237	276
		02	SF	1.0	47	71%	0%	67%	235	360	300	302	302	284
Gagne,Eric	R	02	LA	1.1	228	82%	93%	92%	212	157	204	131	213	163
Garces,Rich	R	00	BOS	1.2	96	75%	20%	84%	217	244	256	153	209	242
		01	BOS	1.1	71	69%	50%	92%	205	238	221	222	188	240
		02	BOS	0.8	17	52%		83%	195	361	290	154	364	205
Ginter,Matt	R	02	CHW	1.6	46	72%	100%	100%	219	336	300	217	342	208
Glover,Gary	R	01	CHW	2.2	40	66%	0%	67%	221	299	185	267	237	269
		02	CHW	3.4	20	65%	100%	56%	236	282	169	241	280	219
Gomes,Wayne	R	00	PHI	1.1	47	70%	64%	60%	310	221	253	282	306	234
		01	SF	1.2	50	68%	20%	71%	254	339	259	363	319	279
		02	BOS	1.1	40	70%	100%	67%	250	233	250	250	103	364
Gordon,Tom	R	01	CHC	1.0	160	70%	87%	82%	200	171	177	237	188	188
		02	HOU	1.2	117	75%		70%	266	254	253	291	269	255
Graves,Danny	R	00	CIN	1.4	42	84%	86%	80%	224	262	242	248	267	220
		01	CIN	1.2	75	68%	82%	76%	238	301	249	322	301	243
		02	CIN	1.4	70	76%	82%	80%	236	295	281	280	272	259
Grimsley,Jason	R	00	NYY	1.5	29	67%	25%	62%	291	243	224	290	228	299
		01	KC	1.1	69	79%	0%	69%	239	245	236	256	261	218
		02	KC	1.0	67	72%	33%	67%	214	257	223	269	248	225
Groom,Buddy	L	00	BAL	0.8	61	66%	36%	79%	297	254	282	269	193	326
		01	BAL	0.9	168	68%	85%	82%	281	222	263	222	194	291
		02	BAL	0.9	130	87%	50%	86%	192	202	201	151	181	208
Gryboski,Kevin	R	02	ATL	0.9	17	83%	0%	81%	283	233	293	154	169	306
Guardado,Eddie	L	00	MIN	0.9	34	80%	82%	80%	233	243	224	268	287	208
		01	MIN	1.0	111	68%	86%	92%	202	194	172	270	167	216
		02	MIN	1.0	118	79%	88%	84%	204	235	225	182	263	200
Guthrie,Mark	L	00	3TM	0.9	56	71%	0%	57%	223	302	254	286	276	253
		01	OAK	1.0	79	69%	33%	83%	277	219	220	263	239	241
		02	NYM	0.7	95	80%	50%	85%	232	176	224	115	187	223
Hammond,Chris	L	02	ATL	1.2	98	92%	0%	86%	212	175	213	160	174	206
Haney,Chris	L	02	BOS	1.3	45	70%	100%	100%	305	241	227	375	286	265
Harper,Travis	R	02	TAM	2.3	41	67%	50%	47%	306	272	336	271	301	280
Hasegawa,Shige	R	00	ANA	1.4	36	79%	50%	72%	244	301	286	288	246	291
		01	ANA	1.2	66	70%	0%	59%	246	250	234	276	221	270
		02	SEA	1.3	50	76%	20%	71%	233	244	219	222	284	199
Hawkins,LaTroy	R	00	MIN	1.3	57	76%	100%	82%	240	275	232	320	242	265
		01	MIN	0.8	31	67%	76%	67%	235	331	321	196	276	305
		02	MIN	1.2	133	81%	0%	86%	209	228	258	155	225	211
Henriquez,Oscar	R	02	DET	0.9	39	69%	100%	92%	177	229	211	158	164	238
Heredia,Felix	L	00	CHC	0.8	65	66%	40%	78%	195	250	217	218	195	236
		01	CHC	0.7	28	67%	0%	67%	339	296	287	355	292	333
		02	TOR	1.0	33	78%	0%	67%	216	299	282	189	224	281
Herges,Matt	R	00	LA	1.9	65	76%	33%	76%	240	258	261	244	265	237
		01	LA	1.3	57	78%	13%	63%	252	268	280	218	280	243
		02	MON	1.0	37	80%	43%	57%	346	267	321	286	315	300

Bullpen Indicators

				BPIs			Results		Runners		Pitch Ct		Platoon	
Pitcher			Tm	IP/g	bpv	S%	Sv%	Eff%	Emp	On	0-15	16-30	vLH	vRH
Hernandez,Rob	R	00	TAM	1.1	23	81%	80%	71%	305	239	289	266	328	223
		01	KC	1.1	50	73%	82%	73%	270	262	249	322	299	230
		02	KC	1.0	78	72%	79%	73%	311	287	302	295	282	317
Hoffman,Trevor	R	00	SD	1.0	11	74%	86%	77%	213	245	244	176	200	246
		01	SD	1.0	87	78%	93%	87%	216	216	216	226	214	218
		02	SD	1.0	146	76%	93%	83%	250	214	229	267	186	275
Holmes,Darren	R	00	2NL	1.1	9	47%	50%	50%	297	500	510	231	483	383
		02	ATL	1.0	133	84%	50%	77%	268	133	222	162	230	198
Holtz,Mike	L	00	ANA	0.7	80	63%	0%	81%	268	231	202	351	213	300
		01	ANA	0.6	74	70%	0%	84%	243	303	263	320	312	227
		02	SD	0.7	6	76%	0%	54%	266	316	305	258	306	284
Howry,Bob	R	00	CHW	1.1	79	75%	58%	72%	223	207	222	181	174	256
		01	CHW	1.1	53	71%	45%	73%	262	295	323	214	306	253
		02	BOS	1.0	80	65%	0%	75%	246	280	265	274	239	280
Irabu,Hideki	R	02	TEX	1.2	14	66%	80%	64%	355	200	212	367	269	289
Isringhausen,Jas	R	00	OAK	1.1	32	75%	83%	78%	238	268	244	280	242	265
		01	OAK	1.1	120	78%	79%	76%	196	212	220	165	240	152
		02	STL	1.1	154	72%	86%	83%	199	200	213	161	247	164
Jackson,Mike	R	01	HOU	1.0	32	71%	44%	78%	268	248	228	351	294	231
		02	MIN	1.0	58	78%	0%	81%	376	196	319	156	275	288
Jimenez,Jose	R	00	COL	1.0	28	76%	80%	79%	248	228	258	206	240	238
		01	COL	1.0	46	74%	77%	79%	278	250	278	240	255	271
		02	COL	1.0	110	73%	87%	73%	218	336	261	232	266	264
Jones,Todd	R	00	DET	1.0	25	78%	91%	85%	302	259	315	158	294	256
		01	MIN	1.0	41	79%	62%	68%	321	303	302	311	325	301
		02	COL	1.0	75	68%	33%	84%	240	303	280	261	233	301
Julio,Jorge	R	01	BAL	1.2	80	78%	0%	67%	333	259	321	269	290	286
		02	BAL	1.0	77	87%	81%	72%	230	195	217	206	213	214
Karsay,Steve	R	00	CLE	1.1	86	73%	69%	67%	241	295	279	215	223	304
		01	ATL	1.2	119	81%	67%	72%	231	224	204	290	257	203
		02	NYY	1.1	70	77%	75%	80%	299	218	267	202	243	269
Kent,Steve	L	02	TAM	1.7	25	70%	50%	40%	260	318	376	274	316	283
Kershner,Jason	L	02	TOR	1.0	37	68%	50%	50%	200	250	148	308	256	192
Kim,Byung-Hyun	R	00	ARI	1.2	115	71%	70%	68%	178	228	196	222	239	170
		01	ARI	1.3	105	76%	83%	78%	151	208	166	207	199	151
		02	ARI	1.2	133	84%	86%	83%	219	196	208	222	220	198
King,Ray	R	00	MIL	0.8	71	89%	0%	73%	200	156	198	71	204	157
		01	MIL	0.7	71	75%	25%	73%	247	236	244	241	210	276
		02	MIL	0.9	72	79%	0%	86%	272	237	257	255	219	280
Kline,Steve	L	00	MON	1.0	65	78%	78%	75%	256	304	290	263	243	297
		01	STL	0.8	82	85%	90%	88%	197	210	194	250	149	237
		02	STL	0.9	73	74%	75%	91%	281	218	275	156	230	266
Knotts,Gary	R	02	FLA	1.1	21	71%	0%	80%	155	263	192	259	191	194
Koch,Billy	R	00	TOR	1.2	93	81%	87%	84%	276	235	278	176	255	261
		01	TOR	1.0	52	68%	82%	75%	254	278	268	276	289	245
		02	OAK	1.1	84	76%	88%	85%	206	225	207	208	237	196
Kolb,Danny	R	01	TEX	0.9	46	74%		100%	182	360	238	313	261	257
		02	TEX	0.9	45	71%	25%	40%	222	231	197	250	291	172
Koplove,Mike	R	02	ARI	1.1	86	69%		94%	217	207	224	131	174	230
Leskanic,Curtis	R	00	MIL	1.1	72	85%	92%	89%	244	182	226	183	214	211
		01	MIL	1.0	56	80%	71%	62%	242	241	245	193	275	220
Levine,Al	R	00	ANA	1.9	15	77%	100%	71%	305	223	206	303	263	268
		01	ANA	1.2	40	86%	33%	66%	217	306	261	153	288	229
		02	ANA	1.2	26	75%	71%	76%	265	238	280	200	240	263
Ligtenberg,Kerry	R	00	ATL	0.9	71	77%	86%	84%	252	193	248	163	206	236
		01	ATL	1.1	78	79%	50%	50%	246	204	213	243	241	216
		02	ATL	1.3	57	81%		63%	229	185	177	227	200	216
Lincoln,Mike	R	01	PIT	1.3	71	79%	0%	75%	238	209	247	186	196	240
		02	PIT	1.3	52	82%	0%	65%	285	296	255	333	276	296
Lloyd,Graeme	L	01	MON	0.8	60	69%	33%	75%	281	262	281	235	252	284
		02	FLA	0.9	72	62%	63%	71%	277	319	320	167	326	281
Looper,Braden	R	00	FLA	0.9	29	71%	40%	86%	245	284	257	293	359	230
		01	FLA	1.0	53	76%	50%	79%	240	245	269	194	250	236
		02	FLA	1.1	62	76%	81%	79%	238	221	204	276	278	191
Lowe,Sean	R	00	CHW	1.4	29	69%	0%	91%	280	287	344	235	345	241
		01	CHW	2.8	61	73%	100%	79%	259	253	236	257	281	233
		02	COL	1.6	66	65%	0%	75%	351	280	315	287	348	294
Magnante,Mike	L	00	OAK	0.7	14	76%	0%	79%	372	253	291	359	288	330
		01	OAK	0.9	38	82%	0%	91%	231	262	260	209	230	254
		02	OAK	0.9	17	64%	0%	50%	304	328	333	300	263	341
Mairena,Oswaldc	L	02	FLA	1.1	15	70%		63%	310	262	263	375	315	269
Mantei,Matt	R	00	ARI	1.0	35	69%	85%	82%	167	221	204	176	183	200
		01	ARI	0.9	82	100%	100%	100%	267	167	263	125	455	62
		02	ARI	0.8	80	71%	0%	57%	222	250	275	67	200	250
Marte,Damaso	L	02	CHW	0.9	143	75%	83%	89%	157	270	227	135	149	252
Matthews,Mike	L	01	STL	1.8	67	78%	33%	54%	194	283	189	205	133	268
		02	MIL	1.0	64	72%	0%	67%	299	210	306	224	208	292

Bullpen Indicators

				BPIs			Results		Runners		Pitch Ct		Platoon	
Pitcher			Tm	IP/g	bpv	S%	Sv%	Eff%	Emp	On	0-15	16-30	vLH	vRH
Mecir,Jim	R	00	2AL	1.4	82	76%	38%	77%	250	206	232	203	204	245
		01	OAK	1.2	93	74%	38%	63%	234	226	255	202	195	267
		02	OAK	1.1	64	71%	17%	75%	294	226	267	211	204	297
Mendoza,Ramiro	R	01	NYY	1.8	91	68%	75%	82%	214	277	241	202	248	236
		02	NYY	1.5	100	75%	50%	75%	277	273	282	289	261	286
Mercado,Hector	L	01	CIN	1.0	69	77%	0%	67%	255	279	254	318	287	252
		02	PHI	1.3	77	67%		71%	179	263	183	342	125	252
Mercker,Kent	L	02	COL	0.8	1	72%	0%	75%	319	278	309	279	209	350
Mesa,Jose	R	00	SEA	1.2	61	69%	33%	67%	238	323	282	296	262	296
		01	PHI	1.0	102	83%	91%	87%	303	180	264	182	236	255
		02	PHI	1.0	67	80%	83%	77%	233	230	248	194	225	237
Mota,Guillermo	R	00	MON	1.0	39	53%	0%	86%	200	311	194	314	244	246
		01	MON	0.9	25	67%	0%	68%	252	294	310	128	310	248
		02	LA	1.4	75	65%	0%	56%	223	183	193	205	188	213
Mullen,Scott	L	02	KC	0.9	35	81%	0%	59%	295	236	290	120	263	270
Myers,Mike	L	00	COL	0.6	96	83%	50%	89%	173	147	152	208	121	220
		01	COL	0.6	71	74%	0%	71%	235	216	244	105	231	216
		02	ARI	0.5	70	70%	44%	76%	281	269	269	333	241	317
Nelson,Jeff	R	00	NYY	1.0	99	80%	0%	74%	184	181	210	133	232	157
		01	SEA	0.9	116	76%	80%	89%	122	153	125	158	167	119
		02	SEA	1.1	89	73%	50%	81%	210	232	258	169	224	218
Nen,Robb	R	00	SF	1.0	19	87%	89%	85%	179	138	175	130	193	128
		01	SF	1.0	149	73%	87%	80%	182	238	220	138	240	162
		02	SF	1.1	150	80%	84%	83%	232	232	214	294	224	242
Nunez,Vladimir	R	01	FLA	1.8	67	81%	0%	57%	233	235	288	176	213	253
		02	FLA	1.3	70	73%	71%	74%	217	234	229	223	191	251
Oropesa,Eddie	L	01	PHI	0.6	41	72%	0%	88%	296	190	245	200	156	297
		02	ARI	0.8	-16	52%	0%	90%	283	423	325	320	340	356
Orosco,Jesse	L	00	STL	0.4	3	100%	0%	100%	333	250	273	0	500	0
		01	LA	0.5	84	81%	0%	77%	261	289	281	250	275	300
		02	LA	0.5	49	84%	100%	90%	302	177	245	91	238	214
Osuna,Antonio	R	00	LA	1.5	35	75%	0%	44%	236	220	261	227	227	230
		02	CHW	1.1	104	69%	79%	85%	223	278	294	224	250	250
Paniagua,Jose	R	00	SEA	1.2	76	75%	63%	88%	239	228	228	247	206	255
		01	SEA	1.1	36	72%	75%	85%	191	268	236	225	257	216
		02	DET	1.0	25	69%	50%	80%	291	298	309	261	276	309
Parra,Jose	R	02	ARI	0.9	41	79%		80%	333	200	263	231	214	270
Patterson,Danny	R	00	DET	1.0	46	73%	0%	85%	330	292	304	314	292	323
		01	DET	1.1	64	75%	20%	73%	315	238	244	356	327	231
Pavano,Carl	R	02	FLA	3.7	67	66%		47%	303	326	286	284	357	276
Percival,Troy	R	00	ANA	0.9	30	72%	76%	71%	176	303	228	217	237	220
		01	ANA	1.0	154	74%	93%	90%	195	174	182	203	176	202
		02	ANA	1.0	112	88%	91%	90%	202	170	231	91	247	138
Perez,Yorkis	L	00	HOU	0.7	14	74%	0%	63%	341	208	286	227	282	255
		02	BAL	1.2	55	81%	100%	100%	236	157	186	172	204	193
Phelps,Travis	R	01	TAM	1.3	77	75%	83%	87%	207	253	208	197	223	227
		02	TAM	1.4	30	74%		67%	292	143	277	217	267	187
Pineda,Luis	R	02	CIN	1.2	46	76%		63%	250	189	222	207	250	200
Plesac,Dan	L	00	ARI	0.7	79	82%	0%	74%	265	198	230	190	260	194
		01	TOR	0.7	125	74%	50%	78%	210	205	220	152	184	234
		02	PHI	0.6	73	72%	25%	79%	200	200	216	105	120	300
Politte,Cliff	R	02	TOR	1.1	101	69%	25%	83%	178	257	211	183	272	159
Porzio,Mike	L	02	CHW	1.3	11	75%		71%	253	244	260	246	269	229
Pote,Lou	R	00	ANA	1.6	17	77%	100%	80%	217	326	270	232	294	245
		01	ANA	2.0	55	73%	67%	80%	249	269	331	153	268	250
Powell,Jay	R	00	HOU	0.9	40	66%	0%	86%	137	393	239	345	233	297
		01	COL	1.0	47	81%	54%	69%	262	259	282	210	296	233
		02	TEX	1.0	43	80%	0%	71%	245	260	270	228	222	270
Prinz,Bret	R	01	ARI	0.9	47	83%	75%	83%	257	188	254	118	293	174
		02	ARI	0.7	18	59%	0%	56%	381	417	341	563	429	395
Quantrill,Paul	L	00	TOR	1.2	42	70%	33%	70%	319	278	314	274	299	296
		01	TOR	1.0	131	76%	22%	79%	310	233	287	257	355	232
		02	LA	0.9	83	79%	33%	87%	292	237	283	233	254	275
Reames,Britt	R	01	MON	2.3	40	68%	0%	53%	255	297	239	333	297	258
		02	MON	1.6	69	70%	0%	58%	237	295	265	309	342	234
Reed,Steve	R	00	CLE	1.0	44	72%	0%	92%	235	298	292	220	271	268
		01	ATL	0.8	65	75%	50%	79%	279	179	267	143	181	259
		02	NYM	1.1	132	79%	25%	71%	279	179	267	143	181	259
Reichert,Dan	R	00	KC	3.5	91	72%	33%	50%	274	267	244	312	275	267
		02	KC	2.2	19	68%		64%	266	354	220	302	295	314
Remlinger,Mike	L	00	ATL	1.0	85	74%	75%	85%	166	256	201	203	203	209
		01	ATL	1.0	130	83%	20%	83%	256	203	246	211	322	194
		02	ATL	0.9	108	84%	0%	82%	210	186	211	175	235	184
Reyes,Al	R	00	2TM	1.0	12	71%	0%	80%	243	176	224	200	111	273
		01	LA	1.3	52	79%	50%	60%	269	269	264	344	292	250
		02	PIT	1.1	134	73%	0%	75%	194	120	189	143	158	162

Bullpen Indicators

				BPIs			Results		Runners		Pitch Ct		Platoon	
Pitcher			Tm	IP/g	bpv	S%	Sv%	Eff%	Emp	On	0-15	16-30	vLH	vRH
Reyes,Dennys	L	00	CIN	0.7	43	75%	0%	86%	177	341	283	161	178	330
		01	CIN	1.5	56	70%		57%	220	289	121	191	167	276
		02	TEX	1.4	28	71%		67%	283	319	325	271	299	299
Rhodes,Arthur	R	00	SEA	1.0	106	64%	0%	66%	167	244	202	230	220	193
		01	SEA	1.0	215	85%	43%	91%	174	208	151	321	198	179
		02	SEA	1.1	203	74%	29%	81%	163	220	182	211	158	215
Riedling,John	R	00	CIN	1.2	8	83%	50%	75%	212	200	206	286	280	143
		01	CIN	1.1	79	77%	33%	70%	230	140	192	184	185	188
		02	CIN	1.4	52	81%		71%	250	213	226	259	320	163
Rincon,Ricardo	R	00	CLE	0.6	81	83%	0%	100%	324	143	250	0	216	240
		01	CLE	0.8	96	77%	50%	84%	269	172	224	222	213	233
		02	OAK	0.8	153	56%	20%	78%	219	242	199	349	203	267
Riske,David	R	01	CLE	1.0	66	91%	100%	100%	244	179	273	125	143	232
		02	CLE	1.0	62	71%	100%	80%	228	283	268	226	253	259
Rivera,Mariano	L	00	NYY	1.1	25	75%	88%	83%	174	254	186	284	210	206
		01	NYY	1.1	206	76%	88%	81%	191	235	200	238	187	229
		02	NYY	1.0	127	74%	88%	79%	185	225	226	156	181	225
Roberts,Willis	L	01	BAL	2.9	46	69%	60%	52%	280	267	285	299	264	289
		02	BAL	1.1	54	78%	33%	76%	286	255	266	310	276	266
Rocker,John	L	00	ATL	0.9	48	86%	89%	85%	247	175	197	224	243	202
		01	CLE	1.0	90	71%	77%	69%	230	238	226	253	239	233
		02	TEX	0.8	54	65%	25%	68%	255	340	324	167	364	266
Rodriguez,Felix	R	00	SF	1.1	105	81%	38%	84%	224	215	237	190	158	270
		01	SF	1.0	133	87%	0%	91%	199	172	189	188	150	213
		02	SF	1.0	79	65%	0%	73%	168	271	231	175	234	196
Rodriguez,Rich	R	01	CLE	0.7	69	71%	0%	71%	250	289	256	370	189	346
		02	TEX	0.5	46	63%	33%	67%	320	176	255	0	214	294
Romero,J.C.	L	02	MIN	1.0	95	85%	20%	88%	228	199	263	82	216	211
Ryan,B.J.	L	00	BAL	1.0	44	65%	0%	60%	271	189	243	262	175	252
		01	BAL	0.9	65	73%	50%	75%	194	273	203	222	198	261
		02	BAL	0.9	58	70%	50%	88%	227	252	253	182	192	283
Sadler,Carl	L	02	CLE	0.8	86	67%	0%	67%	200	222	232	154	205	219
Santana,Johan	L	02	MIN	4.0	119	77%	100%	67%	196	235	203	224	195	216
Santana,Julio	R	02	DET	1.5	32	86%	0%	63%	262	214	263	205	261	219
Santiago,Jose	R	00	KC	1.5	48	74%	25%	56%	219	309	307	263	224	303
		01	PHI	1.3	56	66%	0%	62%	279	306	299	252	352	252
		02	PHI	1.1	37	56%	0%	71%	296	284	287	294	304	282
Sasaki,Kazuhiro	R	00	SEA	1.0	31	81%	93%	83%	197	168	213	119	198	170
		01	SEA	1.0	167	66%	87%	80%	187	208	195	213	218	168
		02	SEA	1.0	131	81%	82%	76%	215	179	207	190	207	194
Sauerbeck,Scott	L	00	PIT	1.0	76	77%	25%	73%	323	229	287	247	222	305
		01	PIT	0.9	90	64%	50%	85%	208	308	241	328	272	248
		02	PIT	0.8	107	84%		89%	241	200	220	226	147	273
Schoeneweis,S	L	02	ANA	2.2	22	69%	25%	66%	238	297	244	188	202	290
Seanez,Rudy	R	00	ATL	0.9	74	67%	67%	67%	163	229	203	143	294	114
		01	ATL	1.0	89	82%	33%	71%	164	191	191	143	151	197
		02	TEX	1.0	58	66%	0%	61%	224	236	195	306	220	238
Shields,Scot	R	02	ANA	1.7	57	83%		73%	198	172	198	160	184	191
Shuey,Paul	R	00	CLE	1.1	101	74%	0%	82%	207	232	240	167	203	235
		01	CLE	1.2	124	79%	40%	73%	293	218	298	187	280	225
		02	LA	1.0	89	74%	20%	82%	214	228	247	160	226	217
Silva,Carlos	R	02	PHI	1.2	60	75%	20%	78%	304	255	330	242	292	276
Smith,Dan	R	02	MON	1.4	50	76%	100%	83%	267	145	207	271	151	239
Smoltz,John	R	01	ATL	1.6	155	73%	91%	82%	238	238	196	229	263	211
		02	ATL	1.1	135	68%	93%	91%	167	261	183	264	213	199
Soriano,Rafael	R	02	SEA	4.7	40	70%	100%	25%	234	262	281	286	297	179
Speier,Justin	R	00	CLE	1.5	83	79%	0%	79%	212	245	202	169	171	274
		01	COL	1.4	74	67%	0%	71%	242	254	283	202	247	247
		02	COL	1.0	67	66%	25%	86%	209	225	216	227	240	197
Spooneybarger,T	R	02	ATL	1.0	49	82%	100%	100%	207	205	228	152	150	234
Stanton,Mike	L	00	NYY	1.0	108	70%	0%	71%	274	250	288	194	339	199
		01	NYY	1.1	101	82%	0%	86%	260	267	239	329	283	251
		02	NYY	1.0	57	77%	67%	88%	283	229	260	274	268	247
Stechschulte,G	R	00	STL	1.3	17	61%	0%	80%	179	341	132	424	186	296
		01	STL	1.0	39	78%	75%	74%	286	260	272	296	284	268
		02	STL	1.1	33	68%	0%	73%	169	320	173	346	263	221
Stein,Blake	R	01	KC	3.6	38	71%	50%	47%	217	252	242	212	229	237
		02	KC	1.7	38	56%	50%	29%	316	296	342	317	319	293
Stewart,Scott	L	01	MON	0.8	90	71%	75%	88%	236	250	215	344	286	215
		02	MON	1.0	118	73%	89%	90%	180	245	205	196	159	235
Stone,Ricky	R	02	HOU	1.0	54	79%	50%	80%	252	281	250	305	288	258
Strickland,Scott	R	00	MON	1.0	111	75%	33%	73%	213	216	226	164	296	163
		01	MON	1.1	77	80%	75%	72%	230	213	256	181	274	189
		02	NYM	1.0	76	77%	33%	64%	256	212	244	217	313	188
Sullivan,Scott	R	00	CIN	1.3	76	76%	50%	76%	255	189	231	211	209	238
		01	CIN	1.3	73	77%	0%	87%	237	250	232	273	252	237
		02	CIN	1.1	54	65%	33%	79%	279	311	293	255	357	253

Bullpen Indicators

				BPIs			Results		Runners		Pitch Ct		Platoon	
Pitcher			Tm	IP/g	bpv	S%	Sv%	Eff%	Emp	On	0-15	16-30	vLH	vRH
Tam,Jeff	R	00	OAK	1.2	64	79%	50%	81%	297	239	274	284	360	209
		01	OAK	1.1	60	77%	50%	81%	257	242	253	186	247	251
		02	OAK	1.0	23	69%	0%	40%	273	385	360	277	300	352
Tejera,Michael	L	02	FLA	3.0	39	72%	33%	63%	270	267	190	297	228	280
Telford,Anthony	R	00	MON	1.2	78	74%	60%	76%	280	227	255	287	281	240
		02	TEX	1.2	25	67%	50%	78%	410	250	347	270	273	353
Thurman,Corey	R	02	TOR	1.6	25	78%	0%	55%	264	233	300	189	236	259
Timlin,Mike	R	00	2TM	1.0	42	77%	67%	70%	230	321	277	271	311	241
		01	STL	1.1	71	70%	43%	68%	247	317	248	382	319	257
		02	PHI	1.3	107	69%	0%	71%	218	198	213	189	208	214
Tucker,T.J.	R	02	MON	1.1	41	76%	57%	82%	354	232	314	232	269	300
Urbina,Ugueth	R	00	MON	1.0	5	67%	80%	73%	120	333	194	308	269	174
		01	BOS	1.0	123	75%	86%	83%	212	257	242	217	278	196
		02	BOS	1.0	118	79%	87%	77%	211	184	199	178	257	143
Van Poppel,Todd	R	00	CHC	1.7	75	78%	40%	62%	275	217	282	171	234	261
		01	CHC	1.3	88	87%		90%	282	158	245	169	281	194
		02	TEX	1.4	74	68%	50%	70%	306	245	319	238	291	262
Venafro,Mike	L	00	TEX	0.7	51	73%	50%	91%	275	313	268	388	252	351
		01	TEX	0.9	44	63%	50%	77%	194	282	266	160	258	227
		02	OAK	0.8	9	74%		89%	284	329	327	250	270	337
Veres,Dave	R	00	STL	1.1	25	79%	81%	73%	243	234	251	219	210	261
		01	STL	0.9	54	79%	79%	81%	241	219	240	228	237	229
		02	STL	1.2	50	79%	50%	68%	234	210	255	163	190	246
Villafuerte,Brand	R	02	SD	1.0	77	92%	100%	83%	275	227	238	290	286	213
Vizcaino,Luis	R	01	OAK	1.0	46	74%	100%	86%	264	268	230	341	241	282
		02	MIL	1.1	104	73%	83%	88%	197	185	209	149	225	170
Voyles,Brad	R	02	KC	1.2	25	66%	50%	40%	302	268	241	316	318	262
Wagner,Billy	L	00	HOU	1.0	18	68%	40%	38%	286	235	261	250	321	232
		01	HOU	1.0	147	76%	95%	85%	182	224	207	182	261	182
		02	HOU	1.1	141	79%	85%	83%	187	213	207	167	180	201
Wakefield,Tim	R	00	BOS	3.1	65	68%	0%	45%	293	245	236	250	244	295
		01	BOS	3.7	75	72%	60%	52%	255	240	213	297	226	264
		02	BOS	3.6	91	77%	60%	73%	201	210	215	188	195	213
Walker,Jamie	L	02	DET	0.8	107	72%	25%	64%	205	193	203	184	202	194
Walker,Pete	R	02	TOR	3.7	33	72%	100%	74%	290	248	306	255	288	254
Weathers,David	R	00	MIL	1.1	48	81%	14%	62%	302	212	274	212	223	278
		01	CHC	1.1	76	82%	40%	69%	291	144	222	183	213	218
		02	NYM	1.1	63	81%	0%	75%	283	208	299	122	267	232
Weber,Ben	R	01	ANA	1.2	46	76%	0%	80%	254	248	249	234	210	278
		02	ANA	1.2	68	80%	64%	84%	253	244	251	268	243	253
Wells,Bob	R	00	MIN	1.1	116	74%	50%	55%	251	241	213	313	233	255
		01	MIN	1.1	55	65%	50%	79%	278	265	278	309	264	277
		02	MIN	1.2	28	65%		89%	293	364	293	356	355	300
White,Gabe	L	00	2NL	1.2	165	78%	56%	85%	197	232	249	157	200	217
		01	COL	1.0	7	63%	0%	50%	249	317	262	293	269	271
		02	CIN	0.9	127	73%	0%	93%	214	269	233	256	202	267
White,Rick	R	00	2TM	1.5	38	73%	43%	48%	236	209	211	231	268	193
		01	NYM	1.3	84	72%	50%	70%	235	285	235	333	271	249
		02	STL	1.0	83	64%	0%	72%	311	200	267	266	295	245
Wickman,Bob	R	00	2TM	1.1	32	75%	81%	73%	228	244	231	238	258	214
		01	CLE	1.0	150	80%	91%	93%	265	206	252	191	279	205
		02	CLE	1.0	109	71%	91%	81%	299	268	311	185	275	294
Williamson,Scott	R	00	CIN	2.3	97	79%	75%	63%	234	214	188	224	256	202
		02	CIN	1.2	106	75%	67%	70%	174	190	207	141	198	170
Williams,Mike	R	00	PIT	1.0	40	77%	83%	75%	201	236	223	205	231	209
		01	HOU	1.0	49	79%	88%	82%	283	206	269	169	256	233
		02	PIT	1.0	64	80%	92%	83%	254	206	241	213	281	180
Witasick,Jay	R	01	NYY	1.3	117	80%	25%	79%	229	274	276	260	288	234
		02	SF	1.6	97	80%		100%	264	192	237	191	228	238
Wohlers,Mark	R	01	NYY	1.1	61	72%	0%	89%	285	335	287	226	236	280
		02	CLE	1.1	55	65%	64%	71%	229	295	246	305	256	265
Worrell,Tim	R	00	CHC	1.2	39	91%	50%	72%	297	222	292	247	225	296
		01	SF	1.1	76	74%	0%	65%	255	223	264	179	248	234
		02	SF	0.9	80	82%	0%	91%	227	198	209	220	204	218
Wunsch,Kelly	L	00	CHW	0.7	74	79%	20%	82%	197	248	223	227	160	275
		01	CHW	0.7	33	42%	0%	63%	190	302	274	83	262	233
		02	CHW	0.6	39	79%	0%	85%	204	250	253	71	208	268
Yan,Esteban	R	00	TAM	3.2	42	60%	0%	50%	304	260	290	266	316	258
		01	TAM	1.2	158	71%	71%	63%	285	230	282	219	272	252
		02	TAM	1.3	44	74%	70%	62%	265	252	280	224	273	246
Zambrano,Victor	R	01	TAM	1.4	112	76%	33%	68%	225	167	252	101	205	198
		02	TAM	2.7	18	68%	33%	60%	289	268	235	303	292	266
Zerbe,Chad	L	02	SF	1.1	44	77%	0%	88%	238	257	235	283	247	248
Zimmerman,Jeff	R	00	TEX	1.1	61	70%	33%	79%	333	257	286	283	297	278
		01	TEX	1.1	133	83%	90%	84%	193	190	215	138	220	163

Off-Season Injury Report

by Rick Wilton, Dr. HQ

Paul Abbott (RHP, SEA) had season-ending surgery in late June and isn't expected to be 100% until late in spring training if not sometime in April.

Brian Anderson (LHP, ARI) suffered a broken bone in his left foot in Sept. He'll be ready at the opening of camp.

Matt Anderson's (RHP, DET) right shoulder will be very close to 100% at the start of spring training.

Ryan Anderson (LHP, SEA) had his second labrum surgery and his career is in doubt due to a repeat of this injury. We might not see him pitching in a minor league game until mid-season.

Danny Bautista (OF, ARI) appears to be almost completely recovered from his torn labrum, but because of the extensive damage to the shoulder, he is at risk to lose some flexibility which might affect his swing and defense.

Kevin Brown (RHP, LA) is recovering from a serious back injury and a flexor tendon problem. There is no guarantee that he'll be 100% by spring training.

Sean Burroughs (3B, SD) had his labrum and rotator cuff repaired this fall. While he could be ready for spring training, the Padres might play it safe and leave him behind to build up his shoulder strength.

Chris Carpenter (RHP, TOR) had surgery to repair a tear in his labrum and he's expected to miss 10-12 months, costing him the 2003 campaign.

Sean Casey (1B, CIN) had both his labrum and rotator cuff repaired, along with some muscle in the rotator cuff area, and could return by mid-season.

Luis Castillo (2B, FLA) underwent arthroscopic surgery on his right hip to repair a torn labrum in the joint. The tear was small and it should not hinder his running.

Frank Catalanotto (UT, TEX) is making solid progress from a broken right hand and he's expected to test it against live pitching before the start of spring training.

Jason Christiansen (LHP, SF) had Tommy John surgery in June and is expected to miss almost all of 2003.

Craig Counsell (UT, ARI) is expected to need extra time to recover next spring from season-ending neck surgery.

Einar Diaz (C, CLE) was shut down late in the year after complaining of swelling in his right elbow. The Indians hope that rest will clear it up in time for spring training.

Darren Dreifort (RHP, LA) showed no ill effects from 2001's Tommy Johns surgery by late last season.

J.D. Drew's (OF, STL) had extensive surgery on his right patellar tendon. Count on him missing the start of the season, and returning mid-year in a reduced role until the knee is strong enough to handle day-to-day action.

Scott Elarton's (RHP, COL) repaired right labrum is healing ahead of schedule and he is now pain free. He will be ready to throw when the pitchers report in February.

Alex Escobar (OF, CLE) played in the instructional league but needed a knee brace to support his left ACL, which he tore in March. Look for the Indians to start him at Triple-A so he can regain the strength in his knee.

Bobby Estalella (C, COL) had his left rotator cuff repaired in late July and could miss the start of the spring.

Chad Fox (RHP, MIL) should be completely recovered from the strained rotator cuff that ended his season. His injury history does not bode well for 2003, however.

Alex Gonzalez' (SS, FLA) left shoulder has responded to treatment and he's regained most of the strength after dislocating his left shoulder in May.

Juan Gonzalez' (OF, FA) strained ligament in his right thumb might need surgery. That decision will have been made by the time you read this.

Luis Gonzalez (OF, ARI) is recovering from a separated left shoulder and could start the 2003 season slowly.

Rusty Greer (OF, TEX) had successful surgery to fuse several discs in his back. Now he's facing surgery on his rotator cuff, knee, hip and elbow, which will likely put an end to his career.

Ken Griffey (OF, CIN) has chronic knee and leg problems and is a high risk for further injury.

Pete Harnisch (RHP, CIN) had Tommy John surgery in April. He is making good progress, but expect a slow start.

Todd Helton (1B, COL) had surgery to remove a bone spur from his left elbow. During the surgery, a benign tumor was found that might have hindered his swing in 2002. He should be close to 100% by April 1.

Oscar Henriquez (RHP, DET) season ended in September when he went down with bone chips in his pitching elbow. He might not return until mid-2003.

Trevor Hoffman (RHP, SD) had a frayed rotator cuff repaired in mid-October and the Padres believe he'll be ready to work at the start of the season.

Hideki Irabu (RHP, TEX) was shut down in July with blood clots in his lungs. Latest word was that he is improving, but no further information was available.

Kazuhisa Ishii (LHP, LA) should be recovered from the skull fracture and complications from being hit in the face in mid-September. His major hurdle will be a mental one.

Jason Isringhausen (RHP, STL) had surgery to repair a slight tear in his right labrum. Early prognosis has him starting slowly in the spring.

Kevin Jarvis (RHP, SD) had surgery to repair the flexor tendon in his right elbow. He could miss the start of spring.

Geoff Jenkins (OF, MIL) is expected to be fully recovered from a dislocated right ankle and subsequent ligament damage by April.

Jason Johnson's (RHP, BAL) right shoulder tendonitis that caused him some problems in 2002 is gone.

Brian Jordan's (OF, FA) patella tendon surgery in October was a success. If there are no setbacks, he could be ready for the start of spring training, or slightly after.

Eric Karros (1B, LA) had scar tissue removed from his shoulder and might be brought along slowly next spring.

Austin Kearns (OF, CIN) suffered a strained left hamstring in August but should be 100% by late January.

Jason Kendall (C, PIT) had bone spurs taken out of his left foot and is expected to be ready by February 1.

Barry Larkin (SS, CIN) had bone spurs removed from his right big toe in late September and should be back in time for spring training.

Brandon Larson (3B, CIN) went down with a broken left hand in early September. He should be 100% by the time spring training starts.

Jason LaRue (C, CIN) had hernia surgery in late September and is expected to be ready when catchers and pitchers report in February.

Matt Lawton (OF, CLE) had surgery late in 2002 to repair his labrum, which was completely torn and required re-attachment. He'll need at least 6-9 months to recover.

Curtis Leskanic (RHP, MIL) continues to recover from surgery to both his labrum and rotator cuff. Considering he's had setbacks in his rehab work, a delay to the start of his season is expected.

Jon Lieber (RHP, FA) underwent Tommy John surgery in August and isn't expected back until spring 2004.

Mike Lieberthal (C, PHI) had surgery to repair cartilage in his right knee and should be ready in February.

Julio Lugo's (SS, HOU) fractured left forearm is healing but his latest X-ray suggested he's now a bit behind in his rehab. Lugo should be ready for spring training, but the odds are high for another setback.

Mark McLemore (UT, SEA) had bone chips removed from his right elbow and continues to rehab a pulled groin muscle. He might not be ready until sometime in April.

Gil Meche (RHP, SEA) is pitching this winter, but he won't likely be ready for Opening Day.

Mitch Meluskey (C, DET) was shut down due to severe back pain for a second time and the Tigers believe he is close to retiring unless the pain subsides quickly.

Denny Neagle (LHP, COL) had surgery in early October to remove bone spurs from his pitching elbow. He'll be brought along slowly and could miss part of spring training.

Nick Neugebauer (RHP, MIL) struggled with a strained rotator cuff twice during the 2002 season. His track record points to more trouble in 2003.

Jose Ortiz (2B, COL) continues to recover from surgery to repair torn cartilage in his right knee. He's expected to be running at full speed before the start of spring training.

Dean Palmer (DH, DET) continues to have neck problems. His sore right shoulder is also a concern. The Tigers hope he will be cleared to play by sometime in April.

Danny Patterson (RHP, DET)) underwent Tommy John surgery in late June and is not expected to return in 2003.

Robert Person (RHP, FA) had season-ending surgery to repair a tear in his right shoulder and might not be ready for the start of spring training.

Luis Pineda's (RHP, CIN) season ended on August 15 when he had arthroscopic surgery to repair both his labrum and rotator cuff. He should return in May or June.

Mark Prior's (RHP, CHC) season ended in early September due to a strained left hamstring. He'll be 100% for spring training.

Luke Prokopec (RHP, FA) had shoulder surgery and is projected to miss the 2003 season.

Mark Quinn (DH, KC) looks to be recovered from a strained left hamstring and ribcage problem.

Shane Reynolds' (RHP, FA) recovery from back surgery is coming along slowly. He's had back woes for three straight seasons and is now a high risk investment for any major league team.

Paul Rigdon (RHP, MIL) had shoulder surgery in June to repair his rotator cuff, and should be ready by March.

Scott Rolen (3B, STL) continues to rehab his sprained left shoulder and is expected to be close to 100% by January 1.

Alex Sanchez (OF, MIL) suffered a broken left fibula in early September and his left leg might not be strong enough for game play until late April.

Kazuhiro Sasaki (RHP, SEA) had bone chips removed from his pitching elbow in mid-October. It's his third elbow surgery and there is a chance he'll start 2003 on the DL.

David Segui (1B/DH) had surgery in May to repair damaged tendons in his left wrist. By season's end he was still struggling could need extra time to rehab this spring.

Aaron Sele (RHP, ANA) had a partial tear in his right rotator cuff repaired at the end of the season and it's likely he'll start the 2003 season slowly.

Mike Sirotka's (LHP, CHC) left shoulder is coming around slowly but he won't be 100% for spring training. He's expected to pitch sometime next year.

Chris Snelling (OF, SEA) tore his left ACL in June and could miss up to the first 30-60 days of the 2003 campaign.

Scott Sullivan (RHP, CIN) had a bout of tendinitis in his right shoulder during the 2002 season and has a ton of innings on his arm. The percentages say to expect more problems in 2003.

B.J. Surhoff (OF, FA) continues to recover from a torn ACL in his right knee and could be ready for the start of spring training.

Eddie Taubensee (CLE, C) had several discs in his lower back fused and won't be ready for the start of the season.

Brian Tollberg (RHP, SD) had reconstructive surgery on his right elbow (TJS) and is projected to miss 2003.

Ryan Vogelsong (RHP, PIT) is throwing restriction free one year after Tommy John surgery and is expected to be ready for the start of spring training.

Turk Wendell (RHP, PHI) has developed chronic tendinitis in his right elbow and might need time after spring training to get ready for the season.

Bob Wickman (RHP, CLE) had Tommy John surgery (TJS) to repair his right elbow and will miss the entire season.

Dave Williams (LHP, PIT) had surgery to repair his torn left labrum and could miss most of spring training as he rehabs the shoulder.

Kevin Young (1B, PIT) had another knee surgery to clean out some cartilage. One has to wonder how much longer his knees will hold up.

Gregg Zaun (C, HOU) had surgery to repair a partially torn flexor tendon in his throwing elbow, which will keep him out of baseball related activity until February. He'll be ready to play by late April.

Jeff Zimmerman (RHP, TEX) underwent Tommy John surgery in late July and will miss the 2003 season.

IV. MINOR LEAGUES

Top Prospects for 2003

For many minor leaguers that have potential to make an impact in the majors in 2003, a narrow focus on statistics is often inadequate to describe their skills and upside.

Sometimes a player's stats will be distorted by the fact that, in a given year, their organization has them focus on a particular element of their game to the exclusion of others. For instance, a pitcher that has already proven the capabilities of his fastball will spend a year working on an off-speed pitch.

And sometimes a player's body type lends itself to future development in an area that the statistics don't reveal early on. For instance, a batter might be viewed as a long-term power threat "once he fills out" but you'd never think he could even reach the warning track by a scan of his yearly home run totals.

For these reasons, it's comforting to know that there are many astute baseball people who can identify a player's true skills and put some perspective on what the statistics seem to say. Some of these people become baseball scouts (but as it turns out, only some baseball scouts actually have this ability), and those that are not allowed into this exclusive network become writers and analysts.

We are fortunate that these analysts exist. They are often far more objective than people who are actually paid to scout for major league clubs. They don't have to follow the often archaic rules that organizations rely on. The growing crop of intelligent minor league analysts would actually consider a right-handed pitcher under 6 feet tall as a player worth pursuing, a possibility that 80% of the major clubs would never even entertain.

And I am personally fortunate that one of these analysts writes for Baseball HQ and has been contributing to this book for the past seven years. Deric McKamey is an amazing repository of information. But more than that, he knows talent.

Over the next six pages, Deric will introduce you to 54 of the names you need to tuck away for 2003. It is important to note that these are players expected to hit the majors this coming year, and does not necessarily represent the prospects with the best long-term upside overall. There are still players in the lower minors that could become bigger names, but will not likely see the majors until 2004 at the earliest. You'll be able to find information on those players at Baseball HQ over the winter. In fact, Deric's annual organizational reports are online at this very moment.

The following section is a minor league extension of the player boxes that appear in the main part of the book. As such, the player boxes themselves will be familiar to you. They contain much of the same information as those for the major league players. Some statistical gauges have been omitted as they are not relevant to an evaluation of prospects, such as Rotisserie values. Other data, like RH/LH splits, were just not available. The number to the left of each player box is his relative rank among the batters and the pitchers.

We have listed a preliminary projection for each player. These are all highly speculative and represent a most likely scenario if three conditions occur in 2003:

1. They make their respective teams.
2. They get the playing time we expect.
3. They overcome the mental hurdle of jumping to the majors and perform at the level they are probably capable of as a first year player.

These unknowns can turn the hottest of prospects into a non-entity. Just ask Hank Blalock. As such, you'll note that there is no Forecast Risk listed for any of these players. It is safe to assume that all of them — all essentially unproven — are high risks.

The snapshot section of each player box contains some new information that helps put each player's potential into better perspective. The following abbreviations pertain to each player's ability, as of the moment, and are subjective assessments.

BATTERS

PWR: The ability to hit for power

SPD: Speed and baserunning ability

BAVG: The ability to hit for batting average and judge the strike zone.

DEF: Overall defense, which includes range, hands, throwing arm and agility. While Rotisserie types might not have direct interest in defense, simulation players certainly do, and Deric often notes that defense is what gets a player to the majors (and offense is what keeps him there). This alone can explain why apparently solid minor league hitters, like Chris Hatcher and Phil Hiatt, never got the chance that many casual observers thought they rightfully deserved. They didn't.

PITCHERS

VEL: Velocity of a pitcher's fastball, with movement factored in slightly

BRE: Quality of breaking pitch(es)

CHG: Ability to change speeds, along with the quality of change-up

PIT: Pitchability. This is the mental aspect of the game, a pitcher's ability to work hitters, set up pitches, establish command, and a pitcher's level of poise.

20 Bard,Josh

Pos CA
Bats S
Age 25 Pre-Peak
PWR +
SPD ++
BAVG ++
DEF +++

Year	Lev	Tm	AB	R	H	HR	RBI	SB	Avg	OB	Slg	OPS	bb%	ct%	Eye	PX	SX	RC/G	BPV
2000	aaa	COL	17	0	4	0	1	0	235	235	235	471	0	88	0.00			1.85	-22
2001	aa	2TM	318	40	86	5	49	0	270	343	393	736	10	84	0.70	93	30	4.99	43
2001	aaa	CLE	4	0	0	0	0	0	0	0	0	0	0	75	0.00			0.00	-100
2002	aaa	CLE	344	36	102	6	53	0	297	335	436	771	5	87	0.44	94	44	5.48	50
2002	MLB	CLE	90	9	20	3	12	0	222	255	378	633	4	86	0.31	99	25	3.26	23
2001	MLE		322	36	82	5	44	0	255	320	373	693	9	86	0.70	85	27	4.30	36
2002	MLE		344	33	98	6	49	0	285	320	416	736	5	88	0.43	92	30	4.91	43
2003	**Projection**		**250**	**27**	**70**	**4**	**37**	**0**	**280**	**328**	**410**	**739**	**7**	**87**	**0.54**	**90**	**40**	**4.97**	**44**

CLE loves his defense and he showed he could hold his own with the bat in his brief Sept trial. Power is not going to be his forte, but can drive the gaps and hit in situations. Platooning him with a RH CA might be the way to go

9 Berroa,Angel

Pos SS
Bats R
Age 23 Growth
PWR ++
SPD +++
BAVG ++
DEF +++

Year	Lev	Tm	AB	R	H	HR	RBI	SB	Avg	OB	Slg	OPS	bb%	ct%	Eye	PX	SX	RC/G	BPV
2001	a	KC	199	43	63	6	25	10	317	346	538	884	4	79	0.22	145	203	6.53	70
2001	aa	KC	304	63	90	8	42	15	296	333	467	800	5	82	0.31	109	166	5.62	52
2001	MLB	KC	53	8	16	0	4	2	302	339	340	679	5	81	0.30	32	80	4.63	21
2002	aaa	KC	297	37	64	8	35	6	215	253	360	613	5	72	0.18	82	146	3.05	12
2002	MLB	KC	75	8	17	0	5	3	227	293	347	639	9	87	0.70	92	121	3.78	30
2001	MLE		304	49	83	6	33	12	273	303	414	717	4	87	0.33	93	131	4.26	38
2002	MLE		297	30	59	7	28	5	199	230	323	553	4	78	0.18	74	106	2.28	2
2003	**Projection**		**450**	**66**	**110**	**11**	**51**	**14**	**244**	**278**	**396**	**674**	**4**	**79**	**0.22**	**92**	**147**	**3.66**	**26**

A meniscus tear in his knee delayed the start of 2002 and he never got on track. His wiry strength, speed, and defense are good enough to get him by, despite his lack of plate discipline. He should improve as the year goes on.

7 Borchard,Joe

Pos CF
Bats S
Age 24 Growth
PWR +++++
SPD +++
BAVG +++
DEF +++

Year	Lev	Tm	AB	R	H	HR	RBI	SB	Avg	OB	Slg	OPS	bb%	ct%	Eye	PX	SX	RC/G	BPV
2000	a	CHW	52	7	15	2	7	0	288	362	462	824	10	83	0.67	111	24	6.38	55
2000	aa	CHW	22	3	5	0	3	0	227	320	318	638	12	64	0.38	39	254	3.73	0
2001	aa	CHW	515	95	152	27	98	5	295	376	509	885	12	69	0.42	125	68	7.24	62
2002	aaa	CHW	438	62	119	20	59	2	272	345	498	843	10	68	0.35	137	60	6.16	59
2002	MLB	CHW	36	5	8	2	5	0	222	243	389	632	3	61	0.07	84	41	3.16	12
2001	MLE		515	79	141	25	82	4	274	346	472	818	10	75	0.44	117	53	5.90	51
2002	MLE		438	55	112	20	52	2	256	326	470	797	10	72	0.37	134	43	5.38	51
2003	**Projection**		**400**	**58**	**104**	**19**	**57**	**2**	**260**	**335**	**474**	**809**	**10**	**71**	**0.38**	**131**	**54**	**5.63**	**52**

His power is unmistakable, and though the K's continue to mount, he is exercising more patience. He is playing out of position in CF, but has handled himself well, owing it to experience. CHW will likely create room for him in 2003.

19 Broussard,Ben

Pos CF
Bats L
Age 26 Pre-Peak
PWR +++
SPD +
BAVG +++
DEF +

Year	Lev	Tm	AB	R	H	HR	RBI	SB	Avg	OB	Slg	OPS	bb%	ct%	Eye	PX	SX	RC/G	BPV
1999	aa	CIN	127	26	27	8	21	1	213	275	441	716	8	68	0.27	141	82	4.17	31
2000	aa	CIN	286	64	73	14	41	15	255	368	458	826	15	73	0.65	120	158	5.58	46
2001	aa	CIN	353	81	113	23	69	10	320	420	592	1012	15	80	0.88	166	79	9.97	96
2001	aaa	CLE	340	61	88	16	51	4	259	362	471	833	14	76	0.69	125	78	6.39	56
2002	MLB	CLE	112	10	27	4	9	0	241	286	384	670	6	78	0.28	85	14	3.84	23
2001	MLE		353	59	95	17	50	7	269	352	479	831	11	83	0.75	129	65	6.13	61
2002	MLE		340	54	82	16	46	4	241	337	447	784	13	78	0.64	125	72	5.49	47
2003	**Projection**		**350**	**64**	**89**	**13**	**53**	**6**	**254**	**351**	**433**	**783**	**13**	**78**	**0.68**	**111**	**85**	**5.59**	**47**

CLE gave him a brief trial to see if he could handle LF, but didn't hit LH pitching and his defense was average. A good spring training should net him 350-400 at bats in a 1B/LF/DH role, but he is the type that needs regular PT.

2 Byrd,Marlon

Pos CF
Bats R
Age 25 Pre-Peak
PWR +++
SPD +++
BAVG ++
DEF ++

Year	Lev	Tm	AB	R	H	HR	RBI	SB	Avg	OB	Slg	OPS	bb%	ct%	Eye	PX	SX	RC/G	BPV
1999	a	PHI	243	40	72	13	50	8	296	369	535	904	10	71	0.40	139	183	7.54	60
2000	a	PHI	515	104	159	17	93	41	309	371	515	886	9	79	0.46	130	231	7.66	64
2001	aa	PHI	510	108	161	28	89	32	316	379	555	934	9	82	0.56	135		8.35	74
2002	aaa	PHI	538	103	160	15	63	15	297	353	476	829	8	82	0.47	111	153	6.51	57
2002	MLB	PHI	35	2	8	1	1	0	229	250	371	621	3	77	0.13	92	38	2.27	19
2001	MLE		510	85	141	20	69	25	276	333	467	799	8	83	0.49	109	162	5.74	50
2002	MLE		538	85	147	12	52	13	273	325	429	754	7	83	0.46	102	136	5.22	45
2003	**Projection**		**500**	**89**	**135**	**14**	**65**	**15**	**270**	**328**	**440**	**769**	**8**	**82**	**0.48**	**105**	**156**	**5.35**	**45**

His '02 numbers were more indicative of his potential than the gaudy stats he has put up in the past. Still, he's a considerable upgrade for PHI in CF. That position should be his for the next five years, before he moves to a corner.

16 Cash,Kevin

Pos CA SS
Bats R
Age 25 Pre-Peak
PWR ++
SPD +
BAVG ++
DEF ++++

Year	Lev	Tm	AB	R	H	HR	RBI	SB	Avg	OB	Slg	OPS	bb%	ct%	Eye	PX	SX	RC/G	BPV
2000	a	TOR	196	28	48	10	27	5	245	321	459	780	10	72	0.41	129	92	5.10	43
2001	a	TOR	371	55	105	12	66	4	283	357	453	810	10	78	0.54	112	54	6.02	54
2002	aa	TOR	213	38	59	8	44	5	277	382	469	851	14	79	0.82	120	89	6.84	62
2002	aaa	TOR	236	27	52	10	26	0	220	295	424	719	10	69	0.35	126	22	4.35	37
2002	MLB	TOR	14	1	2	0	0	0	143	200	143	343	7	71	0.25	0	30	0.96	-47
2001	MLE		0	0	0	0	0	0	0					0		0			
2002	MLE		449	51	100	14	55	4	223	298	392	690	10	80	0.53	111	54	3.99	33
2003	**Projection**		**300**	**41**	**69**	**9**	**45**	**1**	**230**	**315**	**398**	**713**	**11**	**77**	**0.53**	**109**	**54**	**4.36**	**35**

His offense will fail to live up to what he's posted the last two years, as his bat is a bit slow, but he's excellent in the clutch and makes contact. Defensively, he'll be better than anyone TOR has had in some time.

4 Choi,Hee Seop

Pos 1B
Bats L
Age 24 Growth
PWR +++++
SPD +
BAVG +++
DEF ++

Year	Lev	Tm	AB	R	H	HR	RBI	SB	Avg	OB	Slg	OPS	bb%	ct%	Eye	PX	SX	RC/G	BPV
2000	a	CHC	345	60	102	15	70	4	296	364	533	897	10	77	0.47	157	134	7.39	69
2000	aa	CHC	122	25	37	10	25	3	303	422	623	1045	17	69	0.66	203	60	10.34	96
2001	aaa	CHC	266	38	61	13	45	5	229	317	417	734	11	75	0.51	111	64	4.75	34
2002	aaa	CHC	478	94	137	26	97	3	287	405	513	917	17	75	0.80	129	76	8.09	68
2002	MLB	CHC	50	6	9	2	4	0	180	281	320	601	12	70	0.47	77	26	3.11	3
2001	MLE		266	34	56	11	40	4	211	291	368	659	10	79	0.55	91	65	3.74	21
2002	MLE		478	66	115	18	68	2	241	335	404	739	12	82	0.80	96	56	4.86	38
2003	**Projection**		**500**	**78**	**125**	**20**	**85**	**3**	**250**	**348**	**426**	**774**	**13**	**78**	**0.68**	**105**	**67**	**5.44**	**42**

He has light-tower power and improved his walk rate in '02, but seemed lost during his Sept stint and can be had by good pitching. 1B is likely his, but he will have to show a more mature approach to the plate if he wants to stay.

27 Crosby,Bobby

Pos SS
Bats R
Age 23 Growth
PWR ++
SPD +++
BAVG +++
DEF +++

Year	Lev	Tm	AB	R	H	HR	RBI	SB	Avg	OB	Slg	OPS	bb%	ct%	Eye	PX	SX	RC/G	BPV
1999			0	0	0	0	0	0	0					0					
2000			0	0	0	0	0	0	0					0					
2001	a	OAK	38	7	15	1	3	0	395	439	605	1044	7	79	0.38	152	34	11.57	106
2002	a	OAK	280	47	86	2	38	5	307	380	404	784	11	85	0.77	67	105	6.21	48
2002	aa	OAK	228	31	64	7	31	9	281	336	443	779	8	82	0.46	107	79	5.57	49
2001	MLE		0	0	0	0	0	0	0					0		0			
2002	MLE		228	27	57	6	27	8	250	299	390	690	7	85	0.46	93	78	4.17	33
2003	**Projection**		**200**	**28**	**51**	**4**	**25**	**4**	**255**	**316**	**381**	**697**	**8**	**85**	**0.58**	**84**	**87**	**4.37**	**33**

OAK likes the way he plays the game and has adjusted to each level. Mark Ellis would be a better UT player, which might create an opening at 2B, a position he has little experience at. His work ethic should take care of the rest.

3 Cuddyer,Michael

Pos RF
Bats R
Age 24 Growth
PWR ++++
SPD +
BAVG ++
DEF +

Year	Lev	Tm	AB	R	H	HR	RBI	SB	Avg	OB	Slg	OPS	bb%	ct%	Eye	PX	SX	RC/G	BPV
2000	aa	MIN	490	72	129	6	61	5	263	338	394	731	10	81	0.59	88	128	4.84	36
2001	aa	MIN	509	95	153	30	87	5	301	390	560	950	13	79	0.71	156	71	8.05	82
2001	MLB	MIN	18	1	4	0	1	1	222	300	333	633	10	67	0.33	95	54	3.85	22
2002	aaa	MIN	330	70	102	20	53	12	309	377	594	971	10	76	0.46	152	211	8.22	80
2002	MLB	MIN	112	12	29	4	13	3	259	308	429	737	7	73	0.27	108	58	4.89	39
2001	MLE		509	95	153	29	87	5	301	389	558	947	13	79	0.70	156	69	7.99	82
2002	MLE		330	51	90	14	39	9	273	326	482	808	7	82	0.44	119	139	5.25	51
2003	**Projection**		**400**	**72**	**111**	**17**	**59**	**7**	**278**	**351**	**491**	**842**	**10**	**80**	**0.55**	**125**	**125**	**6.04**	**58**

Finding a place for him to play proved difficult in '02, as MIN was full of overachievers in the OF. A spot will certainly open up for him in 2003 and he will display his impressive power and on-base ability on the American League.

12 Cust,Jack

Pos LF
Bats L
Age 24 Growth
PWR +++++
SPD +
BAVG ++
DEF +

Year	Lev	Tm	AB	R	H	HR	RBI	SB	Avg	OB	Slg	OPS	bb%	ct%	Eye	PX	SX	RC/G	BPV
2000	aa	ARI	447	100	131	20	75	12	293	440	526	965	21	66	0.78	154	128	9.03	73
2001	aaa	ARI	442	81	123	27	79	6	278	414	525	938	19	64	0.64	155	79	8.46	68
2001	MLB	ARI	2	0	1	0	1	1	500	667	500	1167	33	50	1.00		45	30.26	87
2002	aaa	COL	359	74	95	23	55	6	265	403	524	926	19	66	0.69	152	61	8.04	69
2002	MLB	COL	65	8	11	1	8	0	169	299	246	545	16	51	0.38	50	41	2.53	-14
2001	MLE		442	67	116	21	65	5	262	380	462	842	16	73	0.71	118	58	6.58	53
2002	MLE		359	47	87	19	35	4	242	340	460	799	13	80	0.75	130	44	5.52	52
2003	**Projection**		**350**	**60**	**89**	**19**	**59**	**4**	**254**	**379**	**485**	**864**	**17**	**72**	**0.71**	**138**	**63**	**6.79**	**59**

His anticipated arrival was a disappointment. His defense was better than advertised and he did show power, but he really hasn't hit well since the first half of '01. He will need to tighten his strike zone and concentrate more.

17 Greene,Khalil

Pos SS
Bats R
Age 23 Growth
PWR +++
SPD +++
BAVG +++
DEF ++

Year	Lev	Tm	AB	R	H	HR	RBI	SB	Avg	OB	Slg	OPS	bb%	ct%	Eye	PX	SX	RC/G	BPV
1998			0	0	0	0	0	0	0					0					
1999			0	0	0	0	0	0	0					0					
2000			0	0	0	0	0	0	0					0					
2001	r	SD	37	5	10	0	6	1	270	357	297	654	12	84	0.83	23	56	4.32	17
2002	a	SD	183	33	58	9	32	0	317	359	525	884	6	82	0.36	121	63	7.26	66
2001	MLE		0	0	0	0	0	0	0					0		0			
2002	MLE		0	0	0	0	0	0	0					0					
2003	**Projection**		**250**	**20**	**63**	**5**	**24**	**3**	**252**	**308**	**328**	**636**	**8**	**90**	**0.83**	**44**	**46**	**3.73**	**20**

Predicting a 2002 draftee to reach the Majors this quickly might be premature, but SD is weak at SS and he has shown an advanced bat. He won't overwhelm you with offensive or defensive tools, but can be appreciated on a daily basis.

13 Hafner,Travis

Pos 1B
Bats L
Age 25 Pre-Peak
PWR ++++
SPD +
BAVG +++
DEF +

Year	Lev	Tm	AB	R	H	HR	RBI	SB	Avg	OB	Slg	OPS	bb%	ct%	Eye	PX	SX	RC/G	BPV
1999	a	TEX	480	94	140	28	111	5	292	378	546	924	12	69	0.44	153	105	7.76	69
2000	a	TEX	436	90	151	22	109	0	346	433	580	1014	13	80	0.78	146	38	10.15	94
2001	aa	TEX	323	59	91	20	74	3	282	393	545	938	15	75	0.72	159	53	8.23	78
2002	aaa	TEX	401	79	137	21	77	2	342	450	559	1009	16	81	1.04	125	54	10.58	91
2002	MLB	TEX	62	6	15	1	6	0	242	329	387	716	11	76	0.53	94	93	4.35	32
2001	MLE		323	47	82	18	59	2	254	350	492	843	13	79	0.72	146	40	6.32	62
2002	MLE		401	60	122	17	58	2	304	395	486	881	13	86	1.03	110	47	7.57	70
2003	**Projection**		**350**	**60**	**101**	**13**	**55**	**2**	**289**	**390**	**469**	**859**	**14**	**80**	**0.85**	**112**	**58**	**7.12**	**62**

Hitting MLB pitching likely won't pose a problem, as he uses the whole field, draws walks, and has good power. Finding a position for him might be, as he isn't proficient on defense and doesn't run well. He'd do well as a DH.

24 Infante,Omar

Pos SS
Bats R
Age 21 Growth
PWR +
SPD +++
BAVG ++
DEF +++

Year	Lev	Tm	AB	R	H	HR	RBI	SB	Avg	OB	Slg	OPS	bb%	ct%	Eye	PX	SX	RC/G	BPV
2000	a	DET	48	7	11	0	5	1	229	302	229	531	9	85	0.71		71	2.67	-9
2000	a	DET	259	35	71	2	24	11	274	326	340	666	7	89	0.69	49	85	4.03	26
2001	aa	DET	540	86	163	2	62	27	302	357	367	723	8	84	0.53	45	123	4.94	31
2002	aaa	DET	436	49	117	4	51	19	268	313	369	682	6	89	0.57	59	144	3.81	28
2002	MLB	DET	72	4	24	1	6	0	333	360	417	777	4	86	0.30	57	13	5.55	42
2001	MLE		540	79	167	1	57	25	309	359	369	728	7	89	0.69	44	101	4.88	36
2002	MLE		436	51	127	3	53	20	291	338	394	733	7	92	0.84	62	146	4.45	41
2003	**Projection**		**150**	**19**	**41**	**1**	**17**	**6**	**273**	**323**	**358**	**681**	**7**	**89**	**0.66**	**55**	**122**	**3.92**	**28**

Doesn't have the offensive or defensive upside of Ramon Santiago, but has played well for a player younger (?) than his competition. For DET, 2B is a trouble spot and he will get a chance to compete. His offense will have to improve.

18 Ludwick,Ryan

Pos CF
Bats R
Age 24 Growth
PWR ++++
SPD +++
BAVG ++
DEF +++

Year	Lev	Tm	AB	R	H	HR	RBI	SB	Avg	OB	Slg	OPS	bb%	ct%	Eye	PX	SX	RC/G	BPV
2000	a	OAK	493	86	130	29	102	10	264	353	505	858	12	74	0.53	143	100	6.43	58
2001	aa	OAK	443	82	119	25	96	9	269	351	503	854	11	74	0.50	137	97	6.12	58
2001	aaa	OAK	57	10	13	1	7	2	228	254	333	588	3	72	0.13	71		3.03	10
2002	aaa	TEX	305	62	87	15	52	2	285	364	548	912	11	75	0.50	157	120	7.40	75
2002	MLB	TEX	81	10	19	1	9	2	235	295	346	641	8	70	0.29	83	67	3.55	20
2001	MLE		500	73	114	21	81	9	228	293	406	699	8	80	0.45	105	79	3.81	31
2002	MLE		305	47	78	12	40	2	256	320	472	792	9	82	0.52	136	90	5.34	55
2003	**Projection**		**150**	**26**	**37**	**5**	**25**	**1**	**247**	**322**	**427**	**749**	**10**	**78**	**0.50**	**113**	**85**	**4.74**	**42**

He likely would have played CF for most of Sept had he not injured his hip. His power continues to develop, but will have to judge the strike zone better. TEX likes his defense and deceptive speed, and may give him a shot to start.

11 Munson,Eric

Pos 1B SS
Bats L
Age 25 Pre-Peak
PWR ++++
SPD +
BAVG ++
DEF ++

Year	Lev	Tm	AB	R	H	HR	RBI	SB	Avg	OB	Slg	OPS	bb%	ct%	Eye	PX	SX	RC/G	BPV
2000	MLB	DET	5	0	0	0	1	0	0	0	0	0	0	80	0.00			0.00	-100
2001	aa	DET	519	88	135	26	102	0	260	363	482	845	14	73	0.60	136	35	6.42	58
2001	MLB	DET	66	4	10	1	6	0	152	188	273	461	4	68	0.14	74	112	1.46	-14
2002	aaa	DET	477	77	125	24	84	1	262	365	493	857	14	76	0.68	133	70	6.59	61
2002	MLB	DET	59	3	11	2	5	0	186	262	288	550	9	81	0.55	51	-1	2.58	-5
2001	MLE		519	70	117	17	81	0	225	313	389	702	11	78	0.57	105	34	4.25	32
2002	MLE		477	69	112	18	76	1	235	336	426	762	13	79	0.74	115	73	5.10	43
2003	**Projection**		**350**	**53**	**86**	**13**	**50**	**0**	**246**	**345**	**432**	**777**	**13**	**77**	**0.66**	**115**	**57**	**5.38**	**45**

His bat was blistering in mid-summer, but was mediocre otherwise. Experience and maturity helped his offense and he has the most power of anyone in the organization. With Carlos Pena at 1B, his only chance may be at DH.

25 Nady,Xavier

Pos LF
Bats R
Age 24 Growth
PWR +++
SPD +
BAVG +++
DEF +

Year	Lev	Tm	AB	R	H	HR	RBI	SB	Avg	OB	Slg	OPS	bb%	ct%	Eye	PX	SX	RC/G	BPV
1999			0	0	0	0	0	0	0					0					
2000			0	0	0	0	0	0	0					0					
2001	a	SD	424	96	158	26	100	6	373	453	651	1104	13	74	0.57	174	82	12.81	110
2002	a	SD	169	41	47	13	37	2	278	381	580	961	14	76	0.70	160	149	8.46	77
2002	aaa	SD	315	46	89	10	43	0	283	325	422	748	6	81	0.33	83	52	5.00	37
2001	MLE		0	0	0	0	0	0	0					0		0			
2002	MLE		315	40	79	8	37	0	251	289	368	657	5	83	0.31	71	52	3.71	21
2003	**Projection**		**200**	**39**	**54**	**8**	**38**	**2**	**270**	**348**	**448**	**795**	**11**	**78**	**0.54**	**109**	**89**	**5.84**	**48**

He finally endured a season without injury, but his offense suffered, mostly due to poor plate discipline. He did play well at his new position (LF). SD will give him a chance to start, but he won't likely be up until the All-Star break.

10 Olivo,Miguel

Pos CA
Bats R
Age 24 Growth
PWR ++
SPD ++
BAVG ++
DEF +++++

Year	Lev	Tm	AB	R	H	HR	RBI	SB	Avg	OB	Slg	OPS	bb%	ct%	Eye	PX	SX	RC/G	BPV
2000	a	OAK	227	40	64	5	35	5	282	329	441	770	7	77	0.30	97	183	5.30	40
2000	aa	OAK	59	8	14	1	9	0	237	297	322	619	8	75	0.33	55	38	3.42	10
2001	aa	CHW	316	45	82	14	55	6	259	337	472	809	10	80	0.60	131	77	5.72	56
2002	aa	CHW	359	51	110	6	49	29	306	376	479	855	10	82	0.61	104	204	6.60	61
2002	MLB	CHW	19	2	4	1	5	0	211	286	421	707	10	74	0.40	125	14	4.14	32
2001	MLE		316	36	74	13	45	5	234	301	427	728	9	83	0.57	120	65	4.42	41
2002	MLE		359	44	98	6	43	25	273	341	423	764	9	82	0.58	95	157	5.01	44
2003	**Projection**		**150**	**20**	**39**	**4**	**21**	**5**	**260**	**329**	**432**	**761**	**9**	**81**	**0.55**	**108**	**123**	**4.89**	**45**

One of the top defensive CA's in the minors, his bat and speed were a surprise in a repeat of AA. He's not ready to catch regularly from an offensive standpoint, so CHW may be wise to platoon him for half the season.

22 Pena,Wily Mo

Pos CF
Bats R
Age 21 Growth
PWR ++++
SPD ++++
BAVG +
DEF +++

Year	Lev	Tm	AB	R	H	HR	RBI	SB	Avg	OB	Slg	OPS	bb%	ct%	Eye	PX	SX	RC/G	BPV
2000	r	NYY	73	17	22	1	13	0	301	370	397	768	10	78	0.50	70	60	5.76	39
2000	a	NYY	249	41	51	10	28	6	205	258	361	620	7	63	0.20	89	114	2.94	11
2001	a	CIN	511	87	135	26	113	26	264	309	485	794	6	65	0.19	129	151	5.18	47
2002	aa	CIN	388	47	99	11	47	8	255	318	405	723	8	68	0.29	95	87	4.79	33
2002	MLB	CIN	18	1	4	1	1	0	222	222	389	611	0	39	0.00	83	-10	2.83	11
2001	MLE		0	0	0	0	0	0	0					0		0			
2002	MLE		388	40	96	9	40	6	247	300	384	684	7	76	0.32	90	80	4.18	28
2003	**Projection**		**150**	**21**	**33**	**3**	**22**	**3**	**220**	**274**	**356**	**630**	**7**	**69**	**0.24**	**87**	**106**	**3.28**	**16**

His Major League contract forces him to remain with CIN and they will use him as their 5th OF. His raw skills are as good as any player in the minors, but his plate discipline is atrocious and he will lose precious developmental time.

1 Phillips,Brandon

Pos 2B
Bats R
Age 21 Growth
PWR ++
SPD ++++
BAVG +++
DEF ++++

Year	Lev	Tm	AB	R	H	HR	RBI	SB	Avg	OB	Slg	OPS	bb%	ct%	Eye	PX	SX	RC/G	BPV
2001	a	MON	194	36	55	4	23	17	284	401	428	829	16	77	0.84	102	138	7.09	51
2001	aa	MON	295	35	79	7	36	13	268	296	403	700	4	86	0.29	99	89	4.10	35
2002	aa	MON	245	40	80	9	35	6	327	368	506	874	6	87	0.48	110	99	7.10	66
2002	aaa	CLE	258	31	72	9	32	8	279	321	453	775	6	83	0.36	109	76	5.34	49
2002	MLB	CLE	31	5	8	0	4	0	258	324	419	743	9	81	0.50	112	162	4.94	44
2001	MLE		265	32	77	6	33	12	291	319	430	749	4	87	0.31	96	79	4.72	45
2002	MLE		503	67	153	18	64	14	304	343	479	822	6	86	0.44	111	80	6.14	58
2003	**Projection**		**400**	**54**	**111**	**13**	**51**	**14**	**278**	**321**	**443**	**763**	**6**	**85**	**0.42**	**105**	**92**	**5.09**	**47**

The top MI in the minors will have to switch to 2B until Vizquel goes. Athleticism helps him on both sides of the baseball and he can beat you in many ways. He will open as a starter and eventually move to the top of the order.

5 Rivera,Juan

Pos RF
Bats R
Age 24 Growth
PWR ++++
SPD ++
BAVG ++
DEF +++

Year	Lev	Tm	AB	R	H	HR	RBI	SB	Avg	OB	Slg	OPS	bb%	ct%	Eye	PX	SX	RC/G	BPV
2000	aa	NYY	62	9	14	2	12	0	226	294	403	697	9	76	0.40	121	40	4.15	33
2001	aa	NYY	316	50	101	14	58	5	320	350	528	879	5	84	0.30	125	96	6.56	67
2001	aaa	NYY	199	39	65	14	40	4	327	374	603	977	7	84	0.48	157	87	8.10	87
2002	aaa	NYY	265	40	86	8	47	5	325	356	502	858	5	85	0.33	114	88	6.94	66
2002	MLB	NYY	83	9	22	1	6	1	265	315	361	676	7	88	0.60	70	48	4.00	31
2001	MLE		515	79	157	27	86	8	305	339	526	866	5	86	0.38	130	75	6.12	65
2002	MLE		265	33	77	7	38	4	291	319	449	768	4	88	0.34	105	76	5.27	49
2003	**Projection**		**350**	**53**	**97**	**12**	**59**	**5**	**277**	**312**	**460**	**772**	**5**	**86**	**0.37**	**114**	**89**	**4.99**	**50**

He matured during 2002 season he was rewarded with post-season playing time. There are still some holes in his swing and he will have to be more patient, but has the power and defense to land and keep a starting role.

23 Romano,Jason

Pos 2B
Bats R
Age 23 Growth
PWR ++
SPD ++++
BAVG ++
DEF ++

Year	Lev	Tm	AB	R	H	HR	RBI	SB	Avg	OB	Slg	OPS	bb%	ct%	Eye	PX	SX	RC/G	BPV
2000	aa	TEX	535	87	145	8	70	25	271	340	389	729	9	84	0.67	84	115	4.85	38
2001	aa	TEX	186	19	45	1	19	8	242	302	317	619	8	83	0.52	55	97	3.42	15
2001	aaa	TEX	149	32	47	4	13	3	315	396	450	846	12	81	0.71	80	97	6.61	55
2002	aaa	2TM	325	48	93	4	37	18	286	337	388	725	7	79	0.37	65	134	4.86	32
2002	MLB	2TM	91	17	23	0	5	6	253	306	319	625	7	74	0.29	47	163	3.71	11
2001	MLE		335	45	89	5	28	9	266	332	364	696	9	87	0.73	66	79	4.21	32
2002	MLE		325	31	84	3	24	12	258	293	338	632	5	88	0.40	54	94	3.33	18
2003	**Projection**		**150**	**21**	**41**	**2**	**14**	**6**	**273**	**329**	**375**	**704**	**8**	**84**	**0.52**	**67**	**102**	**4.37**	**31**

COL is just as undecided about what position he'll play as TEX was. His athleticism is a definite plus, but his bat has stalled for two years, making him a bad choice for the OF. His best usage would be as a utility player or a starter at 2B.

21 Sanchez,Freddy

Pos 2B
Bats R
Age 25 Pre-Peak
PWR +
SPD +++
BAVG +++
DEF ++

Year	Lev	Tm	AB	R	H	HR	RBI	SB	Avg	OB	Slg	OPS	bb%	ct%	Eye	PX	SX	RC/G	BPV
2001	a	BOS	280	40	95	1	24	5	339	387	446	834	7	89	0.73	78	116	6.83	60
2001	aa	BOS	178	25	58	2	19	3	326	358	472	830	5	88	0.43	115	66	6.54	67
2001	aaa	BOS	311	60	102	3	38	19	328	399	437	837	11	86	0.82	80	119	7.31	61
2002	aaa	BOS	183	25	55	4	28	5	301	344	432	775	6	89	0.57	82	87	5.16	48
2002	MLB	BOS	16	3	3	0	2	0	188	278	188	465	11	81	0.67	0	62	1.92	-24
2001	MLE		178	21	53	2	16	3	298	324	433	757	4	89	0.37	105	62	5.19	52
2002	MLE		494	67	141	5	52	19	285	336	387	723	7	89	0.68	73	98	4.83	40
2003	**Projection**		**250**	**35**	**71**	**3**	**29**	**5**	**284**	**332**	**403**	**735**	**7**	**88**	**0.61**	**85**	**84**	**4.80**	**44**

His ability to hit for BA is his only above average skill, but has defensive versatility, is sound, and he plays hard. BOS may give him a shot to start at 2B, but he's really a future utility player.

6 Snelling,Chris

Pos LF
Bats L
Age 21 Growth
PWR ++
SPD ++++
BAVG +++
DEF +++

Year	Lev	Tm	AB	R	H	HR	RBI	SB	Avg	OB	Slg	OPS	bb%	ct%	Eye	PX	SX	RC/G	BPV
1999	r	SEA	265	46	81	10	50	8	306	383	498	881	11	91	1.38	119	111	6.74	78
2000	a	SEA	259	44	79	9	56	7	305	386	483	868	12	87	1.00	100	139	7.09	65
2001	a	SEA	450	90	151	7	73	12	336	396	491	887	9	86	0.71	97		7.73	69
2002	aa	SEA	89	10	29	1	12	5	326	406	506	912	12	88	1.09	120	150	8.40	84
2002	MLB	SEA	27	2	4	1	3	0	148	207	259	466	7	85	0.50	56	14	1.72	-16
2001	MLE		0	0	0	0	0	0	0					0		0			
2002	MLE		89	11	29	1	13	5	326	412	483	895	13	89	1.30	114	105	8.23	84
2003	**Projection**		**200**	**33**	**53**	**5**	**36**	**2**	**265**	**349**	**433**	**782**	**11**	**88**	**1.06**	**105**	**109**	**5.36**	**55**

Chances are he would have secured LF in '02 if he hadn't torn his ACL. He has excellent pop for his size, showing great speed and defense. He plays with reckless abandon, which is fun to watch, but it may hurt him in the long-run.

8 Teixeira,Mark

Pos 3B SS
Bats S
Age 23 Growth
PWR ++++
SPD ++
BAVG ++++
DEF ++

Year	Lev	Tm	AB	R	H	HR	RBI	SB	Avg	OB	Slg	OPS	bb%	ct%	Eye	PX	SX	RC/G	BPV
1999			0	0	0	0	0	0	0					0					
2000			0	0	0	0	0	0	0					0					
2001			0	0	0	0	0	0	0					0					
2002	a	TEX	150	32	48	9	41	2	320	404	593	997	12	84	0.88	155	119	9.63	94
2002	aa	TEX	171	31	54	10	28	3	316	403	591	994	13	79	0.69	159	124	9.18	88
2001	MLE		0	0	0	0	0	0	0					0		0			
2002	MLE		171	28	52	9	25	3	304	387	556	942	12	82	0.74	146	120	8.13	79
2003	**Projection**		**250**	**46**	**75**	**9**	**49**	**3**	**300**	**384**	**499**	**883**	**12**	**83**	**0.79**	**119**	**121**	**7.37**	**68**

The minors' top hitter has it all: power, contact ability, and strike zone judgment from both sides of the plate. TEX is brimming with corner players and his defense is nothing special, but his offense may be too good to ignore.

26 Thurston,Joe

Pos 2B
Bats L
Age 23 Growth
PWR +
SPD ++++
BAVG ++
DEF +++

Year	Lev	Tm	AB	R	H	HR	RBI	SB	Avg	OB	Slg	OPS	bb%	ct%	Eye	PX	SX	RC/G	BPV
1999	r	LA	277	48	79	0	32	27	285	349	343	692	9	88	0.79	44	141	3.97	28
2000	a	LA	551	97	167	4	70	43	303	367	410	778	9	89	0.92	78	157	5.35	51
2001	aa	LA	544	80	145	7	46	20	267	326	377	703	8	88	0.74	71	123	4.12	34
2002	aaa	LA	587	106	196	12	55	22	334	361	506	867	4	90	0.42	106	174	6.95	66
2002	MLB	LA	13	1	6	0	1	0	462	462	538	1000	0	92	0.00	66	11	11.77	83
2001	MLE		544	75	132	7	43	19	243	301	340	641	8	88	0.70	62	118	3.28	22
2002	MLE		587	76	162	9	39	16	276	298	397	694	3	93	0.41	79	120	3.99	35
2003	**Projection**		**150**	**23**	**41**	**2**	**13**	**4**	**273**	**314**	**397**	**711**	**6**	**90**	**0.59**	**80**	**125**	**4.15**	**37**

His 196 hits led the PCL, and despite problems drawing walks and his baserunning, he's probably ready for the Majors. Power and speed improved, and played better defense but LA does not usually promote youngsters.

14 Utley,Chase

Pos 3B
Bats L
Age 24 Growth
PWR +++
SPD ++
BAVG ++
DEF +

Year	Lev	Tm	AB	R	H	HR	RBI	SB	Avg	OB	Slg	OPS	bb%	ct%	Eye	PX	SX	RC/G	BPV
1998			0	0	0	0	0	0	0					0					
1999			0	0	0	0	0	0	0					0					
2000	a	PHI	153	21	47	2	22	5	307	380	444	825	11	85	0.78	100	87	6.39	61
2001	a	PHI	467	65	120	16	59	19	257	312	422	733	7	81	0.42	100	104	4.60	38
2002	aaa	PHI	464	73	122	17	70	8	263	329	461	791	9	81	0.52	129	87	5.50	54
2001	MLE		0	0	0	0	0	0	0					0		0			
2002	MLE		464	64	119	15	61	7	256	320	446	766	8	84	0.57	126	79	5.10	52
2003	**Projection**		**150**	**21**	**39**	**4**	**20**	**4**	**260**	**327**	**429**	**756**	**9**	**84**	**0.60**	**113**	**98**	**4.98**	**48**

His offense is almost ready, but his defense is not going to cut it. Hitting from the left side may help matters in a possible platoon role, but PHI needs to give him some more time in the minors before making him a full-time starter.

15 Werth,Jayson

Pos RF
Bats R
Age 24 Growth
PWR ++
SPD ++
BAVG ++
DEF ++

Year	Lev	Tm	AB	R	H	HR	RBI	SB	Avg	OB	Slg	OPS	bb%	ct%	Eye	PX	SX	RC/G	BPV
2000	aa	BAL	276	47	63	5	26	9	228	355	355	710	16	82	1.08	86	113	4.76	33
2001	a	TOR	70	9	14	2	14	1	200	356	329	685	20	73	0.89	81	41	4.31	19
2001	aa	TOR	369	51	105	18	69	12	285	389	499	888	15	75	0.68	128	79	7.54	65
2002	aaa	TOR	443	65	114	18	82	24	257	355	445	800	13	72	0.54	110	109	5.88	46
2002	MLB	TOR	46	4	12	0	6	1	261	346	348	694	12	76	0.55	56	125	4.69	22
2001	MLE		369	43	99	16	59	10	268	360	466	826	13	79	0.69	122	69	6.30	56
2002	MLE		443	52	103	14	65	19	233	315	388	703	11	78	0.54	99	84	4.28	31
2003	**Projection**		**250**	**33**	**63**	**9**	**40**	**10**	**252**	**348**	**432**	**781**	**13**	**77**	**0.63**	**111**	**89**	**5.54**	**45**

TOR believes his power and overall offense will improve, and backed it up by giving him playing time in Sept. Moving from CA to OF may have helped, but in the end, his best usage may be that of a semi-regular at C/1B/OF.

3 Ainsworth,Kurt

Th R | Role Starter | Age 24 Growth | Type Power | VEL +++ | BRE ++++ | CHG +++ | PIT +++

Year	Lev	Tm	W	L	Sv	IP	ERA	Br/IP	BF/G	OBA	OOB	H%	xERA	Ctl	Dom	Cmd	hr/9	S%	BPV
2000	aa	SF	10	9	0	158	3.30	1.27	23.7	236	311	29%	3.31	3.6	7.4	2.1	0.7	76%	75
2001	aaa	SF	10	9	0	149	5.07	1.30	23.3	249	315	31%	4.15 +	3.3	9.5	2.9	1.3	64%	83
2001	MLB	SF	0	0	0	2	13.50	2.50	5.4	347	470	43%	11.58 +	9.0	13.5	1.5	4.5	50%	-37
2002	aaa	SF	8	6	0	116	3.41	1.24	24.1	236	306	31%	3.11	3.3	9.2	2.8	0.5	73%	105
2002	MLB	SF	1	2	0	25	2.14	1.35	17.9	236	324	27%	3.25 -	4.3	5.4	1.3	0.4	85%	55
2001	MLE		10	9	0	149	4.89	1.27	23.1	253	310	30%	3.92 +	2.8	7.9	2.8	1.1	63%	77
2002	MLE		8	6	0	116	3.96	1.33	24.6	257	320	32%	3.54	3.2	7.9	2.5	0.5	70%	89
2003	Projection		10	7	0	120	4.13	1.28	24.0	247	313	31%	3.55 +	3.2	8.4	2.6	0.8	69%	88

He was squeezed out in a numbers game, but took it in stride and pitched well in AAA. With an improving fastball and a deadly slider, he should be assured of a rotation spot in 2003.

19 Anderson,Jason

Th R | Role Reliever | Age 23 Growth | Type Power | VEL ++++ | BRE +++ | CHG + | PIT +++

Year	Lev	Tm	W	L	Sv	IP	ERA	Br/IP	BF/G	OBA	OOB	H%	xERA	Ctl	Dom	Cmd	hr/9	S%	BPV
2001	a	NYY	5	1	0	48	1.69	0.92	26.3	191	245	27%	1.50	2.3	10.5	4.7	0.4	83%	167
2001	a	NYY	7	9	0	124	3.77	1.35	23.0	266	323	32%	3.91	2.9	7.3	2.5	0.7	73%	79
2002	a	NYY	4	2	1	224	0.44	0.13	57.0	41	45	4%	-2.02 +	0.1	0.9	7.3	0.1	68%	204
2002	aa	NYY	1	1	2	19	0.95	1.00	4.7	207	262	29%	2.04 -	2.4	9.9	4.2	0.5	94%	147
2002	aaa	NYY	5	1	7	34	3.18	1.09	5.2	213	278	25%	2.70	2.9	7.4	2.5	0.8	74%	86
2001	MLE		0	0	0	0	0.00	0.00											
2002	MLE		6	2	9	53	2.71	1.15	5.2	231	289	28%	2.96	2.7	7.4	2.8	0.7	79%	91
2003	Projection		3	2	0	40	3.60	1.20	5.7	237	299	27%	3.37	2.9	6.5	2.2	0.9	73%	67

NYY is conservative with their rookie pitchers, so earning a bullpen spot could be tough. He traversed three levels in 2002 and was able to adjust well with his mid-90's heat and curve. A fiery competitor whose pitches belie his size.

15 Beltran,Francis

Th R | Role Reliever | Age 23 Growth | Type Power | VEL ++++ | BRE +++ | CHG + | PIT ++

Year	Lev	Tm	W	L	Sv	IP	ERA	Br/IP	BF/G	OBA	OOB	H%	xERA	Ctl	Dom	Cmd	hr/9	S%	BPV
2000	a	CHC	2	2	8	44	2.66	1.09	7.1	184	279	27%	1.75 +	4.1	10.6	2.6	0.2	74%	130
2000	a	CHC	1	1	0	18	9.50	2.39	6.0	321	459	41%	6.74 +	9.5	8.0	0.8	0.0	56%	56
2001	a	CHC	6	9	0	95	5.02	1.40	19.5	258	332	31%	3.53 +	3.8	6.8	1.8	0.3	62%	74
2002	aa	CHC	2	2	23	42	2.57	1.12	4.3	191	284	26%	2.15	4.1	9.2	2.3	0.4	78%	107
2002	MLB	CHC	0	0	0	12	7.50	2.50	5.9	293	470	34%	7.98	12.0	8.3	0.7	1.5	71%	15
2001	MLE		0	0	0	0	0.00	0.00											
2002	MLE		2	2	23	41	3.28	1.26	4.4	216	309	28%	2.82	4.4	8.3	1.9	0.4	74%	88
2003	Projection		3	3	7	50	4.32	1.54	7.0	262	353	34%	4.03	4.9	8.3	1.7	0.4	71%	77

As inconsistent as CHC's pen was in 2002, there is certainly room for a hard-thrower of this caliber. His size, velocity, and competitive nature make him an imposing figure on the mound and his command will aid him in his quest to close.

14 Bukvich,Ryan

Th R | Role Reliever | Age 25 Growth | Type Power | VEL ++++ | BRE + | CHG | PIT ++

Year	Lev	Tm	W	L	Sv	IP	ERA	Br/IP	BF/G	OBA	OOB	H%	xERA	Ctl	Dom	Cmd	hr/9	S%	BPV
2001	a	KC	0	1	13	58	1.71	1.24	6.5	200	306	32%	2.20 -	4.8	12.4	2.6	0.2	86%	139
2001	aa	KC	0	0	0	12	3.75	0.92	6.6	210	245	26%	2.86 +	1.5	10.5	7.0	1.5	67%	178
2002	aa	KC	1	1	8	34	1.32	0.94	5.7	151	250	26%	0.83 +	4.0	12.4	3.1	0.0	84%	165
2002	aaa	KC	1	0	8	14	0.00	0.79	4.3	92	218	15%	-0.15	4.5	10.9	2.4	0.0	100%	153
2002	MLB	KC	0	1	0	25	6.12	1.80	4.5	269	390	32%	5.16 +	6.8	7.2	1.1	0.7	65%	45
2001	MLE		0	0	0	0	0.00	0.00											
2002	MLE		2	1	16	48	1.13	1.02	5.4	161	266	24%	1.17	4.3	9.6	2.2	0.0	88%	127
2003	Projection		1	1	21	60	3.90	1.58	6.6	265	360	35%	4.54 -	5.1	10.1	2.0	0.8	77%	81

With an electric fastball, solid BPIs, and a fiery demeanor, he would be the best option to close. Command of his splitter and slider will enable him to take the next step, but he should at least be able to earn a setup role.

21 Chulk,Vinny

Th R | Role Starter | Age 24 Growth | Type Power | VEL +++ | BRE +++ | CHG + | PIT ++

Year	Lev	Tm	W	L	Sv	IP	ERA	Br/IP	BF/G	OBA	OOB	H%	xERA	Ctl	Dom	Cmd	hr/9	S%	BPV
2001	a	TOR	1	2	1	35	3.09	1.46	9.6	278	341	41%	4.57 -	3.3	12.9	3.8	1.0	83%	126
2001	aa	TOR	2	5	2	43	3.14	0.98	7.0	219	257	27%	2.71	1.7	9.0	5.4	1.0	73%	147
2001	aaa	TOR	1	0	0	6	1.50	1.50	5.3	228	347	26%	3.20 -	6.0	4.5	0.8	0.0	89%	52
2002	aa	TOR	13	5	1	152	2.96	1.22	25.2	237	303	27%	3.23	3.1	6.4	2.0	0.7	78%	67
2002	aaa	TOR	0	1	0	5	5.40	2.40	13.3	299	460	35%	6.44 -	10.8	5.4	0.5	0.0	75%	38
2001	MLE		3	5	2	49	3.67	1.16	6.9	246	292	28%	3.59	2.2	7.2	3.3	1.1	73%	84
2002	MLE		13	6	1	156	3.51	1.36	24.7	260	325	29%	3.91	3.3	5.5	1.7	0.7	76%	50
2003	Projection		8	8	0	120	4.05	1.36	24.4	263	325	30%	4.33	3.2	6.9	2.2	1.1	74%	56

TOR used him as a SP in the minors, hoping to improve his pitch selection and Cmd, but he's pitched so well that they may leave him there. More K's would be preferable, but keeps hitters at bay with his arm angles and movement.

12 Cook,Aaron

Th R | Role Starter | Age 24 Growth | Type Power | VEL ++++ | BRE +++ | CHG + | PIT +++

Year	Lev	Tm	W	L	Sv	IP	ERA	Br/IP	BF/G	OBA	OOB	H%	xERA	Ctl	Dom	Cmd	hr/9	S%	BPV
2000	a	COL	10	7	0	143	2.96	1.07	27.2	244	275	30%	2.85	1.4	7.4	5.1	0.6	74%	140
2001	a	COL	1	6	0	43	5.44	1.49	27.1	300	345	36%	4.93 +	2.5	7.7	3.1	0.8	63%	81
2002	aa	COL	7	2	0	95	1.42	0.97	26.4	214	256	25%	1.98 -	1.8	5.5	3.1	0.4	88%	98
2002	aaa	COL	4	4	0	64	3.80	1.33	27.2	271	320	29%	4.12	2.5	4.5	1.8	0.8	73%	40
2002	MLB	COL	2	1	0	36	4.50	1.50	17.7	288	347	30%	4.96	3.3	3.5	1.1	1.0	72%	11
2001	MLE		0	0	0	0	0.00	0.00											
2002	MLE		11	6	0	159	3.00	1.24	27.6	266	306	29%	3.86 -	2.0	4.5	2.3	0.8	79%	50
2003	Projection		7	7	0	120	4.88	1.55	26.8	297	355	32%	5.32	3.2	4.8	1.5	1.1	71%	22

He throw hard (92-95mph) and has movement, but also a tendency to pitch up in the zone, which is a problem in Coors. His arm has proven to be durable and he did win despite marginal BPIs. His selection will always be risky.

17 Foppert,Jesse

Th R | Role Starter | Age 22 Growth | Type Power | VEL ++++ | BRE +++ | CHG ++ | PIT +++

Year	Lev	Tm	W	L	Sv	IP	ERA	Br/IP	BF/G	OBA	OOB	H%	xERA	Ctl	Dom	Cmd	hr/9	S%	BPV
1999			0	0	0	0	0.00	0.00											
2000			0	0	0	0	0.00	0.00											
2001	r	SF	8	1	0	70	1.93	0.83	18.7	151	227	20%	1.35 +	3.0	11.3	3.8	0.9	84%	146
2002	aa	SF	3	3	0	61	2.80	1.07	22.1	204	274	29%	2.16 +	3.1	10.9	3.5	0.4	74%	140
2002	aaa	SF	3	6	0	79	3.99	1.34	24.0	242	322	34%	4.18	4.0	12.4	3.1	1.4	76%	106
2001	MLE		0	0	0	0	0.00	0.00											
2002	MLE		6	9	0	140	3.92	1.28	23.6	243	313	32%	3.58	3.4	10.0	2.9	0.8	71%	103
2003	Projection		9	5	0	120	4.35	1.38	25.8	252	329	32%	4.56	3.9	10.1	2.6	1.5	74%	74

The game's top pitching prospect, he has everything you look for in a staff ace (stuff, command, solid mechanics, and pitchability). He simply overmatched hitters in '02 and will compete for a 5th rotation spot in SF.

1 German,Franklyn

Th R | Role Reliever | Age 23 Growth | Type Power | VEL +++++ | BRE +++ | CHG | PIT ++

Year	Lev	Tm	W	L	Sv	IP	ERA	Br/IP	BF/G	OBA	OOB	H%	xERA	Ctl	Dom	Cmd	hr/9	S%	BPV
2000	a	OAK	5	5	0	72	5.50	1.74	23.9	302	381	36%	5.20	4.6	6.5	1.4	0.5	67%	48
2001	a	OAK	2	4	19	63	4.00	1.56	5.3	274	356	43%	4.27	4.4	13.3	3.0	0.4	74%	130
2002	aa	OAK	1	1	16	41	3.07	1.34	4.7	195	322	33%	2.32 +	5.9	13.0	2.2	0.0	75%	140
2002	aaa	DET	1	1	13	23	1.57	0.96	3.9	188	253	31%	1.24	2.7	12.1	4.4	0.0	82%	183
2002	MLB	DET	1	0	1	6	0.00	0.81	3.3	146	222	21%	0.49	2.9	8.7	3.0	0.0	100%	141
2001	MLE		0	0	0	0	0.00	0.00											
2002	MLE		2	2	29	64	2.95	1.23	4.4	210	304	33%	2.25 +	4.4	11.5	2.6	0.0	73%	138
2003	Projection		2	2	16	50	3.96	1.44	5.6	246	338	34%	3.72	4.7	10.3	2.2	0.5	72%	97

He'll challenge any hitter with serious heat (94-99mph), but also has solid Cmd and complementary pitches. He did not yield a HR all season. His style resembles Benitez and Mesa, and like them, he will eventually close.

26 Gobble,Jimmy

Th L | Role Starter | Age 21 Green | Type Power | VEL ++ | BRE ++++ | CHG ++ | PIT +++

Year	Lev	Tm	W	L	Sv	IP	ERA	Br/IP	BF/G	OBA	OOB	H%	xERA	Ctl	Dom	Cmd	hr/9	S%	BPV
1998			0	0	0	0	0.00	0.00											
1999	r	KC	0	0	0	7	2.57	1.57	7.9	233	358	34%	3.39 -	6.4	10.3	1.6	0.0	82%	104
2000	a	KC	12	10	0	145	3.66	1.23	24.1	260	303	31%	3.50	2.1	7.1	3.4	0.6	71%	98
2001	a	KC	10	6	0	162	2.56	1.03	23.7	227	268	29%	2.34	1.8	8.6	4.7	0.4	76%	146
2002	aa	KC	5	7	0	69	3.39	1.30	22.4	267	316	32%	3.58	2.5	6.8	2.7	0.4	74%	88
2001	MLE		0	0	0	0	0.00	0.00											
2002	MLE		5	7	0	69	4.56	1.52	23.6	306	350	35%	4.83	2.5	5.6	2.3	0.5	69%	59
2003	Projection		8	10	0	120	4.43	1.40	24.7	285	332	33%	4.26	2.5	5.9	2.4	0.6	68%	65

He may still need some seasoning, but is the best pitching prospect KC has, and they may need him more than he needs them. Terrific base skills, a solid repertoire, and the will to win could lead him into the rotation in 2003.

16 Heilman,Aaron

		Year	Lev	Tm	W	L	Sv	IP	ERA	Br/IP	BF/G	OBA	OOB	H%	xERA	Ctl	Dom	Cmd	hr/9	S%	BPV
Th	R	2000			0	0	0	0	0.00	0.00											
Role	Starter	2000			0	0	0	0	0.00	0.00											
Age	24 Growth	2001	a	NYM	0	1	0	38	2.37	1.03	21.4	195	267	26%	1.96	3.1	9.2	3.0	0.5	78%	120
Type	Power	2002	aa	NYM	4	4	0	97	3.80	1.16	23.3	237	292	31%	3.03 +	2.6	9.0	3.5	0.6	68%	115
VEL	+++	2002	aaa	NYM	2	3	0	49	3.31	1.18	20.1	233	296	27%	2.97	2.9	6.4	2.2	0.6	73%	76
BRE	+++	2001	MLE		0	0	0	0	0.00	0.00											
CHG	++	2002	MLE		6	7	0	146	4.19	1.27	22.6	255	310	30%	3.52 +	2.7	6.9	2.5	0.6	67%	80
PIT	++++	2003	Projection		5	7	0	120	4.05	1.23	22.6	244	303	29%	3.24 +	2.9	6.8	2.4	0.6	67%	80

He has nothing to prove in the minors and NYM are expected to give him a shot at a rotation spot. Complements a good fastball with a slider/ splitter that can put the best hitters away. Not a future ace, but certainly a #2 starter.

27 Howard,Ben

		Year	Lev	Tm	W	L	Sv	IP	ERA	Br/IP	BF/G	OBA	OOB	H%	xERA	Ctl	Dom	Cmd	hr/9	S%	BPV
Th	R	2001	a	SD	8	2	0	102	2.82	1.16	23.1	230	291	31%	2.61	2.8	9.4	3.3	0.4	75%	125
Role	Starter	2001	aa	SD	2	0	0	30	2.40	1.07	17.1	167	274	20%	2.21	4.5	8.7	1.9	0.9	83%	87
Age	24 Growth	2002	aa	SD	3	1	0	33	2.18	1.27	23.1	218	311	28%	2.93 -	4.4	8.2	1.9	0.5	85%	83
Type	Power	2002	aaa	SD	0	4	0	45	6.20	1.38	17.6	270	328	27%	5.32 +	3.0	5.0	1.7	2.0	60%	6
VEL	++++	2002	MLB	SD	0	1	0	10	9.71	2.65	18.9	311	484	32%	10.54 -	12.4	8.8	0.7	3.5	70%	-45
BRE	+++	2001	MLE		2	0	0	30	3.00	1.17	17.5	183	293	21%	2.65	4.8	6.9	1.4	0.9	78%	63
CHG	++	2002	MLE		3	5	0	78	5.19	1.46	20.1	272	341	29%	4.98	3.7	5.4	1.5	1.4	68%	23
PIT	++	2003	Projection		2	2	0	50	4.86	1.44	7.0	262	338	28%	5.15	4.0	6.5	1.6	1.8	73%	22

Cmd problems he had early in his career resurfaced and he was less effective in 2002. Not only was he over-hyped, but SD likely rushed him when they had better options. SD's rotation looks to be full, so he could land a relief role.

20 Journell,Jim

		Year	Lev	Tm	W	L	Sv	IP	ERA	Br/IP	BF/G	OBA	OOB	H%	xERA	Ctl	Dom	Cmd	hr/9	S%	BPV
Th	R	2000	a	STL	1	0	0	32	1.97	1.13	10.0	117	285	19%	0.94 +	6.8	11.0	1.6	0.0	81%	131
Role	Starter	2001	a	STL	14	6	0	151	2.50	1.08	23.2	221	277	30%	2.46	2.5	9.3	3.7	0.5	78%	130
Age	25 Growth	2001	aa	STL	1	0	0	7	0.00	0.43	23.4	0	132	0%	-1.80 +	3.9	7.7	2.0			143
Type	Power	2002	aa	STL	3	3	0	67	2.69	1.01	26.4	209	265	28%	2.08 +	2.4	8.9	3.7	0.4	74%	131
VEL	++++	2002	aaa	STL	2	4	0	37	3.65	1.51	23.4	267	349	33%	4.40 -	4.4	7.8	1.8	0.7	77%	64
BRE	+++	2001	MLE		0	0	0	0	0.00	0.00											
CHG	++	2002	MLE		5	7	0	103	3.67	1.34	25.8	260	322	32%	3.75	3.1	7.5	2.4	0.6	73%	80
PIT	+++	2003	Projection		4	3	0	60	3.75	1.40	23.6	252	332	32%	3.64	4.1	8.1	2.0	0.5	73%	82

STL wants him to be a RP with his deadly sinker/slider, but he has shown better stamina and a willingness to change speeds which might force them to rethink their position. He'll begin in the minors, but will be up in '03.

22 Kozlowski,Ben

		Year	Lev	Tm	W	L	Sv	IP	ERA	Br/IP	BF/G	OBA	OOB	H%	xERA	Ctl	Dom	Cmd	hr/9	S%	BPV
Th	L	2001	r	ATL	3	5	0	61	4.72	1.38	21.8	232	328	29%	3.16 +	4.7	7.2	1.5	0.3	63%	75
Role	Starter	2001	a	ATL	1	0	0	8	1.13	1.25	11.1	117	307	15%	1.33	7.9	6.8	0.9	0.0	90%	90
Age	22 Growth	2002	a	TEX	4	4	0	79	2.05	1.11	15.2	220	283	29%	2.31	2.8	8.7	3.0	0.2	81%	120
Type	Power	2002	aa	TEX	4	2	0	52	1.90	0.96	25.2	160	254	19%	1.49	3.8	7.1	1.9	0.5	83%	89
VEL	+++	2002	MLB	TEX	0	0	0	10	6.30	2.20	25.6	281	438	26%	8.21 -	9.9	5.4	0.5	2.7	79%	-38
BRE	+++	2001	MLE		0	0	0	0	0.00	0.00											
CHG	++	2002	MLE		4	2	0	52	2.60	1.08	26.0	188	276	21%	2.30	3.8	6.2	1.6	0.7	79%	68
PIT	+++	2003	Projection		6	8	0	120	4.43	1.48	24.0	278	345	32%	4.57	3.6	6.7	1.9	0.8	71%	54

He throws harder than the normal LHer and pitches aggressively to both sides of the plate. His complementary pitches improved, though he needs to cut down his walk rate. The uncertain TEX rotation may have an opening.

18 Lee,Cliff

		Year	Lev	Tm	W	L	Sv	IP	ERA	Br/IP	BF/G	OBA	OOB	H%	xERA	Ctl	Dom	Cmd	hr/9	S%	BPV
Th	L	2000	a	MON	1	4	0	45	5.20	1.91	19.8	283	404	43%	5.05	7.2	12.6	1.8	0.2	71%	105
Role	Starter	2001	a	MON	6	7	0	110	2.78	1.13	21.2	201	286	26%	2.87	3.8	10.6	2.8	1.1	81%	105
Age	24 Growth	2002	aa	2TM	9	3	0	103	3.58	1.02	22.5	199	266	26%	2.61 +	2.9	10.7	3.7	1.1	70%	124
Type	Power	2002	aaa	CLE	3	2	0	43	3.77	1.35	22.9	229	324	24%	4.15	4.6	6.3	1.4	1.5	78%	32
VEL	+++	2002	MLB	CLE	0	1	0	10	1.78	1.39	21.7	174	330	21%	2.28 -	7.1	5.3	0.8	0.0	86%	68
BRE	+++	2001	MLE		0	0	0	0	0.00	0.00											
CHG	+++	2002	MLE		5	3	0	59	5.78	1.57	24.2	258	358	27%	5.19 +	5.3	6.1	1.1	1.5	66%	18
PIT	+++	2003	Projection		6	9	0	120	4.73	1.49	23.0	252	346	29%	4.58	4.9	7.1	1.5	1.2	71%	42

A number of LHers (Tallet, Traber, and Herrera) could stake their claim in CLE, but Lee has the best potential. He repeated his delivery more often in '02 and with his ability to command and mix four pitches, he'll be tough.

6 Lewis,Colby

		Year	Lev	Tm	W	L	Sv	IP	ERA	Br/IP	BF/G	OBA	OOB	H%	xERA	Ctl	Dom	Cmd	hr/9	S%	BPV
Th	R	2000	a	TEX	11	10	0	164	4.06	1.30	24.7	268	316	34%	3.68	2.5	8.4	3.4	0.6	69%	105
Role	Starter	2001	a	TEX	1	0	0	4	0.00	0.00	11.7	0	0	0%	-2.92 +	0.0	18.0				163
Age	23 Growth	2001	aa	TEX	10	10	0	156	4.50	1.36	26.7	254	325	33%	3.95 +	3.6	9.3	2.6	0.9	68%	89
Type	Power	2002	aaa	TEX	5	6	0	107	3.62	1.20	22.0	249	298	32%	2.95 +	2.4	8.3	3.5	0.3	69%	119
VEL	++++	2002	MLB	TEX	1	3	0	34	6.35	2.00	11.2	305	415	36%	6.50	6.9	7.4	1.1	1.1	69%	29
BRE	+++	2001	MLE		10	10	0	156	5.65	1.51	27.6	285	348	35%	4.98 +	3.5	8.4	2.4	1.1	63%	66
CHG	++	2002	MLE		5	6	0	106	4.07	1.28	22.3	269	312	33%	3.48 +	2.2	7.3	3.3	0.3	67%	104
PIT	++	2003	Projection		8	8	0	140	4.31	1.40	24.2	260	332	31%	4.06	3.7	7.5	2.1	0.8	70%	68

All year, TEX shuttled him between Oklahoma and TEX, and from SP to RP. He commands 4 pitches and has an explosive fastball, though he still needs work in setting up his pitches. He should be a lock for a rotation spot.

7 Lidge,Brad

		Year	Lev	Tm	W	L	Sv	IP	ERA	Br/IP	BF/G	OBA	OOB	H%	xERA	Ctl	Dom	Cmd	hr/9	S%	BPV
Th	R	2000	a	HOU	2	1	0	42	2.79	1.02	20.7	191	266	26%	2.08 +	3.2	9.9	3.1	0.6	75%	121
Role	Reliever	2001	aa	HOU	2	0	0	26	1.73	1.08	20.8	223	276	39%	2.29 -	2.4	14.5	6.0	0.3	85%	213
Age	26 Growth	2002	aa	HOU	1	1	0	11	2.45	1.09	8.8	225	279	41%	1.97	2.5	14.7	6.0	0.0	75%	224
Type	Power	2002	aaa	HOU	5	5	0	112	3.38	1.16	19.0	208	292	26%	2.73 +	3.8	8.8	2.3	0.7	73%	94
VEL	++++	2002	MLB	HOU	1	0	0	8	6.59	2.56	7.5	342	476	52%	7.46 -	9.9	13.2	1.3	0.0	71%	94
BRE	++++	2001	MLE		0	0	0	0	0.00	0.00											
CHG	+	2002	MLE		6	6	0	122	4.49	1.40	18.2	250	332	30%	4.10	4.1	7.7	1.9	1.0	70%	62
PIT	+++	2003	Projection		4	3	0	80	4.05	1.35	15.5	244	324	31%	3.72	3.9	8.9	2.3	0.8	71%	83

His stuff is impressive, but has never been healthy enough to realize his potential. HOU worked him as a SP to build his arm strength, but his destiny will take him to the bullpen, where he'll dominate.

8 Neal,Blaine

		Year	Lev	Tm	W	L	Sv	IP	ERA	Br/IP	BF/G	OBA	OOB	H%	xERA	Ctl	Dom	Cmd	hr/9	S%	BPV
Th	R	2000	aa	FLA	1	1	0	15	3.60	1.47	21.9	274	342	34%	4.23 -	3.6	7.8	2.2	0.6	76%	74
Role	Reliever	2001	aa	FLA	2	3	21	53	2.38	1.21	4.1	223	300	29%	2.54	3.6	7.6	2.1	0.2	79%	96
Age	25 Growth	2001	MLB	FLA	0	0	0	5	7.20	2.40	6.7	332	460	39%	6.91	9.0	5.4	0.6	0.0	67%	34
Type	Power	2002	aaa	FLA	3	1	11	31	2.90	1.35	4.6	236	325	29%	3.45 -	4.4	7.5	1.7	0.6	80%	72
VEL	++++	2002	MLB	FLA	3	0	0	33	2.73	1.39	4.4	256	331	34%	3.51 -	3.8	9.0	2.4	0.3	80%	99
BRE	+++	2001	MLE		2	3	21	53	3.40	1.47	4.3	265	343	32%	3.76	4.1	6.5	1.6	0.2	75%	69
CHG	+	2002	MLE		3	1	11	31	2.90	1.32	4.5	236	319	28%	3.38	4.1	6.7	1.6	0.6	79%	65
PIT	+++	2003	Projection		3	3	18	50	3.78	1.44	4.5	258	338	31%	3.91	4.1	7.0	1.7	0.5	74%	65

If he can ever gain command of his breaking pitches, his status in the FLA pen will improve. He knows how to pitch, likes to work inside, and has a dynamic fastball. He'll begin in match-up situations, but has the goods to close.

5 Patterson,John

		Year	Lev	Tm	W	L	Sv	IP	ERA	Br/IP	BF/G	OBA	OOB	H%	xERA	Ctl	Dom	Cmd	hr/9	S%	BPV
Th	R	2001	a	ARI	0	0	0	9	6.00	1.33	19.1	262	321	27%	5.97	3.0	9.0	3.0	3.0	67%	30
Role	Starter	2001	aa	ARI	1	2	0	25	4.32	1.56	22.4	299	356	35%	4.98 -	3.2	6.8	2.1	0.7	73%	59
Age	25 Growth	2001	aaa	ARI	2	7	0	68	5.82	1.66	24.0	300	371	32%	5.66	4.1	5.3	1.3	1.2	66%	18
Type	Power	2002	aaa	ARI	10	5	0	113	4.22	1.43	25.9	269	337	32%	4.58	3.6	8.3	2.3	1.1	74%	66
VEL	+++	2002	MLB	ARI	2	0	0	30	3.28	1.13	17.5	241	285	27%	4.33 -	2.1	9.2	4.4	2.1	85%	93
BRE	++++	2001	MLE		3	9	0	93	6.00	1.73	24.0	319	380	35%	6.08	3.7	4.9	1.3	1.1	66%	17
CHG	++	2002	MLE		10	5	0	112	4.73	1.51	26.1	288	348	33%	5.06	3.3	7.0	2.1	1.1	71%	50
PIT	+++	2003	Projection		10	9	0	140	4.31	1.44	24.4	277	338	32%	4.70	3.3	7.1	2.2	1.1	73%	55

He looks recovered from his 2000 elbow surgery and may be a low-cost option at the back end of the ARI rotation. His delivery is as clean as you want to see and his curveball is a plus pitch. He just needs to gain confidence in his stuff.

9 Rauch,Jon

Th R · Role Starter · Age 24 Growth · Type Power · VEL +++ · BRE +++ · CHG ++ · PIT ++

Year	Lev	Tm	W	L	Sv	IP	ERA	Br/IP	BF/G	OBA	OOB	H%	xERA	Ctl	Dom	Cmd	hr/9	S%	BPV
2000	a	CHW	11	3	0	110	2.86	1.23	25.3	247	303	33%	3.40 -	2.7	10.1	3.8	0.8	80%	121
2000	aa	CHW	5	1	0	56	2.25	0.93	26.9	186	248	25%	1.81	2.6	10.1	3.9	0.6	79%	142
2001	aaa	CHW	1	3	0	28	5.79	1.25	19.5	262	307	28%	5.39	2.3	8.7	3.9	2.6	63%	59
2002	aaa	CHW	7	8	0	109	4.29	1.22	23.8	228	302	27%	3.52 +	3.5	8.0	2.3	1.2	68%	71
2002	MLB	CHW	2	1	0	28	6.70	1.49	15.5	260	346	26%	5.69 +	4.5	6.1	1.4	2.2	60%	1
2001	MLE		1	3	0	28	8.04	1.50	20.6	307	347	30%	7.91	2.3	7.7	3.4	3.9	57%	-4
2002	MLE		7	8	0	109	5.69	1.40	24.8	262	332	29%	4.84 +	3.6	7.4	2.0	1.6	63%	43
2003	Projection		7	9	0	120	4.65	1.29	24.1	252	314	28%	4.43	3.1	7.6	2.5	1.6	69%	55

His BPIs were better than the end result and did seem to benefit from being sent back to AAA. He also got stronger as the season progressed, which may indicate that his arm is 100%. He could still regain his prospect status.

2 Rodriguez,Francisco

Th R · Role Reliever · Age 21 Green · Type Power · VEL ++++ · BRE ++++ · CHG + · PIT +++

Year	Lev	Tm	W	L	Sv	IP	ERA	Br/IP	BF/G	OBA	OOB	H%	xERA	Ctl	Dom	Cmd	hr/9	S%	BPV
2000	a	ANA	4	4	0	64	2.81	1.17	20.1	192	294	29%	2.06 +	4.5	11.1	2.5	0.3	75%	127
2001	a	ANA	5	7	0	114	5.37	1.60	25.7	283	361	40%	5.09	4.3	11.6	2.7	1.0	67%	93
2002	aa	ANA	3	3	9	41	1.98	1.15	7.2	217	289	35%	2.50 -	3.3	13.4	4.1	0.4	84%	164
2002	aaa	ANA	2	3	6	42	2.57	1.02	6.1	202	266	33%	1.77 +	2.8	12.6	4.5	0.2	74%	179
2002	MLB	ANA	0	0	0	6	0.00	0.83	4.5	151	228	43%	0.49 -	3.0	19.5	6.5	0.0	100%	278
2001	MLE		0	0	0	0	0.00	0.00											
2002	MLE		5	6	15	83	2.38	1.06	6.6	212	273	33%	2.12	2.7	12.2	4.5	0.3	78%	171
2003	Projection		5	6	5	80	3.15	1.16	5.4	221	292	32%	2.61 +	3.3	11.3	3.4	0.5	73%	137

He was so impressive in his few innings that ANA reserved a post-season spot for him. His fastball/slider has always been dominating, but now he seems to have a sense of how to pitch. He could be Percival's prime setup man.

11 Rodriguez,Ricardo

Th R · Role Starter · Age 25 Growth · Type Power · VEL +++ · BRE ++++ · CHG ++ · PIT +++

Year	Lev	Tm	W	L	Sv	IP	ERA	Br/IP	BF/G	OBA	OOB	H%	xERA	Ctl	Dom	Cmd	hr/9	S%	BPV
2000	r	LA	10	3	0	96	1.88	0.93	24.6	196	247	31%	1.44	2.2	12.1	5.6	0.2	79%	201
2001	a	LA	14	6	0	154	3.21	1.25	24.7	234	308	30%	3.33	3.5	9.0	2.6	0.8	77%	93
2002	aa	LA	5	4	0	68	1.99	1.01	24.3	226	265	26%	2.38	1.7	5.8	3.4	0.5	83%	100
2002	aaa	2TM	4	1	0	37	3.65	1.38	26.5	272	328	31%	3.91	2.9	5.1	1.8	0.5	73%	53
2002	MLB	CLE	2	2	0	41	5.69	1.41	25.4	257	334	28%	4.38 +	3.9	5.3	1.3	1.1	60%	30
2001	MLE		0	0	0	0	0.00	0.00											
2002	MLE		9	5	0	104	3.54	1.39	26.4	287	330	31%	4.38 -	2.3	4.7	2.0	0.7	76%	47
2003	Projection		10	9	0	140	4.05	1.41	26.3	274	333	31%	4.22	3.1	5.8	1.9	0.7	72%	53

CLE prematurely put him in the rotation, despite his low dominance, lack of an off-speed pitch and slow delivery. He'll work on his change-up over the winter, as CLE believes he still can be a successful starter.

13 Sanchez,Duaner

Th R · Role Reliever · Age 23 Growth · Type Power · VEL ++++ · BRE ++++ · CHG · PIT ++

Year	Lev	Tm	W	L	Sv	IP	ERA	Br/IP	BF/G	OBA	OOB	H%	xERA	Ctl	Dom	Cmd	hr/9	S%	BPV
2001	a	ARI	2	4	0	59	4.58	1.41	25.5	281	333	34%	4.19	2.7	7.5	2.7	0.6	67%	83
2001	aa	ARI	3	7	0	70	6.81	1.67	24.7	318	372	36%	5.51 +	3.2	5.3	1.6	0.6	57%	38
2002	aa	ARI	4	3	13	36	3.00	1.22	4.8	234	302	32%	2.71	3.3	9.3	2.8	0.3	74%	116
2002	aaa	2TM	1	4	7	28	5.14	1.46	5.1	269	342	34%	4.49 +	3.9	9.3	2.4	1.0	66%	79
2002	MLB	2TM	0	0	0	6	9.00	2.17	3.4	262	434	27%	8.10 +	10.5	9.0	0.9	3.0	64%	-15
2001	MLE		3	7	0	70	7.46	1.76	25.2	336	384	37%	6.04 +	3.0	4.5	1.5	0.6	55%	27
2002	MLE		5	7	20	63	4.84	1.47	5.0	279	343	35%	4.32 +	3.4	8.0	2.3	0.6	66%	79
2003	Projection		4	6	5	60	3.90	1.40	5.4	271	332	34%	3.90	3.2	8.0	2.5	0.5	72%	88

His 92-98mph fastball and slider are excellent pitches, and his use of multiple arm angles makes it tough on the opposition. His style is reminiscent of Octavio Dotel, but he will need better Cmd if he's to get the PIT closer role.

4 Smyth,Steve

Th L · Role Starter · Age 24 Growth · Type Finesse · VEL ++ · BRE +++ · CHG +++ · PIT +++

Year	Lev	Tm	W	L	Sv	IP	ERA	Br/IP	BF/G	OBA	OOB	H%	xERA	Ctl	Dom	Cmd	hr/9	S%	BPV
2000	a	CHC	8	8	0	138	3.26	1.38	24.7	256	329	30%	3.77 -	3.7	6.5	1.8	0.6	77%	62
2001	aa	CHC	9	3	0	120	2.55	1.25	27.8	245	307	29%	3.40 -	3.0	7.0	2.3	0.7	82%	76
2002	aa	CHC	4	4	0	73	3.58	1.10	26.7	231	280	29%	2.94 +	2.2	9.1	4.1	0.9	70%	124
2002	aaa	CHC	3	2	0	31	5.81	1.45	22.6	286	340	33%	4.92 +	2.9	7.3	2.5	1.2	61%	59
2002	MLB	CHC	1	3	0	26	9.35	1.69	15.0	317	375	30%	7.86 +	3.5	5.5	1.6	3.1	49%	-35
2001	MLE		9	3	0	120	2.85	1.37	28.6	268	326	31%	3.95 -	3.0	5.9	2.0	0.6	81%	59
2002	MLE		7	6	0	104	4.76	1.31	25.9	269	317	32%	4.13 +	2.4	7.3	3.0	1.0	65%	79
2003	Projection		10	7	0	140	4.31	1.44	26.6	282	338	32%	4.90 -	3.0	6.9	2.3	1.2	74%	51

Shows good polish for his age and CHC needs a LH pitcher in their RH-dominated staff. Has a nice arsenal of pitches and will throw any of them at any point in the count. Not a lot of upside, but could chew-up a ton of innings.

24 Soriano,Rafael

Th R · Role Starter · Age 23 Growth · Type Power · VEL +++ · BRE +++ · CHG ++ · PIT ++

Year	Lev	Tm	W	L	Sv	IP	ERA	Br/IP	BF/G	OBA	OOB	H%	xERA	Ctl	Dom	Cmd	hr/9	S%	BPV
2000	a	SEA	8	4	0	122	2.88	1.20	24.0	220	299	27%	2.46	3.7	6.6	1.8	0.2	75%	82
2001	a	SEA	6	3	0	89	2.53	0.99	23.2	163	260	23%	1.49 +	3.9	9.9	2.5	0.4	75%	122
2001	aa	SEA	2	2	0	48	3.38	1.00	23.5	201	262	26%	2.44 +	2.6	9.9	3.8	0.9	70%	126
2002	aa	SEA	2	3	0	46	2.34	1.02	18.2	197	265	25%	2.62	2.9	10.1	3.5	1.2	85%	114
2002	MLB	SEA	0	3	0	47	4.59	1.30	19.9	253	315	27%	4.44	3.1	6.1	2.0	1.5	70%	37
2001	MLE		2	2	0	48	3.94	1.13	24.3	224	285	28%	3.04 +	2.8	9.0	3.2	0.9	67%	103
2002	MLE		2	3	0	46	3.12	1.19	19.0	230	297	27%	3.70 -	3.1	8.6	2.8	1.4	81%	77
2003	Projection		8	6	0	120	4.05	1.26	23.9	247	309	29%	3.78	3.0	7.7	2.6	1.1	71%	75

Would have been a fixture in the SEA rotation if not for a strained shoulder. Needs to understand that he can't blow every pitch by hitters. Dynamic stuff and aggressive approach should allow him to succeed in any role.

23 Standridge,Jason

Th R · Role Starter · Age 24 Growth · Type Power · VEL +++ · BRE ++++ · CHG + · PIT ++

Year	Lev	Tm	W	L	Sv	IP	ERA	Br/IP	BF/G	OBA	OOB	H%	xERA	Ctl	Dom	Cmd	hr/9	S%	BPV
2001	aa	TAM	0	2	0	9	5.87	1.74	21.4	316	381	39%	4.95 +	3.9	6.8	1.8	0.0	63%	70
2001	aaa	TAM	5	10	0	102	5.29	1.76	23.9	311	385	33%	6.11 -	4.4	4.2	1.0	1.1	72%	4
2001	MLB	TAM	0	0	0	19	4.71	1.73	9.9	261	380	24%	6.42 -	6.6	4.2	0.6	2.4	82%	-29
2001	aaa	TAM	10	9	0	173	3.12	1.34	25.4	256	322	29%	3.70 -	3.3	5.8	1.7	0.6	78%	56
2002	MLB	TAM	0	0	0	3	9.00	3.67	19.8	453	565	45%	15.48 -	12.0	3.0	0.3	3.0	80%	-102
2001	MLE		5	12	0	112	7.07	2.03	25.2	351	418	37%	7.59 -	4.5	3.9	0.9	1.3	66%	-13
2002	MLE		10	9	0	173	3.90	1.51	26.4	286	349	32%	4.64 -	3.4	4.9	1.4	0.7	75%	37
2003	Projection		6	8	0	120	4.43	1.43	24.8	263	336	29%	4.31	3.8	5.0	1.3	0.9	70%	33

Returning him to the minors was the best thing TAM could have done. His BPIs improved and he learned how to attack hitters and utilize his stuff better. He'll have to perform in spring training, but should lock up a rotation spot.

10 Van Hekken,Andy

Th L · Role Starter · Age 23 Growth · Type Finesse · VEL ++ · BRE +++ · CHG ++++ · PIT +++++

Year	Lev	Tm	W	L	Sv	IP	ERA	Br/IP	BF/G	OBA	OOB	H%	xERA	Ctl	Dom	Cmd	hr/9	S%	BPV
2001	a	DET	5	0	0	48	4.69	1.48	26.4	318	344	35%	5.21 -	1.5	5.4	3.6	0.9	70%	72
2001	a	DET	10	4	0	111	3.16	1.24	24.3	251	306	30%	3.44	2.7	6.6	2.5	0.6	76%	77
2002	aa	DET	4	7	0	134	3.83	1.28	26.8	268	313	31%	3.79	2.3	6.5	2.9	0.7	71%	80
2002	aaa	DET	5	0	0	49	1.84	1.06	27.9	229	273	24%	2.77 -	2.0	3.5	1.7	0.7	88%	44
2002	MLB	DET	1	3	0	30	3.00	1.47	26.3	310	342	31%	4.87 -	1.8	1.5	0.8	0.6	81%	2
2001	MLE		5	0	0	48	5.44	1.63	27.3	344	366	38%	5.94 -	1.3	4.7	3.6	0.8	66%	67
2002	MLE		5	0	0	49	2.20	1.16	28.6	253	292	26%	3.38 -	1.8	3.1	1.7	0.7	85%	37
2003	Projection		5	9	0	140	4.05	1.30	26.9	273	316	30%	3.94	2.2	5.0	2.3	0.7	70%	57

His ability to keep hitters off-balance and win despite 85 mph velocity is incredible. His BPIs remain marginal, but if he can gain consistent command of his curveball, it could be "lights-out".

25 Wayne,Justin

Th R · Role Starter · Age 24 Growth · Type Finesse · VEL ++ · BRE +++ · CHG +++ · PIT ++++

Year	Lev	Tm	W	L	Sv	IP	ERA	Br/IP	BF/G	OBA	OOB	H%	xERA	Ctl	Dom	Cmd	hr/9	S%	BPV
2001	a	MON	2	3	0	42	3.00	0.95	20.3	207	252	27%	1.51 +	1.9	7.5	3.9	0.0	65%	140
2001	aa	MON	9	2	0	93	2.61	1.30	28.0	249	316	30%	3.31 -	3.3	6.8	2.1	0.4	80%	77
2002	aa	2TM	8	5	0	141	3.13	1.15	23.9	227	289	25%	2.88	2.9	4.9	1.7	0.6	74%	56
2002	aaa	FLA	0	1	0	11	6.55	1.27	23.1	205	311	19%	4.61 +	4.9	8.2	1.7	2.5	55%	24
2002	MLB	FLA	2	3	0	23	5.43	1.51	20.5	252	349	28%	4.61 +	5.0	6.2	1.2	1.2	66%	33
2001	MLE		9	2	0	92	3.33	1.48	28.9	280	344	32%	4.30 -	3.4	5.8	1.7	0.5	78%	54
2002	MLE		8	6	0	152	3.43	1.18	24.0	234	295	25%	3.09	2.9	4.6	1.6	0.7	72%	49
2003	Projection		6	6	0	120	4.28	1.43	26.1	259	337	29%	4.32	4.1	6.0	1.5	1.0	72%	41

Doesn't have a dominating pitch, but mixes four pitches with regularity. His upside won't be great, but will soak up innings and keep his team in the game. FLA is breaking in several young pitchers and he'll play a big part.

Major League Equivalents

In his 1985 *Baseball Abstract*, Bill James introduced the concept of major league equivalencies. His assertion was that, with the proper adjustments, a minor leaguer's statistics could be converted to an equivalent major league level performance with a great deal of accuracy.

Because of wide variations in the level of play among different minor leagues, it is difficult to get a true reading on a player's potential. For instance, a .300 AVG achieved in the high-offense Pacific Coast League is not nearly as much of an accomplishment as a similar level in the Eastern League. MLEs normalize these variances, among others.

The actual MLEs are not projections. They represent how a player's previous performance might look at the major league level. However, that MLE stat line can be used in forecasting future performance in just the same way as a major league stat line would.

The model we use contains a few minor variations to James' version and updates all of the minor league and ballpark factors. In addition, we have designed a module to project pitching statistics, which is something James did not do.

Another of the enhancements we made is to include an adjustment for each player's age and relative level reached at that age. This serves to truly separate the prospects from the suspects. In other words, it might seem that Shane Andrews' 22 HR, .256 season may look worthy of another shot in the majors, but a 31-year-old facing young AAA pitching is bound to put up good numbers. His MLE of 15 HRs, .213 shows the appropriate — albeit radical — adjustment facing potential big league pitchers, and diffuses any thought of him being able to help a major league club.

Do MLEs really work?

Used correctly, MLEs are excellent indicators of potential. But, just like we cannot take traditional major league statistics at face value, the same goes for MLEs. The underlying measures of base skill — batting eye ratios, pitching command ratios, etc. — are far more accurate in evaluating future talent than raw home runs, batting averages or ERAs.

The charts we present here also provide the unique perspective of looking at two year's worth of data. These are only short-term trends, for sure. But even here we can find small indications of players improving their skills, or struggling, as they rise through more difficult levels of competition. Since players — especially those with any modicum of talent — are promoted rapidly through major league systems, a two-year scan is often all we get to spot any trends.

Here are some things to look for as you scan these charts:

Target players who...

- spent a full season in Double-A and then a full season at Triple-A
- had consistent playing time from one year to the next
- maintained or improved their base skills levels as they were promoted.

Raise the warning flag for players who...

- were stuck at the same level both years, or regressed
- displayed marked changes in playing time from one year to the next.
- showed large drops in BPIs from one year to the next.

Also be sure to keep an eye on each player's age. While minor leaguers over 26 have officially lost their "prospect" status, there are still some who will make it to the majors. Don't discount them completely or you might end up missing out on a player like Dave Roberts or Jason Simontacchi.

Players are listed on the charts if they spent at least part of 2001 or 2002 in Triple-A or Double-A and had at least 100 at bats or 30 innings pitched within those two levels. Each is listed with the organization they finished the season with.

Only statistics accumulated in Triple-A and Double-A ball are included (and players who split a season are indicated as a/a); major league and Single-A stats are excluded.

Each player's actual AB and IP totals are used as the base for the conversion. However, it is more useful to compare performances using common levels, so rely on the ratios and sabermetric gauges. Complete explanations of these formulas appear in the glossary.

Major League Equivalent Statistics

BATTER	Yr	Age	Pos	Lev	Org	AB	R	H	D	T	HR	RBI	BB	K	SB	CS	BA	OB	Slg	OPS	bb%	ct%	Eye	PX	RC/G	BPV
Abad,Andy	01	29	8	aaa	OAK	462	52	110	15	1	14	59	42	59	3	2	238	302	362	664	8%	87%	0.71	75	3.86	25
	02	30	8	aaa	FLA	352	32	80	22	2	6	46	38	37	0	4	227	303	352	655	10%	89%	1.03	87	3.62	32
Abbott,Jeff	01	29	8	a/a	FLA	201	22	55	8	0	7	22	6	31	1	4	272	294	421	715	3%	85%	0.21	92	4.08	33
	02	30	8	aaa	BOS	367	36	87	24	1	7	32	19	42	3	2	237	275	365	640	5%	89%	0.45	90	3.42	25
Abernathy,Brent	01	24	4	aaa	TAM	252	40	72	20	0	4	21	14	20	10	4	286	323	413	736	5%	92%	0.70	95	4.82	48
Abreu,Dennis	01	23	46	a/a	CHC	343	32	80	7	1	3	27	16	67	12	5	233	267	286	553	4%	80%	0.24	34	2.61	-3
	02	24	4	aa	CHC	402	38	101	15	3	6	43	21	97	15	15	251	288	348	637	5%	76%	0.22	63	3.13	14
Acevas,Jon	02	25	2	a/a	CHW	165	23	35	7	1	3	14	20	32	0	1	212	297	321	619	11%	81%	0.63	71	3.31	13
Agbayani,Benny	02	31	8	aaa	BOS	164	23	36	8	1	8	26	23	37	1	0	220	316	427	742	12%	77%	0.62	124	4.81	37
Aguila,Chris	01	23	8	aa	FLA	241	24	59	16	1	4	28	18	51	5	7	245	297	369	667	7%	79%	0.35	88	3.51	25
	02	24	8	aa	FLA	429	49	109	24	3	5	37	39	89	11	9	254	316	359	675	8%	79%	0.44	74	3.91	24
Ahumada,Alex	02	24	6	aa	BOS	185	23	39	4	2	1	15	12	34	8	4	211	259	270	529	6%	82%	0.35	37	2.32	-7
Airoso,Kurt	01	27	8	a/a	DET	306	38	62	16	2	11	36	29	55	1	1	203	272	371	643	9%	82%	0.53	104	3.41	21
	02	28	0	aa	DET	386	51	80	12	0	11	43	41	100	4	3	207	283	324	607	10%	74%	0.41	72	3.14	7
Akers,Chad	01	29	854	aaa	SEA	316	35	76	13	2	2	25	11	36	5	5	239	264	308	573	3%	89%	0.30	50	2.63	6
Alcantara,Israel	01	28	8	aaa	BOS	451	64	115	23	1	25	72	44	98	7	2	256	321	478	800	9%	78%	0.45	134	5.54	49
	02	29	8	aaa	MIL	410	50	96	18	1	24	54	42	86	7	3	234	305	459	764	9%	79%	0.49	132	4.87	42
Aldridge,Cory	01	22	8	aa	ATL	452	52	105	18	2	17	51	45	125	11	6	232	302	394	696	9%	72%	0.36	97	4.09	25
Alexander,Chad	01	27	8	aaa	SEA	527	64	127	38	0	10	65	47	91	1	1	242	303	373	676	8%	83%	0.51	95	4.01	30
	02	28	8	aaa	DET	313	31	73	20	4	5	29	18	54	2	4	233	275	371	646	5%	83%	0.33	93	3.34	23
Alexander,Manny	01	31	46	aaa	SEA	344	36	77	21	1	6	41	12	57	4	9	222	248	343	591	3%	84%	0.21	84	2.52	13
Alfaro,Jason	01	24	4	aa	HOU	284	20	62	16	2	2	23	6	35	2	1	219	234	307	542	2%	88%	0.17	65	2.37	3
	02	25	5	aa	HOU	455	53	125	32	2	13	55	37	63	9	10	275	329	440	769	8%	86%	0.59	110	4.97	49
Alfonzo,Eliezer	02	24	2	aa	MIL	244	19	57	14	1	6	32	8	48	2	3	234	258	373	631	3%	80%	0.17	92	3.11	19
Allensworth,Jermain	01	30	8	aaa	DET	485	43	110	19	5	6	39	36	62	10	9	227	281	325	606	7%	87%	0.59	64	3.01	14
	02	31	8	aa	ATL	270	27	48	11	1	1	21	27	56	5	1	178	253	237	490	9%	79%	0.48	45	2.10	-13
Allen,Chad	02	28	8	aaa	CLE	311	40	84	20	1	10	55	13	39	0	1	270	299	437	737	4%	87%	0.33	110	4.62	42
Allen,Luke	01	23	8	a/a	LA	495	63	124	28	4	14	61	35	97	11	4	251	300	408	708	7%	80%	0.36	101	4.31	32
	02	24	8	aaa	LA	501	60	137	23	1	8	55	40	56	3	8	273	327	371	698	7%	89%	0.71	67	4.24	33
Almonte,Erick	01	24	6	a/a	NYY	357	50	96	18	2	12	48	40	84	4	6	269	343	431	774	10%	76%	0.48	102	5.21	41
	02	25	6	a/a	NYY	408	45	87	15	1	15	52	39	102	10	3	213	282	365	647	9%	75%	0.38	92	3.56	17
Almonte,Wady	01	26	8	aaa	BAL	316	22	60	7	3	3	28	15	52	6	3	190	226	258	484	4%	84%	0.28	41	1.89	-14
Alvarez,Gabe	01	28	5	aa	CIN	336	39	65	18	1	11	33	42	77	2	4	193	281	348	630	11%	77%	0.54	100	3.23	16
Alvarez,Jimmy	02	23	4	aa	TOR	497	62	120	30	2	6	51	59	96	15	13	241	322	346	668	11%	81%	0.61	76	3.81	24
Alvarez,Tony	01	22	8	aa	PIT	254	32	77	16	1	6	23	8	28	16	12	303	324	445	769	3%	89%	0.29	96	4.64	46
	02	23	8	aa	PIT	507	63	144	35	1	11	48	21	57	23	20	284	313	422	735	4%	89%	0.37	96	4.23	42
Alviso,Jerome	01	26	43	aaa	COL	266	19	56	11	0	1	12	10	29	2	1	212	239	263	502	4%	89%	0.34	41	2.09	-6
	02	27	6	aaa	COL	304	20	82	12	0	1	16	8	18	3	1	270	288	319	608	3%	94%	0.44	40	3.28	15
Amezaga,Alfredo	01	24	6	a/a	ANA	485	60	125	13	6	4	29	28	74	25	25	258	298	334	632	5%	85%	0.38	47	3.01	13
	02	25	6	aaa	ANA	518	58	113	22	4	5	39	34	74	17	17	218	266	305	571	6%	86%	0.46	59	2.50	6
Amezcua,Adan	01	28	2	aa	BAL	135	14	22	5	1	3	16	7	27	0	0	160	199	283	482	5%	80%	0.25	76	1.79	-10
	02	29	2	a/a	SD	229	19	57	9	1	4	26	11	33	0	0	249	283	349	633	5%	86%	0.33	66	3.48	17
Amrhein,Mike	01	26	23	aa	CHC	311	23	57	10	0	3	24	17	45	0	1	185	228	243	471	5%	86%	0.39	43	1.81	-13
	02	27	2	a/a	CHC	317	29	79	15	1	4	30	20	31	3	4	249	294	341	634	6%	90%	0.65	64	3.41	22
Andreopoulos,Alex	01	29	2	aaa	CLE	102	11	19	5	0	3	7	10	15	1	0	187	260	312	572	9%	85%	0.65	81	2.79	9
Andrews,Shane	01	30	3	aaa	STL	193	22	33	7	1	7	22	25	57	2	0	173	268	331	599	12%	71%	0.44	95	3.06	6
	02	31	5	aaa	BOS	390	47	83	17	1	15	48	39	117	1	1	213	284	377	661	9%	70%	0.33	100	3.68	19
Ardoin,Danny	01	27	2	aaa	MIN	302	28	67	16	1	4	28	16	66	2	7	220	260	318	577	5%	78%	0.24	70	2.54	7
	02	28	2	a/a	TEX	183	15	34	7	0	4	16	16	47	1	0	186	251	290	541	8%	74%	0.34	68	2.48	-3
Arias,Alex	02	35	6	aaa	NYY	263	24	50	14	0	1	18	15	23	2	2	190	234	255	489	5%	91%	0.65	53	1.93	-2
Asche,Kirk	02	25	8	aa	OAK	376	39	73	11	6	9	43	31	126	7	6	194	256	327	583	8%	66%	0.25	77	2.68	1
Ashby,Chris	01	27	8	aaa	TEX	318	26	66	14	1	4	22	23	52	2	5	207	261	293	554	7%	84%	0.45	59	2.46	3
Atkins,Garrett	02	23	5	aa	COL	510	51	132	25	2	11	44	43	52	4	7	259	316	380	697	8%	90%	0.83	80	4.17	36
Aven,Bruce	01	30	8	aaa	LA	292	29	57	13	0	5	22	16	51	4	1	196	239	296	535	5%	83%	0.32	68	2.37	-0
	02	31	0	aaa	PHI	324	32	69	14	0	10	44	40	56	3	1	213	299	349	648	11%	83%	0.71	86	3.69	21
Badeaux,Brooks	01	25	485	aa	TAM	470	44	107	10	5	1	25	30	49	12	7	228	275	277	552	6%	89%	0.61	32	2.61	2
	02	26	4	aaa	TAM	340	39	78	14	2	2	25	24	39	7	2	229	280	300	580	7%	89%	0.62	51	2.97	10
Baez,Kevin	01	35	64	aaa	NYM	311	29	57	14	0	3	23	27	67	0	3	182	248	252	499	8%	79%	0.41	52	2.03	-10
Bailey,Jeff	01	23	3	aa	FLA	432	54	99	27	2	12	64	62	138	7	2	229	326	384	710	13%	68%	0.45	102	4.55	28
	02	24	3	aa	MON	309	35	77	16	1	11	41	49	63	2	4	249	352	414	766	14%	80%	0.78	104	5.22	41
Bair,Rod	01	27	8	aa	COL	273	18	61	11	0	7	23	8	46	3	5	223	245	341	586	3%	83%	0.17	76	2.57	9
	02	28	8	aaa	COL	258	20	59	15	1	3	23	11	31	9	7	229	260	329	590	4%	88%	0.35	73	2.68	13
Baldelli,Rocco	02	21	8	a/a	TAM	166	22	56	10	2	4	19	4	27	4	9	337	353	494	847	2%	84%	0.15	101	5.47	57
Balfe,Ryan	01	26	835	aaa	STL	422	46	107	27	2	11	49	35	95	2	4	253	310	404	714	8%	78%	0.36	100	4.34	33
Banks,Brian	01	31	38	aaa	CHC	396	56	87	23	3	17	52	28	106	4	5	220	272	420	692	7%	73%	0.26	123	3.73	30
	02	32	3	aaa	FLA	439	59	104	30	2	12	59	49	66	6	5	237	314	396	710	10%	85%	0.74	107	4.32	38
Barajas,Rod	01	26	32	aaa	ARI	162	17	46	12	0	7	24	7	19	2	1	281	310	479	789	4%	89%	0.37	128	5.32	54
Bard,Josh	01	24	2	a/a	CLE	322	36	82	23	0	5	44	31	44	0	1	255	320	373	693	9%	86%	0.70	87	4.30	35
	02	25	2	aaa	CLE	344	33	98	25	1	6	49	18	42	0	0	285	320	416	736	5%	88%	0.43	94	4.91	42
Barker,Glen	01	30	8	aaa	HOU	168	22	40	2	3	2	15	9	43	5	3	236	275	311	585	5%	74%	0.21	40	2.89	-1
Barker,Kevin	01	26	38	a/a	MIL	391	46	94	19	1	10	49	47	78	0	2	241	321	370	691	11%	80%	0.59	85	4.24	27
	02	27	3	aaa	SD	390	45	82	11	1	10	40	37	66	1	1	210	279	321	599	9%	83%	0.56	67	3.08	9
Barkett,Andy	01	27	3	aaa	PIT	273	28	56	14	0	5	31	28	39	2	2	205	278	310	588	9%	86%	0.71	73	2.94	13
	02	28	3	aa	SEA	421	43	79	18	1	6	47	43	93	7	7	188	263	278	541	9%	78%	0.46	62	2.39	-3
Barmes,Clint	02	24	6	aa	COL	438	44	111	20	2	14	42	21	49	11	13	253	288	404	692	5%	89%	0.43	94	3.66	32
Barnes,John	01	25	8	aaa	MIN	311	33	82	20	1	6	33	21	22	2	2	264	310	392	702	6%	93%	0.94	89	4.31	43
	02	26	8	aaa	COL	269	28	68	17	1	5	18	12	10	3	5	253	285	379	664	4%	96%	1.20	88	3.52	45
Barnes,Larry	01	27	3	aaa	ANA	404	56	99	18	5	13	52	21	69	5	1	245	282	412	693	5%	83%	0.30	101	4.05	29
	02	28	3	aaa	ANA	452	50	116	24	6	16	68	20	72	6	1	257	288	442	731	4%	84%	0.28	114	4.51	38
Barns,B.J.	01	24	8	aa	PIT	109	10	22	6	2	6	13	6	36	3	1	200	240	444	685	5%	67%	0.16	143	3.45	29
Baron,Brian	02	24	8	aa	MIN	390	36	102	21	0	1	27	15	42	2	1	262	289	323	612	4%	89%	0.36	52	3.31	16

Major League Equivalent Statistics

BATTER	Yr	Age	Pos	Lev	Org	AB	R	H	D	T	HR	RBI	BB	K	SB	CS	BA	OB	Slg	OPS	bb%	ct%	Eye	PX	RC/G	BPV
Barry,Jeff	01	33	83	aaa	LA	355	37	71	15	1	8	30	25	63	7	5	200	253	317	570	7%	82%	0.40	76	2.59	6
Bartee,Kimera	01	29	8	aaa	ANA	245	25	49	12	1	5	29	17	45	5	1	201	253	323	576	7%	82%	0.38	81	2.80	8
	02	30	8	aaa	CHC	419	37	79	20	1	6	41	26	88	15	15	189	236	284	520	6%	79%	0.30	67	1.94	-4
Barthol,Blake	01	29	2	aaa	SEA	278	30	63	12	1	7	30	20	67	4	0	227	280	348	628	7%	76%	0.31	78	3.46	14
	02	30	2	aaa	SEA	178	23	35	14	2	2	14	19	43	0	2	197	274	331	606	10%	76%	0.44	97	2.97	14
Basak,Chris	02	24	64	a/a	NYM	437	51	97	17	3	3	34	34	95	20	16	222	278	295	573	7%	78%	0.36	51	2.59	2
Bass,Jayson	01	27	8	a/a	CHC	558	56	137	29	3	11	65	41	143	18	15	245	297	369	666	7%	74%	0.29	83	3.58	22
	02	28	8	aaa	CHC	419	51	94	11	2	14	52	34	70	8	8	224	283	360	643	8%	83%	0.49	79	3.33	17
Bates,Fletcher	02	29	8	a/a	NYM	268	29	60	13	3	6	33	17	46	4	5	224	270	362	632	6%	83%	0.37	87	3.13	18
Battersby,Eric	01	26	3	aa	CHW	438	51	92	15	1	12	50	61	79	5	5	210	306	329	635	12%	82%	0.78	74	3.51	16
	02	27	3	a/a	CHW	385	32	84	16	1	6	31	31	63	4	4	218	276	312	588	7%	84%	0.49	63	2.90	9
Battle,Howard	01	30	5	aaa	ATL	491	43	116	18	0	8	62	21	75	2	5	235	267	322	589	4%	85%	0.28	59	2.85	8
	02	31	5	aaa	MON	193	15	39	10	0	4	14	8	27	0	1	202	234	316	550	4%	86%	0.30	78	2.37	5
Baughman,Justin	01	27	4	aaa	ANA	288	38	74	12	3	2	23	14	41	15	7	257	292	340	632	5%	86%	0.35	57	3.42	16
	02	28	8	aaa	CHW	420	47	83	10	0	6	31	27	72	25	9	198	246	264	510	6%	83%	0.38	43	2.18	-9
Bautista,Rayner	02	24	6	aa	DET	302	27	67	16	2	3	26	18	58	4	2	222	266	318	584	6%	81%	0.31	68	2.87	8
Bay,Jason	02	24	8	aa	SD	188	29	48	8	3	7	27	24	45	14	6	255	340	441	781	11%	76%	0.53	109	5.25	41
Beamon,Trey	01	28	8	aa	SEA	238	25	45	10	1	1	14	14	37	5	2	188	234	248	481	6%	84%	0.38	46	1.90	-11
Beattie,Andy	01	24	4	a/a	CIN	178	26	43	12	0	3	19	17	27	3	2	242	308	360	667	9%	85%	0.63	86	3.87	28
	02	25	8	aa	CIN	166	18	36	9	1	5	14	13	24	2	2	217	274	373	647	7%	86%	0.54	100	3.37	24
Becker,Brian	01	26	3	aa	TAM	411	31	78	19	0	6	35	36	103	0	0	191	255	282	537	8%	75%	0.34	64	2.44	-3
Becker,Rich	01	30	8	aaa	FLA	397	45	75	13	2	7	28	48	82	6	5	188	276	284	560	11%	79%	0.59	61	2.67	-1
Beinbrink,Andy	01	25	5	aa	TAM	443	44	105	20	5	5	42	48	72	4	2	238	312	333	645	10%	84%	0.66	64	3.75	19
	02	26	5	a/a	TAM	426	48	110	23	1	3	49	46	75	17	11	258	331	338	669	10%	82%	0.61	61	3.95	23
Bellhorn,Mark	01	27	8	aaa	OAK	156	23	34	5	0	9	27	16	51	2	0	219	292	414	707	9%	68%	0.32	112	4.27	26
Bellinger,Clay	02	34	8	aaa	ANA	324	31	66	14	3	10	28	9	71	3	2	204	225	358	583	3%	78%	0.13	94	2.58	9
Bell,Mike	01	27	54	aaa	COL	320	28	81	18	1	12	35	11	54	0	5	252	276	424	700	3%	83%	0.20	110	3.78	33
	02	28	5	aaa	COL	240	20	58	16	1	3	21	10	26	3	5	242	272	354	626	4%	89%	0.38	82	3.06	22
Bell,Ricky	01	23	5	aa	LA	188	20	44	8	0	3	21	12	29	1	1	234	280	324	604	6%	85%	0.41	62	3.13	12
	02	24	5	aaa	LA	448	42	98	21	2	9	54	11	54	0	1	219	237	335	572	2%	88%	0.20	77	2.61	9
Benefield,Brian	01	25	8	aa	KC	177	13	29	5	1	3	9	8	28	4	5	163	199	249	449	4%	84%	0.29	55	1.41	-17
Benham,Dave	01	26	2	aa	STL	132	6	26	4	0	1	12	3	33	2	0	198	218	250	469	3%	75%	0.10	39	1.83	-16
Benjamin,Al	01	24	8	aa	SD	374	44	89	20	1	10	44	15	76	7	3	239	268	381	650	4%	80%	0.20	93	3.47	22
	02	25	8	a/a	SD	221	19	41	11	1	3	15	5	46	1	2	186	204	285	489	2%	79%	0.11	69	1.77	-7
Berblinger,Jeff	01	31	4	aaa	KC	288	28	53	11	2	5	17	16	48	6	5	184	228	281	509	5%	83%	0.34	63	1.97	-6
Bergeron,Peter	01	24	8	aaa	MON	206	26	46	5	2	0	7	18	39	14	8	223	286	267	553	8%	81%	0.46	30	2.54	-4
	02	25	8	aaa	MON	340	45	93	9	3	1	25	33	56	6	8	274	338	326	664	9%	84%	0.59	36	3.88	18
Berger,Brandon	01	27	8	aa	KC	454	67	112	23	2	28	80	28	77	10	6	247	291	489	779	6%	83%	0.36	142	4.77	48
	02	28	8	aaa	KC	261	27	67	14	1	10	36	19	36	9	2	257	307	433	740	7%	86%	0.53	110	4.79	42
Berrios,Harry	01	30	8	a/a	TEX	380	40	83	15	3	12	43	19	69	5	1	218	255	366	622	5%	82%	0.28	91	3.18	16
Berroa,Angel	01	22	6	aa	KC	304	49	83	19	3	6	33	13	40	12	7	273	303	414	717	4%	87%	0.33	95	4.26	37
	02	25	6	aaa	KC	297	30	59	10	3	7	28	12	65	5	5	199	230	323	553	4%	78%	0.18	75	2.28	1
Berroa,Cristian	01	22	4	a/a	HOU	128	12	24	3	1	0	2	8	15	5	6	189	239	230	468	6%	88%	0.55	29	1.53	-14
Betemit,Wilson	01	20	6	aa	ATL	183	22	68	14	0	4	19	12	30	6	2	373	412	523	935	6%	84%	0.40	106	8.87	76
	02	22	6	aaa	ATL	343	40	82	17	1	7	32	30	68	7	6	239	300	356	656	8%	80%	0.44	78	3.62	21
Betts,Todd	01	28	35	aaa	SEA	506	72	127	33	3	10	53	44	55	3	5	252	311	388	699	8%	89%	0.80	93	4.21	38
	02	29	3	aaa	BOS	416	46	102	15	2	10	35	47	55	3	5	245	322	363	685	10%	87%	0.85	73	4.10	29
Betzsold,James	01	29	8	aaa	SEA	157	15	19	3	1	5	19	17	71	0	0	122	209	255	464	10%	55%	0.24	74	1.72	-24
Bevins,Andy	01	26	8	a/a	STL	494	55	93	19	1	17	49	43	101	4	10	189	253	338	591	8%	80%	0.42	91	2.63	9
Bierek,Kurt	01	29	83	aaa	DET	394	48	89	24	1	10	40	24	64	2	2	226	270	367	637	6%	84%	0.37	95	3.36	22
	02	30	8	aaa	TEX	220	14	37	8	1	2	14	13	36	1	1	168	215	241	456	6%	84%	0.36	50	1.66	-16
Bigbie,Larry	01	24	8	a/a	BAL	304	42	82	14	2	9	32	41	57	10	9	270	357	418	774	12%	81%	0.72	92	5.21	42
	02	25	8	aaa	BAL	348	37	95	20	1	2	31	30	71	6	3	273	331	353	684	8%	80%	0.42	62	4.31	25
Bikowski,Scott	02	26	8	aa	CHW	395	38	86	14	1	4	29	50	69	14	11	218	306	289	594	11%	83%	0.72	49	3.01	7
Blakely,Darren	01	25	8	aa	SD	135	18	27	4	1	5	15	10	46	6	6	197	255	345	600	7%	66%	0.23	86	2.52	6
	02	26	8	a/a	SD	439	57	82	19	3	8	52	60	125	9	4	187	285	298	583	12%	72%	0.48	73	2.96	2
Blake,Casey	01	28	5	aaa	MIN	375	47	99	21	4	7	35	24	55	10	4	263	308	399	707	6%	85%	0.44	90	4.38	34
	02	29	5	aaa	MIN	482	58	119	22	2	12	38	35	65	16	10	247	298	376	673	7%	87%	0.54	83	3.78	27
Blalock,Hank	01	21	5	aa	TEX	272	44	87	18	3	11	54	36	29	3	3	320	399	525	924	12%	89%	1.25	128	8.11	85
	02	22	5	aaa	TEX	387	53	117	32	1	7	52	29	41	2	1	302	351	444	795	7%	89%	0.71	103	5.92	58
Bledsoe,Hunter	02	27	3	aa	LA	348	32	78	15	1	3	31	45	47	3	3	224	313	299	612	11%	86%	0.96	54	3.34	16
Bloomquist,Willie	01	24	64	aa	SEA	491	52	108	19	1	0	24	26	55	30	10	219	259	263	522	5%	89%	0.48	37	2.36	-2
	02	25	8	aaa	SEA	337	42	82	13	2	5	42	26	39	18	11	243	298	338	636	7%	88%	0.67	62	3.33	20
Bolivar,Papo	01	23	8	aa	MIN	142	15	38	7	0	2	20	9	25	1	1	268	311	359	670	6%	82%	0.36	65	3.98	23
	02	24	8	aa	MIN	547	63	138	34	2	10	70	38	87	15	6	252	301	377	677	6%	84%	0.44	87	3.99	29
Borchard,Joe	01	23	8	aa	CHW	515	79	141	25	1	25	82	57	130	4	5	274	346	472	818	10%	75%	0.44	120	5.90	49
	02	24	8	aaa	CHW	438	55	112	32	1	20	52	46	124	2	4	256	326	470	797	10%	72%	0.37	137	5.38	49
Borders,Pat	01	38	2	aaa	SEA	324	22	60	12	1	2	23	14	63	3	2	186	219	244	463	4%	80%	0.21	43	1.72	-16
	02	39	2	aaa	SEA	317	33	68	14	1	9	22	9	46	3	2	215	236	350	586	3%	85%	0.20	86	2.69	11
Borrego,Ramon	01	23	46	aa	MIN	136	16	24	6	2	1	3	14	31	5	0	178	253	271	524	9%	77%	0.44	62	2.48	-6
Bowers,Jason	01	24	6	aa	STL	460	32	100	17	3	4	30	24	108	9	11	217	256	293	550	5%	76%	0.22	52	2.35	-2
	02	25	6	aa	STL	343	34	83	15	2	2	28	21	40	2	2	242	286	315	601	6%	88%	0.53	53	3.12	13
Bozied,Tagg	02	23	3	aa	SD	234	30	43	12	0	8	28	14	41	1	0	184	230	338	567	6%	82%	0.34	98	2.55	9
Bradley,Milton	01	23	8	aaa	MON	250	35	62	10	2	7	25	37	56	21	3	248	345	388	733	13%	78%	0.66	86	5.25	31
Bragg,Darren	01	32	8	aaa	NYM	298	43	77	13	2	9	23	41	79	6	4	257	347	402	749	12%	74%	0.52	90	5.10	33
Branson,Jeff	01	35	46	aaa	LA	289	19	59	13	0	3	14	17	62	2	3	202	247	274	521	6%	78%	0.27	53	2.20	-5
	02	36	5	aaa	LA	233	19	41	11	0	2	16	13	42	0	1	176	220	249	468	5%	82%	0.31	55	1.75	-12
Bravo,Danny	01	24	64	a/a	CHW	294	29	68	13	1	5	30	21	28	3	3	231	283	333	616	7%	90%	0.75	68	3.19	20
	02	25	5	aa	CHW	138	14	28	6	0	1	13	13	20	5	5	203	272	268	540	9%	86%	0.65	50	2.27	1
Brazell,Craig	02	22	3	aa	NYM	130	12	35	7	0	5	16	1	24	0	2	269	275	438	713	1%	82%	0.04	107	3.91	35
Brewer,Jace	02	23	6	aa	TAM	153	11	30	5	0	1	14	3	24	2	0	196	212	248	460	2%	84%	0.13	39	1.75	-16

Major League Equivalent Statistics

BATTER	Yr	Age	Pos	Lev	Org	AB	R	H	D	T	HR	RBI	BB	K	SB	CS	BA	OB	Slg	OPS	bb%	ct%	Eye	PX	RC/G	BPV
Bridges,Kary	01	29	4	aaa	NYY	408	47	104	15	1	5	31	29	26	4	8	255	304	331	635	7%	94%	1.12	52	3.36	29
	02	31	4	aaa	NYY	502	52	104	6	2	6	29	34	23	5	7	207	257	263	520	6%	95%	1.48	33	2.21	12
Briggs,Stoney	01	30	8	aa	BAL	164	17	27	3	1	5	15	17	48	2	2	165	241	288	529	9%	71%	0.34	70	2.24	-9
Brignac,Junior	01	24	8	aa	ATL	203	18	38	9	1	1	11	19	65	4	2	186	257	253	511	9%	68%	0.30	50	2.22	-11
Brinkley,Darryl	02	34	8	aaa	BAL	509	46	119	24	2	6	58	20	67	15	5	234	263	324	587	4%	87%	0.30	63	2.91	10
Brito,Juan	01	22	2	aa	KC	236	17	58	9	0	3	22	13	21	2	4	246	285	322	607	5%	91%	0.62	53	3.03	16
	02	23	2	a/a	KC	311	37	78	12	0	6	35	19	36	1	1	251	294	347	641	6%	88%	0.53	64	3.60	21
Brock,Tarrik	02	29	8	aa	LA	325	45	64	12	1	7	36	55	113	6	7	197	313	305	618	14%	65%	0.49	69	3.26	4
Broussard,Ben	01	25	3	aa	CIN	353	59	95	23	0	17	50	45	60	7	4	268	351	479	830	11%	83%	0.75	134	6.13	59
	02	26	83	aaa	CLE	340	54	82	20	1	16	46	49	76	4	1	241	337	447	784	13%	78%	0.64	128	5.49	46
Brown,Adrian	02	29	8	aaa	PIT	184	28	53	7	1	2	12	18	15	17	7	288	351	370	721	9%	92%	1.20	55	4.77	43
Brown,Brant	01	30	3	aaa	STL	342	37	66	10	1	7	23	25	98	2	4	192	248	289	537	7%	71%	0.26	61	2.31	-6
Brown,Dee	02	25	8	aaa	KC	458	54	116	21	1	14	61	34	87	8	5	253	305	395	700	7%	81%	0.39	90	4.20	29
Brown,Emil	02	28	8	aaa	TAM	422	48	106	23	3	10	48	28	75	9	2	251	298	391	689	6%	82%	0.37	91	4.16	29
Brown,Jason	01	27	2	a/a	FLA	101	11	28	7	0	2	14	5	22	0	0	273	305	395	700	4%	78%	0.21	87	4.36	31
	02	28	2	aa	MON	106	6	16	6	0	2	8	6	41	0	0	151	196	264	461	5%	61%	0.15	79	1.65	-14
Brown,Kevin	01	28	2	aaa	MIL	290	14	56	14	1	7	25	14	92	0	1	192	229	314	544	5%	68%	0.15	80	2.33	0
	02	29	2	aaa	BOS	246	25	49	12	1	5	19	15	62	0	0	199	245	317	562	6%	75%	0.24	78	2.60	4
Brown,Roosevelt	01	26	8	aaa	CHC	364	57	108	28	1	17	65	12	62	3	6	296	318	522	840	3%	83%	0.19	145	5.72	62
Brown,Tonayne	01	24	8	aa	BOS	396	33	105	19	1	3	26	12	68	3	12	264	286	338	624	3%	83%	0.18	56	2.98	15
	02	25	8	aa	BOS	472	49	101	19	5	8	41	24	76	8	17	214	252	326	578	5%	84%	0.32	71	2.35	7
Bruce,Mo	01	26	45	a/a	MON	185	20	33	7	0	3	15	12	49	12	4	178	227	262	489	6%	73%	0.24	57	1.95	-12
Brumbaugh,Cliff	01	27	85	aaa	TEX	410	55	117	27	3	10	65	55	78	7	7	285	370	433	803	12%	81%	0.71	99	5.91	50
	02	28	8	aaa	COL	505	50	125	30	1	12	48	34	69	4	3	248	295	382	677	6%	86%	0.49	91	3.93	30
Bruntlett,Eric	01	24	6	a/a	HOU	519	73	127	23	2	3	34	43	66	19	8	245	302	314	617	8%	87%	0.65	52	3.38	16
	02	25	6	a/a	HOU	532	75	127	23	2	2	41	54	60	30	15	239	309	301	610	9%	89%	0.90	47	3.26	17
Buck,John	02	22	2	aa	HOU	448	38	108	27	3	10	70	24	74	2	4	241	280	382	661	5%	83%	0.32	94	3.58	26
Budzinski,Mark	01	28	8	aaa	CLE	438	57	99	23	3	2	33	23	114	11	4	225	264	304	568	5%	74%	0.20	59	2.76	4
	02	29	8	a/a	CHC	459	53	108	16	4	3	28	39	79	15	8	235	295	307	602	8%	83%	0.49	49	3.15	8
Buford,Damon	01	31	8	aaa	BAL	203	29	48	12	1	6	22	28	44	3	2	235	327	395	722	12%	78%	0.63	103	4.60	33
	02	32	8	aaa	CHW	169	20	32	7	0	3	10	14	27	5	1	189	251	284	535	8%	84%	0.52	64	2.46	-0
Burford,Kevin	01	24	3	aa	COL	363	42	103	20	3	7	29	38	66	3	1	283	351	412	762	9%	82%	0.57	86	5.47	41
	02	25	3	aa	COL	266	30	67	21	1	3	23	33	36	1	7	252	334	372	707	11%	86%	0.92	91	4.16	40
Burke,Chris	02	23	4	aa	HOU	481	52	116	18	7	3	29	30	49	13	18	241	286	326	612	6%	90%	0.61	56	2.86	16
Burke,Jamie	01	30	2	aaa	ANA	215	17	37	8	2	0	18	13	22	1	0	172	217	226	444	6%	90%	0.57	41	1.63	-15
	02	31	2	aaa	ANA	316	32	77	10	2	6	31	14	31	1	4	244	276	345	621	4%	90%	0.45	63	3.13	16
Burkhart,Lance	01	27	2	aa	MIL	170	27	33	9	0	10	30	17	55	0	1	194	266	415	680	9%	68%	0.30	132	3.61	25
	02	28	2	a/a	MIL	154	16	28	10	0	4	14	27	51	2	3	182	304	325	629	15%	67%	0.53	98	3.30	11
Burkhart,Morgan	01	30	3	aaa	BOS	412	50	94	16	1	17	48	51	105	1	0	228	313	398	710	11%	74%	0.48	102	4.45	28
Burnham,Gary	01	27	3	aa	PHI	371	42	95	23	2	10	55	26	44	1	2	256	305	406	710	7%	88%	0.60	100	4.34	38
	02	28	3	aaa	TOR	537	53	130	32	1	12	67	40	57	1	2	242	295	372	667	7%	89%	0.70	89	3.83	31
Burns,Kevan	02	26	8	aa	ARI	187	25	51	7	4	2	18	15	21	2	5	273	327	385	712	7%	89%	0.71	69	4.20	33
Burns,Kevin	01	26	3	a/a	HOU	404	61	100	24	4	18	54	49	85	2	1	247	328	463	791	11%	79%	0.57	132	5.47	48
	02	27	3	aa	ANA	169	14	22	8	1	3	15	23	48	1	0	130	234	243	477	12%	72%	0.48	75	1.93	-16
Burroughs,Sean	01	21	5	aaa	SD	394	58	125	28	1	8	53	33	45	9	2	318	371	452	823	8%	88%	0.73	94	6.59	60
	02	22	4	aaa	SD	179	26	50	15	1	2	21	19	14	1	0	279	348	408	756	10%	92%	1.36	96	5.40	60
Burton,Darren	01	29	8	aa	PIT	299	25	62	11	2	5	23	16	77	4	1	206	245	306	551	5%	74%	0.20	65	2.54	-1
Butler,Brent	01	24	4	aaa	COL	272	35	84	18	2	6	26	11	17	3	3	309	336	456	792	4%	94%	0.65	99	5.57	57
	02	25	6	aaa	COL	105	13	32	8	1	2	11	4	7	0	0	305	330	457	787	4%	93%	0.57	105	5.66	56
Byas,Mike	01	25	8	a/a	SF	337	47	77	13	1	0	21	43	49	17	12	229	316	273	589	11%	85%	0.86	36	2.99	9
Byrd,Marlon	01	24	8	aa	PHI	510	85	141	23	7	20	69	43	87	25	6	276	332	464	796	8%	83%	0.49	112	5.69	48
	02	25	8	aaa	PHI	538	85	147	38	5	12	52	41	89	13	1	273	325	429	754	7%	83%	0.46	105	5.22	44
Byrnes,Eric	01	26	8	aaa	OAK	415	63	103	20	1	16	40	26	54	20	4	248	292	415	707	6%	87%	0.48	103	4.32	35
	02	27	8	aaa	OAK	119	12	25	6	0	3	12	5	11	4	1	210	242	336	578	4%	91%	0.45	84	2.72	14
Cabrera,Jolbert	02	30	8	aaa	LA	193	25	46	10	0	1	12	15	22	4	6	238	293	306	599	7%	89%	0.68	54	2.86	15
Cabrera,Ray	02	24	8	aa	BAL	243	21	58	17	0	3	24	6	27	5	6	239	257	346	603	2%	89%	0.22	81	2.74	17
Caceres,Wilmy	01	23	6	aaa	ANA	325	29	72	4	2	0	16	9	33	9	7	222	243	246	489	3%	90%	0.27	16	1.89	-14
	02	29	6	aaa	TAM	347	33	76	5	5	0	15	18	45	13	8	219	258	262	520	5%	87%	0.40	25	2.21	-8
Cadiente,Brett	01	24	8	a/a	TEX	267	27	70	15	4	3	20	13	54	7	6	262	296	382	678	5%	80%	0.24	80	3.77	25
	02	25	8	a/a	TEX	319	34	68	15	4	2	20	31	61	11	8	213	283	304	587	9%	81%	0.51	62	2.92	7
Cairo,Miguel	01	27	4	aaa	CHC	123	18	31	6	1	2	11	7	11	3	5	255	293	363	656	5%	91%	0.63	72	3.25	27
Calderon,Henry	01	24	5	aa	KC	327	37	75	18	3	4	36	12	39	3	9	230	258	337	595	4%	88%	0.32	75	2.61	14
Calloway,Ron	01	25	8	a/a	MON	518	66	144	33	3	18	72	34	100	32	9	277	321	455	776	6%	81%	0.34	114	5.29	46
	02	26	8	aaa	MON	447	61	108	21	3	12	50	37	78	14	13	242	300	383	682	8%	83%	0.47	89	3.71	27
Calzado,Napolean	02	26	5	aa	BAL	482	55	108	15	2	3	32	26	49	32	12	224	264	282	546	5%	90%	0.53	41	2.53	2
Cameron,Troy	02	24	54	aa	COL	325	26	67	13	2	8	28	20	66	0	1	206	252	332	584	6%	80%	0.30	79	2.78	7
Camilli,Jason	01	26	4	aa	TEX	213	21	46	8	1	3	21	26	39	3	3	215	301	300	601	11%	82%	0.67	57	3.14	9
	02	27	4	aa	ANA	338	29	61	10	1	3	21	27	61	4	5	180	241	243	484	7%	82%	0.44	43	1.87	-13
Camilo,Juan	01	23	8	aa	DET	110	12	27	3	1	4	14	6	22	1	1	247	285	397	682	5%	80%	0.27	86	3.84	23
	02	26	8	aa	DET	156	12	24	5	3	3	15	11	43	3	0	154	210	282	492	7%	72%	0.26	75	1.96	-13
Cancel,Robinson	01	25	2	a/a	MIL	258	21	48	7	0	1	20	13	46	0	6	184	223	223	446	5%	82%	0.28	30	1.44	-21
	02	26	2	aa	OAK	402	42	88	17	1	9	48	23	69	8	7	219	261	333	595	5%	83%	0.33	74	2.80	10
Candelaria,Ben	01	27	8	a/a	FLA	258	27	70	20	1	5	35	18	28	0	1	271	319	414	733	7%	89%	0.66	102	4.75	46
	02	28	8	a/a	FLA	128	9	29	10	0	1	14	6	19	2	2	227	261	328	589	4%	85%	0.32	81	2.77	15
Canizaro,Jay	02	29	4	aaa	MIN	247	28	56	9	1	9	25	20	38	4	4	227	285	381	665	7%	85%	0.53	92	3.57	24
Cantu,Jorge	01	20	6	aa	TAM	512	62	140	29	3	4	47	18	79	4	10	273	297	367	664	3%	85%	0.22	68	3.62	24
	02	21	6	aa	TAM	512	45	122	32	1	3	39	20	61	2	7	238	267	322	589	4%	88%	0.33	66	2.79	13
Capista,Aaron	01	22	65	aa	BOS	404	41	82	24	3	2	34	16	41	2	1	203	233	292	525	4%	90%	0.39	67	2.25	3
	02	23	4	aa	BOS	174	16	38	9	1	1	8	11	21	4	2	218	265	299	564	6%	88%	0.52	60	2.67	8
Carpenter,Brian	01	31	8	aa	COL	100	7	16	5	0	1	7	10	20	2	1	161	236	231	467	9%	80%	0.49	54	1.85	-14
Carpenter,Bubba	01	33	8	aaa	COL	207	21	43	14	1	3	14	20	30	3	5	209	278	322	600	9%	86%	0.66	82	2.80	16

Major League Equivalent Statistics

BATTER	Yr	Age	Pos	Lev	Org	AB	R	H	D	T	HR	RBI	BB	K	SB	CS	BA	OB	Slg	OPS	bb%	ct%	Eye	PX	RC/G	BPV
Carreno,Jose	01	23	2	aa	MON	120	3	16	1	0	0	7	10	22	0	2	137	202	146	347	7%	82%	0.45	7	0.90	-42
Carroll,Jamey	01	28	465	aaa	MON	267	23	57	8	2	0	14	15	40	5	5	213	256	256	512	5%	85%	0.38	31	2.12	-8
	02	29	45	a/a	MON	430	46	105	18	1	7	39	31	34	5	10	244	295	340	635	7%	92%	0.91	64	3.26	26
Carr,Dustin	01	26	58	aaa	TAM	227	21	49	6	1	4	22	21	42	4	2	218	285	303	589	9%	81%	0.50	53	3.01	5
Carter,Charley	01	26	38	aa	HOU	525	49	116	23	1	21	72	26	99	1	1	221	258	387	645	5%	81%	0.26	102	3.36	21
	02	27	3	aa	DET	492	44	104	23	1	12	65	38	80	1	0	211	268	335	603	7%	84%	0.48	81	3.09	13
Carter,Mike	01	32	8	aaa	ATL	388	44	96	14	2	2	16	8	44	8	10	248	264	306	570	2%	89%	0.18	42	2.52	4
Caruso,Joe	01	27	84	aa	KC	424	50	90	21	1	5	40	32	55	8	6	211	267	302	569	7%	87%	0.58	64	2.67	9
	02	32	58	a/a	KC	354	32	77	14	4	4	36	17	47	3	4	218	253	314	567	5%	87%	0.36	62	2.58	6
Caruso,Mike	01	24	46	aaa	TAM	387	55	106	10	7	0	31	20	19	10	10	274	310	336	645	5%	95%	1.05	39	3.51	28
	02	25	46	a/a	KC	233	27	67	3	2	3	23	11	11	9	3	288	320	356	676	5%	95%	1.00	39	4.20	32
Carvajal,Jhonny	02	29	5	aa	SF	419	37	80	20	3	3	22	23	75	7	4	191	233	274	507	5%	82%	0.31	60	2.08	-6
Cash,Kevin	02	25	2	a/a	TOR	449	51	100	32	1	14	55	48	90	4	4	223	298	392	690	10%	80%	0.53	113	3.99	32
Casillas,Uriel	01	26	5	aa	PHI	384	32	74	16	2	3	28	20	47	3	5	193	233	270	502	5%	88%	0.42	54	1.96	-5
	02	27	54	a/a	PHI	252	31	62	10	2	2	26	25	35	3	1	246	314	325	639	9%	86%	0.71	54	3.73	19
Casimiro,Carlos	01	25	58	a/a	BAL	468	39	96	20	1	8	35	24	112	6	7	205	244	303	547	5%	76%	0.21	66	2.34	-0
Castellano,John	02	25	8	aa	SEA	194	14	44	9	0	1	18	9	32	3	3	227	261	289	550	4%	84%	0.28	49	2.46	1
Castillo,Carlos	02	23	6	aa	DET	112	6	21	4	2	0	5	3	26	1	1	188	209	259	468	3%	77%	0.12	47	1.68	-16
Castillo,Ruben	01	21	6	aa	SEA	126	11	22	4	0	0	6	7	26	1	0	175	218	206	424	5%	79%	0.27	28	1.52	-25
	02	24	6	aa	SEA	394	38	77	11	3	3	34	15	88	10	7	195	225	261	486	4%	78%	0.17	43	1.83	-14
Castro,Bernabel	02	23	4	aa	SD	419	53	95	12	2	0	28	45	65	47	21	227	302	265	567	10%	84%	0.69	30	2.79	2
Castro,Nelson	01	25	6	a/a	SF	502	63	127	25	4	8	49	33	101	31	13	252	298	365	663	6%	80%	0.32	75	3.74	22
	02	26	68	a/a	SF	394	36	74	15	5	6	28	12	70	18	11	188	212	297	509	3%	82%	0.17	68	1.84	-6
Castro,Ramon	01	22	6	a/a	ATL	396	48	114	29	6	7	46	32	70	6	12	289	342	439	781	7%	82%	0.46	102	5.04	47
	02	23	64	a/a	ATL	331	62	92	23	2	9	33	46	53	17	13	278	366	441	807	12%	84%	0.87	109	5.60	55
Castro,Ramon	01	26	2	aaa	FLA	390	56	108	28	0	18	62	27	56	1	1	277	323	485	808	6%	86%	0.48	134	5.68	57
Cepicky,Matt	01	24	8	aa	MON	459	49	109	21	6	16	65	17	88	4	13	237	265	416	681	4%	81%	0.20	108	3.31	27
	02	25	8	aa	MON	419	41	101	24	1	12	58	25	78	6	1	241	284	389	673	6%	81%	0.32	97	3.88	27
Cervenak,Mike	01	25	534	aa	NYY	463	52	109	32	1	10	50	36	76	2	4	235	290	371	662	7%	84%	0.48	95	3.68	27
	02	26	3	aa	NYY	492	57	110	28	1	17	70	24	82	3	2	224	260	388	648	5%	83%	0.29	106	3.38	24
Cesar,Dionys	01	25	6	a/a	MIL	356	43	95	22	1	8	42	30	62	4	3	267	323	400	724	8%	83%	0.48	91	4.65	36
	02	26	4	aaa	MIL	479	46	113	20	2	6	33	26	69	7	8	236	275	324	599	5%	86%	0.38	60	2.93	11
Chamblee,Jim	01	26	4	aaa	HOU	413	35	91	23	0	10	29	28	103	7	6	221	270	348	618	6%	75%	0.27	86	3.09	15
	02	27	53	a/a	STL	444	61	103	27	2	13	57	40	82	7	2	232	295	390	685	8%	82%	0.49	103	4.05	30
Chapman,Travis	02	24	5	aa	PHI	478	50	126	33	1	11	60	46	73	3	1	264	328	406	734	9%	85%	0.63	99	4.89	41
Charles,Frank	01	33	2	aaa	HOU	243	12	50	11	0	1	18	8	53	1	1	204	229	259	489	3%	78%	0.15	45	1.94	-10
	02	34	3	aaa	HOU	332	23	76	9	2	5	39	14	83	1	3	229	260	313	573	4%	75%	0.17	53	2.68	1
Chavez,Endy	01	24	8	a/a	KC	272	36	79	11	1	1	13	12	19	12	11	290	320	349	670	4%	93%	0.63	45	3.67	28
	02	25	8	aaa	MON	405	59	132	29	3	4	36	28	32	18	14	326	370	442	811	6%	92%	0.88	85	5.86	61
Chavez,Raul	01	28	2	aaa	HOU	278	30	75	16	0	7	32	15	31	1	1	270	308	400	708	5%	89%	0.50	88	4.40	36
	02	30	2	aaa	HOU	373	19	74	9	0	3	29	16	49	3	4	198	231	247	478	4%	87%	0.33	34	1.82	-13
Chen,Chin-Feng	01	24	8	aa	LA	224	43	63	14	1	16	46	37	66	5	4	281	383	559	942	14%	71%	0.56	165	7.82	73
	02	25	3	aaa	LA	511	63	119	21	2	18	59	41	115	1	0	233	290	387	677	7%	77%	0.36	94	3.94	24
Chevalier,Virgil	01	28	38	a/a	BOS	483	49	112	25	1	11	58	33	55	3	3	232	282	358	640	6%	89%	0.61	84	3.45	24
	02	29	2	a/a	NYM	397	50	97	21	0	6	42	41	44	4	3	244	315	343	658	9%	89%	0.93	70	3.86	29
Chiaffredo,Paul	01	25	2	aa	TOR	132	8	28	6	1	1	13	16	30	2	2	211	298	293	591	11%	77%	0.54	59	3.01	6
	02	26	2	aa	TOR	258	25	38	6	1	7	25	9	70	3	0	147	176	260	436	3%	73%	0.13	66	1.45	-21
Chiaramonte,Giuser	01	26	2	a/a	SF	144	11	26	7	0	2	12	6	19	0	2	179	211	268	479	4%	87%	0.31	64	1.69	-8
Choi,Hee Seop	01	23	3	aaa	CHC	266	34	56	9	0	11	40	30	55	4	1	209	290	363	654	10%	79%	0.55	93	3.69	19
	02	24	3	aaa	CHC	478	66	115	20	2	18	68	68	85	2	3	241	335	404	739	12%	82%	0.80	99	4.86	37
Christensen,McKay	01	26	8	aaa	LA	330	45	71	14	4	6	20	25	51	15	5	215	270	332	602	7%	85%	0.50	74	3.07	12
	02	27	8	aaa	NYM	377	44	92	20	4	4	26	22	69	17	14	244	286	350	636	6%	82%	0.32	73	3.13	18
Christensen,Mike	01	25	5	aa	ANA	298	23	57	19	1	5	23	14	63	3	2	190	225	305	530	4%	79%	0.21	82	2.21	2
	02	26	5	aa	ANA	413	24	73	15	1	4	25	11	93	1	2	177	198	247	445	3%	77%	0.12	49	1.52	-18
Christenson,Ryan	01	28	8	aaa	ARI	285	29	64	19	0	5	23	20	45	5	2	223	274	340	614	7%	84%	0.44	85	3.20	18
	02	29	8	aaa	MIL	260	32	58	15	1	5	25	15	27	9	5	223	265	346	612	5%	90%	0.56	84	3.00	20
Christianson,Ryan	02	21	2	aa	SEA	190	20	46	11	0	5	17	16	35	0	2	242	301	379	680	8%	82%	0.46	92	3.87	28
Church,Ryan	02	24	8	aa	CLE	291	34	80	16	3	12	45	11	54	1	0	275	301	474	776	4%	81%	0.20	122	5.15	46
Cintron,Alex	01	23	6	aaa	ARI	425	44	118	23	2	2	29	13	35	7	7	277	298	356	653	3%	92%	0.36	60	3.60	24
	02	24	6	aaa	ARI	351	40	103	20	2	3	20	8	24	7	6	293	309	387	697	2%	93%	0.33	69	4.16	33
Clapinski,Chris	01	30	8	a/a	FLA	217	27	42	8	1	5	16	15	42	2	2	195	248	315	563	7%	81%	0.36	75	2.54	3
	02	31	6	aaa	LA	342	37	75	18	1	7	36	25	41	1	0	219	272	339	612	7%	88%	0.61	81	3.20	19
Clapp,Stubby	01	29	4	aaa	STL	299	36	75	12	5	4	24	34	41	6	5	252	329	361	690	10%	86%	0.84	69	4.21	29
	02	30	4	aaa	STL	359	37	72	15	1	2	15	37	65	2	7	201	275	265	540	9%	82%	0.57	48	2.36	-2
Clark,Brady	01	28	8	aaa	CIN	167	18	38	5	1	2	14	14	14	5	2	228	288	301	589	8%	92%	1.00	47	3.05	15
	02	29	8	aaa	CIN	109	12	27	6	0	1	12	2	8	0	2	248	261	330	592	2%	93%	0.25	63	2.70	14
Clark,Doug	01	26	8	aa	SF	414	41	94	14	3	5	40	34	79	15	5	226	285	304	589	8%	81%	0.43	51	3.05	5
	02	27	8	a/a	SF	350	31	81	15	2	5	27	28	76	7	11	231	288	329	617	7%	78%	0.37	65	2.97	11
Clark,Howie	02	29	8	aaa	BAL	418	47	110	18	3	6	35	33	27	3	5	263	317	364	681	7%	94%	1.22	67	4.04	40
Clark,Jermaine	01	25	4	aaa	SEA	216	31	47	6	2	1	23	25	36	11	2	215	296	275	571	10%	83%	0.68	40	3.06	2
	02	26	4	aaa	TEX	425	44	100	14	4	5	29	51	53	26	18	235	317	322	640	11%	88%	0.96	56	3.40	21
Clemente,Edgard	01	26	8	a/a	BOS	345	33	83	16	1	11	36	22	78	2	1	241	286	387	674	6%	77%	0.28	92	3.86	24
	02	27	8	aaa	MIL	373	33	82	17	1	8	35	20	92	5	1	220	260	335	595	5%	75%	0.22	76	2.98	9
Closser,J.D.	02	23	2	aa	COL	315	31	85	25	1	12	45	32	46	6	4	270	337	470	807	9%	85%	0.70	132	5.66	58
Coffie,Ivanon	01	24	5	aaa	BAL	206	31	51	8	1	8	32	14	44	3	0	248	295	413	708	6%	79%	0.32	99	4.38	30
	02	25	5	aaa	CHC	373	38	72	26	3	5	36	29	46	1	6	193	251	319	570	7%	88%	0.63	90	2.49	14
Colangelo,Mike	01	25	8	a/a	SD	214	29	51	10	1	3	23	29	49	4	3	238	329	336	666	12%	77%	0.59	67	3.97	19
	02	26	8	aaa	OAK	217	16	38	7	0	0	16	24	26	2	4	175	257	207	465	10%	88%	0.92	29	1.75	-11
Coleman,Michael	01	26	8	aaa	NYY	101	14	21	3	2	4	14	11	30	3	3	211	287	394	680	10%	70%	0.36	102	3.55	20
	02	27	8	aaa	BOS	204	22	42	7	1	7	18	23	51	0	0	206	286	353	639	10%	75%	0.45	88	3.51	14
Cole,Eric	01	26	8	aaa	HOU	397	40	98	25	2	3	35	32	82	1	4	247	303	342	644	7%	79%	0.39	71	3.56	19
	02	27	8	a/a	TEX	397	30	83	19	2	5	32	21	78	2	3	209	249	305	554	5%	80%	0.27	66	2.48	2

Major League Equivalent Statistics

BATTER	Yr	Age	Pos	Lev	Org	AB	R	H	D	T	HR	RBI	BB	K	SB	CS	BA	OB	Slg	OPS	bb%	ct%	Eye	PX	RC/G	BPV
Colina,Javier	02	24	4	a/a	COL	458	39	107	26	3	4	32	20	47	3	6	234	266	330	595	4%	90%	0.43	70	2.85	15
Collier,Lou	01	28	8	aaa	MIL	312	36	75	15	1	10	27	19	55	7	4	241	284	393	678	6%	82%	0.34	96	3.79	27
	02	29	8	aaa	MON	307	38	84	25	4	5	41	29	65	4	2	274	336	430	766	9%	79%	0.45	109	5.30	45
Collins,Mike	02	26	4	aa	LA	384	34	101	12	1	0	39	38	39	6	1	263	329	299	629	9%	90%	0.97	30	3.76	20
Connacher,Kevin	02	28	4	aa	MIN	356	33	67	21	2	8	32	28	88	17	9	188	247	326	573	7%	75%	0.32	92	2.53	7
Connors,Greg	01	27	3	aa	SEA	455	51	81	10	3	7	51	25	108	4	5	177	220	263	482	5%	76%	0.23	51	1.80	-15
	02	28	38	a/a	SEA	366	33	71	24	0	8	47	25	80	3	3	194	246	325	571	6%	78%	0.31	92	2.59	9
Conti,Jason	01	27	8	aaa	ARI	519	71	147	32	4	10	53	32	68	4	7	284	326	417	742	6%	87%	0.47	90	4.79	41
Cookson,Brent	01	32	8	aaa	LA	190	21	41	9	1	8	32	14	30	1	1	213	269	398	666	7%	84%	0.48	112	3.57	27
Coolbaugh,Mike	01	29	5	aaa	MIL	347	36	76	20	2	7	37	29	80	2	2	220	281	351	632	8%	77%	0.36	88	3.37	17
	02	30	5	aaa	STL	411	47	82	16	1	23	57	41	117	7	3	200	272	411	683	9%	72%	0.35	123	3.74	24
Coquillette,Trace	01	27	84	aaa	DET	263	31	47	10	3	6	25	25	54	1	2	177	248	303	551	9%	80%	0.46	78	2.44	1
	02	28	58	a/a	PIT	254	26	41	10	1	4	24	20	68	2	4	161	223	256	479	7%	73%	0.29	63	1.74	-14
Cordido,Julio	01	21	5	aa	SF	433	39	85	13	1	1	41	26	57	10	3	196	242	238	480	6%	87%	0.46	32	1.97	-12
Coste,Chris	01	29	2	a/a	CLE	295	27	72	14	2	7	42	13	48	0	2	243	275	369	644	4%	84%	0.27	82	3.41	20
	02	30	3	aaa	CLE	478	49	134	28	1	7	56	28	55	0	0	280	320	387	707	6%	88%	0.51	76	4.56	35
Cota,Humberto	01	23	2	aaa	PIT	377	51	105	21	1	12	61	21	56	6	2	279	317	432	748	5%	85%	0.37	99	4.97	41
	02	24	2	aaa	PIT	404	42	99	26	1	7	45	25	82	4	9	245	289	366	655	6%	80%	0.30	86	3.41	23
Cotton,John	01	31	53	a/a	PIT	317	30	60	12	1	14	38	17	91	3	4	190	232	361	592	5%	71%	0.19	101	2.60	9
Cox,Darron	01	34	2	aaa	COL	209	21	48	8	1	3	15	15	30	2	1	228	281	314	595	7%	86%	0.51	58	3.07	10
Crawford,Carl	01	20	8	aa	TAM	537	64	149	25	3	4	51	37	81	36	22	278	324	360	684	6%	85%	0.45	59	3.93	26
	02	21	8	aaa	TAM	353	56	109	19	9	7	50	19	55	25	10	309	344	473	817	5%	84%	0.35	101	5.89	51
Crede,Joe	01	23	5	aaa	CHW	463	61	123	32	1	18	59	43	79	2	1	266	328	456	784	8%	83%	0.54	123	5.44	50
	02	24	5	aaa	CHW	359	50	107	19	0	24	57	25	43	0	1	298	344	552	895	7%	88%	0.58	150	7.03	73
Crespo,Cesar	01	22	48	aaa	SD	273	42	66	17	2	7	26	34	58	21	3	242	325	400	725	11%	79%	0.58	103	4.93	35
	02	23	4	aaa	SD	322	37	73	15	1	7	32	43	70	18	8	227	318	345	663	12%	78%	0.61	78	3.86	20
Cresse,Brad	01	23	2	aa	ARI	429	41	107	35	1	10	60	32	89	0	1	249	301	402	703	7%	79%	0.36	109	4.27	35
	02	24	2	a/a	ARI	366	36	78	22	0	4	28	15	85	1	0	213	244	306	550	4%	77%	0.18	70	2.52	3
Cridland,Mark	01	26	8	aa	MIL	234	20	44	7	1	5	25	10	57	3	3	190	221	294	515	4%	75%	0.17	64	1.99	-7
Cromer,D.T.	01	31	3	aaa	CIN	242	25	58	11	1	8	36	12	42	3	2	238	273	390	664	5%	83%	0.28	95	3.61	24
Cromer,Tripp	02	35	3	aaa	HOU	265	24	59	12	2	6	21	7	42	0	0	223	243	351	594	3%	84%	0.17	82	2.85	11
Crosby,Bobby	02	23	6	aa	OAK	228	27	57	14	0	6	27	16	35	8	2	250	299	390	690	7%	85%	0.46	95	4.17	32
Crosby,Bubba	01	25	8	a/a	LA	426	60	107	20	4	5	44	32	61	19	8	251	303	351	654	7%	86%	0.52	67	3.73	22
	02	26	8	a/a	LA	429	29	87	14	2	8	41	22	63	7	5	203	242	301	542	5%	85%	0.35	62	2.34	0
Crozier,Eric	02	24	3	aa	CLE	142	16	38	8	1	1	11	18	47	1	0	268	350	359	709	11%	67%	0.38	67	4.82	24
Cruz,Ivan	02	34	3	aaa	STL	461	63	106	22	0	28	77	40	90	0	0	230	291	460	751	8%	80%	0.44	136	4.66	42
Cuddyer,Michael	01	23	53	aa	MIN	509	95	153	38	3	29	87	74	105	5	9	301	389	558	947	13%	79%	0.70	159	7.99	80
	02	24	8	aaa	MIN	330	51	90	15	6	14	39	26	59	9	9	273	326	482	808	7%	82%	0.44	122	5.25	50
Cummings,Midre	01	30	8	aaa	ARI	263	27	72	20	5	4	27	17	42	2	4	273	318	433	751	6%	84%	0.41	107	4.76	44
Cunningham,Marco	02	25	8	aa	KC	215	32	34	6	0	4	23	28	37	11	8	158	255	242	497	12%	83%	0.76	54	1.95	-10
Curl,John	01	29	3	aa	SEA	174	17	32	5	0	4	14	18	56	2	1	184	259	280	539	9%	68%	0.31	60	2.48	-8
Curry,Chris	01	24	2	aa	CHC	108	8	19	3	0	1	9	10	31	0	0	180	247	234	481	8%	71%	0.31	38	1.97	-18
Curry,Mike	01	25	8	a/a	NYM	433	60	110	15	3	5	26	43	108	23	19	254	321	337	659	9%	75%	0.40	55	3.55	15
	02	26	8	a/a	CIN	263	30	58	8	1	1	11	31	47	10	7	221	303	270	573	11%	82%	0.66	36	2.83	2
Cust,Jack	01	23	8	aaa	ARI	442	67	116	23	1	21	65	84	118	5	4	261	379	461	840	16%	73%	0.71	122	6.54	52
	02	24	8	aaa	COL	359	47	87	21	0	19	35	53	71	4	4	242	340	460	799	13%	80%	0.75	134	5.52	51
Dalesandro,Mark	01	33	2	aaa	CHW	262	14	59	15	0	4	19	5	24	0	1	223	239	323	562	2%	91%	0.22	73	2.53	9
	02	34	2	aaa	CHW	160	10	30	6	0	2	8	5	13	0	0	188	212	263	475	3%	92%	0.38	53	1.80	-8
Dallimore,Brian	01	28	5	aa	ARI	517	47	125	29	3	5	42	19	51	7	13	242	269	340	610	4%	90%	0.38	70	2.84	17
	02	29	5	aaa	ARI	419	44	103	22	2	5	35	20	56	9	5	246	280	344	624	5%	87%	0.36	69	3.29	18
Darula,Bobby	02	28	8	a/a	CIN	372	37	93	16	2	3	29	34	26	7	3	250	313	328	641	8%	93%	1.31	55	3.71	32
DaVanon,Jeff	01	28	8	aaa	ANA	256	33	67	16	5	8	35	23	44	6	4	263	324	453	776	8%	83%	0.52	118	5.13	47
	02	29	8	aaa	ANA	100	15	27	8	1	4	13	12	19	4	4	270	348	490	838	11%	81%	0.63	142	5.61	61
Davidson,Cleatus	01	25	6	aa	SD	467	34	88	15	3	2	29	19	104	11	9	189	221	246	467	4%	78%	0.18	41	1.68	-17
	02	26	40	aa	NYY	118	15	24	2	2	1	15	9	26	5	6	203	260	280	540	7%	78%	0.35	43	2.06	-7
Davis,Glenn	01	26	3	aa	LA	478	52	95	23	5	17	75	56	156	12	5	200	283	378	662	10%	67%	0.36	109	3.65	19
	02	27	3	aa	MON	114	12	24	3	1	5	12	11	31	1	1	211	280	386	666	9%	73%	0.35	99	3.61	18
Davis,J.J.	01	23	8	aa	PIT	228	19	54	13	2	4	24	19	73	2	5	237	296	364	660	8%	68%	0.26	85	3.49	19
	02	24	8	aa	PIT	348	41	88	16	2	15	49	26	80	6	5	253	305	440	744	7%	77%	0.33	113	4.57	37
Davis,Tommy	01	28	3	aaa	CIN	396	36	92	22	1	5	35	21	83	1	1	233	272	329	601	5%	79%	0.26	70	3.07	12
	02	29	20	aaa	CLE	289	22	66	14	1	9	42	5	71	0	1	228	241	377	619	2%	75%	0.07	94	2.99	16
Dawkins,Travis	01	22	6	aa	CIN	394	47	81	15	2	7	32	26	68	11	5	206	255	307	562	6%	83%	0.38	66	2.60	3
	02	23	6	a/a	CIN	322	28	76	15	2	1	16	28	47	6	9	236	297	304	601	8%	85%	0.60	52	2.94	12
De La Rosa,Tomas	01	24	8	aaa	MON	420	51	94	23	0	7	27	35	58	11	10	224	284	329	612	8%	86%	0.60	74	3.03	17
	02	25	65	aaa	MON	351	33	73	17	1	3	29	22	44	9	6	208	255	288	542	6%	87%	0.50	59	2.39	4
De Los Santos,Eddy	01	24	4	aa	TAM	415	31	100	13	1	2	35	20	58	13	11	241	276	290	566	5%	86%	0.35	36	2.60	2
De Los Santos,Luis	02	25	3	aaa	BAL	187	18	45	7	1	5	14	12	39	0	0	241	286	369	655	6%	79%	0.31	79	3.71	19
De Renne,Keoni	02	23	4	aa	ATL	320	42	77	22	2	2	38	32	33	2	5	241	310	341	650	9%	90%	0.97	76	3.60	31
Deardorff,Jeff	01	23	8	aa	MIL	201	27	51	11	1	13	39	12	61	1	1	256	297	507	803	5%	70%	0.19	148	5.21	50
	02	24	8	aa	MIL	425	57	96	20	1	16	50	48	117	10	7	226	304	391	695	10%	72%	0.41	102	4.04	26
DeCinces,Tim	01	27	2	a/a	SD	198	10	32	4	1	3	21	16	37	0	0	163	226	235	461	8%	81%	0.44	44	1.77	-19
DeHaan,Kory	01	25	8	a/a	SD	463	56	111	15	5	9	46	35	94	22	14	239	292	351	643	7%	80%	0.37	68	3.37	15
	02	26	8	aaa	SD	442	54	108	26	10	2	33	26	90	19	10	244	286	362	648	6%	80%	0.29	79	3.47	20
DeLeon,Jorge	01	27	5	a/a	BOS	141	13	29	8	2	1	10	11	18	2	1	209	268	310	578	7%	87%	0.64	70	2.83	11
Delgado,Wilson	01	26	4	aaa	KC	255	18	56	10	1	3	23	12	33	6	3	221	255	301	555	4%	87%	0.35	55	2.55	3
	02	30	6	aaa	STL	365	23	77	15	1	5	27	18	50	2	5	211	248	299	547	5%	86%	0.36	60	2.35	2
Dellaero,Jason	01	25	6	aaa	CHW	377	29	64	9	0	11	25	16	101	4	4	170	204	281	485	4%	73%	0.16	66	1.75	-13
	02	26	65	a/a	CHW	264	26	52	11	1	9	26	10	76	5	4	197	226	348	575	4%	71%	0.13	93	2.43	7
Demetral,Chris	01	32	4	aaa	TEX	322	25	63	10	1	2	21	26	28	1	1	196	256	249	505	7%	91%	0.94	38	2.17	-0
Dent,Darrell	01	24	8	aa	LA	376	45	91	12	1	4	29	37	95	28	12	243	310	311	621	9%	75%	0.39	47	3.39	8
Depastino,Joe	02	29	2	aaa	NYM	248	19	61	13	2	4	22	10	47	4	0	246	275	363	638	4%	81%	0.21	78	3.55	19

Major League Equivalent Statistics

BATTER	Yr	Age	Pos	Lev	Org	AB	R	H	D	T	HR	RBI	BB	K	SB	CS	BA	OB	Slg	OPS	bb%	ct%	Eye	PX	RC/G	BPV
Depippo,Jeff	01	25	2	aa	CLE	240	26	54	9	2	5	23	12	49	5	8	225	261	345	606	5%	80%	0.24	75	2.65	11
DeRenne,Keoni	01	22	46	aa	ATL	453	38	102	14	2	3	38	41	51	4	2	225	289	285	574	8%	89%	0.80	42	2.92	8
DeRosa,Mark	01	27	6	aaa	ATL	186	27	50	16	0	2	15	16	20	6	3	271	327	391	718	8%	89%	0.79	95	4.60	45
Derosso,Tony	02	27	5	aa	PIT	182	16	27	4	2	5	23	19	43	2	0	148	229	275	504	9%	76%	0.44	72	2.11	-12
	01	26	5	aa	SD	312	24	60	18	0	7	36	22	61	0	1	193	246	320	566	6%	80%	0.35	87	2.59	7
Deschaine,Jim	02	25	5	aa	TOR	405	41	72	12	0	11	46	35	72	2	4	178	243	289	532	8%	82%	0.49	68	2.25	-3
Devore,Doug	01	24	8	aa	ARI	476	49	121	28	7	11	54	34	91	8	4	255	304	410	714	7%	81%	0.37	100	4.39	33
	02	25	8	aaa	ARI	436	44	103	18	5	11	44	20	74	7	7	236	270	376	646	4%	83%	0.27	86	3.30	20
Dewey,Jason	01	24	2	aa	COL	243	19	56	20	0	6	22	19	66	1	0	231	286	383	670	7%	73%	0.29	109	3.85	28
	02	25	2	a/a	COL	358	31	76	22	0	10	41	18	67	3	5	212	250	358	608	5%	81%	0.27	98	2.82	16
Diaz,Alejandro	02	24	8	aa	CIN	150	10	29	7	2	1	14	9	26	5	2	193	239	287	526	6%	83%	0.35	63	2.25	-2
Diaz,Angel	01	25	2	a/a	ANA	143	17	33	10	0	3	15	6	22	0	1	228	259	360	619	4%	84%	0.27	93	3.07	20
Diaz,Edwin	01	27	45	aaa	MIN	381	45	91	23	2	8	43	18	52	2	7	239	274	372	646	5%	86%	0.36	90	3.26	24
Diaz,Juan	01	26	3	aaa	BOS	279	38	68	16	1	15	44	14	73	0	0	245	281	468	749	5%	74%	0.19	136	4.56	41
	02	29	3	aaa	BOS	389	37	86	13	0	15	42	19	97	0	0	221	257	370	628	5%	75%	0.20	89	3.23	14
Diaz,Maikell	02	24	6	a/a	BAL	153	11	21	3	2	0	9	5	28	2	1	137	165	183	348	3%	82%	0.18	29	0.92	-39
Diaz,Matt	02	25	8	aa	TAM	449	58	109	26	1	9	41	28	66	26	10	243	287	365	652	6%	85%	0.42	84	3.58	24
Diaz,Miguel	01	24	8	aa	STL	117	6	29	4	1	0	6	4	20	2	5	244	267	292	560	3%	83%	0.19	36	2.26	-0
Diaz,Victor	02	21	3	aa	LA	152	22	32	6	0	4	24	7	39	7	5	211	245	329	574	4%	74%	0.18	76	2.42	5
Dillon,Joe	01	26	35	aa	KC	369	42	85	16	2	10	40	23	51	3	3	231	277	368	645	6%	86%	0.46	86	3.41	22
	02	27	50	a/a	MIN	362	35	73	17	2	6	37	37	59	3	1	202	276	309	585	9%	84%	0.63	72	2.96	10
Dina,Allen	01	28	8	a/a	NYM	281	27	63	15	1	2	31	14	55	7	7	225	262	304	566	5%	80%	0.25	60	2.54	5
	02	29	8	aa	FLA	182	21	31	11	1	4	12	5	36	3	3	170	193	308	500	3%	80%	0.14	92	1.72	-2
DiSarcina,Gary	02	35	4	aaa	BOS	144	17	30	10	2	1	7	6	14	0	1	208	240	326	566	4%	90%	0.43	84	2.51	13
Dishington,Nate	01	27	8	aa	STL	129	10	21	4	0	6	17	6	66	1	0	162	200	337	537	5%	49%	0.09	103	2.14	-2
Dodson,Jeremy	01	24	8	aa	KC	113	10	20	1	1	1	5	8	24	2	0	177	228	227	455	6%	79%	0.31	28	1.79	-23
Dominique,Andy	01	26	23	a/a	PHI	396	50	90	25	0	12	57	45	75	3	1	228	306	380	686	10%	81%	0.60	102	4.12	30
	02	27	3	aa	BOS	361	27	77	17	1	5	35	23	54	2	1	213	260	307	568	6%	85%	0.43	66	2.72	7
Donnels,Chris	01	35	3	aaa	LA	137	12	23	4	0	5	17	14	21	0	1	171	245	296	541	9%	85%	0.64	74	2.34	0
Donovan,Todd	02	24	8	aa	SD	114	14	21	4	1	2	8	12	31	5	3	184	262	289	551	10%	73%	0.39	66	2.45	-4
Doster,David	02	32	4	aaa	PHI	579	69	142	26	7	7	69	32	87	7	3	245	285	351	635	5%	85%	0.37	69	3.49	18
Dransfeldt,Kelly	01	26	6	aaa	TEX	551	62	124	27	4	8	51	42	95	10	10	225	280	331	611	7%	83%	0.44	72	3.05	13
	02	27	6	aaa	TEX	507	43	98	18	5	10	48	31	102	7	4	193	240	308	547	6%	80%	0.30	71	2.41	-0
Duncan,Carlos	02	25	4	aa	ANA	215	23	50	9	1	5	17	8	40	12	5	233	260	353	614	4%	81%	0.20	77	3.01	13
Dunn,Adam	01	22	8	a/a	CIN	350	66	120	23	0	30	75	57	59	10	6	343	435	663	1098	14%	83%	0.97	190	11.50	112
Dunwoody,Todd	01	27	8	aaa	CHC	251	26	60	15	2	6	26	15	68	5	5	240	281	383	664	5%	73%	0.21	94	3.51	23
	02	28	8	aaa	CLE	363	49	88	29	3	7	26	10	61	7	3	242	263	397	659	3%	83%	0.16	108	3.51	29
Durham,Chad	02	24	8	aa	CHW	366	53	90	10	1	0	30	33	69	33	19	246	308	279	587	8%	81%	0.48	27	2.88	3
Durrington,Trent	01	26	4	a/a	ANA	359	50	91	23	3	11	44	34	69	24	8	254	318	424	743	9%	81%	0.49	111	4.80	40
	02	27	28	a/a	ANA	450	45	84	17	3	9	39	29	77	19	16	187	236	298	534	6%	83%	0.38	70	2.05	-1
Eberwein,Kevin	02	26	5	aaa	SD	320	28	57	15	0	10	31	27	92	0	1	178	242	319	561	8%	71%	0.29	90	2.52	2
Echevarria,Angel	02	31	8	aaa	CHC	217	25	49	9	2	8	29	11	39	0	0	226	263	396	659	5%	82%	0.28	102	3.55	23
Eckelman,Alex	01	27	458	aa	STL	411	25	67	13	0	4	29	17	77	11	4	164	196	226	422	4%	81%	0.22	44	1.41	-23
Edwards,Mike	01	25	3	a/a	CLE	120	20	37	7	2	6	22	12	25	0	0	308	371	550	921	9%	79%	0.48	144	7.88	72
	02	26	8	a/a	CIN	481	48	133	23	2	10	51	34	53	7	12	277	324	395	719	7%	89%	0.64	78	4.32	37
Ellison,Jason	02	25	8	aaa	SF	196	28	56	8	1	2	7	19	24	14	3	286	349	367	716	9%	88%	0.79	56	5.03	34
Ellis,Mark	01	24	8	aaa	OAK	472	56	111	32	0	8	42	43	62	17	9	235	299	354	653	8%	87%	0.69	86	3.63	28
Encarnacion,Angelo	01	28	2	aaa	BOS	155	13	36	5	1	1	8	6	15	1	0	234	261	294	555	3%	90%	0.37	41	2.66	2
Encarnacion,Mario	01	24	8	aaa	OAK	231	29	61	11	1	11	34	17	55	3	5	264	315	463	778	7%	76%	0.31	120	4.85	44
	02	27	8	aaa	CHC	200	16	45	7	0	5	19	11	46	0	3	225	265	335	600	5%	77%	0.24	70	2.83	9
Ensberg,Morgan	01	26	5	aaa	HOU	316	53	90	19	0	20	50	37	54	5	3	285	360	540	900	10%	83%	0.69	154	7.17	72
	02	27	5	aaa	HOU	292	42	77	11	3	7	31	42	53	8	5	264	356	394	750	13%	82%	0.79	80	5.15	37
Erickson,Corey	01	25	5	a/a	CLE	489	61	105	27	2	21	58	29	115	6	4	215	259	407	666	6%	76%	0.25	119	3.46	26
	02	26	5	aa	CLE	345	40	68	18	2	17	51	27	101	3	3	197	255	409	664	7%	71%	0.27	128	3.37	24
Erickson,Matt	01	26	46	aaa	FLA	413	45	103	17	1	1	19	26	53	8	5	249	294	303	597	6%	87%	0.50	43	3.11	11
	02	27	4	aaa	FLA	379	44	87	25	2	1	19	22	51	10	5	230	272	314	586	5%	87%	0.43	67	2.89	13
Escobar,Alex	01	23	8	aaa	NYM	397	51	99	20	3	10	48	32	142	17	3	249	305	390	696	7%	64%	0.23	90	4.35	25
Espada,Joe	02	27	4	aaa	KC	223	14	44	10	0	0	18	14	21	10	5	197	245	242	487	6%	91%	0.67	40	1.95	-5
Espada,Josue	01	26	6	aaa	COL	317	46	83	19	1	4	21	30	37	11	11	263	327	367	694	9%	88%	0.81	76	4.01	35
Espy,Nate	02	24	3	aa	PHI	517	66	120	27	2	11	60	61	78	14	1	232	313	356	669	11%	85%	0.78	83	4.13	27
Estalella,Bobby	01	27	2	aaa	SF	193	21	41	10	1	8	29	15	41	0	3	212	269	389	658	7%	79%	0.37	109	3.32	23
Estrada,Johnny	01	25	2	aaa	PHI	131	12	38	15	0	0	15	5	6	0	0	287	313	401	714	4%	95%	0.82	100	4.60	53
	02	26	2	aaa	PHI	434	40	108	26	0	9	54	22	49	1	0	249	285	371	656	5%	89%	0.45	85	3.73	27
Evans,Lee	01	24	258	aa	PIT	428	47	96	19	6	10	43	32	114	10	5	224	279	362	640	7%	73%	0.28	85	3.43	16
	02	25	52	a/a	CHW	308	34	68	18	2	8	25	19	88	4	1	221	266	370	636	6%	71%	0.22	98	3.37	18
Evans,Tom	01	27	5	aaa	DET	169	21	39	11	1	3	15	20	26	1	3	230	312	360	671	11%	84%	0.76	91	3.78	29
Everett,Adam	01	25	6	aaa	HOU	441	58	103	20	6	5	34	33	64	20	6	234	287	340	627	7%	85%	0.52	70	3.44	17
	02	26	6	aaa	HOU	345	45	91	16	7	2	22	21	54	11	3	264	306	368	674	6%	84%	0.39	68	4.08	24
Fagan,Shawn	02	25	3	aa	TOR	421	52	96	22	0	9	50	75	71	5	4	228	345	344	689	15%	83%	1.06	79	4.36	30
Faison,Vince	02	22	8	aa	SD	359	36	82	20	4	6	40	35	97	5	8	228	297	357	654	9%	73%	0.36	85	3.46	18
Farnsworth,Troy	01	26	53	aa	STL	422	39	83	18	1	16	58	25	109	4	7	196	242	358	600	6%	74%	0.23	99	2.65	11
Fasano,Sal	01	30	2	aaa	KC	128	16	30	5	0	6	22	9	31	0	0	232	282	415	697	7%	76%	0.29	107	4.06	27
	02	31	2	aaa	ANA	173	13	32	9	0	5	14	6	39	1	0	185	212	324	536	3%	77%	0.15	91	2.23	2
Feliciano,Jesus	02	23	8	aa	LA	245	29	52	5	1	0	12	12	28	9	11	212	249	241	490	5%	89%	0.43	22	1.72	-12
Fernandez,Alex	02	21	8	a/a	SD	489	46	134	21	0	8	68	12	71	25	13	274	291	366	657	2%	85%	0.17	63	3.59	21
Fernandez,Jose	01	27	5	aaa	ANA	452	74	133	32	1	23	84	41	69	7	9	294	352	524	876	8%	85%	0.59	144	6.53	69
Figga,Mike	01	31	2	a/a	NYM	146	12	25	5	0	5	18	3	37	0	1	173	188	302	490	2%	75%	0.07	80	1.70	-8
Figgins,Chone	01	24	4	aa	ANA	470	47	95	22	5	2	28	41	76	26	12	202	266	283	549	8%	84%	0.53	58	2.52	2
	02	25	4	aaa	ANA	511	77	136	22	9	6	47	40	62	30	10	266	319	380	699	7%	88%	0.65	72	4.39	31
Figueroa,Franky	01	25	3	aa	BAL	534	52	139	26	0	12	62	19	132	0	4	260	285	377	662	3%	75%	0.14	78	3.67	22
	02	26	3	a/a	BAL	229	26	53	8	1	3	27	9	47	0	0	231	261	314	575	4%	79%	0.19	55	2.81	4

Major League Equivalent Statistics

BATTER	Yr	Age	Pos	Lev	Org	AB	R	H	D	T	HR	RBI	BB	K	SB	CS	BA	OB	Slg	OPS	bb%	ct%	Eye	PX	RC/G	BPV
Figueroa,Luis	01	25	5	a/a	SEA	140	12	31	5	0	0	12	4	13	1	1	221	243	257	500	3%	91%	0.31	32	2.06	-7
	02	26	5	aa	SEA	180	23	52	12	0	1	23	22	16	2	1	289	366	372	739	11%	91%	1.38	68	5.27	52
Figueroa,Luis	01	28	64	aaa	PIT	405	40	102	12	1	4	26	28	27	6	6	251	299	314	613	6%	93%	1.01	44	3.24	22
	02	29	6	a/a	MON	336	37	63	15	3	2	27	20	29	4	9	188	233	268	501	6%	91%	0.69	57	1.83	-0
Fiore,Curtis	02	25	8	aa	ATL	319	31	72	17	1	6	31	29	43	3	0	226	290	342	632	8%	87%	0.67	79	3.54	21
Fischer,Mark	01	25	8	aa	BOS	463	37	87	19	2	7	42	19	140	3	1	189	220	284	504	4%	70%	0.14	64	2.04	-8
	02	26	8	aa	BOS	131	11	15	4	0	2	6	8	39	2	1	115	165	191	356	6%	70%	0.21	51	0.97	-37
Fitzgerald,Jason	01	26	8	aa	CLE	239	18	54	10	1	3	15	8	38	8	2	226	250	320	571	3%	84%	0.21	64	2.74	6
	02	27	8	a/a	CLE	405	36	88	21	0	10	46	32	91	17	7	217	275	343	618	7%	78%	0.35	84	3.18	14
Flaherty,Tim	02	26	2	aa	SF	247	17	42	9	2	3	25	21	77	0	1	170	235	259	494	8%	69%	0.27	58	1.99	-14
Fleming,Ryan	01	26	8	aa	TOR	349	44	82	17	3	8	27	29	46	5	6	235	293	369	662	8%	87%	0.63	86	3.57	26
	02	27	8	a/a	TOR	298	30	64	14	0	3	28	21	24	3	5	215	266	292	558	7%	92%	0.88	57	2.52	13
Flores,Javier	01	26	2	aa	TEX	116	6	23	4	1	0	8	7	9	2	2	202	248	248	497	6%	92%	0.81	34	2.00	-2
Flores,Jose	01	28	654	aaa	COL	316	39	79	18	3	2	23	32	40	5	3	250	318	341	660	9%	87%	0.79	66	3.91	27
	02	29	6	aaa	OAK	363	44	86	15	1	1	25	38	44	11	5	237	309	292	601	9%	88%	0.86	43	3.26	14
Forbes,P.J.	01	34	468	aaa	PHI	514	67	139	31	2	4	51	42	81	5	0	270	325	357	682	8%	84%	0.52	67	4.35	28
	02	35	8	aaa	PHI	355	34	80	16	1	1	32	18	47	3	1	225	263	285	547	5%	87%	0.38	47	2.58	2
Ford,Lew	01	25	8	aa	MIN	252	27	50	8	3	6	23	18	39	5	5	196	250	325	575	7%	85%	0.46	77	2.56	6
	02	26	8	a/a	MIN	566	85	147	33	3	14	52	43	61	20	6	260	312	403	715	7%	89%	0.70	95	4.52	40
Foster,Quincy	01	27	8	aa	FLA	200	29	36	2	2	2	11	21	36	19	8	178	256	231	487	9%	82%	0.59	29	2.01	-17
	02	28	8	aa	MON	264	27	56	7	2	2	22	12	41	17	12	212	246	277	523	4%	84%	0.29	42	2.00	-6
Fox,Jason	01	25	8	aa	MIL	289	29	64	10	2	3	25	16	69	17	7	220	262	296	557	5%	76%	0.23	50	2.60	-1
	02	26	8	aa	MIL	147	9	23	5	2	0	13	5	33	3	1	156	184	218	402	3%	78%	0.15	42	1.26	-27
Francia,Dave	01	26	8	aaa	PHI	347	31	75	15	2	3	33	23	61	17	7	215	265	294	558	6%	82%	0.38	55	2.63	2
	02	27	8	aaa	PHI	117	10	22	7	1	1	8	4	18	3	2	188	215	291	505	3%	85%	0.22	74	1.91	-2
Franco,Matt	01	32	53	aaa	NYM	433	41	89	22	1	6	39	42	78	5	2	206	276	303	580	9%	82%	0.54	69	2.91	8
	02	33	3	aaa	ATL	173	19	41	9	0	5	23	11	18	1	0	237	283	376	658	6%	90%	0.61	91	3.73	29
Franklin,Micah	01	29	85	aaa	MIL	331	40	62	10	3	17	46	35	63	1	3	187	264	390	654	9%	81%	0.55	115	3.34	21
	02	30	8	aaa	ARI	311	43	72	15	0	12	41	32	59	4	4	232	303	395	699	9%	81%	0.54	102	4.08	30
Frank,Mike	01	27	8	aaa	NYY	356	37	81	17	1	9	44	34	45	9	3	226	294	354	648	9%	87%	0.75	84	3.65	25
	02	28	8	a/a	STL	324	26	71	10	2	6	34	19	24	7	3	219	262	318	580	6%	93%	0.79	61	2.82	14
Freel,Ryan	01	26	8	aaa	TOR	319	50	77	21	2	4	28	35	35	19	10	242	316	357	673	10%	89%	0.98	82	3.87	34
	02	27	4	aaa	TAM	448	54	107	25	4	7	41	31	46	31	11	239	288	359	647	6%	90%	0.67	81	3.56	27
Freeman,Choo	02	23	8	aa	COL	430	58	120	17	5	11	46	46	68	11	16	279	349	419	767	10%	84%	0.68	85	4.87	42
Freire,Alejandro	01	27	8	aa	DET	501	51	113	27	0	10	57	32	105	2	2	225	271	338	609	6%	79%	0.30	78	3.10	13
	02	28	3	a/a	SF	322	26	68	14	1	8	29	25	67	0	2	211	268	335	603	7%	79%	0.37	80	2.99	11
Frese,Nate	01	24	6	aa	CHC	233	20	35	4	1	3	15	30	57	0	1	151	249	212	461	12%	76%	0.53	37	1.80	-24
	02	25	6	aa	CHC	230	19	43	8	1	2	14	19	59	4	3	187	249	257	506	8%	74%	0.32	48	2.10	-11
Frias,Hanley	01	28	64	aaa	STL	382	31	69	11	1	2	20	21	62	6	8	182	224	231	455	5%	84%	0.34	36	1.58	-18
	02	29	64	aaa	ARI	427	44	91	16	6	4	26	22	47	5	2	213	252	307	558	5%	89%	0.47	60	2.60	5
Frye,Jeff	02	36	45	aaa	HOU	397	36	98	13	0	1	19	26	37	4	4	247	293	287	580	6%	91%	0.70	33	2.93	10
Furniss,Eddy	01	26	3	aa	OAK	132	8	24	8	1	1	9	13	39	0	0	185	258	277	535	9%	70%	0.33	69	2.44	-4
Gallagher,Shawn	01	25	3	aa	KC	345	32	80	17	3	10	35	18	47	4	8	231	270	380	650	5%	86%	0.38	94	3.20	23
Gall,John	02	25	3	aa	STL	526	62	141	38	2	16	62	30	62	3	1	268	308	439	747	5%	88%	0.48	114	4.85	46
Gandolfo,Rob	02	25	4	a/a	SEA	201	16	35	4	1	1	14	14	25	1	3	174	228	219	447	7%	88%	0.56	30	1.55	-18
Gann,Jamie	01	26	8	a/a	ARI	205	16	39	5	0	2	16	5	34	4	4	189	208	241	449	2%	83%	0.14	36	1.50	-19
Garabito,Eddy	01	23	46	aaa	BAL	517	63	132	26	4	3	34	32	68	23	13	256	299	341	640	6%	87%	0.47	62	3.48	20
	02	26	6	aaa	BAL	434	46	100	18	3	3	28	21	43	10	9	230	266	306	572	5%	90%	0.49	54	2.63	9
Garcia,Amaury	01	26	4	aaa	CHW	118	8	25	4	1	0	6	7	24	4	0	214	257	263	520	5%	80%	0.29	36	2.46	-8
Garcia,Carlos	01	34	5	aaa	NYY	215	17	45	10	0	3	14	11	37	6	1	209	247	293	540	5%	83%	0.29	60	2.51	0
Garcia,Douglas	02	23	8	a/a	TEX	153	8	40	8	0	1	15	2	28	0	0	261	271	333	604	1%	82%	0.07	56	3.15	12
Garcia,Jesse	01	28	6	aaa	ATL	375	42	87	20	2	2	19	19	52	15	7	233	269	310	579	5%	86%	0.36	58	2.82	9
	02	29	4	aaa	ATL	230	24	58	10	1	5	14	13	31	7	5	252	292	370	662	5%	87%	0.42	76	3.60	24
Garcia,Karim	01	26	8	aaa	CLE	462	63	115	15	3	29	74	39	91	4	4	249	307	480	787	8%	80%	0.42	130	5.07	45
	02	27	8	aaa	CLE	379	53	107	21	4	15	63	26	60	1	6	282	328	478	806	6%	84%	0.43	120	5.42	52
Garcia,Luis	02	27	8	aaa	BAL	339	19	70	11	1	3	26	6	42	1	1	206	220	271	492	2%	88%	0.14	45	1.93	-10
Garcia,Luis	01	23	3	aa	BOS	229	30	67	19	1	11	39	23	59	0	1	293	357	528	886	9%	74%	0.39	152	7.02	68
	02	24	8	aa	CLE	474	57	120	23	1	16	50	39	80	4	2	253	310	407	717	8%	83%	0.49	97	4.50	34
Garcia,Luis	01	26	6	aaa	STL	422	32	92	17	1	6	34	7	60	2	1	218	231	306	536	2%	86%	0.11	60	2.32	-0
	02	27	45	aaa	PIT	188	12	34	10	1	2	15	7	26	2	0	181	210	277	487	4%	86%	0.27	68	1.91	-6
Garcia,Osmani	01	27	5	a/a	TEX	433	35	95	23	3	7	45	10	38	1	5	219	238	331	569	2%	91%	0.28	76	2.48	10
Garrett,Shawn	02	24	8	aa	PIT	489	57	125	22	5	8	58	26	70	16	7	256	293	370	663	5%	86%	0.37	74	3.77	23
Garrick,Matt	01	26	2	aa	STL	127	8	23	5	0	2	8	8	28	1	0	178	226	260	486	6%	78%	0.28	58	1.96	-11
Gazarek,Marty	01	28	8	a/a	DET	157	18	33	7	0	1	7	10	17	2	1	213	261	278	540	6%	89%	0.59	51	2.48	4
German,Amado	02	25	8	aa	TAM	344	45	82	10	4	2	28	31	87	12	16	238	301	308	609	8%	75%	0.36	45	2.85	5
German,Esteban	01	23	4	a/a	OAK	485	100	138	25	2	8	37	67	66	40	17	284	371	396	767	12%	86%	1.02	77	5.49	47
	02	25	4	aaa	OAK	458	54	105	14	2	1	32	57	49	19	18	229	315	275	590	11%	89%	1.16	34	2.90	14
Gerut,Jody	02	25	8	a/a	CLE	439	65	120	20	3	10	51	49	48	17	13	273	346	401	747	10%	89%	1.02	82	4.85	45
Gibbs,Kevin	02	29	8	aa	NYY	217	26	47	6	2	2	13	15	36	14	7	217	267	290	558	6%	83%	0.42	47	2.53	-0
Gibralter,Dave	01	26	83	a/a	MIL	452	53	114	25	0	14	54	35	51	1	3	253	307	399	706	7%	89%	0.69	96	4.28	38
	02	27	8	aa	CHC	166	16	30	6	0	2	13	9	30	1	1	181	223	253	476	5%	82%	0.30	51	1.81	-13
Gibralter,Steve	01	29	8	aa	CIN	306	31	58	15	1	10	32	15	68	6	2	189	227	338	565	5%	78%	0.22	95	2.50	6
Gibson,Derrick	01	27	8	a/a	ARI	169	16	43	11	1	3	23	8	29	6	1	253	285	379	664	4%	83%	0.27	88	3.87	26
Gilbert,Shawn	01	37	46	aaa	LA	224	17	56	10	1	5	24	14	38	7	5	249	292	374	665	6%	83%	0.36	80	3.66	23
	02	35	5	aaa	PIT	143	14	32	2	1	1	11	17	27	2	5	224	306	273	579	11%	81%	0.63	29	2.69	-1
Giles,Marcus	01	23	4	aaa	ATL	252	43	79	18	1	5	39	20	43	12	6	313	364	452	816	7%	83%	0.47	97	6.11	54
	02	24	4	aaa	ATL	115	22	34	6	0	3	14	11	13	3	0	296	357	426	783	9%	89%	0.85	87	6.01	51
Gillespie,Eric	01	26	83	aa	FLA	240	23	44	14	2	3	30	24	53	3	1	185	260	301	561	9%	78%	0.46	80	2.66	4
Gil,Geronimo	01	26	2	aaa	LA	363	34	84	16	1	8	40	12	64	0	1	232	256	347	604	3%	82%	0.18	76	2.99	12
Ginter,Keith	01	25	48	aaa	HOU	457	63	115	31	4	15	58	50	127	7	7	251	326	433	759	10%	72%	0.40	117	4.90	40
	02	26	4	aaa	HOU	435	60	108	27	1	12	47	48	90	3	4	248	323	398	721	10%	79%	0.53	100	4.53	35

Major League Equivalent Statistics

BATTER	Yr	Age	Pos	Lev	Org	AB	R	H	D	T	HR	RBI	BB	K	SB	CS	BA	OB	Slg	OPS	bb%	ct%	Eye	PX	RC/G	BPV
Glendenning,Mike	01	25	8	aa	SF	347	29	58	10	0	7	28	29	110	1	0	166	230	257	487	8%	68%	0.26	57	1.97	-16
Gload,Ross	01	26	83	aaa	CHC	475	59	123	27	7	12	79	30	79	8	8	258	302	419	721	6%	83%	0.38	101	4.27	36
	02	27	3	aaa	COL	442	43	123	24	4	13	44	12	36	6	5	278	297	439	736	3%	92%	0.33	102	4.51	41
Goelz,Jim	01	26	6	a/a	CLE	287	27	70	19	2	1	25	12	39	5	3	245	275	335	610	4%	86%	0.30	69	3.13	16
Gomez,Alexis	01	21	8	aa	KC	342	43	88	14	4	3	26	20	51	12	12	257	298	348	646	6%	85%	0.39	60	3.32	18
	02	22	8	aa	KC	461	64	131	20	7	13	67	38	72	32	26	284	339	443	781	8%	84%	0.53	95	4.73	45
Gomez,Chris	01	30	6	aaa	SD	133	16	32	6	1	4	17	10	9	2	1	244	296	386	682	7%	93%	1.11	90	3.99	41
Gomez,Ramon	01	26	8	aa	PHI	105	5	17	6	2	0	7	3	41	2	2	157	184	249	433	3%	61%	0.08	66	1.33	-19
Gomez,Rich	01	24	8	aa	DET	346	48	81	20	1	10	35	20	61	21	8	233	275	379	654	5%	82%	0.33	96	3.50	24
	02	26	8	aaa	SD	334	36	67	13	1	9	45	20	69	11	6	201	246	326	572	6%	79%	0.29	79	2.56	5
Gonzalez,Adrian	02	20	3	aa	FLA	508	60	125	33	1	14	83	47	90	5	4	246	310	398	708	8%	82%	0.52	102	4.32	34
Gonzalez,Jimmy	01	29	2	aaa	MON	215	15	33	7	1	6	16	7	48	0	0	156	181	277	457	3%	77%	0.13	75	1.55	-15
	02	30	2	aa	NYM	299	20	47	7	1	4	23	27	57	2	3	157	227	227	454	8%	81%	0.47	44	1.66	-20
Gonzalez,Luis	01	22	4	aa	CLE	199	37	57	12	2	5	15	6	23	2	3	286	307	442	750	3%	88%	0.26	101	4.66	42
	02	23	4	a/a	CLE	282	38	69	10	2	6	23	12	37	4	0	245	276	358	634	4%	87%	0.32	71	3.50	17
Gonzalez,Manuel	01	25	8	aa	PHI	264	25	63	20	0	2	18	11	40	2	5	239	269	334	603	4%	85%	0.27	77	2.88	17
Gonzalez,Raul	01	28	8	aaa	CIN	539	69	143	36	1	9	51	51	59	5	9	264	328	382	711	9%	89%	0.87	85	4.39	41
	02	29	8	aaa	CIN	432	66	122	24	1	10	50	43	47	7	9	282	347	412	759	9%	89%	0.91	87	5.06	48
Goodell,Steve	01	26	3	aa	BAL	135	21	26	4	1	5	20	19	37	1	3	193	293	354	648	12%	73%	0.52	94	3.37	14
Goodwin,Curtis	01	29	8	aaa	TEX	236	18	46	3	1	2	15	8	38	3	3	193	220	235	455	3%	84%	0.21	26	1.63	-21
Gordon,Brian	02	24	8	aa	ARI	477	54	120	29	8	8	49	26	87	2	7	252	290	396	686	5%	82%	0.30	95	3.81	29
Goudie,Jaime	01	23	4	aa	TOR	154	16	36	7	2	1	13	6	18	3	1	234	263	325	587	4%	88%	0.33	62	2.92	10
Grabowski,Jason	01	25	583	aaa	SEA	394	52	102	28	2	7	50	55	89	6	5	259	350	392	742	12%	77%	0.62	94	5.01	37
	02	26	8	aaa	OAK	265	36	64	18	2	9	38	28	43	4	5	242	314	426	740	10%	84%	0.65	119	4.50	43
Graham,Jess	01	26	8	aa	BOS	124	7	28	6	0	3	14	10	36	0	1	225	285	337	622	8%	71%	0.29	76	3.25	12
Gredvig,Doug	02	23	3	aa	BAL	465	40	112	18	1	12	67	38	86	2	3	241	298	361	660	8%	82%	0.44	76	3.75	21
Greene,Charlie	01	31	2	aaa	SD	277	12	32	3	0	1	11	9	64	0	0	114	142	133	275	3%	77%	0.14	14	0.58	-54
	02	32	2	aaa	FLA	320	23	60	19	0	5	27	7	44	0	0	188	205	294	499	2%	86%	0.16	77	1.93	-3
Greene,Todd	01	30	2	aaa	NYY	131	13	28	6	0	5	13	3	18	3	2	213	229	385	614	2%	86%	0.15	106	2.75	18
	02	31	2	aaa	TEX	277	33	73	17	0	12	49	8	40	2	0	264	284	455	739	3%	86%	0.20	121	4.59	42
Green,Chad	01	26	8	a/a	SD	331	43	69	17	4	5	29	25	96	13	6	208	264	328	592	7%	71%	0.26	80	2.87	8
	02	27	8	a/a	MIN	296	30	57	12	2	6	30	12	66	10	3	193	224	307	531	4%	78%	0.18	73	2.24	-2
Green,Nick	02	24	4	aa	ATL	355	39	72	13	1	11	40	28	79	2	6	203	261	338	599	7%	78%	0.35	83	2.78	9
Green,Scarborough	01	27	8	a/a	PIT	309	26	63	9	1	0	16	29	65	20	6	203	270	237	507	8%	79%	0.44	27	2.33	-12
Gregorio,Tom	01	24	2	aa	ANA	157	11	26	9	0	1	17	5	29	0	0	163	188	236	424	3%	81%	0.16	58	1.40	-19
	02	25	2	a/a	ANA	239	19	51	12	1	3	13	9	39	2	1	213	242	310	552	4%	84%	0.23	68	2.48	4
Grijak,Kevin	01	31	3	aaa	FLA	142	11	26	5	0	3	17	7	10	1	0	184	223	279	502	5%	93%	0.72	63	2.06	2
Grindell,Nate	01	25	8	aa	CLE	229	29	59	15	1	10	39	9	41	5	4	257	284	456	740	4%	82%	0.21	127	4.29	42
	02	26	8	aa	CLE	435	59	105	21	5	10	49	27	61	4	3	241	286	382	667	6%	86%	0.44	88	3.74	26
Gripp,Ryan	01	23	5	aa	CHC	255	26	49	16	0	6	37	20	55	2	0	190	250	320	570	7%	79%	0.37	89	2.71	8
	02	24	5	aa	CHC	380	43	76	21	1	9	41	39	80	4	2	200	274	332	606	9%	79%	0.49	88	3.11	13
Gross,Gabe	02	23	8	aa	TOR	403	44	85	17	3	7	42	41	54	6	2	211	284	320	604	9%	87%	0.76	71	3.18	15
Grummitt,Dan	01	25	3	aa	TAM	244	32	50	10	1	10	35	20	77	2	2	207	266	376	642	8%	69%	0.26	102	3.31	16
	02	26	3	aa	TAM	363	41	74	18	1	6	35	26	94	3	3	204	257	309	566	7%	74%	0.28	72	2.62	3
Gubanich,Creighton	01	30	2	aaa	MIL	197	18	35	6	0	6	17	13	44	0	0	176	226	305	530	6%	78%	0.29	79	2.24	-3
Guerrero,Cristian	02	22	8	aa	MIL	394	41	82	15	1	7	42	22	86	18	10	208	250	305	555	5%	78%	0.26	63	2.42	1
Guerrero,Wilton	01	27	4	aaa	CIN	227	18	62	14	1	0	22	10	25	10	6	273	303	342	645	4%	89%	0.39	57	3.54	22
Guevara,Giomar	01	29	6	aaa	DET	400	38	80	14	2	4	28	25	80	7	2	200	247	272	519	6%	80%	0.32	49	2.28	-7
	02	30	6	aa	OAK	363	32	61	11	2	1	12	24	103	5	5	168	220	218	437	6%	72%	0.23	36	1.51	-24
Guiel,Aaron	01	29	8	aaa	KC	442	56	99	23	2	15	53	35	76	5	5	224	282	389	671	7%	83%	0.47	103	3.67	27
	02	30	8	aaa	KC	215	32	64	9	1	7	37	21	30	6	1	298	360	447	807	9%	86%	0.70	92	6.24	51
Guiel,Jeff	01	28	8	a/a	ANA	400	51	109	22	2	18	52	29	72	4	2	273	321	473	794	7%	82%	0.40	122	5.48	50
	02	29	8	a/a	ANA	330	36	64	17	2	9	33	31	68	5	3	194	263	339	603	9%	79%	0.46	93	2.96	12
Guillen,Jose	01	25	8	aaa	TAM	119	16	33	9	0	6	26	3	24	0	0	275	292	499	791	2%	80%	0.12	144	5.19	53
Gulan,Mike	01	31	5	aaa	FLA	485	50	118	34	1	13	58	23	119	1	7	243	277	395	672	4%	75%	0.19	104	3.54	28
Guzman,Edwards	02	26	2	aaa	SF	390	39	103	21	0	4	48	14	24	1	3	264	290	349	638	3%	94%	0.58	64	3.48	26
Guzman,Elpidio	01	23	8	aa	ANA	459	45	100	19	5	6	36	13	67	14	17	218	239	320	560	3%	85%	0.19	67	2.17	4
	02	26	8	aa	ANA	454	43	92	13	5	4	32	31	84	16	11	203	254	280	533	6%	81%	0.37	49	2.26	-5
Haad,Yamid	01	24	2	a/a	PIT	147	12	34	5	0	2	9	6	23	0	3	231	261	306	568	4%	84%	0.26	51	2.48	3
	02	25	2	a/a	TAM	231	20	41	4	0	3	27	10	40	3	1	177	212	234	445	4%	83%	0.25	35	1.61	-21
Haas,Chris	01	25	3	aa	CHC	417	52	85	13	3	19	59	52	139	2	2	203	292	385	677	11%	67%	0.38	105	3.84	18
	02	26	305	a/a	TEX	289	28	53	15	1	10	28	33	85	0	0	183	267	346	613	10%	71%	0.39	103	3.13	11
Hafner,Travis	01	24	3	aa	TEX	323	47	82	23	0	18	59	48	67	2	1	253	350	491	842	13%	79%	0.72	149	6.31	60
	02	25	3	aaa	TEX	401	60	122	20	1	17	58	60	58	2	1	304	395	486	881	13%	86%	1.03	112	7.57	68
Hallmark,Pat	02	29	8	aa	KC	362	39	70	10	1	2	23	24	68	30	10	193	244	243	487	6%	81%	0.35	35	2.02	-14
Hall,Bill	01	22	6	aa	MIL	160	13	39	8	1	3	13	5	41	5	3	244	267	363	629	3%	74%	0.12	79	3.16	16
	02	23	6	aaa	MIL	465	34	105	20	1	4	29	23	89	16	12	226	262	299	561	5%	81%	0.26	53	2.50	2
Hall,Toby	01	26	2	aaa	TAM	373	52	118	28	1	18	63	26	19	1	3	316	360	539	899	6%	95%	1.34	142	7.25	91
Hall,Victor	02	22	8	aa	ARI	161	14	43	4	4	0	9	5	17	5	5	267	289	342	631	3%	89%	0.29	44	3.16	13
Haltiwanger,Garrick	01	27	8	a/a	TOR	206	25	48	10	2	4	22	23	46	8	7	231	309	353	662	10%	77%	0.50	79	3.57	20
	02	28	0	aa	TOR	133	13	22	7	1	2	12	12	36	5	2	165	234	278	513	8%	73%	0.33	77	2.13	-7
Hamilton,Jon	01	24	8	a/a	CLE	475	54	126	23	3	16	58	38	102	8	13	265	320	427	747	7%	79%	0.37	101	4.50	37
	02	25	8	aa	CHC	386	49	86	17	5	9	46	29	76	8	4	223	277	363	640	7%	80%	0.38	87	3.40	18
Hammock,Rob	02	25	2	aa	ARI	441	48	105	23	3	8	51	30	57	4	5	238	287	358	645	6%	87%	0.53	80	3.47	23
Hammond,Joey	01	24	6	aa	BAL	342	43	83	11	1	1	22	38	55	2	3	244	319	289	609	10%	84%	0.69	35	3.34	9
	02	25	45	a/a	BAL	285	32	63	10	1	1	17	36	42	3	2	221	308	274	582	11%	85%	0.86	40	3.06	7
Hankins,Ryan	02	26	3	aa	CHW	422	40	97	23	1	6	57	38	78	6	6	230	293	332	625	8%	82%	0.49	72	3.31	16
Hannahan,Buzz	02	26	4	aa	PHI	269	34	49	6	2	2	17	32	49	10	4	182	269	242	511	11%	82%	0.65	38	2.29	-11
Hannahan,Jack	02	23	5	aa	DET	226	14	47	10	1	2	16	18	38	2	1	208	266	288	554	7%	83%	0.47	57	2.63	2
Hansen,Jed	01	29	8	a/a	KC	345	38	79	19	1	10	20	30	78	11	8	229	291	377	668	8%	77%	0.38	96	3.60	24
	02	30	5	aaa	KC	339	46	74	14	3	11	36	37	73	13	5	218	295	375	670	10%	78%	0.51	95	3.82	22

Major League Equivalent Statistics

BATTER	Yr	Age	Pos	Lev	Org	AB	R	H	D	T	HR	RBI	BB	K	SB	CS	BA	OB	Slg	OPS	bb%	ct%	Eye	PX	RC/G	BPV
Hardtke,Jason	01	30	48	aaa	CHW	336	42	75	18	2	9	32	29	43	2	2	222	284	367	651	8%	87%	0.66	94	3.56	26
Hardy,J.J.	02	20	6	aa	MIL	145	13	33	6	0	1	12	8	15	1	2	228	268	290	558	5%	90%	0.53	47	2.54	6
Harper,Brandon	01	25	2	aa	FLA	247	18	50	12	0	3	21	23	59	0	0	204	273	284	557	9%	76%	0.40	59	2.70	0
Harris,Brian	01	26	46	aa	PHI	511	50	101	25	3	9	41	33	63	14	9	197	246	312	558	6%	88%	0.52	76	2.45	8
	02	27	4	aa	KC	490	61	109	18	6	2	35	37	78	7	4	222	277	296	573	7%	84%	0.47	50	2.82	4
Harris,Willie	01	23	48	aa	BAL	525	73	142	22	3	8	43	42	67	48	17	270	323	368	691	7%	87%	0.62	65	4.26	29
	02	24	4	aaa	CHW	360	48	95	15	3	5	29	31	55	28	15	264	322	364	686	8%	85%	0.56	66	3.97	26
Hart,Bo	02	26	4	aa	STL	405	42	77	13	3	3	27	31	74	10	7	190	248	259	507	7%	82%	0.42	46	2.09	-9
Hart,Corey	02	21	506	a/a	KC	376	46	91	17	2	3	47	48	51	8	9	242	328	322	650	11%	86%	0.94	57	3.66	23
Hart,Jason	01	24	3	aaa	OAK	494	56	105	22	1	15	59	45	81	2	4	213	278	352	631	8%	84%	0.56	88	3.28	18
	02	25	8	aaa	TEX	514	58	119	28	1	20	62	51	91	1	0	232	301	407	707	9%	82%	0.56	110	4.33	34
Harvey,Ken	01	24	3	aa	KC	314	41	95	18	2	7	48	14	45	2	0	303	332	439	770	4%	86%	0.30	91	5.50	44
	02	25	3	aaa	KC	488	61	124	27	1	17	61	33	68	7	3	254	301	418	719	6%	86%	0.49	105	4.44	38
Hatcher,Chris	01	33	8	aaa	TAM	251	25	57	11	0	9	31	15	61	4	2	226	270	376	647	6%	76%	0.25	94	3.44	19
Haverbusch,Kevin	01	25	48	a/a	PIT	300	35	81	16	3	8	42	8	49	3	3	271	289	422	712	3%	84%	0.16	96	4.19	33
	02	26	8	a/a	PIT	224	19	53	11	1	5	20	5	33	5	3	237	253	362	615	2%	85%	0.15	82	2.99	16
Haynes,Dee	02	25	8	aa	STL	504	57	133	24	3	16	74	20	56	2	2	264	292	419	711	4%	89%	0.36	97	4.28	35
Haynes,Nathan	01	22	8	aa	ANA	316	39	89	10	3	4	18	25	49	26	18	282	334	370	705	7%	84%	0.51	56	4.01	27
	02	23	8	aaa	ANA	283	28	70	12	3	2	9	9	40	8	12	247	271	332	603	3%	86%	0.23	58	2.61	11
Headley,Justin	02	27	8	aa	BOS	377	39	76	18	1	7	37	27	58	2	7	202	255	310	565	7%	85%	0.47	73	2.46	7
Heintz,Chris	01	27	2	a/a	CHW	129	12	26	8	0	2	8	9	23	0	2	199	249	302	551	6%	82%	0.37	75	2.34	5
	02	28	2	aa	STL	373	26	83	20	1	5	29	13	60	1	0	223	249	322	570	3%	84%	0.22	71	2.71	8
Henson,Drew	01	22	5	a/a	NYY	289	30	69	8	0	12	39	11	70	2	2	240	268	392	660	4%	76%	0.16	88	3.51	20
	02	23	5	aaa	NYY	471	58	104	28	2	16	55	33	117	2	1	221	272	391	662	7%	75%	0.28	109	3.62	24
Hermansen,Chad	01	24	8	aaa	PIT	447	60	98	20	4	14	50	32	123	18	6	219	271	376	647	7%	72%	0.26	96	3.45	18
Hernandez,Alex	01	24	38	aaa	PIT	342	36	91	15	1	6	29	10	52	2	5	266	287	368	655	3%	85%	0.19	69	3.52	21
	02	25	8	aaa	CIN	307	29	67	18	1	4	26	27	67	5	0	218	281	322	604	8%	78%	0.40	75	3.25	12
Hernandez,Carlos	01	26	4	a/a	NYM	460	62	116	22	1	4	37	32	69	21	11	252	300	329	629	6%	85%	0.46	57	3.40	17
	02	22	64	aaa	NYM	332	39	103	16	2	0	27	14	49	14	7	310	338	370	709	4%	85%	0.29	48	4.60	29
Hernandez,Michel	01	23	2	aa	NYY	128	9	27	6	0	2	9	9	19	1	0	212	262	303	566	6%	86%	0.47	64	2.76	6
	02	24	2	a/a	NYY	182	18	47	10	1	2	19	11	16	1	5	258	301	357	658	6%	91%	0.69	70	3.42	29
Hessman,Mike	01	24	5	aa	ATL	478	58	100	21	2	22	71	35	115	2	4	209	263	402	665	7%	76%	0.30	115	3.45	23
	02	25	5	aaa	ATL	484	59	117	26	1	22	68	29	93	1	6	242	285	436	721	6%	81%	0.31	120	4.09	36
Hiatt,Phil	01	32	5	aaa	LA	436	73	110	22	3	31	68	35	97	5	5	252	308	524	832	7%	78%	0.36	158	5.52	56
	02	33	8	aaa	LA	355	44	80	10	1	14	52	27	70	1	3	225	280	377	658	7%	80%	0.39	88	3.53	19
Hill,Bobby	01	24	4	aa	CHC	209	25	54	7	1	2	17	26	35	16	9	260	342	330	672	11%	83%	0.75	47	4.01	21
	02	25	4	aaa	CHC	354	56	83	19	2	6	27	35	47	20	7	234	303	350	654	9%	87%	0.74	79	3.76	26
Hill,Jason	01	25	2	a/a	ANA	325	35	78	17	1	9	37	15	46	1	1	240	274	382	655	4%	86%	0.33	92	3.57	24
	02	26	2	aa	ANA	431	32	97	17	1	5	41	11	58	2	5	225	244	304	548	2%	87%	0.19	55	2.36	1
Hill,Koyie	02	24	2	aa	LA	468	62	114	22	1	10	59	71	88	5	3	244	343	359	702	13%	81%	0.81	77	4.56	29
Hill,Mike	02	26	8	aa	HOU	527	51	119	24	4	10	42	26	97	10	8	226	262	343	606	5%	82%	0.27	76	2.93	12
Hinch,A.J.	01	27	2	aaa	KC	168	21	48	12	0	8	25	8	26	1	0	283	314	492	806	4%	84%	0.29	135	5.65	56
Hinske,Eric	01	24	5	aaa	OAK	436	56	106	23	1	20	62	43	90	16	9	243	311	438	749	9%	79%	0.48	120	4.63	40
Hitchcox,Brian	02	24	4	aa	PHI	297	34	69	17	2	5	21	13	28	3	6	232	265	354	618	4%	91%	0.46	83	2.94	21
Hochgesang,Josh	01	24	5	aa	OAK	303	36	57	14	2	5	25	23	69	6	4	188	245	295	540	7%	77%	0.33	71	2.34	-1
	02	25	5	aa	OAK	354	32	67	17	0	10	48	22	89	3	5	189	237	322	559	6%	75%	0.25	86	2.37	4
Hodges,Scott	01	23	4	aa	MON	305	26	77	10	1	5	28	21	49	3	2	252	301	341	642	6%	84%	0.43	57	3.62	16
	02	24	5	aa	MON	526	61	127	34	1	7	53	48	82	2	2	241	305	350	655	8%	84%	0.59	79	3.79	25
Hodge,Kevin	01	25	5	aa	MIN	139	15	23	4	1	1	6	13	41	1	2	164	237	226	463	9%	70%	0.32	41	1.71	-22
Hoffpauir,Josh	02	25	4	aa	BAL	302	24	66	9	2	1	20	16	28	8	6	219	258	272	529	5%	91%	0.57	37	2.27	-0
Holbert,Aaron	01	29	4	aaa	TOR	212	20	45	9	2	2	15	7	29	7	0	211	234	298	532	3%	86%	0.22	60	2.45	-1
	02	30	6	aaa	SEA	399	50	103	20	2	5	35	15	48	14	14	258	285	356	641	4%	88%	0.31	68	3.17	20
Holliday,Matt	02	23	8	aa	COL	463	57	122	18	2	9	46	49	68	12	2	263	334	369	703	10%	85%	0.72	68	4.66	30
Hollins,Damon	01	27	8	aaa	MIN	392	42	91	16	3	8	40	27	64	4	6	233	281	347	628	6%	84%	0.41	73	3.22	16
	02	28	8	aaa	ATL	498	54	120	29	1	9	48	28	72	8	2	241	281	357	639	5%	86%	0.39	81	3.53	22
Hollins,Dave	01	35	3	aaa	CLE	316	40	74	22	2	14	53	36	74	0	0	234	312	441	753	10%	76%	0.48	132	4.89	42
Holt,Daylan	02	24	8	aa	OAK	201	15	48	9	0	3	21	12	45	1	5	239	282	328	610	6%	78%	0.27	63	2.90	11
Honeycutt,Heath	01	25	5	aa	FLA	475	49	98	21	2	7	51	36	146	9	7	207	262	303	566	7%	69%	0.25	65	2.61	1
Hooper,Clay	02	26	6	aa	NYY	236	26	45	5	1	2	13	17	34	0	6	191	245	246	491	7%	86%	0.50	36	1.79	-12
Hooper,Kevin	01	25	4	aa	FLA	468	65	131	18	5	2	36	55	84	22	12	280	356	351	707	11%	82%	0.65	49	4.61	27
	02	26	6	aaa	FLA	452	50	109	18	2	1	28	25	39	12	13	241	281	296	577	5%	91%	0.64	43	2.67	11
Hoover,Paul	01	25	2	aaa	TAM	293	33	58	18	3	3	19	10	58	4	3	199	226	311	536	3%	80%	0.17	78	2.22	2
	02	26	2	aaa	TAM	227	22	46	12	3	4	16	15	60	3	3	203	252	335	587	6%	74%	0.25	86	2.71	8
Hopper,Shane	01	26	8	aa	SD	190	22	39	8	0	2	18	12	57	4	3	206	254	275	529	6%	70%	0.21	51	2.25	-6
	02	27	58	a/a	SD	173	13	36	6	2	3	19	9	48	3	1	208	247	318	565	5%	72%	0.19	68	2.63	1
Horner,Jim	01	28	2	aaa	SEA	236	37	56	13	0	5	24	9	40	1	0	238	264	354	618	3%	83%	0.21	81	3.23	17
	02	29	2	a/a	SEA	229	27	54	16	1	3	25	15	56	1	1	236	283	354	636	6%	76%	0.27	86	3.45	19
Horn,Jeff	01	31	2	aa	ATL	187	11	32	6	0	1	11	17	54	1	0	168	237	225	462	8%	71%	0.31	41	1.82	-21
House,J.R.	01	22	2	aa	PIT	426	47	105	24	1	10	52	34	96	1	1	246	302	378	680	7%	77%	0.35	88	4.05	26
Howe,Matt	02	26	5	aa	OAK	187	15	37	11	1	3	14	18	49	3	3	198	268	316	584	9%	74%	0.37	82	2.76	7
Hubbard,Mike	01	31	2	aaa	TEX	129	16	34	7	1	5	17	9	18	0	1	265	313	460	774	7%	86%	0.51	120	5.04	48
	02	32	2	aaa	BAL	211	21	49	9	0	4	23	14	24	1	2	232	280	332	612	6%	89%	0.58	67	3.13	17
Hubbard,Trenidad	01	35	8	aaa	KC	346	52	87	17	3	12	42	46	51	18	11	252	340	419	759	12%	85%	0.90	103	4.91	45
Huckaby,Ken	01	31	23	a/a	ARI	366	32	91	16	1	3	33	7	66	1	4	248	263	320	583	2%	82%	0.11	53	2.76	7
Hudson,Orlando	01	24	4	a/a	TOR	500	70	144	36	9	7	67	50	63	16	7	288	353	438	791	9%	87%	0.79	101	5.74	54
	02	25	4	aaa	TOR	417	50	115	27	2	8	30	28	43	6	6	276	321	408	729	6%	90%	0.65	91	4.60	43
Huffman,Royce	01	25	5	aa	HOU	511	59	140	33	1	4	39	40	80	10	9	273	326	364	690	7%	84%	0.50	71	4.21	30
	02	26	3	aa	HOU	522	56	139	31	3	10	65	29	62	9	6	266	305	395	700	5%	88%	0.47	87	4.21	34
Huff,Aubrey	02	26	3	aaa	TAM	126	16	38	9	0	3	17	10	11	0	0	302	353	444	797	7%	91%	0.91	100	5.99	60
Huisman,Jason	01	25	48	aa	ANA	371	39	84	18	0	7	36	28	53	3	10	226	280	332	612	7%	86%	0.52	73	2.89	16
	02	26	8	aa	ANA	263	30	51	12	1	4	26	10	31	8	6	194	223	293	516	4%	88%	0.32	67	1.97	-1

Major League Equivalent Statistics

BATTER	Yr	Age	Pos	Lev	Org	AB	R	H	D	T	HR	RBI	BB	K	SB	CS	BA	OB	Slg	OPS	bb%	ct%	Eye	PX	RC/G	BPV
Hummel,Tim	01	23	46	aa	CHW	524	69	139	30	4	7	53	53	57	12	3	265	333	378	711	9%	89%	0.93	78	4.69	39
	02	24	6	aaa	CHW	523	49	126	30	0	4	36	48	85	5	6	241	305	321	626	8%	84%	0.56	63	3.41	17
Hunter,Brian	01	34	3	aaa	TOR	105	16	21	5	0	3	13	12	19	1	0	197	278	317	595	10%	82%	0.62	78	3.09	10
	02	35	3	aaa	TAM	101	6	17	5	1	3	14	7	21	0	0	168	222	327	549	6%	79%	0.33	99	2.35	3
Hunter,Scott	01	26	8	a/a	NYM	492	58	122	20	3	14	63	13	82	17	10	248	267	384	651	3%	83%	0.16	85	3.33	21
	02	27	8	aa	BAL	386	37	68	18	0	5	32	17	74	8	5	176	211	262	473	4%	81%	0.23	61	1.72	-11
Huskey,Butch	01	30	3	aaa	COL	458	47	126	25	1	15	55	26	68	1	3	274	314	433	747	5%	85%	0.39	102	4.82	41
Hutchins,Norm	01	26	8	a/a	TAM	366	42	78	11	2	9	34	14	86	17	4	214	242	327	570	4%	77%	0.16	69	2.68	3
Hyzdu,Adam	01	30	8	aaa	PIT	261	27	62	15	1	8	28	13	60	1	4	237	273	394	667	5%	77%	0.21	101	3.48	25
	02	31	8	aaa	PIT	243	24	49	14	0	7	37	22	51	1	2	202	268	346	614	8%	79%	0.43	96	3.06	15
Iapoce,Anthony	02	29	8	aa	FLA	280	26	53	11	2	2	19	17	52	12	3	189	236	264	500	6%	81%	0.33	52	2.12	-9
Infante,Omar	01	20	6	aa	DET	540	79	167	23	3	1	57	42	61	25	15	310	359	371	730	7%	89%	0.69	46	4.90	36
	02	21	6	aaa	DET	436	51	127	16	10	3	53	31	37	20	18	291	338	394	733	7%	92%	0.84	63	4.45	40
Inglin,Jeff	01	26	8	aaa	CHW	481	58	122	23	5	24	66	39	95	3	4	254	310	474	784	7%	80%	0.41	130	5.09	46
	02	27	8	aaa	CHW	152	15	38	4	0	6	18	8	21	2	2	250	288	395	682	5%	86%	0.38	84	3.82	26
Ingram,Darron	01	25	8	aa	CHW	514	58	113	28	3	19	68	40	171	5	6	219	275	394	669	7%	67%	0.23	110	3.54	23
	02	26	0	a/a	CHW	434	44	85	18	1	18	56	46	161	7	7	196	273	366	639	10%	63%	0.29	103	3.23	13
Izturis,Cesar	01	22	64	aaa	TOR	342	30	102	18	2	2	33	9	16	22	11	299	317	383	699	3%	95%	0.54	61	4.20	36
Izturis,Maicer	02	22	4	aa	CLE	253	30	66	12	5	0	29	15	25	7	4	261	302	348	650	6%	90%	0.60	59	3.66	23
Jackson,Nic	02	23	8	aa	CHC	131	16	34	8	1	3	17	5	22	7	2	260	287	405	691	4%	83%	0.23	96	4.06	31
Jackson,Ryan	02	31	8	aaa	DET	420	33	94	28	1	5	41	11	80	5	3	224	244	331	575	3%	81%	0.14	80	2.65	10
Jacobsen,Bucky	01	26	3	a/a	MIL	393	53	104	25	1	18	68	35	79	1	2	264	324	474	798	8%	80%	0.44	132	5.48	51
	02	27	3	aa	STL	300	29	59	14	1	10	39	22	63	2	2	197	252	350	602	7%	79%	0.35	96	2.88	12
Jacobson,Russ	02	25	2	aa	PHI	282	15	48	14	0	2	27	15	73	1	0	170	212	241	453	5%	74%	0.21	55	1.67	-17
James,Kenny	02	26	8	aa	TOR	414	37	85	15	1	2	23	18	57	28	14	205	238	261	499	4%	86%	0.32	42	1.95	-8
Jennings,Robin	01	30	8	aaa	OAK	296	37	70	14	2	11	34	14	51	5	5	237	270	406	676	4%	83%	0.27	103	3.58	27
	02	31	8	aaa	CIN	351	20	63	18	0	3	33	18	46	3	5	179	220	256	476	5%	87%	0.39	59	1.73	-8
Jensen,Marcus	01	29	2	aaa	TEX	290	41	70	15	2	10	29	42	62	0	0	241	336	410	747	13%	78%	0.67	106	5.06	37
	02	30	2	aaa	MIL	183	20	36	6	0	4	21	27	38	0	0	197	300	295	595	13%	79%	0.71	63	3.18	6
Jester,Joe	01	23	4	aa	SF	150	22	43	13	1	5	23	10	29	4	1	285	328	479	807	6%	81%	0.34	130	5.79	55
	02	24	4	aa	SF	359	43	86	18	2	8	32	24	58	11	6	240	287	368	655	6%	84%	0.41	84	3.57	23
Jimenez,D'Angelo	01	24	4	aaa	NYY	214	28	52	10	1	5	16	21	26	4	7	243	311	369	680	9%	88%	0.81	82	3.67	31
	02	25	6	aaa	CHW	157	21	41	10	1	6	16	23	13	5	2	261	356	452	808	13%	92%	1.77	121	5.92	72
Johnson,Adam	01	26	8	a/a	CHW	166	12	42	10	0	2	13	8	25	0	1	251	285	345	629	4%	85%	0.31	70	3.37	19
Johnson,Ben	02	21	8	aa	SD	456	52	98	20	3	8	50	57	119	10	10	215	302	325	627	11%	74%	0.48	72	3.29	11
Johnson,Brian	01	34	23	aaa	LA	166	14	38	9	0	5	21	7	34	0	0	228	260	363	623	4%	79%	0.21	90	3.21	17
	02	25	2	aa	KC	109	12	23	5	0	1	11	5	16	3	0	211	246	284	530	4%	85%	0.31	55	2.47	-1
Johnson,Gary	01	26	8	aa	ANA	466	44	92	19	1	8	50	42	78	5	7	197	264	294	557	8%	83%	0.54	65	2.51	3
	02	27	8	a/a	ANA	532	56	112	20	3	8	58	46	110	10	10	211	273	305	578	8%	79%	0.42	62	2.72	4
Johnson,Gary	01	25	8	aa	CHC	463	68	95	22	3	5	50	45	102	12	5	206	276	299	576	9%	78%	0.44	65	2.84	4
Johnson,Jason	01	24	8	aa	PHI	197	20	46	10	0	0	8	8	38	7	5	231	260	285	545	4%	81%	0.20	47	2.38	1
	02	25	8	aa	PHI	411	30	96	14	0	0	34	13	76	14	11	234	257	268	525	3%	82%	0.17	30	2.18	-6
Johnson,Keith	01	30	65	aaa	LA	435	37	80	23	2	8	33	12	76	3	5	184	206	302	508	3%	83%	0.15	80	1.86	-2
	02	31	5	aaa	ANA	367	38	82	17	2	11	38	7	53	5	4	223	238	371	609	2%	86%	0.13	92	2.82	15
Johnson,Lance	01	38	8	aaa	COL	135	16	39	6	1	2	10	3	10	5	5	287	301	387	687	2%	93%	0.27	68	3.78	29
Johnson,Mark	01	26	2	aaa	CHW	196	21	49	5	2	4	21	26	32	2	1	252	341	356	697	12%	84%	0.82	61	4.51	26
Johnson,Mark	01	34	3	aaa	NYM	152	23	41	13	0	6	21	18	22	2	1	266	344	474	818	11%	85%	0.81	138	5.97	62
	02	35	3	aaa	NYM	270	38	60	14	1	11	31	27	52	1	0	222	293	404	697	9%	81%	0.52	112	4.15	31
Johnson,Nick	01	23	3	aaa	NYY	359	58	86	18	0	17	42	69	88	8	2	240	362	432	794	16%	75%	0.78	118	5.87	44
Johnson,Reed	01	25	8	aa	TOR	554	85	155	28	3	11	60	36	69	34	13	280	324	401	725	6%	87%	0.52	80	4.64	37
	02	26	8	aaa	TOR	159	21	33	8	2	2	8	10	18	1	5	208	254	321	575	6%	89%	0.56	75	2.37	11
Johnson,Rontrez	01	25	8	a/a	BOS	442	69	121	30	3	11	46	26	64	21	12	274	314	430	744	6%	86%	0.41	105	4.59	43
	02	26	8	aaa	KC	403	57	111	25	3	8	43	39	40	25	13	275	339	412	751	9%	90%	0.98	92	4.90	49
Jones,Chris	01	36	8	aaa	TOR	315	33	65	7	2	8	31	24	79	5	5	206	263	317	580	7%	75%	0.31	65	2.68	2
	02	37	8	aaa	MIL	273	28	66	11	3	3	24	21	50	5	5	242	296	337	633	7%	82%	0.42	62	3.36	15
Jones,Damien	02	23	8	aa	ATL	211	16	40	7	1	1	10	18	46	7	6	190	253	246	500	8%	78%	0.39	41	1.97	-12
Jones,Jason	01	25	3	aa	TEX	107	7	20	6	0	2	7	3	14	0	0	186	208	293	501	3%	87%	0.21	75	1.95	-3
	02	26	3	aa	TEX	471	66	120	28	2	11	60	70	93	10	7	255	351	393	744	13%	80%	0.75	93	5.02	38
Jones,Jeremy	01	24	2	aa	TEX	311	27	63	12	0	4	23	25	51	1	3	202	260	278	538	7%	84%	0.49	54	2.39	-1
	02	25	2	aa	TEX	132	14	25	4	0	2	6	13	20	1	1	189	262	265	527	9%	85%	0.65	50	2.34	-3
Jones,Mitch	02	25	5	aa	NYY	216	27	41	14	0	9	23	15	56	1	4	190	242	380	622	6%	74%	0.27	122	2.77	19
Jones,Ryan	02	28	3	aa	SD	266	29	42	7	1	9	40	22	63	2	1	158	222	293	515	8%	76%	0.35	79	2.10	-8
Jordan,Kevin	02	33	45	aaa	CIN	270	19	50	7	1	2	15	12	28	1	0	185	220	241	461	4%	90%	0.43	38	1.75	-14
Jorgensen,Ryan	01	22	2	aa	CHC	109	7	11	3	0	2	6	9	33	0	0	101	169	183	353	8%	70%	0.27	53	0.99	-39
	02	23	2	aa	FLA	144	12	27	4	0	1	11	10	29	2	1	188	240	236	476	6%	80%	0.34	35	1.90	-16
Kata,Matt	02	25	4	aa	ARI	578	70	150	29	8	9	43	27	63	9	8	260	293	384	677	4%	89%	0.43	81	3.82	28
Kaup,Nathan	02	25	5	aa	TAM	272	19	58	12	0	2	22	21	42	1	4	213	270	279	549	7%	85%	0.50	50	2.45	2
Kearns,Austin	01	21	8	aa	CIN	205	24	51	11	1	5	29	21	33	6	6	249	319	385	704	9%	84%	0.64	90	4.08	33
Keck,Brian	01	28	65	aa	COL	327	25	72	12	1	3	29	16	45	8	4	221	257	294	551	5%	86%	0.35	52	2.52	2
Keith,Rusty	01	24	8	aa	OAK	201	20	42	10	1	2	24	24	30	1	5	212	295	294	589	11%	85%	0.80	62	2.90	15
	02	25	8	aa	OAK	358	41	77	13	0	1	17	20	42	5	5	215	257	260	516	5%	88%	0.48	36	2.19	-4
Kelly,Heath	02	27	5	aa	FLA	180	17	27	6	1	4	17	11	71	2	0	150	199	261	460	6%	61%	0.15	69	1.69	-19
Kelly,Kenny	01	23	8	aa	SEA	478	65	111	18	3	9	42	43	107	16	13	232	296	339	634	8%	78%	0.40	68	3.30	14
	02	24	8	aaa	SEA	391	45	87	12	6	9	47	23	82	10	3	223	266	353	619	6%	79%	0.28	76	3.20	11
Kelly,Roberto	01	37	8	aaa	COL	212	20	51	8	0	10	30	12	34	1	3	242	282	420	702	5%	84%	0.34	106	3.90	31
Kelton,Dave	01	22	5	aa	CHC	224	29	62	8	3	10	39	21	49	1	3	277	339	473	812	9%	78%	0.43	113	5.65	47
	02	23	3	aa	CHC	498	60	119	26	4	18	69	47	116	11	7	239	305	416	720	9%	77%	0.41	109	4.34	33
Kielty,Bobby	01	25	8	aaa	MIN	341	45	88	24	1	9	39	41	60	4	0	258	337	412	750	11%	83%	0.68	105	5.21	43
Kieschnick,Brooks	01	29	8	aaa	COL	252	27	63	7	2	11	28	15	52	2	3	249	293	423	715	6%	80%	0.30	99	4.18	30
	02	30	0	aaa	CHW	189	25	44	9	0	12	32	12	46	0	0	233	279	471	750	6%	76%	0.26	140	4.51	41
Kinchen,Jason	02	27	0	aa	NYY	123	10	22	4	1	5	14	12	29	1	1	179	252	350	601	9%	76%	0.41	99	2.85	9

Major League Equivalent Statistics

BATTER	Yr	Age	Pos	Lev	Org	AB	R	H	D	T	HR	RBI	BB	K	SB	CS	BA	OB	Slg	OPS	bb%	ct%	Eye	PX	RC/G	BPV
Kingsale,Eugene	01	25	8	aaa	SEA	459	52	97	23	4	2	34	31	65	24	7	211	261	291	552	6%	86%	0.47	58	2.63	4
	02	26	8	aaa	SEA	188	21	43	14	2	5	22	13	27	9	3	229	279	404	683	6%	86%	0.48	116	3.82	34
King,Brad	01	27	2	aa	SEA	262	27	64	12	0	8	44	28	37	3	3	246	318	382	700	10%	86%	0.76	87	4.24	33
	02	28	25	a/a	TEX	198	27	40	4	0	3	14	31	31	1	1	202	310	268	578	14%	84%	1.00	41	3.02	4
King,Brennan	02	22	5	aa	LA	435	59	110	18	1	7	60	56	47	1	1	253	338	347	685	11%	89%	1.19	64	4.37	34
Kinkade,Mike	02	29	8	aaa	LA	287	41	74	16	3	7	33	19	40	4	3	258	304	408	712	6%	86%	0.48	96	4.31	35
Kirby,Scott	01	24	8	aa	MIL	184	24	38	12	0	6	20	19	59	3	0	207	281	367	647	9%	68%	0.32	107	3.62	20
Klassen,Danny	02	27	6	a/a	ARI	426	35	81	19	3	3	32	18	109	4	1	190	223	270	493	4%	74%	0.17	57	1.98	-10
Klimek,Josh	01	28	58	a/a	MIL	414	50	101	16	1	15	46	46	81	2	1	243	318	397	715	10%	80%	0.56	93	4.55	31
	02	29	5	aaa	TOR	424	37	94	26	1	6	44	30	58	1	2	222	273	330	603	7%	86%	0.52	78	3.06	17
Knorr,Randy	02	34	2	aaa	MON	338	24	74	23	1	6	30	24	50	0	0	219	271	346	617	7%	85%	0.48	90	3.22	20
Knox,Ryan	02	25	8	aa	MIL	217	20	39	6	1	0	7	19	41	14	7	180	246	217	462	8%	81%	0.46	29	1.76	-19
Knupfer,Jason	01	27	4	aaa	PHI	276	36	62	13	2	1	22	28	63	9	5	224	294	296	590	9%	77%	0.44	54	3.03	6
	02	28	64	a/a	PHI	299	37	61	11	2	2	23	31	75	10	3	204	279	274	553	9%	75%	0.41	49	2.72	-4
Koonce,Graham	01	26	38	a/a	SD	334	49	78	16	0	12	44	77	88	0	0	232	376	386	762	19%	74%	0.87	98	5.56	35
	02	27	3	aa	OAK	470	61	95	21	0	17	69	95	122	2	0	202	336	355	692	17%	74%	0.78	96	4.41	22
Kopitzke,Casey	02	24	2	aa	CHC	244	13	48	5	0	0	16	11	32	2	3	197	231	217	449	4%	87%	0.34	18	1.60	-20
Krause,Scott	01	28	8	aa	CLE	303	34	59	12	1	11	38	18	91	0	2	195	241	351	593	6%	70%	0.20	95	2.69	8
	02	29	8	a/a	SEA	140	8	24	6	0	2	10	7	30	2	1	171	211	257	468	5%	79%	0.23	60	1.73	-13
Kremblas,Mike	02	27	2	aa	OAK	141	11	21	2	0	0	5	12	36	1	2	149	216	163	379	8%	74%	0.33	13	1.13	-39
Krynzel,Dave	02	21	8	aa	MIL	129	12	30	2	2	2	12	3	24	12	6	233	250	326	576	2%	81%	0.13	51	2.44	1
Kuzmic,Craig	01	24	45	aa	SEA	479	68	114	27	3	12	79	61	135	6	4	238	324	383	707	11%	72%	0.45	94	4.43	27
	02	25	5	a/a	SEA	454	50	85	21	4	9	45	60	144	9	2	187	282	311	593	12%	68%	0.42	79	3.08	4
LaForest,Pete	02	25	2	a/a	TAM	425	53	103	20	1	19	66	51	110	8	8	242	324	428	752	11%	74%	0.46	113	4.73	37
Laird,Gerald	02	23	2	aa	TEX	442	62	116	20	3	10	60	40	82	7	7	262	324	389	713	8%	81%	0.49	81	4.40	31
Laker,Tim	01	32	2	aaa	CLE	320	36	68	11	0	17	45	23	50	2	1	211	263	405	668	7%	84%	0.45	113	3.57	26
	02	33	2	aaa	CLE	216	19	42	9	0	4	23	17	53	2	0	194	253	292	545	7%	75%	0.32	66	2.54	-2
Lamb,David	01	26	64	a/a	COL	363	35	93	20	0	6	28	36	40	2	4	257	323	361	684	9%	89%	0.89	74	4.13	34
	02	27	6	aaa	MIN	440	50	114	23	2	7	50	31	45	1	8	259	308	368	676	7%	90%	0.69	75	3.79	31
Lamb,Mike	01	26	5	aaa	TEX	273	28	74	17	2	8	33	11	26	0	2	270	297	433	731	4%	91%	0.41	107	4.46	42
Landaeta,Luis	01	25	8	aa	COL	241	22	65	10	3	1	19	13	23	7	6	268	306	347	653	5%	90%	0.57	55	3.60	23
Landry,Jacques	01	28	8	aa	OAK	506	64	84	10	2	22	60	40	183	23	6	166	227	327	554	7%	64%	0.22	90	2.41	-3
	02	29	8	a/a	OAK	290	32	54	11	1	9	40	34	96	7	5	186	272	324	596	10%	67%	0.35	85	2.89	4
Lane,Jason	01	25	8	aa	HOU	526	81	149	34	2	33	98	48	87	11	2	284	343	545	888	8%	83%	0.54	159	6.98	71
	02	26	8	aaa	HOU	426	56	111	36	2	15	72	27	82	11	3	261	305	460	765	6%	81%	0.33	133	4.99	48
Lane,Ryan	01	27	8	aaa	OAK	186	12	31	7	0	3	10	15	33	5	1	169	231	250	482	8%	82%	0.47	55	1.97	-12
Langaigne,Selwyn	01	26	83	a/a	TOR	263	31	60	11	1	3	25	17	54	4	4	230	276	312	588	6%	80%	0.31	57	2.86	7
	02	27	8	a/a	TOR	277	18	53	11	1	4	16	12	57	1	5	191	225	282	507	4%	79%	0.21	61	1.89	-7
Langerhans,Ryan	02	23	8	aa	ATL	391	48	88	21	1	7	52	55	68	8	6	225	321	338	658	12%	83%	0.81	78	3.81	23
Langston,James	01	24	5	aa	PIT	103	8	27	3	1	0	7	2	21	0	1	264	277	311	588	2%	80%	0.09	33	2.89	4
LaRocca,Greg	01	29	56	a/a	CLE	320	46	89	19	1	13	47	25	43	2	3	279	331	465	796	7%	87%	0.58	117	5.52	53
	02	30	5	aaa	CLE	382	58	98	25	1	6	35	40	49	15	4	257	327	374	701	9%	87%	0.82	85	4.53	37
LaRoche,Adam	02	23	3	aa	ATL	173	14	45	8	0	3	16	15	31	1	1	260	319	358	678	8%	82%	0.48	68	4.12	24
Larson,Brandon	01	25	5	aaa	CIN	424	49	99	21	1	12	45	20	98	4	7	233	268	371	639	4%	77%	0.20	89	3.19	19
	02	26	5	aaa	CIN	297	36	89	18	1	20	52	17	54	1	1	300	338	569	907	5%	82%	0.31	161	7.10	73
Latham,Chris	01	28	8	aaa	TOR	288	45	70	19	7	10	43	40	80	11	11	242	335	459	793	12%	72%	0.50	132	4.95	45
	02	29	8	aaa	NYM	405	48	76	18	4	5	35	49	103	21	9	188	275	289	564	11%	75%	0.48	67	2.71	-0
Lawrence,Joe	01	25	2	aaa	TOR	318	23	65	11	3	1	22	30	51	5	10	204	273	267	540	9%	84%	0.59	44	2.26	-2
	02	26	4	aaa	TOR	108	10	16	4	1	2	9	11	18	2	0	148	227	259	486	9%	83%	0.61	70	2.01	-10
Leach,Jalal	01	33	8	aaa	SF	467	46	103	23	2	10	47	20	77	9	7	220	251	341	593	4%	84%	0.26	81	2.75	12
	02	34	8	aaa	NYY	287	25	57	11	3	5	21	14	44	5	5	199	236	310	546	5%	85%	0.32	70	2.27	1
Leach,Nick	01	24	3	aa	NYY	167	15	32	12	0	3	19	25	36	2	2	192	298	314	611	13%	78%	0.70	89	3.21	14
Lebron,Juan	01	24	8	aa	NYM	363	34	75	14	3	13	42	30	113	2	5	207	268	372	640	8%	69%	0.27	98	3.21	15
	02	25	8	aa	SEA	311	40	63	16	1	5	30	22	79	5	4	203	255	309	564	7%	75%	0.28	73	2.57	3
LeCroy,Matthew	01	26	2	aaa	MIN	396	42	117	16	0	15	62	28	75	0	2	295	341	448	789	7%	81%	0.37	93	5.63	44
	02	27	0	aaa	MIN	174	26	52	7	1	8	36	12	27	1	0	299	344	489	833	6%	84%	0.44	112	6.37	55
Lemonis,Chris	01	28	4	a/a	ARI	381	36	94	18	1	1	38	19	49	6	4	247	282	305	587	5%	87%	0.38	47	2.96	9
Leon,Carlos	02	23	4	aa	BOS	265	33	65	10	1	1	16	20	25	12	11	245	298	302	600	7%	91%	0.80	43	2.87	15
Leon,Donny	01	25	5	a/a	NYY	479	43	110	25	1	15	67	19	113	1	2	229	259	378	637	4%	76%	0.17	96	3.26	19
	02	26	5	a/a	CIN	476	50	110	30	1	16	57	33	89	10	8	231	281	399	680	6%	81%	0.37	110	3.69	30
Leon,Jose	01	25	5	a/a	BAL	511	66	137	25	3	15	67	31	108	7	4	268	310	417	727	6%	79%	0.29	94	4.59	34
	02	26	5	aaa	BAL	312	34	78	14	1	7	35	16	49	0	0	250	287	369	655	5%	84%	0.33	77	3.72	22
Lesher,Brian	01	31	8	aaa	MIL	346	38	79	14	3	5	46	30	69	1	1	229	290	333	623	8%	80%	0.43	68	3.38	13
	02	32	8	aaa	TOR	248	24	53	12	1	5	20	14	48	5	1	214	256	331	586	5%	81%	0.29	78	2.89	9
Levis,Jesse	01	34	2	aaa	ATL	232	18	53	6	0	3	27	22	21	2	0	229	295	291	586	9%	91%	1.02	42	3.11	14
	02	34	2	aaa	CIN	254	17	59	10	1	2	17	21	16	1	1	232	291	303	594	8%	94%	1.31	51	3.10	25
Lewis,Mark	01	32	5	aaa	CLE	184	18	47	9	1	4	23	14	24	0	1	254	308	372	680	7%	87%	0.59	78	4.05	29
Lidle,Kevin	01	30	2	aaa	ANA	123	7	23	6	0	1	8	7	33	2	1	185	231	259	489	6%	73%	0.22	57	1.95	-10
Liefer,Jeff	01	27	3	aaa	CHW	119	20	31	7	0	6	18	13	39	3	1	263	337	463	801	10%	67%	0.34	124	5.71	46
Linden,Todd	02	22	8	a/a	SF	492	72	134	27	3	11	54	70	117	10	6	272	363	407	769	12%	76%	0.60	89	5.51	39
Lindsey,Rodney	01	26	8	aa	DET	385	38	81	13	1	1	25	17	66	22	13	210	244	255	499	4%	83%	0.26	35	1.95	-10
	02	27	8	a/a	DET	402	36	87	12	6	1	17	24	88	24	10	216	261	284	544	6%	78%	0.27	43	2.47	-4
Lindstrom,Dave	01	27	2	aaa	DET	203	16	46	15	1	1	17	8	19	1	1	225	253	323	576	4%	91%	0.40	78	2.72	15
Liniak,Cole	01	25	5	aaa	TOR	344	34	77	21	1	9	41	27	45	1	2	224	280	368	649	7%	87%	0.59	96	3.50	26
Lockwood,Mike	01	25	8	aa	OAK	493	53	105	29	2	5	52	37	67	7	5	212	267	308	575	7%	86%	0.55	71	2.76	11
	02	26	8	aa	OAK	501	52	96	20	5	3	38	46	63	4	6	192	260	269	529	8%	87%	0.73	53	2.30	1
Lofton,James	01	28	6	a/a	BOS	262	33	74	14	0	8	20	16	46	5	4	283	324	424	749	6%	82%	0.35	93	4.87	40
	02	29	6	a/a	BOS	426	32	82	12	1	3	26	17	79	7	5	192	223	246	470	4%	81%	0.22	38	1.75	-16
Logan,Kyle	01	26	8	aa	HOU	258	26	66	19	2	4	23	14	43	9	3	256	294	395	689	5%	84%	0.33	98	4.10	32
	02	27	8	aaa	HOU	335	46	92	19	3	11	38	20	45	18	9	275	315	448	763	6%	87%	0.44	109	4.83	45
Logan,Matt	01	22	3	aa	TOR	277	27	53	12	1	8	29	23	67	3	1	191	253	329	582	8%	76%	0.34	86	2.79	6
	02	23	3	aa	TOR	345	34	73	24	0	2	37	26	49	6	1	212	267	299	565	7%	86%	0.53	71	2.79	10

Major League Equivalent Statistics

BATTER	Yr	Age	Pos	Lev	Org	AB	R	H	D	T	HR	RBI	BB	K	SB	CS	BA	OB	Slg	OPS	bb%	ct%	Eye	PX	RC/G	BPV
Loggins,Josh	01	25	8	aa	SD	265	29	56	13	0	4	29	18	82	2	2	212	262	305	567	6%	69%	0.22	67	2.67	2
Lomasney,Steve	01	24	2	a/a	BOS	272	29	65	17	2	9	33	22	82	2	1	239	296	415	711	7%	70%	0.27	113	4.29	32
	02	25	2	a/a	BOS	368	33	63	16	2	6	44	43	126	4	6	171	258	274	532	10%	66%	0.34	69	2.28	-8
Lopez-Cao,Mike	01	26	2	a/a	BAL	175	16	30	9	0	4	17	16	32	0	2	172	239	288	528	8%	82%	0.49	78	2.17	-1
Lopez,Felipe	01	21	64	a/a	TOR	430	72	120	23	7	18	45	36	88	15	11	279	335	486	821	8%	79%	0.41	124	5.60	53
	02	22	6	aaa	TOR	173	29	53	12	1	2	14	24	28	11	0	306	391	422	813	12%	84%	0.86	84	7.06	54
Lopez,Luis	01	28	3	aaa	TOR	339	46	97	24	2	8	58	31	28	1	1	285	345	442	786	8%	92%	1.10	106	5.67	61
	02	29	5	aaa	OAK	516	45	111	22	0	6	49	43	52	1	4	215	275	293	568	8%	90%	0.83	56	2.72	11
Lopez,Mendy	01	27	4	aaa	HOU	208	30	53	11	1	13	29	15	43	2	2	256	305	499	804	7%	79%	0.34	143	5.24	51
	02	28	6	aaa	PIT	385	47	85	24	0	8	56	27	81	3	1	221	272	345	617	7%	79%	0.33	87	3.23	16
Lopez,Mickey	01	28	468	aa	PHI	382	48	80	17	4	7	32	45	61	14	6	209	292	326	618	11%	84%	0.73	75	3.30	15
	02	29	64	a/a	CHC	400	39	78	20	1	3	31	30	51	9	7	195	251	273	524	7%	87%	0.59	58	2.21	1
Lopez,Pee Wee	02	26	2	a/a	ATL	127	12	25	3	0	3	13	10	20	1	1	197	255	291	547	7%	84%	0.50	57	2.47	-1
Lopez,Rafael	01	25	2	a/a	CHC	123	12	28	6	1	1	12	7	18	0	0	228	269	317	586	5%	85%	0.39	63	2.95	10
Lorenzana,Luis	02	24	6	aa	SD	288	28	61	7	1	2	17	35	40	0	1	212	297	264	561	11%	86%	0.88	35	2.80	3
Lorenzo,Juan	01	23	65	aa	MIN	319	31	74	9	3	3	23	5	33	2	2	231	243	304	547	1%	90%	0.15	46	2.42	-1
	02	24	6	aa	MIN	215	26	52	6	1	2	16	7	20	1	2	242	266	307	573	3%	91%	0.35	43	2.71	5
Lowery,Terrell	01	31	8	aaa	TAM	253	23	56	13	2	1	14	23	67	5	3	221	284	295	579	8%	74%	0.34	56	2.90	3
Loyd,Brian	01	28	2	a/a	SD	138	10	28	5	0	3	10	5	22	2	0	200	226	296	522	3%	84%	0.21	62	2.25	-3
	02	29	2	a/a	SD	257	22	47	8	0	3	23	10	44	0	1	183	213	249	463	4%	83%	0.23	46	1.69	-16
Lucca,Lou	01	31	5	aaa	STL	479	41	101	26	1	7	46	21	61	2	4	210	243	314	557	4%	87%	0.34	73	2.47	7
Luderer,Brian	01	23	2	aa	OAK	307	23	66	16	1	4	26	17	40	1	1	215	257	313	570	5%	87%	0.43	70	2.71	9
	02	24	2	aa	CLE	155	25	34	10	1	3	14	10	31	0	0	219	267	355	622	6%	80%	0.32	93	3.24	18
Ludwick,Ryan	01	23	8	a/a	OAK	500	73	114	22	2	21	81	46	102	9	12	228	293	406	699	8%	80%	0.45	108	3.81	29
	02	24	8	aaa	TEX	305	47	78	24	3	12	40	29	56	2	2	256	320	472	792	9%	82%	0.52	139	5.34	53
Luke,Matt	02	32	3	aaa	TAM	106	11	21	5	0	1	9	11	27	0	0	198	274	274	547	9%	75%	0.41	56	2.61	-3
Lunar,Fernando	02	25	2	aaa	BAL	145	6	25	1	0	2	7	3	24	1	0	172	189	221	410	2%	83%	0.13	27	1.34	-29
Lunsford,Trey	02	23	2	a/a	SF	267	25	62	13	0	2	25	30	49	4	2	232	310	303	613	10%	82%	0.61	55	3.39	12
Luster,Jeremy	01	24	3	aa	SF	506	45	120	29	1	3	63	27	84	5	3	237	275	315	590	5%	83%	0.32	62	2.98	11
Luther,Ryan	01	25	42	aa	SF	453	45	110	23	1	3	35	26	69	5	9	243	284	317	600	5%	85%	0.37	56	2.95	12
	02	26	2	a/a	SF	116	10	28	6	0	1	14	11	25	4	0	241	307	319	626	9%	78%	0.44	59	3.73	14
Luuloa,Keith	01	27	436	aaa	SD	310	38	67	17	1	5	22	20	39	1	1	216	264	325	590	6%	87%	0.52	77	2.91	14
	02	28	5	a/a	MIL	340	45	68	10	3	7	32	45	53	3	3	200	294	309	602	12%	84%	0.85	66	3.13	11
Lydy,Scott	01	33	83	aaa	HOU	283	28	64	18	1	6	32	35	59	6	5	226	311	363	674	11%	79%	0.60	94	3.84	26
Machado,Albenis	01	23	4	aa	MON	341	49	82	12	2	3	29	37	49	9	8	240	315	314	629	10%	86%	0.76	50	3.40	16
	02	24	4	a/a	MON	281	33	62	11	2	3	28	45	38	6	6	221	328	306	634	14%	86%	1.18	57	3.54	21
Machado,Andy	01	21	6	aa	PHI	101	11	14	2	0	1	6	11	21	4	2	135	217	187	404	9%	79%	0.50	34	1.34	-31
	02	22	6	aa	PHI	450	59	103	24	2	10	64	63	105	33	13	229	324	358	681	12%	77%	0.60	86	4.11	24
Machado,Rob	01	28	2	aaa	CHC	180	16	42	8	0	6	24	8	34	0	0	233	267	372	639	4%	81%	0.24	89	3.40	19
Mackowiak,Rob	01	25	8	aaa	PIT	118	11	28	5	0	3	11	6	31	1	1	235	272	352	624	5%	73%	0.19	76	3.21	13
Maddox,Garry	01	27	8	a/a	BOS	314	40	81	23	4	8	41	32	73	3	6	259	328	432	760	9%	77%	0.44	115	4.85	43
Madonna,Chris	01	29	2	aa	OAK	106	13	18	2	1	2	10	10	31	0	1	166	241	264	505	9%	71%	0.33	55	2.05	-15
Magruder,Chris	01	24	8	a/a	TEX	490	73	135	26	6	16	52	47	72	8	7	276	339	451	790	9%	85%	0.65	108	5.45	50
	02	25	8	aaa	CLE	191	26	49	10	1	5	15	24	32	3	2	257	340	398	737	11%	83%	0.75	91	4.90	38
Mahoney,Mike	01	29	2	aaa	CHC	289	18	53	11	1	2	21	18	59	1	3	183	230	248	478	6%	80%	0.30	47	1.81	-14
	02	30	2	aaa	CHC	223	21	43	9	1	1	12	11	34	1	1	193	231	256	486	5%	85%	0.32	47	1.93	-10
Maier,T.J.	01	27	4	a/a	STL	272	42	67	18	1	4	30	36	56	8	5	246	334	364	698	12%	80%	0.64	85	4.34	30
Maldonado,Carlos	01	23	2	aa	HOU	262	24	70	14	0	4	27	22	47	1	2	267	324	366	690	8%	82%	0.47	71	4.26	28
	02	24	2	a/a	HOU	152	12	34	8	0	4	18	19	25	0	0	224	310	355	665	11%	84%	0.76	87	3.95	26
Malloy,Marty	01	29	46	aaa	CIN	468	51	120	32	3	5	36	21	45	6	7	257	288	366	654	4%	90%	0.46	80	3.53	28
	02	30	4	aaa	CIN	180	17	36	6	1	3	11	14	20	5	5	200	258	294	552	7%	89%	0.70	60	2.35	6
Marsters,Brandon	01	27	2	aa	MIN	349	30	67	15	1	8	31	24	86	2	1	192	245	307	551	7%	75%	0.28	74	2.50	0
	02	28	2	aa	MIN	260	26	54	14	0	4	24	13	51	0	0	208	245	308	553	5%	80%	0.25	71	2.53	4
Martinez,Belvani	01	23	84	aa	COL	430	39	113	21	6	6	32	6	48	25	14	263	273	381	654	1%	89%	0.13	77	3.31	22
Martinez,Eddy	01	24	6	a/a	BAL	436	57	110	13	1	8	39	33	89	11	3	252	305	342	647	7%	80%	0.37	57	3.78	15
Martinez,Felix	02	28	6	a/a	LA	386	39	70	11	2	3	30	20	67	4	4	181	222	244	465	5%	83%	0.30	42	1.71	-16
Martinez,Gabby	01	28	4	a/a	NYM	236	25	54	10	2	1	13	12	33	14	8	229	268	302	570	5%	86%	0.38	53	2.61	6
Martinez,Greg	01	30	8	aaa	TAM	242	29	61	5	2	1	17	24	44	11	7	252	319	301	619	9%	82%	0.54	32	3.34	8
	02	31	8	aa	TAM	101	5	14	1	1	0	6	4	19	4	1	139	171	168	340	4%	81%	0.21	18	0.94	-42
Martinez,Louis	01	25	4	a/a	ATL	123	11	18	3	0	0	4	4	15	1	1	146	173	171	344	3%	88%	0.27	22	0.90	-37
Martinez,Sandy	02	32	2	aaa	MON	133	9	25	3	1	3	14	8	39	2	0	188	234	293	527	6%	71%	0.21	62	2.33	-8
Martinez,Victor	02	24	2	aa	CLE	443	73	139	38	0	20	74	50	58	3	3	314	383	535	918	10%	87%	0.86	146	7.88	82
Martine,Chris	01	26	2	aa	STL	180	17	30	5	0	0	4	10	51	2	2	169	215	198	413	5%	72%	0.21	26	1.36	-29
Martin,Billy	02	26	8	aa	ARI	264	23	45	13	0	5	26	21	79	0	0	170	232	277	508	7%	70%	0.27	73	2.12	-8
Martin,Justin	01	26	4	aa	PIT	161	17	46	6	0	0	11	12	22	14	5	285	334	324	658	7%	86%	0.53	35	3.98	20
Martin,Norberto	01	35	48	aaa	FLA	333	28	77	15	2	3	23	9	33	5	4	230	250	311	561	3%	90%	0.27	58	2.55	6
Mashore,Damon	01	32	8	aaa	STL	289	25	68	14	1	5	27	14	57	2	5	237	273	346	619	5%	80%	0.25	73	3.06	14
Mashore,Justin	01	30	8	aa	COL	172	14	33	9	0	3	15	8	45	2	2	192	226	297	522	4%	74%	0.17	73	2.08	-2
Mateo,Henry	01	25	4	aaa	MON	500	65	126	14	9	5	39	29	82	43	15	252	293	346	639	5%	84%	0.35	56	3.52	14
	02	26	4	aaa	MON	285	31	67	10	4	4	22	15	45	13	7	235	273	340	614	5%	84%	0.33	65	3.05	12
Mateo,Ruben	01	24	8	aaa	CIN	302	31	69	18	3	3	27	12	42	2	2	228	258	338	596	4%	86%	0.29	77	2.90	14
	02	25	8	aaa	CIN	209	29	57	14	0	7	18	8	29	5	2	273	300	440	740	4%	86%	0.28	111	4.65	42
Mathis,Jared	01	26	8	aa	MIL	204	12	41	10	1	2	14	5	25	1	1	200	220	281	502	2%	88%	0.21	58	1.99	-5
	02	27	5	aa	MIL	203	17	37	4	2	2	13	7	27	3	5	182	210	251	461	3%	87%	0.26	41	1.51	-17
Matos,Julius	01	27	6	a/a	SD	450	47	113	16	1	6	31	13	53	6	11	252	273	330	602	3%	88%	0.24	52	2.84	10
	02	28	6	aaa	SD	186	17	49	14	0	3	22	8	19	1	2	263	294	387	681	4%	90%	0.42	92	3.88	34
Matos,Luis	02	24	8	aa	BAL	218	28	52	12	1	8	34	26	41	12	5	239	320	413	733	11%	81%	0.63	110	4.60	37
Matos,Pascual	01	27	2	aaa	NYY	256	18	49	11	1	4	21	10	52	1	3	193	223	288	511	4%	80%	0.19	64	1.98	-6
Matranga,Dave	01	25	4	a/a	HOU	403	68	115	35	2	10	53	37	82	15	8	285	345	457	802	8%	80%	0.45	120	5.68	54
	02	26	4	aaa	HOU	300	41	78	15	3	7	35	24	72	6	2	260	315	400	715	7%	76%	0.33	89	4.55	30
Matthews,Lamont	02	24	8	aa	LA	317	37	53	15	1	8	29	61	99	3	3	167	302	297	598	16%	69%	0.62	84	3.12	3

Major League Equivalent Statistics

BATTER	Yr	Age	Pos	Lev	Org	AB	R	H	D	T	HR	RBI	BB	K	SB	CS	BA	OB	Slg	OPS	bb%	ct%	Eye	PX	RC/G	BPV
Maule,Jason	02	25	5	aa	HOU	171	23	37	3	0	2	11	14	24	9	5	216	276	269	545	8%	86%	0.58	34	2.48	-2
Maxwell,Jason	02	31	6	aaa	CIN	269	31	66	18	2	2	22	24	37	4	5	245	307	349	657	8%	86%	0.65	77	3.64	27
Maynard,Scott	01	24	2	aa	SEA	229	14	35	10	0	0	16	19	59	3	0	153	218	195	413	8%	74%	0.32	37	1.47	-27
McCarty,Dave	02	33	3	aaa	TAM	114	20	32	6	1	6	17	11	32	0	1	281	344	509	853	9%	72%	0.34	136	6.28	56
McClure,Brian	01	28	54	aa	DET	255	20	49	12	1	1	15	16	41	0	0	192	239	254	493	6%	84%	0.38	48	2.04	-8
McCracken,Quinton	01	32	8	aaa	MIN	361	38	101	23	3	3	32	14	47	5	11	279	307	381	688	4%	87%	0.31	76	3.77	30
McDonald,Darnell	01	23	8	a/a	BAL	508	50	120	23	2	5	54	38	90	16	14	236	289	320	609	7%	82%	0.42	60	3.02	12
	02	24	8	a/a	BAL	476	56	125	26	5	9	44	46	94	17	7	263	328	395	723	9%	80%	0.49	87	4.67	33
McDonald,Donzell	01	27	8	aaa	NYY	374	49	86	10	6	8	30	35	68	16	5	231	297	350	647	9%	82%	0.51	69	3.69	16
	02	28	8	aaa	KC	452	48	105	13	12	6	27	42	83	23	7	232	298	354	652	9%	82%	0.51	69	3.73	16
McDonald,John	01	27	6	aaa	CLE	410	44	89	15	1	2	28	28	64	14	10	218	267	273	540	6%	84%	0.43	42	2.37	-1
McDonald,Keith	01	29	2	aaa	STL	333	31	72	19	1	8	31	20	53	1	0	215	259	352	610	6%	84%	0.37	91	3.10	17
	02	30	2	aaa	STL	267	25	60	16	0	10	28	12	51	1	2	225	258	397	655	4%	81%	0.24	111	3.36	25
McDougall,Marshall	02	24	5	aa	OAK	341	55	92	21	4	8	50	37	53	6	5	270	341	425	766	10%	84%	0.70	101	5.19	46
McDowell,Arturo	02	23	8	aa	SF	221	15	35	3	1	0	9	13	39	8	6	158	205	181	386	6%	82%	0.33	16	1.13	-34
McGee,Tom	01	27	2	aa	BAL	156	11	19	4	0	2	10	10	33	0	1	123	173	184	357	6%	79%	0.29	42	0.97	-36
McGowan,Sean	01	24	83	a/a	SF	516	56	132	33	1	13	66	22	90	1	1	256	286	399	685	4%	83%	0.24	97	4.00	30
	02	25	3	a/a	SF	217	11	45	15	2	1	15	5	40	1	1	207	225	309	534	2%	82%	0.13	76	2.24	3
McGuire,Ryan	01	30	3	aaa	FLA	239	28	55	11	1	5	26	16	40	0	1	228	278	339	617	6%	83%	0.41	73	3.22	15
	02	31	3	aaa	BAL	315	35	74	12	1	9	37	23	69	0	1	235	287	365	652	7%	78%	0.33	81	3.62	18
McKay,Cody	01	28	2	aaa	OAK	350	27	75	15	0	5	30	20	54	1	0	214	257	299	555	5%	85%	0.37	59	2.62	3
	02	29	2	aaa	OAK	378	38	86	13	1	8	40	15	47	1	1	228	257	331	588	4%	88%	0.32	66	2.87	9
McKeel,Walt	01	30	2	a/a	COL	147	16	30	5	1	4	9	14	29	0	0	204	272	328	600	8%	81%	0.48	77	3.07	9
	02	31	2	aaa	COL	130	5	26	5	0	2	6	9	18	0	0	200	252	285	536	6%	86%	0.50	58	2.43	1
McKinley,Dan	01	25	8	aaa	MON	360	28	94	17	5	5	36	18	80	11	6	261	296	377	673	5%	78%	0.22	75	3.84	22
	02	26	8	a/a	MON	294	24	54	12	3	3	24	10	51	4	5	184	211	276	486	3%	83%	0.20	61	1.73	-10
McKinley,Josh	02	23	4	aa	MON	325	31	67	16	0	6	25	32	65	2	5	206	277	311	588	9%	80%	0.49	72	2.82	8
McMillon,Billy	02	31	8	aaa	NYY	442	53	106	26	2	6	33	44	64	2	5	240	309	348	657	9%	86%	0.69	77	3.71	25
McNally,Sean	01	29	5	aaa	ARI	427	35	83	13	2	9	42	34	122	3	2	194	254	298	552	7%	72%	0.28	65	2.54	-3
	02	30	5	aa	TEX	243	15	39	5	1	5	27	19	83	3	2	160	221	251	472	7%	66%	0.23	54	1.79	-20
McNamara,Rusty	01	27	3	aa	PHI	118	13	27	10	0	1	11	4	10	0	1	229	256	332	588	4%	91%	0.42	83	2.78	19
	02	28	5	aa	ATL	448	37	91	14	1	4	37	23	47	5	1	203	242	266	508	5%	90%	0.49	43	2.18	-5
McNaughton,Troy	01	27	8	a/a	STL	410	51	82	28	2	8	33	35	102	5	11	201	264	336	600	8%	75%	0.34	94	2.70	13
McNeal,Aaron	01	23	3	aa	SD	484	48	104	17	1	15	49	23	132	1	4	214	250	345	595	5%	73%	0.18	80	2.80	8
	02	24	3	a/a	NYM	434	49	104	15	0	16	64	42	107	1	2	240	307	385	692	9%	75%	0.39	88	4.15	24
Meadows,Randy	01	25	4	aa	CHC	140	13	29	5	1	0	12	5	34	1	3	206	230	257	488	3%	75%	0.13	40	1.78	-12
	02	26	6	aa	PIT	111	11	11	2	0	1	5	4	25	2	1	99	130	144	275	3%	77%	0.16	30	0.56	-51
Meadows,Tydus	01	24	8	aa	CHC	197	34	44	9	2	8	24	32	53	0	2	222	331	400	732	14%	73%	0.61	107	4.63	30
	02	25	8	aa	KC	119	19	36	10	3	4	16	11	22	4	2	303	362	538	899	8%	82%	0.50	149	7.16	72
Medrano,Jesus	02	24	4	aa	FLA	414	60	105	23	5	2	25	63	74	30	20	254	352	348	700	13%	82%	0.85	67	4.23	29
Medrano,Steve	01	24	6	aa	KC	140	11	29	5	0	0	11	10	17	2	2	210	261	244	505	6%	88%	0.56	30	2.12	-6
Medrano,Tony	01	27	486	aaa	CLE	466	58	124	26	1	7	45	47	35	18	8	266	333	371	704	9%	92%	1.33	74	4.51	46
	02	28	6	aaa	MON	438	40	93	17	2	2	35	30	42	10	1	212	263	274	537	6%	90%	0.71	45	2.56	4
Meier,Dan	01	24	83	aa	PIT	312	38	72	13	3	11	33	39	78	1	1	231	317	402	719	11%	75%	0.50	102	4.52	29
	02	25	8	aa	PIT	237	20	48	9	1	5	24	17	57	2	3	203	256	312	568	7%	76%	0.30	70	2.58	2
Melhuse,Adam	01	30	2	aaa	COL	184	16	41	8	1	5	20	20	30	0	1	223	299	366	665	10%	84%	0.67	90	3.78	25
	02	31	2	aaa	COL	341	33	87	23	1	10	34	25	47	3	5	255	306	416	722	7%	86%	0.53	108	4.32	40
Meliah,Dave	01	25	45	a/a	TEX	370	41	98	21	3	12	45	29	47	5	7	265	318	435	753	7%	87%	0.62	108	4.70	45
	02	26	8	a/a	TEX	328	35	71	16	2	8	35	16	40	2	5	216	253	351	604	5%	88%	0.40	86	2.79	16
Melian,Jackson	01	22	8	aa	CIN	426	51	93	21	0	13	41	29	74	8	8	218	268	359	627	6%	83%	0.39	91	3.09	18
	02	23	8	aa	CHC	418	52	104	21	1	9	44	47	112	18	10	249	325	368	693	10%	73%	0.42	80	4.19	24
Melo,Juan	01	25	4	aaa	SF	375	35	100	19	3	6	41	14	47	7	11	267	293	380	673	4%	87%	0.29	76	3.54	26
	02	26	4	aaa	SF	479	59	119	27	2	12	55	29	82	5	8	248	291	388	680	6%	83%	0.35	92	3.75	28
Mench,Kevin	01	24	8	aa	TEX	475	63	114	32	1	23	67	28	61	3	7	241	283	459	743	6%	87%	0.46	137	4.25	46
Mendez,Carlos	01	27	32	aaa	DET	398	35	85	25	1	12	60	7	42	0	0	212	225	372	598	2%	89%	0.16	105	2.75	17
	02	28	2	aaa	OAK	404	41	103	20	1	8	52	8	42	2	1	255	269	369	638	2%	90%	0.19	77	3.43	20
Mendez,Donaldo	02	24	6	a/a	SD	441	58	82	21	1	8	31	27	109	22	10	186	233	293	525	6%	75%	0.25	72	2.16	-3
Mendoza,Carlos	02	23	6	aa	SF	377	37	83	19	2	1	24	57	35	10	10	220	323	289	612	13%	91%	1.63	53	3.24	28
Menechino,Frank	02	32	6	aaa	OAK	314	33	59	9	0	4	33	31	48	6	4	188	261	255	516	9%	85%	0.65	45	2.24	-6
Mensik,Todd	01	27	3	aa	OAK	502	48	107	26	1	15	55	41	95	0	1	213	272	357	629	8%	81%	0.43	93	3.31	18
	02	28	0	aa	OAK	251	27	44	9	0	4	22	28	66	2	1	175	258	259	517	10%	74%	0.42	56	2.29	-10
Meran,Jorge	01	24	2	a/a	DET	138	9	32	4	0	2	16	5	35	1	0	232	259	304	563	3%	75%	0.14	48	2.73	-0
	02	28	2	aa	DET	184	12	33	3	2	2	11	11	53	1	0	179	226	250	476	6%	71%	0.21	41	1.88	-19
Merloni,Lou	01	31	6	aaa	BOS	195	23	43	11	0	3	15	11	34	2	0	222	262	318	581	5%	82%	0.31	70	2.90	9
Merrill,Ronnie	01	23	4	aa	DET	147	18	40	14	0	3	15	10	21	0	1	272	318	429	747	6%	86%	0.48	116	4.83	48
Metcalfe,Mike	01	29	48	a/a	CIN	494	52	120	22	3	3	35	33	54	25	12	243	290	316	606	6%	89%	0.61	54	3.13	15
	02	30	4	aaa	KC	149	20	31	5	0	1	11	8	10	7	2	208	248	262	510	5%	93%	0.80	40	2.24	2
Metzler,Rod	01	27	4	aa	KC	381	42	87	17	2	3	42	30	68	9	11	228	284	301	585	7%	82%	0.44	53	2.72	7
Meyers,Chad	01	26	48	aaa	CHC	446	77	114	26	3	7	46	49	65	22	10	257	330	374	704	10%	85%	0.75	81	4.42	34
	02	27	8	aaa	STL	412	54	93	16	1	8	29	53	57	34	10	226	314	328	642	11%	86%	0.93	67	3.77	21
Michaels,Jason	01	25	8	aaa	PHI	418	53	105	22	3	15	63	36	129	10	3	251	310	424	734	8%	69%	0.28	107	4.69	34
Miles,Aaron	01	25	5	aa	CHW	343	42	78	14	2	8	33	21	31	2	6	227	272	346	618	6%	91%	0.68	76	3.02	21
	02	26	4	aa	CHW	531	55	145	33	1	8	56	35	46	21	15	273	318	384	702	6%	91%	0.76	80	4.15	39
Miller,Corky	01	26	2	a/a	CIN	314	44	89	22	0	14	55	29	40	2	2	284	344	486	829	8%	87%	0.71	130	6.11	62
	02	27	2	aaa	CIN	134	11	27	5	0	5	16	12	15	1	2	201	267	351	618	8%	89%	0.80	91	3.00	21
Miller,Ryan	01	29	6	a/a	NYM	116	8	17	5	0	2	5	3	30	1	0	144	164	233	397	2%	74%	0.09	60	1.19	-25
Minor,Damon	01	28	3	aaa	SF	406	53	102	18	2	16	50	30	64	1	1	250	303	424	726	7%	84%	0.47	105	4.53	36
Minor,Ryan	01	28	8	aaa	MON	143	17	31	6	2	5	16	13	40	0	0	219	286	385	671	9%	72%	0.33	98	3.82	20
	02	29	5	aaa	SEA	157	12	30	6	1	1	7	9	27	0	0	191	235	261	496	5%	83%	0.33	49	2.04	-9
Mitchell,Derek	01	27	6	aa	CHW	237	27	39	6	1	2	15	25	64	3	4	165	246	220	466	10%	73%	0.39	37	1.75	-22
	02	28	46	a/a	CIN	184	17	29	5	0	2	17	21	46	3	3	158	244	217	461	10%	75%	0.46	41	1.74	-21

Major League Equivalent Statistics

BATTER	Yr	Age	Pos	Lev	Org	AB	R	H	D	T	HR	RBI	BB	K	SB	CS	BA	OB	Slg	OPS	bb%	ct%	Eye	PX	RC/G	BPV
Moeller,Chad	01	27	2	aaa	ARI	274	31	66	18	0	6	27	19	43	1	5	241	291	372	663	7%	84%	0.45	92	3.53	27
	02	28	2	aaa	ARI	211	27	58	7	2	8	34	20	36	1	0	275	338	441	778	9%	83%	0.56	96	5.56	43
Mohr,Dustan	01	25	8	aa	MIN	518	81	158	39	3	21	82	43	122	8	8	304	358	509	867	8%	76%	0.35	133	6.63	63
Molina,Izzy	01	30	2	aaa	TOR	256	26	67	18	1	13	29	14	48	1	0	260	297	485	782	5%	81%	0.28	142	5.13	51
	02	31	2	a/a	BAL	342	23	54	8	0	5	23	19	64	2	1	158	202	225	427	5%	81%	0.30	43	1.46	-24
Molina,Jose	01	26	2	aaa	ANA	213	21	55	10	1	4	23	11	37	1	2	260	295	369	664	5%	83%	0.29	73	3.74	22
	02	27	2	aaa	ANA	290	22	75	11	1	3	31	9	47	0	4	259	281	334	615	3%	84%	0.19	53	3.09	12
Monahan,Shane	01	27	8	a/a	PIT	112	10	27	6	1	3	10	5	19	1	2	238	269	382	650	4%	83%	0.25	92	3.28	22
	02	28	8	aa	KC	391	39	92	20	2	7	42	12	56	8	9	235	258	350	608	3%	86%	0.21	78	2.82	15
Monroe,Craig	01	25	8	aaa	TEX	410	50	108	24	4	19	63	40	67	8	9	263	329	480	809	9%	84%	0.60	132	5.36	54
	02	26	8	aaa	DET	358	55	105	27	5	7	45	34	49	6	3	293	355	455	810	9%	86%	0.69	109	6.05	57
Montgomery,Ray	01	31	8	aaa	NYM	194	31	52	6	1	5	28	23	39	4	2	269	345	394	739	10%	80%	0.58	76	5.04	33
Moon,Brian	01	24	2	aa	MIL	287	15	40	10	2	0	14	17	47	0	2	139	187	189	376	6%	83%	0.36	38	1.09	-31
	02	25	2	a/a	MIL	221	18	42	8	0	1	15	23	49	4	1	190	266	240	506	9%	78%	0.47	39	2.27	-11
Moore,Frank	02	24	4	aa	TAM	331	33	83	16	0	2	28	24	57	8	8	251	301	317	619	7%	83%	0.42	52	3.21	14
Moore,Jason	02	25	6	aa	TEX	417	46	91	19	3	11	58	41	85	3	4	218	288	357	646	9%	80%	0.48	88	3.48	18
Morales,Andy	01	27	5	aa	NYY	160	12	30	3	1	1	11	8	26	1	1	190	228	234	462	5%	83%	0.30	28	1.74	-19
Morales,Steve	02	24	2	aa	FLA	164	12	36	9	0	4	19	4	20	0	1	220	238	348	586	2%	88%	0.20	86	2.66	13
Morales,Willie	01	29	2	aaa	COL	215	14	38	6	0	2	8	4	29	3	1	178	191	233	424	2%	87%	0.13	39	1.41	-22
	02	30	2	aaa	ARI	315	30	79	20	0	5	36	10	47	3	5	251	274	362	636	3%	85%	0.21	81	3.23	21
Moreta,Ramon	01	26	8	a/a	SEA	185	19	41	6	1	2	24	11	44	11	11	220	263	294	556	5%	76%	0.24	49	2.15	-2
	02	27	8	aa	SF	273	24	53	9	2	2	27	14	52	12	15	194	233	264	497	5%	81%	0.27	47	1.61	-11
Morgan,Scott	01	28	8	aaa	ANA	501	65	110	32	2	20	59	29	91	2	0	219	262	412	674	5%	82%	0.32	122	3.66	30
	02	29	8	aaa	SD	384	33	79	14	0	7	35	15	99	3	1	206	236	297	532	4%	74%	0.15	60	2.32	-3
Moriarty,Mike	01	28	6	aaa	MIN	404	48	84	15	1	10	37	42	77	4	5	207	281	320	601	9%	81%	0.54	72	3.01	9
	02	29	6	aaa	BAL	311	39	73	15	1	4	21	30	48	4	1	235	302	328	630	9%	85%	0.63	65	3.57	18
Morneau,Justin	02	21	3	aa	MIN	494	60	137	31	3	13	66	35	75	6	0	277	325	431	756	7%	85%	0.47	102	5.23	44
Morrissey,Adam	02	21	4	aa	OAK	302	33	63	13	1	2	19	32	61	3	2	209	284	278	563	10%	80%	0.52	51	2.77	1
Morris,Bobby	01	29	48	aa	CIN	224	22	46	14	1	6	28	26	40	2	4	207	291	361	651	11%	82%	0.66	101	3.43	24
Morris,Warren	01	28	4	aaa	PIT	223	20	58	14	1	4	30	10	18	2	5	260	290	383	674	4%	92%	0.53	87	3.60	33
	02	29	4	aaa	BOS	356	41	86	20	4	5	35	17	46	3	3	242	276	362	638	5%	87%	0.37	81	3.38	21
Mosquera,Julio	01	30	2	a/a	NYY	309	30	70	17	0	8	28	12	70	2	1	227	255	362	618	4%	77%	0.17	91	3.11	16
	02	31	82	a/a	TEX	278	27	59	10	0	5	21	10	51	9	1	212	240	302	542	3%	82%	0.20	60	2.50	-1
Mota,Tony	01	24	8	aaa	LA	442	47	109	23	5	6	43	30	62	12	9	247	294	362	656	6%	86%	0.48	77	3.57	24
	02	25	8	aaa	STL	136	18	27	6	0	3	11	13	23	3	2	199	268	309	577	9%	83%	0.57	73	2.75	8
Mottola,Chad	01	30	8	aaa	FLA	457	42	102	18	1	9	42	19	68	7	6	223	254	327	581	4%	85%	0.28	68	2.68	8
	02	31	8	aaa	TOR	476	55	102	32	1	9	48	36	76	9	2	214	270	342	612	7%	84%	0.47	91	3.19	18
Mouton,James	02	34	8	aaa	ARI	333	41	77	20	2	5	29	23	78	7	6	231	281	348	629	6%	77%	0.29	82	3.23	17
Mouton,Lyle	01	32	8	aaa	HOU	271	46	74	17	2	16	38	22	66	3	1	272	326	528	854	7%	76%	0.33	154	6.24	61
Munoz,Billy	01	26	3	aa	CLE	114	3	17	3	0	3	10	10	21	0	0	153	218	275	493	8%	82%	0.46	74	1.95	-9
	02	27	3	aa	CLE	248	27	49	17	1	4	32	31	51	0	1	198	287	323	609	11%	79%	0.61	89	3.18	15
Munoz,Juan	01	28	3	aa	STL	456	30	98	15	2	7	43	20	55	7	7	215	248	304	552	4%	88%	0.36	58	2.41	3
Munson,Eric	01	24	3	aa	DET	519	70	117	32	1	17	81	66	115	0	3	225	312	390	702	11%	78%	0.57	108	4.24	31
	02	25	3	aaa	DET	477	69	112	27	5	18	76	73	99	1	3	235	336	426	762	13%	79%	0.74	118	5.10	42
Murphy,Mike	01	30	8	aa	COL	410	37	82	14	1	6	28	41	124	14	4	199	271	282	553	9%	70%	0.33	55	2.69	-4
Murphy,Nate	01	26	8	a/a	ANA	299	37	66	14	3	7	29	26	63	5	5	221	283	354	637	8%	79%	0.42	84	3.31	16
	02	27	8	aaa	ARI	245	29	59	11	4	8	23	25	45	6	5	241	311	416	727	9%	82%	0.56	105	4.36	35
Murray,Calvin	01	30	8	aaa	SF	138	12	28	5	1	3	8	8	27	2	4	202	246	307	553	6%	81%	0.30	65	2.26	0
	02	31	8	aaa	TEX	139	15	30	5	1	2	10	7	17	3	0	216	253	309	563	5%	88%	0.41	60	2.75	5
Myers,Adrian	01	26	8	a/a	SEA	389	38	81	12	7	0	42	32	87	9	9	209	270	274	544	8%	78%	0.37	42	2.40	-5
	02	27	8	aa	SEA	449	51	96	22	5	3	41	25	89	13	7	214	255	305	560	5%	80%	0.28	64	2.56	3
Myers,Tootie	01	23	84	aa	MON	396	41	93	14	6	9	41	28	107	15	8	235	286	365	651	7%	73%	0.26	77	3.50	16
Myrow,Brian	02	26	5	aa	NYY	188	29	46	13	0	3	23	33	44	3	0	245	357	362	719	15%	77%	0.75	86	5.02	32
Nady,Xavier	02	24	8	aaa	SD	315	40	79	11	1	8	37	17	54	0	1	251	289	368	657	5%	83%	0.31	73	3.71	20
Ndungidi,Ntema	01	23	8	aa	BAL	339	30	64	14	1	3	31	34	81	3	6	189	263	263	525	9%	76%	0.42	53	2.22	-7
Neal,Steve	02	26	3	aa	ARI	407	41	95	24	0	12	53	43	89	2	1	233	307	381	688	10%	78%	0.48	98	4.15	28
Neill,Mike	01	31	8	aaa	BOS	208	21	43	9	2	4	17	23	66	2	1	208	285	320	605	10%	68%	0.34	73	3.17	6
Nelson,Bryant	01	28	54	aaa	ARI	511	45	134	20	0	8	42	19	29	9	10	262	289	346	634	4%	94%	0.64	58	3.32	24
	02	29	8	aaa	BOS	223	20	57	7	2	6	19	11	17	1	6	256	291	386	676	5%	92%	0.65	77	3.51	30
Nettles,Jeff	02	24	6	a/a	NYY	168	12	39	9	1	3	18	16	36	1	2	232	299	351	650	9%	79%	0.44	80	3.57	19
Neuberger,Scott	01	24	8	aa	TAM	419	45	103	24	1	4	39	33	82	5	3	245	300	333	634	7%	80%	0.40	66	3.54	17
	02	25	8	aa	TAM	348	32	83	11	2	4	26	29	57	3	4	239	297	316	613	8%	84%	0.51	51	3.23	11
Nevers,Tom	01	30	56	a/a	CIN	421	45	86	30	1	13	50	32	92	3	5	203	260	368	628	7%	78%	0.35	111	3.06	20
	02	31	3	aa	CIN	444	33	90	18	1	8	44	20	84	5	5	203	237	302	539	4%	81%	0.24	66	2.28	-1
Nicholson,Derek	02	26	80	a/a	DET	326	42	76	22	5	5	50	46	73	1	1	233	328	377	705	12%	78%	0.63	97	4.48	30
Nicholson,Kevin	01	26	6	aaa	SD	109	13	32	5	0	1	11	7	9	1	2	291	333	363	696	6%	92%	0.76	54	4.26	35
	02	27	6	a/a	STL	392	39	84	20	3	4	41	31	57	4	10	214	272	311	583	7%	85%	0.54	68	2.63	10
Niekro,Lance	02	24	3	aa	SF	297	27	81	18	1	3	28	6	28	0	2	273	287	370	657	2%	91%	0.21	72	3.66	25
Nieves,Jose	01	26	4	aaa	ANA	258	37	74	13	3	9	27	6	27	6	9	286	301	459	760	2%	90%	0.22	106	4.36	43
Nieves,Wil	01	24	2	aa	SD	330	25	86	21	0	3	36	15	42	1	0	262	294	351	646	4%	87%	0.36	69	3.71	23
	02	25	2	aaa	SD	237	21	64	18	1	6	25	4	36	0	0	270	282	430	713	2%	85%	0.11	110	4.29	38
Niles,Drew	01	25	64	aa	FLA	194	20	42	7	2	4	16	16	59	2	7	215	276	328	604	8%	70%	0.27	69	2.70	6
	02	26	5	aa	FLA	259	20	47	8	6	0	12	11	64	2	2	181	215	259	474	4%	75%	0.17	48	1.75	-16
Norris,Dax	01	29	2	aaa	ATL	317	21	78	22	0	3	32	14	42	2	2	246	278	343	621	4%	87%	0.33	76	3.27	20
	02	30	2	aaa	ATL	262	24	57	12	0	3	20	12	26	1	1	218	252	298	550	4%	90%	0.46	58	2.51	6
Nunez,Abraham	01	22	8	aa	FLA	467	72	106	14	7	15	51	81	158	25	20	227	341	383	725	15%	66%	0.51	90	4.35	23
	02	26	8	aaa	FLA	428	49	88	21	4	14	43	38	85	22	8	206	270	371	642	8%	80%	0.45	102	3.35	20
Nunez,Jorge	01	24	6	aa	LA	473	57	109	13	1	4	25	30	90	40	12	230	276	285	561	6%	81%	0.34	38	2.80	-1
	02	28	4	aaa	MON	282	35	73	9	3	0	17	10	39	23	8	259	284	312	596	3%	86%	0.26	38	3.10	7
Nunnally,Jon	01	30	8	aaa	KC	316	36	56	7	0	14	38	37	89	8	3	176	263	328	591	11%	72%	0.42	87	2.91	3
	02	31	8	aaa	STL	360	42	71	15	1	14	44	33	93	11	5	197	265	361	626	8%	74%	0.35	100	3.15	14

Major League Equivalent Statistics

BATTER	Yr	Age	Pos	Lev	Org	AB	R	H	D	T	HR	RBI	BB	K	SB	CS	BA	OB	Slg	OPS	bb%	ct%	Eye	PX	RC/G	BPV
Nunnari,Talmadge	01	27	3	a/a	MON	375	33	72	16	1	5	33	32	80	11	2	191	255	277	532	8%	79%	0.40	59	2.46	-4
Nye,Rodney	01	25	5	aa	NYM	366	36	85	20	0	6	36	38	76	4	6	231	303	332	636	9%	79%	0.50	72	3.43	17
	02	26	5	aa	NYM	394	38	73	14	0	9	39	40	92	3	2	185	260	289	550	9%	77%	0.43	67	2.54	-2
O'Keefe,Mike	02	24	3	aa	ANA	468	58	115	29	4	18	63	49	64	8	3	246	317	440	757	9%	86%	0.77	122	4.97	48
Ojeda,Augie	02	28	6	aaa	CHC	291	36	52	15	2	1	18	21	22	3	4	179	234	254	488	7%	92%	0.95	57	1.88	2
Olivares,Teuris	01	23	6	aa	NYY	439	50	88	14	2	4	27	20	84	5	4	200	235	269	504	4%	81%	0.24	46	2.05	-9
	02	24	4	aa	NYY	142	19	33	6	1	2	13	12	28	4	3	232	292	331	623	8%	80%	0.43	65	3.24	13
Oliver,Brian	02	26	4	aa	TEX	356	46	82	15	1	3	21	26	52	3	4	230	283	303	586	7%	85%	0.50	53	2.90	9
Olivo,Miguel	01	23	2	aa	CHW	316	36	74	20	1	13	45	30	53	5	3	233	300	424	724	9%	83%	0.57	122	4.37	39
	02	24	2	aa	CHW	359	44	98	22	7	6	43	37	64	25	13	273	341	423	764	9%	82%	0.58	97	5.01	43
Olmedo,Ranier	02	21	6	aa	CIN	478	50	108	21	1	3	24	42	66	12	19	226	288	293	581	8%	86%	0.64	50	2.60	9
Olson,Tim	01	23	6	aa	ARI	167	21	46	12	0	1	17	8	28	3	5	273	305	360	665	4%	83%	0.28	71	3.57	26
	02	24	6	aa	ARI	433	46	103	21	2	8	48	19	72	7	12	238	270	351	621	4%	83%	0.26	76	2.91	16
Ordaz,Luis	02	27	6	aaa	KC	330	36	84	18	3	2	26	13	31	7	3	255	283	345	628	4%	91%	0.42	66	3.40	20
Orie,Kevin	01	29	5	aaa	PHI	509	66	133	35	2	10	38	68	70	9	5	261	348	397	745	12%	86%	0.97	95	5.08	46
	02	30	5	aaa	CHC	294	32	67	12	2	13	40	16	32	0	1	228	268	415	683	5%	89%	0.50	111	3.73	32
Orr,Pete	02	23	6	aa	ATL	305	29	67	9	1	2	29	16	39	18	5	220	259	275	534	5%	87%	0.41	39	2.49	-2
Ortega,Bill	01	26	8	aaa	STL	495	43	121	22	3	5	49	34	63	5	7	245	293	331	625	6%	87%	0.54	60	3.30	17
	02	27	8	aaa	STL	293	37	64	14	1	6	29	30	38	1	5	218	291	334	625	9%	87%	0.79	77	3.19	20
Ortiz,Hector	01	32	2	aaa	KC	150	14	32	6	0	2	11	10	22	0	3	216	265	294	559	6%	85%	0.45	56	2.45	4
	02	33	2	aaa	KC	181	10	35	5	0	1	9	15	27	1	1	193	255	238	493	8%	85%	0.56	33	2.06	-11
Ortiz,Jose	01	24	4	aaa	OAK	256	32	60	14	3	6	31	20	40	6	5	234	290	383	673	7%	84%	0.50	95	3.67	27
	02	25	6	aaa	COL	111	15	34	8	1	5	12	3	8	1	1	306	325	532	856	3%	93%	0.38	141	6.23	68
Ortiz,Luis	02	32	3	aaa	MON	382	37	95	35	0	4	50	17	33	1	0	249	281	372	652	4%	91%	0.52	97	3.66	33
Ortiz,Nick	01	28	6	aaa	KC	316	29	68	18	1	5	30	23	53	2	7	215	269	321	589	7%	83%	0.44	75	2.71	11
Otanez,Willis	01	28	3	aa	ATL	308	29	62	10	2	9	31	31	68	2	2	200	274	330	603	9%	78%	0.46	79	3.06	8
Ottavinia,Paul	01	28	38	a/a	NYY	449	59	102	26	4	7	39	36	57	11	6	228	286	352	638	7%	87%	0.64	84	3.44	23
	02	29	8	aa	TEX	522	51	97	23	2	5	40	35	67	10	6	186	237	266	503	6%	87%	0.52	57	2.05	-4
Overbay,Lyle	01	25	38	aa	ARI	532	60	160	43	2	9	73	48	73	5	5	300	358	436	794	8%	86%	0.67	99	5.85	54
	02	26	3	aaa	ARI	525	62	161	37	0	15	82	31	64	0	0	307	345	463	808	6%	88%	0.48	107	6.07	56
Owens,Jeremy	01	25	8	aa	SD	395	41	73	17	4	6	23	45	154	29	12	185	268	291	559	10%	61%	0.29	69	2.59	-4
Owens,Ryan	01	24	5	aa	ARI	448	51	102	19	1	6	35	49	96	9	6	227	304	314	618	10%	79%	0.52	60	3.35	11
	02	25	45	a/a	COL	337	27	79	19	1	9	36	30	70	5	5	234	297	377	674	8%	79%	0.43	94	3.78	25
Ozuna,Pablo	02	28	4	aaa	FLA	261	25	67	13	1	5	22	12	30	11	4	257	289	372	661	4%	89%	0.40	77	3.74	25
Pachot,John	01	27	2	a/a	LA	174	12	37	13	1	4	18	3	21	1	2	212	225	362	587	2%	88%	0.14	104	2.52	16
	02	28	2	aa	PIT	321	21	64	23	0	2	30	4	29	1	0	199	209	290	499	1%	91%	0.14	73	1.96	-1
Paciorek,Pete	01	25	8	aa	LA	150	14	26	6	1	4	17	13	46	3	1	174	238	300	538	8%	70%	0.28	80	2.36	-4
Padgett,Matt	02	25	8	aa	FLA	406	38	75	21	1	11	46	32	123	5	5	185	244	323	567	7%	70%	0.26	90	2.51	4
Padilla,Jorge	02	23	8	aa	PHI	484	57	111	29	2	6	52	34	70	26	13	229	280	335	615	7%	86%	0.49	76	3.10	17
Parrish,Dave	02	23	2	aa	NYY	341	33	72	16	1	4	36	35	59	12	7	211	285	299	584	9%	83%	0.59	62	2.88	8
Pascucci,Val	01	23	8	aa	MON	476	68	107	16	1	19	58	54	100	7	9	225	304	382	686	10%	79%	0.54	93	3.86	24
	02	24	8	aa	MON	459	56	95	14	1	21	64	71	93	2	0	207	313	379	692	13%	80%	0.76	100	4.25	25
Patterson,Corey	01	22	8	aaa	CHC	367	57	85	20	2	6	28	26	54	17	9	232	283	349	632	7%	85%	0.48	80	3.26	20
Patterson,Jarrod	01	28	5	a/a	DET	283	46	78	19	2	9	33	32	48	2	1	276	349	453	802	10%	83%	0.65	115	5.89	52
	02	29	5	aaa	DET	447	55	111	27	6	9	58	40	67	3	1	248	310	396	706	8%	85%	0.60	97	4.40	35
Paul,Josh	02	27	2	aaa	CHW	231	15	55	13	1	0	14	15	42	9	4	238	285	303	588	6%	82%	0.36	54	2.99	9
Paz,Rich	01	24	45	aa	PIT	248	27	53	14	1	4	27	46	54	6	6	215	337	326	662	16%	78%	0.85	78	3.85	21
	02	25	5	aa	KC	479	67	117	23	0	5	59	62	76	4	6	244	331	324	654	11%	84%	0.82	59	3.84	22
Pecci,Jay	01	25	46	aa	OAK	469	51	95	23	4	2	35	30	50	12	7	201	249	278	527	6%	89%	0.59	57	2.26	3
	02	26	4	aa	SEA	271	26	62	9	1	1	22	22	37	8	8	229	287	280	567	8%	86%	0.59	38	2.62	4
Peeples,Mike	01	25	8	aaa	COL	424	48	117	21	3	17	47	19	41	6	11	276	306	458	764	4%	90%	0.45	111	4.56	47
	02	26	8	a/a	FLA	314	30	59	15	2	5	31	15	54	6	6	188	225	296	521	5%	83%	0.28	73	2.02	-2
Pelaez,Alex	01	26	5	aa	SD	416	37	97	18	1	8	44	25	57	2	0	234	277	340	617	6%	86%	0.44	70	3.30	16
	02	27	5	aaa	SD	411	40	110	26	1	9	54	16	37	0	1	268	295	401	697	4%	91%	0.43	92	4.18	36
Pellow,Kit	01	28	3	aaa	KC	484	60	122	13	0	15	60	26	82	3	4	252	290	371	661	5%	83%	0.32	71	3.70	20
	02	29	5	aaa	KC	402	48	97	21	2	21	56	15	70	3	2	241	269	460	729	4%	83%	0.21	132	4.17	39
Pena,Angel	01	27	2	aaa	LA	198	28	50	6	1	12	30	13	42	1	0	255	299	470	770	6%	79%	0.30	121	5.01	41
	02	28	2	aaa	SF	248	23	56	10	2	6	29	12	51	2	2	226	262	355	616	5%	79%	0.24	80	3.08	13
Pena,Carlos	01	23	3	aaa	TEX	431	69	117	37	2	21	62	69	100	9	3	271	372	513	885	14%	77%	0.69	156	7.17	68
	02	24	3	aaa	OAK	175	22	35	8	1	7	24	18	36	2	0	200	275	377	652	9%	79%	0.50	107	3.59	21
Pena,Elvis	01	25	6	aaa	MIL	437	45	93	14	2	1	23	24	61	10	6	213	254	261	514	5%	86%	0.39	36	2.20	-6
	02	28	4	a/a	MIL	397	44	86	11	3	2	23	36	79	24	12	217	282	275	556	8%	80%	0.46	39	2.62	-3
Pena,Wily Mo	02	21	8	aa	CIN	388	40	96	24	1	9	40	29	92	6	0	247	300	384	684	7%	76%	0.32	93	4.18	27
Peoples,Danny	01	27	3	aaa	CLE	370	53	76	18	1	16	41	48	115	0	3	204	295	385	680	11%	69%	0.41	111	3.83	22
Peralta,John	02	20	6	aa	CLE	470	58	132	28	3	15	58	42	84	4	2	281	340	449	789	8%	82%	0.50	108	5.64	48
Perez,Antonio	02	23	4	aa	SEA	240	30	59	8	1	2	24	11	63	15	9	246	279	313	591	4%	74%	0.17	46	2.79	4
Perez,Jerson	01	26	6	a/a	TOR	438	51	112	24	3	4	42	26	86	12	3	255	297	350	647	6%	80%	0.30	68	3.74	19
	02	27	6	aaa	TOR	203	21	43	7	1	3	12	11	40	2	2	212	252	300	553	5%	80%	0.28	58	2.48	-0
Perez,Jhonny	01	25	46	a/a	DET	413	51	100	19	4	4	36	24	53	14	7	242	284	337	620	5%	87%	0.45	64	3.25	16
	02	26	4	aa	DET	343	33	84	11	2	2	34	23	43	6	6	245	292	306	598	6%	87%	0.53	43	3.03	10
Perez,Josue	01	24	8	aa	PHI	167	10	24	4	0	1	5	11	35	2	3	142	197	182	379	6%	79%	0.33	29	1.09	-34
	02	25	8	aa	PHI	196	11	34	7	0	1	13	10	40	5	5	173	214	224	438	5%	80%	0.25	40	1.42	-21
Perez,Robert	01	32	8	aaa	MIL	230	24	61	14	2	7	32	6	30	5	6	266	286	434	720	3%	87%	0.21	107	3.92	37
	02	33	8	aaa	NYY	460	40	93	23	2	11	45	11	51	6	7	202	221	333	553	2%	89%	0.22	85	2.23	7
Perez,Santiago	01	26	8	aaa	SD	184	27	45	11	0	4	9	12	55	16	3	242	288	366	654	6%	70%	0.22	86	3.84	20
Perez,Timo	01	25	8	aaa	NYM	192	35	65	10	2	5	18	11	18	14	2	339	374	490	864	5%	91%	0.61	96	7.50	65
Pernalete,Marco	01	23	4	a/a	SF	194	16	53	12	2	3	20	16	30	1	1	271	325	401	726	8%	85%	0.53	87	4.72	37
	02	24	53	a/a	SF	314	30	73	8	1	4	26	12	56	3	1	232	261	303	563	4%	82%	0.21	45	2.71	0
Perry,Chan	01	29	2	aaa	ATL	350	31	82	13	2	6	32	15	58	1	6	234	266	335	602	4%	83%	0.27	65	2.82	10
	02	30	3	aa	KC	399	37	85	13	1	9	46	18	54	4	4	213	247	318	565	4%	86%	0.33	66	2.55	5
Peterman,Tommy	01	26	2	aa	MIN	302	30	64	15	1	3	30	18	46	1	1	210	255	291	546	6%	85%	0.40	59	2.50	2

Major League Equivalent Statistics

BATTER	Yr	Age	Pos	Lev	Org	AB	R	H	D	T	HR	RBI	BB	K	SB	CS	BA	OB	Slg	OPS	bb%	ct%	Eye	PX	RC/G	BPV
Petersen,Chris	01	31	46	a/a	ARI	278	23	55	11	0	3	25	19	44	2	5	197	249	265	514	6%	84%	0.43	49	2.08	-5
	02	32	4	aaa	ATL	223	23	42	5	1	0	12	14	38	0	2	188	236	220	456	6%	83%	0.37	24	1.67	-20
Peters,Tony	01	27	8	aa	TOR	256	34	51	8	1	9	24	18	79	6	1	201	254	340	594	7%	69%	0.23	83	2.95	6
Petrick,Ben	02	26	8	aaa	COL	265	33	77	16	3	13	35	26	46	6	8	291	354	521	875	9%	83%	0.57	139	6.28	66
Phelps,Josh	01	23	2	aa	TOR	486	79	130	35	1	26	81	65	108	3	3	267	354	505	859	12%	78%	0.60	149	6.53	63
	02	24	2	aaa	TOR	257	40	68	20	1	19	51	26	66	0	0	265	332	572	904	9%	74%	0.39	187	6.89	73
Phillips,Andy	01	25	4	aa	NYY	183	20	45	9	2	6	22	18	52	1	0	244	312	405	717	9%	72%	0.35	99	4.56	29
	02	26	4	a/a	NYY	477	73	118	30	2	24	70	36	93	3	5	247	300	470	770	7%	81%	0.39	137	4.78	47
Phillips,Brandon	01	20	6	aa	MON	265	32	77	19	0	6	33	11	35	12	7	289	316	432	748	4%	87%	0.30	100	4.65	44
	02	21	6	a/a	CLE	503	67	153	32	1	18	64	30	68	14	5	304	343	479	822	6%	86%	0.44	113	6.14	57
Phillips,Dan	02	24	8	aa	COL	287	18	57	9	4	2	16	9	49	6	8	199	223	279	502	3%	83%	0.18	51	1.79	-9
Phillips,Jason	01	25	2	a/a	NYM	383	44	102	22	0	11	60	33	31	0	1	266	324	408	732	8%	92%	1.04	94	4.79	49
	02	26	2	aaa	NYM	323	30	80	19	1	11	56	20	28	1	0	248	292	415	706	6%	91%	0.71	108	4.27	41
Phillips,J.R.	01	31	3	aa	COL	119	11	25	6	0	6	13	7	39	0	1	212	256	418	673	6%	68%	0.18	124	3.48	25
Phoenix,Wynter	01	27	8	aa	FLA	327	35	62	16	3	4	22	24	90	10	5	189	245	293	538	7%	73%	0.27	70	2.32	-3
Piatt,Adam	01	26	8	aaa	OAK	109	11	24	8	0	1	12	9	21	2	0	218	277	318	595	8%	81%	0.42	78	3.15	13
	02	27	8	aaa	OAK	234	33	56	13	0	6	32	25	23	3	4	239	313	372	685	10%	90%	1.09	89	3.96	38
Pickering,Calvin	01	25	3	aaa	BAL	465	57	120	21	0	21	91	61	142	0	1	258	344	436	781	12%	69%	0.43	109	5.52	39
Pickler,Jeff	01	26	4	aa	MIL	523	61	129	15	2	0	27	50	51	28	14	246	312	282	595	9%	90%	0.99	29	3.16	14
	02	27	4	a/a	TEX	418	48	101	16	0	0	23	41	41	14	8	242	309	280	589	9%	90%	1.00	34	3.09	15
Piedra,Jorge	01	22	8	aa	CHC	441	47	94	22	4	6	46	32	70	10	6	213	266	322	588	7%	84%	0.46	73	2.85	10
Pigott,Tony	01	25	8	aa	TAM	250	25	52	9	1	2	24	6	41	7	3	209	228	274	502	2%	84%	0.15	46	2.04	-8
Piniella,Juan	01	24	8	aa	TEX	373	42	87	22	1	3	27	32	79	11	3	234	295	322	617	8%	79%	0.40	67	3.41	14
	02	25	8	aa	CHW	153	19	42	8	0	1	10	16	33	10	8	275	343	346	690	9%	78%	0.48	56	3.95	24
Podsednik,Scott	01	26	8	aaa	SEA	269	40	68	13	3	2	26	12	43	11	6	254	285	346	631	4%	84%	0.27	64	3.32	16
	02	27	8	aaa	SEA	438	54	107	22	4	7	52	37	64	30	15	244	303	361	664	8%	85%	0.58	77	3.67	25
Pogue,Jamie	02	25	2	aa	STL	208	14	32	9	0	2	18	24	32	1	1	154	241	226	467	10%	85%	0.75	53	1.84	-12
Polcovich,Kevin	01	31	46	aaa	STL	183	25	43	8	1	3	14	9	36	3	0	236	272	334	606	5%	81%	0.25	66	3.22	11
Pond,Simon	01	25	3	aa	CLE	388	40	94	27	2	10	40	26	64	2	3	242	289	402	691	6%	83%	0.40	107	3.97	33
Porter,Bo	01	29	8	aaa	TEX	224	30	47	8	1	11	30	20	52	7	5	211	276	402	678	8%	77%	0.39	111	3.59	24
	02	30	8	a/a	ATL	447	42	94	22	2	6	46	37	136	14	10	210	271	309	579	8%	70%	0.27	68	2.72	4
Porter,Colin	01	26	8	a/a	HOU	412	51	98	19	5	8	38	32	112	10	10	238	292	365	658	7%	73%	0.28	81	3.48	18
	02	27	8	aaa	HOU	461	50	114	29	5	6	32	39	118	24	8	247	306	371	677	8%	74%	0.33	85	4.03	24
Pose,Scott	02	36	8	aaa	TEX	158	11	25	4	1	0	10	16	10	4	5	158	236	196	432	9%	94%	1.60	28	1.42	-4
Post,Dave	01	28	3	a/a	LA	194	21	46	12	1	2	27	20	23	2	4	235	308	336	643	10%	88%	0.91	74	3.48	27
	02	29	4	aaa	PIT	345	45	88	15	1	5	29	28	48	8	5	255	311	348	659	8%	86%	0.58	63	3.81	23
Powell,Dante	01	28	8	aaa	SF	426	51	95	19	2	15	43	22	96	18	6	223	261	380	641	5%	78%	0.23	97	3.33	19
Powers,Jeff	01	26	4	a/a	COL	100	5	17	2	1	1	6	5	11	0	1	168	208	238	445	5%	89%	0.45	42	1.50	-18
Powers,John	01	27	45	aa	SD	315	32	66	12	3	3	27	27	69	6	4	211	272	300	573	8%	78%	0.39	58	2.74	2
	02	28	4	aa	CHC	198	23	43	6	1	4	16	22	34	6	2	217	295	318	614	10%	83%	0.65	63	3.34	11
Pratt,Scott	01	25	4	aa	CLE	264	29	67	11	3	4	21	22	44	13	11	255	312	363	676	8%	83%	0.49	70	3.63	24
	02	26	8	a/a	CLE	466	71	113	16	3	15	49	54	86	16	5	242	321	386	707	10%	82%	0.63	86	4.49	29
Pressley,Josh	01	22	3	aa	TAM	111	10	30	2	1	1	12	6	21	0	0	270	308	333	641	5%	81%	0.29	38	3.74	11
	02	23	3	a/a	TAM	389	42	104	20	0	3	43	42	46	4	8	267	339	342	681	10%	88%	0.91	57	4.07	31
Pride,Curtis	02	34	8	aaa	PIT	385	53	95	19	1	7	34	24	64	16	8	247	291	356	647	6%	83%	0.38	74	3.52	20
Prieto,Alejandro	01	25	546	aaa	KC	376	36	98	20	2	7	35	28	44	7	2	261	311	379	691	7%	88%	0.62	80	4.28	32
	02	26	4	aaa	MIN	276	27	62	13	1	5	20	14	36	3	5	225	262	333	595	5%	87%	0.39	73	2.77	13
Prieto,Chris	01	29	8	aaa	LA	446	67	98	20	3	13	40	46	68	17	8	220	293	363	656	9%	85%	0.67	89	3.61	24
Prieto,Rick	01	29	8	a/a	CHW	339	44	68	10	3	4	27	47	49	7	6	201	299	279	578	12%	85%	0.96	50	2.88	7
Pritchett,Chris	01	32	3	aaa	ANA	476	45	115	29	2	13	51	31	83	2	2	242	288	389	677	6%	82%	0.37	98	3.88	28
	02	33	3	aaa	PIT	397	40	95	14	1	6	45	34	82	2	0	239	299	325	624	8%	79%	0.41	57	3.51	12
Punto,Nick	01	24	6	aaa	PHI	463	53	104	22	5	1	36	66	115	31	9	225	321	300	622	12%	75%	0.57	55	3.63	9
	02	25	6	aaa	PHI	443	62	110	12	4	1	24	68	76	35	9	248	348	300	649	13%	83%	0.89	35	4.16	15
Quatraro,Matt	01	28	23	aa	TAM	271	30	71	20	2	5	28	13	67	3	1	263	298	404	702	5%	75%	0.20	99	4.30	33
	02	29	3	aaa	TAM	101	9	18	4	1	0	6	4	25	0	0	178	210	238	447	4%	75%	0.16	44	1.61	-19
Quinlan,Robb	01	25	3	aa	ANA	492	62	124	29	5	11	59	40	67	0	5	253	309	400	709	8%	86%	0.59	96	4.25	36
	02	26	8	aaa	ANA	528	72	154	28	7	17	85	31	71	6	2	292	331	468	799	6%	87%	0.44	109	5.73	51
Quintero,Humberto	02	23	2	a/a	CHW	178	13	42	8	0	1	20	8	19	1	3	236	269	298	567	4%	89%	0.42	48	2.58	7
Rabe,Josh	02	24	8	aa	MIN	183	16	39	10	0	1	15	8	27	3	1	213	246	284	530	4%	85%	0.30	57	2.36	0
Rachels,Wes	02	27	4	aa	BAL	199	14	31	4	1	0	14	16	33	3	0	156	219	186	405	7%	83%	0.48	22	1.42	-29
Radmanovich,Ryan	01	30	8	aaa	SD	390	48	85	20	1	14	51	51	111	3	5	217	308	383	691	12%	72%	0.46	104	4.02	24
	02	31	8	aaa	PIT	271	26	50	14	0	5	20	22	50	2	5	185	246	292	537	8%	82%	0.44	74	2.21	1
Raines,Tim	01	22	8	a/a	BAL	387	62	104	17	1	6	40	45	79	39	15	269	345	366	711	10%	80%	0.57	66	4.63	28
	02	23	8	aa	BAL	491	55	112	15	3	4	21	28	92	27	16	228	270	295	565	5%	81%	0.30	45	2.57	1
Ramirez,Dan	02	29	8	aaa	ARI	236	22	60	5	3	1	14	11	39	5	10	254	287	314	601	4%	83%	0.28	37	2.69	5
Ramirez,Julio	01	24	8	aaa	CHW	319	33	66	10	1	8	23	19	72	14	6	207	251	320	571	6%	77%	0.26	69	2.63	3
	02	25	8	aaa	ANA	139	13	33	3	3	2	8	3	23	6	4	237	254	345	599	2%	83%	0.13	60	2.71	7
Ramirez,Omar	01	31	8	aaa	HOU	363	31	77	18	0	2	30	22	40	7	4	211	255	275	530	6%	89%	0.54	52	2.36	2
Ramos,Kelly	01	25	2	a/a	BOS	195	12	38	6	1	5	23	5	44	0	0	195	215	313	528	3%	77%	0.11	71	2.18	-3
Randolph,Jaisen	01	23	8	aa	CHC	404	43	80	10	1	0	14	47	58	20	22	198	282	228	509	10%	86%	0.81	24	1.97	-8
Ransom,Cody	01	26	6	aaa	SF	469	56	94	18	4	16	57	31	100	13	2	201	250	357	606	6%	79%	0.31	93	3.02	12
	02	27	6	aaa	SF	449	46	81	16	4	9	40	40	134	5	4	180	247	294	541	8%	70%	0.30	70	2.38	-5
Reding,Josh	01	25	65	a/a	MON	390	22	71	10	3	3	32	16	90	9	5	182	214	246	460	4%	77%	0.18	41	1.67	-19
Redman,Prentice	02	23	8	aa	NYM	491	63	117	30	1	8	50	46	98	34	11	238	304	352	656	9%	80%	0.47	81	3.80	22
Redman,Tike	01	25	8	aaa	PIT	398	43	109	16	7	2	34	19	30	17	8	274	307	364	671	5%	92%	0.63	59	3.92	28
	02	26	8	aaa	PIT	311	33	76	9	2	2	17	17	19	13	8	244	284	305	589	5%	94%	0.89	41	2.89	16
Reed,Keith	01	23	8	a/a	BAL	141	16	36	8	1	3	17	10	22	3	3	255	305	390	695	7%	84%	0.45	89	3.98	31
	02	24	8	aa	BAL	488	47	103	16	1	12	52	32	99	3	10	211	260	322	581	6%	80%	0.32	69	2.59	5
Reese,Kevin	02	25	8	aa	NYY	514	68	130	21	4	4	38	67	83	19	14	253	339	333	672	12%	84%	0.81	55	4.00	23
Restovich,Michael	01	23	8	aa	MIN	501	69	136	34	4	22	84	53	124	15	7	271	341	487	828	10%	75%	0.43	135	5.98	55
	02	24	8	aaa	MIN	518	69	130	30	5	20	71	38	113	8	9	251	302	444	746	7%	78%	0.34	120	4.48	40

Major League Equivalent Statistics

BATTER	Yr	Age	Pos	Lev	Org	AB	R	H	D	T	HR	RBI	BB	K	SB	CS	BA	OB	Slg	OPS	bb%	ct%	Eye	PX	RC/G	BPV
Reyes,Jose	02	19	6	aa	NYM	275	44	79	16	6	2	23	15	31	25	15	287	324	411	735	5%	89%	0.48	82	4.28	39
Reyes,Rene	02	25	8	aa	COL	455	44	121	29	3	12	37	20	48	7	12	266	297	422	719	4%	89%	0.42	103	4.02	39
Richardson,Corey	02	26	8	aa	DET	377	39	76	10	1	1	16	46	68	22	5	202	288	241	530	11%	82%	0.68	30	2.64	-7
Rich,Dominic	02	23	4	aa	TOR	132	11	31	4	1	1	11	14	19	2	5	235	308	303	611	10%	86%	0.74	45	2.94	12
Rifkin,Aaron	02	24	3	aa	NYY	235	35	52	12	1	4	29	25	60	4	3	221	296	332	628	10%	74%	0.42	75	3.38	13
Riggs,Adam	01	29	4	aaa	SD	394	33	84	15	1	15	51	9	79	6	3	212	230	372	602	2%	80%	0.12	96	2.77	13
	02	30	8	aaa	STL	122	20	23	7	0	2	8	18	26	4	1	189	293	295	588	13%	79%	0.69	76	3.12	8
Riggs,Eric	01	25	5	aa	LA	394	44	83	23	1	5	31	35	53	6	4	210	275	313	588	8%	86%	0.66	74	2.93	14
	02	26	6	aa	LA	455	57	91	29	1	6	57	52	83	3	3	200	282	308	590	10%	82%	0.63	79	2.98	12
Rigsby,Randy	02	26	8	aa	FLA	156	7	30	8	0	3	15	7	46	3	2	192	227	301	528	4%	71%	0.15	75	2.16	-2
Rios,Brian	01	27	5	aaa	DET	372	37	106	27	4	10	49	17	54	2	5	286	317	455	772	4%	86%	0.32	112	5.02	48
	02	28	5	aaa	DET	262	23	60	10	4	2	23	16	41	0	2	229	273	321	594	6%	84%	0.39	59	2.93	9
Risinger,Ben	02	25	5	aa	SD	466	37	115	22	0	3	38	34	61	1	2	247	298	313	611	7%	87%	0.56	52	3.30	15
Rivera,Carlos	01	23	3	aa	PIT	389	40	84	28	0	9	45	12	68	0	2	217	240	357	596	3%	83%	0.17	99	2.77	16
	02	24	3	aa	PIT	494	52	129	26	1	16	66	21	61	1	1	261	291	415	706	4%	88%	0.34	99	4.25	35
Rivera,Juan	01	23	8	a/a	NYY	515	79	157	27	3	27	86	27	71	8	13	305	339	526	866	5%	86%	0.38	133	6.12	64
	02	24	8	aaa	NYY	265	33	77	19	1	7	38	11	32	4	1	291	319	449	768	4%	88%	0.34	108	5.27	48
Rivera,Mike	01	25	2	aa	DET	415	58	97	17	1	21	77	33	83	2	2	234	291	429	720	7%	80%	0.40	116	4.30	34
	02	26	2	aaa	DET	265	38	56	10	1	15	48	33	57	0	1	211	299	426	725	11%	78%	0.58	124	4.36	33
Rivera,Roberto	01	25	8	aa	ATL	392	43	84	17	1	5	24	27	74	8	4	213	263	298	561	6%	81%	0.36	60	2.65	3
Rivera,Ruben	02	29	8	a/a	TEX	303	40	71	14	5	12	46	26	65	4	3	234	295	432	727	8%	79%	0.40	117	4.34	34
Roberge,J.P.	01	29	538	a/a	PHI	439	56	116	22	1	14	65	28	60	9	5	265	310	413	722	6%	86%	0.47	94	4.48	37
	02	30	83	a/a	PHI	431	39	94	23	1	6	37	24	74	5	1	218	259	318	577	5%	83%	0.32	71	2.83	8
Robertson,Mike	01	31	38	aaa	ATL	434	33	100	16	4	5	32	24	54	4	12	230	271	315	586	5%	87%	0.45	56	2.62	9
Roberts,Brian	01	24	64	a/a	BAL	242	26	61	9	1	2	17	35	31	30	3	252	347	322	669	13%	87%	1.13	49	4.78	27
	02	25	4	aaa	BAL	313	43	77	8	5	3	26	34	41	19	4	246	320	332	652	10%	87%	0.83	52	4.02	20
Roberts,Dave	01	29	8	a/a	CLE	305	35	75	15	3	0	20	22	49	17	6	245	295	310	605	7%	84%	0.44	50	3.25	11
Robinson,Bo	01	26	53	aa	SEA	474	59	108	18	1	10	59	67	62	3	0	228	323	330	654	12%	87%	1.08	67	3.95	25
	02	27	3	aa	SEA	420	32	81	16	0	2	34	37	60	1	2	193	258	245	503	8%	86%	0.62	41	2.15	-6
Rodriguez,Guillermc	01	23	2	aa	SF	216	17	39	6	0	4	21	7	35	3	0	180	205	260	465	3%	84%	0.19	52	1.75	-15
	02	24	2	a/a	SF	156	11	33	6	2	2	12	9	29	1	3	212	255	314	569	5%	81%	0.31	65	2.48	4
Rodriguez,John	01	24	8	aa	NYY	393	56	105	28	1	21	58	23	108	2	3	267	308	506	814	6%	72%	0.22	150	5.42	55
	02	25	8	aa	NYY	354	43	67	16	2	13	53	30	88	11	3	189	253	356	609	8%	75%	0.34	102	3.00	12
Rodriguez,Liu	01	25	4	aaa	CHW	444	48	122	24	0	0	34	38	54	6	4	275	332	329	661	8%	88%	0.70	48	4.03	25
Rodriguez,Luis	01	28	2	a/a	BOS	262	31	53	10	2	7	22	10	56	3	1	203	231	334	565	3%	79%	0.17	81	2.53	5
	02	29	2	aaa	BOS	259	19	51	11	4	5	24	9	57	0	3	197	224	328	552	3%	78%	0.16	81	2.24	2
Rodriguez,Luis	02	29	6	aa	MIN	455	40	86	14	2	5	26	40	48	2	2	189	255	262	516	8%	89%	0.83	48	2.25	-0
Rodriguez,Sammy	01	26	2	aa	NYM	159	15	30	10	0	3	10	13	39	1	0	192	253	317	570	8%	75%	0.33	87	2.72	6
Rodriguez,Tony	01	31	6	aa	CHC	131	8	23	3	0	1	9	2	29	2	2	176	189	214	403	2%	78%	0.07	27	1.19	-29
Rodriguez,Victor	01	25	4	aa	NYY	218	29	58	9	1	3	15	13	17	2	3	266	308	353	661	6%	92%	0.79	59	3.77	29
	02	26	4	aa	PIT	188	22	45	5	0	2	14	6	17	2	0	239	263	298	561	3%	91%	0.35	40	2.75	3
Rogers,Ed	01	20	6	aa	BAL	191	11	36	8	1	0	13	6	34	9	2	187	213	242	455	3%	82%	0.18	44	1.73	-16
	02	24	6	aa	BAL	422	48	94	22	1	9	47	13	65	11	5	223	246	344	590	3%	85%	0.20	81	2.77	12
Rolison,Nate	02	26	3	aaa	SEA	411	49	95	19	1	14	47	32	124	1	0	231	287	384	671	7%	70%	0.26	96	3.86	22
Rolls,Damian	02	25	8	a/a	TAM	251	34	61	6	4	5	29	18	40	12	1	243	294	359	652	7%	84%	0.45	66	3.91	17
Romano,Jason	01	22	4	a/a	TEX	335	45	89	16	1	5	28	33	45	9	8	266	331	367	698	9%	87%	0.73	69	4.22	32
	02	23	8	aaa	COL	325	31	84	13	2	3	24	16	40	12	8	258	293	338	632	5%	88%	0.40	55	3.33	17
Romero,Armando	02	35	2	aaa	PIT	283	30	69	22	0	12	38	18	41	1	1	244	289	449	738	6%	86%	0.44	134	4.48	46
Romero,Mandy	01	34	2	a/a	OAK	169	12	33	9	0	2	12	14	23	0	0	197	256	282	539	7%	86%	0.58	64	2.47	3
Roneberg,Brett	01	23	8	aa	FLA	164	16	41	11	0	5	18	17	25	1	0	250	320	409	729	9%	85%	0.68	107	4.78	41
	02	24	8	a/a	FLA	219	29	56	13	2	3	28	23	31	2	2	256	326	374	701	10%	86%	0.74	82	4.38	34
Rosamond,Mike	01	23	8	aa	HOU	107	12	28	5	2	1	10	10	24	2	6	263	324	372	696	8%	78%	0.41	70	3.58	25
	02	24	8	aa	HOU	422	35	85	20	4	10	36	21	100	5	10	201	239	339	578	5%	76%	0.21	87	2.41	7
Rosario,Melvin	01	28	2	aaa	ARI	188	14	39	11	1	4	20	6	41	1	1	208	231	336	567	3%	78%	0.14	88	2.50	8
Rose,Mike	01	25	2	a/a	ARI	284	31	59	13	2	3	25	42	51	3	6	209	310	300	610	13%	82%	0.82	62	3.15	12
	02	26	2	a/a	KC	265	28	57	15	3	4	23	30	52	2	4	215	295	340	635	10%	80%	0.58	83	3.34	18
Rose,Pete	01	32	5	aa	CIN	121	7	25	6	0	1	8	5	21	0	0	208	239	278	517	4%	82%	0.23	55	2.22	-3
Roskos,John	01	27	3	aaa	SD	224	21	48	12	1	4	28	18	48	0	0	212	272	325	597	8%	78%	0.38	77	3.05	10
Ross,Cody	02	22	8	aa	DET	400	60	97	24	3	13	59	38	66	13	2	243	308	415	723	9%	84%	0.58	110	4.64	38
Ross,Dave	01	25	2	aa	LA	246	31	57	10	1	10	40	30	75	1	1	232	316	398	714	11%	70%	0.41	101	4.46	27
	02	26	2	aaa	LA	293	34	70	13	1	11	48	25	63	1	1	239	299	403	701	8%	78%	0.40	100	4.21	29
Ross,Jason	01	27	8	a/a	ATL	312	36	66	10	2	13	31	35	94	15	9	210	290	384	674	10%	70%	0.38	101	3.63	19
Rouse,Michael	02	22	6	aa	TOR	231	27	53	11	0	7	33	22	36	5	7	229	296	368	664	9%	84%	0.61	89	3.46	25
Rowand,Aaron	01	24	8	aaa	CHW	329	49	93	26	0	17	44	20	42	7	2	283	324	517	840	6%	87%	0.48	150	6.09	66
Royster,Aaron	01	29	8	a/a	PHI	165	18	38	5	3	6	16	9	43	5	0	231	272	395	667	5%	74%	0.22	92	3.83	19
Ruan,Wilken	01	22	8	aa	MON	117	12	27	7	0	0	5	3	16	5	0	231	250	291	541	3%	86%	0.19	53	2.65	3
	02	24	8	a/a	LA	477	49	111	19	5	2	49	16	42	27	4	233	258	306	564	3%	91%	0.38	51	2.82	6
Rumfield,Toby	01	29	3	aaa	CHW	463	40	110	24	0	19	57	24	63	0	0	238	275	413	688	5%	86%	0.38	109	3.92	32
	02	30	2	aaa	STL	198	16	45	6	0	3	21	14	29	0	2	227	278	303	581	7%	85%	0.48	50	2.81	6
Rushford,Jim	01	28	8	aa	MIL	187	27	51	13	1	6	23	17	24	2	2	271	333	444	777	9%	87%	0.72	115	5.33	52
	02	29	8	a/a	MIL	424	43	105	27	2	6	53	36	47	1	2	248	307	363	670	8%	89%	0.77	82	3.93	32
Rust,Brian	01	27	38	a/a	BAL	315	34	67	14	0	12	42	25	80	5	5	211	268	374	642	7%	75%	0.31	101	3.25	18
Ryan,Mike	01	24	84	aaa	MIN	527	69	138	34	5	14	57	40	94	1	7	262	314	425	739	7%	82%	0.43	107	4.56	40
	02	25	8	aaa	MIN	540	66	122	34	4	21	72	39	93	3	6	226	278	420	698	7%	83%	0.42	122	3.84	34
Ryan,Rob	01	28	8	aaa	ARI	434	59	100	21	6	13	60	49	71	2	7	231	310	396	706	10%	84%	0.69	101	4.13	33
	02	29	8	aaa	OAK	442	53	86	23	2	11	39	40	65	3	1	195	261	330	592	8%	85%	0.62	89	2.93	14
Sagmoen,Marc	01	30	8	aaa	TEX	324	23	60	13	1	4	20	11	67	3	2	186	212	264	476	3%	79%	0.16	54	1.78	-12
Salazar,Jeremy	01	26	2	aaa	PHI	160	15	37	15	0	1	15	10	35	0	0	229	274	340	614	6%	78%	0.28	92	3.23	20
	02	27	2	aaa	PHI	129	8	24	6	0	0	8	10	31	1	0	186	245	233	477	7%	76%	0.32	41	1.97	-15
Salazar,Oscar	01	23	65	a/a	OAK	537	59	120	26	3	14	76	39	83	8	4	223	276	361	637	7%	85%	0.47	88	3.40	20
	02	24	46	a/a	DET	285	18	50	16	1	5	26	19	46	2	3	175	227	291	518	6%	84%	0.41	80	2.07	-0

Major League Equivalent Statistics

BATTER	Yr	Age	Pos	Lev	Org	AB	R	H	D	T	HR	RBI	BB	K	SB	CS	BA	OB	Slg	OPS	bb%	ct%	Eye	PX	RC/G	BPV
Salazar,Ruben	01	24	4	aa	MIN	530	68	154	29	2	10	64	35	78	6	1	291	335	408	743	6%	85%	0.45	80	5.15	39
	02	25	40	a/a	MIN	397	39	95	22	2	3	31	20	62	5	0	239	276	327	603	5%	84%	0.32	65	3.21	13
Salzano,Jerry	01	27	5	aa	BOS	453	49	106	26	1	4	41	36	89	11	6	234	290	325	615	7%	80%	0.40	68	3.25	14
	02	28	8	a/a	BOS	445	50	89	23	0	8	47	37	72	13	5	200	261	306	567	8%	84%	0.51	74	2.70	7
Samuels,Scott	01	30	8	aaa	BOS	125	11	27	8	1	3	11	10	20	4	2	216	274	360	634	7%	84%	0.50	97	3.29	22
Sanchez,Alex	01	25	8	aaa	MIL	335	43	94	13	3	1	21	18	35	22	9	281	317	346	663	5%	89%	0.50	46	3.92	23
Sanchez,Freddy	01	24	6	aa	BOS	178	21	53	18	0	2	16	7	19	3	1	300	325	436	761	4%	90%	0.37	108	5.26	52
	02	25	6	a/a	BOS	494	67	141	31	2	5	52	38	56	19	7	285	336	387	723	7%	89%	0.68	75	4.83	40
Sanchez,Tino	02	24	8	aa	COL	272	22	71	15	1	3	18	30	20	8	5	261	334	357	691	10%	93%	1.50	69	4.29	46
Sanchez,Wellington	01	24	68	aa	MIL	212	25	44	10	0	1	12	19	53	4	3	206	271	264	536	8%	75%	0.36	47	2.43	-5
Sandberg,Jared	01	24	5	a/a	TAM	350	40	81	18	0	16	50	41	82	0	1	231	312	420	732	10%	77%	0.50	116	4.61	35
	02	25	5	aaa	TAM	114	17	30	9	0	3	18	12	37	1	0	263	333	421	754	10%	68%	0.32	111	5.23	40
Sanders,Anthony	02	29	8	aaa	CIN	335	23	67	13	2	9	34	12	75	5	4	200	228	331	559	3%	78%	0.16	81	2.37	3
Sanders,Deion	01	34	8	aaa	TOR	181	21	51	10	5	2	12	7	14	8	7	283	311	418	729	4%	92%	0.50	86	4.15	40
Sandoval,Danny	01	23	68	aa	CHW	203	20	52	6	1	0	24	15	21	14	5	256	307	296	603	7%	90%	0.71	31	3.31	12
	02	24	6	aa	CHW	504	76	121	27	1	5	40	43	53	34	25	240	300	327	627	8%	89%	0.81	65	3.08	23
Sandusky,Scott	01	26	2	aa	MON	387	28	79	17	1	2	18	26	74	5	2	205	255	267	522	6%	81%	0.35	48	2.33	-5
	02	27	2	aa	MON	354	26	57	14	1	2	24	21	59	0	2	161	208	223	431	6%	83%	0.36	46	1.46	-20
Santana,Pedro	01	25	4	aaa	DET	432	37	89	10	2	3	25	22	75	30	9	206	244	259	503	5%	83%	0.29	35	2.17	-11
	02	28	4	aa	CIN	350	27	75	14	2	4	20	17	73	8	8	214	251	300	551	5%	79%	0.23	58	2.34	0
Santangelo,F.P.	01	34	84	aaa	OAK	188	23	29	5	1	4	12	21	42	4	5	153	237	249	486	10%	78%	0.49	59	1.82	-15
	02	35	68	aaa	OAK	101	7	12	3	0	1	4	12	19	2	4	119	212	178	391	11%	81%	0.63	42	1.08	-31
Santiago,Ramon	02	23	6	a/a	DET	103	15	30	1	2	2	11	5	13	5	2	291	324	398	722	5%	87%	0.38	56	4.66	28
Santora,Jack	01	25	64	aa	ARI	265	23	50	12	0	0	9	23	39	3	5	187	253	231	484	8%	85%	0.60	39	1.86	-10
	02	26	64	a/a	ARI	190	18	31	3	2	1	5	14	29	2	5	163	221	216	436	7%	85%	0.48	31	1.39	-23
Santos,Angel	01	22	4	a/a	BOS	525	68	140	34	0	12	48	47	89	24	11	266	327	396	723	8%	83%	0.53	91	4.62	37
	02	23	4	aaa	BOS	350	34	84	15	2	8	42	32	60	10	9	240	304	363	667	8%	83%	0.53	78	3.65	23
Santos,Deivis	02	23	83	a/a	SF	495	54	139	35	5	4	61	17	48	7	5	281	305	396	701	3%	90%	0.35	84	4.25	35
Santos,Jose	02	29	5	aa	FLA	214	15	31	6	1	2	22	15	60	2	2	145	201	210	411	7%	72%	0.25	43	1.32	-29
Sapp,Damian	02	26	2	aa	CIN	137	13	26	9	0	3	9	17	39	0	1	190	279	321	600	11%	72%	0.44	92	3.01	10
Sardinha,Dane	02	24	2	aa	CIN	394	26	72	19	0	3	31	11	90	0	2	183	205	254	459	3%	77%	0.12	54	1.62	-14
Sasser,Rob	01	27	5	aaa	MON	181	17	38	9	2	3	22	18	39	6	1	209	282	327	609	9%	78%	0.47	77	3.29	11
	02	28	5	aaa	MIL	185	16	38	8	0	3	15	16	28	6	0	205	269	297	566	8%	85%	0.57	63	2.90	6
Saturria,Luis	01	25	8	a/a	STL	442	57	91	17	4	12	45	31	108	5	9	206	258	343	600	6%	76%	0.28	83	2.74	9
Saunders,Chris	01	31	5	a/a	CHW	478	60	116	29	0	11	56	51	88	3	1	243	316	371	687	10%	82%	0.58	88	4.25	29
	02	32	53	a/a	CHW	352	23	58	14	0	4	30	18	90	0	1	165	205	239	444	5%	74%	0.20	53	1.55	-19
Saylor,Jamie	01	27	4	a/a	FLA	183	17	31	5	1	4	18	14	46	2	5	171	231	270	501	7%	75%	0.31	60	1.83	-12
	02	28	6	aaa	HOU	237	19	47	7	3	3	10	17	58	4	1	198	252	291	543	7%	76%	0.29	57	2.50	-5
Scales,Bobby	02	25	4	aa	SD	250	32	56	11	2	3	22	22	59	5	3	224	287	320	607	8%	76%	0.37	65	3.15	9
Scanlon,Matt	02	24	8	aa	MIN	197	19	33	6	2	2	20	12	35	3	1	168	215	249	464	6%	82%	0.34	52	1.75	-16
Scarborough,Steve	02	25	64	a/a	MIL	438	50	106	32	1	8	45	49	87	9	10	242	318	374	693	10%	80%	0.56	95	4.03	31
Schall,Gene	01	31	3	aaa	PHI	263	33	66	21	1	11	45	27	64	0	0	250	320	459	778	9%	75%	0.42	136	5.27	48
Scheschuk,John	02	26	3	aa	SD	153	14	33	8	1	1	22	26	20	1	2	216	330	301	630	15%	87%	1.30	62	3.55	24
Schneider,Brian	01	25	2	aaa	MON	338	30	88	26	1	6	39	24	51	2	0	260	309	396	706	7%	85%	0.47	98	4.46	37
Schrager,Tony	02	25	4	aa	CHC	350	45	66	19	3	8	38	63	92	7	3	189	312	329	641	15%	74%	0.68	91	3.66	14
Schumacher,Shawn	01	25	2	aa	STL	122	5	22	5	0	1	8	3	10	3	1	177	195	236	431	2%	92%	0.27	44	1.46	-17
Scott,Bill	02	24	3	aa	MIL	249	14	53	8	0	3	22	13	55	3	2	213	252	281	533	5%	78%	0.24	47	2.36	-5
Scutaro,Marcos	01	26	4	aaa	MIL	495	70	131	27	2	9	41	50	67	9	13	264	332	380	712	9%	87%	0.76	79	4.29	36
	02	27	4	aaa	NYM	354	42	100	19	4	6	24	25	58	6	9	282	330	410	739	7%	84%	0.43	84	4.59	37
Seabol,Scott	01	26	5	a/a	NYY	410	41	98	23	1	14	52	16	77	4	6	239	268	400	668	4%	81%	0.21	104	3.48	27
	02	27	3	aaa	NYY	428	43	93	25	1	12	52	23	77	2	4	217	257	364	622	5%	82%	0.30	97	3.05	18
Seal,Scott	01	26	8	aa	COL	186	17	34	6	1	3	19	25	32	2	2	182	280	281	561	12%	83%	0.78	62	2.69	2
Sears,Todd	01	26	3	aaa	MIN	408	48	115	24	1	10	39	32	56	2	1	281	333	417	751	7%	86%	0.57	91	5.15	43
	02	27	3	aaa	MIN	484	62	129	33	3	14	71	42	110	1	1	267	325	434	759	8%	77%	0.38	111	5.13	42
Secrist,Reed	01	31	582	a/a	PIT	352	48	86	17	1	17	48	38	83	3	0	245	319	445	764	10%	76%	0.45	120	5.13	41
	02	32	5	aaa	PIT	358	44	76	21	2	8	41	38	74	5	5	212	288	349	637	10%	79%	0.51	91	3.36	19
Sefcik,Kevin	01	31	84	aaa	COL	432	41	89	20	1	5	28	26	33	5	10	206	251	294	545	6%	92%	0.78	62	2.27	10
	02	32	4	aa	PIT	467	40	93	22	1	1	29	25	47	7	6	199	240	257	497	5%	90%	0.53	47	1.99	-4
Seguignol,Fernando	01	27	3	aaa	MON	242	32	69	12	0	14	40	13	46	0	1	285	320	501	821	5%	81%	0.27	129	5.77	54
Selby,Bill	01	31	43	aaa	CIN	330	34	71	15	1	11	41	19	41	1	0	215	258	365	623	5%	88%	0.46	94	3.20	20
	02	32	8	aaa	CLE	184	23	48	13	1	5	18	16	34	4	1	261	320	424	744	8%	82%	0.47	109	4.94	41
Sell,Chip	01	30	83	a/a	ARI	366	32	77	15	2	4	31	13	66	5	2	209	235	290	526	3%	82%	0.19	57	2.26	-3
Sequea,Jorge	02	22	4	aa	DET	397	45	93	20	3	3	32	35	60	11	2	234	296	322	619	8%	85%	0.58	63	3.47	16
Sergio,Tom	02	27	80	a/a	BOS	486	55	104	23	2	9	54	32	77	4	6	214	263	325	588	6%	84%	0.42	74	2.78	10
Servais,Scott	01	34	2	aaa	HOU	148	17	42	9	1	5	23	9	20	0	0	286	327	468	795	6%	86%	0.45	116	5.65	52
	02	35	2	aaa	SF	136	18	32	11	0	1	21	5	21	0	0	235	262	338	601	4%	85%	0.24	83	3.04	17
Sexton,Chris	01	30	6	aaa	CIN	409	43	95	22	2	2	34	30	50	4	5	233	285	308	593	7%	88%	0.59	57	2.96	13
	02	31	5	aaa	CIN	414	56	107	25	3	5	34	29	33	2	2	258	307	370	677	7%	92%	0.88	79	4.03	36
Shabala,Adam	02	25	8	aa	SF	148	11	28	8	0	1	13	5	31	3	1	189	216	264	479	3%	79%	0.16	58	1.85	-10
Shackelford,Brian	01	25	8	aa	KC	366	43	78	15	2	14	50	23	64	3	5	214	259	384	643	6%	82%	0.35	102	3.19	20
	02	26	0	aa	KC	244	23	44	8	0	4	24	17	41	3	3	180	234	262	496	7%	83%	0.41	54	1.95	-9
Shaffer,Josh	02	22	5	aa	CHW	210	23	45	7	1	0	15	32	54	1	5	214	318	257	575	13%	74%	0.59	34	2.80	-3
Shave,Jon	01	34	64	aaa	BOS	308	27	67	9	0	5	21	16	46	3	3	216	255	289	545	5%	85%	0.36	48	2.44	-1
Sheets,Andy	01	30	6	aaa	TAM	225	23	54	13	2	4	18	20	43	6	3	239	301	360	661	8%	81%	0.47	82	3.80	23
	02	31	5	aaa	TAM	374	43	94	23	5	11	54	22	70	5	2	251	293	428	721	6%	81%	0.31	112	4.38	36
Sheff,Chris	01	31	8	aaa	CIN	312	40	72	16	1	7	37	30	64	3	3	231	298	358	655	9%	79%	0.46	84	3.68	21
Sherrod,Justin	02	25	8	aa	BOS	243	28	52	17	1	6	35	21	67	6	5	214	277	366	643	8%	72%	0.31	104	3.27	20
Shipp,Brian	02	24	4	aa	NYM	375	39	69	22	2	6	38	17	84	6	9	184	219	301	521	4%	78%	0.20	81	1.92	-1
Short,Rick	01	29	5	a/a	CHC	332	34	74	15	1	4	27	21	41	2	2	224	271	308	579	6%	88%	0.52	59	2.84	10
	02	30	0	aaa	ANA	410	50	118	24	1	5	47	15	35	2	2	288	313	388	701	4%	91%	0.43	73	4.38	35
Silvestre,Juan	01	24	8	aa	SEA	372	25	73	12	0	7	34	19	111	0	2	196	235	282	517	5%	70%	0.17	56	2.14	-8

Major League Equivalent Statistics

BATTER	Yr	Age	Pos	Lev	Org	AB	R	H	D	T	HR	RBI	BB	K	SB	CS	BA	OB	Slg	OPS	bb%	ct%	Eye	PX	RC/G	BPV
Simmons,Brian	01	28	8	aaa	TOR	201	19	46	9	1	2	16	15	32	3	6	227	280	310	590	7%	84%	0.46	59	2.72	9
	02	29	8	aaa	SF	319	36	77	16	4	7	33	27	73	5	4	241	301	382	683	8%	77%	0.37	89	3.94	25
Simons,Mitch	01	33	4	aaa	TEX	121	11	24	6	0	0	5	9	20	0	2	201	256	253	509	7%	83%	0.45	46	2.07	-5
Simon,Randall	01	26	3	aaa	DET	222	22	67	13	0	7	25	16	16	0	3	301	350	450	800	7%	93%	1.00	98	5.68	61
Sisco,Steve	01	32	43	aaa	PHI	351	32	73	18	0	5	24	24	79	6	5	208	259	297	556	6%	78%	0.31	65	2.54	2
Sitzman,Jay	02	25	8	aa	PHI	385	47	85	20	5	7	45	24	77	14	10	221	267	353	620	6%	80%	0.31	86	2.98	15
Skrehot,Shaun	01	26	6	a/a	PIT	526	58	126	31	4	6	45	32	65	21	19	239	282	346	629	6%	88%	0.49	76	3.04	21
	02	27	6	aa	PIT	312	29	59	12	2	2	17	17	53	6	4	189	231	260	491	5%	83%	0.32	50	1.92	-10
Sledge,Termel	01	25	3	aa	MON	448	54	109	20	4	8	40	41	66	25	9	244	307	356	663	8%	85%	0.62	73	3.89	24
	02	26	8	a/a	MON	476	68	123	22	5	8	43	51	74	10	10	258	330	376	706	10%	84%	0.69	76	4.32	31
Smith,Bobby	01	28	84	aaa	TAM	396	57	107	24	2	19	59	38	84	9	2	271	335	485	820	9%	79%	0.45	132	5.98	54
	02	28	5	aaa	MIL	293	22	61	19	0	7	26	20	55	9	2	208	259	345	603	6%	81%	0.36	94	3.05	16
Smith,Bubba	01	32	3	aa	FLA	122	8	15	3	0	4	15	4	41	0	0	120	150	230	379	3%	66%	0.10	65	1.04	-31
Smith,Jason	01	24	6	aaa	CHC	271	28	54	8	4	3	15	10	71	5	3	199	228	292	519	4%	74%	0.14	56	2.12	-8
	02	25	6	aaa	TAM	206	25	52	11	2	3	24	8	39	4	1	252	280	369	649	4%	81%	0.21	78	3.64	21
Smith,Jeff	01	27	2	aa	MIN	351	32	84	13	1	6	35	12	69	0	0	239	265	331	596	3%	80%	0.18	61	3.02	8
	02	28	2	a/a	MIN	324	26	69	14	0	7	33	15	52	1	2	213	248	321	569	4%	84%	0.29	72	2.60	6
Smith,Mark	01	31	8	aaa	MON	145	16	25	7	0	5	14	12	39	4	2	174	235	335	571	7%	73%	0.30	102	2.51	6
	02	32	8	aaa	FLA	389	40	86	23	0	7	36	27	67	4	3	221	272	334	606	6%	83%	0.40	80	3.07	15
Smith,Nestor	01	24	8	aa	MIN	294	28	72	5	7	3	16	8	75	5	6	244	264	337	600	3%	74%	0.10	50	2.83	4
Smothers,Stewart	01	25	8	aa	ATL	120	8	23	6	0	0	5	12	34	1	2	195	267	248	514	9%	71%	0.34	46	2.18	-9
	02	26	8	a/a	ATL	105	7	14	1	0	2	7	13	33	0	3	133	229	200	429	11%	69%	0.39	38	1.35	-32
Snead,Esix	01	25	8	aa	STL	520	59	102	18	5	1	27	40	121	53	23	196	253	253	505	7%	77%	0.33	41	2.08	-11
	02	26	8	aa	NYM	401	44	77	7	3	2	30	31	69	47	18	192	250	239	489	7%	83%	0.45	30	2.00	-15
Snopek,Chris	01	31	65	aaa	CHC	470	50	103	25	0	10	44	24	66	5	5	218	257	335	592	5%	86%	0.37	80	2.79	13
Snusz,Chris	01	29	2	a/a	CLE	133	14	38	4	2	2	19	7	23	1	0	287	324	385	709	5%	83%	0.33	59	4.67	26
Snyder,Earl	01	25	3	a/a	NYM	424	64	111	36	1	17	68	52	105	4	3	262	343	469	812	11%	75%	0.50	138	5.83	54
	02	26	5	aaa	CLE	400	61	98	27	1	18	59	38	92	0	2	245	311	453	763	9%	77%	0.41	132	4.90	44
Solano,Danny	01	23	6	aa	TEX	423	48	96	15	4	6	37	40	60	2	5	227	294	324	618	9%	86%	0.67	62	3.23	14
	02	27	6	aa	TOR	249	26	45	10	2	3	24	30	45	4	3	181	269	273	542	11%	82%	0.67	61	2.48	-1
Soler,Ramon	02	25	4	a/a	NYM	185	23	37	6	0	1	10	20	33	13	8	200	278	249	527	10%	82%	0.61	37	2.26	-6
Sollmann,Scott	01	26	8	aa	CIN	121	16	30	3	1	0	5	14	15	9	6	252	329	288	616	10%	88%	0.93	25	3.21	13
Sorensen,Zach	01	25	6	a/a	CLE	201	23	45	6	1	5	15	10	26	9	9	224	261	338	599	5%	87%	0.38	69	2.54	11
	02	26	4	aaa	CLE	455	50	114	12	9	7	50	22	68	12	6	251	285	363	648	5%	85%	0.32	65	3.54	17
Sosa,Juan	01	26	64	a/a	ARI	335	24	63	11	1	0	16	16	38	8	5	188	224	226	450	4%	89%	0.41	31	1.62	-16
Specht,Brian	01	21	6	aa	ANA	155	12	39	8	1	2	13	11	23	2	2	251	298	359	657	6%	85%	0.46	75	3.66	24
	02	22	6	aa	ANA	476	54	109	22	2	12	51	41	107	15	5	229	290	359	649	8%	78%	0.38	84	3.64	19
Spehr,Tim	01	35	2	aaa	CIN	184	16	25	6	0	4	18	14	63	2	1	137	196	230	426	7%	66%	0.21	61	1.43	-25
Spencer,Shane	01	30	8	aaa	NYY	173	13	34	8	1	3	11	18	20	3	1	195	271	300	571	10%	89%	0.92	71	2.81	13
Spivey,Junior	01	27	4	aaa	ARI	194	19	39	6	0	4	20	20	26	7	7	200	276	290	566	10%	87%	0.79	58	2.50	6
Sprague,Ed	02	35	0	aaa	TEX	400	35	86	21	1	7	44	28	76	0	1	215	266	325	591	7%	81%	0.37	76	2.93	10
Stankiewicz,Andy	01	37	4	aaa	LA	202	12	40	5	0	0	9	17	26	4	3	196	259	223	482	8%	87%	0.67	24	1.95	-12
Stanley,Henri	02	25	8	aa	HOU	456	67	126	32	9	13	53	53	72	10	10	276	352	471	823	10%	84%	0.74	124	5.83	58
Steed,Dave	01	29	2	aaa	TEX	227	21	46	9	0	7	22	20	52	0	1	201	267	328	595	8%	77%	0.40	81	2.93	8
Stefanski,Mike	01	32	2	aaa	STL	164	18	34	6	1	5	19	10	28	1	2	209	254	340	594	6%	83%	0.36	81	2.77	10
	02	33	2	aaa	CIN	203	16	46	7	1	5	16	9	21	0	0	227	259	345	604	4%	90%	0.43	73	3.05	14
Stenson,Dernell	01	23	8	aaa	BOS	464	45	102	17	1	12	59	35	98	0	0	220	275	338	613	7%	79%	0.36	74	3.21	11
	02	24	8	aaa	BOS	368	37	85	20	1	7	30	31	82	3	3	231	291	348	639	8%	78%	0.38	80	3.48	18
Stevens,Tony	01	23	6	aa	MIN	245	18	41	7	1	1	20	10	30	3	3	166	198	214	412	4%	88%	0.32	34	1.30	-24
Stoner,Mike	01	28	8	aa	COL	290	27	61	11	2	5	33	11	40	0	2	210	239	314	554	4%	86%	0.28	67	2.39	3
Stratton,Rob	01	24	8	a/a	NYM	490	63	110	28	1	25	76	46	188	8	6	224	291	439	730	9%	62%	0.24	131	4.27	34
	02	25	8	aaa	NYM	336	50	71	9	1	22	52	21	116	5	4	211	258	440	698	6%	65%	0.18	128	3.65	27
Strong,Jamal	02	24	8	aa	SEA	503	60	126	15	3	1	29	58	89	44	16	250	328	298	626	10%	82%	0.65	35	3.65	11
St. Pierre,Maxim	02	22	2	a/a	DET	209	21	49	8	0	2	25	15	25	0	1	234	286	301	587	7%	88%	0.60	49	2.98	10
Sutton,Larry	01	31	38	aaa	STL	246	25	50	10	2	4	26	34	43	1	2	201	299	300	599	12%	82%	0.79	65	3.13	10
	02	32	3	aaa	OAK	431	56	95	31	1	8	55	62	90	1	0	220	318	353	671	13%	79%	0.69	94	4.08	26
Swann,Pedro	01	31	8	aaa	ATL	488	55	120	28	4	6	58	42	93	10	6	245	305	356	661	8%	81%	0.45	77	3.79	23
	02	32	8	aaa	TOR	368	37	83	15	2	10	44	27	68	1	4	226	278	359	637	7%	82%	0.40	83	3.30	17
Sweeney,Mark	01	32	8	aaa	MIL	404	48	95	28	1	5	50	41	62	2	1	234	305	341	646	9%	85%	0.67	80	3.72	24
Sykes,Jamie	01	27	8	aa	ARI	216	15	42	5	0	2	10	9	63	6	2	193	225	242	466	4%	71%	0.14	34	1.81	-19
t'Hoen,E.J.	01	26	4	a/a	ANA	157	14	26	9	1	3	11	10	36	4	5	164	214	290	504	6%	77%	0.27	85	1.73	-5
Taguchi,So	02	33	8	a/a	STL	411	38	78	19	0	4	34	15	60	6	4	190	218	265	484	4%	85%	0.25	56	1.83	-9
Tamargo,John	01	26	4	a/a	NYM	262	20	62	10	1	2	18	21	33	3	3	237	294	304	598	8%	87%	0.65	48	3.09	12
	02	27	4	aaa	NYM	101	10	17	3	0	2	8	10	9	2	0	168	243	257	501	9%	91%	1.11	57	2.19	2
Tarasco,Tony	01	31	8	aaa	NYM	366	44	90	27	3	5	48	40	47	12	8	246	320	379	698	10%	87%	0.85	95	4.17	38
	02	32	8	aaa	NYM	153	17	35	5	1	1	14	7	16	4	3	229	263	294	557	4%	90%	0.44	45	2.51	3
Taveras,Luis	01	24	2	a/a	TEX	213	28	40	4	1	5	21	18	37	4	1	188	251	286	537	8%	83%	0.49	57	2.45	-4
	02	27	2	aa	ATL	156	7	30	7	1	3	17	12	24	1	1	192	250	308	558	7%	85%	0.50	75	2.53	5
Taylor,Reggie	01	25	8	aaa	PHI	464	52	120	23	9	6	46	23	95	29	16	259	294	386	679	5%	80%	0.24	81	3.70	24
Taylor,Seth	02	25	4	aa	COL	161	13	36	12	0	3	17	9	24	1	1	224	265	354	619	5%	85%	0.38	95	3.14	21
Tebbs,Nate	01	29	648	aaa	ATL	219	14	34	7	0	0	7	12	56	5	2	157	201	187	388	5%	74%	0.22	26	1.23	-32
Teixeira,Mark	02	22	5	aa	TEX	171	28	52	10	3	9	25	23	31	3	2	304	387	556	942	12%	82%	0.74	149	8.13	78
Terrero,Luis	01	21	8	aa	ARI	147	22	39	12	2	2	6	3	33	7	2	265	280	415	695	2%	78%	0.09	105	4.04	34
	02	22	8	aa	ARI	360	38	95	18	5	6	42	17	67	14	26	264	297	392	689	5%	81%	0.25	82	3.05	27
Terveen,Bryce	02	25	2	aa	ATL	172	18	31	7	0	2	10	22	36	0	2	180	273	256	529	11%	79%	0.61	54	2.33	-5
Thames,Marcus	01	25	8	aa	NYY	520	99	153	39	3	29	85	64	96	9	4	294	371	550	921	11%	82%	0.66	159	7.70	77
	02	26	8	aaa	NYY	386	41	69	19	2	11	36	35	58	4	5	179	247	324	571	8%	85%	0.60	92	2.54	10
Theodorou,Nick	01	26	8	a/a	LA	103	13	25	4	0	0	9	20	14	2	1	245	370	283	652	17%	86%	1.41	33	4.15	24
	02	27	46	a/a	LA	198	15	35	7	0	0	17	28	28	3	0	177	279	212	491	12%	86%	1.00	31	2.22	-8
Thomas,Chuck	02	24	8	aa	ATL	229	32	47	7	0	2	15	22	36	4	3	205	275	262	537	9%	84%	0.61	41	2.46	-3
Thomas,Juan	01	29	3	aaa	SEA	503	60	121	31	1	17	76	34	144	2	2	241	288	409	697	6%	71%	0.23	109	4.08	30
	02	30	0	aaa	SEA	429	38	92	28	1	13	46	34	100	3	1	214	272	375	647	7%	77%	0.34	107	3.49	22

Major League Equivalent Statistics

BATTER	Yr	Age	Pos	Lev	Org	AB	R	H	D	T	HR	RBI	BB	K	SB	CS	BA	OB	Slg	OPS	bb%	ct%	Eye	PX	RC/G	BPV
Thompson,Andy	01	26	8	aaa	TOR	178	13	37	5	1	6	23	12	36	2	4	207	256	343	599	6%	80%	0.32	80	2.70	8
	02	27	80	a/a	TAM	282	23	53	10	2	5	33	12	55	1	1	188	221	291	512	4%	80%	0.22	65	2.07	-6
Thompson,Rich	02	23	8	aa	TOR	554	82	134	13	2	2	33	38	68	34	16	242	291	283	574	6%	88%	0.56	30	2.84	4
Thompson,Ryan	01	34	8	aaa	FLA	385	37	79	23	0	13	49	11	70	3	6	206	227	362	590	3%	82%	0.15	102	2.48	14
	02	35	8	aaa	MIL	273	30	68	10	2	11	32	9	46	0	4	249	273	421	694	3%	83%	0.20	101	3.71	29
Thrower,Jake	01	26	4	a/a	SD	440	44	104	24	1	3	29	39	71	4	3	236	298	315	613	8%	84%	0.55	60	3.31	15
	02	27	4	aaa	SD	362	38	83	26	1	3	28	19	49	1	0	229	268	331	599	5%	86%	0.39	79	3.07	17
Thurston,Joe	01	22	4	aa	LA	544	75	132	22	5	7	43	45	64	19	19	243	301	340	641	8%	88%	0.70	64	3.28	21
	02	23	4	aaa	LA	587	76	162	32	6	9	39	18	44	16	12	276	298	397	694	3%	93%	0.41	81	3.99	34
Timmons,Ozzie	02	32	8	aaa	ATL	496	43	106	19	1	12	60	30	87	5	1	214	259	329	587	6%	82%	0.34	73	2.90	8
Toca,Jorge	01	27	38	aaa	NYM	407	48	98	12	1	10	46	20	63	11	2	241	277	346	622	5%	85%	0.32	64	3.38	13
	02	28	3	aaa	NYM	195	18	42	8	0	2	12	8	29	2	1	215	246	287	533	4%	85%	0.28	52	2.36	-1
Tolentino,Juan	01	26	8	aaa	ANA	452	52	110	31	2	9	50	19	64	13	5	243	273	379	652	4%	86%	0.30	94	3.53	26
Tonis,Mike	01	23	2	aa	KC	226	28	56	10	1	7	33	16	30	1	1	248	298	394	691	7%	87%	0.53	91	4.10	31
Topolski,Jon	02	26	8	aa	HOU	300	29	59	5	2	7	24	33	78	2	6	197	276	297	573	10%	74%	0.42	57	2.63	-3
Torcato,Tony	01	22	8	a/a	SF	297	30	89	17	1	2	28	10	25	0	2	300	323	385	708	3%	91%	0.39	64	4.48	34
	02	23	8	aaa	SF	490	60	135	24	3	11	60	27	54	4	7	276	313	404	717	5%	89%	0.50	84	4.37	36
Torrealba,Steve	01	24	2	aa	ATL	295	33	74	19	0	7	30	30	51	0	0	250	319	385	704	9%	83%	0.60	94	4.46	34
	02	25	2	aaa	ATL	191	17	41	10	0	3	16	16	27	0	0	215	275	314	589	8%	86%	0.59	71	3.00	13
Torrealba,Yorvit	01	23	2	aaa	SF	394	42	92	20	2	6	27	14	47	1	4	234	260	340	600	3%	88%	0.30	73	2.88	14
Torres,Andres	01	24	8	aa	DET	252	44	67	16	2	1	18	29	39	16	13	266	342	354	696	10%	84%	0.74	67	4.01	31
	02	25	8	aaa	DET	462	72	115	15	9	3	38	50	99	38	13	249	322	340	662	10%	79%	0.51	56	3.99	16
Torres,Gabby	01	24	2	aa	MIN	133	23	40	12	1	2	13	10	11	0	2	299	347	445	792	7%	91%	0.86	106	5.51	61
	02	25	2	aa	MIN	191	16	47	12	1	2	19	22	23	0	2	246	324	351	675	10%	88%	0.96	76	4.00	33
Tracy,Andy	01	28	5	aaa	MON	190	14	35	10	1	4	16	20	69	4	2	185	262	310	572	10%	63%	0.29	84	2.72	2
	02	29	5	aaa	NYM	432	50	72	13	1	15	50	45	120	4	1	167	245	306	551	9%	72%	0.38	82	2.50	-3
Tracy,Chad	02	22	5	aa	ARI	514	63	163	36	4	6	58	29	38	2	4	317	354	438	791	5%	93%	0.76	87	5.81	57
Treanor,Matt	02	27	2	a/a	FLA	251	23	51	10	1	6	32	28	41	3	1	203	283	323	606	10%	84%	0.68	76	3.19	13
Tremie,Chris	01	32	2	a/a	HOU	237	21	43	7	0	5	23	20	33	0	5	182	245	270	515	8%	86%	0.59	56	2.02	-4
	02	33	2	aa	HOU	134	9	20	2	0	1	11	7	20	0	1	149	191	187	378	5%	85%	0.35	25	1.10	-33
Truby,Chris	01	28	53	aaa	HOU	321	43	90	24	5	10	57	19	60	8	6	281	321	482	804	6%	81%	0.32	129	5.38	53
Tyler,Brad	02	34	8	aaa	LA	148	22	26	6	1	1	8	26	29	0	3	176	299	250	549	15%	80%	0.90	52	2.51	-2
Tyler,Josh	01	28	8	a/a	SF	274	18	64	15	1	2	21	14	41	6	6	234	271	316	587	5%	85%	0.34	62	2.77	10
Tyner,Jason	01	24	8	aaa	TAM	157	22	46	2	1	0	11	13	9	10	6	293	347	318	666	8%	94%	1.44	17	3.98	34
	02	25	8	aaa	TAM	351	50	95	12	4	0	23	29	24	17	8	271	326	328	654	8%	93%	1.21	40	3.87	31
Tyson,Torre	01	26	8	aa	NYY	224	35	47	7	0	0	12	28	49	7	3	209	297	241	538	11%	78%	0.57	28	2.63	-7
Ullery,Dave	01	27	2	a/a	KC	146	12	31	6	1	2	16	9	31	1	0	213	257	306	563	6%	79%	0.28	62	2.70	2
	02	28	2	aa	BAL	106	8	15	3	0	1	4	11	34	0	0	142	222	198	420	9%	68%	0.32	40	1.49	-30
Umbria,Jose	02	25	2	a/a	TOR	116	8	23	3	0	0	7	6	23	1	1	198	238	224	462	5%	80%	0.26	23	1.75	-19
Unroe,Tim	02	32	3	aaa	ATL	264	26	53	11	1	8	32	22	82	1	2	201	262	341	603	8%	69%	0.27	87	2.94	8
Uribe,Juan	01	22	6	a/a	COL	294	33	91	28	5	7	39	9	32	9	9	311	332	518	850	3%	89%	0.29	140	5.78	67
Urquhart,Derick	01	26	8	aa	ANA	250	30	54	9	1	4	32	23	31	3	1	216	283	302	586	9%	88%	0.75	57	3.01	11
	02	27	8	a/a	ANA	287	23	48	10	2	3	16	22	37	5	6	167	227	247	474	7%	87%	0.59	53	1.71	-10
Urquiola,Carlos	01	21	8	aa	ARI	285	33	74	11	1	0	14	19	23	10	9	260	306	305	611	6%	92%	0.83	37	3.11	18
Ust,Brant	01	23	5	aa	DET	323	29	69	16	1	4	25	12	64	1	1	213	241	303	544	3%	80%	0.18	64	2.41	1
	02	24	5	aa	DET	209	22	33	9	1	6	15	16	44	0	1	158	218	297	514	7%	79%	0.36	87	2.03	-4
Utley,Chase	02	23	5	aaa	PHI	464	64	119	41	1	15	61	43	76	7	3	256	320	446	766	8%	84%	0.57	130	5.10	50
Valderrama,Carlos	01	24	8	aa	SF	159	24	44	11	1	1	7	15	26	10	6	275	335	372	707	8%	84%	0.56	74	4.32	33
	02	25	0	aa	SF	135	10	28	3	1	3	12	8	20	3	0	207	252	311	563	6%	85%	0.40	61	2.74	2
Valdez,Jerry	01	27	2	a/a	PHI	255	28	58	15	2	8	33	10	49	1	2	227	255	391	646	4%	81%	0.19	105	3.26	23
Valdez,Mario	02	28	3	aaa	OAK	304	30	63	14	1	2	18	41	44	1	0	207	301	280	581	12%	86%	0.93	54	3.07	10
Valdez,Wilson	02	24	6	aa	FLA	375	40	83	16	4	1	23	11	42	14	7	221	244	293	537	3%	89%	0.26	51	2.31	0
Valencia,Vic	01	24	2	aa	CIN	230	18	47	8	1	5	25	21	48	2	0	202	269	306	574	8%	79%	0.43	65	2.87	3
Valentin,Javier	01	26	253	aaa	MIN	431	40	107	26	1	13	53	35	87	0	1	248	304	401	705	7%	80%	0.40	101	4.30	32
	02	27	2	aaa	MIN	455	48	108	29	1	14	55	29	76	0	1	237	283	398	681	6%	83%	0.38	106	3.88	30
Valent,Eric	01	25	83	aaa	PHI	448	60	119	35	2	18	72	48	106	0	1	266	337	473	810	10%	76%	0.45	135	5.81	53
	02	26	8	aaa	PHI	546	57	125	34	2	7	69	43	85	0	2	229	285	337	622	7%	84%	0.51	78	3.32	19
Valenzuela,Mario	01	25	8	a/a	CHW	517	60	137	22	3	22	69	26	82	5	6	265	300	447	747	5%	84%	0.32	109	4.59	40
Valera,Yohanny	01	25	2	aa	TAM	250	23	56	18	3	5	28	11	70	0	2	223	255	382	637	4%	72%	0.15	107	3.17	22
	02	26	2	a/a	DET	146	12	28	7	1	1	5	5	37	0	0	192	219	274	493	3%	75%	0.14	59	1.95	-9
Van Iten,Bobby	01	24	238	aa	PHI	404	35	81	24	1	5	40	29	111	1	1	200	254	299	553	7%	73%	0.27	72	2.55	2
	02	25	2	aa	PHI	313	31	59	11	2	3	24	16	77	4	2	188	228	265	493	5%	75%	0.21	52	1.97	-12
Vazquez,Ramon	01	25	6	aaa	SEA	466	74	122	25	1	8	68	69	79	8	8	261	357	370	727	13%	83%	0.88	75	4.82	36
Velandia,Jorge	01	27	6	aaa	NYM	260	22	58	19	0	4	33	14	47	8	4	224	262	343	606	5%	82%	0.29	89	2.98	17
	02	28	6	aaa	NYM	407	36	69	17	1	5	31	25	76	4	2	170	218	253	471	6%	81%	0.33	58	1.78	-13
Velazquez,Gil	01	22	6	aa	NYM	358	28	66	10	1	2	16	21	73	1	1	184	230	235	464	6%	80%	0.29	36	1.78	-18
	02	23	4	a/a	NYM	105	7	19	3	0	0	5	9	21	0	3	181	246	210	455	8%	80%	0.43	25	1.53	-21
Vento,Mike	02	24	8	aa	NYY	227	25	47	14	1	4	22	22	46	3	3	207	277	330	608	9%	80%	0.48	86	3.04	14
Veras,Wilton	01	24	5	aaa	BOS	521	37	113	15	2	6	44	11	53	4	7	217	233	288	521	2%	90%	0.21	47	2.09	-4
	02	25	5	a/a	BOS	471	42	127	30	2	5	66	26	34	0	2	270	308	374	682	5%	93%	0.76	77	4.09	37
Victorino,Shane	02	22	8	aa	LA	481	58	116	14	1	4	32	45	48	43	17	241	306	299	605	9%	90%	0.94	40	3.25	16
Vinas,Julio	01	29	3	aaa	BAL	142	15	26	4	1	3	18	11	23	0	0	183	243	282	525	7%	84%	0.49	59	2.29	-4
Vitiello,Joe	02	33	3	aaa	MON	431	45	122	32	0	13	65	30	56	1	0	283	330	448	778	7%	87%	0.54	112	5.48	51
Wakeland,Chris	01	27	8	aaa	DET	547	67	135	30	2	15	67	30	101	6	9	247	286	393	679	5%	82%	0.30	95	3.71	28
	02	28	8	aaa	DET	297	33	60	9	1	7	27	21	98	5	3	202	255	310	564	7%	67%	0.21	66	2.61	-1
Walbeck,Matt	01	32	2	aaa	PHI	338	32	77	19	0	4	39	30	52	1	2	226	289	314	603	8%	85%	0.57	66	3.15	14
Waldron,Jeff	02	26	2	a/a	ARI	214	16	53	9	0	1	19	20	33	0	2	248	312	304	616	9%	85%	0.61	44	3.33	13
Ward,Turner	01	37	8	aaa	PHI	222	23	55	23	4	3	23	26	34	7	0	247	326	418	744	11%	84%	0.76	123	5.14	48
Ware,Jeremy	01	26	8	a/a	MON	234	22	59	18	0	5	26	11	34	3	1	254	287	393	680	4%	85%	0.32	100	3.96	32
	02	27	8	a/a	CLE	230	25	56	14	1	6	29	11	41	2	1	243	278	391	669	5%	82%	0.27	98	3.75	27
Warner,Michael	02	31	8	aaa	OAK	103	6	14	2	1	2	8	10	22	4	4	136	212	233	445	9%	79%	0.45	56	1.39	-23

Major League Equivalent Statistics

BATTER	Yr	Age	Pos	Lev	Org	AB	R	H	D	T	HR	RBI	BB	K	SB	CS	BA	OB	Slg	OPS	bb%	ct%	Eye	PX	RC/G	BPV
Warren,Chris	02	26	4	aa	COL	205	20	38	5	1	6	14	15	44	1	2	185	241	307	548	7%	79%	0.34	71	2.36	-2
Warriax,Brandon	02	23	6	aa	ANA	316	26	52	8	2	5	16	25	77	3	2	165	226	250	476	7%	76%	0.32	53	1.84	-17
Washington,Rico	01	23	54	aa	PIT	291	28	81	16	0	4	26	18	47	5	5	280	323	377	700	6%	84%	0.39	71	4.27	30
	02	24	5	aa	PIT	359	41	68	10	2	6	27	47	54	2	5	189	283	279	562	12%	85%	0.87	55	2.64	3
Waszgis,B.J.	01	31	23	aaa	FLA	311	31	57	14	0	14	41	19	72	0	1	182	229	356	585	6%	77%	0.26	106	2.62	10
Wathan,Derek	01	25	6	aa	FLA	469	60	106	11	7	4	32	42	88	23	16	227	290	304	594	8%	81%	0.47	47	2.88	4
	02	26	6	aaa	FLA	329	31	77	15	5	3	30	17	33	5	14	234	272	337	609	5%	90%	0.52	68	2.62	16
Wathan,Dusty	01	28	2	aa	FLA	134	18	27	8	0	2	16	10	36	0	1	203	260	299	559	7%	73%	0.29	71	2.58	3
	02	29	2	a/a	KC	185	16	39	8	1	1	20	12	40	1	1	211	259	281	540	6%	78%	0.30	51	2.45	-3
Watkins,Pat	01	29	8	aaa	KC	245	21	52	10	1	5	21	9	34	2	7	212	240	327	567	4%	86%	0.27	74	2.24	6
Watson,Matt	02	24	8	aa	NYM	441	44	102	22	1	8	52	29	46	10	9	231	279	340	619	6%	90%	0.63	74	3.10	20
Weber,Jake	01	25	8	aa	SEA	451	54	106	23	3	3	48	34	57	9	6	235	289	315	605	7%	87%	0.60	59	3.13	15
	02	26	8	a/a	SEA	255	23	59	6	0	2	22	17	31	5	4	231	279	278	558	6%	88%	0.55	33	2.63	2
Weekly,Chris	01	25	5	aa	TOR	131	13	30	4	1	4	19	11	31	0	2	232	294	363	656	8%	77%	0.37	77	3.52	17
	02	26	5	a/a	CHC	139	14	28	9	0	0	7	15	34	0	4	201	279	266	545	10%	76%	0.44	57	2.30	-0
Wells,Vernon	01	23	8	aaa	TOR	413	50	114	28	3	12	46	25	53	14	13	277	319	445	764	6%	87%	0.47	111	4.69	48
Werth,Jayson	01	22	23	aa	TOR	369	43	99	23	1	16	59	53	77	10	3	268	360	466	826	13%	79%	0.69	125	6.30	55
	02	23	8	aaa	TOR	443	52	103	25	1	14	65	53	98	19	8	233	315	388	703	11%	78%	0.54	101	4.28	30
Wesson,Barry	01	25	8	aa	HOU	472	52	105	22	5	14	43	32	120	15	10	223	273	380	654	6%	75%	0.27	97	3.34	20
	02	26	8	aaa	HOU	413	38	116	25	5	11	53	14	91	4	8	281	304	446	750	3%	78%	0.15	106	4.53	40
West,Todd	02	24	4	aa	MIL	120	11	23	5	0	0	7	7	21	5	3	192	236	233	470	6%	83%	0.33	37	1.76	-14
Whitaker,Chad	01	25	8	aa	CLE	155	13	32	8	1	5	14	11	32	2	1	203	255	372	627	7%	79%	0.34	105	3.14	18
White,Walt	01	30	46	a/a	ARI	165	13	25	5	1	0	7	10	40	1	1	149	198	188	385	6%	76%	0.25	29	1.18	-33
Whitmore,Darrell	01	33	8	aaa	STL	328	34	73	18	0	8	37	17	56	2	4	222	261	351	612	5%	83%	0.31	87	2.98	16
Widger,Chris	02	31	2	aaa	NYY	217	19	42	11	1	7	28	13	28	0	4	194	239	350	589	6%	87%	0.46	99	2.51	15
Wigginton,Ty	01	24	54	a/a	NYM	288	30	66	14	0	6	21	28	66	4	3	229	297	340	638	9%	77%	0.42	75	3.50	16
	02	25	5	aaa	NYM	383	44	104	24	2	5	43	38	46	4	3	272	337	384	721	9%	88%	0.83	80	4.75	40
Wilcox,Luke	01	28	8	a/a	NYY	260	24	53	13	0	10	39	20	44	1	2	205	261	376	638	7%	83%	0.45	108	3.22	22
Wilkerson,Brad	01	24	8	aaa	MON	233	39	60	10	0	12	44	53	63	11	5	258	395	455	850	19%	73%	0.84	118	6.79	51
Wilkins,Rick	01	34	2	aaa	SD	222	14	37	12	1	5	25	11	78	0	1	166	205	288	493	5%	65%	0.14	82	1.84	-8
Williams,Gerald	02	36	8	aaa	STL	278	31	53	11	2	3	12	11	41	6	5	191	221	277	498	4%	85%	0.27	58	1.88	-7
Williams,Glenn	01	24	54	aa	TOR	487	51	110	27	0	10	52	36	104	1	6	226	280	339	619	7%	79%	0.35	79	3.14	15
	02	25	5	aaa	TOR	339	39	83	18	2	12	37	16	64	2	0	245	279	416	695	5%	81%	0.25	107	4.06	31
Williams,Peanut	01	24	3	aa	SEA	125	10	21	8	0	1	8	12	37	1	1	167	242	251	493	9%	71%	0.34	66	2.00	-11
Wilson,Craig	01	31	53	aaa	KC	473	56	117	23	2	8	50	31	49	5	5	247	293	354	647	6%	90%	0.63	72	3.57	25
	02	32	4	aaa	DET	415	40	91	17	2	1	38	39	37	2	2	219	286	277	563	9%	91%	1.05	44	2.78	12
Wilson,Desi	01	32	3	aaa	ARI	320	32	86	17	1	2	27	10	41	3	2	270	292	346	638	3%	87%	0.24	58	3.56	19
Wilson,Jack	01	24	6	aaa	PIT	103	16	34	6	1	1	5	7	11	2	2	330	373	437	810	6%	89%	0.64	75	6.09	54
Wilson,Tom	01	31	2	aaa	OAK	259	31	57	12	1	5	34	35	54	0	1	219	312	334	646	12%	79%	0.64	75	3.71	17
Wilson,Travis	01	24	48	a/a	ATL	506	42	125	28	3	4	53	9	94	5	8	247	260	338	598	2%	81%	0.10	66	2.82	12
	02	25	8	aaa	ATL	494	51	119	21	3	11	62	11	93	9	3	241	257	362	620	2%	81%	0.12	77	3.16	15
Wilson,Vance	01	29	2	aaa	NYM	228	20	48	12	0	5	27	10	35	0	1	212	246	326	572	4%	84%	0.29	79	2.63	9
Wise,Dewayne	01	24	8	a/a	TOR	364	38	81	13	5	7	37	18	54	11	7	223	259	343	603	5%	85%	0.33	74	2.87	11
	02	25	8	aa	TOR	340	44	86	20	2	8	36	22	40	11	10	253	298	394	692	6%	88%	0.55	94	3.80	34
Witt,Kevin	01	26	38	aaa	SD	456	57	117	25	3	22	75	18	118	1	1	256	284	467	751	4%	74%	0.15	128	4.61	41
	02	27	3	aaa	CIN	509	57	118	30	1	19	81	24	106	0	1	232	266	407	673	5%	79%	0.23	112	3.67	28
Woods,Ken	01	31	8	aaa	CHC	185	14	36	6	1	0	10	13	22	5	3	195	246	238	484	6%	88%	0.57	34	1.94	-10
	02	32	8	a/a	PHI	241	26	50	10	2	3	19	8	33	5	4	207	233	303	536	3%	86%	0.24	63	2.20	0
Woodward,Chris	01	25	5	aaa	TOR	193	25	55	14	2	10	26	13	33	0	0	287	332	533	865	6%	83%	0.39	152	6.54	66
Wood,Jason	01	32	56	aaa	PIT	379	33	74	15	1	5	27	19	64	0	0	195	233	283	516	5%	83%	0.29	60	2.18	-5
	02	33	5	aaa	FLA	457	51	110	29	2	9	46	25	78	2	0	241	280	372	652	5%	83%	0.32	91	3.65	24
Wright,Corey	01	22	8	aa	TEX	418	52	98	18	2	0	22	50	81	19	17	234	316	287	603	11%	81%	0.62	42	3.03	8
Wright,Mike	01	26	2	a/a	SF	190	12	41	9	0	3	18	9	51	0	2	214	249	307	556	4%	73%	0.18	66	2.44	2
Wright,Ron	01	26	3	aaa	TAM	439	55	107	27	0	18	66	45	91	2	2	244	313	426	739	9%	79%	0.49	117	4.71	39
	02	27	0	aaa	SEA	359	45	86	18	1	12	49	33	80	0	1	240	304	396	699	8%	78%	0.41	99	4.22	29
Youkilis,Kevin	02	24	5	aa	BOS	160	26	49	10	0	4	19	23	14	4	5	306	393	444	837	13%	91%	1.64	94	6.36	74
Young,Ernie	01	32	8	aaa	SD	409	51	90	17	1	15	52	28	118	0	3	220	270	378	648	6%	71%	0.24	97	3.39	18
	02	33	8	aaa	ARI	160	20	42	7	1	10	33	16	27	0	4	263	330	506	836	9%	83%	0.59	141	5.46	58
Young,Mike	01	25	4	aaa	TEX	189	23	51	8	0	7	23	17	27	3	3	270	330	423	753	8%	86%	0.63	95	4.91	42
Zamora,Junior	01	25	5	a/a	ANA	164	14	32	5	1	5	17	8	26	1	1	193	230	326	556	5%	84%	0.30	79	2.41	3
Zapp,A.J.	01	23	3	aa	ATL	292	32	62	16	0	7	30	18	80	5	1	213	259	336	595	6%	72%	0.23	83	2.98	10
	02	24	3	a/a	ATL	392	38	78	16	0	15	44	33	94	1	0	199	261	355	616	8%	76%	0.35	95	3.14	13
Zech,Scott	01	27	5	a/a	MON	121	13	25	5	0	0	9	14	21	3	7	204	288	243	531	11%	83%	0.68	35	2.05	-4
Zinter,Alan	01	33	32	aaa	HOU	332	44	75	14	0	16	50	25	81	1	1	225	280	415	694	7%	76%	0.31	114	3.96	28
	02	34	3	aaa	HOU	225	23	45	13	0	10	31	17	63	2	0	200	256	391	647	7%	72%	0.27	120	3.39	22
Zoccolillo,Peter	02	26	8	aa	MIL	227	33	57	10	1	10	35	31	48	5	7	251	341	436	777	12%	79%	0.65	111	4.96	42
Zuber,Jon	02	33	3	aaa	MIL	385	44	78	11	2	2	21	55	49	5	2	203	302	257	559	13%	87%	1.12	38	2.85	6
Zuleta,Julio	01	27	3	aaa	CHC	146	16	39	11	0	6	24	6	30	3	1	266	294	458	752	4%	80%	0.19	126	4.74	45
	02	28	8	aaa	CHC	444	53	104	16	0	21	69	29	80	0	1	234	281	412	693	6%	82%	0.36	105	3.98	29
Zuniga,Tony	01	27	5	aaa	SF	413	56	92	14	1	17	53	39	63	4	1	223	290	388	677	9%	85%	0.62	97	3.92	27
	02	28	5	aaa	SF	304	18	63	15	1	4	28	15	35	0	4	207	245	303	547	5%	88%	0.43	67	2.32	5
Zywica,Mike	01	27	8	aa	TEX	163	16	30	7	0	4	15	4	57	0	1	183	204	306	509	2%	65%	0.07	80	1.92	-4
	02	28	38	a/a	CHW	189	17	33	5	0	5	18	13	49	3	0	175	228	280	508	6%	74%	0.27	64	2.16	-10

Major League Equivalent Statistics

					Actual				Major League Equivalents														
PITCHER	Yr	Age	Lev	Org	W	L	G	Sv	IP	H	ER	HR	BB	K	ERA	Br/IP	BF/G	OOB	CTL	DOM	CMD	hr/9	BPV
Abreu,Winston	01	25	aa	ATL	3	5	34	0	73	71	53	12	49	78	6.47	1.64	9.8	360	6.1	9.6	1.6	1.4	53
	02	26	aa	KC	4	0	34	2	55	51	40	4	46	54	6.52	1.76	7.6	376	7.5	8.8	1.2	0.7	65
Acevedo,Jose	01	24	aa	CIN	4	4	16	0	78	80	40	7	26	71	4.64	1.36	20.9	318	3.0	8.2	2.7	0.8	85
	02	25	aaa	CIN	12	7	23	0	154	158	60	17	31	107	3.50	1.23	27.8	296	1.8	6.2	3.5	1.0	83
Achilles,Matt	01	25	aa	CHC	3	4	9	0	52	68	29	2	23	30	4.98	1.75	27.1	374	4.0	5.1	1.3	0.4	39
	02	26	aa	CHC	8	7	41	1	115	166	71	8	45	54	5.55	1.83	13.3	386	3.5	4.2	1.2	0.6	21
Adams,Brian	02	25	aa	BOS	1	0	16	1	31	36	12	1	20	13	3.48	1.81	9.2	382	5.8	3.8	0.7	0.3	26
Adkins,Jonathan	01	24	a/a	OAK	9	8	27	0	150	181	81	10	43	68	4.89	1.50	24.5	339	2.6	4.1	1.6	0.6	35
	02	25	aaa	OAK	11	8	28	0	143	193	83	11	41	90	5.22	1.64	23.3	359	2.6	5.7	2.2	0.7	51
Adkins,Tim	01	27	a/a	NYY	3	1	41	0	80	99	46	10	36	64	5.17	1.68	9.0	365	4.0	7.1	1.8	1.2	41
	02	28	a/a	DET	2	3	34	0	74	101	56	6	41	46	6.80	1.92	10.5	396	5.0	5.6	1.1	0.7	27
Affeldt,Jeremy	01	22	aa	KC	10	6	25	0	145	171	73	10	42	106	4.53	1.47	25.5	335	2.6	6.6	2.5	0.6	71
Agamennone,Brand	01	26	a/a	MON	5	0	53	3	72	80	42	13	28	46	5.26	1.50	6.0	340	3.5	5.7	1.6	1.6	20
	02	27	a/a	MON	7	1	35	2	67	89	36	10	24	38	4.82	1.68	8.8	365	3.2	5.1	1.6	1.3	16
Agosto,Stevenson	01	25	a/a	TAM	8	10	33	0	135	151	87	19	67	97	5.82	1.61	18.6	356	4.5	6.5	1.4	1.3	31
	02	27	aa	TAM	3	1	7	0	38	60	17	5	16	20	4.02	1.99	26.8	406	3.8	4.7	1.3	1.2	4
Ahearne,Pat	01	32	aaa	FLA	6	10	28	0	144	221	97	12	34	67	6.04	1.77	24.1	377	2.1	4.2	2.0	0.7	31
	02	33	aaa	DET	5	4	12	0	82	95	38	3	13	42	4.16	1.31	29.0	310	1.4	4.6	3.2	0.3	84
Ainsworth,Kurt	01	23	aaa	SF	10	9	27	0	149	142	81	18	47	130	4.89	1.27	23.1	303	2.8	7.9	2.8	1.1	78
	02	24	aaa	SF	8	6	20	0	116	113	51	6	41	102	3.96	1.33	24.6	313	3.2	7.9	2.5	0.5	91
Aldred,Scott	01	33	aa	NYY	4	3	11	0	37	52	25	5	8	31	6.01	1.62	15.3	357	2.0	7.7	3.8	1.1	82
	02	34	aaa	LA	2	2	42	2	44	52	21	2	18	40	4.28	1.58	4.7	352	3.7	8.1	2.2	0.4	81
Almanzar,Carlos	01	28	aaa	NYY	2	1	35	18	33	44	12	3	6	22	3.15	1.53	4.2	343	1.7	5.9	3.5	0.9	75
Almonte,Ed	01	25	aa	CHW	1	4	54	36	66	72	15	5	17	52	2.01	1.34	5.2	314	2.3	7.1	3.1	0.7	87
	02	26	aaa	CHW	2	3	50	26	60	63	20	8	13	51	3.00	1.26	5.0	302	1.9	7.6	3.9	1.2	94
Altman,Gene	02	24	aa	MIL	0	3	24	1	33	38	42	4	44	19	11.42	2.48	7.4	459	12.0	5.2	0.4	1.1	6
Alvarado,Carlos	01	24	aa	PIT	5	7	26	0	83	92	42	7	33	60	4.58	1.50	14.1	340	3.6	6.5	1.8	0.8	54
Alvarez,Juan	01	28	aaa	ANA	2	2	48	0	67	80	44	15	27	35	5.91	1.59	6.3	352	3.6	4.7	1.3	2.0	-7
Alvarez,Victor	01	25	a/a	LA	9	4	28	0	163	158	69	13	49	112	3.81	1.27	24.4	303	2.7	6.2	2.3	0.7	67
	02	26	aaa	LA	10	7	34	3	122	131	58	9	34	91	4.27	1.35	15.3	316	2.5	6.7	2.7	0.7	78
Alvarez,Wilson	01	32	a/a	TAM	2	4	9	0	38	59	23	6	13	26	5.51	1.90	20.4	394	3.1	6.2	2.0	1.3	25
Anderson,Craig	02	22	aa	SEA	7	7	27	0	152	173	73	14	67	80	4.32	1.58	25.3	351	4.0	4.7	1.2	0.8	28
Anderson,Jason	02	23	a/a	NYY	6	2	42	9	53	45	16	4	16	44	2.71	1.15	5.2	282	2.7	7.4	2.8	0.7	92
Anderson,Luke	02	25	aa	SF	2	4	26	11	32	36	12	1	13	38	3.38	1.53	5.5	344	3.7	10.7	2.9	0.3	116
Andra,Jeff	01	26	a/a	SF	4	12	27	0	135	197	90	19	47	59	5.99	1.80	23.6	381	3.1	4.0	1.3	1.3	1
Andrews,Clayton	01	23	a/a	CIN	3	5	14	0	79	113	58	13	29	34	6.61	1.80	26.6	381	3.3	3.9	1.2	1.5	-7
Aramboles,Ricardo	01	20	a/a	NYY	1	5	6	0	33	39	18	3	3	20	4.95	1.28	23.3	305	0.9	5.3	5.6	0.9	119
Arias,Pablo	02	26	aa	DET	5	8	29	0	106	167	98	22	60	43	8.31	2.14	18.5	423	5.1	3.6	0.7	1.9	-34
Arnold,Jamie	01	28	aaa	SF	1	4	44	9	76	103	51	12	33	45	5.98	1.79	8.1	380	3.9	5.3	1.4	1.4	11
	02	29	aaa	FLA	3	8	16	0	67	89	57	9	29	20	7.66	1.76	19.6	376	3.9	2.7	0.7	1.2	-13
Arnold,Jason	02	23	aa	NYY	6	3	13	0	75	70	30	4	31	61	3.60	1.34	24.6	315	3.7	7.3	2.0	0.5	77
Arroyo,Bronson	01	25	aaa	PIT	6	2	9	0	66	69	32	6	15	42	4.36	1.27	30.8	303	2.0	5.7	2.8	0.8	71
	02	26	aaa	PIT	8	6	22	0	143	145	58	10	26	98	3.65	1.20	26.8	291	1.6	6.2	3.8	0.6	101
Arteaga,J.D.	01	27	aaa	HOU	8	6	32	1	138	178	64	15	31	73	4.19	1.51	19.1	341	2.0	4.8	2.4	1.0	44
	02	28	aaa	HOU	9	10	42	3	119	177	85	27	47	61	6.42	1.88	13.6	392	3.5	4.6	1.3	2.0	-19
Atchison,Scott	01	26	aa	SEA	9	10	24	0	136	216	84	12	32	68	5.59	1.82	26.9	384	2.1	4.5	2.1	0.8	31
	02	27	aaa	SEA	5	10	27	2	124	143	78	13	31	93	5.66	1.40	19.9	324	2.2	6.7	3.0	0.9	74
Austin,Jeff	01	25	aaa	KC	3	7	28	2	70	101	64	16	25	46	8.21	1.79	11.8	381	3.2	5.9	1.8	2.1	1
	02	26	aaa	KC	4	0	39	2	52	63	23	2	14	36	3.97	1.48	5.9	336	2.4	6.2	2.6	0.3	77
Averette,Robert	01	25	aaa	COL	6	14	27	0	166	241	145	44	47	109	7.88	1.74	28.7	373	2.6	5.9	2.3	2.4	-0
	02	26	aa	COL	1	6	11	0	61	124	76	11	25	25	11.18	2.43	29.8	455	3.7	3.7	1.0	1.6	-32
Aybar,Manny	01	27	aaa	CHC	2	5	19	0	75	94	51	13	25	49	6.05	1.58	17.8	351	3.0	5.9	2.0	1.5	26
	02	30	aaa	SF	1	4	45	24	50	57	27	6	19	41	4.85	1.52	4.9	342	3.4	7.4	2.2	1.1	56
Babula,Shaun	01	24	aa	BAL	2	4	28	2	38	45	18	2	13	23	4.22	1.52	6.1	342	3.0	5.4	1.8	0.5	53
Backe,Brandon	02	25	aa	TAM	4	6	20	2	92	111	63	11	40	36	6.16	1.64	21.0	360	3.9	3.5	0.9	1.1	4
Bacsik,Mike	01	24	a/a	CLE	13	6	25	0	149	162	66	19	28	86	3.98	1.27	25.0	304	1.7	5.2	3.1	1.1	62
	02	25	aaa	NYM	5	5	25	0	108	153	54	13	26	63	4.50	1.66	19.8	362	2.2	5.2	2.4	1.1	40
Baerlocher,Ryan	01	24	aa	KC	13	8	28	0	180	212	98	29	54	98	4.89	1.47	28.3	335	2.7	4.9	1.8	1.5	21
	02	25	a/a	KC	8	4	24	0	110	129	67	16	47	61	5.47	1.60	20.7	354	3.8	5.0	1.3	1.3	16
Baez,Benito	01	24	aaa	FLA	7	1	49	1	59	53	18	4	6	49	2.74	1.00	4.7	255	0.9	7.5	8.2	0.6	206
Bailie,Matt	01	26	a/a	PHI	1	6	36	2	68	99	72	16	38	59	9.54	2.01	9.3	407	5.0	7.7	1.5	2.1	6
Baisley,Brad	01	22	aa	PHI	5	4	12	0	62	93	53	14	15	34	7.68	1.74	24.1	373	2.2	4.9	2.3	2.0	3
	02	23	aa	PHI	7	9	21	0	116	130	67	13	56	57	5.19	1.60	25.0	354	4.3	4.4	1.0	1.0	17
Baker,Brad	02	22	aa	SD	4	4	12	0	64	53	38	5	46	48	5.34	1.54	23.8	346	6.5	6.7	1.0	0.7	52
Baker,Chris	01	24	aa	TOR	15	6	28	1	179	199	88	27	44	98	4.45	1.36	27.4	318	2.2	4.9	2.2	1.4	35
	02	25	aaa	TOR	4	7	18	0	89	106	51	13	28	36	5.15	1.50	21.9	340	2.8	3.6	1.3	1.3	7
Bale,John	01	27	aaa	BAL	1	1	9	0	30	39	9	1	5	35	2.82	1.46	14.7	334	1.6	10.5	6.7	0.3	187
Balfour,Grant	01	24	a/a	MIN	4	3	46	13	66	53	22	4	34	76	3.00	1.32	6.1	311	4.6	10.3	2.2	0.5	105
	02	25	aaa	MIN	2	4	58	8	71	65	35	3	29	75	4.43	1.32	5.2	312	3.7	9.5	2.6	0.4	107
Banks,Willie	01	33	aaa	TOR	10	5	26	0	159	195	73	15	58	107	4.11	1.59	27.6	352	3.3	6.1	1.9	0.8	46
Baptist,Travis	01	30	a/a	CHW	3	9	43	5	99	162	70	13	35	62	6.31	1.99	11.3	405	3.2	5.6	1.7	1.2	17
Bartosh,Cliff	02	23	aa	SD	2	4	62	25	70	63	31	4	34	57	3.97	1.38	4.9	321	4.4	7.3	1.7	0.5	72
Bauer,Greg	02	25	aa	LA	2	4	38	1	70	76	29	6	33	31	3.73	1.56	8.2	348	4.2	4.0	0.9	0.8	21
Bauer,Peter	01	23	aa	TOR	6	8	21	0	128	171	92	14	37	60	6.46	1.62	27.7	357	2.6	4.2	1.6	1.0	22
	02	24	aa	TOR	6	13	28	0	177	237	101	14	53	78	5.14	1.64	28.8	359	2.7	4.0	1.5	0.7	25
Bauer,Rick	01	25	a/a	BAL	12	10	28	0	174	206	95	23	40	107	4.90	1.42	27.0	326	2.1	5.5	2.7	1.2	51
Baugh,Kenny	01	23	aa	DET	1	3	5	0	30	26	12	4	5	26	3.59	1.03	23.8	261	1.5	7.8	5.2	1.2	129
Bausher,Andy	02	26	a/a	SD	5	1	42	0	74	98	33	8	21	37	4.01	1.61	8.0	355	2.6	4.5	1.8	1.0	27
Bazzell,Shane	02	24	aa	OAK	5	7	39	3	97	116	60	3	47	73	5.56	1.68	11.5	365	4.4	6.8	1.6	0.3	62
Beal,Andy	02	24	a/a	NYY	6	9	18	0	107	119	62	10	43	82	5.21	1.51	26.4	341	3.6	6.9	1.9	0.8	56
Beasley,Ray	01	25	aaa	ATL	1	3	65	0	55	69	30	5	23	33	4.91	1.67	3.9	364	3.8	5.4	1.4	0.8	33
	02	26	aaa	ATL	6	5	64	4	55	64	20	3	16	38	3.26	1.45	3.8	332	2.6	6.2	2.4	0.5	71

Major League Equivalent Statistics

					Actual				Major League Equivalents														
PITCHER	Yr	Age	Lev	Org	W	L	G	Sv	IP	H	ER	HR	BB	K	ERA	Br/IP	BF/G	OOB	CTL	DOM	CMD	hr/9	BPV
Bechler,Steve	01	22	a/a	BAL	4	6	14	0	86	86	49	21	20	60	5.08	1.23	25.5	296	2.1	6.3	3.0	2.2	39
	02	23	a/a	BAL	8	12	28	0	173	204	90	18	58	76	4.68	1.51	27.4	341	3.0	4.0	1.3	0.9	21
Beckett,Josh	01	21	aa	FLA	8	1	13	0	74	60	20	9	21	89	2.43	1.09	22.9	272	2.6	10.8	4.2	1.1	133
Bedard,Erik	02	24	aa	BAL	6	3	13	0	68	49	18	0	31	54	2.38	1.17	21.5	287	4.1	7.1	1.7	0.0	95
Beech,Matt	01	30	a/a	TEX	4	7	18	0	106	177	84	27	40	61	7.13	2.04	29.3	412	3.4	5.1	1.5	2.3	-23
	02	31	a/a	NYY	6	8	23	0	120	179	81	10	71	74	6.07	2.08	26.1	416	5.3	5.5	1.0	0.7	20
Beirne,Kevin	02	29	aaa	LA	10	3	22	0	125	137	56	11	39	72	4.03	1.41	24.6	325	2.8	5.2	1.8	0.8	47
Belflower,Jay	02	23	aa	ARI	5	3	36	2	55	75	29	5	13	44	4.73	1.59	6.9	353	2.1	7.2	3.4	0.8	81
Belisle,Matt	02	22	aa	ATL	5	9	26	0	159	181	89	19	37	103	5.03	1.37	26.3	319	2.1	5.8	2.8	1.1	60
Belitz,Todd	01	26	aaa	OAK	4	4	52	2	64	77	45	8	18	52	6.37	1.48	5.4	336	2.5	7.4	2.9	1.1	68
	02	27	aaa	COL	1	3	22	2	44	62	30	8	19	24	6.14	1.84	9.5	387	3.9	4.9	1.3	1.6	-3
Bell,Heath	01	24	aa	NYM	3	1	43	4	61	95	48	13	20	44	7.13	1.88	6.8	391	2.9	6.4	2.2	1.9	14
	02	25	a/a	NYM	4	4	46	11	69	71	24	2	16	62	3.12	1.26	6.3	301	2.1	8.1	3.9	0.3	125
Bell,Rob	02	26	a/a	TEX	6	0	13	0	83	89	44	12	25	49	4.77	1.37	27.4	320	2.7	5.3	2.0	1.3	35
Beltran,Francis	02	22	aa	CHC	2	2	39	23	41	32	15	2	20	38	3.28	1.26	4.4	302	4.4	8.3	1.9	0.4	90
Beltran,Rigo	01	32	aaa	PHI	2	5	37	2	115	112	55	12	51	98	4.28	1.41	13.5	325	3.9	7.6	1.9	0.9	65
Benes,Alan	01	30	aaa	STL	7	6	25	0	142	199	69	15	56	82	4.39	1.80	26.8	381	3.6	5.2	1.5	1.0	23
	02	31	aaa	CHC	10	9	28	0	113	147	76	17	53	68	6.05	1.77	18.9	377	4.2	5.4	1.3	1.4	12
Benoit,Joaquin	01	22	a/a	TEX	10	5	28	0	153	158	87	19	76	148	5.11	1.53	24.3	343	4.5	8.7	1.9	1.1	62
	02	25	aaa	TEX	8	4	16	0	98	82	44	8	35	89	4.03	1.19	25.2	290	3.2	8.2	2.5	0.7	91
Bergman,Dusty	01	24	aa	ANA	7	13	27	0	153	225	103	11	52	70	6.06	1.80	26.8	382	3.0	4.1	1.4	0.7	21
	02	25	a/a	ANA	6	1	56	4	85	95	43	11	16	53	4.55	1.30	6.4	309	1.7	5.6	3.3	1.2	68
Bernero,Adam	01	25	aaa	DET	6	11	26	0	140	193	93	12	49	84	5.97	1.73	25.0	372	3.1	5.4	1.7	0.8	36
	02	26	aaa	DET	2	2	9	0	57	54	12	2	12	44	1.89	1.16	25.8	284	1.9	6.9	3.7	0.3	115
Bertotti,Mike	01	32	aaa	NYY	1	2	19	0	41	45	23	5	29	35	5.07	1.82	10.2	384	6.5	7.7	1.2	1.2	37
Bevel,Bobby	01	28	a/a	LA	2	4	56	6	81	99	35	9	32	45	3.92	1.61	6.6	355	3.5	5.0	1.4	1.0	25
	02	29	a/a	SEA	6	2	51	1	55	84	46	10	26	36	7.50	1.99	5.3	406	4.2	5.9	1.4	1.6	2
Beverlin,Jason	01	28	a/a	ANA	10	4	25	0	122	149	67	16	43	78	4.91	1.57	21.9	350	3.1	5.8	1.8	1.2	34
	02	29	aaa	DET	13	8	27	0	137	154	73	11	46	100	4.79	1.46	22.2	333	3.0	6.6	2.2	0.7	63
Bevis,P.J.	02	22	aa	ARI	5	5	53	11	70	61	24	3	30	64	3.08	1.30	5.6	307	3.8	8.2	2.1	0.4	92
Bierbrodt,Nick	01	23	a/a	ARI	6	2	11	0	65	67	16	1	14	64	2.22	1.25	24.6	299	1.9	8.9	4.6	0.1	148
Billingsley,Brent	01	26	a/a	MON	7	9	20	0	115	174	102	28	41	75	7.99	1.87	27.6	391	3.2	5.8	1.8	2.2	-5
	02	27	a/a	MON	4	9	34	1	108	149	92	15	47	69	7.66	1.81	15.0	383	3.9	5.7	1.5	1.2	19
Blair,Willie	01	36	aaa	CLE	4	3	11	0	72	89	31	4	7	41	3.82	1.35	27.9	315	0.9	5.1	5.5	0.5	127
Blank,Matt	01	26	aaa	MON	6	7	14	0	81	107	63	16	32	48	6.94	1.72	26.9	370	3.6	5.3	1.5	1.8	2
	02	27	aaa	MON	11	7	31	0	147	164	71	15	58	76	4.35	1.51	21.0	341	3.6	4.7	1.3	0.9	28
Bleazard,Dave	01	28	a/a	TOR	0	2	8	0	34	40	26	5	18	13	6.96	1.71	19.8	370	4.8	3.4	0.7	1.2	-3
Blevins,Jeremy	01	24	aa	NYY	1	6	50	6	63	59	31	3	28	52	4.35	1.38	5.4	322	4.1	7.5	1.8	0.5	76
	02	25	a/a	NYY	5	3	36	1	50	60	24	4	29	34	4.32	1.78	6.5	379	5.2	6.1	1.2	0.7	36
Bochtler,Doug	01	31	a/a	MIN	2	5	49	7	77	90	37	8	33	79	4.27	1.60	7.1	354	3.9	9.2	2.4	0.9	76
	02	32	aaa	MIN	7	4	34	0	88	80	41	6	45	65	4.19	1.42	11.2	327	4.6	6.6	1.4	0.6	59
Bohannan,Brad	01	24	aa	CHW	3	5	29	0	51	75	43	13	22	21	7.62	1.90	8.5	394	3.9	3.7	0.9	2.2	-37
Bohanon,Brian	02	34	aaa	CIN	3	0	14	0	44	59	27	7	19	19	5.51	1.77	14.8	377	3.9	3.9	1.0	1.4	-6
Bones,Ricky	02	34	aaa	LA	0	2	30	9	30	35	13	2	12	12	3.89	1.56	4.5	348	3.6	3.6	1.0	0.6	23
Bong,Jung	02	22	aa	ATL	7	8	27	2	122	152	51	6	43	90	3.76	1.60	20.4	354	3.2	6.6	2.1	0.4	66
Booker,Chris	01	25	aa	CHC	4	6	61	2	68	60	37	7	48	83	4.88	1.59	5.0	353	6.4	10.9	1.7	1.0	81
Bootcheck,Chris	01	23	aa	ANA	3	3	6	0	36	43	25	3	10	19	6.23	1.47	26.4	335	2.5	4.7	1.9	0.7	43
	02	24	a/a	ANA	12	10	28	0	174	217	101	18	49	109	5.22	1.53	27.6	344	2.5	5.6	2.2	0.9	48
Borland,Toby	01	32	aaa	ANA	7	3	45	3	74	61	22	2	28	76	2.68	1.21	6.8	293	3.5	9.2	2.7	0.3	115
	02	33	aaa	FLA	5	2	56	14	70	59	23	2	29	63	2.96	1.26	5.2	301	3.7	8.1	2.2	0.3	97
Borowski,Joe	01	30	aaa	CHC	8	7	39	1	110	104	39	10	28	101	3.18	1.20	11.6	292	2.3	8.2	3.6	0.8	107
Borrell,Danny	02	24	aa	NYY	9	4	21	0	128	138	42	6	41	79	2.95	1.40	26.3	324	2.9	5.6	1.9	0.4	62
Boskie,Shawn	01	35	aaa	ARI	4	6	12	0	62	111	58	8	17	26	8.39	2.05	25.7	413	2.4	3.7	1.5	1.2	-3
Bost,Heath	01	27	aaa	COL	2	2	45	0	75	99	47	21	24	55	5.69	1.64	7.6	359	2.8	6.6	2.3	2.5	7
	02	28	aaa	OAK	1	5	52	12	78	73	29	7	18	56	3.35	1.17	6.1	285	2.1	6.5	3.1	0.8	86
Bowers,Cedrick	01	24	aaa	TAM	6	5	42	0	94	98	41	12	57	58	3.93	1.65	10.2	361	5.5	5.6	1.0	1.1	23
	02	25	aaa	TAM	4	3	47	0	69	87	30	10	44	67	3.91	1.90	7.1	394	5.7	8.7	1.5	1.3	40
Bowe,Brandon	02	27	aa	FLA	6	4	45	4	75	111	39	7	26	41	4.68	1.83	7.9	385	3.1	4.9	1.6	0.8	25
Bowie,Micah	01	27	aaa	OAK	6	8	38	3	116	136	71	13	43	85	5.52	1.55	13.6	346	3.4	6.6	2.0	1.0	48
	02	28	aaa	OAK	3	2	46	4	54	43	20	2	23	52	3.32	1.22	4.9	294	3.8	8.6	2.3	0.3	102
Bowles,Brian	01	25	aaa	TOR	3	5	66	6	77	66	31	4	43	68	3.66	1.41	5.1	326	5.1	8.0	1.6	0.5	77
	02	26	aaa	TOR	4	7	59	14	59	54	27	4	32	45	4.12	1.46	4.4	333	4.9	6.9	1.4	0.6	60
Boyd,Jason	01	29	aaa	PHI	2	7	52	12	59	58	19	5	28	56	2.95	1.46	5.0	333	4.3	8.5	2.0	0.8	73
	02	30	aaa	SD	1	1	28	5	42	38	12	5	18	28	2.57	1.33	6.4	313	3.9	6.0	1.6	1.1	44
Bradley,Ryan	01	26	aa	NYY	4	5	16	0	58	63	66	11	57	41	10.15	2.07	18.1	414	8.8	6.4	0.7	1.7	3
Braswell,Bryan	02	27	aa	NYM	3	1	24	1	34	63	31	1	13	13	8.18	2.23	7.3	433	3.4	3.4	1.0	0.3	11
Brazelton,Dewon	02	22	a/a	TAM	6	9	27	0	151	155	67	8	70	97	3.99	1.49	24.7	338	4.2	5.8	1.4	0.5	52
Brea,Lesli	01	23	aaa	BAL	2	6	63	1	82	90	43	7	34	92	4.70	1.51	5.8	341	3.8	10.1	2.7	0.7	96
	02	24	aaa	BAL	3	7	60	3	86	91	37	4	37	63	3.86	1.48	6.3	337	3.9	6.6	1.7	0.4	65
Brewington,Jamie	01	30	aaa	MIN	2	8	35	0	67	110	58	13	34	41	7.76	2.16	9.7	425	4.6	5.4	1.2	1.8	-13
	02	31	aaa	BOS	5	6	18	0	91	105	59	19	38	49	5.83	1.57	22.7	350	3.8	4.8	1.3	1.9	-2
Bridges,Donnie	01	23	a/a	MON	4	7	16	0	72	87	66	16	58	53	8.25	2.01	22.2	408	7.3	6.6	0.9	2.0	-5
	02	24	aa	FLA	4	8	20	0	78	103	75	7	62	47	8.63	2.11	19.7	419	7.1	5.4	0.8	0.8	17
Brink,Jim	01	25	a/a	OAK	0	1	21	2	34	41	17	6	20	24	4.45	1.79	7.6	380	5.3	6.3	1.2	1.7	9
	02	26	aa	TEX	7	5	42	0	85	141	72	17	24	31	7.61	1.94	9.9	399	2.5	3.3	1.3	1.8	-24
Brittan,Corey	01	27	aaa	NYM	4	2	58	4	81	103	24	4	29	37	2.63	1.63	6.4	358	3.2	4.1	1.3	0.5	32
	02	28	aaa	COL	3	6	35	0	97	144	76	21	44	58	7.04	1.94	13.5	399	4.1	5.4	1.3	1.9	-11
Brock,Chris	01	31	aaa	PHI	6	2	13	0	78	102	48	11	21	46	5.50	1.58	27.1	351	2.4	5.3	2.2	1.3	32
Brohawn,Troy	02	30	aaa	SF	3	3	56	1	69	87	35	7	22	43	4.57	1.58	5.5	351	2.9	5.6	2.0	0.9	42
Brownson,Mark	01	26	aa	MIL	10	5	24	0	131	198	100	25	41	87	6.87	1.83	25.9	385	2.8	6.0	2.1	1.7	15
Brown,Derek	01	25	a/a	BAL	6	5	43	2	86	116	61	13	27	49	6.37	1.66	9.2	363	2.9	5.2	1.8	1.3	21
	02	26	aa	BAL	3	6	41	0	87	148	64	11	29	39	6.62	2.03	10.5	411	3.0	4.0	1.3	1.1	-0

Major League Equivalent Statistics

					Actual				Major League Equivalents														
PITCHER	Yr	Age	Lev	Org	W	L	G	Sv	IP	H	ER	HR	BB	K	ERA	Br/IP	BF/G	OOB	CTL	DOM	CMD	hr/9	BPV
Brown,Elliot	01	26	a/a	SF	2	10	22	0	96	163	71	10	36	37	6.66	2.07	21.8	415	3.3	3.5	1.0	0.9	-4
	02	27	aa	SF	8	4	25	0	111	173	72	6	39	27	5.83	1.91	21.5	395	3.2	2.2	0.7	0.5	-1
Brown,Jamie	02	26	aa	CLE	9	5	18	0	103	129	47	7	20	56	4.10	1.44	25.0	331	1.7	4.9	2.8	0.6	65
Bruback,Matt	01	23	aa	CHC	2	5	9	0	38	63	42	3	20	37	9.95	2.18	21.6	428	4.7	8.8	1.9	0.7	53
	02	24	aa	CHC	9	7	28	0	174	187	77	10	51	135	3.98	1.37	26.6	319	2.6	7.0	2.6	0.5	83
Brueggemann,Dean	02	27	aa	COL	0	3	34	0	51	84	62	7	37	27	10.90	2.36	8.0	447	6.5	4.7	0.7	1.2	-10
Brummett,Sean	01	24	aa	ANA	2	4	25	0	65	74	48	9	27	38	6.69	1.55	11.7	347	3.7	5.2	1.4	1.3	21
Brunette,Justin	01	26	a/a	NYM	5	3	47	4	56	107	61	10	26	42	9.79	2.35	6.3	446	4.1	6.8	1.7	1.6	4
	02	27	a/a	NYM	3	2	48	2	81	102	46	5	24	33	5.11	1.56	7.6	348	2.7	3.7	1.4	0.6	29
Brunson,Will	01	32	aaa	ANA	2	2	39	0	69	84	40	11	19	43	5.20	1.49	7.8	338	2.5	5.6	2.3	1.4	36
Bruske,Jim	01	37	aaa	ANA	5	3	37	1	106	148	71	17	24	88	5.98	1.63	13.0	358	2.1	7.5	3.6	1.4	69
Buddie,Mike	01	31	aaa	MIL	4	1	27	3	46	44	16	4	27	24	3.03	1.54	7.6	345	5.2	4.7	0.9	0.9	27
	02	32	aaa	MON	4	4	29	2	42	42	26	2	24	14	5.57	1.57	6.5	350	5.1	3.0	0.6	0.4	21
Bukvich,Ryan	02	24	a/a	KC	2	1	35	16	48	26	6	0	23	51	1.13	1.02	5.4	259	4.3	9.6	2.2	0.0	128
Buller,Sean	01	26	a/a	DET	3	1	21	2	32	41	20	2	8	16	5.61	1.54	6.8	345	2.4	4.5	1.9	0.6	44
Bullinger,Jim	01	36	aaa	STL	1	8	10	0	53	79	48	13	32	32	8.22	2.09	26.5	417	5.4	5.5	1.0	2.1	-23
Bullinger,Kirk	01	32	a/a	CHW	0	4	39	6	54	66	32	8	26	31	5.37	1.69	6.4	366	4.3	5.1	1.2	1.3	13
	02	33	aaa	HOU	4	1	55	4	75	78	34	8	13	38	4.07	1.21	5.6	293	1.6	4.6	2.9	1.0	62
Bump,Nate	01	25	aa	FLA	4	5	11	0	54	73	48	12	12	32	7.93	1.58	22.2	351	2.0	5.4	2.7	2.0	19
	02	26	aa	FLA	7	6	20	0	127	138	61	6	33	62	4.32	1.34	27.1	315	2.3	4.4	1.9	0.4	54
Burnside,Adrian	01	25	aa	LA	4	5	19	0	100	87	43	11	49	81	3.88	1.37	22.6	319	4.5	7.3	1.6	0.9	58
	02	26	aa	PIT	6	9	32	0	130	152	89	20	70	94	6.15	1.71	18.8	369	4.8	6.5	1.3	1.4	24
Bynum,Mike	01	24	aa	SD	2	7	16	0	84	106	59	15	38	53	6.29	1.72	24.4	370	4.1	5.7	1.4	1.7	9
	02	25	a/a	SD	7	2	13	0	74	61	23	6	14	52	2.80	1.01	22.4	258	1.7	6.3	3.7	0.7	105
Byrd,Paul	01	31	aaa	PHI	1	3	5	0	37	46	23	6	9	29	5.68	1.47	32.5	335	2.2	7.0	3.2	1.4	65
Calero,Kiko	01	27	aa	KC	14	5	27	0	124	141	61	13	54	68	4.42	1.57	20.7	350	3.9	4.9	1.3	0.9	27
	02	28	a/a	KC	8	7	25	0	141	164	76	17	45	90	4.84	1.48	24.9	336	2.9	5.7	2.0	1.1	42
Callaway,Mickey	01	26	aaa	TAM	11	7	29	0	129	159	58	11	25	68	4.03	1.42	19.3	328	1.7	4.7	2.7	0.8	58
	02	27	aaa	ANA	9	2	17	0	91	91	20	8	21	61	1.98	1.23	22.2	296	2.1	6.0	2.9	0.8	77
Cameron,Ryan	01	24	aa	COL	7	6	18	0	89	157	91	20	53	62	9.13	2.35	26.1	446	5.3	6.2	1.2	2.0	-19
	02	25	a/a	COL	5	8	38	0	119	107	67	14	58	116	5.06	1.39	13.5	322	4.4	8.8	2.0	1.1	71
Cammack,Eric	02	27	a/a	NYM	3	4	47	5	64	72	52	6	63	51	7.30	2.11	6.9	419	8.8	7.2	0.8	0.8	34
Camp,Jared	01	26	aa	KC	2	3	44	5	65	77	48	10	54	44	6.68	2.02	7.3	408	7.5	6.1	0.8	1.4	8
Camp,Shawn	01	26	a/a	SD	11	2	58	0	96	99	48	6	35	72	4.54	1.39	7.1	323	3.3	6.8	2.1	0.6	69
	02	27	aaa	PIT	4	1	39	2	58	59	27	5	14	49	4.18	1.26	6.2	301	2.2	7.6	3.5	0.8	99
Cannon,Jon	01	27	aa	SF	2	0	17	1	36	30	17	5	21	28	4.29	1.40	9.2	324	5.1	6.9	1.3	1.1	46
	02	28	a/a	SF	2	5	41	4	67	76	39	6	49	43	5.24	1.87	7.8	390	6.6	5.8	0.9	0.8	28
Capuano,Chris	01	23	aa	ARI	10	11	28	0	159	206	106	12	72	139	6.01	1.75	26.5	375	4.1	7.8	1.9	0.7	60
	02	24	aaa	ARI	4	1	6	0	36	33	12	1	10	24	2.99	1.19	24.7	290	2.5	6.0	2.4	0.2	86
Caraballo,Angel	01	22	aa	TOR	3	3	26	1	52	59	40	8	21	31	6.90	1.53	8.9	344	3.6	5.3	1.5	1.4	21
Caraccioli,Lance	01	24	aa	LA	8	4	28	1	130	166	86	8	49	72	5.92	1.66	21.3	362	3.4	5.0	1.5	0.6	37
	02	25	a/a	CLE	12	5	28	1	164	193	87	10	78	101	4.77	1.65	26.8	361	4.3	5.5	1.3	0.5	42
Carlson,Dan	01	32	a/a	STL	5	2	39	5	72	100	43	9	23	64	5.41	1.71	8.6	369	2.9	8.0	2.7	1.1	63
Carnes,Matt	01	26	aa	MIN	4	5	28	2	64	97	49	7	26	47	6.93	1.92	11.1	396	3.7	6.6	1.8	1.0	35
	02	27	a/a	MIN	11	6	42	1	124	176	97	9	49	63	7.03	1.81	14.0	383	3.6	4.6	1.3	0.7	24
Carrasco,Dan	01	25	aa	PIT	2	2	27	1	37	43	24	2	29	29	5.89	1.96	6.7	402	7.2	6.9	1.0	0.5	44
Carter,Lance	02	28	aaa	TAM	12	2	33	1	132	136	54	18	13	72	3.68	1.13	16.2	279	0.9	4.9	5.5	1.2	112
Casadiego,Gerardo	02	22	aa	MON	1	3	9	0	35	52	32	8	15	21	8.21	1.91	18.8	395	3.8	5.4	1.4	2.1	-12
Casey,Joe	01	23	aa	TOR	4	3	42	1	61	86	40	10	16	36	5.90	1.67	6.7	364	2.4	5.3	2.3	1.5	25
	02	24	a/a	TOR	1	1	29	1	35	47	28	5	27	10	7.18	2.11	6.1	419	6.9	2.6	0.4	1.3	-23
Cash,David	02	23	aa	SF	5	8	34	5	109	106	42	7	38	73	3.46	1.32	13.6	311	3.1	6.0	1.9	0.6	64
Cassidy,Scott	01	26	a/a	TOR	9	9	27	0	160	179	78	21	58	99	4.37	1.48	26.1	336	3.2	5.6	1.7	1.2	33
Castellanos,Hugo	01	21	aa	TOR	5	2	43	2	64	62	23	5	33	40	3.22	1.48	6.6	336	4.6	5.6	1.2	0.7	43
	02	22	a/a	TOR	3	5	52	18	57	55	39	6	29	31	6.15	1.47	4.8	335	4.6	4.9	1.1	0.9	29
Castillo,Carlos	01	26	aaa	BOS	9	11	28	0	163	214	80	12	25	91	4.43	1.47	25.6	334	1.4	5.0	3.7	0.7	80
Cedeno,Blas	01	29	a/a	PHI	4	4	42	2	71	94	48	13	34	48	6.10	1.80	8.0	381	4.3	6.0	1.4	1.6	9
Cercy,Rick	02	26	aa	COL	3	4	47	1	65	93	56	9	51	59	7.75	2.22	7.1	431	7.1	8.2	1.2	1.2	25
Cerda,Jaime	02	24	a/a	NYM	5	1	26	1	52	34	10	0	17	42	1.72	0.98	7.8	251	2.9	7.2	2.5	0.0	114
Cerros,Juan	01	25	a/a	NYM	2	5	51	1	75	106	44	7	32	37	5.30	1.84	7.0	386	3.8	4.4	1.2	0.9	14
	02	26	a/a	NYM	1	3	28	2	40	49	18	2	12	20	4.03	1.52	6.4	342	2.7	4.5	1.7	0.4	45
Cervantes,Chris	01	23	aa	ARI	3	7	45	1	96	119	63	13	33	75	5.91	1.58	9.6	352	3.1	7.0	2.3	1.2	49
	02	24	aa	ARI	6	4	33	0	121	151	54	7	23	72	4.01	1.44	16.0	330	1.7	5.3	3.1	0.5	77
Chacin,Gustavo	01	21	aa	TOR	11	8	25	0	140	153	74	19	37	77	4.77	1.36	24.0	318	2.4	4.9	2.1	1.2	37
	02	22	aa	TOR	6	5	35	1	119	145	70	12	56	59	5.29	1.69	15.7	366	4.2	4.5	1.1	0.9	18
Chantres,Carlos	01	26	aaa	MIL	7	11	28	0	167	199	96	16	89	74	5.17	1.72	27.7	371	4.8	4.0	0.8	0.9	12
	02	27	a/a	TAM	9	10	28	0	147	208	101	21	80	60	6.18	1.96	25.6	401	4.9	3.7	0.8	1.3	-11
Chapman,Jake	01	28	aa	MON	7	3	53	2	67	77	27	7	34	48	3.55	1.65	5.8	361	4.5	6.4	1.4	1.0	38
Chavez,Anthony	01	31	aaa	ARI	7	6	51	1	86	134	56	6	39	59	5.80	2.01	8.3	408	4.1	6.1	1.5	0.6	36
Chavez,Wilton	02	24	aa	CHC	8	5	18	0	103	118	56	8	42	72	4.89	1.55	25.6	347	3.7	6.3	1.7	0.7	51
Chiasson,Scott	01	24	a/a	CHC	3	4	63	34	73	61	16	3	20	63	2.03	1.10	4.7	274	2.4	7.8	3.2	0.4	113
	02	25	a/a	CHC	1	4	30	7	31	44	29	9	14	26	8.39	1.86	5.0	390	4.1	7.5	1.9	2.6	-4
Chiavacci,Ron	01	24	aa	MON	3	11	25	0	147	166	85	15	82	128	5.22	1.69	27.1	366	5.0	7.8	1.6	0.9	52
	02	25	aa	MON	6	9	35	0	111	132	70	8	70	75	5.67	1.82	15.0	384	5.7	6.1	1.1	0.6	37
Childers,Jason	01	27	aa	MIL	7	6	40	2	87	105	43	10	36	64	4.39	1.61	9.9	355	3.7	6.6	1.8	1.1	43
	02	28	a/a	MIL	3	4	40	0	79	108	49	10	49	38	5.58	1.98	9.7	405	5.6	4.3	0.8	1.1	-1
Childers,Matt	01	23	aa	MIL	2	2	7	0	39	49	20	4	12	18	4.60	1.56	25.0	348	2.8	4.1	1.5	0.9	24
	02	24	a/a	MIL	2	5	37	12	86	123	54	8	30	52	5.65	1.78	10.9	379	3.1	5.4	1.7	0.8	33
Choate,Randy	02	27	aaa	NYY	3	2	31	1	36	28	8	0	16	27	1.99	1.22	4.8	294	4.0	6.7	1.7	0.0	89
Chouinard,Bobby	01	29	aaa	COL	3	1	39	1	39	57	22	9	14	38	5.06	1.83	4.8	385	3.3	8.8	2.7	2.0	37
Cho,Jin Ho	01	26	aaa	BOS	3	10	37	10	117	160	76	14	18	62	5.86	1.51	14.0	341	1.3	4.8	3.5	1.1	61
	02	27	aaa	BOS	3	6	20	2	54	91	44	11	13	16	7.32	1.92	13.1	397	2.2	2.7	1.2	1.8	-31
Christensen,Ben	02	25	aa	CHC	2	6	12	0	64	88	59	7	38	30	8.30	1.97	26.1	403	5.3	4.2	0.8	1.0	3

Major League Equivalent Statistics

PITCHER	Yr	Age	Lev	Org	Actual				Major League Equivalents														
					W	L	G	Sv	IP	H	ER	HR	BB	K	ERA	Br/IP	BF/G	OOB	CTL	DOM	CMD	hr/9	BPV
Christman,Tim	01	27	aaa	COL	2	5	38	2	40	63	37	6	22	36	8.35	2.11	5.3	420	4.9	8.1	1.7	1.4	27
Chrysler,Clint	01	26	a/a	PIT	4	3	58	3	59	80	27	6	18	30	4.17	1.66	4.7	362	2.7	4.6	1.7	1.0	26
	02	27	aa	PIT	3	2	51	3	56	72	34	8	23	19	5.44	1.69	5.1	367	3.7	3.0	0.8	1.3	-9
Chulk,Vinny	01	23	a/a	TOR	3	5	29	2	49	45	20	6	12	39	3.67	1.16	6.9	285	2.2	7.2	3.3	1.1	85
	02	24	a/a	TOR	13	6	27	1	156	155	61	12	57	95	3.51	1.36	24.7	317	3.3	5.5	1.7	0.7	51
Cisar,Mark	01	26	aa	BOS	1	1	21	3	31	40	22	2	8	15	6.32	1.55	6.6	347	2.3	4.3	1.8	0.7	38
Clark,Chris	01	27	aa	ANA	4	3	32	0	72	99	69	11	44	30	8.62	1.98	11.0	404	5.5	3.8	0.7	1.4	-15
Clark,Jeff	02	22	aa	SF	2	2	6	0	35	49	22	4	2	17	5.63	1.45	25.6	332	0.5	4.3	8.5	1.0	164
Claussen,Brandon	01	22	aa	NYY	9	2	21	0	131	123	43	8	58	131	2.95	1.38	26.8	321	4.0	9.0	2.3	0.5	91
	02	23	aaa	NYY	2	8	15	0	93	93	38	4	44	65	3.67	1.47	27.3	335	4.3	6.3	1.5	0.4	61
Cloude,Ken	02	28	aaa	SEA	9	4	15	0	92	87	31	9	21	42	3.03	1.17	25.1	286	2.0	4.1	2.0	0.9	46
Coco,Pasqual	01	24	a/a	TOR	8	7	25	0	138	169	91	18	56	79	5.91	1.63	25.1	358	3.6	5.1	1.4	1.1	22
	02	25	aaa	TOR	4	9	30	0	141	165	92	18	56	84	5.87	1.57	21.1	349	3.6	5.4	1.5	1.1	27
Cogan,Tony	02	26	aa	KC	4	6	17	0	90	123	52	6	29	46	5.19	1.69	24.4	366	2.9	4.6	1.6	0.6	34
Coggin,Dave	01	25	aaa	PHI	5	5	15	0	97	113	46	7	36	48	4.26	1.53	28.8	344	3.3	4.4	1.3	0.6	33
Cole,Joey	02	25	a/a	NYM	2	4	11	0	48	69	35	6	24	24	6.55	1.93	21.2	398	4.5	4.5	1.0	1.1	3
Collazo,William	02	23	aa	ATL	4	2	51	4	72	78	32	7	26	62	3.99	1.44	6.2	330	3.2	7.7	2.4	0.9	71
Collins,Pat	02	25	aa	MON	3	0	29	7	50	51	13	3	19	41	2.33	1.39	7.5	323	3.4	7.4	2.2	0.5	77
Colon,Jose	02	28	aa	CLE	5	4	46	5	76	102	31	10	10	31	3.67	1.47	7.3	335	1.2	3.7	3.1	1.2	44
Colyer,Steve	02	24	aa	LA	5	4	59	21	62	60	31	7	43	57	4.49	1.66	4.8	362	6.2	8.2	1.3	1.0	52
Condrey,Clay	01	26	a/a	SD	3	5	66	14	87	114	56	8	31	50	5.76	1.65	6.0	362	3.2	5.2	1.6	0.9	33
	02	27	aaa	SD	10	4	25	0	133	145	61	11	41	60	4.12	1.40	23.0	324	2.8	4.1	1.5	0.7	33
Connelly,Steve	01	27	aaa	SF	2	3	33	4	58	51	24	2	21	31	3.74	1.23	7.3	296	3.3	4.8	1.5	0.3	60
Coogan,Patrick	01	26	aa	STL	8	8	33	0	148	231	129	29	54	94	7.82	1.92	21.8	397	3.3	5.7	1.7	1.7	4
Cook,Aaron	02	24	a/a	COL	11	6	24	0	159	163	53	15	35	79	3.00	1.24	27.6	299	2.0	4.5	2.3	0.8	52
Cook,Andy	01	25	aa	NYM	2	2	22	1	47	59	29	3	17	27	5.63	1.61	9.7	355	3.2	5.1	1.6	0.6	41
	02	26	aa	NYM	6	3	30	0	55	78	38	7	24	30	6.22	1.85	8.8	388	3.9	4.9	1.3	1.1	11
Cook,B.R.	01	24	aa	STL	5	8	20	0	121	142	74	14	41	77	5.51	1.51	26.9	341	3.1	5.7	1.9	1.1	39
	02	25	aa	STL	7	13	28	0	163	209	99	16	65	96	5.46	1.68	26.8	365	3.6	5.3	1.5	0.9	30
Cooper,Brian	01	27	aaa	ANA	12	8	28	0	173	208	103	29	56	89	5.37	1.53	27.5	343	2.9	4.6	1.6	1.5	12
	02	28	aaa	TOR	9	9	27	0	155	212	111	22	48	57	6.44	1.68	26.4	365	2.8	3.3	1.2	1.3	-2
Coppinger,Rocky	01	28	a/a	MIL	8	1	31	4	78	70	24	3	36	50	2.78	1.35	10.8	317	4.1	5.7	1.4	0.4	60
Corbin,Archie	01	34	aaa	CHW	6	7	58	4	77	75	40	4	61	54	4.67	1.76	6.2	376	7.1	6.3	0.9	0.5	47
Corcoran,Tim	02	24	aa	BAL	0	5	35	1	49	72	24	5	31	39	4.41	2.10	7.0	419	5.7	7.2	1.3	0.9	30
Cordova,Jorge	02	25	a/a	CIN	5	2	37	13	40	44	21	4	13	26	4.71	1.42	4.7	327	2.9	5.8	2.0	0.9	50
Corey,Bryan	01	28	aaa	SD	8	7	47	6	106	144	65	13	34	50	5.54	1.68	10.4	365	2.9	4.3	1.5	1.1	16
	02	29	aaa	LA	5	4	37	1	53	84	25	4	17	27	4.23	1.90	6.9	394	2.9	4.6	1.6	0.7	25
Corey,Mark	01	27	a/a	NYM	9	4	53	27	72	59	17	2	39	70	2.08	1.35	5.8	317	4.8	8.8	1.8	0.3	93
Cornejo,Nate	01	22	a/a	DET	16	3	23	0	154	147	51	12	43	108	2.98	1.23	27.8	297	2.5	6.3	2.5	0.7	75
	02	23	aaa	DET	9	8	21	0	132	188	80	10	29	78	5.45	1.64	28.7	360	2.0	5.3	2.7	0.7	57
Cornett,Brad	01	33	aaa	TOR	5	2	39	2	73	89	29	4	18	49	3.62	1.47	8.2	334	2.2	6.1	2.8	0.5	75
Correa,Cristobal	02	23	aa	STL	6	9	26	0	137	158	78	9	56	69	5.12	1.56	23.6	349	3.7	4.5	1.2	0.6	34
Cotton,Joe	01	27	a/a	OAK	6	3	53	7	71	68	31	6	34	54	3.94	1.44	5.8	330	4.4	6.8	1.6	0.7	59
Coughenour,Jory	02	24	aa	HOU	3	2	32	3	61	86	31	2	28	38	4.57	1.87	9.1	390	4.1	5.6	1.4	0.3	43
Coward,Chad	02	24	aa	TAM	9	4	37	0	87	100	38	7	36	48	3.92	1.56	10.6	348	3.7	5.0	1.3	0.7	35
Cox,Ryan	01	25	aa	SF	8	8	24	0	136	171	68	8	24	48	4.52	1.43	24.7	329	1.6	3.2	2.0	0.6	40
	02	26	aa	SF	7	9	27	0	145	201	87	13	33	56	5.39	1.61	24.4	356	2.0	3.5	1.7	0.8	23
Cozier,Vance	02	25	aa	SF	3	7	21	0	67	104	56	8	40	19	7.50	2.14	16.2	423	5.4	2.5	0.5	1.1	-21
Crabtree,Robbie	01	29	aaa	SF	8	10	63	6	114	127	49	10	32	76	3.90	1.39	7.8	323	2.5	6.0	2.4	0.8	63
	02	30	aaa	TOR	4	8	56	2	84	100	74	8	38	49	7.92	1.64	6.8	360	4.1	5.2	1.3	0.9	30
Crawford,Joe	01	31	a/a	ARI	2	8	15	0	82	130	60	9	26	48	6.59	1.90	26.3	394	2.8	5.2	1.9	1.0	26
Crawford,Paxton	02	25	a/a	BOS	3	3	10	0	53	76	36	9	21	23	6.11	1.83	25.2	385	3.6	3.9	1.1	1.5	-10
Croushore,Rick	02	32	aaa	TAM	5	4	36	7	64	67	32	6	28	49	4.50	1.48	7.8	337	3.9	6.9	1.8	0.8	55
Crowder,Chuck	01	25	aa	COL	6	6	32	0	101	187	110	16	78	57	9.80	2.62	17.5	473	6.9	5.1	0.7	1.4	-18
Crudale,Mike	01	25	aa	STL	4	9	62	9	80	96	41	9	25	75	4.61	1.51	5.7	341	2.8	8.4	3.0	1.1	78
Crumpton,Chuck	01	25	aa	MON	2	6	52	4	66	88	42	7	27	35	5.72	1.75	5.9	375	3.7	4.8	1.3	1.0	18
	02	26	a/a	MON	2	5	40	3	84	116	52	5	29	34	5.56	1.72	9.8	371	3.1	3.6	1.2	0.5	21
Cruz,Juan	01	21	aa	CHC	9	6	23	0	121	110	56	6	56	124	4.18	1.38	22.6	320	4.2	9.2	2.2	0.4	96
Cubillan,Darwin	01	27	aaa	TEX	3	3	26	4	44	62	43	8	27	32	8.82	2.01	8.4	407	5.5	6.5	1.2	1.7	4
	02	30	aaa	MON	1	1	29	6	36	36	20	5	23	27	5.00	1.64	5.7	359	5.8	6.8	1.2	1.3	32
Cueto,Jose	02	26	aa	FLA	1	4	9	0	43	43	24	6	24	36	5.00	1.55	21.5	347	5.0	7.5	1.5	1.3	43
Cumberland,Chris	01	29	a/a	ATL	5	10	33	1	142	208	88	8	56	71	5.58	1.86	20.6	389	3.6	4.5	1.3	0.5	26
	02	30	a/a	TOR	0	5	37	1	45	70	29	1	27	18	5.77	2.15	6.2	424	5.4	3.6	0.7	0.2	15
Cummings,Jeremy	02	26	aa	STL	4	3	14	0	78	83	40	7	24	42	4.62	1.37	23.9	320	2.8	4.8	1.8	0.8	43
Cummings,Ryan	01	25	aa	ANA	6	3	42	6	65	76	33	3	22	32	4.60	1.50	6.9	339	3.1	4.5	1.5	0.5	42
	02	26	a/a	ANA	7	5	43	1	62	82	32	8	30	26	4.64	1.80	6.8	382	4.3	3.8	0.9	1.2	-1
Cunnane,Will	02	28	aaa	CHC	4	1	43	2	73	73	18	3	23	57	2.21	1.31	7.2	310	2.8	7.0	2.5	0.4	87
Curtis,Daniel	02	23	aa	ATL	4	2	10	0	54	68	34	7	17	24	5.66	1.57	24.3	350	2.8	4.0	1.4	1.2	13
Cyr,Eric	02	24	a/a	SD	4	6	23	0	86	85	36	6	45	64	3.76	1.51	16.6	341	4.7	6.7	1.4	0.6	56
D'Amico,Jeff	01	27	aaa	KC	5	7	32	0	140	176	67	22	38	74	4.31	1.53	19.5	344	2.5	4.7	1.9	1.4	22
	02	28	aaa	CIN	6	10	27	1	118	148	75	19	37	58	5.72	1.57	19.6	349	2.8	4.4	1.6	1.4	11
Daigle,Casey	02	22	aa	ARI	3	2	7	0	44	51	18	5	8	24	3.67	1.34	26.8	314	1.6	4.9	3.0	1.0	60
Daneker,Pat	01	26	a/a	CHC	5	6	28	0	73	136	85	11	28	20	10.50	2.25	13.5	435	3.5	2.5	0.7	1.3	-32
Darnell,Paul	01	25	a/a	CIN	5	1	42	0	59	65	22	5	25	64	3.37	1.53	6.3	344	3.8	9.7	2.5	0.8	87
	02	26	a/a	CIN	3	4	39	0	68	73	32	11	32	46	4.23	1.54	7.8	346	4.2	6.1	1.4	1.5	24
Darrell,Tommy	01	25	aa	MON	0	2	24	0	34	58	41	6	22	12	10.82	2.34	7.5	445	5.8	3.1	0.5	1.5	-33
Darwin,Dave	01	28	a/a	CLE	3	3	23	0	74	113	48	10	30	42	5.87	1.93	15.6	397	3.6	5.1	1.4	1.3	9
Davenport,Joe	01	26	aaa	COL	2	2	31	0	34	74	41	5	15	20	10.96	2.61	6.1	472	4.0	5.2	1.3	1.3	-11
Davey,Tom	02	29	aaa	SD	2	1	22	4	32	20	8	1	13	17	2.25	1.03	5.7	261	3.7	4.8	1.3	0.3	67
Davis,Allen	01	26	aa	MON	2	2	8	0	53	64	24	6	10	26	4.10	1.41	28.7	326	1.8	4.4	2.5	1.0	47
Davis,Doug	02	27	aaa	TEX	4	3	9	0	61	81	40	7	11	40	5.89	1.51	30.0	340	1.6	5.9	3.6	1.0	73
Davis,Jason	02	22	aa	CLE	6	2	10	0	59	75	30	3	17	39	4.58	1.56	26.4	348	2.6	5.9	2.3	0.5	64

Major League Equivalent Statistics

					Actual				Major League Equivalents														
PITCHER	Yr	Age	Lev	Org	W	L	G	Sv	IP	H	ER	HR	BB	K	ERA	Br/IP	BF/G	OOB	CTL	DOM	CMD	hr/9	BPV
Davis,Lance	01	25	aaa	CIN	7	2	13	0	79	95	34	8	15	42	3.90	1.39	26.3	323	1.7	4.7	2.7	0.9	55
	02	26	a/a	CIN	4	10	23	0	127	183	71	17	34	59	5.03	1.71	25.6	369	2.4	4.2	1.7	1.2	14
Davis,Tim	01	24	aa	MIL	1	2	28	2	37	44	16	1	19	27	3.99	1.69	6.1	367	4.5	6.6	1.5	0.2	60
Dawley,Joey	01	30	a/a	ATL	8	5	25	0	134	145	74	24	60	95	4.95	1.53	23.9	343	4.0	6.4	1.6	1.6	25
	02	31	aaa	ATL	9	7	24	0	140	137	53	12	38	108	3.40	1.25	24.3	300	2.4	6.9	2.8	0.8	83
Day,Zach	01	23	a/a	MON	12	12	29	0	169	192	89	12	56	94	4.74	1.47	25.6	334	3.0	5.0	1.7	0.6	45
	02	24	aaa	MON	5	6	17	0	90	91	46	6	33	58	4.60	1.38	22.8	321	3.3	5.8	1.8	0.6	57
De La Rosa,Jorge	01	21	aa	BOS	1	3	29	0	37	63	30	4	19	23	7.18	2.21	6.5	431	4.6	5.6	1.2	0.9	13
	02	22	aa	BOS	3	7	35	6	51	62	35	1	23	25	6.18	1.67	6.7	363	4.1	4.4	1.1	0.2	40
De La Rosa,Maximo	01	30	aa	CIN	2	6	38	2	46	94	47	7	19	32	9.18	2.44	6.5	456	3.6	6.3	1.7	1.4	5
De Los Santos,Luis	02	25	aaa	TAM	9	2	24	0	115	122	39	9	22	58	3.05	1.25	20.0	300	1.7	4.5	2.6	0.7	63
DeHart,Blair	02	24	aa	SD	2	3	7	0	32	53	20	2	9	24	5.61	1.93	22.2	398	2.5	6.7	2.7	0.6	62
DeHart,Casey	02	25	aa	CIN	1	3	21	1	30	38	26	4	15	19	7.77	1.76	6.7	376	4.5	5.7	1.3	1.2	19
DeHart,Rick	02	33	aaa	KC	1	0	49	1	57	66	32	5	21	36	5.03	1.52	5.2	342	3.3	5.7	1.7	0.8	45
Del La Ratta,Pete	01	28	aa	NYM	4	2	22	0	30	48	29	4	10	21	8.67	1.93	6.6	398	2.9	6.2	2.2	1.1	34
DeLucia,Rich	01	36	aaa	DET	1	1	28	5	39	32	14	3	15	36	3.16	1.19	5.7	289	3.4	8.3	2.4	0.7	91
Demouy,Chris	01	26	aa	ANA	2	0	25	0	35	52	31	4	23	13	7.98	2.15	7.1	424	6.0	3.2	0.5	1.1	-16
Denney,Kyle	02	25	aa	CLE	3	1	6	0	34	30	9	3	6	25	2.37	1.05	22.6	265	1.6	6.6	4.2	0.8	112
DePaula,Julio	02	23	aa	NYY	14	6	27	0	175	204	104	16	66	108	5.35	1.54	28.9	346	3.4	5.6	1.6	0.8	41
DePaula,Sean	02	29	aaa	CLE	2	3	34	9	57	71	37	9	20	43	5.84	1.60	7.6	353	3.2	6.8	2.2	1.4	38
Deschenes,Marc	01	29	a/a	CLE	4	4	44	0	61	88	42	7	48	43	6.25	2.24	7.1	434	7.1	6.4	0.9	1.0	15
DeSilva,John	01	34	aaa	LA	2	3	40	1	64	87	36	6	15	46	5.02	1.59	7.2	353	2.1	6.4	3.1	0.9	68
Devey,Phil	01	24	a/a	LA	8	4	27	1	127	163	72	13	31	69	5.11	1.53	20.9	343	2.2	4.9	2.2	0.9	42
	02	25	a/a	LA	5	5	34	0	122	178	65	9	41	45	4.79	1.79	16.9	380	3.0	3.3	1.1	0.7	11
Dewitt,Matt	01	24	aaa	TOR	3	2	53	27	58	52	23	5	17	37	3.56	1.19	4.5	289	2.6	5.7	2.2	0.8	65
DeWitt,Scott	01	27	aa	COL	2	6	43	1	63	106	49	12	37	38	7.06	2.28	7.6	438	5.3	5.5	1.0	1.7	-16
Diaz,Felix	02	22	aa	SF	7	5	19	0	91	86	33	4	29	67	3.26	1.26	20.0	302	2.9	6.6	2.3	0.4	83
Dickey,R.A.	01	27	aaa	TEX	11	7	24	0	163	197	89	19	44	104	4.90	1.48	29.9	336	2.4	5.7	2.3	1.0	49
	02	28	aaa	TEX	8	7	37	0	154	203	82	8	46	90	4.79	1.62	18.9	356	2.7	5.3	2.0	0.5	51
Dickson,Jason	01	29	a/a	TOR	6	8	16	0	90	144	86	16	35	44	8.58	1.98	27.6	405	3.5	4.4	1.3	1.6	-12
	02	30	aaa	TAM	3	4	9	0	47	69	41	11	26	25	7.83	2.02	25.8	409	5.0	4.8	1.0	2.1	-26
Difelice,Mark	01	25	a/a	COL	9	6	27	0	169	215	106	43	34	119	5.66	1.47	27.5	335	1.8	6.3	3.5	2.3	37
Diggins,Ben	02	23	aa	MIL	2	1	7	0	37	31	10	0	15	28	2.42	1.24	22.1	297	3.6	6.8	1.9	0.0	90
Dillinger,John	01	28	aaa	TOR	11	7	26	0	155	187	92	13	61	86	5.36	1.60	27.0	354	3.6	5.0	1.4	0.7	33
	02	29	a/a	NYY	5	2	22	0	97	172	94	18	40	55	8.70	2.18	22.5	428	3.7	5.1	1.4	1.7	-11
Dingman,Craig	01	28	aaa	COL	3	5	46	7	48	71	27	6	9	47	5.13	1.67	4.8	363	1.8	8.7	4.9	1.2	108
Diorio,Mike	01	29	aa	PIT	1	4	18	0	33	60	49	8	26	10	13.30	2.61	10.1	472	7.2	2.6	0.4	2.0	-60
Dittfurth,Ryan	02	23	aa	TEX	1	3	9	0	41	51	35	1	24	28	7.66	1.82	21.7	385	5.3	6.1	1.2	0.2	50
Donaldson,Bo	01	27	a/a	SD	6	2	36	5	54	34	13	3	22	40	2.11	1.04	5.9	263	3.6	6.7	1.8	0.6	80
	02	28	a/a	NYY	5	5	46	0	106	128	62	11	38	71	5.26	1.57	10.3	349	3.2	6.0	1.9	0.9	44
Donnelly,Brendan	01	30	a/a	ANA	9	2	56	13	70	81	26	9	25	60	3.37	1.52	5.6	342	3.2	7.7	2.4	1.1	61
	02	31	aaa	ANA	4	0	25	6	33	31	15	5	11	34	4.07	1.27	5.6	302	3.0	9.2	3.1	1.4	86
Dougherty,Jim	01	34	aaa	LA	4	5	59	14	81	87	38	7	34	69	4.21	1.49	6.1	339	3.7	7.7	2.1	0.8	66
	02	35	a/a	PIT	3	4	40	4	55	68	39	7	26	32	6.37	1.71	6.4	369	4.2	5.2	1.2	1.1	18
Douglass,Sean	01	22	aaa	BAL	8	9	27	0	162	180	77	15	60	147	4.28	1.48	26.4	336	3.3	8.2	2.5	0.8	75
	02	23	aaa	BAL	4	6	14	0	66	74	41	4	35	60	5.57	1.65	21.6	361	4.8	8.2	1.7	0.5	68
Drese,Ryan	01	26	a/a	CLE	10	8	25	0	147	156	82	15	48	102	5.02	1.39	25.4	322	3.0	6.2	2.1	0.9	56
Drew,Tim	01	23	aaa	CLE	8	6	18	0	108	136	61	16	27	64	5.08	1.51	26.6	341	2.3	5.3	2.4	1.3	37
	02	24	aaa	MON	14	7	28	0	181	206	81	13	48	61	4.03	1.40	27.9	325	2.4	3.0	1.3	0.6	24
Driskill,Travis	01	30	aaa	HOU	11	5	28	0	178	230	109	30	39	113	5.50	1.51	28.2	341	2.0	5.7	2.9	1.5	43
Drumright,Mike	01	27	a/a	FLA	5	13	37	1	133	162	74	15	59	94	4.97	1.66	16.5	362	4.0	6.4	1.6	1.0	38
	02	28	aaa	BAL	6	8	30	0	150	189	85	12	54	86	5.10	1.62	22.7	357	3.2	5.2	1.6	0.7	38
Dubose,Eric	02	26	a/a	BAL	5	3	42	3	65	59	24	2	26	50	3.32	1.31	6.5	309	3.6	6.9	1.9	0.3	81
Duchscherer,Justin	01	24	a/a	TEX	13	6	25	0	168	158	58	19	33	157	3.10	1.14	27.3	280	1.8	8.4	4.8	1.0	126
	02	25	aaa	OAK	2	4	14	0	63	75	38	6	15	44	5.43	1.43	19.6	329	2.1	6.3	2.9	0.9	71
Duckworth,Brandon	01	26	aaa	PHI	13	2	22	0	147	151	60	16	42	135	3.65	1.31	28.3	310	2.6	8.2	3.2	1.0	90
Duff,Matt	02	28	a/a	STL	11	1	51	5	69	53	15	5	28	72	1.95	1.17	5.6	286	3.6	9.4	2.6	0.7	104
Duncan,Courtney	02	28	aaa	CHC	3	5	55	6	68	77	35	5	32	53	4.62	1.60	5.6	354	4.2	7.0	1.7	0.7	56
Dunn,Scott	01	23	aa	CIN	7	2	17	0	98	113	57	12	72	75	5.20	1.89	27.8	393	6.6	6.9	1.0	1.1	27
	02	24	aa	CIN	5	7	37	1	110	116	58	12	53	91	4.74	1.53	13.3	345	4.3	7.4	1.7	1.0	53
Durocher,Jayson	01	27	a/a	TEX	4	1	34	6	43	46	32	7	29	44	6.72	1.73	5.9	373	6.0	9.1	1.5	1.4	45
Duvall,Mike	01	27	aaa	MIN	2	2	55	3	62	87	39	7	22	51	5.64	1.76	5.3	376	3.2	7.4	2.3	1.1	51
Dykhoff,Radhames	01	27	aa	ANA	2	3	27	0	80	114	57	5	40	27	6.35	1.92	14.4	397	4.5	3.0	0.7	0.5	5
Eason,Clay	02	27	a/a	CHW	5	2	40	4	88	93	38	9	41	61	3.89	1.52	9.8	343	4.2	6.2	1.5	0.9	43
Ebert,Derrin	01	25	a/a	BOS	9	12	30	0	160	226	109	17	35	97	6.16	1.63	24.3	358	2.0	5.5	2.8	0.9	53
	02	26	aaa	MIL	6	4	50	4	74	81	40	14	27	38	4.85	1.46	6.5	333	3.3	4.6	1.4	1.7	7
Eckenstahler,Eric	01	25	aa	DET	4	2	46	4	64	77	35	6	29	59	4.87	1.66	6.4	362	4.1	8.3	2.0	0.9	62
	02	26	aaa	DET	2	4	52	0	67	67	41	7	33	62	5.51	1.49	5.7	338	4.4	8.3	1.9	0.9	65
Edmondson,Brian	01	29	a/a	FLA	4	8	37	1	56	75	42	11	24	26	6.78	1.76	7.1	376	3.8	4.2	1.1	1.7	-10
	02	30	aa	DET	5	2	43	6	52	79	29	5	16	29	5.02	1.83	5.7	385	2.8	5.0	1.8	0.9	29
Eibey,Scott	01	28	aa	BAL	0	3	38	0	69	117	70	13	27	36	9.11	2.08	9.1	416	3.5	4.7	1.3	1.7	-14
Eischen,Joey	01	31	aaa	MON	2	3	34	7	52	53	18	8	13	43	3.09	1.25	6.4	300	2.2	7.4	3.4	1.5	75
Elder,Dave	01	26	a/a	TEX	9	10	28	0	130	153	79	7	92	108	5.45	1.89	22.3	392	6.4	7.5	1.2	0.5	53
	02	27	a/a	CLE	5	2	45	14	70	70	28	3	39	64	3.60	1.56	7.0	348	5.0	8.2	1.6	0.4	76
Ellison,Jason	01	26	aa	SEA	2	8	46	9	65	99	37	3	33	45	5.09	2.03	7.0	411	4.6	6.3	1.4	0.5	38
	02	25	aa	SEA	1	6	36	2	73	102	47	1	37	37	5.79	1.90	9.8	395	4.6	4.6	1.0	0.1	35
Ellis,Robert	02	32	aaa	LA	9	7	29	0	172	201	75	15	34	91	3.92	1.36	25.4	319	1.8	4.8	2.7	0.8	59
Elmore,Chris	01	24	aa	BOS	5	3	14	0	78	94	27	4	20	44	3.15	1.45	24.4	332	2.3	5.0	2.2	0.5	58
	02	25	a/a	BOS	8	5	21	0	114	141	54	4	36	70	4.26	1.55	24.3	347	2.8	5.5	1.9	0.3	60
Emanuel,Brandon	02	27	a/a	ANA	7	6	21	0	119	168	71	23	31	57	5.37	1.67	26.0	364	2.3	4.3	1.8	1.7	2
Emiliano,Jamie	01	27	aa	COL	3	6	50	2	64	90	47	10	40	28	6.59	2.03	6.4	410	5.6	4.0	0.7	1.4	-12
	02	28	aa	ATL	3	3	42	3	54	48	15	5	29	26	2.50	1.42	5.6	328	4.8	4.3	0.9	0.8	28

Major League Equivalent Statistics

					Actual				Major League Equivalents														
PITCHER	Yr	Age	Lev	Org	W	L	G	Sv	IP	H	ER	HR	BB	K	ERA	Br/IP	BF/G	OOB	CTL	DOM	CMD	hr/9	BPV
Enders,Trevor	01	27	a/a	TAM	5	8	45	0	94	136	78	23	22	50	7.44	1.68	9.6	365	2.1	4.7	2.2	2.2	-3
Ennis,John	02	23	aa	ATL	9	9	26	0	148	146	80	7	59	86	4.86	1.38	24.5	321	3.6	5.2	1.5	0.4	54
Enochs,Chris	01	26	aa	OAK	5	4	39	1	99	126	59	10	43	50	5.32	1.70	11.8	368	3.9	4.6	1.2	0.9	18
	02	27	a/a	OAK	7	13	29	0	164	220	110	19	77	87	6.04	1.81	26.8	383	4.2	4.8	1.1	1.0	13
Erdos,Todd	01	28	aaa	BOS	5	1	49	7	67	73	31	3	25	43	4.09	1.46	6.0	333	3.4	5.7	1.7	0.4	58
	02	29	aaa	BOS	4	4	52	10	78	109	38	4	23	38	4.38	1.69	6.9	367	2.7	4.4	1.7	0.5	37
Espina,Rendy	01	23	aaa	ANA	6	1	38	0	49	46	22	5	16	29	4.03	1.26	5.4	302	2.9	5.3	1.8	0.9	49
	02	24	aaa	BAL	2	2	45	0	53	73	47	13	31	32	7.97	1.96	5.8	401	5.3	5.4	1.0	2.2	-21
Esslinger,Cam	01	25	aa	COL	1	1	40	16	42	45	40	0	36	43	8.57	1.93	5.1	398	7.7	9.2	1.2	0.0	81
	02	26	a/a	COL	0	2	35	2	39	44	32	3	20	24	7.38	1.64	5.1	360	4.6	5.5	1.2	0.7	37
Estrada,Horacio	01	26	aaa	COL	8	4	16	0	91	121	62	17	20	67	6.09	1.55	25.5	347	2.0	6.7	3.3	1.7	51
	02	27	aaa	ARI	8	7	29	1	163	188	81	23	38	87	4.47	1.38	24.2	322	2.1	4.8	2.3	1.3	37
Estrella,Leo	01	27	a/a	NYM	3	2	45	1	95	130	61	10	46	47	5.78	1.84	10.1	387	4.3	4.4	1.0	0.9	11
	02	28	a/a	CHC	4	4	32	1	74	98	46	5	39	38	5.58	1.85	11.1	387	4.7	4.6	1.0	0.6	23
Estrella,Luis	01	27	a/a	SF	9	3	37	0	124	163	74	21	60	58	5.33	1.80	15.8	381	4.3	4.2	1.0	1.5	-6
	02	28	aaa	SF	7	13	38	7	144	201	88	15	66	78	5.50	1.85	18.1	388	4.1	4.9	1.2	0.9	16
Evans,Dave	01	34	a/a	HOU	2	1	26	1	47	73	50	19	31	34	9.57	2.22	9.3	432	6.0	6.5	1.1	3.6	-61
Evans,Keith	01	26	aaa	MON	7	3	45	1	83	113	49	9	14	59	5.35	1.53	8.2	344	1.5	6.4	4.2	1.0	89
Evert,Brett	02	22	aa	ATL	5	8	16	0	93	105	59	15	34	70	5.70	1.49	25.7	338	3.3	6.8	2.1	1.4	40
Eyre,Scott	01	29	aaa	TOR	4	6	62	0	79	86	38	10	29	75	4.38	1.44	5.6	331	3.3	8.5	2.6	1.1	73
Eyre,Willie	02	24	aa	MIN	6	4	28	2	50	48	24	1	23	35	4.32	1.42	7.8	327	4.1	6.3	1.5	0.2	70
Falkenborg,Brian	01	24	a/a	SEA	7	10	20	0	114	146	74	15	44	75	5.84	1.67	26.2	363	3.5	5.9	1.7	1.2	30
	02	25	aaa	SEA	4	4	9	0	49	58	18	3	13	36	3.30	1.45	23.8	331	2.4	6.6	2.8	0.5	79
Falteisek,Steve	01	30	aa	BAL	1	6	11	0	42	91	61	17	20	17	13.11	2.63	21.2	474	4.3	3.5	0.8	3.7	-103
Farmer,Tom	02	23	a/a	LA	9	9	25	0	145	175	82	14	41	70	5.08	1.49	25.6	338	2.5	4.3	1.7	0.9	32
Farnsworth,Jeff	01	26	aa	SEA	11	10	27	0	155	237	102	11	56	89	5.94	1.89	27.6	393	3.3	5.1	1.6	0.7	30
Feliciano,Pedro	01	25	a/a	LA	5	5	60	17	69	65	23	5	17	48	3.02	1.19	4.7	290	2.2	6.3	2.9	0.7	84
	02	26	a/a	CIN	3	2	53	6	74	100	33	6	17	42	4.01	1.58	6.3	351	2.1	5.1	2.5	0.7	52
Felix,Miguel	01	25	a/a	BAL	5	6	16	0	85	94	59	10	39	53	6.21	1.56	23.9	348	4.1	5.6	1.4	1.1	30
Ferguson,Ian	02	23	aa	KC	6	2	11	0	76	74	31	9	18	49	3.67	1.21	28.5	293	2.1	5.8	2.7	1.1	65
Fernandez,Jared	01	30	aaa	CIN	10	9	33	0	196	279	124	32	59	96	5.70	1.73	27.6	371	2.7	4.4	1.6	1.5	6
	02	31	aaa	CIN	12	5	26	1	128	182	68	17	31	60	4.78	1.66	22.6	363	2.2	4.2	1.9	1.2	20
Fernandez,Osvaldo	01	33	aaa	CIN	3	2	9	0	53	66	31	7	13	27	5.16	1.48	26.0	337	2.1	4.5	2.1	1.2	29
	02	34	aaa	MON	7	6	28	0	103	138	72	9	34	52	6.28	1.67	16.9	363	3.0	4.5	1.5	0.8	28
Ferrari,Anthony	02	24	aa	MON	7	4	44	6	75	95	42	2	35	43	5.03	1.73	7.9	372	4.2	5.2	1.2	0.2	44
Fesh,Sean	02	30	aa	FLA	1	1	24	5	42	51	29	1	29	32	6.18	1.90	8.5	394	6.2	6.8	1.1	0.2	54
Field,Nathan	01	26	aa	KC	4	2	52	19	73	76	16	3	19	50	1.92	1.29	5.9	307	2.3	6.2	2.7	0.4	84
	02	27	aaa	NYY	2	2	39	7	55	76	40	6	29	33	6.55	1.91	6.8	395	4.7	5.4	1.1	1.0	18
Figueroa,Juan	01	22	aa	BAL	3	10	18	0	99	146	67	16	27	47	6.08	1.75	25.7	374	2.5	4.3	1.7	1.5	7
	02	23	aa	BAL	1	6	24	1	89	114	60	15	27	56	6.07	1.58	16.7	352	2.7	5.7	2.1	1.5	26
Figueroa,Nelson	01	27	aaa	PHI	4	2	13	0	87	95	35	7	22	64	3.59	1.34	28.6	315	2.3	6.6	2.9	0.8	78
	02	28	aaa	MIL	5	0	6	0	39	51	23	3	14	20	5.28	1.66	29.9	362	3.2	4.6	1.4	0.7	30
Fikac,Jeremy	01	27	a/a	SD	6	0	54	18	72	71	21	3	23	57	2.63	1.31	5.7	309	2.9	7.1	2.4	0.4	86
File,Bob	02	26	aaa	TOR	0	0	33	2	36	44	28	2	15	20	6.98	1.63	5.0	359	3.7	5.0	1.3	0.5	39
Fiore,Tony	01	30	aaa	MIN	6	0	47	4	101	116	43	4	37	53	3.86	1.51	9.5	340	3.3	4.7	1.4	0.4	46
Fischer,Rich	02	22	aa	ANA	1	3	7	0	44	46	26	10	10	31	5.29	1.27	26.4	303	2.0	6.3	3.1	2.0	44
Fisher,Pete	01	24	aa	MIN	5	2	9	0	52	72	18	4	14	31	3.09	1.64	26.4	359	2.4	5.4	2.3	0.7	50
Fitzgerald,Brian	01	27	0	SEA	6	2	50	1	76	93	31	6	32	41	3.68	1.65	6.9	361	3.8	4.8	1.3	0.7	31
	02	28	aaa	COL	3	4	36	2	57	77	42	7	25	34	6.62	1.79	7.5	380	3.9	5.4	1.4	1.1	19
Flohr,Adam	01	25	aa	MIN	3	5	18	0	74	129	66	12	18	40	8.07	1.99	20.2	405	2.2	4.9	2.2	1.4	14
	02	26	aa	MIN	4	5	43	0	82	107	31	4	22	36	3.40	1.57	8.6	350	2.4	3.9	1.6	0.4	38
Flores,Randy	01	26	a/a	NYY	14	7	28	0	164	213	77	22	74	93	4.20	1.75	27.4	375	4.1	5.1	1.2	1.2	13
	02	27	aaa	COL	3	3	22	1	56	68	32	3	22	36	5.14	1.61	11.5	355	3.5	5.8	1.6	0.5	51
Florie,Bryce	02	32	aaa	OAK	4	6	18	0	83	98	48	11	36	56	5.20	1.61	20.9	356	3.9	6.1	1.6	1.2	31
Flury,Pat	01	29	a/a	MON	4	3	48	3	65	56	31	8	35	60	4.22	1.41	5.9	325	4.9	8.2	1.7	1.1	60
Fogg,Josh	01	25	aaa	CHW	4	7	40	4	114	159	86	28	32	79	6.78	1.67	13.1	364	2.5	6.2	2.5	2.2	13
Foppert,Jesse	02	22	a/a	SF	6	9	25	0	140	127	61	13	53	156	3.92	1.28	23.6	306	3.4	10.0	2.9	0.8	105
Fordham,Tom	01	28	aaa	MIL	1	2	18	0	38	29	14	6	13	29	3.23	1.11	8.5	275	3.0	6.7	2.3	1.5	56
Ford,Ben	02	27	aaa	CHC	6	11	32	0	142	167	78	12	69	70	4.94	1.66	20.3	363	4.4	4.4	1.0	0.8	23
Fortunato,Bartolome	02	28	a/a	TAM	4	0	12	0	30	31	12	4	15	25	3.60	1.53	11.1	344	4.5	7.5	1.7	1.2	47
Fossum,Casey	01	24	aa	BOS	3	7	20	0	117	124	48	5	30	105	3.72	1.31	24.8	310	2.3	8.0	3.5	0.4	112
Foster,John	01	23	aa	ATL	8	7	50	7	68	88	31	7	35	54	4.08	1.80	6.4	381	4.6	7.2	1.5	1.0	41
	02	24	aaa	ATL	8	4	55	8	62	77	36	5	28	40	5.23	1.69	5.2	367	4.1	5.8	1.4	0.7	38
Foster,Kevin	01	33	aaa	TEX	3	1	16	0	54	41	22	8	22	55	3.67	1.17	13.8	285	3.7	9.1	2.5	1.4	79
Foster,Kris	01	27	a/a	LA	3	2	47	25	49	52	21	2	14	43	3.80	1.34	4.4	314	2.5	7.8	3.1	0.4	101
Franco,Martire	02	25	aa	PHI	4	8	16	0	89	131	72	15	28	44	7.28	1.79	26.2	380	2.8	4.4	1.6	1.5	2
Franklin,Wayne	01	28	aaa	HOU	2	1	41	0	49	59	28	8	20	42	5.20	1.60	5.4	355	3.7	7.6	2.1	1.5	40
	02	29	aaa	HOU	13	9	29	0	179	201	92	22	69	113	4.63	1.51	27.3	341	3.5	5.7	1.6	1.1	35
Franks,Lance	01	26	aa	STL	2	8	28	0	90	118	63	16	60	58	6.31	1.98	15.8	404	6.0	5.8	1.0	1.6	0
Frascatore,John	01	32	aaa	TOR	1	4	37	2	37	58	22	5	9	14	5.38	1.82	4.7	384	2.3	3.5	1.5	1.3	-1
Frederick,Kevin	01	25	aa	MIN	6	2	44	7	82	77	25	7	34	88	2.77	1.34	8.0	315	3.7	9.7	2.6	0.8	95
	02	26	aaa	MIN	3	6	46	22	55	69	30	7	20	40	4.91	1.62	5.4	357	3.3	6.5	2.0	1.1	42
Freed,Mark	02	24	aa	CHC	9	11	29	0	132	193	99	17	63	88	6.74	1.94	22.1	399	4.3	6.0	1.4	1.2	19
Freeman,Kai	01	25	aa	CHW	5	3	28	0	83	123	63	5	35	32	6.84	1.90	14.3	394	3.8	3.5	0.9	0.6	11
Frendling,Neal	02	23	aa	TAM	5	6	22	0	112	128	72	16	69	56	5.79	1.76	23.8	376	5.5	4.5	0.8	1.3	4
Fuentes,Brian	01	26	aaa	SEA	3	2	35	6	52	40	20	4	27	61	3.39	1.29	6.3	306	4.6	10.6	2.3	0.7	103
	02	27	aaa	COL	3	3	41	1	49	52	24	0	31	51	4.40	1.69	5.5	367	5.7	9.3	1.6	0.0	92
Fussell,Chris	01	25	aaa	KC	2	6	9	0	39	67	51	17	22	29	11.63	2.27	22.6	438	5.1	6.6	1.3	4.0	-71
	02	26	aaa	KC	12	6	28	0	164	195	101	26	70	82	5.54	1.61	26.6	356	3.8	4.5	1.2	1.4	6
Fyhrie,Mike	02	33	aaa	OAK	7	2	13	0	77	66	21	3	22	55	2.45	1.14	24.1	281	2.6	6.4	2.5	0.4	90
Gaal,Bryan	02	26	aa	SD	4	1	32	3	36	50	16	1	12	24	3.98	1.71	5.2	370	3.0	6.0	2.0	0.2	61
Gagliano,Steve	01	24	aa	CHC	1	2	35	0	48	56	26	5	23	36	4.91	1.64	6.3	359	4.3	6.7	1.6	1.0	42

Major League Equivalent Statistics

					Actual				Major League Equivalents														
PITCHER	Yr	Age	Lev	Org	W	L	G	Sv	IP	H	ER	HR	BB	K	ERA	Br/IP	BF/G	OOB	CTL	DOM	CMD	hr/9	BPV
Galva,Claudio	01	22	a/a	OAK	2	2	59	11	66	65	21	6	29	45	2.85	1.41	4.9	326	3.9	6.1	1.6	0.8	52
	02	26	aa	OAK	3	3	62	4	65	80	34	9	36	41	4.71	1.78	4.9	379	5.0	5.7	1.1	1.2	16
Galvez,Randy	01	23	aa	PIT	5	6	15	0	86	114	45	4	26	37	4.75	1.63	26.1	358	2.7	3.9	1.4	0.4	33
Gandarillas,Gus	01	30	aaa	BOS	4	3	40	2	81	104	38	4	26	44	4.19	1.60	9.2	354	2.8	4.9	1.7	0.5	45
Garcia,Gerardo	02	23	a/a	TAM	4	8	25	0	102	119	72	10	43	66	6.35	1.59	18.4	352	3.8	5.8	1.5	0.9	39
Garcia,Jose	01	23	aa	MIL	6	5	21	0	111	123	64	7	52	71	5.18	1.57	23.7	350	4.2	5.7	1.4	0.6	46
	02	24	a/a	MIL	5	11	28	0	144	175	93	11	71	66	5.81	1.71	23.8	369	4.4	4.1	0.9	0.7	20
Garcia,Reynaldo	02	28	a/a	TEX	7	3	43	4	100	116	54	18	51	65	4.86	1.67	10.7	364	4.6	5.9	1.3	1.6	11
Garcia,Rosman	02	24	aa	TEX	8	5	53	6	74	93	35	1	34	32	4.25	1.71	6.5	370	4.1	3.9	0.9	0.1	34
Garcia,Sonny	02	26	aa	OAK	4	3	21	1	59	87	34	6	22	28	5.18	1.84	13.4	387	3.4	4.3	1.3	0.9	13
Gardner,Lee	01	27	a/a	TAM	5	2	57	2	78	101	34	14	27	43	3.96	1.63	6.2	359	3.1	5.0	1.6	1.7	8
	02	28	aaa	TAM	2	1	45	25	49	61	17	1	16	42	3.11	1.57	4.9	349	2.9	7.7	2.6	0.2	91
Garibaldi,Cecilio	01	24	aa	TAM	5	6	35	1	104	140	75	22	40	55	6.51	1.73	13.8	372	3.5	4.8	1.4	1.9	-7
Garland,Jon	01	22	aaa	CHW	0	3	5	0	33	36	13	1	11	24	3.64	1.44	28.8	331	3.1	6.6	2.1	0.3	76
Garrett,Josh	01	24	aa	BOS	3	6	46	0	81	102	67	10	46	54	7.44	1.83	8.4	385	5.1	6.0	1.2	1.1	21
Garza,Alberto	02	25	aa	CLE	2	0	20	1	36	20	10	3	33	35	2.49	1.46	7.9	334	8.2	8.7	1.1	0.7	75
Gassner,Dave	02	24	a/a	TOR	1	3	5	0	30	32	11	1	9	13	3.29	1.36	25.8	318	2.7	3.9	1.4	0.3	46
Geary,Geoff	01	25	a/a	PHI	9	10	36	2	134	167	83	18	32	94	5.58	1.48	16.4	337	2.1	6.3	3.0	1.2	59
	02	26	aaa	PHI	4	2	38	1	101	128	42	10	35	73	3.74	1.61	12.1	356	3.1	6.5	2.1	0.9	51
George,Chris	01	22	aaa	KC	11	3	20	0	117	111	52	15	46	74	4.03	1.34	25.0	315	3.5	5.6	1.6	1.2	38
	02	23	aaa	KC	6	12	22	0	127	166	101	17	63	78	7.15	1.80	27.3	382	4.5	5.5	1.2	1.2	16
German,Franklyn	02	23	a/a	DET	2	2	60	29	64	48	21	0	31	82	2.95	1.23	4.4	297	4.4	11.5	2.6	0.0	139
Giese,Dan	02	25	aa	BOS	5	7	55	3	102	133	48	10	23	68	4.24	1.53	8.3	344	2.0	6.0	3.0	0.9	65
Gilfillan,Jason	02	26	a/a	KC	4	4	54	4	76	88	38	9	44	44	4.49	1.73	6.6	372	5.2	5.2	1.0	1.1	19
Gil,Dave	01	23	aa	CIN	6	1	11	1	61	77	27	5	31	48	3.95	1.77	26.0	378	4.6	7.0	1.5	0.8	46
	02	24	a/a	CIN	12	7	27	0	132	148	76	27	44	98	5.18	1.45	21.4	333	3.0	6.7	2.2	1.8	31
Ginter,Matt	01	24	aaa	CHW	2	3	22	0	76	76	31	4	26	59	3.67	1.34	14.7	315	3.1	7.0	2.3	0.5	79
Giron,Isabel	01	24	a/a	SD	4	1	58	0	83	100	46	16	32	72	4.99	1.59	6.5	353	3.5	7.8	2.3	1.7	39
Giron,Roberto	02	27	a/a	MIL	2	4	51	11	70	76	39	6	48	60	5.01	1.77	6.4	378	6.2	7.7	1.3	0.8	50
Gissell,Chris	01	24	aa	CHC	5	11	28	0	159	178	91	12	63	113	5.13	1.52	25.2	342	3.6	6.4	1.8	0.7	55
	02	25	aaa	CHC	8	12	28	0	154	180	100	16	55	117	5.84	1.52	24.5	343	3.2	6.8	2.1	0.9	55
Glaser,Eric	02	25	aa	BOS	2	9	33	1	113	168	85	15	33	65	6.76	1.78	16.1	378	2.6	5.2	2.0	1.2	24
Glauber,Keith	01	30	a/a	CIN	5	4	45	0	81	138	67	24	22	39	7.45	1.97	8.8	403	2.4	4.4	1.8	2.7	-36
Glover,Gary	01	25	aaa	CHW	2	1	6	0	38	26	11	4	5	26	2.60	0.81	23.7	218	1.2	6.1	5.2	0.9	135
Glynn,Ryan	01	27	aaa	TEX	2	6	13	0	79	105	74	13	40	46	8.46	1.84	28.9	387	4.6	5.2	1.1	1.5	2
	02	28	aaa	FLA	8	11	26	0	141	189	89	12	52	70	5.67	1.71	25.1	369	3.3	4.5	1.3	0.8	24
Gobble,Jimmy	02	21	aa	KC	5	7	13	0	69	86	35	4	19	43	4.56	1.52	23.6	342	2.5	5.6	2.3	0.5	61
Gomes,Wayne	02	30	aaa	BOS	5	4	48	4	81	104	51	10	45	47	5.67	1.84	8.0	386	5.0	5.2	1.0	1.1	14
Gonzalez,Alfredo	02	23	a/a	LA	2	4	27	4	41	38	10	1	10	36	2.18	1.17	6.2	285	2.2	7.9	3.6	0.2	123
Gonzalez,Dicky	01	23	aaa	NYM	6	5	17	0	96	107	40	10	20	62	3.75	1.32	23.9	311	1.9	5.8	3.1	1.0	70
	02	24	aaa	MON	8	5	23	0	124	170	68	13	36	67	4.93	1.66	24.7	362	2.6	4.9	1.9	0.9	31
Gonzalez,Jeremi	02	28	aaa	TEX	6	5	46	14	92	99	40	8	38	77	3.91	1.49	8.8	338	3.7	7.5	2.0	0.8	65
Gonzalez,Mike	01	23	aa	PIT	5	4	14	0	87	100	49	6	41	54	5.11	1.62	28.3	357	4.3	5.6	1.3	0.6	41
	02	24	aa	PIT	8	4	16	0	85	93	46	4	46	67	4.86	1.63	24.2	359	4.9	7.1	1.5	0.4	61
Gooch,Arnie	01	25	aaa	CIN	7	10	28	1	148	204	117	19	43	85	7.11	1.67	24.3	363	2.6	5.2	2.0	1.2	29
	02	26	aa	CIN	3	3	7	0	37	56	33	2	17	21	7.98	1.96	25.9	402	4.1	5.1	1.2	0.5	29
Goodrich,Randy	01	25	aa	SF	1	1	19	0	33	54	34	7	12	15	9.16	1.97	8.5	403	3.1	4.1	1.3	2.0	-24
Good,Andrew	01	22	aa	ARI	2	3	10	0	56	86	40	2	19	40	6.41	1.87	26.9	390	3.0	6.4	2.1	0.3	59
	02	23	aa	ARI	13	6	28	0	178	195	82	23	25	103	4.15	1.24	26.4	297	1.3	5.2	4.1	1.2	83
Gosling,Mike	02	22	aa	ARI	14	5	27	0	166	166	67	7	58	96	3.63	1.35	26.3	316	3.1	5.2	1.7	0.4	59
Grabow,John	01	23	aa	PIT	2	5	10	0	50	36	25	1	43	36	4.48	1.57	22.6	350	7.7	6.5	0.8	0.2	66
	02	24	aa	PIT	8	13	28	0	146	213	111	10	45	81	6.84	1.77	24.5	377	2.8	5.0	1.8	0.6	38
Gracesqui,Frank	02	23	a/a	TOR	4	2	41	1	42	45	26	3	34	40	5.55	1.87	4.9	391	7.3	8.5	1.2	0.6	58
Grace,Mike	01	31	aa	CIN	3	2	21	0	33	60	31	2	18	20	8.32	2.35	8.3	445	4.8	5.5	1.2	0.6	17
Graham,Tom	02	25	a/a	TEX	1	2	26	0	44	56	27	3	13	43	5.50	1.56	7.6	348	2.6	8.8	3.3	0.6	98
Graman,Alex	01	24	aa	NYY	12	9	28	0	166	219	93	14	65	116	5.03	1.71	27.4	369	3.5	6.3	1.8	0.8	45
	02	25	a/a	NYY	11	11	28	0	174	216	97	14	52	112	5.02	1.54	27.7	345	2.7	5.8	2.2	0.7	54
Gray,Brett	02	26	aa	CIN	6	6	48	0	94	113	38	6	22	44	3.64	1.44	8.5	330	2.1	4.2	2.0	0.6	47
Gray,Mike	01	25	aa	ARI	6	2	54	4	72	83	26	5	21	29	3.28	1.44	5.8	331	2.6	3.6	1.4	0.7	28
	02	26	a/a	ARI	1	2	25	0	36	67	24	2	15	22	5.97	2.27	7.5	437	3.7	5.5	1.5	0.5	26
Green,Steve	01	24	aaa	ANA	6	2	10	0	59	64	27	3	12	35	4.12	1.29	24.8	306	1.8	5.3	2.9	0.5	80
Gregg,Kevin	01	23	aa	OAK	5	5	44	1	81	98	45	5	39	60	5.03	1.69	8.5	367	4.3	6.7	1.5	0.6	52
	02	24	a/a	OAK	5	8	27	0	96	125	73	9	39	75	6.84	1.71	16.5	369	3.7	7.0	1.9	0.8	51
Greisinger,Seth	02	27	a/a	DET	3	1	7	0	36	34	14	1	17	25	3.49	1.41	22.3	326	4.2	6.2	1.5	0.2	67
Grezlovski,Ben	02	26	aa	ANA	0	2	38	1	59	90	47	4	38	23	7.15	2.16	7.9	425	5.8	3.5	0.6	0.6	2
Griffiths,Jeremy	02	25	aa	NYM	8	6	27	0	152	180	76	12	56	102	4.49	1.55	25.2	347	3.3	6.0	1.8	0.7	50
Grilli,Jason	01	25	a/a	FLA	1	3	9	0	51	55	25	5	21	32	4.37	1.48	24.9	336	3.6	5.6	1.6	0.9	41
Gross,Kip	01	37	aaa	LA	4	8	28	0	100	147	65	14	16	46	5.86	1.63	16.3	358	1.4	4.1	2.9	1.2	36
Gryboski,Kevin	01	28	aaa	SEA	2	5	58	22	60	75	32	8	21	43	4.74	1.60	4.7	353	3.2	6.4	2.0	1.3	38
Guerra,Mark	01	30	a/a	HOU	9	8	37	0	144	216	84	18	33	58	5.26	1.73	18.1	372	2.1	3.6	1.8	1.1	12
	02	31	aaa	HOU	6	11	28	0	173	248	118	24	42	68	6.14	1.68	28.4	365	2.2	3.5	1.6	1.2	7
Guerrier,Matt	01	23	a/a	CHW	18	4	27	0	180	192	88	21	52	104	4.40	1.36	28.5	317	2.6	5.2	2.0	1.1	43
	02	24	aaa	PIT	7	12	27	0	157	176	97	20	44	111	5.56	1.40	25.1	324	2.5	6.4	2.5	1.1	56
Guillory,Dan	02	26	aa	CLE	3	3	19	2	32	28	6	1	24	26	1.68	1.62	7.7	357	6.7	7.3	1.1	0.3	67
Gulin,Lindsay	01	25	aa	LA	7	5	26	0	126	156	48	12	52	90	3.46	1.64	22.1	360	3.7	6.4	1.7	0.8	46
	02	26	a/a	LA	10	4	33	3	130	149	62	14	43	114	4.29	1.48	17.3	336	3.0	7.9	2.7	1.0	73
Gunderson,Eric	01	36	aaa	NYY	2	4	58	7	76	88	34	8	25	52	3.98	1.49	5.8	338	3.0	6.2	2.1	1.0	49
Guttormson,Rick	01	25	a/a	SD	5	17	28	0	148	179	98	19	56	61	5.95	1.59	23.8	352	3.4	3.7	1.1	1.1	8
Guy,Brad	01	26	a/a	PIT	5	6	50	4	98	127	58	7	37	53	5.32	1.68	9.0	365	3.4	4.9	1.4	0.7	33
	02	27	aa	PIT	3	2	26	1	76	114	38	8	17	30	4.49	1.72	13.6	371	2.0	3.5	1.8	0.9	17
Guzman,Geraldo	01	29	aaa	ARI	3	6	20	0	94	110	62	10	30	68	5.96	1.48	20.7	337	2.9	6.5	2.3	0.9	57
Guzman,Juan	01	35	a/a	TAM	6	2	12	0	72	78	49	10	39	40	6.10	1.62	27.3	357	4.9	4.9	1.0	1.2	15

Major League Equivalent Statistics

PITCHER	Yr	Age	Lev	Org	W	L	G	Sv	IP	H	ER	HR	BB	K	ERA	Br/IP	BF/G	OOB	CTL	DOM	CMD	hr/9	BPV
					Actual				Major League Equivalents														
Guzman,Leiby	01	25	aa	TEX	4	1	36	1	63	84	48	10	18	36	6.80	1.62	8.0	356	2.5	5.1	2.0	1.4	23
Haines,Talley	01	25	a/a	TAM	6	6	59	9	74	91	40	9	31	62	4.88	1.64	5.7	360	3.8	7.5	2.0	1.1	50
	02	26	aaa	TAM	4	7	48	0	75	98	47	10	25	51	5.63	1.64	7.1	359	3.0	6.1	2.0	1.2	37
Hale,Beau	01	23	aa	BAL	1	5	12	0	61	86	44	9	15	36	6.47	1.65	23.3	361	2.2	5.3	2.4	1.3	32
Halladay,Roy	01	24	a/a	TOR	3	1	7	0	48	44	16	5	6	35	3.09	1.05	27.2	265	1.2	6.5	5.6	1.0	136
Hall,Josh	02	22	aa	CIN	7	8	22	0	132	156	63	8	46	97	4.30	1.53	26.7	344	3.1	6.6	2.1	0.5	65
Hamann,Rob	02	26	a/a	TOR	0	0	19	1	35	48	17	3	12	10	4.37	1.71	8.5	370	3.1	2.6	0.8	0.8	1
Hamilton,Jimmy	01	26	a/a	BAL	3	4	49	2	85	114	54	7	40	58	5.76	1.81	8.2	383	4.2	6.1	1.4	0.7	38
	02	27	aa	PHI	3	2	46	4	71	76	31	7	49	42	3.93	1.76	7.2	376	6.2	5.3	0.9	0.9	25
Hammond,Chris	01	36	aaa	ATL	10	4	49	1	82	105	37	6	26	69	4.04	1.60	7.6	354	2.9	7.6	2.6	0.7	74
Hampton,Matt	02	25	aa	SD	6	5	57	0	94	116	49	11	32	75	4.69	1.57	7.4	350	3.1	7.2	2.3	1.1	56
Hamulack,Tim	02	26	aa	FLA	8	4	38	6	78	89	31	7	32	42	3.58	1.55	9.2	347	3.7	4.8	1.3	0.8	31
Hancock,Josh	01	24	aa	BOS	8	6	24	0	130	167	70	8	39	96	4.85	1.58	24.4	352	2.7	6.6	2.5	0.6	68
	02	24	a/a	BOS	7	6	23	1	129	141	62	11	45	81	4.33	1.44	24.5	331	3.1	5.7	1.8	0.8	49
Harang,Aaron	01	23	aa	OAK	10	8	27	0	150	192	76	9	36	93	4.58	1.52	24.7	342	2.2	5.6	2.6	0.6	65
	02	24	a/a	OAK	5	3	11	0	55	59	18	1	15	49	2.94	1.34	21.4	315	2.5	8.0	3.3	0.2	113
Harden,Rich	02	21	aa	OAK	8	3	16	0	85	71	31	2	49	91	3.28	1.41	23.0	326	5.2	9.6	1.9	0.2	101
Harikkala,Tim	01	30	aaa	MIL	11	10	31	0	172	261	117	18	44	75	6.10	1.78	26.1	378	2.3	3.9	1.7	0.9	17
	02	31	aaa	MIL	8	10	31	1	162	218	88	11	25	73	4.89	1.50	23.1	339	1.4	4.1	2.9	0.6	59
Harper,Travis	01	25	aaa	TAM	12	6	25	0	155	167	83	30	38	99	4.80	1.32	26.3	312	2.2	5.7	2.6	1.8	37
Harrell,Tim	01	26	aa	LA	5	4	47	5	81	90	38	14	34	55	4.20	1.54	7.7	345	3.8	6.1	1.6	1.6	22
Harriger,Mark	01	26	aa	ANA	2	3	10	0	50	67	34	9	25	23	6.19	1.84	23.8	386	4.5	4.2	0.9	1.7	-12
Hartmann,Pete	01	30	aa	ARI	0	4	19	0	31	71	41	4	41	16	11.99	3.63	10.7	554	12.0	4.7	0.4	1.2	-34
Harvey,Ian	02	26	aa	SD	6	1	12	0	57	68	16	2	17	33	2.53	1.49	21.0	338	2.7	5.2	1.9	0.3	60
Harville,Chad	01	25	aaa	OAK	5	2	33	8	40	38	19	5	11	47	4.30	1.23	5.1	297	2.5	10.4	4.2	1.1	122
	02	26	aaa	OAK	1	2	24	5	30	34	19	4	12	21	5.70	1.53	5.6	344	3.6	6.3	1.8	1.2	38
Hasselhoff,Derek	01	28	aaa	SF	8	1	59	14	72	58	23	9	25	50	2.82	1.15	5.0	282	3.1	6.3	2.0	1.1	60
	02	29	aaa	BOS	0	4	39	11	44	59	34	5	9	23	6.92	1.54	5.1	345	1.8	4.7	2.6	1.0	43
Hazlett,Andy	01	26	a/a	BOS	8	1	23	2	75	84	37	8	18	42	4.39	1.36	14.0	318	2.1	5.1	2.4	0.9	52
	02	27	a/a	SD	1	1	27	0	54	63	37	10	18	31	6.14	1.49	8.9	339	3.0	5.1	1.7	1.7	15
Hearns,Shane	01	26	a/a	DET	6	5	50	6	72	52	40	4	64	59	4.99	1.62	6.5	357	8.0	7.4	0.9	0.6	62
	02	27	a/a	COL	2	3	34	0	40	54	53	11	55	24	11.90	2.72	6.6	482	12.3	5.4	0.4	2.5	-41
Heaverlo,Jeff	01	24	aa	SEA	11	6	27	0	178	192	76	12	43	152	3.85	1.32	28.0	311	2.2	7.7	3.5	0.6	102
Hebson,Bryan	01	26	aa	MON	2	8	26	0	75	100	51	16	22	41	6.13	1.63	13.1	358	2.7	4.9	1.8	1.9	4
	02	27	a/a	MON	11	1	43	7	103	88	32	7	30	66	2.79	1.14	9.8	281	2.6	5.8	2.2	0.6	72
Heilman,Aaron	02	24	a/a	NYM	6	7	27	0	146	141	68	10	44	112	4.19	1.27	22.6	303	2.7	6.9	2.5	0.6	82
Heiserman,Rick	01	29	a/a	STL	1	1	32	0	61	98	45	15	22	31	6.60	1.97	9.3	403	3.3	4.6	1.4	2.3	-26
	02	30	aaa	STL	1	1	22	1	38	53	29	15	11	13	6.85	1.68	8.0	365	2.6	3.1	1.2	3.5	-73
Henderson,Rod	01	31	aaa	OAK	4	1	8	0	36	60	38	10	19	23	9.39	2.18	23.1	427	4.7	5.8	1.2	2.5	-31
Henderson,Scott	01	27	aa	FLA	5	7	39	4	56	71	46	11	29	42	7.36	1.78	6.8	379	4.6	6.7	1.5	1.8	10
Hendrickson,Ben	02	22	aa	MIL	4	2	13	0	69	67	29	2	35	43	3.77	1.47	23.4	335	4.6	5.6	1.2	0.3	57
Hendrickson,Mark	01	27	aaa	TOR	2	9	38	0	73	98	51	16	19	27	6.22	1.60	8.7	354	2.3	3.3	1.4	1.9	-17
	02	28	aaa	TOR	7	5	19	0	92	109	45	13	23	55	4.40	1.43	21.1	329	2.3	5.4	2.4	1.3	42
Henkel,Rob	02	24	aa	FLA	5	4	13	0	70	62	35	6	28	57	4.50	1.29	22.6	306	3.6	7.3	2.0	0.8	72
Henriquez,Oscar	01	28	aaa	NYM	2	4	39	19	38	37	16	1	21	35	3.73	1.52	4.3	342	5.0	8.3	1.7	0.2	83
	02	29	aaa	DET	2	1	33	17	32	38	16	4	14	33	4.47	1.61	4.4	356	3.9	9.2	2.4	1.1	69
Henry,Butch	01	33	aaa	TOR	8	8	18	0	116	172	85	18	19	63	6.61	1.64	29.4	360	1.5	4.9	3.3	1.4	45
Hensley,Matt	02	24	aaa	ANA	7	5	19	0	117	143	71	17	36	91	5.45	1.53	27.4	343	2.8	7.0	2.5	1.3	52
Hernandez,Adrian	01	22	aaa	NYY	8	7	21	0	117	130	88	16	58	88	6.73	1.60	25.2	354	4.5	6.8	1.5	1.2	35
	02	28	aaa	NYY	6	7	20	0	109	132	75	9	46	92	6.18	1.63	24.8	358	3.8	7.6	2.0	0.7	62
Hernandez,Buddy	02	24	aa	ATL	4	0	40	1	59	41	9	0	23	66	1.37	1.08	5.9	271	3.5	10.1	2.9	0.0	137
Hernandez,Carlos	01	21	aa	HOU	12	3	24	0	139	135	72	14	72	143	4.66	1.49	25.5	338	4.7	9.3	2.0	0.9	75
Hernandez,Runelvys	02	22	aa	KC	8	3	16	0	106	116	43	4	24	71	3.65	1.32	28.1	311	2.0	6.0	3.0	0.3	89
Herndon,Junior	01	23	aaa	SD	9	5	21	0	116	145	66	17	40	38	5.12	1.59	24.9	353	3.1	2.9	1.0	1.3	-7
	02	24	aaa	SD	7	13	28	0	159	190	105	27	52	50	5.94	1.52	25.2	343	2.9	2.8	1.0	1.5	-12
Herrera,Alex	02	26	a/a	CLE	0	3	35	5	68	72	45	11	42	57	5.95	1.67	8.9	364	5.6	7.5	1.4	1.5	32
High,Andy	02	28	aa	MIL	1	1	16	1	31	51	16	3	14	20	4.62	2.08	9.8	416	4.0	5.8	1.4	0.9	22
Hiles,Cary	01	26	aa	PHI	2	3	51	11	81	76	29	7	26	50	3.20	1.25	6.6	299	2.8	5.6	2.0	0.7	59
	02	27	a/a	PHI	5	8	47	8	83	119	51	3	39	41	5.52	1.90	8.5	394	4.2	4.4	1.1	0.3	28
Hiljus,Erik	01	29	aaa	OAK	8	5	15	0	101	91	47	19	27	86	4.21	1.17	27.6	286	2.4	7.7	3.2	1.7	70
	02	30	aaa	OAK	1	3	9	0	37	62	34	3	15	24	8.23	2.07	20.6	415	3.6	5.8	1.6	0.7	29
Hill,Jeremy	02	25	aa	KC	4	7	56	19	76	81	30	6	36	59	3.55	1.54	6.1	345	4.3	7.0	1.6	0.7	57
Hill,Ken	01	36	aaa	BOS	4	2	14	0	63	92	52	9	24	26	7.37	1.84	21.4	386	3.5	3.7	1.1	1.4	-8
Hill,Terry	01	26	aa	BOS	3	1	22	0	38	50	22	3	11	32	5.26	1.61	7.8	355	2.6	7.5	2.8	0.8	73
	02	27	aa	BOS	6	5	45	3	83	137	71	10	40	64	7.70	2.13	9.3	422	4.3	6.9	1.6	1.1	25
Hinchliffe,Brett	01	27	aaa	NYM	3	2	11	0	59	82	26	8	19	37	4.00	1.71	24.9	369	2.9	5.6	2.0	1.3	27
Hoard,Brent	02	26	aa	MIN	11	8	31	0	161	198	92	13	60	97	5.14	1.60	23.5	354	3.4	5.4	1.6	0.7	40
Hodges,Kevin	01	28	aaa	SEA	5	5	14	0	86	115	49	9	28	47	5.16	1.66	28.2	362	2.9	4.9	1.7	0.9	29
Hodges,Trey	02	24	aaa	ATL	15	9	28	0	172	182	75	10	55	97	3.92	1.38	26.4	320	2.9	5.1	1.8	0.5	54
Hodge,Kevin	02	26	aa	MIN	3	2	24	6	30	29	14	3	9	22	4.19	1.26	5.2	302	2.7	6.6	2.4	0.9	69
Holt,Chris	02	31	aaa	COL	6	3	12	1	70	80	36	14	16	44	4.62	1.37	25.1	319	2.1	5.6	2.8	1.8	37
Holzemer,Mark	02	33	aaa	ARI	2	3	51	2	34	41	23	4	19	27	6.09	1.76	3.1	377	5.0	7.1	1.4	1.1	38
Hooten,Dave	01	26	a/a	MIN	6	1	25	4	61	88	27	7	20	28	3.93	1.77	11.4	377	3.0	4.1	1.4	1.0	13
	02	27	aa	CHC	5	1	65	9	76	69	17	5	24	48	2.01	1.22	4.8	295	2.8	5.7	2.0	0.6	66
Horgan,Joe	01	24	a/a	SF	3	5	34	1	111	119	52	10	28	53	4.18	1.32	13.8	311	2.3	4.3	1.9	0.8	43
	02	25	a/a	SF	6	5	37	0	113	156	77	12	41	59	6.12	1.74	14.3	373	3.3	4.7	1.4	1.0	21
House,Craig	01	24	aaa	COL	2	2	54	6	58	59	37	6	30	55	5.72	1.53	4.8	344	4.6	8.5	1.8	0.9	65
Howard,Ben	01	23	aa	SD	2	0	7	0	30	19	10	3	16	23	3.00	1.17	17.5	285	4.8	6.9	1.4	0.9	64
	02	24	a/a	SD	3	5	17	0	78	82	45	12	32	47	5.19	1.46	20.1	334	3.7	5.4	1.5	1.4	24
Howington,Ty	01	21	aa	CIN	1	3	7	0	41	39	17	4	23	36	3.75	1.51	26.0	340	5.0	7.8	1.6	0.8	61
	02	22	aa	CIN	1	5	15	0	65	72	42	5	31	43	5.82	1.58	19.5	352	4.3	6.0	1.4	0.7	44

Major League Equivalent Statistics

					Actual				Major League Equivalents														
PITCHER	Yr	Age	Lev	Org	W	L	G	Sv	IP	H	ER	HR	BB	K	ERA	Br/IP	BF/G	OOB	CTL	DOM	CMD	hr/9	BPV
Hudson,Luke	01	24	aa	COL	7	12	29	0	165	223	134	39	80	122	7.29	1.84	27.1	386	4.4	6.6	1.5	2.1	-0
	02	25	aaa	CIN	5	9	30	3	117	112	65	6	52	107	4.99	1.40	16.9	324	4.0	8.2	2.1	0.5	84
Hughes,Travis	01	23	aa	TEX	5	7	47	8	87	109	58	10	44	75	5.97	1.76	8.7	377	4.6	7.7	1.7	1.1	45
	02	24	aa	TEX	9	7	26	0	143	176	79	15	88	114	4.97	1.84	26.2	387	5.5	7.2	1.3	0.9	38
Huisman,Rick	01	32	aaa	STL	0	2	23	1	32	48	28	9	19	26	7.99	2.11	7.0	419	5.3	7.2	1.4	2.7	-21
Hundley,Jeff	01	25	aa	ANA	2	6	10	0	54	74	45	8	24	26	7.54	1.81	25.6	383	4.0	4.3	1.1	1.4	-3
	02	26	a/a	ANA	1	5	42	1	69	81	40	9	26	37	5.21	1.55	7.4	347	3.4	4.8	1.4	1.2	21
Hunter,Johnny	01	26	aa	SD	3	6	19	0	98	138	74	8	45	43	6.75	1.86	24.7	390	4.1	3.9	1.0	0.7	11
	02	27	a/a	SD	5	5	33	1	113	152	72	11	51	44	5.73	1.79	16.2	381	4.1	3.5	0.9	0.9	5
Hurtado,Edwin	02	33	aaa	KC	4	4	11	0	60	83	38	6	19	36	5.70	1.70	25.2	368	2.9	5.4	1.9	0.9	36
Husted,Brent	01	26	a/a	LA	3	3	37	1	57	87	36	7	21	26	5.64	1.90	7.4	394	3.3	4.0	1.2	1.2	1
Hutchinson,Chad	01	25	aaa	STL	4	9	27	0	97	109	97	9	104	104	8.98	2.19	18.4	429	9.6	9.6	1.0	0.8	53
Hutchison,Wesley	02	23	a/a	SF	3	13	39	3	101	136	79	10	42	53	7.04	1.76	12.1	376	3.7	4.7	1.3	0.9	20
Ireland,Eric	01	25	aaa	OAK	8	11	29	0	168	231	105	23	53	88	5.62	1.69	26.7	367	2.8	4.7	1.7	1.2	17
Izquierdo,Hansel	01	25	aa	FLA	7	2	10	0	56	59	34	12	12	37	5.39	1.25	23.5	301	1.9	5.9	3.2	1.9	49
	02	26	a/a	FLA	4	6	14	0	78	105	46	9	24	33	5.31	1.65	25.5	362	2.8	3.8	1.4	1.0	12
Jacome,Jason	01	31	aaa	ARI	1	8	35	0	120	183	90	12	39	56	6.75	1.85	16.4	388	2.9	4.2	1.4	0.9	14
	02	32	aaa	STL	8	6	28	1	105	138	62	17	24	60	5.30	1.54	16.8	345	2.1	5.1	2.5	1.5	33
Jacquez,Tom	01	26	aaa	PHI	10	6	33	0	109	123	53	9	34	77	4.33	1.44	14.4	331	2.8	6.4	2.2	0.7	62
	02	27	aaa	CHW	0	7	14	0	61	97	63	10	23	41	9.28	1.96	21.3	402	3.4	6.0	1.8	1.5	14
James,Delvin	01	24	a/a	TAM	5	7	38	0	128	149	71	11	37	71	4.99	1.45	14.7	332	2.6	5.0	1.9	0.8	45
	02	25	a/a	TAM	3	3	10	0	47	63	26	7	6	32	4.98	1.47	20.6	335	1.1	6.1	5.3	1.3	101
James,Mike	02	35	aaa	COL	1	1	24	1	31	45	35	7	16	21	10.16	1.97	6.3	403	4.6	6.1	1.3	2.0	-8
Jamison,Ryan	01	24	aa	HOU	5	2	10	0	46	59	24	6	25	26	4.63	1.81	21.8	383	4.8	5.1	1.1	1.2	11
	02	25	aa	HOU	3	6	42	1	94	125	54	6	42	73	5.16	1.77	10.5	378	4.0	7.0	1.7	0.6	54
Janke,Cheyenne	01	25	aa	STL	1	4	17	0	44	82	38	6	16	18	7.75	2.22	13.3	432	3.2	3.7	1.1	1.3	-16
	02	26	aa	STL	12	8	28	0	150	174	73	16	43	92	4.38	1.45	23.4	331	2.6	5.5	2.1	1.0	47
Jarvis,Matt	01	30	a/a	SEA	3	1	35	8	40	48	23	1	23	20	5.20	1.76	5.4	377	5.2	4.4	0.8	0.3	33
	02	31	aaa	SF	5	4	43	3	56	71	27	3	21	38	4.32	1.64	6.0	359	3.4	6.1	1.8	0.5	55
Jean,Domingo	01	33	a/a	NYY	5	6	56	9	71	94	32	8	30	68	4.08	1.75	5.9	375	3.8	8.7	2.3	1.0	63
	02	34	a/a	NYY	0	6	55	19	70	83	44	11	28	46	5.65	1.58	5.7	352	3.6	5.9	1.6	1.4	25
Jenks,Bobby	02	22	aa	ANA	3	6	10	0	58	57	37	2	44	50	5.74	1.74	27.0	374	6.8	7.8	1.1	0.3	66
Jennings,Jason	01	23	a/a	COL	9	8	26	0	157	212	111	17	51	118	6.35	1.67	27.8	364	2.9	6.8	2.3	1.0	52
Jensen,Ryan	01	26	aaa	SF	11	2	20	0	106	102	41	9	31	77	3.50	1.25	22.1	301	2.6	6.5	2.5	0.8	73
Jimenez,Jason	01	26	a/a	TAM	3	4	50	11	74	87	42	8	41	59	5.12	1.74	6.9	373	5.0	7.2	1.4	1.0	40
	02	27	aaa	TAM	2	2	44	3	51	57	20	3	16	46	3.52	1.43	5.1	329	2.8	8.1	2.9	0.5	93
Jodie,Brett	01	25	a/a	SD	14	5	26	0	164	192	69	16	37	72	3.79	1.40	27.2	323	2.0	3.9	1.9	0.9	35
Johnson,Adam	01	22	a/a	MIN	6	7	22	0	137	150	85	12	52	115	5.58	1.47	27.4	335	3.4	7.5	2.2	0.8	69
	02	23	aaa	MIN	13	8	27	0	151	196	99	23	53	96	5.90	1.65	25.6	361	3.2	5.7	1.8	1.4	25
Johnson,Barry	01	32	a/a	NYY	5	3	46	1	75	101	51	10	28	41	6.13	1.72	7.6	370	3.3	5.0	1.5	1.2	17
Johnson,James	01	25	aa	CLE	4	0	31	0	46	47	22	3	21	42	4.34	1.47	6.5	335	4.1	8.3	2.0	0.7	76
Johnson,Jeremy	02	20	aa	DET	6	1	8	0	48	52	22	6	12	25	4.11	1.33	25.6	313	2.2	4.7	2.1	1.1	39
Johnson,Jonathan	01	27	aaa	ARI	4	4	15	0	73	74	52	7	42	42	6.34	1.58	22.0	351	5.2	5.1	1.0	0.9	28
	02	28	a/a	SD	0	4	29	1	66	100	68	11	22	38	9.26	1.85	10.9	387	3.0	5.2	1.7	1.5	9
Johnson,Mark	01	26	aaa	DET	7	11	24	0	141	196	90	20	23	65	5.72	1.55	26.3	347	1.4	4.1	2.9	1.3	38
	02	27	a/a	DET	4	2	17	0	52	77	36	3	20	24	6.21	1.86	14.7	389	3.4	4.1	1.2	0.5	22
Johnson,Mike	01	26	aaa	TEX	5	5	25	2	98	130	65	18	25	65	5.96	1.58	17.6	351	2.3	6.0	2.6	1.6	35
	02	27	aaa	LA	2	1	8	0	44	56	19	5	17	29	3.89	1.66	25.2	362	3.5	5.9	1.7	1.0	35
Johnson,Rett	02	23	aa	SEA	10	4	21	0	117	133	65	6	57	86	5.00	1.62	25.3	357	4.4	6.6	1.5	0.5	56
Jones,Bobby M.	02	31	aaa	NYM	1	4	13	0	40	53	24	4	17	27	5.39	1.75	14.4	374	3.8	6.1	1.6	0.9	35
Jones,Chris	02	37	aa	SF	1	7	36	0	84	124	78	14	44	42	8.35	2.00	11.5	406	4.7	4.5	1.0	1.5	-10
Jones,Greg	02	26	aaa	ANA	7	4	39	2	62	75	33	5	20	47	4.77	1.53	7.1	343	2.9	6.8	2.4	0.7	65
Jones,Marcus	01	27	aaa	OAK	2	3	27	1	73	90	41	4	20	43	5.08	1.49	12.0	339	2.4	5.3	2.2	0.5	58
	02	28	aa	OAK	1	4	7	0	31	49	27	4	20	17	7.79	2.21	22.9	431	5.8	4.9	0.9	1.2	-2
Jongejan,Ferenc	02	24	aa	CHC	3	4	62	2	67	70	32	4	30	44	4.29	1.49	4.8	338	4.0	5.9	1.5	0.5	52
Joseph,Jake	02	25	a/a	NYM	6	5	15	0	90	100	39	4	28	35	3.90	1.42	26.1	327	2.8	3.5	1.3	0.4	35
Joseph,Kevin	01	25	a/a	STL	2	4	41	1	54	58	33	4	31	31	5.42	1.63	6.0	358	5.1	5.2	1.0	0.7	33
	02	26	aaa	STL	1	1	31	2	35	44	9	2	11	13	2.30	1.56	5.1	349	2.8	3.3	1.2	0.5	24
Journell,Jimmy	02	25	a/a	STL	5	7	17	0	103	102	42	7	36	86	3.67	1.34	25.8	314	3.1	7.5	2.4	0.6	81
Judd,Mike	02	27	aaa	FLA	8	6	23	0	125	146	74	9	49	84	5.32	1.56	24.4	348	3.5	6.0	1.7	0.6	51
Juden,Jeff	01	31	aaa	CHW	5	5	12	0	65	60	38	8	54	50	5.23	1.76	25.4	376	7.5	7.0	0.9	1.1	36
Julio,Jorge	01	23	a/a	BAL	1	2	46	19	56	51	24	5	22	55	3.84	1.30	5.2	308	3.5	8.8	2.5	0.8	89
Junge,Eric	01	25	aa	LA	10	11	27	0	164	175	82	23	63	94	4.51	1.45	26.5	332	3.5	5.2	1.5	1.3	26
	02	26	aaa	PHI	12	6	29	0	180	196	87	17	73	114	4.35	1.49	27.4	338	3.6	5.7	1.6	0.8	42
Kalinowski,Josh	01	25	aa	COL	7	8	25	0	137	212	107	31	76	97	7.05	2.10	27.5	418	5.0	6.4	1.3	2.0	-9
Kalita,Tim	01	23	aa	DET	15	9	30	0	200	214	100	22	44	125	4.50	1.29	28.1	306	2.0	5.6	2.8	1.0	65
	02	24	aaa	DET	1	9	15	0	87	107	59	9	21	43	6.09	1.47	25.5	335	2.2	4.4	2.0	0.9	38
Kamieniecki,Scott	01	37	aaa	CHC	1	4	8	0	37	39	17	3	11	31	4.10	1.34	19.7	314	2.6	7.6	3.0	0.8	87
Kane,Kyle	01	26	a/a	CHW	2	1	27	3	37	31	13	1	7	36	3.07	1.02	5.4	260	1.8	8.8	4.9	0.3	159
Karl,Scott	01	30	aaa	PIT	4	3	14	0	84	97	44	10	33	41	4.75	1.54	26.8	346	3.6	4.4	1.2	1.1	19
Karnuth,Jason	01	25	aaa	STL	4	4	55	3	73	92	40	8	24	39	4.97	1.59	6.0	352	3.0	4.7	1.6	1.0	27
	02	26	a/a	STL	3	4	59	4	71	93	37	9	24	38	4.69	1.65	5.5	361	3.0	4.8	1.6	1.1	21
Karp,Josh	02	23	aa	MON	7	5	16	0	86	97	45	7	34	56	4.70	1.52	23.9	342	3.5	5.8	1.6	0.7	47
Kaye,Justin	01	25	aaa	SEA	3	2	56	4	77	58	28	5	47	96	3.31	1.36	5.9	318	5.5	11.2	2.0	0.6	106
	02	26	aaa	SEA	3	7	47	6	62	63	34	2	42	54	4.93	1.69	6.1	367	6.1	7.8	1.3	0.3	69
Keisler,Randy	01	26	aaa	NYY	5	7	18	0	97	131	72	13	40	75	6.65	1.77	25.3	377	3.7	7.0	1.9	1.2	36
Keller,Kris	01	24	aaa	DET	5	2	52	4	68	72	40	9	34	51	5.29	1.56	5.9	348	4.5	6.7	1.5	1.2	38
	02	25	aaa	ATL	3	0	46	2	61	53	25	5	30	34	3.69	1.36	5.7	318	4.4	5.0	1.1	0.7	41
Kelley,Rich	02	32	aaa	ANA	6	5	40	0	119	146	62	17	39	59	4.69	1.55	13.3	347	2.9	4.5	1.5	1.3	16
Kennedy,Joe	01	22	a/a	TAM	6	0	11	0	73	61	11	3	12	65	1.36	1.00	26.0	255	1.5	8.0	5.4	0.4	161
Kent,Nathan	01	23	aa	ATL	8	10	26	0	154	229	96	14	40	95	5.60	1.74	27.7	374	2.3	5.5	2.4	0.8	45

Major League Equivalent Statistics

PITCHER	Yr	Age	Lev	Org	Actual				Major League Equivalents														
					W	L	G	Sv	IP	H	ER	HR	BB	K	ERA	Br/IP	BF/G	OOB	CTL	DOM	CMD	hr/9	BPV
Kershner,Jason	01	25	a/a	PHI	6	10	32	0	139	192	95	23	33	68	6.13	1.61	19.7	356	2.1	4.4	2.1	1.5	16
	02	26	aaa	SD	7	2	31	0	86	73	33	8	26	69	3.45	1.15	11.3	283	2.7	7.2	2.7	0.8	84
Kessel,Kyle	01	25	a/a	HOU	4	10	31	0	107	187	111	19	58	57	9.29	2.29	18.0	440	4.9	4.8	1.0	1.6	-18
Kibler,Ryan	01	21	aa	COL	4	1	8	0	47	51	18	0	21	36	3.45	1.53	26.2	344	4.0	6.9	1.7	0.0	78
	02	22	aa	COL	7	8	25	0	143	190	105	10	63	51	6.61	1.77	26.8	377	4.0	3.2	0.8	0.6	10
Kiefer,Mark	01	33	aaa	LA	11	7	32	1	145	135	68	20	45	142	4.24	1.24	18.9	298	2.8	8.8	3.1	1.2	88
Kieschnick,Brooks	02	30	aaa	CHW	0	1	25	0	31	40	13	1	12	25	3.76	1.67	5.7	364	3.5	7.2	2.1	0.3	72
Kimball,Andrew	01	26	aa	MIL	8	6	48	2	71	101	37	10	33	30	4.66	1.89	7.1	393	4.2	3.7	0.9	1.3	-9
Kim,Sun-Woo	01	24	aaa	BOS	6	7	19	0	89	108	67	10	27	65	6.78	1.52	20.8	342	2.7	6.6	2.4	1.0	56
	02	25	aaa	MON	7	2	15	0	89	76	29	7	33	54	2.93	1.22	24.6	295	3.3	5.5	1.6	0.7	56
Kingrey,Jarrod	01	25	aa	TOR	5	3	51	27	54	53	21	8	36	40	3.51	1.64	4.8	360	5.9	6.6	1.1	1.3	29
	02	26	aaa	TOR	4	1	26	1	41	37	27	6	20	23	5.91	1.39	6.8	322	4.4	5.0	1.2	1.3	23
Kinney,Matt	01	25	aaa	MIN	6	11	29	0	161	202	108	26	73	124	6.03	1.71	25.7	369	4.1	6.9	1.7	1.5	29
	02	26	a/a	MIN	2	1	6	0	31	54	37	11	5	20	10.71	1.90	25.0	394	1.4	5.8	4.0	3.2	4
Kirsten,Rick	01	23	aa	DET	14	8	28	0	161	187	100	21	49	118	5.58	1.46	25.2	334	2.8	6.6	2.4	1.2	54
Klepacki,Ed	02	24	aa	FLA	2	1	19	2	33	26	15	2	24	17	4.08	1.51	7.7	341	6.5	4.6	0.7	0.5	39
Knight,Brandon	01	26	aaa	NYY	12	7	25	0	162	210	87	22	47	146	4.81	1.59	29.2	353	2.6	8.1	3.1	1.2	70
	02	27	aaa	NYY	2	7	36	12	80	77	41	6	38	68	4.60	1.43	9.7	329	4.3	7.6	1.8	0.7	69
Knoll,Brian	01	28	a/a	SF	0	3	24	0	67	116	64	13	34	35	8.51	2.24	14.5	434	4.6	4.7	1.0	1.7	-22
Knotts,Gary	01	25	aaa	FLA	6	7	21	0	118	135	66	12	39	90	5.03	1.47	24.7	335	3.0	6.9	2.3	0.9	61
	02	26	aaa	FLA	5	3	42	3	53	55	24	3	30	39	4.08	1.60	5.7	355	5.1	6.6	1.3	0.5	54
Knott,Eric	01	27	a/a	ARI	10	3	42	1	99	140	52	9	17	47	4.70	1.59	10.6	352	1.6	4.3	2.7	0.8	47
	02	28	aaa	ARI	8	10	31	1	150	220	97	13	23	74	5.82	1.62	22.0	357	1.4	4.4	3.2	0.8	59
Kofler,Ed	01	24	aa	TAM	2	7	13	0	59	102	75	9	28	33	11.44	2.19	23.3	429	4.2	5.0	1.2	1.4	-7
Kohlmeier,Ryan	01	24	aaa	BAL	1	4	14	4	42	42	14	5	8	25	3.00	1.19	12.3	290	1.7	5.4	3.1	1.1	70
	02	25	aaa	CHW	2	1	38	0	65	79	48	17	21	53	6.64	1.54	7.6	345	2.9	7.3	2.5	2.4	23
Kolb,Brandon	01	28	aaa	MIL	3	5	40	14	54	58	32	7	22	47	5.24	1.48	6.0	336	3.7	7.7	2.1	1.2	55
	02	29	aaa	CHC	3	3	53	1	64	76	35	3	37	43	4.91	1.76	5.7	376	5.2	6.0	1.2	0.4	45
Komiyama,Satoru	02	37	aaa	NYM	3	1	17	0	44	33	8	4	9	34	1.63	0.95	10.0	246	1.8	6.9	3.8	0.8	111
Koplove,Mike	01	25	a/a	ARI	7	3	51	13	66	71	23	4	28	53	3.15	1.50	5.7	339	3.9	7.2	1.9	0.6	67
	02	26	aaa	ARI	1	2	23	3	30	24	4	1	4	25	1.19	0.93	5.1	241	1.2	7.5	6.3	0.3	179
Koronka,John	01	21	aa	CIN	1	5	9	0	55	71	43	8	28	39	7.04	1.80	28.8	381	4.6	6.4	1.4	1.3	22
	02	22	aa	CIN	2	8	16	0	95	121	61	11	48	58	5.77	1.78	27.9	378	4.5	5.5	1.2	1.0	21
Kozlowski,Ben	02	22	aa	TEX	4	2	8	0	52	34	15	4	22	36	2.60	1.08	26.0	269	3.8	6.2	1.6	0.7	69
Kramer,Aaron	01	26	aa	CHC	2	7	25	0	51	70	40	13	14	32	7.10	1.65	9.3	360	2.4	5.7	2.3	2.2	7
Krawczyk,Jack	01	26	aa	MIL	6	2	47	1	81	93	48	13	18	50	5.36	1.37	7.4	320	2.0	5.5	2.7	1.4	46
	02	27	a/a	MIL	5	3	46	5	69	78	33	6	21	54	4.30	1.43	6.5	329	2.7	7.0	2.6	0.8	72
Krivda,Rick	01	32	aaa	STL	4	6	14	0	80	101	46	11	21	41	5.20	1.52	25.4	343	2.4	4.6	1.9	1.2	28
Kubes,Greg	02	26	aa	PHI	13	7	28	0	174	223	89	19	53	87	4.60	1.59	28.0	352	2.7	4.5	1.6	1.0	26
Kusiewicz,Mike	01	25	a/a	BOS	6	7	26	0	126	151	69	9	32	99	4.93	1.45	21.2	331	2.3	7.1	3.1	0.7	84
	02	26	a/a	BOS	7	8	23	0	114	131	63	9	35	69	4.97	1.45	21.7	333	2.8	5.4	2.0	0.7	51
Lackey,John	01	23	a/a	ANA	12	11	28	0	185	200	104	17	42	118	5.06	1.31	27.9	309	2.0	5.7	2.8	0.8	70
	02	24	aaa	ANA	8	2	16	0	101	97	32	5	26	70	2.85	1.22	26.2	294	2.3	6.2	2.7	0.4	86
Lail,Denny	01	27	aaa	NYY	6	6	33	0	136	178	94	15	49	86	6.19	1.67	18.9	364	3.3	5.7	1.7	1.0	35
	02	28	aaa	STL	1	3	10	0	41	52	28	3	28	20	6.13	1.95	20.0	400	6.1	4.4	0.7	0.7	16
Lakman,Jason	01	25	a/a	BAL	1	2	37	1	61	96	54	8	23	33	7.88	1.94	8.0	399	3.3	4.9	1.5	1.2	8
Lambert,Jeremy	01	23	a/a	STL	7	3	59	17	64	63	27	13	26	81	3.80	1.39	4.7	323	3.7	11.4	3.1	1.8	83
Lamber,Justin	01	25	aa	KC	0	2	19	1	36	52	28	8	24	15	6.94	2.13	9.6	422	6.1	3.8	0.6	1.9	-34
	02	26	aa	SEA	1	2	34	0	33	48	18	1	18	18	4.89	1.99	4.8	406	4.9	4.9	1.0	0.3	31
Langen,Brian	02	25	aa	STL	2	0	46	0	53	56	28	3	32	29	4.75	1.66	5.3	362	5.4	4.9	0.9	0.5	35
Langone,Steve	02	25	aa	LA	2	2	14	1	32	26	6	0	14	14	1.68	1.24	9.6	298	3.9	3.9	1.0	0.0	56
Lankford,Frank	01	31	aaa	OAK	5	5	40	2	69	103	44	9	24	29	5.79	1.85	8.2	388	3.2	3.8	1.2	1.2	-0
	02	32	aaa	OAK	6	6	46	0	80	99	42	8	21	46	4.72	1.50	7.7	339	2.4	5.2	2.2	0.9	46
Lantigua,Delvis	01	22	aa	CHW	4	0	7	0	43	47	23	3	18	30	4.79	1.50	27.3	340	3.8	6.3	1.7	0.6	54
	02	23	a/a	CHW	7	7	31	0	137	136	90	22	68	99	5.90	1.49	19.5	337	4.5	6.5	1.5	1.4	31
Larkin,Andy	01	27	aaa	COL	4	8	26	0	120	165	97	27	42	83	7.26	1.73	21.5	372	3.2	6.2	2.0	2.1	8
Larson,Ryan	02	23	a/a	CLE	2	3	33	8	37	48	12	5	7	27	2.92	1.49	4.9	337	1.7	6.6	3.9	1.2	77
Lavigne,Tim	02	24	aa	NYM	2	3	23	9	34	34	13	1	16	20	3.42	1.46	6.5	334	4.2	5.3	1.3	0.3	54
Lawrence,Brian	01	25	aaa	SD	1	3	9	1	45	46	21	3	17	34	4.24	1.41	21.7	326	3.4	6.7	2.0	0.6	66
Lawrence,Sean	01	31	aaa	ARI	1	6	43	0	58	61	27	3	22	62	4.24	1.43	5.9	329	3.4	9.6	2.8	0.5	103
Laxton,Brett	01	28	aaa	KC	3	7	45	2	96	112	55	9	35	58	5.14	1.53	9.5	344	3.3	5.4	1.6	0.8	40
	02	29	aaa	KC	9	13	29	0	156	229	115	16	52	78	6.63	1.80	25.4	381	3.0	4.5	1.5	0.9	19
Layfield,Scotty	02	26	aa	STL	6	4	58	24	65	69	22	6	26	50	3.05	1.46	4.9	334	3.6	6.9	1.9	0.8	59
Leach,Bryan	01	24	aa	BOS	2	2	23	1	40	52	27	7	12	31	6.16	1.58	7.8	351	2.6	7.1	2.7	1.7	43
Leek,Randy	01	24	a/a	DET	11	7	30	1	186	228	96	25	25	104	4.64	1.36	26.5	317	1.2	5.0	4.2	1.2	78
	02	25	aa	LA	7	5	15	0	95	122	32	7	12	44	3.03	1.41	27.5	325	1.1	4.2	3.7	0.7	76
Leese,Brandon	01	26	aaa	FLA	3	3	9	0	44	69	32	6	6	25	6.54	1.71	22.6	369	1.3	5.2	4.1	1.3	64
Lee,Cliff	02	24	a/a	CLE	5	3	11	0	59	58	38	10	35	40	5.78	1.57	24.2	350	5.3	6.1	1.1	1.5	20
Lee,Corey	01	27	a/a	TEX	5	12	27	0	128	158	112	21	59	84	7.88	1.69	21.9	367	4.1	5.9	1.4	1.5	16
	02	28	aaa	CHW	7	6	38	0	111	163	67	18	41	81	5.43	1.84	13.9	386	3.3	6.6	2.0	1.5	25
Lee,Dave	02	30	aaa	MIN	9	1	51	5	64	95	38	5	33	55	5.33	1.99	6.2	406	4.6	7.7	1.7	0.7	48
Lee,Derek	01	27	aa	MIL	7	11	28	0	162	251	99	14	48	78	5.49	1.84	27.6	387	2.7	4.3	1.6	0.8	22
	02	28	aa	MIL	5	10	34	0	127	203	69	9	56	71	4.89	2.04	18.5	411	4.0	5.0	1.3	0.6	22
Lee,Garrett	01	25	aa	ATL	4	9	32	0	92	137	69	16	20	50	6.74	1.70	13.3	368	2.0	4.9	2.5	1.5	24
	02	26	a/a	KC	8	2	37	2	92	120	42	9	21	35	4.11	1.53	11.1	344	2.1	3.4	1.7	0.9	22
Lee,Sang	01	31	aaa	BOS	3	5	43	4	53	68	44	12	18	32	7.55	1.61	5.6	356	3.0	5.5	1.8	2.1	3
Lehr,Chuck	01	24	aa	OAK	11	12	29	0	155	233	106	21	43	85	6.17	1.78	25.1	378	2.5	4.9	2.0	1.2	21
Lehr,Justin	02	25	aa	OAK	8	3	58	4	80	110	47	8	33	45	5.29	1.79	6.5	380	3.7	5.1	1.4	0.9	23
Levrault,Allen	01	24	aaa	MIL	2	1	5	0	30	25	10	1	8	26	2.98	1.09	24.2	272	2.4	7.7	3.3	0.3	117
	02	25	aaa	OAK	7	8	24	0	111	151	79	13	41	68	6.40	1.73	21.5	372	3.3	5.5	1.7	1.1	28
Lewis,Colby	01	22	aa	TEX	10	10	25	0	156	175	98	19	60	145	5.65	1.51	27.6	340	3.5	8.4	2.4	1.1	68
	02	23	aaa	TEX	5	6	20	0	106	110	48	4	26	86	4.07	1.28	22.3	305	2.2	7.3	3.3	0.3	106

Major League Equivalent Statistics

					Actual				Major League Equivalents														
PITCHER	Yr	Age	Lev	Org	W	L	G	Sv	IP	H	ER	HR	BB	K	ERA	Br/IP	BF/G	OOB	CTL	DOM	CMD	hr/9	BPV
Lewis,Derrick	01	25	aaa	ATL	4	4	12	0	60	60	39	2	38	44	5.89	1.63	22.8	358	5.7	6.5	1.1	0.3	58
	02	26	a/a	ATL	4	5	19	0	83	101	51	11	40	41	5.53	1.70	20.2	368	4.3	4.4	1.0	1.2	9
Lewis,Richie	01	36	aaa	NYM	9	4	24	1	122	125	63	13	67	62	4.65	1.58	22.9	351	5.0	4.5	0.9	0.9	22
Lidge,Brad	02	26	a/a	HOU	6	6	29	0	122	115	61	13	56	105	4.49	1.40	18.2	324	4.1	7.7	1.9	1.0	63
Lidle,Kevin	02	31	aa	DET	2	11	23	0	91	187	91	13	37	29	9.00	2.46	21.3	457	3.7	2.9	0.8	1.3	-33
Lincoln,Mike	01	27	aaa	PIT	5	4	18	0	91	102	40	10	27	59	3.97	1.41	22.0	326	2.6	5.8	2.2	1.0	50
Linebrink,Scott	01	25	aaa	HOU	7	6	50	8	72	63	36	5	25	61	4.55	1.22	6.0	295	3.2	7.7	2.4	0.6	87
Linton,Doug	01	36	aaa	NYM	7	3	12	0	75	91	36	9	12	54	4.28	1.36	26.8	317	1.4	6.5	4.7	1.1	100
	02	38	aaa	ATL	9	11	28	0	174	202	63	16	27	127	3.26	1.32	26.3	311	1.4	6.6	4.7	0.8	111
Lira,Felipe	01	29	aaa	PHI	5	5	44	6	69	98	29	5	13	44	3.72	1.61	7.1	355	1.7	5.7	3.3	0.7	72
	02	30	aaa	CIN	4	6	32	1	99	130	66	8	30	43	6.00	1.62	14.0	356	2.7	3.9	1.4	0.7	25
Lira,James	01	23	aa	HOU	0	1	27	2	39	38	18	3	10	22	4.04	1.24	6.0	298	2.4	5.1	2.2	0.7	60
	02	25	aa	HOU	3	4	28	3	43	44	21	7	19	23	4.40	1.47	6.7	334	4.0	4.8	1.2	1.5	13
Loewer,Carlton	01	28	aaa	SD	5	4	14	0	81	115	42	8	16	47	4.65	1.62	26.3	356	1.8	5.3	2.9	0.8	58
Lohse,Kyle	01	23	a/a	MIN	7	3	14	0	87	99	37	10	18	68	3.83	1.34	26.5	315	1.9	7.0	3.8	1.0	89
Loiselle,Rich	01	30	aaa	PIT	0	2	26	0	33	40	29	2	26	14	7.75	1.99	6.3	405	7.1	3.7	0.5	0.6	12
Lontayo,Alejandro	01	26	aa	ATL	3	5	9	0	50	79	42	4	30	34	7.58	2.17	28.4	427	5.4	6.1	1.1	0.8	22
Looney,Brian	02	33	a/a	BAL	1	2	19	0	35	40	23	7	17	17	5.88	1.62	8.4	357	4.3	4.3	1.0	1.8	-8
Looper,Aaron	02	26	aa	SEA	6	1	57	0	90	106	36	6	36	54	3.59	1.57	7.1	350	3.6	5.4	1.5	0.6	43
Lopez,Aquilino	01	21	aa	SEA	4	3	42	2	62	54	25	4	26	71	3.62	1.29	6.2	306	3.8	10.3	2.7	0.6	111
	02	27	aaa	SEA	4	4	34	5	109	106	37	6	28	84	3.05	1.23	13.3	296	2.3	6.9	3.0	0.5	95
Lopez,Javier	01	24	aa	ARI	1	0	22	0	40	73	38	6	14	17	8.53	2.16	9.2	425	3.1	3.8	1.2	1.4	-15
	02	25	aa	ARI	2	2	61	6	46	42	18	3	17	35	3.51	1.28	3.2	305	3.3	6.8	2.1	0.6	74
Lopez,Jose	01	26	aa	PIT	1	2	6	0	31	50	26	4	13	18	7.37	2.03	25.7	410	3.8	5.2	1.4	1.3	5
Lopez,Rodrigo	01	26	aaa	SD	2	2	11	0	52	51	22	7	15	30	3.84	1.26	19.8	301	2.6	5.1	2.0	1.2	40
Lorraine,Andrew	01	29	aaa	FLA	9	5	30	0	150	227	90	16	36	80	5.41	1.76	23.4	376	2.2	4.8	2.2	1.0	32
	02	30	aaa	MIL	7	11	25	0	165	210	83	20	48	67	4.53	1.56	29.6	349	2.6	3.7	1.4	1.1	13
Loux,Shane	01	22	aaa	DET	10	11	28	0	151	216	108	19	63	64	6.41	1.85	25.7	388	3.7	3.8	1.0	1.1	-1
	02	23	aaa	DET	11	10	26	0	158	227	103	10	36	79	5.86	1.66	27.9	363	2.0	4.5	2.2	0.6	45
Lovingier,Kevin	01	30	a/a	NYY	3	7	60	0	100	103	40	1	49	72	3.59	1.51	7.4	341	4.4	6.5	1.5	0.1	70
	02	31	a/a	NYY	0	4	40	1	48	78	32	1	39	25	6.00	2.44	6.4	455	7.3	4.7	0.6	0.2	19
Lowe,Benny	01	27	aa	CIN	3	2	26	0	38	40	27	1	29	26	6.24	1.80	6.9	381	6.8	6.1	0.9	0.3	49
Luebbers,Larry	01	32	a/a	CIN	9	9	29	0	175	228	91	13	40	86	4.68	1.53	26.9	344	2.1	4.4	2.2	0.7	45
	02	33	aaa	OAK	11	11	28	0	168	218	95	16	53	65	5.08	1.61	27.2	356	2.8	3.5	1.2	0.9	14
Lugo,Ruddy	02	22	aa	LA	3	1	11	1	33	40	19	3	14	20	5.17	1.63	13.7	358	3.8	5.4	1.4	0.8	35
Lukasiewicz,Mark	01	29	aaa	ANA	3	0	20	2	30	14	6	4	2	33	1.93	0.54	5.2	155	0.6	9.7	15.1	1.3	365
	02	30	aaa	ANA	3	2	35	0	43	55	23	7	18	37	4.81	1.70	5.7	368	3.8	7.7	2.1	1.5	40
Lundberg,Spike	01	24	a/a	TEX	8	8	31	6	122	176	87	15	24	62	6.38	1.64	18.0	359	1.7	4.6	2.6	1.1	37
	02	25	a/a	TEX	11	9	29	0	164	227	100	18	42	78	5.49	1.64	25.8	360	2.3	4.3	1.9	1.0	26
Lundquist,Dave	01	28	aaa	SD	4	7	50	7	63	70	27	6	22	50	3.83	1.45	5.5	331	3.1	7.2	2.3	0.9	64
	02	29	aaa	SD	1	4	30	21	32	34	25	7	16	24	7.03	1.56	4.8	349	4.5	6.8	1.5	2.0	15
Lyon,Brandon	01	22	a/a	TOR	10	3	20	0	127	145	65	17	19	83	4.61	1.29	26.7	307	1.3	5.9	4.4	1.2	90
	02	23	aaa	TOR	4	9	14	0	75	111	50	4	18	30	5.98	1.72	24.9	370	2.2	3.6	1.7	0.5	30
MacDougal,Mike	01	25	aaa	KC	8	8	28	0	144	163	89	15	71	91	5.56	1.62	23.4	357	4.4	5.7	1.3	0.9	32
	02	26	a/a	KC	4	6	16	0	70	78	53	6	82	34	6.79	2.28	22.8	438	10.5	4.4	0.4	0.8	12
MacRae,Scott	01	27	a/a	CIN	7	4	30	2	81	99	38	7	23	44	4.20	1.50	12.0	339	2.5	4.9	1.9	0.8	43
	02	28	aaa	CIN	4	2	49	2	72	86	31	5	27	42	3.86	1.57	6.6	349	3.4	5.2	1.6	0.6	42
Madson,Ryan	02	22	aa	PHI	16	4	26	0	171	171	73	12	57	121	3.84	1.33	28.0	313	3.0	6.4	2.1	0.6	68
Maduro,Calvin	01	27	aaa	BAL	2	7	12	0	67	76	41	12	24	41	5.51	1.49	24.6	338	3.3	5.5	1.7	1.6	21
Magrane,Jim	01	23	aa	TAM	8	12	29	0	182	210	87	21	61	106	4.28	1.49	27.7	338	3.0	5.2	1.7	1.0	36
	02	24	a/a	TAM	7	11	29	0	156	204	115	23	73	64	6.63	1.77	25.3	378	4.2	3.7	0.9	1.3	-6
Mahay,Ron	01	30	aaa	SD	4	3	50	14	63	51	23	8	17	50	3.33	1.07	5.0	269	2.4	7.2	3.0	1.1	85
	02	31	aaa	CHC	0	1	39	2	46	34	11	3	15	42	2.14	1.06	4.7	266	2.9	8.2	2.8	0.6	105
Mahomes,Pat	02	32	aaa	CHC	4	5	44	14	72	61	28	11	19	59	3.50	1.11	6.6	275	2.4	7.4	3.1	1.4	78
Mairena,Ozwaldo	01	26	a/a	FLA	7	4	53	3	74	94	47	7	23	56	5.66	1.59	6.3	352	2.8	6.8	2.4	0.8	61
Majewski,Gary	02	23	aa	CHW	5	3	57	3	74	74	30	4	36	69	3.64	1.48	5.7	337	4.4	8.4	1.9	0.5	80
Malaska,Mark	02	25	aa	TAM	4	5	12	1	70	100	38	4	31	39	4.87	1.87	28.0	390	4.0	5.0	1.3	0.5	30
Mallette,Brian	01	27	a/a	MIL	7	3	56	19	72	68	19	8	34	73	2.36	1.42	5.6	327	4.3	9.1	2.1	1.0	76
	02	28	aaa	MIL	3	2	45	25	45	49	20	5	19	41	3.99	1.51	4.4	341	3.8	8.2	2.2	1.0	65
Malone,Corwin	02	22	aa	CHW	10	7	22	0	124	140	88	8	95	82	6.38	1.89	27.2	393	6.9	5.9	0.9	0.6	36
Maness,Nick	01	23	aa	NYM	6	12	28	0	143	185	89	12	66	90	5.60	1.76	23.9	375	4.2	5.7	1.4	0.8	34
	02	24	a/a	NYM	7	9	28	1	149	151	84	15	80	102	5.07	1.55	23.8	347	4.8	6.2	1.3	0.9	40
Mangrum,Micah	02	25	aa	KC	1	2	23	1	38	61	22	2	10	14	5.21	1.87	7.9	390	2.4	3.3	1.4	0.5	19
Mangum,Mark	01	23	aa	MON	7	8	26	0	140	192	92	18	38	48	5.89	1.64	24.6	360	2.5	3.1	1.2	1.1	2
	02	24	aa	MON	7	5	18	2	80	101	46	14	25	32	5.18	1.58	20.0	350	2.8	3.6	1.3	1.6	-4
Manning,Charlie	02	24	aa	NYY	4	2	11	0	63	66	32	1	28	52	4.57	1.49	25.3	338	4.0	7.4	1.9	0.1	81
Manning,David	02	30	aaa	MIN	3	3	11	0	62	114	57	4	40	22	8.26	2.48	30.5	459	5.8	3.2	0.6	0.6	-9
Mann,Jim	01	27	aaa	HOU	6	3	53	27	68	64	26	9	19	68	3.41	1.21	5.3	293	2.5	9.0	3.7	1.2	100
	02	28	a/a	HOU	0	3	34	22	36	46	25	10	9	23	6.22	1.52	4.7	342	2.2	5.7	2.6	2.5	8
Manon,Julio	01	28	a/a	MON	5	7	25	1	136	167	71	25	61	79	4.67	1.68	25.0	365	4.0	5.2	1.3	1.6	5
	02	29	a/a	MON	13	7	34	2	144	170	82	16	60	92	5.12	1.60	19.1	353	3.7	5.7	1.5	1.0	34
Markwell,Diegomar	02	22	aa	TOR	13	9	28	1	168	192	93	23	57	87	4.98	1.48	26.4	337	3.1	4.7	1.5	1.2	22
Maroth,Mike	01	24	aaa	DET	7	10	24	0	131	177	79	10	45	54	5.42	1.69	25.2	367	3.1	3.7	1.2	0.7	19
	02	25	aaa	DET	8	1	11	0	73	62	28	6	21	46	3.45	1.14	27.0	280	2.6	5.7	2.2	0.7	68
Marquez,Rob	01	28	aaa	MON	6	0	34	0	60	73	28	6	14	21	4.18	1.45	7.7	331	2.1	3.2	1.5	1.0	19
	02	29	aaa	MIL	4	7	47	8	68	80	43	14	27	34	5.68	1.57	6.5	350	3.6	4.5	1.3	1.9	-4
Marrero,Darwin	02	22	aa	MON	6	5	19	0	105	135	56	18	20	46	4.80	1.47	24.3	336	1.7	3.9	2.3	1.5	20
Marr,Jason	01	26	aa	STL	3	4	51	0	61	94	52	7	31	22	7.61	2.05	6.0	412	4.6	3.2	0.7	1.0	-11
Marshall,Lee	01	25	a/a	MIN	5	5	50	13	72	89	25	4	26	42	3.15	1.61	6.5	355	3.3	5.2	1.6	0.5	44
	02	26	aaa	BAL	4	6	59	4	78	118	52	6	33	29	6.00	1.94	6.4	399	3.8	3.3	0.9	0.7	5
Marsonek,Sam	02	24	aa	NYY	5	8	19	0	100	136	74	7	37	64	6.65	1.73	24.5	372	3.3	5.7	1.7	0.6	43
Marte,Damaso	01	27	a/a	PIT	3	1	27	1	41	41	21	7	8	31	4.62	1.19	6.3	289	1.7	6.7	3.9	1.5	83

Major League Equivalent Statistics

PITCHER	Yr	Age	Lev	Org	Actual				Major League Equivalents														
					W	L	G	Sv	IP	H	ER	HR	BB	K	ERA	Br/IP	BF/G	OOB	CTL	DOM	CMD	hr/9	BPV
Martines,Jason	01	26	a/a	ARI	4	6	63	2	87	107	48	7	26	52	5.01	1.54	6.2	345	2.7	5.4	2.0	0.8	47
	02	27	aa	ARI	2	1	27	2	40	57	28	3	14	18	6.28	1.77	7.0	377	3.1	4.0	1.3	0.7	21
Martinez,Anastacio	02	22	aa	BOS	5	12	27	0	139	168	93	11	73	107	6.02	1.73	24.0	373	4.7	6.9	1.5	0.7	47
Martinez,Gustavo	02	27	a/a	SEA	3	6	22	0	102	126	53	8	52	61	4.67	1.74	21.6	374	4.6	5.4	1.2	0.7	31
Martinez,Jesus	01	28	aa	NYM	2	0	17	0	30	43	23	2	19	17	6.87	2.09	8.8	417	5.8	5.0	0.9	0.7	15
Martinez,Jose	01	27	a/a	TEX	6	6	25	0	100	128	69	17	42	50	6.20	1.70	18.5	368	3.8	4.5	1.2	1.5	0
Martinez,Luis	02	23	aa	MIL	8	8	29	1	109	134	80	7	65	91	6.61	1.83	17.8	385	5.4	7.5	1.4	0.6	53
Martinez,Willie	01	24	aaa	MIN	7	8	21	0	112	167	83	19	39	73	6.66	1.84	25.4	386	3.1	5.9	1.9	1.5	16
Martin,Chandler	02	29	a/a	COL	8	8	27	0	141	202	92	15	61	71	5.87	1.86	25.0	390	3.9	4.5	1.2	1.0	12
Masaoka,Onan	01	24	aaa	LA	8	5	45	6	88	100	50	10	31	71	5.10	1.49	8.6	337	3.2	7.2	2.3	1.0	60
Mateo,Julio	02	25	a/a	SEA	5	2	32	6	48	57	20	4	11	33	3.74	1.41	6.5	326	2.1	6.2	3.0	0.7	75
Matos,Josue	02	25	a/a	SEA	5	7	28	0	150	218	127	30	43	90	7.62	1.74	25.0	373	2.6	5.4	2.1	1.8	11
Mattes,Troy	01	26	aaa	MON	5	5	15	0	82	92	44	4	36	57	4.86	1.56	24.5	348	4.0	6.3	1.6	0.5	57
Matz,Brian	01	27	aa	MON	1	8	37	0	96	161	88	31	35	43	8.23	2.04	12.9	411	3.3	4.0	1.2	2.9	-56
Maurer,Dave	01	27	aaa	OAK	0	1	46	2	53	47	30	10	24	54	5.07	1.34	4.9	314	4.0	9.2	2.3	1.7	59
	02	28	aaa	CLE	5	1	36	5	68	63	32	8	27	60	4.23	1.32	8.0	312	3.6	7.9	2.2	1.1	69
Mayo,Blake	02	30	a/a	ARI	1	5	19	0	55	93	55	5	34	28	8.98	2.30	15.2	441	5.6	4.6	0.8	0.8	2
McAvoy,Jeff	02	26	a/a	MON	3	3	17	3	39	55	33	5	13	18	7.58	1.73	10.7	373	3.0	4.1	1.4	1.1	10
McClaskey,Tim	01	26	aa	FLA	2	2	37	2	50	51	23	7	12	41	4.19	1.26	5.7	302	2.2	7.3	3.3	1.2	81
McClellan,Matt	01	25	a/a	TOR	3	4	48	3	71	81	32	8	29	51	4.00	1.56	6.6	348	3.7	6.5	1.7	1.1	42
McClendon,Matt	01	24	a/a	ATL	0	7	12	0	57	71	64	7	39	35	10.11	1.93	23.0	398	6.2	5.5	0.9	1.1	14
McClung,Seth	02	22	aa	TAM	5	7	20	0	114	160	85	13	54	54	6.71	1.88	27.3	391	4.3	4.3	1.0	1.0	6
McConnell,Sam	01	26	aaa	PIT	7	10	26	0	134	177	102	20	42	83	6.85	1.63	23.5	359	2.8	5.6	2.0	1.4	27
	02	27	a/a	PHI	2	7	36	3	104	151	57	16	41	54	4.92	1.84	13.8	387	3.5	4.7	1.3	1.4	3
McCrotty,Will	02	23	aa	LA	1	4	43	6	52	44	19	3	32	49	3.28	1.46	5.3	333	5.5	8.4	1.5	0.5	78
McDade,Neal	01	25	a/a	PIT	3	6	27	0	88	119	48	4	35	51	4.95	1.74	15.2	374	3.5	5.2	1.5	0.4	41
	02	26	aa	PIT	8	3	49	3	78	111	47	13	17	38	5.42	1.64	7.3	359	2.0	4.4	2.2	1.5	18
McDill,Allen	01	30	aaa	BOS	3	3	47	2	71	80	38	8	21	54	4.79	1.42	6.6	328	2.7	6.8	2.6	1.0	65
McDonald,Jon	01	24	aa	MIN	8	3	17	0	96	119	60	10	40	56	5.59	1.65	25.9	361	3.8	5.3	1.4	1.0	28
	02	25	aa	MIN	3	8	21	0	72	94	64	4	52	23	7.99	2.02	17.0	410	6.5	2.9	0.4	0.5	5
McKnight,Tony	01	24	aaa	HOU	9	5	18	0	92	123	64	13	25	52	6.25	1.61	23.2	355	2.4	5.1	2.1	1.3	28
	02	25	aaa	PIT	11	14	30	0	175	229	125	22	42	102	6.42	1.55	26.1	346	2.2	5.2	2.4	1.1	42
McLeary,Marty	01	27	a/a	BOS	10	8	53	2	85	112	43	7	51	46	4.58	1.92	7.8	396	5.4	4.8	0.9	0.7	20
	02	28	a/a	BOS	1	3	29	0	52	83	52	7	36	22	8.98	2.28	9.3	439	6.2	3.8	0.6	1.2	-16
McNichol,Brian	01	27	a/a	CIN	8	1	47	0	54	56	11	1	16	42	1.91	1.34	4.9	314	2.7	6.9	2.6	0.2	93
Meacham,Rusty	01	34	aaa	TAM	2	1	27	15	31	21	4	2	5	25	1.22	0.85	4.3	225	1.5	7.2	4.7	0.6	141
Meadows,Brian	01	26	aaa	KC	6	5	18	0	105	164	87	23	19	60	7.45	1.74	27.2	374	1.6	5.2	3.1	2.0	23
	02	27	aaa	PIT	9	8	23	0	126	156	75	15	26	81	5.35	1.44	23.9	331	1.9	5.8	3.1	1.1	63
Mears,Chris	02	25	aa	SEA	6	9	30	0	143	176	71	19	42	84	4.47	1.52	21.2	343	2.6	5.3	2.0	1.2	34
Meche,Gil	02	24	aa	SEA	4	6	26	0	65	86	66	9	35	46	9.14	1.86	12.4	389	4.8	6.4	1.3	1.2	21
Medina,Carlos	01	24	aa	NYM	0	1	24	1	33	42	16	2	14	13	4.31	1.69	6.3	367	3.7	3.6	1.0	0.6	19
Medina,Rafael	01	27	aaa	STL	3	1	27	0	38	34	19	7	16	33	4.37	1.32	6.0	312	3.9	7.8	2.0	1.7	46
Mendoza,Geronimo	01	24	a/a	CHW	10	12	29	0	166	224	123	32	61	94	6.66	1.71	26.6	370	3.3	5.1	1.5	1.7	3
	02	23	aaa	CHW	1	9	11	0	53	77	61	13	25	35	10.36	1.92	23.3	397	4.2	5.9	1.4	2.2	-13
Mendoza,Hatuey	02	25	aa	ANA	3	10	29	0	90	138	73	14	38	36	7.29	1.95	15.1	401	3.8	3.6	0.9	1.4	-14
Mendoza,Marcos	02	22	aa	CLE	2	5	21	0	37	36	13	3	25	23	3.15	1.64	8.1	360	6.1	5.6	0.9	0.7	36
Mendoza,Mario	02	24	a/a	ANA	0	5	13	1	54	76	32	5	19	32	5.32	1.76	19.5	376	3.2	5.3	1.7	0.8	32
Mercado,Hector	02	28	aaa	PHI	3	1	26	3	33	27	8	2	14	36	2.18	1.24	5.3	298	3.8	9.8	2.6	0.5	108
Meyers,Mike	01	24	aaa	CHC	7	4	25	0	147	140	58	8	62	106	3.55	1.37	25.3	320	3.8	6.5	1.7	0.5	66
Meyer,Jake	01	27	a/a	SEA	1	4	34	1	52	72	46	8	28	43	7.88	1.92	7.4	397	4.8	7.5	1.6	1.3	28
	02	28	a/a	SEA	2	1	29	0	50	54	29	6	29	31	5.21	1.66	7.9	362	5.2	5.6	1.1	1.1	25
Miadich,Bart	01	26	aaa	ANA	4	4	55	27	59	44	18	4	27	62	2.77	1.22	4.4	294	4.2	9.5	2.3	0.6	101
	02	27	aaa	ANA	4	3	59	14	80	67	37	5	62	77	4.15	1.61	6.2	355	7.0	8.6	1.2	0.6	72
Michalak,Chris	02	32	aaa	BOS	5	9	18	0	94	153	79	17	34	43	7.55	1.99	25.7	405	3.2	4.1	1.3	1.6	-14
Middlebrook,Jason	01	26	a/a	SD	10	4	25	0	143	152	52	7	37	85	3.29	1.32	24.3	311	2.3	5.3	2.3	0.4	69
	02	27	aaa	NYM	4	6	15	0	60	66	38	7	15	44	5.69	1.35	17.1	316	2.2	6.6	2.9	1.0	70
Mieses,Jose	01	22	a/a	MIL	0	3	8	0	38	49	18	7	10	44	4.26	1.52	21.2	342	2.2	10.4	4.6	1.6	107
Miller,Benji	01	25	aa	SF	1	6	37	2	66	78	40	8	37	29	5.45	1.73	8.3	373	5.0	3.9	0.8	1.1	6
Miller,Greg	01	22	aa	HOU	5	3	14	0	55	44	25	4	37	32	4.08	1.47	17.3	335	6.0	5.2	0.9	0.7	42
	02	23	aa	HOU	3	6	14	0	68	91	47	7	21	43	6.21	1.64	22.2	360	2.8	5.7	2.0	0.9	42
Miller,Justin	01	24	aaa	OAK	7	10	29	0	165	187	93	25	61	115	5.07	1.50	25.2	340	3.3	6.3	1.9	1.4	35
	02	25	aaa	TOR	3	2	8	0	44	38	9	0	16	25	1.83	1.22	22.9	295	3.3	5.1	1.6	0.0	73
Miller,Matt	01	30	aaa	SD	1	7	44	17	44	53	22	1	15	32	4.48	1.54	4.5	346	3.1	6.5	2.1	0.2	73
	02	31	aaa	OAK	3	7	54	6	71	92	37	4	28	49	4.69	1.69	6.1	367	3.5	6.2	1.8	0.5	52
Miller,Matt	01	27	aaa	DET	1	2	50	4	62	71	24	3	17	40	3.50	1.40	5.4	325	2.4	5.8	2.4	0.5	70
Miller,Travis	02	30	aaa	CLE	1	3	40	1	55	84	37	5	21	29	6.03	1.90	6.7	394	3.4	4.7	1.4	0.8	19
Miller,Trever	01	28	aaa	BOS	3	11	33	0	116	177	90	17	37	72	7.01	1.84	16.7	387	2.8	5.6	2.0	1.3	21
	02	29	aaa	CIN	9	5	65	0	82	90	35	7	23	61	3.84	1.38	5.4	321	2.5	6.7	2.7	0.8	73
Mills,Ryan	01	24	aa	MIN	2	5	8	0	40	62	48	4	17	24	10.84	1.96	24.5	402	3.8	5.3	1.4	0.9	19
	02	25	aa	MIN	3	11	26	0	105	151	88	12	79	52	7.53	2.19	20.7	428	6.8	4.4	0.7	1.0	-1
Milo,Tony	01	23	aa	ANA	1	2	19	1	30	33	22	6	16	29	6.47	1.64	7.2	360	4.9	8.7	1.8	1.8	34
	02	24	aa	ANA	2	4	15	0	44	69	51	7	25	29	10.41	2.13	14.9	422	5.1	5.9	1.2	1.4	2
Minix,Travis	02	25	aa	TAM	5	7	38	0	68	90	32	3	33	37	4.24	1.81	8.5	383	4.4	4.9	1.1	0.4	34
Mintz,Steve	01	33	aaa	ANA	1	2	13	0	37	58	28	5	11	17	6.89	1.84	13.6	387	2.6	4.1	1.6	1.3	6
Mitchell,Scott	01	29	a/a	MON	1	3	15	0	41	56	28	7	20	17	6.18	1.86	13.1	389	4.4	3.7	0.9	1.5	-15
Mobley,Kevin	01	27	aa	TEX	3	0	36	0	75	95	47	9	36	45	5.66	1.75	9.7	374	4.3	5.4	1.3	1.1	20
Mohler,Mike	01	33	aaa	ARI	5	0	40	3	45	61	19	4	14	39	3.78	1.66	5.2	362	2.7	7.8	2.8	0.8	73
	02	34	aaa	BAL	1	2	34	1	49	61	19	2	16	35	3.49	1.57	6.5	350	2.9	6.4	2.2	0.4	69
Molina,Gabe	01	26	aaa	FLA	5	9	40	0	107	129	66	11	37	88	5.55	1.55	12.0	347	3.1	7.4	2.4	1.0	62
	02	27	aaa	STL	5	4	56	12	71	73	22	8	25	47	2.78	1.38	5.5	321	3.2	5.9	1.9	1.0	48
Montalbano,Greg	01	24	aa	BOS	3	3	10	0	48	62	33	8	15	35	6.12	1.60	21.7	354	2.8	6.6	2.4	1.6	36
Montane,Ivan	01	28	a/a	NYM	3	6	36	2	70	94	39	6	41	42	4.98	1.93	9.4	398	5.3	5.3	1.0	0.8	23

Major League Equivalent Statistics

					Actual				Major League Equivalents														
PITCHER	Yr	Age	Lev	Org	W	L	G	Sv	IP	H	ER	HR	BB	K	ERA	Br/IP	BF/G	OOB	CTL	DOM	CMD	hr/9	BPV
Montero,Agustin	02	25	aa	LA	1	3	31	0	41	49	26	7	33	20	5.71	2.00	6.5	407	7.2	4.4	0.6	1.5	-10
Montgomery,Matt	02	26	aa	PIT	3	0	44	3	66	82	43	3	28	37	5.85	1.66	6.9	363	3.8	5.0	1.3	0.4	41
Moody,Eric	01	31	aaa	PIT	5	6	42	0	112	137	53	17	16	39	4.28	1.36	11.4	317	1.2	3.1	2.5	1.3	27
Moore,Trey	01	29	aaa	ATL	9	8	26	0	163	181	86	11	46	98	4.73	1.40	27.1	323	2.5	5.4	2.1	0.6	59
Moraga,David	01	26	a/a	COL	4	6	26	0	96	142	84	29	33	53	7.90	1.82	17.6	385	3.1	5.0	1.6	2.7	-30
Moreno,Orber	01	24	a/a	KC	1	1	22	4	30	26	13	4	9	28	3.99	1.16	5.6	284	2.8	8.4	3.0	1.2	87
Moseley,Dustin	02	21	aa	CIN	5	6	13	0	80	96	40	5	32	46	4.49	1.60	27.9	353	3.6	5.2	1.4	0.6	41
Moskau,Ryan	01	24	aa	FLA	3	2	39	2	103	131	57	15	34	65	4.96	1.59	11.9	353	2.9	5.6	1.9	1.3	30
Moss,Damian	01	25	a/a	ATL	5	5	20	0	98	100	46	15	40	89	4.25	1.43	21.3	328	3.7	8.2	2.2	1.4	56
Mota,Danny	01	26	aaa	LA	4	5	46	3	59	71	40	7	30	42	6.13	1.71	5.9	370	4.6	6.4	1.4	1.1	31
Mota,Guillermo	02	29	aaa	LA	1	3	20	1	36	36	12	1	8	30	2.98	1.22	7.5	294	2.0	7.5	3.8	0.2	120
Mounce,Tony	02	28	a/a	TEX	5	4	13	0	62	91	43	10	18	37	6.22	1.75	22.4	375	2.6	5.4	2.1	1.4	20
Mullen,Scott	01	27	aaa	KC	5	4	48	5	53	77	47	9	22	31	8.05	1.87	5.3	390	3.7	5.3	1.4	1.6	3
	02	28	aaa	KC	1	2	19	0	31	39	12	0	9	16	3.48	1.55	7.3	347	2.6	4.6	1.8	0.0	60
Munoz,Arnaldo	02	20	aa	CHW	6	0	51	6	72	71	28	8	30	76	3.50	1.40	6.1	324	3.7	9.5	2.5	1.0	85
Munoz,Bobby	01	34	aaa	MON	4	6	19	0	110	123	58	6	43	52	4.74	1.51	25.7	341	3.5	4.3	1.2	0.5	35
	02	35	aaa	NYM	1	4	18	0	47	94	63	7	32	36	12.06	2.68	14.6	479	6.1	6.9	1.1	1.3	-2
Munro,Pete	01	26	aaa	TEX	8	6	33	0	88	107	60	15	42	63	6.10	1.69	12.3	367	4.3	6.4	1.5	1.6	19
	02	27	aaa	HOU	7	1	19	0	94	87	37	4	17	60	3.54	1.11	19.9	275	1.6	5.7	3.5	0.4	104
Murray,Dan	01	28	aaa	KC	3	3	48	8	98	125	54	12	29	55	4.93	1.58	9.2	351	2.7	5.1	1.9	1.1	32
	02	29	aaa	TEX	5	7	39	2	109	156	91	16	52	43	7.50	1.90	13.5	395	4.3	3.5	0.8	1.3	-12
Murray,Heath	01	28	aaa	DET	1	1	11	1	36	27	10	4	2	34	2.42	0.81	12.2	216	0.5	8.6	16.0	1.1	370
Myers,Aaron	01	25	aa	MIL	3	4	34	2	70	71	41	6	46	53	5.29	1.67	9.4	363	5.9	6.8	1.2	0.7	47
Myers,Brett	01	21	aa	PHI	13	4	26	0	156	176	79	21	46	118	4.56	1.42	26.1	328	2.7	6.8	2.6	1.2	58
	02	22	aaa	PHI	9	6	19	0	128	131	59	10	20	93	4.15	1.18	27.6	288	1.4	6.5	4.7	0.7	119
Myers,Rodney	02	33	aaa	SD	5	2	42	4	48	56	24	2	14	29	4.48	1.45	5.0	332	2.6	5.4	2.1	0.4	63
Myette,Aaron	01	24	a/a	TEX	5	3	13	0	76	80	38	6	31	68	4.52	1.47	25.6	334	3.7	8.0	2.2	0.7	74
	02	25	aaa	TEX	7	4	16	0	106	95	41	5	41	91	3.48	1.28	27.8	305	3.5	7.7	2.2	0.4	88
Nagy,Charles	01	34	aaa	CLE	5	1	6	0	38	49	15	0	9	14	3.47	1.54	28.4	346	2.2	3.4	1.5	0.0	45
	02	35	aaa	CLE	1	2	5	0	36	48	19	8	4	15	4.72	1.44	31.5	330	1.0	3.7	3.8	2.0	34
Nakamura,Micheal	01	25	aa	MIN	5	1	48	5	86	109	30	4	30	84	3.14	1.61	8.1	356	3.1	8.7	2.8	0.5	92
	02	26	aaa	MIN	4	3	46	2	87	94	51	7	22	66	5.27	1.33	8.1	313	2.3	6.8	3.0	0.7	83
Nance,Shane	01	24	aa	LA	7	0	28	1	45	38	11	5	19	36	2.10	1.26	6.7	301	3.8	7.2	1.9	1.1	62
	02	25	aaa	MIL	14	3	46	1	75	85	36	6	33	53	4.32	1.57	7.3	350	4.0	6.4	1.6	0.7	49
Nannini,Mike	02	22	aa	HOU	7	10	29	0	141	173	110	17	65	103	7.02	1.69	22.4	366	4.1	6.6	1.6	1.1	36
Natale,Mike	02	23	aa	KC	4	3	24	0	48	48	39	7	46	42	7.30	1.95	9.8	401	8.6	7.9	0.9	1.3	31
Nathan,Joe	01	27	a/a	SF	3	11	31	0	109	161	103	24	71	41	8.52	2.13	17.8	421	5.9	3.3	0.6	2.0	-41
	02	28	aaa	SF	6	12	31	0	146	196	111	18	75	95	6.84	1.85	22.5	388	4.6	5.9	1.3	1.1	20
Nation,Joey	01	23	aaa	CHC	3	2	14	0	44	42	16	5	13	41	3.26	1.24	13.1	299	2.6	8.3	3.2	1.0	92
Navarro,Jason	01	26	aa	STL	1	2	52	0	61	89	55	16	46	39	8.11	2.20	6.0	429	6.8	5.8	0.9	2.4	-30
Neal,Blaine	01	24	aa	FLA	2	3	54	21	53	54	20	1	24	38	3.32	1.46	4.3	333	4.0	6.4	1.6	0.2	70
	02	25	aaa	FLA	3	1	29	11	31	27	10	2	14	23	2.90	1.32	4.5	312	4.1	6.7	1.6	0.6	66
Nelson,Joe	01	27	aaa	ATL	1	2	29	8	39	28	6	1	14	34	1.42	1.08	5.4	270	3.3	7.8	2.4	0.2	105
Neugebauer,Nick	01	21	a/a	MIL	7	7	25	0	131	114	53	8	57	159	3.66	1.31	22.2	309	3.9	10.9	2.8	0.5	117
Neu,Mike	02	25	a/a	CIN	3	3	61	23	67	65	26	4	26	69	3.49	1.36	4.7	317	3.5	9.3	2.7	0.5	100
Nichting,Chris	01	35	aaa	CIN	2	1	27	17	33	29	15	6	11	38	4.01	1.21	5.1	293	2.9	10.3	3.6	1.7	95
	02	36	aaa	COL	1	4	22	1	32	63	45	11	21	18	12.66	2.63	8.1	473	5.9	5.1	0.9	3.1	-70
Nickle,Doug	01	27	aaa	PHI	9	3	47	7	85	80	23	2	45	52	2.45	1.47	8.0	335	4.8	5.5	1.2	0.2	57
	02	28	aaa	STL	6	6	48	10	76	88	37	9	25	40	4.38	1.48	7.0	337	3.0	4.7	1.6	1.1	28
Nickoli,Michael	02	23	aa	ANA	3	10	17	0	82	134	69	11	45	27	7.56	2.18	24.6	427	4.9	3.0	0.6	1.2	-23
Nina,Elvin	01	26	aaa	ANA	10	11	29	0	158	215	107	20	74	86	6.10	1.83	25.9	385	4.2	4.9	1.2	1.2	11
	02	27	aaa	ANA	5	9	26	0	108	129	63	16	48	56	5.24	1.64	19.0	359	4.0	4.7	1.2	1.3	10
Nitkowski,C.J.	02	30	aaa	TEX	3	5	49	2	47	64	31	4	21	35	5.92	1.80	4.5	382	4.0	6.7	1.7	0.8	44
Nomura,Takahito	02	34	aaa	MIL	1	2	31	0	33	48	29	5	12	19	7.91	1.82	5.0	384	3.3	5.2	1.6	1.4	12
Norris,Ben	01	24	aa	ARI	1	6	16	0	58	116	53	1	29	20	8.14	2.50	19.7	461	4.5	3.2	0.7	0.2	3
Norton,Phil	01	26	aaa	CHC	6	3	46	2	73	72	24	3	40	63	2.98	1.53	7.1	344	5.0	7.8	1.6	0.4	73
Noyce,Dave	01	25	aa	CHC	3	8	50	1	96	113	49	8	49	71	4.64	1.69	8.8	366	4.6	6.7	1.4	0.8	44
	02	26	aa	CHC	3	2	53	0	76	82	31	9	41	43	3.67	1.62	6.5	357	4.9	5.1	1.0	1.1	22
Nunez,Franklin	01	25	aa	PHI	8	7	39	3	110	127	67	9	58	97	5.51	1.68	13.0	366	4.7	7.9	1.7	0.8	58
O'Brien,Matt	02	26	aa	OAK	1	3	54	2	63	59	27	8	22	38	3.85	1.28	4.9	305	3.1	5.4	1.7	1.1	41
O'Connor,Brian	01	25	aaa	PIT	6	9	37	1	111	136	86	15	59	63	6.96	1.75	14.0	375	4.8	5.1	1.1	1.2	13
	02	26	a/a	PIT	5	8	28	0	90	112	65	6	56	47	6.49	1.86	15.4	390	5.6	4.7	0.8	0.6	23
Obermueller,Wes	02	26	aa	KC	9	5	17	0	105	131	51	8	44	49	4.36	1.66	28.4	363	3.8	4.2	1.1	0.7	23
Ochoa,Pablo	01	26	aaa	NYM	3	4	19	0	73	84	38	8	29	41	4.72	1.55	17.2	346	3.6	5.0	1.4	1.0	28
Ohka,Tomo	01	26	aaa	BOS	2	5	8	0	42	65	33	5	9	27	7.14	1.76	24.5	375	1.9	5.7	2.9	1.1	50
Ohman,Will	01	24	aaa	CHC	5	2	40	4	51	55	25	8	18	57	4.41	1.43	5.5	329	3.2	10.1	3.2	1.4	86
Ohme,Kevin	02	31	aaa	STL	4	3	56	2	87	124	57	13	22	48	5.88	1.67	7.2	364	2.3	5.0	2.2	1.3	25
Olsen,Kevin	01	25	aa	FLA	10	3	26	0	154	164	69	14	26	113	4.02	1.23	24.6	297	1.5	6.6	4.4	0.8	108
	02	26	aaa	FLA	2	5	8	0	49	47	21	5	13	21	3.86	1.22	25.4	295	2.4	3.9	1.6	0.9	35
Ontiveros,Steve	01	41	aaa	OAK	9	8	23	0	126	142	63	14	37	75	4.51	1.42	23.8	327	2.6	5.4	2.0	1.0	45
Oquist,Mike	01	33	aaa	MIN	5	8	21	0	110	158	64	14	31	62	5.24	1.71	24.3	369	2.5	5.0	2.0	1.1	28
Orloski,Joe	02	23	aa	TOR	6	5	54	4	60	79	41	4	29	38	6.15	1.80	5.2	381	4.4	5.7	1.3	0.6	37
Ortiz,Omar	02	25	aa	FLA	4	8	33	3	103	130	76	18	77	59	6.63	2.01	15.4	407	6.7	5.1	0.8	1.6	-5
Osting,Jimmy	01	25	a/a	SD	11	8	24	0	128	149	80	12	59	68	5.65	1.63	24.3	358	4.1	4.8	1.2	0.9	25
	02	26	aaa	MIL	5	7	22	0	126	139	67	9	39	95	4.78	1.41	24.8	326	2.8	6.8	2.4	0.6	73
Oswalt,Roy	01	24	aaa	HOU	2	3	5	0	31	38	20	5	6	29	5.81	1.42	26.9	327	1.7	8.4	4.8	1.5	104
Outlaw,Mark	01	25	aa	PHI	4	6	49	7	64	88	45	5	32	51	6.35	1.87	6.3	390	4.4	7.2	1.6	0.7	46
	02	26	aa	PHI	6	2	41	2	50	57	33	3	40	24	5.92	1.93	5.9	398	7.2	4.3	0.6	0.5	21
Ozias,Todd	01	25	aa	TEX	3	3	39	0	68	80	38	11	32	34	4.99	1.65	8.0	361	4.3	4.5	1.1	1.5	3
	02	26	aa	PHI	3	1	46	3	59	74	28	3	25	48	4.26	1.68	5.9	365	3.8	7.3	1.9	0.5	65
Ozuna,Francisco	02	21	aa	TOR	2	2	44	0	70	81	41	12	18	30	5.27	1.41	6.9	326	2.3	3.9	1.7	1.5	10
Pacheco,Alex	01	28	aa	NYY	5	4	43	26	50	39	13	4	21	46	2.25	1.20	4.8	291	3.8	8.2	2.1	0.7	87

Major League Equivalent Statistics

PITCHER	Yr	Age	Lev	Org	Actual W	L	G	Sv	Major League Equivalents IP	H	ER	HR	BB	K	ERA	Br/IP	BF/G	OOB	CTL	DOM	CMD	hr/9	BPV
Pacheco,Delvis	01	23	aaa	ATL	1	4	22	0	58	92	44	5	25	45	6.83	2.02	13.0	409	3.9	7.0	1.8	0.8	41
Padilla,Juan	02	26	aa	MIN	3	5	54	29	65	89	33	2	21	40	4.56	1.69	5.6	367	2.9	5.5	1.9	0.3	56
Padilla,Vicente	01	24	aaa	PHI	7	0	16	0	81	78	30	9	13	68	3.33	1.12	20.5	277	1.4	7.5	5.2	1.0	131
Palki,Jeromy	01	25	aa	MIN	3	1	31	1	60	72	33	1	28	45	4.99	1.66	8.9	363	4.2	6.7	1.6	0.2	66
	02	26	a/a	MIN	6	6	56	3	91	119	48	11	37	77	4.74	1.71	7.5	369	3.7	7.6	2.1	1.1	50
Palma,Rick	01	22	aa	CHC	4	9	57	0	70	66	26	6	24	60	3.33	1.28	5.2	305	3.1	7.7	2.5	0.8	82
	02	23	a/a	CHC	2	3	55	0	71	72	16	3	20	60	2.03	1.30	5.4	307	2.5	7.6	3.0	0.4	101
Paradis,Mike	01	23	aa	BAL	8	13	27	0	137	188	93	15	65	94	6.09	1.84	24.2	387	4.3	6.2	1.4	1.0	28
	02	24	aa	BAL	8	13	27	0	151	204	116	13	69	76	6.90	1.81	26.5	382	4.1	4.5	1.1	0.8	19
Parker,Matt	02	24	aa	MIL	4	4	40	2	77	89	43	6	35	66	5.02	1.61	8.7	355	4.1	7.7	1.9	0.7	63
Paronto,Chad	01	26	aaa	BAL	3	3	33	1	43	54	29	6	26	34	6.03	1.84	6.2	387	5.4	7.1	1.3	1.3	27
Parque,Jim	02	27	aaa	CHW	7	9	20	0	105	162	104	30	41	56	8.90	1.93	25.5	398	3.5	4.8	1.4	2.6	-34
Parra,Christian	01	24	aa	ATL	3	8	18	0	89	107	74	11	60	70	7.50	1.87	23.7	391	6.0	7.1	1.2	1.1	29
Parrish,John	01	24	aaa	BAL	7	7	26	0	133	136	67	13	53	113	4.53	1.42	22.2	327	3.6	7.6	2.1	0.9	67
Parrish,Wade	01	24	aa	LA	5	1	20	0	33	31	10	1	11	16	2.81	1.28	6.9	305	3.1	4.5	1.5	0.3	55
	02	25	a/a	CHW	9	9	28	0	160	224	101	20	63	64	5.67	1.79	27.0	380	3.5	3.6	1.0	1.1	-1
Parrott,Rhett	02	23	aa	STL	4	1	9	0	66	59	24	3	12	34	3.27	1.08	29.3	269	1.6	4.6	2.8	0.4	83
Patterson,John	01	24	a/a	ARI	3	9	18	0	93	123	62	11	38	51	6.00	1.73	24.0	372	3.7	4.9	1.3	1.1	19
	02	25	aaa	ARI	10	5	19	0	112	128	59	14	41	87	4.73	1.51	26.1	340	3.3	7.0	2.1	1.1	52
Pautz,Brad	02	26	aa	PHI	4	6	43	3	79	89	36	9	31	49	4.10	1.52	8.2	342	3.5	5.6	1.6	1.0	35
Pavlas,Dave	01	39	aaa	PIT	1	4	41	6	41	39	14	4	8	32	3.00	1.15	4.1	283	1.8	7.1	3.8	0.9	101
Pavlovich,Tony	01	27	aa	PIT	0	3	31	12	42	54	23	0	17	18	4.89	1.69	6.3	366	3.6	3.9	1.1	0.0	40
Payne,Jerrod	02	25	a/a	TOR	2	0	27	0	35	34	18	3	15	15	4.60	1.39	5.6	323	3.8	3.8	1.0	0.8	26
Pearce,Josh	01	24	a/a	STL	10	12	28	0	185	216	102	27	49	119	4.97	1.44	28.8	330	2.4	5.8	2.4	1.3	44
Pearsall,J.J.	01	28	aa	TEX	6	4	43	10	58	79	33	11	21	42	5.04	1.72	6.3	371	3.3	6.5	2.0	1.7	19
	02	29	a/a	FLA	3	3	45	1	63	76	35	6	34	47	4.99	1.74	6.5	374	4.8	6.7	1.4	0.9	40
Pearson,Jason	01	26	aa	SD	5	5	54	1	86	112	54	6	36	49	5.69	1.72	7.4	370	3.7	5.1	1.4	0.6	35
	02	27	aaa	SF	3	0	57	0	66	69	24	7	25	38	3.27	1.42	5.0	328	3.4	5.2	1.5	1.0	37
Pearson,Terry	01	30	aa	DET	4	4	59	23	61	97	31	1	19	40	4.52	1.90	5.0	394	2.7	5.9	2.1	0.2	58
	02	31	a/a	DET	3	8	55	6	61	108	45	3	23	30	6.62	2.14	5.6	423	3.4	4.4	1.3	0.4	20
Peavy,Jake	02	21	aa	SD	4	5	14	0	80	73	30	4	31	75	3.37	1.30	24.1	308	3.5	8.4	2.4	0.4	95
Peguero,Darwin	02	24	aa	HOU	3	2	54	1	60	77	37	7	30	34	5.54	1.78	5.2	379	4.5	5.1	1.1	1.0	17
Pember,David	02	24	aa	MIL	10	6	27	0	156	194	74	17	56	90	4.27	1.60	26.1	354	3.2	5.2	1.6	1.0	31
Pena,Jesus	01	27	a/a	BOS	5	9	40	1	104	179	100	18	51	58	8.65	2.21	13.3	431	4.4	5.0	1.1	1.5	-12
	02	28	a/a	TEX	3	9	46	2	79	128	76	11	56	55	8.66	2.33	9.0	444	6.4	6.3	1.0	1.3	4
Pena,Juan	01	22	aa	OAK	11	9	27	0	148	176	72	13	44	91	4.38	1.49	24.2	337	2.7	5.5	2.1	0.8	50
	02	25	aaa	BOS	4	11	17	0	82	97	61	21	37	50	6.68	1.63	22.0	358	4.1	5.5	1.4	2.3	-10
Penney,Mike	01	25	a/a	MIL	8	6	43	8	106	143	67	14	45	54	5.69	1.78	11.6	379	3.9	4.6	1.2	1.2	8
	02	26	aa	MIL	7	4	37	3	57	69	21	6	24	29	3.30	1.63	7.0	358	3.8	4.6	1.2	0.9	21
Perez,Beltran	02	21	aa	ARI	3	8	20	0	97	121	65	10	30	68	6.03	1.56	21.7	348	2.8	6.3	2.3	0.9	53
Perez,Carlos	01	31	aaa	LA	2	1	6	0	30	48	23	3	11	15	6.98	1.96	24.5	401	3.3	4.6	1.4	1.0	11
Perez,Frank	02	24	aa	PHI	2	0	28	5	45	53	21	6	13	26	4.18	1.46	7.1	333	2.6	5.2	2.0	1.2	35
	02	27	aa	DET	0	4	20	1	33	46	23	4	17	25	6.27	1.91	8.0	395	4.6	6.8	1.5	1.1	29
Perez,Yorkis	02	35	aaa	BAL	1	1	28	0	40	49	21	4	21	35	4.71	1.75	6.7	374	4.7	7.9	1.7	0.9	51
Perisho,Matt	01	26	aaa	DET	2	3	25	9	42	48	9	3	10	23	1.99	1.40	7.3	324	2.2	5.0	2.3	0.7	56
	02	27	aaa	DET	4	4	51	1	66	76	23	4	19	38	3.14	1.44	5.6	330	2.6	5.2	2.0	0.5	55
Persails,Mark	01	26	a/a	DET	3	7	22	0	88	138	79	9	37	32	8.07	1.99	19.6	405	3.8	3.3	0.9	1.0	-6
Peterson,Kyle	01	26	aaa	MIL	2	10	21	0	115	162	85	18	25	62	6.64	1.62	24.9	358	2.0	4.9	2.5	1.4	28
Peters,Chris	01	27	aaa	CIN	5	5	17	0	84	123	63	11	44	39	6.74	1.99	24.3	405	4.7	4.2	0.9	1.2	-5
	02	31	aa	DET	3	3	43	0	59	109	49	4	31	36	7.47	2.37	7.3	448	4.7	5.5	1.2	0.6	17
Pettyjohn,Adam	01	24	aaa	DET	5	8	17	0	107	120	48	8	23	66	4.03	1.34	26.8	314	1.9	5.5	2.9	0.7	73
Phelps,Tommy	01	28	a/a	DET	4	3	44	3	92	138	49	5	28	63	4.83	1.80	9.9	381	2.7	6.1	2.3	0.4	58
	02	29	aaa	FLA	4	2	51	2	74	83	27	6	20	51	3.28	1.39	6.3	323	2.4	6.2	2.6	0.7	68
Phelps,Travis	02	25	aaa	TAM	3	2	27	8	31	34	19	2	14	29	5.52	1.55	5.1	347	4.1	8.4	2.1	0.6	77
Phillips,Jason	01	28	a/a	CLE	4	4	24	0	68	86	52	7	31	37	6.85	1.72	13.2	371	4.1	4.8	1.2	0.9	21
	02	26	aaa	CLE	7	4	16	0	98	109	52	11	19	59	4.77	1.30	25.9	309	1.7	5.4	3.1	1.0	67
Pickford,Kevin	02	28	aaa	SD	4	7	20	1	69	92	55	5	33	32	7.15	1.81	16.4	382	4.3	4.2	1.0	0.7	18
Piersoll,Chris	01	24	aa	CIN	1	4	50	19	56	58	27	2	32	66	4.40	1.60	5.1	354	5.1	10.5	2.1	0.3	99
Pina,Rafael	01	30	a/a	BAL	1	4	17	0	49	75	20	3	16	25	3.66	1.85	13.8	388	3.0	4.5	1.5	0.5	32
	02	31	aaa	BAL	6	5	50	10	111	139	54	11	33	60	4.38	1.55	9.9	347	2.7	4.9	1.8	0.9	36
Pineda,Isauro	02	24	aa	BOS	9	13	28	0	156	196	114	20	68	99	6.58	1.69	25.7	367	3.9	5.7	1.5	1.2	25
Pineda,Luis	01	23	a/a	DET	7	2	18	0	94	80	34	7	25	83	3.25	1.11	21.1	276	2.4	7.9	3.3	0.7	107
Pineiro,Joel	01	23	aaa	SEA	6	3	18	0	77	75	35	8	34	58	4.09	1.42	18.5	327	4.0	6.8	1.7	0.9	53
Pine,Chris	02	26	a/a	ANA	2	9	36	1	79	117	67	12	40	29	7.61	1.98	10.8	404	4.5	3.3	0.7	1.4	-18
Poe,Ryan	01	24	aa	MIL	1	2	7	0	35	38	21	6	7	33	5.41	1.29	21.1	307	1.9	8.6	4.5	1.6	98
Porzio,Mike	01	29	a/a	CHW	7	6	33	0	147	206	110	26	76	84	6.72	1.92	21.6	396	4.6	5.2	1.1	1.6	-2
	02	30	aaa	CHW	6	5	14	0	75	110	56	13	34	50	6.70	1.91	26.0	396	4.1	6.0	1.5	1.6	8
Pote,Lou	02	31	aaa	ANA	2	1	7	0	39	48	29	3	9	35	6.69	1.46	24.4	334	2.1	8.1	3.9	0.7	105
Powell,Brian	01	28	aaa	HOU	9	8	24	0	144	181	71	18	44	76	4.43	1.56	26.9	348	2.8	4.8	1.7	1.1	26
	02	29	aaa	DET	10	3	20	0	119	162	70	8	27	67	5.29	1.59	26.8	352	2.0	5.1	2.5	0.6	56
Powell,Jeremy	01	25	aaa	SD	4	2	11	0	73	47	15	2	14	50	1.86	0.84	25.0	224	1.7	6.2	3.6	0.2	123
Prather,Scott	01	25	aa	STL	1	3	23	0	48	69	30	7	20	32	5.60	1.84	10.0	387	3.7	6.0	1.6	1.2	22
Pratt,Andy	01	22	aa	TEX	8	10	27	0	168	204	108	23	55	118	5.79	1.54	27.8	346	2.9	6.3	2.1	1.2	42
	02	23	a/a	ATL	8	11	26	0	133	144	69	7	52	86	4.66	1.47	22.5	335	3.5	5.8	1.7	0.5	56
Pridie,Jon	02	23	aa	MIN	5	3	16	0	94	110	66	7	48	60	6.32	1.68	27.0	365	4.6	5.7	1.3	0.7	38
Priest,Eddie	01	28	aaa	LA	4	8	23	0	93	141	64	13	31	54	6.21	1.84	19.3	387	3.0	5.2	1.8	1.2	19
Prinz,Bret	02	25	aaa	ARI	1	0	37	18	39	46	14	4	8	28	3.22	1.38	4.5	321	1.8	6.4	3.5	0.9	82
Prior,Mark	02	22	a/a	CHC	5	2	9	0	51	42	14	1	17	70	2.47	1.16	23.1	284	3.0	12.4	4.1	0.2	166
Proctor,Scott	01	25	aa	LA	4	3	10	0	49	47	31	7	35	39	5.58	1.67	22.6	364	6.4	7.1	1.1	1.3	31
	02	26	aa	LA	7	9	26	0	133	144	73	12	99	103	4.94	1.83	24.3	385	6.7	7.0	1.0	0.8	40
Pruett,Jason	01	23	aa	TAM	2	5	38	1	51	72	40	7	20	25	7.06	1.80	6.3	382	3.5	4.4	1.3	1.2	5
Puffer,Brandon	01	26	aa	HOU	6	1	56	8	82	70	28	6	43	68	3.02	1.37	6.3	319	4.7	7.4	1.6	0.6	69

Major League Equivalent Statistics

					Actual				Major League Equivalents														
PITCHER	Yr	Age	Lev	Org	W	L	G	Sv	IP	H	ER	HR	BB	K	ERA	Br/IP	BF/G	OOB	CTL	DOM	CMD	hr/9	BPV
Pulsipher,Bill	01	28	aaa	BOS	1	1	24	10	31	33	14	1	11	18	4.05	1.42	5.6	327	3.1	5.1	1.6	0.3	57
Pumphrey,Ken	01	25	a/a	MIN	9	8	29	1	142	183	92	11	49	56	5.80	1.64	22.3	359	3.1	3.5	1.1	0.7	19
	02	26	a/a	PHI	13	9	28	0	171	219	108	13	54	80	5.68	1.59	27.6	353	2.8	4.2	1.5	0.7	30
Purvis,Rob	01	24	aa	CHW	5	9	24	0	140	203	109	13	75	45	7.04	1.98	28.6	405	4.8	2.9	0.6	0.8	-6
Putz,Joe	01	25	aa	SEA	7	9	27	0	148	173	79	12	65	116	4.80	1.61	24.8	355	4.0	7.0	1.8	0.7	56
Putz,J.J.	02	26	a/a	SEA	5	14	24	0	138	166	76	13	53	81	4.96	1.59	25.9	352	3.5	5.3	1.5	0.8	35
Qualls,Chad	02	24	aa	HOU	6	13	29	0	163	209	101	12	72	116	5.58	1.72	26.1	371	4.0	6.4	1.6	0.7	46
Quevedo,Ruben	01	23	aaa	CHC	9	5	22	0	141	129	49	11	45	135	3.10	1.23	26.6	296	2.9	8.6	3.0	0.7	101
Radinsky,Scott	01	34	a/a	CLE	2	3	39	4	39	57	23	1	4	20	5.36	1.56	4.5	348	1.0	4.5	4.5	0.3	102
Rain,Steve	01	26	aaa	CHC	2	2	34	2	43	51	44	6	40	36	9.28	2.11	6.4	419	8.4	7.5	0.9	1.3	23
Rakers,Aaron	01	25	aa	BAL	4	4	51	14	60	64	21	9	21	63	3.15	1.42	5.1	327	3.2	9.4	3.0	1.4	78
	02	26	aa	BAL	5	1	36	10	48	48	14	3	13	34	2.63	1.27	5.6	303	2.4	6.4	2.6	0.6	80
Rakers,Jason	01	28	aaa	KC	6	4	44	5	97	122	61	19	16	76	5.69	1.42	9.6	327	1.5	7.1	4.7	1.8	83
Ramirez,Erasmo	01	25	aa	TEX	4	1	34	1	50	54	22	6	11	46	3.98	1.31	6.2	309	2.0	8.2	4.1	1.0	107
	02	26	a/a	TEX	8	3	59	3	75	84	29	1	13	40	3.48	1.29	5.4	307	1.6	4.8	3.1	0.1	89
Ramirez,Horacio	02	23	aa	ATL	9	5	16	0	92	95	36	5	31	54	3.52	1.37	24.7	319	3.0	5.3	1.7	0.5	56
Ramirez,Jose	02	27	aa	DET	0	3	28	0	45	71	40	7	30	28	8.00	2.24	8.3	435	6.0	5.6	0.9	1.4	-4
Ramirez,Santiago	02	24	a/a	HOU	7	2	51	5	84	75	35	7	40	74	3.74	1.37	7.1	319	4.3	7.9	1.9	0.7	72
Ramos,Mario	01	24	a/a	OAK	16	4	28	0	174	156	64	12	52	129	3.31	1.20	25.6	290	2.7	6.7	2.5	0.6	82
	02	25	aaa	TEX	3	8	34	0	121	178	112	21	49	65	8.32	1.87	17.1	391	3.6	4.8	1.3	1.6	-2
Ramsay,Rob	01	28	aaa	SEA	10	11	26	0	149	186	96	26	65	97	5.78	1.69	26.4	366	3.9	5.8	1.5	1.6	14
Randall,Scott	01	26	a/a	COL	6	5	20	0	77	103	65	20	37	42	7.61	1.81	18.3	383	4.3	4.9	1.1	2.3	-25
	02	27	a/a	MIN	14	0	24	0	136	168	64	10	31	56	4.23	1.46	24.9	334	2.0	3.7	1.8	0.7	36
Randolph,Steve	01	27	a/a	ARI	7	6	36	0	96	117	75	14	78	61	7.00	2.03	13.2	410	7.3	5.7	0.8	1.3	8
	02	28	aaa	ARI	15	7	28	0	163	177	75	16	80	100	4.14	1.58	26.2	350	4.4	5.5	1.3	0.9	34
Rath,Fred	01	29	a/a	STL	4	5	28	0	80	144	88	18	44	45	9.90	2.33	15.0	444	4.9	5.1	1.0	2.0	-28
Ratliff,Jon	01	30	aaa	OAK	1	7	18	0	63	99	65	10	40	32	9.26	2.20	17.9	429	5.7	4.6	0.8	1.4	-13
	02	31	aaa	TOR	2	4	28	1	37	60	29	3	24	14	7.04	2.26	6.9	437	5.8	3.4	0.6	0.7	-5
Rauch,Jon	01	23	aaa	CHW	1	3	6	0	28	35	25	12	7	24	8.04	1.50	20.6	339	2.3	7.7	3.4	3.9	-2
	02	24	aaa	CHW	7	8	19	0	109	109	69	19	44	90	5.69	1.40	24.8	324	3.6	7.4	2.0	1.6	44
Reames,Britt	01	28	aaa	MON	4	3	8	0	54	60	30	5	15	30	5.02	1.39	29.1	323	2.5	5.0	2.0	0.9	44
	02	29	aaa	MON	3	2	7	0	42	41	19	4	15	20	4.07	1.33	25.5	313	3.2	4.3	1.3	0.9	33
Redding,Tim	01	24	a/a	HOU	14	3	20	0	128	101	53	12	46	133	3.72	1.15	26.1	282	3.2	9.3	2.9	0.8	104
	02	25	aaa	HOU	3	3	11	0	38	39	30	8	14	43	7.11	1.39	14.9	323	3.3	10.2	3.1	1.9	72
Reed,Brandon	01	27	aaa	NYY	1	2	24	1	33	33	18	3	8	25	4.75	1.24	5.8	298	2.2	6.8	3.1	0.8	84
Regilio,Nick	01	23	aa	TEX	1	3	10	0	52	74	41	3	20	35	7.14	1.80	24.6	382	3.4	6.0	1.8	0.5	47
	02	24	a/a	TEX	7	8	20	0	109	126	58	10	53	53	4.78	1.64	24.9	360	4.4	4.4	1.0	0.8	21
Reichert,Dan	01	25	aaa	KC	1	5	10	0	32	52	36	4	15	25	10.16	2.07	16.1	415	4.2	6.9	1.6	1.1	26
Reid,Justin	01	24	aa	PIT	5	5	17	0	110	131	43	6	17	57	3.53	1.34	27.6	315	1.4	4.7	3.4	0.5	81
	02	25	aa	PIT	11	8	25	0	153	191	99	23	29	83	5.82	1.44	26.7	330	1.7	4.9	2.9	1.4	44
Reimers,Cameron	01	23	aa	TOR	1	2	5	0	30	38	29	10	5	16	8.66	1.44	26.2	331	1.5	4.7	3.0	3.1	-7
	02	24	a/a	TOR	5	9	25	0	116	192	81	18	30	41	6.28	1.91	22.4	396	2.3	3.2	1.4	1.4	-11
Reinike,Chris	01	25	a/a	CLE	1	3	28	5	53	68	43	6	22	34	7.34	1.69	8.7	366	3.7	5.8	1.6	1.0	30
Reith,Brian	01	24	a/a	CIN	6	4	19	0	109	127	60	12	43	85	4.95	1.56	25.7	348	3.5	7.0	2.0	1.0	52
	02	25	aaa	CIN	8	13	27	0	150	177	92	17	51	94	5.51	1.52	24.7	342	3.1	5.6	1.8	1.0	39
Rekar,Bryan	02	30	aaa	COL	7	10	25	0	147	253	121	28	41	85	7.41	2.00	28.9	407	2.5	5.2	2.1	1.7	4
Revenig,Todd	01	32	aaa	ARI	4	5	46	0	65	96	44	9	12	34	6.10	1.65	6.5	361	1.6	4.7	3.0	1.3	39
Reyes,Al	02	32	aaa	PIT	7	3	43	1	66	48	25	5	22	73	3.40	1.06	6.1	266	3.0	9.9	3.3	0.7	124
Reyes,Carlos	01	33	aaa	ARI	2	1	25	0	40	52	36	6	19	27	8.01	1.75	7.5	375	4.2	6.0	1.4	1.4	17
Reyes,Dennys	01	24	aaa	CIN	4	2	7	0	34	40	18	4	16	30	4.75	1.64	22.2	360	4.2	7.9	1.9	1.1	53
Reyes,Eddy	01	25	aa	TAM	2	3	31	1	43	61	40	3	31	22	8.37	2.14	7.0	423	6.5	4.5	0.7	0.7	10
Rheinecker,John	02	23	aa	OAK	7	7	20	0	128	158	58	7	25	83	4.08	1.43	27.8	329	1.8	5.8	3.3	0.5	86
Ricketts,Chad	01	27	aaa	LA	1	3	48	3	58	52	19	4	24	58	2.87	1.29	5.1	307	3.7	9.0	2.5	0.6	95
Riggan,Jerrod	01	27	aaa	NYM	2	0	28	13	32	32	9	4	4	29	2.66	1.11	4.6	276	1.2	8.3	7.0	1.2	166
	02	28	aaa	CLE	4	1	27	3	45	52	17	4	13	30	3.39	1.44	7.3	330	2.6	6.0	2.3	0.8	59
Rijo,Fernando	02	25	aa	LA	8	8	27	0	142	160	79	16	79	87	5.01	1.68	24.2	366	5.0	5.5	1.1	1.0	25
Riley,Matt	02	23	aa	BAL	4	10	22	0	109	157	92	12	49	86	7.59	1.89	23.8	393	4.0	7.1	1.8	1.0	39
Riley,Mike	01	27	a/a	SF	5	6	35	0	96	136	69	16	46	64	6.45	1.88	13.2	392	4.3	6.0	1.4	1.5	12
Rincon,Juan	01	23	aa	MIN	14	6	29	0	153	170	77	13	65	113	4.53	1.53	23.5	345	3.8	6.6	1.7	0.8	53
	02	24	aaa	MIN	7	4	19	0	101	119	58	11	34	64	5.16	1.51	23.6	341	3.0	5.7	1.9	1.0	42
Riske,David	01	25	aaa	CLE	1	2	38	15	53	53	18	3	17	62	3.05	1.32	5.9	311	2.9	10.5	3.6	0.5	128
Rivera,Homero	01	23	aa	DET	1	2	16	2	30	40	20	4	10	16	5.86	1.68	8.7	365	3.1	4.6	1.5	1.2	15
	02	25	a/a	DET	6	4	52	8	82	87	34	5	23	39	3.73	1.34	6.7	315	2.5	4.3	1.7	0.5	47
Rivera,Saul	01	24	aa	MIN	5	2	33	13	42	47	25	4	22	46	5.28	1.64	5.8	359	4.6	9.7	2.1	0.9	76
	02	25	aa	MON	2	5	45	16	57	55	25	2	33	38	3.93	1.54	5.7	345	5.2	6.0	1.2	0.3	56
Rizzo,Todd	01	30	aaa	LA	4	4	49	6	63	74	32	6	38	45	4.60	1.78	6.1	379	5.4	6.4	1.2	0.8	37
Roach,Jason	01	25	a/a	NYM	9	9	26	0	132	179	68	8	38	62	4.66	1.64	23.2	360	2.6	4.2	1.6	0.6	34
	02	26	a/a	NYM	9	10	27	0	150	194	66	13	48	67	3.95	1.61	25.2	356	2.9	4.0	1.4	0.8	24
Roa,Joe	01	30	a/a	FLA	6	8	26	0	160	230	90	21	19	74	5.06	1.55	27.5	347	1.1	4.2	4.0	1.2	62
	02	31	aaa	PHI	14	0	17	0	111	100	29	4	18	65	2.35	1.06	26.0	267	1.5	5.3	3.6	0.3	106
Robbins,Jake	01	25	aaa	ATL	5	3	57	1	78	87	63	1	53	47	7.22	1.78	6.4	379	6.1	5.4	0.9	0.1	47
	02	26	aaa	ATL	2	6	58	3	68	91	59	7	57	43	7.79	2.17	6.0	426	7.5	5.7	0.8	0.9	14
Robertson,Jeriome	01	25	aa	HOU	5	1	57	3	73	109	43	14	23	59	5.31	1.81	6.1	383	2.8	7.2	2.5	1.7	34
	02	26	aaa	HOU	12	8	27	0	180	197	72	18	49	97	3.60	1.37	28.6	319	2.5	4.9	2.0	0.9	44
Robertson,Nathan	02	25	aa	FLA	10	9	27	0	163	189	76	12	56	86	4.20	1.50	26.7	340	3.1	4.7	1.5	0.7	39
Roberts,Grant	01	24	aaa	NYM	3	5	30	2	67	93	43	4	20	46	5.76	1.68	10.3	365	2.7	6.2	2.3	0.5	60
Roberts,Mark	01	26	aaa	FLA	6	3	33	8	36	48	16	4	14	29	4.12	1.75	5.1	374	3.6	7.3	2.0	1.0	47
Roberts,Nick	01	25	aa	HOU	2	4	8	0	45	64	35	8	11	21	6.93	1.66	25.8	362	2.1	4.2	2.0	1.7	6
	02	26	aa	HOU	12	7	28	0	172	248	112	20	48	76	5.86	1.72	28.5	371	2.5	4.0	1.6	1.0	15
Roberts,Rick	02	23	aa	LA	8	2	51	2	87	79	40	6	45	72	4.13	1.42	7.4	328	4.6	7.4	1.6	0.6	67
Rodgers,Bobby	01	27	a/a	FLA	4	5	44	4	77	80	43	11	36	50	4.96	1.51	7.8	340	4.2	5.9	1.4	1.3	27
	02	28	a/a	FLA	5	5	28	2	104	138	73	18	65	61	6.31	1.95	18.1	400	5.6	5.3	0.9	1.6	-3

Major League Equivalent Statistics

					Actual				Major League Equivalents														
PITCHER	Yr	Age	Lev	Org	W	L	G	Sv	IP	H	ER	HR	BB	K	ERA	Br/IP	BF/G	OOB	CTL	DOM	CMD	hr/9	BPV
Rodney,Fernando	02	26	a/a	DET	2	1	41	15	42	32	6	1	14	37	1.28	1.09	4.1	272	3.0	7.9	2.6	0.2	110
Rodriguez,Francisco	02	21	a/a	ANA	5	6	50	15	83	63	22	3	25	113	2.38	1.06	6.6	266	2.7	12.2	4.5	0.3	172
Rodriguez,Frank	01	29	aaa	CIN	8	6	43	5	80	84	30	6	26	47	3.38	1.37	8.0	319	2.9	5.2	1.8	0.7	50
Rodriguez,Jose	01	27	aaa	STL	2	1	54	1	60	59	28	8	32	49	4.16	1.51	4.9	340	4.8	7.3	1.5	1.2	43
Rodriguez,Nerio	01	31	a/a	NYM	8	5	23	1	110	142	79	18	39	50	6.45	1.65	21.8	361	3.2	4.1	1.3	1.4	2
	02	32	aaa	ATL	7	3	21	0	126	118	40	15	23	69	2.86	1.12	24.2	277	1.6	4.9	3.0	1.1	67
Rodriguez,Ricardo	02	24	a/a	CLE	9	5	17	0	104	118	41	8	27	54	3.54	1.39	26.4	323	2.3	4.7	2.0	0.7	48
Rodriguez,Wil	01	23	aa	HOU	5	9	42	0	92	110	62	13	59	81	6.06	1.83	10.4	386	5.8	7.9	1.4	1.3	35
Rogers,Brian	01	25	aa	NYY	10	9	29	0	177	240	114	31	71	124	5.78	1.75	28.5	375	3.6	6.3	1.8	1.6	19
	02	25	a/a	NYY	13	8	27	0	139	173	79	14	44	85	5.11	1.56	23.1	348	2.8	5.5	1.9	0.9	42
Rojas,Chris	02	26	aa	SD	6	8	25	0	126	157	96	11	84	61	6.85	1.91	24.4	395	6.0	4.4	0.7	0.8	13
Rojas,Jose	02	21	aa	LA	3	4	10	0	54	62	35	9	30	37	5.83	1.70	25.0	368	5.0	6.2	1.2	1.5	16
Romero,J.C.	01	25	aaa	MIN	3	3	12	0	63	77	31	4	24	47	4.46	1.60	23.8	354	3.5	6.6	1.9	0.6	59
Roney,Matt	02	23	aa	COL	3	6	13	0	70	88	65	10	32	53	8.33	1.71	25.0	369	4.1	6.8	1.7	1.3	32
Roque,Rafael	01	30	aaa	BOS	8	5	20	0	98	130	64	16	38	51	5.84	1.71	22.7	370	3.5	4.7	1.3	1.5	3
Rosario,Juan	01	26	aa	TAM	1	3	44	3	68	94	42	4	31	43	5.58	1.84	7.4	387	4.1	5.7	1.4	0.6	36
	02	27	a/a	BAL	4	10	27	0	130	184	96	13	61	68	6.65	1.88	23.1	392	4.2	4.7	1.1	0.9	14
Rosario,Rodrigo	02	23	aa	HOU	11	6	26	0	130	121	55	6	60	81	3.80	1.39	21.6	323	4.2	5.6	1.4	0.4	56
Rose,Brian	01	26	aaa	TAM	9	2	19	1	98	105	44	13	19	75	4.07	1.27	21.6	302	1.8	6.9	3.9	1.2	89
Rose,Ted	01	28	aaa	MON	7	9	37	0	120	160	76	12	40	76	5.72	1.66	14.9	363	3.0	5.7	1.9	0.9	40
	02	29	a/a	CLE	4	3	11	0	57	80	39	10	22	22	6.16	1.79	24.4	380	3.5	3.5	1.0	1.6	-15
Ruffin,Johnny	01	30	aaa	FLA	2	3	46	27	41	48	17	1	13	45	3.65	1.49	3.9	337	2.9	9.9	3.4	0.2	121
Ruhl,Nathan	01	25	aa	TAM	3	3	31	6	51	73	34	10	27	42	6.08	1.96	8.0	402	4.7	7.5	1.6	1.8	14
	02	26	aa	CIN	1	5	44	19	48	60	34	5	36	30	6.38	2.00	5.4	407	6.8	5.6	0.8	0.9	18
Runser,Greg	02	24	aa	TEX	1	4	61	25	61	92	36	4	31	22	5.31	2.02	4.9	408	4.6	3.2	0.7	0.6	4
Ryan,Jason	01	26	aaa	PIT	3	8	14	0	67	89	55	10	27	27	7.32	1.73	22.3	372	3.7	3.6	1.0	1.4	-6
Saarloos,Kirk	02	23	a/a	HOU	12	1	17	0	99	71	22	3	24	87	2.00	0.96	22.6	247	2.2	7.9	3.6	0.3	131
Sabel,Erik	01	27	aaa	ARI	2	2	18	2	39	40	15	3	7	26	3.55	1.21	9.0	293	1.7	6.0	3.6	0.7	94
	02	28	aaa	DET	5	5	39	1	77	100	53	6	23	46	6.18	1.59	8.9	353	2.7	5.4	2.0	0.7	47
Sadler,Carl	02	26	a/a	CLE	5	2	33	3	65	73	22	1	22	41	3.05	1.46	8.6	334	3.0	5.7	1.9	0.1	68
Saenz,Jason	01	25	aa	NYM	8	15	28	0	143	194	106	16	85	76	6.69	1.95	24.9	400	5.4	4.8	0.9	1.0	9
	02	26	a/a	NYM	6	3	41	2	78	93	58	6	68	40	6.68	2.06	9.5	414	7.8	4.6	0.6	0.7	16
Saipe,Mike	01	28	aa	ATL	4	2	7	0	49	64	21	3	16	26	3.90	1.63	31.9	359	3.0	4.7	1.6	0.5	41
	02	29	aaa	ATL	4	6	42	1	94	135	54	5	29	48	5.17	1.74	10.4	374	2.8	4.6	1.7	0.5	37
Saladin,Miguel	02	27	a/a	HOU	4	5	55	24	58	53	21	6	31	36	3.25	1.44	4.6	331	4.8	5.6	1.2	0.9	37
Sampson,Benj	02	27	a/a	MIN	6	8	29	0	149	206	102	20	31	46	6.16	1.59	23.2	353	1.9	2.8	1.5	1.2	2
Sanches,Brian	01	23	aa	KC	7	9	29	0	134	175	106	13	58	77	7.13	1.74	21.5	373	3.9	5.1	1.3	0.9	25
	02	24	aa	KC	10	6	33	0	116	141	81	11	46	80	6.27	1.61	15.9	355	3.6	6.2	1.7	0.9	44
Sanchez,Duaner	01	22	aa	ARI	3	7	13	0	70	100	58	5	23	35	7.45	1.75	25.2	375	3.0	4.5	1.5	0.6	29
	02	23	a/a	PIT	5	7	55	20	63	69	34	4	24	56	4.84	1.47	5.0	335	3.4	8.0	2.3	0.6	80
Sanchez,Jesus	01	27	aaa	FLA	6	1	16	0	75	63	26	3	32	48	3.15	1.26	19.6	301	3.8	5.7	1.5	0.4	65
	02	28	aaa	CHC	8	9	26	0	125	154	82	24	62	79	5.90	1.73	22.3	372	4.5	5.7	1.3	1.7	5
Sanders,Dave	01	22	aa	CHW	3	0	36	0	34	32	13	1	25	22	3.44	1.68	4.3	365	6.6	5.8	0.9	0.3	52
	02	23	aa	CHW	3	1	47	0	63	70	19	4	31	54	2.71	1.60	6.1	354	4.4	7.7	1.7	0.6	66
Sansom,Trevor	02	26	aa	STL	4	4	47	0	79	99	47	14	32	40	5.34	1.65	7.7	362	3.6	4.5	1.3	1.6	1
Santana,Johan	02	24	aaa	MIN	5	2	11	0	48	40	18	7	26	64	3.36	1.37	18.8	319	4.9	12.0	2.5	1.3	95
Santana,Julio	01	29	aaa	SF	8	8	25	0	132	176	89	25	47	97	6.08	1.69	24.4	367	3.2	6.6	2.0	1.7	24
Santos,Alex	02	25	aa	TAM	1	4	7	0	31	63	40	4	10	11	11.54	2.34	23.4	445	2.9	3.2	1.1	1.2	-19
Santos,Victor	01	25	aaa	DET	2	1	6	0	35	57	29	5	11	19	7.51	1.93	28.4	398	2.8	4.8	1.7	1.3	10
	02	26	aaa	COL	4	9	21	0	118	170	91	25	40	113	6.94	1.78	26.4	379	3.1	8.6	2.8	1.9	43
Scanlan,Bob	01	35	aaa	MON	0	5	32	23	32	52	19	4	12	17	5.31	1.97	4.9	403	3.2	4.8	1.5	1.2	8
	02	36	aaa	NYY	2	3	51	3	70	115	42	3	23	27	5.39	1.97	6.7	403	3.0	3.5	1.2	0.4	17
Scheffer,Aaron	01	26	aa	FLA	2	1	24	1	35	21	6	2	11	31	1.42	0.92	5.6	239	2.8	7.8	2.8	0.6	109
	02	27	aaa	OAK	4	1	35	1	52	58	28	1	23	29	4.84	1.55	6.7	347	4.0	5.0	1.3	0.2	51
Schmack,Brian	01	28	aaa	TEX	2	2	40	1	53	68	32	6	14	29	5.36	1.55	5.9	347	2.3	4.8	2.1	1.1	34
	02	29	a/a	TEX	1	7	41	1	92	149	78	9	28	48	7.63	1.92	10.9	397	2.7	4.7	1.7	0.9	21
Schoening,Brent	01	24	aa	MIN	2	6	12	0	45	65	39	8	19	30	7.80	1.85	18.0	388	3.7	6.0	1.6	1.6	10
	02	25	aa	MIN	3	1	21	0	62	74	47	14	25	47	6.80	1.59	13.4	353	3.6	6.8	1.9	2.0	17
Schrenk,Steve	01	33	aaa	OAK	7	4	46	5	61	66	21	5	19	53	3.10	1.39	5.7	323	2.8	7.8	2.8	0.8	84
	02	34	aaa	CHW	2	7	38	0	77	93	48	12	27	39	5.60	1.55	9.1	347	3.1	4.5	1.4	1.4	12
Schurman,Ryan	02	26	aa	STL	0	3	18	0	51	85	52	11	22	31	9.18	2.10	14.2	418	3.9	5.5	1.4	1.9	-13
Seale,Dustin	02	25	a/a	MON	1	2	30	0	68	80	35	13	16	43	4.62	1.41	9.8	325	2.1	5.7	2.7	1.7	37
Seay,Bobby	01	23	aa	TAM	2	5	15	0	64	102	62	12	28	41	8.67	2.02	21.2	409	3.9	5.7	1.5	1.7	-3
	02	24	a/a	TAM	2	0	25	0	50	55	30	3	18	31	5.38	1.45	8.8	332	3.2	5.6	1.7	0.5	54
Secoda,Jason	01	27	aaa	CHW	3	9	34	1	139	218	119	26	63	88	7.70	2.02	20.2	409	4.1	5.7	1.4	1.7	-2
	02	28	aaa	FLA	6	3	35	0	116	117	60	11	41	52	4.65	1.36	14.2	318	3.2	4.0	1.3	0.9	29
Sedlacek,Shawn	01	24	a/a	KC	11	11	28	0	168	212	97	23	34	88	5.19	1.46	26.3	334	1.8	4.7	2.6	1.2	41
	02	25	a/a	KC	8	6	14	0	98	100	48	7	20	65	4.40	1.22	29.1	295	1.8	6.0	3.3	0.6	88
Seelbach,Chris	01	29	aaa	ATL	7	7	22	1	88	108	70	11	40	67	7.14	1.67	18.4	364	4.1	6.8	1.7	1.1	39
Seibel,Phil	02	24	aa	NYM	10	8	28	0	149	165	74	16	49	93	4.46	1.43	23.2	329	3.0	5.6	1.9	1.0	45
Seifert,Ryan	01	26	aa	COL	4	6	33	1	103	157	68	22	36	68	5.92	1.87	15.0	391	3.1	5.9	1.9	1.9	5
	02	27	aaa	COL	1	5	21	0	62	95	60	21	27	29	8.68	1.96	14.5	402	3.9	4.2	1.1	3.0	-57
Sekany,Jason	01	26	a/a	BOS	1	8	22	0	72	121	74	16	29	37	9.31	2.08	16.4	416	3.6	4.6	1.3	1.9	-22
Seo,Jae Weong	01	24	a/a	NYM	7	3	21	0	108	113	38	7	19	59	3.17	1.22	21.3	295	1.5	4.9	3.2	0.6	81
	02	25	a/a	NYM	6	9	27	0	133	176	73	15	24	75	4.93	1.50	21.8	340	1.6	5.1	3.1	1.0	58
Sequea,Jacobo	02	21	a/a	BAL	2	10	20	0	100	102	67	18	44	47	6.02	1.46	21.9	333	4.0	4.2	1.1	1.6	3
Serafini,Dan	01	28	aaa	SF	8	5	47	1	83	102	47	6	25	51	5.14	1.53	7.9	344	2.7	5.6	2.0	0.7	51
Sergent,Joe	02	24	aa	FLA	3	6	20	0	70	98	58	13	23	34	7.46	1.73	16.3	372	3.0	4.4	1.5	1.7	-3
Serrano,Elio	01	23	aa	PHI	1	1	30	2	37	25	14	3	10	27	3.40	0.94	4.8	244	2.4	6.5	2.7	0.7	92
	02	24	aaa	PHI	1	3	43	5	71	73	28	7	18	41	3.55	1.28	6.9	305	2.3	5.2	2.3	0.9	55
Serrano,Jim	01	25	a/a	MON	6	4	56	20	62	51	23	5	33	67	3.35	1.34	4.7	314	4.7	9.6	2.0	0.8	89
	02	26	aaa	NYM	8	6	53	3	74	103	41	3	33	62	4.99	1.84	6.6	386	4.0	7.5	1.9	0.4	64

Major League Equivalent Statistics

PITCHER	Yr	Age	Lev	Org	Actual				Major League Equivalents														
					W	L	G	Sv	IP	H	ER	HR	BB	K	ERA	Br/IP	BF/G	OOB	CTL	DOM	CMD	hr/9	BPV
Serrano,Wascar	01	23	aaa	SD	6	5	27	0	93	108	53	10	36	59	5.12	1.55	15.4	346	3.5	5.7	1.6	1.0	38
	02	25	aaa	SEA	1	3	41	5	71	97	61	6	29	48	7.72	1.77	8.1	378	3.7	6.1	1.7	0.8	40
Serrano,Willy	02	26	aa	BAL	4	4	27	0	48	93	52	11	33	22	9.71	2.61	9.9	472	6.2	4.1	0.7	2.1	-48
Service,Scott	02	36	aaa	PIT	4	4	47	6	61	57	29	8	24	57	4.26	1.32	5.5	312	3.5	8.4	2.4	1.2	72
Sessions,Doug	01	25	aa	HOU	6	4	41	1	103	128	71	19	39	60	6.21	1.62	11.4	357	3.4	5.3	1.6	1.7	10
	02	26	a/a	HOU	2	2	41	0	58	82	53	14	29	33	8.20	1.91	6.9	395	4.5	5.1	1.1	2.2	-21
Severino,Ronni	01	26	aa	TAM	3	8	38	0	90	163	80	18	57	48	8.05	2.45	12.7	456	5.7	4.8	0.8	1.8	-31
	02	27	aa	TAM	0	4	25	0	35	48	26	1	25	35	6.67	2.08	7.0	416	6.4	9.0	1.4	0.3	67
Shaffar,Ben	02	25	a/a	PIT	9	7	19	0	116	141	53	7	42	82	4.11	1.58	27.5	351	3.3	6.4	2.0	0.5	59
Shearn,Tom	01	24	aa	HOU	5	6	43	1	110	116	63	9	56	111	5.17	1.56	11.5	348	4.6	9.1	2.0	0.8	75
	02	25	aaa	HOU	4	6	57	8	83	95	37	10	45	68	4.01	1.68	6.7	366	4.9	7.4	1.5	1.1	42
Shepard,David	02	29	a/a	NYY	8	8	43	1	92	124	65	11	31	51	6.35	1.68	9.9	366	3.0	5.0	1.6	1.1	24
Sheredy,Kevin	01	27	aa	STL	0	7	48	1	64	63	32	9	43	47	4.53	1.65	6.1	361	6.0	6.6	1.1	1.3	28
	02	28	aaa	STL	1	2	35	2	41	51	28	3	23	30	6.12	1.80	5.6	381	5.0	6.6	1.3	0.7	43
Shibilo,Andy	02	26	a/a	BOS	5	4	56	6	82	107	51	3	28	65	5.60	1.65	6.7	361	3.1	7.1	2.3	0.3	75
Shields,Scot	01	26	aaa	ANA	6	11	21	0	137	159	87	26	29	87	5.68	1.37	28.0	319	1.9	5.7	3.0	1.7	45
	02	27	aaa	ANA	2	2	28	1	47	44	18	5	6	41	3.45	1.06	6.7	267	1.1	7.9	6.8	1.0	168
Shiell,Jason	01	25	aa	SD	2	3	45	0	81	109	52	5	36	46	5.73	1.79	8.5	380	4.0	5.1	1.3	0.6	31
	02	26	aaa	SD	4	3	56	6	74	70	26	6	29	62	3.16	1.34	5.6	314	3.5	7.5	2.1	0.7	74
Shouse,Brian	01	33	aaa	HOU	2	2	56	1	53	63	23	5	17	46	3.93	1.51	4.2	341	2.9	7.7	2.7	0.9	74
Shumaker,Tony	01	28	aaa	BAL	8	7	53	4	72	89	44	10	34	44	5.50	1.71	6.3	370	4.3	5.4	1.3	1.2	19
Sikorski,Brian	01	27	aaa	TEX	6	4	14	0	87	109	46	11	23	62	4.79	1.52	27.6	343	2.4	6.4	2.7	1.1	56
Silva,Carlos	01	22	aa	PHI	15	8	28	0	180	222	92	20	29	91	4.60	1.39	27.7	323	1.5	4.6	3.1	1.0	59
Silva,Jose	02	29	aaa	CIN	1	2	20	1	35	47	11	1	4	21	2.81	1.45	7.7	332	1.0	5.4	5.3	0.3	127
Simas,Bill	02	31	aaa	CHW	1	3	28	2	40	61	23	7	9	18	5.18	1.75	6.7	375	2.0	4.1	2.0	1.6	5
Simontacchi,Jason	01	28	aaa	MIN	7	13	32	0	143	228	106	23	24	67	6.69	1.77	21.0	377	1.5	4.2	2.8	1.5	25
	02	29	aaa	STL	5	1	6	0	42	55	14	2	5	23	2.99	1.43	30.5	328	1.1	4.9	4.6	0.4	106
Simon,Ben	01	27	a/a	LA	9	12	27	0	134	150	88	22	49	92	5.90	1.48	21.9	337	3.3	6.2	1.9	1.5	31
	02	28	a/a	LA	7	0	38	1	116	140	60	14	51	59	4.66	1.65	13.9	361	4.0	4.6	1.2	1.1	16
Simpson,Allan	01	24	aa	SEA	2	1	22	9	38	29	11	1	17	31	2.48	1.21	7.2	293	4.0	7.4	1.9	0.2	89
	02	25	aa	SEA	10	5	56	7	82	71	42	6	58	77	4.60	1.57	6.6	350	6.4	8.4	1.3	0.7	68
Sims,Ken	01	26	aa	BAL	8	4	24	1	112	163	72	13	31	40	5.82	1.73	21.7	373	2.5	3.2	1.3	1.0	4
	02	27	aa	BAL	5	11	28	0	107	176	93	7	48	37	7.82	2.09	19.2	417	4.0	3.1	0.8	0.6	0
Sinclair,Steve	01	30	aaa	CHW	4	6	53	1	63	90	51	8	28	45	7.29	1.87	5.7	390	4.0	6.4	1.6	1.1	29
	02	31	aaa	CHC	6	2	52	1	73	76	33	4	32	49	4.06	1.48	6.2	336	3.9	6.0	1.5	0.5	56
Sismondo,Bobby	01	25	aa	MIL	1	3	34	3	55	71	29	11	25	35	4.81	1.74	7.6	373	4.1	5.7	1.4	1.7	6
Skrmetta,Matt	01	29	aaa	CIN	2	4	46	6	54	52	20	6	22	48	3.40	1.35	5.0	316	3.6	8.0	2.2	1.1	69
	02	30	aaa	LA	9	1	47	1	68	67	24	5	35	51	3.17	1.50	6.4	339	4.6	6.7	1.5	0.7	56
Sloan,Brandon	02	25	a/a	FLA	2	8	45	8	73	89	38	7	33	40	4.67	1.67	7.5	363	4.1	4.9	1.2	0.9	25
Slusarski,Joe	01	35	aaa	HOU	5	2	37	1	48	58	18	5	12	24	3.36	1.45	5.7	331	2.2	4.5	2.1	1.0	37
Small,Aaron	01	30	aaa	ANA	10	8	44	0	102	126	51	18	32	52	4.45	1.55	10.4	347	2.8	4.6	1.6	1.5	11
	02	31	aaa	ATL	0	3	14	0	31	61	30	2	16	14	8.71	2.48	12.0	460	4.6	4.1	0.9	0.6	-0
Smith,Brian	01	27	a/a	PIT	2	2	38	11	43	53	22	7	8	28	4.56	1.41	4.9	326	1.7	5.8	3.5	1.4	60
	02	30	aaa	PIT	3	3	33	7	37	47	21	2	11	19	5.08	1.56	5.0	348	2.7	4.6	1.7	0.5	44
Smith,Bud	01	22	aaa	STL	8	5	17	0	108	115	34	6	25	80	2.80	1.30	26.8	307	2.1	6.7	3.2	0.5	92
	02	23	aaa	PHI	3	1	9	0	55	59	20	1	19	43	3.27	1.42	26.5	327	3.1	7.0	2.3	0.2	86
Smith,Cam	01	28	a/a	LA	1	6	37	0	65	78	52	8	65	43	7.17	2.19	9.0	429	9.0	5.9	0.7	1.1	12
Smith,Clint	02	26	aa	DET	5	13	38	0	120	210	105	17	61	60	7.86	2.25	16.4	436	4.6	4.5	1.0	1.3	-10
Smith,Dan	01	26	aaa	CLE	6	4	21	0	106	135	71	22	45	56	6.04	1.70	23.3	368	3.9	4.8	1.2	1.8	-6
	02	27	aaa	MON	5	4	14	0	83	88	41	13	19	49	4.44	1.29	25.0	306	2.1	5.3	2.6	1.4	46
Smith,Hans	02	24	aa	TAM	2	4	46	0	54	66	33	2	31	36	5.49	1.79	5.5	380	5.2	6.0	1.2	0.3	46
Smith,Matt	02	23	aa	NYY	3	8	17	0	89	134	69	9	39	60	6.97	1.94	25.5	399	3.9	6.1	1.5	0.9	28
Smith,Mike	01	24	aa	TOR	6	2	14	0	93	98	33	8	27	63	3.16	1.35	28.3	316	2.6	6.1	2.3	0.8	62
	02	25	aaa	TOR	8	4	20	0	121	120	56	10	42	65	4.16	1.34	25.8	314	3.1	4.8	1.5	0.7	44
Smith,Roy	01	25	aaa	CLE	0	5	48	18	74	71	24	3	29	73	2.95	1.35	6.6	316	3.6	8.9	2.5	0.4	101
	02	26	aaa	CLE	5	4	36	1	70	80	42	3	32	54	5.39	1.60	8.8	354	4.1	6.9	1.7	0.4	64
Smith,Travis	01	29	a/a	HOU	15	8	30	1	162	218	84	11	33	62	4.64	1.55	24.1	346	1.8	3.4	1.9	0.6	35
	02	30	aaa	STL	4	7	16	0	85	96	30	9	15	51	3.17	1.30	22.5	309	1.6	5.4	3.4	1.0	75
Smyth,Steve	01	23	aa	CHC	9	3	18	0	120	124	38	8	40	78	2.86	1.36	28.6	319	3.0	5.8	1.9	0.6	60
	02	24	a/a	CHC	7	6	17	0	104	108	55	11	28	84	4.76	1.31	25.9	309	2.4	7.3	3.0	1.0	81
Snare,Ryan	02	24	aa	FLA	4	2	16	0	61	58	26	6	23	48	3.84	1.33	16.2	313	3.4	7.1	2.1	0.9	66
Sneed,John	02	26	a/a	MIN	3	7	40	1	92	119	66	13	50	62	6.46	1.84	10.9	386	4.9	6.1	1.2	1.3	18
Snyder,Bill	01	27	aa	OAK	1	3	31	0	42	72	32	10	23	18	6.88	2.27	7.0	437	4.9	3.9	0.8	2.2	-45
Snyder,John	01	27	aaa	MIL	3	11	32	0	147	238	111	17	37	69	6.76	1.87	22.0	390	2.3	4.2	1.9	1.0	18
	02	28	aaa	SD	7	12	26	0	144	185	81	12	54	73	5.06	1.66	25.4	362	3.4	4.6	1.4	0.7	27
Snyder,Matt	01	27	a/a	CHC	3	1	39	1	53	80	60	7	34	37	10.13	2.16	6.9	426	5.8	6.2	1.1	1.2	11
Sobkowiak,Scott	01	24	aa	ATL	2	5	12	0	65	88	55	12	42	41	7.57	2.00	26.6	406	5.9	5.6	1.0	1.7	-5
	02	25	a/a	ATL	3	2	17	0	39	35	22	3	31	35	5.06	1.69	10.6	366	7.1	8.1	1.1	0.7	59
Sollecito,Gabe	02	31	a/a	ARI	3	3	50	6	51	61	26	6	15	27	4.58	1.49	4.5	337	2.6	4.8	1.8	1.1	32
Song,Seung	02	22	aa	MON	7	7	22	0	113	126	63	12	36	102	5.01	1.43	22.4	329	2.9	8.1	2.8	1.0	79
Sonnier,Shawn	01	25	aaa	KC	5	5	47	6	71	79	45	17	31	51	5.76	1.55	6.8	347	4.0	6.5	1.6	2.2	8
Soriano,Rafael	01	22	aa	SEA	2	2	8	0	48	39	21	5	15	48	3.93	1.12	24.3	278	2.8	9.0	3.2	0.9	105
	02	23	aa	SEA	2	3	10	0	46	39	16	7	16	44	3.12	1.19	19.0	290	3.1	8.6	2.8	1.4	78
Sparks,Steve	01	27	a/a	PIT	4	9	38	3	113	138	78	14	106	73	6.19	2.15	15.1	424	8.4	5.8	0.7	1.2	11
Spencer,Corey	01	25	aa	BOS	3	5	55	20	77	111	56	10	36	61	6.48	1.90	6.8	394	4.1	7.1	1.7	1.2	33
	02	26	a/a	BOS	2	4	47	7	74	112	62	8	44	55	7.52	2.10	7.9	419	5.3	6.7	1.3	1.0	24
Spencer,Sean	01	26	aaa	MON	2	1	52	0	64	65	29	5	30	48	4.05	1.48	5.4	336	4.2	6.7	1.6	0.7	55
Spencer,Stan	01	32	aaa	SD	5	6	20	0	99	127	66	12	33	62	6.03	1.62	22.5	356	3.0	5.6	1.9	1.1	36
Spiegel,Mike	02	27	a/a	CLE	7	3	26	0	95	96	53	11	64	68	5.01	1.68	16.8	365	6.1	6.4	1.1	1.0	33
Spille,Ryan	02	26	aa	TOR	7	12	27	0	159	231	116	24	57	76	6.56	1.81	27.9	383	3.2	4.3	1.3	1.4	2
Spooneybarger,Tim	01	22	a/a	ATL	4	1	57	5	72	60	20	2	25	76	2.49	1.17	5.2	287	3.1	9.4	3.1	0.2	124
Spradlin,Jerry	01	34	aaa	STL	4	1	29	14	32	20	9	2	7	25	2.65	0.85	4.2	225	2.1	6.9	3.4	0.6	114

Major League Equivalent Statistics

					Actual				Major League Equivalents														
PITCHER	Yr	Age	Lev	Org	W	L	G	Sv	IP	H	ER	HR	BB	K	ERA	Br/IP	BF/G	OOB	CTL	DOM	CMD	hr/9	BPV
Springer,Dennis	01	37	aaa	LA	7	7	19	0	114	152	67	15	27	42	5.31	1.57	27.0	349	2.2	3.3	1.5	1.2	9
	02	38	aaa	LA	7	8	26	1	143	209	87	18	34	31	5.48	1.70	25.4	368	2.1	2.0	0.9	1.1	-15
Spurgeon,Jay	01	25	aaa	BAL	3	5	15	0	87	101	58	15	28	54	5.96	1.49	25.6	337	2.9	5.6	1.9	1.6	25
	02	26	aaa	BAL	4	14	29	0	154	214	111	18	43	69	6.49	1.67	24.4	364	2.5	4.0	1.6	1.1	17
Spurling,Chris	01	24	aa	PIT	5	7	34	1	121	167	59	12	33	51	4.38	1.65	16.3	361	2.4	3.8	1.6	0.9	21
	02	25	aa	PIT	4	3	51	20	70	69	23	9	12	46	2.96	1.16	5.6	284	1.5	5.9	3.8	1.2	86
Stamler,Keith	02	23	aa	TEX	6	7	30	0	134	196	91	6	29	50	6.11	1.68	20.6	365	1.9	3.4	1.7	0.4	33
Standridge,Jason	01	23	a/a	TAM	5	12	22	0	112	171	88	16	56	48	7.07	2.03	25.2	410	4.5	3.9	0.9	1.3	-11
	02	24	aaa	TAM	10	9	29	0	173	195	75	13	66	94	3.90	1.51	26.4	341	3.4	4.9	1.4	0.7	38
Stanford,Jason	01	25	a/a	CLE	7	11	25	0	151	191	88	14	33	98	5.22	1.48	26.6	336	2.0	5.8	3.0	0.9	66
	02	26	a/a	CLE	10	7	24	0	138	178	69	11	49	89	4.50	1.64	26.2	360	3.2	5.8	1.8	0.7	45
Stanifer,Rob	01	30	aaa	CHC	7	8	54	6	74	101	42	9	30	62	5.07	1.76	6.4	377	3.6	7.5	2.1	1.1	48
Stark,Dennis	01	27	a/a	SEA	15	2	25	0	158	157	52	13	51	112	2.97	1.31	26.8	310	2.9	6.3	2.2	0.8	66
	02	28	aaa	COL	1	2	7	0	37	41	20	6	14	31	4.84	1.48	23.4	336	3.4	7.5	2.2	1.5	48
Steenstra,Kennie	01	31	aaa	ARI	9	6	28	0	170	218	95	15	42	93	5.02	1.53	27.0	344	2.2	4.9	2.2	0.8	47
	02	32	aaa	ARI	2	3	18	0	53	97	57	5	18	25	9.66	2.17	15.0	426	3.1	4.2	1.4	0.8	7
Stemle,Steve	01	24	aa	STL	7	10	26	0	134	201	100	16	49	67	6.72	1.87	24.7	390	3.3	4.5	1.3	1.1	10
	02	25	a/a	STL	12	6	28	0	137	168	73	13	39	69	4.80	1.51	21.7	341	2.6	4.5	1.8	0.9	35
Stephens,Jason	01	26	aa	ANA	6	7	19	0	119	149	69	15	28	57	5.21	1.49	27.6	337	2.1	4.3	2.0	1.1	30
	02	27	a/a	ANA	1	8	10	0	57	95	49	13	16	23	7.74	1.95	27.7	400	2.5	3.6	1.4	2.1	-27
Stephens,John	01	22	a/a	BAL	13	9	27	0	190	164	64	17	39	180	3.02	1.07	28.1	268	1.8	8.5	4.6	0.8	133
	02	23	aaa	BAL	11	5	21	0	142	135	54	10	22	105	3.42	1.10	27.2	274	1.4	6.6	4.8	0.6	127
Stevens,Dave	01	32	a/a	ATL	2	2	48	3	70	93	71	19	42	43	9.13	1.93	7.1	398	5.4	5.5	1.0	2.4	-26
Stevens,Josh	02	23	aa	NYY	1	1	24	0	40	60	22	2	8	28	4.95	1.70	7.7	368	1.8	6.3	3.5	0.5	85
Stewart,Josh	01	23	aa	CHW	3	4	16	0	82	129	78	9	43	42	8.55	2.10	25.7	418	4.7	4.6	1.0	1.0	4
	02	24	aa	CHW	11	7	26	0	150	180	82	16	62	82	4.92	1.61	26.2	356	3.7	4.9	1.3	1.0	25
Stewart,Paul	02	24	aa	MIL	12	9	27	0	161	177	77	15	43	103	4.30	1.36	25.6	319	2.4	5.8	2.4	0.8	60
Stocks,Nick	01	23	aa	STL	2	12	16	0	82	110	65	13	37	57	7.13	1.80	24.2	381	4.1	6.3	1.5	1.5	18
Stokley,Billy	02	25	aa	ANA	4	14	38	1	131	200	87	14	38	32	5.98	1.82	16.3	384	2.6	2.2	0.8	1.0	-12
Stone,Ricky	01	27	aaa	HOU	6	3	51	2	95	120	51	10	30	65	4.78	1.57	8.4	350	2.8	6.2	2.2	1.0	48
Strange,Pat	01	21	a/a	NYM	12	6	27	0	159	189	94	17	52	100	5.33	1.51	26.1	342	3.0	5.6	1.9	1.0	42
	02	22	aaa	NYM	10	10	29	0	165	179	80	11	58	97	4.36	1.44	24.8	330	3.2	5.3	1.7	0.6	50
Strong,Joe	01	39	aaa	FLA	6	3	46	1	59	83	39	7	17	40	5.94	1.69	5.9	367	2.6	6.1	2.4	1.1	42
Stull,Everett	02	31	aaa	MIL	11	11	24	0	151	188	92	18	54	97	5.48	1.60	28.5	354	3.2	5.8	1.8	1.1	35
Sturdy,Tim	02	24	aa	MIN	1	0	35	0	53	77	51	5	32	17	8.63	2.05	7.6	412	5.4	2.9	0.5	0.8	-8
Suarez,Felipe	01	26	aa	ANA	2	5	34	3	66	96	42	14	19	36	5.74	1.73	9.1	372	2.6	4.9	1.9	2.0	-1
Surkont,Keith	02	26	aa	OAK	2	3	27	1	65	87	37	6	38	28	5.12	1.92	11.7	397	5.3	3.9	0.7	0.8	6
Suzuki,Mac	02	27	a/a	KC	0	4	30	0	58	85	39	8	26	36	6.03	1.91	9.4	395	4.0	5.6	1.4	1.2	14
Sweeney,Brian	01	27	aa	SEA	7	4	37	1	104	160	63	10	29	72	5.42	1.82	13.3	384	2.5	6.2	2.5	0.8	51
	02	28	aaa	SEA	9	5	30	2	142	191	76	17	29	90	4.82	1.55	21.2	347	1.8	5.7	3.1	1.1	59
Sylvester,Billy	01	25	a/a	ATL	1	4	62	23	67	58	40	6	56	68	5.37	1.69	5.0	367	7.5	9.2	1.2	0.8	65
	02	26	a/a	ATL	2	3	58	26	58	51	30	8	40	40	4.64	1.56	4.5	349	6.2	6.2	1.0	1.2	30
Taglienti,Jeff	01	26	aa	CIN	5	5	51	7	55	82	40	4	16	36	6.53	1.77	5.1	378	2.5	5.9	2.3	0.7	49
	02	27	aa	CIN	2	0	24	0	30	47	16	1	7	13	4.77	1.79	5.9	380	2.1	3.9	1.9	0.3	39
Takeoka,Kazuhiro	01	27	aa	ATL	5	3	45	3	74	105	33	2	25	36	4.05	1.76	7.7	375	3.1	4.3	1.4	0.3	37
	02	28	a/a	ATL	2	3	44	4	65	84	41	1	34	30	5.68	1.82	7.0	383	4.7	4.2	0.9	0.1	33
Tallet,Brian	02	25	a/a	CLE	12	4	26	0	146	177	69	14	54	81	4.25	1.58	25.3	351	3.3	5.0	1.5	0.9	32
Tankersley,Dennis	01	23	a/a	SD	5	3	16	0	84	67	32	8	33	84	3.43	1.19	21.6	290	3.5	9.0	2.5	0.9	94
	02	24	a/a	SD	6	7	19	0	101	101	45	7	52	91	4.00	1.51	23.6	341	4.6	8.1	1.8	0.6	71
Taylor,Aaron	02	25	aa	SEA	4	3	61	24	77	69	30	7	40	72	3.51	1.42	5.5	327	4.7	8.4	1.8	0.8	72
Tejera,Mike	01	25	aa	FLA	9	8	25	0	141	181	79	20	47	108	5.04	1.62	25.6	357	3.0	6.9	2.3	1.3	45
Tekavec,Nate	02	23	aa	DET	6	9	27	0	141	220	125	27	48	49	7.98	1.90	25.2	394	3.1	3.1	1.0	1.7	-26
Telford,Anthony	01	36	aaa	MON	3	5	28	1	76	99	53	9	19	49	6.23	1.55	12.1	347	2.2	5.9	2.6	1.1	50
	02	37	aaa	TEX	8	2	35	5	50	55	22	3	21	29	3.95	1.52	6.4	342	3.8	5.2	1.4	0.5	44
Tessmer,Jay	01	30	aaa	COL	8	5	45	4	72	102	40	12	16	39	4.93	1.64	7.3	360	2.1	4.9	2.4	1.5	24
	02	31	aaa	NYY	5	4	63	4	78	132	47	7	16	43	5.42	1.90	6.0	394	1.8	5.0	2.7	0.8	44
Teut,Nate	01	26	aaa	CHC	13	8	29	0	167	202	105	26	68	106	5.66	1.61	26.1	356	3.6	5.7	1.6	1.4	21
	02	27	aaa	FLA	5	6	27	0	116	138	67	15	49	70	5.20	1.61	19.5	356	3.8	5.4	1.4	1.2	25
Thames,Charlie	02	23	aa	ANA	1	3	38	4	53	54	38	5	36	35	6.43	1.69	6.5	367	6.1	5.9	1.0	0.8	34
Thomas,Brad	01	24	aa	MIN	10	3	19	0	119	123	42	6	31	81	3.19	1.29	26.4	306	2.3	6.1	2.6	0.5	80
	02	25	aaa	MIN	6	12	28	0	152	188	104	19	52	83	6.16	1.58	24.4	351	3.1	4.9	1.6	1.1	25
Thomas,Evan	01	27	aaa	PHI	3	13	19	0	104	158	88	17	44	64	7.65	1.94	26.6	400	3.8	5.5	1.4	1.5	6
	02	28	aaa	PHI	10	2	22	0	113	130	63	8	43	64	5.02	1.53	22.9	344	3.4	5.1	1.5	0.6	41
Thompson,Doug	01	25	aa	COL	2	5	26	1	38	49	29	4	23	26	6.82	1.90	7.1	394	5.5	6.2	1.1	1.0	23
	02	26	aa	COL	6	2	50	6	70	86	49	9	29	51	6.29	1.64	6.4	360	3.7	6.5	1.8	1.2	37
Thompson,Eric	01	24	aa	OAK	1	4	35	2	64	84	35	9	21	56	4.87	1.64	8.4	360	3.0	7.9	2.7	1.3	56
	02	25	a/a	OAK	6	5	35	3	114	142	60	11	36	65	4.74	1.56	14.6	348	2.8	5.1	1.8	0.9	38
Thompson,Mark	01	31	aa	COL	3	2	8	0	48	81	63	11	24	24	11.79	2.20	30.7	430	4.6	4.5	1.0	2.1	-35
	02	32	a/a	COL	1	4	20	0	58	104	50	17	16	32	7.75	2.07	14.5	414	2.5	5.0	2.0	2.6	-28
Thompson,Travis	01	27	a/a	COL	1	3	37	5	46	81	58	16	22	30	11.30	2.25	6.4	435	4.3	5.8	1.3	3.0	-49
Thompson,Travis	01	24	aa	CIN	12	10	28	0	167	206	93	13	47	100	4.99	1.52	26.5	342	2.6	5.4	2.1	0.7	52
	02	25	a/a	CIN	1	7	23	0	81	122	58	5	21	52	6.44	1.76	16.5	377	2.3	5.8	2.5	0.6	57
Thomson,John	01	28	aaa	COL	5	3	12	0	68	94	34	10	14	43	4.55	1.58	25.5	351	1.9	5.7	3.1	1.3	51
Thornton,Matt	02	26	aa	SEA	1	5	12	0	62	72	39	3	34	33	5.66	1.71	23.9	369	4.9	4.8	1.0	0.4	34
Thurman,Corey	01	23	a/a	KC	13	5	26	0	160	138	72	18	62	126	4.05	1.25	25.7	300	3.5	7.1	2.0	1.0	64
Thurman,Mike	02	29	aaa	NYY	7	3	12	0	76	100	36	9	15	41	4.25	1.51	28.1	341	1.8	4.8	2.7	1.1	48
Tokarse,Brian	01	27	aa	CHW	2	6	39	0	65	76	43	6	46	63	5.87	1.87	8.0	390	6.3	8.6	1.4	0.8	55
Tolar,Kevin	01	31	aaa	DET	3	4	44	7	56	61	22	3	21	56	3.57	1.47	5.6	335	3.4	9.0	2.6	0.5	94
	02	32	aaa	PIT	6	1	44	1	78	80	28	5	26	67	3.23	1.36	7.6	318	3.0	7.7	2.6	0.6	86
Tomko,Brett	01	29	aaa	SEA	10	6	19	0	127	147	70	13	28	99	4.95	1.38	28.7	321	2.0	7.0	3.5	0.9	87
Torres,Salomon	02	31	aaa	PIT	8	5	26	0	162	216	93	13	41	104	5.16	1.59	28.1	352	2.3	5.8	2.5	0.7	59
Totten,Heath	02	24	aa	LA	3	3	9	0	49	56	21	2	16	25	3.86	1.47	23.9	335	2.9	4.6	1.6	0.4	48

Major League Equivalent Statistics

					Actual				Major League Equivalents													
PITCHER	Yr	Age	Lev	Org	W	L	G	Sv	IP	H	ER	HR	BB	K	ERA	Br/IP	BF/G	OOB	CTL	DOM	CMD	hr/9	BPV
Towers,Josh	01	25	aaa	BAL	3	1	6	0	41	47	21	2	8	24	4.61	1.34	29.1	315	1.8	5.3	3.0	0.4	80
	02	26	aaa	BAL	0	9	15	0	69	124	69	17	14	36	9.00	2.00	22.6	407	1.8	4.7	2.6	2.2	-6
Traber,Billy	01	22	a/a	NYM	4	4	9	0	50	62	26	4	14	38	4.66	1.51	24.7	341	2.5	6.8	2.7	0.7	72
	02	23	a/a	CLE	17	5	27	0	162	188	70	14	34	99	3.89	1.37	25.8	319	1.9	5.5	2.9	0.8	69
Trujillo,J.J.	01	26	aa	SD	3	3	43	6	51	57	21	1	24	30	3.65	1.60	5.4	354	4.3	5.4	1.3	0.2	52
	02	27	a/a	SD	5	0	49	20	68	70	22	3	23	57	2.91	1.37	6.0	319	3.0	7.5	2.5	0.4	88
Tucker,Julien	01	28	aa	DET	1	6	28	0	54	88	50	3	40	18	8.33	2.36	10.2	447	6.7	3.1	0.5	0.4	-1
Tucker,T.J.	01	23	a/a	MON	8	10	27	0	166	170	80	26	73	100	4.34	1.46	27.0	334	4.0	5.4	1.4	1.4	22
Turman,Jason	01	26	aaa	SEA	7	5	29	1	75	61	22	6	27	76	2.66	1.17	10.6	286	3.3	9.1	2.8	0.7	103
Ulacia,Dennis	02	22	aa	CHW	6	14	28	1	145	209	106	21	55	81	6.57	1.82	24.6	384	3.4	5.0	1.5	1.3	11
Ulloa,Enmanuel	01	23	aa	SEA	2	2	45	4	80	92	32	3	22	58	3.60	1.43	7.7	328	2.5	6.5	2.6	0.3	83
	02	24	aaa	SEA	4	7	38	2	77	103	61	13	28	35	7.13	1.70	9.4	368	3.3	4.1	1.3	1.5	-3
Urban,Jeff	01	25	aa	SF	7	11	27	0	156	209	83	17	33	92	4.79	1.55	25.9	347	1.9	5.3	2.8	1.0	54
	02	26	aaa	SF	5	7	35	0	103	128	45	8	34	61	3.93	1.57	13.2	350	3.0	5.3	1.8	0.7	44
Valdes,Marc	01	30	aaa	ATL	9	11	29	2	123	173	88	16	46	77	6.42	1.78	19.9	378	3.4	5.7	1.7	1.2	23
Valentine,Joe	02	23	aa	CHW	4	1	55	36	59	44	18	1	32	58	2.74	1.29	4.5	306	4.9	8.8	1.8	0.2	101
Valverde,Jose	01	22	aa	ARI	2	2	39	13	41	39	20	1	25	62	4.38	1.56	4.7	348	5.5	13.6	2.5	0.2	133
	02	23	aaa	ARI	2	4	49	5	47	49	34	8	21	54	6.48	1.48	4.2	337	4.0	10.3	2.6	1.5	73
Van Dusen,Derrick	02	21	aa	TEX	2	3	8	0	37	54	31	5	15	19	7.54	1.86	22.1	390	3.6	4.6	1.3	1.2	6
Van Hekken,Andy	01	22	aa	DET	5	0	8	0	48	71	29	4	7	25	5.44	1.63	27.3	358	1.3	4.7	3.6	0.8	68
	02	23	a/a	DET	9	7	28	0	183	202	76	12	41	102	3.74	1.33	27.8	313	2.0	5.0	2.5	0.6	65
Vance,Cory	02	23	aa	COL	10	8	25	0	150	176	88	13	77	96	5.28	1.69	27.7	366	4.6	5.8	1.2	0.8	35
Vargas,Claudio	01	22	aa	FLA	8	9	27	0	159	147	99	28	74	131	5.60	1.39	25.4	322	4.2	7.4	1.8	1.6	41
	02	23	a/a	FLA	6	13	25	0	109	132	76	17	42	84	6.27	1.59	19.7	353	3.5	6.9	2.0	1.4	38
Vargas,Jose	02	26	aa	CLE	4	1	18	2	39	56	28	1	19	26	6.43	1.91	10.5	396	4.4	6.0	1.4	0.2	47
Vargas,Martin	01	24	a/a	CLE	1	8	54	13	68	86	45	3	40	49	5.94	1.85	6.0	388	5.3	6.5	1.2	0.4	47
	02	26	aaa	CLE	3	2	22	8	35	43	12	3	12	16	3.09	1.57	7.1	350	3.1	4.1	1.3	0.8	25
Vasquez,Leo	01	28	aaa	OAK	0	1	36	0	44	60	30	4	31	29	6.14	2.07	6.1	415	6.4	5.9	0.9	0.9	20
Vega,Rene	01	25	aa	NYM	3	6	41	2	106	143	53	13	36	52	4.52	1.69	11.9	366	3.0	4.4	1.5	1.1	15
	02	26	aa	NYM	1	6	26	2	45	76	45	7	21	25	8.98	2.15	8.8	424	4.2	5.0	1.2	1.4	-5
Vent,Kevin	02	25	aa	SF	9	4	45	3	81	101	38	6	30	24	4.22	1.62	8.2	356	3.3	2.7	0.8	0.7	8
Veras,Dario	01	29	aaa	CLE	5	1	48	6	67	88	47	14	23	55	6.36	1.65	6.4	361	3.0	7.4	2.4	1.9	32
Veronie,Shanin	02	26	aa	ATL	2	2	29	0	52	69	31	6	24	23	5.34	1.78	8.5	379	4.1	4.0	1.0	1.0	6
Verplancke,Jeff	01	24	a/a	SF	3	9	51	23	61	63	30	4	24	49	4.43	1.43	5.2	328	3.5	7.2	2.0	0.6	71
	02	25	aaa	SF	3	5	51	3	64	67	31	5	24	44	4.35	1.42	5.5	327	3.4	6.2	1.8	0.7	57
Viera,Rolando	02	29	a/a	BOS	5	1	48	10	84	128	63	20	46	34	6.75	2.07	8.7	415	4.9	3.6	0.7	2.1	-40
Villafuerte,Brandon	01	26	aaa	TEX	5	5	38	10	63	75	25	5	25	57	3.60	1.58	7.5	351	3.6	8.2	2.3	0.7	73
	02	27	aaa	SD	8	4	47	1	58	49	15	2	23	45	2.33	1.24	5.1	298	3.6	7.0	2.0	0.3	84
Villano,Mike	01	30	aa	KC	6	7	44	9	77	136	59	14	40	27	6.83	2.28	9.1	438	4.7	3.2	0.7	1.7	-37
Villarreal,Oscar	01	20	aa	ARI	6	9	27	0	140	152	68	8	54	102	4.38	1.47	22.8	334	3.4	6.6	1.9	0.5	65
	02	21	aa	ARI	9	6	24	0	148	141	67	9	40	116	4.07	1.22	25.6	295	2.4	7.0	2.9	0.5	93
Villegas,Ismael	01	25	aaa	ATL	4	7	34	1	134	153	81	24	40	87	5.42	1.44	17.2	330	2.7	5.8	2.2	1.6	30
Vining,Ken	01	27	aaa	CHW	2	3	41	4	46	44	14	3	21	41	2.82	1.41	4.9	326	4.0	8.0	2.0	0.6	77
	02	28	aaa	CHW	2	5	44	1	47	46	21	6	27	30	4.02	1.55	4.8	347	5.2	5.7	1.1	1.1	28
Vizcaino,Luis	01	24	aaa	OAK	2	2	27	7	42	38	11	5	9	48	2.36	1.12	6.3	277	1.9	10.3	5.3	1.1	149
Vogelsong,Ryan	01	24	aaa	PIT	5	6	16	0	90	67	36	8	34	74	3.59	1.12	22.8	277	3.4	7.4	2.2	0.8	81
	02	25	aa	PIT	1	5	8	0	43	60	37	6	10	27	7.71	1.62	24.5	357	2.1	5.6	2.7	1.3	43
Voyles,Brad	01	25	aa	KC	1	0	26	10	32	22	2	0	19	35	0.59	1.28	5.2	305	5.3	9.9	1.9	0.0	115
	02	26	aaa	KC	3	4	26	5	32	33	18	2	21	28	5.05	1.68	5.7	366	5.9	7.9	1.3	0.6	61
Wade,Travis	01	26	aa	HOU	2	3	60	23	65	90	33	10	26	42	4.60	1.78	5.1	379	3.6	5.8	1.6	1.4	16
	02	27	a/a	HOU	3	8	48	1	68	102	57	14	38	35	7.54	2.06	7.1	414	5.0	4.6	0.9	1.9	-21
Wainhouse,Dave	01	34	aaa	CHC	3	5	49	6	75	98	40	8	24	49	4.79	1.62	7.0	357	2.9	5.9	2.0	1.0	41
Waligora,Tom	01	25	aa	CHC	4	1	22	0	31	27	14	3	14	28	4.19	1.33	6.0	312	4.2	8.1	1.9	1.0	70
Walker,Adam	01	25	aa	PHI	7	4	17	0	95	67	24	2	36	72	2.32	1.08	22.3	269	3.4	6.8	2.0	0.2	93
Walker,Jamie	01	30	aaa	CLE	7	2	38	2	93	137	58	17	30	40	5.59	1.79	11.5	380	2.9	3.8	1.3	1.6	-10
Walker,Pete	01	33	aaa	NYM	13	4	26	0	168	178	75	14	52	86	4.00	1.37	27.7	319	2.8	4.6	1.7	0.7	42
Walker,Tyler	01	25	a/a	NYM	4	2	12	0	63	52	24	8	23	39	3.45	1.18	21.6	288	3.3	5.5	1.7	1.2	44
	02	26	aaa	NYM	10	5	28	1	142	178	78	13	40	89	4.94	1.54	22.6	345	2.5	5.6	2.2	0.8	51
Walk,Mitch	02	25	aa	SF	6	5	33	1	124	152	46	5	49	55	3.33	1.62	17.1	357	3.6	4.0	1.1	0.4	33
Walling,Dave	01	23	aa	NYY	3	3	6	0	38	59	30	3	4	27	7.07	1.65	29.1	361	0.9	6.4	6.8	0.7	145
	02	24	aaa	NYY	2	7	11	0	67	80	38	8	11	41	5.10	1.36	26.1	317	1.5	5.5	3.7	1.1	76
Walrond,Les	01	25	aa	STL	2	8	16	0	81	86	49	6	53	60	5.49	1.71	23.5	370	5.8	6.6	1.1	0.7	44
	02	26	a/a	STL	10	8	32	0	145	173	92	25	75	123	5.71	1.71	21.0	369	4.7	7.6	1.6	1.6	31
Ward,Bryan	01	30	aaa	BOS	0	3	19	0	33	60	22	2	7	14	5.96	2.02	8.6	409	1.8	3.7	2.1	0.6	26
	02	31	aaa	COL	1	2	6	0	38	47	28	7	16	21	6.63	1.66	29.0	362	3.8	5.0	1.3	1.7	3
Ward,Jeremy	01	24	a/a	ARI	3	4	46	13	54	60	21	3	17	35	3.50	1.43	5.1	328	2.8	5.8	2.1	0.5	63
	02	25	aaa	ARI	4	6	54	1	62	74	33	5	13	34	4.77	1.40	5.0	324	1.9	4.9	2.6	0.7	60
Watkins,Steve	01	23	aa	SD	4	8	23	0	97	128	77	15	58	43	7.17	1.91	20.4	396	5.4	4.0	0.7	1.4	-11
	02	24	aa	SD	4	8	37	0	116	147	61	8	53	70	4.72	1.72	14.6	371	4.1	5.4	1.3	0.6	36
Watson,Mark	01	28	a/a	SEA	3	3	36	5	47	61	33	5	22	30	6.37	1.76	6.1	376	4.2	5.7	1.4	0.9	30
	02	29	aaa	COL	6	0	44	3	60	81	48	9	32	35	7.18	1.88	6.6	391	4.8	5.2	1.1	1.3	6
Wayne,Justin	01	22	aa	MON	9	2	14	0	92	101	34	5	35	59	3.32	1.48	28.9	336	3.4	5.8	1.7	0.5	56
	02	23	a/a	FLA	8	6	26	0	152	131	58	11	49	77	3.43	1.18	24.0	288	2.9	4.6	1.6	0.7	50
Weaver,Eric	01	28	aa	CHW	3	3	24	2	31	36	19	5	20	22	5.43	1.81	6.1	382	5.8	6.3	1.1	1.4	15
	02	29	aa	PHI	5	4	37	7	45	57	33	11	37	32	6.60	2.09	6.1	417	7.4	6.4	0.9	2.2	-15
Webb,Brandon	02	23	a/a	ARI	10	7	27	0	159	161	63	4	58	106	3.57	1.38	25.3	321	3.3	6.0	1.8	0.2	71
Webb,John	02	23	aa	CHC	4	5	11	0	61	62	39	6	24	39	5.74	1.41	24.1	325	3.5	5.7	1.6	0.9	46
Wedel,Jeremy	01	25	aa	PHI	5	3	45	5	63	80	33	4	18	37	4.66	1.55	6.3	347	2.6	5.3	2.1	0.6	52
	02	26	aaa	PHI	7	1	43	1	60	70	22	1	21	31	3.29	1.51	6.2	341	3.1	4.6	1.5	0.1	52
Weibl,Clint	02	28	aaa	STL	5	8	24	0	110	147	56	19	25	54	4.57	1.56	20.6	348	2.0	4.4	2.2	1.6	18
Wellemeyer,Todd	02	24	aa	CHC	3	3	8	0	46	40	32	2	20	31	6.26	1.30	24.3	309	3.9	6.1	1.6	0.4	66

Major League Equivalent Statistics

					Actual				Major League Equivalents														
PITCHER	Yr	Age	Lev	Org	W	L	G	Sv	IP	H	ER	HR	BB	K	ERA	Br/IP	BF/G	OOB	CTL	DOM	CMD	hr/9	BPV
Wengert,Don	01	32	aaa	PIT	7	7	18	0	112	156	60	17	21	54	4.82	1.58	28.0	351	1.7	4.4	2.6	1.4	30
	02	33	aaa	BOS	8	12	29	0	169	265	112	20	36	60	5.96	1.78	27.4	379	1.9	3.2	1.7	1.1	7
Westbrook,Jake	01	24	aaa	CLE	8	1	12	0	64	71	30	3	23	39	4.21	1.46	23.5	334	3.2	5.5	1.7	0.4	56
West,Brian	02	22	aa	CHW	9	11	27	0	149	156	98	13	76	84	5.92	1.56	24.7	348	4.6	5.1	1.1	0.8	32
Wheeler,Dan	01	24	a/a	TAM	3	7	21	0	81	104	57	16	18	44	6.33	1.50	17.1	340	2.0	4.9	2.4	1.8	21
	02	25	aaa	ATL	9	6	27	0	155	188	98	25	41	92	5.69	1.48	25.2	336	2.4	5.3	2.2	1.5	32
Whisenant,Matt	01	30	aaa	LA	1	7	24	1	60	93	52	4	38	32	7.82	2.18	12.8	428	5.7	4.9	0.9	0.7	13
Whiteside,Matt	02	35	aaa	COL	4	7	60	26	70	101	53	18	15	66	6.80	1.65	5.3	362	1.9	8.5	4.4	2.3	63
White,Bill	01	23	aa	ARI	0	4	7	0	37	41	21	2	19	22	5.08	1.61	24.1	356	4.6	5.3	1.2	0.5	42
White,Matt	01	23	aaa	TAM	0	5	7	0	30	39	33	5	25	14	9.90	2.13	21.7	422	7.5	4.2	0.6	1.5	-15
	02	25	a/a	TAM	7	4	41	1	140	186	91	20	69	76	5.85	1.82	16.2	384	4.4	4.9	1.1	1.3	6
White,Matt	01	24	aa	CLE	8	10	25	0	144	191	108	24	63	59	6.78	1.76	27.0	376	3.9	3.7	0.9	1.5	-11
Wiggins,Scott	02	27	a/a	TOR	5	2	52	1	61	47	17	1	22	46	2.51	1.13	4.8	279	3.2	6.8	2.1	0.1	93
Wilkins,Marc	01	31	aaa	PIT	4	1	32	1	36	47	23	2	14	19	5.83	1.70	5.2	368	3.6	4.7	1.3	0.6	33
	02	32	aaa	CHC	2	0	31	1	41	45	22	1	12	24	4.81	1.38	5.7	321	2.6	5.2	2.0	0.2	67
Williams,Brian	01	33	aaa	BOS	5	6	19	0	62	91	46	5	28	29	6.72	1.92	15.8	397	4.1	4.1	1.0	0.8	11
Williams,Dave	01	23	a/a	PIT	6	3	11	0	69	62	26	12	18	38	3.39	1.16	25.6	284	2.3	4.9	2.1	1.6	35
Williams,Jeff	01	29	aaa	LA	7	5	16	0	90	114	42	12	24	47	4.17	1.54	25.1	345	2.4	4.7	2.0	1.2	28
	02	30	aaa	LA	6	4	56	28	79	88	23	2	21	59	2.61	1.38	6.1	320	2.4	6.7	2.8	0.2	92
Williams,Jerome	01	20	aa	SF	9	7	23	0	130	117	60	13	29	77	4.15	1.13	22.9	278	2.0	5.3	2.6	0.9	69
	02	21	aaa	SF	6	11	28	0	160	136	64	12	42	128	3.60	1.11	23.1	276	2.4	7.2	3.0	0.7	97
Williams,Matt	01	31	aaa	MIL	2	2	51	0	72	81	40	4	44	35	5.00	1.74	6.6	374	5.6	4.4	0.8	0.6	26
Williams,Shad	01	31	a/a	ANA	3	4	19	1	49	94	51	13	24	24	9.38	2.39	13.7	450	4.3	4.4	1.0	2.3	-45
Williams,Todd	02	32	aaa	MON	3	5	46	24	48	71	27	5	13	17	5.06	1.75	4.9	375	2.4	3.2	1.3	0.9	6
Wilson,C.J.	02	22	aa	TEX	1	0	5	0	30	28	8	0	12	15	2.40	1.33	25.5	313	3.6	4.5	1.3	0.0	60
Wilson,Jeff	01	25	a/a	BAL	3	12	33	0	134	184	109	25	56	74	7.34	1.79	19.1	380	3.7	5.0	1.3	1.7	-2
	02	26	aa	BAL	4	4	50	10	91	92	29	6	36	58	2.87	1.41	7.9	325	3.6	5.7	1.6	0.6	54
Wilson,Kris	02	26	a/a	KC	5	3	21	1	74	111	27	6	6	37	3.28	1.58	15.9	351	0.7	4.5	6.2	0.7	122
Wilson,Phil	02	22	aa	ANA	2	4	7	0	42	66	42	12	14	13	8.96	1.90	29.0	394	3.0	2.8	0.9	2.6	-55
Wimberly,Larry	01	26	a/a	PIT	5	3	28	0	83	116	54	14	26	35	5.89	1.70	13.7	367	2.8	3.8	1.4	1.6	-5
	02	27	aa	PIT	1	2	26	1	53	67	35	5	20	26	5.93	1.64	9.3	359	3.4	4.4	1.3	0.8	23
Winchester,Scott	01	28	aaa	CIN	6	3	23	0	53	62	28	6	11	31	4.74	1.38	9.9	320	1.8	5.2	2.9	1.1	56
	02	29	aaa	TOR	2	4	44	2	63	91	54	11	21	32	7.69	1.77	6.7	378	3.0	4.6	1.5	1.6	1
Winkelsas,Joe	01	28	aa	ATL	4	2	20	3	33	36	20	0	19	10	5.45	1.67	7.6	363	5.1	2.6	0.5	0.0	27
Wise,Matt	01	26	aaa	ANA	9	9	21	0	123	147	77	20	16	95	5.61	1.33	24.9	313	1.2	6.9	5.9	1.5	118
	02	27	aaa	ANA	3	4	16	0	78	114	53	13	14	63	6.12	1.64	22.2	360	1.6	7.3	4.5	1.5	81
Wolff,Bryan	01	30	a/a	MIN	4	7	23	0	127	218	122	32	48	69	8.64	2.09	27.7	417	3.4	4.9	1.4	2.2	-27
Woodards,Orlando	02	25	a/a	FLA	5	9	29	1	103	118	42	6	35	52	3.67	1.48	15.7	337	3.1	4.5	1.5	0.5	41
Woodard,Steve	01	26	a/a	CLE	4	2	7	0	41	52	17	3	2	26	3.64	1.32	25.0	312	0.5	5.7	11.7	0.7	253
	02	27	aaa	PHI	5	4	22	5	65	84	43	9	11	48	5.95	1.46	12.9	334	1.5	6.6	4.4	1.2	88
Wood,Mike	02	22	aa	OAK	11	3	17	0	105	115	43	8	28	54	3.68	1.36	26.5	318	2.4	4.6	1.9	0.7	48
Wooten,Greg	01	28	aaa	SEA	11	8	27	0	169	235	89	18	35	100	4.76	1.59	28.3	353	1.8	5.3	2.9	1.0	54
	02	29	aaa	SEA	4	6	14	0	73	108	52	6	17	20	6.40	1.71	24.2	369	2.1	2.5	1.2	0.7	5
Wright,Chris	02	25	aa	SEA	6	4	37	0	70	102	40	7	32	32	5.13	1.91	9.2	395	4.1	4.1	1.0	0.9	7
Wright,Danny	01	24	aa	CHW	7	7	20	0	134	135	55	8	43	110	3.67	1.33	28.5	313	2.9	7.4	2.5	0.6	84
Wright,Jaret	01	26	a/a	CLE	3	1	8	0	36	34	22	5	14	26	5.50	1.31	19.1	309	3.4	6.4	1.9	1.3	45
	02	27	aaa	CLE	5	3	10	0	55	71	33	7	27	36	5.38	1.78	25.9	378	4.4	5.9	1.3	1.1	23
Wrigley,Jase	01	26	aa	COL	6	6	47	2	64	138	82	9	34	26	11.54	2.69	7.6	479	4.8	3.7	0.8	1.2	-29
	02	27	a/a	COL	2	3	53	10	71	92	32	3	37	31	4.04	1.81	6.4	383	4.7	3.9	0.8	0.4	23
Wuertz,Mike	01	23	aa	CHC	4	9	27	0	160	174	78	19	57	116	4.39	1.44	25.9	331	3.2	6.5	2.0	1.1	51
	02	24	aaa	CHC	9	5	28	0	154	188	91	21	63	115	5.32	1.63	25.0	358	3.7	6.7	1.8	1.2	38
Wylie,Mitch	01	25	aa	CHW	15	4	24	0	141	171	88	18	49	104	5.64	1.56	26.3	348	3.2	6.6	2.1	1.1	46
	02	26	aaa	CHW	2	3	6	0	34	52	24	8	5	21	6.35	1.68	26.0	365	1.3	5.6	4.2	2.1	44
Yates,Tyler	01	24	a/a	OAK	5	6	60	18	68	76	33	4	28	53	4.37	1.53	5.0	344	3.7	7.1	1.9	0.5	66
	02	25	aaa	NYM	2	2	24	6	34	33	6	1	13	29	1.59	1.35	6.1	317	3.4	7.7	2.2	0.3	90
Young,Jason	02	23	a/a	COL	13	9	27	0	168	184	88	16	64	131	4.71	1.48	27.4	336	3.4	7.0	2.0	0.9	60
Young,Tim	02	29	aaa	BOS	5	3	57	4	72	70	39	5	41	49	4.86	1.54	5.6	345	5.1	6.1	1.2	0.6	48
Zambrano,Carlos	01	20	aaa	CHC	10	5	26	0	150	117	62	7	57	153	3.70	1.16	23.6	285	3.4	9.2	2.7	0.4	111
Zambrano,Victor	01	27	aaa	TAM	1	2	29	12	30	33	9	2	13	24	2.83	1.50	4.6	340	3.8	7.1	1.9	0.6	64
Zamora,Pete	01	26	aaa	PHI	8	4	45	3	89	80	41	8	49	70	4.17	1.46	8.7	333	5.0	7.1	1.4	0.8	55
	02	27	aaa	PHI	5	2	55	15	62	76	31	2	33	28	4.50	1.76	5.3	376	4.8	4.1	0.8	0.3	29
Zancanaro,Dave	01	33	a/a	STL	6	14	28	1	148	223	131	37	60	95	7.96	1.91	25.6	396	3.6	5.7	1.6	2.2	-12
Zimmerman,Jordan	01	26	aaa	SEA	4	3	41	4	58	95	53	8	25	40	8.14	2.06	7.1	413	3.8	6.2	1.6	1.3	16

V.
RATINGS
and
RANKINGS

Draft Guide History

A few months ago, I was adding some content pages to the BaseballForecaster.com web site when I decided to do a history of this book. I pulled out all my old copies and took a stroll down Memory Lane. It was very sentimental, recalling my first brush with skills analysis, getting doe-eyed over my first set of projections... I'm sure you know the feeling.

And there it was, all the way back in 1988 — the first Draft Guide History. The longest, continuously running feature in this book began at a time when Ronald Reagan was lucid, Bill Clinton was monogamous and George W. Bush was not yet sober. And here, 15 years later, it still occupies a very special place in the heart of the 2003 edition.

Sniff.

The draft guide history (DGH) provides a capsule summary of each player's last few seasons along with their projection for 2003 using several different measures of performance. The players are then ranked by primary position. The true value of this exercise is not so much the projections themselves (which will change over the next few months, as uniforms and playing time expectations change), but the historical ratings. They keep every player's performance in perspective.

The DGH summarizes the tons of information in the forecast boxes. So, you can look at potential draft picks here, and if you're undecided about any player, you can refer back to their forecast box for more detailed information.

UNIVERSAL DISCLAIMER... This section is intended solely as a preliminary look based on current factors. Do not treat this guide as the Draft Day gospel. Use the ratings and rankings as a rough guide to get a general sense of where a player falls. For Draft Day, you will need to make your own adjustments based upon about seven thousand different criteria that can impact the world between now and then. Updates will appear next spring online at BaseballHQ.com. And don't forget the free projections update at BaseballForecaster.com.

Standard Rotisserie

The standard Rotisserie listings are provided for leagues that use the 4x4 statistical categories (HR, RBI, SB, BA for batters; W, Sv, ERA, WHIP for pitchers) but can also be used as rough guides by leagues with other formats.

Runs Created per Game

This category can be used for many any other fantasy formats, from point systems to simulation leagues to table/computer games. RC/G gives you a sense of overall value, but it does not take playing time into account. As such, a platoon or bench player projected to post a 5.00 RC/G will be ranked right up there with a 600 AB regular.

The value of this? It allows you to do some cherry-picking. Players with high value, but low-playing time, are your best late-round roster fillers. When a Mark DeRosa or a Greg Zaun finish in the Top 10 of *anything,* you might scratch your head. But when it's two in the morning and you have the catcher and middle infielder slots open and $2 left to spend, you'll thank this list.

Power and Speed

These are rankings using our league-normalized power and speed indices (PX and SX). They are very insightful, but they, too, do not account for playing time. They just tell you where each player falls on the skills scale.

There are plenty of no-brainer rankings on these lists, but there are plenty of surprises as well. The value is in picking out the high-ranked lesser names. These are players who may be prime fodder for further analysis, or again, could be excellent late-round cherry-picking targets.

For example, if you have one last catcher slot open and have drafted a team short on speed, you can use the SX ranking to pick out that one backstop whose one extra potential stolen base might put you over the top come October. Who woulda thunk that Eli Marrero could be your man?

Base Performance Value

For pitchers, BPV gets you beyond the erratic trends and noise inherent in ERA. Just pure skills. No playing time is taken into account here either. The relievers list will go a long way to helping you fill out a LIMA Plan pitching staff.

Within each of the above five categories, players are rated as part of the entire population, not within each position. So those who qualify at multiple positions may be moved around freely without affecting their ratings. Of course, their ranking within a new position will likely change.

Runs Above Replacement (RAR)

The most important use for RAR is that it allows us to integrate batters and pitchers in the ranking process. To those who play Scoresheet Baseball, or some other simulation game, RAR is probably the single best gauge for your draft — if you've got a firm handle on projected playing time. Which we don't. Not yet, anyway. Consider these lists preliminary, but probably the best you'll find for your early stage drafts. Come March, the RAR updates online at Baseball HQ provide no better evaluator.

Catchers

Std Rotisserie	'98	'99	'00	'01	'02	'03Prj
Rodriguez,Ivan	26	39	25	23	19	24
Piazza,Mike	33	30	32	26	23	23
Posada,Jorge	11	6	18	18	17	16
LoDuca,Paul	8	3	10	25	13	16
Kendall,Jason	30	19	25	12	13	15
Hall,Toby		2	13	23	9	14
Lieberthal,Mike	7	23	12	0	12	13
Barrett,Michael	19	9	2	3	10	12
Varitek,Jason	5	12	5	6	11	11
Santiago,Benito	1	3	6	7	16	10
Hernandez,Ramon	11	8	5	9	3	10
Davis,Ben	8	7	4	6	7	10
Pierzynski,A.J.	11	(0)	10	10	11	9
Miller,Damian	4	7	8	9	6	9
Lopez,Javy	27	11	18	12	5	8
Schneider,Brian		5	0	2	5	8
LaRue,Jason	14	2	5	5	7	7
Miller,Corky		(1)	(0)	13	2	7
Wilson,Tom	3	2	5	1	6	7
Molina,Ben	11	7	11	5	4	6
Gonzalez,Wiki	5	10	1	6	(1)	6
Greene,Todd	2	7	4	1	15	6
Johnson,Charles	5	7	22	12	1	6
Redmond,Mike	4	5	(0)	5	7	5
Wilson,Dan	5	6	1	8	9	5
Rivera,Mike		0	(4)	11	6	5
Ausmus,Brad	10	11	8	1	6	5
Diaz,Einar	12	8	4	8	(3)	5
Mayne,Brent	5	7	11	6	3	5
Alomar Jr.,Sandy	1	8	7	2	6	5
Torrealba,Yorvit	(2)	(0)	4	1	2	5
Zaun,Gregg	(1)	1	7	6	1	4
Pratt,Todd	7	4	5	(2)	5	4
Widger,Chris	8	9	4		2	4
Flaherty,John	(3)	11	4	2	5	4
Gil,Geronimo	1	4	6	3	6	4
Hundley,Todd	(2)	6	15	0	4	4
Estalella,Bobby	8	2	7	2	5	3
Matheny,Mike	2	(1)	4	0	2	3
Haselman,Bill	5	3	4	3	2	3
Paul,Josh		4	2	7	4	3
Hinch,A.J.	3	4	2	6	5	3
Bennett,Gary	1	2	8	2	4	3
Mirabelli,Doug	1	8	2	4	3	3
Stinnett,Kelly	6	5	1	5	(2)	3
Lampkin,Tom	3	7	3	1	3	3
Meluskey,Mitch	12	0	14		(0)	2
Wilson,Vance	0	1	4	1	3	2
Johnson,Mark L.	4	0	0	6	(1)	2
Moeller,Chad	2	(1)	0	2	10	2
Castro,Ramon	1	(0)	8	13	3	2
Barajas,Rod		10	(1)	4	3	2
Myers,Greg	2	3	(0)	4	2	2
Machado,Robert	(0)	(2)	6	2	2	2
Kreuter,Chad	2	(0)	4	0	2	1
Casanova,Raul	1	(3)	5	6	(2)	1
Fordyce,Brook	2	10	11	(2)	0	1
Prince,Tom	(2)	(1)	1	2	2	1
Molina,Jose	(5)	(1)	(4)	3	4	1
Fabregas,Jorge	(2)	(3)	3	(0)	(2)	1
Perez,Eddie	9	2	(0)	2	(1)	1
Osik,Keith	(1)	(3)	5	(0)	(2)	1
Inge,Brandon			3	(2)	2	0
Huckaby,Ken	(3)	(2)	(0)	2	1	0
Nieves,Wilbert			1	4	3	0
Girardi,Joe	4	2	6	2	(2)	0
DiFelice,Mike	(0)	6	1	(2)	1	0
Walbeck,Matt	5	0	(1)	1	(1)	(0)
Blanco,Henry	0	3	2	0	(1)	(0)
Bako,Paul	4	(0)	(1)	(0)	0	(0)

RC/Gm	'98	'99	'00	'01	'02	'03Prj
Piazza,Mike	8.87	7.90	9.56	8.34	7.10	7.40
Rodriguez,Ivan	7.18	7.40	9.64	6.93	7.11	7.29
Pratt,Todd	5.05	5.48	6.36	3.54	9.23	6.61
Posada,Jorge	6.19	5.01	8.48	6.16	6.54	6.31
Schneider,Brian		3.74	2.89	7.57	5.65	6.09
Miller,Damian	5.08	5.08	5.64	5.15	5.32	6.02
Lieberthal,Mike	4.14	7.43	6.09	3.72	5.42	5.84
Meluskey,Mitch	6.99	3.97	7.69		3.05	5.64
LoDuca,Paul	3.93	4.44	5.06	7.66	4.74	5.57
Kendall,Jason	7.37	8.88	7.31	3.84	4.50	5.33
Torrealba,Yorvit	2.28	2.79	4.17	2.97	5.20	5.32
Barrett,Michael	5.92	5.52	3.75	3.71	5.08	5.30
Kreuter,Chad	4.09	3.40	6.87	4.97	4.75	5.29
Hall,Toby		3.00	5.02	6.47	4.18	5.24
Wilson,Tom	3.41	4.07	4.91	3.71	4.63	5.24
Hernandez,Ramo	4.46	4.54	4.20	4.52	3.71	5.18
Varitek,Jason	4.35	5.80	4.80	6.92	4.60	5.17
Davis,Ben	4.11	4.39	4.19	4.36	4.50	5.03
Zaun,Gregg	2.76	3.87	6.13	7.56	2.98	5.03
Redmond,Mike	4.26	5.11	3.19	6.17	5.18	4.99
Estalella,Bobby	5.32	3.71	6.21	3.45	5.21	4.96
Gonzalez,Wiki	11.92	5.13	3.69	5.51	3.68	4.88
Mirabelli,Doug	3.43	5.18	4.57	5.21	4.39	4.80
Johnson,Charles	3.74	5.12	8.60	5.15	4.00	4.76
Hundley,Todd	2.29	4.40	8.21	3.08	4.36	4.70
Miller,Corky		3.14	2.77	5.70	3.70	4.67
Santiago,Benito	6.06	4.20	4.53	3.81	5.15	4.59
Haselman,Bill	6.82	4.92	5.41	3.70	3.44	4.58
Moeller,Chad	4.04	3.00	3.35	3.53	5.95	4.56
Pierzynski,A.J.	4.78	3.03	5.11	4.75	5.11	4.52
Lampkin,Tom	4.09	5.79	5.93	3.55	4.02	4.49
LaRue,Jason	6.37	3.21	3.73	3.97	4.28	4.47
Widger,Chris	3.84	4.79	4.59		2.88	4.46
Lopez,Javy	6.34	7.25	6.03	4.79	3.68	4.39
Rivera,Mike		3.71	1.83	4.34	3.81	4.35
Myers,Greg	4.14	4.90	3.21	4.95	4.80	4.34
Johnson,Mark L.	5.17	4.32	3.63	4.58	3.02	4.31
Alomar Jr.,Sandy	3.12	6.22	4.69	3.33	4.46	4.23
Castro,Ramon	2.96	3.00	5.14	5.57	5.43	4.16
Hinch,A.J.	3.51	3.44	3.52	3.97	4.28	4.12
Greene,Todd	4.02	3.86	4.96	2.49	4.91	4.07
Bennett,Gary	3.25	3.89	5.89	4.06	3.67	4.04
Ausmus,Brad	4.82	5.17	4.83	3.39	3.98	4.02
Casanova,Raul	4.00	1.76	4.45	5.25	2.46	3.98
Stinnett,Kelly	5.48	4.32	3.21	5.11	2.79	3.97
Wilson,Dan	4.25	4.43	3.39	4.31	4.88	3.91
Mayne,Brent	4.95	6.25	6.24	4.30	3.37	3.89
Flaherty,John	2.26	4.53	3.99	3.36	3.88	3.86
Molina,Ben	4.99	4.46	4.85	3.67	3.03	3.82
Matheny,Mike	3.03	2.84	4.14	2.83	3.52	3.75
Diaz,Einar	4.82	4.26	4.21	4.18	2.32	3.73
Machado,Robert	2.97	1.98	4.20	3.26	4.36	3.71
Fordyce,Brook	4.02	5.89	6.44	2.80	3.14	3.68
Barajas,Rod		4.34	2.15	3.62	3.99	3.62
Wilson,Vance	2.56	3.23	2.90	2.85	3.41	3.54
Paul,Josh		3.60	3.41	5.06	3.04	3.53
Girardi,Joe	4.16	3.36	4.75	3.91	2.83	3.46
Gil,Geronimo	3.27	4.34	3.91	3.17	3.30	3.44
Perez,Eddie	8.62	3.78	1.29	6.28	2.41	3.44
Bako,Paul	4.09	3.85	3.47	3.88	3.33	3.42
Prince,Tom	2.30	1.34	4.09	3.21	3.80	3.41
DiFelice,Mike	3.21	5.96	3.95	2.19	3.83	3.40
Blanco,Henry	3.04	4.46	4.40	3.45	2.97	3.33
Osik,Keith	2.69	1.98	6.55	2.98	1.67	3.20
Fabregas,Jorge	2.19	2.93	3.71	2.53	1.91	3.16
Nieves,Wilbert			2.71	3.71	3.61	3.13
Inge,Brandon			3.14	2.39	3.27	3.06
Molina,Jose	2.01	3.13	2.00	3.75	3.14	3.01
Walbeck,Matt	4.22	3.22	2.66	3.27	2.06	2.84
Huckaby,Ken	1.97	2.55	2.51	2.75	2.59	2.61

Power	'98	'99	'00	'01	'02	'03Prj
Rodriguez,Ivan	121	130	180	137	152	148
Piazza,Mike	159	155	163	157	150	148
Estalella,Bobby	135	100	141	108	172	136
Miller,Damian	110	113	109	94	120	131
Posada,Jorge	128	95	141	121	137	129
Schneider,Brian		86	46	99	125	126
Hundley,Todd	70	130	165	104	119	119
Meluskey,Mitch	125	73	115		0	118
Johnson,Charles	105	96	155	121	105	118
Lieberthal,Mike	96	151	123	82	104	118
Greene,Todd	119	128	115	78	144	116
Mirabelli,Doug	94	101	83	133	118	111
Pratt,Todd	131	58	106	74	133	109
Barrett,Michael	121	99	62	83	97	107
Widger,Chris	102	113	121		96	105
Lampkin,Tom	102	119	156	80	88	105
Rivera,Mike		169	71	115	112	104
LaRue,Jason	131	99	111	104	96	104
Castro,Ramon	78	90	105	128	125	103
Torrealba,Yorvit	31	67	59	73	86	103
Wilson,Tom	69	114	111	78	84	103
Hall,Toby		105	92	129	83	102
Pierzynski,A.J.	85	41	94	107	100	101
Varitek,Jason	99	134	92	121	90	100
Hernandez,Ramo	80	89	87	98	74	98
Miller,Corky		118	75	128	101	97
Davis,Ben	96	94	89	75	94	97
Haselman,Bill	136	90	123	62	63	97
LoDuca,Paul	69	77	86	134	85	95
Flaherty,John	46	83	69	87	89	95
Moeller,Chad	99	60	73	81	106	95
Hinch,A.J.	66	67	64	118	95	93
Barajas,Rod		92	79	104	92	93
Myers,Greg	93	64	75	120	99	92
Stinnett,Kelly	117	115	74	123	74	92
Blanco,Henry	89	90	109	86	81	89
Santiago,Benito	150	83	88	71	103	89
Lopez,Javy	156	136	113	92	86	88
Prince,Tom	69	54	87	76	111	85
Kreuter,Chad	50	63	94	101	78	85
Inge,Brandon			83	77	97	85
Gil,Geronimo	86	104	81	68	87	84
Casanova,Raul	94	85	95	131	46	82
Kendall,Jason	105	115	93	59	53	81
Perez,Eddie	141	83	39	130	71	81
Alomar Jr.,Sandy	82	129	71	63	86	80
Zaun,Gregg	71	44	83	135	62	80
Machado,Robert	80	77	79	87	83	79
Fordyce,Brook	91	108	120	79	69	79
DiFelice,Mike	71	103	100	49	90	78
Gonzalez,Wiki	179	109	74	107	57	77
Johnson,Mark L.	69	74	64	70	56	76
Wilson,Vance	48	90	88	72	84	75
Wilson,Dan	90	77	65	88	71	72
Bennett,Gary	82	57	109	82	57	72
Nieves,Wilbert			32	68	94	71
Paul,Josh		72	66	110	50	69
Bako,Paul	59	81	56	91	59	69
Diaz,Einar	76	59	77	83	65	68
Ausmus,Brad	56	87	64	73	63	68
Osik,Keith	38	39	97	54	56	67
Molina,Ben	85	85	82	57	58	62
Girardi,Joe	69	84	62	61	47	61
Redmond,Mike	92	39	36	67	63	60
Walbeck,Matt	71	42	89	66	39	55
Matheny,Mike	69	59	68	55	50	54
Fabregas,Jorge	38	65	52	56	53	54
Mayne,Brent	69	96	80	41	48	53
Molina,Jose	38	66	33	73	52	52
Huckaby,Ken	47	46	53	52	37	43

Speed	'98	'99	'00	'01	'02	'03Prj
Rodriguez,Ivan	106	105	103	92	85	95
Inge,Brandon			98	58	132	94
Kendall,Jason	122	146	120	83	87	91
Ausmus,Brad	114	117	93	100	72	86
Paul,Josh		89	144	72	85	81
Lampkin,Tom	71	80	65	53	67	78
Pierzynski,A.J.	73	30	84	58	95	75
Santiago,Benito	27	57	47	80	92	69
Girardi,Joe	106	86	53	43	56	65
Moeller,Chad	43	56	80	52	69	62
Diaz,Einar	76	85	94	51	44	60
Barrett,Michael	77	49	52	59	63	58
Bako,Paul	52	54	36	87	46	56
Hinch,A.J.	45	93	72	42	77	56
Estalella,Bobby	42	63	100	58	29	54
Davis,Ben	59	68	69	46	56	54
Greene,Todd	33	41	43	61	52	52
Blanco,Henry	58	64	20	96	38	52
Gonzalez,Wiki	47	38	40	41	43	52
Mayne,Brent	37	38	22	37	74	51
Varitek,Jason	56	55	44	35	63	51
Rivera,Mike		21	38	59	54	50
Alomar Jr.,Sandy	52	77	69	44	37	49
Wilson,Dan	60	85	43	60	48	48
Fabregas,Jorge		51	47	60	28	47
LaRue,Jason	97	71	63	73	51	47
LoDuca,Paul	85	51	72	37	62	46
Johnson,Mark L.	45	55	65	76	48	46
Bennett,Gary			33	46	57	46
Gil,Geronimo	78	53	44	33	33	45
Pratt,Todd	72	50	43	36	44	45
Prince,Tom	85	39	46	71	77	44
Stinnett,Kelly	41	47	22	55	50	44
Posada,Jorge	30	62	48	32	50	43
Schneider,Brian		45	50		71	41
Huckaby,Ken	62	38	67	46	45	41
Zaun,Gregg	73	90	66	30	67	40
Matheny,Mike	34	27	33	33	43	40
Barajas,Rod		66	49	47	34	40
Lieberthal,Mike	92	36	49	54	32	39
Osik,Keith	39	42	73	35	15	37
Flaherty,John		28		50	46	37
Meluskey,Mitch	45	51	32		25	36
Hall,Toby		37	36	48	41	36
Piazza,Mike	43	45	51		34	34
Wilson,Vance	36	87	75	26	41	33
Hernandez,Ramo	55	53	42	36	33	33
Kreuter,Chad	53	22	35	39	34	32
DiFelice,Mike	64	23	49	72	21	31
Torrealba,Yorvit	29	51	52	68	28	30
Fordyce,Brook		54	39	42	31	30
Molina,Jose	45	36	31	56	29	30
Haselman,Bill		44	30	24	22	29
Nieves,Wilbert			30	32	59	29
Castro,Ramon	34		24	41	10	29
Machado,Robert	52	34	32	24	38	29
Walbeck,Matt	64	51	45	34	13	27
Lopez,Javy	64	39	28	41	19	27
Molina,Ben	43	34	58	24	22	27
Wilson,Tom	68		39	46	26	26
Widger,Chris	65	37	58		37	26
Miller,Damian	95	23	42	24	26	24
Mirabelli,Doug	63	73	67		19	24
Perez,Eddie	33	22			16	24
Hundley,Todd	30	50	21		17	22
Johnson,Charles		36	50	21	10	22
Miller,Corky		51	43	48	26	20
Myers,Greg	30			24	12	19
Redmond,Mike			38	26	14	19
Casanova,Raul		33	61		4	17

1Bmen

Std Rotisserie	'98	'99	'00	'01	'02	'03Prj
Helton,Todd	27	32	46	45	34	**38**
Thome,Jim	21	20	20	31	35	**36**
Sweeney,Mike	5	25	34	28	30	**34**
Giambi,Jason	23	28	35	36	34	**32**
Fullmer,Brad	15	15	23	16	19	**31**
Klesko,Ryan	16	19	26	32	27	**29**
Palmeiro,Rafael	33	37	25	28	27	**28**
Delgado,Carlos	27	26	36	25	24	**27**
Bagwell,Jeff	36	40	37	33	27	**26**
Martinez,Tino	22	17	11	24	14	**23**
Sexson,Richie	24	18	18	28	22	**23**
Lee,Derrek	10	5	17	18	25	**22**
McGriff,Fred	17	25	18	26	22	**22**
Durazo,Erubiel	27	30	5	8	12	**22**
Konerko,Paul	19	18	18	22	25	**22**
Huff,Aubrey		13	12	6	25	**21**
Vaughn,Mo	35	21	21		14	**20**
Olerud,John	32	20	14	22	22	**20**
Surhoff,B.J.	20	26	16	12	2	**15**
Pena,Carlos			22	16	13	**15**
Colbrunn,Greg	7	6	14	4	11	**15**
Casey,Sean	11	27	21	20	7	**15**
Spiezio,Scott	6	10	7	11	17	**15**
Simon,Randall	4	7	8	15	19	**14**
Daubach,Brian	15	16	9	13	15	**13**
Karros,Eric	23	29	17	7	13	**13**
Cox,Steve	7	16	7	8	13	**12**
Mientkiewicz,Doug	21	(1)	16	18	9	**12**
Conine,Jeff	6	12	10	24	15	**11**
Hatteberg,Scott	8	0	5	1	13	**10**
Lee,Travis	18	9	6	14	12	**9**
Lamb,Mike		17	7	14	9	**9**
Clark,Tony	25	20	7	14	(0)	**8**
Johnson,Nick		18		9	9	**7**
Young,Kevin	26	29	15	11	8	**7**
Minor,Damon	2	5	10	7	6	**7**
Grace,Mark	23	20	12	17	6	**6**
Franco,Julio	19	26	24	43	8	**6**
Snow,J.T.	11	17	17	4	4	**6**
Stevens,Lee	11	16	13	14	3	**6**
Kinkade,Mike	10	7	13	4	10	**5**
Snyder,Earl				12	10	**5**
Mabry,John	5	4	3	1	8	**5**
Galarraga,Andres	36		24	11	7	**5**
Offerman,Jose	30	17	3	9	5	**5**
Helms,Wes	11	3	10	4	2	**4**
Saenz,Olmedo	10	7	8	1	5	**3**
Hansen,Dave	7	1	6	1	4	**3**
Franco,Matt	2	1	(2)	(1)	11	**3**
Leon,Jose		5	5	13	6	**1**
Sweeney,Mark	0	3	(0)	5	(1)	**(0)**

RC/Gm	'98	'99	'00	'01	'02	'03Prj
Thome,Jim	9.48	9.11	8.14	10.05	11.98	**11.80**
Helton,Todd	7.68	8.80	13.96	11.78	10.22	**10.78**
Giambi,Jason	7.25	9.36	13.05	13.32	10.18	**10.22**
Delgado,Carlos	8.60	7.81	12.85	8.30	8.47	**9.59**
Sweeney,Mike	4.52	7.80	8.45	7.84	9.13	**8.99**
Palmeiro,Rafael	7.91	10.53	8.61	8.02	8.50	**8.59**
Colbrunn,Greg	5.67	7.64	8.02	6.49	9.18	**8.19**
Klesko,Ryan	6.28	7.72	7.86	8.12	8.04	**7.96**
Durazo,Erubiel	10.29	10.42	6.38	7.45	8.24	**7.92**
Fullmer,Brad	5.12	5.69	6.95	5.23	6.64	**7.89**
Bagwell,Jeff	9.26	10.65	9.95	8.68	8.00	**7.78**
Olerud,John	10.45	8.00	6.75	7.54	7.92	**7.53**
McGriff,Fred	6.35	8.94	6.61	8.07	6.53	**7.12**
Huff,Aubrey		6.03	5.62	3.92	7.02	**7.01**
Sexson,Richie	7.51	5.42	6.38	6.60	6.78	**6.60**
Vaughn,Mo	9.42	6.59	6.63		5.63	**6.50**
Martinez,Tino	6.70	5.64	4.91	5.96	5.41	**6.47**
Lee,Derrek	4.45	3.46	6.84	5.97	6.88	**6.43**
Konerko,Paul	6.08	6.79	6.52	6.47	6.71	**6.28**
Hatteberg,Scott	5.93	4.68	6.03	4.08	6.11	**5.98**
Grace,Mark	7.33	7.36	6.58	7.05	5.15	**5.94**
Casey,Sean	5.96	8.39	7.75	6.38	4.59	**5.90**
Mientkiewicz,Dou	7.61	3.82	5.87	6.70	5.34	**5.69**
Daubach,Brian	5.46	7.41	4.93	6.54	5.83	**5.68**
Spiezio,Scott	4.49	6.56	5.46	5.11	5.99	**5.65**
Kinkade,Mike	4.41	4.01	5.05	4.69	5.04	**5.56**
Hansen,Dave	4.41	6.32	9.06	5.04	5.61	**5.53**
Simon,Randall	2.96	5.45	3.78	5.70	5.37	**5.52**
Pena,Carlos			7.94	7.17	4.48	**5.49**
Johnson,Nick		9.00		5.34	4.50	**5.34**
Snow,J.T.	5.15	6.18	6.21	5.33	4.55	**5.30**
Surhoff,B.J.	5.51	6.55	5.72	4.80	4.53	**5.29**
Lamb,Mike		6.16	4.44	4.89	5.52	**5.29**
Franco,Julio	6.66	17.10	8.55	13.50	5.29	**5.23**
Cox,Steve	4.20	6.01	6.39	4.59	4.77	**5.23**
Karros,Eric	6.42	7.47	5.27	4.13	4.62	**5.09**
Saenz,Olmedo	4.05	5.73	7.81	3.41	5.60	**5.07**
Minor,Damon	3.33	4.82	5.23	4.10	6.47	**5.00**
Lee,Travis	5.61	4.69	4.71	5.37	4.78	**4.98**
Conine,Jeff	4.77	5.51	5.49	6.56	5.14	**4.92**
Snyder,Earl				5.85	4.62	**4.91**
Clark,Tony	6.96	6.78	6.85	6.95	2.63	**4.90**
Stevens,Lee	5.89	6.21	5.93	5.52	4.12	**4.82**
Mabry,John	4.04	4.20	3.83	3.43	5.81	**4.71**
Franco,Matt	4.96	5.15	2.80	2.89	5.90	**4.66**
Galarraga,Andres	8.33		6.70	4.92	4.68	**4.52**
Helms,Wes	4.43	4.92	4.10	4.33	3.89	**4.49**
Offerman,Jose	7.17	6.50	4.54	4.82	3.76	**4.38**
Young,Kevin	5.47	7.40	4.65	3.89	4.49	**4.19**
Leon,Jose		3.61	3.59	4.59	3.68	**3.53**
Sweeney,Mark	3.92	4.31	4.14	4.04	2.06	**3.39**

Power	'98	'99	'00	'01	'02	'03Prj
Thome,Jim	175	150	148	186	215	**222**
Delgado,Carlos	181	173	191	151	171	**186**
Palmeiro,Rafael	157	171	148	166	185	**175**
Giambi,Jason	116	141	173	192	176	**174**
Helton,Todd	144	159	197	207	150	**171**
Fullmer,Brad	127	137	149	107	160	**171**
Colbrunn,Greg	103	108	127	133	186	**157**
Durazo,Erubiel	145	138	109	157	170	**154**
Sweeney,Mike	99	125	109	150	147	**152**
Klesko,Ryan	135	144	139	148	146	**147**
Bagwell,Jeff	162	169	174	165	136	**144**
Sexson,Richie	152	139	131	152	137	**140**
Lee,Derrek	123	93	125	119	133	**135**
Huff,Aubrey		129	119	93	127	**133**
McGriff,Fred	102	140	96	136	135	**131**
Snyder,Earl				136	128	**129**
Vaughn,Mo	147	127	128		113	**128**
Daubach,Brian	140	159	120	148	127	**127**
Pena,Carlos			134	151	122	**127**
Saenz,Olmedo	109	125	116	107	127	**125**
Martinez,Tino	136	113	101	126	107	**123**
Konerko,Paul	120	128	110	135	125	**120**
Olerud,John	132	109	103	106	129	**114**
Stevens,Lee	141	122	128	126	103	**114**
Mabry,John	94	97	101	98	139	**113**
Helms,Wes	91	126	91	121	110	**113**
Minor,Damon	95	111	110	94	131	**111**
Spiezio,Scott	76	133	120	106	107	**109**
Galarraga,Andres	177		129	127	82	**105**
Conine,Jeff	112	105	91	82	115	**102**
Cox,Steve	92	124	103	109	97	**102**
Casey,Sean	106	130	124	101	75	**101**
Young,Kevin	141	138	106	110	102	**101**
Kinkade,Mike	86	85	89	65	102	**100**
Mientkiewicz,Dou	125	72	97	106	94	**99**
Johnson,Nick		113		108	98	**98**
Clark,Tony	139	133	148	121	61	**97**
Karros,Eric	113	150	121	95	82	**97**
Grace,Mark	113	113	102	107	91	**96**
Simon,Randall	68	93	96	94	98	**93**
Hatteberg,Scott	109	66	105	76	98	**93**
Snow,J.T.	121	106	108	81	79	**90**
Lee,Travis	101	79	86	110	82	**90**
Surhoff,B.J.	111	112	98	91	58	**89**
Lamb,Mike		126	72	90	80	**88**
Franco,Matt	63	79	39	67	108	**86**
Leon,Jose		113	94	91	79	**80**
Franco,Julio	112	139	112	138	63	**76**
Sweeney,Mark	71	87	90	82	62	**74**
Offerman,Jose	76	90	61	69	71	**67**
Hansen,Dave	75	102	155	83	69	**63**

Speed	'98	'99	'00	'01	'02	'03Prj
Fullmer,Brad	67	62	63	72	144	**113**
Lee,Derrek	74	63	46	89	131	**106**
Offerman,Jose	177	147	54	80	102	**103**
Klesko,Ryan	69	66	98	143	67	**99**
Colbrunn,Greg	106	125	34	21	71	**93**
Pena,Carlos			100	80	87	**91**
Conine,Jeff	49	32	69	72	104	**90**
Franco,Julio	77	104	26	113	81	**89**
Kinkade,Mike	126	94	100	47	102	**89**
Helton,Todd	48	91	69	76	88	**77**
Spiezio,Scott	45	42	68	88	73	**77**
Bagwell,Jeff	94	86	80	110	71	**71**
Sweeney,Mike	41	84	63	70	67	**68**
Franco,Matt	77	21		66	83	**67**
Saenz,Olmedo	52	51	90	44	58	**65**
Durazo,Erubiel	80	75	48	34	88	**62**
Lee,Travis	79	108	79	56	60	**61**
Snyder,Earl				65	45	**59**
Surhoff,B.J.	66	70	85	87	32	**58**
Helms,Wes	65	37	59	109	39	**57**
Martinez,Tino	57	60	81	48	49	**57**
Young,Kevin	96	122	79	77	55	**56**
Cox,Steve	57	53	44	38	69	**55**
Daubach,Brian	89	61	49	63	66	**54**
Grace,Mark	56	74	37	51	53	**54**
Stevens,Lee	83	48	41	53	69	**54**
Snow,J.T.	49	37	49	44	42	**53**
Giambi,Jason	39	46	49	55	52	**53**
Karros,Eric	61	46	48	43	53	**52**
Lamb,Mike		71	66	54	38	**50**
Delgado,Carlos	62	43	30	55	64	**50**
Thome,Jim	64	48	49	29	47	**48**
Casey,Sean	58	47	51	50	50	**48**
Palmeiro,Rafael	62	31	62	27	45	**48**
Huff,Aubrey		55	43	43	55	**46**
Leon,Jose		41	89	88	52	**45**
McGriff,Fred	55	35	41	36	40	**44**
Hatteberg,Scott	33	27		40	49	**43**
Sexson,Richie	61	117	61	61	41	**42**
Minor,Damon	55	68	30	57	42	**42**
Galarraga,Andres	66		44	45	35	**41**
Johnson,Nick		88		64	39	**41**
Mabry,John	26	55	51	36	60	**41**
Clark,Tony	37	37	25	56	42	**37**
Sweeney,Mark	92	59	26	71	7	**37**
Konerko,Paul	33	67	54	41	26	**36**
Mientkiewicz,Dou	69	71	74	36	40	**34**
Hansen,Dave	30	53	93		43	**32**
Simon,Randall	52	41	71	29	28	**32**
Olerud,John	61	52	23	51	23	**29**
Vaughn,Mo	41		44		23	**28**

2Bmen

Std Rotisserie	'98	'99	'00	'01	'02	'03Prj
Soriano,Alfonso		16	10	27	44	**39**
Kent,Jeff	32	23	37	25	34	**32**
Castillo,Luis	8	22	32	15	28	**25**
Vidro,Jose	3	13	28	19	26	**25**
Durham,Ray	26	24	21	20	25	**24**
Walker,Todd	22	12	17	18	19	**21**
Boone,Bret	20	12	12	38	25	**21**
Alomar,Roberto	17	39	33	37	14	**19**
Hairston Jr.,Jerry	9	17	8	11	13	**19**
Giles,Marcus			14	19	7	**15**
Kennedy,Adam	14	17	14	9	19	**15**
Young,Eric	24	22	28	18	16	**15**
Vina,Fernando	22	3	11	20	11	**15**
Spivey,Junior	5	4	3	6	23	**14**
Hudson,Orlando			(0)	17	13	**14**
Rivas,Luis		11	10	16	7	**13**
DeRosa,Mark	1	2	6	9	7	**12**
Harris,Willie				22	18	**12**
Jimenez,D'Angelo	16	23	(0)	8	10	**12**
Hill,Bobby				7	12	**11**
Bellhorn,Mark	4	0	14	1	15	**11**
Biggio,Craig	44	24	9	20	13	**11**
Anderson,Marlon	21	7	14	16	7	**10**
Ortiz,Jose	9	11	31	11	5	**10**
Gutierrez,Ricky	8	2	12	14	6	**9**
Roberts,Brian				15	12	**9**
Graffanino,Tony	(1)	18	4	5	6	**9**
Butler,Brent		4	7	10	10	**9**
Vazquez,Ramon		0	5	11	7	**9**
Reese,Pokey	2	22	15	10	10	**9**
Febles,Carlos	24	12	7	8	8	**9**
Grudzielanek,Mark	16	15	11	11	9	**8**
Young,Mike			9	12	11	**8**
Abernathy,Brent		12	10	15	5	**7**
Ellis,Mark			1	7	9	**7**
Deshields,Delino	18	7	26	9	1	**7**
Menechino,Frank	3	7	5	6	1	**6**
Easley,Damion	23	14	11	9	2	**6**
Sanchez,Rey	5	11	5	9	7	**6**
Jackson,Damian	10	12	12	9	6	**6**
Sheets,Andy	6	(3)	(0)	2	13	**5**
Gil,Benji	2	3	4	9	6	**4**
Nieves,Jose	7	5	3	9	4	**4**
Canizaro,Jay	(0)	10	12		4	**3**
Berg,Dave	6	5	2	1	6	**3**
Belliard,Ron	19	13	8	8	(2)	**3**
Shumpert,Terry	3	22	8	10	2	**3**
Nunez,Abraham	4	0	4	4	(0)	**3**
Alicea,Luis	6	(1)	10	7	1	**3**
Perez,Tomas	3	(0)	7	4	3	**3**
Guerrero,Wilton	10	7	5	12	0	**2**
Cintron,Alex			7	7	7	**2**
Hocking,Denny	(1)	8	10	3	2	**2**
Merloni,Lou	8	5	2	3	2	**2**
Ordaz,Luis	3	1	0	2	5	**1**
Bush,Homer	5	23	(1)	10	(0)	**1**
McDonald,John	(1)	7	1	1	1	**1**
Garcia,Jesse	8	1	(3)	3	3	**0**
Lockhart,Keith	6	2	4	(0)	(1)	**0**
Matos,Julius		1	(6)	4	4	**0**
Lawrence,Joe		1	0	(2)	(2)	**(1)**

RC/Gm	'98	'99	'00	'01	'02	'03Prj
Kent,Jeff	7.34	6.96	9.90	6.93	7.97	**7.94**
Vidro,Jose	3.63	5.95	7.96	6.76	7.20	**7.11**
Durham,Ray	6.23	6.19	5.87	5.61	6.44	**6.17**
Walker,Todd	6.79	4.95	5.97	5.88	5.69	**6.06**
Alomar,Roberto	5.50	9.44	7.25	9.31	4.64	**5.93**
Soriano,Alfonso		4.06	3.87	4.58	6.34	**5.84**
Graffanino,Tony	2.81	5.96	4.73	5.98	5.07	**5.68**
Giles,Marcus			5.35	5.53	4.89	**5.66**
Hudson,Orlando			2.93	5.74	4.71	**5.53**
Spivey,Junior	6.91	4.36	5.23	3.75	6.82	**5.36**
DeRosa,Mark	3.48	2.87	4.10	4.68	4.56	**5.35**
Boone,Bret	5.26	4.37	4.87	8.19	5.68	**5.35**
Jimenez,D'Angelc	5.67	5.90	2.70	4.37	4.65	**5.32**
Bellhorn,Mark	4.91	4.41	6.06	3.30	6.83	**5.25**
Biggio,Craig	7.91	6.51	5.70	6.18	4.63	**5.04**
Hairston Jr.,Jerry	5.33	4.29	4.66	3.48	4.45	**5.00**
Castillo,Luis	3.55	5.62	6.69	4.28	5.14	**4.97**
Butler,Brent		3.49	5.16	4.82	4.14	**4.89**
Ortiz,Jose	4.01	4.94	7.56	4.03	4.48	**4.84**
Deshields,Delino	6.08	4.35	6.44	4.83	3.43	**4.76**
Gil,Benji	2.83	2.83	3.75	5.59	5.28	**4.66**
Kennedy,Adam	4.33	5.17	4.24	4.04	5.79	**4.63**
Vazquez,Ramon		3.67	4.43	4.58	4.72	**4.57**
Gutierrez,Ricky	4.09	4.23	5.73	5.07	3.93	**4.56**
Perez,Tomas	3.07	2.81	4.06	5.40	4.52	**4.53**
Anderson,Marlon	4.77	3.77	4.27	5.23	4.31	**4.53**
Vina,Fernando	5.69	4.00	5.07	5.23	3.81	**4.51**
Young,Eric	5.23	4.86	5.93	4.56	4.53	**4.51**
Canizaro,Jay	3.37	4.31	5.44		3.34	**4.51**
Menechino,Frank	3.76	4.42	5.63	4.83	2.61	**4.43**
Ellis,Mark			5.25	3.63	4.99	**4.40**
Shumpert,Terry	3.11	10.30	5.32	5.45	3.94	**4.37**
Roberts,Brian				4.09	3.85	**4.34**
Berg,Dave	6.70	4.89	4.32	3.60	4.34	**4.30**
Easley,Damion	5.42	5.22	5.17	4.15	3.16	**4.28**
Febles,Carlos	6.53	4.96	3.86	4.26	3.93	**4.19**
Reese,Pokey	3.81	5.15	4.59	3.49	4.42	**4.17**
Sheets,Andy	4.63	2.12	2.99	3.23	4.16	**4.13**
Rivas,Luis		3.71	4.32	4.12	4.09	**4.11**
Jackson,Damian	4.34	4.10	4.92	3.89	4.18	**4.06**
Nunez,Abraham	3.28	2.93	3.01	4.09	3.38	**4.05**
Young,Mike			3.85	4.43	4.14	**4.04**
Merloni,Lou	7.19	4.59	4.23	3.42	4.05	**4.01**
Grudzielanek,Mar	3.96	6.05	4.75	4.26	3.92	**3.97**
Belliard,Ron	5.71	5.45	5.14	5.40	2.42	**3.95**
Alicea,Luis	5.76	3.64	5.57	4.06	3.31	**3.92**
Nieves,Jose	3.44	3.06	3.64	4.33	3.70	**3.91**
Sanchez,Rey	4.26	4.42	3.65	3.74	3.99	**3.90**
Hill,Bobby				3.95	3.95	**3.90**
Hocking,Denny	2.56	4.00	5.98	3.90	3.58	**3.86**
Harris,Willie				4.07	3.68	**3.80**
Cintron,Alex			3.62	3.67	4.05	**3.70**
Abernathy,Brent		3.85	3.70	4.71	3.05	**3.50**
Lockhart,Keith	4.29	4.00	4.45	2.90	3.20	**3.31**
Ordaz,Luis	3.19	3.21	2.08	3.72	3.21	**3.11**
McDonald,John	2.32	3.60	3.12	2.37	3.22	**2.97**
Guerrero,Wilton	3.86	4.50	3.84	4.23	2.36	**2.95**
Garcia,Jesse	3.74	2.22	2.14	2.82	2.99	**2.69**
Bush,Homer	7.75	5.66	2.25	4.49	2.15	**2.66**
Matos,Julius		2.89	1.92	2.83	3.26	**2.58**
Lawrence,Joe		4.27	3.82	2.26	2.12	**2.42**

Power	'98	'99	'00	'01	'02	'03Prj
Kent,Jeff	168	141	153	132	151	**150**
Soriano,Alfonso		100	97	103	161	**148**
Vidro,Jose	61	120	133	108	114	**123**
Gil,Benji	81	91	71	110	142	**116**
Bellhorn,Mark	105	57	116	96	147	**115**
Durham,Ray	104	85	100	123	108	**112**
Boone,Bret	130	106	98	146	120	**112**
Hudson,Orlando			60	99	99	**104**
Walker,Todd	107	83	82	104	91	**102**
Graffanino,Tony	77	108	52	75	107	**100**
Giles,Marcus			93	96	96	**98**
Biggio,Craig	128	115	72	102	98	**98**
Spivey,Junior	116	87	126	74	110	**97**
Canizaro,Jay	88	119	99		89	**96**
Merloni,Lou	105	85	71	80	97	**94**
Alomar,Roberto	91	129	103	122	70	**94**
Shumpert,Terry	96	162	109	92	87	**92**
Ortiz,Jose	81	99	120	102	79	**92**
Butler,Brent		69	93	88	97	**92**
Nieves,Jose	96	80	97	109	65	**91**
Easley,Damion	128	103	96	79	84	**86**
Kennedy,Adam	92	94	84	70	98	**86**
Rivas,Luis		80	86	60	99	**85**
Deshields,Delino	92	61	98	75	73	**84**
Sheets,Andy	98	45	62	73	103	**84**
Ellis,Mark			38	84	85	**83**
Hairston Jr.,Jerry	86	83	76	72	80	**83**
Perez,Tomas	56	62	85	84	89	**83**
Jimenez,D'Angelc	88	92	43	72	77	**82**
Berg,Dave	75	70	68	80	86	**81**
Anderson,Marlon	104	75	73	84	81	**81**
Belliard,Ron	98	82	79	123	55	**79**
Menechino,Frank	65	85	119	83	58	**78**
Young,Mike			82	93	80	**78**
Jackson,Damian	96	85	79	66	86	**75**
Gutierrez,Ricky	58	45	76	71	52	**74**
Febles,Carlos	102	91	41	81	72	**72**
DeRosa,Mark	66	45	58	80	74	**71**
Reese,Pokey	40	89	77	76	66	**71**
Grudzielanek,Mar	63	72	73	74	63	**68**
Young,Eric	81	56	74	82	65	**68**
Hocking,Denny	54	71	78	62	59	**66**
Vazquez,Ramon		68	76	68	61	**65**
Hill,Bobby				47	76	**65**
Abernathy,Brent		85	68	84	51	**64**
Lockhart,Keith	94	31	57	54	73	**63**
Harris,Willie				63	60	**60**
Cintron,Alex			60	59	68	**59**
Alicea,Luis	96	79	67	60	46	**56**
Vina,Fernando	86	50	65	73	50	**53**
Nunez,Abraham	50	22	33	48	63	**53**
Garcia,Jesse	49	53	29	59	62	**52**
Lawrence,Joe		86	57	43	57	**52**
McDonald,John	41	46	54	41	55	**50**
Roberts,Brian				54	54	**50**
Ordaz,Luis	61	61	16	46	58	**44**
Matos,Julius		53	46	53	60	**43**
Sanchez,Rey	58	49	36	38	43	**41**
Bush,Homer	58	68	27	55	25	**41**
Castillo,Luis	29	48	37	47	38	**40**
Guerrero,Wilton	56	71	37	53	19	**32**

Speed	'98	'99	'00	'01	'02	'03Prj
Durham,Ray	159	152	155	152	150	**153**
Roberts,Brian				136	151	**152**
Deshields,Delino	171	96	132	162	133	**145**
Castillo,Luis	124	130	126	166	132	**140**
Rivas,Luis		136	138	130	144	**140**
Febles,Carlos	182	182	116	115	141	**133**
Soriano,Alfonso		103	127	126	137	**131**
Jackson,Damian	166	126	149	172	113	**130**
Bellhorn,Mark	109	40	183	111	112	**129**
Kennedy,Adam	126	110	166	86	145	**127**
Nieves,Jose	108	72	116	115	112	**125**
Harris,Willie				129	122	**123**
Graffanino,Tony	57	147	115	70	131	**121**
Hairston Jr.,Jerry	114	122	94	125	124	**120**
Young,Eric	125	118	126	132	114	**119**
Alomar,Roberto	90	135	126	167	105	**119**
Biggio,Craig	130	90	138	95	125	**119**
Shumpert,Terry	98	141	192	190	86	**118**
Spivey,Junior	113	174	150	113	124	**118**
Hudson,Orlando			105	144	94	**116**
Hill,Bobby				102	133	**113**
McDonald,John	97	74	68	90	126	**112**
Vina,Fernando	120	66	116	133	103	**110**
Young,Mike			128	87	118	**109**
Ellis,Mark			58	81	124	**107**
Guerrero,Wilton	160	146	99	96	116	**107**
Gil,Benji	126	103	77	109	99	**107**
Anderson,Marlon	151	114	120	80	105	**106**
Abernathy,Brent		98	92	93	107	**106**
Vazquez,Ramon		91	61	70	112	**104**
Reese,Pokey	132	138	152	127	81	**102**
Jimenez,D'Angelc	105	95	67	61	124	**98**
Ortiz,Jose	111	106	118	110	83	**96**
Sanchez,Rey	64	125	89	118	85	**95**
Bush,Homer	106	137	94	100	97	**94**
Boone,Bret	63	91	78	75	95	**93**
Giles,Marcus			89	101	78	**91**
Nunez,Abraham	103	80	88	122	67	**89**
Sheets,Andy	164	48	86	82	103	**88**
Kent,Jeff	100	89	109	91	74	**87**
Alicea,Luis	114	79	95	98	80	**84**
Cintron,Alex			86	83	82	**82**
Canizaro,Jay	81	92	83		79	**82**
DeRosa,Mark	77	76	101	83	85	**81**
Walker,Todd	106	102	114	52	78	**81**
Merloni,Lou	70	64	74	71	86	**80**
Butler,Brent		35	42	87	99	**80**
Belliard,Ron	133	83	115	119	54	**76**
Garcia,Jesse	118	94	85	111	82	**75**
Ordaz,Luis	65	47	111	60	100	**69**
Lockhart,Keith	53	79	96	40	74	**69**
Grudzielanek,Mar	88	92	124	88	57	**69**
Menechino,Frank	113	93	92	64	69	**68**
Vidro,Jose	81	41	66	77	70	**67**
Perez,Tomas	87	54	89	48	58	**63**
Easley,Damion	94	88	104	111	43	**57**
Berg,Dave	47	61	75	59	51	**57**
Hocking,Denny	102	95	103	87	31	**51**
Matos,Julius		98	58	63	43	**51**
Lawrence,Joe		75	73	77	86	**49**
Gutierrez,Ricky	92	105	87	79	30	**46**

3Bmen

Std Rotisserie	'98	'99	'00	'01	'02	'03Prj
Rolen,Scott	31	19	23	28	24	**29**
Boone,Aaron	12	19	11	16	23	**28**
Nevin,Phil	2	15	25	33	13	**27**
Lowell,Mike	18	7	16	18	20	**26**
Beltre,Adrian	19	17	21	14	15	**24**
Chavez,Eric	30	6	16	27	27	**24**
Glaus,Troy	19	12	30	24	23	**23**
Ramirez,Aramis	6	14	10	30	8	**23**
Alfonzo,Edgardo	18	27	26	8	19	**23**
Hinske,Eric		0	10	15	23	**21**
Batista,Tony	11	21	22	13	18	**20**
Crede,Joe		1	19	12	26	**19**
Zeile,Todd	17	19	14	9	16	**19**
Koskie,Corey	19	13	13	28	16	**18**
Ventura,Robin	14	26	11	9	17	**15**
Valentin,Jose	8	4	22	17	15	**15**
Hillenbrand,Shea		2	9	8	20	**15**
Randa,Joe	7	21	20	10	15	**15**
Burroughs,Sean			4	16	6	**13**
Mueller,Bill	14	7	8	6	6	**12**
Blalock,Hank				14	12	**12**
Loretta,Mark	17	11	7	6	8	**12**
Perry,Herbert	0	7	13	5	18	**11**
Williams,Matt	16	30	9	13	8	**11**
Cirillo,Jeff	24	24	24	25	8	**11**
Bell,David	7	14	4	10	13	**10**
Sandberg,Jared			4	6	12	**10**
Polanco,Placido	4	3	11	15	13	**9**
Norton,Greg	4	8	5	8	3	**8**
Ensberg,Morgan				15	10	**8**
Castilla,Vinny	42	21	0	16	5	**7**
Counsell,Craig	4	(2)	5	8	10	**7**
Tatis,Fernando	14	32	10	1	6	**7**
Blum,Geoff	3	8	9	6	11	**6**
Wigginton,Ty			9	2	13	**6**
Bell,Jay	12	28	13	6	(1)	**6**
Ginter,Keith			27	10	7	**6**
Stynes,Chris	8	2	16	8	3	**5**
Houston,Tyler	6	2	8	9	8	**5**
Pellow,Kit	8	13	5	9	12	**4**
Coomer,Ron	12	10	11	7	3	**3**
Truby,Chris	8	12	13	15	(2)	**2**
Donnels,Chris	6		14	(2)	2	**2**
LaRocca,Greg	4	0	7	10	11	**2**
Selby,Bill	4	4	6	3	7	**2**
Johnson,Russ	6	7	1	7	3	**2**
Mordecai,Mike	(0)	2	4	6	0	**2**
Paquette,Craig	2	15	8	14	(1)	**1**
Smith,Bobby	10	12	12	14	1	**1**
Feliz,Pedro	5	6	12	2	1	**1**
Smith,Jason			4	(2)	5	**1**
Carroll,Jamey	1	8	5	(2)	6	**1**
Wilson,Enrique	10	3	6	(2)	(0)	**0**
Benjamin,Mike	5	4	4		(5)	**(1)**

RC/Gm	'98	'99	'00	'01	'02	'03Prj
Alfonzo,Edgardo	5.69	7.63	9.32	4.70	7.09	**7.62**
Rolen,Scott	7.74	7.34	7.72	7.07	6.36	**7.47**
Nevin,Phil	3.60	6.97	7.80	8.62	5.46	**7.19**
Lowell,Mike	5.56	4.49	6.01	5.51	6.03	**6.79**
Mueller,Bill	5.95	5.56	4.70	7.07	5.34	**6.64**
Zeile,Todd	5.61	6.47	6.09	5.04	5.71	**6.63**
Glaus,Troy	5.77	5.31	8.96	7.16	5.86	**6.55**
Ventura,Robin	5.66	7.73	5.22	5.45	6.35	**6.38**
Chavez,Eric	7.66	5.16	6.57	6.74	6.58	**6.23**
Koskie,Corey	5.09	6.81	6.86	6.50	5.72	**6.11**
Beltre,Adrian	5.26	5.53	6.42	4.50	4.46	**5.99**
Boone,Aaron	3.89	5.09	6.01	6.14	4.75	**5.90**
Hinske,Eric		6.71	5.10	4.63	6.78	**5.89**
Ensberg,Morgan				7.09	5.07	**5.89**
Ramirez,Aramis	4.49	6.21	4.88	6.79	3.68	**5.82**
Norton,Greg	4.07	5.54	5.08	6.08	4.00	**5.79**
Blalock,Hank				8.19	5.18	**5.76**
Crede,Joe		3.00	6.47	5.13	6.50	**5.70**
Loretta,Mark	6.11	5.16	5.20	4.40	5.97	**5.61**
Valentin,Jose	4.41	5.28	6.32	5.97	5.20	**5.60**
Perry,Herbert	5.63	4.92	5.99	4.51	5.69	**5.57**
Wigginton,Ty			3.86	3.50	5.19	**5.53**
Bell,Jay	5.41	7.86	5.64	5.12	2.63	**5.52**
Donnels,Chris	7.89		6.61	2.55	5.01	**5.46**
Blum,Geoff	4.95	5.17	5.31	3.71	6.23	**5.46**
Batista,Tony	5.84	6.24	5.47	4.16	4.75	**5.26**
Randa,Joe	4.04	6.57	5.63	4.15	5.36	**5.25**
Williams,Matt	5.20	7.02	4.79	5.27	5.33	**5.24**
Burroughs,Sean			4.14	6.61	4.54	**5.12**
Ginter,Keith			8.28	4.89	4.67	**4.84**
Bell,David	4.66	5.23	4.16	4.44	5.06	**4.76**
Hillenbrand,Shea		2.80	4.01	3.77	5.38	**4.67**
LaRocca,Greg	3.64	2.33	4.07	5.49	4.57	**4.66**
Cirillo,Jeff	7.15	7.38	7.39	6.74	3.40	**4.62**
Counsell,Craig	4.97	2.55	6.37	4.78	4.57	**4.60**
Tatis,Fernando	4.86	8.19	6.50	4.37	4.03	**4.60**
Stynes,Chris	4.13	3.41	7.62	4.55	4.19	**4.55**
Sandberg,Jared			4.44	3.97	4.82	**4.47**
Polanco,Placido	3.52	3.63	5.38	4.90	4.71	**4.39**
Houston,Tyler	3.97	4.00	5.01	6.00	4.96	**4.38**
Coomer,Ron	4.33	4.68	4.79	4.50	3.87	**4.22**
Pellow,Kit	3.73	4.27	3.36	3.70	4.14	**4.21**
Johnson,Russ	4.23	5.72	3.53	6.32	3.51	**4.05**
Selby,Bill	3.86	3.92	4.32	3.29	4.35	**3.90**
Castilla,Vinny	7.74	5.75	2.57	4.93	3.12	**3.89**
Mordecai,Mike	3.04	3.49	5.33	4.75	3.18	**3.84**
Smith,Bobby	5.19	4.58	4.50	5.63	2.79	**3.83**
Truby,Chris	3.96	3.82	4.32	4.84	2.63	**3.47**
Carroll,Jamey	3.51	3.62	3.56	2.13	3.66	**3.42**
Feliz,Pedro	3.41	3.29	4.65	3.28	3.35	**3.40**
Paquette,Craig	3.34	4.91	4.40	5.40	2.27	**3.12**
Wilson,Enrique	4.97	3.91	5.38	2.01	2.27	**2.83**
Smith,Jason			2.52	2.12	3.35	**2.70**
Benjamin,Mike	4.11	3.76	4.11		0.95	**2.31**

Power	'98	'99	'00	'01	'02	'03Prj
Rolen,Scott	161	155	147	130	137	**146**
Glaus,Troy	134	124	179	165	126	**144**
Valentin,Jose	114	107	128	144	144	**142**
Nevin,Phil	84	156	141	161	79	**142**
Chavez,Eric	146	110	121	155	148	**140**
Ramirez,Aramis	92	115	90	142	96	**132**
Boone,Aaron	86	100	114	118	122	**131**
Lowell,Mike	123	89	128	107	125	**131**
Donnels,Chris	133		149	76	108	**130**
Batista,Tony	155	142	143	115	137	**130**
Crede,Joe		65	113	112	152	**125**
Ventura,Robin	106	140	120	107	128	**125**
Beltre,Adrian	128	95	112	88	100	**122**
Koskie,Corey	121	100	91	130	125	**121**
Perry,Herbert	213	105	106	104	130	**118**
Williams,Matt	114	140	94	122	122	**118**
Hinske,Eric		158	106	117	134	**117**
Sandberg,Jared			96	98	132	**114**
Pellow,Kit	134	138	94	70	124	**110**
Ensberg,Morgan				147	83	**110**
Norton,Greg	101	106	80	144	102	**110**
Blalock,Hank				128	101	**110**
Alfonzo,Edgardo	100	124	134	97	96	**108**
Selby,Bill	110	100	103	95	114	**108**
Wigginton,Ty			101	73	93	**108**
Zeile,Todd	108	122	121	70	93	**106**
Ginter,Keith			138	115	100	**105**
Smith,Bobby	87	99	116	123	88	**104**
Tatis,Fernando	96	150	141	74	103	**103**
Randa,Joe	73	98	81	88	101	**99**
Bell,David	100	100	83	100	104	**99**
Houston,Tyler	87	88	139	102	96	**95**
LaRocca,Greg	91	34	92	115	86	**95**
Hillenbrand,Shea		75	72	80	114	**93**
Truby,Chris	115	111	89	127	75	**93**
Bell,Jay	118	155	102	96	92	**91**
Blum,Geoff	127	113	102	77	98	**90**
Paquette,Craig	73	133	116	109	81	**89**
Castilla,Vinny	163	117	52	126	74	**87**
Mueller,Bill	75	58	77	96	86	**87**
Stynes,Chris	58	35	103	84	83	**80**
Loretta,Mark	85	71	83	44	77	**80**
Coomer,Ron	81	99	89	84	76	**78**
Cirillo,Jeff	88	90	106	97	58	**77**
Johnson,Russ	67	96	42	98	75	**77**
Burroughs,Sean			70	94	64	**76**
Feliz,Pedro	103	84	123	87	51	**74**
Polanco,Placido	72	48	63	54	79	**69**
Smith,Jason			76	55	78	**68**
Mordecai,Mike	89	80	116	82	46	**65**
Wilson,Enrique	85	68	87	47	66	**63**
Benjamin,Mike	75	82	86		22	**58**
Carroll,Jamey	48	65	46	32	71	**57**
Counsell,Craig	87	35	70	60	53	**55**

Speed	'98	'99	'00	'01	'02	'03Prj
Smith,Jason			129	141	158	**139**
Wilson,Enrique	86	75	57	46	169	**116**
Rolen,Scott	108	88	129	92	118	**115**
LaRocca,Greg	111	57	122	58	118	**113**
Truby,Chris	125	116	102	118	119	**109**
Hinske,Eric		353	141	84	106	**108**
Boone,Aaron	127	119	73	87	114	**102**
Benjamin,Mike	69	163	101		75	**98**
Carroll,Jamey	121	100	103	89	84	**96**
Koskie,Corey	105	42	90	110	87	**95**
Ensberg,Morgan				59	113	**93**
Johnson,Russ	74	48	72	72	114	**93**
Beltre,Adrian	100	116	81	117	91	**90**
Bell,Jay	79	114	103	37	18	**89**
Burroughs,Sean			66	84	78	**83**
Valentin,Jose	71	134	150	87	89	**83**
Polanco,Placido	105	93	93	117	77	**82**
Chavez,Eric	88	59	82	72	85	**80**
Pellow,Kit	96	97	71	49	72	**79**
Blum,Geoff	126	93	51	73	86	**79**
Counsell,Craig	112	62	78	87	75	**79**
Glaus,Troy	68	63	76	78	85	**77**
Hillenbrand,Shea		69	64	61	91	**76**
Williams,Matt	73	60	54	50	90	**74**
Cirillo,Jeff	73	62	64	105	67	**73**
Stynes,Chris	115	85	79	78	65	**73**
Donnels,Chris	33		76	22	51	**72**
Norton,Greg	83	46	60	83	67	**72**
Randa,Joe	76	101	87	53	77	**72**
Selby,Bill	65	60	84	58	90	**70**
Ginter,Keith			113	97	52	**70**
Batista,Tony	62	68	74	98	68	**69**
Blalock,Hank				87	55	**67**
Alfonzo,Edgardo	87	80	63	70	69	**67**
Perry,Herbert		51	85	64	66	**67**
Feliz,Pedro	38	95	48	74	53	**66**
Wigginton,Ty			69	52	71	**66**
Mueller,Bill	52	53	94	64	66	**65**
Sandberg,Jared			62	31	76	**62**
Smith,Bobby	89	116	92	93	70	**61**
Houston,Tyler	58	47	34	31	77	**55**
Mordecai,Mike	115	81	49	79	62	**55**
Castilla,Vinny	69	39	38	39	75	**54**
Tatis,Fernando	110	95	60	35	52	**53**
Bell,David	41	79	60	50	55	**52**
Paquette,Craig	99	80	76	59	62	**51**
Nevin,Phil	46	30	54	46	60	**50**
Lowell,Mike	70		59	31	51	**45**
Ramirez,Aramis	28	59	65	49	44	**44**
Crede,Joe		60	42	63	21	**42**
Zeile,Todd	69	38	53	45	29	**37**
Loretta,Mark	60	93	39	53	34	**35**
Ventura,Robin	62	30	41	34	43	**27**
Coomer,Ron	44	51	54	20	24	**25**

Shortstops

Std Rotisserie	'98	'99	'00	'01	'02	'03Prj
Rodriguez,Alex	48	32	36	45	43	**43**
Tejada,Miguel	5	13	21	24	34	**32**
Garciaparra,Nomar	35	35	31	4	29	**31**
Renteria,Edgar	20	21	20	13	26	**26**
Jeter,Derek	33	36	29	30	30	**25**
Eckstein,David		14	4	17	20	**23**
Cabrera,Orlando	8	4	6	22	15	**21**
Rollins,Jimmy		15	14	27	15	**20**
Aurilia,Rich	9	16	14	32	9	**19**
Guzman,Cristian	14	(1)	11	21	14	**18**
Vizquel,Omar	20	31	17	7	20	**15**
Womack,Tony	28	29	22	13	18	**15**
Furcal,Rafael			21	12	17	**13**
Gonzalez,Alex S.	10	4	8	15	10	**12**
Uribe,Juan				24	4	**12**
Lugo,Julio		13	22	10	8	**12**
Lopez,Felipe			3	21	13	**11**
Woodward,Chris	1	1	4	6	11	**10**
Hernandez,Jose	15	14	6	14	20	**10**
Guillen,Carlos	8		7	6	9	**9**
Izturis,Cesar			3	18	(0)	**9**
Relaford,Desi	5	2	3	14	10	**8**
Fox,Andy	13	4	3	2	13	**8**
Cruz,Deivi	5	10	14	7	6	**7**
Gonzalez,Alex	6	11	(0)	5	1	**7**
Larkin,Barry	29	24	17	3	7	**6**
Vizcaino,Jose	6	1	1	3	11	**6**
Perez,Neifi	11	15	13	13	3	**6**
Bordick,Mike	9	15	18	7	5	**6**
Wilson,Jack			5	1	4	**6**
Martinez,Ramon	6	5	7	3	5	**5**
Gomez,Chris	5	0	(1)	10	8	**5**
Cora,Alex	2	4	6	(3)	9	**5**
Halter,Shane	1	(3)	4	13	4	**4**
Clayton,Royce	13	13	7	11	6	**3**
Everett,Adam		9	2	7	5	**2**
Valentin,John	11	7	1	(1)	2	**2**
Santiago,Ramon					9	**2**
Escalona,Felix					1	**2**
Ordonez,Rey	2	5	(3)	3	3	**1**
Castro,Juan	(3)	(3)	3	(1)	(0)	**1**
Lopez,Luis M.	2	(0)	4	3	(0)	**1**
Ojeda,Augie	(2)	3	6	(1)	(8)	**(1)**

RC/Gm	'98	'99	'00	'01	'02	'03Prj
Rodriguez,Alex	7.38	7.66	10.20	9.57	9.14	**9.65**
Garciaparra,Nom.	7.88	10.31	11.11	6.97	7.05	**8.24**
Tejada,Miguel	3.64	4.71	6.25	5.31	6.64	**6.59**
Jeter,Derek	7.33	9.79	8.11	7.05	6.24	**6.09**
Renteria,Edgar	4.16	5.09	5.32	4.28	6.11	**5.98**
Aurilia,Rich	4.60	5.38	5.55	8.12	4.43	**5.68**
Cabrera,Orlando	3.58	4.01	3.70	5.01	4.48	**5.41**
Martinez,Ramon	4.28	4.71	6.36	4.05	4.97	**5.30**
Eckstein,David		5.15	3.64	4.67	4.79	**5.23**
Woodward,Chris	3.26	4.52	4.76	5.23	5.77	**5.13**
Larkin,Barry	8.14	6.55	7.30	5.11	4.00	**4.92**
Vizquel,Omar	5.10	7.26	5.44	3.85	5.09	**4.83**
Relaford,Desi	3.44	3.46	3.97	6.37	4.66	**4.72**
Guillen,Carlos	4.42		4.78	4.47	4.56	**4.71**
Gonzalez,Alex S.	3.44	5.60	4.37	3.99	4.64	**4.68**
Rollins,Jimmy		4.52	4.73	5.13	4.01	**4.59**
Valentin,John	5.24	4.47	4.22	3.19	4.03	**4.54**
Hernandez,Jose	5.00	5.24	3.88	4.59	6.14	**4.51**
Lugo,Julio		4.85	5.30	4.17	4.51	**4.50**
Cora,Alex	2.38	3.26	3.95	2.83	5.88	**4.49**
Lopez,Felipe			2.96	5.26	4.81	**4.43**
Guzman,Cristian	3.94	2.42	4.05	5.79	3.73	**4.35**
Clayton,Royce	4.12	5.55	3.94	4.32	3.82	**4.31**
Halter,Shane	2.77	2.11	3.92	5.77	4.11	**4.26**
Uribe,Juan				5.96	3.41	**4.25**
Vizcaino,Jose	3.77	3.27	3.14	3.95	4.94	**4.17**
Fox,Andy	4.81	4.74	3.38	4.53	4.15	**4.10**
Gomez,Chris	4.74	3.69	2.61	4.24	4.22	**4.10**
Furcal,Rafael			5.95	4.48	4.34	**4.02**
Cruz,Deivi	3.38	4.47	5.12	3.82	3.74	**3.99**
Gonzalez,Alex	3.84	4.40	2.40	3.84	3.20	**3.93**
Everett,Adam		4.00	3.96	3.39	3.75	**3.91**
Womack,Tony	4.54	4.87	4.26	3.78	4.14	**3.88**
Wilson,Jack			4.52	3.05	3.59	**3.82**
Bordick,Mike	4.50	5.01	5.49	4.21	3.78	**3.68**
Lopez,Luis M.	3.63	3.11	4.27	4.34	2.97	**3.57**
Izturis,Cesar			2.37	4.11	2.50	**3.57**
Castro,Juan	2.13	2.40	4.13	2.72	2.84	**3.54**
Perez,Neifi	4.24	4.46	4.83	4.34	2.59	**3.51**
Ordonez,Rey	2.79	3.74	2.28	3.56	3.32	**3.24**
Escalona,Felix					2.25	**2.79**
Ojeda,Augie	3.13	3.67	3.57	2.48	1.91	**2.52**
Santiago,Ramon					3.80	**2.38**

Power	'98	'99	'00	'01	'02	'03Prj
Rodriguez,Alex	144	168	163	173	190	**198**
Garciaparra,Nom.	153	150	143	120	150	**152**
Tejada,Miguel	96	106	118	123	125	**133**
Woodward,Chris	69	73	116	142	118	**126**
Aurilia,Rich	101	98	102	144	102	**120**
Gonzalez,Alex S.	79	91	94	81	107	**110**
Hernandez,Jose	135	95	81	114	112	**104**
Halter,Shane	67	46	68	115	102	**97**
Lopez,Felipe			61	113	98	**95**
Larkin,Barry	128	82	108	85	88	**95**
Martinez,Ramon	86	80	115	65	91	**93**
Renteria,Edgar	46	85	92	69	91	**93**
Guillen,Carlos	77		84	64	89	**92**
Uribe,Juan				129	65	**91**
Cabrera,Orlando	67	96	98	98	87	**90**
Jeter,Derek	92	120	86	105	82	**90**
Gomez,Chris	88	40		93	103	**89**
Lopez,Luis M.	65	63	104	70	86	**88**
Rollins,Jimmy		77	94	86	85	**84**
Guzman,Cristian	57	34	78	104	78	**84**
Valentin,John	126	93	108	73	84	**83**
Cora,Alex	64	52	74	59	90	**81**
Bordick,Mike	99	81	96	95	91	**81**
Cruz,Deivi	65	95	98	86	71	**81**
Lugo,Julio		83	89	68	81	**80**
Relaford,Desi	70	61	53	117	72	**80**
Gonzalez,Alex	89	94	74	88	66	**79**
Clayton,Royce	81	93	82	81	76	**78**
Vizquel,Omar	60	73	58	53	96	**74**
Castro,Juan	45	61	91	54	57	**70**
Furcal,Rafael			58	69	72	**69**
Everett,Adam		64	67	67	59	**67**
Perez,Neifi	72	75	88	73	49	**63**
Ojeda,Augie	42	63	70	46	55	**62**
Wilson,Jack			81	56	54	**61**
Escalona,Felix					59	**59**
Eckstein,David		60	57	52	64	**59**
Fox,Andy	80	78	58	77	52	**57**
Womack,Tony	55	60	65	52	54	**56**
Izturis,Cesar			45	64	55	**54**
Vizcaino,Jose	56	35	38	43	64	**52**
Ordonez,Rey	44	47	32	62	54	**50**
Santiago,Ramon					67	**41**

Speed	'98	'99	'00	'01	'02	'03Prj
Guzman,Cristian	116	105	224	205	111	**167**
Rollins,Jimmy		120	150	189	156	**159**
Escalona,Felix					167	**158**
Woodward,Chris	58	85	105	93	123	**151**
Uribe,Juan				177	132	**145**
Womack,Tony	159	186	199	151	132	**144**
Everett,Adam		93	100	152	155	**138**
Lopez,Felipe			77	148	131	**133**
Fox,Andy	124	85	112	111	148	**132**
Santiago,Ramon					185	**127**
Cora,Alex	121	124	127	56	134	**126**
Eckstein,David		120	85	111	130	**124**
Furcal,Rafael			137	100	144	**119**
Jeter,Derek	157	141	125	118	115	**118**
Vizquel,Omar	135	137	102	115	114	**117**
Lugo,Julio		131	150	112	94	**107**
Guillen,Carlos	100		103	98	112	**105**
Perez,Neifi	103	139	107	130	99	**105**
Relaford,Desi	86	107	113	86	117	**102**
Renteria,Edgar	118	118	89	106	100	**101**
Cabrera,Orlando	149	97	60	109	96	**101**
Wilson,Jack			112	73	103	**100**
Gonzalez,Alex	127	111	119	55	89	**100**
Ojeda,Augie	48	88	91	83	91	**99**
Halter,Shane	70	87	102	102	87	**98**
Larkin,Barry	167	116	125	72	105	**97**
Clayton,Royce	115	110	115	106	109	**97**
Gonzalez,Alex S.	103	69	69	105	95	**96**
Izturis,Cesar			135	117	85	**95**
Martinez,Ramon	37	63	101	69	105	**94**
Rodriguez,Alex	136	102	104	93	81	**82**
Vizcaino,Jose	78	47	93	114	65	**80**
Garciaparra,Nom.	127	112	83	36	95	**79**
Tejada,Miguel	79	94	83	98	72	**77**
Lopez,Luis M.	92	44	45	81	53	**71**
Bordick,Mike	62	127	72	86	94	**68**
Aurilia,Rich	72	39	46	70	61	**62**
Cruz,Deivi	77	39	65	62	53	**61**
Ordonez,Rey	57	68	19	67	68	**58**
Hernandez,Jose	124	94	48	72	57	**57**
Castro,Juan	42	57	60	38	13	**56**
Gomez,Chris	61	44		78	62	**55**
Valentin,John	70	40	66	30	17	**29**

Outfielders

Std Rotisserie	'98	'99	'00	'01	'02	'03Prj
Guerrero,Vladimir	39	38	41	42	52	47
Giles,Brian	15	32	32	33	34	40
Ordonez,Magglio	15	29	33	35	37	38
Ramirez,Manny	33	38	32	31	31	36
Berkman,Lance	17	10	18	37	35	36
Bonds,Barry	41	23	34	51	44	36
Abreu,Bobby	26	34	32	37	33	35
Green,Shawn	33	37	24	41	32	35
Jones,Chipper	36	41	33	36	32	34
Pujols,Albert				36	34	34
Anderson,Garret	18	19	25	29	31	34
Suzuki,Ichiro	28	25	31	43	28	33
Sosa,Sammy	54	39	40	47	32	32
Floyd,Cliff	29	12	27	35	25	32
Damon,Johnny	21	29	37	14	25	30
Jones,Andruw	30	24	34	22	23	29
Sheffield,Gary	28	28	33	32	28	29
Cameron,Mike	8	22	19	29	24	29
Gonzalez,Luis	17	32	28	43	27	29
Hunter,Torii	13	7	22	19	31	28
Pierre,Juan			31	33	23	28
Beltran,Carlos	12	29	7	34	34	28
Ibanez,Raul	0	8	0	10	24	27
Winn,Randy	15	14	12	11	27	27
Walker,Larry	33	40	13	42	33	27
Williams,Bernie	32	32	29	27	30	26
Edmonds,Jim	24	4	31	28	26	25
Kearns,Austin				5	21	25
Roberts,Dave	24	12	16	6	21	25
Salmon,Tim	20	12	21	7	21	25
Jones,Jacque	22	14	16	14	25	24
Stewart,Shannon	27	27	26	26	18	24
Wilson,Preston	11	19	32	22	17	24
Dunn,Adam				40	19	23
Nixon,Trot	24	10	11	21	18	23
Burrell,Pat		18	15	16	27	23
Mondesi,Raul	27	28	20	24	18	23
Encarnacion,Juan	25	21	18	8	24	22
Lee,Carlos	17	20	24	21	17	22
Wells,Vernon		12	13	17	22	22
Kotsay,Mark	16	8	19	16	20	21
Dye,Jermaine	10	23	28	24	15	21
Lawton,Matt	20	14	24	21	10	21
Catalanotto,Frank	11	8	10	22	6	21
Gibbons,Jay			11	6	15	21
Finley,Steve	12	21	25	16	26	20
Alou,Moises	37		33	31	15	19
Gonzalez,Juan	38	33	14	34	8	18
Payton,Jay	4	7	15	6	19	18
Millar,Kevin	0	13	7	21	16	18
Cruz,Jose	16	11	15	31	13	18
Higginson,Bobby	19	5	27	20	16	18
Erstad,Darin	24	9	41	14	21	18
Crawford,Carl				19	26	18
Giambi,Jeremy	21	11	6	11	9	18
Kapler,Gabe	21	12	16	20	10	17
Sanders,Reggie	18	28	10	24	19	17
Cedeno,Roger	3	31	13	28	13	17
Garcia,Karim	10	5	9	18	26	17
Hidalgo,Richard	9	7	37	16	7	17
Griffey Jr.,Ken	41	38	26	16	5	17
Drew,J.D.	11	14	19	27	12	17
Tucker,Michael	9	9	12	13	16	16
Ward,Daryle	11	18	10	6	13	16
Patterson,Corey			17	9	13	16
Marrero,Eli	6	0	3	6	17	15
Chavez,Endy				6	22	15
Quinn,Mark	13	26	17	14	1	15
Sanchez,Alex		7	15	12	19	15
Matthews Jr.,Gary	8	4	(0)	6	11	14
Wilkerson,Brad		(1)	15	10	14	14
Lofton,Kenny	29	17	21	15	17	14

RC/Gm	'98	'99	'00	'01	'02	'03Prj
Bonds,Barry	10.32	9.10	12.15	18.50	21.62	15.27
Giles,Brian	6.56	10.31	10.46	9.19	11.08	11.82
Ramirez,Manny	8.52	11.60	13.35	9.43	10.90	10.85
Jones,Chipper	8.79	11.64	8.99	10.09	9.71	10.03
Berkman,Lance	6.48	5.36	8.55	10.19	8.97	9.59
Sosa,Sammy	9.13	8.43	10.16	13.01	9.20	9.30
Walker,Larry	11.72	13.55	7.64	12.05	9.94	9.26
Guerrero,Vladimir	8.04	8.45	10.31	7.65	9.37	9.19
Sheffield,Gary	8.96	8.40	11.13	9.61	8.07	8.98
Pujols,Albert				9.54	8.36	8.89
Edmonds,Jim	7.02	5.09	9.38	9.03	9.23	8.82
Abreu,Bobby	7.96	10.14	9.24	8.14	8.45	8.66
Ordonez,Magglio	4.66	6.63	8.06	7.78	8.55	8.66
Floyd,Cliff	5.67	7.04	7.82	8.72	7.68	8.40
Gonzalez,Luis	5.70	8.70	8.10	11.55	7.81	8.35
Salmon,Tim	8.75	7.04	8.36	5.13	7.21	8.31
Green,Shawn	6.02	8.42	6.51	8.45	8.05	8.12
Williams,Bernie	9.65	9.39	8.46	8.01	8.26	7.63
Giambi,Jeremy	9.29	6.74	5.22	6.54	7.93	7.59
Ibanez,Raul	3.33	5.24	3.37	5.93	6.87	7.45
Nixon,Trot	6.41	6.38	6.57	7.07	5.74	7.36
Lee,Carlos	4.58	5.35	6.26	5.22	6.37	7.33
Burrell,Pat		7.94	6.45	5.91	7.81	7.28
Jones,Andruw	6.03	6.25	7.40	5.11	6.81	7.27
Dunn,Adam				9.74	6.75	7.06
Anderson,Garret	5.46	5.88	5.70	5.43	6.70	7.04
Suzuki,Ichiro	8.73	9.31	10.76	6.93	6.33	6.97
Kearns,Austin				4.08	8.15	6.83
Millar,Kevin	21.42	5.50	6.42	7.94	6.74	6.81
Catalanotto,Frank	6.17	4.93	6.37	7.39	5.05	6.81
Damon,Johnny	5.32	7.21	7.75	4.16	6.02	6.75
Kapler,Gabe	5.88	5.33	6.47	5.72	4.64	6.72
Drew,J.D.	9.98	5.26	7.16	10.11	5.41	6.61
Cameron,Mike	3.10	6.02	5.93	6.40	5.39	6.55
Griffey Jr.,Ken	8.22	8.23	7.93	7.35	5.52	6.48
Alou,Moises	9.11		10.66	8.86	5.40	6.46
Stewart,Shannon	5.60	5.73	7.18	6.36	6.27	6.43
Gonzalez,Juan	8.88	8.88	6.18	8.63	5.40	6.41
Gibbons,Jay			5.92	4.72	5.18	6.37
Dye,Jermaine	4.35	6.97	8.62	6.08	5.22	6.32
Greer,Rusty	6.83	7.83	6.76	5.68	5.34	6.25
Finley,Steve	4.28	6.34	7.11	5.22	7.02	6.25
Justice,David	6.66	7.73	8.36	5.18	5.96	6.24
Kielty,Bobby			5.02	5.23	7.73	6.24
Wilkerson,Brad		3.73	6.85	5.58	6.24	6.22
Lawton,Matt	6.69	4.92	7.38	6.00	4.34	6.12
Cruz,Jose	6.26	5.52	5.33	6.40	5.06	6.03
Jones,Jacque	5.51	4.83	5.26	4.85	6.31	6.01
Hunter,Torii	4.48	3.97	5.91	4.88	6.26	6.01
Branyan,Russ	9.63	3.79	5.75	5.34	5.09	6.01
Marrero,Eli	4.03	2.37	4.46	4.88	5.52	5.96
Kotsay,Mark	4.63	4.38	5.72	6.12	5.92	5.94
Hidalgo,Richard	6.16	4.79	9.04	5.66	4.58	5.84
Beltran,Carlos	7.25	5.72	4.32	7.39	6.49	5.82
Ochoa,Alex	3.48	7.13	8.28	4.66	4.74	5.80
Stairs,Matt	7.09	6.90	5.03	5.80	5.81	5.80
Grieve,Ben	6.67	6.31	6.61	5.48	5.52	5.78
Ward,Daryle	4.54	6.75	5.65	5.41	4.94	5.76
Jenkins,Geoff	4.71	7.88	7.71	5.55	4.67	5.76
Winn,Randy	4.43	4.75	5.09	4.63	6.24	5.75
Higginson,Bobby	6.25	4.75	7.85	6.05	5.27	5.74
Matthews Jr.,Gary	5.37	3.42	2.85	4.38	5.69	5.70
Trammell,Bubba	6.70	6.15	5.91	5.49	4.87	5.69
Payton,Jay	3.14	6.89	5.07	3.73	6.26	5.66
Benard,Marvin	6.80	5.83	4.94	4.89	4.74	5.65
Lane,Jason				6.95	5.32	5.53
Mondesi,Raul	5.41	5.80	6.13	5.45	4.56	5.51
Ledee,Ricky	5.67	5.40	4.36	3.58	5.04	5.47
Buchanan,Brian	4.04	3.82	5.17	5.99	5.15	5.47
McLemore,Mark	4.61	5.11	4.20	6.52	5.62	5.43
Wilson,Preston	3.82	6.32	5.53	5.69	4.73	5.41
Gant,Ron	5.96	5.97	5.77	5.88	5.70	5.34

Power	'98	'99	'00	'01	'02	'03Prj
Bonds,Barry	196	200	209	292	244	213
Giles,Brian	115	175	160	162	189	191
Berkman,Lance	136	98	159	178	166	188
Ramirez,Manny	176	186	195	175	181	186
Ordonez,Magglio	84	122	132	139	179	182
Sosa,Sammy	197	190	178	225	167	178
Floyd,Cliff	138	137	139	158	159	167
Guerrero,Vladimir	166	165	173	155	152	166
Burrell,Pat		142	126	125	157	164
Nixon,Trot	108	119	110	133	141	163
Walker,Larry	184	189	119	180	163	161
Hunter,Torii	106	77	109	129	151	159
Pujols,Albert				168	149	157
Jones,Andruw	153	126	136	119	148	156
Green,Shawn	135	165	126	167	157	153
Salmon,Tim	140	135	144	94	146	153
Edmonds,Jim	126	116	160	157	150	151
Anderson,Garret	104	103	135	116	159	150
Ibanez,Raul	88	103	72	122	158	149
Jones,Chipper	146	186	150	157	129	148
Jones,Jacque	133	99	103	90	138	147
Branyan,Russ	213	120	157	146	133	147
Abreu,Bobby	122	130	142	155	138	146
Cameron,Mike	77	128	100	126	127	146
Jenkins,Geoff	103	162	165	123	127	145
Dye,Jermaine	90	139	140	112	132	145
Gibbons,Jay			113	139	149	141
Lane,Jason				154	132	141
Lee,Carlos	97	104	107	121	138	141
Gonzalez,Juan	187	160	128	157	120	141
Millar,Kevin		98	136	151	136	137
Sheffield,Gary	145	126	174	155	123	135
Stairs,Matt	132	154	110	128	138	135
Larson,Brandon		134	109	85	157	134
Gonzalez,Luis	127	134	142	201	118	134
Cruz,Jose	109	105	127	152	124	133
Dunn,Adam				185	122	133
Wilkerson,Brad		67	147	102	120	133
Petrick,Ben	148	152	113	114	131	130
Sanders,Reggie	94	140	108	159	119	129
Mondesi,Raul	135	133	142	117	131	128
Berger,Brandon			54	151	115	128
Mench,Kevin				133	127	127
Garcia,Karim	109	111	106	137	139	127
Wells,Vernon		91	113	105	119	126
Perez,Eduardo	60	89	116	84	149	125
Wilson,Preston	123	128	130	132	109	124
Wilson,Craig	104	130	152	133	106	124
Giambi,Jeremy	134	88	95	104	149	124
Kearns,Austin				87	126	124
Griffey Jr.,Ken	184	159	156	143	97	124
Buchanan,Brian	95	78	112	130	119	124
Fick,Robert	121	67	76	121	112	122
Thompson,Ryan	89	82	134	105	119	121
Catalanotto,Frank	113	114	96	103	114	121
Drew,J.D.	181	104	106	161	105	121
Marrero,Eli	101	67	106	104	113	121
Ward,Daryle	107	152	152	124	100	121
Ledee,Ricky	118	108	84	91	120	120
Alou,Moises	169		155	133	90	119
Hidalgo,Richard	121	121	186	109	106	118
Finley,Steve	107	150	147	96	123	118
Burnitz,Jeromy	147	173	129	146	87	117
Vander Wal,John	165	101	157	107	120	116
Winn,Randy	54	83	73	84	110	114
Trammell,Bubba	156	123	112	117	101	114
Grissom,Marquis	80	91	64	105	139	113
Hollandsworth,T	82	100	106	194	117	113
Beltran,Carlos	145	93	70	121	147	113
Quinn,Mark	112	132	117	117	86	113
Bocachica,Hiram	92	70	113	100	112	112
Kapler,Gabe	135	127	108	107	74	112

Speed	'98	'99	'00	'01	'02	'03Prj
Goodwin,Tom	123	173	188	203	171	168
Beltran,Carlos	180	143	139	181	160	167
Robinson,Kerry	133	186	135	130	177	164
Taylor,Reggie	149	143	149	171	156	164
Damon,Johnny	148	161	173	118	181	161
Torres,Andres			63	127	191	160
Roberts,Dave	153	176	121	126	175	159
Crawford,Carl				111	195	156
Winn,Randy	197	129	108	118	153	154
Pierre,Juan			111	173	149	153
Lombard,George	132	129	148	172	170	150
Sanchez,Alex		114	125	151	174	149
Singleton,Chris	143	139	147	120	168	148
Tucker,Michael	101	162	153	164	146	148
Cedeno,Roger	103	155	179	188	115	146
Hunter,Brian L.	123	171	136	109	150	145
Little,Mark	156	163	124	91	175	144
Sadler,Donnie	187	127	132	105	164	140
Cameron,Mike	161	171	128	147	146	139
Kingsale,Gene	134	107	132	138	140	139
Lofton,Kenny	146	161	142	117	170	139
Catalanotto,Frank	111	59	108	118	215	139
Stewart,Shannon	132	113	133	127	136	137
Gipson,Charles	117	181	176	256	262	137
Rolls,Damian	70		41	115	157	136
Byrnes,Eric		74	103	117	158	135
Glanville,Doug	140	138	136	121	127	134
Abreu,Bobby	119	165	154	128	130	131
Owens,Eric	123	122	132	82	139	130
Tyner,Jason		126	97	139	134	129
Cruz,Jose	116	131	116	131	120	129
Suzuki,Ichiro	93	95	90	151	137	128
Erstad,Darin	111	114	123	91	138	127
Patterson,Corey			136	134	134	126
Bergeron,Peter	144	124	122	143	126	125
Encarnacion,Juan	156	159	131	138	115	125
Benard,Marvin	90	126	140	115	153	125
Brown,Adrian	143	111	141	73	124	125
McCracken,Quint	122	110	84	88	160	125
Chavez,Endy				80	134	122
Michaels,Jason			93	107	152	121
Sanders,Reggie	152	160	112	121	142	120
Hubbard,Trenidad	94	117	177	126	100	120
Conti,Jason	170	134	133	77	105	116
Wilson,Preston	121	104	120	111	105	115
Hunter,Torii	93	100	142	106	128	114
Bautista,Danny	54	93	147	87	112	114
Crisp,Covelli					120	113
Matthews Jr.,Gary	124	97	128	93	126	111
Bradley,Milton		115	76	135	110	111
Knoblauch,Chuck	127	124	113	117	114	111
Perez,Timo	62	25	118	112	115	109
Murray,Calvin	129	120	114	101	147	109
Bocachica,Hiram	140	123	81	113	83	109
Guerrero,Vladimir	112	96	123	127	95	108
Henderson,Rickey	122	96	122	134	127	106
Kotsay,Mark	114	118	120	95	108	105
Giles,Brian	61	81	110	123	104	105
McLemore,Mark	86	131	100	192	107	105
Wise,DeWayne				130	118	104
Hermansen,Chad	121	88	116	136	90	103
Harris,Lenny	60	44	161	91	97	103
Macias,Jose	98	107	124	131	86	103
Cairo,Miguel	111	132	128	91	106	103
Mateo,Ruben	119	93	90	100	74	103
Wilkerson,Brad		59	89	98	137	102
Mora,Melvin	59	98	121	69	113	102
Finley,Steve	129	131	111	99	112	101
Wells,Vernon		97	141	96	104	100
Ochoa,Alex	116	102	130	128	76	100
Marrero,Eli	87	102	155	156	104	100
Grissom,Marquis	76	100	90	86	127	100

Outfielders

Std Rotisserie	'98	'99	'00	'01	'02	'03Prj
Jenkins,Geoff	13	21	28	14	4	14
Grieve,Ben	17	16	19	12	14	14
Lane,Jason				26	18	13
White,Rondell	21	22	16	15	8	13
Larson,Brandon		6	11	4	19	13
Fick,Robert	15	2	0	12	13	13
Rowand,Aaron			16	19	5	13
Bradley,Milton		14	8	12	9	13
Singleton,Chris	1	22	13	14	15	12
Hollandsworth,T	4	8	16	9	16	12
Trammell,Bubba	17	12	8	17	8	12
Perez,Timo	8	(1)	14	15	15	12
Owens,Eric	7	18	19	5	14	12
Long,Terrence	17	12	19	17	9	12
Branyan,Russ	10	6	14	8	10	12
Knoblauch,Chuck	20	24	9	16	7	12
Ochoa,Alex	4	10	16	15	8	12
Justice,David	19	16	25	8	10	12
Benard,Marvin	13	22	14	12	4	12
Jordan,Brian	32	24	14	23	17	11
Burnitz,Jeromy	28	22	14	18	6	11
Cordova,Marty	8	16	2	17	11	11
Everett,Carl	21	34	27	11	12	11
Mench,Kevin				11	12	11
Mora,Melvin	(1)	6	12	8	14	11
Rios,Armando	13	11	8	10	2	10
Torres,Andres			(2)	7	16	10
Lombard,George	18	4	12	3	7	10
Kingsale,Gene	11	9	2	5	11	10
Wilson,Craig	5	9	12	11	11	10
Kielty,Bobby			5	7	12	10
Grissom,Marquis	14	20	11	9	15	10
Piatt,Adam		24	10	(1)	8	10
Crisp,Covelli					23	9
Buchanan,Brian	12	6	13	7	6	9
McLemore,Mark	7	10	10	22	13	9
Stairs,Matt	24	19	8	10	8	9
Taylor,Reggie	7	14	10	15	9	9
Liefer,Jeff	9	7	12	13	3	9
Glanville,Doug	17	30	18	18	8	9
Sierra,Ruben	1	20	11	18	12	9
Macias,Jose	7	(4)	0	14	6	8
Mackowiak,Rob		1	12	6	10	8
Mohr,Dustan		(2)		23	11	8
Bautista,Danny	2	10	12	7	9	8
Brown,Adrian	11	6	12	0	11	8
O'Leary,Troy	15	19	7	6	10	8
Brown,Roosevelt	2	19	10	19	(0)	7
Gant,Ron	15	14	12	7	13	7
Merced,Orlando	7	5	1	6	8	7
Hammonds,Jeffrey	9	11	29	5	6	7
Berger,Brandon			(0)	19	11	7
Robinson,Kerry	16	15	11	7	3	6
Hunter,Brian L.	15	12	8	7	5	6
Palmeiro,Orlando	7	4	5	3	8	6
Tyner,Jason		17	12	18	10	6
Shinjo,Tsuyoshi	(1)	9	22	10	4	6
Greer,Rusty	21	20	12	6	4	6
Petrick,Ben	10	23	14	7	13	6
Agbayani,Benny	7	18	14	7	5	6
Brown,Dee		14	16	6	13	5
Ledee,Ricky	11	9	9	2	2	5
Conti,Jason	19	9	11	11	4	5
Cordero,Wil	9	7	11	2	5	5
Goodwin,Tom	19	15	24	8	7	5
Spencer,Shane	19	4	7	7	4	5
Dellucci,David	6	6	0	8	3	5
Gonzalez,Raul	12	15	1	9	16	5
Michaels,Jason			7	12	3	4
Wise,DeWayne				4	11	4
McCracken,Quint	17	3	(3)	6	11	4
Rolls,Damian	(3)		(1)	5	9	4

RC/Gm	'98	'99	'00	'01	'02	'03Prj
Vander Wal,John	7.55	5.86	9.18	5.96	5.13	5.34
Cordero,Wil	4.98	6.68	5.34	3.80	5.50	5.34
Jordan,Brian	7.37	5.73	4.88	6.06	5.71	5.32
Encarnacion,Juar	5.91	4.11	5.21	3.94	5.17	5.31
Sanders,Reggie	5.10	7.15	4.32	6.21	5.04	5.30
Rios,Armando	4.29	6.01	6.43	5.61	3.23	5.29
Petrick,Ben	5.69	8.17	6.78	4.89	5.55	5.29
Wells,Vernon			5.79	4.72	4.89	4.97	5.26
Fick,Robert	5.57	4.86	3.57	5.73	5.13	5.25
Brown,Roosevelt	3.73	6.27	4.95	5.75	3.13	5.23
Larson,Brandon		4.06	4.22	2.99	7.13	5.22
Wilson,Craig	5.81	5.14	5.66	7.36	5.05	5.19
Lofton,Kenny	6.18	7.07	6.08	4.57	5.30	5.18
Merced,Orlando	4.85	6.10	2.67	5.54	5.94	5.17
Piatt,Adam		8.45	5.57	3.20	4.02	5.10
Everett,Carl	6.06	8.78	8.10	4.74	5.11	5.08
Tucker,Michael	4.87	5.20	6.84	4.72	4.75	5.06
Pierre,Juan			5.20	5.89	4.20	5.06
Garcia,Karim	4.04	4.41	4.22	5.44	5.71	5.04
Quinn,Mark	6.04	7.40	6.18	4.22	2.71	5.04
Hollandsworth,T	4.17	5.72	5.37	11.62	5.65	5.03
Agbayani,Benny	4.27	7.29	6.88	5.13	4.27	5.03
White,Rondell	6.64	6.56	6.93	7.27	3.61	5.02
Roberts,Dave	5.40	3.36	4.28	3.36	5.07	5.01
O'Leary,Troy	5.19	6.22	4.70	4.31	5.25	4.93
Mench,Kevin				4.20	4.80	4.92
Bautista,Danny	3.92	4.70	5.82	5.56	7.05	4.90
Liefer,Jeff	4.57	5.23	5.23	5.66	3.89	4.90
Echevarria,Angel	4.65	6.55	4.69	4.60	4.34	4.89
Burnitz,Jeromy	6.10	8.22	5.69	6.16	3.73	4.88
Vaughn,Greg	7.90	6.80	6.83	5.10	3.01	4.88
Michaels,Jason			4.04	4.72	5.06	4.86
Sierra,Ruben	2.79	8.10	5.07	6.04	4.94	4.83
Palmeiro,Orlando	4.67	4.40	6.36	3.48	5.23	4.83
Henderson,Ricke	5.33	7.87	4.47	4.70	4.88	4.81
Perez,Timo	5.36	1.73	5.62	4.78	5.20	4.78
Cordova,Marty	4.37	6.25	3.69	6.22	4.82	4.74
McCarty,Dave	4.87	3.17	5.85	4.90	4.13	4.74
Bragg,Darren	5.41	5.31	3.70	4.91	5.01	4.73
Crisp,Covelli					5.16	4.71
Hunter,Brian L.	3.55	3.14	4.29	4.93	5.13	4.69
Lombard,George	5.96	2.95	4.50	7.28	4.36	4.68
Lankford,Ray	8.28	7.23	6.61	6.47	4.08	4.63
Berger,Brandon			1.58	5.21	4.21	4.63
Grissom,Marquis	4.01	4.90	3.49	3.22	5.97	4.61
Dellucci,David	4.46	10.24	3.40	6.06	4.23	4.59
Long,Terrence	5.66	4.01	5.97	5.19	3.95	4.57
Chavez,Endy				3.13	5.59	4.56
Hyzdu,Adam	5.95	4.81	4.12	3.45	3.95	4.55
Hammonds,Jeffre	6.15	6.19	8.10	4.39	4.73	4.54
Brown,Adrian	3.96	5.16	6.57	2.50	3.63	4.52
Conti,Jason	5.97	4.05	4.25	4.76	4.26	4.52
Rowand,Aaron			4.13	6.16	3.92	4.51
Anderson,Brady	5.17	7.27	5.79	3.23	3.22	4.51
Singleton,Chris	2.87	6.02	4.10	4.92	4.41	4.50
Mohr,Dustan		1.55		6.26	5.05	4.47
Tarasco,Tony	4.51	3.48	4.67	4.17	3.45	4.47
Bradley,Milton		5.62	4.11	4.17	4.43	4.45
Kingsale,Gene	3.46	3.16	3.50	2.67	4.47	4.42
Erstad,Darin	6.34	4.07	9.12	4.23	4.57	4.42
Brown,Dee		7.60	4.98	3.57	4.18	4.41
Gonzalez,Raul	4.76	5.35	2.75	4.42	4.82	4.40
Knoblauch,Chuck	5.17	6.61	5.14	4.29	3.17	4.40
Perez,Eduardo	3.81	3.24	5.79	3.78	4.33	4.40
Spencer,Shane	7.75	4.55	5.51	3.97	4.17	4.37
McCracken,Quint	5.08	3.74	2.17	3.62	6.35	4.37
Mackowiak,Rob		3.36	3.81	4.05	4.85	4.36
Cedeno,Roger	3.80	6.59	5.72	5.05	4.15	4.33
Mora,Melvin	2.20	3.58	4.85	4.11	4.45	4.24
Harris,Lenny	3.80	4.90	4.72	2.44	5.54	4.21
Magruder,Chris		3.79	4.30	5.12	3.85	4.19
Mateo,Ruben	6.54	5.98	5.53	3.12	4.56	4.17

Power	'98	'99	'00	'01	'02	'03Prj
Liefer,Jeff	113	112	139	144	92	112
Justice,David	125	109	166	110	93	112
Hyzdu,Adam	111	133	116	102	112	112
Payton,Jay	70	134	94	74	107	111
Gant,Ron	155	104	134	115	131	111
Grieve,Ben	111	123	124	82	121	111
Encarnacion,Juar	99	116	85	98	103	110
White,Rondell	138	114	116	132	92	110
Michaels,Jason			89	106	117	110
Williams,Bernie	140	112	149	134	109	110
Echevarria,Angel	112	120	86	127	103	110
Matthews Jr.,Gar	87	70	65	88	105	109
Benard,Marvin	89	107	82	103	90	109
McCarty,Dave	99	105	115	96	113	109
Cordova,Marty	78	111	59	121	118	108
Kielty,Bobby			95	103	122	108
Tucker,Michael	119	95	136	94	105	108
Rowand,Aaron			100	130	92	108
Rivera,Ruben	106	122	108	103	102	107
Tarasco,Tony	105	94	105	91	81	107
Rios,Armando	104	99	137	120	49	107
Kotsay,Mark	83	81	92	100	96	106
Jordan,Brian	141	110	97	121	113	106
Ochoa,Alex	68	103	163	82	96	105
Piatt,Adam		167	92	67	100	105
Damon,Johnny	97	106	102	72	103	104
Cordero,Wil	109	128	116	61	109	104
Mackowiak,Rob		99	84	89	113	103
Higginson,Bobby	120	88	141	102	93	102
Hermansen,Chad	144	120	77	91	107	102
Everett,Carl	129	150	161	111	109	101
Macias,Jose	84	48	46	78	91	100
Brown,Dee		119	111	72	95	100
Guillen,Jose	105	88	125	101	93	100
Stewart,Shannon	89	69	122	97	98	99
Mohr,Dustan		41		121	111	99
Agbayani,Benny	96	148	115	77	101	99
Brown,Roosevelt	104	150	100	140	73	99
Lawton,Matt	123	64	102	92	102	99
Greer,Rusty	93	121	108	125	59	98
Sierra,Ruben	88	149	89	141	101	96
Long,Terrence	100	76	105	85	101	95
Byrnes,Eric		67	105	105	98	94
Hammonds,Jeffre	100	142	114	111	91	94
Mateo,Ruben	135	131	94	70	105	93
Singleton,Chris	67	115	76	84	103	93
Merced,Orlando	91	122	40	110	92	93
Lombard,George	111	83	84	162	94	93
Bradley,Milton		102	74	81	97	93
Vaughn,Greg	195	160	140	120	96	92
Taylor,Reggie	67	77	75	79	105	92
Mora,Melvin	32	62	82	80	111	92
Dellucci,David	89	78	67	117	93	92
Wise,DeWayne				68	94	91
Cepicky,Matt				103	96	91
Patterson,Corey			113	73	87	91
Spencer,Shane	163	92	100	91	88	91
Conti,Jason	107	67	79	87	93	90
Guiel,Aaron	99	124	103	100	86	88
Magruder,Chris		61	68	100	95	88
Anderson,Brady	113	114	98	58	66	87
O'Leary,Troy	120	127	93	114	71	87
Perez,Timo	70		86	79	92	86
Lofton,Kenny	84	85	84	83	98	86
Lankford,Ray	162	123	140	144	78	85
Bragg,Darren	98	75	76	91	88	84
Little,Mark	100	68	100	91	69	83
Shinjo,Tsuyoshi	75	96	121	89	79	83
McCracken,Quint	81	50	47	72	100	81
Bautista,Danny	106	98	112	84	99	81
Magee,Wendell	118	87	82	99	81	80
Gonzalez,Raul	92	95	60	84	82	79

Speed	'98	'99	'00	'01	'02	'03Prj
Payton,Jay	109	83	50	73	127	99
Cabrera,Jolbert	88	140	126	139	71	99
Rivera,Ruben	143	104	145	93	115	98
Shinjo,Tsuyoshi	69	125	82	60	102	98
Gant,Ron	89	128	86	134	77	98
Lane,Jason				90	106	98
Mondesi,Raul	115	132	140	115	98	97
Kapler,Gabe	103	125	70	97	134	95
McEwing,Joe	105	88	117	125	102	94
Petrick,Ben	82	104	87	108	92	94
Bragg,Darren	85	69	92	90	111	94
Kearns,Austin				80	97	93
Magruder,Chris		102	97	106	89	93
Higginson,Bobby	70	43	110	110	94	92
Mohr,Dustan		116		81	93	91
Ibanez,Raul	72	64	69	92	104	90
Green,Shawn	128	97	114	120	68	90
Hollandsworth,T	170	96	99	121	65	90
Lawton,Matt	111	100	93	101	88	90
Berger,Brandon			96	109	97	90
Rowand,Aaron			122	80	72	89
Gonzalez,Luis	105	86	49	84	88	89
Magee,Wendell	97	65	104	138	54	89
Merced,Orlando	30	60	72	108	115	88
Long,Terrence	151	104	93	93	71	88
Hidalgo,Richard	57	78	104	66	112	88
Tarasco,Tony	53	73	37	102	92	87
Brown,Dee		121	121	54	80	86
Dunn,Adam				78	86	86
Walker,Larry	120	111	145	103	92	85
Dellucci,David	171	110	92	86	86	85
Lankford,Ray	100	95	94	132	59	84
Drew,J.D.	107	166	97	145	79	83
Palmeiro,Orlando	113	71	93	78	87	81
Kielty,Bobby			67	73	102	81
Floyd,Cliff	110	66	100	136	77	80
Berkman,Lance	55	73	85	88	72	80
Quinn,Mark	110	55	80	85	97	79
Branyan,Russ	106	67	84	76	61	78
Nixon,Trot	102	114	150	92	82	78
Mackowiak,Rob		69	112	92	78	77
Garcia,Karim	173	98	65	70	58	76
Bonds,Barry	136	122	112	84	78	75
Vaughn,Greg	106	100	85	68	92	75
Thompson,Ryan	35	61	83	55	74	75
Ledee,Ricky	109	145	116	80	68	75
Williams,Bernie	112	94	126	69	74	75
Sheffield,Gary	94	62	62	81	75	74
Burnitz,Jeromy	64	77	68	67	68	74
Anderson,Garret	97	59	79	77	80	72
Gonzalez,Juan	62	63	58	51	75	71
Cepicky,Matt				97	70	70
Grieve,Ben	56	62	62	76	64	70
Cordero,Wil	89	69	75	41	56	70
Alou,Moises	104		58	63	72	69
Anderson,Brady	118	140	77	97	53	69
Hammonds,Jeffre	117	47	102	94	84	68
Ordonez,Maggio	78	93	105	88	76	68
Rios,Armando	88	81	142	85	42	68
Dunston,Shawon	188	133	104	141	31	68
Justice,David	87	29	48	47	82	67
Greer,Rusty	74	67	93	45	77	67
Agbayani,Benny	104	105	64	67	61	65
Dye,Jermaine	80	96	44	78	64	65
Jones,Chipper	113	89	78	89	65	65
O'Leary,Troy	105	59	61	116	46	65
White,Rondell	106	108	62	48	48	64
Piatt,Adam		79	99	69	63	64
Edmonds,Jim	76	115	79	60	73	64
Buchanan,Brian	99	88	73	39	71	64
Larson,Brandon		58	81	62	48	63
Jones,Jacque	103	106	99	60	77	63

Outfielders

Std Rotisserie	'98	'99	'00	'01	'02	'03Prj
Harris,Lenny	6	5	7	(0)	6	4
Vaughn,Greg	34	26	15	14	(0)	4
Magee,Wendell	12	5	5	1	7	4
Guillen,Jose	14	10	12	7	7	4
Vander Wal,John	4	6	23	14	4	4
Byrnes,Eric		(2)	18	15	5	4
Echevarria,Angel	7	8	5	2	7	4
Bragg,Darren	10	4	2	7	5	4
Tarasco,Tony	5	3	7	8	4	4
Lankford,Ray	35	19	14	13	2	3
Hyzdu,Adam	3	12	5	4	6	3
Henderson,Rickey	26	25	11	11	4	3
Mateo,Ruben	23	17	7	1	7	3
Hubbard,Trenidad	10	11	(1)	12	4	3
Cepicky,Matt				8	9	3
Thompson,Ryan	3	2	11	3	9	3
Rivera,Ruben	3	8	5	7	9	3
Little,Mark	8	2	8	7	1	3
Cairo,Miguel	11	14	11	6	2	3
Perez,Eduardo	3	4	14	1	2	3
Magruder,Chris		7	7	13	6	2
Bergeron,Peter	15	14	3	2	6	2
McCarty,Dave	8	1	8	3	3	2
Bocachica,Hiram	11	10	14	1	2	2
Clark,Brady	1	11	10	6	(0)	2
Cabrera,Jolbert	14	4	6	6	(2)	2
Guiel,Aaron	4	1	5	6	13	2
McEwing,Joe	17	9	3	9	(1)	2
Anderson,Brady	12	28	13	2	(0)	2
Gipson,Charles	0	4	5	(0)	2	1
Hermansen,Chad	19	15	1	8	2	1
Rushford,Jim				5	2	1
Dunston,Shawon	4	12	7	7	(1)	1
Murray,Calvin	10	14	4	4	(3)	0
Sadler,Donnie	5	4	(1)	(3)	(0)	(0)

RC/Gm	'98	'99	'00	'01	'02	'03Prj
Guillen,Jose	4.17	4.90	5.74	4.51	3.68	4.15
Macias,Jose	4.10	2.30	3.38	4.46	3.62	4.13
Crawford,Carl				3.92	4.81	4.07
Patterson,Corey			4.12	3.19	3.83	4.05
Owens,Eric	3.89	4.76	4.79	3.52	4.33	4.05
Torres,Andres			0.93	4.03	3.69	3.98
Shinjo,Tsuyoshi	3.04	4.27	5.52	4.36	3.63	3.96
Rivera,Ruben	4.39	3.95	3.81	4.62	3.88	3.94
Cairo,Miguel	3.88	4.52	3.87	4.61	3.72	3.93
Thompson,Ryan	4.95	3.02	4.46	2.68	4.17	3.91
Glanville,Doug	4.47	7.02	4.22	3.80	3.69	3.89
Guiel,Aaron	4.68	3.55	4.88	3.62	4.44	3.89
Wise,DeWayne				2.72	3.37	3.88
Goodwin,Tom	4.84	4.16	4.91	3.33	3.68	3.87
Magee,Wendell	4.66	3.55	4.89	3.90	3.80	3.85
Little,Mark	3.99	2.84	3.89	5.65	3.39	3.81
Bocachica,Hiram	4.06	3.65	4.50	3.70	3.39	3.79
Robinson,Kerry	3.38	3.20	3.39	4.12	3.72	3.78
Tyner,Jason		4.19	2.92	3.86	3.23	3.78
Rushford,Jim				5.35	3.43	3.76
Byrnes,Eric		2.02	5.13	4.45	3.33	3.72
Taylor,Reggie	3.22	2.91	3.45	3.70	3.99	3.71
Clark,Brady	3.08	4.65	4.94	4.26	2.37	3.67
Sanchez,Alex		1.82	2.79	3.70	4.50	3.56
Hubbard,Trenidad	5.46	5.52	2.34	4.87	3.07	3.46
Bergeron,Peter	4.15	5.53	3.80	2.51	3.60	3.40
Cepicky,Matt				3.28	3.79	3.31
Rolls,Damian	1.58		2.89	3.52	3.80	3.28
Hermansen,Chad	5.66	4.07	2.55	3.18	3.35	3.25
Murray,Calvin	3.75	3.70	4.41	3.28	2.28	3.24
Gipson,Charles	2.88	2.78	3.69	2.70	4.53	3.04
McEwing,Joe	5.14	4.76	3.24	5.10	2.01	3.03
Cabrera,Jolbert	4.89	3.15	4.07	3.71	2.24	3.03
Dunston,Shawon	3.11	5.42	4.50	5.17	2.41	2.89
Sadler,Donnie	3.92	4.43	2.77	1.64	1.74	2.07

Power	'98	'99	'00	'01	'02	'03Prj
McEwing,Joe	114	81	93	103	62	78
Erstad,Darin	122	73	110	71	73	77
Henderson,Ricke	66	102	46	76	81	77
Crisp,Covelli					80	76
Hubbard,Trenidad	101	77	45	101	67	75
Hunter,Brian L.	57	41	27	56	105	75
Crawford,Carl				56	92	75
Suzuki,Ichiro	110	138	94	70	70	74
Kingsale,Gene	33	50	59	55	91	72
McLemore,Mark	47	57	51	71	86	71
Rushford,Jim				113	75	70
Chavez,Endy				39	88	70
Glanville,Doug	68	88	63	70	61	67
Knoblauch,Chuck	85	101	68	64	60	67
Murray,Calvin	80	85	72	70	61	66
Dunston,Shawon	116	82	134	133	40	65
Cairo,Miguel	67	46	49	76	68	63
Clark,Brady	63	92	107	67	55	62
Harris,Lenny	82	69	69	38	67	61
Torres,Andres				68	54	61
Brown,Adrian	50	56	77	48	56	60
Owens,Eric	70	81	53	55	61	58
Rolls,Damian	38		66	57	70	57
Cedeno,Roger	60	66	58	59	56	57
Roberts,Dave	78	48	63	51	54	55
Palmeiro,Orlando	65	40	76	55	46	54
Goodwin,Tom	33	49	49	60	51	53
Cabrera,Jolbert	71	43	66	63	44	53
Robinson,Kerry	41	46	39	37	61	49
Gipson,Charles	48	44	47	54	90	47
Bergeron,Peter	62	96	67	40	35	45
Pierre,Juan			29	56	39	45
Sadler,Donnie	77	70	48	36	40	42
Sanchez,Alex		30	40	48	41	42
Tyner,Jason		34	19	25	34	30

Speed	'98	'99	'00	'01	'02	'03Prj
Wilson,Craig	51	58	57	104	54	62
Everett,Carl	109	120	107	124	39	62
Pujols,Albert				64	59	62
Gonzalez,Raul	74	87	79	53	74	60
Clark,Brady	104	90	88	90	56	60
Salmon,Tim	34	83	43	66	73	60
Jenkins,Geoff	82	88	130	73	66	58
Guiel,Aaron	111	83	86	77	73	58
Jordan,Brian	138	102	80	75	70	58
Vander Wal,John	63	35	75	94	67	57
Cordova,Marty	56	108	56	48	45	56
Sosa,Sammy	78	60	56	75	70	56
Sierra,Ruben	83	70	67	80	58	56
Spencer,Shane	55	38	88	88	55	55
Stairs,Matt	75	58	61	38	51	52
Mench,Kevin				56	62	52
Perez,Eduardo	29	47	85	61	30	51
Jones,Andruw	164	112	126	98	63	51
Trammell,Bubba	67	27	87	65	41	51
Lee,Carlos	79	78	107	97	50	51
Guillen,Jose	55	49	116	45	50	50
Millar,Kevin	53	84	66	68	23	50
Griffey Jr.,Ken	105	111	79	72	19	49
Fick,Robert	93	56	86	48	40	46
Brown,Roosevelt	49	72	81	74	35	44
Liefer,Jeff	83	86	41	50	36	43
Burrell,Pat		68	51	56	52	42
McCarty,Dave	73	64	55	24	66	41
Rushford,Jim				74	49	39
Hyzdu,Adam	74	74	51	46	35	35
Giambi,Jeremy	79	54	69	29	26	34
Ward,Daryle	62	41	54		22	34
Ramirez,Manny	70	73	55	39	23	32
Gibbons,Jay			52	22	45	32
Echevarria,Angel	34	38	43	23	56	30

DH

Std Rotisserie	'98	'99	'00	'01	'02	'03Prj
Thomas,Frank	20	16	35	1	18	22
Phelps,Josh			1	17	25	20
Burks,Ellis	22	22	27	19	26	17
Martinez,Edgar	27	26	33	25	12	17
Richard,Chris	(0)	15	20	13	4	15
Ortiz,David	8	15	9	8	15	15
Young,Dmitri	20	13	19	22	7	13
LeCroy,Matt		4	5	18	13	11
Segui,David	19	12	24	11	2	10
Palmer,Dean	26	20	16	6	(1)	7
Wooten,Shawn	1	5	14	9	4	7
Cruz,Jacob	19	7	0	4	2	6
Clark,Howie	8	3	3	18	7	2
Baerga,Carlos	7	(2)		11	6	1

RC/Gm	'98	'99	'00	'01	'02	'03Prj
Martinez,Edgar	9.93	10.29	10.01	9.19	7.54	7.93
Thomas,Frank	7.08	7.67	11.01	5.03	6.37	7.75
Burks,Ellis	6.63	8.26	10.63	7.58	7.16	6.88
Ortiz,David	5.97	6.37	6.32	5.51	6.18	6.60
Phelps,Josh			3.22	6.24	7.25	6.20
Segui,David	6.81	6.26	7.95	7.50	4.68	5.68
Young,Dmitri	6.63	6.72	6.28	6.18	5.52	5.30
Palmer,Dean	6.27	6.12	5.81	4.65	0.04	5.24
Richard,Chris	2.43	5.12	5.40	4.95	3.99	5.16
Clark,Howie	4.52	4.19	4.48	7.07	4.15	5.16
LeCroy,Matt		4.95	4.59	6.20	5.49	5.10
Cruz,Jacob	5.57	4.69	4.84	3.83	4.08	4.50
Wooten,Shawn	6.17	3.58	6.10	5.79	4.28	4.49
Baerga,Carlos	3.87	2.44		7.26	4.53	3.12

Power	'98	'99	'00	'01	'02	'03Prj
Ortiz,David	116	128	110	141	152	163
Phelps,Josh			102	141	179	153
Burks,Ellis	131	164	147	156	150	151
Thomas,Frank	130	109	171	127	139	146
Martinez,Edgar	154	133	144	150	139	136
Richard,Chris	69	133	124	108	129	126
Palmer,Dean	134	143	119	121	0	120
Young,Dmitri	128	132	116	108	121	116
LeCroy,Matt		125	117	104	120	112
Segui,David	117	106	111	108	73	102
Wooten,Shawn	153	80	123	90	91	97
Cruz,Jacob	121	88	87	100	67	89
Clark,Howie	98	77	70	101	72	80
Baerga,Carlos	74	47		118	74	47

Speed	'98	'99	'00	'01	'02	'03Prj
Cruz,Jacob	89	82	52	64	138	95
Clark,Howie	51	70	59	101	63	76
Wooten,Shawn		50	93	61	54	69
Richard,Chris	67	70	93	94	29	69
Palmer,Dean	80	66	66	68	-10	62
Phelps,Josh			66	62	46	62
Burks,Ellis	114	54	106	73	48	59
Baerga,Carlos	30	52		128	77	57
Young,Dmitri	50	82	61	79	55	53
Thomas,Frank	86	40	28		58	52
Ortiz,David	47	50	51	54	40	43
Segui,David	59	58	38	50	20	42
LeCroy,Matt		73	40		59	40
Martinez,Edgar	33	65	49	57	25	24

Starting Pitchers

Std Rotisserie	'98	'99	'00	'01	'02	'03Prj
Johnson,Randy	29	42	39	41	49	38
Schilling,Curt	28	25	20	37	44	35
Martinez,Pedro	36	50	54	20	36	34
Oswalt,Roy			20	24	32	33
Millwood,Kevin	16	39	11	6	30	31
Miller,Wade	9	7	5	22	20	28
Mulder,Mark		2	-0	29	24	27
Colon,Bartolo	16	24	19	12	29	23
Zito,Barry		2	23	23	32	23
Mussina,Mike	25	27	24	30	19	22
Maddux,Greg	40	24	38	31	29	22
Hudson,Tim	2	30	27	25	20	22
Vazquez,Javier	-10	7	12	27	14	22
Morris,Matt	14		7	28	22	22
Weaver,Jeff		4	17	14	16	21
Washburn,Jarrod	4	-0	13	14	24	21
Prior,Mark					21	21
Perez,Odalis	9	-4		3	34	20
Wood,Kerry	18		5	17	18	20
Lidle,Cory	1	-0	12	20	11	20
Buehrle,Mark			21	28	21	19
Beckett,Josh				19	7	19
Pineiro,Joel	-0	-5	10	19	17	19
Radke,Brad	14	20	14	21	7	18
Pettitte,Andy	14	8	18	15	15	18
Wolf,Randy	7	3	10	14	24	18
Schmidt,Jason	8	12	-4	16	23	18
Halladay,Roy	6	7	-15	17	26	18
Padilla,Vicente		8	4	13	23	17
Lawrence,Brian			27	9	15	16
Ohka,Tomokazu	-0	23	22	-8	21	16
Moyer,Jamie	26	23	8	29	22	16
Milton,Eric	-2	13	17	15	11	16
Reed,Rick	25	9	16	16	18	16
Leiter,Al	29	12	27	18	18	15
Foulke,Keith	7	24	33	36	12	15
Roa,Joe	2		-4	-3	29	15
Lopez,Rodrigo		5	1	3	18	14
Glavine,Tom	32	12	33	16	27	14
Ortiz,Russ	6	16	6	22	17	14
Clement,Matt	12	5	4	-0	20	14
Burnett,A.J.		-3	0	11	22	14
Nomo,Hideo	-0	13	6	10	21	14
Williams,Woody	11	12	17	16	21	14
Astacio,Pedro	-5	11	4	2	8	14
Thomson,John	3	-18		8	6	13
Wells,Kip		17	-7	3	15	13
Garcia,Freddy	9	17	11	31	13	13
Armas Jr.,Tony		16	8	8	9	13
Graves,Danny	10	29	32	25	32	13
Lackey,John			5	8	19	13
Saarloos,Kirk					23	13
Ortiz,Ramon	-1	15	12	8	18	13
Trachsel,Steve	10	1	4	13	15	12
Sheets,Ben			19	6	8	12
Daal,Omar	15	23	-11	9	15	12
Santana,Johan			-7	-1	16	12
Appier,Kevin	-8	9	11	18	12	11
Rueter,Kirk	13	6	11	9	21	11
Munro,Peter	-16	5	7	-2	18	11
Byrd,Paul	11	13	-4	2	20	11
Dessens,Elmer	-2	-1	12	7	16	10
Wright,Danny			3	7	5	10
Wells,David	32	17	26	3	20	10
Soriano,Rafael				4	4	10
Stephens,John				25	14	10
Jarvis,Kevin	0	6	6	11	3	10
Clemens,Roger	38	12	21	25	11	10

Base Perf Value	'98	'99	'00	'01	'02	'03Prj
Schilling,Curt	148	88	91	186	246	186
Martinez,Pedro	117	259	256	215	187	172
Johnson,Randy	137	164	157	184	154	149
Prior,Mark					138	140
Oswalt,Roy			134	152	105	117
Mussina,Mike	113	96	115	141	95	105
Vazquez,Javier	35	53	84	128	86	98
Wood,Kerry	126		60	106	85	98
Stephens,John				132	92	98
Beckett,Josh				116	86	97
Foulke,Keith	81	174	128	127	119	97
Lieber,Jon	80	96	80	85	156	96
Millwood,Kevin	86	107	69	40	90	94
Santana,Johan			26	31	113	94
Schmidt,Jason	56	45	42	90	103	89
Perez,Odalis	93	45		66	108	88
Mulder,Mark		45	13	85	82	86
Miller,Wade	49	50	54	66	81	86
Morris,Matt	73		64	104	82	85
Milton,Eric	24	66	74	52	87	84
Lawrence,Brian			103	71	77	84
Peavy,Jake				120	84	83
Burnett,A.J.		47	42	50	98	82
Clement,Matt	67	47	49	54	97	82
Weaver,Jeff		35	58	62	81	80
Zambrano,Carlos			78	99	69	80
Clemens,Roger	129	59	69	96	101	80
Pettitte,Andy	48	32	43	108	93	79
Wolf,Randy	67	51	52	94	82	79
Radke,Brad	77	52	56	116	67	76
Duckworth,Brandon			77	77	65	74
Finley,Chuck	73	72	62	67	82	74
Halladay,Roy	32	18	-8	127	89	74
Maddux,Greg	136	87	122	156	72	73
Hernandez,Carlos				77	56	72
Zito,Barry		82	72	91	75	72
Soriano,Rafael				103	57	71
Lidle,Cory	73	37	63	60	68	71
Pineiro,Joel	-36	25	48	76	61	71
Leiter,Al	101	57	91	84	72	70
Perez,Oliver					79	70
Hudson,Tim	35	96	66	78	67	70
Sheets,Ben			72	33	66	70
Padilla,Vicente		58	65	107	67	67
Nomo,Hideo	72	59	53	81	64	67
Williams,Woody	37	34	48	55	94	66
Saarloos,Kirk					83	66
Ohka,Tomokazu	40	72	44	41	64	66
Roa,Joe	28		-3	59	79	66
Reed,Rick	115	42	70	98	88	66
Washburn,Jarrod	32	48	23	51	68	64
Colon,Bartolo	66	62	84	67	61	64
Lackey,John			77	68	68	63
Munro,Peter	21	59	46	17	76	61
Hernandez,Orlando	91	55	55	33	84	61
Burkett,John	66	40	58	90	49	61
Benoit,Joaquin			61	61	61	61
Garcia,Freddy	61	63	32	78	70	60
Armas Jr.,Tony		58	34	70	48	60
Harang,Aaron				64	71	60
Rupe,Ryan		52	19	42	69	59
Ishii,Kazuhisa	101	103	114	82	50	59
Affeldt,Jeremy				70	56	58
Torres,Salomon				-99	50	58
Jarvis,Kevin	53	13	13	46	62	57
Meadows,Brian	29	-3	-1	7	56	55
Dempster,Ryan	34	41	65	50	53	55
Thomson,John	45	-8		54	40	54

Relief Pitchers

Std Rotisserie	'98	'99	'00	'01	'02	'03Prj
Smoltz,John	26	24		13	46	41
Nen,Robb	40	24	39	37	41	39
Gagne,Eric		30	4	11	51	39
Kim,Byung-Hyun		13	14	24	41	36
Wagner,Billy	24	39	3	31	36	36
Hoffman,Trevor	44	34	37	31	32	32
Benitez,Armando	19	26	36	32	31	32
Rivera,Mariano	30	41	35	41	18	31
Percival,Troy	28	26	23	31	27	29
Isringhausen,Jason		12	27	28	32	29
Guardado,Eddie	2	4	14	17	27	28
Williams,Mike	5	12	20	18	36	27
Koch,Billy	-3	21	35	19	33	27
Stewart,Scott	-1	3	6	6	20	27
Sasaki,Kazuhiro	36	15	29	31	26	26
Jimenez,Jose	19	-3	22	15	33	26
Urbina,Ugueth	33	32	5	18	24	25
Mesa,Jose	5	16	0	32	36	25
Lowe,Derek	7	27	37	18	35	25
Williamson,Scott	5	32	10		14	23
Julio,Jorge				13	21	23
Cordero,Francisco		27	-4	-0	10	22
Dotel,Octavio	19	11	7	14	25	19
Looper,Braden	12	2	4	6	16	19
DeJean,Mike	6	-10	1	8	21	18
Vizcaino,Luis	-1	3	2	11	16	18
Baez,Danys			3	9	7	18
Escobar,Kelvim	10	3	6	12	20	18
Acevedo,Juan	23	0	5	-2	18	17
Rhodes,Arthur	9	1	9	19	17	15
Alfonseca,A	6	18	30	22	13	15
Hernandez,Roberto	17	30	26	19	12	13
Wakefield,Tim	16	10	1	11	21	13
Mendoza,Ramiro	17	12	8	15	10	13
Marte,Damaso	-7	-7	0	3	10	12
Rodriguez,Felix	-2	2	11	18	10	12
Karsay,Steve	-1	15	19	15	13	12
Quantrill,Paul	11	4	2	16	9	10
Fossum,Casey				6	4	10
Weber,Ben	17	9	10	6	14	10
Shuey,Paul	8	14	8	7	11	10
Bradford,Chad	15	20	15	10	8	10
Osuna,Antonio	12	-0	4	-3	12	10
Lilly,Ted	1	5	3	0	8	10
Groom,Buddy	3	2	8	11	11	9
Franklin,Ryan	-5	-3	8	7	8	9
Gordon,Tom	40	5		20	1	9
Brown,Kevin	37	37	36	17	3	9
Borowski,Joe	3	-1	11	11	12	9
White,Gabe	12	1	24	-4	10	8
Politte,Cliff	-6	8	16	4	7	8
Hawkins,LaTroy	-1	-7	15	9	13	8
Kline,Steve	5	9	11	16	9	8
Remlinger,Mike	-1	17	15	8	14	8
Nunez,Vladimir	-0	8	-5	10	24	7
Koplove,Mike			7	14	18	7
Embree,Alan	3	7	3	-6	12	7
Weathers,David	-1	5	7	13	9	7
Romero,J.C.	8	10	3	-4	14	7
Hasegawa,Shige	16	4	17	5	9	7
Veres,Dave	11	17	26	13	10	7
Eischen,Joey	-1	-13	-5	6	20	7
Rincon,Ricardo	11	2	3	6	3	7
Durocher,Jayson		11	12	1	9	7
Yan,Esteban	7	-3	0	18	14	7
Middlebrook,Jason		-9	-12	14	2	7
Timlin,Mike	19	23	11	5	15	7
Crudale,Mike				6	16	7

Base Perf Value	'98	'99	'00	'01	'02	'03Prj
Rhodes,Arthur	90	52	106	208	196	180
Nen,Robb	164	87	182	146	145	144
Wagner,Billy	154	212	30	145	138	136
Smoltz,John	130	113		147	132	136
Hoffman,Trevor	164	155	209	86	142	135
Dotel,Octavio	100	71	56	139	158	134
Gagne,Eric		94	35	77	222	124
Urbina,Ugueth	149	120	172	121	116	124
Kim,Byung-Hyun		110	115	109	130	124
Marte,Damaso	33	-4	-1	84	140	121
Isringhausen,Jason		54	62	117	151	120
Gordon,Tom	127	89		159	103	118
Percival,Troy	116	84	59	152	115	114
Rivera,Mariano	74	112	88	197	121	114
Sasaki,Kazuhiro	218	197	94	159	129	111
Guardado,Eddie	44	77	34	110	113	110
Rincon,Ricardo	87	32	81	95	131	109
Groom,Buddy	52	70	61	158	123	108
Benitez,Armando	91	165	123	84	114	106
Sauerbeck,Scott	40	62	76	96	109	106
Shuey,Paul	88	105	101	125	94	103
Embree,Alan	48	78	69	57	142	103
Williamson,Scott	90	112	97	55	111	102
Osuna,Antonio	86	100	79	-82	103	99
Bradford,Chad	54	106	99	167	121	99
Crudale,Mike				79	113	97
Stewart,Scott	15	58	75	85	116	97
White,Gabe	71	86	165	4	118	96
Rodriguez,Felix	42	62	105	132	80	93
Julio,Jorge				85	77	93
Borowski,Joe	39	32	84	95	104	91
Politte,Cliff	37	45	69	93	100	91
Riske,David	131	112	-9	102	72	89
Fossum,Casey				85	94	89
Vizcaino,Luis	-8	37	43	92	104	88
Nelson,Jeff	73	85	99	129	96	87
Mantei,Matt	114	125	87	87	70	87
Witasick,Jay	58	16	31	116	94	87
Strickland,Scott		111	111	80	78	86
Remlinger,Mike	47	83	85	126	110	85
Fox,Chad	112	100		106	59	84
Cordero,Francisco		85	15	24	104	83
Rocker,John	94	136	98	96	83	83
Swindell,Greg	43	69	93	96	60	83
Reed,Steve	94	39	44	64	117	83
Koplove,Mike			79	69	100	82
Mercado,Hector		56	61	74	93	80
Spooneybarger,Tim				119	66	79
Hawkins,LaTroy	23	13	57	38	125	79
Van Poppel,Todd	24	35	75	91	71	78
Shields,Scot		61	46	40	81	78
Lowe,Derek	63	102	108	85	85	78
Durocher,Jayson		43	45	43	87	78
Holmes,Darren	59	53	19		127	78
Karsay,Steve	63	80	86	115	67	77
Plesac,Dan	120	85	79	130	77	77
Mecir,Jim	90	76	82	93	63	76
Hammond,Chris	16			73	99	76
Almanza,A	91	78	69	52	83	76
Creek,Doug	39	25	75	65	80	75
King,Ray	60	66	71	72	69	75
Komiyama,Satoru	97	85	59	65	78	75
Koch,Billy	36	60	93	53	88	74
Pineda,Luis				85	60	74
Middlebrook,Jason		-2	2	53	74	73
Seanez,Rudy	143	75	74	95	72	73
Villafuerte,Brandon	52	56	40	53	80	73
Myers,Mike	62	55	96	77	70	72

Starting Pitchers

Std Rotisserie	'98	'99	'00	'01	'02	'03Prj
Benson,Kris	-2	13	14		6	9
Helling,Rick	20	11	16	2	11	9
Callaway,Mickey	-4	2	1	9	15	9
Zambrano,Carlos			18	12	6	9
Penny,Brad		0	8	17	2	9
Duckworth,Brandon			15	19	-1	9
Tomko,Brett	13	5	7	6	8	9
Simontacchi,Jason	17			-12	18	9
Rusch,Glendon	-6	-2	16	2	3	9
Reitsma,Chris			12	-1	10	9
Redman,Mark	-3	2	11	-2	7	9
Hernandez,Orlando	22	23	18	1	13	8
Peavy,Jake				3	10	8
Ishii,Kazuhisa	19	9	23	17	7	8
Moss,Damian		-9	8	4	18	8
Eaton,Adam		13	15	8	1	8
Ashby,Andy	23	20	9	2	10	8
Finley,Chuck	15	14	18	1	9	8
Jennings,Jason			-1	-6	10	8
Hernandez,Carlos				9	3	8
Mays,Joe	-4	7	2	28	1	8
Torres,Salomon				-5	-0	7
Hernandez,Livan	-3	2	21	-1	8	7
Batista,Miguel	-0	4	-9	15	8	7
Meadows,Brian	-0	1	6	-15	5	7
Myers,Brett				8	15	7
Burkett,John	1	1	4	22	7	6
Valdes,Ismael	10	12	-4	6	9	6
Kim,Sun Woo		-1	-10	-8	13	6
Rupe,Ryan		13	-6	-7	2	6
Anderson,Brian	14	9	17	-1	4	6
Walker,Pete	-6	3	8	13	8	6
Jensen,Ryan	-0	6	-5	12	8	6
Wilson,Paul	2		12	3	-3	5
Ponson,Sidney	3	10	10	0	5	5
Kennedy,Joe				20	5	5
Sele,Aaron	14	12	18	20	-0	5
Rogers,Kenny	29	11	12	-8	11	5
Johnson,Jason	-1	6	1	9	2	5
Hendrickson,Mark		-7	3	-6	9	5
Maroth,Mike			4	-5	13	5
Haynes,Jimmy	-0	-5	-1	-0	10	4
Suppan,Jeff	2	12	6	7	-1	4
Hernandez,Runelvy:					11	4
Person,Robert	8	7	13	16	-2	4
Garland,Jon		1	13	5	6	4
May,Darrell	7	13	27	11	-2	4
Ritchie,Todd	-0	20	7	10	-9	4
Figueroa,Nelson	7	12	18	7	-1	3
Perez,Oliver					10	3
Stark,Dennis		-7	6	17	11	3
Lohse,Kyle		-7	-22	6	9	3
Loaiza,Esteban	2	9	11	3	0	3
Dempster,Ryan	1	1	19	3	-4	3
Neagle,Denny	21	15	15	-1	0	3
Pavano,Carl	8	1	13	-4	-2	3
Davis,Doug		14	9	6	-1	3
Miller,Justin			14	-1	5	3
Bacsik,Mike		2	9	12	-1	3
Jones,Bobby J.	11	4	7	-2	1	3
Reynolds,Shane	21	23	2	12	0	2
Castillo,Frank	-9	-3	18	11	-1	2
Park,Chan Ho	16	2	26	23	-7	2
Lyon,Brandon				14	-9	2
Cornejo,Nate			1	22	-4	2
Tejera,Michael				-1	4	2
Lieber,Jon	9	12	18	27	12	2
Quevedo,Ruben		10	-2	16	-7	1

Base Perf Value	'98	'99	'00	'01	'02	'03Prj
Hernandez,Runelvys					70	54
Wells,David	129	60	121	54	74	54
Lopez,Rodrigo		51	48	39	59	53
Rusch,Glendon	25	62	95	84	36	53
Wells,Kip		58	9	46	50	53
Penny,Brad		90	42	88	37	53
Davis,Doug		66	23	48	37	53
Graves,Danny	53	49	41	68	64	53
Park,Chan Ho	75	42	76	86	39	52
Cornejo,Nate			41	74	41	52
Ortiz,Russ	67	45	42	73	53	52
Eaton,Adam		73	56	67	29	52
Trachsel,Steve	44	45	23	67	43	51
Douglass,Sean			40	69	45	51
Bere,Jason	22	27	39	70	46	50
Drese,Ryan				56	43	50
Kim,Sun Woo		55	35	49	52	50
Astacio,Pedro	38	62	60	67	51	50
Buehrle,Mark			60	65	51	50
Wright,Danny			41	50	35	49
Castillo,Frank	29	25	55	63	46	48
Myers,Brett				56	62	48
Burba,Dave	37	48	67	53	41	48
Appier,Kevin	-25	31	32	80	50	48
Callaway,Mickey	3	34	14	51	69	48
Neugebauer,Nick			83	114	15	48
Ortiz,Ramon	63	55	41	40	49	47
Redman,Mark	41	58	56	26	55	46
Loaiza,Esteban	30	53	46	44	50	46
Hernandez,Livan	25	45	60	35	49	46
Benson,Kris	40	56	66		36	46
Johnson,Jason	24	29	42	27	51	46
Moyer,Jamie	92	67	33	63	72	46
Pavano,Carl	47	56	59	37	39	46
May,Darrell	56	92	123	97	29	45
James,Delvin			85	44	35	45
Valdes,Ismael	54	48	17	41	41	45
Tomko,Brett	71	44	33	59	38	45
Myette,Aaron		37	17	56	58	45
Estes,Shawn	62	46	51	53	42	44
Daal,Omar	85	58	11	33	50	44
Zambrano,Victor		47	32	91	27	43
Figueroa,Nelson	35	54	53	59	14	42
Helling,Rick	55	15	35	38	48	42
Jennings,Jason			30	49	37	42
Batista,Miguel	43	52	-23	51	54	41
Jensen,Ryan	57	62	35	54	33	41
Byrd,Paul	59	16	11	41	63	41
Tejera,Michael				44	38	40
Sabathia,C.C.			72	70	57	40
Miller,Justin			66	34	40	40
Lyon,Brandon				73	12	39
Tollberg,Brian	76	57	67	48	4	39
Quevedo,Ruben		82	32	86	10	39
Reitsma,Chris			58	33	40	39
Moss,Damian		-19	38	54	41	38
Glavine,Tom	74	45	62	28	45	38
Neagle,Denny	73	34	38	45	32	38
Ponson,Sidney	35	13	41	36	40	38
Wilson,Paul	75		72	52	23	37
Rincon,Juan			33	49	37	37
Ashby,Andy	66	55	25	126	40	37
Lohse,Kyle		10	15	57	38	37
Ritchie,Todd	64	52	48	54	17	37
Dessens,Elmer	29	4	51	39	35	35
Simontacchi,Jason	108			23	34	35
Sele,Aaron	64	73	53	47	23	35
D'Amico,Jeff		-13	58	8	58	34

Relief Pitchers

Std Rotisserie	'98	'99	'00	'01	'02	'03Prj
Day,Zach			4	5	9	7
Reed,Steve	11	3	3	5	11	7
Speier,Justin	2	-2	14	8	9	7
Mantei,Matt	12	23	10	1	3	7
Stanton,Mike	7	2	4	12	11	6
Sauerbeck,Scott	-4	10	1	-3	10	6
Strickland,Scott		12	13	9	8	6
Witasick,Jay	10	-3	-6	9	7	6
Fyhrie,Mike	-16	5	8	2	12	6
Villafuerte,Brandon	-6	10	-11	6	18	6
Walker,Jamie	-1	-1	-12	-3	6	6
Mecir,Jim	12	1	19	6	4	6
Hammond,Chris	-5			7	18	6
Ligtenberg,Kerry	26		11	5	6	6
Cruz,Juan				12	2	6
Fikac,Jeremy				26	-1	6
Shields,Scot		6	-7	1	13	6
Redding,Tim			1	17	-3	6
Guthrie,Mark	1	0	2	6	10	5
King,Ray	4	6	8	1	6	5
Grimsley,Jason	1	9	2	5	3	5
Donnelly,Brendan	13	8	-9	15	12	5
White,Rick	1	4	12	6	3	5
Riedling,John	-7	17	17	5	-0	5
Spooneybarger,Tim				12	16	5
Van Poppel,Todd	-6	-2	10	7	-2	5
Marquis,Jason		1	-2	7	1	4
Worrell,Tim	1	2	11	3	14	4
Halama,John	10	13	8	12	2	4
Roberts,Grant		3	8	-1	7	4
Mota,Guillermo		10	11	-1	6	4
Fox,Chad	1	-2		15	-0	4
Boehringer,Brian	1	8	-2	2	8	4
Nelson,Jeff	5	2	13	11	3	4
Levine,Al	-5	7	5	13	4	4
Irabu,Hideki	16	11	-5	-2	8	4
Carrara,Giovanni	1	13	5	12	10	4
Riske,David	1	21	1	15	-0	4
Howry,Bob	16	22	12	4	2	4
Almanza,A	10	-1	0	0	4	4
Holmes,Darren	3	4	-4		11	4
Komiyama,Satoru	17	14	14	19	6	4
de los Santos,Val	12	-2	-0	-0	6	4
Adams,Terry	4	14	9	10	5	4
Stone,Ricky	8	-5	6	2	3	3
Mullen,Scott	8	-8	11	-4	5	3
Fultz,Aaron	7	5	5	3	1	3
Myers,Mike	5	0	6	2	5	3
Schoeneweis,Scott	-11	-12	2	1	4	3
Lincoln,Mike	8	-10	-1	9	5	3
Plesac,Dan	9	-0	6	5	4	3
Olsen,Kevin			-1	15	0	3
Fiore,Tony	-2	6	14	6	12	3
Knotts,Gary		5	-2	0	8	3
Smith,Dan	-9	-0	-4	-6	9	3
Farnsworth,Kyle	4	5	-2	11	-3	3
Biddle,Rocky			4	-0	3	3
Santiago,Jose	13	8	13	1	5	3
Thurman,Corey			1	15	-2	3
Hamilton,Joey	6	-1	4	-9	-1	2
Arrojo,Rolando	20	1	3	12	2	2
Tam,Jeff	17	4	12	7	-2	2
Phelps,Travis			14	12	3	2
Lloyd,Graeme	9	10		8	3	2
Silva,Carlos				10	10	2
Sullivan,Scott	2	14	11	10	-2	2
Yoshii,Masato	7	14	-4	1	4	2
Cormier,Rheal	-2	5	4	5	0	2

Base Perf Value	'98	'99	'00	'01	'02	'03Prj
Cruz,Juan				88	51	72
Redding,Tim			43	85	54	71
Roberts,Grant		60	54	76	67	71
Baez,Danys			55	100	57	71
Jimenez,Jose	36	47	58	44	100	71
Guthrie,Mark	71	38	56	77	95	71
Brown,Kevin	163	115	134	98	68	71
Donnelly,Brendan	60	63	-5	59	109	71
Grimsley,Jason	23	43	29	67	68	70
Quantrill,Paul	78	37	42	121	79	70
Mendoza,Ramiro	46	66	21	84	91	70
Kline,Steve	89	77	65	82	71	69
White,Rick	32	60	58	77	62	69
Escobar,Kelvim	77	40	40	97	69	69
Eischen,Joey	36	-15	-14	48	120	68
Hiljus,Erik	79	133	100	78	9	68
Wakefield,Tim	41	35	15	75	88	67
Mota,Guillermo		45	39	22	87	67
Boehringer,Brian	46	48	-20	67	79	67
Ryan,B.J.	85	105	44	69	62	67
Phelps,Travis			68	86	54	67
Wickman,Bob	73	57	81	142	103	66
Fikac,Jeremy				93	39	66
Walker,Jamie	26	48	-49	-12	92	66
Nunez,Vladimir	43	56	45	64	70	65
Romero,J.C.	75	52	34	41	97	65
Howry,Bob	82	84	79	50	76	65
Williams,Mike	75	71	72	52	62	65
Adams,Terry	69	58	51	87	59	65
Ligtenberg,Kerry	121		71	81	61	64
Stanton,Mike	65	96	108	98	55	64
Fyhrie,Mike	0	51	67	59	72	63
Weathers,David	76	42	48	76	64	63
Looper,Braden	84	40	29	53	59	63
Jones,Todd	58	66	88	39	72	63
Fultz,Aaron	55	43	68	87	51	63
Farnsworth,Kyle	54	12	36	133	37	62
Chen,Bruce	107	65	68	47	69	61
Day,Zach			81	44	58	61
Eyre,Scott	0	43	62	74	61	61
Sullivan,Scott	63	60	76	71	50	61
Veres,Dave	96	38	91	54	52	61
Lilly,Ted	61	73	55	60	64	60
Riedling,John	39	73	77	81	51	60
Hernandez,Roberto	63	97	69	48	63	60
DeJean,Mike	29	-20	15	74	64	60
Mesa,Jose	49	6	61	97	71	59
Speier,Justin	19	33	83	69	57	59
de los Santos,Val	91	1	44	78	61	59
Tam,Jeff	123	31	64	59	44	59
Fassero,Jeff	62	-1	44	115	68	58
Smith,Bud			103	76	49	58
Tankersley,Dennis				93	46	58
Weber,Ben	74	58	69	47	64	57
Lincoln,Mike	43	-4	33	54	60	57
Alfonseca,A	26	53	47	63	65	57
Westbrook,Jake		25	50	55	36	57
Hitchcock,Sterling	77	70	51	48	24	56
Darensbourg,Vic	103	30	68	84	0	56
Franklin,Ryan	25	26	48	53	63	55
Stone,Ricky	59	30	36	46	54	55
Lloyd,Graeme	93	42		55	67	54
Reames,Britt			82	42	58	54
Bailey,Cory	106	55	47	84	29	54
Yan,Esteban	60	29	45	149	43	54
Cormier,Rheal	-63	66	59	63	51	53
Cruz,Nelson	36	41	55	86	36	53
Thurman,Mike	31	39	18	33	45	53

Starting Pitchers

Std Rotisserie	'98	'99	'00	'01	'02	'03Prj
Harang,Aaron				4	6	**1**
Burba,Dave	16	17	13	-5	-2	**1**
Hermanson,Dustin	22	10	8	10	-3	**1**
D'Amico,Jeff		-4	27	-3	3	**1**
Drese,Ryan				7	-4	**1**
Benes,Andy	15	7	8	-9	10	**1**
Phillips,Jason	1	-5	-1	-6	3	**1**
Fogg,Josh		-5	11	-6	9	**1**
Affeldt,Jeremy				5	-1	**1**
Greisinger,Seth	5				1	**1**
Zambrano,Victor		-2	1	18	-0	**0**
Tollberg,Brian	3	-1	17	8	-8	**0**
Williams,David				14	-0	**0**
James,Delvin			4	-0	-3	**0**
Sabathia,C.C.			4	14	9	**0**
Bere,Jason	-6	-6	3	10	-4	**0**
Moehler,Brian	20	6	11	-0	0	**-0**
Abbott,Paul	6	10	13	13	-10	**-0**
Estes,Shawn	-2	2	10	7	-6	**-0**
Sturtze,Tanyon	0	11	4	7	-11	**-0**
Benoit,Joaquin			2	1	5	**-0**
Parris,Steve	9	13	5	-1	-2	**-0**
Smith,Travis	-3	-4	5	7	3	**-1**
Maduro,Calvin	-6	5	-4	4	-2	**-1**
Carpenter,Chris	12	8	-3	9	-8	**-1**
Driskill,Travis	-2	-5	-5	-0	5	**-1**
Hampton,Mike	10	33	23	-1	-17	**-1**
Hentgen,Pat	3	8	10	5	-4	**-1**
Douglass,Sean			5	4	-8	**-1**
Rincon,Juan			-7	6	-3	**-1**
Bell,Rob		5	8	-10	-1	**-1**
Wright,Jamey	-8	-13	6	1	-3	**-1**
Powell,Brian	8	-3	-1	1	-1	**-2**
Neugebauer,Nick			0	9	-8	**-2**
Sparks,Steve	1	-4	16	17	-14	**-2**
Sedlacek,Shawn			11	3	2	**-2**
Kinney,Matt		-10	11	-11	-8	**-3**
Asencio,Miguel					-5	**-3**
Chacon,Shawn			-2	0	-5	**-3**
Myette,Aaron		9	0	-3	-3	**-3**
Anderson,Jimmy	-3	9	-1	-2	-5	**-4**
Erickson,Scott	16	11	-10		-8	**-6**
Oliver,Darren	-5	9	-12	-4	-5	**-8**

Base Perf Value	'98	'99	'00	'01	'02	'03Prj
Jones,Bobby J.	49	56	21	35	34	**34**
Maroth,Mike			25	17	52	**34**
Mays,Joe	35	35	36	47	13	**34**
Abbott,Paul	99	70	28	40	-9	**34**
Kennedy,Joe				83	41	**33**
Greisinger,Seth	27				37	**33**
Garland,Jon		33	41	27	31	**32**
Haynes,Jimmy	30	18	11	34	38	**32**
Rogers,Kenny	60	52	38	18	35	**32**
Hendrickson,Mark		30	26	-19	49	**32**
Hermanson,Dustin	80	56	14	24	30	**32**
Reynolds,Shane	101	131	38	52	24	**32**
Anderson,Brian	57	49	35	6	40	**32**
Bacsik,Mike		5	37	58	31	**31**
Fogg,Josh		17	60	30	29	**30**
Phillips,Jason	46	13	5	20	41	**29**
Walker,Pete	-53	2	51	44	32	**29**
Suppan,Jeff	65	25	18	33	19	**28**
Moehler,Brian	42	33	49	38	18	**28**
Driskill,Travis	16	8	14	42	30	**28**
Person,Robert	14	46	77	60	28	**28**
Sedlacek,Shawn			26	39	44	**27**
Benes,Andy	60	27	39	-12	40	**27**
Sturtze,Tanyon	26	71	35	30	21	**27**
Stark,Dennis		13	70	59	12	**26**
Wright,Jamey	8	10	39	29	25	**26**
Bell,Rob		90	31	12	33	**25**
Powell,Brian	22	23	4	22	35	**23**
Sparks,Steve	40	5	36	40	13	**23**
Carpenter,Chris	63	52	14	47	2	**22**
Kinney,Matt		14	49	27	-5	**21**
Smith,Travis	8	15	27	32	41	**20**
Chacon,Shawn			46	41	-1	**19**
Parris,Steve	79	45	21	6	19	**19**
Rueter,Kirk	30	18	9	14	23	**18**
Williams,David				27	21	**17**
Maduro,Calvin	16	34	42	29	-5	**16**
Hampton,Mike	47	71	64	18	-4	**15**
Hentgen,Pat	11	24	28	45	-26	**12**
Oliver,Darren	19	47	-2	24	13	**11**
Erickson,Scott	70	16	-10		9	**7**
Anderson,Jimmy	21	51	30	24	-9	**5**
Asencio,Miguel					6	**2**

Relief Pitchers

Std Rotisserie	'98	'99	'00	'01	'02	'03Prj
Lima,Jose	24	30	-11	-2	-5	**-0**
Morgan,Mike	1	1	3	-1	-0	**-0**
Cassidy,Scott			-5	4	-0	**-0**
Cressend,Jack	-7	-5	6	7	-4	**-0**
Wickman,Bob	19	24	24	28	9	**-0**
Riggan,Jerrod			27	15	-0	**-1**
Paniagua,Jose	12	6	10	4	1	**-1**
Bailey,Cory	20	13	5	6	5	**-1**
Mulholland,Terry	12	9	3	-1	-3	**-1**
Fernandez,Jared	-17	6	11	-10	1	**-1**
Rijo,Jose				-2	1	**-1**
Stein,Blake	-3	5	11	3	-10	**-1**
Villone,Ron	1	16	0	-5	-2	**-1**
Farnsworth,Jeff			6	-10	-7	**-2**
Reyes,Dennys	6	3	-0	-0	-4	**-2**
Holtz,Mike	2	1	3	-1	-3	**-2**
Porzio,Mike		0	-19	-16	-6	**-2**
Alvarez,Juan	6	7	3	-4	-4	**-2**
Flores,Randy			2	3	-5	**-2**
Tavarez,Julian	3	-3	9	4	-6	**-2**
Beimel,Joe			-3	-1	-3	**-2**

Base Perf Value	'98	'99	'00	'01	'02	'03Prj
Reichert,Dan	-0	60	30	26	15	**28**
Glover,Gary	8	66	23	53	18	**28**
Orosco,Jesse	67	61	1	111	50	**27**
Buddie,Mike	45	77	16	39	24	**27**
Jackson,Mike	135	52		28	51	**27**
Gryboski,Kevin	2	15	43	39	29	**26**
Levine,Al	2	16	15	38	29	**25**
Mlicki,Dave	41	33	10	-6	38	**25**
Cassidy,Scott			15	32	30	**23**
Bauer,Rick			16	42	12	**23**
Wells,Bob	6	42	116	49	15	**22**
Farnsworth,Jeff			43	29	6	**21**
Prokopec,Luke	82	60	108	31	-8	**21**
Rijo,Jose				21	18	**21**
Brock,Chris	66	28	21	29	10	**20**
Fernandez,Jared	7	3	21	5	23	**20**
Alvarez,Juan	40	67	32	-10	24	**19**
Flores,Randy			25	13	21	**18**
Benes,Alan		-18	-5	15	26	**18**
Baldwin,James	43	18	26	22	18	**18**
Beimel,Joe			-9	21	31	**17**

Relief Pitchers

Std Rotisserie	'98	'99	'00	'01	'02	'03Prj
Cruz,Nelson	-4	9	9	6	-1	**2**
Bauer,Rick			-8	6	4	**2**
Zerbe,Chad		4	4	8	6	**2**
Harper,Travis		0	18	7	-4	**2**
Westbrook,Jake		6	1	4	-3	**2**
Fassero,Jeff	18	-16	5	14	2	**2**
Cabrera,Jose	-1	21	1	10	-8	**2**
Stephenson,Garrett	-11	8	16	0	-3	**2**
Izquierdo,Hansel				5	-4	**2**
Banks,Willie	-0	7	-4	5	4	**2**
Stechschulte,Gene		11	20	4	10	**2**
Mercado,Hector		1	2	2	8	**2**
Mairena,Oswaldo		6	2	2	-1	**2**
Heredia,Felix	-1	1	7	-3	0	**2**
Beirne,Kevin	9	-2	-1	-3	11	**2**
Buddie,Mike	10	11	6	7	-1	**2**
Brower,Jim	11	8	7	7	2	**2**
Ryan,B.J.	3	13	-2	2	-0	**1**
Venafro,Mike	6	7	4	6	-1	**1**
Jones,Todd	14	21	29	8	0	**1**
Lopez,Albie	12	4	14	1	-2	**1**
Chen,Bruce	23	7	15	5	-6	**1**
Eyre,Scott	-5	1	10	4	-1	**1**
Wunsch,Kelly	-3	6	11	-1	2	**1**
Wohlers,Mark	-19	-5	-2	3	4	**1**
Glover,Gary	-7	11	-3	10	2	**1**
Reames,Britt			13	-1	-1	**1**
Pineda,Luis				11	-0	**1**
Swindell,Greg	8	10	8	4	-2	**1**
Jackson,Mike	33	28		6	3	**1**
Hitchcock,Sterling	12	14	-1	1	-8	**1**
Thurman,Mike	6	10	-12	-0	2	**1**
Paronto,Chad	-6	-14	3	-3	2	**1**
Matthews,Mike	-2	-9	5	8	0	**1**
Roberts,Willis	1	-10	-6	6	4	**1**
Kolb,Danny	-10	-0	6	3	1	**1**
Brock,Chris	9	-0	8	1	-0	**1**
Mahomes,Pat	-7	14	-3	-2	17	**1**
Lowe,Sean	4	6	-1	14	-8	**1**
Smith,Bud			31	19	-4	**1**
Pote,Lou	-11	-4	13	3	0	**1**
Tucker,T.J.		7	1	4	5	**1**
Borbon,Pedro	-7	5	-5	5	1	**1**
Seanez,Rudy	15	10	4	3	-2	**0**
Haney,Chris	-6	2	11	-0	3	**0**
Creek,Doug	-2	0	3	-1	-3	**0**
Darensbourg,Vic	3	-8	5	2	-6	**0**
Hackman,Luther	-30	0	1	3	1	**0**
Smith,Mike				8	2	**0**
Hiljus,Erik	2	10	6	16	-9	**0**
Santana,Julio	3	-6	-1	-6	5	**0**
Prokopec,Luke	5	3	19	4	-6	**0**
Wells,Bob	-0	13	13	7	-4	**0**
Colome,Jesus			14	1	-4	**0**
Rocker,John	8	32	15	16	-0	**0**
Bottalico,Ricky	-3	8	17	6	-2	**0**
Herges,Matt	-7	8	17	9	3	**0**
Orosco,Jesse	10	-0	-0	2	3	**0**
Bernero,Adam			15	-10	1	**0**
Powell,Jay	12	4	-2	10	-1	**0**
Puffer,Brandon				12	4	**0**
Baldwin,James	6	6	15	5	-2	**-0**
Ginter,Matt			16	4	-2	**-0**
Coggin,Dave	-5	-8	1	5	-1	**-0**
Sosa,Jorge					-3	**-0**
Fetters,Mike	4	-2	12	4	0	**-0**
Alvarez,Wilson	5	9		2	-1	**-0**
Tankersley,Dennis				8	-7	**-0**

Base Perf Value	'98	'99	'00	'01	'02	'03Prj
Pote,Lou	20	32	73	52	57	**53**
Coggin,Dave	22	-29	35	41	66	**52**
Olsen,Kevin			30	113	35	**51**
Biddle,Rocky			35	36	48	**51**
Fetters,Mike	53	14	54	33	67	**51**
Alvarez,Wilson	46	43		98	31	**51**
Lowe,Sean	24	40	29	57	48	**51**
Wunsch,Kelly	40	36	74	32	44	**50**
Worrell,Tim	62	66	39	76	81	**50**
Santiago,Jose	10	7	48	48	50	**49**
Halama,John	70	41	24	42	59	**48**
Puffer,Brandon				67	59	**48**
Paronto,Chad	42	0	29	18	62	**47**
Hamilton,Joey	49	20	35	30	46	**47**
Heredia,Felix	74	57	65	26	35	**47**
Arrojo,Rolando	66	31	39	75	52	**47**
Wohlers,Mark	-6	-41	25	58	52	**46**
Riggan,Jerrod			107	75	37	**46**
Marquis,Jason		22	29	54	33	**46**
Knotts,Gary		33	31	64	43	**46**
Stephenson,Garrett	8	47	33	57	55	**45**
Timlin,Mike	106	60	42	64	73	**45**
Matthews,Mike	14	-5	68	66	40	**45**
Reyes,Dennys	100	88	43	58	29	**44**
Bernero,Adam			61	31	58	**44**
Smith,Mike				63	34	**44**
Ginter,Matt			56	73	21	**43**
Roberts,Willis	40	-0	4	44	53	**43**
Holtz,Mike	91	51	80	72	23	**43**
Borbon,Pedro	15	44	20	90	42	**42**
Irabu,Hideki	40	62	48	81	10	**42**
Acevedo,Juan	61	3	37	41	62	**41**
Herges,Matt	35	41	65	58	34	**41**
Powell,Jay	69	84	40	46	26	**41**
Colome,Jesus			60	43	43	**41**
Izquierdo,Hansel				43	16	**40**
Hasegawa,Shige	57	10	36	64	50	**40**
Brower,Jim	42	5	26	44	63	**40**
Carrara,Giovanni	47	35	48	81	34	**40**
Banks,Willie	37	59	-4	50	45	**40**
Haney,Chris	1	38	64	-6	62	**39**
Cressend,Jack	40	47	63	53	4	**39**
Silva,Carlos				57	56	**39**
Venafro,Mike	30	51	51	45	23	**38**
Bottalico,Ricky	5	45	32	58	51	**38**
Villone,Ron	33	66	7	52	44	**38**
Santana,Julio	11	2	42	23	40	**37**
Beirne,Kevin	57	22	49	-7	39	**36**
Schoeneweis,Scott	26	7	16	27	21	**36**
Mullen,Scott	40	8	59	0	43	**36**
Stein,Blake	32	51	36	44	29	**36**
Lopez,Albie	65	31	22	38	42	**35**
Mairena,Oswaldo		55	45	59	16	**35**
Zerbe,Chad		28	36	45	44	**34**
Fiore,Tony	44	41	28	50	35	**34**
Thurman,Corey			13	63	31	**34**
Kolb,Danny	10	21	57	70	43	**34**
Kent,Steve					29	**33**
Mahomes,Pat	-1	42	27	11	59	**33**
Stechschulte,Gene		49	17	39	44	**32**
Smith,Dan	-3	41	10	-9	43	**32**
Paniagua,Jose	80	68	76	41	38	**32**
Harper,Travis		45	34	25	29	**31**
Tucker,T.J.		51	-17	21	41	**31**
Yoshii,Masato	52	36	7	36	47	**30**
Hackman,Luther	-30	38	27	49	31	**30**
Cabrera,Jose	94	106	43	60	0	**30**
Tavarez,Julian	45	21	29	47	21	**29**

Runs Above Replacement

RAR	Pos	'02Prj
Bonds,Barry	LF	**188.8**
Giles,Brian	LF	**137.1**
Rodriguez,Alex	SS	**118.5**
Thome,Jim	1B	**108.8**
Ramirez,Manny	LF	**105.3**
Helton,Todd	1B	**104.0**
Jones,Chipper	LF	**103.5**
Berkman,Lance	CF	**100.0**
Johnson,Randy	SP	**88.6**
Giambi,Jason	1B	**87.4**
Garciaparra,Nomar	SS	**85.7**
Guerrero,Vladimir	RF	**82.1**
Sosa,Sammy	RF	**81.3**
Pujols,Albert	LF	**76.2**
Oswalt,Roy	SP	**75.2**
Edmonds,Jim	CF	**74.5**
Martinez,Pedro	SP	**73.9**
Abreu,Bobby	RF	**72.9**
Kent,Jeff	2B	**72.5**
Sheffield,Gary	RF	**68.2**
Delgado,Carlos	1B	**67.4**
Schilling,Curt	SP	**66.9**
Gonzalez,Luis	LF	**65.8**
Miller,Wade	SP	**65.3**
Ordonez,Magglio	RF	**64.1**
Millwood,Kevin	SP	**64.1**
Walker,Larry	RF	**64.1**
Green,Shawn	RF	**63.0**
Mulder,Mark	SP	**61.7**
Lowe,Derek	RP	**59.4**
Sweeney,Mike	1B	**58.7**
Colon,Bartolo	SP	**58.3**
Zito,Barry	SP	**56.9**
Maddux,Greg	SP	**56.9**
Morris,Matt	SP	**56.9**
Hudson,Tim	SP	**56.9**
Vidro,Jose	2B	**56.2**
Tejada,Miguel	SS	**55.5**
Floyd,Cliff	RF	**55.4**
Jones,Andruw	CF	**55.1**
Palmeiro,Rafael	1B	**54.6**
Halladay,Roy	SP	**54.5**
Mussina,Mike	SP	**54.5**
Rolen,Scott	3B	**54.0**
Wood,Kerry	SP	**53.3**
Williams,Bernie	CF	**53.2**
Prior,Mark	SP	**53.1**
Vazquez,Javier	SP	**52.3**
Washburn,Jarrod	SP	**52.2**
Lawrence,Brian	SP	**52.1**
Salmon,Tim	RF	**51.1**
Lidle,Cory	SP	**51.0**
Pineiro,Joel	SP	**49.8**
Perez,Odalis	SP	**49.7**
Buehrle,Mark	SP	**49.7**
Wolf,Randy	SP	**49.7**
Alfonzo,Edgardo	3B	**49.4**
Piazza,Mike	CA	**49.1**
Weaver,Jeff	SP	**48.7**
Burrell,Pat	LF	**47.8**
Bagwell,Jeff	1B	**46.9**
Klesko,Ryan	1B	**46.9**
Rodriguez,Ivan	CA	**46.2**
Leiter,Al	SP	**46.0**
Padilla,Vicente	SP	**46.0**
Nevin,Phil	3B	**45.9**
Schmidt,Jason	SP	**44.8**
Beckett,Josh	SP	**44.6**
Pettitte,Andy	SP	**43.7**
Dunn,Adam	LF	**43.6**
Jeter,Derek	SS	**43.6**
Durazo,Erubiel	1B	**43.1**

RAR	Pos	'02Prj
Lowell,Mike	3B	**42.1**
Radke,Brad	SP	**41.3**
Ohka,Tomokazu	SP	**41.2**
Glavine,Tom	SP	**41.2**
Giambi,Jeremy	LF	**40.2**
Clement,Matt	SP	**40.0**
Burnett,A.J.	SP	**40.0**
Armas Jr.,Tony	SP	**40.0**
Ortiz,Russ	SP	**40.0**
Sheets,Ben	SP	**40.0**
Nomo,Hideo	SP	**40.0**
Thomas,Frank	DH	**39.9**
Ibanez,Raul	LF	**39.7**
Fossum,Casey	RP	**39.0**
Lopez,Rodrigo	SP	**38.9**
Garcia,Freddy	SP	**38.8**
Wells,Kip	SP	**38.8**
Renteria,Edgar	SS	**38.3**
Foulke,Keith	SP	**38.0**
Durham,Ray	2B	**37.8**
Lackey,John	SP	**37.7**
Zambrano,Carlos	SP	**37.3**
Glaus,Troy	3B	**37.3**
Anderson,Garret	LF	**37.1**
Posada,Jorge	CA	**37.1**
Dotel,Octavio	RP	**36.9**
Santana,Johan	SP	**36.7**
Moyer,Jamie	SP	**36.5**
Walker,Todd	2B	**36.5**
Dessens,Elmer	SP	**36.4**
Damon,Johnny	CF	**36.3**
Trachsel,Steve	SP	**36.3**
Nixon,Trot	RF	**35.9**
Lee,Carlos	LF	**35.6**
Wakefield,Tim	RP	**35.5**
Penny,Brad	SP	**35.2**
Suzuki,Ichiro	RF	**34.8**
Olerud,John	1B	**34.7**
Fullmer,Brad	1B	**34.3**
Kearns,Austin	RF	**34.2**
Reed,Rick	SP	**34.1**
Benson,Kris	SP	**34.0**
Astacio,Pedro	SP	**33.8**
Alomar,Roberto	2B	**33.6**
Zeile,Todd	3B	**33.6**
Martinez,Edgar	DH	**33.0**
Milton,Eric	SP	**32.9**
Rueter,Kirk	SP	**32.8**
Rusch,Glendon	SP	**32.8**
Aurilia,Rich	SS	**32.7**
Graves,Danny	SP	**32.5**
Thomson,John	SP	**32.5**
Roa,Joe	SP	**32.5**
Williams,Woody	SP	**32.4**
Millar,Kevin	LF	**32.3**
Kim,Byung-Hyun	RP	**32.0**
Soriano,Alfonso	2B	**31.9**
Ishii,Kazuhisa	SP	**31.3**
Mueller,Bill	3B	**30.8**
Griffey Jr.,Ken	CF	**30.7**
Nen,Robb	RP	**30.7**
Smoltz,John	RP	**30.7**
Wilkerson,Brad	CF	**30.7**
Appier,Kevin	SP	**30.5**
Chavez,Eric	3B	**29.6**
Cameron,Mike	CF	**29.5**
Finley,Steve	CF	**29.5**
Cabrera,Orlando	SS	**29.4**
Peavy,Jake	SP	**28.9**
Wagner,Billy	RP	**28.3**
McGriff,Fred	1B	**28.2**
Hernandez,Livan	SP	**28.2**

RAR	Pos	'02Prj
Redman,Mark	SP	**28.1**
Ortiz,Ramon	SP	**28.1**
Kotsay,Mark	CF	**28.0**
Moss,Damian	SP	**27.8**
Daal,Omar	SP	**27.7**
Hernandez,Carlos	SP	**27.5**
Ventura,Robin	3B	**27.1**
Benitez,Armando	RP	**27.1**
Eckstein,David	SS	**26.7**
Batista,Miguel	SP	**26.6**
Reitsma,Chris	SP	**26.5**
Ashby,Andy	SP	**26.5**
Catalanotto,Frank	LF	**26.3**
Colbrunn,Greg	1B	**26.2**
Lieberthal,Mike	CA	**26.0**
Quantrill,Paul	RP	**25.9**
Wells,David	SP	**25.8**
Wilson,Paul	SP	**25.8**
Saarloos,Kirk	SP	**25.3**
Drew,J.D.	RF	**25.2**
Boone,Aaron	3B	**25.1**
Jarvis,Kevin	SP	**25.0**
Rhodes,Arthur	RP	**25.0**
Rivera,Mariano	RP	**25.0**
Karsay,Steve	RP	**24.9**
Callaway,Mickey	SP	**24.8**
Gagne,Eric	RP	**24.7**
Lilly,Ted	RP	**24.7**
Clemens,Roger	SP	**24.6**
Wright,Danny	SP	**24.5**
Valdes,Ismael	SP	**24.5**
Koskie,Corey	3B	**24.5**
Stewart,Shannon	LF	**24.3**
LoDuca,Paul	CA	**24.3**
Alou,Moises	LF	**24.3**
Helling,Rick	SP	**24.2**
Beltre,Adrian	3B	**24.2**
Munro,Peter	SP	**23.8**
Bradford,Chad	RP	**23.8**
Brown,Kevin	RP	**23.8**
Julio,Jorge	RP	**23.8**
Fyhrie,Mike	RP	**23.7**
Borowski,Joe	RP	**23.5**
Weathers,David	RP	**23.4**
Rodriguez,Felix	RP	**23.4**
Ramirez,Aramis	3B	**23.1**
Duckworth,Brandon	SP	**23.0**
Simontacchi,Jason	SP	**22.9**
Hinske,Eric	3B	**22.8**
Miller,Damian	CA	**22.8**
Sexson,Richie	1B	**22.6**
Weber,Ben	RP	**22.6**
Torres,Salomon	SP	**22.6**
Mendoza,Ramiro	RP	**22.5**
Soriano,Rafael	SP	**22.4**
Cruz,Juan	RP	**22.4**
Franklin,Ryan	RP	**22.4**
Vizcaino,Luis	RP	**22.3**
Witasick,Jay	RP	**22.2**
Johnson,Jason	SP	**22.2**
Isringhausen,Jason	RP	**22.2**
Giles,Marcus	2B	**22.2**
Byrd,Paul	SP	**22.1**
Spivey,Junior	2B	**22.1**
Finley,Chuck	SP	**22.0**
Haynes,Jimmy	SP	**21.9**
Tomko,Brett	SP	**21.8**
Perez,Oliver	SP	**21.5**
Percival,Troy	RP	**21.4**
Eaton,Adam	SP	**21.4**
Acevedo,Juan	RP	**21.4**
Boone,Bret	2B	**21.3**

RAR	Pos	'02Prj
Stephens,John	SP	**21.2**
Kendall,Jason	CA	**21.2**
Hernandez,Orlando	SP	**21.2**
Looper,Braden	RP	**21.1**
Williamson,Scott	RP	**21.0**
Eischen,Joey	RP	**21.0**
Huff,Aubrey	1B	**20.9**
Hoffman,Trevor	RP	**20.9**
Ponson,Sidney	SP	**20.9**
Shuey,Paul	RP	**20.6**
Hudson,Orlando	2B	**20.4**
Romero,J.C.	RP	**20.2**
Hawkins,LaTroy	RP	**20.2**
Groom,Buddy	RP	**20.2**
Rincon,Ricardo	RP	**20.2**
Timlin,Mike	RP	**19.9**
Lee,Derrek	1B	**19.9**
DeJean,Mike	RP	**19.8**
Sele,Aaron	SP	**19.8**
Remlinger,Mike	RP	**19.8**
Strickland,Scott	RP	**19.8**
Reed,Steve	RP	**19.7**
Sauerbeck,Scott	RP	**19.7**
Suppan,Jeff	SP	**19.6**
Jennings,Jason	SP	**19.5**
Politte,Cliff	RP	**19.4**
Payton,Jay	CF	**19.2**
Estes,Shawn	SP	**19.2**
Jensen,Ryan	SP	**19.2**
Marquis,Jason	RP	**19.1**
Gibbons,Jay	RF	**19.0**
Cordero,Francisco	RP	**19.0**
Bellhorn,Mark	2B	**19.0**
Martinez,Tino	1B	**19.0**
Grimsley,Jason	RP	**18.9**
Stanton,Mike	RP	**18.9**
Koch,Billy	RP	**18.9**
Burkett,John	SP	**18.7**
Nunez,Vladimir	RP	**18.7**
Riedling,John	RP	**18.7**
Stewart,Scott	RP	**18.6**
Mesa,Jose	RP	**18.6**
Kline,Steve	RP	**18.6**
Crede,Joe	3B	**18.6**
Williams,Mike	RP	**18.6**
Veres,Dave	RP	**18.6**
King,Ray	RP	**18.5**
Mays,Joe	SP	**18.5**
Koplove,Mike	RP	**18.5**
Rogers,Kenny	SP	**18.5**
Woodward,Chris	SS	**18.4**
Hunter,Torii	CF	**18.4**
Beltran,Carlos	CF	**18.0**
Vaughn,Mo	1B	**18.0**
Guardado,Eddie	RP	**17.8**
Sasaki,Kazuhiro	RP	**17.8**
Urbina,Ugueth	RP	**17.8**
Vizquel,Omar	SS	**17.8**
Middlebrook,Jason	RP	**17.7**
Burks,Ellis	DH	**17.6**
Jimenez,Jose	RP	**17.4**
Boehringer,Brian	RP	**17.4**
Crudale,Mike	RP	**17.3**
Hammond,Chris	RP	**17.3**
Spooneybarger,Tim	RP	**17.3**
Walker,Pete	SP	**17.2**
Dempster,Ryan	SP	**17.1**
Dye,Jermaine	RF	**16.8**
Anderson,Brian	SP	**16.8**
Meadows,Brian	SP	**16.7**
Myers,Brett	SP	**16.7**
Osuna,Antonio	RP	**16.6**

Runs Above Replacement

RAR	Pos	'02Prj
Castillo,Luis	2B	16.6
Figueroa,Nelson	SP	16.5
Baez,Danys	RP	16.5
Day,Zach	RP	16.4
Barrett,Michael	CA	16.3
Rollins,Jimmy	SS	16.2
White,Rick	RP	16.2
Hernandez,Runelvys	SP	16.1
Durocher,Jayson	RP	16.1
Ligtenberg,Kerry	RP	16.1
Kennedy,Joe	SP	16.0
Winn,Randy	CF	16.0
Wilson,Preston	CF	16.0
Gonzalez,Juan	RF	15.9
Valentin,Jose	3B	15.9
Hall,Toby	CA	15.8
Lawton,Matt	RF	15.7
Jimenez,D'Angelo	2B	15.7
Varitek,Jason	CA	15.6
Stark,Dennis	SP	15.5
Redding,Tim	RP	15.5
Kapler,Gabe	LF	15.4
Jones,Jacque	LF	15.4
DeRosa,Mark	2B	15.3
Miller,Justin	SP	15.1
Carrara,Giovanni	RP	15.0
Loretta,Mark	3B	15.0
Stone,Ricky	RP	15.0
Fikac,Jeremy	RP	15.0
Silva,Carlos	RP	15.0
Rupe,Ryan	SP	15.0
Worrell,Tim	RP	15.0
Lincoln,Mike	RP	15.0
Maroth,Mike	SP	14.9
Roberts,Grant	RP	14.9
White,Gabe	RP	14.9
Mantei,Matt	RP	14.9
Justice,David	LF	14.8
Hidalgo,Richard	RF	14.8
Fogg,Josh	SP	14.7
Blalock,Hank	3B	14.7
Gonzalez,Alex S.	SS	14.4
Cruz,Jose	LF	14.3
Benes,Andy	SP	14.3
Mecir,Jim	RP	14.2
Howry,Bob	RP	14.2
Shields,Scot	RP	14.2
Marte,Damaso	RP	14.2
Yoshii,Masato	RP	14.1
Van Poppel,Todd	RP	14.1
Neugebauer,Nick	SP	14.1
Ortiz,David	DH	14.1
Graffanino,Tony	2B	14.0
Jenkins,Geoff	LF	14.0
Ward,Daryle	LF	14.0
Affeldt,Jeremy	SP	14.0
Davis,Doug	SP	14.0
Hernandez,Ramon	CA	13.9
Kim,Sun Woo	SP	13.5
Pratt,Todd	CA	13.5
Eyre,Scott	RP	13.4
Embree,Alan	RP	13.4
Biggio,Craig	2B	13.3
Larkin,Barry	SS	13.1
Pavano,Carl	SP	13.1
Schneider,Brian	CA	13.1
Person,Robert	SP	12.9
Bacsik,Mike	SP	12.9
Guillen,Carlos	SS	12.9
Tejera,Michael	SP	12.9
Cornejo,Nate	SP	12.8
Halama,John	RP	12.8
May,Darrell	SP	12.7
Olsen,Kevin	RP	12.6
Lopez,Albie	RP	12.6

RAR	Pos	'02Prj
Mota,Guillermo	RP	12.5
Villafuerte,Brandon	RP	12.5
Hairston Jr.,Jerry	2B	12.4
Garland,Jon	SP	12.4
Sturtze,Tanyon	SP	12.4
Gordon,Tom	RP	12.4
Pierre,Juan	CF	12.1
Phelps,Josh	DH	12.0
Batista,Tony	3B	12.0
Hernandez,Jose	SS	11.8
Nelson,Jeff	RP	11.8
Donnelly,Brendan	RP	11.8
Riske,David	RP	11.8
Fiore,Tony	RP	11.7
Hasegawa,Shige	RP	11.7
Marrero,Eli	RF	11.6
Lugo,Julio	SS	11.6
Reynolds,Shane	SP	11.6
Zambrano,Victor	SP	11.5
Ritchie,Todd	SP	11.4
Kielty,Bobby	RF	11.4
Alfonseca,A	RP	11.4
Adams,Terry	RP	11.4
Jones,Todd	RP	11.4
Konerko,Paul	1B	11.3
Fultz,Aaron	RP	11.3
Park,Chan Ho	SP	11.2
Zerbe,Chad	RP	11.2
Holmes,Darren	RP	11.2
Fox,Chad	RP	11.1
Randa,Joe	3B	11.0
Ensberg,Morgan	3B	10.9
Hampton,Mike	SP	10.8
Quevedo,Ruben	SP	10.7
Levine,Al	RP	10.6
Phelps,Travis	RP	10.6
Walker,Jamie	RP	10.6
Biddle,Rocky	RP	10.5
Escobar,Kelvim	RP	10.5
Davis,Ben	CA	10.5
Williams,David	SP	10.5
Arrojo,Rolando	RP	10.5
Perry,Herbert	3B	10.4
Thurman,Corey	RP	10.3
Hendrickson,Mark	SP	10.3
Buddie,Mike	RP	10.2
Chen,Bruce	RP	10.2
Lohse,Kyle	SP	10.2
Hamilton,Joey	RP	10.2
Loaiza,Esteban	SP	10.2
Trammell,Bubba	RF	10.1
Gonzalez,Wiki	CA	10.1
Norton,Greg	3B	10.0
Guthrie,Mark	RP	10.0
de los Santos,Val	RP	10.0
Komiyama,Satoru	RP	9.9
Burroughs,Sean	3B	9.8
Guzman,Cristian	SS	9.8
Roberts,Dave	CF	9.7
Higginson,Bobby	LF	9.7
Martinez,Ramon	SS	9.6
Wunsch,Kelly	RP	9.4
Wilson,Tom	CA	9.3
Roberts,Willis	RP	9.3
Thurman,Mike	RP	9.3
Stephenson,Garrett	RP	9.3
Harang,Aaron	SP	9.1
Burba,Dave	SP	9.1
Cruz,Nelson	RP	9.0
Coggin,Dave	RP	9.0
Izquierdo,Hansel	RP	9.0
Hermanson,Dustin	SP	9.0
Matthews,Mike	RP	8.8
Hentgen,Pat	SP	8.8
Stairs,Matt	RF	8.8

RAR	Pos	'02Prj
Santiago,Jose	RP	8.8
Ledee,Ricky	CF	8.8
Grieve,Ben	RF	8.7
Myers,Mike	RP	8.7
Relaford,Desi	SS	8.7
Mercado,Hector	RP	8.7
Neagle,Denny	SP	8.4
Casey,Sean	1B	8.3
Butler,Brent	2B	8.3
Tam,Jeff	RP	8.3
Pote,Lou	RP	8.2
Uribe,Juan	SS	8.2
Hernandez,Roberto	RP	8.2
Schoeneweis,Scott	RP	8.2
Creek,Doug	RP	8.2
Santana,Julio	RP	8.2
Mullen,Scott	RP	8.2
Wright,Jamey	SP	8.1
Bailey,Cory	RP	8.1
Kolb,Danny	RP	8.1
Yan,Esteban	RP	8.1
Lyon,Brandon	SP	8.1
Benard,Marvin	RF	8.1
Tavarez,Julian	RP	8.1
Vina,Fernando	2B	7.9
Bell,Jay	3B	7.9
Castillo,Frank	SP	7.9
Ortiz,Jose	2B	7.9
Redmond,Mike	CA	7.8
Powell,Brian	SP	7.8
Lopez,Felipe	SS	7.8
Hackman,Luther	RP	7.8
Reames,Britt	RP	7.7
Sullivan,Scott	RP	7.7
Speier,Justin	RP	7.7
Brower,Jim	RP	7.7
Darensbourg,Vic	RP	7.6
Smith,Dan	RP	7.6
Stechschulte,Gene	RP	7.6
Almanza,A	RP	7.6
Miller,Corky	CA	7.6
Lofton,Kenny	CF	7.5
Vazquez,Ramon	2B	7.5
Santiago,Benito	CA	7.4
Johnson,Charles	CA	7.4
Williams,Matt	3B	7.4
Blum,Geoff	3B	7.2
Greer,Rusty	LF	7.2
Paronto,Chad	RP	7.1
Ryan,B.J.	RP	7.0
Ginter,Matt	RP	7.0
Banks,Willie	RP	7.0
Heredia,Felix	RP	7.0
D'Amico,Jeff	SP	6.9
Wohlers,Mark	RP	6.9
Jones,Bobby J.	SP	6.9
Bauer,Rick	RP	6.9
Encarnacion,Juan	RF	6.9
Lane,Jason	RF	6.8
Drese,Ryan	SP	6.7
James,Delvin	SP	6.7
Brown,Roosevelt	CF	6.6
Tankersley,Dennis	RP	6.6
Benoit,Joaquin	SP	6.6
Herges,Matt	RP	6.5
Beirne,Kevin	RP	6.5
Tucker,T.J.	RP	6.5
Cormier,Rheal	RP	6.5
Rijo,Jose	RP	6.5
Anderson,Marlon	2B	6.5
Wells,Vernon	CF	6.5
Knotts,Gary	RP	6.4
Lloyd,Graeme	RP	6.4
Kennedy,Adam	2B	6.4
Puffer,Brandon	RP	6.3

RAR	Pos	'02Prj
Estalella,Bobby	CA	6.3
Young,Eric	2B	6.3
Torrealba,Yorvit	CA	6.2
Orosco,Jesse	RP	6.2
Jordan,Brian	LF	6.1
Wigginton,Ty	3B	6.1
Branyan,Russ	LF	6.0
Pierzynski,A.J.	CA	6.0
Rocker,John	RP	5.9
Seanez,Rudy	RP	5.9
Matthews Jr.,Gary	RF	5.8
Cora,Alex	SS	5.7
Sanders,Reggie	RF	5.7
Hitchcock,Sterling	RP	5.7
Cabrera,Jose	RP	5.4
Fassero,Jeff	RP	5.3
LaRue,Jason	CA	5.3
Mairena,Oswaldo	RP	5.3
Deshields,Delino	2B	5.3
Sparks,Steve	SP	5.3
Meluskey,Mitch	CA	5.2
Ochoa,Alex	RF	5.2
Gutierrez,Ricky	2B	5.1
Moehler,Brian	SP	5.1
Mahomes,Pat	RP	5.1
Furcal,Rafael	SS	5.0
Reyes,Dennys	RP	5.0
Larson,Brandon	LF	4.9
Zaun,Gregg	CA	4.9
Plesac,Dan	RP	4.9
Gant,Ron	LF	4.8
Perez,Timo	CF	4.8
Grace,Mark	1B	4.7
Mondesi,Raul	RF	4.7
Hundley,Todd	CA	4.6
Jackson,Mike	RP	4.6
Westbrook,Jake	RP	4.6
Brock,Chris	RP	4.6
Bernero,Adam	RP	4.5
Vizcaino,Jose	SS	4.5
Harper,Travis	RP	4.5
Alvarez,Wilson	RP	4.5
Kreuter,Chad	CA	4.4
Lopez,Javy	CA	4.4
Halter,Shane	SS	4.3
Hatteberg,Scott	1B	4.3
Rios,Armando	RF	4.3
Farnsworth,Kyle	RP	4.1
Lowe,Sean	RP	4.1
Gryboski,Kevin	RP	4.0
Sabathia,C.C.	SP	4.0
Bottalico,Ricky	RP	3.9
Fox,Andy	SS	3.9
Lieber,Jon	SP	3.8
Valentin,John	SS	3.8
McLemore,Mark	LF	3.5
Mirabelli,Doug	CA	3.5
Smith,Mike	RP	3.4
Sosa,Jorge	RP	3.4
Parris,Steve	SP	3.4
Powell,Jay	RP	3.4
Colome,Jesus	RP	3.4
Petrick,Ben	LF	3.4
Venafro,Mike	RP	3.4
Riggan,Jerrod	RP	3.4
Phillips,Jason	SP	3.4
Paniagua,Jose	RP	3.4
Haney,Chris	RP	3.4
Irabu,Hideki	RP	3.4
Douglass,Sean	SP	3.3
Bell,David	3B	3.3
Wells,Bob	RP	3.3
Ginter,Keith	3B	3.3
Bere,Jason	SP	3.3
Baldwin,James	RP	3.3

Runs Above Replacement

RAR	Pos	'02Prj
Gomez,Chris	SS	3.2
Cruz,Deivi	SS	3.2
Wilson,Craig	RF	3.1
Anderson,Jimmy	SP	3.1
Donnels,Chris	3B	2.9
Moeller,Chad	CA	2.8
Fetters,Mike	RP	2.8
Swindell,Greg	RP	2.7
Fernandez,Jared	RP	2.7
Menechino,Frank	2B	2.6
Smith,Bud	RP	2.5
Holtz,Mike	RP	2.5
Pineda,Luis	RP	2.5
Borbon,Pedro	RP	2.5
Ellis,Mark	2B	2.5
Agbayani,Benny	CF	2.5
Lampkin,Tom	CA	2.4
Womack,Tony	SS	2.4
Gonzalez,Alex	SS	2.4
Grissom,Marquis	CF	2.3
Chavez,Endy	CF	2.3
Haselman,Bill	CA	2.3
Clayton,Royce	SS	2.3
Merced,Orlando	RF	2.2
Cassidy,Scott	RP	2.2
Alvarez,Juan	RP	2.2
Hiljus,Erik	RP	2.2
Rivera,Mike	CA	2.2
Rincon,Juan	SP	2.2
Greisinger,Seth	SP	2.2
Stein,Blake	RP	2.2
Michaels,Jason	CF	2.1
Segui,David	DH	2.1
Glover,Gary	RP	2.1
Gil,Benji	2B	2.1
Alomar Jr.,Sandy	CA	2.1
O'Leary,Troy	LF	2.0
Buchanan,Brian	RF	2.0
Perez,Tomas	2B	2.0
Myette,Aaron	SP	1.9
Hammonds,Jeffrey	CF	1.9
Hunter,Brian L.	CF	1.9
Johnson,Mark L.	CA	1.9
Widger,Chris	CA	1.8
Shumpert,Terry	2B	1.7
Morgan,Mike	RP	1.5
Canizaro,Jay	2B	1.4
Hillenbrand,Shea	3B	1.3
Myers,Greg	CA	1.3
Flores,Randy	RP	1.3
Tollberg,Brian	SP	1.3
Wickman,Bob	RP	1.2
Cressend,Jack	RP	1.1
Roberts,Brian	2B	1.1
Prokopec,Luke	RP	1.1
Brown,Adrian	CF	1.1
Easley,Damion	2B	1.0
Farnsworth,Jeff	RP	1.0
Wilson,Jack	SS	1.0
Reese,Pokey	2B	1.0
Asencio,Miguel	SP	0.9
Driskill,Travis	SP	0.9
Kinkade,Mike	1B	0.9
Castro,Ramon	CA	0.8
Everett,Adam	SS	0.8
Hansen,Dave	1B	0.8
Hyzdu,Adam	CF	0.8
Counsell,Craig	3B	0.7
Berg,Dave	2B	0.7
Tatis,Fernando	3B	0.6
Benes,Alan	RP	0.6
Vander Wal,John	RF	0.6
Mientkiewicz,Doug	1B	0.6
Ausmus,Brad	CA	0.5
Bennett,Gary	CA	0.5

RAR	Pos	'02Prj
Daubach,Brian	1B	0.4
Cirillo,Jeff	3B	0.3
Beimel,Joe	RP	0.3
Hinch,A.J.	CA	0.2
LaRocca,Greg	3B	0.2
Casanova,Raul	CA	0.2
Fick,Robert	RF	0.1
Gonzalez,Raul	CF	0.1
Smith,Travis	SP	0.1
Mulholland,Terry	RP	0.1
Spiezio,Scott	1B	0.0
Stynes,Chris	3B	0.0
Greene,Todd	CA	0.0
Bautista,Danny	RF	0.0
Stinnett,Kelly	CA	-0.1
Echevarria,Angel	RF	-0.1
Febles,Carlos	2B	-0.1
Carpenter,Chris	SP	-0.1
Burnitz,Jeromy	RF	-0.2
Maduro,Calvin	SP	-0.2
Lima,Jose	RP	-0.3
Piatt,Adam	LF	-0.3
Chacon,Shawn	SP	-0.3
Nunez,Abraham	2B	-0.4
Lombard,George	CF	-0.5
Sheets,Andy	2B	-0.5
Abbott,Paul	SP	-0.5
Cordero,Wil	LF	-0.8
Snow,J.T.	1B	-0.8
Merloni,Lou	2B	-0.9
Castro,Juan	SS	-1.0
Lankford,Ray	LF	-1.0
Franco,Julio	1B	-1.1
Jackson,Damian	2B	-1.1
Clark,Howie	DH	-1.1
Bragg,Darren	RF	-1.1
Belliard,Ron	2B	-1.2
McCarty,Dave	LF	-1.2
Crisp,Covelli	CF	-1.2
Surhoff,B.J.	1B	-1.3
Anderson,Brady	CF	-1.3
Tarasco,Tony	LF	-1.3
Houston,Tyler	3B	-1.3
Nieves,Jose	2B	-1.3
Bordick,Mike	SS	-1.5
White,Rondell	LF	-1.5
Simon,Randall	1B	-1.6
Barajas,Rod	CA	-1.6
Rivas,Luis	2B	-1.6
Flaherty,John	CA	-1.6
Berger,Brandon	CF	-1.7
Wilson,Dan	CA	-1.7
Pellow,Kit	3B	-1.7
Coomer,Ron	3B	-1.7
Vaughn,Greg	LF	-1.7
Machado,Robert	CA	-1.7
Fordyce,Brook	CA	-1.8
Mlicki,Dave	RP	-1.8
Cintron,Alex	2B	-1.8
Villone,Ron	RP	-1.8
Mayne,Brent	CA	-1.9
Wilson,Vance	CA	-2.0
Sandberg,Jared	3B	-2.1
Grudzielanek,Mark	2B	-2.1
Pickford,Kevin	RP	-2.1
Prince,Tom	CA	-2.1
Everett,Carl	RF	-2.1
Palmer,Dean	DH	-2.1
Alicea,Luis	2B	-2.2
Young,Mike	2B	-2.2
Henderson,Rickey	LF	-2.2
Smith,Bobby	3B	-2.3
Girardi,Joe	CA	-2.4
Polanco,Placido	3B	-2.4
Osik,Keith	CA	-2.4

RAR	Pos	'02Prj
Izturis,Cesar	SS	-2.4
Perez,Eduardo	RF	-2.4
Dellucci,David	RF	-2.4
Matheny,Mike	CA	-2.5
Liefer,Jeff	LF	-2.5
Nieves,Wilbert	CA	-2.5
Nagy,Charles	RP	-2.6
Porzio,Mike	RP	-2.6
Kent,Steve	RP	-2.6
Lopez,Luis M.	SS	-2.7
DiFelice,Mike	CA	-2.7
Hocking,Denny	2B	-2.7
Johnson,Russ	3B	-2.7
Kinney,Matt	SP	-2.7
Bell,Rob	SP	-2.7
Saenz,Olmedo	1B	-2.7
Reichert,Dan	RP	-2.8
Pena,Carlos	1B	-2.9
Perez,Eddie	CA	-2.9
Brown,Dee	CF	-3.0
Young,Dmitri	DH	-3.0
Molina,Ben	CA	-3.0
Sanchez,Rey	2B	-3.1
Tucker,Michael	RF	-3.1
Selby,Bill	3B	-3.2
Sierra,Ruben	LF	-3.2
Quinn,Mark	RF	-3.2
Hill,Bobby	2B	-3.2
Garcia,Karim	RF	-3.2
Mordecai,Mike	3B	-3.3
Mateo,Ruben	RF	-3.3
Harris,Lenny	LF	-3.3
Ordaz,Luis	2B	-3.3
Mercker,Kent	RP	-3.3
Guillen,Jose	RF	-3.4
Palmeiro,Orlando	RF	-3.4
Carroll,Jamey	3B	-3.5
Rushford,Jim	RF	-3.5
Fabregas,Jorge	CA	-3.5
Bako,Paul	CA	-3.6
Diaz,Einar	CA	-3.6
Johnson,Nick	1B	-3.7
Walbeck,Matt	CA	-3.7
Lockhart,Keith	2B	-3.7
Ojeda,Augie	SS	-3.8
Perez,Neifi	SS	-3.8
Cairo,Miguel	LF	-3.8
Thompson,Ryan	LF	-3.8
Karros,Eric	1B	-3.9
Mench,Kevin	RF	-4.0
McCracken,Quint	RF	-4.1
Minor,Damon	1B	-4.1
Goodwin,Tom	LF	-4.1
Blanco,Henry	CA	-4.1
Guiel,Aaron	RF	-4.2
Garcia,Jesse	2B	-4.2
LeCroy,Matt	DH	-4.2
Paul,Josh	CA	-4.2
Harris,Willie	2B	-4.3
Magruder,Chris	LF	-4.4
Escalona,Felix	SS	-4.4
Rivera,Ruben	CF	-4.5
Murray,Calvin	CF	-4.5
Lamb,Mike	1B	-4.5
Shinjo,Tsuyoshi	CF	-4.6
Singleton,Chris	CF	-4.7
Richard,Chris	DH	-4.8
Molina,Jose	CA	-4.8
Lee,Travis	1B	-4.9
Little,Mark	RF	-5.0
Clark,Brady	LF	-5.0
Feliz,Pedro	3B	-5.1
Guerrero,Wilton	2B	-5.2
Erickson,Scott	SP	-5.2
Sedlacek,Shawn	SP	-5.3

RAR	Pos	'02Prj
Hermansen,Chad	CF	-5.3
Glanville,Doug	CF	-5.3
Galarraga,Andres	1B	-5.3
Helms,Wes	1B	-5.4
Cordova,Marty	LF	-5.4
Conti,Jason	RF	-5.6
Long,Terrence	CF	-5.6
Lawrence,Joe	2B	-5.7
Franco,Matt	1B	-5.7
Rowand,Aaron	CF	-5.8
Snyder,Earl	1B	-5.9
Robinson,Kerry	LF	-5.9
Patterson,Corey	CF	-6.1
Taylor,Reggie	CF	-6.1
Tyner,Jason	LF	-6.2
Hollandsworth,T	LF	-6.2
Wise,DeWayne	RF	-6.2
Sweeney,Mark	1B	-6.3
Macias,Jose	CF	-6.3
Byrnes,Eric	LF	-6.4
Oliver,Darren	SP	-6.4
Leon,Jose	1B	-6.4
Huckaby,Ken	CA	-6.4
Cedeno,Roger	LF	-6.5
Gipson,Charles	LF	-6.6
Paquette,Craig	3B	-6.6
Gil,Geronimo	CA	-6.6
Mackowiak,Rob	RF	-6.7
Cox,Steve	1B	-6.7
Benjamin,Mike	3B	-6.8
Matos,Julius	2B	-6.8
Hubbard,Trenidad	RF	-6.8
Bush,Homer	2B	-7.0
Ordonez,Rey	SS	-7.0
Baerga,Carlos	DH	-7.1
McDonald,John	2B	-7.4
Mabry,John	1B	-7.5
Bocachica,Hiram	LF	-7.7
Bradley,Milton	CF	-7.8
Cruz,Jacob	DH	-7.8
Inge,Brandon	CA	-7.8
Bergeron,Peter	CF	-7.8
Magee,Wendell	CF	-7.9
Castilla,Vinny	3B	-7.9
Wilson,Enrique	3B	-8.1
Truby,Chris	3B	-8.2
Spencer,Shane	RF	-8.2
Mohr,Dustan	RF	-8.5
Smith,Jason	3B	-8.5
Owens,Eric	LF	-8.6
Cepicky,Matt	LF	-8.6
Sadler,Donnie	CF	-8.8
Dunston,Shawon	RF	-8.8
Rolls,Damian	RF	-8.8
Conine,Jeff	1B	-9.0
Kingsale,Gene	RF	-9.1
Erstad,Darin	CF	-9.1
Knoblauch,Chuck	LF	-9.3
Nichting,Chris	RP	-9.4
Clark,Tony	1B	-9.5
Abernathy,Brent	2B	-9.6
Offerman,Jose	1B	-10.2
Torres,Andres	CF	-10.2
Wooten,Shawn	DH	-10.7
Stevens,Lee	1B	-10.7
McEwing,Joe	RF	-11.2
Sanchez,Alex	CF	-12.6
Cabrera,Jolbert	CF	-12.9
Mora,Melvin	LF	-14.2
Santiago,Ramon	SS	-14.9
Crawford,Carl	LF	-16.0
Young,Kevin	1B	-16.7

VI. Managing the LIMA Plan
2002 Greatest Hits

This section is my annual quest for immortality. Sort of.

You see, I write a weekly column for about 10 months of the year that appears on BaseballHQ.com. Each week, I get to conduct new research, rehash old research and make up stuff out of thin air. Keeps me off the streets.

The problem is, at Baseball HQ, these essays have a life of about three weeks, and then disappear forever. For the real good stuff, this is unfortunate, because I hate to expend all that effort for a shelf life of three weeks. For the not so good stuff, three weeks is often about 22 days too long.

But here we have this nice little book with a shelf life of more than three weeks. In fact, some people keep these books for many years. At this past year's Fantasy Baseball Symposium in Phoenix, one attendee pulled out a copy of the 1988 Forecaster for me to autograph. Admittedly, that was a little weird, even for me.

Anyway, the best columns from 2002 appear here, and in a variety of other spots in this book as well. The new look at batting eye, the PQS studies and my bullpen rantings were all HQ columns from this past year. And in this section, we take a comprehensive look at managing the LIMA Plan.

For those of you who have never experienced the joys and wonders of a subscription to Baseball HQ, these essays should provide you with some exposure to what you've been missing. For those of you who already subscribe to Baseball HQ, don't think of this as rehashed content. All of these essays have been updated based on subsequent events; at minimum, all are worth re-reading and owning for good.

But no autographs in 2017, please.

LIMA Grading

The LIMA (Low Investment Mound Aces) Plan, in a nutshell (a more detailed description is in the Glossary)...

> Budget a maximum of $60 for pitching, of which about half should be targeted to acquiring saves. The remaining $30 should be spent on pitchers who have a minimum statistical profile of 2.0 K/BB ratio, 6.0 K/9 IP, 1.0 HR/9, without regard to role or ERA. Draft the minimum number of innings your league will allow, and then maximize your offense with the remaining $200.

For the past three years in the *Baseball Forecaster,* we've been providing LIMA grades for every player. These are intended to give you a sense of how well that batter or pitcher would fit onto a roster employing the LIMA Plan. Grade A's are players that are perfect fits; Grade F's should come nowhere near a LIMA roster, no matter how desirable they might be otherwise.

The grades look at three essential elements...

1. Performance... as measured by our leading indicators. This is the element of the plan that has value for any type of game, not just Rotisserie. By focusing on leading indicators rather than traditional stat categories, we gain an advantage in uncovering true skills potential.

For batters, we look at walk and contact rates, and power and speed indices. The better these gauges, the higher the grade. For pitchers, base performance value does a fine job of capturing the skills measured in the command ratio, strikeout rate and HR rate, so we need to look no further than BPV.

2. Playing time... is a part of the LIMA grade for batters only. As our goal is to maximize our offensive investments, we need to separate those high-skilled players that are on the field every day versus those that tend to ride the bench. Ultimately, you want to amass as many at bats as you possibly can. The truism is that, if you succeed in drafting the most at bats in your league, you will immediately fare well in the Runs and RBI categories, no matter what caliber of player you draft. Of course, in LIMA, caliber is important too.

For pitchers, innings are our enemy. Higher grades tend to go more to relievers as a matter of course. For starters, we have to do more cherry-picking to find the few standouts who merit a spot on our LIMA rosters.

3. Rotisserie value... is the element of the LIMA grade that presents the most difficulty. Value is a matter of in-draft market forces and the perception of your competition. I may tell you that Raul Mondesi is worth $27, but if the other owners in your league see him as returning to the 30-30 plateau, his value could break $30. If they are extremely risk-averse and fear either injury or a trade out of the league, his value could drop below $25.

LIMA grading uses a player's Rotisserie value to determine his "fit" for your team. If that value is over $30 — the ceiling level for LIMA's risk-spreading approach — his grade would typically drop. So, in assigning a LIMA grade, how can we account for perception?

In this book, the LIMA grades for pitchers are run off of last season's Rotisserie value. The assumption is that market forces will more likely associate a pitcher's value with last year's performance. While there will be natural variations in perception, most people frame their perspective in this way, which is why we set the book's LIMA grades up as such.

A look at the percentage of players that receive each LIMA grade, on average, provides some interesting insight...

	BATTERS		PITCHERS	
GRADE	AL	NL	AL	NL
=====	===	===	===	===
A/A+	1%	1%	5%	4%
B/B+	19%	17%	20%	24%
C/C+	26%	23%	24%	25%
D/D+	22%	24%	11%	11%
F	32%	35%	40%	36%

More than one third of all players are just not worth drafting at all. In fact, between the "D's" and "F's," over half of the player population has no value. This is one of the prime assertions of the "high target drafting" strategy. It is tough to keep track of so many players and maintain focus; this proves that we can cut our workload down by perhaps half and just ignore those players that have no place on our rosters. While this particular analysis focuses on the LIMA Plan, the concept really applies to all drafting approaches.

How to best use all this information...

For drafting purposes, your goal should be to stock your roster with as many players that have at least a grade of "B" as possible. In shallow leagues, this should be an easy task. In standard and deep leagues, it will be more of a challenge.

The 20%-25% of the player pool that has a grade of "B" or better works out to about eight players per team in a standard 12 or 13-team league (note that the percentages above are based on a large player population — about 1000 players — but the draftable population in typical leagues is less than that). Hypothetically, if *everyone* in your league followed the LIMA Plan, eight Grade "B" or above players would be the best you could expect to have on your roster.

But everyone does not follow LIMA, nor do they likely hold the same opinion on every player as you do. So that average of eight high-grade players should be easy to exceed. For every high-grade player you draft above eight, you start to shift the balance of power towards your team. Ideally, you'd like to see all 23 of your players with high grades, but that's probably unrealistic. However, if you can draft 15-20 of these LIMA studs, you'll position yourself just fine for a run at a title.

8 Myths of the LIMA Plan

It's like a game of telephone.

Somebody starts and tries to explain a new concept to somebody else. Person #2 then passes on his interpretation to person #3, who then adds his own take to person #4. By the time the original concept reaches person #20, "grand slam home run" has become "ground ham on a bun."

And so it has become with the LIMA Plan. This was the first year that I have seen so many references to the concept in so many diverse places. And half of the time, they get it wrong.

I suppose, this is good news for you. Since you know the truth, you can leverage that knowledge over all those people who *think* they know the truth. For me, the news isn't quite as good. For those sources that see fit to attribute the concept to its rightful purveyor, I'd much prefer that they get it right. I swear I'm gonna throw something if I read one more time that "Ron Shandler's Lima Plan tells you to draft a $60 staff of middle relievers." Of course, all those people who follow, and fail, with that advice will undoubtedly look back at Ron Shandler as some type of crackpot.

I also suppose that there are a bunch of you reading this right now who may have come to us for the first time this year under those false LIMA pretenses. So I'd like to set the record straight, and provide some insight even to those who are LIMA vets.

There are three basic elements of the plan. First is the resource allocation of your dollars. Second is the targeting of skills rather than stats. And finally, there is risk management. All three are important, but to varying degrees, and dependent upon the particular league in which LIMA is being implemented. It is often the interpretation of these elements, and their interaction, where perception goes awry.

MYTH #1: LIMA means... Low Innings Mound Aces

I saw this a few times last winter. It is one of several misinterpretations that focus on a single element of the plan. In this case, it leads people to believe that LIMA requires you to ignore starting pitching. But minimizing innings was intended purely to remind us that you do not necessarily need a lot of innings to contend, or even to meet minimum IP requirements. (Even I was surprised to learn that, in order to meet a 900 IP requirement, you only needed two 180 IP starting pitchers!) For me, this has morphed into a risk management tool, nothing more; certainly not the core concept of the Plan.

To be honest, this element of LIMA was an afterthought. It was the final element included, and only because it provided more in-season management flexibility.

MYTH #2: LIMA means... a pitching staff filled with middle relievers.

Another myth associated with the low innings element. Stocking your pitching staff with middle relievers may be an end result if you cannot acquire other more valuable arms, but it is certainly not the intent of LIMA. There are many starters and conditional saves sources that are inexpensive and far more valuable than middle relievers. However, if the price tags of these arms are too high, there are *tons* of middle relievers who can fill out a staff nicely without doing too much damage. A LIMA staff will typically end up with at least a few of these pitchers, only because they are the cheapest end-game fillers. But to target middle relievers specifically is not only unnecessary, it's foolish.

MYTH #3: LIMA means... you have to punt wins.

This is probably the greatest myth of the plan. The assumption is that, since you are not drafting many innings, there is no way to compete in Wins. Perception of a pure innings-to-wins correlation is pervasive, but reality is different. Sure, the more innings you accumulate, the more likely it is that there will be wins, but better correlations can be found elsewhere. In fact, the two highest correlating elements to Wins are team offense and pitching skill.

The entire foundation of the LIMA Plan is that the focus on skill will yield its just rewards. Most times, this alone will lead to an acceptable ranking in the Wins category. Last year's LIMA gods, like J.C. Romero and Arthur Rhodes, provided more boost in Wins than dozens of starting pitchers. That's a pure LIMA benefit.

However, it's true that the lack of innings does put a strain on the Wins category. There's less margin for error. Still, there is no reason to go into a season expecting the worst. LIMA's upside is that, even if you do fare poorly in Wins, you should have enough points from everywhere else to still contend. But punting Wins outright? *Never* at the draft table. During the season, it's an option you might have to consider at some point, but only if you absolutely have to.

MYTH #4: LIMA means... don't spend for saves.

This appeared in one place over the winter and it astounded me. The fact is, you *have to spend for saves,* if for no other reason than the riskiness of the Wins category. However, you should try to cap that spending at about $30, which could be one stud or several second tier sources. This is designed so that you have at least $30 to fill your other 7-8 pitching roster spots.

Every time I failed using the LIMA Plan, it was because I did not draft the right saves guys. Saves are fickle, as any Vladimir Nunez owner already knows. Acquiring those precious saves is probably the single biggest challenge to pulling off LIMA. So, if you have to spend $35, do it. In the right scenario, if you have to spend $40, do it.

Ah..... but....

MYTH #5: If you don't spend that $200 on offense, you've blown it.

Or alternatively, "blow the rules, punt the plan." LIMA provides a series of targets, but just because you miss a few doesn't mean that your efforts have gone to waste.

Clearly, buying a staff of pitchers with 1.0 command ratios runs in direct opposition to the plan, but snaring a few slightly under 2.0 won't kill you. Drafting Randy Johnson, Robb Nen and seven $1 pitchers won't cut it either, but it's okay to go after a $15-$20 arm if you need the comfort of a "staff anchor." And spending only $170 on offense won't do the job, but anything above $190 is fine. In keeper leagues, 5x5 leagues, and other hybrids, the rules may have to be fudged much more.

LIMA is a framework. You need to mold it to fit your own individual league. There is a strong undercurrent, however, convinced of facts such as...

MYTH #6: LIMA will not work in a 5x5 league.

Here again, it's a matter of molding the framework to fit the needs of your particular league. Yes, the innings restriction and budget allocations may be a problem, so you move them. Don't use the foundation to weigh you down, use it as a springboard. There are several 5x5 variations that are very doable.

MYTH #7: LIMA only works in Rotisserie leagues.

AskRotoman's Peter Kreutzer provided the best perspective on the LIMA Plan in Baseball HQ's Think Tank back in March. He noted that there was really only one element of the plan that was truly innovative. Most of the elements are nothing new — spending heavily on offense, spreading risk — but the focus on player evaluation skills is what provides the greatest benefit and is what sets LIMA apart from any other strategy.

Given that, the core LIMA concepts become applicable to just about any fantasy game. Even simulation games like Scoresheet can benefit by forcing owners to focus on pitching skills when selecting their staff. In fact, this is even more valuable in Scoresheet-type games as it properly devalues situational stats like saves. In 2002, the Rhodes and Romeros would have made far better closers than half of the arms that were designated with the role. Similarly, cherry-picking the late-round Washburns and Lawrences would have provided solid rotation anchors and freed up early draft picks for more productive bats. All based on LIMA concepts.

MYTH #8: The LIMA Plan won't work if more than one person is doing it.

If LIMA is vulnerable, the risk is *not* in other people trying to employ it concurrently. There are plenty of LIMA-caliber pitchers to go around, and certainly more than enough offense. Two owners going at it will make little difference in the results; even three, and possibly four, can successfully go LIMA at the same time.

However, as more and more owners build large offenses and wait for pitching bargains, there will be an economic shift you need to be cognizant of. In this scenario, certain players must end up going under value, and those players will most likely be second tier starting pitchers. The Randy Johnsons and Mike Mussinas will continue to draw high salaries, if for no other reason than a need to price-enforce. But the hurlers who should go in the low $20's — the Hudson and Wade Miller-types — might slide into the high teens. Alert bidders might consider these opportunities to grab bargains, even if it means exceeding your pitching budget.

But that would not mean the LIMA Plan has failed, not so long as the pitchers you have on your roster are still skills-worthy. Grabbing a $17 Javier Vazquez is far different than grabbing a $17 Aaron Sele. And those extra dollars spent won't likely make that much of a difference anyway; at the draft table, we play the game with projections, after all.

There *is* one reality amidst all this, however. It's no myth... the LIMA Plan *can* be beaten.

How to Beat the LIMA Plan

A post-LABR interview with Steve Moyer of Baseball Info Solutions:

BASEBALL WEEKLY: "When I talked to Ron Shandler, he said that you knew his strategy. You might have thrown out a few guys that he would go for. Was there any chance to play off of his strategy, to counter-program against him?"

MOYER: "Totally, on purpose. I wrote down all his A and B+ LIMA Players and that's all I brought out all night long."

BW: "So do you feel your strategy worked?"

MOYER: "There's plenty of players for Ron to find. He's good enough that he always finds somebody else. At least maybe I ruined it a little bit."

Just a little.

Beating the LIMA Plan has become a popular pursuit. Beyond Steve's proclamation, even John Hunt wrote in his column, "LIMA Must Die." But so far, anti-LIMA efforts have been largely ineffective. In the ten times I've used the Plan in expert league play, I've pulled down four titles and two second place finishes, good results for leagues that draft from scratch every year. Others have fared similarly, and even better in keeper leagues.

Steve's efforts did not go unnoticed, however. I found it interesting to see him bring out names like Felix Rodriguez and Mike Remlinger in the first few rounds. I suppose he was hoping that I'd bite on some of the early openers, but I let them pass; I knew there was still a large pool to draw from. The only time I blinked was when he came out with Aaron Fultz, about 10 rounds into the draft. I decided to test his interest and bid $2. Of course, I owned him. Steve rostered virtually none of these openers.

In the end, his ploy flushed out many low cost, high skills pitchers far earlier in the draft than would have otherwise occurred. While the execution was perfect from his end, the result was unsuccessful. Why? Two key reasons...

1. Working alone, his efforts only served to draw out about 20 names. Of those, maybe half came out earlier than they should have. Depleting 10 LIMA-worthy arms was not enough to make a dent in the available pool of hurlers.

2. By focusing exclusively on Grade A and B+ pitchers, the names he drew out were almost all relievers. The available pool of relievers is very deep, so this effort also made little dent.

Even though Steve Moyer's anti-LIMA strategy failed, it did reveal that LIMA could be beaten given the right set of circumstances.

First, if several owners collude to open bidding only on LIMA-worthy names, that would deplete the availability of arms quicker. If Steve could bring out 10-20 names working alone, two or three owners working in tandem could easily derail the Plan. Of course, if your league has several owners willing to engage in collusion, there are worse problems afoot then just combating the anti-LIMA militia.

However, there is another, potentially more damaging approach to shooting down LIMA, and it only requires the efforts of a single owner. If even one owner limited his opening bids to LIMA-caliber *starting* pitchers... that is where the most vulnerability exists. In this year's drafts, there were only 10 AL and 17 NL starting pitchers with a LIMA grade of B or better who were projected to cost $15 or less. That is a very small pool that could be quickly depleted by the anti-LIMA faction.

For those owners married to LIMA, especially those who tend to be inflexible during the draft, this can be fatal. For those able to adjust quickly on the fly, there are ways to combat these tactics and still draft a LIMA-worthy pitching staff. Tuck these tips away for next year; odds are, you may have to use them.

1. Maintain your patience, but don't be afraid to pay a little extra for your pitching staff.

With LIMA hurlers being offered up in earlier than normal rounds, there may be a slight economic shift. With more money available in the early-going, the LIMA-quality pitchers might garner higher bids. For instance, I purchased Brian Lawrence for $7 in Round 16 of LABR; had an anti-LIMA-ite thrown him out in Round 5, it's unlikely he would have gone for less than double-digits.

In these cases, continue to focus on offense early, but you'll probably have to budget a bit more for your targeted pitchers. Allotting $6 for your last five slots might not cut it; you might have to spend $10 or $12. You might even have to take another arm in the $15-$20 range.

Those extra dollars will likely have to come from your offense. If you're only spending $185-$190 on bats, there is less wiggle-room. Be *very* risk-averse, avoiding any players with an injury history, erratic trends or soft skills.

2. Be prepared to jump in and grab your pitchers early. Rather than waiting for the second half of the draft to roster your pitchers, recognize the early trends and grab your needed arms when they come out.

Be careful, though. The anti-LIMAs may try to draw you into bidding wars. Resist. If they see that you're not chasing their offerings, they might pull back.

There's one exception, however... pitchers whose *market value* is significantly lower than your projected value. As long as you have faith in your projections, it is okay to chase a player a few dollars over market value. But be cautious, and selective in who you decide to chase.

3. Draft a staff of relievers and acquire starters later. If all else fails and you are unable to draft a balanced LIMA staff without grossly overpaying, let the anti-LIMAs have their day. Or, let them *think* so.

This circumstance is actually not a bad one to be in, especially in a league where there is active trading. Draft your pitching staff exclusively from available relievers (do buy saves, however). A roster containing a closer, a second tier closer and seven middle relief types (all LIMA caliber) should only cost you about $40-$45, leaving a whopping $220 for offense. Through active trading, you should be able to deal off some of that excess offense for starting pitching during the season. And there are always free agent pickups to be had.

Of course, this approach leaves a narrower margin for error. You'd be coming out of the draft extremely weak in the Wins category, and any efforts to correct that situation could put other categories at risk. You could opt to punt Wins, but then again, everything else has to go right. In 5x5, you'd be coming out of the draft having essentially punted both Wins and Strikeouts, which is not insurmountable, but forces you to pretty much ace everything else.

In the Xperts Fantasy League (XFL), a new experts keeper league that debuted in Phoenix in November, owner Doug Dennis did just that. But in a shallow, 12-team mixed league with a plentiful free agent pool, he might just be able to pull it off.

I suppose what this all means is that a strong draft is important, but it does not have to be perfect. The LIMA Plan does not stop after that last player is rostered in March. LIMA concepts continue during the season with your roster management, and might be considered a second stage to the Plan.

Troubleshooting LIMA

There is no crying in fantasy baseball.

Yes, maybe you have found success with the LIMA Plan. Maybe it has even won you a few titles. But there are never any guarantees. Stuff goes wrong. You can curse the Plan's founder, or cancel your subscription, but it won't turn your team around any faster.

The fact is, no matter how you've built your team, titles are rarely won on draft day. You have to work your roster constantly, all season long. There are always holes to fill, injuries to weather, and unexpected performances to do reality checks on.

Thankfully, when things go awry, one of the nice things about LIMA is that there are built-in safety nets. When you spend $200 on offense, you can easily withstand an injury or two to a front-liner. Minimizing innings allows you to deal for a stud pitcher in June and still be able to make up significant ground in the ratio categories.

But sometimes, even the safety nets are not enough. The best constructed LIMA pitching staffs can still end up wallowing in the depths of the ERA category. The many components of a $200 offense can pull up lame, all at once. Assuming that you had at least a moderately successful LIMA draft, it probably looks a lot worse now than it really is, but it doesn't hurt to do a little trouble-shooting...

PROBLEM 1: My offense stinks.

It takes a fair bit of bad luck to not find any redeeming qualities in a $200 offense. This was supposed to be the part of your draft that was a no-brainer. This was supposed to be the wealth of riches from which you could deal off excess to fill holes. Ah, fate can be cruel.

When it comes to veteran players who have a history of demonstrated success, you have to exercise excruciating patience. Any other course of action is a poor percentage play. It doesn't matter what type of numbers have been compiled up until now; seasons are evaluated based on the numbers in the books at the end of the year. Those stats don't have to be spread evenly over six months; they are worth just as much if the bulk of them are compiled in four months, or even two.

With a LIMA offense, there are far too many batters to give up hope on any one, barring a definite role downgrade. The odds are so highly stacked against a complete meltdown that you have to assume at least a few will eventually return to normal levels of productivity.

While the patience tactic goes for the power and tightly-linked RBI categories, it also can apply to batting average.

The perception is that the BA standings stabilize by the end of May and little can be done to make up ground after that.. However, **it is still very doable to add 5-10 points to your team BA by season's end**. For veteran bats — once again — patience is in order. Of course, you *can* nudge things along. **Maintain focus on base skills** when you move players on to and off of your roster. High contact rates, walk rates and eye ratios are always good targets, and are often cheap acquisitions from owners focused more on traditional categories.

Of course, you always need to **focus on team context.** Everything is driven by projected playing time, so if you're saddled with a player like Lee Stevens, you have to consider where the AB's will come from for him to turn things around.

And finally, remember that **small moves can add up**. You don't always have to replace your worst hitter with a superstar; replacing him with a moderate upgrade can provide incremental gains. These gains have a cumulative effect over time... as long as you can exercise patience.

Bottom line is that, unless you are hit with an overwhelming rash of injuries or drafted poorly, **$200 worth of offense is going to eventually provide a reasonable return**. Patience, combined with periodic tweaks should be all you need.

PROBLEM 2: I'm last in Wins.

This is an inherent hazard with employing the LIMA Plan. The goal is to fare well enough in the other categories that a good showing in Wins is not necessary, however, sometimes it would really help to pick up a few points in that category.

I've often said that chasing wins is a fool's quest, but a methodical approach can at least lower your risk a bit. The greatest danger, of course, is to your ERA/WHIP, which is why Wins are often considered the antithesis to LIMA.

Obviously, the best way to add wins is to shop for starting pitchers.

In a 4x4 league, you would add arms to the three or four who you've drafted, likely replacing some middle relievers who are expendable. In a 5x5 league, you would add arms to the five or six who you've drafted, likely replacing some bottom-feeding starters or closer-wannabes.

The best starters are already rostered somewhere, so most of your opportunity will likely come from the free agent pool, and most often from recently promoted minor leaguers. Many analysts will tell you to stay away from this mine field, but there are things you can look for to minimize your risk with young arms.

As usual, **check minor league BPI's**, especially converted to their major league equivalents. Rule of thumb... *No matter how much the hype or how low the ERA, if a young pitcher has a command ratio under 2.0, stay away. Any arm with superb BPI's, even if he is very young, or not a media darling, or not expected to remain in a rotation for long, is worth taking a flyer on.*

Why? Because **skills win roles, no matter what a manager says or what is written in the media.**

Of course, you can also trade for starting pitchers, and for those teams that have managed to build an excess in offense, this is a fine path. In 2001, I dealt Luis Gonzalez (and Ruben Quevedo) for Curt Schilling (and Marvin Benard), which is something a $180 offense would be harder-pressed to pull off.

PROBLEM 3: I've blown the saves category.

I've done a fair amount of writing about those fickle saves, but it has always been true that drafting the correct closers is key to a successful LIMA Plan. If you were unlucky enough to draft Matt Anderson and Jeff Zimmerman as your primary closers, you're immediately in a hole that's tough to get out of.

When it comes to unearthing saves, you have to be vigilant. **Follow the news on possible opportunities,** and **keep a list of high-skills candidates in your back pocket**. You won't always be able to foresee a pitcher coming out of nowhere, but at least you give yourself a fighting chance.

Remember to **exercise self-control when MLB teams go through their typical gyrations**. No matter what any manager says, every bullpen decision can change with a single blown save.

Finally, **saves are one area where desperation moves can pay off.** Since new sources of saves often come out of nowhere, taking some risks on conditional speculations might make sense in certain circumstances.

For instance, if there are rumblings about a frontline closer getting dealt, you could quickly grab up several of the high-skilled relievers from that team's bullpen. Typically, these would be players who are still available in the free agent pool.

In 2002, an astute fantasy leaguer might have been able to FAAB both Braden Looper and Vladimir Nunez at the first leak of an Antonio Alfonseca deal. That move would have panned out. Around the All Star Break in 2001, my saves-starved AL Tout Wars club FAABed nearly the entire Angels bullpen when rumors came down about an impending Troy Percival trade. That move did not pan out.

Because Hail Mary passes don't always reach their intended targets. But sometimes they do.

(Football?! How did *that* get in here??)

PROBLEM 4: My team ERA... ARRRRGH!

When it comes down to it, the whole point of the LIMA Plan is to provide your team with a competitive ERA, at a low cost. So, it's naturally disheartening to find yourself floundering in the ERA and WHIP categories. The good news is, if you've successfully minimized your innings damage, even July is still early enough to make up at least a half run in ERA.

Here are a few quick tips for dealing with the struggling hurlers already on your roster...

You must exercise patience with:

- Veterans who have a proven track record.
- Pitchers who have otherwise solid BPI's.
- Pitchers whose struggles are tied to their underachieving teams.

You can employ a quicker hook with:

- Pitchers who have demonstrated fewer than two years of solid BPI's
- Pitchers with a spotty injury history, even if they are claiming perfect health
- Pitchers with poor BPI's, especially if they are taking a regular turn in a rotation
- Low cost, easily replaceable arms, especially middle relievers

You can cautiously ride pitchers with solid ERAs but soft support skills, but be prepared to jump ship at the slightest provocation. This was particularly tough to do for all us Jason Simontacchi owners this year, but he is *exactly* the type of pitcher that has to be handled with kid gloves.

And as for free agent pickups, as always, focus on skills, even speculative skills. For instance, if you are in a league that has fairly flexible roster movement rules, you can afford to take more risks. In these cases, feel free to take chances on a pitcher who...

- has a history of solid BPI's but is struggling this year, especially if there is a chance he might move to another team.
- has a history of solid BPI's but has spent more time on the DL than on the mound. Periods of health can come in small bunches.
- is coming out of the minors with solid BPI's but mediocre or lousy traditional stats.

And of course, any undrafted middle reliever with solid skills makes a great place-holder until something better comes along... and might be able to provide some value as well. Low cost FAAB pickups I personally grabbed last year included Alan Embree, Tim Worrell, Mark Hendrickson, Brandon Villafuerte and Scott Williamson — each for a $1 FAAB bid.

And one final, non-LIMA column dedicated especially to those who might peruse this book in the middle of next season...

Fixating on Today

Vladimir Nunez recorded his first save on April 11, 2002, at a time when the Marlins were still trying to figure out who was in their bullpen. It wasn't until April 25 that Nunez notched save #2, which started a string of 7 saves in 8 outings over the next two weeks. He had "officially" claimed the role of closer.

And at Baseball HQ, all our analysts, who are tasked with updating the player projections each week, shrugged their collective shoulders and said, "so what?"

Or so it seemed.

The posts on the subscriber forum ("Your Braden Looper projection is a joke.") and the comments in the reader survey ("You take way too long to make changes in your playing time projections.") made clear your displeasure. But it was not our intent to incur your wrath. It's all a by-product of our prognosticating philosophy.

There are two ways to do in-season player projections...

1. Consider the current reality as fixed.

2. Assume that reality is fluid.

There is a natural tendency for people to be fixated on the here and now. Today's reality is the only thing that you can count on as being true. We all know subconsciously that things might change tomorrow, but we don't know what those changes will look like. So we rely on the security of "what is" rather than the uncertainty of "what might be."

But what if we embrace a new reality? What if we define what reality truly means in the world of baseball?

In our new baseball reality, nothing is real. Nothing is permanent. Nothing can be counted on.

When a media bite reports that someone has won a job, all that means is that the job has been won for today. There is no assumption of any long-term implication. All it can take is just a short string of 0-fers at the plate or back-to-back blown saves to cost him that spot.

How real is this reality? Had we created fixed projections based on the prevailing conditions of Opening Day 2002, this is what we would have locked in on...

- Homer Bush and Frank Menechino would be the starting 2Bmen for their respective clubs.
- Hank Blalock, Morgan Ensberg and Sean Burroughs would all be fixtures at the hot corner.
- John Rocker would be the closer for the Rangers.
- Brady Anderson would be batting lead-off for the Indians.
- Opening Day starters Joey Hamilton and Ron Villone would still be leading their teams' rotations.
- Peter Bergeron would be patrolling CF for the Expos.
- Kyle Farnsworth and Jeff Fassero would be the RH/LH closing tandem for the Cubs.
- Eric Gagne would represent only a third of LA's closing committee, with Giovanni Carrara and Paul Quantrill.
- Ben Petrick would be the starting catcher at Coors.

And for all those other information services that provide pre-season projections but never update them, every one of these statements remained true all year long, stuck in time.

Things change all the time, which brings to light the critical unknown variable. When an event occurs or a decision is made, how long can we count on it? What is the expected duration of any individual baseball reality? The easy answer is, "as long as the player remains successful in the role." But how can we project the potential for success?

- A history of success in that role
- A history of success in similar roles
- Skills levels that support success in that role

For Vlad Nunez, he had no history as a closer. Over his career, he only had two saves, a dozen holds and five blown saves. His one year of success in a non-stress bullpen role (in 2001) represented a slight overachievement due to a 26% hit rate, a 81% strand rate and an ERA near 4.00 whenever he was put on the mound with less than two days rest. And while 2002's two-week stretch of solid performance — that allegedly cemented the closer's role for him — was admirable, it was hardly sufficient to project anything for the long-term.

So, in our May 15 update, we projected that Nunez would get 55% of the Marlins' saves, with the other 45% going to Looper, the only other arm in the pen with any closing experience. Over the ensuing months, those percentages shifted up and down, but always seemed to come back down to rest with Nunez at 55%.

Most of you would have preferred us approaching it differently. Perhaps Nunez should have gotten 90% of the saves with the remaining 10% being distributed to a few other arms in the pen. We could have done that, and it would have represented the reality of May 15. Had you made your roster management decisions based on that, however, you might have grossly overvalued Nunez's projected contribution.

"But it's only July and Nunez is still the Marlins' best option," you might have rightly said. "He's still good enough to turn it around and grab 90% of the saves from here on out."

Sure, anything can happen in our baseball reality. But our projections will still hedge his potential, because of his...

- Command ratio under 2.0
- BPV under 75
- Saves percentage under 80%
- .292 opposition batting average after pitch #15
- .273 opposition batting average against right-handed batters

Those are not the numbers of a 90% closer. And treating Nunez as such just because he happens to have the job right now is not a good percentage play.

Reader Andrew Cleary came to our defense on the Nunez/Looper projection, and posted a note that explains our position as well as any of us could...

"What often throws people off when they see this kind of projection is that they are imposing their own *mistake* onto the projection... They are in essence throwing away the advantage that a more measured approach gives you.

"Basically, Ron's projections are attempts to project an *average expectation* for the entire season. Sure, Looper isn't saving games now, and if your form of projection is to take what has happened in the last week and assume it will happen all year, you will necessarily think that a projection that takes a longer look at things is a "joke."

"But Ron's projections are *expected values*. They average the possibility that Looper will get no saves with the possibility that he will take over the closer role. Nunez is no sure thing. He could get injured, obviously, but even beyond that, being named "closer" is a fickle thing, especially for a guy with pretty average BPI's.

"The sad thing is that one of the best advantages you can get from Baseball HQ is the ability to look *past* short-term results and instead look at what is expected for the entire season. I find this constantly gives me advantages, as people panic based on short-term results and as long as I show patience and bet instead on what is expected over the entire season, I gain an advantage."

And you might rightly say, "Ron, this is all well and good, but how do you deal with the Eric Gagnes of the world, players whose change in performance or role becomes permanent?"

I grant you that there is a downside to our approach, but these cases are more the exception rather than the rule. In Gagne's case, however, his BPI's have *always* indicated the potential for better things, so it would have been a strong percentage play to stick with him. And in fact, our weekly projections did reflect that fact nearly immediately last April.

But typically, permanence is just not a core element of baseball reality.

It's Time to Kill Off Fantasy Baseball:
The 2003 Crusade

It's a simple question...

"What do you do for a living?"

For most of you, I assume that this is a no-brainer of a question. For me, it's agonizing. How do I answer that? Based on the way that people see me these days, I suppose I should respond with, "I am a fantasy baseball analyst."

(Shudder.)

For most of the real world, "fantasy" means Dungeons and Dragons, not Dodgers and Diamondbacks. "Rotisserie" is no better, as most folks free-associate that term more with chicken than baseball. And a "fantasy baseball analyst," well, that's like calling Hans Christian Andersen a "fairy tale technician."

So I tell people that I drive a truck.

This fantasy baseball problem has not gone away. In fact, it has gotten worse. The major sports leagues have started to embrace the fantasy step-child, as the trickle-down dollar signs cloud their vision. And as they welcome these non-threatening fantasy people into their home, the term is becoming accepted, and ingrained into our collective consciousness. This is not a good thing.

In *Wise Guy Baseball 2002,* Gene McCaffrey writes, "Can we please turf this 'fantasy' word? People ask me what I do, then look at me like I'm peddling webcam shots of Andruw Jones at the club. Who decided to call it this? How could they get it more wrong? The games we play are won by predicting reality... What we play is personal baseball, admittedly not as catchy a moniker. The true appeal of the games is that they provide an arena in which we can be provably correct."

Gene is right. What we do is no fantasy. **But its legitimacy goes unacknowledged because people cannot see past That Word.**

One of my readers wrote: "*Fantasy* refers to something that is never expected to occur. *Fantasy baseball* deals with events and happenings that *are* expected to occur. We deal with the real world, facts, the manipulation of those facts, the extrapolation of those facts, probabilities, trends, predictability, and expected outcomes. Fantasy leaguers deal with statistics and with real world events, all in the setting of a competition."

Arguably, it's been the evolution of the "real" game that has driven us to fantasy in the first place. And that's why it's so important. Another reader wrote:

"While I have always enjoyed the game of baseball, the business of baseball was threatening my passion for the sport. To give your heart to any of the established "real" teams also meant taking the risk of having it ripped out by either meddling owners, incompetent management and/or mercenary-like demands of players.

"Though this lack of individual fan control has always been present in "real sports," the development of our spin-off sport has given fans a choice. Now I can enjoy the beauty of the game for what it is, but also reorganize the real results into a team approach that I can more readily root for, and have control over as well."

Fantasy sports have spawned a new type of fandom that is, in fact, *more grounded in reality.* With the growth of sabermetric research, today's new, intelligent fan has a better understanding of the intricacies of the game than ever before.

Another reader defined what we do in pure terms, and perhaps best described its legitimacy:

"We use game theory principles to construct models of successful performing teams. Specifically, we examine the individual performances of baseball players to predict a successful team model. These models are then tested by the actual performances of players and teams during the current season."

This is a terrific description and also helps bridge the gap between the sabermetric world and us fantasy types. The perception of the collective intelligence level of fantasy leaguers has been distorted by That Word; in fact, many have viewed us as a bane to intelligent analysis. However, if we can show how we approach these contests as statistical and economic game models, then it would be clear how legitimate this all is.

I worry that we're stuck with That Word, however. I fear we will forever be looked at as stat geeks, relegated to the back room, playing with our G.I. Joes and adorning our bicycle spokes with baseball cards.

So I need your help.

We have to rename this thing before it's too late. Yes, yes, I know, this crusade should have occurred about 15 years ago, but it doesn't get any better by just letting the years continue to pile up.

We have to strip away the fantasy and find a fitting moniker that truly describes the important things we are doing. Not only for our own self-esteem, mind you, but also to legitimize it with everyone else we know... "Sorry Hon, I can't take you to the mall tonight; I have to work on my fantasy team" just doesn't cut it any more. And forget trying to explain this to your mother-in-law.

Despite outward appearances, it *is* possible to start a grass roots effort and create a groundswell of support. In our internet world, you, personally, are just an e-mail away from the industry's top movers and shakers. A few hundred thousand e-mails to the heads of ESPN.com or MLB.com would certainly open up some eyes. Heck, if there are 10+ million of us fantasy leaguers out there, as the research studies suggest, a few hundred thousand should be a piece of cake.

But first we have to come up with a new name.

Shadow baseball, statistical baseball, boxscore baseball... They've all been offered and rejected. We need something with impact, something that exudes importance. Something that I can feel confident saying to people when asked what I do for a living.

And we need it now. As baseball rebounds from the latest labor unrest, this is the perfect time to ride the wave of momentum into 2003. This is the perfect time to proclaim that "Cvnsdjk Baseball" is a viable, legitimate part of the baseball landscape.

We can do it. We can.

I first kicked off this crusade in my last column of 2002 at Baseball HQ. Within days, I had received over 200 e-mails from subscribers, packed full of support and many with suggestions. Admittedly, several readers wrote that I was taking things too seriously, an odd thing for me to do given my penchant for *not* taking things too seriously. However, over 200 e-mails were in clear support of the need for a change. And if that percentage is representative of the fantasy universe as a whole, heck, this undercurrent would potentially be large enough to sway the largest media company.

So, let's get out our trusty Thesauruses and create the perfect descriptor for this important avocation. Write me at **newname@baseballhq.com** with your ideas.

Below is the beginnings of a list, compiled from the e-mails and letters I've received to date. There are some interesting ideas already here, and some that are head-scratchers. But for this brainstorming exercise, every idea is a good idea. Feel free to use this as a springboard to other ideas. I'll continue to collect these over the winter and post the best ones to the Baseball HQ home page.

We'll vote. We'll decide. And then we'll tell everyone. As an added incentive, whoever creates the winning name will get a free one-year subscription to Baseball HQ.

It's time to kill off this fantasy.

It's time to make it all real.

________ BASEBALL

________ SPORTS

________ LEAGUE BASEBALL

________ LEAGUE SPORTS

(AAAA) Four A
Actuarial
Alternative
Alternative Reality
Analytic
Basil
Bleacher
BOP (Baseball on Paper)
Calvinball
Competitive Statistical
Contest
Data
Database
Derivative
Doppelganger
Expansion Team
Fan-Control
Fan-Managed
Fan Challenge
Fan League
Fantastic
Forecast
Free Agent
Futurist
Game Theory
Grandstand
Index
Inferential
Intelligent
Management Simulation
Maven
Mercenary
Muscle
Paper
Paradigm
Parallel
Peoples'
Perfection (PERFormance ProjECTION)
Personal
Personal Power
POP (Power of Prognostication)
Power
Prediction
Predictive
Predictive Management
Premier
Primary
Prognostication
PUBS (Parallel Universe of Baseball Statistics)
Pure
Radical
Real Hardball
Realistic
Reality
Reality-Based
Remunerative
Sabermetric
Scientific
Select
Shadow
Stat
Statistical Management
Statistical Performance
Statistical Prophecy
Strategy
Study League
Systematic
Systematic Categorical
Systems
Transcendental Transmutable
Virtual
Visionary

VII. SABERMETRIC TOOLS

Glossary

Avg: Batting Average (see also BA)

BA: Batting Average (see also Avg)

Base Performance Index (BPX): A comparison of a player's Base Performance Value to the overall level of talent in his league in a given year. This accounts for changes in overall talent level from one year to the next. A BPX value of 100 represents a skill set that is exactly at the league average. Values above 100 are above average performances; below 100 are below average performances.

Base Performance Indicator (BPI): A statistical formula that measures a single, isolated aspect of a player's raw skill and is almost always a situation independent evaluator. Although there are many such formulas, there are only a few that we are referring to when the term is used in this book. For batters, our BPIs are linear weighted power index (PX), speed score index (SX), walk rate (bb%), contact rate (ct%), batting eye (Eye) and expected batting average (xBA). For pitchers, our BPI's are control (bb/9), dominance (k/9), command (k/bb), opposition on base average (OOB), hit rate on balls in play (H%), strand rate (S%), and expected earned run average (xERA).

Base Performance Value (BPV): A single value that describes a player's overall raw skill level. This is more useful than any traditional statistical gauge to track player performance trends and project future statistical output. The actual BPV formula combines and weights several BPIs.

Batting BPV: *(Batting Eye x 20) + ((Batting Average - .300) / .003) + (Linear Weighted Power x 1.25)*

This formula combines the individual raw skills of batting eye, the ability to hit safely, and the ability to hit with power. **BENCHMARKS:** The best hitters will have a BPV of 50 or greater, and represent approximately the top 20% of all offensive players. (Note: Batting BPV does not appear in this edition of the *Forecaster*.)

Pitching BPV: *(Dominance Rate x 6) + (Command Ratio x 21) - (Opposition HR Rate x 30) - ((Opp. Batting Average - .275) x 200)*

This formula combines the individual raw skills of power, command, the ability to keep batters from reaching base, and the ability to prevent long hits, all characteristics that are unaffected by most external team factors. In tandem with a pitcher's strand rate, it provides a complete picture of the elements that contribute to a pitcher's ERA, and therefore serves as an accurate tool to project likely changes in ERA.

BENCHMARKS: We generally consider a BPV of 50 to be the minimum level required for long-term success. There are some veteran pitchers who rarely reach this level, but they are generally the types who are workhorse inning-eaters and post high ERA's. The elite of the bullpen aces will have BPV's in excess of 100 and it is rare for these stoppers to enjoy long term success with consistent levels under 75.

Baserunners per Innings Pitched: The ratio of hits and walks to innings pitched. Decreed as a base Rotisserie category, is also alternately called WHIP (walks, hits, innings pitched), BRIP, and the highly-descriptive "Ratio." **BENCHMARKS:** Usually, a Br/IP of under 1.20 is considered top level and over 1.50 is indicative of poor performance. Levels under 1.00 — allowing fewer runners than IP — represent extraordinary performance and are rarely maintained over time.

Batters Faced per Game *(Craig Wright)*

((IP x 2.82) + H + BB) / G

A measure of pitcher usage and one of the leading indicators for potential pitcher burnout. (See Usage Warning Flags in the Forecaster's Toolbox.)

Batting Average (BA, or Avg): A grand old nugget that has long outgrown its usefulness, leaving its true value as nothing more than a link to baseball's past. But this remains deceptive. We revere .300 hitting superstars and scoff at .250 hitters, yet the difference between the two is 1 hit every 20 ABs. This 1 hit every four or five games is not nearly the wide variance that exists in our perceptions of what it means to be a .300 or .250 hitter. The bottom line is that BA is a poor evaluator of overall baseball performance. BA neglects the offensive value of the base on balls and assumes that all hits are created equal.

Batting Eye (Eye)

(Walks / Strikeouts)

A measure of a player's strike zone judgment, the raw ability to distinguish between balls and strikes.

BENCHMARKS: The best hitters have eye ratios over 1.00 (indicating more walks than strikeouts) and are the most likely to be among a league's .300 hitters. At the other end of the scale are ratios less than 0.50, which represent batters who likely also have lower BA's. (See Forecaster's Toolbox for more research.)

bb%: Walk rate (hitters)

bb/9: Opposition Walks per 9 IP

BF/Gm: Batters Faced Per Game

BPI: Base Performance Indicator

BPV: Base Performance Value

BPX: Base Performance Index

Br/IP: Baserunners per Innings Pitched

Cmd: Command ratio

Command Ratio (Cmd)

(Strikeouts / Walks)

This is a measure of a pitcher's raw ability to get the ball over the plate. There is no more fundamental a skill than this, and so it is accurately used as a leading indicator to project future rises and falls in other gauges, such as ERA. Command is one of the best gauges to use to evaluate minor league performance. It is a prime component of a pitcher's base performance value.

BENCHMARKS: Baseball's upper echelon of command pitchers will have ratios in excess of 3.0. Pitchers with ratios under 1.0 — indicating that they walk more batters than they strike out — have virtually no potential for long term success. If you make no other changes in your approach to drafting a pitching staff, limiting your focus to only pitchers with a command ratio of 2.0 or better will substantially improve your odds of success. (See the Forecaster's Toolbox for more command ratio research.)

Contact Rate (ct%)

((AB - K) / AB)

Measures a batter's ability to get wood on the ball.

BENCHMARK: Those batters with the best contact skill will have levels of 90% or better. The hackers of society will have levels of 75% or less.

Control Rate (bb/9), or Opposition Walks per Game

BB Allowed x 9 / IP

Measures how many walks a pitcher allows per game equivalent. **BENCHMARK:** The best pitchers will have bb/9 levels of 3.0 or less.

Crickets: The sound heard when someone's opening draft bid on a player is also the only bid.

Ct%: Contact rate

Ctl: Control Rate

DIS%: PQS Disaster Rate

Dom: Dominance Rate

DOM%: PQS Domination Rate

Dominance Rate (k/9), or Opposition Strikeouts per Game

(K Allowed x 9 / IP)

Used in the BPV formula, it measures how many strikeouts a pitcher allows per game equivalent. **BENCHMARK:** The best pitchers will have k/9 levels of 6.0 or higher.

ERA Variance: The variance between a pitcher's ERA and his XERA, which is a measure of over or underachievement. A positive variance indicates the potential for a pitcher's ERA to rise. A negative variance indicates the potential for ERA improvement. (See Expected Earned Run Average.)

BENCHMARKS: Discount variances that are under 0.50. Any variance over 1.00 (one run per game) is regarded as a clear indicator of future change. Note that all variances over 0.50 are indicated by a "+" or "-" in the player boxes.

Expected Batting Average *(John Burnson)*

AL: CT% x [(.00077 x PX) + (.00005 x SX) + .245]

NL: CT% x [(.00065 x PX) + (.00012 x SX) + .252]

A hitter's batting average as calculated by multiplying the percentage of balls put in play (contact rate) by the chance that a ball in play falls for a hit. The likelihood that a ball in play falls for a hit is a product of the speed of the ball and distance it is hit (PX), and the speed of the batter (SX).

BENCHMARKS: In general, xBA's should approximate a hitter's batting average fairly closely. However, those hitters who have large variances between the two gauges are candidates for further analysis. (Note that the variables shown in the above equation are for the 2002 season only.)

Expected Earned Run Average *(Gill and Reeve)*

(.575 x H [per 9 IP]) + (.94 x HR [per 9 IP]) + (.28 x BB [per 9 IP]) - (.01 x K [per 9 IP]) - Normalizing Factor

"xERA represents the expected ERA of the pitcher based on a normal distribution of his statistics. It is not influenced by situation-dependent factors." xERA erases the inequity between starters' and relievers' ERA's, eliminating the effect that a pitcher's success or failure has on another pitcher's ERA.

Similar to other gauges, the accuracy of this formula changes with the level of competition from one season to the next. The normalizing factor allows us to better approximate a pitcher's actual ERA. This value is usually somewhere around 2.77 and varies by league and year.

BENCHMARKS: In general, xERA's should approximate a pitcher's ERA fairly closely. However, those pitchers who have large variances between the two gauges are candidates for further analysis. (See ERA Variance.)

There is some confusion about how to interpret a pitcher's projected xERA as compared to his projected ERA.

The projected xERA is probably the more accurate gauge for looking ahead, as it is constructed solely from skills-related variables and situationally independent events.

The projected ERA is constructed from a trend analysis of historical ERAs, with some adjustments for leading indicators. The reason we include this at all is that pitching performance is also impacted by situationally *dependent* events — bullpen support, park factors, etc. — which are reflected better by ERA. The optimal approach, however, is to use *both* gauges as a range of the expectation for the coming year.

Eye: Batting Eye

G/F: Ground Ball to Fly Ball Ratio

Gopheritis (also, Acute Gopheritis and Chronic Gopheritis): The dreaded malady in which a pitcher is unable to keep the ball in the ballpark. Pitchers with gopheritis allow over 15% of their hits to leave the park, an approximate hr/9 level of 1.3 or higher.

Ground Ball / Fly Ball Ratio (G/F): A simple ratio of ground balls to fly balls. This has a variety of uses for both batters and pitchers. For batters, increased fly ball tendency may foretell a rise in power skills. For pitchers, the ability to keep the ball on the ground is usually necessary for long-term success.

BENCHMARKS: For batters, a G/F ratio over 1.80 may indicate a low ceiling for power potential. A G/F ratio under 1.00 may indicate a high ceiling. *(Mat Olkin)* Further study is needed to determine appropriate pitching benchmarks.

H%: Hits Allowed per Balls in Play

Hits Allowed per Balls in Play *(Voros McCracken)*

(H—HR) / ((IP x 2.82) + H - K - HR)

See Forecaster's Toolbox for a complete discussion on this gauge. **BENCHMARK:** The league average H% is 30%. Any +/- variance of 3% or more can affect a pitcher's ERA.

hr/9: Opposition Home Runs per 9 IP

IP/G: Innings Pitched per Game Appearance

k/9: Dominance rate (opposition strikeouts per 9 IP)

Leading Indicator: A statistical formula (usually a base performance indicator) that can be used to project likely future performance.

LIMA Plan: A strategy for Rotisserie leagues that allows you to target high skills pitchers at very low cost, thereby freeing up dollars for offense. LIMA is an acronym for Low Investment Mound Aces, and also pays tribute to Jose Lima, a $1 pitcher in 1998 who exemplified the power of the strategy. There are six steps to the strategy:

1. Budget a maximum of $60 (out of $260) for your pitching staff. This figure may vary slightly; keeper leagues can probably budget less, 5x5 leagues would need to budget more.

2. Allot no more than $30 of that budget for acquiring saves. That might mean one $30 stud, or several lower-priced closers.

3. Completely ignore the remaining pitching categories. When assembling the rest of your staff, only draft pitchers who:

- have a command ratio (K/BB) of 2.0 or better.
- have a strikeout rate of 6.0 or better.
- have a home run rate of 1.0 or less.

4. Draft as few innings as your league rules will allow. This enables you to better manage your staff during the season. And plan ahead; if your league has a 900 minimum innings rule, for instance, you only need two 180 IP starters to meet that requirement, surprisingly enough.

5. Maximize your batting acquisitions. With $200 or more to spend on hitters, you should be able to assemble an offense that ranks at or near the top of every batting category. But spend every penny and make sure all categories are covered.

6. Spread your risk. Risk minimization is an important element of value maximization, so spend no more than $29 for any player and try to keep the $1 picks to a minimum.

The overall goal is to ace the batting categories and carefully pick your pitching staff so that it will finish in the upper third in ERA/WHIP, in the upper third in saves, and somewhere around 9th-12th in wins. In a competitive league, that should usually generate enough points to win, and definitely enough to finish in the money. Worst case, you should have an excess of offense available that you can deal for arms.

The LIMA Plan works because it focuses on better allocation of resources. When fantasy leaguers pay big bucks for pitchers, they are not only paying for expected performance. They are also paying for better defined roles, which translates into more innings, more wins and more saves. But roles are highly variable, changing often during the course of a season. The LIMA Plan says, let's invest in skill and let the roles fall where they may. In the long run, better skills should translate into more innings, wins and saves anyway. And as it turns out, pitching skill costs much less than pitching roles do.

Linear Weights *(Pete Palmer)*

((Singles x .46) + (Doubles x .8) + (Triples x 1.02) + (Home runs x 1.4) + (Walks x .33) + (Stolen Bases x .3) - (Caught Stealing x .6) - ((At bats - Hits) x Normalizing Factor)

LW is also referred to as Batting Runs. Formula whose premise is that all events in baseball are linear, that is, the output (runs) is directly proportional to the input (offensive events). Each of these offensive events is then weighted according to its relative value in producing runs. Positive events — hits, walks, stolen bases — have positive values. Negative events — outs, caught stealing — have negative values.

The normalizing factor, representing the value of an out, is an offset to the particular level of offense in a given year. As such it changes every season, growing larger in high offense years and smaller in low offense years. The value is usually somewhere around .26 and varies by league.

LW is no longer included in the player forecast boxes, but the LW concept is used with the linear weighted power gauge.

Linear Weighted Power (LWPwr)

(((Doubles x .8) + (Triples x .8) + (Home runs x 1.4)) / At bats) x 365

An excerpt/variation of the LW formula that only considers events that are measures of a batter's raw power. A prime base performance indicator.

BENCHMARKS: Baseball's top sluggers usually top the 50 mark. Weak hitters will have a LWPwr level of under 20.

Linear Weighted Power Index (PX)

(Batter's LWPwr / League LWPwr) x 100

LWPwr is presented in this book in its normalized form to get a better read on a batter's accomplishment in each year. For instance, a 30-HR season today is not nearly as much of an accomplishment as 30 HRs hit in a lower offense year like 1995. A level of 100 equals league average power skills. Any player with a value over 100 has above average power skills, and those over 175 are the slugging elite.

LW: Linear Weights

LWPwr: Linear Weighted Power

Major League Equivalency *(Bill James):* A formula that converts a player's minor league statistics into a comparable performance in the major leagues. These are not projections, but rather conversions of current performance. Contains adjustments for the level of play in individual leagues and teams. Works best with Triple-A stats, not quite as well with Double-A stats, and hardly at all with the lower levels. James' formula only addressed batting. Our research has devised a similar methodology for pitchers, however, its best use comes when looking at MLE levels of BPI's, not traditional stats.

Mendoza Line: Named for Mario Mendoza, it represents the benchmark for batting futility. Usually refers to a .200 batting average, but can also be used for low levels of other statistical categories. Despite the "Mendoza Line" being used to describe a .200 hitter, Mendoza's lifetime batting average was actually a much loftier .215.

MLE: Major League Equivalency

Noise: Irrelevant or meaningless pieces of information that can distort the results of an analysis. In news, this is opinion or rumor that can invalidate valuable information. In forecasting, these are unimportant elements of statistical data that can invalidate a set of numbers.

OB: On Base Average (batters)

OBA: Opposition On Base Average (pitchers)

On Base Average (OBA)

(H + BB) / (AB + BB)

Addressing one of the two deficiencies in BA, OB gives value to those events that get batters on base, but are not hits. By adding walks (and often, hit batsmen) into the basic batting average formula, we have a better gauge of a batter's ability to reach base safely. An OB of .350 can be read as "this batter gets on base 35% of the time."

Why this is a more important gauge than batting average... When a run is scored, there is no distinction made as to how that runner reached base. So, two thirds of the time — about how often a batter comes to the plate with the bases empty — a walk really is as good as a hit.

BENCHMARKS: We all know what a .300 hitter is, but what represents "good" for OB? That comparable level would likely be .400, with .275 representing the level of futility.

On Base Plus Slugging Average (OPS): A simple sum of the two gauges, it is considered as one of the better evaluators of overall performance. OPS combines the two basic elements of offensive production — the ability to get on base (OB) and the ability to advance baserunners (Slg).

BENCHMARKS: The game's top batters will have OPS levels over .900. The worst batters will have levels under .600.

Opposition Batting Average (OBA)

(Hits Allowed / ((IP x 2.82) + Hits Allowed))

A close approximation of the batting average achieved by opposing batters against a particular pitcher.

BENCHMARKS: The converse of the benchmark for batters, the best pitchers will have levels under .250; the worst pitchers levels over .300.

Opposition Home Runs per Game (hr/9)

(HR Allowed x 9 / IP)

Used in the BPV formula, it measures how many home runs a pitcher allows per game equivalent. **BENCHMARK**: The best pitchers will have hr/9 levels of under 1.0.

Opposition On Base Average (OOB)

(Hits Allowed + BB) / ((IP x 2.82) + H + BB)

A close approximation of the on base average achieved by opposing batters against a particular pitcher. **BENCHMARK**: The best pitchers will have levels under .300; the worst pitchers levels over .375.

Opposition Strikeouts per Game: See Dominance Rate.

Opposition Walks per Game: See Control Rate.

OPS: On Base Plus Slugging Average

Pitching Contact Rate

(BB + K) / IP

Measures the level by which a pitcher allows balls to be put into play. Pitching contact rate helps to tie a pitcher's success to his team's level of defensive ability. In general, extreme power pitchers can be successful even with poor defensive teams. Extreme contact pitchers usually cannot. Power pitchers tend to have greater longevity in the game. Contact pitchers with poor defenses behind them are high risks to have poor won-loss records — even if they have acceptable ERAs.

BENCHMARKS: A level of 1.1 or greater describes the extreme power pitchers, or more aptly described as pure throwers. A level of .95 or lower describes an extreme finesse style, or a high contact pitcher. Tip... if you have to draft a pitcher from a poor defensive team, going with power over contact will usually net you more wins in the long run.

PQS: Pure Quality Starts

PQS Disaster Rate (Gene McCaffrey): The percentage of a starting pitcher's outings that rate as a PQS-0 or PQS-1. See the Pitching Logs section for more information on DIS%.

PQS Domination Rate (Gene McCaffrey): The percentage of a starting pitcher's outings that rate as a PQS-4 or PQS-5. See the Pitching Logs section for more information on DOM%.

Pure Quality Starts: See page 129 for a complete description.

Pw: Linear Weighted Power

PX: Linear Weighted Power Index

R$: Rotisserie value

RAR: Runs Above Replacement

RC: Runs Created

RC/G: Runs Created Per Game

REff%: Relief Efficiency Per Cent

Reliever Efficiency Per Cent (REff%)

(Wins + Saves + Holds) / (Wins + Losses + SaveOpps + Holds)

This is a measure of the effectiveness of relief pitchers in pressure situations. How often does a reliever contribute positively to the outcome of the game? A record of consistent, positive impact on game outcomes breeds managerial confidence, and that confidence could pave the way to save opportunities. For those pitchers that are suddenly thrust into a closer's role, this formula helps gauge their potential to succeed based on past successes in similar roles.

BENCHMARK: Minimum of 80%.

Rotisserie Value (R$): The dollar value placed on a player's performance in a Rotisserie league, and designed to measure the impact that player has on the standings. These values are highly variable depending upon a variety of factors. In other words, a $30 player is only a $30 player if

- there is a 260-unit salary cap
- there are 12 teams in the league
- each team has a 23-man roster
- there are no freeze lists
- every other player is drafted at optimal value

Any variation in these factors will inflate or deflate a player's value. In addition, a player's value will also be affected by the stage of the draft you are in, the position and category demands when the player comes up for bid, and the prevailing winds of the media.

In other words, a $30 player is only a $30 player if someone in your draft pays $30 for him.

There are a variety of methods to calculate value, most involving a delineation of a least valuable performance level (given league size and structure), and then assigning a certain dollar amount for incremental improvement from that base. The method we use is a variation of the Standings Gain Points method described in the book, *How to Value Players for Rotisserie Baseball,* by Art McGee.

Research has been showing a shift in how people play Rotisserie. The 5x5 game (adding runs scored and pitching strikeouts) has become very popular, and as many as 40% of you currently play in at least one mixed league.

Does this invalidate the ratings in this book? No. Since values are driven by playing time, and our playing time projections are preliminary anyway, the best use for this data is to get a *general sense of value* no matter how you play the game.

In fact, since we currently have no idea whether Brandon Phillips will really break camp as the Indians' starting secondbaseman, or who is going to be playing the outfield in Colorado next year, all the projected values are slightly inflated. They are roughly based on a 12-team AL and 13-team NL league. We've attempted to take into account as many contingencies as prudent, but the values will not total to anywhere near $3120, so don't waste your time adding them up, and save your irate e-mails.

A $25 player in this book might actually be worth $21. Or maybe $28. This level of precision is irrelevant in a process that is going to be driven by market forces anyway. So, don't obsess over it.

I always wonder how other writers manage to publish perfect Rotisserie values over the winter. Do they make their own arbitrary decisions as to which free agents are going to sign where, and who is going to land jobs in spring training? I'm not about to make those massive leaps of faith.

Bottom line... Some things you can predict, to other things you have to react. As roles become more defined closer to Opening Day, our online updates will provide better approximations of playing time, and projected Roto values that add up to $3120.

Runs Above Replacement (RAR): An estimate of the number of runs a player contributes above a "replacement level" player. "Replacement" is defined as the level of performance at which another player can easily be found at little or no cost to a team. What constitutes replacement level is a topic that is hotly debated. There are a variety of formulas and rules of thumb used to determine this level for each position (replacement level for a shortstop will be very different from replacement level for an outfielder). Our estimates appear below.

One of the major values of RAR for fantasy applications is that it can be used to assemble an integrated ranking of batters and pitchers for drafting purposes.

Batters create runs; pitchers save runs. But are batters and pitchers who have comparable RAR levels truly equal in value? In fact, pitchers might be considered to have higher value. Saving an additional run is more important than producing an additional run. A pitcher who throws a shutout is guaranteed to win that game, whereas no matter how many runs a batter produces, his team can still lose given a poor pitching outing.

To calculate RAR for batters:

- Start with a batter's runs created per game (RC/G).
- Subtract his position's replacement level RC/G.
- Multiply by number of games played, calculated as (plate appearances / 35).

Replacement levels used in this book, for 2002:

POS	AL	NL
C	3.69	4.20
1B	5.98	5.71
2B	4.12	4.50
3B	4.56	4.68
SS	4.67	3.98
LF	4.93	6.51
CF	4.87	4.97
RF	5.12	5.41
DH	5.64	

To calculate RAR for pitchers:

- Start with the replacement level league ERA.
- Subtract the pitcher's ERA. (To calculate *projected* RAR, use the pitcher's XERA.)
- Multiply by number of games played, calculated as plate appearances (IP x 4.34) divided by 35.
- Multiply the resulting RAR level by 1.08 to account for the variance between earned runs and total runs.

RAR can also be used to calculate rough *projected team won-loss records.* (Roger Miller) Total the RAR levels for all the players on a team, divide by 10 and add to 53 wins.

Runs Created *(Bill James)*

(H + BB - CS) x (Total bases + (.52 x SB) + (.26 x BB)) / (AB + BB)

A formula that converts all offensive events into a total of runs scored. As calculated for individual teams, the result approximates a club's actual run total with great accuracy.

Runs Created Per Game *(Bill James)*

Runs Created / ((AB - H + CS) / 25.5)

RC expressed on a per-game basis might be considered the hypothetical ERA compiled against a particular batter. Another way to look at it... a batter with a RC/G of 7.00 would be expected to score 7 runs per game if he were cloned nine times and faced an average pitcher in every at bat. Cloning batters is not a practice we recommend.

BENCHMARKS: Few players surpass the level of a 10.00 RC/G in any given season, but any level over 7.50 can still be considered very good. At the bottom of the scale are those who post RC/G levels below 3.00.

S%: Strand Rate

Save: There are six events that need to occur in order for a pitcher to post a single save...

1. The starting pitcher and middle relievers must pitch well.
2. The offense must score enough runs.
3. It must be a reasonably close game.
4. The manager must choose to put the pitcher in for a save opportunity.
5. The pitcher must pitch well and hold the lead.
6. The manager must let him finish the game.

Of these six events, only one is within the control of the relief pitcher. As such, projecting saves for a reliever has little to do with skill and a lot to do with opportunity. However, pitchers with excellent skills sets may create opportunity for themselves.

Situation Independent: Describing a statistical gauge that measures performance apart from the context of team, ballpark, or other outside variables. Home runs, inasmuch as they are unaffected by the performance of a batter's team, are often considered a situation independent stat (they are, however, affected by park dimensions). Strikeouts and Walks are better examples.

Conversely, RBI's are situation dependent because individual performance varies greatly by the performance of other batters on the team (you can't drive in runs if there is nobody on base). Similarly, pitching wins are as much a measure of the success of a pitcher as they are a measure of the success of the offense and defense performing behind that pitcher, and are therefore a poor measure of pitching performance alone.

Situation independent gauges are important for us to be able to separate a player's contribution to his team and isolate his performance so that we may judge it on its own merits.

Slg: Slugging Average

Slugging Average (Slg)

(Singles + (2 x Doubles) + (3 x Triples) + (4 x HR)) / AB

A measure of the total number of bases accumulated (or the minimum number of runners' bases advanced) per at bat. It is a misnomer; it is not a true measure of a batter's slugging ability because it includes singles. Slg also assumes that each type of hit has proportionately increasing value (i.e. a double is twice as valuable as a single, etc.) which is not true. For instance, with the bases loaded, a HR always scores four runs, a triple always scores three, but a double could score two or three and a single could score one, or two, or even three.

BENCHMARKS: The top 10%-15% of batters will have levels over .500. The bottom 5%-10% will have levels under .300.

Soft stats (also, Soft Skills): Batting eyes less than 0.50. Command ratios under 2.0. Strikeout rates below 5.0. Etc.

Soft-tosser: Pitcher with a strikeout rate of 5.0 or less.

Spd: Speed Score

Speed Score *(Bill James):* A measure of the various elements that comprise a runner's speed skills. Although this formula (a variation of James' original version) may be used as a leading indicator for stolen base output, SB attempts are controlled by managerial strategy which makes Spd somewhat less valuable.

The speed scores in this book are calculated as the mean value of the following four elements...

Stolen base efficiency = *(((SB + 3)/(SB + CS + 7)) - .4) x 20*

Stolen base frequency = *Square root of ((SB + CS)/(Singles + BB)) / .07*

Triples rating = *(3B / (AB - HR - K)) / .0016*

Runs scored as a percentage of times on base = *(((R - HR)/(H + BB - HR)) - .1) / .04*

Speed Score Index (SX)

(Batter's Spd / League Spd) x 100

Normalized speed scores are presented in this book to get a better read on a runner's accomplishment in context. A level of 100 equals league average speed skill. Values over 100 indicate above average skill, over 200 represent the Elite Fleet of Feet.

Strand Rate (S%)

(H + BB - ER) / (H + BB - HR)

This represents the percentage of allowed runners a pitcher strands, and measures both individual pitcher skill and bullpen effectiveness.

BENCHMARKS: The most adept at stranding runners will have S% levels over 75%. Once a pitcher's S% starts dropping down below 70%, he's going to have problems with his ERA. Those pitchers with strand rates over 80% will have artificially low ERAs, which will be prone to relapse. (See the Forecaster's Toolbox for more strand rate research.)

Strikeouts per Game: See Opposition Strikeouts per game.

SX: Speed Score Index

Vintage Eck Territory: A base performance value (BPV) level of 200 or over. Over the course of his career, Dennis Eckersely posted levels this high four times:

1989	345
1990	347
1991	226
1992	210

Vulture: A pitcher, typically a middle reliever, who accumulates an unusually high number of wins by preying on other pitchers' misfortunes. More accurately, this is a pitcher typically brought into a game after a starting pitcher has put his team behind, and then pitches well enough and long enough to allow his offense to take the lead, thereby "vulturing" a win from his starting pitcher.

Walk rate (bb%)

(BB / (AB + BB))

A measure of a batter's eye and plate patience.

BENCHMARKS: The best batters will have levels of over 10%. Those with the least plate patience will have levels of 5% or less.

Walks per Game: See Opposition Walks per Game.

Wasted talent: A player with a high level skill that is negated by a deficiency in another skill. For instance, basepath speed can be negated by poor on base ability. Pitchers with strong arms can be wasted because home plate is an elusive concept to them.

Wins: There are five events that need to occur in order for a pitcher to post a single win...

1. He must pitch well, allowing few runs.

2. The offense must score enough runs.

3. The defense must successfully field all batted balls.

4. The bullpen must hold the lead.

5. The manager must leave the pitcher in for 5 innings, and not remove him if the team is still behind.

Of these five events, only one is within the control of the pitcher. As such, projecting wins can be an exercise in futility.

XBA: Expected Batting Average

XERA: Expected ERA

CHEATER'S BOOKMARK

BATTING STATISTICS

Abbrv	Term	Formula / Descr.	BAD UNDER	'02 LG AVG AL	'02 LG AVG NL	BEST OVER
Avg	Batting Average	h/ab	250	259	264	300
xBA	Expected Batting Average	*See glossary*		270	274	
OB	On Base Average	(h+bb)/(ab+bb)	300	327	327	375
Slg	Slugging Average	total bases/ab	350	410	424	500
OPS	On Base plus Slugging	OB+Slg	650	738	751	875
bb%	Walk Rate	bb/(ab+bb)	5%	9%	9%	10%
ct%	Contact Rate	(ab-k) / ab	75%	80%	82%	85%
Eye	Batting Eye	bb/k	0.50	0.52	0.51	1.00
PX	Power Index	Normalized power skills	80	100	100	120
SX	Speed Index	Normalized speed skills	80	100	100	120
G/F	Groundball/Flyball Ratio	gb / fb		1.14	1.22	
RC/G	Runs Created per Game	*See glossary*	3.00	4.86	5.02	7.50
RAR	Runs Above Replacement	*See glossary*	-0			+25
BPV	Base Performance Value	*See glossary*	35	36	41	75
BPX	Base Performance Index	*See glossary*	80	100	100	120

PITCHING STATISTICS

Abbrev	Term	Formula / Descr.	BAD OVER	'02 LG AVG AL	'02 LG AVG NL	BEST UNDER
ERA	Earned Run Average	er*9/ip	5.00	4.11	4.46	4.00
Br/IP	Baserunners per Inning	(h+bb)/ip	1.50	1.37	1.38	1.25
BF/G	Batters Faced per Game	((ip*2.82)+h+bb)/g	28.0			
OBA	Opposition Batting Avg	Opp. h/ab	290	259	265	250
OOB	Opposition On Base Avg	Opp. (h+bb)/(ab+bb)	350	327	329	300
H%	Hits per balls in play	(h-hr)/((ip*2.82)+h-k-hr)		29.5%	29.8%	
xERA	Expected ERA	*See glossary*	5.00	4.10	4.46	4.00
Ctl	Control Rate	bb*9/ip		3.5	3.3	3.0
hr/9	Homerun Rate	hr*9/ip		1.0	1.1	1.0
S%	Strand Rate	(h+bb-er)/(h+bb-hr)		73%	70%	
DIS%	PQS Disaster Rate	% GS that are PQS 0/1		25%	23%	20%

Abbrev	Term	Formula / Descr.	BAD UNDER	'01 LG AVG AL	'01 LG AVG NL	BEST OVER
RAR	Runs Above Replacement	*See glossary*	-0			+25
Dom	Dominance Rate	k*9/ip		6.7	6.4	6.5
Cmd	Command Ratio	k/bb		1.9	1.9	2.2
G/F	Groundball/Flyball Ratio	gb / fb		1.16	1.27	
BPV	Base Performance Value	*See glossary*	50	53	48	75
BPX	Base Performance Index	*See glossary*	80	100	100	120
DOM%	PQS Dominance Rate	% GS that are PQS 4/5		38%	42%	50%

NOTES

10 reasons why <u>winners</u> rely on BaseballHQ.com

BaseballHQ.com is where fantasy leaguers go for the information they need to WIN. Not just news and stats, BHQ provides the fantasy implications, analysis of what the future may hold, and all the tools you need to take your team to victory.

1 NO OTHER RESOURCE gives you more in-depth analysis, more tools and more vital intelligence to help you win. Compare BHQ's offerings with any other information source:

- Daily market watch
- Daily buyers guides
- Weekly player projections
- Advisory forums
- Top 10 hot lists
- Expert columnists
- Interactive think tank
- Expert and reader exhibitions
- Team analyses
- Starting pitcher logs
- Bullpen indicator charts
- Searchable player database
- Personal team profiler
- Trade analyzer
- Weekly minors column
- Daily call-ups analyses
- Major league equivalent statistics
- Fantasy draft guides
- Rotisserie bidding grid
- Customized Rotisserie values
- Roster analysis service
- Forecasting research results

2 NO OTHER RESOURCE provides more exclusive information — features you won't find anywhere else — such as:

- Cutting edge component skills analyses, as revolutionized in *Ron Shandler's Baseball Forecaster*
- Innovative roster management strategies like the LIMA Plan
- Specialized online charts and tools, like the MACK Engine, PlayerLink and the PQS Pitching Logs.

3 NO OTHER RESOURCE has as consistent a track record of success in national experts competitions... 7 first place and 3 second place finishes since 1998. No other expert comes remotely close.

- *LABR:* 1st place-NL (2001), 2nd place-AL (2001)
- *Tout Wars:* 1st place-AL (1998), 1st place-NL (1998), 1st place-AL (2000), 2nd place-AL (1999)
- *Fantasy Sports Trade Association:* 1st place tie (1999), 2nd place (2001)
- *CBS Sportsline:* 1st place (2000)
- *MLB.com:* 1st place-NL (2002)

4 NO OTHER RESOURCE has as solid a track record in projecting impact performances... In 2002, our subscribers knew about the following tidbits, and dozens more:

- the huge draftability of Eric Gagne, Eddie Guardado and Damaso Marte
- the 20-win potential of Bartolo Colon
- the SB rebound of Eric Owens
- the upside of journeymen Randy Winn, Scott Hatteberg and Randall Simon
- the riskiness of Hank Blalock and Josh Beckett
- the breakdown of Scott Sullivan
- the ERA upsides of Hideo Nomo and Andy Pettitte
- the huge potential of John Smoltz and Vicente Padilla
- the SB drop-offs of Roger Cedeno, Cristian Guzman and Jimmy Rollins
- the sleeper upsides of Mark DeRosa and Steve Trachsel
- the new performance levels of Ted Lilly and Jarrod Washburn
- the expected backslides of Marty Cordova and Chris Singleton

5 NO OTHER RESOURCE is supported by over two dozen top writers and analysts — paid professionals and proven winners, not weekend hobbyists or corporate staffers. Every contributor to BHQ goes through an intense application and screening process, and we typically hire fewer than 2% of those who apply for openings.

6 NO OTHER RESOURCE has a wider scope, providing valuable information not only for Rotisserie, but for alternative game formats as well. BHQ readers participate in such contests as:

- Scoresheet Baseball
- National challenge games
- Bill James Fantasy Baseball
- Strat-O-Matic, APBA, other sim games
- and many other formats

7 NO OTHER RESOURCE is 100% dedicated to baseball. BHQ doesn't spread itself to other sports, taking resources away from baseball. For 12 months of the year, the focus is purely, exclusively and absolutely on baseball, and providing the valuable information you need to win.

8 NO OTHER RESOURCE is as highly regarded by its peers in the fantasy baseball industry. Many members of the LABR experts league use Baseball HQ. They said: "For cutting-edge fantasy advice and analysis, HQ earns raves across the board.... For the advanced player, the gourmet stats and theories are indispensable." In fact, BHQ's player projections are often used as source material and as a sanity check by other fantasy information services!

No sense going anywhere else when the original source is right here.

9 NO OTHER RESOURCE has been creating fantasy baseball winners for as long as we have. Shandler Enterprises' 17 years of stability <u>guarantees</u> your investment. No other information source – anywhere – can make that type of guarantee.

10 Year after year, over 90% of our subscribers report that Baseball HQ has helped them improve their performance in their fantasy leagues. That's the bottom line, as over 300 dedicated readers attest on BHQ's testimonials page. One summed it up best: "I come here. I win here."

With a subscription to Baseball HQ, you simply can't lose.

Subscription Plans

ONE YEAR (Best deal!)	$99
Six months	$69
Three months	$39

TO ORDER

SECURELY ONLINE:
https://www.baseballhq.com
/subscribe.html

TOLL FREE PHONE: 1-800-422-7820

MAIL: Send check or money order to:
Shandler Enterprises LLC
P.O. Box 20303
Roanoke, VA 24018.